Issues Regarding Items in Financial Statements (under various GAAPs) *(continued)*	Chapters
• Fair value and cash flow hedges	16
• Foreign currency translation	NA
• Business combination	12
• Consolidated statements on date of acquisition	NA
• Consolidated financial statements subsequent to acquisition date	NA
• Joint ventures: proportionate consolidation or equity method	NA
• Complex financial instruments (e.g., perpetual debt, convertible debt, derivatives)	16
Financial Statement Analysis	
• Vertical and horizontal analysis	5A, 23, and all chapters
• Ratios and benchmarking	5A, 23, and all chapters
• Financial statement results for various users	5A, 23, and all chapters
• Pro forma statements	NA
• Impact of financial results on the whole organization	5A, 23, and all chapters

Meeting Financial Reporting Technical Competencies in the CPA Competency Map—The following table maps the financial reporting technical competencies from the CPA Competency Map to *Intermediate Accounting, Eleventh Canadian Edition* (Volume 1). The textbook in its entirety covers the Financial Reporting competencies as noted below. Detailed mapping of specific CPA Financial Reporting competencies to specific textbook Learning Objectives is provided in the charts at the beginning of each chapter. Coverage of other technical competencies (that is, Strategy and Governance, Management Accounting, Audit and Assurance, Finance and Taxation competencies) has also been identified in the charts at the beginning of each chapter and in the end-of-chapter material. Selected enabling competencies have also been identified throughout.

FINANCIAL REPORTING

1.1 Financial Reporting Needs and Systems	Chapters
1.1.1 Evaluates financial reporting needs	1, 2, 3, 4, 5, 6, 7, 8, 9, 10, 11, 12
1.1.2 Evaluates the appropriateness of the basis of financial reporting	1, 2, 3, 4, 5, 6, 7, 8, 9, 10, 11, 12
1.1.3 Evaluates reporting processes to support reliable financial reporting	3, 8, 12
1.1.4 Explains implications of current trends and emerging issues in financial reporting	2, 3, 4, 5, 6, 7, 8, 9, 10, 11, 12
1.1.5 Identifies financial reporting needs for the public sector	10
1.1.6 Identifies specialized financial reporting requirements for specified regulatory and other filing requirements	NA
1.2 Accounting Policies and Transactions	
1.2.1 Develops or evaluates appropriate accounting policies and procedures	1, 2, 3, 4, 5, 6, 7, 8, 9, 10, 11, 12
1.2.2 Evaluates treatment for routine transactions	2, 3, 4, 5, 6, 7, 8, 9, 10, 11, 12
1.2.3 Evaluates treatment for non-routine transactions	2, 3, 4, 5, 6, 7, 8, 9, 10, 11, 12
1.2.4 Analyzes treatment for complex events or transactions	7, 8, 10, 12
1.3 Financial Report Preparation	
1.3.1 Prepares financial statements	1, 3, 4, 5, 6
1.3.2 Prepares routine financial statement note disclosure	4, 5, 6, 7, 8, 9, 10, 11, 12
1.4 Financial Statement Analysis	
1.4.1 Analyzes complex financial statement note disclosure	4, 5, 7, 8, 9, 11, 12
1.4.2 Evaluates financial statements including note disclosures	4, 5, 7, 8, 9, 11, 12
1.4.3 Analyzes and provides input in the preparation of the management communication (e.g., management discussion and analysis (MD&A))	5
1.4.4 Interprets financial reporting results for stakeholders (external or internal)	4, 5, 7, 8, 9, 11, 12
1.4.5 Analyzes and predicts the impact of strategic and operational decisions on financial results	3, 4, 5, 6, 7, 8, 9

WileyPLUS with ORION

Quickly identify areas of strength and weakness before the first exam, and use the information to build a learning path to success.

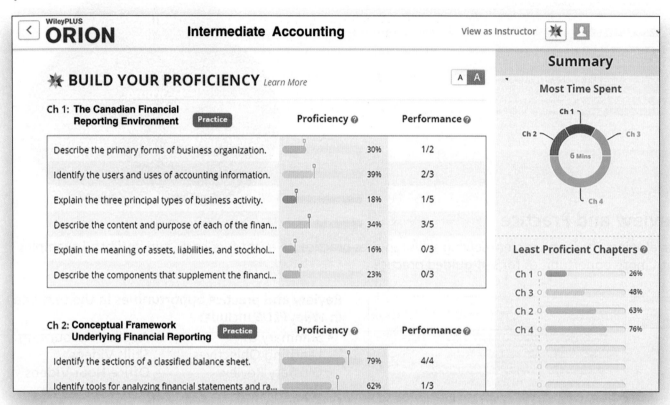

A little time with ORION goes a long way.

Based on usage data, students who engage in ORION adaptive practice—just a few minutes per week—get better outcomes. In fact, students who used ORION five or more times over the course of a semester reported the following results:

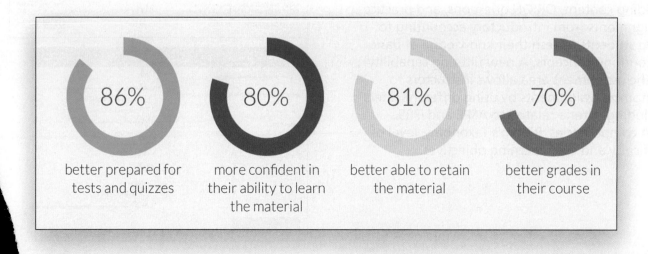

Streamlined Learning Objectives

Easy to follow learning objectives help students make the best use of their time outside of class. Each learning objective is addressed by reading content, watching educational videos, and answering a variety of practice questions, so that no matter where students begin their work, the relevant resources and practice are readily accessible. Learning objectives include references to the CPA competency map. This lets students know which of the CPA competencies they are mastering when they study a particular topic.

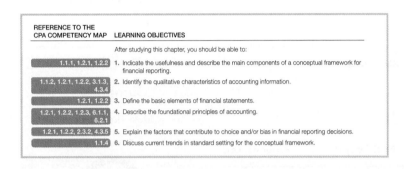

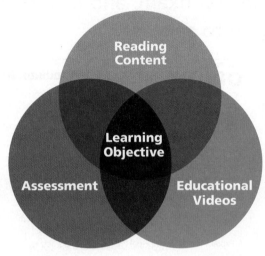

Review and Practice

Developing effective problem-solving skills requires practice, relevant feedback, and insightful examples with more opportunities for self-guided practice.

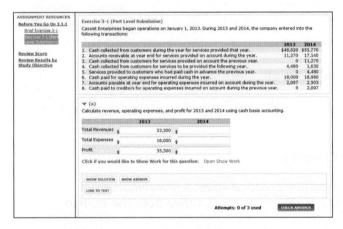

A new bridge course in *WileyPLUS* includes reading content, ORION questions, and practice assignments from introductory accounting to help students refresh their knowledge of basic accounting concepts. A new filtering capability in the assignment area allows instructors to customize assignments by using different filters including criteria related to ASPE and IFRS, CPA competencies, Bloom's Taxonomy, level of difficulty and even learning objectives.

Review and practice opportunities in the text and in *WileyPLUS* include:

- Summary of Learning Objectives
- Glossary Review
- Practice Exercises
- Demonstration Problems
- Applied Accounting Skills Videos
- Office Hour Videos Featuring Core Concept and Problem Walkthroughs

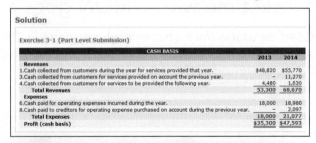

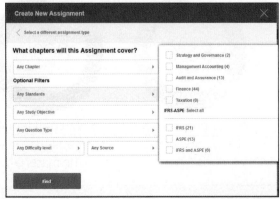

INTERMEDIATE ACCOUNTING

ELEVENTH CANADIAN EDITION

INTERMEDIATE ACCOUNTING

Donald E. Kieso, Ph.D., CPA
KPMG Peat Marwick Emeritus Professor of Accounting
Northern Illinois University
DeKalb, Illinois

Jerry J. Weygandt, Ph.D., CPA
Arthur Andersen Alumni Professor of Accounting
University of Wisconsin
Madison, Wisconsin

Terry D. Warfield, Ph.D.
PWC Professor in Accounting
University of Wisconsin
Madison, Wisconsin

Nicola M. Young, M.B.A., FCPA, FCA
Saint Mary's University
Halifax, Nova Scotia

Irene M. Wiecek, FCPA, FCA
University of Toronto
Toronto, Ontario

Bruce J. McConomy, Ph.D., CPA, CA
Wilfrid Laurier University
Waterloo, Ontario

Library and Archives Canada Cataloguing in Publication

Kieso, Donald E., author

Intermediate accounting / Donald E. Kieso, PhD, CPA (KPMG Peat Marwick Emeritus Professor of Accounting, Northern Illinois University, DeKalb, Illinois), Jerry J. Weygandt, PhD, CPA (Arthur Andersen Alumni Professor of Accounting, University of Wisconsin-Madison, Wisconsin), Terry D. Warfield, PhD (Associate Professor, University of Wisconsin-Madison, Wisconsin), Nicola M. Young, MBA, FCA (Saint Mary's University, Halifax, Nova Scotia), Irene M. Wiecek, FCPA, FCA (University of Toronto, Toronto, Ontario), Bruce J. McConomy, PhD, CPA, CA (Wilfrid Laurier University, Waterloo, Ontario). — Eleventh Canadian edition.

Includes bibliographical references and indexes.
ISBN 978-1-119-04853-4 (volume 1: bound).—ISBN 978-1-119-04854-1 (volume 2: bound)

1. Accounting—Textbooks. I. Weygandt, Jerry J., author II. Warfield, Terry D., author III. Young, Nicola M., author IV. Wiecek, Irene M., author V. McConomy, Bruce J. (Bruce Joseph), 1958-, author VI. Title.

HF5636.K54 2015   657'.044   C2015-906298-5

Production Credits
Executive Editor: Zoë Craig
Vice President and Director, Market Solutions: Veronica Visentin
Senior Marketing Manager: Anita Osborne
Editorial Manager: Karen Staudinger
Developmental Editor: Daleara Jamasji Hirjikaka
Media Editor: Luisa Begani
Assistant Editor: Ashley Patterson
Production and Media Specialist: Meaghan MacDonald
Typesetting: Aptara
Cover and Interior Design: Joanna Vierra
Cover Photo: Rolf Hicker/All Canada Photos/Getty
Printing and Binding: Quad Graphics

Dedicated to accounting educators in Canada
who, as mentors, are helping the next generation of accountants
develop ethical and integrative frameworks for decision-making.

About the Authors

Canadian Edition

Nicola (Nickie) M. Young, M.B.A., FCPA, FCA, is a Professor of Accounting in the Sobey School of Business at Saint Mary's University, with teaching responsibilities varying from introductory to advanced financial accounting courses to the survey course in the Executive M.B.A. program. She has received teaching awards, and has contributed to the life of the university through membership on the Board of Governors, and the Pension and other committees. Nickie was associated with the Atlantic School of Chartered Accountancy for over 25 years in roles varying from teaching to program development and reform. She has been active in the provincial and national accounting profession, including having served on boards of the CICA (now CPA Canada) dealing with licensure, education, and governance; and has been associated with the Canadian Public Sector Accounting Board and many of its related task forces for almost 25 years. She and Irene Wiecek co-authored the *IFRS Primer: International GAAP Basics* (Canadian and U.S. editions). Nickie is currently working on a phased retirement.

Irene M. Wiecek, FCPA, FCA, is an Associate Professor, Teaching Stream at the University of Toronto, where she is cross-appointed to the Joseph L. Rotman School of Management. She teaches financial reporting in various programs, including the Commerce Program (Accounting Specialist) and the CPA-accredited Master of Management & Professional Accounting Program (MMPA). The Associate Director of the MMPA Program for many years, she co-founded and is Director of the CPA/Rotman Centre for Innovation in Accounting Education, which supports and facilitates innovation in accounting education. Irene has been involved in professional accounting education for over 25 years, sitting on various provincial and national professional accounting organization committees as well as developing and directing the CICA IFRS Immersion Programs for practising accountants. She was appointed a member of the E&Y Academic Resource Center, where she helped to author a new IFRS curriculum for the Americas. In the area of standard setting, she has chaired the CAAA Financial Reporting Exposure Draft Response Committee and is currently a member of the IFRS Discussion Group (IDG). Irene co-authored the *IFRS Primer: International GAAP Basics* (Canadian and U.S. editions) and was the co-editor and contributor for the books *Leveraging Change—The New Pillars of Accounting Education* and *Educating Professionals: Ethics and Judgment in a Changing Learning Environment.* Currently, she co-authors the *Guide to IFRS in Canada* series, which is published by CPA Canada.

Bruce J. McConomy, Ph.D., CPA, CA, is a Professor of Accounting at Wilfrid Laurier University in Waterloo, Ontario. He was a Senior Audit Manager with Deloitte and Touche before returning to Queen's University to obtain his Ph.D. in accounting. Bruce has been the Director of the CPA/Laurier Centre for the Advancement of Accounting Research and Education since it was created in 2005, and is the CPA Ontario Professor of Accounting at Laurier. He has been teaching intermediate financial accounting since the mid-1990s to undergraduates, and since the start of Laurier's CPA Accredited CPA/M.B.A. program (and its predecessor the CMA/M.B.A.) to graduate students. He also teaches in Laurier's Ph.D. in Management program. Bruce has published articles in *Contemporary Accounting Research, Journal of Accounting, Auditing and Finance, Journal of Business, Finance and Accounting,* and *Accounting, Auditing & Accountability Journal.* He has also published cases in *Accounting Perspectives, Issues in Accounting Education,* and *Journal of Accounting Case Research.* Bruce was elected to and served on Council at the Institute of Chartered Accountants of Ontario from 2006 to 2010. Bruce is an Associate Editor of *Accounting Perspectives.*

U.S. Edition

Donald E. Kieso, Ph.D., CPA, received his bachelor's degree from Aurora University and his doctorate in accounting from the University of Illinois. He has served as chair of the Department of Accountancy and is currently the KPMG Emeritus Professor of Accountancy at Northern Illinois University. He has public accounting experience with Price Waterhouse & Co. (San Francisco and Chicago) and Arthur Andersen & Co. (Chicago) and research experience with the Research Division of the American Institute of Certified Public Accountants (New York). He has done post-doctorate work as a Visiting Scholar at the University of California at Berkeley and is a recipient of NIU's Teaching Excellence Award and four Golden Apple Teaching Awards. Professor Kieso is the author of other accounting and business books and is a member of the American Accounting Association, the American Institute of Certified Public Accountants, and the Illinois CPA Society. He is the recipient of the Outstanding Accounting Educator Award from the Illinois CPA Society, the FSA's Joseph A. Silvoso Award of Merit, the NIU Foundation's Humanitarian Award for Service to Higher Education, the Distinguished Service Award from the Illinois CPA Society, and in 2003 received an honorary doctorate from Aurora University.

Jerry J. Weygandt, Ph.D., CPA, is Arthur Andersen Alumni Professor of Accounting at the University of Wisconsin-Madison. He holds a Ph.D. in accounting from the University of Illinois. His articles have appeared in *Accounting Review, Journal of Accounting Research, Accounting Horizons, Journal of Accountancy,* and other academic and professional journals. Professor Weygandt is the author of other accounting and financial reporting books and is a member of the American Accounting Association, the American Institute of Certified Public Accountants, and the Wisconsin Society of Certified Public Accountants. He has been actively involved with the American Institute of Certified Public Accountants and has been a member of the Accounting Standards Executive Committee (AcSEC) of that organization. He also served on the FASB task force that examined the reporting issues related to accounting for income taxes. He is the recipient of the Wisconsin Institute of CPAs' Outstanding Educator's Award and the Lifetime Achievement Award. In 2001, he received the American Accounting Association's Outstanding Accounting Educator Award.

Terry D. Warfield, Ph.D., is the PWC Professor in Accounting at the University of Wisconsin-Madison. He received a B.S. and M.B.A. from Indiana University and a Ph.D. in accounting from the University of Iowa. Professor Warfield's area of expertise is financial reporting, and prior to his academic career, he worked for five years in the banking industry. He served as the Academic Accounting Fellow in the Office of the Chief Accountant at the U.S. Securities and Exchange Commission in Washington, D.C., from 1995–1996. Professor Warfield's primary research interests concern financial accounting standards and disclosure policies. He has published scholarly articles in *The Accounting Review, Journal of Accounting and Economics, Research in Accounting Regulation,* and *Accounting Horizons,* and he has served on the editorial boards of *The Accounting Review, Accounting Horizons,* and *Issues in Accounting Education.* Professor Warfield has served on the Financial Accounting Standards Committee of the American Accounting Association (Chair 1995–1996) and the AAA-FASB Research Conference Committee. He currently serves on the Financial Accounting Standards Advisory Council of the Financial Accounting Standards Board. Professor Warfield has received teaching awards at both the University of Iowa and the University of Wisconsin, and he was named to the Teaching Academy at the University of Wisconsin in 1995. Professor Warfield has developed and published several case studies based on his research for use in accounting classes. These cases have been selected for the AICPA Professor-Practitioner Case Development Program and have been published in *Issues in Accounting Education.*

Preface

In the last decade, we have come through a period of unprecedented change in accounting standards. More recently, in Canada, we have witnessed the evolution of the accounting profession from three main accounting bodies (representing Chartered Accountants, Certified Management Accountants, and Certified General Accountants) into one unified group: Chartered Professional Accountants Canada (CPA Canada). We now have a freshly minted CPA education program, a new CPA Competency Map (CM), a new CPA Knowledge Supplement (KS), and new CPA Common Final Examinations. Many of us have remapped our curricula to the CPA CM and created new courses and programs (some of which have been accredited by the CPA profession). The pace of change for standard setting and related educational requirements for professional accountants sometimes seems staggering! Change has become the new norm for us and things don't seem to be slowing down.

This state of flux has made many of us rethink our learning environments. Some fundamental questions are being revisited. How can we and our students keep up with the changing standards? What does it mean to be a competent accountant? How much do we emphasize the use of technology as a learning platform? And finally, how does what we do fit with the changing professional landscape?

From our perspective, we see the need for

- increased emphasis on helping faculty and students understand how to cope with changes in standards,

- a broadened perspective on what it means to be competent,

- increased use of a variety of technologies to promote learning, and

- renewed acknowledgement that what we do in our classrooms is only part of the journey that students embark on to become professional accountants.

In our roles as educators, many of us increasingly see ourselves as facilitators as opposed to purveyors of knowledge. At the heart of things, we still want to produce good, ethical decision-makers as well as to encourage thoughtfulness and reflection. We also want our graduates to be competent and skilled. Our students have to at least begin to master our complex body of knowledge and also to be competent in applying it. This is a lot to ask, especially when things keep shifting.

This edition is about learning to live with a constantly changing body of knowledge. To this end, we have incorporated new accounting standards where the standards have already been issued (even if they are not yet mandatory). In addition, we have included the "Looking Ahead" section again at the end of each chapter, which signals changes in accounting standards coming down the pipe. We are committed to helping our accounting faculty and students steer their way through standards changes that are issued between editions of this text. To this end, we will continue to issue supplements and updates between editions as we have done for the past few years.

This edition is also about integration along the following dimensions:

- integration of financial reporting with other areas (such as assurance and finance);

- integration of our learning environments and frameworks with those of the accounting profession, including a competency-based framework; and

- increased integration with a learning environment that features technology, including *WileyPLUS* and our new Office Hour Videos.

We have also included charts showing how the textbook integrates with the CPA Competency Map and Knowledge Supplement throughout the text and within *WileyPLUS*. This is discussed in the New Features section that follows. We encourage you to have a quick look. Below is a brief overview that highlights our new and continuing features.

New Features

As noted above, several new features have been added to this edition.

Emphasis on Integration with Related Areas

We have included integration icons in each chapter to help identify key areas of integration (in addition to our existing finance and law icons). Many of our end-of-chapter questions have an integration aspect. For those problems that most directly focus on integration, we also include integration icons so that they are easily identified. We have added an Office Hour Video feature, which provides a short video discussion of selected end-of-chapter questions per chapter, and an additional integration-related topic in most chapters.

Augmented End-of-Chapter Material

End-of-chapter material has been expanded to include questions that provide students with Excel spreadsheets to help them prepare solutions. We also continued our emphasis on having students evaluate the differences in solutions prepared using IFRS versus ASPE. Our new Office Hour Video feature provides a short walkthrough of select questions and solutions.

CPA Competency Map Integration

At the start of each chapter, we now provide a chart linking that chapter's Learning Objectives with the related requirements of the CPA Competency Map. This information will help students planning to obtain their Advanced Certificate in Accounting and Finance (ACAF) or write the Common Final Evaluation (CFE) to link the coverage of intermediate accounting topics to the CPA educational requirements. We have also mapped the content of the book against the Competency Map and Knowledge Supplement. These appear on the inside front cover of the text. In addition, the material in *WileyPLUS* has been more comprehensively mapped.

Task-Based Simulations

We have added a new type of question to our end-of-chapter material that is in a format similar to questions used in the CPA Professional Education program. Task-Based Simulations after Chapters 5, 9, 12, 15, 17, and 23 combine material from the current chapter with previous chapters and present it in this new hands-on format. This allows students to become familiar with the new exam format while getting a sense of how the various concepts fit together.

Continuing Features

Many features have contributed to the success of this textbook over the years. The following points outline just a few.

Emphasis on Business

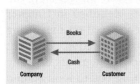

The focus of the feature story that starts each chapter in this edition is on the business models of various companies and industries, along with accounting issues that affect them. The first section of most chapters focuses on **Understanding the Business**, which introduces the accounting topic in the context of everyday business. Many chapters have a **business transactions example box**. In most business transactions, you give something up and receive something. These boxes are meant to help you understand what has been given up and what has been received in the transaction. This is tremendously helpful when you are trying to decide how to account for a transaction or economic event.

Emphasis on IFRS and ASPE

Icons: Individual IFRS and ASPE icons call attention to items treated differently by the two sets of standards. The joint IFRS-ASPE icon indicates a direct comparison between the two approaches.

Side-by-side journal entries: These journal entries illustrate differences in treatment between IFRS and ASPE.

Enhanced comparison charts: The end-of-chapter charts that identify the major differences between IFRS and ASPE include a column with cross-references to relevant illustrations and brief exercises that describe the differences outlined in the comparison chart. As before, where there is a new standard being proposed, we have added a column to the end-of-chapter charts so that you understand what may be in store in the near future, or provided a discussion within the chapter's Looking Ahead feature to alert you to upcoming changes expected.

Emphasis on Professional and Ethical Behaviour

ETHICS

Rather than featuring ethics coverage and problem material in isolation, we use an ethics icon to highlight ethical issues as they are discussed within each chapter. This icon also appears beside exercises, problems, or cases where ethical issues must be dealt with in relation to all kinds of accounting situations.

Emphasis on Readability

The readability of the text has been improved by using fewer abbreviations, plainer language, shorter sentences, numbered lists, and clearer headings. An **end-of-book glossary** provides definitions of key terms highlighted in the text. **Alternative Terminology** notes within the chapter familiarize students with other commonly used terms.

Grounding in Accounting Research and Theory

THEORY

We have always emphasized concepts and principles, including those that span other disciplines, such as law and finance. In addition to this, the **Accounting Theory** icon calls attention to accounting theory that underpins much of the accounting body of knowledge, introducing students to an accounting research perspective.

Real World Emphasis

REAL WORLD EMPHASIS

Because intermediate accounting is a course in which students must understand the application of accounting principles and techniques in practice, we strive to include as many real-world examples as possible.

Reinforcement of the Concepts

WHAT DO THE NUMBERS MEAN?

UNDERLYING CONCEPT

Throughout each chapter, you are asked What Do the Numbers Mean? and are presented with discussions applying accounting concepts to business contexts. This feature builds on the opening feature stories in making the accounting concepts relevant to you. Through current examples of how accounting is applied, you will be better able to relate to and understand the material. The underlying concepts icons in each chapter alert you to remember that the issue under discussion draws on concepts identified in Chapter 2 as part of the conceptual framework. More emphasis has been placed on measuring fair values using the new IFRS 13 standard. In addition, an Analysis section is present in most chapters. This section discusses the effect on the financial statements of many of the accounting choices made by corporate management, alerting you to look behind the numbers. Finally, the accounting equation appears in the margin next to key journal entries to help you understand the impact of each transaction on the company's financial position and cash flows.

Helping Students Practise

The end-of-chapter material is comprehensive. Brief exercises, exercises, and problems focus on quantitative material. Case material allows you to analyze business transactions and apply both IFRS and ASPE, with particular attention to integration being provided by Integrated Case questions. Research and Analysis questions allow you to explore the nature of GAAP differences and understand how different accounting standard setters can arrive at different solutions in terms of standards.

A summary of the Case Primer guiding you through the case study method appears inside the back cover of this text. This is in addition to the full Case Study Primer available on *WileyPLUS* and the Student Website.

Analysis doesn't have to be just part of the cases. Our Digging Deeper feature asks you to look more closely at the results you obtain in the problems and exercises. For instance, you might be asked to comment on results or determine how things might be different if one of the original variables were to change. Digging Deeper questions are identified using the icon shown here.

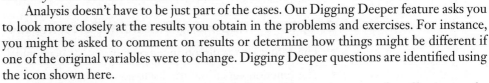

WileyPLUS is an innovative, research-based on-line environment for effective teaching and learning. *WileyPLUS* builds students' confidence because it takes the guesswork out of studying by providing students with a clear roadmap: **what to do, how to do it, and if they did it right**. Students will take more initiative so you'll have a greater impact on their achievement in the classroom and beyond.

Among its many features, this on-line learning interface allows students to study and practise using the digital textbook, quizzes, and algorithmic exercises. The immediate feedback helps students understand where they need to focus their study efforts. We have standardized the chart of accounts to reduce complexity and to facilitate on-line practice.

Based on cognitive science, **WileyPLUS with Orion** is a personalized adaptive learning experience that gives students the practice they need to build proficiency on topics while using their study time more effectively. The adaptive engine is powered by hundreds of unique questions per chapter, giving students endless opportunities for practice throughout the course. Orion is available with this text.

Currency and Accuracy

As in past editions, we have endeavoured to make this edition the most current and accurate text available. Everywhere there has been a significant change in the accounting standard or how it is applied, it has been highlighted with a significant change icon. Where change is on the horizon, we have noted this at the end of each chapter under the Looking Ahead section. We are also committed to issuing brief update supplements on *WileyPLUS* when new standards are issued.

The following list outlines the revisions and improvements made to the chapters in Volume One of this text.

Chapter 2   Conceptual Framework Underlying Financial Reporting

- The revenue recognition principle has been updated to incorporate IFRS 15.

- New information has been added on common forms of business including those for professionals.

- A section on how the concept of materiality is used in audits has been added.

- The material on measurement has been moved from the appendix to Chapter 3.

- The Looking Ahead feature gives a brief update on the impact of proposed changes to the conceptual framework and the June 2014 IASB Exposure Draft entitled the "Disclosure Initiative (Proposed amendments to IAS 1)."

Chapter 3   The Accounting Information System and Measurement Issues

- The revised chapter has been split into two parts plus appendices for ease of use and flexibility.

- The start of this chapter continues to provide students with an overview and review of accounting transactions, journal entries, and other aspects of the accounting cycle. For instructors who like to emphasize a 10-column work sheet approach to assist with financial statement presentation, this material is now in the self-contained Appendix 3A.

- A new section (Part II) has been developed for this chapter emphasizing measurement issues. This section covers valuation techniques, how to calculate value in use, and measuring fair value under IFRS 13.

- A new appendix has been added on present value techniques. Appendix 3B illustrates how to perform present value calculations using formulas, tables, financial calculators, and spreadsheets.

Chapter 4   Reporting Financial Performance

- The definition for discontinued operations has been updated.

- The function versus nature discussion has been streamlined and examples given, illustrating the fact that many companies use a mixed approach.

- The example and discussion relating to the statement of changes in shareholders' equity has been updated.

- Material on calculating a price/earnings ratio has been added.

Chapter 5   Financial Position and Cash Flows

- More emphasis has been placed on presentation under IFRS. (For instance, there are more examples of Canadian companies using IFRS.)

- A detailed discussion has been added in the Looking Ahead section of the impact of proposed changes to the conceptual framework and the June 2014 IASB Exposure Draft entitled the "Disclosure Initiative (Proposed amendments to IAS 1)."

Chapter 6   Revenue Recognition

- The chapter has been rewritten to incorporate IFRS 15 *Revenue from Contracts with Customers*. The chapter includes more detailed discussions of how to identify performance obligations, how to measure them, and when to recognize revenues. Select material on the earnings approach under ASPE has been retained.

- The discussion on accounting for long-term contracts has been moved to an appendix.

- The chapter includes more detailed discussion on specific items, such as rights of returns, repurchase agreements, principal and agent, and warranties.

- Summaries have been added, which capture the new 5-step revenue recognition process as well as other more complex revenue recognition issues.

Chapter 7   Cash and Receivables

- There is more focus on the requirements of IFRS 9 and a reduced emphasis on IAS 39 for areas such as impairment, as the IASB continues to move toward a forward-looking impairment model.

- A discussion has been added of the IFRS standards on derecognition of financial assets, which are now complete. A brief discussion of the likely impact of the IFRS changes for companies following ASPE has also been added.

Chapter 8   Inventory

- The chapter has been refreshed and streamlined, including updating for an interface with Chapter 6 and IFRS 15.

- The section on biological assets has been updated to introduce the concept of bearer biological assets.

Chapter 9 Investments

- The chapter has been rewritten to incorporate changes to IFRS 9 *Financial Instruments*. Select references to IAS 39 have been retained but de-emphasized.

- Material has been added to deal with FV-OCI accounting for debt instruments (with recycling).

- The section on impairments has been updated and augmented as it relates to the expected loss model. Numerical examples and a decision tree have been added.

- Additional information has been included regarding disclosure requirements.

Chapter 10 Property, Plant, and Equipment: Accounting Model Basics

- A more detailed discussion of the full cost and successful efforts methods of accounting for natural resource properties is now included.

- Appendix 10B—Revaluation: The Proportionate Method has been expanded to provide more details of the calculations behind the numerical example of this method.

- The chapter and Looking Ahead section discuss a change to IAS 16 regarding accounting for *Agriculture: Bearer Plants*, effective for annual periods beginning on or after January 1, 2016.

Chapter 11 Depreciation, Impairment, and Disposition

- The chapter and Looking Ahead section discuss a change to IAS 16 regarding restrictions on the use of depreciation methods based on revenue generated by companies.

- Changes to disclosure requirements for impairment of assets under IAS 36 are discussed. (The changes became effective on January 1, 2014, and tie in to new requirements for the fair value hierarchy under IFRS 13.)

Chapter 12 Intangible Assets and Goodwill

- The chapter and Looking Ahead section discuss a change to IAS 38 regarding additional items that could indicate commercial or technological obsolescence.

- New (and updated) examples have been provided, including a discussion of challenges faced by companies as set out in a recent Financial Executives Institute Goodwill Impairment Study.

Special Student Supplements

The *Study Guide to Accompany Intermediate Accounting*, Eleventh Canadian Edition, provides a solid review of the concepts presented in the intermediate accounting course, and gives students strategies for dealing with the complexities of applying those concepts. The following are included in this guide to help you make your way through each chapter.

To Help Gain a Solid Understanding of the Concepts

- A chapter **Overview** introduces the reader to the topics covered and their importance.

- **Study Steps** review the business transaction under discussion; show how to recognize, measure, and disclose issues related to that transaction; and demonstrate how to then make the appropriate calculations and apply the appropriate accounting methods.

- **Tips** alert learners to common pitfalls and misconceptions and to remind students of important terminology, concepts, and relationships.

- A **Toolkit** printed on cards can be detached from the guide and referred to throughout the course. These cards present material such as a review of the conceptual triangle from the book, a glossary of definitions, and summary of key ratios.

To Aid in Applying Concepts Successfully

- **Exercises and Multiple-Choice Questions** allow students to practise using material that is representative of homework assignments and exam questions they are likely to encounter.

- **Purposes** identify the essence of each exercise or question and link it to the text material.

- **Solutions** show students the appropriate worked-out solutions for each exercise and multiple-choice question.

- **Explanations** give users the details of how selected solutions were derived and explain why things are done as shown.

- **Approaches** coach students on the particular model, computational format, or other strategy to be used to solve particular problems.

The Intermediate Accounting Simulation Practice Set by Fred Pries will help students see how the individual topics they study in intermediate accounting are related to the accounting systems of an organization and to the financial statements as a whole. Students play the role of a newly hired accountant for Woodlawn Engineering, an owner-managed company, and prepare a full set of financial statements starting from an unadjusted trial balance. Each module of the simulation is linked to a particular topic covered in the intermediate accounting course and introduces new information. Students analyze this information, recommend what adjustments are needed to the books and financial statements of the company, and write reports to the chief financial officer explaining the basis for their recommendations.

Canadian Financial Accounting Cases by Camillo Lento and Jo-Anne Ryan provides additional cases at the intermediate level that may be used either for assignment purposes or for in-class discussion. The cases are keyed to various topics covered by the two volumes of *Intermediate Accounting* and have been developed using IFRS and ASPE.

Acknowledgements

We thank the users of our tenth edition, including the many instructors, faculty, and students who contributed to this revision through their comments and instructive criticism.

Appreciation is also extended to colleagues at the University of Toronto and the Lazaridis School of Business and Economics, Wilfrid Laurier University, who provided input, suggestions, and support, especially Peter Thomas, for his professionalism and wisdom.

It takes many people and coordinated efforts to get an edition off the ground. Many thanks to the team at John Wiley & Sons Canada, Ltd., who are superb: Zoë Craig, Executive Editor; Daleara Hirjikaka, Developmental Editor; Veronica Visentin, V.P. and Director, Market Solutions; Karen Staudinger, Editorial Manager, who has been an integral part of the last six editions; Luisa Begani, Media Editor, for managing this increasingly important aspect of the text; Deanna Durnford, Supplements Coordinator; Anita Osborne, Senior Marketing Manager; Kaitlyn Sykes, Editorial Intern; and Sara Veltkamp, Kristen Vanderkooy, and Duncan Moore, Digital Solutions Managers. Their enthusiasm and support have been invaluable. The editorial contributions of Laurel Hyatt, Zofia Laubitz, Merrie-Ellen Wilcox, and Belle Wong are also very much appreciated.

We are grateful to Peter Alpaugh, Robert Collier, Catherine Duffy, Peter Martin, Carrie McMillan, and Don Smith for reviewing selected chapters of the text.

We are particularly grateful to Sandra Daga, Cécile Laurin, Camillo Lento, Marisa Moriello, Sandra Scott, Laura Simeoni, and Heather Sceles for all their help with the end-of-chapter material and solutions. Thanks also go to Darrin Ambrose, Ann-Marie Cederholm, Laura Cumming, Angela Davis, Amy Hoggard, Debra Lee Hue, Mark Magee, Lisa Ricci, Ouafa Sakka, Joel Shapiro, Marie Sinnot, Ruth Ann Strickland, and Ralph Tassone, who contributed so much to the related supplements.

We thank CPA Canada and the IFRS Foundation for allowing us to quote from their materials and Brookfield Asset Management for permitting us to use its 2014 financial statements for our specimen financial statements.

We appreciate the opportunity to reach out to so many colleagues and students through this book. Your conversations and input have greatly helped shape the book and make it all it can be. We are thankful to be part of a group of such dedicated educators! Let's keep the conversation going.

Suggestions and comments are always appreciated. We have striven to produce an error-free text, but if anything has slipped through the variety of checks undertaken, please let us know so that corrections can be made to subsequent printings.

Irene M. Wiecek
TORONTO, ONTARIO
wiecek@rotman.utoronto.ca

Bruce McConomy
WATERLOO, ONTARIO
bmcconomy@wlu.ca

November 2015

Brief Contents

VOLUME ONE

CHAPTER 1
The Canadian Financial Reporting Environment

CHAPTER 2
Conceptual Framework Underlying Financial Reporting

CHAPTER 3
The Accounting Information System

CHAPTER 4
Reporting Financial Performance

CHAPTER 5
Financial Position and Cash Flows

CHAPTER 6
Revenue Recognition

CHAPTER 7
Cash and Receivables

CHAPTER 8
Inventory

CHAPTER 9
Investments

CHAPTER 10
Property, Plant, and Equipment: Accounting Model Basics

CHAPTER 11
Depreciation, Impairment, and Disposition

CHAPTER 12
Intangible Assets and Goodwill

SPECIMEN FINANCIAL STATEMENTS
Brookfield Asset Management

TABLES

VOLUME TWO

CHAPTER 13
Non-Financial and Current Liabilities

CHAPTER 14
Long-Term Financial Liabilities

CHAPTER 15
Shareholders' Equity

CHAPTER 16
Complex Financial Instruments

CHAPTER 17
Earnings Per Share

CHAPTER 18
Income Taxes

CHAPTER 19
Pensions and Other Employee Future Benefits

CHAPTER 20
Leases

CHAPTER 21
Accounting Changes and Error Analysis

CHAPTER 22
Statement of Cash Flows

CHAPTER 23
Other Measurement and Disclosure Issues

SPECIMEN FINANCIAL STATEMENTS
Brookfield Asset Management

TABLES

Contents

CHAPTER 1 The Canadian Financial Reporting Environment p. 2

FINANCIAL STATEMENTS AND
FINANCIAL REPORTING **p. 3**
Accounting and Capital Allocation p. 4
Stakeholders p. 5
Objective of Financial Reporting p. 8
Information Asymmetry p. 9

STANDARD SETTING **p. 11**
Need for Standards p. 11
Parties Involved in Standard Setting p. 12

GENERALLY ACCEPTED
ACCOUNTING PRINCIPLES **p 16**
GAAP Hierarchy p. 16
Professional Judgement p. 17

CHALLENGES AND OPPORTUNITIES FOR
THE ACCOUNTING PROFESSION **p. 18**
Oversight in the Capital Marketplace p. 18
Centrality of Ethics p. 19
Standard Setting in a Political
Environment p. 20
Principles versus Rules p. 21
Impact of Technology p. 22
Integrated Reporting p. 22
Conclusion p. 23

CHAPTER 2 Conceptual Framework Underlying Financial Reporting p. 34

CONCEPTUAL FRAMEWORK **p. 35**
Rationale for Conceptual Framework p. 35
Development of the Conceptual Framework p. 36
Information Asymmetry Revisited p. 37

OBJECTIVE OF FINANCIAL REPORTING **p. 37**
Qualitative Characteristics of Useful
Information p. 37
Elements of Financial Statements p. 43

FOUNDATIONAL PRINCIPLES **p. 45**
Recognition/Derecognition p. 46
Measurement p. 50
Presentation and Disclosure p. 55

FINANCIAL REPORTING ISSUES **p. 57**
Principles-Based Approach p. 57
Financial Engineering p. 58
Fraudulent Financial Reporting p. 58

IFRS/ASPE COMPARISON **p. 59**
Looking Ahead p. 60

CHAPTER 3 The Accounting Information System and Measurement Issues p. 76

ACCOUNTING INFORMATION SYSTEM **p. 78**
Basic Terminology and Double-Entry
Rules p. 78
Accounting Equation p. 79

THE ACCOUNTING CYCLE AND THE
RECORDING PROCESS **p. 80**
Identifying and Recording Transactions
and Other Events p. 80
Journalizing p. 81
Posting p. 82
Trial Balance p. 83
Adjusting Entries p. 84

FINANCIAL STATEMENTS AND OWNERSHIP
STRUCTURE **p. 93**

THE CLOSING PROCESS **p. 94**
Preparing Closing Entries p. 94
Reversing Entries p. 96

MEASURING FINANCIAL STATEMENT
ELEMENTS **p. 97**
Valuation Techniques p. 98
Value in Use Measurements p. 101
Measuring Fair Value Using IFRS 13 p. 102

IFRS/ASPE COMPARISON **p. 104**
A Comparison of IFRS and ASPE p. 104
Looking Ahead p. 105

APPENDIX 3A—USING A WORK SHEET **p. 107**
Adjustments Entered on the Work
Sheet p. 107
Work Sheet Columns p. 108
Completing the Work Sheet p. 108
Preparing Financial Statements from a
Work Sheet p. 110

APPENDIX 3B—PRESENT VALUE
CONCEPTS **p. 113**
The Nature of Interest p. 113
Fundamental Variables in Present
Value Calculations p. 113
Different Ways to Perform the Calculations p. 115
Some Additional Calculations p. 122

CHAPTER 4   Reporting Financial Performance   p. 148

PERFORMANCE   **p. 150**
Business Models and Industries   p. 150
Communicating Information about
Performance   p. 153
Quality of Earnings/Information   p. 153

THE STATEMENT OF INCOME AND
THE STATEMENT OF COMPREHENSIVE
INCOME   **p. 156**
Measurement   p. 156
Discontinued Operations   p. 158
Presentation   p. 162

THE STATEMENT OF RETAINED EARNINGS AND
THE STATEMENT OF CHANGES IN EQUITY   **p. 173**
Presentation of the Statement of
Retained Earnings   p. 173
Presentation of the Statement of
Changes in Equity   p. 174

DISCLOSURE AND ANALYSIS   **p. 176**
Disclosures   p. 176
Analysis   p. 176
Non-GAAP Measures   p. 177
Other Key Measures   p. 177

IFRS/ASPE COMPARISON   **p. 178**
A Comparison of IFRS and ASPE   p. 178
Looking Ahead   p. 179

APPENDIX 4A—CASH BASIS VERSUS ACCRUAL
BASIS EARNINGS   **p. 181**
Differences Between Cash and Accrual Bases   p. 181
Conversion from Cash Basis to Accrual Basis   p. 182
Theoretical Weaknesses of the Cash Basis   p. 185

CHAPTER 5   Financial Position and Cash Flows   p. 208

USEFULNESS OF THE STATEMENTS OF FINANCIAL
POSITION AND CASH FLOWS FROM A BUSINESS
PERSPECTIVE   **p. 210**
Analyzing a Statement of Financial Position   p. 210
Assessing Earnings Quality   p. 210
Assessing the Creditworthiness of
Companies   p. 210

STATEMENT OF FINANCIAL POSITION   **p. 211**
Usefulness and Limitations of the Statement
of Financial Position   p. 211
Classification in the Statement
of Financial Position   p. 213
Preparation of the Classified Statement
of Financial Position (Balance Sheet)   p. 216
Additional Information Reported   p. 226
Techniques of Disclosure   p. 228

STATEMENT OF CASH FLOWS   **p. 230**
Purpose, Content, and Format of a
Statement of Cash Flows   p. 230
Preparation of the Statement of Cash Flows   p. 232
Usefulness of the Statement of Cash Flows   p. 235
Perspectives   p. 237

IFRS/ASPE COMPARISON   **p. 239**
A Comparison of IFRS and ASPE   p. 239
Looking Ahead   p. 240

APPENDIX 5A—RATIO ANALYSIS:
A REFERENCE   **p. 242**
Business Risks   p. 242
Financial Ratios   p. 243
Cumulative Coverage and Task-Based
Simulation: Chapters 3 to 5

CHAPTER 6   Revenue Recognition   p. 272

UNDERSTANDING THE NATURE OF
SALES TRANSACTIONS FROM A
BUSINESS PERSPECTIVE   **p. 274**
Economics of Sales Transactions   p. 274
Legalities of Sales Transactions   p. 278
Information for Decision-Making   p. 279

RECOGNITION AND MEASUREMENT   **p. 280**
Asset-Liability Approach   p. 280
Five-Step Revenue Recognition
Process—Example   p. 281
Identifying the Contract with
Customers—Step 1   p. 282
Identifying Separate Performance
Obligations—Step 2   p. 283
Determining the Transaction Price—Step 3   p. 285
Allocating the Transaction Price to Separate
Performance Obligations—Step 4   p. 289
Recognizing Revenue When (or as) Each
Performance Obligation is
Satisfied—Step 5   p. 291
Summary of the Five-Step Revenue
Recognition Process   p. 292
Earnings Approach   p. 293

OTHER REVENUE RECOGNITION ISSUES   **p. 295**
Right of Return   p. 295
Repurchase Agreements   p. 296
Bill-and-Hold Arrangements   p. 298
Principal-Agent Relationships   p. 298
Consignments   p. 300
Warranties   p. 300
Non-refundable Upfront Fees   p. 302
Summary of Other Revenue Recognition
Issues   p. 302

PRESENTATION AND DISCLOSURE   **p. 304**
Presentation   p. 304
Disclosure   p. 306

IFRS/ASPE Comparison   p. 307
A Comparison of IFRS and ASPE   p. 307
Looking Ahead   p. 309

Appendix 6A—Long-Term Contracts   p. 310
Percentage-of-Completion Method   p. 311
Completed-Contract Method   p. 315

CHAPTER 7   Cash and Receivables   p. 338

**Understanding Cash and
Accounts Receivable   p. 340**
How Do Companies Manage and Control Cash?   p. 340
What Types of Companies Have
Extensive Accounts Receivable?   p. 340
What Are the Types of Accounts Receivable?   p. 341
How Do Companies Manage Accounts
Receivable?   p. 341

Cash Recognition and Measurement   p. 342
What Is Cash?   p. 342
Reporting Cash   p. 343
Summary of Cash-Related Items   p. 345

**Receivables—Recognition and
Measurement   p. 345**
Definition and Types   p. 346
Recognition and Measurement of
Accounts Receivable   p. 347
Impairment of Accounts Receivable   p. 350
Recognition and Measurement of
Short-Term Notes and Loans Receivable   p. 356
Recognition and Measurement of
Long-Term Notes and Loans Receivable   p. 357
Derecognition of Receivables   p. 364

**Presentation, Disclosure, and
Analysis of Receivables   p. 371**
Presentation and Disclosure   p. 371
Analysis   p. 373

IFRS/ASPE Comparison   p. 374
A Comparison of IFRS and ASPE   p. 374
Looking Ahead   p. 375

Appendix 7A—Cash Controls   p. 378
Management and Control of Cash   p. 378
Using Bank Accounts   p. 378
The Imprest Petty Cash System   p. 379
Physical Protection of Cash Balances   p. 380
Reconciliation of Bank Balances   p. 380

CHAPTER 8   Inventory   p. 408

Understanding Inventory   p. 410
What Types of Companies Have Inventory?   p. 410
Inventory Categories   p. 410
Inventory Planning and Control   p. 410
Information for Decision-Making   p. 411

Recognition   p. 412
Accounting Definition of Inventory   p. 413
Physical Goods Included in Inventory   p. 413
Inventory Errors   p. 419

Measurement   p. 421
Costs Included in Inventory   p. 421
Inventory Accounting Systems   p. 426
Cost Formulas   p. 428
Lower of Cost and Net Realizable Value   p. 434
Exceptions to Lower of Cost and Net Realizable
Value Model   p. 438
Estimating Inventory   p. 442

Presentation, Disclosure, and Analysis   p. 444
Presentation and Disclosure of Inventories   p. 444
Analysis   p. 446

IFRS/ASPE Comparison   p. 446
A Comparison of IFRS and ASPE   p. 446
Looking Ahead   p. 448

**Appendix 8A—The Retail Inventory Method
of Estimating Inventory Cost   p. 450**
Retail Method Terminology   p. 451
Retail Inventory Method with Markups
and Markdowns—Conventional Method   p. 452
Special Items   p. 454
Evaluation of Retail Inventory Method   p. 455

**Appendix 8B—Accounting Guidance for
Specific Inventory   p. 456**

CHAPTER 9   Investments   p. 484

Understanding Investments   p. 486
Types of Investments   p. 486
Types of Companies That Have Investments   p. 487
Information for Decision-Making   p. 488

Measurement   p. 489
Cost/Amortized Cost Model   p. 490
Fair Value through Net Income (FV-NI) Model   p. 495
Fair Value through Other Comprehensive
Income (FV-OCI) Model   p. 500
Impairment Models   p. 507

Strategic Investments   p. 511
Investments in Associates   p. 512
Investments in Subsidiaries   p. 517

Presentation, Disclosure, and Analysis   p. 518
Presentation and Disclosure   p. 518
Analysis   p. 523

IFRS/ASPE Comparison   p. 524
A Comparison of IFRS and ASPE   p. 524
Looking Ahead   p. 526
Cumulative Coverage and Task-Based
Simulation: Chapters 6 to 9   p. 553

CHAPTER 10 Property, Plant, and Equipment: Accounting Model Basics p. 556

DEFINITION AND RECOGNITION OF PROPERTY, PLANT, AND EQUIPMENT p. 557
Property, Plant, and Equipment—Business Perspective p. 557
Property, Plant, and Equipment—Characteristics p. 558

COST ELEMENTS p. 560
Self-Constructed Assets p. 561
Borrowing Costs p. 561
Dismantling and Restoration Costs p. 562

MEASUREMENT OF COST p. 563
Determining Asset Cost when Cash is Not Exchanged at Acquisition p. 563
Costs Associated with Specific Assets p. 572

MEASUREMENT AFTER ACQUISITION p. 574
Cost and Revaluation Models p. 575
Fair Value Model p. 578
Costs Incurred after Acquisition p. 580

IFRS/ASPE COMPARISON p. 585
A Comparison of IFRS and ASPE p. 585
Looking Ahead p. 587

APPENDIX 10A—CAPITALIZATION OF BORROWING COSTS p. 590
Qualifying Assets p. 590
Capitalization Period p. 590
Avoidable Borrowing Costs p. 591
Disclosures p. 595

APPENDIX 10B—REVALUATION: THE PROPORTIONATE METHOD p. 596

CHAPTER 11 Depreciation, Impairment, and Disposition p. 626

THE IMPORTANCE OF DEPRECIATION, IMPAIRMENT, AND DISPOSITION FROM A BUSINESS PERSPECTIVE p. 628

DEPRECIATION—A METHOD OF ALLOCATION p. 628
Factors Considered in the Depreciation Process p. 629
Depreciation—Methods of Allocation and Calculation p. 631
Depletion of Mineral Resources p. 636
Other Depreciation Issues p. 638

IMPAIRMENT p. 641
Indicators of Impairment p. 642
Impairment—Recognition and Measurement Models p. 642
Asset Groups and Cash-Generating Units p. 646

HELD FOR SALE AND DERECOGNITION p. 648
Long-Lived Assets to Be Disposed of by Sale p. 648
Derecognition p. 649

PRESENTATION, DISCLOSURE, AND ANALYSIS p. 651
Presentation and Disclosure p. 651
Analysis p. 653

IFRS/ASPE COMPARISON p. 655
A Comparison of IFRS and ASPE p. 655
Looking Ahead p. 657

APPENDIX 11A—DEPRECIATION AND INCOME TAX p. 659
Capital Cost Allowance Method p. 659

CHAPTER 12 Intangible Assets and Goodwill p. 692

THE BUSINESS IMPORTANCE AND CHARACTERISTICS OF GOODWILL AND INTANGIBLE ASSETS p. 694
Characteristics of Goodwill p. 694
Characteristics of Intangible Assets p. 695

RECOGNITION AND MEASUREMENT OF INTANGIBLE ASSETS p. 696
Recognition and Measurement at Acquisition p. 696
Recognition and Measurement of Internally Developed Intangible Assets p. 698
Recognition and Measurement after Acquisition p. 701
Specific Intangibles p. 704

IMPAIRMENT AND DERECOGNITION p. 708
Impairment of Limited-Life Intangibles p. 708
Impairment of Indefinite-Life Intangibles p. 710
Derecognition p. 710

GOODWILL p. 711
Recognition and Measurement of Goodwill p. 711
Bargain Purchase p. 713

Valuation after Acquisition   p. 713
Impairment of Goodwill   p. 714

**PRESENTATION, DISCLOSURE,
AND ANALYSIS   p. 716**
Presentation and Disclosure   p. 716
Analysis   p. 719

IFRS/ASPE COMPARISON   p. 720
A Comparison of IFRS and ASPE   p. 720
Looking Ahead   p. 721

APPENDIX 12A—VALUING GOODWILL   p. 724
Excess-Earnings Approach   p. 724
Total-Earnings Approach   p. 727

Other Valuation Methods   p. 728
Cumulative Coverage and Task-Based
    Simulation: Chapters 3 to 5   p. 753

APPENDIX: SPECIMEN FINANCIAL STATEMENTS   757
Brookfield Asset Management

TABLES   784

GLOSSARY   G-1

COMPANY INDEX   I-1

SUBJECT INDEX   I-3

THE CANADIAN FINANCIAL REPORTING ENVIRONMENT

LEARNING OBJECTIVES

**REFERENCE TO THE
CPA COMPETENCY MAP** **LEARNING OBJECTIVES**

After studying this chapter, you should be able to:

1.1.1, 1.2.1, 5.2.3	**1.** Explain how accounting makes it possible to use scarce resources more efficiently.
1.1.1, 1.1.2	**2.** Explain the meaning of "stakeholder" and identify key stakeholders in financial reporting, explaining what is at stake for each one.
1.1.1, 1.1.2	**3.** Identify the objective of financial reporting.
1.1.1, 1.1.2	**4.** Explain how information asymmetry and bias interfere with the objective of financial reporting.
1.1.1, 1.1.2	**5.** Explain the need for accounting standards and identify the major entities that influence standard setting and financial reporting.
1.1.1, 1.1.2, 1.2.1	**6.** Explain the meaning of generally accepted accounting principles (GAAP) and the significance of professional judgement in applying GAAP.
1.1.1, 1.1.2, 1.2.1, 1.3.1	**7.** Discuss some of the challenges and opportunities for accounting.

CAPITALIZING ON FINANCIAL REPORTING

EVERY BUSINESS—from the lawn-mowing service you may have operated in high school to a multinational corporation—needs capital to survive. You likely borrowed money from your parents to buy a weed trimmer, while the corporation issued millions of shares to raise capital from the public. But what about all the small and medium-sized enterprises (SMEs) in the middle? How do they get money to launch and grow?

The TMX Group, which operates the Toronto Stock Exchange (TSX) for publicly traded companies and the TSX Venture Exchange for companies to raise money from venture capital funds, recognizes the need to help SMEs raise capital through other means. While there are 3,900 companies listed on the TMX's two public exchanges, there are about 1.1 million private companies—more than 98% of them considered SMEs.

In late 2014, the TMX Group launched TSX Private Markets, which allows companies to trade securities in the exempt market. This means these companies, called private issuers, are exempt from the rigorous requirements of public issuers to file a prospectus, a document disclosing financial and other business information. "For companies that don't wish to go public, exempt markets fill an important need for capital and liquidity," said Thomas Kloet, then-CEO of the TMX Group. "The private companies that access the platform are vetted, but there are fewer requirements than for exchange-listed companies."

The TMX Group is looking into another way that SMEs can get capital: crowdfunding. It started as an on-line way for the

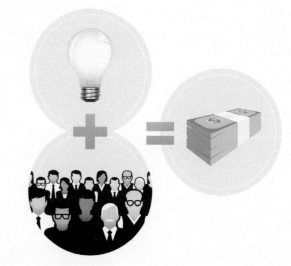

Matt Chalwell/Getty Images

public to donate to a cause or project without expecting to get anything in return. Now, both not-for-profits and businesses raise billions of dollars through crowdfunding sites such as Kickstarter and Indiegogo. The Ontario Securities Commission recently proposed rules that would allow small companies to issue shares in exchange for money on on-line portals registered with securities regulators, raising up to $1.5 million a year. At the time that Mr. Kloet spoke to the Economic Club of Canada in the spring of 2014, the TMX Group wanted to somehow get involved in this burgeoning equity crowdfunding. "It is generally understood that we don't know exactly where this financing method will go, but it is also understood that, in time, this will be a very important capital raising tool for Canadian entrepreneurs, particularly for the smallest companies. Given that Canada is truly a nation of SMEs, it could be transformational," Mr. Kloet said.

What does raising capital have to do with financial reporting? No matter how big the company, no matter how it raises money, it needs to present its financial information to potential investors and other stakeholders accurately and consistently with financial reporting standards—using a common "language" that investors understand. "Investor confidence is the cornerstone of financing small businesses," Mr. Kloet said.

Sources: "TMX Group Launches TSX Private Markets," TMX Group news release, November 14, 2014; Speech by Thomas Kloet to the Economic Club of Canada, May 27, 2014; "Exempt Market Review," Ontario Securities Commission backgrounder, March 20, 2014.

PREVIEW OF CHAPTER 1

North American financial reporting systems are among the best in the world. Our commitment to keeping our financial reporting systems strong is as intense as ever, because in this changing business world, information must be relevant and reliable for our capital markets to work efficiently. This chapter explains the environment of financial reporting and the many factors that affect it. It provides the theory and concepts underpinning the topics covered in the rest of the chapters, giving you the foundation to exercise professional judgement in the many issues that require it.

The chapter is organized as follows:

THE CANADIAN FINANCIAL REPORTING ENVIRONMENT			
Financial Statements and Financial Reporting	**Standard Setting**	**Generally Accepted Accounting Principles**	**Challenges and Opportunities for the Accounting Profession**
▪ Accounting and capital allocation ▪ Stakeholders ▪ Objective of financial reporting ▪ Information asymmetry	▪ Need for standards ▪ Parties involved in standard setting	▪ GAAP hierarchy ▪ Professional judgement	▪ Oversight in the capital marketplace ▪ Centrality of ethics ▪ Standard setting in a political environment ▪ Principles versus rules ▪ Impact of technology ▪ Integrated reporting ▪ Conclusion

FINANCIAL STATEMENTS AND FINANCIAL REPORTING

Like other human activities and disciplines, accounting is largely a product of its environment. This environment includes conditions, constraints, and influences that are social, economic, political, and legal—all of which change over time. As a result, accounting theory and practices have always evolved and need to continue to evolve in order to remain relevant.

Over the past decade or two, the accounting landscape has changed dramatically, being shaped by many things—some good and some not so good. These include:

REAL WORLD EMPHASIS

- spectacular business failures, including **WorldCom Inc.**, **Enron**, and **Arthur Andersen**;
- capital market failures, including the subprime lending crisis and bank failures;
- near bankruptcies of several countries;

- globalization of capital and other markets;
- globalization of financial reporting standards;
- increasing use of more sophisticated technology; and
- increasing access to information.[1]

All of these factors, as well as many others, provide accountants with great challenges but also great opportunities!

Accounting is defined best by describing its three essential characteristics. Accounting is (1) the identification, measurement, and communication of financial information (2) about economic entities (3) to interested persons.

Financial accounting (financial reporting) is the process that culminates in the preparation of financial reports that cover all of the enterprise's business activities and that are used by both **internal and external** parties. Users of these financial reports include investors, creditors, and others. In contrast, **managerial accounting** is the process of identifying, measuring, analyzing, and **communicating financial information** to **internal** decision-makers. This information may take varied forms, such as cost-benefit analyses and forecasts that management uses to plan, evaluate, and control an organization's operations. This textbook focuses on financial accounting, while managerial accounting is covered in other courses.

Financial statements are the principal way of communicating financial information to those who are outside an enterprise. These statements give the firm's history, quantified in terms of money. The most frequently provided financial statements are the:

1. **statement of financial position,**
2. **statement of income/comprehensive income,**
3. **statement of cash flows,** and
4. **statement of changes in equity.**

ALTERNATIVE TERMINOLOGY

These financial statements are also sometimes called:

1. balance sheet,
2. income statement, and
3. cash flow statement.

Under ASPE, the comparable statement to the statement of changes in equity is the statement of retained earnings, which is a different statement.

In addition, **note disclosures** are an important part of each financial statement. Some financial information cannot be expressed in the financial statements or is better expressed through other means. Examples include the president's letter and supplementary schedules in the corporate annual report, prospectuses, reports filed with government agencies, news releases, management forecasts, and descriptions of an enterprise's social or environmental impact. Such information may be required by a pronouncement by an authority, or a regulatory rule[2] or custom, or because management wants to disclose it voluntarily. The main focus of this textbook is the basic financial statements (including notes).

Accounting and Capital Allocation

Objective 1
Explain how accounting makes it possible to use scarce resources more efficiently.

Because **resources** are limited, people try to conserve them, use them effectively, and identify and encourage those who can make efficient use of them. Through an **efficient use of resources,** our standard of living increases.

Markets, free enterprise, and competition determine whether a business will succeed and thrive. The accounting profession has the important responsibility of **measuring**

TREASURY MANAGEMENT
5.2.3

company performance accurately and fairly on a timely basis. The information provided by accounting enables investors and creditors to **compare** the income and assets of companies and thus **assess the relative risks and returns** of different investment opportunities. Based on their assessments, investors and creditors can then channel their resources (that is, invest in these companies or lend them money) more effectively. Illustration 1-1 shows the process of **capital allocation**.

Illustration 1-1

Capital Allocation Process

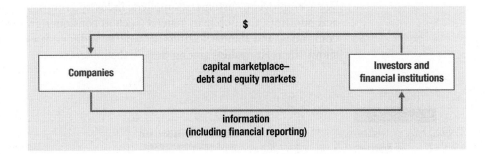

In Canada, the primary exchange mechanisms for allocating resources are **debt and equity markets**,[3] as well as **financial institutions** such as banks.[4] The debt and equity marketplace includes both public stock markets/exchanges and private sources.

Illustration 1-2 shows the sources of capital in Canada for various stages of company growth.

Illustration 1-2

Sources of Capital

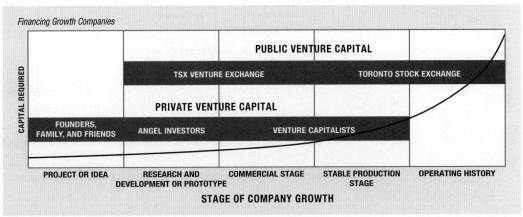

Providing an effective system to facilitate capital allocation is critical to a healthy economy. Efficient capital markets promote productivity, encourage innovation, and provide a platform for buying and selling securities and obtaining and granting credit.[5] Unreliable and irrelevant information leads to **poor capital allocation**, which hurts the securities markets and economic growth. The accounting numbers that companies report affect the **transfer of resources** among companies and individuals. Consider the fact that stock prices generally rise when positive news (including financial information) is unexpectedly released. In addition, **credit rating agencies** use accounting and other information to rate companies' financial stability.[6] This gives investors and creditors **additional independent information** to use when making decisions. For companies, a good rating can mean greater access to capital and at lower costs.

Objective 2

Explain the meaning of "stakeholder" and identify key stakeholders in financial reporting, explaining what is at stake for each one.

Stakeholders

Stakeholders are parties who have something at risk in the financial reporting environment, such as their salary, job, investment, or reputation. Key stakeholders in the financial reporting environment include **traditional users** of financial information as well as others. In the stakeholder context, **users** may be more broadly defined to include not only parties who are relying directly on the financial information for resource allocation (such as investors and creditors) but also others who help in the efficient allocation of resources (such as financial analysts and regulators).

The broader definition of users includes anyone who **prepares, relies on, reviews, audits, or monitors financial information**. It includes investors, creditors, analysts, managers, employees, customers, suppliers, industry groups, unions, government departments and ministers, the public in general (such as consumer groups), regulatory agencies, other companies, and standard setters, as well as auditors, lawyers, and others. Illustration 1-3 shows the relationships among these stakeholders.

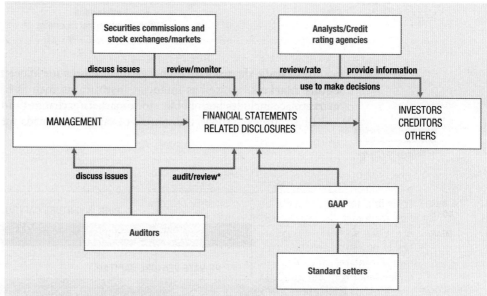

Illustration 1-3

Selected Key Stakeholders in the Financial Reporting Environment

* Not all financial statements are required to be audited. In general, all companies whose shares or debt are **publicly traded** must have an audit and therefore comply with generally accepted accounting principles (GAAP). Private companies may decide not to have an audit but must have unanimous shareholder consent according to the Canada Business Corporations Act. For private companies, the decision to have an audit or not may depend on whether the statements' users would find audited GAAP statements more useful.

Various stakeholders have specific functions in the financial reporting environment. Company management **prepares** the financial statements. It has the best insight into the business and therefore knows what should be included in the financial statements. The statements are then **audited** by auditors, who may discuss with management how economic events and transactions have been communicated in the financial statements. The value that auditors add to the statements lies in the auditors' independence. They act on behalf of the shareholders to ensure that management is accounting properly for the economic transactions. The auditors also **review** the information to ensure that it reflects sound accounting choices.

Investors and creditors **rely on** the financial statements to make decisions. It is up to these parties to carefully examine the information given. Standard setters **set generally accepted accounting principles (GAAP)**. Securities commissions and stock exchanges **monitor** the financial statements to ensure full and plain disclosure of material information and to determine whether the companies may continue to list their shares on stock exchanges. Finally, the credit rating agencies and analysts **monitor and analyze** the information produced by the company, looking for signs of change; that is, an improved or weakened financial condition.

LAW

Illustration 1-4 identifies what is at stake for each stakeholder. This is not meant to be a complete list. Rather, it identifies the major stakeholder groups.

Illustration 1-4

What Is at Stake for Each Stakeholder?

STAKEHOLDER	WHAT IS AT STAKE?
Investors/creditors	Investment/loan
Management	Job, bonus, reputation, salary increase, access to capital markets by company
Securities commissions and stock exchanges	Reputation, effective and efficient capital marketplace
Analysts and credit rating agencies	Reputation, profits
Auditors	Reputation, profits (companies are their clients)
Standard setters	Reputation
Others	Various

As noted in Illustration 1-3, the system provides **checks and balances** to ensure that the people with capital—the investors and creditors—have good information to use when deciding where best to invest or allocate their capital. The system does not always work, however. Because the system involves people, human behaviour is often a key unpredictable variable. People often act in their own **self-interest** rather than in the **best interest of the capital marketplace, and by extension, the economy.**

WHAT DO THE NUMBERS MEAN?

ETHICS

Consider the much-publicized crisis that arose when large numbers of borrowers with lower-quality, "subprime" mortgages defaulted, which was partly responsible for destabilizing the capital markets and the economy, starting in 2007. What was this all about and how did it trigger a global recession? Much has to do with individuals and entities acting in their own self-interest and a lack of transparency or lack of understanding of the true risks involved.

Financial institutions regularly securitize pools of assets in order to access the cash that is tied up in the assets. As a general rule, the securitization involves selling the assets to a separate entity, often for cash. The entity then sells units or shares in the pool of assets to investors. The following are the steps in a normal securitization of mortgage assets:

1. Lender lends money to customers to buy homes.
2. Lender sells pool of mortgage assets from the above loans to a separate entity (often referred to as a special purpose entity or SPE).
3. SPE sells units or shares in the pool of mortgages to investors.

There is nothing inherently wrong with this structure and it can work very well for all parties as long as they understand the risks involved. It is good for borrowers because it makes funds more accessible. It is good for lenders because they are able to get their cash out of the mortgage assets. It is good for SPEs because they earn interest on the pool of assets. Finally, it is good for investors because they earn a return on their investment. What went wrong in the subprime lending situation, then?

First, the lenders or their designated mortgage brokers loaned money aggressively, in the hopes of higher profits, to borrowers who may not have been creditworthy.

Second, many of the loans were adjustable-rate notes, which meant that, initially, the interest rates were low—often below the prime lending rate, which is where the term "subprime" comes from. But afterwards, the rates reset themselves according to the loan agreement, often becoming significantly higher. Therefore, even though the borrowers may have been able to afford the loan payments initially, many could no longer afford them once the interest rates became higher. The borrowers borrowed the funds anyway because they wanted to buy houses, even though they knew or should have known that they might not be able to keep up with the loan payments in future.

Third, many investors in the SPE did not understand the risks they were taking on by investing in this type of pool of assets, which was systemically risky due to the creditworthiness of the borrowers and the mortgages' interest rate reset feature.

Things began to unwind when the mortgages' interest rates were set higher. This caused many borrowers to default on their mortgages and lose their homes. These homes were repossessed and flooded the market, driving house prices down. Many borrowers found that the amounts of their mortgages were now higher than the value of their homes and they walked away from their debt, causing more homes to go on sale in an already depressed market. The investors in the SPE suffered large losses due to the defaulted loans. All this contributed to a depressed housing market and economy.

From a financial reporting perspective, a few lessons were learned:

1. Many capital market participants act in their own self-interest to the potential harm of others.
2. The amount and nature of risk are not always properly communicated to investors.
3. Investors do not always understand what they are investing in.

Stakeholders in the capital marketplace are working to ensure that this type of situation does not happen again.

Objective of Financial Reporting

Objective 3
Identify the objective of financial reporting.

THEORY

What is the **objective of financial reporting**? The objective of **general-purpose financial statements** is to **provide financial information about the reporting entity that is useful to present and potential equity investors, lenders, and other creditors in making decisions in their capacity as capital providers.** (This is referred to as the **decision-usefulness approach** to financial reporting.) Information that is decision-useful to capital providers may also be useful to other users of financial reporting who are not investors and creditors. Let's examine each of the elements of this objective.[7]

As part of the objective of general-purpose financial reporting, an **entity perspective** is adopted. Companies are viewed as separate and distinct from their owners (present shareholders) using this perspective. The assets of incorporated entities such as companies listed on stock exchanges are viewed as assets of the company and not of a specific creditor or shareholder. Investors and creditors have claims on a company's assets in the form of equity or liability claims. The entity perspective is common today, because most companies that report their financial information have substance distinct from their investors (both shareholders and creditors). Thus, the perspective that financial reporting should be focused only on the needs of shareholders—often referred to as the **proprietary perspective**—is not considered appropriate.

As mentioned earlier, investors are interested in assessing (1) the company's ability to generate net cash inflows and (2) management's ability to protect and enhance the capital providers' investments. Financial reporting should therefore help investors assess the amounts, timing, and uncertainty of prospective cash inflows from dividends or interest, and the proceeds from the sale, redemption, or maturity of securities or loans. In order for investors to make these assessments, they must understand the economic resources of an enterprise, the claims to those resources, and the changes in them. Financial statements and related explanations should be a primary source for determining this information.

The emphasis on "assessing cash flow prospects" does not mean that the cash basis is preferred over the accrual basis of accounting. Information based on accrual accounting generally better indicates a company's present and future ability to generate favourable cash flows than does information limited to the financial effects of cash receipts and payments. Recall from your first accounting course the objective of **accrual-basis accounting**. It ensures that a company records events that change its financial statements in the periods in which the events occur, rather than only in the periods in which it receives or pays cash. Using the accrual basis to determine net income means that a company recognizes revenues when it provides the goods or services rather than when it receives cash. Similarly, it recognizes expenses when it incurs them rather than when it pays them. Under accrual accounting, a company generally recognizes revenues when it makes sales. The company can then relate the revenues to the economic environment of the period in which they occurred. Over the long run, trends in revenues and expenses are generally more meaningful than trends in cash receipts and disbursements.

Providing information that is useful to users is a challenging task since they have **different needs and levels of knowledge. Institutional investors,**[8] such as the Canada Pension Plan, hold an increasing percentage of equity share holdings[9] and generally put a lot of their resources into managing their investment portfolios. Can those who prepare financial information therefore assume that the average individual investor has the same needs and knowledge level as an institutional investor when it comes to business and financial reporting? Likely not. We will discuss this issue further in Chapter 2.

**WHAT
DO THE
NUMBERS
MEAN?**

**REAL WORLD
EMPHASIS**

The Canada Pension Plan (CPP) is one of the top 10 largest retirement funds in the world according to its website. Over 18 million Canadians participate in the plan. The plan is managed by the Canada Pension Plan Investment Board (CPPIB), which decides how to invest the CPP funds. Its mandate is to "maximize returns without undue risk of loss."

The chart below shows where the money is invested by region and then by type of asset.

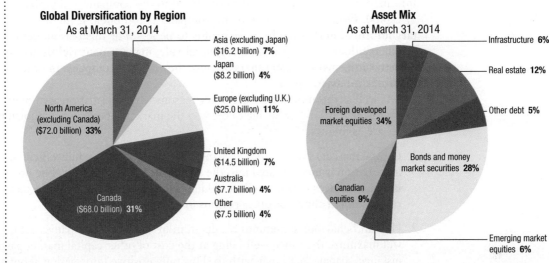

The fund stood at $219.1 billion as at March 31, 2014 and experienced a 16.5% rate of return for 2014. CPPIB had 1,000 full-time employees in 2014, many of whom are professionals, including accountants and lawyers. As you can see below, the composition of types of assets has shifted from primarily fixed income to primarily equities—shares in publicly traded corporations. As a large institutional investor with substantial equities holdings, the CPP is a significant stakeholder in how publicly traded companies report their financial information.

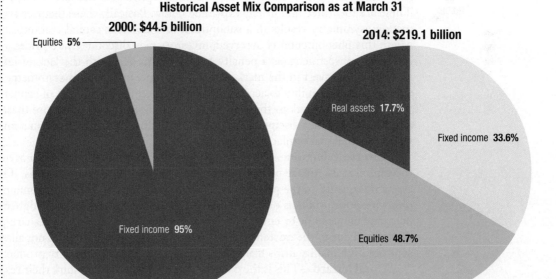

Information Asymmetry

Objective 4

Explain how information asymmetry and bias interfere with the objective of financial reporting.

Ideally, to facilitate the flow of capital in the most efficient and effective manner, all stakeholders should have equal access to all relevant information. In other words, there should be symmetry of access to information (**information symmetry**). This is nice in theory but it does not always work in practice. Management may feel that disclosure of too much information may hurt the company's competitive advantage or position. For instance, if the company were in the middle of a lawsuit, management would want to be careful about how much information was disclosed because it might affect the outcome of the lawsuit. In cases such as this, the company must weigh the costs and benefits of sharing information. On the one hand, if the company is known to be open and forthright, revealing information may facilitate the flow of capital to the company and perhaps lower the cost of capital. On the other hand, if the company is too open, it might give away proprietary information that might cause profits to be less. For this reason, perfect information symmetry does not exist and, as a general rule, management rightly has access to more or better information than others because they run the company. In other words, there is **information asymmetry**.

As well as the above, there are other reasons why information asymmetry exists in the marketplace. This might be due to the way the markets operate or to human nature. Some issues are as follows:

1. Capital markets such as stock exchanges are not necessarily fully efficient; that is, not all information is incorporated into the stock prices of companies. The problem of course is that the prices may not reflect hidden or insider information. This may be due to the reasons noted above, or other reasons in point 2 below.

2. Human behaviour sometimes results in individuals and companies acting in ways that will maximize their own well-being at the cost of other capital market participants. For instance, management may wish to show only positive information about a company in order to ensure access to capital markets or maximize their own personal bonuses.

Accounting and economic theory tries to help us understand these issues. The **efficient markets hypothesis** proposes that market prices reflect all publicly available information about a company.[10]

THEORY

In addition to researching whether market mechanisms are efficient or not, accounting theorists look at the issue of information asymmetry from other perspectives. There are two common types of information asymmetry problems that are studied by academics. These are identified and briefly explained below. Basically these theories argue that information asymmetry results in a suboptimal or inefficient capital marketplace. In markets where this phenomenon is observed, investors may discount share prices, require higher returns on investment (as a penalty for having to deal with the lack of information), or choose not to invest in the market. In the extreme, information asymmetry may interfere with a company's ability to access capital and/or minimize the cost of capital.

We will refer back to these concepts throughout the text. Because these concepts are also studied in other disciplines, the examples below look at them from a financial reporting and capital marketplace perspective.

Adverse selection—Basically, this means that where information asymmetry exists, the capital marketplace may attract the wrong type of company; that is, if buyers cannot assess the quality of the product they are buying, the market could contain only companies with poor products or it could fail. In addition, companies with higher quality products may choose not to enter the capital marketplace knowing that share prices may be discounted due to the existence of information asymmetry that does not allow investors to separate high quality firms from "lemons" that produce low quality products.

Moral hazard—This is the concept that people will often shirk their responsibilities if they think that no one is watching. For instance, a manager of a pharmaceutical company may choose not to work as hard, if investors cannot tell the level of effort being made due to information asymmetry. Similarly, he may choose not to disclose negative information about ongoing drug trials, knowing that it will result in a decline in share prices and perhaps his bonus. In addition, he may engage in greater risk-taking. Accountants sometimes refer to this as **management bias**. Managers may decide to downplay the negative and focus on the positive (referred to as **aggressive accounting**). This bias might take the form of overstated assets and/or net income, understated liabilities and/or expenses, or carefully selected note disclosures that emphasize only positive events.[11] **Conservative accounting** would be the opposite.[12] Any bias in financial reporting results in less useful information.

There are many reasons why management may present biased information in the financial statements. Illustration 1-5 examines these possible motivations. We will revisit the issue of bias in Chapter 2 and throughout the text.

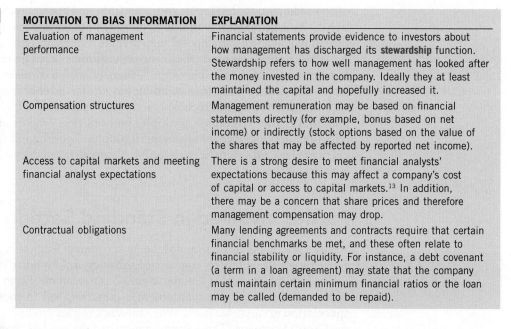

Illustration 1-5

Possible Motivations for Management Bias

ETHICS

MOTIVATION TO BIAS INFORMATION	EXPLANATION
Evaluation of management performance	Financial statements provide evidence to investors about how management has discharged its **stewardship** function. Stewardship refers to how well management has looked after the money invested in the company. Ideally they at least maintained the capital and hopefully increased it.
Compensation structures	Management remuneration may be based on financial statements directly (for example, bonus based on net income) or indirectly (stock options based on the value of the shares that may be affected by reported net income).
Access to capital markets and meeting financial analyst expectations	There is a strong desire to meet financial analysts' expectations because this may affect a company's cost of capital or access to capital markets.[13] In addition, there may be a concern that share prices and therefore management compensation may drop.
Contractual obligations	Many lending agreements and contracts require that certain financial benchmarks be met, and these often relate to financial stability or liquidity. For instance, a debt covenant (a term in a loan agreement) may state that the company must maintain certain minimum financial ratios or the loan may be called (demanded to be repaid).

WHAT DO THE NUMBERS MEAN?

In their book *Freakonomics*, Levitt and Dubner acknowledge that it is very common in most transactions for one party to have more or better information than the other. Often, in a transaction, one party is an expert and the other not. In the capital marketplace, experts, including accountants, bankers, institutional investors, and company managers, all have more and better information than the average consumer or investor. Levitt and Dubner go on to argue, however, that the Internet allows information to pass very freely from experts to non-experts. They argue that the Internet has "vastly shrunk the gap between experts and the public."

Shifting to another discipline, for example, consider your own relationship with your family doctor. Several decades ago, if something was wrong with you, you would have made an appointment and sat passively in the doctor's office while he or she analyzed your symptoms and made a diagnosis. At that time, the doctor might have shared the analysis and diagnosis with you and might have handed you an illegible prescription to fill. The Internet has changed this. Now, most people do a bit of research before they go to the doctor. By doing a quick search on the Internet, patients are able to get information so that they know what questions to ask and what options might be available for treatment. Patients can now freely access information about side effects and new drugs. Many people keep their own medical histories. Doctors understand that their role is to help their patients navigate the significant amount of information that is available, not necessarily to dictate a diagnosis and treatment.

Returning to the business world, the real question is: As people turn more and more to the Internet and the information there becomes more and more robust, what is the role of experts in the capital marketplace and how will the issue of information asymmetry evolve?

Source: Steven Levitt and Stephen Dubner, *Freakonomics*, HarperCollins Publishers, New York, 2005.

STANDARD SETTING

Objective 5

Explain the need for accounting standards and identify the major entities that influence standard setting and financial reporting.

Need for Standards

Accounting standards help reduce the information asymmetry problem in financial reporting. They do this by requiring that transactions and events be recognized, measured, presented, and disclosed in a specific way. But the main controversy in financial reporting is this: Whose rules should we play by, and what should they be? The answer is not immediately clear. This is because the users of financial statements have both similar and conflicting needs for information of various types.

Accounting professions in various countries have tried to develop a set of standards that are generally accepted and universally practised. Without these standards, each enterprise would have to develop its own standards, and readers of financial statements would have to become familiar with every company's particular accounting and reporting practices. It would be almost impossible to prepare statements that could be compared.

This common set of standards and procedures is called **generally accepted accounting principles (GAAP)**. The term "generally accepted" means either that an authoritative rule-making body in accounting has created a reporting principle in a particular area or that, over time, a specific practice has been accepted as appropriate because it is used universally.[14] Although principles and practices have resulted in both debate and criticism, most members of the financial community recognize them as the standards that over time have proven to be most useful. A more detailed discussion of GAAP is presented later in this chapter.

Parties Involved in Standard Setting

Before 1900, single ownership was the most common form of business organization in our economy. Financial reports emphasized **solvency and liquidity** and were only for **internal use** or for banks and other lending institutions to examine. From 1900 to 1929, the growth of large corporations and their absentee ownership led to **increasing investment and speculation** in corporate stock. When the stock market crashed in 1929, this contributed to the Great Depression. These events emphasized the need for **standardized and increased corporate disclosures** that would allow shareholders to make informed decisions.

Several organizations play a role in developing financial reporting standards in Canada. The major standard-setting organizations are:

1. Canadian **Accounting Standards Board (AcSB)**: *www.frascanada.ca*

2. **International Accounting Standards Board (IASB)**: *www.ifrs.org*

3. The **Financial Accounting Standards Board (FASB)**: *www.fasb.org;* and the U.S. **Securities and Exchange Commission (SEC)**: *www.sec.gov*

4. **Provincial securities commissions** such as the **Ontario Securities Commission (OSC)**: *www.osc.gov.on.ca*

Illustration 1-6 shows how these organizations influence GAAP for Canadian entities. We will discuss each in greater detail below.

	Standard-Setting Body	GAAP Development	How GAAP Applies to Canadian Entities
Illustration 1-6 *Various Entities Responsible for GAAP*	AcSB	GAAP for Canadian private companies (referred to as **Accounting Standards for Private Enterprises** or **ASPE**), pension plans, and not-for-profit entities	ASPE is effective for periods beginning on or after January 1, 2011. Not-for-profit entities in the public sector may have to follow public sector GAAP, which is the responsibility of the Public Sector Accounting Board (PSAB).
	IASB	GAAP for public companies, referred to as **International Financial Reporting Standards (IFRS)**	IFRS is effective for periods beginning on or after January 1, 2011. Private companies and not-for-profit entities may choose to use IFRS.
	FASB	GAAP for U.S. entities (referred to as U.S. GAAP)	Canadian public companies may choose to follow U.S. GAAP (see text directly below under Securities commissions).
	Securities commissions	Not responsible for GAAP but often require additional disclosures for public companies	The Ontario Securities Commission requires that public companies follow IFRS or U.S. GAAP (where public companies list on U.S. stock exchanges or markets and choose to follow U.S. GAAP instead of IFRS) for periods beginning on or after January 1, 2011.

Canadian Accounting Standards Board (AcSB)

The first official recommendations on standards of financial statement disclosure were published in 1946 by the **Canadian Institute of Chartered Accountants (CICA)**. The CICA was the predecessor organization of **Chartered Professional Accountants Canada (CPA Canada)**. Today, the Accounting Standards Board (AcSB) has primary responsibility for setting GAAP in Canada. The AcSB produces a variety of authoritative material, including the most important source of GAAP, the *CPA Canada Handbook*.[15] The *CPA Canada Handbook* was originally published in 1968[16] and now consists of several volumes of accounting and assurance guidance.[17]

The objectives of the AcSB are as follows:

a. To establish financial reporting standards and guidance that improve the quality of information reported by Canadian entities, principally annual and interim general purpose financial statements, with due consideration for the costs and the benefits to the preparers and users of financial statements of different categories of reporting entity, and changes in the economic environment.

b. To facilitate the capital allocation process in both the business and not-for-profit sectors through improved information.

c. To participate with other standard setters in the development of a single set of high-quality internationally accepted financial reporting standards.

d. To support the implementation of financial reporting standards and the resolution of emerging application issues.[18]

Two basic premises underlie the process of establishing financial accounting standards:

1. The AcSB should **respond to the needs and viewpoints** of the **entire economic community**, not just the public accounting profession.

2. The AcSB should **operate in full public view** through a **due process** system that gives interested persons enough opportunity to make their views known.

The **Accounting Standards Oversight Council (AcSOC)** oversees AcSB activities. Its duties include providing input to AcSB activities and reporting to the public, among other things. Members of the AcSB and the AcSOC come from a wide range of groups that are interested or involved in the financial reporting process.[19]

The AcSB is responsible for setting standards for public and private entities as well as not-for-profit entities (including some profit-oriented government entities). As noted in Illustration 1-6, from 2011 onward, the AcSB has been responsible for developing standards for private enterprises, not-for-profit entities, and pension plans only. Standards for publicly accountable entities (public companies) are developed by the International Accounting Standards Board even though they are still adopted into Canadian GAAP by the AcSB. This approach makes sense for a number of reasons, including the following:

1. Public companies often operate globally and often raise funds in global capital markets; therefore, it makes sense to have a common language for reporting financial position and performance so that users can compare companies internationally.

2. Private companies often operate locally and have less complex business models and fewer users, who are often close to the company and can gain other information about the business first-hand. Therefore, it makes sense to have a separate GAAP that is less complicated, has fewer disclosures, and is geared toward fewer users who have access to additional information about the company.

Note that there are some private companies that are global and complex. These entities have the option to use IFRS. Private entities that are planning to go public may find it easier to follow IFRS right from the beginning.[20]

International Accounting Standards Board (IASB)

Most countries agree that more uniform standards are needed. As a result, the International Accounting Standards Committee (IASC) was formed in 1973 to try to lessen the areas of difference among countries' own standards. The IASC's objective in standard setting was to work generally to improve and harmonize regulations, accounting standards, and procedures relating to the presentation of financial statements. Eliminating differences is not easy: the financial reporting objectives in each country are different, the institutional structures are often not comparable, and there are strong national tendencies in most countries. Nevertheless, much progress has been made since the IASC's early days. In 2001, a new International Accounting Standards Board (IASB) was created.

According to the IASB website, its aims are as follows:

(a) to develop, in the public interest, a single set of high quality, understandable, enforceable and globally accepted financial reporting standards based upon clearly articulated principles. These standards should require high quality, transparent and comparable information in financial statements and other financial reporting to help investors, other participants in the world's capital markets and other users of financial information make economic decisions.

(b) to promote the use and rigorous application of those standards.

(c) in fulfilling the objectives associated with (a) and (b), to take account of, as appropriate, the needs of a range of sizes and types of entities in diverse economic settings.

(d) to promote and facilitate adoption of International Financial Reporting Standards (IFRSs), being the standards and interpretations issued by the IASB, through the convergence of national accounting standards and IFRSs.[21]

Illustration 1-7 shows the governing structure of the IASB. As shown in the diagram, the **IFRS Foundation** monitors, reviews the effectiveness of, appoints members to, and funds the IASB. The **International Financial Reporting Interpretation Committee (IFRIC)** studies issues where guidance in IASB is insufficient or non-existent. If necessary, it produces additional guidance in the form of IFRIC interpretations, which are part of IFRS.

The **IFRS Advisory Council** is composed of various user groups, such as preparers of financial statements, analysts, auditors, regulators, professional accounting bodies, and academics. As its name suggests, it provides guidance and feedback to the IASB.

Illustration 1-7

How the IASB Is Set Up[22]

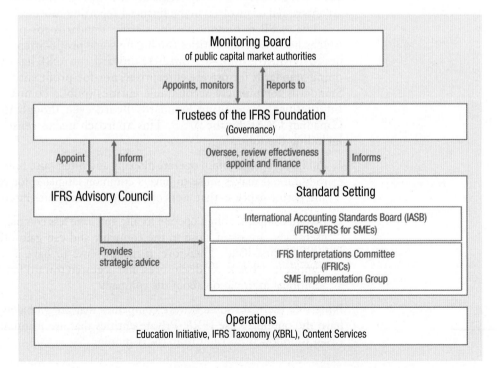

Illustration 1-8 shows the various stages in producing an international standard.

Illustration 1-8

Evolution of a New or Revised IFRS[23]

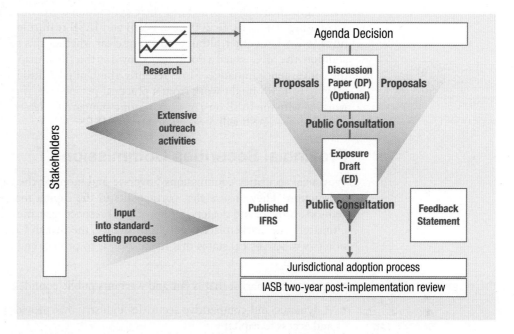

The process is very similar to the Canadian and U.S. processes. One difference is the increased and more common use of discussion papers (DPs). DPs are often the predecessors of exposure drafts (EDs). When IFRS are being formulated, the IASB may issue a DP and ask for comment letters just as it does for EDs. Therefore, by the time the proposed standard gets to the ED stage, many key decisions have already been made.[24]

The IASB is quickly becoming the dominant standard-setting body in the world. As of December 2014, over 131 countries required or allowed the use of IFRS (with 95 of these countries requiring IFRS for all domestic-listed companies).[25]

Financial Accounting Standards Board and the Securities and Exchange Commission

In the United States, the Financial Accounting Standards Board (FASB) is the major standard-setting body, although it does not have final authority over standards—instead, the Securities and Exchange Commission (SEC) does. (Note that the SEC is a national body, whereas in Canada, the securities commissions are provincial.) The SEC has confirmed its support for the FASB by stating that financial statements that conform to FASB standards will be presumed to have substantial authoritative support. The SEC has also indicated in its reports to the U.S. government that it continues to believe that the private sector (for example, the FASB) should stay responsible for establishing and improving accounting standards, although the commission must oversee any changes. Like the Canadian securities commissions, the SEC also indicates its position on various financial reporting issues through what it calls financial reporting releases.

U.S. GAAP has and will continue to have a significant impact on GAAP in Canada for several reasons. First, because Canadian GAAP is based on principles and is fairly open to interpretation, **accounting professionals have often relied on the more prescriptive, specific guidance** provided in U.S. GAAP.

Second, many Canadian companies are also listed on U.S. stock markets and exchanges, such as NASDAQ (National Association of Securities Dealers Automated Quotation) and the NYSE (New York Stock Exchange). To be listed on a U.S. exchange, these companies must follow U.S. GAAP[26] or IFRS.[27] As we move toward international harmonization in accounting standards, the U.S. standards will continue to influence Canadian and international standards due to the significant capital pool of these markets.

This brings us to the third point, which concerns the fact that the United States has not adopted IFRS. In October 2002, the FASB and IASB signed an agreement (the Norwalk Agreement) that formalized their commitment to converge U.S. and international accounting standards. In 2008, the FASB and IASB reaffirmed their commitment to continue to work together, although it is not clear whether this relationship will continue. In addition, the SEC issued a document known as the "Roadmap"[28] outlining issues regarding the convergence initiative. More recently, the United States has been examining just how moving to IFRS might work from a practical perspective, if at all. The FASB is currently working with the IASB on a new accounting standard for leases. Beyond that, it is uncertain as to how the FASB will proceed in terms of IFRS.

Provincial Securities Commissions

Provincial securities commissions[29] oversee and monitor the capital marketplace in their jurisdiction. They ensure that participants in the capital markets (including companies, auditors, brokers and dealers, and investors) respect securities law and legislation so that, ultimately, the marketplace is fair. For instance, the British Columbia Securities Commission (www.bcsc.bc.ca) states that its mission is to protect and promote the public interest by fostering:

LAW

- A securities market that is fair and warrants public confidence

- A dynamic and competitive securities industry that provides investment opportunities and access to capital

As part of ensuring that investors have access to the information that they need in order to make informed decisions, securities law and legislation require that companies that issue shares to the public and whose shares trade on a Canadian stock exchange or stock market produce GAAP financial statements.

Ontario is home to the largest stock exchange in Canada, the **Toronto Stock Exchange (TSX)**, and most large Canadian public companies are therefore registered with the Ontario Securities Commission (OSC). The OSC reviews and monitors the financial statements of companies whose shares are publicly traded on the TSX so that it can judge whether the statements present the financial position and results of operations of these companies fairly.[30] It also issues its own Management Discussion and Analysis disclosure requirements.[31] Stock exchanges, as well as securities commissions, can fine a company and/or delist the company's shares from the stock exchange, which removes a company's access to capital markets.

GENERALLY ACCEPTED ACCOUNTING PRINCIPLES

Objective 6

Explain the meaning of generally accepted accounting principles (GAAP) and the significance of professional judgement in applying GAAP.

GAAP includes **not only specific rules, practices, and procedures** for particular circumstances but also **broad principles and conventions that apply generally**, including underlying concepts.

GAAP Hierarchy

ASPE

The **GAAP hierarchy** identifies the sources of GAAP and lets users know which ones should be consulted first in asking the question: What is GAAP?

Under ASPE, GAAP is divided into **primary sources** and **other sources**. Based on the *CPA Canada Handbook*, Part II, Section 1100, the **primary** sources of GAAP (in descending order of authority) are as follows:

- *Handbook* Sections 1400 to 3870, including Appendices; and

- **Accounting guidelines**, including Appendices.

Other sources of GAAP noted in Section 1100 include:

- **Background information and basis for conclusion documents issued by the AcSB**

- **Pronouncements** by accounting standard-setting bodies in other jurisdictions, although it is not necessary to comply with guidance in IFRS or other GAAP in order to comply with Canadian GAAP for private entities[32]

- **Approved drafts of primary sources** of GAAP where no primary sources apply (such as exposure drafts)

- **Research studies**

- Accounting **textbooks, journals, studies, and articles**

- Other sources, including industry practice

In general, primary sources must be looked at **first** for how to treat an issue. If primary sources do not deal with the specific issue, the entity should use accounting policies that are **consistent with the primary sources.** The policies should also be developed through the use of professional judgement in accordance with the concepts in Section 1000, which is the **conceptual framework.** (The conceptual framework is the foundation of financial reporting and is examined in greater detail in Chapter 2.) As business is constantly changing and new business transactions and contracts are regularly being entered into, the other listed sources are also important sources of GAAP.

Under IFRS, GAAP incorporates the following which includes guidance that is integral to the standard:[33]

- IFRS

- International Accounting Standards (IAS) (standards that were issued by the IASB's predecessor)[34]

- Interpretations (IFRIC or the former Standards Interpretation Committee [SIC])

What happens when a company has an accounting issue but the above do not specifically apply? In that case, management uses professional judgement, considering the conceptual framework and the applicability of similar IFRS in similar situations, as long as the resulting information is relevant and reliable. The following sources would be considered, in descending order:

- Pronouncements of other standard-setting bodies

- Other accounting literature

- Accepted industry practices

In essence, although the wording is different, both hierarchies are similar, as follows:

- They provide guidance that helps answer the question "What is GAAP?"

- They rank sources and consider certain sources as more important.

- They are grounded in the conceptual framework.

- They establish the value of and expect the use of professional judgement.

Professional Judgement

Professional judgement plays an especially important role in ASPE and IFRS.[35] This is due to the basic philosophy of Canadian and international accountants on standard setting: **there cannot be a rule for every situation.** ASPE and IFRS are therefore based primarily on **general principles** rather than **specific rules.** The basic premise is that professional accountants with significant education and experience will be able to apply these principles appropriately to any situation.

In a principles-based standard-setting system, the conceptual framework underlies the standards. Therefore, accountants either apply specific standards that are based on the conceptual framework, or, if no specific standard exists, the accountant uses the conceptual framework and professional judgement to reason through to an answer, as noted previously as part of the GAAP hierarchy.[36]

Challenges and Opportunities for the Accounting Profession

Objective 7
Discuss some of the challenges and opportunities for accounting.

During 2001 and 2002, the future of the capital market system was challenged by several major corporate scandals, as mentioned earlier in this chapter. This was followed by the subprime lending and banking crisis starting in 2007, which triggered a period of significant global economic instability. The resulting turmoil has given stakeholders a chance to re-examine their roles in the capital marketplace and to question if and how they add value to the system. Advancements in technology and the way we view information are also having a profound impact on accounting. It is useful to continually review the role accountants play in the capital markets in light of constant change. Are we doing what we should? Can we do better? Do others understand what we do?

Oversight in the Capital Marketplace

ETHICS AND LAW

While most stakeholders fulfill their roles in the capital marketplace in a very positive and productive manner, some do not. Should the markets be self-regulating? Accounting scandals at companies such as Enron, **Cendant**, **Sunbeam**, **Rite-Aid**, and **Livent** have prompted governments to increase regulation in the capital marketplace. In the United States, the Sarbanes-Oxley Act (SOX), enacted in 2002, gave more resources to the SEC to fight fraud and poor business practices.[37] The SEC was able to increase its policing efforts and approve new auditor independence rules and materiality guidelines for financial reporting. In addition, SOX introduced sweeping changes to the institutional structure of the accounting profession. The following are some of the legislation's key provisions:

- An **accounting oversight board** was established and given oversight and enforcement authority. It was mandated to establish auditing, quality control, and independence standards and rules, and is known as the **Public Company Accounting Oversight Board (PCAOB)**.

- Stronger **independence rules** were made for auditors. Audit partners, for example, are required to rotate every five years.

- Chief executive officers (CEOs) and chief financial officers (CFOs) are required to **certify** that the financial statements and company disclosures are appropriate and fairly presented. They must **forfeit bonuses and profits** if there is a restatement of their companies' accounting disclosures.

- Company management must **report on the effectiveness of the financial reporting internal control systems** and the auditors must assess and report on these internal controls.

- Audit committees must have **independent members** and members with financial expertise.

- Companies must disclose whether they have a **code of ethics** for their senior financial officers.

Stakeholders in Canada were faced with the question of whether similar reforms should be put in place in our capital markets. Companies that issue shares in the United States are bound by SOX[38] and these companies therefore have no choice. Many stakeholders felt that unless Canada matched the standard set by SOX, Canadian capital markets would be seen as inferior. As a result, many of the SOX requirements have now been put in place in Canada, as follows:

- The **Canadian Public Accountability Board (CPAB)**[39] was formed to look after similar issues to the PCAOB.

- The **Canadian Securities Administrators** (CSA) issued rules that, among other things, require company management to take **responsibility for the appropriateness and fairness of the financial statements**, public companies to have **independent audit committees**, and public accounting firms to be subject to the CPAB.[40]

- The **CSA** issued a harmonized statement that requires much **greater disclosures**, including ratings from rating agencies, payments by companies to stock promoters, legal proceedings, and details about directors, including their previous involvement with bankrupt companies.[41]

- The **Province of Ontario** made amendments to its Securities Act.

The impact of these reforms on North American capital markets has been to put more emphasis on government regulation and less on self-regulation. Do we have the balance right? At a minimum, there is greater understanding of the roles that the various stakeholders play. However, stakeholders should be doing things because they are the right things to do, not just because they must do so by law.

Centrality of Ethics

ETHICS

Accountants play significant roles in the capital marketplace. Illustration 1-3 shows that they are part of every stakeholder group, including preparers, auditors, regulators, investors, and others. They are therefore central in making the capital marketplace efficient and effective. However, decision-making is a complicated and human process. In accounting, as in other areas of business, **ethical dilemmas** are common. Some of these dilemmas are simple and easy to resolve. Many, however, are complex, and solutions are not obvious. Management biases—either internally prompted (by the desire to maximize bonuses, for example) or externally prompted (by the desire to meet analysts' earnings expectations, for example)—are the starting point of many ethical dilemmas. These biases sometimes lead to an emphasis on short-term results over long-term results and place accountants (both inside and outside the company) in an environment of conflict and pressure. Basic questions such as "Is this way of communicating financial information transparent?", "Does it provide useful information?", and "What should I do in this circumstance?" cannot always be answered by simply following GAAP or the rules of the profession. Technical competence is not enough when decisions have an ethical side.

Doing the **right thing** and making the right decision is not always easy. What is right is not always evident and the pressures to "bend the rules," "play the game," or "just ignore it" can be considerable. In these cases, self-interest must be balanced with the interests of others. The decision is more difficult because no consensus has emerged among business professionals as to what constitutes a comprehensive ethical system.

This process of **ethical sensitivity** and choosing among alternatives can also be complicated by time pressures, job pressures, client pressures, personal pressures, and peer pressures. Throughout this textbook, ethical considerations are presented to make you aware of the types of situations that you may encounter in your professional responsibility. Many believe that accountants play the role of a conscience in the capital marketplace. That is our challenge and opportunity. Throughout the text, we will refer to specific ethics-related issues with an ethics icon. The cases at the end of each chapter focus on professional judgement and accounting policy choices. They also include ethical considerations.

Standard Setting in a Political Environment

When it comes to influencing the development of accounting standards, the most powerful force may be the stakeholder. **Accounting standards result as much from political action as they do from careful logic or research findings.** As part of their mandate, standard setters include stakeholders as members, giving them a **formal voice** in the process. Furthermore, through due process, interested parties can comment on proposed changes or new standards. This is a good thing.

However, stakeholders may want particular economic events to be accounted for or reported in a particular way, and they may fight hard to get what they want. They know that the most effective way to influence the standards that dictate accounting practice is to participate in formulating them or to try to influence or persuade the formulator. This is not necessarily optimal since the stakeholders who make themselves heard the loudest may get their way, to the detriment of others.

Should politics play a role in setting financial accounting and reporting standards? The AcSB and IASB do not exist in isolation. Standard setting is part of the real world, and it cannot escape politics and political pressures. That is not to say that politics in standard setting is necessarily bad. Since many accounting standards do have economic consequences,[42] it is not surprising that special interest groups become vocal and critical (some supporting, some opposing) when standards are being formulated. Given this reality, a standard-setting body must pay attention to the economic consequences of its actions; at the same time, however, it should not issue pronouncements that are motivated mainly by politics. While paying attention to their constituencies, standard setters should base their standards on sound research and a conceptual framework that is grounded in economic reality. Recent work by the European Financial Reporting Advisory Group has resulted in some widely supported conclusions that standard setters should undertake an analysis of the impact of potential changes during the standard-setting process.

The standard-setting process is difficult enough when a standard setter is a national one such as the AcSB. The political nature of standard setting has increased as more and more countries have adopted IFRS. The IASB, for instance, has 16 members from many countries. It must consider the needs of all users when creating or changing standards. These user needs become more diverse as we consider the different political, cultural, economic, social, and legal settings of an increasing number of countries.

One political factor is how the standard-setting bodies are financed. The IASB has committed to four principles to ensure that the nature and amount of funding for standard setting does not result in politicization of the process. The principles are as follows per the IASB website.

Funding should be:

1. Broad-based: It should not rely on one or a few sources.

2. Compelling: Constituents should not be allowed to benefit from the standards without contributing to the process of standard setting.

3. Open-ended: Financial commitments for funding should not be contingent upon any particular outcomes that may infringe upon independence in the standard-setting process.

4. Country-specific: Funding should be shared by the major economies on a proportionate basis.[43]

The challenge for standard setters is to find a balance between letting stakeholders have a voice while not bowing to undue political pressures. You might find it very interesting to follow along as a standard is being set. Information such as IASB minutes, presentations to the IASB, exposure drafts, discussion papers, and comment letters are all available on the IASB website (www.ifrs.org). You will see that some spirited discussion takes place and there are many dissenting views.

Principles versus Rules

As mentioned in this chapter, Canadian, U.S., and international accounting standards are becoming increasingly interrelated. All parties are committed to converging toward a high quality set of standards, but there are still many issues that standard setters must deal with. One key issue is the **principles versus rules** debate regarding GAAP.

U.S. GAAP has historically been more prescriptive (even though it is based on principles) and thus has leaned toward the rules-based approach. **In a rules-based approach—much like the Canadian tax system**—there is a rule for most things (even though the rule may be based on a principle). The result is that the body of knowledge in a rules-based approach is significantly larger than that in a principles-based approach. There is also a tendency for companies to interpret the rules literally. Many companies take the view that, if there is no rule for a particular situation, they are free to choose whatever treatment they think is appropriate (within reason). Similarly, many believe that as long as they comply with a rule, even in a narrow sense, they are in accordance with GAAP. Some accountants, auditors, lawyers, and companies favour a GAAP body of knowledge that is more prescriptive because it may be easier to **defend** how to account for a particular item.

Unfortunately, the rules-based approach does not always emphasize the importance of communicating the **best** information for users. Just because a practice is defensible does not mean it provides the best information. This particular issue is a significant one for the United States as it decides whether to adopt IFRS.[44]

IFRS and ASPE are more principles-based. The body of knowledge is smaller and the idea is that one or more principles form the basis for decision-making in many differing scenarios. In addition, professional judgement is fundamental. There is less emphasis on right and wrong answers. Rather, the financial reporting is a result of carefully reasoned application of the principle to the business facts. In a principles-based body of knowledge, bright-line tests are minimized. **Bright-line tests** are often numeric benchmarks for determining accounting treatment. For instance, when determining how to account for a lease under Section 3065 (ASPE), there is a test that looks at whether the lease term is greater than or equal to 75% of the economic life of the asset. The trouble with bright-line tests is that they create a distinctive threshold that is either met or not. Reality is not so clear-cut.

The challenge is for standard setters to ensure that the body of knowledge:

1. rests on a cohesive set of principles and a conceptual framework that are consistently applied,

2. is sufficiently flexible to be of use in many differing business situations and industries, and

3. is sufficiently detailed to provide good guidance but not so big as to be unwieldy.

Throughout the text, we will focus on the development of professional judgement within a principles-based GAAP system (IFRS and ASPE). The cases at the end of each chapter are particularly good for helping you understand how to apply GAAP and deal with choice and ambiguity.

WHAT DO THE NUMBERS MEAN?

Will the United States migrate to IFRS? That is a big question. As mentioned previously, there is a significant difference philosophically between IFRS, which is a high-level, principles-based system, and U.S. GAAP, which is a more detailed, prescriptive system of GAAP. While IFRS consists of between 2,000 and 3,000 pages, prior to 2009 U.S. GAAP had more than 2,000 separate standards, many containing multiple pages. The bodies of knowledge are different in size and level of detailed guidance. The FASB has since restructured the U.S. body of knowledge, reorganizing the separate standards into one large set of U.S. GAAP. This initiative is known as the codification project and it brings all of U.S. GAAP under one roof. This is a giant move forward in helping to make U.S. GAAP more accessible and user-friendly.

Prior to the codification, the FASB surveyed more than 1,400 people who use U.S. GAAP. Some 80% felt it was confusing and 85% felt the required level of research to determine how to account for something was excessive.

While the codification project makes U.S. GAAP more user-friendly, it is still fundamentally different from IFRS. For a number of years, the FASB and the IASB have been working together to harmonize various specific standards so that they are worded essentially the same. Moving from a prescriptive, detailed body of knowledge to a more high-level, principles-based body of knowledge may not be so easy, however. In a speech in December 2010, the deputy chief accountant of the SEC, Paul Beswick, was asked what a reasonable approach would be for the United States to move over to IFRS. Mr. Beswick proposed what he called a "condorsement" approach: part endorsement and part convergence. Under this approach, U.S. GAAP would continue to exist and the FASB would continue to work through each IFRS standard to ensure it was suitable for the U.S. capital market. (This is the convergence aspect.) In addition, the FASB would consider new IASB standards and make a decision whether to endorse them or not. Whether U.S. companies will ever be allowed to use IFRS remains to be seen.

Currently, the FASB has implemented a three-part strategy for seeking greater comparability in accounting standards internationally:

1. Develop high-quality GAAP standards.

2. Actively participate in the development of IFRS.

3. Enhance relationships and communications with other national standard setters.

There are significant divergent views between the IASB and FASB in the areas of impairment of financial instruments, accounting for certain lease contracts, and treatment of insurance contracts. The list of areas where the two standard-setting bodies differ in their views is growing. Thus it seems less and less likely that the United States will adopt IFRS for U.S. companies.

Source: Financial Accounting Foundation, FASB Accounting Standards Codification, 2011, and current FASB website, 2014.

Impact of Technology

As **providers of information**, accountants **identify, measure, and communicate useful information to users**. Technology affects this process in many profound ways. Information is becoming increasingly abundant and available through technology. Companies now file required disclosures electronically with securities commissions. Investors can tap into conversations, including earnings calls, briefings with analysts, and interviews with senior management and market regulators. This gives stakeholders easy access to a significant amount of very timely company information. The Internet allows users to quickly find related information about a company. Companies can disclose more detail on-line, which the user can then aggregate and analyze. From the company's perspective, providing information over the Internet gives it access to a much larger group of users. Information can also be targeted to specific users, and costs are greatly reduced as well.

Some of the main drawbacks of technology concern accessibility: Will all users have the knowledge and ability to access the information? Equal access is certainly important to ensure fairness for all stakeholders. Another issue is the quality and reliability of the information, especially since the information may not be audited. Are certain sites and content more reliable than others? Finally, will making increasing amounts of information available in this way leave companies open to information theft or manipulation?

As technology advances at a dramatic pace, will this lead to on-line real-time and/or continuous reporting with access for all users? The industry is experimenting with the use of extensible business reporting language (XBRL). This system allows a company to tag its information so that users can more easily extract it for analyzing and other use. With XBRL companies can streamline financial information collecting and reporting, while consumers of financial data such as investors, analysts, financial institutions, and regulators can find, receive, compare, and analyze data more quickly and efficiently.

The challenge is to embrace technological opportunities without losing the quality and content of traditional financial reporting.

Integrated Reporting

Financial performance is rooted in a company's business model (that is, the earnings process, how companies finance the process, and what resources companies invest in). Historically, this has not always been the focus of financial accounting. However, a company's ability to articulate its strategic vision and carry out that vision does affect financial performance. The accounting information system is also part of a larger system of information management—a system that contains a significant amount of non-financial information.

Institutional investors are increasingly looking for more information about how a company deals with environmental, social, and governance issues.[45]

The **International Integrated Reporting Committee (IIRC)** has been established to look at this broader view of reporting and includes in its membership corporations, investors, accountants, regulators, academics, standard setters, and others. Its goal is to work toward a more integrated framework for business reporting that includes management information, governance and compensation, and financial and sustainability reporting.[46]

The opportunity is to view financial reporting as part of a larger integrated "ecosystem" and not in isolation.

Conclusion

Financial reporting is standing at the threshold of some significant changes. Is the accounting profession up to the challenge? We believe that the profession is reacting responsibly and effectively to correct the shortcomings that have been identified and to move forward with a new vision. Because of its great resources and expertise, the profession should be able to develop and maintain high standards. This is and will continue to be a difficult process that requires time, logic, and diplomacy. Through a well-chosen mix of these three ingredients, however, the accounting profession will continue to be a leader on the global business stage.

SUMMARY OF LEARNING OBJECTIVES

1 Explain how accounting makes it possible to use scarce resources more efficiently.

Accounting provides reliable, relevant, and timely information to managers, investors, and creditors so that resources are allocated to the most efficient enterprises. Accounting also provides measurements of efficiency (profitability) and financial soundness.

2 Explain the meaning of "stakeholder" and identify key stakeholders in financial reporting, explaining what is at stake for each one.

Investors, creditors, management, securities commissions, stock exchanges, analysts, credit rating agencies, auditors, and standard setters are some of the major stakeholders. Illustration 1-4 explains what is at stake for each one.

3 Identify the objective of financial reporting.

The objective of financial reporting is to communicate information that is useful to key decision-makers such as investors and creditors in making resource allocation decisions (including assessing management stewardship) about the resources and claims to resources of an entity and how these are changing.

4 Explain how information asymmetry and bias interfere with the objective of financial reporting.

Ideally, all stakeholders should have access to the same information in order to ensure that good decisions are made in the capital marketplace. This is known as information symmetry. However, this is not the case—there is often information asymmetry. Of necessity,

management has access to more information so that it can run the company. It must also make sure that it does not give away information that might harm the company, such as in a lawsuit where disclosure might cause the company to lose. Aside from this, information asymmetry exists because of management bias whereby management acts in its own self-interest, such as wanting to maximize management bonuses. This is known as moral hazard in accounting theory. Information asymmetry causes markets to be less efficient. It may cause stock prices to be discounted or costs of capital to increase. In addition, it might restrict good companies from raising capital in the particular market where relevant information is not available (referred to as adverse selection in accounting theory). The efficient markets hypothesis is felt to exist only in a semi-strong form, meaning that only publicly available information is assimilated into stock prices.

5 Explain the need for accounting standards and identify the major entities that influence standard setting and financial reporting.

The accounting profession has tried to develop a set of standards that is generally accepted and universally practised. This is known as GAAP (generally accepted accounting principles). Without this set of standards, each enterprise would have to develop its own standards, and readers of financial statements would have to become familiar with every company's particular accounting and reporting practices. As a result, it would be almost impossible to prepare statements that could be compared. In addition, accounting standards help deal with the information asymmetry problem.

The Canadian Accounting Standards Board (AcSB) is the main standard-setting body in Canada for private companies, pension plans, and not-for-profit entities. Its mandate comes from the Canada Business Corporations Act and Regulations as well as provincial acts of incorporation. For public companies, GAAP is International Financial Reporting Standards (IFRS) as established by the International Accounting Standards Board (IASB). Public companies are required to follow GAAP in order to access capital markets, which are monitored by provincial securities commissions. The U.S. Financial Accounting Standards Board (FASB) is also important because it influences IFRS standard setting. Private companies may choose to follow IFRS. Public companies that list on U.S. stock exchanges may choose to follow U.S. GAAP.

6 Explain the meaning of generally accepted accounting principles (GAAP) and the significance of professional judgement in applying GAAP.

Generally accepted accounting principles are either principles that have substantial authoritative support, such as the *CPA Canada Handbook*, or those arrived at through the use of professional judgement and the conceptual framework.

Professional judgement plays an important role in Accounting Standards for Private Enterprises (ASPE) and IFRS since much of GAAP is based on general principles, which need to be interpreted.

7 Discuss some of the challenges and opportunities for accounting.

Some of the challenges facing accounting are oversight in the capital markets, centrality of ethics, standard setting in a political environment, principles- versus rules-based standard setting, the impact of technology, and integrated reporting. All of these require the accounting profession to continue to strive for excellence and to understand how accounting adds value in the capital marketplace.

KEY TERMS

Accounting Standards Board (AcSB), p. 12
Accounting Standards for Private Enterprises (ASPE), p. 12
Accounting Standards Oversight Council (AcSOC), p. 13
accrual-basis accounting, p. 8
adverse selection, p. 10
aggressive accounting, p. 10
bright-line tests, p. 21
Canadian Institute of Chartered Accountants (CICA), p. 13
Canadian Public Accountability Board (CPAB), p. 19
capital allocation, p. 5
Chartered Professional Accountants Canada (CPA Canada), p. 13
conservative accounting, p. 10
CPA Canada Handbook, p. 13
decision-usefulness approach, p. 8
due process, p. 13
efficient markets hypothesis, p. 10

entity perspective, p. 8
ethical dilemmas, p. 19
financial accounting, p. 4
Financial Accounting Standards Board (FASB), p. 12
financial reporting, p. 4
financial statements, p. 4
GAAP hierarchy, p. 16
generally accepted accounting principles (GAAP), p. 6
general-purpose financial statements, p. 8
IFRS Advisory Council, p. 14
IFRS Foundation, p. 14
information asymmetry, p. 10
information symmetry, p. 9
institutional investors, p. 8
International Accounting Standards Board (IASB), p. 12
International Financial Reporting Interpretation Committee (IFRIC), p. 14

International Financial Reporting Standards (IFRS), p. 12
International Integrated Reporting Committee (IIRC), p. 23
management bias, p. 10
managerial accounting, p. 4
moral hazard, p. 10
objective of financial reporting, p. 8
Ontario Securities Commission (OSC), p. 12
professional judgement, p. 17
proprietary perspective, p. 8
provincial securities commissions, p. 12
Public Company Accounting Oversight Board (PCAOB), p. 18
Securities and Exchange Commission (SEC), p. 12
stakeholders, p. 5
stewardship, p. 11
Toronto Stock Exchange (TSX), p. 16

Note: Completion of this end-of-chapter material will help develop CPA enabling competencies (such as ethics and professionalism, problem-solving and decision-making and communication) and technical competencies. We have highlighted selected items with an integration icon and material in *WileyPLUS* has been linked to the competencies. All cases emphasize integration, especially of the enabling competencies. The brief exercises, exercises and problems generally emphasize problem-solving and decision-making.

Brief Exercises

(LO 1) BE1-1 How does accounting help the capital allocation process?

(LO 2) BE1-2 Identify at least three major stakeholders that use financial accounting information and briefly explain how these stakeholders might use the information from financial statements.

(LO 3) BE1-3 What are the major objectives of financial reporting?

(LO 4) BE1-4 Describe what is meant by information asymmetry.

(LO 4) BE1-5 How does information asymmetry hurt investors in the capital marketplace?

(LO 5) BE1-6 What is the value of having a common set of standards in financial accounting and reporting?

(LO 5) BE1-7 What is the likely limitation on "general-purpose financial statements"?

(LO 5) BE1-8 What are some of the developments or events that occurred between 1900 and 1930 that helped bring about changes in accounting theory or practice?

(LO 5) BE1-9 Which organization is currently dominant in the world for setting accounting standards?

(LO 5) BE1-10 Explain the role of the Canadian Accounting Standards Board (AcSB) in establishing generally accepted accounting principles.

(LO 5) BE1-11 What is the role of the Ontario Securities Commission (OSC) in standard setting?

(LO 5) BE1-12 What are some possible reasons why another organization, such as the OSC or the Securities and Exchange Commission (SEC), should not issue financial reporting standards?

(LO 5) BE1-13 What are the sources of pressure that change and influence the development of accounting principles and standards?

(LO 5) BE1-14 Some individuals have argued that the AcSB and the International Accounting Standards Board (IASB) need to be aware of the economic consequences of their pronouncements. What is meant by "economic consequences"? What are some of the dangers if politics play too much of a role in the development of financial reporting standards?

(LO 5) BE1-15 Some individuals have argued that all Canadian companies should follow the same set of accounting principles. Explain why there are multiple sets of standards in Canada.

(LO 5) BE1-16 If you were given complete authority to decide this, how would you propose that accounting principles or standards be developed and enforced?

(LO 6) BE1-17 If you had to explain or define "generally accepted accounting principles," what essential characteristics would you include in your explanation?

(LO 6) BE1-18 Explain the difference between primary and other sources of GAAP.

(LO 6) BE1-19 The chair of the Financial Accounting Standards Board (FASB) at one time noted that "the flow of standards can only be slowed if (1) producers focus less on quarterly earnings per share and tax benefits and more on quality products, and (2) accountants and lawyers rely less on rules and law and more on professional judgement and conduct." Explain his comment.

(LO 6, 7) BE1-20 What is the difference between principles-based and rules-based accounting standards? In which category does IFRS belong? ASPE? Explain.

(LO 7) BE1-21 One writer recently noted that 99.4% of all companies prepare statements that are in accordance with GAAP. Why then is there such concern about fraudulent financial reporting?

(LO 7) BE1-22 Some foreign countries have reporting standards that are different from standards in Canada. What are some of the main reasons why reporting standards are often different among countries?

(LO 7) BE1-23 How are financial accountants pressured when they need to make ethical decisions in their work? Is having technical mastery of GAAP enough to practise financial accounting?

(LO 7) BE1-24 What are some of the major challenges facing the accounting profession?

(LO 7) BE1-25 The Sarbanes-Oxley Act was enacted to combat fraud and curb poor reporting practices. What are some key provisions of this legislation? Are these provisions in effect in Canada?

ENABLING COMPETENCIES

Cases

Refer to the Case Primer on the Student Website and in *WileyPLUS* to help you answer these cases.

CA1-1 Sherry Chan has just started up a small corporation that produces jewellery. She has applied for and received a government grant. The grant will automatically be renewed as long as the business shows a profit at year end. Because she is trying to control costs, Sherry will prepare the financial statements. The bank has loaned Sherry money and is also waiting for the year-end statements. It will decide whether to renew the loan or not.

Instructions

Discuss the ethical issues of Sherry preparing her own financial statements.

ETHICS

CA1-2 When the AcSB issues new standards, the implementation date is usually 12 months after the issue date, but early implementation is encouraged. In this case, Paula Popov, controller, is discussing with her financial vice-president the need for early implementation of a standard that would result in a fairer presentation of the company's financial condition and earnings. When the financial vice-president determines that early implementation of the standard will lower the reported net income for the year, he discourages Popov from implementing the standard until it is required.

Instructions

Discuss the ethical issues of the financial VP's request.

(CMA adapted)

ETHICS

CA1-3 Boston Clothing Limited was a private company that experienced cash flow difficulties and hired new management to turn the company around. The company then went public and the shares sold at $15 per share. Within months, however, the share price plummeted and Beatle Clothing Inc. acquired the company for $1 per share when Boston was on the threshold of bankruptcy.

Instructions

(a) Who were the stakeholders in this situation?

(b) Explain what was at stake and why and how stakeholders were affected when the share price plummeted.

FINANCE

CA1-4 The National Credit Rating Agency downgraded the credit rating of Grand Limited by two levels from BB to B+. The credit rating agency was concerned about the company's ability to refinance portions of its debt. Both BB and B+ are considered "junk" bonds and are below the BBB– category, which is the lowest grade that many pension and mutual funds are allowed to hold.

Financial statement analysts said the company's financial profile had weakened due to tight debt covenants and resulting cash flow restrictions.

Instructions

(a) Discuss whether the credit rating agency is a stakeholder from Grand Limited's perspective.

(b) Discuss any bias that Grand might have when it issues its financial statements.

CA1-5 Save the Trees (STT) is a not-for-profit organization whose mandate is to keep our cities green by planting and looking after trees. STT is primarily funded by government grants and must comply with a significant number of criteria in order to obtain additional funds. One such requirement is that the entity prepare financial statements in accordance with GAAP.

Instructions

(a) Identify who the stakeholders are in this case and explain why they are stakeholders.

(b) Which GAAP should the entity follow and why?

RESEARCH AND ANALYSIS

RA1-1 Standardized versus Voluntary Disclosure

Some critics argue that having different organizations establish accounting principles is wasteful and inefficient. Instead of mandating accounting standards, each company could voluntarily disclose the type of information it considered important. In addition, if an investor wanted additional information, the investor could contact the company and pay to receive the desired information.

Instructions

Comment on the appropriateness of this viewpoint.

RA1-2 Politicization of Standard Setting

Some accountants have said that the development and acceptance of generally accepted accounting principles (that is, standard setting) is undergoing a "politicization." Some use the term "politicization" in a narrow sense to mean the influence by government agencies, particularly the securities commissions, on the development of generally accepted accounting principles. Others use it more broadly to mean the compromise that results when the bodies that are responsible for developing generally accepted accounting principles are pressured by interest groups (securities commissions, stock exchanges, businesses through their various organizations, financial analysts, bankers, lawyers, and so on).

Instructions

(a) What are the arguments in favour of the politicization of accounting standard setting?

(b) What are the arguments against the politicization of accounting standard setting?   (CMA adapted.)

RA1-3   Accounting Standard-Setting Models

Three models for setting accounting standards follow:

1. The purely political approach, where national legislative action decrees accounting standards

2. The private, professional approach, where financial accounting standards are set and enforced by private, professional actions only

3. The public/private mixed approach, where standards are set by private-sector bodies that behave as though they were public agencies and the standards are mostly enforced through government agencies

Instructions

(a) Which of these three models best describes standard setting in Canada? Explain your choice.

(b) Why are companies, financial analysts, labour unions, industry trade associations, and others actively interested in standard setting?

(c) Cite an example of a group other than the AcSB that tries to establish accounting standards. Speculate on why such a group might want to set its own standards.

RA1-4   Continuous Reporting Model

The increased availability and accessibility of information has had a major impact on the process of financial reporting. Most companies have websites and make available to stakeholders a significant amount of financial information, including annual reports and other financial data. This has sparked the question of whether companies should use a continuous reporting model instead of the current discrete model where financial statements are generally issued only quarterly and annually. Under a continuous reporting model, the company would make more information available to users in real time or perhaps on a "delayed" real-time basis (such as weekly).

Instructions

What are the pros and cons of a continuous reporting model? Consider the various stakeholders in the capital marketplace.

REAL WORLD EMPHASIS

RA1-5   Fair Presentation

Nortel Networks Inc., the former telecommunications giant, was accused of misstating its financial statements. The auditors for the company signed audit reports in which they stated that Nortel's financial statements were fairly presented.

Instructions

How is it possible that a company can misrepresent its financial statements and still receive a "clean" audit opinion from its auditors?

RA1-6   Government Regulation

As mentioned in the chapter, the capital marketplace's reaction to recent corporate failures has been to increase the amount of government regulation.

Instructions

(a) Identify what steps Canada and the United States have taken to increase government regulation of the capital marketplace.

(b) What other options to strengthen the capital marketplace might have been available to stakeholders?

(c) What are the strengths and weaknesses of government regulation in this area?

RA1-7   Disclosures

Hans Hoogervorst, Chair of the IASB, delivered a speech at the Korean Accounting Review International Symposium in Seoul, Korea, on March 31, 2015, entitled "Mind the Gap (Between non-GAAP and GAAP)." In this presentation, he spoke of issues related to the IASB's disclosure initiative, particularly corporate reporting of non-GAAP measures and the need for professional judgement when making disclosure decisions.

Instructions

Access Mr. Hoogervorst's March 31, 2015 speech and IAS 1 *Presentation of Financial Statements* on the IASB website (www. ifrs.org).

(a) What is meant by "non-GAAP measures"? Explain Mr. Hoogervorst's position on such measures and why they are a concern to the IASB.

(b) What disclosure issues does Mr. Hoogervorst identify that require professional judgement? What does he mean by "boilerplate" disclosures? What is meant by professional judgement?

(c) Review the requirements of IAS 1 and identify three requirements where preparers of the financial statements would need to exercise professional judgement.

RA1-8   Stakeholder Information Needs

Financial statements can be a valuable tool for many parties interested in a company's performance. Consider a public company in Alberta that drills oil and sells it to refineries in the United States. The company prepares its financial statements using IFRS and publishes the statements on its website.

Instructions

(a) Who are the stakeholders who would be interested in the company's financial reporting?

(b) What information would be most relevant to these stakeholders?

RA1-9   Limits on Disclosure

There are many situations in which management of a company may want to disclose more or less information about its operations. Consider a manufacturer that is preparing for the launch of a new product line. The information available to management may include the product's projected release date, the associated costs, the price at which the product will be sold, and the results of any market research performed as to the expected sales.

Instructions

Why might management want to share the information above with the public? Why might they try to keep this information private? Also consider the impact of management's decision on those outside of the organization.

ETHICS

RA1-10   Disclosure Decision

It is a goal of standard setters to develop accounting standards that will provide comparability across organizations and over time. However, there are instances when professional judgement must be used in determining the correct amount of disclosure. Assume the role of the ethical accountant working as an advisor for ABC Inc., a toy manufacturer. ABC Inc. has received reports that a particular toy may have led to children's injuries. At this time, the information available is inconclusive as to whether the toy actually caused the injury or whether it was a result of user error. Management must now decide whether to communicate the potential malfunction to the public or to wait for additional information.

Instructions

(a) Describe the reasons for management to await additional information before making a public statement about the toy's safety.

(b) Describe the reasons management might communicate the potential defect to the public immediately.

(c) In your role as the ethical accountant, what course of action would you recommend and why?

ETHICS

RA1-11   Users of Integrated Reporting

The integrated reporting initiative discussed in this chapter focuses on extending the disclosure of financial statements to include more information about a company and its objectives and performance.

Instructions

Discuss what type of financial statement users would be in favour of the additional disclosure required for integrated reporting.

RA1-12   Funding Principles

The IASB has instituted four principles related to its funding to ensure that funding does not lead to politicization of standard setting. The standards specify that funding should be broad-based, compelling, open-ended, and country-specific. This differs from the funding processes for the AcSB and FASB.

Instructions

(a) Discuss the four principles and what impact they have on the standard-setting process.

(b) What issues might arise if these principles did not exist?

(c) The AcSB and FASB do not have the same funding principles in place. Why might the same principles not work for the AcSB and FASB?

RA1-13   Materiality

Materiality has always been an elusive concept in IFRS. It is defined in a general sense, but, in the past, there has been little guidance to help preparers and others apply the concept. For this reason, the IASB decided it was important to issue a Practice Statement on materiality (in late 2015) as part of its disclosure initiative.

While a Practice Statement does not form an authoritative part of IFRS, it has been subject to due process, having received public exposure and input. It falls somewhere between educational guidance and implementation guidance as far as its authority is concerned.

Instructions

Read the Practice Statement on materiality and respond to the following questions:

(a) What was the reason for undertaking the project on materiality?

(b) How is materiality defined?

(c) What general guidance is provided on how to apply the materiality concept to financial reporting decisions?

RA1-14   IASB

Michael Sharpe, then-deputy chairman of the International Accounting Standards Committee, made the following comments before the Financial Executives International 63rd Annual Conference:

There is an irreversible movement toward the harmonization of financial reporting throughout the world. The international capital markets require an end to:

1. The confusion caused by international companies announcing different results depending on the set of accounting standards applied. Recent announcements by

Daimler-Benz (now DaimlerChrysler) highlight the confusion that this causes.

2. Companies in some countries obtaining unfair commercial advantages from the use of particular national accounting standards.

3. The complications in negotiating commercial arrangements for international joint ventures caused by different accounting requirements.

4. The inefficiency of international companies having to understand and use myriad accounting standards depending on the countries in which they operate and the countries in which they raise capital and debt. Executive talent is wasted on keeping up to date with numerous sets of accounting standards and the never-ending changes to them.

5. The inefficiency of investment managers, bankers, and financial analysts as they seek to compare financial reporting drawn up in accordance with different sets of accounting standards.

6. Failure of many stock exchanges and regulators to require companies subject to their jurisdiction to provide comparable, comprehensive, and transparent financial reporting frameworks giving international comparability.

7. Difficulty for developing countries and countries entering the free market economy, such as China and Russia, in accessing foreign capital markets because of the complexity of and differences between national standards.

8. The restriction on the mobility of financial service providers across the world as a result of different accounting standards.

Clearly, eliminating these inefficiencies by having comparable high-quality financial reporting used across the world would benefit international businesses.

Instructions

Research the issue using the Internet and answer the following questions:

(a) What is the International Accounting Standards Board and what is its relationship with the International Accounting Standards Committee?

(b) Which stakeholders might benefit from the use of international accounting standards?

(c) What do you believe are some of the major obstacles to harmonization?

REAL WORLD EMPHASIS

RA1-15   Canadian Coalition for Good Governance (CCGG)

The Canadian Coalition for Good Governance (www.ccgg.ca) was formed in 2002 and represents a significant number of institutional investors in Canada.

Instructions

(a) What is the purpose of the CCGG?

(b) How does an institutional investor differ from other investors?

(c) In your opinion, what impact would the presence of a large number of investors have on management's financial reporting decisions?

(d) Identify three current members of the CCGG. Go to these member companies' websites and identify some of their most significant investments. What total dollar value of investments does each have under management?

RA1-16   SOX and the CPAB

In 2002, the Sarbanes-Oxley Act (SOX) was passed in the United States to strengthen the capital marketplace. In the following year, there were many debates in Canada about whether the securities commissions here should adopt the same regulations. In the end, Canada did adopt a similar level of regulation with the introduction of the Canadian Public Accountability Board (CPAB).

Instructions

(a) Why was the Sarbanes-Oxley Act issued and what are its key components?

(b) What impact do you think the Act had on the U.S. capital marketplace?

(c) What was the major spillover effect in the Canadian regulatory environment?

(d) Since SOX and the CPAB have been in place, continuing pressure has been felt in a number of areas relating to auditor independence requirements. Identify three current and emerging issues the CPAB has studied and reported on. What is the CPAB's position?

RA1-17   Convergence of IASB and FASB GAAP

From the IFRS website (www.ifrs.org), locate the "Update by the IASB and FASB" to the meeting of the G20 finance ministers and central bank governors on February 15 and 16, 2013, as well as the update on convergence included in the "Report of the Chair of the IASB" in the 2014 IASB Annual Report. These reports provide a picture of the extent to which convergence was achieved on significant accounting and reporting issues as the work originating from the 2002 Norwalk Agreement (memorandum of understanding) between the two boards came to a close. Some of the significant differences between U.S. GAAP and IFRS are related to the perceived rules-based approach taken by the United States compared with the principles-based approach of IFRS.

Instructions

Review the reports and respond to the following questions:

(a) In your own words, state the differences between a rules-based approach and a principles-based approach.

(b) Refer to the updates related to the revenue standard. What are the reasons provided for needing convergence on this standard? Have the differences been resolved in the converged revenue standard?

(c) Refer to the updates on the work undertaken on the impairment model within the financial instruments standard. Identify whether the proposed amendments resulted in a converged impairment standard.

(d) Refer to the updates on the leases project. What are the reasons provided for needing convergence on this standard? Have the differences been resolved in a converged lease standard?

(e) Refer to the updates on the joint efforts on the insurance contracts project. Have any differences been resolved in a converged insurance contracts standard? Explain briefly.

REAL WORLD
EMPHASIS

ETHICS

RA1-18   Financial Reporting Pressures

What follows is part of the testimony from Troy Normand in the **WorldCom** case. He was a manager in the corporate reporting department and is one of five individuals who pleaded guilty. He testified in the hope of receiving no prison time when he was ultimately sentenced.

Q: Mr. Normand, if you could just describe for the jury how the meeting started and what was said during the meeting?

A: I can't recall exactly who initiated the discussion, but right away Scott Sullivan acknowledged that he was aware we had problems with the entries, David Myers had informed him, and we were considering resigning.

He said that he respected our concerns but that we weren't being asked to do anything that he believed was wrong. He mentioned that he acknowledged that the company had lost focus quite a bit due to the preparations for the Sprint merger, and that he was putting plans in place and projects in place to try to determine where the problems were, why the costs were so high.

He did say he believed that the initial statements that we produced, that the line costs in those statements could not have been as high as they were, that he believed something was wrong and there was no way that the costs were that high.

I informed him that I didn't believe the entry we were being asked to do was right, that I was scared, and I didn't want to put myself in a position of going to jail for him or the company. He responded that he didn't believe anything was wrong, nobody was going to be going to jail, but that if it later was found to be wrong, that he would be the person going to jail, not me.

He asked that I stay, don't jump off the plane, let him land softly, that's basically how he put it. And he mentioned that he had a discussion with Bernie Ebbers asking Bernie to reduce projections going forward and Bernie had refused.

Q: Mr. Normand, you said that Mr. Sullivan said something about don't jump out of the plane. What did you understand him to mean when he said that?

A: Not to quit.

Q: During this meeting, did Mr. Sullivan say anything about whether you would be asked to make entries like this in the future?

A: Yes, he made a comment that from that point going forward we wouldn't be asked to record any entries, high-

level late adjustments, that the numbers would be the numbers.

Q: What did you understand that to mean, the numbers would be the numbers?

A: That after the preliminary statements were issued, with the exception of any normal transactions, valid transactions, we wouldn't be asked to be recording any more late entries.

Q: I believe you testified that Mr. Sullivan said something about the line cost numbers not being accurate. Did he ask you to conduct any analysis to determine whether the line cost numbers were accurate?

A: No, he did not.

Q: Did anyone ever ask you to do that?

A: No.

Q: Did you ever conduct any such analysis?

A: No, I didn't.

Q: During this meeting, did Mr. Sullivan ever provide any accounting justification for the entry you were asked to make?

A: No, he did not.

Q: Did anything else happen during the meeting?

A: I don't recall anything else.

Q: How did you feel after this meeting?

A: Not much better actually. I left his office not convinced in any way that what we were asked to do was right. However, I did question myself to some degree after talking with him wondering whether I was making something more out of what was really there.

Instructions

Answer the following questions:

(a) What appears to be the ethical issue in this case?

(b) Was Troy Normand acting improperly or immorally?

(c) What would you do if you were Troy Normand?

(d) Who are the major stakeholders in this case?

RA1-19   Prudence

In 2012, Hans Hoogervorst, Chairman of the IASB, gave a speech at the FEE Conference on Corporate Reporting of the Future entitled "The Concept of Prudence: Dead or Alive?" This speech was in answer to many who opposed the elimination of "prudence" from the recently revised qualitative characteristics of useful financial statement information. The speech can be found on the IFRS website at www.ifrs.org. Subsequently, in the May 2015 Exposure Draft "Conceptual Framework for Financial Reporting," the notion of "prudence" was reintroduced into the conceptual framework, with an explanation in the basis for conclusions that accompanied the Exposure Draft.

Instructions

(a) Mr. Hoogervorst indicated in his 2012 speech that there are many instances that demonstrate that IFRS implementation has not led to a loss of prudence. Discuss some specific examples he provides in which the revised conceptual framework of IFRS continues to instill the concept of prudence, although in practice not definition, in financial reporting.

(b) Why was the idea of prudence originally removed from the earlier version of the qualitative characteristics of the conceptual framework? Why was the concept reintroduced in the 2015 Exposure Draft?

(c) How does professional judgement affect the application of the concept of prudence? Will it be applied any differently than it was originally?

ENDNOTES

1 Julia Christensen Hughes and Joy Mighty, in their book entitled *Taking Stock* (Queen's School of Policy Studies, Kingston, 2010), refer to this as the ubiquity of information, meaning that information is now more freely, openly, and readily available. In the book, Christensen Hughes and Mighty discuss the impact of this phenomenon on education; however, it applies equally to the capital marketplace.

2 All public companies must disclose certain information under provincial securities law. This information is collected by the provincial securities commissions under the Canadian umbrella organization, the Canadian Securities Administrators (CSA), and is available electronically at www.sedar.com.

3 The largest, most senior equity market in Canada is the Toronto Stock Exchange (TSX). The junior market—the TSX Venture Exchange (formerly the CDNX Stock Market and now referred to as the TSXV)—was created in 2001 to handle start-up companies. The Montreal Exchange (MX), known also as the Canadian Derivatives Exchange, is the main market for derivatives and futures trading. As noted at the beginning of the chapter, a new market has opened up to help private companies raise capital (TSX Private Market).

4 According to Bloomberg in an article entitled "Big 5 Canadian Banks Now Big 3 as Assets Diverge" on July 7, 2014, what were previously known as the "Big 5"—the Royal Bank of Canada, Toronto Dominion Bank, Bank of Nova Scotia, Bank of Montreal, and Canadian Imperial Bank of Commerce—have now become the "Big 3" with the first three listed being the largest.

5 AICPA Special Committee on Financial Reporting, "Improving Business Reporting: A Customer Focus," supplement in *Journal of Accountancy* (October 1994).

6 For example, institutions such as Dominion Bond Rating Service, Moody's, and Standard & Poor's rate issuers of bonds and preferred shares in the Canadian and global marketplaces.

7 IASB *Conceptual Framework*, Chapter 1, and *CPA Canada Handbook*, Part II, Section 1000.12.

8 Institutional investors are corporate investors such as insurance companies, pension plans, mutual funds, and others. They are considered a separate class of investors because of their size and financial expertise, and the large size of the investments that they hold in other companies. In general, for these reasons, institutional investors have greater power than the average investor.

9 The Canadian Coalition for Good Governance (CCGG) is a group of institutional investors that controls over $3.0 trillion in investments (including investments in private and public equities and bonds). Its members include many significant pension funds in Canada, such as Alberta Teachers' Retirement Fund, Ontario Teachers' Pension Plan, OPSEU Pension Trust, and Ontario Municipal Employees Retirement System, as well as many significant mutual funds and financial institutions, such as Mackenzie Financial Corp., RBC Global Asset Management Inc., and TD Asset Management Inc. According to its website (www.ccgg.ca), CCGG was started in 2002 "to represent Canadian institutional shareholders in the promotion of corporate governance practices that best align the interests of boards and management with those of the shareholder." As a comparison point, the total market capitalization of the TSX is estimated at $2.5 trillion (as at December 2014).

10 There are three forms of the efficient markets hypothesis: (1) the weak form (market prices incorporate all historic publicly available information), (2) the semi-strong form (market prices incorporate all public information), and (3) the strong form (market prices incorporate all information whether public or not). Historically, economists have argued that North American markets are less than perfectly efficient and that they are efficient in the semi-strong form only. This hypothesis has come under attack in recent years. Many feel that we have put too much faith in the belief that markets are efficient and may need other mechanisms to deal with information asymmetry.

11 This is not a new problem. David Brown, then-chairman of the Ontario Securities Commission (OSC), spoke at length on this topic in a speech in 1999 entitled "Public Accounting at a Crossroads." Arthur Levitt, then-chair of the U.S. Securities and Exchange Commission (SEC), discussed his concerns over this issue in "Numbers Game," a major address to New York University in 1998. Both the OSC and the SEC review financial statements and financial reporting practices to ensure that investors have "full and plain disclosure" of all material facts that are needed to make investment decisions. In their speeches, Mr. Brown and Mr. Levitt both cited specific cases where they felt that financial reporting practices were problematic.

12 As noted earlier, conservative accounting would generally result in ensuring that assets and income are not overstated and all relevant information is disclosed.

13 Financial analysts monitor earnings announcements carefully and compare them with their earlier expectations. They and others (including certain stock markets) post what they refer to as earnings surprises each day on their websites. Earnings surprises occur when a company reports net income figures that are different from what the market expected. The focus is on net income or earnings. If net income is higher than expected, this is a positive earnings surprise. If net income is lower than expected, this is a negative earnings surprise and the market will generally react unfavourably, resulting in declining share prices. For instance, for quarterly earnings numbers released on January 23, 2015, the NASDAQ website noted that there were nine positive earnings surprises and five negative earnings surprises. Positive earnings surprises included McDonald's Corporation, Honeywell International Inc., and General Electric Company. Selected negative earnings surprises noted for the same day included Kimberly-Clark Corporation and Rockwell Collins, Inc.

[14] The terms "principle" and "standard" are used interchangeably in practice and throughout this textbook.

[15] The Canada Business Corporations Act and Regulations (CBCA), Part XIV Financial Disclosure and Part 8 (paras. 70 and 71), as well as provincial corporations acts, require that most companies incorporated under these acts prepare financial statements in accordance with Canadian GAAP. This textbook usually refers to this document as the *CPA Canada Handbook* or just the *Handbook*.

[16] The *Handbook* is also available to students and members on-line. With the rapid pace of change in standard setting, most members use the on-line version as their main source of GAAP.

[17] Technically, IFRS is considered to be part of the Canadian *CPA Canada Handbook—Accounting* for legal reasons. However, the *CPA Canada Handbook* as it relates to IFRS will exactly mirror the IASB standards as long as the AcSB continues to officially accept any updates or changes into Canadian GAAP. This was done because many Canadian laws refer to Canadian GAAP.

[18] AcSB Terms of Reference (www.frascanada.ca).

[19] AcSOC membership consists of senior members from business, finance, government, academe, the accounting and legal professions, regulators, and the financial analyst community. The members have a broad perspective on the complex issues facing standard setters. The goal is to achieve full representation across the spectrum of stakeholders (www.frascanada.ca).

[20] Actually, there are at least seven sets of GAAP in Canada. The *CPA Canada Handbook—Accounting* is divided into five parts: Part I—IFRS (for publicly accountable enterprises), Part II—Accounting Standards for Private Enterprises, Part III—Accounting Standards for Not-for-profit Organizations, Part IV—Accounting Standards for Pension Plans, and Part V—Pre-changeover Canadian GAAP (pre-2011). In addition, the *Public Sector Accounting Standards Handbook* contains GAAP for governments. Finally, as mentioned earlier, the Ontario Securities Commission allows Canadian public companies that are U.S. reporting issuers to use U.S. GAAP.

[21] According to the IFRS Foundation Constitution: www.ifrs.org. Note that the IASB also establishes standards for small and medium-sized private entities (referred to as IFRS for SMEs). Since the AcSB produces separate standards for Canadian private entities, Canadian companies do not follow IFRS for SMEs. Copyright © International Financial Reporting Standards Foundation. All rights reserved. Reproduced by John Wiley & Sons Canada, Ltd with the permission of the International Financial Reporting Standards Foundation®. Reproduction and use rights are strictly limited. No permission granted to third parties to reproduce or distribute.

[22] IFRS, *Who We Are and What We Do*, November 2011, p. 2. Copyright © International Financial Reporting Standards Foundation. All rights reserved. Reproduced by John Wiley & Sons Canada, Ltd with the permission of the International Financial Reporting Standards Foundation®. Reproduction and use rights are strictly limited. No permission granted to third parties to reproduce or distribute.

[23] IFRS, *Who We Are and What We Do*, November 2011, p. 5. Copyright © International Financial Reporting Standards Foundation. All rights reserved. Reproduced by John Wiley & Sons Canada, Ltd with the permission of the International Financial Reporting Standards Foundation®. Reproduction and use rights are strictly limited. No permission granted to third parties to reproduce or distribute.

[24] For instance, the IASB issued a DP for revenue recognition, financial statement presentation, and fair value measurement and received 221, 227, and 136 comment letters, respectively. These comment letters were used to draft the subsequent ED.

[25] www.iasplus.com, "Use of IFRSs by Jurisdiction." A complete up-to-date list is on the website. Some of these countries allow companies to alter IFRS (that is, not follow certain standards or follow alternate standards). The IASB has also done an analysis, which may be found at www.ifrs.org under "Analysis of IFRS Jurisdictional Profiles."

[26] The make-up of U.S. GAAP is discussed in the "What do the Numbers Mean" feature.

[27] Before 2007, Canadian companies that were listed on U.S. exchanges could use IFRS or pre-changeover Canadian GAAP but had to reconcile their reporting to U.S. GAAP. This reconciliation was difficult and cumbersome and many Canadian entities decided to just use U.S. GAAP for their U.S. filings. The OSC allows Canadian reporting issuers who list on U.S. stock exchanges or markets to use U.S. GAAP or IFRS according to Canadian Securities Administrators National Instrument 52-107. Note that many non-U.S. companies that list on U.S. exchanges use IFRS. According to a PwC publication entitled "IFRS and U.S. GAAP: Similarities and Differences" published in October 2014, there are 450 foreign firms that file in the United States, with a total market capitalization in the multiple trillions of U.S. dollars.

[28] SEC, *Roadmap for the Potential Use of Financial Statements Prepared in Accordance with International Financial Reporting Standards by U.S. Issuers*, November 2008.

[29] In Canada, securities regulation is carried out by each province, with each of the 10 provinces and three territories being responsible for the companies in its jurisdiction. Many critics feel that this is cumbersome and costly, and are therefore lobbying for a national securities commission. There has been some movement in this direction. The provincial and territorial regulators have formed the Canadian Securities Administrators (CSA). The CSA is mainly responsible for developing a harmonized approach to securities regulation across the country (www.csa-acvm.ca). For now, the CSA collects and archives all filings that are required under the securities regulations of each province and territory (www.sedar.com).

[30] The OSC has a Continuous Disclosure Team that regularly reviews public companies' financial statements and other regulatory findings. The team plans to review each company at least every four years. Results of the review are published on the OSC website.

[31] For instance, in 2002, Staff Accounting Notice 52-303 on "Non-GAAP Earnings Measures" was issued.

[32] *CPA Canada Handbook—Accounting*, Part II, Section 1100.20.

[33] IAS 8. Copyright © International Financial Reporting Standards Foundation. All rights reserved. Reproduced by John Wiley & Sons Canada, Ltd with the permission of the International Financial Reporting Standards Foundation®. Reproduction and use rights are strictly limited. No permission granted to third parties to reproduce or distribute.

[34] The IASB decided to retain the old numbering system for these standards for familiarity and to signal that these standards are older and originated from the IASB's predecessor, the IASC.

[35] As mentioned earlier, U.S. GAAP is often said to be more prescriptive, and provides significantly more detailed guidance than IFRS and ASPE.

[36] Neither ASPE nor IFRS is a perfect principles-based system. The conceptual frameworks for both were written after many of the other standards were written. Therefore, there may be inconsistencies. Standard setters are working to get rid of these inconsistencies in the standards.

[37] Sarbanes-Oxley Act of 2002, H. R. Rep. No. 107-610 (2002).

[38] Sarbanes-Oxley Act of 2002, Section 106 (2002).

[39] www.cpab-ccrc.ca.

[40] CSA Multilateral Instrument 52-109, 52-110, and 52-108. A multilateral instrument is an instrument that has been adopted by one or more CSA jurisdictions.

[41] CSA revised National Instrument 51-102, "Continuous Disclosure Obligations." A national instrument is an instrument that has been adopted by all CSA jurisdictions.

[42] "Economic consequences" in this context means the impact of accounting reports on the wealth positions of issuers and users of financial information and the decision-making behaviour resulting from that impact. The resulting behaviour of these individuals and groups could have harmful financial effects on the providers of the financial information (enterprises). For a more detailed discussion of this phenomenon, see Stephen A. Zeff, "The Rise of Economic Consequences," *Journal of Accountancy* (December 1978), pp. 56–63.

[43] These principles were established in 2006. The IASB's 2014 revenue, including contributions and revenues from sale of products, was £28.4 million.

[44] Note that adoption of IFRS is not necessarily the same as convergence with IFRS. Under convergence, the two sets of standards might still exist side by side and have differing aspects.

[45] In March 2014, CPA Canada and the TMX Group (which operates the Toronto Stock Exchange) issued a publication entitled "A Primer for Environmental & Social Disclosure." It is available on-line (www.cpacanada.ca).

[46] See the publication entitled "The International IR Framework", published by the IIRC (December 2013) (available at http://integratedreporting.org).

CONCEPTUAL FRAMEWORK UNDERLYING FINANCIAL REPORTING

REFERENCE TO THE CPA COMPETENCY MAP | **LEARNING OBJECTIVES**

After studying this chapter, you should be able to:

1.1.1, 1.2.1, 1.2.2	**1.** Indicate the usefulness and describe the main components of a conceptual framework for financial reporting.
1.1.2, 1.2.1, 1.2.2, 3.1.3, 4.3.4	**2.** Identify the qualitative characteristics of accounting information.
1.2.1, 1.2.2	**3.** Define the basic elements of financial statements.
1.2.1, 1.2.2, 1.2.3, 6.1.1, 6.2.1	**4.** Describe the foundational principles of accounting.
1.2.1, 1.2.2, 2.3.2, 4.3.5	**5.** Explain the factors that contribute to choice and/or bias in financial reporting decisions.
1.1.4	**6.** Discuss current trends in standard setting for the conceptual framework.

HOW SHOULD A GRAPEVINE BE VALUED?

HOW TO VALUE A COMPANY'S ASSETS in its financial statements has long been debated. Standard setters and corporations are increasingly favouring the fair value principle, which measures an asset based on what a company could expect to sell it for on the market today.

One of the most challenging types of assets to measure is agricultural resources, partly because the prices they fetch can vary widely over short periods. How do you measure the value of grapevines, for example, especially when newly planted ones take years before they can be harvested?

Until June 2014, the international standard covering agricultural resources, IAS 41 *Agriculture*, required all biological agricultural assets (live plants or animals) to be measured at fair value less costs to sell. "This is based on the principle that the biological transformation that these assets undergo during their lifespan is best reflected by fair value measurement," the IFRS Foundation explained. However, the IASB recognized that there is a particular type of biological assets, such as rubber trees and grapevines, whose sole purpose is to grow produce over a certain number of years. These assets are called bearer plants because they bear produce. "At the end of their productive lives they are usually scrapped. Once a bearer plant is mature, apart from bearing produce, its biological transformation is no longer significant in generating future economic benefits. The only

Getty Images/Thanasis Zovoilis

significant future economic benefits it generates come from the agricultural produce that it creates," the IFRS Foundation stated.

Consequently, the IASB amended IAS 41 so that bearer plants are accounted for as property, plant, and equipment, and therefore fall under IAS 16 *Property, Plant, and Equipment*, "because their operation is similar to that of manufacturing." IAS 41 still covers the produce growing on bearer plants.

What was the thinking behind these amendments? The IASB consulted stakeholders, who said that bearer plants are more like pieces of manufacturing equipment. "Many of these respondents also expressed concerns about the cost, complexity and practical difficulties of fair value measurements of bearer biological assets in the absence of markets for these assets, and about the volatility that arises from recognising changes in the fair value less costs to sell in profit or loss. Furthermore, some respondents asserted that investors, analysts and other users of financial statements adjust the reported profit or loss to eliminate the effects of changes in the fair values of these bearer biological assets."

In changing IAS 16 and 41 so that bearer plants had a more consistent accounting treatment, the IASB was applying the conceptual framework, the accepted objectives and foundation of financial reporting that lead to a coherent set of standards. You could say that the conceptual framework in this case bore fruit.

Sources: "Agriculture: Bearer Plants" (Amendments to IAS 16 and IAS 41), Project Summary and Feedback Statement, IFRS Foundation, June 2014; "IAS 41 – Agriculture," IAS Plus, Deloitte, retrieved from http://www.iasplus.com/en/standards/ias/ias41.

PREVIEW OF CHAPTER 2

Users of financial statements need relevant and reliable information. To help develop this type of financial information, accountants use a conceptual framework that guides financial accounting and reporting. In this chapter, we discuss the basic concepts that underlie this conceptual framework.

The chapter is organized as follows:

CONCEPTUAL FRAMEWORK UNDERLYING FINANCIAL REPORTING				
Conceptual Framework	**Objective of Financial Reporting**	**Foundational Principles**	**Financial Reporting Issues**	**IFRS/ASPE Comparison**
■ Rationale for conceptual framework ■ Development of the conceptual framework ■ Information asymmetry revisited	■ Qualitative characteristics of useful information ■ Elements of financial statements	■ Recognition/ derecognition ■ Measurement ■ Presentation and disclosure	■ Principles-based approach ■ Financial engineering ■ Fraudulent financial reporting	■ Looking ahead

CONCEPTUAL FRAMEWORK

Objective 1
Indicate the usefulness and describe the main components of a conceptual framework for financial reporting.

A **conceptual framework** is like a constitution: it is a "coherent system of interrelated objectives and fundamentals that can lead to consistent standards and that prescribes the nature, function, and limits of financial accounting and financial statements."[1] Many observers believe that the real contribution of standard-setting bodies, and even their continued existence, depends on the quality and usefulness of the conceptual framework.

Rationale for Conceptual Framework

Why is a conceptual framework necessary? First, to be useful, **standard setting should build on an established body of concepts and objectives.** Having a soundly developed conceptual framework as their starting point, standard setters are then able to issue additional **useful and consistent** standards over time. The result is a **coherent** set of standards and rules, because they have all been built upon the same foundation. It is important that such a framework **increases** financial statement users' **understanding** of and **confidence** in financial reporting, and that it **enhances the comparability** of different companies' financial statements.

Second, by referring to an existing framework of basic theory, it should be possible to solve **new and emerging practical problems** more quickly. It is difficult, if not impossible, for standard setters to quickly state the proper accounting treatment for highly complex situations. Practising accountants, however, must solve such problems on a day-to-day basis. By using **good judgement**, and with the help of a **universally accepted conceptual framework**, it is hoped that accountants will be able to decide against certain alternatives quickly and to focus instead on a logical and acceptable treatment.

Development of the Conceptual Framework

Over the years, many organizations, committees, and interested individuals have developed and published their own conceptual frameworks, but no single framework has been universally accepted and relied on in practice. Realizing there was a need for a generally accepted framework, in 1976 the FASB issued a three-part discussion memorandum entitled "Conceptual Framework for Financial Accounting and Reporting: Elements of Financial Statements and Their Measurement." It stated the major issues that would need to be addressed in establishing a conceptual framework for setting accounting standards and resolving financial reporting controversies. Based on this, six Statements of Financial Accounting Concepts were then published. A seventh statement, on accounting measurement, was added in 2000.

SIGNIFICANT CHANGE

The AcSB and IASB followed the FASB's example and issued their own respective frameworks. At the time this text was going to press, the IASB was continuing to work on the conceptual framework to promote global consistency and comparability. The first part of the new joint framework has been issued by both the IASB and FASB and deals with the objective of general-purpose financial reporting and the qualitative characteristics of useful information. This chapter incorporates ideas from the newly emerging framework. The AcSB has signalled that it will likely adopt the framework for private entities as well.

Illustration 2-1 shows an overview of a conceptual framework.[2] At the first level, the objectives identify accounting's **goals and purposes**: these are the conceptual framework's

Illustration 2-1

Conceptual Framework for Financial Reporting

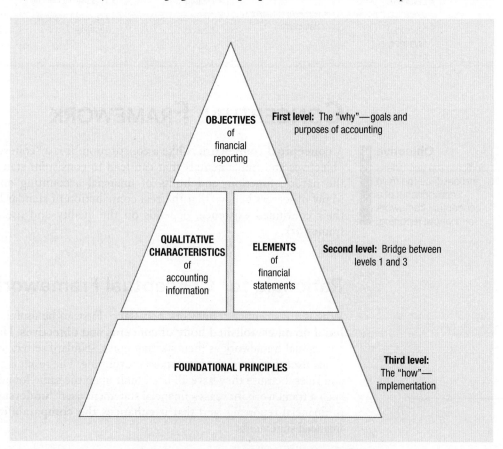

First level: The "why"—goals and purposes of accounting

OBJECTIVES of financial reporting

QUALITATIVE CHARACTERISTICS of accounting information

ELEMENTS of financial statements

Second level: Bridge between levels 1 and 3

FOUNDATIONAL PRINCIPLES

Third level: The "how"— implementation

building blocks. At the second level are the **qualitative characteristics** that make accounting information useful and the **elements of financial statements** (assets, liabilities, equity, revenues, expenses, gains, and losses).[3] At the third and final level are the **foundational principles** used in establishing and applying accounting standards.

Information Asymmetry Revisited

THEORY

As discussed in Chapter 1, investors and creditors need information in order to make sound resource allocation decisions. However, information in the capital marketplace is not always evenly accessible or available to investors and creditors. Stock markets and regulators go to great lengths to ensure information symmetry for all capital market participants so that no one is at a disadvantage. Despite this, various stakeholders often do not have the same information. This can be a problem because stakeholders may make suboptimal decisions because they are lacking good or complete information.

Financial statements play a large part in helping to ensure that investors, creditors, and others have access to information they need to make decisions. However, because of **adverse selection** and/or **moral hazard** (see Chapter 1), problems may arise. The moral hazard issue is worse where certain stakeholders such as accountants and owner-managers have expert knowledge that the rest of the capital marketplace does not. They may use this expertise to act in their own self-interest to the detriment of other capital marketplace participants such as investors.

A well-written conceptual framework based on sound principles may help address these information asymmetry concerns.

OBJECTIVE OF FINANCIAL REPORTING

According to the conceptual framework, the **objective of financial reporting** is to communicate information that is **useful** to investors, creditors, and other users. Financial information is useful in making decisions about how to **allocate resources** (including **assessing management stewardship**). For example, a bank may need information in order to decide whether to lend a company money or call a loan. Similarly, an investor may need information about a company's profitability in order to decide whether to invest in it or divest.

Consequently, companies should provide information about their financial position, changes in financial position, and performance. They should also show how efficiently and effectively management and the board of directors have discharged their responsibilities to use the entity's resources.[4]

Companies provide this information to users of financial statements through **general-purpose financial statements**. These are basic financial statements that give information that meets the needs of **key users**.[5] The statements are intended to provide the most **useful information possible in a manner whereby benefits exceed costs** to the different kinds of users.

Qualitative Characteristics of Useful Information

Objective 2
Identify the qualitative characteristics of accounting information.

Choosing an acceptable accounting method, the amount and types of information to be disclosed, and the format in which information should be presented involves determining **which alternative gives the most useful information for decision-making purposes** (**decision usefulness**). The conceptual framework's second level has identified the **qualitative characteristics** of accounting information that distinguish information that is better (more useful) for making decisions from information that is inferior (less useful). These characteristics are explained next.

Fundamental Qualitative Characteristics

Relevance and **representational faithfulness** (sometimes referred to as faithful representation) are fundamental qualities that make accounting information useful for decision-making. Above all else, these two characteristics must be present.

Relevance

To be relevant, accounting information must be capable of **making a difference in a decision**. If a piece of information has no impact on a decision, it is irrelevant to that decision. Care should be taken to ensure that relevant information is included in financial reporting. Relevant information helps users make predictions about the final outcome of past, present, and future events; that is, it has **predictive value**. For example, separating income from continuing operations from that of operations that have been discontinued may help users predict future income. Relevant information also helps users confirm or correct their previous expectations; it has **feedback/confirmatory value**. For instance, providing information about rental income and the value of the investment in rental properties might help users assess how well management is managing the investment in rental properties.

When discussing relevance, we often hear about the notion of materiality. **Materiality** refers to how important a piece of information is. It is generally thought to be material if it would make a difference to the decision-maker. For instance, a major product defect would be of interest to a potential investor. Material information is relevant and should be included in the financial statements. When determining whether something is material or not, the amount in question is often compared with the entity's amounts of other revenues and expenses, assets and liabilities, or net income.

It is hard to give firm guidelines to decide when an item is or is not material because materiality depends on both a relative amount and relative importance.

For example, the two sets of numbers in Illustration 2-2 show relative size.

Illustration 2-2

Materiality Comparison

	Company A	Company B
Sales	$10,000,000	$100,000
Costs and expenses	9,000,000	90,000
Income from operations	1,000,000	10,000
Unusual gain	20,000	5,000

During the particular period, the revenues and expenses, and therefore the net incomes, of Company A and Company B are proportional. That is, the amounts for Company A are 10 times larger than those for Company B. Each has an unusual gain.

In looking at the abbreviated income figures for Company A, it does not appear significant whether the amount of the unusual gain is presented separately or is merged with the regular operating income. It is only 2% of the operating income and, if merged, would not seriously distort the income figure. Company B has had an unusual gain of only $5,000, but it is relatively much more significant than the larger gain recognized by A. For Company B, an item of $5,000 amounts to 50% of its operating income. Obviously, including such an item in ordinary operating income would affect the amount of that income materially. In this example, we can therefore see the importance of an item's relative size in determining its materiality.

Current auditing standards (CAS 320.A7) define what is material by using benchmark examples from different types of organizations. This standard considers 5% of pre-tax income from continuing operations for manufacturing companies and 1% of revenues for not-for-profit entities to be material. This is not a definitive rule and is a fairly simplistic view of materiality. We need to consider the item's impact on other factors, such as on key financial statement ratios and management compensation; in other words, on **any sensitive number on the financial statements**. In addition, both

**AUDIT AND
ASSURANCE
4.3.4**

quantitative and **qualitative** factors must be considered in determining whether an item is material.

Qualitative factors might include illegal acts, failure to comply with regulations, or inadequate or inappropriate description of an accounting policy. Materiality is also a factor in a large number of internal accounting decisions. Judgements should be determined based on reasonableness and practicality with, for example, the amount of classification required in a subsidiary expense ledger, the degree of accuracy required in prorating expenses among the departments of a business, and the extent to which adjustments should be made for accrued and deferred items. In other words, we must sensibly apply the materiality constraint. Only by exercising good judgement and professional expertise can we find reasonable and appropriate answers.

WHAT DO THE NUMBERS MEAN?

REAL WORLD EMPHASIS

As noted earlier, the concept of materiality is used in financial reporting to help determine if the way something is accounted for would influence decisions made by users of financial statements. How is this concept used in auditing? The overall objective of the audit is to determine whether the financial statements are materially misstated or not. The auditor must complete audit procedures to gain this assurance.

An auditor would use the concept of materiality as follows:

1. In the planning stages: to help decide how much and what type of audit procedures to perform on particular transactions or balances. More work would be done on balances and transactions that are thought to be material.

2. During the audit: to refine the amount and type of audit procedures being done, given the findings. For instance, in the planning stages, the auditor might not think something is material but when the audit is being performed, some new information might come to light.

3. In assessing whether the financial statements are materially misstated and whether they can give an unqualified audit opinion, which states that the financial statements are fairly presented. The auditor will generally find things that need adjusting in the financial statements. A decision must be made as to whether these adjustments need to be made or not. As long as the financial statements are not materially misstated, an unqualified opinion may be given.

Below is an excerpt from the audit report for **Air Canada**. Note the reference to materiality. PwC gave Air Canada an unqualified audit opinion.

Opinion

In our opinion, the consolidated financial statements present fairly in all material respects the financial position of Air Canada and its subsidiaries as at December 31, 2014 and December 31, 2013 and their financial performance and their cash flows for the years ended December 31, 2013 and December 31, 2014 in accordance with International Financial Reporting Standards.

Representational Faithfulness

ECONOMICS

Accounting information is representationally faithful to the extent that it faithfully reflects or represents the underlying **economic substance** of an event or transaction. This notion of representing economic reality is sometimes referred to as **transparency**. If financial statement users read the financial statements, can they see what lies beneath the numbers? This is critical since the statements are meant to tell a story about the business. Is this a risky business? Is it a mature business? Is it capital-intensive? How do we ensure that this information is appropriately presented? Information that is representationally faithful is **complete, neutral,** and **free from material error**.

Completeness refers to the idea that the statements should include all information necessary to portray the underlying events and transactions. Care must be taken to ensure that pertinent information is included since it is possible to misrepresent something by not including all pertinent information. Often this is a question of the amount of details to be presented. For instance, it is important to note the nature of capital assets that an entity has under its control, including property, plant, and equipment. But presenting the amortized cost of such investments are might not be sufficient if some of these assets are leased. The presumption about most property, plant, and equipment that is reported on a statement of financial position is that the company has legal title to the property. Therefore, if this is not the case—in other words, the assets are leased—this additional information should be presented.

Neutrality means that information cannot be selected to **favour one set of interested parties over another.**[6] The information should not be manipulated in any way. Factual, truthful, unbiased information needs to be the overriding consideration when preparing financial information.

WHAT DO THE NUMBERS MEAN?

REAL WORLD EMPHASIS

Livent Inc. was a Canadian company that produced and presented large Broadway-style musicals. In 1993, the company went public, listing its shares on the TSX. By 1998, it filed for bankruptcy protection while it was being accused of accounting irregularities, and in 2001 it was investigated by the Ontario Securities Commission (OSC). The following excerpt is from the OSC Notice of Hearing and Allegation about manipulation of the financial statements. The respondents mentioned below were company management, including Garth Drabinsky, Myron Gottlieb, Gordon Eckstein, and Robert Topol.

... at the end of each financial reporting period, Livent accounting staff circulated to the Respondents a management summary reflecting actual results (including net income, on a show-by-show basis, compared to budget), as well as any improper adjustments carried forward from a prior financial period in connection with each show. Having regard to the actual results, the Respondents then provided instructions, directly or indirectly, to the Livent accounting staff specifying changes to be made to the actual results reflected in the company's books and records. In order to give effect to the Respondents' instructions, Livent accounting

staff manipulated Livent's books and records by various means which did not accord with GAAP. The effect of the manipulations was to improve the presentation of Livent's financial results for the reporting period. Draft financial statements would then be generated for the reporting period incorporating the manipulations. These draft financial statements were then distributed to the Livent audit committee and, thereafter the Livent board of directors, for their review and approval. The Respondents attended meetings of the audit committee and the board of directors where these draft financial statements were discussed and ultimately approved. The Respondents did not disclose to the audit committee or the board of directors that, to their knowledge, the financial statements were false or misleading.

Among other things, management was charged with deliberately and systematically biasing the information. This contributed to the company's eventual downfall. Garth Drabinsky and Myron Gottlieb, co-founders of Livent, were found guilty in 2009 of two counts of fraud and one of forgery. Drabinsky's lawyers argued that he was not motivated by personal greed but rather by a desire to save the company.

In practice, management needs to use many assumptions because of uncertainty in financial reporting, such as uncertainty caused by accrual accounting. For instance, revenues are recorded when earned and not necessarily when cash is received. Thus, companies must estimate the amount of revenue that will be realized or eventually collected. When choosing these assumptions, management must use its best estimates (**management best estimate**) in order to portray the economic reality. Management best estimate assumptions are unbiased, and involve management making diligent efforts to obtain and use all information that it has access to in order to come up with the best-quality information.

ETHICS

As we can see in the Livent example, producing financial statements with biased information can have significant negative consequences, not only for investors and creditors, but also for financial statement preparers and company management.

There is also another aspect to neutrality: neutrality in standard setting. Some observers argue that standards should not be issued if they cause undesirable economic effects on an industry or company. (This is the **economic consequences argument**, which we mentioned in Chapter 1.) Standards must be free from bias, however, or we will no longer have **credible financial statements**. Standard setters should therefore choose the best standards regardless of economic consequences. If the accounting results in users changing their decisions, then by definition, the information is decision-relevant.[7]

Freedom from material error means that the information must be reliable. The task of converting economic events (which are constantly changing and difficult to measure) to numbers in a set of financial statements is complex. Management must make estimates and use judgement in determining how to portray events and transactions. This does not mean that information must be **"perfectly accurate in all respects."**[8] Often, there is no correct or single right way to portray economic reality. For instance, how does a company portray the impact of a major ecological disaster such as an oil spill? Significant assumptions must be made about cleanup activities in order to estimate potential costs and liabilities.

How much effort should be put into obtaining information? Do we need to incur costs such as hiring engineers to help estimate? When is a mismeasurement an error? Information is more useful if it is free from material error, so every attempt should be made to achieve this. Companies must ensure that they invest in good information systems so that they can capture necessary information and must also have strong internal controls to ensure that errors and omissions are minimized.

Enhancing Qualitative Characteristics

Enhancing qualitative characteristics include **comparability**, **verifiability**, **timeliness**, and **understandability**.

Comparability

Information that has been measured and reported in a similar way (both company to company and consistently from year to year) is considered comparable. **Comparability** enables users to **identify the real similarities and differences in economic phenomena** because these have not been obscured by accounting methods that cannot be compared. For example, the accounting for inventory is different under IFRS and FASB. FASB allows the use of last-in, first-out (LIFO) accounting, for instance, whereas IFRS does not. The result is that in times of rising prices, companies using LIFO, such as **Walmart Stores Inc.**, will have a net income that is lower than companies not using LIFO, such as **Loblaw Companies Limited**.

It is important to remember that **resource allocation decisions involve evaluations of alternatives** and it is easier to make a valid evaluation if comparable information is available. Although it is not a substitute for comparable information, a full disclosure of information sometimes allows users to overcome inconsistencies in how information is presented.

Verifiability

Verifiability exists when knowledgeable, independent users achieve similar results or reach consensus regarding the accounting for a particular transaction. Some numbers are more easily verified than others; for example, cash can be verified by confirming with the bank where the deposit is held. Other numbers—such as accruals for future pension liabilities—are more difficult (although not necessarily impossible) to verify, as many assumptions are made to arrive at an estimate. Numbers that are easy to verify with a reasonable degree of accuracy are often referred to as "hard" numbers. Those that have more measurement uncertainty are called "soft" numbers.

Timeliness

Timeliness is also important. Information should be available to decision-makers before it loses its ability to influence their decisions. Quarterly reporting (involving the issuance of financial information every three months) provides information on a more timely basis. Thus, users have information throughout the year as opposed to having to wait until after the year end for the annual financial statements.

Understandability

Users need to have **reasonable knowledge** of business and financial accounting matters in order to understand the information in financial statements. However, financial information must also be of sufficient quality and clarity that it allows reasonably informed users to see its significance. This is the information's **understandability**. In addition, standard setters assume that users have the responsibility to review and analyze the information with reasonable diligence. This point is important: it means that the onus to prepare under-standable statements and to be able to understand them rests with both the financial state-ment preparer and the user. This characteristic affects both how information is reported and how much is reported.

Where the underlying transactions or economic events are more complex, the as-sumption is that users will seek the aid of an advisor.[9] The preparer must also have a clear understanding of the legalities and economics of transactions in order to be able to portray them in the most meaningful way to users.

WHAT DO THE NUMBERS MEAN?

REAL WORLD EMPHASIS

An excerpt follows from the notes to the financial statements of **Enron Corp.** for the year ended Decem-ber 31, 2000 (all figures are in U.S. dollars). The complexity of the business arrangements makes it difficult to understand the nature of the underlying transactions. It contributes to a set of financial state-ments that lack transparency. The choice of words also makes the note difficult to read.

In 2000 and 1999, Enron sold approximately $632 million and $192 million, respectively, of merchant investments and other assets to White-wing. Enron recognized no gains or losses in con-nection with these transactions. Additionally, in 2000, ECT Merchant Investments Corp., a wholly owned Enron subsidiary, contributed two pools of merchant investments to a limited partnership that

is a subsidiary of Enron. Subsequent to the contri-butions, the partnership issued partnership inter-ests representing 100% of the beneficial, economic interests in the two asset pools, and such interests were sold for a total of $545 million to a limited liability company that is a subsidiary of Whitew-ing. See Note 3. These entities are separate legal entities from Enron and have separate assets and liabilities. In 2000 and 1999, the Related Party, as described in Note 16, contributed $33 million and $15 million, respectively, of equity to Whitew-ing. In 2000, Whitewing contributed $7.1 million to a partnership formed by Enron, Whitewing, and a third party. Subsequently, Enron sold a portion of its interest in the partnership through a securitization. See Note 3.[10]

Trade-Offs

In general, preparers of financial information should identify all **relevant** information, then consider how best to ensure that the financial statements are presented such that they reflect the economic substance **(representational faithfulness)**. Both characteristics must be present in order to ensure the information is decision-relevant.

However, it is not always possible for financial information to have all the enhancing qualities of useful information. Trade-offs may exist. For instance, in the interest of provid-ing more relevant information, a new standard may be applied prospectively. In this case, comparability (or **consistency** year to year) is temporarily sacrificed for better information in the future.

The accounting profession is constantly striving to produce financial information that meets all of the qualitative characteristics of useful information.

Too often, users assume that information is a cost-free commodity. But preparers and providers of accounting information know this is not true. This is why the **cost-benefit relationship** must be considered: the costs of providing the information must be weighed against the benefits that can be had from using the information. In order to justify requir-ing a particular measurement or disclosure, the costs must be justified by the benefits. In other words, the benefits must outweigh the costs.

The difficulty in cost-benefit analysis is that the costs and, especially, the benefits are not always evident or measurable. There are several kinds of costs, including the costs of:

MANAGEMENT REPORTING NEEDS AND SYSTEMS

3.1.3

- Collecting and processing

- Distributing

- Auditing

- Potential litigation

- Disclosure of proprietary information to competitors

- Analysis and interpretation

The benefits are enjoyed by both preparers (in terms of greater management control and access to capital) and users (in terms of allocation of resources, tax assessment, and rate regulation). Benefits are generally more difficult to quantify than costs.

The AcSB has taken some steps to reduce the cost of providing information by developing separate standards for private entities that are less onerous and costly. This model allows these companies to follow a simplified version of GAAP based on cost-benefit considerations. In many cases, the shareholders and creditors of private companies have greater access to information and do not necessarily rely solely on the external financial statements. In addition, for smaller private companies, the business and business model are not as complicated and therefore less complex accounting standards are required. Private entities have the option to use IFRS if they wish.

Elements of Financial Statements

Objective 3
Define the basic elements of financial statements.

At present, accounting uses many terms that have specific meanings. These terms make up the **language of accounting and business**. There are many **elements** that users expect to find on the financial statements, including **assets**, **liabilities**, **equity**, **revenues**, **expenses**, **gains**, and **losses**. In addition, within each of these categories there are many subcategories, such as current and non-current assets, cash, inventory, and so on. The conceptual framework's second level defines the basic elements so that users have a common understanding of the main items presented on the financial statements.

The **basic elements** of financial statements that are most directly related to measuring an enterprise's performance and financial status are listed below. We will explain and examine each of these elements in more detail in later chapters.[11]

Assets

Assets have three essential characteristics:

1. There is some economic benefit to the entity.

2. The entity has control over that benefit.

3. The benefits result from a past transaction or event.[12]

For instance, consider a manufacturing plant that is owned by a company. The economic benefits are represented by the cash flows that the plant will generate. The entity has access to (control over) those benefits through legal ownership of the property itself (a tangible asset), thus allowing the company to decide whether to sell it or use it in order to generate cash flows. The transaction giving rise to the benefits would have been the acquisition of the asset.

An asset may also be represented by a contractual or other right. For instance, a purchased patent has value because it gives the holder access to future cash flows from the sale of the patented product. Another example of an asset generated through contractual rights is a leased machine. The lease contract gives the company contractual rights to use the asset despite the fact that the company does not have legal title to the machine.

When determining if an economic resource exists, we must take care to review not only items such as inventory, cash, land, and patents (which represent both tangible and intangible properties) but also contractual and other rights (such as forward contracts, insurance, and others).

Liabilities

Liabilities have three essential characteristics:

1. They represent a present duty or responsibility.

2. The duty or responsibility obligates the entity, leaving it little or no discretion to avoid it.

3. The transaction or event results from a past transaction or event.[13]

Similar but opposite to an asset, a liability has a negative economic value and requires that the entity give up economic resources to settle the obligation. For instance, assume that a company hires employees and agrees to pay them a salary for services provided. Once the employee accepts the offer of employment and starts to provide services, a liability is created. The company has a duty to pay the salary according to the predetermined employment arrangement with the employee once the employee has rendered services. The entity must pay the salary; otherwise there will be negative consequences. For example, the employee will quit and may sue the company for unpaid wages.

Liabilities may arise through contractual obligations, as noted in the case above, or through statutory requirements, such as for illegally polluting. In addition, they may arise through other means, including constructive and equitable obligations.

LAW

Constructive obligations are obligations that arise through past or present practice that signal that the company acknowledges a potential economic burden. For instance, the entity might make a statement that it stands behind its products. Therefore, if a product is defective, even though the entity might not be required to replace it under the terms of the sales contract, the expectation is that the entity will replace it because of the policy to stand behind its products.

Equitable obligations arise due to moral or ethical considerations. For instance, a company might feel a moral obligation to retrain an employee who is being downsized. Care should be taken to ensure that all obligations are identified and properly accounted for. We will discuss these further in subsequent chapters, including Chapters 13, 14, and 16.

Liabilities may be further categorized by standard setters as either financial (as defined in IAS 32 regarding contractual obligations to deliver cash or other financial assets) or non-financial (everything else).[14]

Equity

Equity is a **residual interest** in an entity that remains after deducting its liabilities from its assets. This is also known as its net worth. In a business enterprise, the equity is the **ownership** interest.[15] Equity would normally consist of common or ordinary shares, preferred shares, retained earnings, and, under IFRS, accumulated other comprehensive income.

Revenues

Revenues are increases in economic resources, either by inflows or other enhancements of an entity's assets or by settlement of its liabilities, which result from an entity's **ordinary activities**. For instance, assume that a real estate company owns 10 buildings and leases them out under long-term leases. For this company, revenues would include rental income.

Expenses

Expenses are decreases in economic resources, either by outflows or reductions of assets or by the incurrence of liabilities that result from an entity's **ordinary revenue-generating activities**. For instance, for the real estate company above, this would include heating and property taxes.

Gains/Losses

Gains are increases in equity (net assets) from an entity's **peripheral or incidental transactions** and from all other transactions and other events and circumstances affecting the entity during a period, except those that result from revenues or investments by owners.[16]

Losses are decreases in equity (net assets) from an entity's **peripheral or incidental transactions** and from all other transactions and other events and circumstances affecting the entity during a period, except those that result from expenses or distributions to owners.

For the same real estate company, this might include gains and losses on the sale of the buildings. As noted in the above example, the company's business model includes purchasing buildings and renting them out on a long-term basis, not buying and selling buildings.

The financial statements include the following items:

1. Income statement and/or statement of comprehensive income (IFRS only)

2. Statement of financial position

3. Statement of retained earnings (ASPE only) or changes in shareholders' equity (IFRS only)

4. Statement of cash flows

The term **comprehensive income** is a relatively new income concept and includes more than the traditional notion of net income. It includes net income and **other comprehensive income** (all other changes in equity except for owners' investments and distributions). Other comprehensive income is made up of revenues, expenses, gains, and losses that, in accordance with primary sources of GAAP, are recognized in comprehensive income, but excluded from net income. For example, the following would be included as other comprehensive income in the comprehensive income statement:

- Unrealized holding gains and losses on certain securities (such as Fair Value—OCI investments)

- Changes in the revaluation surplus when using the revaluation method to account for capital assets

- Certain gains and losses related to the translation of foreign operations, and cash flow hedges

- Certain gains and losses related to remeasurement of defined benefit plans and liabilities measured at fair value

Note that IFRS does not require companies to use the terms "comprehensive income" or "other comprehensive income." We will discuss this further in Chapter 4. The concepts of comprehensive income and other comprehensive income do not exist under ASPE. Items would either be booked through net income or straight to shareholders' equity.

FOUNDATIONAL PRINCIPLES

Objective 4
Describe the foundational principles of accounting.

The conceptual framework's third level consists of **foundational principles** that implement the basic objectives of the first level. These concepts help explain which, when, and how financial elements and events should be **recognized, measured**, and **presented/disclosed** by the accounting system. They act as guidelines for developing rational responses to controversial financial reporting issues. They have evolved over time, and the specific accounting standards issued by standard setters are based on these concepts in a fundamental way.

Basic **foundational principles** underlying the financial accounting structure also include assumptions and conventions. It is often difficult to put a label onto the items noted below and accounting practices vary, and so we have grouped them together. The label is not important—it is the substance of the concept and how it provides a solid foundation for accounting standard setting that is important. We will discuss the 10 foundational principles and assumptions under the groupings of recognition/derecognition, measurement, and presentation and disclosure, as follows:

Recognition/Derecognition	Measurement	Presentation and Disclosure
1. Economic entity assumption	5. Periodicity assumption	10. Full disclosure principle
2. Control	6. Monetary unit assumption	
3. Revenue recognition and realization principles	7. Going concern assumption	
4. Matching principle	8. Historical cost principle	
	9. Fair value principle	

Recognition/Derecognition

Recognition deals with the act of including something on the entity's statement of financial position or income statement. At a macro level, decisions need to be made about whether to consolidate investments in other entities. At a micro level, decisions need to be made about whether and when to include assets, liabilities, revenues, expenses, gains, and losses in the financial statements. In addition, once recognized, decisions need to be made about when to derecognize these elements (remove them from the financial statements). These are significant decisions.

The conceptual framework provides general recognition and measurement criteria, and underlying principles may be used to justify whether something should be reflected in the financial statements or not.

Historically, elements of financial statements have been recognized when they:

- meet the definition of an element (for example, a liability),

- are probable, and

- are reliably measurable.

For instance, an entity must use all information to make a neutral decision as to whether the liability or asset exists or not (that is, whether the definition is met). It must then decide whether it is probable that an outflow or inflow of resources will occur and whether it is measurable. We will discuss measurement in greater detail in the next section.

The term "probable" may have differing meanings under IFRS and ASPE when dealing with recognition of losses and liabilities. Under IFRS, "**probable**" is defined as "**more likely than not**" (often interpreted to mean a greater than 50% chance).[17] Under ASPE, it is defined as "likely" (that is, there is a high chance of occurrence).[18] Note that this may cause more losses and liabilities to be recognized under IFRS due to a perceived lower threshold.

Derecognition is the act of taking something off the statement of financial position or income statement. In the past, derecognition criteria were discussed in the context of financial instruments only, and primarily focused on financial assets. We will discuss derecognition as it pertains to financial instruments in Chapters 7 and 14. Having said this, just as the conceptual framework includes general recognition criteria for all elements, it makes sense that it should include general derecognition criteria for all elements. The IASB has included derecognition criteria in the Exposure Draft relating to the conceptual framework.[19]

Several additional underlying principles help determine whether something should be recognized or not. A discussion of these follows.

Economic Entity Assumption and Control

The **economic entity assumption** (or entity concept) allows us to **identify an economic activity** with a particular **unit of accountability** (for example, a company, a part of a company such as a division, or an individual). If all the economic events that occur could not be separated in a meaningful way, there would be no basis for accounting. This concept helps accountants determine what to include or recognize in a particular set of financial statements (as well as what not to recognize). As you may have learned in introductory accounting, there are many different ways that companies are organized. The organizational structure is often driven by tax and legal reasons.

**LAW/
CORPORATE TAX**

6.1.1, 6.2.1

Three common forms of organization are sole proprietorship, partnership, and corporation. Illustration 2-3 looks at some pros and cons of each type of business structure.

	Brief Description	Pros	Cons
Proprietorship	Small business owned and run by one person (sole proprietor)	– Simple to set up and maintain records – Does not have to file a separate tax return since the income is treated as income of the owner for tax purposes	– Not a separate legal entity and therefore any lawsuits against the business would be directed against the sole proprietor – Personal assets may be required to pay off business debts
Partnership	Business usually owned and/or run by more than one person (the partners)	– A basic partnership is simple to set up and maintain records for – Does not have to file separate tax returns because the income is treated as income of the partners for tax purposes	– Not a separate legal entity and therefore any lawsuits against the business would be directed against the partners – Personal assets may be required to pay off business debts
Corporation	Business is incorporated as a separate legal entity	– Limited liability protection – Any obligations are the obligations of the corporation and not the owners	– More complex to set up and maintain records – Separate tax returns must be completed and filed for the corporation – Covered by the Canada Business Corporations Act or provincial corporations act—legal requirements for reporting and maintaining records

Illustration 2-3

Some Common Forms of Business Organization

WHAT DO THE NUMBERS MEAN?

REAL WORLD EMPHASIS

There are two additional types of organizational structures that are used by professionals in Canada: professional corporations and limited liability partnerships (LLP). These have evolved for two main reasons:

1. For tax planning, and

2. To limit liability of the partners for negligence by other partners.

According to CPA Canada:

The LLP legislation provides that a partner is not personally liable for any debts, obligations or liabilities of the LLP that arise from any negligent act by another partner or by any person under that partner's direct supervision and control. The law does not reduce or limit the liability of the Firm. All of the Firm's assets and insurance protection remain at risk. In addition, all partners of an LLP remain personally liable for their own actions and for the actions of those they directly supervise and control.

Note that the partners are still held accountable for their own actions—just not those of the other partners.

Professional corporations may allow for greater flexibility in tax planning than limited liability partnerships.

LAW CORPORATE TAX

6.1.1

This text deals mostly with corporations. We will revisit issues relating to unincorporated businesses in Chapter 23. For tax and legal purposes, the **legal entity** is the relevant unit for an incorporated company. Tax returns are filed and taxes are paid based on taxable income for each corporation. Lawsuits pertaining to the business are generally filed against the corporation since it is a separate legal entity (although the shareholders and management may also be sued as individuals).

GAAP, however, considers a broader definition when preparing consolidated financial statements. A parent and its subsidiaries may be separate **legal entities (such as separate corporations)**, but merging their activities for accounting and reporting purposes gives more meaningful information. Thus, the consolidated financial statements are prepared from the perspective of the **economic entity**. This allows the company to recognize and group together the assets, liabilities, and other financial statement elements that are under the parent's **control** into one set of statements. Several separate corporations may therefore be grouped together to produce the consolidated financial statements.

Historically, for most situations, the definition of control has been anchored in the number of common shares held. That is, control existed where the entity held more than 50% of the voting common shares of another entity.[20] However, the concept has been changing as business practices have been changing.[21] The IASB has included additional guidance on the reporting entity in the Exposure Draft relating to the conceptual framework.[22]

In the meantime, the standard setters issued revised standards[23] dealing with consolidation that define **control** that became effective in 2013. IFRS 10 notes that an investor has control over an investee when it has the following:

1. **power over the investee;**

2. **exposure, or rights, to variable returns from its involvement with the investee; and**

3. **the ability to use its power over the investee to affect the amount of the investors' returns.**

This standard is principles-based and broadens the concept so that control is assessed not only through ownership of common shares but through other means, including exposure to the risks and rewards of the entity.

Under ASPE, control is defined as the continuing power to determine strategic decisions without the co-operation of others—a similarly broad concept.[24] For the most part, ASPE standards are similar where the company owns voting common shares in another company. However, in some situations (for instance, when dealing with sales of financial instruments to certain trusts or other legal entities), the ASPE standards are significantly different. ASPE focuses more on whether the other entity is "demonstrably distinct" from the company. In assessing this, the company looks at the following (as well as other factors):

• whether the entity in question can be unilaterally dissolved by the company, and

• whether others have more than a 10% ownership interest.[25]

Consolidation of financial statements is generally covered in advanced accounting courses and will not be dealt with further here for that reason. It is important, however, to have a high-level view of which entities are included as part of the economic entity for financial reporting purposes. As mentioned earlier, this will also have an impact on accounting for derecognition of financial instruments in situations where assets are transferred.[26]

WHAT DO THE NUMBERS MEAN?

REAL WORLD EMPHASIS

Many companies use what are known as special purpose entities (SPEs). SPEs are sometimes referred to as variable interest entities or structured entities. They are often separate legal entities (for instance, they could be a limited partnership or corporation) set up for a specific purpose, such as to hold leases, pension funds, or perhaps certain investments and/or to create investment opportunities for investors. Are SPEs part of the economic entity for consolidated financial reporting purposes? This was the centre of much of the controversy surrounding the Enron scandal. Enron created many SPEs that it did not consolidate. It sold assets to these SPEs, often at a profit. As it turned out, Enron should have consolidated them since the liabilities and losses of these SPEs ended up being liabilities and losses of Enron. In other words, Enron was exposed to the risks of ownership.

Enron's accounting had the impact of understating liabilities as well as overstating income in its consolidated financial statements. Under revised accounting standards, SPEs that were not previously included may now be included in the consolidated financial statements. Similarly, some may be excluded since the detailed guidance has changed.

Revenue Recognition and Realization Principles

A crucial question for many enterprises is when revenue should be recognized. This is governed loosely by what is known as the **revenue recognition principle**. Although this is a principle in transition, historically, revenue has generally been recognized when the following three conditions are met:

1. **risks and rewards** have passed and/or the **earnings process is substantially complete (significant acts have been performed and there is no continuing involvement)**;

2. **the revenue is measurable**; and

3. **the revenue is collectible** (realized or realizable).[27]

This is an income statement approach in that it focuses more on the earnings process. ASPE continues to follow this.

The new IFRS 15 standard entitled *Revenue from Contracts with Customers* is effective for fiscal years beginning on or after January 1, 2018, although earlier application is allowed. This new standard follows a five-step approach in determining when revenue is recognized:

1. Identify the contract with the customer.

2. Identify the performance obligations in the contract (promises to transfer goods and/or services that are distinct).

3. Determine the transaction price.

4. Allocate the transaction price to each performance obligation.

5. Recognize revenue when each performance obligation is satisfied.

SIGNIFICANT CHANGE

This new IFRS approach is a **balance sheet approach,** which recognizes that a transaction has occurred when the entity enters into a contract. The entity has rights and performance obligations under the contract. Collectible revenues are recognized when **performance obligations** are settled (when control over goods/services passes to the customer). There is a presumption that the contract is measurable. We will examine this in greater detail in Chapter 6.

Revenues are **realized** when products (goods or services), merchandise, or other assets are **exchanged** for cash or claims to cash. Revenues are **realizable** if the assets received or held can be readily converted into cash or claims to cash. Assets are readily convertible if they can be sold or interchanged in an active market at prices that are readily determinable and there is no significant additional cost.

Matching Principle

Assets such as property, plant, and equipment contribute to a company's ability to generate revenues. Therefore, accounting attempts to match these costs with the revenues that they produce. This practice is called **matching** because it dictates that effort (expenditures) be matched with accomplishment (revenues) whenever this is reasonable and can be done. It also illustrates the **cause and effect relationship** between the money spent to earn revenues and the revenues themselves.

It may be difficult to establish exactly how much of a contribution is made to each period, however, so often an estimation technique must be used. GAAP requires that a **rational and systematic** allocation policy be used that will approximate the asset's contribution to the revenue stream. Selection of a rational and systematic allocation technique involves making assumptions about the benefits that are being received as well as the costs associated with those benefits. The cost of a long-lived asset, for example, must be allocated over all accounting periods during which the asset is used because the asset contributes to revenue generation throughout its useful life.

Assets such as inventory similarly contribute to a company's ability to generate revenues, but in a different way. While property, plant, and equipment are normally used up in generating revenues, inventory is sold to generate revenues. Operating expenditures incurred during the year are often classified into two groups depending on whether they are seen to be part of the inventory production process or not. These two groups are labelled **product costs** and **period costs**.

Product costs such as material, labour, and overhead attach to the product and are carried into future periods as inventory (if not sold) because they are seen to be part of the inventory production process and because inventory meets the definition of an asset. Period costs such as officers' salaries and other administrative expenses are recognized immediately—even though the benefits associated with these costs occur in the future. This is because they are not seen as part of the production process and therefore are not inventory costs, and because the costs do not meet the definition of an asset by themselves. Period costs are seen to be a normal ongoing annual expense of running the business as opposed to part of the inventory production process. This same analysis occurs for self-constructed or internally generated assets other than inventory.

WHAT DO THE NUMBERS MEAN?

ETHICS

Livent Inc., mentioned earlier, followed the policy of deferring pre-production costs for the creation of each separate show until the show was opened. The company felt that this was acceptable because it was creating an asset: the show. On opening night, the show would start to produce revenues and then the costs were amortized and matched with those revenues. Such costs included advertising, publicity and promotions, set construction, props, costumes, and salaries paid to the cast, crew, musicians, and creative workers during rehearsal. In short, anything to do with the production was deferred.

On the one hand, one might argue that this was aggressive. One could also argue that this treatment was acceptable because of the direct and incremental nature of these costs in terms of future production revenues. The trouble began when Livent started to reclassify some of these costs as fixed assets and also to reallocate these costs to different and unrelated shows that had higher revenue. The company even had spreadsheets to keep track of actual results as compared with those that were publicly reported.[28] As noted earlier, there was more going on than a simple accounting policy choice.

While in the past, it may have been acceptable to capitalize certain costs on the basis of matching, there are no grounds for recognizing assets and liabilities that do not specifically meet the definitions of these elements under the current conceptual framework. If a cost or expenditure does not meet the definition of an asset, it is expensed (matching notwithstanding). Care should be taken also to ensure that only costs directly related to the creation of assets such as inventory or property, plant, and equipment are included. Similarly, there are no grounds for deferral of revenues as liabilities based exclusively on matching.[29]

Measurement

Because **accrual accounting** is followed, many estimates must be used when preparing financial statements. Most numbers on a statement of financial position and income statement are in fact quite "soft" and inexact. In order to communicate information about economic events, accountants must convert the economic events into the language of business: numbers. Some things are easy to measure, such as cash in the bank. Others are not so easy to measure. For instance, how do you measure the potential cost of selling what proves to be a dangerous product?

Too much uncertainty may make it inappropriate to recognize a financial statement element. As a general rule, **elements cannot be recognized** in the financial statements if they cannot be **measured**. We will first discuss a few underlying concepts, such as periodicity, unit of measure, and going concern. Then we will look at basic measurement choices. The key for accountants is to **determine an acceptable level of uncertainty**, use **measurement tools** that help deal with the uncertainty, and **disclose enough information** to signal the uncertainty.

Measurability is a big issue for many financial statement elements. When there is a **variance** between the recognized amount and another reasonably possible amount, this is called **measurement uncertainty**. Accountants are continually working to develop and make use of **measurement tools** such as option pricing and discounted cash flow models. When observable values are not available (such as market prices and cost), these models are used as a way of dealing with measurement uncertainty. There is a trade-off with uncertainty. Too much measurement uncertainty undermines the reliability of the financial statements. However, if the element is not recognized at all in the financial statements, then some relevant information has not been included and the statements are incomplete. A compromise is to measure and recognize the elements in the body of the financial statements and to disclose the measurement uncertainty and its significance in the notes to the financial statements.

Chapter 3 looks in greater detail at measurement models that incorporate uncertainty.

Periodicity Assumption

The most accurate way to measure the results of an enterprise's activity would be to do the measurement at the time of the enterprise's eventual liquidation. At that point, there is complete certainty about all of the company's cash flows. Business, government, investors, and various other user groups, however, cannot wait that long for such information. Users need to be informed about performance and economic status on a **timely basis** so that they can evaluate and compare firms. For this reason, information must be reported periodically. The **periodicity assumption** (or time period assumption) implies that an enterprise's economic activities can be divided into **artificial time periods**. These time periods vary, but the most common are one month, one quarter, and one year.

The shorter the time period, the more difficult it becomes to **determine the proper net income** for the period. A month's results are usually less reliable than a quarter's results, and a quarter's results are likely less reliable than a year's results. This is because more estimates are needed to accrue costs and revenues in accrual accounting when the time period is shorter. Investors want and demand information that has been processed and distributed quickly, yet the more quickly the information is released, the more likely errors become.

The question of what time period is appropriate is becoming more serious because product cycles are shorter and products become obsolete more quickly. Many observers believe that, given the advances in technology, more on-line, **real-time financial information** needs to be provided to ensure that relevant information is available. The issue of continuous financial reporting was introduced in Chapter 1.

Monetary Unit Assumption

The **monetary unit assumption** means that money is the common denominator of economic activity and is an appropriate **basis for accounting measurement** and analysis. This assumption implies that the monetary unit is the most effective way of expressing to interested parties changes in capital and exchanges of goods and services. The monetary unit is relevant, simple, universally available, understandable, and useful. Applying this assumption depends on the even more basic assumption that **quantitative data** are useful in communicating economic information and in making rational economic decisions.

In Canada and the United States, accountants have generally chosen to ignore the phenomenon of **price-level change** (inflation and deflation) by assuming that the unit of measure, the dollar, remains reasonably **stable**. This assumption about the monetary unit has been used to justify adding 1970 dollars to 2016 dollars without any adjustment. Only if circumstances change dramatically (such as if Canada or the United States were to experience extremely high inflation) would the standard setters consider "inflation accounting." IAS 29 deals with hyperinflation. There is no comparable standard under ASPE.

Going Concern Assumption

Most accounting methods are based on the **going concern assumption**. This is the assumption that a business enterprise will **continue to operate for the foreseeable future**; that is, it will not be forced to end its operations. Although there are many business failures, experience indicates that companies do have a fairly high continuance rate. While accountants do not believe that business firms will last indefinitely, they do expect them to last long enough to fulfill their commitments. Management must assess the company's ability to continue as a going concern and take into account all available information, looking out at least 12 months from the date of the statement of financial position.

The implications of this assumption are profound. The **historical cost principle** would have limited usefulness if **liquidation** were assumed to be likely. Under a liquidation approach, for example, asset values are better stated at **net realizable value** (sales price less costs of disposal) than at **acquisition cost**. Amortization and amortization policies are justifiable and appropriate only if we assume some permanence to the enterprise; this is what justifies allocating the costs of the amortized assets to future periods to match them against future revenues. If a liquidation approach were adopted, the **current versus non-current classification** of assets and liabilities would lose much of its significance. Labelling anything a **fixed or long-term** asset would be difficult to justify. Indeed, listing liabilities according to their likely liquidation date would be more reasonable.

The going concern assumption applies in most business situations. The only time when the assumption does not apply is when **there is intent to liquidate the company's net assets and cease operations or cease trading in the company's shares or when the company has no realistic alternative but to liquidate or cease operations.** In these cases, a total revaluation of assets and liabilities can provide information that closely approximates the entity's **net realizable value**. The accounting problems that arise when an enterprise is in liquidation are presented in advanced accounting courses.

How do we measure things when we assume the entity is a going concern? Management must continually assess the likelihood of outcomes (such as whether the company will lose a lawsuit) based on history and supporting evidence. Often, companies rely on specialists such as lawyers and engineers for help with such assessments.

Historical Cost Principle

Transactions are initially measured at the amount of cash (or cash equivalents) that was paid or received or the fair value that was ascribed to the transactions when they took place. This is often called the **historical cost principle**. The historical cost principle has three underlying assumptions that support its value and usefulness:

1. It represents a value at a **point in time**.

2. It results from a **reciprocal exchange** (in other words, a two-way exchange).

3. The exchange includes **an outside arm's-length party**.

Initial Recognition

For non-financial assets, the value includes any **laid-down costs**; that is, any cost that is incurred to get the asset ready (whether for sale or for generating income by using it). Inventory, for instance, might include the **cost of material, labour, and a reasonable allocation of overhead**. Similarly, for a self-constructed asset, cost would include any expenditure made to get the asset **ready for its intended use**, including transportation and installation costs.

Sometimes it is not possible or not appropriate to determine a value using the historical cost principle. Transactions that have some or all of the following characteristics present challenges:

- **Nonmonetary** or **barter transactions** where **no cash or monetary consideration** is exchanged. Here it may be more difficult to determine the value of the assets exchanged.

- **Nonmonetary, non-reciprocal transactions** where there is **no exchange**, such as donations.

- **Related party transactions** where the parties to the transaction are not acting at arm's length (in other words, there is **no outside party**). In these cases, the exchange price may not reflect the true value of the assets exchanged.

As a default, an attempt may be made to estimate the **fair value** if possible, and this may become the cost basis going forward.

The historical cost principle also applies to financial instruments. Bonds, notes, and accounts payable and receivable are issued by a business enterprise in exchange for assets, or perhaps services. This price, established by the exchange transaction, is the "cost" of the financial instrument and gives the figure at which the instrument should be recognized in the financial statements as long as it is equal to the fair value of the financial instrument issued. Where the instruments are issued in exchange for cash, the cost is straightforward but where they are issued for goods or services, the value may be more difficult to determine. Measurement techniques such as discounting are used to measure the fair value.

Subsequent Remeasurement

Historical cost has an important advantage over other valuation methods. Because it generally comes from an **arm's-length transaction** or exchange, it represents a bargained, fairly arrived-at value at a specific point in time. When it is first recognized, cost usually represents fair value. Over time, however, it often becomes irrelevant in terms of **predictive value**.

Later remeasurements also have limitations, however. They can be based on different measurement values, such as fair value, and give information that is more relevant, but they often involve **measurement uncertainty**. Furthermore, because there is often no external exchange (exchange with an outside party), the values may be **subjective**. Despite these limitations, the trend is toward an increasingly **mixed valuation model**. What used to be primarily a **historical cost-based model**, modified by the application of conservatism (that is, revaluations occurred if the asset's value declined below cost), is moving more toward a **market valuation model**. The use of fair value will be discussed below.

Fair Value Principle

IFRS has increasingly called for the use of standardized fair value measurements in the financial statements. This is an emerging principle that we will call the **fair value principle**. Fair value information may be more useful than historical cost for certain types of assets and liabilities and in certain industries. For example, companies report many financial instruments, including derivatives, at fair value. Brokerage houses and mutual funds prepare their financial statements using fair value.

Fair value is defined under IFRS as "the price that would be received to **sell** an asset or paid to transfer a liability in an orderly transaction between market participants at the measurement date."[30] Accordingly, fair value is an **exit price**. Exit price refers to a selling price, as opposed to an "entry price," which reflects the entity's purchase price. According to the definition, fair value is also a **market-based measure**, as opposed to an **entity-specific measure**. As such, it is meant to be more objective. It seeks to determine value by looking at how market participants would value the item in question. It does not look at value from the perspective of the entity itself and as such it does not consider company-specific synergies.[31]

Illustration 2-4 illustrates the various ways to define "value" or price.

Illustration 2-4

Defining Value or Price

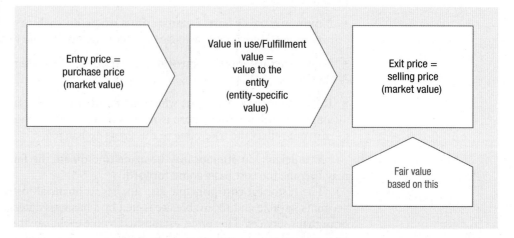

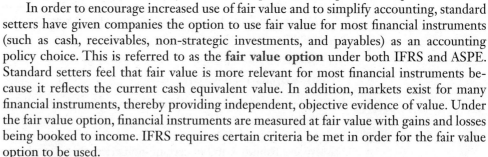

For instance, assume that a restaurant has a fully integrated industrial kitchen, and the grills are built in but are now broken. The restaurant may attribute a higher value to the grills since they are an integrated part of the kitchen and already in place. This value represents an entity-specific value. Market participants might view the value of broken, used equipment as being lower—perhaps at scrap value—especially if the grills are too costly to fix. This latter value is the fair value under IFRS. Where a liquid market does not exist, the entity may use a model such as a discounted cash flow model to estimate fair value.

Which value is better for use in the financial statements? Good question. There is a trade-off. Entity-specific value may be more relevant for operating assets where the entity plans to hold on to them and use them to produce revenues, but it may be more subjective. As noted above, the market-based view is more objective and verifiable and thus, where fair value is called for under IFRS, the market-based view must be applied.

At initial acquisition, historical cost generally equals fair value. In subsequent periods, as market and economic conditions change, historical cost and fair value often diverge. These fair value measures or estimates often provide more relevant information about the expected cash flows related to the asset or liability. For example, when a long-lived asset declines in value, a fair value measure may be used to help determine a potential impairment loss.

In order to encourage increased use of fair value and to simplify accounting, standard setters have given companies the option to use fair value for most financial instruments (such as cash, receivables, non-strategic investments, and payables) as an accounting policy choice. This is referred to as the **fair value option** under both IFRS and ASPE. Standard setters feel that fair value is more relevant for most financial instruments because it reflects the current cash equivalent value. In addition, markets exist for many financial instruments, thereby providing independent, objective evidence of value. Under the fair value option, financial instruments are measured at fair value with gains and losses being booked to income. IFRS requires certain criteria be met in order for the fair value option to be used.

Certain standards under IFRS explicitly allow the use of fair value for some non-financial assets (such as investment properties and property, plant, and equipment) or require it for others (such as certain biological assets). ASPE does not refer to the use of fair value for these items, although it does acknowledge that fair value measures might be used in certain industries, including agriculture and mining.[32] Note that ASPE has defined fair value as the "amount of consideration that would be agreed upon in an arm's length transaction between knowledgeable, willing parties who are under no compulsion to act."[33]

There are some subtle differences here, including the fact that the ASPE definition does not refer to an orderly market, nor does it stipulate that the price is an exit price.

We will expand upon the use of the fair value principle in future chapters, including Chapter 3.

Presentation and Disclosure

Full Disclosure Principle

Accountants follow the general practice of providing information that is important enough to influence an informed user's judgement and decisions. This is referred to as the **full disclosure principle**. The principle recognizes that the nature and amount of information included in financial reports reflects a series of judgemental trade-offs. These trade-offs aim for information that is:

- **detailed enough** to disclose matters that make a difference to users, but

- **condensed enough** to make the information understandable, and also appropriate in terms of the costs of preparing and using it.

More information is not always better. Too much information may result in the user being unable to digest or process it. This is called **information overload**. Information about a company's financial position, income, cash flows, and investments can be found in one of three places:

1. The **main body of financial statements**

2. The **notes to the financial statements**

3. Supplementary information, including the **Management Discussion and Analysis (MD&A)**

The financial statements are a **formalized, structured way of communicating financial information**. Disclosure is not a substitute for proper accounting.[34] Certain numbers, such as earnings per share, send signals to the capital marketplace. For example, cash basis accounting for cost of goods sold is misleading, even if accrual-based amounts have been disclosed in the notes to the financial statements. As we mentioned in Chapter 1, the market watches and listens for signals about earnings in particular and does not usually react well to negative earnings surprises.

The **notes to financial statements** generally **amplify or explain** the items presented in the main body of the statements. If the information in the main body of the statements gives an incomplete picture of the enterprise's performance and position, additional information that is needed to complete the picture should be included in the notes.

Information in the notes does not have to be quantifiable, nor does it need to qualify as an element. Notes can be partially or totally narrative. Examples of notes are:

- **Descriptions** of the accounting policies and methods used in measuring the elements reported in the statements

- **Explanations** of uncertainties and contingencies

- **Details** that are too voluminous to include in the statements

The notes are not only helpful to understanding the enterprise's performance and position, they are essential.

Supplementary information may include details or amounts that present a different perspective from what appears in the financial statements. They may include quantifiable information that is high in relevance but low in reliability, or information that is helpful but not essential. One example of supplementary information is the data and schedules provided by oil and gas companies: typically they give information on proven reserves as well as the related discounted cash flows.

Supplementary information also includes management's explanation of the financial information and a discussion of its significance in the **MD&A**. CPA Canada's publication *MD&A: Guidance on Preparation and Disclosure* lays out six general disclosure principles.

MD&A should:

1. enable readers to view the entity through management's eyes;

2. supplement and complement the information in the financial statements;

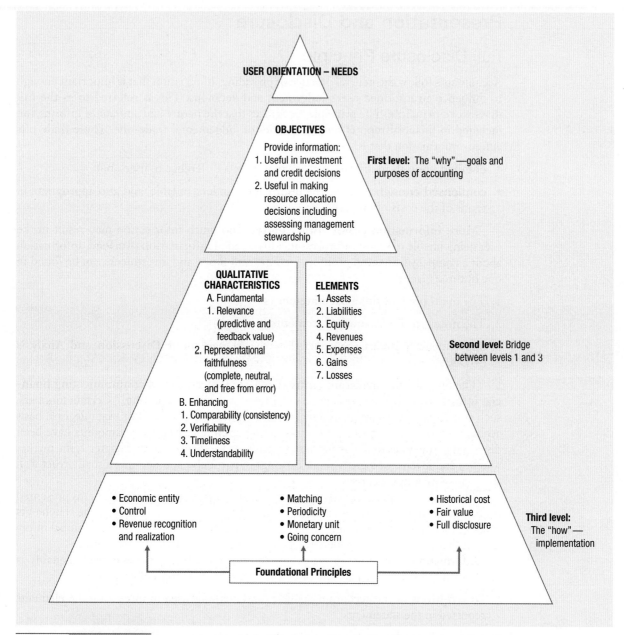

Expanded Conceptual Framework for Financial Reporting

3. provide fair, complete, and balanced information that is material to the decision-making needs of users;

4. outline key trends, risks, and uncertainties that are likely to affect the company in the future; and provide information about its quality of earnings and cash flows;

5. explain management's plan for accomplishing short-term and long-term goals; and

6. be understandable, relevant, comparable, verifiable, and timely.[35]

Thus, the MD&A is a step toward a more broadly based business reporting model that also contains forward-looking information. The guidance also includes a framework that identifies five key elements that should be included in the MD&A:

1. core businesses

2. objectives and strategy

3. capability to deliver results

4. results and outlook

5. key performance measure and indicators

It is hoped that these additional disclosures will give users of the financial information a greater insight into a company's business.[36]

We discuss the content, arrangement, and display of financial statements, along with other facets of full disclosure, specifically in Chapters 4, 5, and 23, and more generally throughout the text. Note that under IFRS there is a general trend toward increased disclosures in a bid for greater transparency.

Illustration 2-5 presents the conceptual framework discussed in this chapter. It is similar to Illustration 2-1, except that it gives additional information for each level. We cannot overemphasize the usefulness of this conceptual framework in helping to understand many of the problem areas that are examined in later chapters.

FINANCIAL REPORTING ISSUES

Objective 5

Explain the factors that contribute to choice and/or bias in financial reporting decisions.

Making financial reporting decisions is complex. This section examines the factors that make this process challenging. As mentioned earlier in the chapter, the main objective of financial reporting is to **provide reliable, decision-relevant financial information** to users so that they can make well-informed capital allocation decisions. Capital that is invested in good investments fuels the economy and encourages job growth and wealth creation. To achieve this objective, well-judged choices must be made between alternative accounting concepts, methods, and means of disclosure. Accounting principles and rules must be **selected and interpreted and professional judgement must be applied**.

As mentioned, accounting is **influenced by its environment**—in many cases in a negative way. It is also influenced by decisions made by individuals who often act in **self-interest** or in the interests of the company (at the expense of other stakeholders). Because of this, it is unrealistic to believe that the financial reporting system will always work properly. Instead of wealth creation in the capital markets and the economy, financial reporting decisions sometimes lead to wealth and value destruction. Bias may exist and this is not a good thing.

Principles-Based Approach

IFRS and ASPE are **principles-based**; that is, they are based on a few foundational principles and concepts like those in the conceptual framework noted earlier in the chapter.

The benefit of this approach is that all decisions should theoretically be **consistent** if they start from the same foundational reasoning.[37] Another benefit is that principles-based GAAP is **flexible**. The most appropriate accounting for any new situation or novel business transaction may be arrived at through reason by going back to these principles (sometimes referred to as **first principles**). However, principles-based GAAP is sometimes criticized for being too flexible. Some critics feel that it allows too much choice and therefore results in **lack of comparability**.

Care should therefore be taken to ensure that this flexibility is not abused. The key foundational concept of **neutrality** is of the greatest importance. **The conceptual framework developed in this chapter is the anchor that should ground all financial reporting decisions.** In the absence of specific GAAP guidance, an entity should adopt accounting policies that are:

ETHICS

1. consistent with specific GAAP guidance, and

2. **developed** through exercising professional judgement and applying the conceptual framework.[38]

Financial Engineering

A practice known as **financial engineering** became more visible during the past two decades. Financial engineering is the process of legally structuring a business arrangement or transaction so that it meets the company's financial reporting objective (such as maximizing earnings or minimizing a debt to equity ratio). This is often done by creating complex legal arrangements and financial instruments. These arrangements and instruments are created so that the resulting accounting meets the desired objective within GAAP. For example, a company that is raising debt financing might want the instrument structured so that it meets the GAAP definition of equity rather than debt. In this way, the debt to equity ratio is not negatively affected.

ETHICS

Many financial institutions develop and market these financial instruments to their clients. These arrangements are often called **structured financings**. Since Enron, this practice has been reduced. Are financial engineering and the practice of structured financings ethically acceptable? Financial engineering has moved from being an accepted practice and commodity to a potentially fraudulent activity.

Illustration 2-6 looks at the various shades of grey in accounting for transactions.

Choice in Accounting Decision-Making

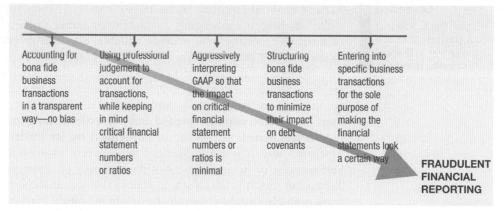

Fraudulent Financial Reporting

ETHICS

The role of accountants who are responsible for preparing a company's financial records is to capture business and economic events and transactions as they occur and communicate them to interested parties. They should not use the financial statements to portray something that is not there. Similarly, good financial reporting should be a result of **well-reasoned and supported analysis** that is grounded in a conceptual framework. It should not be influenced by external pressures. Pressures in the capital marketplace are everywhere, however, and their potentially negative impact on financial reporting must be acknowledged. Pressures may arise from various sources, including the ones discussed below.

Economic or Business Environment

STRATEGY DEVELOPMENT 2.3.2 AND ECONOMICS

Sometimes a company experiences sudden drops in revenue or market share. The underlying reason may be unique to the company and due to some poor strategic and business decisions or it may result from an industry or economic downturn. This may put pressure on a company to "prop up" its revenues. There may be pressure to recognize revenues before they should be recognized or to defer the recognition of some expenses.

Some companies use an industry or economic downturn as an opportunity to "clean up" their financial statements and generally take large writedowns on assets such as inventory or goodwill.

The markets expect a loss and the company's share price is therefore not overly affected in a negative way. This "purging" of the statement of financial position has the positive impact of making future earnings look better.

Other Pressures

Budgets put tremendous pressure on company management. Since bonuses and even jobs may depend on meeting budget targets, sometimes this negative influence leaks inappropriately into accounting decisions. Other pressures were discussed in Chapter 1.

If these and other pressures are not monitored and controlled properly, they are a major problem. In order to lessen the chances of fraudulent financial reporting, various controls and a solid governance structure may be put in place by a company. These could include:

**INTERNAL AUDIT
AND ASSURANCE
4.3.5
AND ETHICS**

- Vigilant, knowledgeable top management

- An independent audit committee

- An internal audit function

- Strong internal control systems

**WHAT
DO THE
NUMBERS
MEAN?**

The U.S.-based Committee of Sponsoring Organizations of the Treadway Commission (COSO) is composed of professional accounting organizations such as the American Accounting Association, the American Institute of Certified Public Accountants, Financial Executives International, the Institute of Internal Auditors, and the National Association of Accountants (now the Institute of Management Accountants). COSO's mandate, according to its website (www.coso.org), is as follows:

> . . . to provide thought leadership through the development of comprehensive frameworks and guidance on enterprise risk management, internal control and fraud deterrence designed to improve organizational performance and governance and to reduce the extent of fraud in organizations.

In 2010, COSO released a report entitled *Fraudulent Financial Reporting: 1998–2007*. The report updated a prior report that it had released looking at fraud for the period 1987 to 1997. The 2010 report found that there were 347 alleged cases of fraud that were investigated by the U.S. Securities and Exchange Commission (SEC) from 1998 to 2007 (as compared with 294 cases for the prior 10-year period). COSO calculated the amount of the misappropriations to be around U.S. $120 billion.

The most common area of fraud involved revenue recognition (alleged in 61% of the frauds). This was followed by overstatement of assets including overcapitalization of expenses (51% of the cases). Understatement of liabilities was much lower (31% of the cases). Approximately 26% of the firms allegedly involved in fraud changed auditors. The average period the alleged frauds took place was 31 months.

Although the report stated that more study was needed to determine why the frauds were committed, it noted that the SEC identified in its proceedings the following motivations for fraud:

- the need to meet internal or external earnings expectations,

- an attempt to conceal the company's deteriorating financial condition,

- the need to increase the stock price,

- the need to bolster financial performance for pending equity or debt financing, or

- the desire to increase management compensation based on financial results.

It will be interesting to see what the next decade brings.

Source: M.S. Beasley, J. V. Carcello, D. R. Hermanson, and T. L. Neal, *Fraudulent Financial Reporting: 1998–2007, An Analysis of U.S. Public Companies*, Committee of Sponsoring Organizations of the Treadway Commission, 2010.

IFRS/ASPE COMPARISON

Objective **6**
Discuss current trends in standard setting for the conceptual framework.

IFRS and ASPE are fundamentally similar since they are both principles-based. So far, the IASB has issued new guidance on the objectives of financial reporting and qualitative characteristics of useful information. We have noted some differences throughout the chapter but we will look at these in more detail in subsequent chapters.

Looking Ahead

The IASB issued an Exposure Draft relating to the conceptual framework in 2015. Some items that are included in the Exposure Draft are the following:

1. Measurement: description of different measurement bases and the information they provide (including historical cost and current value [fair value and fulfillment value/value in use])

2. Presentation and disclosure
   The IASB is proposing to rename the statement of profit or loss as the statement of financial performance

3. Elements
   (a) Clearer definitions of assets and liabilities, including more detailed guidance for interpreting the definitions
   (b) Deleted references to the word "ordinary" (when discussing income and expenses)

4. Recognition and derecognition: detailed guidance

5. Reporting entity: additional guidance

6. Objectives and qualitative characteristics: limited changes including the reintroduction of the reference to prudence (conservatism) and "substance over form"

It is hoped that the revised conceptual framework will be released in 2016.

The IASB is also working on a research project relating to disclosures. The IASB hopes to identify and develop a set of disclosure principles. It is reviewing existing standards to identify and assess disclosure conflicts, duplication, and overlaps.

Finally, the IASB was working on a research project to clarify the concept of materiality and to determine how the concept is used in financial reporting. It hopes to augment IAS 1 with a paragraph that sets out key characteristics of materiality.

SUMMARY OF LEARNING OBJECTIVES

1 Indicate the usefulness and describe the main components of a conceptual framework for financial reporting.

A conceptual framework is needed to (1) create standards that build on an established body of concepts and objectives, (2) provide a framework for solving new and emerging practical problems, (3) increase financial statement users' understanding of and confidence in financial reporting, and (4) enhance comparability among different companies' financial statements.

The first level of the framework deals with the objective of financial reporting. The second level includes the qualitative characteristics of useful information and elements of financial statements. The third level includes foundational principles and conventions.

2 Identify the qualitative characteristics of accounting information.

The overriding criterion by which accounting choices can be judged is decision usefulness; that is, the goal is to provide the information that is the most useful for decision-making. Fundamental characteristics include relevance and faithful representation. These two characteristics must be present. Enhancing characteristics include comparability, verifiability, timeliness, and understandability. There may be trade-offs.

3 Define the basic elements of financial statements.

The basic elements of financial statements are (1) assets, (2) liabilities, (3) equity, (4) revenues, (5) expenses, (6) gains, and (7) losses.

4 Describe the foundational principles of accounting.

(1) Economic entity: the assumption that the activity of a business enterprise can be kept separate and distinct from its owners and any other business unit. (2) Control: the entity has the power to make decisions and reap the benefits or be exposed to the losses (which are variable). (3) Revenue recognition: revenue is generally recognized when it is (a) earned, (b) measurable, and (c) collectible (realizable). (4) Matching: the assumption assists in the measurement of income by ensuring that costs (relating to long-lived assets) incurred in earning revenues are booked in the same period as the revenues earned. (5) Periodicity: the assumption that an enterprise's economic activities can be divided into artificial time periods to facilitate timely reporting. (6) Monetary unit: the assumption that money is the common denominator by

which economic activity is conducted, and that the monetary unit gives an appropriate basis for measurement and analysis. (7) Going concern: the assumption that the business enterprise will have a long life. (8) Historical cost principle: existing GAAP requires that many assets and liabilities be accounted for and reported based on their acquisition price. (9) Fair value principle: assets and liabilities are valued at fair value—that is, an exit price—and viewed from a market participant perspective. (10) Full disclosure principle: accountants follow the general practice of providing information that is important enough to influence an informed user's judgement and decisions.

5 Explain the factors that contribute to choice and/or bias in financial reporting decisions.

Choice is the result of many things, including principles-based standards, measurement uncertainty, and increasingly complex business transactions. The conceptual framework is the foundation that GAAP is built on. If there is no primary source of GAAP for a specific decision, then professional judgement must be used, making sure that the accounting policies chosen are consistent with the primary sources of GAAP and the conceptual framework.

Financial engineering is the process of legally structuring a business arrangement or transaction so that it meets the company's financial reporting objective. This can be a dangerous practice since it often results in biased information.

Fraudulent financial reporting often results from pressures on individuals or the company. These pressures may come from various sources, including worsening company, industry, or economic conditions; unrealistic internal budgets; and financial statement focal points related to contractual, regulatory, or capital market expectations. Weak internal controls and governance also contribute to fraudulent financial reporting.

6 Discuss current trends in standard setting for the conceptual framework.

The IASB was in the stages of issuing a new conceptual framework, which was expected to be issued in final form in 2016. It was also working on projects relating to disclosure and materiality.

KEY TERMS

assets, p. 43
basic elements, p. 43
comparability, p. 41
completeness, p. 39
comprehensive income, p. 45
conceptual framework, p. 35
conservatism, p. 74
consistency, p. 42
constructive obligations, p. 44
control, p. 48
cost-benefit relationship, p. 42
decision usefulness, p. 37
derecognition, p. 46
economic entity assumption, p. 46
economic substance, p. 39
elements of financial statements, p. 37
equitable obligations, p. 44
equity, p. 44
exit price, p. 53
expenses, p. 44
fair value option, p. 54
fair value principle, p. 53

feedback/confirmatory value, p. 38
financial engineering, p. 58
first principles, p. 57
freedom from material error, p. 40
full disclosure principle, p. 55
gains, p. 44
general-purpose financial statements, p. 37
going concern assumption, p. 52
historical cost principle, p. 52
information overload, p. 55
laid-down costs, p. 52
liabilities, p. 43
losses, p. 44
management best estimate, p. 40
matching, p. 49
materiality, p. 38
measurement uncertainty, p. 51
monetary unit assumption, p. 51
neutrality, p. 40
nonmonetary/barter transactions, p. 53
nonmonetary, non-reciprocal transactions, p. 53

notes to financial statements, p. 55
objective of financial reporting, p. 37
other comprehensive income, p. 45
performance obligation, p. 49
periodicity assumption, p. 51
predictive value, p. 38
qualitative characteristics, p. 37
realizable (revenue), p. 49
realized (revenue), p. 49
reciprocal exchange, p. 52
recognition, p. 46
related party transactions, p. 53
relevance, p. 38
representational faithfulness, p. 38
revenue recognition principle, p. 49
revenues, p. 44
supplementary information, p. 55
timeliness, p. 41
transparency, p. 39
understandability, p. 41
verifiability, p. 41

Note: Completion of this end-of-chapter material will help develop CPA enabling competencies (such as ethics and professionalism, problem-solving and decision-making and communication) and technical competencies. We have highlighted selected items with an integration icon and material in *WileyPLUS* has been linked to the competencies. All cases emphasize integration, especially of the enabling competencies. The brief exercises, exercises and problems generally emphasize problem-solving and decision-making.

Brief Exercises

(LO 2) BE2-1 Indicate the qualitative characteristic of financial information being described in each item below:

(a) Financial statements should include all information necessary to portray the underlying transactions.

(b) Financial information should make a difference in a user's decision-making.

(c) Financial information should not favour one user or stakeholder over another.

(d) Financial information should reflect the economic substance of business events or transactions.

(e) Financial information should help users assess the impact of past, present, or future events.

(f) Financial information must be reliable and without errors or omissions.

(g) Financial information should help users confirm or correct their previous expectations.

(h) Financial information should be reported and measured in a similar way within a company and between different companies.

(i) Financial information should be of sufficient quality and clarity to permit reasonably informed users to assess the information's significance.

(j) Financial information should be available to users before it loses its ability to be decision-useful.

(k) Knowledgeable, independent users should be able to achieve similar results and consensus when accounting for a particular financial transaction.

(LO 2) BE2-2 Identify which specific qualitative characteristic of accounting information is best described in each item below.

(a) The annual financial reports of Treelivingo Corp. are audited by public accountants.

(b) Able Corp. and Mona, Inc., both use the straight-line depreciation method.

(c) Global Corp. issues its quarterly reports within five days after each quarter ends.

(d) Philips Inc. segregates information that relates to one of its two subsidiaries, which was disposed of in the year but was included in its consolidated statements for prior years.

(e) The CFO of WebDesign stresses that factual, truthful, unbiased information is the overriding consideration when preparing WebDesign's financial information.

(f) EB Energy Inc. realizes that financial information may be misrepresented or misinterpreted if all pertinent information is not included.

(g) Wright Industries exercises due care and professional judgement in developing all estimates and assumptions used to prepare its financial information.

(LO 2) BE2-3 Presented below are four different transactions related to materiality. Explain whether you would classify these transactions as material.

(a) Blair Inc. has reported a positive trend in earnings over the last three years. In the current year, it reduces its allowance for bad debts and corresponding bad debt expense recovery to ensure another positive earnings year. The impact of this adjustment is equal to 2% of net income.

(b) Heney Limited has a gain of $3.1 million on the sale of plant assets and a $3.3 million loss on the sale of investments. It decides to net the gain and loss because the net effect is considered immaterial. Heney Limited's income for the current year was $10 million.

(c) Manion Corp. expenses all capital equipment under $10,000 on the basis that it is immaterial. The company has followed this practice for a number of years.

(d) Sidney Inc. decided that a note payable of a very small balance should be classified as non-current on its statement of financial position, although the maturity of the note was five months after the year end. The reason given by management was that the current ratio had to be maintained at a certain level to satisfy creditors and that the note would likely be refinanced at maturity.

(LO 2, 4) BE2-4 What principle(s) from the conceptual framework does Henday Limited use in each of the following situations?

(a) Henday includes the activities of its subsidiaries in its financial statements.

(b) Henday was involved in litigation with Kinshasa Ltd. over a product malfunction. This litigation is disclosed in the financial statements.

(c) Henday allocates the cost of its tangible assets over the period when it expects to receive revenue from these assets.

(d) Henday records the purchase of a new packaging machine at its cash equivalent price.

(e) Henday prepares quarterly financial statements for its users.

(f) In preparing its financial statements, Henday assesses its ability to continue to operate for the foreseeable future.

(g) Henday records revenue when risks and rewards are passed to the purchaser.

(LO 3) BE2-5 Discuss whether the following items would meet the definition of an asset using the IFRS definitions currently in place. If so, explain with reference to the appropriate criteria.

(a) MBI Ltd. owns a corporate fleet of cars for senior management's use in performing work duties.

(b) A franchisee has a licence to operate a Tim Hortons restaurant.

(c) Customized manufacturing machinery can only be used for one product line and has a small and limited customer market.

(d) The parent company has guaranteed the operating line of credit of its subsidiary, which resulted in the subsidiary obtaining a lower interest rate than it would otherwise receive. Is the guarantee an asset for the subsidiary?

(e) FreshWater Inc. bottles and sells the spring water from a natural spring near its property. Is the natural spring an asset of the company?

(f) Mountain Ski Resort Ltd. often has to use its snow-making machine to make snow for its hills and trails when there is not enough natural snowfall. Is the snow an asset for Mountain Ski?

(LO 3) BE2-6 Discuss whether the following items would meet the definition of a liability using the criteria currently in place under IFRS. If so, explain with reference to the appropriate criteria.

(a) Environmental remediation when a chemical spill has occurred. This spill has violated an existing law and statute. Does a liability for cleanup exist?

(b) Environmental remediation after a chemical spill has occurred. No existing law or statute has been broken. Does a liability for cleanup exist?

LAW

(c) As part of its contract with the government, a logging company must replant one tree for each tree it cuts. Does a liability for replanting exist?

(d) A logging company has a corporate policy of always replanting trees and advertises this fact in its corporate and marketing brochures. Does a liability for replanting exist?

(e) An airline collects cash for tickets issued for future charter flights to exotic locations.

(LO 3) BE2-7 Explain how you would decide whether to record each of the following expenditures as an asset or an expense. Assume all items are material.

(a) Legal fees paid in connection with the purchase of land are $1,500.

(b) Eduardo, Inc., paves the driveway leading to the office building at a cost of $21,000.

(c) A meat market purchases a meat-grinding machine at a cost of $3,500.

(d) On June 30, the partnership Monroe and Moore, medical doctors, pays six months' office rent to cover the month of July and the next five months.

(e) Smith's Hardware Ltd., a public company, pays $9,000 in wages to labourers for construction on a building to be used in the business.

(f) Alvarez's Florists Ltd. pays wages of $2,100 for the month to an employee who serves as driver of their delivery truck.

(LO 3) BE2-8 Assets are the cornerstone of financial reporting; often it is unclear whether an expenditure is an asset or an expense. For each of the transactions described below, consider whether the expenditure should be recorded as an asset or as an expense. Be sure to include a discussion of the specific criteria in your response. Assume all items are material.

(a) Akamu Limited operates an oil change shop and buys windshield washer fluid to top up customers' reservoirs.

(b) John & John Massage Therapists pay $600 to a receptionist for taking appointments and issuing receipts to clients.

(c) On October 1, Alan & Cheng, Chartered Professional Accountants, pays $500 to a local snow removal service for the upcoming winter season.

(d) Luca, Inc., is a contractor that cuts trees for the local sawmill. Luca pays $1,000 for a chainsaw.

(e) Pharma Inc. incurs legal fees of $5,500 for registering a patent for its product.

(f) Delhi's Florists pays $4,500 for flowers to be delivered to its premises.

(g) Sports Starts Here Inc. spent $4,500 installing hardwood floors in their leased store located in a mall.

(LO 3) BE2-9 For each item that follows, indicate which element of the financial statements it belongs to:

(a) Retained earnings

(b) Sales revenue

(c) Acquired goodwill

(d) Inventory

(e) Depreciation expense

(f) Loss on sale of equipment

(g) Interest payable

(h) Dividends

(i) Issuance of common shares

(LO 4) BE2-10   For each item that follows, identify the foundational principle of accounting that best describes it.

(a) For its annual reports, Sumsong Corp. divides its economic activities into 12-month periods.

(b) Sullivan, Inc., does not adjust amounts in its financial statements for the effects of inflation.

(c) Kiran Ltd. reports current and non-current classifications in its statement of financial position.

(d) In preparing its consolidated financial statements, Paddy Corporation assesses whether it has the power to direct the other entity's activities.

(e) Jaspreet Corporation reports revenue in its income statement when it is earned, even if cash has not been collected.

(f) Duong Enterprises normally includes business transactions in its general ledger when the item meets the definition of an element (as defined in the conceptual framework) and the item is measurable.

(g) Gomez, Inc., provides information about pending lawsuits in the notes to its financial statements.

(h) D&H Farms reports land on its statement of financial position at the amount paid to acquire it, even though the estimated fair value is higher.

(i) King Corporation uses fair value measurements for its financial instruments portfolio.

(j) Magic Inc. assumes that it will continue to operate into the foreseeable future.

(k) Donaldson Corp. operates a chain of restaurants and divides its fiscal year into 13 four-week accounting periods.

(LO 1, 2, 5) BE2-11   What is the objective of financial reporting? For each of the situations discussed below, explain the qualitative characteristics of financial information that help provide decision-useful information to users.

(a) Marcus Corp. has a management bonus plan based on net income. Marcus records revenue only after the risks and rewards of ownership of the goods it sells have passed to the customer.

(b) Beliveau Ltd. is a real estate company that holds land for eventual sale to developers. Beliveau provides fair value information on its property holdings to its users.

(c) Mohawk Inc. has entered into a rental agreement that will eventually transfer ownership of the manufacturing equipment to Mohawk at the end of three years. Irrespective of the legal documentation, Mohawk will account for this transaction based on its economic impact to the company.

(d) Standard setters must ensure that accounting standards do not favour one set of users over another or one industry over another.

Exercises

(LO 1) E2-1   (Usefulness, Objective of Financial Reporting) The conceptual framework has been created to make accounting information useful.

Instructions

Indicate whether the following statements about the conceptual framework are true or false. If false, provide a brief explanation supporting your position.

(a) Accounting standards that rely on a body of concepts will result in useful and consistent pronouncements.

(b) General-purpose financial reports are most useful to company insiders in making strategic business decisions.

(c) Accounting standards based on individual conceptual frameworks will generally result in consistent and comparable accounting reports.

(d) Capital providers are the only users who benefit from general-purpose financial reporting.

(e) Accounting reports should be developed so that users without knowledge of economics and business can become informed about the financial results of a company.

(LO 2, 5) E2-2 (Qualitative Characteristics) The conceptual framework identifies the fundamental and enhancing qualitative characteristics that make accounting information useful.

Instructions

Answer the following questions related to these qualitative characteristics.

(a) Which quality of financial information makes it possible for users to confirm or correct prior expectations?

(b) Identify some of the trade-offs and constraints in financial reporting.

(c) The U.S. Securities and Exchange Commission chairman once noted that if it becomes accepted or expected that accounting principles are determined or modified in order to achieve goals that do not involve economic measurement, we risk a serious loss in confidence in the credibility of our financial information system. Which qualitative characteristic of accounting information should ensure that this situation will not occur?

(d) Milner Corp. chooses to account for a transaction based simply on its legal form. Is this acceptable?

(e) Companies in the mining industry defer losses on their properties because recognizing such losses immediately could have adverse economic consequences for the industry. Which qualitative characteristic of accounting information is not followed?

(f) Only Once Ltd. provides overly complicated descriptions and explanations in its statement notes and provides only aggregated totals on the face of its financial statements. Which qualitative characteristic of accounting information is not followed?

(g) Baskins does not issue its first-quarter report until after the second quarter's results are reported. Which qualitative characteristic of accounting information is not followed?

(h) Predictive value is an ingredient of which qualitative characteristic of useful information?

(i) Vittorio Inc. is the only company in its industry to depreciate its plant assets on a straight-line basis. Which qualitative characteristic is not present?

(j) Green Gable Corp. has tried to determine the replacement cost of its inventory. Three different appraisers arrive at substantially different amounts for this value. The president then decides to use the middle value for external reports. Which qualitative characteristic of information is lacking in these data? (Do not use representational faithfulness.)

(k) The controller at Owens Inc. noticed that a material transaction was not included in the year-end financial results. Which qualitative characteristic is not present?

(LO 2) E2-3 (Qualitative Characteristics) The qualitative characteristics that make accounting information useful include:

Relevance	Neutrality	Representational faithfulness
Verifiability	Completeness	Understandability
Freedom from error	Timeliness	Comparability
Feedback value	Consistency	Predictive value

Instructions

Identify the appropriate qualitative characteristic(s) to be used given the information provided below.

(a) The qualitative characteristic being employed when companies in the same industry are using the same accounting policies.

(b) Quality of information that confirms users' earlier expectations.

(c) Necessary for providing comparisons of a company from period to period.

(d) Ignores the economic consequences of a standard.

(e) Requires a high degree of consensus among individuals on a given measurement.

(f) Predictive value is an ingredient of this fundamental quality of information.

(g) Four qualitative characteristics that are related to both relevance and faithful representation.

(h) Neutrality is an ingredient of this fundamental quality of accounting information.

(i) Two fundamental qualities that make accounting information useful for decision-making purposes.

(j) Issuance of interim reports is an example of what enhancing quality of relevance?

(LO 3) E2-4 (Elements of Financial Statements) The elements that are most directly related to measuring an enterprise's performance and financial status follow:

Assets	Expenses	Liabilities
Gains	Equity	Revenues
Losses		

Instructions

(a) Indicate which element is being described below. For any item that is an asset or liability, consider if the item qualifies under the definition currently in place under IFRS:

1. Arises from peripheral or incidental transactions.

2. Obliges a transfer of resources because of a present, enforceable obligation.

3. Increases in the ownership interest through issuance of shares.

4. Cash dividends to owners (declared and paid).

5. An expenditure that has future economic benefit.

6. Decreases in assets during the period for the payment of income taxes.

7. Arises from income-generating activities that are the entity's ongoing major or central operations.

8. Is the residual interest in the enterprise's assets after deducting its liabilities.

9. Increases assets during the period through the sale of inventory.

10. Decreases assets during the period by purchasing the company's own shares.

(b) Indicate which element listed above is being illustrated in the examples that follow. Consider the current definitions of both assets and liabilities.

1. Notes Co. has a written contract to receive money from the sale of copies of future recordings of music yet to be written.

2. ReadyMart Inc. has inventory out on consignment at a local retailer waiting for sale to the final customer.

3. Music Corp. has a written contract to deliver a percentage of future music revenues (royalties) from the sale of existing recordings.

(LO 4) E2-5   (Forms of Organizations)

LAW AND TAX

Instructions

(a) Identify three common forms of business organizations. Briefly outline the pros and cons of setting up a company using each form of organization.

(b) Identify why accounting professionals use LLPs and PCs.

(LO 4) E2-6   (Foundational Principles) The foundational principles of accounting are as follows:

Recognition/Derecognition	Measurement	Presentation and Disclosure
1. Economic entity	5. Periodicity	10. Full disclosure
2. Control	6. Monetary unit	
3. Revenue recognition and realization	7. Going concern	
4. Matching	8. Historical cost	
	9. Fair value	

Instructions

For each situation that follows, identify by its number the foundational principle above that is described.

(a) Allocates expenses to revenues in the proper period. matching

(b) Indicates that market value changes after the purchase are not recorded in the accounts unless impairment exists. (Do not use the revenue recognition principle.) historical cost

(c) Ensures that all relevant financial information is reported. full disclosure

(d) Is why plant assets are not reported at their liquidation value. (Do not use the historical cost principle.) going concern

(e) Related to the economic entity principle, defines the entities that should be consolidated in the financial statements. control

(f) Indicates that personal and business record-keeping should be separately maintained. economic entity

(g) Separates financial information into time periods for reporting purposes. periodicity

(h) Permits the use of market valuation in certain specific situations. fair value

(i) Requires passing of risks and rewards, measurability, and collectibility before recording the transaction. revenue recognition

(j) Assumes that the dollar is the measuring unit for reporting financial performance. monetary unit

(LO 4) E2-7 (Foundational Principles) The following are operational guidelines and practices that have developed over time for financial reporting.

1. Price-level changes (inflation and deflation) are not recognized in the accounting records.

2. Sufficient financial information is presented so that reasonably prudent investors will not be misled.

3. and equipment are capitalized and depreciated over the periods that they benefit.

4. There is no intent to liquidate the company's operations or activities.

5. Market value is used by companies for the valuation of certain securities that are regularly bought and sold.

6. After initial acquisition, the entity values land at its original transaction price.

7. All significant post–balance sheet events are reported.

8. Revenue is recorded at the point of sale.

9. All important aspects of bond indentures are presented in financial statements.

10. The rationale for accrual accounting is stated.

11. The use of consolidated statements is justified.

12. Reporting must be done at defined time intervals.

13. An allowance for doubtful accounts is established.

14. Goodwill is recorded only at the time of a business combination and does not change unless the goodwill becomes impaired.

15. Sales commission costs are charged to expense in the period of the sale.

Instructions

Select the foundational principle that best justifies each of these procedures and practices.

(LO 1, 2, 4) E2-8 (Foundational Principles) Examples of operational guidelines used by accountants follow.

1. The treasurer of Sweet Grapes Corp. would like to prepare financial statements only during downturns in the company's wine production, which occur periodically when the grape crop fails. He states that it is at such times that the statements could be most easily prepared. The company would never allow more than 30 months to pass without statements being prepared. *periodicity, timeliness, relevance.*

2. Tower Manufacturing Ltd. decided to manufacture its own widgets because it would be cheaper than buying them from an outside supplier. In an attempt to make its statements comparable with those of its competitors, Tower charged its inventory account for what it felt the widgets would have cost if they had been purchased from an outside supplier. (Do not use the revenue recognition principle.) *historical cost, verifiability, relevance*

3. Cargo Discount Centres buys its merchandise by the truckload and train carload. Cargo does not include any transportation costs in calculating the cost of its ending inventory. Such costs, although they vary from period to period, are always material in amount. *matching, historical cost, representational faithfulness (not complete)*

4. Quick & Healthy, a fast-food company, sells franchises for $100,000, accepting a $5,000 down payment and a 25-year note for the remainder. Quick & Healthy promises to assist in site selection, building, and management training for three years. Quick & Healthy records the full $100,000 franchise fee as revenue when the contract is signed. *revenue recognition, representational faithfulness (error)*

5. Kalil Corp. faces a possible government expropriation (i.e., takeover) of its foreign facilities and possible losses on sums that are owed by various customers who are almost bankrupt. The company president has decided that these possibilities should not be noted on the financial statements because Kalil still hopes that these events will not take place. *relevance, full disclosure, representational faithfulness*

6. Maurice Norris, owner of Rare Bookstore, Inc., bought a computer for his own use. He paid for the computer by writing a cheque on the bookstore chequing account and charged the Office Equipment account. *economic entity, free from error*

7. Brock Inc. decides that it will be selling its subsidiary, Breck Inc., in a few years. Brock has excluded Breck's activities from its consolidated financial results. *control, representational faithfulness.*

8. Wilhelm Corporation expensed the purchase of new manufacturing equipment. *matching, free from error, relevance. Is asset. (should be depreciation expense.*

9. A large lawsuit has been filed against Mahoney Corp. Mahoney has recorded a loss and related estimated liability that is equal to the maximum possible amount that it feels it might lose. Mahoney is confident, however, that either it will win the suit or it will owe a much smaller amount. *full disclosure, representational faithfulness.*

Instructions

(a) Discuss the usefulness of a conceptual framework. *– helps you make decisions when recording – consistency / standards / guide – enhances comparability / confidence*

(b) For each of the situations above, list the foundational principle or qualitative characteristic of financial information that has been violated.

(LO 2) E2-9 (Qualitative Characteristics) In general, financial information should include all relevant information that faithfully represents the economic substance of business transactions.

Instructions

Discuss whether it is possible for financial information to have all of the qualitative characteristics.

(LO 2, 3, 4) †E2-10   (Conceptual Framework—Comprehensive) The following are transactions recorded by Trimm Corporation during the current year.

1. Ordinary operating maintenance on equipment was recorded as follows:

Equipment	2,500	
Accounts Payable		2,500

2. Trimm received an advance on a custom order for merchandise that will be shipped during the next accounting year.

Cash	8,000	
Sales Revenue		8,000

3. Trimm Corporation is holding inventory on consignment for Rubber Ltd. Trimm will only pay Rubber when a sale is made to a customer. Trimm made the following entry when it received the inventory:

Inventory	15,000	
Accounts Payable		15,000

4. On the last day of the accounting period, a 12-month insurance policy was purchased. The insurance coverage is for the next accounting year.

Insurance Expense	4,000	
Cash		4,000

Instructions

For each transaction, determine which component of the conceptual framework (i.e., qualitative characteristic, element, or principle) was violated, if any, and give the entry that should have been recorded if there was a violation.

(LO 4, 5) E2-11   (Full Disclosure Principle) The following information is for Brittany, Inc.

1. To be more concise, the company decided that only net income should be reported on the income statement. Details on revenues, cost of goods sold, and expenses were also omitted from the notes to the financial statements.

2. Equipment purchases of $270,000 were partly financed during the year by issuing a $110,000 note payable. The company offset the equipment against the note payable and reported plant assets at $160,000. No information has been provided in the notes.

3. During the year, an assistant controller for the company embezzled $50,000. Brittany's net income for the year was $2.3 million. Neither the assistant controller nor the money has been found. No information has been provided in the notes.

4. Brittany has reported its ending inventory at $2.7 million in the financial statements. No other information on inventories is presented in the financial statements and related notes.

5. The company changed its method of depreciating equipment from the double-declining balance to the straight-line method. This change is not mentioned anywhere in the financial statements or in the related notes.

Instructions

(a) Explain the meaning and implications of the full disclosure principle and how such information may be provided to users.

(b) For each of the situations above, discuss whether Brittany has followed acceptable accounting and disclosure practices.

(LO 4) E2-12   (Going Concern Assumption)

Instructions

(a) Explain the meaning and implications of the going concern assumption in financial accounting.

---

†This item was originally published by the *Certified General Accountants Association of Canada* (CGA Canada), as an examination question. Adapted with permission of the Chartered Professional Accountants of Canada, Toronto, Canada. Any changes to the original material are the sole responsibility of the publisher and have not been reviewed or endorsed by the Chartered Professional Accountants of Canada.

(b) If the going concern assumption did not apply in accounting, how would this affect the amounts shown in the financial statements for the following items?

1. Equipment

2. Unamortized bond premium

3. Depreciation expense

4. Inventory

5. Prepaid insurance

(LO 4, 6) **E2-13** **(Revenue Recognition Principle)** The following independent situations require professional judgement for determining when to recognize revenue from the transactions.

1. Air Yukon sells you an advance purchase airline ticket in September for your flight home at Christmas.

2. Better Buy Ltd. sells you a home theatre on a "no money down, no interest, and no payments for one year" promotional deal.

3. The Centurions baseball team sells season tickets to games on-line. Fans can purchase the tickets at any time, although the season doesn't officially begin until April. It runs from April through October.

4. River's End Ltd. sells you a sweater. In August, you placed the order using River's End's on-line catalogue. The sweater arrives in September and you charge it to your River's End credit card. You receive and pay the credit card bill in October.

Instructions

(a) Explain when revenue is recognized in each of these situations under ASPE.

(b) Identify when revenue should be recognized in each of the situations under the new IFRS 15 model.

Problems

P2-1 Foundational principles of financial reporting may be grouped into four categories: recognition/derecognition, measurement, presentation, and disclosure.

Instructions

Briefly describe what is meant by these terms.

P2-2 Fusters, Inc., provides audited financial statements to its creditors and is required to maintain certain covenants based on its debt to equity ratio and return on assets. In addition, management of Fusters receives a bonus partially based on revenues for the year. Information related to Fusters, Inc., follows.

1. Depreciation expense on the building for the year was $45,000. Because the building was increasing in value during the year, the controller decided not to record any depreciation expense in the current year.

2. New legislation was discussed by the government that would require new pollution control technology for companies such as Fusters. Prior to this, Fusters had been complying with all current requirements and otherwise believed that it was acting in an environmentally responsible manner. In anticipation of this legislation being passed next year, Fusters expects it will need to upgrade its equipment and has booked the following entry:

Equipment	121,000	
Accounts Payable		121,000

3. During the year, the company sold certain equipment for $285,000, recognizing a gain of $45,000. Because the controller believed that new equipment would be needed in the near future, the controller decided to defer the gain and amortize it over the life of the new equipment that would soon be purchased.

4. An order for $61,500 was received from a customer on January 2, 2017, for products on hand. This order was shipped f.o.b. shipping point on January 9, 2017. The company made the following entry for 2016:

Accounts Receivable	61,500	
Sales Revenue		61,500

Instructions

(a) Discuss the reporting objectives of the users of Fusters' financial statements.

(b) Comment on the appropriateness of Fusters' accounting procedures and their impact on the company's financial statement users, applying the current conceptual framework.

ETHICS (c) Discuss whether there are alternatives available under IFRS to provide the reporting desired by Fusters' management.

P2-3   Transactions from Gravenhurst Inc.'s current year follow. Gravenhurst follows IFRS.

1. Gravenhurst Inc. thinks it should dispose of its excess land. While the carrying value is $50,000, current market prices are depressed and only $25,000 is expected upon disposal. The following journal entry was made:

Loss on Disposal of Land	25,000	
Land		25,000

2. Merchandise inventory that cost $630,000 was reported on the statement of financial position at $690,000, which is the expected selling price less estimated selling costs. The following entry was made to record this increase in value:

Inventory	60,000	
Sales Revenue		60,000

3. The company is being sued for $500,000 by a customer who claims damages for personal injury that was allegedly caused by a defective product. Company lawyers feel extremely confident that the company will have no liability for damages resulting from the situation. Nevertheless, the company decides to make the following entry:

Litigation Expense	450,000	
Litigation Liability		450,000

4. Because the general level of prices increased during the current year, Gravenhurst Inc. determined that there was a $15,000 understatement of depreciation expense on its equipment and decided to record it in its accounts. The following entry was made:

Depreciation Expense	15,000	
Accumulated Depreciation—Equipment		15,000

5. Gravenhurst Inc. has been concerned about whether intangible assets could generate cash in case of liquidation. As a result, goodwill arising from a business acquisition during the current year and recorded at $800,000 was written off as follows:

Retained Earnings	800,000	
Goodwill		800,000

6. Because of a "fire sale," equipment that was obviously worth $200,000 was acquired at a bargain price of $155,000. The following entry was made:

Equipment	200,000	
Cash		155,000
Gain		45,000

DIGGING
DEEPER

Instructions

In each of the above situations, discuss the appropriateness of the journal entries in terms of generally accepted accounting principles. For the purposes of your discussion, assume that the financial statements, particularly net income, will be used by the court in a divorce settlement for the company president's spouse.

P2-4   Accounting information provides useful data about business transactions and events. The people who provide and use financial reports must often select and evaluate accounting alternatives. The conceptual framework that was discussed in this chapter examines the characteristics of accounting information that make it useful for decision-making. It also points out that various limitations that are part of the measurement and reporting process can make it necessary to trade off or sacrifice some of the characteristics of useful information.

Instructions

(a) For each of the following pairs of qualitative characteristics, give an example of a situation in which one of the characteristics may be sacrificed for a gain in the other:

1. Relevance and verifiability

2. Relevance and comparability

3. Relevance and timeliness

4. Relevance and understandability

(b) What criterion should be used to evaluate trade-offs between information characteristics?

P2-5   You are hired to review the accounting records of Sheridan Inc. (a public corporation) before it closes its revenue and expense accounts as at December 31, 2017, the end of its current fiscal year. The following information comes to your attention.

1. During the current year, Sheridan Inc. changed its shipment policy from f.o.b. destination to f.o.b shipping point. This would result in an additional $50,000 of revenue being recorded for fiscal 2017.

2. The estimated remaining useful life of its manufacturing equipment was reviewed by management and increased by five years. This reduced depreciation expense by $30,000 during fiscal 2017.

3. When the statement of financial position was prepared, detailed information about the amount of cash on deposit in each of several banks was omitted. Only the total amount of cash under a caption "Cash in banks" was presented.

4. During the current year, Sheridan Inc. purchased an undeveloped piece of land for $320,000. The company spent $80,000 on subdividing the land and getting it ready for sale. A property appraisal at the end of the year indicated that the land was now worth $500,000. Although none of the lots was sold, the company recognized revenue of $180,000, less related expenses of $80,000, for a net income on the project of $100,000. The company has historically used the cost model for this type of property.

5. For several years, the company used the FIFO method for inventory valuation purposes. During the current year, the president noted that all the other companies in the industry had switched to the moving average method. Sheridan Inc. decided not to switch to moving average because net income would decrease by $600,000.

6. During fiscal 2017, new government legislation was passed requiring companies like Sheridan to install additional health and safety devices in their offices by 2022. Although Sheridan does not intend to retrofit the required new devices until 2022, an accrual for $375,500 has been established in the year-end financial statements for the future installation costs.

7. To maintain customer goodwill, Sheridan voluntarily recalled some products during the year. Sheridan has not established an accrual and is recording the sales returns as they happen.

Instructions

State whether or not you agree with each of the accounting decisions made by Sheridan Inc. Explain your reasoning and, wherever possible, support your answers by referring to the generally accepted accounting principles that apply to the circumstances.

P2-6   The following transactions fall somewhere in continuum of choices in accounting decision-making that is shown in Illustration 2-6.

1. The company president approaches one of the company's creditors to ask for a modification of the repayment terms so that they extend beyond the current year. This would make the liabilities long-term rather than short-term and would improve the company's current ratio.

2. The controller determines that significant amounts of capital assets are impaired and should be written off. Coincidentally, the company is currently showing lower levels of net income but expects better results in the following years.

3. The company management decides to use FIFO as opposed to weighted average, since it more closely approximates the flow of costs.

4. The vice-president of finance decides to capitalize interest during the self-construction of its properties. This policy will increase net income and several profitability ratios.

5. The business owner enters into an arrangement with a business associate whereby they will buy each other's merchandise before year end. The merchandise will then be shipped to customers after year end from the holding company's warehouse.

6. The assets and liabilities of an investment have been consolidated into Maher Company's annual financial statements. Maher Company does not have the power to direct the investee's activities.

7. The corporate litigation lawyer representing the business in its defence against a patent infringement lawsuit is uncertain about the possible outcome of the case, as he has just recently been engaged in the matter. Although there is considerable work to be done to establish the merits of the case, management has decided to accrue in the current period half of the amount claimed under the lawsuit. Management is worried that the Board of Directors may declare dividends in the current year that will have to be reduced in a subsequent year, when the case is ultimately settled.

Instructions

ETHICS For each situation, state where it falls in the continuum of choices in decision-making.

P2-7   A Special Committee on Financial Reporting proposed the following constraints related to financial reporting.

1. Business reporting should exclude information outside of management's expertise or for which management is not the best source, such as information about competitors.

2. Management should not be required to report information that would significantly harm the company's competitive position.

3. Management should not be required to provide forecast financial statements. Rather, management should provide information that helps users forecast for themselves the company's financial future.

4. Other than for financial statements, management need report only the information it knows. That is, management should be under no obligation to gather information it does not have, or does not need, in order to manage the business.

5. Companies should present certain elements of business reporting only if users and management agree they should be reported—a concept of flexible reporting.

Instructions

For each item, briefly discuss how the proposed constraint addresses concerns about the costs and benefits of financial reporting.

P2-8   Recently, your Uncle Warren, who knows that you always have your eye out for a profitable investment, has discussed the possibility of your purchasing some corporate bonds that he just learned of. He suggests that you may wish to get in on the ground floor of this deal. The bonds being issued by Jingle Corp. are 10-year debentures, which promise a 40% rate of return. Jingle manufactures novelty and party items.

You have told Uncle Warren that unless you can take a look at Jingle's financial statements, you would not feel comfortable about such an investment. Thinking that this is the chance of a lifetime, Uncle Warren has obtained a copy of Jingle's most recent, unaudited financial statements, which are a year old. These statements were prepared by Mrs. Jingle. You look over these statements, and they are quite impressive.

The statement of financial position showed a debt to equity ratio of 1:10 and, for the year shown, the company reported net income of $2,424,240.

The financial statements are not shown in comparison with amounts from other years. In addition, there are no significant note disclosures about inventory valuation, depreciation methods, loan agreements, and so on.

Instructions

Write a letter to Uncle Warren explaining why it would be unwise to base an investment decision on the financial statements that he has given you. Refer to the concepts developed in this chapter.

ENABLING COMPETENCIES

Cases

Refer to the Case Primer on the Student Website and in *WileyPLUS* to help you answer these cases.

REAL WORLD EMPHASIS

CA2-1   Bre-X Minerals (Bre-X), a small mining company, announced in the early 1990s that it had discovered a fairly significant gold deposit in Indonesia. The company's shares skyrocketed from pennies a share to over $280 per share. Subsequently, it was discovered that the company had been "salting the samples" and that there was little, if any, gold there. This information was not disclosed to the market until long after it was discovered that there was no gold. Certain parties who had access to this information benefited; however, many investors lost a significant amount of money. For example, the Ontario Municipal Employees Retirement System and the Ontario Teachers' Pension Plan lost millions of dollars. Investors sued the company and its management for providing misleading information.

Instructions

Using the conceptual framework, identify and analyze the financial reporting issues.

ETHICS

REAL WORLD EMPHASIS

CA2-2   Bennett Environmental Inc. operates in North America. Its basic business is high-temperature treatment services for contaminated soil. In its 2011 financial statements, the company had a loss of $9.3 million (and an accumulated deficit of $43.7 million).

In the notes to the financial statements, the company stated that it deferred certain transportation costs and recorded them as assets. These costs relate to shipping contaminated materials to the treatment plant. They are reimbursable under the terms of the contract. Per note 19, the company can only run efficiently when it operates continuously for extended periods; however, demand for the services is sporadic. Therefore, the company's business model is structured such that it shuts down operations and otherwise stockpiles inventory. These shutdown periods are followed by active periods during which it processes the stockpiled inventory. Revenues for 2011, a shutdown period, were $0.

In addition, the company received a subpoena from the U.S. Department of Justice regarding conspiracy to commit fraud with respect to the bidding process on a government project. During 2009, the courts stayed proceedings, essentially halting them for the time being.

Instructions

Assume that the financial statements must be issued prior to the resolution of the lawsuit. Discuss the financial reporting issues. The company's shares trade on the TSX.

FINANCE

CA2-3 The statement that follows about Timber Company appeared in a financial magazine:

The land and timber holdings are now carried on the company's books at a mere $100 million (U.S.). The value of the timber alone is variously estimated at $1 billion to $3 billion and is rising all the time. The understatement is pretty severe, conceded company management, who noted, "We have a whole stream of profit nobody sees and there is no way to show it on our books."

Instructions

Act as an analyst and discuss the financial reporting issues. Use the principles noted in chapter 2 (only) to analyze the issues.

RESEARCH AND ANALYSIS

REAL WORLD EMPHASIS

RA2-1   Teck Resources Limited

Obtain the 2014 financial statements of **Teck Resources Limited** from SEDAR (www.sedar.com).

Instructions

(a) Using the notes to the consolidated financial statements, determine the company's revenue recognition policy. Comment on whether the company uses an aggressive or conservative method for reporting revenue.

(b) Give two examples of where historical cost information is reported in the financial statements and related notes. Give two examples where fair value information is reported in either the financial statements or the related notes.

(c) Did Teck adopt any new accounting policies during the current year? What treatment were these changes given in the financial statements? Explain how the conceptual framework became the basis for the adoption and treatment of this policy. What effect, if any, did the changes have on Teck's financial statements?

(d) Did Teck implement any new pronouncements under IFRS ahead of the implementation deadlines? What were the reasons given for the adoption or non-adoption? From the perspective of a user of the financial statements, would you be in agreement with the treatment given by Teck?

REAL WORLD EMPHASIS

RA2-2   Air Canada

In its 2014 financial statements (Note 3), **Air Canada** has disclosed its critical estimates and judgements used in preparing the financial statements.

Instructions

Access the 2014 audited annual financial statements for Air Canada for the year ended December 31, 2014, from the company's website or SEDAR (www.sedar.com). Read Note 3 and related notes and answer the following questions.

(a) What are the main critical accounting estimates and judgements that the company discloses? Briefly outline each.

(b) Why is it important that the company disclose these types of judgements? Consider this question from a user perspective.

(c) How significant are the related financial statement elements?

RA2-3   Retrieval of Information on Public Company

There are several commonly available indexes and reference products that help individuals locate articles that have appeared in business publications and periodicals. Articles can generally be searched by company or by subject matter. Several common sources are *Canadian Business and Current Affairs (CBCA Fulltext Business)*, *Investex Plus*, *The Wall Street Journal Index*, *Business Abstracts* (formerly the *Business Periodical Index*), *EBSCO Business Source Premier*, and *ABI/Inform*.

Instructions

Use one of these resources to find an article about a company that interests you. Read the article and answer the following questions. (*Note:* Your library may have hard-copy or CD-ROM versions of these sources or they may be available through your library's electronic database.)

(a) What is the article about?

(b) What specific information about the company is included in the article?

(c) Identify any accounting-related issues that are discussed in the article.

RA2-4   Fair Values

Using fair values came under attack in light of the credit crunch of the last decade and the related financial crisis. Some have even accused fair value accounting of exacerbating the crisis. Access the following articles: "Discussing the Credit Crunch," *IASB INSIGHT Journal*, Q1 and Q2 (from www.ifrs.org), and "Fair Values: When the Engine Overheats, Don't Blame the Oil Light," by Paul Cherry and Ian Hague, *CA Magazine*, June/July 2009 (from http://www.cpacanada.ca/en/connecting-and-news/cpa-magazine/cpa-magazine-archives/CA-Magazine-archives).

Instructions

Using the articles, address the following questions:

(a) What impact does using fair values to report assets and liabilities have on the financial statements?

(b) Why do some people believe that using fair values is not appropriate for financial reporting? Discuss this in light of the financial crisis that began in 2007.

(c) What are the arguments in support of using fair values in financial reporting?

(d) Do you think fair value accounting should be used in the preparation of financial statements?

(e) Does IFRS allow for greater use of fair values than ASPE? Discuss, giving examples.

RA2-5   Conservatism/Neutrality

Access the *Investor Perspectives* article written by Steve Cooper, a member of the IASB, in June 2015, entitled "A tale of 'prudence'?" (www.ifrs.org). Mr. Cooper states that two different meanings have been attributed to the term "prudence" when it is used as part of the conceptual framework of financial reporting.

Instructions

(a) What two meanings does Steve Cooper describe as having been attributed to the term "prudence"? Explain each briefly.

(b) Identify which meaning was being supported by the IASB when the May 15, 2015 Exposure Draft *Conceptual*

Framework for Financial Reporting was issued for comment. What major arguments support the IASB's position?

RA2-6   Faithful Representation

In the IASB standard-setting conceptual framework, the word "reliability" has been replaced with "faithful representation." This has caused much discussion among preparers of financial information. The change has led to other implications related to substance over form, neutrality, conservatism, and the ability of entities to "override" a standard in very rare circumstances.

Instructions

Discuss the following questions. (You may find the IASB's *Basis for Conclusions to the Exposure Draft: Conceptual Framework for Financial Reporting: The Objective of Financial Reporting and Qualitative Characteristics and Constraints of Decision-Useful Financial Reporting Information*, of May 29, 2008, and *Summary of the Discussion Paper: A Review of the Conceptual Framework for Financial Reporting*, of January 2015, helpful in your discussion. They are available on the IASB website at www.ifrs.org.)

(a) "Faithful representation" has replaced the term "reliability" as a fundamental qualitative characteristic of financial information. What does faithful representation mean and how does this differ from reliability? Why was the term "reliability" replaced?

(b) What does "substance over form" mean? Give examples of where this might be relevant.

ENDNOTES

[1] "Conceptual Framework for Financial Accounting and Reporting: Elements of Financial Statements and Their Measurement," FASB discussion memorandum (Stamford, CT: FASB, 1976), p. 1 of the "Scope and Implications of the Conceptual Framework Project" section.

[2] Adapted from William C. Norby, "Accounting for Financial Analysis." *The Financial Analysts Journal*, March/April 1982, p. 22.

[3] IFRS does not define other comprehensive income as a separate element of the financial statements because it simply contains other elements, such as revenues, expenses, gains, and losses. It is considered to be a subclassification of the income statement. In addition, IFRS defines income as including both revenues and gains in paragraph 4.29 of the conceptual framework. It defines expenses as also including losses (4.33).

[4] IASB *IFRS Conceptual Framework*, Chapter 1 OB4.

[5] Investors and creditors are assumed to be the primary or key users. For not-for-profit entities, key users include members and contributors rather than investors.

[6] How does the concept of **neutrality** fit with the notion of **conservatism**? Few conventions in accounting are as misunderstood as conservatism. In situations involving uncertainty and professional judgement, historically, the concept of conservatism has meant that **net assets and net income would not be overstated**. Conservatism acknowledges a **pre-existing tendency** of companies to overstate net assets and net income and acts to counterbalance this tendency. Users of financial statements are more tolerant of understated net assets and net income than overstated balances. Does the use of conservatism represent a bias? Many believe that it does. The concept of conservatism is currently being downplayed in the existing conceptual framework in favour of neutrality. Having said that, there are many existing standards, both in IFRS and ASPE, where conservatism is embedded. For instance, where cost is used as a measurement basis (as opposed to fair value), accountants feel quite justified and even compelled to override the historical cost principle and write down the carrying value of an impaired asset. However, accountants are not always so quick to recognize an increase in the asset's value. The IASB was planning to bring the concept back into the conceptual framework in the next Exposure Draft.

[7] As a matter of fact, when the IASB issued its standard on joint arrangements in July 2011, it produced a document that assessed the effects of the standard (*IASB Effect Analysis*). In the document the IASB noted the following: "We expect our standards to have economic effects, and we expect those effects to be beneficial for some entities and detrimental to others. For example, a change in financial reporting requirements might affect the cost of capital for individual entities by changing the absolute or relative level of information asymmetry associated with those entities."

[8] IASB, *IFRS Conceptual Framework*, Chapter 3 QC15. Copyright © International Financial Reporting Standards Foundation. All rights reserved. Reproduced by John Wiley & Sons Canada, Ltd with the permission of the International Financial Reporting Standards

Foundation®. Reproduction and use rights are strictly limited. No permission granted to third parties to reproduce or distribute.

[9] IASB, *IFRS Conceptual Framework*, Chapter 3 QC32. This represents a subtle shift in the level of knowledge required. Prior to the joint IASB/FASB conceptual framework project, users were expected to have only a reasonable understanding of business and a willingness to study the statements.

[10] Consolidated financial statements of Enron Corp. for the year ended December 31, 2000.

[11] The elements are defined in the respective conceptual frameworks under IFRS and ASPE and, even though the wording differs, they are essentially very close in meaning.

[12] *CPA Canada Handbook—Accounting*, Part II, Section 1000.25 and IFRS *Conceptual Framework* 4.4 and 4.8-4.14.

[13] *CPA Canada Handbook—Accounting*, Part II, Section 1000.29 and IFRS *Conceptual Framework* 4.4 and 4.15-4.19.

[14] The terms "financial" and "non-financial" are somewhat vague and are meant to draw a line between liabilities that represent financial instruments (financial liabilities) and all other liabilities. Therefore, the term "non-financial" includes items such as contractual nonmonetary performance obligations (such as warranties to fix assets or provide services) and non-contractual monetary obligations (such as lawsuits).

[15] The IASB and FASB are currently looking at the definition of "equity" because the line between liabilities and equity is not well defined for complex financial instruments and business structures.

[16] Under IFRS, revenues and gains are grouped together under the heading of Income in the framework. Similarly, expenses and losses are grouped together under the heading of Expenses. Thus, although acknowledging the existence of and the potential for separate disclosure of gains and losses, IFRS defines fewer elements. ASPE defines these items separately.

[17] IFRS 37.16 and .23. Copyright © International Financial Reporting Standards Foundation. All rights reserved. Reproduced by John Wiley & Sons Canada, Ltd with the permission of the International Financial Reporting Standards Foundation®. Reproduction and use rights are strictly limited. No permission granted to third parties to reproduce or distribute.

[18] *CPA Canada Handbook—Accounting*, Part II, Section 3290.06.

[19] As we will see later in the text, derecognition is linked with how we define the entity, especially where the entity is transferring or selling assets to another entity that it may control. For instance, if an entity transfers investments to another entity that it controls, there is essentially no derecognition since the entity will end up consolidating the combined entity and the entity is just seen to be transferring things between the two related entities.

[20] That is, if the parent owns more than 50% of the (voting) common shares, it can exercise voting control.

[21] For example, it is now harder to define the boundaries of companies. There are public companies with multiple public subsidiaries, each with joint ventures, licensing arrangements, and other affiliations and strategic alliances. Increasingly, loose affiliations of enterprises in joint ventures or customer-supplier relationships are formed and dissolved in a matter of months or weeks. These virtual companies raise accounting issues about how to account for the entity.

[22] See the IASB project on the conceptual framework.

[23] IFRS 10 *Consolidated Financial Statements*. This standard was issued in 2011 and was effective for years beginning on or after January 1, 2013. Copyright © International Financial Reporting Standards Foundation. All rights reserved. Reproduced by John Wiley & Sons Canada, Ltd with the permission of the International Financial Reporting Standards Foundation®. Reproduction and use rights are strictly limited. No permission granted to third parties to reproduce or distribute.

[24] *CPA Canada Handbook—Accounting*, Part II, Section 1591.03.

[25] See *CPA Canada Handbook—Accounting*, Part II, Section 3856. B14 and B15. The 10% test is an example of a bright-line test discussed in Chapter 1. The IASB is, in principle, trying to purge bright-line tests from IFRS due the fact that, in most cases, the "line drawn" is an arbitrary one.

[26] For instance, this may be the case where entity A transfers an asset to entity B and entity A controls entity B. Entity A may be able to derecognize the asset and perhaps recognize a gain/loss, but when the consolidated statements are prepared, the asset will be included in the consolidated financial statements and any gain/loss eliminated.

[27] *CPA Canada Handbook—Accounting*, Part II, Section 3400.04-.06 and IAS 18.14.

[28] OSC Notice of Hearing and Statement of Allegations concerning Livent Inc., July 3, 2001.

[29] Many would argue that accounting standard setters are migrating toward a balance sheet emphasis. Thus the concept of matching is not as central as it would be if the statement of comprehensive income were the main focus. In addition, the use of fair value in measuring assets renders the concept of matching—as historically defined—useless.

[30] IFRS 13.9. The term "market" refers to any mechanism whereby parties objectively determine price, usually through bargaining and supply and demand. IFRS 13 includes the following as examples: exchange markets (such as the London Stock Exchange), dealer markets (such as commodities markets and used-equipment markets), brokered markets (such as real estate markets), and others.

[31] This is different from the way accountants have historically viewed fair values, which often considered the value from the entity's perspective, including any company-specific synergies. The objective of moving to a market-based fair value measure is to reduce subjectivity. For instance, an entity may believe that the asset is worth more than the market thinks it is worth and often attributes this to past entity-specific synergies, which are difficult to prove.

[32] *CPA Canada Handbook—Accounting*, Part II, Section 3031.04. The standard acknowledges that certain assets may be held at net realizable value or fair value less cost to sell. These assets are excluded from the requirements of Section 3031, which essentially requires the use of historical cost for unimpaired inventory.

[33] *CPA Canada Handbook—Accounting*, Part II, various sections including Sections 1582, 3055, 3063, 3064, 3065, 3462, and others.

[34] According to GAAP, recognition means including an item in one or more individual statements and does not mean disclosure in the notes to the financial statements. Some critics might argue, however, that if markets are assumed to be efficient, then as long as the information is disclosed, the market will absorb and use the information in pricing the shares. Whether the markets are fully efficient or not is a question that researchers seek to answer. There is evidence that efficient markets exist at least in a semi-strong form.

[35] CPA Canada's Canadian Performance Reporting Board, *MD&A: Guidance on Preparation and Disclosure*. This material is part of the CPA Canada Standards and Guidance Collection.

[36] Although MD&A disclosures are mandated for public companies, the *CPA Canada Guidance*, in its executive summary, notes that the MD&A can also be used by other organizations to communicate more effectively.

[37] Because the framework was developed after many of the standards were created, there may be some standards that are inconsistent with the framework. Note that the framework does not override any specific standard. The standard setters are working to get rid of inconsistencies between the older standards and the framework.

[38] The IASB continues to work on the new conceptual framework. It is an iterative process since the board must continually test the concepts against the existing and constantly changing body of knowledge to ensure the concepts stand up to current practice and needs.

THE ACCOUNTING INFORMATION SYSTEM AND MEASUREMENT ISSUES

REFERENCE TO THE CPA COMPETENCY MAP | **LEARNING OBJECTIVES**

After studying this chapter, you should be able to:

1.2.2, 1.3.1	**1.** Understand basic accounting terminology and explain double-entry rules.
1.2.2, 1.3.1	**2.** Explain how transactions affect the accounting equation.
1.2.2, 1.3.1, 4.1.2	**3.** Identify the steps in the accounting cycle and the steps in the recording process.
1.2.2, 1.3.1	**4.** Explain the reasons for and prepare adjusting entries.
1.1.1, 1.2.1, 1.2.2, 1.3.1	**5.** Explain how the type of ownership structure affects the financial statements.
1.2.2, 1.3.1	**6.** Prepare closing entries and consider other matters relating to the closing process.
1.1.2, 1.1.3, 1.2.1, 1.2.2, 5.4.1, 5.4.2, 5.4.3	**7.** Use valuation techniques to measure financial statement elements.
1.1.2, 1.1.3, 1.2.1, 1.2.2, 1.2.3, 1.4.5, 5.4.1, 5.4.2, 5.4.3	**8.** Use IFRS 13 to measure fair value.
1.1.4	**9.** Identify differences in accounting between ASPE and IFRS, and what changes are expected in the near future.

After studying Appendix 3A, you should be able to:

1.2.2, 1.3.1	**10.** Prepare a 10-column work sheet and financial statements.

After studying Appendix 3B, you should be able to:

1.1.3, 1.2.2, 5.4.1, 5.4.2, 5.4.3	**11.** Understand and apply present value concepts.

MEASURING ASSETS AND LIABILITIES IS A MOVING TARGET

WHEN TARGET CORPORATION opened to great fanfare in Canada in 2013, the American discount retailer was confident that shoppers north of the border would flock to its stores. Instead, not even two years later, Target announced it was closing all 133 of its Canadian locations.

What happened? The company itself and retail analysts blamed several things. These included stores in lacklustre former Zellers locations, problems plaguing its supply chain that often left shelves empty, and difficulties in offering the same products at the same prices as Canadians experienced when shopping at Target in the United States.

As losses mounted—Target's Canadian segment had an operating loss of U.S. $1.0 billion in 2013 and U.S. $869 million in 2014—the company estimated that it couldn't become profitable until at least 2021. On January 15, 2015, Target

THE CANADIAN PRESS/Andrew Vaughan

Canada Co. filed for court protection from creditors, having spent about U.S. $7.0 billion on its rollout.

In its 2014 annual report, the parent company reported a loss on discontinued operations of its Canadian segment of U.S. $4.1 billion. This included "exit costs"—the costs to exit Canada—of U.S. $5.1 billion. The exit costs included an investment impairment of $4.8 billion. As the parent company owned 100% of the shares of Target Canada Co., this amount represents the loss on that investment. The estimated amount of Target Canada's liabilities exceeded the estimated fair value of its assets available to distribute to creditors.

To estimate the fair value of Target Canada's assets, the parent company valued its inventory by estimating the selling price of its liquidation sales less costs to sell, estimated the value of its owned property using the income approach based on estimated market rents, and estimated the value of its leased property by using discounted cash flow analysis of the difference between the estimated market rent and contractual rent payments. Target Canada's outstanding liabilities included accounts payable and lease liabilities.

Measuring assets and liabilities is challenging for any company, as it almost always involves estimates. Target admitted that by the time the Canadian operations wound down for good, the company could suffer even more losses. "Our estimates involve significant judgment and are based on currently available information," the 2014 annual report stated. "We believe that it is reasonably possible that future changes to our estimates of loss and the ultimate amount paid on these claims could be material to our results of operations in future periods."

Sources: Graham F. Scott, "Target Announces It Will Close All 133 Canadian Stores," *Canadian Business*, January 15, 2015; Marina Strauss, "How Target Botched a $7-Billion Rollout," *The Globe and Mail*, January 15, 2015; Susan Taylor, Solarina Ho, and Andrea Hopkins, "Target's First Misstep in Canada May Have Been Wrong Footprint," Reuters, May 8, 2014; Target Corporation 2014 annual report.

PREVIEW OF CHAPTER 3

This chapter is divided into two parts. The first part deals with bookkeeping systems for capturing and recording transactions. The second part discusses the tools and techniques that will help you measure elements of the financial statements that present the results of those transactions.

It is important to understand how companies measure and record transactions, update their accounting records, and prepare financial statements. Part I of this chapter explains the features of an accounting information system and introduces tools for dealing with measurement issues faced by accountants. Part I assumes that we are able to measure transactions in a straightforward manner; for instance, where the transaction is a cash transaction, such as the company paying $100 for supplies. However, in other cases, measurement is not so straightforward. For example, how do we measure the value of an asset that is impaired?

The second part of the chapter presents the tools and techniques that will help you measure financial statement elements. This part of the chapter provides foundational knowledge that you will need in subsequent chapters.

The chapter is organized as follows:

THE ACCOUNTING INFORMATION SYSTEM AND MEASUREMENT ISSUES

PART I

PART II

Accounting Information System	The Accounting Cycle and the Recording Process	Financial Statements and Ownership Structure	The Closing Process	Measuring Financial Statement Elements	IFRS/ASPE Comparison	Appendix 3A—Using a Work Sheet	Appendix 3B—Present Value Concepts
▪ Basic terminology and double-entry rules ▪ Accounting equation	▪ Identifying and recording transactions and other events ▪ Journalizing ▪ Posting ▪ Trial balance ▪ Adjusting entries		▪ Preparing closing entries ▪ Reversing entries	▪ Valuation techniques ▪ Value in use measurements ▪ Measuring fair value using IFRS 13	▪ A comparison of IFRS and ASPE ▪ Looking ahead	▪ Adjustments entered on the work sheet ▪ Work sheet columns ▪ Completing the work sheet ▪ Preparing financial statements from a work sheet	▪ The nature of interest ▪ Fundamental variables in present value calculations ▪ Different ways to perform the calculations ▪ Some additional calculations

PART I

ACCOUNTING INFORMATION SYSTEM

The system for collecting and processing transaction data to make financial information available to interested parties is known as the **accounting information system**.

Accounting information systems can be very different from one business to another. Many factors shape these systems, including the type of business and the kinds of transactions it engages in, the firm's size, the amount of data handled, and the kind of information that management and others need to get from the system.

Even though most companies have sophisticated computerized accounting systems, it is still important to understand the mechanics of bookkeeping. How do transactions get captured in the accounting system? How do the accounting records get updated at the end of each period? How and when are the financial statements produced? At the end of the fiscal year, what do we do to ready the books of account to start a new fiscal year and a new accounting cycle? What tools should accountants use to approach measurement issues, such as those related to the time value of money and the estimation of fair value? We will now address these questions.

Basic Terminology and Double-Entry Rules

Objective 1
Understand basic accounting terminology and explain double-entry rules.

Financial accounting is built on a set of concepts (discussed in Chapters 1 and 2) for identifying, recording, classifying, and interpreting transactions and other events relating to enterprises. It is important to understand the **basic terminology** that is used in collecting accounting data. The following terms should be familiar to you from your introductory financial accounting course. Each is defined in the Glossary found at the end of this Volume of the textbook (just before the Company Index and the Subject Index). You should refer to the Glossary definitions for any terms that require further explanation.

BASIC TERMINOLOGY

Event (including an external event or *transaction*).

Account (including *permanent accounts* and *temporary accounts*).

Ledger[1] (for example, the *general ledger* or *subsidiary ledger*).

Journal.

Posting.

Trial balance (including an *adjusted trial balance* and a *post-closing trial balance*).

Journal entries (including *adjusting entries*, *closing entries*, and *reversing entries*).

Financial statements, including (1) the *statement of financial position* (or *balance sheet* under ASPE); (2) the *statement of comprehensive income* (or *income statement* under ASPE); (3) the *statement of cash flows*; and (4) the *statement of changes in shareholders' equity* (alternatively, a *statement of retained earnings* is used under ASPE). These financial statements are discussed further in Chapters 4 and 5.

The terms **debit** and **credit** refer to the left and right sides of a general ledger account, respectively. They are commonly abbreviated as Dr. for debit and Cr. for credit. These terms do not mean "increase" or "decrease." The terms "debit" and "credit" are used repeatedly in the recording process to describe where entries are made. For example, the act of entering an amount on the left side of an account is called **debiting** the account. Making an entry on the right side is **crediting** the account. When the totals of the two sides are compared, an account will have a debit balance if the total of the debit amounts is more than the credits. Conversely, an account will have a credit balance if the credit amounts exceed the debits. The procedure of having debits on the left and credits on the right is an accounting custom. We could function just as well if debits and credits were reversed. However, the custom of having debits on the left side of an account and credits on the right side (like the custom of driving on the right-hand side of the road) has been adopted for accounting. This rule applies to all accounts.

The equality of debits and credits is the basis for the double-entry system of recording transactions (also sometimes called double-entry bookkeeping). Under the **double-entry accounting** system, which is used for accounting around the world, the two-sided (dual) effect of each transaction is recorded in the appropriate accounts. This system gives a logical method for recording transactions. It also offers a way to help prove the accuracy of the recorded amounts. Every transaction is recorded with total debits equal to total credits, so the sum of all the debits posted to the accounts must equal the sum of all the credits.

All **asset** and **expense** accounts are increased on the left (or debit side) and decreased on the right (or credit side). Conversely, all **liability** and **revenue** accounts are increased on the right (or credit side) and decreased on the left (or debit side). Shareholders' equity accounts, such as Common Shares, and Retained Earnings, are increased on the credit side, whereas the Dividends account is increased on the debit side. The basic guidelines for an accounting system are presented in Illustration 3-1.

Illustration 3-1

Double-Entry (Debit and Credit) Accounting System

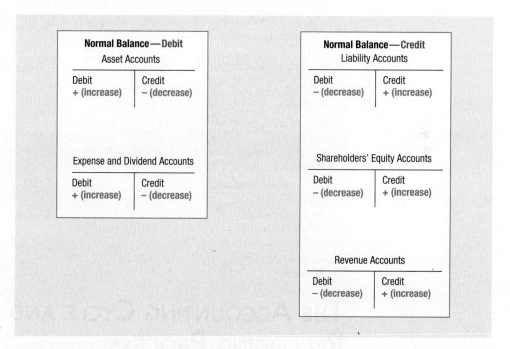

Accounting Equation

Objective 2
Explain how transactions affect the accounting equation.

In a double-entry system, for every debit there must be a credit, and vice versa. This leads us to the basic accounting equation for corporations shown in Illustration 3-2.

Illustration 3-2

The Basic Accounting Equation

| Assets | = | Liabilities | + | Shareholders' Equity |

Illustration 3-3 expands this equation to include shareholders' equity accounts. In addition, it shows the debit/credit rules and effects on each type of account. Study this diagram carefully. It will help you understand the fundamentals of the double-entry system. Like the basic equation, the expanded basic equation must balance. That is, total debits **must** equal total credits.[2]

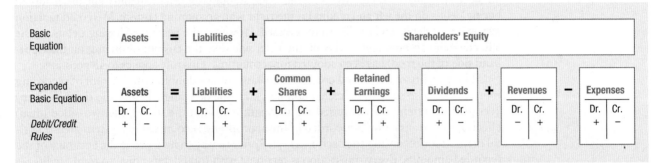

Every time a transaction occurs, the elements in the equation change, but the basic equality of the two sides remains. To illustrate, here are eight different transactions for Perez Inc.:

TRANSACTION	ASSETS	=	LIABILITIES	+	SHAREHOLDERS' EQUITY
1. Owners invest $40,000 in exchange for common shares	+40,000				+40,000
2. Disburse $600 cash for administrative support wages	−600				−600 (expense)
3. Purchase office equipment priced at $5,200, giving a 10% promissory note in exchange	+5,200		+5,200		
4. Services are rendered for $4,000 cash	+4,000				+4,000 (revenue)
5. Pay off a short-term liability of $7,000	−7,000		−7,000		
6. Declare a cash dividend of $5,000			+5,000		−5,000
7. Pay off a long-term liability of $80,000 by issuing common shares			−80,000		+80,000
8. Pay $16,000 cash for a delivery van	−16,000 +16,000				

THE ACCOUNTING CYCLE AND THE RECORDING PROCESS

Objective 3

Identify the steps in the accounting cycle and the steps in the recording process.

Illustration 3-4 charts the steps in the **accounting cycle.** These are the accounting procedures normally used by enterprises to record transactions and prepare financial statements.

Identifying and Recording Transactions and Other Events

The first step in the accounting cycle is to **analyze transactions** and other selected **events.** The problem is determining what to **record.** There are no simple rules for whether an event should be recorded. It is generally agreed that changes in personnel, changes in managerial policies, and the value of human resources, though important, should not be recorded in the accounts. On the other hand, when the company makes a cash sale or purchase—no matter how small—it should be recorded. The treatment relates to the accounting concepts presented in Chapter 2. An item should be **recognized** in the financial statements if it meets the definition of an **element** (such as a liability or asset), and is **measurable**. What happens when there is uncertainty about the future event occurring or not, such as the potential loss from a lawsuit? In that case, the entity must use all available information to make a neutral decision as to whether the liability/asset exists or not. The entity would take that uncertainty into account when it measures the element. We discussed recognition and measurement criteria in Chapter 2.

Illustration 3-4

The Accounting Cycle

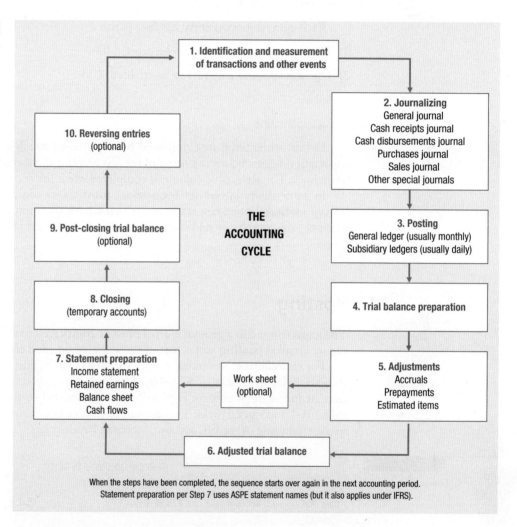

When the steps have been completed, the sequence starts over again in the next accounting period. Statement preparation per Step 7 uses ASPE statement names (but it also applies under IFRS).

Journalizing

The effects of transactions on the basic business elements (assets, liabilities, and equities) are categorized and collected in accounts. The **general ledger** then collects all of the asset, liability, shareholders' equity, revenue, and expense accounts.

In practice, transactions and other selected events are not first recorded in the ledger. This is because each transaction affects two or more accounts, and since each account is on a different page in the ledger, it would be inconvenient to record each transaction this way. The risk of error would also be greater.[3] To overcome this limitation and to have a complete record of each transaction or other selected event in one place, a journal (the book of original entry) is used. The simplest journal form is a chronological listing of transactions and other events that expresses the transactions and events as debits and credits to particular accounts. This is called a **general journal**. Let's look at a page from the general journal of Marra Co., shown in Illustration 3-5. The general journal page shows the following transactions:

Nov. 11 Marra Co. buys a new delivery truck on account from Auto Sales Inc., $22,400.

Nov. 13 Receives an invoice from the *Evening Graphic* for advertising, $280.

Nov. 14 Returns merchandise to Canuck Supply for credit, $175.

Nov. 15 Receives a $95 debit memo from Confederation Ltd., indicating that freight on merchandise purchased from Confederation Ltd. was prepaid by the supplier but is the buyer's obligation.

Each general journal entry has four parts:

1. The accounts and amounts to be debited (Dr.)

2. The accounts and amounts to be credited (Cr.)

3. A date

4. An explanation

Debits are entered first, followed by the credits, which are slightly indented. The explanation begins below the name of the last account to be credited and may take one or more lines. The Reference column is completed when the accounts are posted.

In some cases, businesses use **special journals** in addition to the general journal. Special journals summarize transactions that have a common characteristic (such as cash receipts, sales, purchases, and cash payments), which saves time in doing the various bookkeeping tasks.

Posting

The items entered in a general journal must be transferred to the general ledger. This procedure is called **posting** and is part of the summarizing and classifying process.

For example, the November 11 entry in Marra Co.'s general journal in Illustration 3-5 shows a debit to Trucks of $22,400 and a credit to Accounts Payable of $22,400. The amount in the debit column is posted from the journal to the debit side of the general ledger (GL) account Trucks. The amount in the credit column is posted from the journal to the credit side of the GL account Accounts Payable.

Illustration 3-5

General Journal with Sample Entries

GENERAL JOURNAL PAGE 12

Date 2017	Account Title and Explanation	Ref.	Amount Debit	Amount Credit
Nov. 11	Trucks	8	22,400	
	Accounts Payable	34		22,400
	(Purchased delivery truck on account)			
Nov. 13	Advertising Expense	65	280	
	Accounts Payable	34		280
	(Received invoice for advertising)			
Nov. 14	Accounts Payable	34	175	
	Purchase Returns and Allowances	53		175
	(Returned merchandise for credit)			
Nov. 15	Freight-In	55	95	
	Accounts Payable	34		95
	(Received debit memo for freight on merchandise purchased)			

The numbers in the Ref. column of the general journal refer to the GL accounts to which the items are posted. For example, the 34 placed in the column to the right of Accounts Payable indicates that this $22,400 item was posted to Account No. 34 in the ledger.

The general journal posting is completed when all the posting reference numbers have been recorded opposite the account titles in the journal. This means that the number in the posting reference column serves two purposes: (1) it indicates the ledger account number of the account involved, and (2) it indicates that the posting has been completed for that item. Each business chooses its own numbering system for its ledger accounts. One practice is to begin numbering with asset accounts and to follow with liabilities, shareholders' equity, revenue, and expense accounts, in that order.

Trial Balance

INTERNAL CONTROL
4.1.2

A trial balance is a list of general ledger accounts and their balances at a specific time. Customarily, an entity prepares a trial balance at the end of an accounting period. The accounts are listed in the order in which they appear in the general ledger, with debit balances listed in the left column and credit balances in the right column. The totals of the two columns must agree.

The main purpose of a trial balance is to prove the mathematical equality of debits and credits after posting. Under the double-entry system, this equality will occur when the sum of the debit account balances equals the sum of the credit account balances. A trial balance also uncovers errors in journalizing and posting, and serves as a basic internal control. In addition, it is useful when preparing financial statements. To prepare a trial balance, an entity:

1. Lists the account titles and their balances.

2. Totals the debit and credit columns.

3. Proves the equality of the two columns.

Illustration 3-6 shows the trial balance prepared from the ledger of Pioneer Advertising Agency Inc. at the end of its first month of operations.

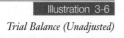

Illustration 3-6

Trial Balance (Unadjusted)

PIONEER ADVERTISING AGENCY INC. Unadjusted Trial Balance October 31, 2017		
	Debit	Credit
Cash	$ 80,000	
Accounts receivable	72,000	
Supplies	25,000	
Prepaid insurance	6,000	
Fair value-NI investments	10,000	
Office equipment	50,000	
Notes payable		$ 50,000
Accounts payable		35,000
Unearned revenue		12,000
Common shares		100,000
Dividends	5,000	
Service revenue		100,000
Salaries and wages expense	40,000	
Rent expense	9,000	
	$297,000	$297,000

Note that the total debits, $297,000, equal the total credits, $297,000. In the trial balance, the account numbers of the account titles are also often shown to the left of the titles.

Adjusting Entries

Objective 4
Explain the reasons for
and prepare adjusting
entries.

Recall that revenues must be recorded in the period in which they are earned, and expenses must be recognized in the period in which they are incurred, regardless of when payment occurs and they must match. In order to do this, **adjusting entries** are made at the end of the accounting period. In short, **adjustments are needed to ensure that the revenue recognition principle is followed and that proper matching occurs.**

The use of adjusting entries makes it possible to report on the statement of financial position the appropriate assets, liabilities, and shareholders' equity at the statement date and to report on the statement of comprehensive income the proper net income (or loss) and comprehensive income for the period. However, the trial balance—the first pulling together of the transaction data—may not contain up-to-date and complete data. This is true for the following reasons:

1. Some events are **not journalized daily** because it is not efficient to do so. Examples are the consumption of supplies and the earning of wages by employees.

2. Some costs are not journalized during the accounting period because these costs **expire with the passage of time** rather than as a result of recurring daily transactions. Examples of such costs are building and equipment deterioration, rent, and insurance.

3. Some items may be **unrecorded.** An example is a utility service bill that will not be received until the next accounting period.

Adjusting entries are required every time financial statements are prepared. The starting point to preparing adjusting entries is to analyze each trial balance account to determine whether it is complete and up to date for financial statement purposes. The analysis requires a thorough understanding of the company's operations and the relationships between its accounts. Preparing adjusting entries is often a complicated process that requires the services of a skilled professional. In accumulating the adjustment data, the company may need to take inventory counts of supplies and repair parts. It may also be desirable to prepare supporting schedules of insurance policies, rental agreements, and other contractual commitments. Adjustments are often prepared after the end of the period, but the entries are dated as at the statement of financial position date.

Adjusting entries can be classified as one of (1) **prepayments,** (2) **accruals,** or (3) **estimated items** (including fair value estimates).[4] Each of these classes has subcategories as shown in Illustration 3-7.

Illustration 3-7

Types of Adjusting Entries

PREPAYMENTS	ACCRUALS	ESTIMATED ITEMS
Prepaid expenses. Expenses paid in cash and recorded as assets before they are used or consumed.	**Accrued revenues.** Revenues earned but not yet received in cash or recorded.	**Bad debts.** Expenses for impaired accounts receivable estimated in the period the related revenue is earned.
Unearned revenues. Revenues received in cash and recorded as liabilities before they are earned.	**Accrued expenses.** Expenses incurred but not yet paid in cash or recorded.	**Unrealized holding gain or loss—NI.** Gain (or loss) on fair value through net income (NI) investments is estimated at the end of an accounting period and recorded as an increase (or decrease) to the investment account with a corresponding gain (or loss) on the statement of comprehensive income.
		Unrealized holding gain or loss—OCI. Gain (or loss) on fair value through other comprehensive income (OCI) investments estimated at the end of an accounting period and recorded as an increase (or decrease) to the investment account with a corresponding gain (or loss) in OCI on the statement of comprehensive income.

We give specific examples and explanations of each type of adjustment later in this chapter. Each example is based on the October 31 trial balance of Pioneer Advertising Agency Inc. (Illustration 3-6). We assume that Pioneer Advertising uses an accounting period of one month. Thus, the company will make monthly adjusting entries. The entries will be dated October 31.

Adjusting Entries for Prepayments

As mentioned in Illustration 3-7, prepayments are either **prepaid expenses** or **unearned revenues**. Adjusting entries for prepayments are required at the statement date to record the portion of the prepaid expense incurred or unearned revenue earned in the current accounting period. Assuming an adjustment is needed for both types of prepayments, the asset and liability involved are overstated and the related expense and revenue are understated. For example, in the trial balance, the balance in the asset account Supplies shows only supplies purchased. This balance is overstated; the related expense account, Supplies Expense, is understated because the cost of supplies used has not been recognized. Thus, the adjusting entry for prepayments will decrease a statement of financial position account and increase a statement of comprehensive income account. Illustration 3-8 shows the effects of adjusting entries for prepayments.

Illustration 3-8

Adjusting Entries for Prepayments

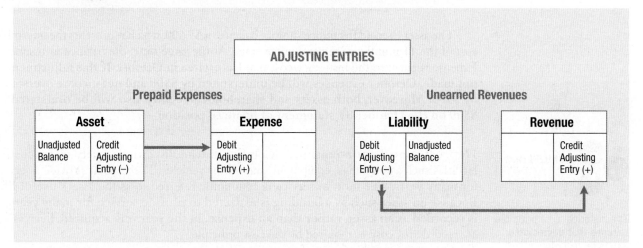

Prepaid Expenses

As shown in Illustration 3-7, expenses that have been paid in cash and recorded as assets before they are used or consumed are identified as **prepaid expenses**. When a cost is incurred, an asset account is debited to show the service or benefit that will be received in the future. Prepayments often occur for such things as insurance, supplies, advertising, and rent.

Prepaid expenses expire either with the passage of time (such as rent and insurance) or by being used and consumed (such as supplies). The expiration of these costs does not require an entry each day, which would be unnecessary and impractical. Instead, it is customary to postpone the recognition of such cost expirations until financial statements are prepared. At each statement date, adjusting entries are made to record the expenses that apply to the current accounting period and to show the remaining unexpired costs in the asset accounts.

Before adjustment, assets are overstated and expenses are understated. **Thus, the prepaid expense adjusting entry results in a debit to an expense account and a credit to an asset account.**

Two common types of prepaid expenses are insurance and depreciation/amortization, whose adjusting entries we'll discuss next.

Insurance. There are many types of insurance. Most companies have fire and theft insurance on inventory and equipment, personal liability insurance for accidents suffered by customers, and automobile insurance on company cars and trucks. The cost of insurance protection is the amount paid as insurance premiums. The term (duration) and coverage (what the company is insured against) are specified in the insurance policy. The minimum term is usually one year, but three- to five-year terms may be available and could result in lower annual premiums. Insurance premiums are normally charged to the asset account Prepaid Insurance when they are paid. At the financial statement date, it is necessary to debit Insurance Expense and credit Prepaid Insurance for the cost that has expired during the period.

On October 4, Pioneer Advertising Agency Inc. paid $6,000 for a one-year fire insurance policy. The coverage began as of October 1. The premium was charged to Prepaid Insurance when it was paid, and this account shows a balance of $6,000 in the October 31 trial balance. An analysis of the policy reveals that $500 of insurance expires each month ($6,000 ÷ 12). Thus, the following adjusting entry is made:

A = L + SE
−500   −500

Cash flows: No effect

	Oct. 31		
Insurance Expense		500	
Prepaid Insurance			500
(To record insurance expired)			

The asset Prepaid Insurance shows a balance of $5,500, which represents the unexpired cost of the 11 months of remaining coverage. At the same time, the balance in Insurance Expense is equal to the insurance cost that has expired in October. **If this adjustment is not made, October expenses will be understated by $500 and net income overstated by $500. Moreover, both assets and shareholders' equity also will be overstated by $500 on the October 31 statement of financial position.**

UNDERLYING CONCEPT

The historical cost principle requires that depreciable assets be recorded at cost. Matching allows this cost to be allocated to periods of use.

Depreciation/Amortization.   Companies typically own a variety of productive facilities such as buildings, equipment, and motor vehicles. These assets provide a service for many years. The term of service is commonly referred to as the asset's **useful life. Because an asset such as a building is expected to provide service for many years, it is recorded as an asset, rather than an expense, in the year it is acquired.** Such assets are recorded at cost, as required by the cost principle.

In order to match the cost of the asset with the revenues that it is generating, a portion of the cost of a long-lived asset should be reported as an expense during each period of the asset's useful life. **Depreciation/amortization** is the process of **allocating the cost of an asset** to expense over its useful life in a rational and systematic manner.

From an accounting standpoint, when productive facilities are acquired, the transaction is viewed essentially as a long-term prepayment for services. Periodic adjusting entries for depreciation are therefore needed for the same reasons described earlier for other prepaid expenses. In other words, it is necessary to recognize the cost that has expired during the period (the expense) and to report the unexpired cost at the end of the period (the asset).

In determining a productive facility's useful life, there are three main causes of depreciation:

1. Actual use

2. Deterioration due to the elements

3. Obsolescence

When an entity acquires an asset, it cannot know the effects of these factors with certainty, so they must instead be estimated. Thus, depreciation is an estimate rather than an exact measurement of the cost that has expired. A common procedure in calculating depreciation expense is to divide the asset's cost by its useful life. For example, if the cost is $10,000 and the useful life is expected to be 10 years, annual depreciation is $1,000.

For Pioneer Advertising, depreciation on the office equipment is estimated at $4,800 a year (cost of $50,000 less a residual value of $2,000 divided by a useful life of 10 years), or $400 per month. Accordingly, depreciation for October is recognized by the following adjusting entry:

A = L + SE
−400   −400

Cash flows: No effect

	Oct. 31		
Depreciation Expense		400	
Accumulated Depreciation—Office Equipment			400
(To record monthly depreciation)			

After the adjusting entry is posted, the balance in the relevant accumulated depreciation account will increase by $400 each month. Therefore, after journalizing and posting the adjusting entry at November 30, the balance in the accumulated depreciation account will then be $800.

Accumulated Depreciation—Office Equipment is a contra asset account. A **contra asset account** is an account that is offset against an asset account on the statement of financial position. In the case of accumulated depreciation, this account is offset against Office Equipment on the statement of financial position and its normal balance is therefore a credit. This account is used instead of crediting Office Equipment so that the equipment's original cost and the total cost that has expired to date can both be disclosed. In the statement of financial position, Accumulated Depreciation—Office Equipment is deducted from the related asset account (which is normally a debit), as shown in Illustration 3-9.

Illustration 3-9

Statement of Financial Position Presentation of Accumulated Depreciation

Office equipment	$50,000	
Less: Accumulated depreciation—office equipment	400	$49,600

The difference between any depreciable asset's cost and its related accumulated depreciation is known as its **book value**. In Illustration 3-9, the equipment's book value, or **carrying amount**, at the statement of financial position date is $49,600. It is important to realize that the asset's **book value and market value are generally two different values**.

Note also that depreciation expense identifies that portion of the asset's cost that has expired in October. What would happen if Pioneer Advertising did not make an adjusting entry for this? As in the case of other prepaid adjustments, **if this adjusting entry is not made, then total shareholders' equity and net income will be overstated and the expense will be understated**.

If additional equipment is involved, such as delivery or store equipment, or if the company has buildings, depreciation expense is recorded on each of these items. Related accumulated depreciation accounts also are created. These accumulated depreciation accounts would be described in the ledger as follows: Accumulated Depreciation—Trucks, Accumulated Depreciation—Office Equipment, and Accumulated Depreciation—Buildings.

Unearned Revenues

As shown in Illustration 3-7, revenues that have been received in cash and recorded as liabilities before they are earned are called **unearned revenues**. Items such as rent, magazine subscriptions, and customer deposits for further service may result in unearned revenues.

WHAT DO THE NUMBERS MEAN?

Companies that receive revenue before providing a service include sports teams, live theatres, and transportation companies. Airlines such as **Air Canada** and **WestJet** treat receipts from the sale of tickets as unearned revenue until the flight service is provided. (For example, "Advance Ticket Sales" totalled $576 million on WestJet's December 31, 2014 financial statements.) The growth in Advance Ticket Sales of $24.7 million (or 4.5% as compared with 2013) was part of the reason WestJet's cash flow from operating activities totalled over $570 million in 2014. In fact, one of the ratios that WestJet tracks is cash and cash equivalents on hand divided by advance ticket sales, which was 2.36 in 2014. This is a key indicator that the company has sufficient cash on hand to meet its liabilities as they come due.

Source: WestJet's Annual Report for the year 2014.

REAL WORLD EMPHASIS

Tuition fees received by a university before the start of a semester are also considered unearned revenue. Unearned revenues are the opposite of prepaid expenses. Indeed, unearned revenue on the books of one company is likely to be a prepayment on the books of the company that has made the advance payment. For example, if identical accounting periods are assumed, a landlord will have unearned rent revenue when a tenant has prepaid rent.

When the payment is received for services that will be provided in a future accounting period, an unearned revenue account (a liability) should be credited to recognize the obligation that exists. Unearned revenues are later earned by performing the service for the customer (which discharges the liability). During the accounting period, it may not be practical to make an entry each day that the revenue is earned. In such cases, the recognition of earned revenue is delayed until the adjustment process. At that time, an adjusting entry is then made to record the revenue that has been earned and to show the liability that remains. Typically, liabilities are overstated and revenues are understated prior to adjustment. Thus, the adjusting entry for unearned revenues results in a debit (decrease) to a liability account and a credit (increase) to a revenue account.

Let's look at an example of unearned revenues for Pioneer Advertising Agency. It received $12,000 on October 2 from R. Knox for advertising services that Pioneer expected to complete by December 31. The payment was credited to Unearned Revenue, and this account shows a balance of $12,000 in the October 31 trial balance. When Pioneer determines that $4,000 of these services have been earned in October, it makes the following adjusting entry:

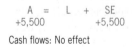

A = L + SE
     −4,000 +4,000

Cash flows: No effect

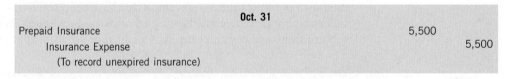

Oct. 31		
Unearned Revenue	4,000	
Service Revenue		4,000
(To record revenue for services provided.)		

The account Unearned Revenue now shows a balance of $8,000, which represents the remaining advertising services that Pioneer expects to perform in the future. At the same time, Service Revenue shows total revenue earned in October of $104,000. **If this adjustment is not made, revenues and net income will be understated by $4,000 in the statement of comprehensive income. Moreover, liabilities will be overstated and shareholders' equity will be understated by $4,000 on the October 31 statement of financial position.**

Alternative Method for Adjusting Prepayments

So far, the assumption has been that an asset (such as prepaid rent) or liability (such as unearned revenue) is recorded when the company initially pays or receives the cash. An alternative treatment is to record the initial entry through the related income statement account and adjust it later. For example, if Pioneer Advertising Agency Inc. paid $6,000 for a one-year fire insurance policy on October 1, it could initially have recorded the whole amount in Insurance Expense. Thus at October 31, the adjusting entry would be as follows:

A = L + SE
+5,500   +5,500

Cash flows: No effect

Oct. 31		
Prepaid Insurance	5,500	
Insurance Expense		5,500
(To record unexpired insurance)		

The same could be done for other prepayments, such as supplies and rent.

Adjusting Entries for Accruals

Another category of adjusting entries is **accruals**. Adjusting entries for accruals are needed to record revenues earned and expenses incurred in the current accounting period that have not been recognized through daily entries. If an accrual adjustment is needed, the revenue account (and the related asset account) and/or the expense account (and the related liability account) are understated. Thus, adjusting entries for accruals will increase both a statement of financial position and a statement of comprehensive income account. Adjusting entries for accruals are shown in Illustration 3-10.

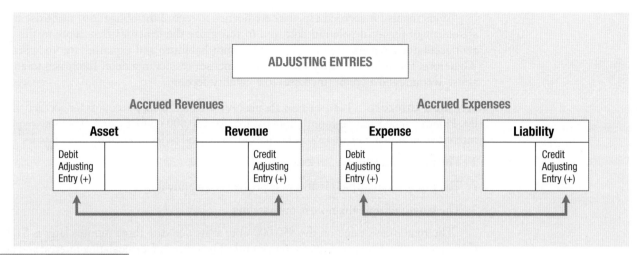

Adjusting Entries for Accruals

Accrued Revenues

As shown in Illustration 3-7, revenues that have been **earned but not yet received** in cash or recorded at the statement date are **accrued revenues**. ("Accrued" means accumulated.) There are two common types of accrued revenues.

1. Accrued revenues may **accumulate (accrue) with the passing of time**, as in the case of interest income and rent revenue. These types of accrued revenues are unrecorded because earning interest and rent does not involve daily transactions.

2. Accrued revenues may also result from **services that have been performed but neither billed nor collected**, as in the case of commissions and fees. These types of accrued revenues may be unrecorded because only a portion of the total service has been provided.

An adjusting entry is required to show the receivable that exists at the statement of financial position date and to record the revenue that has been earned during the period. Before adjustment, both assets and revenues are understated. Accordingly, an adjusting entry for accrued revenues results in a debit (increase) to an asset account and a credit (increase) to a revenue account.

Let's look at an example of accrued revenues for Pioneer Advertising Agency. In October, Pioneer earned $2,000 for advertising services that were not billed to clients before October 31. Because these services have not yet been billed, they have not been recorded in any way. Thus, the following adjusting entry is made:

A = L + SE
+2,000   +2,000

Cash flows: No effect

	Oct. 31		
Accounts Receivable		2,000	
Service Revenue			2,000
(To record revenue for services provided)			

The asset Accounts Receivable shows that $74,000 is owed by clients at the statement of financial position date. The balance of $106,000 in Service Revenue is the total revenue earned during the period ($100,000 + $4,000 + $2,000). If the adjusting entry is not made, assets and shareholders' equity on the statement of financial position, and revenues and net income on the statement of comprehensive income, will all be understated.

Accrued Expenses

UNDERLYING CONCEPT

As indicated in Illustration 3-7, expenses that have been incurred but not yet paid or recorded at the statement date are called **accrued expenses**. Examples of possible accrued expenses are interest, rent, taxes, and salaries. Accrued expenses result from the same causes as accrued revenues. In fact, an accrued expense on the books of one company is accrued revenue for another company. For example, the $2,000 accrual of service revenue by Pioneer is an accrued expense to the client that received the service.

Accrual accounting requires that expenses be accrued when they are incurred.

Adjustments for accrued expenses are needed to record the obligations that exist at the statement of financial position date and to recognize the expenses that apply to the current accounting period. Before adjustment, both liabilities and expenses are understated. Therefore, the adjusting entry for accrued expenses results in a debit (increase) to an expense account and a credit (increase) to a liability account.

Accrued Interest.   Let's see how Pioneer Advertising Agency accounts for accrued interest. Pioneer signed a three-month note payable for $50,000 on October 1. The note requires interest at an annual rate of 12%. The interest to be paid is determined by three factors:

1. The note's face value

2. The interest rate, which is always expressed as an annual rate

3. The length of time the note is outstanding

The total interest due on the $50,000 note at its due date three months later is $1,500 ($50,000 $\times$ 12% $\times$ $^3/_{12}$), or $500 for one month. The formula for calculating interest and how it applies to Pioneer Advertising for the month of October are shown in Illustration 3-11.

Illustration 3-11

Formula for Calculating Interest

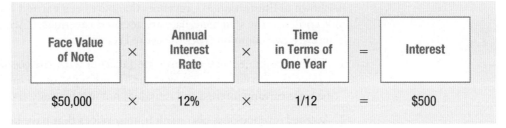

Note that the time period is expressed as a fraction of a year. The accrued expense adjusting entry at October 31 is as follows:

A = L + SE
+500 −500

Cash flows: No effect

	Oct. 31		
Interest Expense		500	
Interest Payable			500
(To record interest on notes payable.)			

Interest Expense shows the interest charges that apply to the month of October. The amount of interest owed at the statement date is shown in Interest Payable. It will not be paid until the note comes due at the end of three months. The Interest Payable account is used instead of crediting Notes Payable in order to disclose the two types of obligations (interest and principal) in the accounts and statements. **If this adjusting entry is not made, liabilities and interest expense will be understated, and net income and shareholders' equity will be overstated.**

Accrued Salaries.   Some types of expenses, such as employee salaries and commissions, are paid for after the services have been performed. At Pioneer Advertising, salaries were last paid on October 20; the next payment of salaries will not occur until November 3. Seven working days remain in October (October 23, 24, 25, 26, 27, 30, and 31).

At October 31, the salaries for these days represent an accrued expense and a related liability to Pioneer Advertising. The employees receive total salaries of $10,000 for a five-day workweek, or $2,000 per day. Thus, accrued salaries at October 31 are $14,000 ($2,000 $\times$ 7), and the adjusting entry is:

A = L + SE
+14,000 −14,000

Cash flows: No effect

	Oct. 31		
Salaries and Wages Expense		14,000	
Salaries and Wages Payable			14,000
(To record accrued salaries)			

After this adjustment, the balance in Salaries and Wages Expense of $44,000 (22 days $\times$ $2,000) is the actual salary expense for October. The balance in Salaries and Wages Payable of $14,000 is the amount of liability for salaries owed as at October 31. **If the $14,000 adjustment for salaries is not recorded, Pioneer's expenses will be understated by $14,000, and its liabilities will be understated by $14,000.**

At Pioneer Advertising, salaries are payable every two weeks. Consequently, the next payday is November 3, when total salaries of $20,000 will again be paid. The payment consists of $14,000 of salaries and wages payable at October 31 plus $6,000 of salaries and wages expense for November (3 working days in November × $2,000). Therefore, Pioneer makes the following entry on November 3:

A   =   L   + SE
−20,000 −14,000 −6,000

Cash flows: ↓20,000 outflow

	Nov. 3		
Salaries and Wages Payable		14,000	
Salaries and Wages Expense		6,000	
Cash			20,000
(To record November 3 payroll)			

This entry eliminates the liability for Salaries and Wages Payable that was recorded in the October 31 adjusting entry and records the proper amount of Salaries and Wages Expense for the period November 1 to November 3.

Adjusting Entries for Estimated Items

The third category of adjusting entries is **estimated items**. Adjusting entries for estimated items are required in order to record expenses, gains, and losses incurred in the current accounting period that have not been recognized through daily entries. If an estimated adjustment is needed for anticipated bad debts, the expense account is understated. So, the adjusting entry will typically increase both a contra account on the statement of financial position and an income statement account. Similarly, an adjusting entry for fair value through net income investments for an unrealized gain would increase an investment account and affect unrealized gains on the statement of comprehensive income. Adjusting entries for estimated items are shown in Illustration 3-12.

Illustration 3-12

Adjusting Entries for Estimated Items

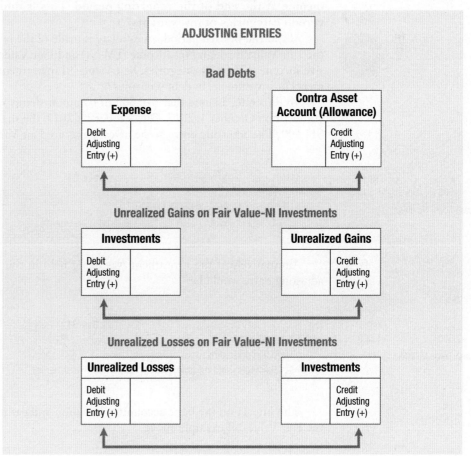

Bad Debts

An estimate of bad debts must be recorded as an expense of the period in which the revenue was earned. It cannot be recorded in the period when the accounts or notes are written off. This is so that expenses are properly matched with revenues. Estimated uncollectible receivables must be recognized so that the receivable balance shows its proper value. Proper matching and valuation therefore require an adjusting entry.

At the end of each period, an estimate is made of the amount of current period revenue on account that will later be uncollectible. The estimate is based on the amount of bad debts experienced in past years, general economic conditions, how long the receivables are past due, and other factors that indicate the likelihood of collection. Often the estimate is expressed as a percentage of revenue each month, followed by a detailed analysis at the end of the fiscal year. As we will see in Chapter 7, the Allowance for Doubtful Accounts contra account may also be calculated by applying different percentages to the aged trade accounts receivable and trade notes receivable balances at the end of the period.

To illustrate, assume that experience shows that a reasonable estimate for bad debt expense for the month is $1,600. The adjusting entry for bad debts is:

A = L + SE
1,600   1,600

Cash flows: No effect

	Oct. 31		
Bad Debt Expense		1,600	
Allowance for Doubtful Accounts			1,600
(To record monthly bad debt expense)			

Unrealized Holding Gains or Losses (NI and OCI)

An unrealized gain or loss must be recorded in the statement of comprehensive income at the end of the reporting period. This is done to adjust to fair value for certain categories of investments.

At the end of each period, an estimate is made of the fair value of investments held in the Fair Value through Net Income (FV-NI) and Fair Value through Other Comprehensive Income (FV-OCI) categories. Fair Value-NI investments could include equity investments or investments in debt securities.[5]

To illustrate, assume that $10,000 of common shares were acquired as an equity investment on October 1, 2017. On October 31, 2017, the shares' fair value had increased to $11,500. The adjusting entry, if the investments are Fair Value-NI, is:

A = L + SE
+1,500   +1,500

Cash flows: No effect

	Oct. 31		
FV-NI Investments		1,500	
Unrealized Holding Gain or Loss-NI			1,500
(To record holding gain on Fair Value-NI investment)			

Alternatively, if the investment was being held in the Fair Value-OCI category, the adjusting entry would be:

A = L + SE
+1,500   +1,500

Cash flows: No effect

	Oct. 31		
FV-OCI Investments		1,500	
Unrealized Holding Gain or Loss-OCI			1,500
(To record holding gain on Fair Value-OCI investments)			

The impact on the basic accounting equation and cash flows would be the same as in the Fair Value-NI example above.

FINANCIAL STATEMENTS AND OWNERSHIP STRUCTURE

Objective 5

Explain how the type of ownership structure affects the financial statements.

After the adjusting entries have been prepared and posted, an adjusted trial balance is prepared. The adjusted trial balance greatly helps when preparing the financial statements. Where are various financial statement elements reported?

1. Assets and liabilities are reported on the statement of financial position, often grouped into current and non-current classifications.

2. Common shares, retained earnings, and accumulated other comprehensive income are reported in the shareholders' equity section of the statement of financial position.

3. Dividends are reported on the statement of changes in shareholders' equity.

4. Revenues and expenses are reported on the statement of comprehensive income. Revenues and expenses are eventually transferred to retained earnings at the end of the period while other comprehensive income is transferred to **accumulated other comprehensive income.**[6]

The relationships within shareholders' equity are shown in Illustration 3-13.

The type of ownership structure that a business enterprise uses determines the types of accounts that are part of the equity section or that affect it. In a **corporation,**[7] **Common Shares, Contributed Surplus, Dividends, Retained Earnings,** and **Accumulated Other Comprehensive Income** are commonly used accounts. In a **proprietorship** or **partnership,** a **Capital** account is used to indicate the investment in the company by the owner(s). An **Owners' Drawings** or withdrawal account may be used to indicate withdrawals by the partners. These two accounts are grouped or netted under **Owners' Equity.** We focus on the corporate organization structure in this text. Companies may use a work sheet to facilitate the preparation of financial statements. We summarize the use of a work sheet for the preparation of corporate financial statements in Appendix 3A.

Illustration 3-13

Financial Statements and Shareholders' Equity Classifications

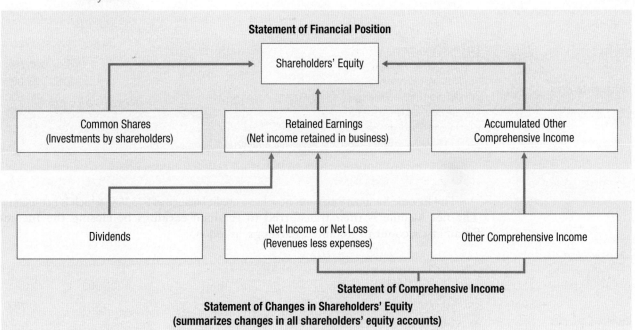

THE CLOSING PROCESS

Objective 6
Prepare closing entries
and consider other
matters relating to the
closing process.

The **closing process** reduces the balance of temporary accounts to zero in order to prepare the accounts for the next period's transactions. In the closing process, all of the revenue and expense account balances (the statement of comprehensive income items) are transferred to a clearing account called **Income Summary**, which is used only at year end. Revenues and expenses are matched in the Income Summary account. The net result of this matching is the net income or net loss for the period. This is then transferred to a shareholders' or owners' equity account. For a corporation, this would be Retained Earnings or, for OCI items, an Accumulated Other Comprehensive Income (AOCI) account. For proprietorships and partnerships, this would normally be the capital accounts or owners' equity accounts.

Preparing Closing Entries

Closing entries are journal entries that close the temporary accounts in order to prepare for the start of a new financial reporting period. All closing entries are posted to the appropriate general ledger accounts.

For example, assume that Collegiate Apparel Shop Inc. (CASI) has three revenue accounts, after adjustments, at year end. CASI would close these accounts by making the following closing journal entry:

A = L + SE
−312,000
+312,000

Cash flows: No effect

Sales Revenue	280,000	
Rent Revenue	27,000	
Interest Income	5,000	
Income Summary		312,000
(To close revenue accounts to Income Summary)		

Similarly, CASI's expense accounts would be closed and the balances transferred through the following closing journal entry:

A = L + SE
−289,000
+289,000

Cash flows: No effect

Income Summary	289,000	
Cost of Goods Sold		206,000
Selling Expenses		25,000
Administrative Expenses		40,600
Interest Expense		4,400
Income Tax Expense		13,000
(To close expense accounts to Income Summary)		

The Income Summary account now has a credit balance of $23,000, which is net income. **The net income is then transferred to retained earnings by closing the Income Summary account to Retained Earnings,** as follows:

A = L + SE
−23,000
+23,000

Cash flows: No effect

Income Summary	23,000	
Retained Earnings		23,000
(To close Income Summary to Retained Earnings)		

Any items posted to Other Comprehensive Income would similarly be closed out to Accumulated Other Comprehensive Income, which acts like a second retained earnings account for certain gains and losses booked to Other Comprehensive Income. Assuming CASI had holding gains on Fair Value through Other Comprehensive Income investments of $12,000, the holding gain would be closed to Accumulated Other Comprehensive Income as follows:

A = L + SE
    −12,000
    +12,000

Cash flows: No effect

Unrealized Holding Gain or Loss-OCI	12,000	
Accumulated Other Comprehensive Income		12,000
(To close holding gains on Fair Value-OCI investments to		
Accumulated Other Comprehensive Income)		

Assuming that dividends of $7,000 were declared and distributed during the year, the Dividends account is closed directly to Retained Earnings, as follows:

A = L + SE
    −7,000
    +7,000

Cash flows: No effect

Retained Earnings	7,000	
Dividends		7,000
(To close Dividends to Retained Earnings)		

After the closing process is completed, each statement of comprehensive income account has a zero balance and is ready to be used in the next accounting period.

Inventory and Cost of Goods Sold

The closing procedures we just showed assume that an entity uses a perpetual inventory system. With a **perpetual inventory system**, purchases and sales are recorded directly in the Inventory account as they occur. Therefore, the balance in Inventory should represent the ending inventory amount, and no adjusting entries are needed to update the inventory account. To be sure that the inventory amount is accurate, a **physical count** of the items in the inventory is generally done each year.

In the perpetual inventory system, since all purchases are debited directly to the Inventory account, there is no separate Purchases account. However, a Cost of Goods Sold account is used to accumulate what is issued from inventory. That is, when inventory items are sold, the cost of the sold goods is credited to Inventory and debited to Cost of Goods Sold.

What about entities using a **periodic inventory system**? In that case, a Purchases account is used, and the Inventory account is unchanged during the period. The Inventory account therefore represents the beginning inventory amount throughout the period. At the end of the accounting period, the Inventory account must be adjusted by **closing out the beginning inventory amount and recording the ending inventory amount**. The entity determines ending inventory by physically counting the items on hand and valuing them at cost or at the lower of cost or market. Under the periodic inventory system, cost of goods sold is therefore determined by adding the beginning inventory to net purchases and deducting the ending inventory.

To illustrate how cost of goods sold is calculated with a periodic inventory system, let's assume that Collegiate Apparel Shop Inc. has a beginning inventory of $30,000, purchases of $200,000, freight-in of $6,000, purchase returns and allowances of $1,000, purchase discounts of $3,000, and ending inventory of $26,000. CASI would close out each of these accounts to Cost of Goods Sold (as illustrated in Chapter 8) and then would close the Cost of Goods Sold account to the Income Summary account.

Post-Closing Trial Balance

We already mentioned that a trial balance is taken after the period's regular transactions have been entered and that a second trial balance (the adjusted trial balance) is taken after the adjusting entries have been posted. A third trial balance may be taken after posting the closing entries. The trial balance after closing, often called the **post-closing trial balance**, shows that equal debits and credits have been posted to the Income Summary account. The post-closing trial balance consists only of asset, liability, and shareholders' equity accounts (that is, the permanent accounts).

Reversing Entries

After the financial statements have been prepared and the books have been closed, it is often helpful to reverse some of the adjusting entries before recording the next period's regular transactions. Such entries are called **reversing entries**. A reversing entry is made at the beginning of the next accounting period and is the exact opposite of the related adjusting entry made in the previous period. The recording of reversing entries is an optional step in the accounting cycle that may be done at the beginning of the next accounting period. The purpose of reversing entries is to make it easier to record transactions in the next accounting period. The use of reversing entries does not change the amounts reported in the previous period's financial statements.

Reversing entries are usually used for reversing two types of adjusting entries: accrued revenues and accrued expenses. Let's illustrate reversing entries for accrued expenses, using the following transaction and adjustment data:

1. October 10 and October 24 (initial salary entries): $4,000 of salaries and wages expense incurred between October 1 and October 24 is paid.

2. October 31 (adjusting entry): $1,200 of salaries and wages expense is incurred between October 25 and October 31. This will be paid in the November 7 payroll.

3. November 7 (subsequent salary entry): $2,500 of salaries and wages expense is paid. Of this amount, $1,200 applies to accrued salaries and wages payable at October 31 and $1,300 was incurred between November 1 and November 7.

The comparative entries are shown in Illustration 3-14.

Reversing Entries Not Used				Reversing Entries Used			
Adjusting Entry				Adjusting Entry			
Oct. 31	Salaries and Wages Expense	1,200		Oct. 31	Salaries and Wages Expense	1,200	
	Salaries and Wages Payable		1,200		Salaries and Wages Payable		1,200
Closing Entry				Closing Entry			
Oct. 31	Income Summary	5,200		Oct. 31	Income Summary	5,200	
	Salaries and Wages Expense		5,200		Salaries and Wages Expense		5,200
Reversing Entry				Reversing Entry			
Nov. 1	No entry is made.			Nov. 1	Salaries and Wages Payable	1,200	
					Salaries and Wages Expense		1,200
Subsequent Salary Entry				Subsequent Salary Entry			
Nov. 7	Salaries and Wages Payable	1,200		Nov. 7	Salaries and Wages Expense	2,500	
	Salaries and Wages Expense	1,300			Cash		2,500
	Cash		2,500				

Illustration 3-14

Comparison of Entries for Accruals, with and without Reversing Entries

Although reversing entries reduce potential errors and are therefore often used, they do not have to be used. Many accountants avoid them entirely. Reversing entries add an extra step to the bookkeeping process. Also there may be instances where it does not make sense to use them. As an example, assume a company with a December 31 year end has accrued six months' worth of interest on a bond that pays interest annually (June 30 interest payment date) at year end. If the company releases financial information monthly, it would not make sense to reverse the entry in January because this would show a credit balance when the monthly reports are prepared.

We have now completed our summary of the steps in the accounting cycle. Refer back to Illustration 3-4 to ensure that you are comfortable with the entire accounting cycle including preparing journal entries, adjusting entries and financial statements. In Part II of this chapter, we'll discuss measurement issues and provide you with the tools needed to account for more complex transactions that you will encounter in later chapters and in the business world. But keep in mind, once you resolve the measurements issues that you face, the transactions will still need to be recorded using the techniques presented in Part I of this chapter!

Part II

MEASURING FINANCIAL STATEMENT ELEMENTS

Objective 7
Use valuation techniques to measure financial statement elements.

A significant part of accounting is measurement. As we discussed in Chapter 2, we have a mixed-attribute measurement model. That is, many items are measured based on historical cost (such as property, plant, and equipment; inventory), but many are based on fair value (such as certain financial instruments). Some measurements fall in between: they are not quite fair value measurements but neither are they completely historical cost measurements. Determining an item's fair value is fairly straightforward when market prices are available. However, when a market price is not available, accountants must rely on valuation models to develop a fair value estimate.

Illustration 3-15 lists some examples of the three measurement categorizations.

Illustration 3-15

Measurement Categorizations and Some Examples of Each

Cost-based measures (for example, historical cost)	Hybrid measures (for example, those that have some attributes of cost-based and current value)	Current value measures (for example, fair value measures)
Property, plant, and equipment carried at cost or net book value (depreciated cost)	Impaired property, plant, and equipment measured at the recoverable amount (higher of the value in use and fair value less costs of disposal) (under IAS 36)	Financial instruments including investments carried at fair value (under IFRS 9)
Financial instruments carried at cost or amortized cost using the effective interest or straight-line methods to amortize premiums and discounts	Inventory measured at the lower of cost and net realizable value (under ASPE 3031 and IAS 2)	Biological assets (IAS 41)
Inventory using various cost flow assumptions, such as weighted average and FIFO	Impaired notes receivable measured using management best estimates of revised cash flows discounted at the original historical discount rate (under IAS 36)	Investment properties (option to measure at fair value under IAS 40)

In addition, we need to think about measurement on initial recognition of the asset, liability, or other element and then again subsequently (for instance, at subsequent financial reporting dates). It is generally easier to measure an initial exchange transaction—usually the transaction is measured at fair value on the transaction date as long as it is arm's length. However, it may be more difficult to determine the subsequent value. Valuation techniques may need to be used.

Historical cost measures, including depreciation and the effective interest method, have a long history and are well developed. We will discuss these further in subsequent chapters. The rest of this chapter will deal with some basic measurement techniques.

Valuation Techniques

VALUATION
5.4.1, 5.4.2, 5.4.3

Whether we are trying to come up with a cost-based measure, a current value measure, or something in between, there are many techniques that may be used to measure value.

Two common types of valuation techniques are noted below:[8]

1. Income models: These techniques convert future amounts (such as future cash flows to be generated by an asset) to current amounts (that is, amounts adjusted for the time value of money). Examples include discounted cash flows and options pricing models. Both of these use present value concepts. Present value concepts are very commonly used in measurement and we will revisit them throughout the text.

2. Market models: These techniques use prices and other information generated from market transactions involving identical or similar transactions. An example is the earnings multiples model. Under this example, an investment in a privately owned company may be valued using publicly available earnings numbers for similar companies as well as multiples that are generated by comparing publicly available earnings numbers with share prices. We will look at earnings multiples in more detail in Chapter 4.

A measurement may be thought of as having three components: the inputs or assumptions, the model or technique, and the measurement itself. This is shown in Illustration 3-16.

Illustration 3-16

Using Models to Measure Elements

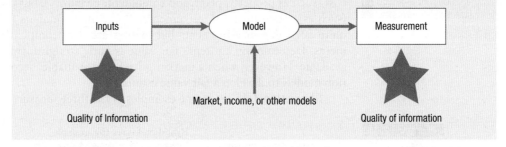

When measuring the value of a financial statement element, accountants must ask and answer three questions:

1. Which model or technique should be used?

2. Which inputs should be used?

3. Does the resulting measurement result in useful information?

Note that the quality of the measurement depends on the quality of the information used and the choice of the model. Certain measurements are seen to be of higher quality because they produce more useful information.

We will discuss each of these three questions below.

Which Model?

How do we decide which model to use? It depends on the item being measured. For instance, in measuring the impairment value of a unique manufacturing facility, it might make sense to use a discounted cash flow calculation (income model). It is likely that comparable market information would not be available for the manufacturing facility given its uniqueness. Thus a market model would not be a good choice. Management is likely able to determine cash flow projections and a suitable discount rate. Income models are frequently used in practice and we will therefore emphasize them in this and subsequent chapters. Many market models are beyond the scope of this text.

You were likely exposed to present value calculations in an introductory accounting or finance course. We have included an overview of basic present value concepts in

Appendix 3B. You should review this material as a refresher before proceeding with the rest of the chapter.

Illustration 3-17 gives examples of measurements using present values and discounted cash flows. We will discuss many of these in greater detail in the following chapters. As you can see, present value concepts to measure financial statement elements are used in many situations, whether these are cost-based measures, current value measures, or something in between.

Illustration 3-17

Some Present Value-Based Accounting Measurements

Financial statement elements	When present value may be used as a tool to help measure the financial statement element
Notes	Valuing non-current receivables and payables that carry no stated interest rate or a lower-than-market interest rate (see Chapters 7, 10, 14, and 16)
Investments	Valuing investments at amortized cost as well as impairment (see Chapter 9)
Derivatives	Valuing derivatives using various models, including option pricing models (see Chapter 16, including Appendix 16C)
Leases	Valuing assets and obligations to be capitalized under long-term leases, calculating annual amortization of the lease obligation, or calculating interest rates and lease payments (see Chapter 20)
Pensions and other post-retirement benefits	Measuring service cost components relating to employers' post-retirement benefits expense and defined benefits obligations (see Chapter 19)
Tangible capital assets	Determining the value of assets acquired under deferred payment contracts. Measuring impairment of assets (see Chapters 10 and 11)
Goodwill	Determining the value of goodwill in business combinations and for impairment purposes (see Chapter 12 and Appendix 12A)
Environmental liabilities	Determining the amount of future obligations for asset retirements (see Chapters 8, 10, and 13).

Which Inputs?

Which inputs to the various models are the best to use? Inputs and assumptions that are more reliable are better. For instance, a risk-free interest rate is generally available[9] whereas a risk-adjusted rate may be more difficult to determine and may be more subjective. Objectively determined information is generally more reliable.

Inputs to income models include the following:

1. Estimates of cash flows: Management makes its best estimates of expected cash flows incorporating contractual cash flows as well as estimated cash flows. When valuing an asset, assumptions may need to be made about how the asset is used (which will affect the cash flows).

2. Time value of money: An interest rate is used to discount the cash flows. This rate may be the risk-free rate or it may be a risk-adjusted rate (see point 3 below). The choice of discount rate is a major issue and we will look at it frequently in subsequent chapters.

3. Uncertainty or risk: Since not all cash flows are the same in terms of amount, timing, and riskiness, discounted cash flow models reflect the risk or uncertainty by adjusting either the cash flows or the discount rate but generally not both in the same calculation. Uncertainty may be reflected in the numerator by applying probabilities to various cash flow scenarios. It may be incorporated in the discount rate by applying a risk premium such that the rate exceeds the risk-free rate.

Quality of the Measurement?

What is the resulting quality of the measurement? Does the measurement provide high-quality information to the users of the financial statements? For instance, is it relevant and does it faithfully represent the asset or liability being valued? Better quality information is obviously better for decision-making. When measuring the value of financial statement elements, the goal is to provide the best information possible within the cost/benefit constraint. At some point the cost of obtaining the information may outweigh the benefits and so a judgement call must be made.

We will discuss quality of information further in Chapter 4.

A Closer Look at Discounted Cash Flows

The **discounted cash flow model** is a very robust, widely accepted tool for dealing with uncertainty and the time value of money.

Two approaches are generally accepted:[10]

1. Traditional approach: The discount rate reflects all risks in the cash flows but the cash flows are assumed to be certain. This is sometimes referred to as the "discount rate adjustment technique."

2. Expected cash flow approach: A risk-free discount rate is used to discount cash flows that have been adjusted for uncertainty. This is sometimes referred to as the "expected present value technique."

Traditional Approach

Under the **traditional discounted cash flow approach**, the stream of contracted cash flows is discounted, and the discount rate is adjusted to accommodate the riskiness of the cash flows. This model is best used where the cash flows are otherwise fairly certain. For instance, if the company is trying to determine the value of a note receivable, it would adjust the discount rate for the credit risk that is associated with the party that is paying the cash flows to the company. This method is useful for instruments where the cash flows are specified in the contract, such as fixed interest and principal payments. It is not very useful for more complex instruments where the cash flows may be variable for other reasons than the credit risk.

To illustrate the traditional discounted cash flow approach, let's assume that Company A has issued a 10% bond that is due in 10 years and has a face value of $100. Assume further that the risk-adjusted market rate that reflects the credit risk of Company A is 10%. This rate would be the rate that the market would demand of Company A, given the specific credit risk. The credit risk is the risk that the company will not be able to repay the bond. This would be influenced by factors such as the economy (whether things are good or bad), the company's business model (whether it is sustainable or not), and the company's cash position. If the market feels that the company is riskier, then the market will demand a premium.

The bond's present value would be calculated as follows:

> PV $1 at 10% × Principal (10 years) + PV of an annuity of $10 for 10 years at 10%
> (All discounted at 10%) = $100

Expected Cash Flow Approach

QUANTITATIVE METHODS/ STATISTICS

Under the **expected cash flow approach**, the discount rate is the risk-free rate and the cash flow uncertainty is dealt with by using probabilities. The projected cash flows reflect the uncertainty in terms of amount and timing using probability weighting. This model is more flexible and is useful where the element being measured has variable cash flows.

To illustrate the expected cash flow approach, let's assume that Al's Auto has several minor lawsuits outstanding. To determine the amount of liability to recognize on the statement of financial position, Al's Auto decides to use expected cash flow techniques.

Based on discussions with the company's lawyers, Al's Auto estimates the expected cash outflows associated with the lawsuits, as shown in Illustration 3-18.

Illustration 3-18

Expected Cash Outflows

	Cash Flow Estimate	×	Probability Assessment	=	Expected Cash Flow
2017	$3,800		20%		$ 760
	6,300		50%		3,150
	7,500		30%		2,250
			Total		$6,160
2018	$5,400		30%		$1,620
	7,200		50%		3,600
	8,400		20%		1,680
			Total		$6,900

Applying expected cash flow concepts to these data, the company estimates cash outflows of $6,160 in 2017 and $6,900 in 2018.

Illustration 3-19 shows the present value of these cash flows, assuming a risk-free rate of 5% and cash flows occurring at the end of the year.

Illustration 3-19

Present Value of Expected Cash Flows

Year	Expected Cash Flow	×	PV Factor, $i = 5\%$	=	Present Value
2017	$6,160		0.95238		$ 5,866.66
2018	6,900		0.90703		6,258.51
			Total		$12,125.17

Value in Use Measurements

We introduced the notion of value in use in Chapter 2. It is an **entity-specific measure** that values assets based on how the company plans to use them. This is different from a fair value measure under IFRS 13, which is based on a **market participant view** of the value. That is, potential buyers in the market might decide to use the asset differently than the company is currently using it. Companies are required to regularly determine whether the value of property, plant, and equipment has been impaired. Under IFRS, an asset is impaired if the carrying amount reported on the statement of financial position is greater than its recoverable amount. The recoverable amount is the greater of the asset's fair value less costs to dispose and its value in use. Present value techniques may be used to measure both value in use and fair value. Let's assume that the value in use and fair value are the same, although they would not necessarily be so if the market values the asset using different assumptions about its potential use.

Determining the value in use requires applying present value concepts. Value in use is calculated in two steps: (1) estimate the future cash flows, and (2) calculate the present value of these cash flows.

For example, assume JB Company owns a specialized piece of equipment used in its manufacturing process. JB needs to determine the asset's value in use to test for impairment. JB follows the two steps to determine value in use. First, JB's management estimates that the equipment will last for another five years and that it will generate the following future cash flows at the end of each year:

Year 1	Year 2	Year 3	Year 4	Year 5
$9,000	$10,000	$13,000	$10,000	$7,000

In the second step of determining value in use, JB calculates the present value of each of these future cash flows. Using a discount rate of 8%, the present value of each future cash flow is shown in Illustration 3-20.

Illustration 3-20

Using Present Value Concepts to Measure Value in Use

	Year 1	Year 2	Year 3	Year 4	Year 5
Future cash flows	$9,000	$10,000	$13,000	$10,000	$7,000
Present value factor[a]	0.92593	0.85734	0.79383	0.73503	0.68058
Present value amount	$8,333	$8,573	$10,320	$7,350	$4,764

[a] The appropriate interest rate to be used is based on current market rates; however, adjustments for uncertainties related to the specific asset may be made. Further discussion on this topic is covered in more advanced texts.

The value in use of JB's specialized equipment is the sum of the present value of each year's cash flow, $39,340 ($8,333 + $8,573 + $10,320 + $7,350 + $4,764). If this amount is less than the asset's carrying amount, JB will be required to record an impairment loss.

The present value method of estimating the value in use of an asset can also be used for intangible assets. For example, assume JB purchases a licence from Redo Industries for the right to manufacture and sell products using Redo's processes and technologies. JB estimates it will earn $6,000 per year from this licence over the next 10 years. What is the value in use to JB of this licence?

Since JB expects to earn the same amount each year, Table PV-2 is used to find the present value factor of the annuity after determining the appropriate discount rate. As pointed out in the previous example, JB should choose a rate based on current market rates; however, adjustments for uncertainties related to the specific asset may be required. Assuming JB uses 8% as the discount rate, the present value factor from Table PV-2 for 10 periods is 6.71008. The value in use of the licence is $40,260 ($6,000 × 6.71008).

Measuring Fair Value Using IFRS 13

Objective 8

Use IFRS 13 to measure fair value.

VALUATION
5.4.1, 5.4.2, 5.4.3

SIGNIFICANT CHANGE

In Chapter 2 we introduced the fair value principle. This section delves a bit deeper in this principle as presented in IFRS 13. According to IFRS 13, in order to measure fair value, an entity must determine (1) the item being measured; (2) how the item would be or could be used by market participants; (3) the market that the item would be (or was) bought and sold in; (4) and finally, if a model is being used to measure fair value, which model it is. Recall that the fair value measurement under IFRS is an exit price. So, for instance, when measuring the value of an asset, the fair value measurement would look at the value that potential buyers would attribute to the asset.

We'll look at these items in more detail below using tangible assets as an example.

1. The particular asset being measured: Consider the specific nature, condition, and location of the asset being measured. Is it old, damaged, obsolete?

2. How the item would/could be used: Many non-financial assets are used for different purposes. For instance, a building may be rented out, used as part of a manufacturing facility, or held for capital appreciation purposes. The perceived value of the building might be different depending on what the company might use it for. This is sometimes referred to as the "valuation premise." Generally, the asset is valued based on what is referred to as its **highest and best use** in the market **regardless of how the entity is actually using the asset**. The highest and best use concept values the asset based on the highest value that the market would place on the asset considering all possible uses that are physically possible, legally permissible, and financially feasible. For example, suppose your company owns a piece of land that is zoned by the local municipality as residential, meaning that it can only be developed for residential purposes. In trying to measure the land's fair value, you would not consider a value that assumed that the land was zoned as a commercial property, because legally, only residential development is allowed at the measurement date.

3. The market: The measurement would consider the value based on the market that the entity normally buys and sells in (referred to as the **principal market**). This would usually also be the **most advantageous market**; that is, the market in which the price would be the highest. Many entities buy and sell in different markets so this concept looks at the main market that the company deals in. For instance, if a company buys and sells shares for investment purposes through the TSX, then the company would use market values as quoted by the TSX.

4. The valuation technique/model: In many cases, a liquid market for the item being measured will be available and this best represents fair value. For example, when valuing common shares that trade on the TSX, the dollar amount that the shares are traded at would provide the best evidence of fair value. In other cases, however, a valuation technique or model would be used to value the item. Any time that pure market values are not used, you are essentially estimating the value using a model. Examples of models include those mentioned earlier in the "Valuation Techniques" section—market and income models—and one additional model: the cost model. The cost model attempts to reflect the amount that would be required to replace the asset's service capacity. The cost model is used to value older non-financial assets where there is no longer a market for the asset, perhaps because it is obsolete.

Because estimating a fair value using a model introduces measurement uncertainty, IFRS 13 attempts to offset this by using good-quality input information. Inputs are classified into three categories depending on their quality: level 1 inputs, level 2 inputs, and level 3 inputs. Level 1 inputs are the highest-quality inputs and will produce the best-quality fair value measurement. Level 3 inputs are at the other end and are used where level 1 and/or 2 inputs are not available.

This categorization of inputs is often referred to as the **fair value hierarchy**. Level 1 and 2 inputs are generally observable in various markets and are therefore more objective, whereas level 3 inputs are generally not observable and hence more subjective. Level 1 inputs require the existence of liquid markets that generate good information that may be used as the inputs.

Assets and liabilities are also categorized into one of the three levels based on the various levels of inputs. For instance, if the fair value of an impaired asset is calculated using level 3 inputs, the asset itself is categorized as a level 3 asset. A company must disclose information about which models and input levels are used. The lower the level of input (for instance, level 3), the greater the required disclosures. This gives additional information to financial statement users about the measurement uncertainty. Illustration 3-21 summarizes the inputs to the IFRS 13 valuation model.

Illustration 3-21 *Inputs to the IFRS 13* *Valuation Model*	**Level 1:** Observable inputs that reflect quoted prices for identical assets or liabilities in active markets. *(Least Subjective)* **Level 2:** Inputs other than quoted prices included in Level 1 that are observable for the asset or liability either directly or through corroboration with observable data. **Level 3:** Unobservable inputs (for example, a company's own data or assumptions). *(Most Subjective)*

Some examples of the various levels of inputs are in Illustration 3-22.

	Level of input	**Example**
Illustration 3-22 *Examples of the Various Input* *Levels under IFRS 13*	Level 1 input	Assume you are measuring the fair value of a share that is traded on the TSX. A level 1 input would be the price for the exact class of share as evidenced by the price it is being traded at currently on the TSX. The shares would be categorized as level 1 assets.
	Level 2 input	Assume that you are measuring the fair value of a new issue of bonds. A level 2 input would be interest rates that are observable in the market (that is, for similar or identical bonds already trading in the market). The bonds would be categorized as level 2 assets (indicating greater measurement uncertainty).
	Level 3 input	Assume you are trying to measure the fair value of a manufacturing division for purposes of impairment. A level 3 input would be the estimated cash flows. The manufacturing division would be categorized as a level 3 asset (and therefore greater disclosures would be required focusing on the increased measurement uncertainty).

Fair value measures may be calculated using any of these models and using different types of inputs. Assume we are trying to determine the fair value of a piece of machinery in order to decide if an impairment loss needs to be recognized. Which model should we use? As a rule of thumb, you should use the one that provides the **best-quality fair value measure**. This is a judgement call and depends on the characteristics of the asset itself and available information. In most cases, only one model may work, but in some cases, more than one may be used.

In the example above, if the machinery is older and obsolete, the market model will not work because you will likely not be able to get any market information for the exact or a similar machine, especially if the machines are no longer produced. Nor would it make sense for management to try to estimate market values for the exact or a similar machine, because too much judgement is involved. In this case, you might use an income model or alternatively, a cost model (which looks at valuing the service capacity as opposed to the asset). Inputs from various levels might be needed to do the calculation. As noted above, the lower the level of the inputs (for instance, level 3), the greater the disclosures required.

However, if you are valuing a company that is planning on going public, you may be able to use both the market and income models. You might use the income model to measure the value by focusing on the discounted cash flows. Alternatively, you might look at recent market transactions for similar companies (or perhaps earnings multiples). There is no perfect answer, just better or worse information. If you are able to measure fair value by using more than one model, this will help because you can compare the estimates to see if they are both reasonable or not. However, keep in mind that using more than one model requires more effort, so the costs might exceed the benefits.

WHAT DO THE NUMBERS MEAN?

When fair values are used to value a company's own debt, interesting results may arise. Where the company's own risk of not being able to repay the debt has increased, using fair value to revalue the debt results in a gain!

For instance, assume a company that is normally profitable has suffered losses in the current year. As a result of being less profitable, it has less cash and is now cash squeezed. Its ability to repay its own debt may now be in jeopardy. The company's liquidity risk has increased. From a creditor perspective, the credit risk for this company has increased. In other words, there is a greater risk that the company will not repay the amount owed. If the company uses amortized cost to value the liability, the debt is not revalued in the financial statements. However, if fair value is used to measure the liability, the debt must be revalued.

Where the fair value is measured using discounted cash flows, the entity must now use a higher discount rate to reflect the increased risk. The higher discount rate means a lower present value.

Therefore, the debt is written down with the following journal entry: debit long-term liability and credit gain. This results in a better debt to equity ratio and higher income even though the company is worse off. Standard setters have recognized this issue. The IASB has implemented a change in the current accounting standard. IFRS 9 requires that any gains resulting from the revaluation of a company's own debt (that are due to deteriorating ability to repay the debt) must be booked through other comprehensive income (OCI). Note that the OCI gains do not increase earnings per share, but they still increase comprehensive income.

IFRS/ASPE COMPARISON

Objective 9

Identify differences in accounting between ASPE and IFRS, and what changes are expected in the near future.

Financial statements prepared under ASPE do not include Other Comprehensive Income (OCI), Accumulated Other Comprehensive Income (AOCI) and Revaluation Surplus (OCI) accounts. Under IFRS, OCI and AOCI accounts are included for items such as Fair Value-OCI Investments, and the Revaluation Surplus (OCI) account is used for Property, Plant and Equipment for companies using the revaluation model. These differences are discussed further in later chapters (including Chapters 9 and 10).

The main difference in the accounting for measurement issues is that IFRS has a well-developed framework for measuring fair values (IFRS 13), whereas ASPE does not. Under IFRS, most of the guidance is in IFRS 13, which provides a standardized definition and guidance. The guidance relating to fair value is spread throughout the ASPE body of knowledge. Chapter 2 also covers more general guidance as it relates to measurement.

A Comparison of IFRS and ASPE

Illustration 3-23 sets out the major differences between the accounting standards under IFRS and ASPE regarding the measurement of fair values.

Illustration 3-23

IFRS and ASPE Comparison Chart

	IFRS—Conceptual Framework for Financial Reporting, IFRS 13	Accounting Standards for Private Enterprises (ASPE)—*CPA Canada Handbook*, Part II, Section 1000	Reference to related illustrations and select brief exercises
Measurement of fair value	Guidance is concentrated in IFRS 13	Guidance is spread throughout the ASPE standards	The guidance in ASPE is not inconsistent with IFRS 13, although there is significantly less detail. Specific differences in measurement as they relate to financial statements and elements will be covered in subsequent chapters.

Looking Ahead

The IASB has issued an Exposure Draft for the conceptual framework. This proposed conceptual framework has considerably increased coverage regarding measurement issues. More detail on this was included in Chapter 2.

SUMMARY OF LEARNING OBJECTIVES

1 Understand basic accounting terminology and explain double-entry rules.

It is important to understand the following terms: (1) event, (2) transaction, (3) account, (4) permanent and temporary accounts, (5) ledger, (6) journal, (7) posting, (8) trial balance, (9) adjusting entries, (10) financial statements, (11) closing entries, and (12) reversing entries.

The left side of any account is the debit side; the right side is the credit side. All asset and expense accounts are increased on the left or debit side and decreased on the right or credit side. Conversely, all liability and revenue accounts are increased on the right or credit side and decreased on the left or debit side. Shareholders' equity accounts, Common Stock, and Retained Earnings are increased on the credit side, whereas Dividends is increased on the debit side.

2 Explain how transactions affect the accounting equation.

In a double-entry accounting system, for every debit there must be a credit, and vice versa. This leads us to the basic accounting equation for corporations: Assets = Liabilities + Shareholders' Equity. The effect of individual transactions on the statement of financial position can be explained using the basic accounting equation. The shareholders' equity portion of the equation can also be expanded to illustrate the effect of transactions on components of equity such as common shares and retained earnings. Whenever a transaction occurs, the elements of the equation change, but the equality of the two sides of the equation remains unaffected.

3 Identify the steps in the accounting cycle and the steps in the recording process.

The basic steps in the accounting cycle are (1) identification and measurement of transactions and other events, (2) journalizing, (3) posting, (4) the unadjusted trial balance, (5) adjustments, (6) the adjusted trial balance, (7) statement preparation, and (8) closing. The first three steps in the accounting cycle form the basis of the recording process used by most medium-sized companies on a daily basis. The simplest journal form is a chronological listing of transactions and events that are expressed as debits and credits to particular accounts. The items entered in a general journal must then be transferred (posted) to the general ledger.

To help prepare financial statements, an unadjusted trial balance should be prepared at the end of a specific period (usually a month, quarter, or year) after the entries have been recorded in the journals and posted to the general ledger.

4 Explain the reasons for and prepare adjusting entries.

Adjustments achieve a proper matching of expenses and revenues, which is needed to determine the correct net income for the current period and to achieve an accurate statement of the end-of-the-period balances in assets, liabilities, and shareholders' equity accounts. When preparing adjusting journal entries, you must first determine how the original transaction was recorded. For example, was an asset created earlier in the fiscal year (such as prepaid rent) when the initial payment was made? If so, an adjustment for the related expense is required. Alternatively, if an income statement account was used initially, an adjustment may be required to set up the proper statement of financial position account at the end of the period.

5 Explain how the type of ownership structure affects the financial statements.

The type of ownership structure that a business uses determines the types of accounts that are part of the equity section. In a corporation, ordinary or common shares, contributed surplus, retained earnings, and accumulated other comprehensive income are commonly shown separately on the statement of financial position. In a proprietorship or partnership, an owner's capital account is used to indicate the investment in the company by the owner(s). An owner's drawings or withdrawal account may be used to indicate withdrawals by the owner(s). These two accounts are grouped or netted under owners' equity.

6 Prepare closing entries and consider other matters relating to the closing process.

In the closing process, all of the revenue and expense account balances (income statement items) are transferred to a clearing account called Income Summary, which is used only at the end of the fiscal year. Revenues and expenses are matched in the Income Summary account. The net result of this matching, which represents the net income or net loss for the period, is then transferred to a shareholders' equity account (Retained Earnings for a corporation and capital accounts for proprietorships and partnerships). Reversing entries may be used for reversing accrued revenues and accrued expenses. Prepayments may also be reversed if the initial entry to record the transaction is made to an expense or revenue account.

7 Use valuation techniques to measure financial statement elements.

IFRS and ASPE incorporate a mixed-attribute measurement model including measurements that are cost-based (such as historical cost), those that are based on current value (such as fair value), and many hybrid measures that have attributes of both cost-based and current value measurements. Valuation techniques are used to help with measurement of financial statement elements. Common examples include market models and income models. Income models are widely used and include discounted cash flow methods and present value concepts. When using models, you must determine what inputs should be used. Common inputs include discount rates and cash flow estimates. The quality of these inputs affects the quality of the final measurement. Accountants often use probabilities to help deal with risk and uncertainty.

8 Use IFRS 13 to measure fair value.

IFRS 13 establishes a fairly detailed body of knowledge relating to measurement of fair value. Fair value measurement under IFRS 13 is a market-based approach that incorporates the specific attributes of the asset/liability being measured, the valuation premise (how the asset/liability is to be used), the principal market, and the valuation technique. Since market prices are not always available, valuation models are used to measure the value. Inputs to these models are either observable in the market or not. Observable inputs are most useful since they are more objective. The fair value hierarchy establishes three levels of inputs, with level 1 being the highest and best type of input (based on observable market prices). Because level 3 inputs are more subjective, additional disclosures are required.

9 Identify differences in accounting between ASPE and IFRS, and what changes are expected in the near future.

The main difference is that IFRS contains specific guidance in IFRS 13 regarding fair value measurements. Under ASPE, guidance is spread throughout the body of knowledge and is less detailed.

KEY TERMS

account, p. 78
accounting cycle, p. 80
accounting information system, p. 78
accrued expenses, p. 89
accrued revenues, p. 89
accumulated other comprehensive income, p. 93
adjusted trial balance, p. 78
adjusting entries, p. 78
balance sheet, p. 78
book value, p. 87
carrying amount, p. 87
closing entries, p. 78
closing process, p. 94
contra asset account, p. 87
credit, p. 78
debit, p. 78
depreciation/amortization, p. 86

discounted cash flow model, p. 100
double-entry accounting, p. 79
event, p. 78
expected cash flow approach, p. 100
fair value hierarchy, p. 103
financial statements, p. 78
general journal, p. 82
general ledger, p. 78
highest and best use, p. 102
income statement, p. 78
journal, p. 78
journal entries, p. 78
most advantageous market, p. 102
periodic inventory system, p. 95
permanent accounts, p. 78
perpetual inventory system, p. 95
post-closing trial balance, p. 78
posting, p. 78

prepaid expenses, p. 85
principal market, p. 102
reversing entries, p. 78
special journals, p. 82
statement of cash flows, p. 78
statement of changes in shareholders' equity, p. 78
statement of comprehensive income, p. 78
statement of financial position, p. 78
statement of retained earnings, p. 78
subsidiary ledger, p. 78
temporary accounts, p. 78
traditional discounted cash flow approach, p. 100
transaction, p. 78
trial balance, p. 78
unearned revenues, p. 85
useful life, p. 86

APPENDIX 3A

USING A WORK SHEET

Objective 10
Prepare a 10-column work sheet and financial statements.

In Illustration 3-4 we discuss the accounting cycle, including the preparation of a trial balance, adjustments and financial statements. Companies will often use a **work sheet** to make the end-of-period (monthly, quarterly, or annually) accounting and reporting process easier. A work sheet is a spreadsheet that managers use to adjust the account balances and prepare financial statements. Using a work sheet helps accountants prepare financial statements on a timelier basis. They do not need to delay preparing the financial statements until the adjusting and closing entries are journalized and posted. The **10-column work sheet** shown later in this appendix (Illustration 3A-1) has columns for the first trial balance, adjustments, an adjusted trial balance, the statement of comprehensive income, and the statement of financial position.

The work sheet does not replace the financial statements. Instead, it is an informal tool for accumulating and sorting the information that is needed for the financial statements. Completing the work sheet makes it more certain that all of the details of the end-of-period accounting and statement preparation have been brought together properly.

Adjustments Entered on the Work Sheet

The following items, (a) through (g), are the basis for the adjusting entries made in the work sheet in Illustration 3A-1:

(a) Office equipment is amortized at the rate of 10% per year based on an original cost of $67,000.

(b) Estimated bad debts are 0.25% of sales ($400,000).

(c) Insurance of $360 expired during the year.

(d) Interest of $800 accrued on notes receivable as at December 31.

(e) The Rent Expense account contains $500 of rent paid in advance, which is applicable to next year.

(f) Property taxes of $2,000 accrued to December 31.

(g) The Fair Value through Other Comprehensive Income (FV-OCI) Investments account is based on the original cost of an equity investment acquired on July 1. On December 31, the fair value of the investment is $15,000. We will cover tax calculations for OCI items in Chapter 18. To simplify matters for Chapter 3, assume that changes in fair value for FV-OCI investments are non-taxable.

The adjusting entries shown on the December 31, 2017 work sheet are as follows:

(a)	Depreciation Expense—Office Equipment	6,700	
	Accumulated Depreciation—Office Equipment		6,700
(b)	Bad Debt Expense	1,000	
	Allowance for Doubtful Accounts		1,000
(c)	Insurance Expense	360	
	Prepaid Insurance		360
(d)	Interest Receivable	800	
	Interest Income		800
(e)	Prepaid Rent	500	
	Rent Expense		500

(f)	Property Tax Expense	2,000	
	Property Tax Payable		2,000
(g)	FV-OCI Investments	3,000	
	Unrealized Holding Gain or Loss-OCI		3,000

These adjusting entries are transferred to the work sheet's Adjustments columns and each adjustment can be named by letter. The accounts that are set up from the adjusting entries and that are not already in the trial balance are listed below the totals of the trial balance, as shown on the work sheet. The Adjustments columns are then totalled and balanced.

Work Sheet Columns

The 10-column work sheet for Uptown Cabinet Corp., a retail company, is shown in Illustration 3A-1. Each of the columns is explained below.

Trial Balance Columns

Data for the trial balance are obtained from the ledger balances of Uptown Cabinet Corp. at December 31. The amount for Inventory, $40,000, is the year-end inventory amount under a perpetual inventory system.

Adjustments Columns

After entering all adjustment data on the work sheet, verify that the total amounts in each adjustment column are equal. Then extend the balances in all accounts to the adjusted trial balance columns.

Adjusted Trial Balance Columns

The adjusted trial balance shows the balance of all accounts after adjustment at the end of the accounting period. For example, the $2,000 shown opposite Allowance for Doubtful Accounts in the Trial Balance Cr. column is added to the $1,000 in the Adjustments Cr. column. The $3,000 total is then extended to the Adjusted Trial Balance Cr. column.

Similarly, the $900 debit opposite Prepaid Insurance is reduced by the $360 credit in the Adjustments column. The result, $540, is shown in the Adjusted Trial Balance Dr. column.

Statement of Comprehensive Income and Statement of Financial Position Columns

All the debit items in the Adjusted Trial Balance columns are extended into the Statement of Comprehensive Income or Statement of Financial Position columns to the right. All the credit items are also extended. The next step is to total the Statement of Comprehensive Income columns; the amount that is needed in order to balance the debit and credit columns is the total of the pre-tax income or loss for the period and OCI. The income (before tax and OCI) of $18,640 is shown in the Statement of Comprehensive Income Dr. column because revenues and gains exceeded expenses and losses by that amount. The Unrealized Holding Gain or Loss-OCI would eventually be closed out to Accumulated Other Comprehensive Income, whereas all other revenue and expense accounts would be closed to Retained Earnings.

Completing the Work Sheet

Income Taxes

The federal and provincial income tax expense and related tax liability are calculated next (item [h] in Illustration 3A-1). We will assume that Uptown Cabinet Corp. uses a tax rate of 22% to arrive at $3,440. (To simplify the example, no allocation is made for deferred taxes on Other Comprehensive Income.) This adjustment is entered in the Statement of Comprehensive

	A	B		C		D		E		F	
1		**UPTOWN CABINET CORP.** **Ten-Column Work Sheet** **For the Year Ended December 31, 2017**										
2	**Accounts**	**Trial Balance**		**Adjustments**		**Adjusted Trial Balance**		**Statement of Comp. Income**		**Statement of Financial Position**	
		Dr.	**Cr.**	**Dr.**	**Cr.**	**Dr.**	**Cr.**	**Dr.**	**Cr.**	**Dr.**	**Cr.**
3	Cash	1,200				1,200				1,200	
4	Notes receivable	16,000				16,000				16,000	
5	Accounts receivable	41,000				41,000				41,000	
6	Allowance for doubtful accounts		2,000		(b)1,000		3,000				3,000
7	Inventory	40,000				40,000				40,000	
8	Prepaid insurance	900			(c)360	540				540	
9	FV-OCI investments	12,000		(g)3,000		15,000				15,000	
10	Office equipment	67,000				67,000				67,000	
11	Accumulated depreciation— office equipment		12,000		(a)6,700		18,700				18,700
12	Notes payable		20,000				20,000				20,000
13	Accounts payable		13,500				13,500				13,500
14	Bonds payable		30,000				30,000				30,000
15	Common shares		50,000				50,000				50,000
16	Retained earnings, Jan. 1, 2017		26,200				26,200				26,200
17	Sales revenue		400,000				400,000		400,000		
18	Cost of goods sold	316,000				316,000		316,000			
19	Salaries and wages expense	20,000				20,000		20,000			
20	Advertising expense	2,200				2,200		2,200			
21	Travel expense	8,000				8,000		8,000			
22	Office expense	19,000				19,000		19,000			
23	Internet expense	600				600		600			
24	Rent expense	4,800			(e)500	4,300		4,300			
25	Property tax expense	3,300		(f)2,000		5,300		5,300			
26	Interest expense	1,700				1,700		1,700			
27	**Totals**	**553,700**	**553,700**								
28	Depreciation expense			(a)6,700		6,700		6,700			
29	Bad debt expense			(b)1,000		1,000		1,000			
30	Insurance expense			(c)360		360		360			
31	Interest receivable			(d)800		800				800	
32	Interest income				(d)800		800		800		
33	Prepaid rent			(e)500		500				500	
34	Property tax payable				(f)2,000		2,000				2,000
35	Unrealized holding gain or loss-OCI				(g)3,000		3,000		3,000		
36	**Totals**			**14,360**	**14,360**	**567,200**	**567,200**	**385,160**	**403,800**		
37	Income (before tax) and OCI							18,640			
38	**Totals**							**403,800**	**403,800**		
39	Income (before tax) and OCI								18,640		
40	Income tax expense			(h)3,440		3,440		3,440			
41	Income tax payable				(h)3,440		3,440				3,440
42	Net income and OCI							15,200			15,200
43	**Totals**					**570,640**	**570,640**	**18,640**	**18,640**	**182,040**	**182,040**

Illustration **3A-1**

Work Sheet

Income Dr. column as Income Tax Expense and in the Statement of Financial Position Cr. column as Income Tax Payable. The following adjusting journal entry is recorded on December 31, 2017, posted to the general ledger, and then entered on the work sheet:

(h)	Income Tax Expense	3,440	
	Income Tax Payable		3,440
	(To record income tax expense on income before tax)		

Net Income

Next, the Statement of Comprehensive Income columns are balanced with the income taxes included. The $15,200 difference between the debit and credit columns in this illustration represents the total of net income plus OCI, or comprehensive income. The comprehensive income of $15,200 is entered in the Statement of Comprehensive Income Dr. column to achieve equality and in the Statement of Financial Position Cr. column.

Preparing Financial Statements from a Work Sheet

The work sheet gives the information that is needed to prepare financial statements without referring to the ledger or other records. In addition, the data have been sorted into appropriate columns, which makes it easier to prepare the statements. The financial statements being prepared using this work sheet are for a corporation that follows IFRS. The work sheet could also be used to prepare financial statements of a corporation following ASPE, or the financial statements for a sole proprietorship or partnership.

The financial statements prepared from the 10-column work sheet are as follows: **Statement of Comprehensive Income for the Year Ended December 31, 2017 (Illustration 3A-2), Statement of Changes in Shareholders' Equity for the Year Ended December 31, 2017 (Illustration 3A-3), and Statement of Financial Position as at December 31, 2017 (Illustration 3A-4).**

Statement of Comprehensive Income

The statement of comprehensive income in Illustration 3A-2 is for a trading or merchandising (retailing) business. If Uptown were a manufacturing business, it would use three inventory accounts: raw materials, work-in-process, and finished goods. Salaries and wages are assumed to relate to selling. Earnings per share is based on net income (not comprehensive income), which we will cover in more detail in Chapter 4.

Statement of Changes in Shareholders' Equity

The net income earned by a corporation may be retained in the business or distributed to shareholders by paying dividends. In Illustration 3A-3, Uptown's net income earned during the year was added to the balance of Retained Earnings on January 1, increasing the balance to $38,400 on December 31. Uptown did not declare any dividends during the year. A statement of changes in shareholders' equity is required for public companies instead of a statement of changes in retained earnings (for companies following ASPE, for instance). The statement of changes in shareholders' equity includes changes in all equity accounts, including Accumulated Other Comprehensive Income, Retained Earnings, and Common Shares. We will cover this statement in more detail in Chapter 4.

Statement of Financial Position

The statement of financial position prepared from the 10-column work sheet has new items, such as property tax payable, created by year-end adjusting entries. Interest receivable, prepaid insurance, and prepaid rent are included as current assets. These assets are considered current because they will be converted into cash or consumed in the ordinary routine of the business in a relatively short period. The amount of Allowance for Doubtful Accounts is deducted from the total of accounts, notes, and interest receivable because it is estimated that only $54,800 of the $57,800 will be collected in cash. If the allowance relates only to Accounts Receivable, it could be set up as a contra account for just Accounts Receivable. The Fair Value-OCI Investments are typically considered a non-current (or long-term) asset, which we will discuss in Chapter 9.

In the property, plant, and equipment section, accumulated depreciation is deducted from the cost of the office equipment; the difference in the two amounts is the book value or carrying amount of the office equipment.

Illustration **3A-2**

Statement of Comprehensive Income

UPTOWN CABINET CORP.
Statement of Comprehensive Income
For the Year Ended December 31, 2017

Sales revenue			$400,000
Cost of goods sold			316,000
Gross profit on sales			84,000
Selling expenses			
Salaries and wages expense		$20,000	
Advertising expense		2,200	
Travel expense		8,000	
Total selling expenses		30,200	
Administrative expenses			
Office expense	$19,000		
Internet expense	600		
Rent expense	4,300		
Property tax expense	5,300		
Depreciation expense—office equipment	6,700		
Bad debt expense	1,000		
Insurance expense	360		
Total administrative expenses		37,260	
Total selling and administrative expenses			67,460
Income from operations			16,540
Other revenues and gains			
Interest income			800
			17,340
Other expenses and losses			
Interest expense			1,700
Income before income taxes			15,640
Income tax expense			3,440
Net income			12,200
Other comprehensive income			3,000
Comprehensive income			$ 15,200
Earnings per share			$ 1.22

Illustration **3A-3**

Statement of Changes in Shareholders' Equity

UPTOWN CABINET CORP.
Statement of Changes in Shareholders' Equity
For the Year Ended December 31, 2017

	Total	Common Shares	Comprehensive Income	Retained Earnings	Accumulated OCI
Beginning, Jan. 1, 2017	$76,200	$50,000	$ -0-	$26,200	$ -0-
Net income for 2017	12,200		12,200	12,200	
Other comprehensive income	3,000		3,000		3,000
Comprehensive income			$15,200		
Ending balance, Dec. 31, 2017	**$91,400**	**$50,000**		**$38,400**	**$3,000**

Property tax payable is shown as a current liability because it is an obligation that is payable within a year. Other short-term accrued liabilities would also be shown as current liabilities.

The bonds payable, due in 2021, are non-current liabilities and are shown in a separate section. (Interest on the bonds was paid on December 31.) Accumulated Other Comprehensive Income is included in the shareholders' equity section.

Illustration **3A-4**

Statement of Financial Position

UPTOWN CABINET CORP.
Statement of Financial Position
As at December 31, 2017

Assets

Current assets			
Cash			$ 1,200
Notes receivable	$16,000		
Accounts receivable	41,000		
Interest receivable	800	$57,800	
Less: Allowance for doubtful accounts		3,000	54,800
Inventory			40,000
Prepaid insurance			540
Prepaid rent			500
Total current assets			97,040
Non-current assets			
Long-term investments			
Fair value-OCI investments			15,000
Property, plant, and equipment			
Office equipment		67,000	
Less: Accumulated depreciation		18,700	
Total property, plant, and equipment			48,300
Total assets			$160,340

Liabilities and Shareholders' Equity

Current liabilities			
Notes payable			$ 20,000
Accounts payable			13,500
Property tax payable			2,000
Income tax payable			3,440
Total current liabilities			38,940
Non-current liabilities			
Bonds payable, due June 30, 2021			30,000
Total liabilities			68,940
Shareholders' equity			
Common shares, issued and outstanding, 10,000 shares		$50,000	
Retained earnings		38,400	
Accumulated other comprehensive income		3,000	
Total shareholders' equity			91,400
Total liabilities and shareholders' equity			$160,340

SUMMARY OF LEARNING OBJECTIVE FOR APPENDIX 3A

10 Prepare a 10-column work sheet and financial statements.

The 10-column work sheet provides columns for the first trial balance, adjustments, adjusted trial balance, statement of comprehensive income, and statement of financial position. The work sheet does not replace the financial statements. Instead, it is the accountant's informal device for accumulating and sorting the information that is needed for the financial statements.

KEY TERM

work sheet, p. 107

APPENDIX 3B

PRESENT VALUE CONCEPTS

Objective 11
Understand and apply present value concepts.

Time value concepts are widely used by accountants when preparing financial statements under both IFRS and ASPE. This appendix will explain the basics that you must be aware of to understand related topics in this text. This appendix will also serve as a foundation for doing more complex measurement calculations. In addition, it will give some basic examples of how time value concepts are incorporated into financial statement measurements. Finally, this appendix briefly touches on different tools available for doing present value calculations, including formulas, present value tables, calculators, and spreadsheets.

The Nature of Interest

You are no doubt familiar with the concept of interest, but what exactly does it represent? Interest is recognition of the fact that the value of one dollar today is not equal to the value of one dollar in the future. There is some utility in having the dollar "in hand" today versus waiting until the end of the year. For instance, if a company borrows money from a bank today, the bank will expect to be repaid this amount plus some additional amount (interest) for the use of the funds and to reflect the fact that the dollar today is worth more than the dollar in the future, because of the time value of money. The company that borrows money incurs interest expense, while the company that lends the money receives interest revenue. For example, let's assume that Corner Bank lends Hillfarm Company $10,000 with the understanding that Hillfarm will repay $11,500. The excess of the repayment amount ($11,500) over $10,000 (the amount loaned) is equal to $1,500 and represents interest expense for Hillfarm and interest revenue for Corner Bank.

The lender generally states the amount of interest as a rate over a specific period of time. For example, if Hillfarm borrowed $10,000 for one year before repaying $11,500, the rate of interest is 15% per year ($1,500 ÷ $10,000). The custom of expressing interest as a percentage rate is an established business practice. In fact, business managers make investing and borrowing decisions based on the rate of interest involved, rather than on the actual dollar amount of interest to be received or paid.

How is the interest rate determined? One important factor is the level of credit risk (risk of nonpayment) involved. Other factors being equal, the higher the credit risk, the higher the interest rate. Low-risk borrowers like **Microsoft** or **Intel** can probably obtain a loan at or slightly below the going market rate of interest. However, a bank would probably charge the neighbourhood delicatessen several percentage points above the prime or base interest rate, if granting the loan at all. Macroeconomic factors also affect interest rates. For instance, when the government wants to encourage savings, it may decide to increase interest rates. Similarly, when it wants to encourage spending, it may decrease interest rates.

VALUATION
5.4.1, 5.4.2, 5.4.3

Fundamental Variables in Present Value Calculations

Where money is borrowed or invested, interest is usually paid.[11] It reflects payment for the use of money. The amount of interest paid is a function of three variables:

1. Principal (p): the amount borrowed or invested.

2. Interest rate (*i*): a percentage of the outstanding principal. The rate of interest is generally stated as an annual rate and is sometimes referred to as the "coupon rate" on a bond or the "contractual rate."

3. Time or number of periods (*n*): the number of years or fractional portion of a year that the principal is outstanding.

Thus, the following three relationships apply:

1. The larger the principal amount, the larger the dollar amount of interest.

2. The higher the interest rate, the larger the dollar amount of interest.

3. The longer the time period, the larger the dollar amount of interest.

Simple Interest

Companies calculate **simple interest** on the amount of the principal only. It is the return on (or growth of) the principal for one time period. The following equation in Illustration 3B-1 expresses simple interest.[12]

Illustration **3B-1**

Simple Interest Formula

$$\text{Interest} = p \times i \times n$$
where
p = principal
i = rate of interest for a single period
n = number of periods

For example, if you borrowed $1,000 for three years at a simple interest rate of 9% annually, you would pay $270 in total interest, calculated as follows:

			Year 1		Year 2		Year 3		
Interest	$= p \times i \times n$								
	$= \$1,000 \times 9\% \times 3$		$90	+	$90	+	$90	=	$270
	$= \$270$								

Compound Interest

Compound interest is the return on (or growth of) the principal for two or more time periods. Compounding calculates interest not only on the principal but also on the interest earned to date on that principal, assuming the interest is left on deposit (that is, added to the original principal amount).

To illustrate the difference between simple and compound interest, assume that you deposit $1,000 in the Last Canadian Bank, where it will earn simple interest of 9% per year, and you deposit another $1,000 in the First Canadian Bank, where it will earn interest of 9% per year compounded annually. Also assume that in both cases you will not withdraw any interest until three years from the date of deposit. The calculation of interest to be received and the accumulated year-end balances are given in Illustration 3B-2.

Illustration **3B-2**

Simple versus Compound Interest

Last Canadian Bank				First Canadian Bank		
Simple Interest Calculation	Simple Interest	Accumulated Year-End Balance		Compound Interest Calculation	Compound Interest	Accumulated Year-End Balance
Year 1 $1,000.00 × 9%	$ 90.00	$1,090.00		Year 1 $1,000.00 × 9%	$ 90.00	$1,090.00
Year 2 $1,000.00 × 9%	90.00	$1,180.00		Year 2 $1,090.00 × 9%	98.10	$1,188.10
Year 3 $1,000.00 × 9%	90.00	$1,270.00		Year 3 $1,188.10 × 9%	106.93	$1,295.03
	$270.00		$25.03 Difference		$295.03	

Note in Illustration 3B-2 that simple interest uses the initial principal of $1,000 to calculate the interest in all three years. Compound interest uses the accumulated balance (principal plus interest to date) at each year end to calculate interest in the following year. This explains why your compound interest account is larger: you are earning interest on interest. For practical purposes, compounding assumes that unpaid interest earned becomes a part of the principal. The accumulated balance at the end of each year becomes the new principal on which interest is earned during the next year.

Assuming all else is equal (especially risk), if you had a choice between investing your money at simple interest or at compound interest, you would choose compound interest. In the example, compounding provides $25.03 of additional interest income.

Compound interest is used in most business situations. Simple interest is generally applicable only to short-term situations of one year or less.

Different Ways to Perform the Calculations

In the previous section on compound and simple interest, the initial principal was given. It was used to calculate the interest earned and the value of the investment at the end of three years. The initial principal, invested at the beginning of year one, is the present value of the investment. The value of the investment at the end of three years is the future value of the investment. The process of determining the present value is often referred to as **discounting the future cash flows**. The word "discount" has many meanings in accounting, each of which varies with the context in which it is used. Be careful not to confuse the use of this term.

There are many different ways to calculate present value, including using the following four tools:

1. Present value formulas

2. Present value tables

3. Financial calculators

4. Spreadsheets such as Excel

Calculating Present Value of a Single Future Amount Using Different Tools

In the following section, we will show four methods of calculating the present value of a single future amount, using each of the above four tools.

To illustrate present value concepts, assume that you want to invest a sum of money at 5% in order to have $1,000 at the end of one year. The amount that you would need to invest today is called the present value of $1,000 discounted for one year at 5%. The variables in this example are shown in the time diagram in Illustration 3B-3.

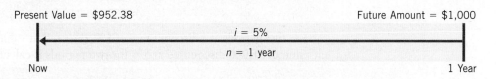

Present Value = $952.38   Future Amount = $1,000

$i = 5\%$

$n = 1$ year

Now   1 Year

Present Value = $952.38   *Future Amount = $1,000*

The next section will show how to use the different tools to calculate the present values.

Present Value Formula

The formula used to determine the present value for any interest (discount) rate (i), number of periods (n), and future amount (FV) is shown in Illustration 3B-4.

$$\text{Present value } (PV) = \frac{\text{Future value } (FV)}{(1 + i)^n}$$
$$= FV \div (1 + i)^n$$

In applying this formula to calculate the present value (PV) for the above example, the future value (FV) of $1,000, the interest (discount) rate (i) of 5%, and the number of periods (n) of one are used as follows:

$$PV = \$1,000 \div (1 + 5\%)^1$$
$$= \$1,000 \div 1.05$$
$$= \$952.38$$

If the single future cash flow of $1,000 is to be received in two years and discounted at 5%, its present value is calculated as follows:

$$PV = \$1,000 \div (1 + 5\%)^2$$
$$= \$1,000 \div 1.1025 \text{ or } [\$1,000 \div (1.05 \times 1.05)]$$
$$= \$907.03$$

The time diagram in Illustration 3B-5 shows the variables used to calculate the present value when cash is received in two years.

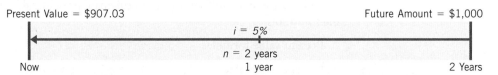

Present Value = $907.03   Future Amount = $1,000

$i = 5\%$

$n = 2$ years

Now   1 year   2 Years

Present Value Tables

The present value may also be determined through tables that show the present value of 1 for n periods for different periodic interest rates or discount rates. In Table A-2 in the Time Value of Money tables at the end of this text, the rows represent the number of discounting periods and the columns the periodic interest or discount rates. The five-digit decimal numbers in the respective rows and columns are the factors for the present value of 1.

When present value tables are used, the present value is calculated by multiplying the future cash amount by the present value factor specified at the intersection of the number of periods and the discount rate. For example, if the discount rate is 5% and the number of periods is 1, Table PV-1 shows that the present value factor is 0.95238. Then the present value of $1,000 discounted at 5% for one period is calculated as follows:

$$PV = \$1,000 \times 0.95238$$
$$= \$952.38$$

For two periods at a discount rate of 5%, the present value factor is 0.90703. The present value of $1,000 discounted at 5% for two periods is calculated as follows:

$$PV = \$1,000 \times 0.90703$$
$$= \$907.03$$

Note that the present values in these two examples are identical to the amounts determined previously when using the present value formula. This is because the factors in a present value table have been calculated using the present value formula. The benefit of using a present value table is that it can be quicker than using the formula. If you are using a simple calculator (not a financial calculator) or doing the calculations by hand, there are more calculations involved as the number of periods increase, making it more tedious than using the present value tables.

Table PV-1 can also be used if you know the present value and wish to determine the future cash flow. The present value amount is divided by the present value factor specified at the intersection of the number of periods and the discount rate in Table PV-1. (The full set of present value tables is at the end of the textbook.) For example, you can easily determine that an initial investment of $907.03 will grow to yield a future amount of $1,000 in two periods, at an annual discount rate of 5% ($1,000 = $907.03 divided by 0.90703).

Table PV-1

PRESENT VALUE OF 1

(*n*) periods	2%	2½%	3%	4%	5%	6%	7%	8%	9%	10%	11%	12%	15%
1	0.98039	0.97561	0.97087	0.96156	0.95238	0.94340	0.93458	0.92593	0.91743	0.90909	0.90090	0.89286	0.86957
2	0.96117	0.95181	0.94260	0.92456	0.90703	0.89000	0.87344	0.85734	0.84168	0.82645	0.81162	0.79719	0.75614
3	0.94232	0.92860	0.91514	0.88900	0.86384	0.83962	0.81630	0.79383	0.77218	0.75132	0.73119	0.71178	0.65752
4	0.92385	0.90595	0.88849	0.85480	0.82270	0.79209	0.76290	0.73503	0.70843	0.68301	0.65873	0.63552	0.57175
5	0.90583	0.88385	0.86261	0.82193	0.78353	0.74726	0.71299	0.68058	0.64993	0.62092	0.59345	0.56743	0.49718
6	0.88797	0.86230	0.83748	0.79031	0.74622	0.70496	0.66634	0.63017	0.59627	0.56447	0.53464	0.50663	0.43233
7	0.87056	0.84127	0.81309	0.75992	0.71068	0.66506	0.62275	0.58349	0.54703	0.51316	0.48166	0.45235	0.37594
8	0.85349	0.82075	0.78941	0.73069	0.67684	0.62741	0.58201	0.54027	0.50187	0.46651	0.43393	0.40388	0.32690
9	0.83676	0.80073	0.76642	0.70259	0.64461	0.59190	0.54393	0.50025	0.46043	0.42410	0.39092	0.36061	0.28426
10	0.82035	0.78120	0.74409	0.67556	0.61391	0.55839	0.50835	0.46319	0.42241	0.38554	0.35218	0.32197	0.24719
11	0.80426	0.76214	0.72242	0.64958	0.58468	0.52679	0.47509	0.42888	0.38753	0.35049	0.31728	0.28748	0.21494
12	0.78849	0.74356	0.70138	0.62460	0.55684	0.49697	0.44401	0.39711	0.35554	0.31863	0.28584	0.25668	0.18691
13	0.77303	0.72542	0.68095	0.60057	0.53032	0.46884	0.41496	0.36770	0.32618	0.28966	0.25751	0.22917	0.16253
14	0.75788	0.70773	0.66112	0.57748	0.50507	0.44230	0.38782	0.34046	0.29925	0.26333	0.23199	0.20462	0.14133
15	0.74301	0.69047	0.64186	0.55526	0.48102	0.41727	0.36245	0.31524	0.27454	0.23939	0.20900	0.18270	0.12289
16	0.72845	0.67362	0.62317	0.53391	0.45811	0.39365	0.33873	0.29189	0.25187	0.21763	0.18829	0.16312	0.10687
17	0.71416	0.65720	0.60502	0.51337	0.43630	0.37136	0.31657	0.27027	0.23107	0.19785	0.16963	0.14564	0.09293
18	0.70016	0.64117	0.58739	0.49363	0.41552	0.35034	0.29586	0.25025	0.21199	0.17986	0.15282	0.13004	0.08081
19	0.68643	0.62553	0.57029	0.47464	0.39573	0.33051	0.27651	0.23171	0.19449	0.16351	0.13768	0.11611	0.07027
20	0.67297	0.61027	0.55368	0.45639	0.37689	0.31180	0.25842	0.21455	0.17843	0.14864	0.12403	0.10367	0.06110

Financial Calculators

Present values can also be calculated using financial calculators. A financial calculator will perform the same calculation as a simple calculator, but it requires fewer steps and less input. Basically, with a financial calculator, you input the future value, the discount rate, and the number of periods, and then tell it to calculate the present value. Illustration 3B-6 shows the required inputs for a present value calculation using a financial calculator.

Illustration **3B-6**

Calculating the Present Value of a Single Future Amount Using a Financial Calculator

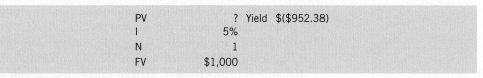

PV	?	Yield $($952.38)
I	5%	
N	1	
FV	$1,000	

Where:

PV = present value
I = interest rate
N = number of periods
FV = future value

Details vary with different financial calculators; however, they generally ask for these variables.

You should know that the present value amounts calculated with a financial calculator can be slightly different than those calculated with present value tables. That is because the numbers in a present value table are rounded. For example, in Table PV-1 the factors are rounded to five digits. In a financial calculator, only the final answer is rounded to the number of digits you have specified.

A major benefit of using a financial calculator is that you are not restricted to the interest rates or numbers of periods on a present value table. In Table PV-1, present value factors have been calculated for 13 interest rates (there are 13 columns in that table) and the maximum number of periods is 20. With a financial calculator you could, for example, calculate the present value of a future amount to be received in 25 periods using 5.75% as the discount rate. Later in this appendix, we will illustrate how to partly overcome this limitation of present value tables through a method called interpolation.

Spreadsheets

Using a spreadsheet is very similar to using financial calculators; however, many spreadsheets such as Excel are significantly more robust. Using Excel as an example to calculate the present value in our example, first select "Formulas," and then "Financial," and then, in the drop-down menu, select "PV." Illustration 3B-7 shows the variables that need to be input.

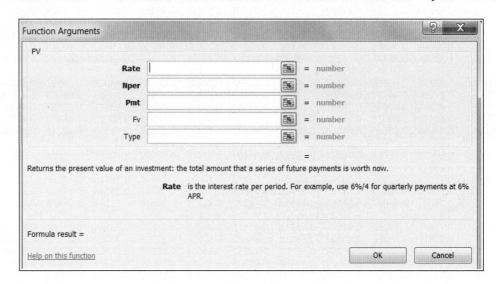

Where:

PV = present value = amount to be calculated
Rate = interest rate = 5% or .05
Nper = number of periods = 1
Pmt = payment = 0
FV = future value = $1,000
Type = type of annuity

In this case, since there are no additional payments aside from one interest payment and one principal payment, the amount included beside "Pmt" is 0. The section entitled "Type" relates to annuities and is not relevant here since this is a single payment. If you input 0 or leave blank, this will suffice. We will cover annuities in the next section.

Regardless of the method used in calculating present values, a higher discount rate produces a smaller present value. For example, using an 8% discount rate, the present value of $1,000 due one year from now is $925.93 versus $952.38 at 5%. It should also be recognized that **the further away from the present the future cash flow is, the smaller the present value**. For example, using the same discount rate of 5%, the present value of $1,000 due in five years is $783.53. The present value of $1,000 due in one year is $952.38.

Calculating the Present Value of a Series of Future Cash Flows (Annuities) Using Different Tools

The preceding discussion was for the discounting of only a single future amount. Businesses and individuals frequently engage in transactions in which a series of equal dollar amounts are to be received or paid periodically. Examples of series of periodic receipts or payments are loan agreements, instalment sales, mortgage notes, lease (rental) contracts, and pension obligations. These series of periodic receipts or payments are called "annuities." In calculating the present value of an annuity, it is necessary to know (1) the discount rate (i), (2) the number of discount periods (n), (3) the amount of the periodic receipts or payments (FV), and (4) when the payments are made (at the end of a period or the beginning). When dealing with payments at the end of a period, this is called an "ordinary annuity." When the payments are made at the beginning of a period, they are called an "annuity due" or "annuity in arrears."

To illustrate the calculation of the present value of an annuity, assume that you will pay $1,000 cash annually for three years (at the end of the year), and that the discount rate is 4%. This situation is shown in the time diagram in Illustration 3B-8.

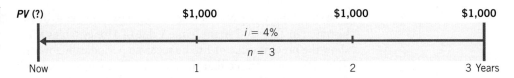

| Illustration **3B-8** |
| *Time Diagram for a Three-Year Annuity* |

Now let's look at the calculation using the four tools.

Present Value Formula

One method of calculating the present value of this annuity is to use the present value formula to determine the present value of each of the three $1,000 payments and then add those amounts as follows:

$$PV = [\$1,000 \text{ divided by } (1 + 4\%)^1] + [\$1,000 \text{ divided by } (1 + 4\%)^2]$$
$$+ [\$1,000 \text{ divided by } (1 + 4\%)^3]$$
$$= \$961.56 + \$924.56 + \$889.00$$
$$= \$2,775.12$$

The same result is achieved by using present value factors from Table PV-1, as shown in Illustration 3B-9.

| Illustration **3B-9** |
| *Present Value of a Series of Future Cash Flows* |

Future Value	×	Present Value of 1 Factor at 4%	=	Present Value
$1,000 (one year away)		0.96156		$961.56
1,000 (two years away)		0.92456		924.56
1,000 (three years away)		0.88900		889.00
		2.77512		$2,775.12

Determining the present value of each single future cash flow, and then adding the present values, is required when the periodic cash flows are not the same in each period. But when the future receipts are the same in each period, an annuity formula may be used to calculate present value. The annuity formula differs depending on whether it is an ordinary annuity (payments at the end of the period) or an annuity due (payments at the beginning of the period).

The present value of an ordinary annuity formula is shown in Illustration 3B-10.

$$Present\ value\ (PV) = Future\ value\ (FV) \times \frac{1 - \dfrac{1}{(1 + i)^n}}{i}$$

$$= \$1{,}000 \times [(1 - (1 \div (1 + 4\%)^3)) \div 4\%]$$
$$= \$1{,}000 \times [(1 - (1 \div (1.04)^3)) \div 0.04]$$
$$= \$1{,}000 \times [(1 - (1 \div 1.124864)) \div 0.04]$$
$$= \$1{,}000 \times [(1 - 0.888996359) \div 0.04]$$
$$= \$1{,}000 \times 2.77509$$
$$= \$2{,}775.09$$

The formula for an annuity due is shown at the top of the present value tables at the end of the textbook. Differences are due to rounding and are not significant.

Present Value Tables

The calculation may also be done using a present value of an ordinary annuity table. As illustrated in Table A-2 in the Time Value of Money tables at the end of this text, these tables show the present value of 1 to be received periodically for a given number of periods. From Table PV-2 we can see that the present value factor of an annuity of 1 for three periods at 4% is 2.77509. This present value factor is the total of the three individual present value factors, as shown in Illustration 3B-10. Applying this present value factor to the annual cash flow of $1,000 produces a present value of $2,775.09 ($1,000 × 2.77509). Recall that there is a separate present value table for annuity due/annuity in arrears.

Table PV-2

PRESENT VALUE OF AN ANNUITY OF 1

$$PV = \frac{1 - \dfrac{1}{(1 + i)^n}}{i}$$

(n) periods	2%	2½%	3%	4%	5%	6%	7%	8%	9%	10%	11%	12%	15%
1	0.98039	0.97561	0.97087	0.96154	0.95238	0.94340	0.93458	0.92593	0.91743	0.90909	0.90090	0.89286	0.86957
2	1.94156	1.92742	1.91347	1.88609	1.85941	1.83339	1.80802	1.78326	1.75911	1.73554	1.71252	1.69005	1.62571
3	2.88388	2.85602	2.82861	2.77509	2.72325	2.67301	2.62432	2.57710	2.53130	2.48685	2.44371	2.40183	2.28323
4	3.80773	3.76197	3.71710	3.62990	3.54595	3.46511	3.38721	3.31213	3.23972	3.16986	3.10245	3.03735	2.85498
5	4.71346	4.64583	4.57971	4.45182	4.32948	4.21236	4.10020	3.99271	3.88965	3.79079	3.69590	3.60478	3.35216
6	5.60143	5.50813	5.41719	5.24214	5.07569	4.91732	4.76654	4.62288	4.48592	4.35526	4.23054	4.11141	3.78448
7	6.47199	6.34939	6.23028	6.00205	5.78637	5.58238	5.38929	5.20637	5.03295	4.86842	4.71220	4.56376	4.16042
8	7.32548	7.17014	7.01969	6.73274	6.46321	6.20979	5.97130	5.74664	5.53482	5.33493	5.14612	4.96764	4.48732
9	8.16224	7.97087	7.78611	7.43533	7.10782	6.80169	6.51523	6.24689	5.99525	5.75902	5.53705	5.32825	4.77158
10	8.98259	8.75206	8.53020	8.11090	7.72173	7.36009	7.02358	6.71008	6.41766	6.14457	5.88923	5.65022	5.01877
11	9.78685	9.51421	9.25262	8.76048	8.30641	7.88687	7.49867	7.13896	6.80519	6.49506	6.20652	5.93770	5.23371
12	10.57534	10.25776	9.95400	9.38507	8.86325	8.38384	7.94269	7.53608	7.16073	6.81369	6.49236	6.19437	5.42062
13	11.34837	10.98319	10.63496	9.98565	9.39357	8.85268	8.35765	7.90378	7.48690	7.10336	6.74987	6.42355	5.58315
14	12.10625	11.69091	11.29607	10.56312	9.89864	9.29498	8.74547	8.24424	7.78615	7.36669	6.98187	6.62817	5.72448
15	12.84926	12.38138	11.93794	11.11839	10.37966	9.71225	9.10791	8.55948	8.06069	7.60608	7.19087	6.81086	5.84737
16	13.57771	13.05500	12.56110	11.65230	10.83777	10.10590	9.44665	8.85137	8.31256	7.82371	7.37916	6.97399	5.95424
17	14.29187	13.71220	13.16612	12.16567	11.27407	10.47726	9.76322	9.12164	8.54363	8.02155	7.54879	7.11963	6.04716
18	14.99203	14.35336	13.75351	12.65930	11.68959	10.82760	10.05909	9.37189	8.75563	8.20141	7.70162	7.24967	6.12797
19	15.67846	14.97889	14.32380	13.13394	12.08532	11.15812	10.33560	9.60360	8.95012	8.36492	7.83929	7.36578	6.19823
20	16.35143	15.58916	14.87747	13.59033	12.46221	11.46992	10.59401	9.81815	9.12856	8.51356	7.96333	7.46944	6.25933

Financial Calculators

Recall that when using a financial calculator, you must input the number of periods, the interest rate, and the amount of the annual payment. When using a financial calculator to calculate the present value of an annuity, you also need to specify if the annual cash flow is an ordinary annuity or an annuity due (in arrears). Illustration 3B-11 shows the inputs needed using a financial calculator. In this case, you do not need to enter a future amount because you are entering a payment value of $1,000, which will be paid at the end of each year.

Illustration **3B-11**

Calculating the Present Value of an Ordinary Annuity Using a Financial Calculator

PV	?	Yield $2,775.09
I	4%	
N	3	
PMT	−$1,000	
FV		
Type	0	

Where:

PV = present value
I = interest rate
N = number of periods
PMT = the payment at the end of each period
FV = future value
Type = ordinary annuity (enter 0) or annuity due (enter 1)

Spreadsheets

Using Excel as an example to calculate the present value of an ordinary annuity in our example, first select "Formulas," and then "Financial," and then, in the drop-down menu, select "PV." Illustration 3B-12 shows the variables that need to be input.

Illustration **3B-12**

Calculating the Present Value of an Ordinary Annuity Using a Spreadsheet Such as Excel

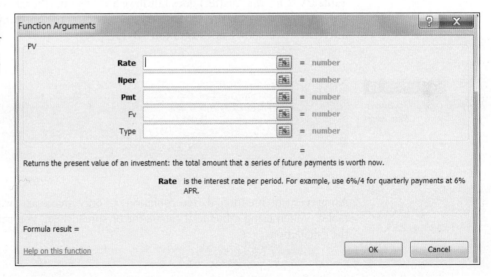

Where:

PV = present value = amount to be calculated
Rate = interest rate = 4% or .04
Nper = number of periods = 3
Pmt = −1000
FV = future value = no need to input
Type = 0

In this case, there is no need to input the FV since you are inputting a payment of $1,000, which is paid at the end of each of the three years. Since this is an ordinary annuity, the Type = 0. If it were an annuity due, the Type = 1.

Interest Rates and Time Periods

In the preceding calculations, the discounting has been done on an annual basis using an annual interest rate. There are situations where adjustments may be required to the interest rate, the time period, or both.

Using Time Periods of Less Than One Year

Discounting may be done over shorter periods of time than one year, such as monthly, quarterly, or semi-annually. When the time frame is less than one year, it is necessary to convert the annual interest rate to the applicable time frame. Assume, for example, that the investor in Illustration 3B-8 received $500 semi-annually for three years instead of $1,000 annually. In this case, the number of periods (n) becomes six (three annual periods $\times$ 2), and the discount rate (i) is 2% (4% $\times$ $^6/_{12}$ months).

If present value tables are used to determine the present value, the appropriate present value factor from Table PV-2 is 5.60143. The present value of the future cash flows is $2,800.72 (5.60143 $\times$ $500). This amount is slightly higher than the $2,775.09 calculated in Illustration 3B-10 because interest is calculated twice during the same year. Thus, interest is compounded on the first half-year's interest.

Interpolation

As previously discussed, one of the limitations of the present value tables is that the tables contain a limited number of interest rates. But in certain situations where the factor for a certain interest rate is not available, it can be deduced or interpolated from the tables. For example, if you wished to find the factor to determine the present value of 1 for a $3^1/_2$% interest rate and five periods, it would be difficult to use Table PV-1 to do so. Table PV-1 (or Table PV-2 for that matter) does not have a $3^1/_2$% interest rate column. We can, however, average the factors for the 3% and 4% interest rates to approximate the factor for a $3^1/_2$% interest rate, as shown in Illustration 3B-13.

Illustration **3B-13**	
Interpolation of $3^1/_2$% Interest Rate Factor	

Factor, n = 5, i = 3%		0.86261
Factor, n = 5, i = 4%	+	0.82193
Sum of two factors	=	1.68454
Average two factors	÷	2
Factor, n = 5, i = $3^1/_2$%	=	0.84227

As previously mentioned, interpolation is only necessary when using present value tables. When using a financial calculator or spreadsheet, you can use any interest rate in the calculations.

Some Additional Calculations

Often you need to calculate the present value, but sometimes one of the other variables (such as interest rate or annuity payments) needs to be calculated. The next section looks at how this might be done.

Calculation of the Interest Rate

Many shoppers use credit cards to make purchases. When you receive the statement for payment, you may pay the total amount due or you may pay the balance in a certain number of payments. For example, assume you receive a statement from MasterCard with a balance due of $528.77. You may pay it off in 12 equal monthly payments of $50 each, with the first payment due one month from now. What rate of interest would you be paying?

The $528.77 represents the present value of the 12 payments of $50 each at an unknown rate of interest. The time diagram in Illustration 3B-14 depicts this situation.

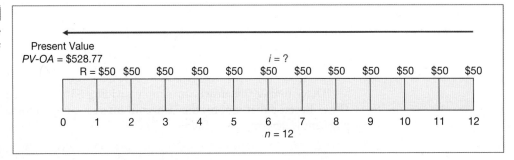

Illustration 3B-14

Solving for the Interest Rate Using a Formula

You calculate the rate as follows:

$$\text{Present value of an ordinary annuity} = R\,(PVF\text{-}OA_{n,i})$$
$$\$528.77 = \$50\,(PVF\text{-}OA_{12,i})$$
$$(PVFOA_{12,i}) = \frac{\$528.77}{\$50} = 10.57540$$

Referring to Table PV-2 and reading across the 12-period row, you find 10.57534 in the 2% column. Therefore, you are paying 2% per month. Obviously, you are better off paying the entire bill now if possible.

When using a spreadsheet such as Excel, you would select "Formula," then "Financial," and then "Rate." Illustration 3B-15 shows the factors that need to be input for both a spreadsheet and a financial calculator.

Illustration 3B-15

Solving for the Interest Rate Using a Spreadsheet or Financial Calculator

Excel		Financial calculator	
Nper	12	PV	−528.77
Pmt	50	N	12
PV	−528.77	PMT	50
FV	0	FV	0
Type	0	Type	0

Where:

PV = present value
Nper or N = number of periods
Pmt or PMT = the payment at the end of each period
FV = future value
Type = ordinary annuity (enter 0) or annuity due (enter 1)

Note that if you have a situation whereby you know the present value and future value (and there are no payments) you input the future value amount as a negative amount.

Calculation of the Periodic Payment

Assume that Norm Inc. is considering leasing a car from Jackie Inc. The fair value of the car today is $36,000. The current market interest rate for financing such a vehicle is 4% compounded semi-annually. Calculate the semi-annual lease payment assuming that the payment is made at the end of the period. Illustration 3B-16 shows a time diagram of this situation.

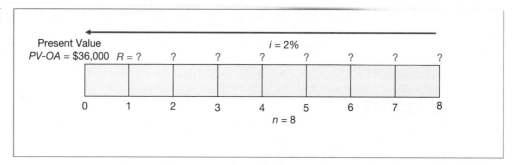

Illustration 3B-16

Time Diagram for Ordinary Annuity for a Lease

Determining the answer by simply dividing $36,000 by eight payments is incorrect. Why? Because that ignores the impact of interest compounding. Thus, the amount of the payment is determined as follows.

$$\text{Present value of an ordinary annuity} = R\,(PVF\text{-}OA_{n,i})$$
$$\$36,000 = R\,(PVF\text{-}OA_{8,2\%})$$
$$\$36,000 = R\,(7.32548)$$
$$R = \$4,914.35$$

When using a spreadsheet such as Excel, you would select "Formula," then "Financial," and then "Pmt." Illustration 3B-17 shows the factors that need to be input for both a spreadsheet and a financial calculator.

Illustration 3B-17

Solving for the Payment Using a Spreadsheet or Financial Calculator

Excel		Financial calculator	
Rate	2%	PV	36000
Nper	8	I	2%
PV	36000	N	8
FV	0	FV	0
Type	0	Type	0

Where:

PV = present value
Nper or N = number of periods
Rate or I = the interest rate per period
FV = future value
Type = ordinary annuity (enter 0) or annuity due (enter 1)

SUMMARY OF LEARNING OBJECTIVE FOR APPENDIX 3B

11 Understand and apply present value concepts.

Present value concepts are used to acknowledge the time value of money. There are various techniques and tools to calculate present value, including formulas, tables, financial calculators, and spreadsheets. Inputs to the calculation include interest, payments, number of periods, and if the calculation involves an annuity, information about whether it is an ordinary annuity or an annuity due. Present value concepts are frequently used in measuring financial statement elements.

KEY TERMS

simple interest, p. 114
compound interest, p. 114

Note: All assignment material with an asterisk (*) relates to the appendices to the chapter.

Completion of this end-of-chapter material will help develop CPA enabling competencies (such as ethics and professionalism, problem-solving and decision-making and communication) and technical competencies. We have highlighted selected items with an integration icon and material in *WileyPLUS* has been linked to the competencies. The brief exercises, exercises and problems generally emphasize problem-solving and decision-making. For chapter 3, since much of the end-of-chapter material dealing with measurement relates also to the finance technical competency area, we have highlighted only selected items relating to finance.

Brief Exercises

(LO 1) BE3-1 Plant Inc. uses the following accounts in its trial balance:

1. Sales
2. Investment Loss
3. Dividends
4. Salaries and Wages Payable
5. Fair Value-OCI Investments

6. Cost of Goods Sold
7. Accumulated Other Comprehensive Income
8. Allowance for Doubtful Accounts

9. Fair Value-Net Income Investments
10. Retained Earnings
11. Interest Receivable
12. Unrealized Gain or Loss-OCI

Indicate whether each account is (a) a permanent account or a temporary account; and (b) an asset, contra-asset, liability, revenue, expense, gain, loss, or shareholders' equity account.

(LO 2) BE3-2 Kothari Ltd. made the following transactions:

1. Payment of a $200 invoice on account
2. Increase in the fair value of a Fair Value-Net Income Investment by $250
3. Sale on account for $100
4. Purchase of equipment paid for with $500 cash and a $1,000 note payable
5. Increase in the fair value of a Fair Value-OCI Investment by $150
6. Repayment of a $2,000 bank loan

Indicate the effect of each of the transactions on (a) the basic accounting equation and (b) the expanded basic accounting equation.

(LO 3) BE3-3 One Wiser Corp. had the following transactions during the first month of business. Journalize the transactions.

Aug.	2	Invested $12,000 cash and $2,500 of equipment in the business in exchange for common shares.
	7	Purchased supplies on account for $600. (Debit asset account.)
	12	Performed services for clients, collecting $1,300 in cash and billing the clients $670 for the remainder.
	15	Paid August rent, $600.
	19	Counted supplies and determined that only $270 of the supplies purchased on August 7 were still on hand.

(LO 3, 4) BE3-4 On August 1, Secret Sauce Technologies Inc. paid $12,600 in advance for two years' membership in a global technology association. Prepare two sets of journal entries for Secret Sauce, with each set of journal entries recording the August 1 journal entry and the December 31 adjusting entry. Treat the expenditure as an asset in the first set of journal entries, and treat the expenditure as an expense in the second set of journal entries.

(LO 3, 4) BE3-5 Store-it-Here owns a warehouse. On September 1, it rented storage space to a lessee (tenant) for six months for a total cash payment of $12,000 received in advance. Prepare two sets of journal entries for Store-it-Here, with each set of journal entries recording the September 1 journal entry and the December 31 adjusting entry. Treat the receipt of cash as a liability in the first set of journal entries, and treat the receipt of cash as a revenue in the second set of journal entries.

(LO 4) BE3-6 Included in Carville Corp.'s December 31, 2017 trial balance is a note payable of $20,000. The note is an eight-month, 12% note dated October 1, 2017. Prepare Carville's December 31, 2017 adjusting entry to record the accrued interest, and June 1, 2018 journal entry to record payment of principal and interest due to the lender.

(LO 4) BE3-7 Jerry Holiday is the maintenance supervisor for Ray's Insurance Co. and has recently purchased a riding lawn mower and accessories that will be used in caring for the grounds around corporate headquarters. He sent the following information to the accounting department:

Cost of mower and accessories	$9,600	Date purchased	July 1, 2017
Estimated useful life	8 years	Monthly salary of groundskeeper	$1,100
		Estimated annual fuel cost	$150

Calculate the amount of depreciation expense (for the mower and accessories) that should be reported on Ray's Insurance Co.'s December 31, 2017 income statement. Assume straight-line depreciation.

(LO 4) BE3-8 Pelican Inc. made a December 31 adjusting entry to debit Salaries and Wages Expense and credit Salaries and Wages Payable for $2,700. On January 2, Pelican paid the weekly payroll of $5,000. Prepare Pelican's (a) January 1 reversing entry, (b) January 2 entry (assuming the reversing entry was prepared), and (c) January 2 entry (assuming the reversing entry was not prepared).

(LO 6) BE3-9 Willis Corporation has Beginning Inventory $76,000; Purchases $486,000; Freight-in $16,200; Purchase Returns $5,800; Purchase Discounts $5,000; and Ending Inventory $69,500. Calculate Willis's cost of goods sold.

(LO 6) BE3-10 Tiger Inc. has the following year-end account balances: Sales Revenue $928,900; Interest Income $17,500; Cost of Goods Sold $406,200; Operating Expenses $129,000; Income Tax Expense $55,100; and Dividends $15,900. Prepare the year-end closing entries.

(LO 7) BE3-11 Below are some financial statement elements and their basis of measurement for a public company that follows IFRS. Complete the third column by noting whether the basis of measurement is a cost-based measure, a current value measure, or a hybrid measure. Explain your choice.

Element	Basis of measurement	Measurement categorization
Building	Depreciated cost unless impaired	
Manufacturing inventory	Lower of cost and net realizable value	
Biological assets	Fair value less (estimated) costs to sell	
Bonds payable	Amortized cost	

(LO 7) BE3-12 In the chapter, there are two common types of valuation techniques noted. Explain the differences between these two models. Note when each of these techniques might be used in measuring financial statement elements.

(LO 7) BE3-13 Present value concepts are often used for measurement in financial reporting. List five situations where present value techniques are used to measure assets and explain how. List five situations where present value techniques are used to measure liabilities.

(LO 7) BE3-14 When using the discounted cash flow model, there are two approaches that are generally accepted. List these two approaches and explain when each might be used to measure a financial statement element.

(LO 7) BE3-15 Assume that Enter Inc. just issued a $1,000, 10-year bond bearing annual interest of 4%. The company would like to determine the amount that should be recognized on the financial statements. The bond carries a fixed interest rate of 4% (interest is payable annually), which is lower than the market interest rate of 5%. Identify and explain what inputs would be required in measuring the bond. Would you recommend using the traditional approach or the expected cash flow approach to measure this liability? Why?

(LO 7) BE3-16 Lucky Enterprises is using a discounted cash flow model. Identify which model Lucky might use to estimate the discounted fair value under each scenario, and calculate the fair value:

Scenario 1: Cash flows are fairly certain	Scenario 2: Cash flows are uncertain
$100/year for five years	75% probability that cash flows will be $100 in five years
Risk-adjusted discount rate is 6%	25% probability that cash flows will be $75 in five years
Risk-free discount rate is 3%	Risk-adjusted discount rate is 6%
	Risk-free discount rate is 3%

(LO 7) BE3-17 Chang Company must perform an impairment test on its equipment. The equipment will produce the following cash flows: Year 1, $35,000; Year 2, $45,000; Year 3, $55,000. The discount rate is 10%. What is the value in use for this equipment?

(LO 7) BE3-18 Alpha Company signs a contract to sell the use of its patented manufacturing technology to Delta Corp for 15 years. The contract for this transaction stipulates that Delta Corp pays Alpha $18,000 at the end of each year for the use of this technology. Using a discount rate of 9%, what is the value in use of the patented manufacturing technology?

(LO 8) BE3-19 Assume that you are following IFRS 13 and measuring the fair value of a building. The building is currently being rented out. Under IFRS 13, the entity must determine the following:

(a) how the item could be/is used

(b) the market and

(c) the valuation technique/model

Briefly explain each of these and note how they would apply to measuring the building.

(LO 8) BE3-20 Medici Patriarchs purchased the following investments during 2017:

(a) 1,000 shares of Private Limited, a start-up company. The value of this investment was based on an internally developed model.

(b) 5,000 shares of CIBC, a public company listed on the TSX.

(c) $15,000 of corporate bonds. Although these bonds do not trade in an active market, their value closely resembles movements in the Bank of Canada bond rate.

Based on the IFRS 13 guidance, indicate at which level in the fair value hierarchy these investment values will fall (level 1, 2, or 3). Explain your choice.

(LO 11) *BE3-21 Determine the amount of interest that will be earned on each of the following investments:

	Investment	(*i*) Interest Rate	(*n*) Number of Periods	Type of Interest
(a)	$100	5%	1	Simple
(b)	$500	6%	2	Simple
(c)	$500	6%	2	Compound

(LO 11) *BE3-22 Smolinski Company is considering an investment that will return a lump sum of $500,000 five years from now. What amount should Smolinski Company pay for this investment in order to earn a 4% return? Show calculations using all four methods (formulas, tables, financial calculator, and Excel).

(LO 11) *BE3-23 If Kerry Dahl invests $3,152 now, she will receive $10,000 at the end of 15 years. What annual rate of interest will Kerry earn on her investment? Round your answer to the nearest whole number. Show calculations using three methods (tables, financial calculator, and Excel).

(LO 11) *BE3-24 Kilarny Company is considering investing in an annuity contract that will return $25,000 at the end of each year for 15 years. What amount should Kilarny Company pay for this investment if it earns a 6% return? Show calculations using three methods (tables, Excel, and financial calculator).

(LO 11) *BE3-25 For each of the following cases, indicate in the chart below the appropriate discount rate (*i*) and the appropriate number of periods (*n*) to be used in present value calculations. Show calculations. The first one has been completed as an example.

	Annual Interest Rate	Number of Years	Frequency of Payment	(*n*) Number of Periods	(*i*) Discount Rate
1.	8%	3	Quarterly	3 × 4 = 12	8% ÷ 4 = 2%
2.	5%	4	Semi-annually		
3.	7%	5	Annually		
4.	4%	3	Quarterly		
5.	6%	6	Semi-annually		
6.	6%	15	Monthly		

(LO 11) *BE3-26 Insert the appropriate discount factor into the table below for each of the situations given. These factors have to be interpolated from Tables PV-1 and PV-2.

	PV of 1 (Table PV-1)	PV of an Annuity of 1 (Table PV-2)
(a) $n = 4$, $i = 4\frac{1}{2}\%$		
(b) $n = 6$, $i = 6\frac{1}{2}\%$		

(LO 11) *BE3-27 Cross Country Railroad Co. is about to issue $100,000 of 10-year bonds that pay a 5.5% annual interest rate, with interest payable semi-annually. The market interest rate is 5%. How much can Cross Country expect to receive for the sale of these bonds? Show calculations using two methods (tables and financial calculator).

(LO 11) *BE3-28 Assume the same information as BE3-27, except that the market interest rate is 6% instead of 5%. In this case, how much can Cross Country expect to receive from the sale of these bonds? Show calculations using three methods (tables, financial calculator, and Excel).

(LO 11) *BE3-29 Caledonian Company receives a six-year, $50,000 note that bears interest at 8% (paid annually) from a customer at a time when the market interest rate is 6%. What is the present value of the note received by Caledonian? Show calculations using three methods (tables, financial calculator, and Excel).

(LO 11) *BE3-30 Hung-Chao Yu Company issues a six-year, 8% mortgage note on January 1, 2017, to obtain financing for new equipment. The terms provide for semi-annual instalment payments of $112,825. What were the cash proceeds received from the issue of the note? Show calculations using three methods (tables, financial calculator, and Excel).

(LO 11) *BE3-31 You are told that a note has repayment terms of $4,000 per year for five years, with a stated interest rate of 4%. How much of the total payment is for principal, and how much is for interest? Show calculations using two methods (financial calculator and Excel).

(LO 11) *BE3-32 You would like to purchase a car with a list price of $30,000, and the dealer offers financing over a five-year period at 8%. If repayments are to be made annually, what would your annual payments be? Show calculations using three methods (tables, financial calculator, and Excel).

(LO 11) *BE3-33 Assume the same information as in BE3-32, except that you can afford to make annual payments of only $6,000. If you decide to trade in your current car to help reduce the amount of financing required, what trade-in value would you need to negotiate to ensure your annual payment is $6,000? Show calculations using three methods (tables, financial calculator, and Excel).

FINANCE

(LO 11) *BE3-34 As CFO of a small manufacturing firm, you have been asked to determine the best financing for the purchase of a new piece of equipment. If the vendor is offering repayment options of $10,000 per year for five years, or no payment for two years followed by one payment of $46,000, which option would you recommend? The current market rate of interest is 8%.

FINANCE (LO 11) *BE3-35 If the market rate of interest in BE3-34 were 10%, would you choose the same option?

Exercises

(LO 3) E3-1 **(Transaction Analysis—Service Company)** Bill Rosenberg recently opened his legal practice as a sole proprietorship. During the first month of operations, the following events and transactions occurred:

Apr.	2	Invested $15,000 cash along with equipment valued at $10,000 in the business.
	2	Hired an administrative assistant at a salary of $480 per week payable monthly.
	3	Purchased $1,200 of supplies on account. (Debit an asset account.)
	7	Paid office rent of $750 for the month.
	11	Completed the preparation of a will and billed the client $1,500 for services rendered. (Use the Service Revenue account.)
	12	Received cash of $4,200 as a retainer for future services.
	17	Received cash of $2,900 for services completed for Botticelli Limited.
	21	Paid insurance expense of $180.
	30	Paid the administrative assistant $1,920 for the month.
	30	A count of supplies indicated that $220 of supplies had been used during the month.
	30	Purchased a new computer for $4,100 paid for with personal funds. (The computer will be used only for business purposes.)

Instructions

Journalize the transactions in the general journal. (Omit explanations.)

(LO 3, 10) *E3-2 **(Trial Balance)** The trial balance of Mis-Match Inc. on June 30, 2017 is as follows:

	Debit	Credit
Cash	$ 2,870	
Accounts receivable	3,231	
Office supplies	800	
Equipment	3,800	
Accounts payable		$ 2,666
Unearned revenue		1,200
Common shares		6,000
Retained earnings		2,795
Service revenue		2,380
Salaries and wages expense	3,400	
Office expense	940	
	$15,041	$15,041

The following transactions took place in July 2017:

1. Payments received from customers on account amounted to $1,320.

2. A computer printer was purchased on account for $500.

3. Services provided to clients and billed on account amounted to $3,890.

4. $400 of supplies was purchased on account in July, and a physical count on July 31 showed that there was $475 of supplies on hand on July 31.

5. When the Unearned Revenue account was reviewed, it was found that $825 of the balance was earned in July.

6. Salaries and Wages Expense of $670 related to employee services provided in July was not yet recorded as at July 31 (will be paid in August).

7. Payments to suppliers on account amounted to $2,125.

8. Received invoices totalling $1,160 related to office expenses incurred in July.

9. Declared a dividend of $575 on July 31.

Instructions

Prepare the trial balance as at July 31, 2017, assuming that Mis-Match did not record closing entries at the end of June 2017. (*Note:* It may be necessary to add one or more accounts to the trial balance.)

(LO 3, 4) E3-3 (Transactions of a Corporation, Including Investment and Dividend) LD Driving Range Inc. was opened on March 1 by Phil Woods. The following selected events and transactions occurred during March:

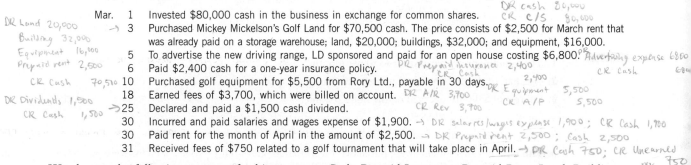

Mar.	1	Invested $80,000 cash in the business in exchange for common shares.
	3	Purchased Mickey Mickelson's Golf Land for $70,500 cash. The price consists of $2,500 for March rent that was already paid on a storage warehouse; land, $20,000; buildings, $32,000; and equipment, $16,000.
	5	To advertise the new driving range, LD sponsored and paid for an open house costing $6,800.
	6	Paid $2,400 cash for a one-year insurance policy.
	10	Purchased golf equipment for $5,500 from Rory Ltd., payable in 30 days.
	18	Earned fees of $3,700, which were billed on account.
	25	Declared and paid a $1,500 cash dividend.
	30	Incurred and paid salaries and wages expense of $1,900.
	30	Paid rent for the month of April in the amount of $2,500.
	31	Received fees of $750 related to a golf tournament that will take place in April.

Handwritten annotations:
DR Land 20,000
Building 32,000
Equipment 16,000
Prepaid rent 2,500
CR Cash 70,510

DR Dividends 1,500
CR Cash 1,500

DR cash 80,000
CR C/S 80,000

Advertising expense 6800
CR Cash 680

DR Prepaid insurance 2,400
CR Cash 2,400

DR Equipment 5,500
CR A/P 5,500

DR A/R 3,700
CR Rev 3,700

DR salaries/wages expense 1,900; CR Cash 1,900
DR Prepaid rent 2,500; Cash 2,500
DR Cash 750; CR Unearned rev 750

Woods uses the following accounts for his company: Cash; Prepaid Insurance; Prepaid Rent; Land; Buildings; Equipment; Accounts Payable; Unearned Revenue; Common Shares; Dividends; Service Revenue; Advertising Expense; Rent Expense; and Salaries and Wages Expense.

Instructions

(a) Journalize the March transactions.

(b) Identify any adjusting entries that should be recorded before preparing financial statements for the month of March. *(handwritten: — depre. equipment, rent expense for march, insurance expense, bad debt?,)*

(LO 3, 4) E3-4 (Alternative Treatment of Prepayment) At Sugarland Ltd., prepaid costs are debited to expense when cash is paid and unearned revenues are credited to revenue when the cash is received. During January of the current year, the following transactions occurred.

Jan.	2	Received $11,100 for services to be performed in the future.
	2	Paid $3,600 for casualty insurance protection for the year.
	10	Paid $5,700 for supplies.

On January 31, it is determined that $3,500 of the service revenue has been earned and that there is $2,800 of supplies on hand.

Instructions

(a) Journalize and post the January transactions. Use T accounts.

(b) Journalize and post the adjusting entries at January 31. Use T accounts.

(c) Determine the ending balance in each of the T accounts.

(d) How would account balances on January 31 be affected if Sugarland records prepayments by debiting an asset when prepaid costs are paid in cash, and crediting a liability when unearned revenues are collected in advance?

(LO 4) E3-5 (Adjusting Entries) Alex Roddick is the new owner of Ace Computer Services. At the end of August 2017, his first month of ownership, Roddick is trying to prepare monthly financial statements. Below is some information related to unrecorded expenses that the business incurred during August.

1. At August 31, Roddick owed his employees $1,900 in wages that will be paid on September 1.

2. At the end of the month, he had not yet received the month's utility bill. Based on past experience, he estimated the bill would be approximately $600.

3. On August 1, Roddick borrowed $30,000 from a local bank on a 15-year mortgage, with the principal being repaid at the end of 15 years. The annual interest rate is 8%.

4. A telephone bill in the amount of $117 covering August charges is unpaid at August 31.

Instructions

Prepare the adjusting journal entries as at August 31, 2017, suggested by the information above.

(LO 4) E3-6 (Adjusting Entries) The ledger of Rainy Day Umbrella Ltd. on March 31 of the current year includes the following selected accounts before quarterly adjusting entries have been prepared:

	Debit	Credit
Prepaid Insurance	$ 3,600	
Supplies	2,800	
Equipment	25,000	
FV-OCI Investments	150,000	
Accumulated Depreciation—Equipment		$ 8,400
Notes Payable		20,000
Unearned Rent Revenue		9,300
Rent Revenue		60,000
Interest Expense	–0–	
Salaries and Wages Expense	14,000	

An analysis of the accounts shows the following:

(350 × 3)

1. The equipment depreciation is $350 per month.   DR Deprec. Expense $1050 , CR accum-deprec.-equipment $1050

2. One half of the unearned rent was earned during the quarter. DR unearned rev $4650 , CR rev $4650

3. Interest of $300 has accrued on the notes payable.   DR Interest expense $300 ; CR Interest payable. $300

4. Supplies on hand total $950.   DR Supplies expense $1850 ; CR Supplies $1850

5. Insurance expires at the rate of $300 per month. DR Insurance expense $900 ; CR Prepaid expense $900

6. The FV-OCI Investments were purchased for $150,000 on March 1. No investments were purchased or sold after that date. The fair value on March 31 was $170,000. DR FV-OCI Investments $20,000; CR Unrealized Gain-OCI $20,000

(handwritten margin, left side: 7 / 2800 / 950 / 1850)

Instructions

(a) Prepare the adjusting entries at March 31, assuming that adjusting entries are made quarterly. Additional accounts are Unrealized Gain or Loss-OCI; Depreciation Expense; Insurance Expense; Interest Payable; and Supplies Expense.

(b) If the notes payable have been outstanding since January 1 of the current year, what is the annual interest rate on the note payable?   3 months → $\frac{20,000 \times X}{4} = 300$ → $\frac{(300 \times 4)}{20,000} = 6\%$

(LO 4) E3-7 (Adjusting Entries) The trial balance for Hanna Resort Limited on August 31 is as follows:

HANNA RESORT LIMITED
Trial Balance
August 31, 2017

	Debit	Credit
Cash	$ 6,700	
Prepaid insurance	3,500	
Supplies	1,800	
Land	20,000	
Buildings	142,000	
Accumulated depreciation—buildings		$ 20,448
Equipment	16,000	
Accumulated depreciation—equipment		4,320
Accounts payable		4,800
Unearned rent revenue		4,600
Notes payable		77,000
Common shares		81,000
Retained earnings		4,680
Dividends	5,000	
Rent revenue		68,002
Salaries and wages expense	43,200	
Insurance expense	12,250	
Interest expense	3,080	
Utilities expense	7,720	
Repairs and maintenance expense	3,600	
	$264,850	$264,850

Additional information:

1. The balance in Prepaid Insurance includes the cost of an insurance policy that will expire on September 30, 2017.

2. An inventory count on August 31 shows $650 of supplies on hand.

3. Buildings and equipment are depreciated straight-line. From the date of purchase, the buildings have an estimated useful life of 25 years, and the equipment has an estimated useful life of 10 years. For both asset categories, residual value is estimated to be 10% of cost.

4. (i) Rent revenue includes amounts received for September rentals in the amount of $8,000. (ii) Of the unadjusted Unearned Rent Revenue of $4,600, one half was earned prior to August 31.

5. Salaries of $375 were unpaid at August 31.

6. Rental fees of $800 were due from tenants at August 31.

7. The note payable interest rate is 8% per year, and the note has been outstanding since December 1, 2016. No principal repayments are due.

Instructions

(a) Journalize the adjusting entries on August 31 for the three-month period June 1 to August 31.

(b) Prepare an adjusted trial balance as at August 31.

(LO 4) E3-8 (Adjusting and Reversing Entries) On December 31, adjusting information for Big & Rich Corporation is as follows:

1. Estimated depreciation on equipment is $3,400.

2. Property taxes amounting to $2,525 have been incurred but are unrecorded and unpaid.

3. Employee wages that have been earned by employees but are unpaid and unrecorded amount to $3,900.

4. The Service Revenue account includes amounts that have been paid by customers for services that have not yet been completed. The amount has been determined to be $5,500.

5. Interest of $200 on a $25,000 note payable has not been recorded or paid.

Instructions

(a) Prepare the adjusting entries.

(b) Prepare the reversing entries, where appropriate.

(LO 4, 6) E3-9 (Closing and Reversing Entries) On December 31, the adjusted trial balance of Domino Inc. shows the following selected data:

Accounts receivable	$ 9,700	Service revenue	$110,000
Interest expense	12,800	Interest payable	6,400

Analysis shows that adjusting entries had been made, and included above, for (1) $9,700 of services performed but not billed, and (2) $6,400 of accrued but unpaid interest.

Instructions

(a) Prepare the closing entries for the temporary accounts at December 31.

(b) Prepare the reversing entries on January 1.

(c) Enter the adjusted trial balance data in the four accounts using T accounts, and post the entries in parts (a) and (b).

(d) Prepare the entries to record (1) collection of the service revenue on January 10, and (2) the $6,400 payment of interest due on January 15.

(e) Post the entries in part (d) to the temporary accounts.

(LO 4, 6) E3-10 (Adjusting and Reversing Entries) A review of the accounts of Tucker and Wu Pan Accountants reflected the following transactions, which may or may not require adjustment for the year ended December 31, 2017.

1. The Prepaid Rent account shows a debit of $7,200 paid October 1, 2017, for a one-year lease that started on that day. The payment was for the last month's rent plus five months' rent starting on October 1, 2017.

2. On November 1, 2017, Services Revenue was credited $2,400 that was paid by a client for audit services to be performed in January.

3. On June 1, 2017, a cheque in the amount of $6,000 was issued for a two-year subscription to a trade publication starting on June 1, 2017. The amount was charged to Operating Expenses.

4. Interest of $1,270 has accrued on notes payable.

Instructions

Prepare (a) the adjusting entry for each item and (b) the reversing entry for each item, where appropriate.

(LO 6) E3-11   (Closing Entries) Selected accounts for Winslow Inc. as at December 31, 2017, are as follows:

Inventory	$ 60,000	Sales Discounts	$ 5,000
FV-NI Investments	22,000	Sales Returns and Allowances	2,000
FV-OCI Investments	11,000	Cost of Goods Sold	222,700
Retained Earnings	45,000	Administrative Expenses	31,000
Dividends	18,000	Income Tax Expense	30,000
Accumulated Other		Investment Income	3,000
Comprehensive Income	17,000	Unrealized Gain or Loss-OCI	
Sales Revenue	390,000	(Note: debit balance)	1,500

Instructions

Prepare closing entries for Winslow Inc. on December 31, 2017.

(LO 6) E3-12   (Find Missing Amounts—Periodic Inventory) Financial information follows for four different companies:

	Pamela's Cosmetics Inc.	Scheibli Grocery Inc.	Berthault Wholesalers Ltd.	Kaiserman Supply Ltd.
Sales Revenue	$98,000	(c)	$144,000	$120,000
Sales Returns and Allowances	(a)	$ 5,000	12,000	9,000
Net Sales Revenue	74,000	101,000	132,000	(g)
Beginning Inventory	21,000	(d)	44,000	24,000
Purchases	63,000	105,000	(e)	90,000
Purchase Returns and Allowances	6,000	10,000	8,000	(h)
Ending Inventory	(b)	48,000	30,000	28,000
Cost of Goods Sold	64,000	72,000	(f)	72,000
Gross Profit	10,000	29,000	18,000	(i)

Instructions

Determine the missing amounts for parts (a) to (i). Show all calculations.

(LO 7) E3-13   (Discounted Cash Flow Models) Hoda Inc. owns 25% of the common shares of Willard Corp. The other 75% are owned by the Willard family. Hoda acquired the shares eight years ago through a financing transaction. Each year, Hoda has received a dividend from Willard. Willard has been in business for 60 years, and continues to have strong operations and cash flows. Hoda must determine the fair value of this investment at its year end. Since there is no market on which the shares are traded, Hoda must use a discounted cash flow model to determine fair value.

FINANCE

Hoda management intends to hold the shares for five more years, at which time they will sell the shares to the Willard family under an existing agreement for $1 million. There is no uncertainty in this amount. Management expects to receive dividends of $80,000 for each of the five years, although there is a 20% chance that dividends could be $50,000 each year. The risk-free rate is 4% and the risk-adjusted rate is 6%.

Instructions

(a) Identify some of the items Hoda will need to consider in determining the fair value of the investment.

(b) Calculate the fair value of the investment in Willard using the traditional approach.

(c) Calculate the fair value of the investment using the expected cash flow approach.

(d) In this case, which discounted cash flow model is the best and why?

(LO 8) E3-14   (Fair Value Principle under IFRS 13) Khalfan Industries would like to determine the fair value of its manufacturing facility in London, Ontario. The facility consists of land, building, and manufacturing equipment.

Instructions

(a) Identify some of the considerations that are involved in a fair value measurement.

(b) Explain the various levels of input in the fair value hierarchy.

(c) Using the fair value hierarchy, discuss the level 1, 2, and 3 types of inputs that Khalfan could use to value each asset as well as its facility altogether.

(LO 8) E3-15   (Fair Value Estimate) Killroy Company owns a trade name that was purchased in an acquisition of McClellan Company. The trade name has a book value of $3.5 million, but according to IFRS, it is assessed for impairment on an annual basis. To perform this impairment test, Killroy must estimate the fair value of the trade name (using IFRS 13). It has developed the following cash flow estimates related to the trade name based on internal information. Each cash flow estimate reflects Killroy's estimate of annual cash flows over the next eight years. The trade name is assumed to have no salvage value after the eight years. (Assume the cash flows occur at the end of each year.)

Cash Flow Estimate	Probability Assessment
$380,000	20%
630,000	50%
750,000	30%

Instructions

(a) What is the estimated fair value of the trade name? Killroy determines that the appropriate discount rate for this estimation is 8%.

(b) Is the estimate developed for part (a) a level 1, level 2 or level 3 fair value estimate? Explain.

(LO 10) *E3-16 (Work Sheet) Selected accounts follow for Kings Inc., as reported in the work sheet at the end of May 2017:

Accounts	Adjusted Trial Balance Dr.	Adjusted Trial Balance Cr.	Income Statement Dr.	Income Statement Cr.	Balance Sheet Dr.	Balance Sheet Cr.
Cash	9,000					
Inventory	80,000					
Accounts payable		26,000				
Sales revenue		480,000				
Sales returns and allowances	10,000					
Sales discounts	5,000					
Cost of goods sold	290,000					
Salaries and wages expense	62,000					
Interest income		12,000				

Instructions

Extend the amounts reported in the adjusted trial balance to the appropriate columns in the work sheet. Do not total individual columns.

(LO 10) *E3-17 (Work Sheet Preparation) The trial balance of Airbourne Travel Inc. on March 31, 2017, is as follows:

AIRBOURNE TRAVEL INC.
Trial Balance
March 31, 2017

	Debit	Credit
Cash	$ 1,800	
Accounts receivable	2,600	
Supplies	600	
Equipment	6,000	
Accumulated depreciation—equipment		$ 400
Accounts payable		1,100
Unearned revenue		500
Common shares		6,400
Retained earnings		600
Sales revenue		2,600
Salaries and wages expense	500	
Miscellaneous expense	100	
	$11,600	$11,600

Additional information:

1. A physical count reveals only $520 of supplies on hand.

2. Equipment is depreciated at a rate of $100 per month.

3. Unearned ticket revenue amounted to $100 on March 31.

4. Accrued salaries are $850.

Instructions

Enter the trial balance on a work sheet and complete the work sheet, assuming that the adjustments relate only to the month of March. (Ignore income taxes.)

(LO 10) *E3-18 (Work Sheet and Statement of Financial Position Presentation) The adjusted trial balance of North Bay Corporation is provided in the following work sheet for the year ended December 31, 2017.

NORTH BAY CORPORATION
Work Sheet (Partial)
For the Year Ended December 31, 2017

Account Titles	Adjusted Trial Balance		Statement of Comprehensive Income		Statement of Financial Position	
	Dr.	Cr.	Dr.	Cr.	Dr.	Cr.
Cash	117,600					
FV-NI investments	42,150					
Accounts receivable	56,720					
Prepaid rent	11,000					
FV-OCI investments	33,990					
Equipment	219,000					
Accumulated depreciation—equipment		81,000				
Accounts payable		54,470				
Interest payable		4,800				
Notes payable		60,000				
Common shares		100,000				
Retained earnings		133,440				
Service revenue		211,190				
Salaries and wages expense	73,090					
Rent expense	66,000					
Depreciation expense	27,000					
Bad debt expense	5,250					
Interest expense	5,100					
Investment income		5,800				
Unrealized gain or loss-OCI		6,200				

Instructions

The note payable is due in four months. Complete the work sheet and prepare a statement of financial position as illustrated in this chapter.

(LO 11) ***E3-19 (Unknown Rate)** LEW Company purchased a machine at a price of $100,000 by signing a note payable, which requires a single payment of $123,210 in two years. Assuming annual compounding of interest, what rate of interest is being paid on the loan?

(LO 11) ***E3-20 (Evaluation of Purchase Options)** Sosa Excavating Inc. is purchasing a bulldozer. The equipment has a price of $100,000. The manufacturer has offered a payment plan that would allow Sosa to make 10 equal annual payments of $16,274.53, with the first payment due one year after the purchase.

Instructions

(a) How much total interest will Sosa pay on this payment plan?

(b) Sosa could borrow $100,000 from its bank to finance the purchase at an annual rate of 9%. Should Sosa borrow from the bank or use the manufacturer's payment plan to pay for the equipment?

(LO 11) ***E3-21 (Analysis of Alternatives)** The Black Knights Inc., a manufacturer of low-sugar, low-sodium, low-cholesterol TV dinners, would like to increase its market share in Western Canada. In order to do so, Black Knights has decided to locate a new factory in Kelowna, BC. Black Knights will either buy or lease a site depending upon which is more advantageous. The site location committee has narrowed down the available sites to the following three buildings.

Building A: Purchase for a cash price of $600,000, useful life 25 years.

FINANCE Building B: Lease for 25 years with annual lease payments of $69,000 being made at the beginning of the year.

Building C: Purchase for $650,000 cash. This building is larger than needed; however, the excess space can be sublet for 25 years at a net annual rental of $7,000. Rental payments will be received at the end of each year. The Black Knights Inc. has no aversion to being a landlord.

Instructions

In which building would you recommend that The Black Knights Inc. locate, assuming a 12% cost of funds?

(LO 11) ***E3-22 (Calculation of Bond Liability)** Viavélo Inc. manufactures cycling equipment. Recently, the company's vice-president of operations has requested construction of a new plant to meet the increasing demand for the company's bikes. After a careful evaluation of the request, the board of directors has decided to raise funds for the new plant by issuing $2 million of 11% term corporate bonds on March 1, 2017, due on March 1, 2031, with interest payable each March 1 and September 1. At the time of issuance, the market interest rate for similar financial instruments is 10%.

[handwritten notes: lower so sell @ premium]

[handwritten: $n = 30$ (15 yrs × 2)]

[handwritten: $i = \frac{10\%}{2} = 5\%$ (market)]

[handwritten: use contractual rate for int. pymts]

[handwritten: PV = 2,153,724.51]

[handwritten: FV = -2,000,000]

[handwritten: PMT = -110,000 (int. pymts → 2,000,000 × 5.5%)]

[handwritten annotations at top:]
or using PV tables: lump   2,000,000 × 0.23138 = 462,760   ← n=30, i=5%.
annuity   110,000 × 15.37245 = 1,690,970
    ↓   ← n=30
    2,000,000 × 5.5%   i=5% $ 2,153,730

Instructions

As Viavélo's controller, determine the selling price of the bonds.

(LO 11) ***E3-23**   **(Calculation of Amount of Rentals)** Your client, Danyleyko Leasing Company, is preparing a contract to lease a machine to Souvenirs Corporation for a period of 25 years. Danyleyko has an investment cost of $365,755 in the machine, which has a useful life of 25 years and no salvage value at the end of that time. Your client is interested in earning an 11% return on its investment and has agreed to accept 25 equal rental payments at the end of each of the next 25 years.

Instructions

You are requested to provide Danyleyko with the amount of each of the 25 rental payments that will yield an 11% return on investment.

(LO 7, 11) ***E3-24**   **(Expected Cash Flows)**

Instructions

For each of the following, determine the expected cash flows.

	Cash Flow Estimate	Probability Assessment
(a)	$4,800	20%
	6,300	50%
	7,500	30%
(b)	5,400	30%
	7,200	50%
	8,400	20%
(c)	(1,000)	10%
	3,000	80%
	5,000	10%

(LO 7, 11) ***E3-25**   **(Expected Cash Flows and Present Value)** Keith Nobrega is trying to determine the amount to set aside so that he will have enough money on hand in two years to overhaul the engine on his vintage used car. While there is some uncertainty about the cost of engine overhauls in two years, by conducting some research on-line, Keith has developed the following estimates.

Engine Overhaul Estimated Cash Outflow	Probability Assessment
$200	10%
450	30%
600	50%
750	10%

Instructions

How much should Keith deposit today in an account earning 6%, compounded annually, so that he will have enough money on hand in two years to pay for the overhaul?

Problems

P3-1   Transactions follow for Emily Cain, D.D.S., for the month of September:

Sept. 1   Cain begins practice as a dentist and invests $32,000 of her own cash.
2   Purchases dental equipment on account from Dig Deep Drill Limited for $12,500.
4   Pays rent for office space, $1,300 in total for the months of September and October (that is, $650 per month).
4   Employs a receptionist, Wanda Micelli.
5   Purchases dental supplies for cash, $900.
8   Receives cash of $1,960 from patients for services performed and $1,600 for referrals to specialists.
10   Pays miscellaneous expenses, $680.
14   Bills patients $4,740 for services performed.
18   Pays Dig Deep Drill Limited on account, $6,300.
19   Withdraws $2,000 cash from the business for personal use.
20   Receives $2,100 from patients on account.
25   Bills patients $2,780 for services performed.
30   Pays the following expenses in cash: salaries and wages, $1,400; and miscellaneous expense, $85.
30   Dental supplies used during September amount to $330.

Instructions

(a) Enter the transactions in appropriate T accounts, using the following account titles: Cash; Accounts Receivable; Prepaid Rent; Supplies; Equipment; Accumulated Depreciation—Equipment; Accounts Payable; Owner's Drawings; Service Revenue; Rent Expense; Miscellaneous Expense; Salaries and Wages Expense; Supplies Expense; Depreciation Expense; Income Summary; and Owner's Capital. Allow 10 lines for the Cash and Income Summary accounts, and five lines for each of the other accounts that are needed. Record depreciation on the equipment using the straight-line method, with a five-year useful life, and no residual value.

(b) Prepare an adjusted trial balance.

(c) Prepare an income statement, balance sheet, and statement of owner's equity.

(d) Prepare a post-closing trial balance at September 30.

P3-2   Mason Advertising Agency Inc. was founded in January 2013. Presented below are adjusted and unadjusted trial balances as at December 31, 2017.

MASON ADVERTISING AGENCY INC.
TRIAL BALANCE
DECEMBER 31, 2017

	Unadjusted		Adjusted	
	Dr.	Cr.	Dr.	Cr.
Cash	$ 11,000		$ 11,000	
Accounts receivable	20,000		23,500	
Supplies	8,400		3,000	
Prepaid insurance	3,350		2,500	
Equipment	60,000		60,000	
Accumulated depreciation—equipment		$ 28,000		$ 33,000
Accounts payable		5,000		5,000
Interest payable		–0–		150
Notes payable		5,000		5,000
Unearned revenue		7,000		5,600
Salaries and wages payable		–0–		1,300
Common shares		10,000		10,000
Retained earnings		3,500		3,500
Service revenue		58,600		63,500
Salaries and wages expense	10,000		11,300	
Insurance expense			850	
Interest expense	350		500	
Depreciation expense			5,000	
Supplies expense			5,400	
Rent expense	4,000		4,000	
	$117,100	$117,100	$127,050	$127,050

Instructions

(a) Journalize the annual adjusting entries that were made. (Omit explanations.)

(b) Prepare an income statement and a statement of retained earnings for the year ending December 31, 2017, and an unclassified balance sheet at December 31.

(c) Answer the following questions.

1. If the note has been outstanding three months, what is the annual interest rate on that note?

2. If the company paid $12,500 in salaries and wages in 2017, what was the balance in Salaries and Wages Payable on December 31, 2016?

P3-3   A review of the ledger of Rolling Resort Inc. at December 31 produces the following data for the preparation of annual adjusting entries:

1. Salaries and Wages Payable, $0. There are eight salaried employees. Five employees receive a salary of $1,200 each per week, and three employees earn $800 each per week. Employees do not work weekends. All employees worked two days after the last pay period and before December 31.

2. Unearned Rent Revenue, $415,200. The company began subleasing condos in its new building on November 1. Each tenant has to make a $5,000 security deposit that is not refundable until occupancy is ended. At December 31, the company had the following rental contracts that were paid in full for the entire term of the lease:

Date	Term (in months)	Monthly Rent	Number of Leases
Nov. 1	6	$ 4,100	5
Dec. 1	6	$10,300	4

3. Prepaid Advertising, $16,200. This balance consists of payments on two advertising contracts. The contracts provide for monthly advertising in two trade magazines. The terms of the contracts are as follows:

Contract	Date	Amount	Number of Magazine Issues
A650	May 1	$7,200	12
B974	Oct. 1	9,000	24

The first advertisement runs in the month in which the contract is signed.

4. Notes Payable, $80,000. This balance consists of a one year, 9%, note that is dated June 1.

DIGGING DEEPER

Instructions

(a) Prepare the adjusting entries at December 31. (Show all calculations.)

(b) Rolling Resort is preparing for a meeting with potential investors. What is the net effect of the adjusting entries on net income? Explain why Rolling Resort's potential investors should be willing to wait for Rolling Resort to complete its year-end adjustment process before deciding whether or not to invest in the company.

P3-4 Second-Hand Almost New Department Store Inc. is located near a shopping mall. At the end of the company's fiscal year on December 31, 2017, the following accounts appeared in two of its trial balances:

	Unadjusted	Adjusted
Accounts payable	$ 79,300	$ 79,300
Accounts receivable	95,300	95,300
Accumulated depreciation—building	42,100	52,500
Accumulated depreciation—equipment	29,600	42,900
Buildings	190,000	190,000
Cash	68,000	68,000
Common shares	160,000	160,000
Cost of goods sold	412,700	412,700
Depreciation expense	–0–	23,700
Dividends	28,000	28,000
Equipment	110,000	110,000
Insurance expense	–0–	7,200
Interest expense	3,000	11,000
Interest income	4,000	4,000
Interest payable	–0–	8,000
Inventory	75,000	75,000
Mortgage payable	80,000	80,000
Prepaid insurance	9,600	2,400
Property tax expense	–0–	4,800
Property tax payable	–0–	4,800
Retained earnings	16,600	16,600
Salaries and wages expense	108,000	108,000
Sales commission expense	11,000	14,500
Sales commission payable	–0–	3,500
Sales returns and allowances	8,000	8,000
Sales revenue	718,000	718,000
Utilities expense	11,000	11,000

Analysis reveals the following additional information:

1. Insurance expense and utilities expense are 60% selling and 40% administrative.

2. In the next year, $20,000 of the mortgage payable will be due for payment.

3. Property tax expense and depreciation on the building are administrative expenses; depreciation on the equipment is a selling expense; and $32,000 of the salaries and wages expense related to office salaries and the remainder related to sales salaries. Depreciation expense includes $10,400 relating to the building and $13,300 relating to equipment.

Instructions

(a) Prepare a multiple-step income statement, statement of retained earnings, and classified balance sheet. (*Hint:* Use Illustrations 3A-2 to 3A-4 as models or look ahead to Chapter 4 to see what a multiple-step income statement is.)

(b) Journalize the adjusting entries that were made.

(c) Journalize the closing entries that are necessary.

P3-5 The following accounts appeared in the December 31 trial balance of the Majestic Theatre:

	Debit	Credit
Equipment	$960,000	
Accumulated depreciation—equipment		$120,000
Notes payable		186,000
Sales revenue		750,000
Advertising expense	62,000	
Salaries and wages expense	80,000	
Interest expense	9,000	

Instructions

(a) From the account balances above and the information that follows, prepare the annual adjusting entries necessary on December 31:

1. The equipment has an estimated life of 16 years and a residual value of $40,000. (Use the straight-line method.)

2. The note payable is a 90-day note given to the bank on October 20 and bearing interest at 10%.

3. In December, 2,000 coupon admission books were sold at $25 each. They can be used for admission any time after January 1.

4. Of the Advertising Expense balance, $1,100 is paid in advance.

5. Salaries accrued but unpaid are $11,800.

(b) What amounts should be shown for each of the following on the income statement for the year?

1. Interest expense

2. Sales revenue

3. Advertising expense

4. Salaries and wages expense

P3-6 The trial balance and other information for consulting engineers Mustang Rovers Consulting Limited follow:

MUSTANG ROVERS CONSULTING LIMITED
Trial Balance
December 31, 2017

	Debit	Credit
Cash	$ 83,700	
Accounts receivable	81,100	
Allowance for doubtful accounts		$ 750
Supplies	1,960	
Equipment	85,000	
Accumulated depreciation—equipment		6,250
Notes payable		7,200
Common shares		35,010
Retained earnings		161,100
Service revenue		100,000
Rent expense	9,750	
Salaries and wages expense	28,500	
Insurance expense	18,500	
Utilities expense	1,080	
Miscellaneous expense	720	
	$310,310	$310,310

Additional information:

1. Service revenue includes fees received in advance from clients of $6,900.

2. Services performed for clients that were not recorded by December 31 were $7,300.

3. Bad debt expense for the year is $6,300.

4. Insurance expense includes a premium paid on December 31 in the amount of $6,000 for the period starting on January 1, 2018.

5. Equipment is depreciated on a straight-line basis over 10 years. Residual value is $15,000.

6. Mustang gave the bank a 90-day, 12% note for $7,200 on December 1, 2017.

7. Rent is $750 per month. The rent for 2017 and for January 2018 has been paid.

8. Salaries and wages earned but unpaid at December 31, 2017 are $2,598.

9. Dividends of $80,000 were declared for payment on February 1, 2018.

Instructions

(a) From the trial balance and other information given, prepare annual adjusting entries as at December 31, 2017.

(b) Prepare an adjusted trial balance for Mustang Rovers as at December 31, 2017.

(c) Prepare an income statement for 2017, a balance sheet as at December 31, 2017, and a statement of retained earnings for 2017.

(d) Explain how the financial statement in part (c) would change if Mustang Rovers operated as a sole proprietorship, rather than operating with a corporate ownership structure.

P3-7 The following information relates to Joachim Anderson, Realtor, at the close of the fiscal year ending December 31:

1. Joachim paid the local newspaper $335 for an advertisement to be run in January of the next year, and charged it to Advertising Expense.

2. On November 1, Joachim signed a three-month, 10% note to borrow $15,000 from Yorkville Bank.

3. The following salaries and wages are due and unpaid at December 31: sales, $1,420; office clerks, $1,060.

4. Interest of $500 has accrued to date on a note that Joachim holds from Grant Muldaur.

5. The estimated loss on bad debts for the period is $1,560.

6. Stamps and stationery are charged to the Office Expense account when purchased; $110 of these supplies remain on hand.

7. Joachim has not yet paid the December rent of $1,000 on the building his business uses.

8. Insurance was paid on November 1 for one year and charged to Prepaid Insurance, $1,170.

9. Property tax accrued, $1,670.

10. On December 1, Joachim accepted Alana Zipursky's two-month, 15% note in settlement of her $6,000 account receivable.

11. On October 31, Joachim received $2,580 from Tareq Giza in payment of six months' rent for Giza's office space in the building and credited Unearned Rent Revenue.

12. On September 1, Joachim paid six months' rent in advance on a warehouse, $8,300, and debited the asset account Prepaid Rent.

13. The bill from Light & Power Limited for December has been received but not yet entered or paid, $510.

14. The estimated depreciation on equipment is $1,400.

Instructions

Prepare annual adjusting entries as at December 31.

P3-8 The trial balance follows of the Masters Golf Club, Inc. as at December 31. The books are closed annually on December 31.

MASTERS GOLF CLUB, INC.
Trial Balance
December 31

	Debit	Credit
Cash	$ 115,000	
Accounts receivable	63,000	
Allowance for doubtful accounts		$ 9,000
Land	350,000	
Buildings	600,000	
Accumulated depreciation—buildings		40,000
Equipment	300,000	

	Debit	Credit
Accumulated depreciation—equipment		120,000
Prepaid insurance	12,000	
Common shares		880,000
Retained earnings		152,000
Sales revenue		413,000
Rent revenue		44,000
Utilities expense	74,000	
Salaries and wages expense	90,000	
Repairs and maintenance expense	54,000	
	$1,658,000	$1,658,000

Instructions

(a) Enter the balances in ledger accounts. Allow five lines for each account.

(b) From the trial balance and the information that follows, prepare annual adjusting entries and post to the ledger accounts:

1. The buildings have an estimated life of 30 years with no residual value. (The company uses the straight-line method.)

2. The equipment is depreciated at 10% of its year-end carrying value per year.

3. Insurance expired during the year was $5,300.

4. The rental revenue is the amount received for 11 months for dining facilities. The December rent of $4,000 has not yet been received. A Rent Receivable account is used.

5. It is estimated that 24% of the accounts receivable will be uncollectible.

6. Salaries and wages earned but not paid by December 31 amounted to $3,600.

7. Sales revenue included dues paid in advance by members and totalled $9,900.

(c) Prepare an adjusted trial balance.

(d) Prepare closing entries and post to the ledger.

P3-9   The unadjusted trial balance of Clancy Inc. at December 31, 2017, is as follows:

	Debit	Credit
Cash	$ 17,740	
Accounts receivable	103,000	
Allowance for doubtful accounts		$ 3,500
Inventory	60,000	
Prepaid insurance	4,620	
Bond investment at amortized cost	40,000	
Land	30,000	
Buildings	154,000	
Accumulated depreciation—buildings		12,400
Equipment	33,600	
Accumulated depreciation—equipment		5,600
Goodwill	16,600	
Accounts payable		101,050
Bonds payable (20-year, 7%)		180,000
Common shares		121,000
Retained earnings		21,360
Sales revenue		200,000
Rent revenue		10,800
Advertising expense	22,500	
Supplies expense	10,800	
Purchases	98,000	
Purchase discounts		900
Salaries and wages expense	53,500	
Interest expense	12,250	
	$656,610	$656,610

Additional information:

1. Actual advertising costs amounted to $1,500 per month. The company has already paid for advertisements in *Montezuma Magazine* for the first quarter of 2018.

2. The building was purchased and occupied on January 1, 2015, with an estimated useful life of 20 years, and residual value of $30,000. (The company uses straight-line depreciation.)

3. Prepaid insurance contains the premium costs of several policies, including Policy A, cost of $2,640, one-year term, taken out on April 1, 2017; and Policy B, cost of $1,980, three-year term, taken out on September 1, 2017.

4. A portion of Clancy's building has been converted into a snack bar that has been rented to the Ono Food Corp. since July 1, 2016, at a rate of $7,200 per year payable each July 1 in advance.

5. One of the company's customers declared bankruptcy on December 30, 2017. It is now certain that the $2,700 the customer owes will never be collected. This fact has not been recorded. In addition, Clancy estimates that 4% of the Accounts Receivable balance on December 31, 2017, will become uncollectible.

6. An advance of $600 to a salesperson on December 31, 2017, was charged to Salaries and Wages Expense.

7. On November 1, 2015, Clancy issued 180 $1,000 bonds at par value. Interest is paid semi-annually on April 30 and October 31.

8. The equipment was purchased on January 1, 2015, with an estimated useful life of 12 years, and no residual value. (The company uses straight-line depreciation.)

9. On August 1, 2017, Clancy purchased at par value 40 $1,000, 9% bonds maturing on July 31, 2019. Interest is paid on July 31 and January 31.

10. The inventory on hand at December 31, 2017, was $90,000 after a physical inventory count.

Instructions

(a) Prepare adjusting and correcting entries for December 31, 2017, using the information given. Record the adjusting entry for inventory using a Cost of Goods Sold account.

(b) Indicate which of the adjusting entries could be reversed.

P3-10 The unadjusted trial balance of Imagine Ltd. at December 31, 2017 is as follows:

	Debit	Credit
Cash	$ 10,850	
Accounts receivable	56,500	
Allowance for doubtful accounts		$ 750
FV-NI investments	8,600	
Inventory	58,000	
Prepaid insurance	2,940	
Prepaid rent	13,200	
FV-OCI investments	14,000	
Bond investment at amortized cost	18,000	
Land	10,000	
Equipment	104,000	
Accumulated depreciation		18,000
Accounts payable		9,310
Bonds payable		50,000
Common shares		100,000
Retained earnings		103,260
Sales revenue		223,310
Rent revenue		10,200
Purchases	170,000	
Purchase discounts		2,400
Freight-out	9,000	
Freight-in	3,500	
Salaries and wages expense	31,000	
Interest expense	6,750	
Miscellaneous expense	890	
	$517,230	$517,230

Additional information:

1. On November 1, 2017, Imagine received $10,200 rent from its lessee for a 12-month lease beginning on that date. This was credited to Rent Revenue.

2. Imagine estimates that 7% of the Accounts Receivable balances on December 31, 2017, will be uncollectible. On December 28, 2017, the bookkeeper incorrectly credited Sales Revenue for a receipt of $1,000 on account. This error had not yet been corrected on December 31.

3. After a physical count, inventory on hand at December 31, 2017, was $77,000.

4. Prepaid insurance contains the premium costs of two policies: Policy A, cost of $1,320, two-year term, taken out on April 1, 2017; Policy B, cost of $1,620, three-year term, taken out on September 1, 2017.

5. The regular rate of depreciation is 10% of cost per year. Acquisitions and retirements during a year are depreciated at half this rate. There were no retirements during the year. On December 31, 2016, the balance of Equipment was $90,000.

6. On April 1, 2017, Imagine issued at par value 50 $1,000, 11% bonds maturing on April 1, 2020. Interest is paid on April 1 and October 1.

7. On August 1, 2017, Imagine purchased at par value 18 $1,000, 12% Legume Inc. bonds, maturing on July 31, 2019. Interest is paid on July 31 and January 31.

8. On May 30, 2017, Imagine rented a warehouse for $1,100 per month and debited Prepaid Rent for an advance payment of $13,200.

9. Imagine's FV-NI investments consist of shares with total market value of $9,400 as at December 31, 2017.

10. The FV-OCI investment is an investment of 500 shares in Yop Inc., with current market value of $25 per share as at December 31, 2017.

Instructions

(a) Prepare the year-end adjusting and correcting entries for December 31, 2017, using the information given. Record the adjusting entry for inventory using a Cost of Goods Sold account.

(b) Indicate which of the adjusting entries could be reversed.

P3-11   Mona Kamaka, CPA, was retained by Downtown TV Repair Ltd. to prepare financial statements for the month of March 2017. Mona accumulated all the ledger balances from the business records and found the following:

DOWNTOWN TV REPAIR LTD.
Trial Balance
March 31, 2017

	Debit	Credit
Cash	$ 7,200	
Accounts receivable	3,500	
Supplies	900	
Equipment	15,000	
Accumulated depreciation—equipment		$ 3,000
Accounts payable		5,950
Salaries and wages payable		600
Unearned revenue		1,500
Common shares		10,000
Retained earnings		4,160
Service revenue		8,000
Salaries and wages expense	3,600	
Advertising expense	800	
Utilities expense	310	
Depreciation expense	700	
Repairs and maintenance expense	1,200	
	$33,210	$33,210

Mona reviewed the records and found the following errors:

1. Cash received from a customer on account was recorded as $570 instead of $750.

2. The purchase, on account, of equipment that cost $900 was recorded as a debit to Supplies and a credit to Accounts Payable for $900.

3. A payment of $30 for advertising expense was entered as a debit to Utilities Expense, $30, and a credit to Cash, $30.

4. The first salary payment this month was for $1,800, which included $600 of salaries and wages payable on February 28. The payment was recorded as a debit to Salaries and Wages Expense of $1,800 and a credit to Cash of $1,800. The business does not use reversing entries.

5. A cash payment for Repairs and Maintenance Expense on equipment for $90 was recorded as a debit to Equipment, $90, and a credit to Cash, $90.

Instructions

(a) Prepare an analysis of each error that shows (1) the incorrect entry, (2) the correct entry, and (3) the correcting entry.

(b) Prepare a corrected trial balance.

P3-12 Samuels Corp. began operations on January 1, 2017. Its fiscal year end is December 31. Samuels has decided that prepaid costs are debited to an asset account when paid, and all revenues are credited to revenue when the cash is received. During 2017, the following transactions occurred.

1. On January 1, 2017, Samuels bought office supplies for $4,100 cash. A physical count at December 31, 2017 revealed $1,900 of supplies still on hand.

2. Samuels bought a $6,000, one-year insurance policy for cash on August 1, 2017. The policy came into effect on this date.

3. On November 15, 2017, Samuels received a $1,200 advance cash payment from a client for services to be provided in the future. As at December 31, 2017, one third of these services had not been performed.

4. On December 1, 2017, Samuels rented out excess office space for a six-month period starting on this date, and received a $1,100 cheque for the first and last month's rent.

Instructions

DIGGING DEEPER

(a) For each of the above transactions, prepare the journal entry for the original transaction and any adjusting entry required at December 31, 2017.

(b) In a business where accounting is performed at several divisions or office locations, is it possible that prepayments would be treated as assets in some offices and as expenses in others when initially recorded? Why or why not? Does the business have to have a consistent approach in all of its offices? Why or why not?

P3-13 James Halabi is a financial executive with McDowell Enterprises. Although James has not had any formal training in finance or accounting, he has a "good sense" for numbers and has helped the company grow from a very small company ($500,000 sales) to a large operation ($45 million in sales). With the business growing steadily, however, the company needs to make a number of difficult financial decisions in which James Halabi feels a little "over his head." He therefore has decided to hire a new employee with "numbers" expertise to help him. As a basis for determining whom to employ, he has decided to ask each prospective employee to prepare answers to questions relating to situations he has encountered recently.

Instructions

Answer James's following questions.

FINANCE

(a) In 2016, McDowell Enterprises negotiated and closed a long-term lease contract for newly constructed truck terminals and freight storage facilities. On January 1, 2017, McDowell took possession of the leased property. The 20-year lease is effective for the period January 1, 2017, through December 31, 2036. Advance rental payments of $800,000 are payable to the lessor (owner of facilities) on January 1 of each of the first 10 years of the lease term. Advance payments of $400,000 are due on January 1 for each of the last 10 years of the lease term. McDowell has an option to purchase all the leased facilities for $1 on December 31, 2036. At the time the lease was negotiated, the fair value of the truck terminals and freight storage facilities was approximately $7.2 million. If the company had borrowed the money to purchase the facilities, it would have had to pay 10% interest. Should the company have purchased rather than leased the facilities?

(b) Last year the company exchanged a piece of land for a non–interest-bearing note. The note is to be paid at the rate of $15,000 per year for nine years, beginning one year from the date of disposal of the land. An appropriate rate of interest for the note was 11%. At the time the land was originally purchased, it cost $90,000. What is the fair value of the note under IFRS 13?

(c) The company has always followed the policy to take any cash discounts on goods purchased. Recently, the company purchased a large amount of raw materials at a price of $800,000 with terms 1/10, n/30 on which it took the discount. McDowell has recently estimated its cost of funds at 10%. Should McDowell continue this policy of always taking the cash discount?

*P3-14 Below are the completed financial statement columns of the work sheet for Canned Heat Limited:

CANNED HEAT LIMITED
Work Sheet
For the Year Ended December 31, 2017

Account No.	Account Titles	Statement of Comprehensive Income		Statement of Financial Position	
		Dr.	Cr.	Dr.	Cr.
101	Cash			18,000	
112	Accounts receivable			42,000	
130	Prepaid insurance			1,800	
140	FV-OCI investments			25,500	
157	Equipment			98,000	
167	Accumulated depreciation—equipment				28,600
201	Accounts payable				31,600
212	Salaries and wages payable				7,200
301	Common shares				80,000
306	Retained earnings				60,000
400	Service revenue		142,000		
622	Repairs and maintenance expense	13,200			
711	Depreciation expense	38,800			
722	Insurance expense	8,800			
726	Salaries and wages expense	106,600			
732	Utilities expense	3,500			
801	Unrealized gain or loss-OCI		6,800		
	Totals	170,900	148,800	185,300	207,400
	Net loss and OCI		22,100	22,100	
		170,900	170,900	207,400	207,400

Instructions

(a) Prepare a statement of comprehensive income, statement of changes in equity, and statement of financial position. During 2017, Canned Heat's shareholders invested $24,000 in exchange for common shares. Accumulated other comprehensive income had a balance of $0 on January 1, 2017.

(b) Prepare closing entries for the year ended December 31, 2017, and a post-closing trial balance.

(c) Briefly discuss how the financial statement in part (a) would change if Canned Heat followed ASPE rather than IFRS.

(d) Assume that Canned Heat operates as a partnership. What additional changes, beyond those discussed in part (c), would affect the financial statement prepared in part (a)?

*P3-15 The trial balance of Slum Dog Fashion Centre Inc. contained the following accounts at November 30, the company's fiscal year end:

SLUM DOG FASHION CENTRE INC.
Trial Balance
November 30, 2017

	Debit	Credit
Cash	$ 29,200	
Accounts receivable	82,000	
Inventory	105,000	
Supplies	8,600	
Equipment	225,000	
Accumulated depreciation—equipment		$ 86,000
Trucks	128,000	
Accumulated depreciation—trucks		39,000
Notes payable		85,000
Accounts payable		78,500
Common shares		300,000
Retained earnings		38,000
Sales revenue		950,200
Sales returns and allowances	24,200	
Cost of goods sold	611,500	

Salaries and wages expense	150,000	
Advertising expense	46,400	
Utilities expense	24,000	
Repairs and maintenance expense	32,100	
Delivery expense	46,700	
Rent expense	64,000	
	$1,576,700	$1,576,700

Adjustment data:

1. Store supplies on hand totalled $3,100.

2. Depreciation is $40,000 on the store equipment and $30,000 on the delivery trucks.

3. Interest of $9,000 is accrued on notes payable at November 30.

Additional information:

1. Salaries and wages expense is 60% selling and 40% administrative.

2. Rent expense and utilities expense are 90% selling and 10% administrative.

3. Of the notes payable, $35,000 is due for payment next year.

4. Repairs and maintenance expense is 100% administrative.

5. The income tax rate for the company is 20%. No taxes have been accrued or paid during the year.

Instructions

(a) Enter the trial balance on a work sheet and complete the work sheet.

(b) Prepare a multiple-step income statement, and statement of retained earnings for the year, and a classified balance sheet as at November 30, 2017. (*Hint*: Look ahead to Chapter 4 to see what a multiple-step income statement is.)

FINANCE

P3-16   Dunn Inc. owns and operates a number of hardware stores in the Atlantic region. Recently, the company has decided to open another store in a rapidly growing area of Nova Scotia. The company is trying to decide whether to purchase or lease the building and related facilities.

Purchase: The company can purchase the site, construct the building, and purchase all store fixtures. The cost would be $1,850,000. An immediate down payment of $400,000 is required, and the remaining $1,450,000 would be paid off over five years with payments of $350,000 per year (including interest payments made at the end of the year). The property is expected to have a useful life of 12 years, and then it will be sold for $500,000. As the owner of the property, the company will have the following out-of-pocket expenses each period.

Property taxes (to be paid at the end of each year)	$40,000
Insurance (to be paid at the beginning of each year)	27,000
Other (primarily maintenance, which occurs at the end of each year)	16,000
	$83,000

Lease: First National Bank has agreed to purchase the site, construct the building, and install the appropriate fixtures for Dunn Inc. if Dunn will lease the completed facility for 12 years. The annual cost for the lease would be $270,000. Dunn would have no responsibility related to the facility over the 12 years. The terms of the lease are that Dunn would be required to make 12 annual payments. (The first payment is to be made at the time the store opens and then one each following year.) In addition, a deposit of $100,000 is required when the store is opened. This deposit will be returned at the end of the twelfth year, assuming there is no unusual damage to the building structure or fixtures.

Instructions

Which of the two approaches should Dunn Inc. follow? (Currently, the cost of funds for Dunn Inc. is 10%.)

RESEARCH AND ANALYSIS

REAL WORLD EMPHASIS

RA3-1 Brookfield Asset Management Inc.

The financial statements of **Brookfield Asset Management Inc.** are presented at the end of the book. Complete the following instructions by referring to these financial statements and the accompanying notes.

Instructions

(a) What were the company's total assets at the end of the two periods that are presented?

(b) How much cash (and cash equivalents) did the company have at December 31, 2014?

(c) What were the company's revenues for the current and preceding year?

(d) By what percentage did 2014 revenues change over those of 2013? Did net income change at the same rate? Explain.

(e) Using the financial statements and related notes, identify at least three different types of adjusting entries Brookfield would have made in preparing its financial statements for the year ended December 31, 2014.

(f) Identify all the items causing changes in retained earnings, including amounts, for the company's year ended December 31, 2014.

(g) Briefly summarize what management's responsibilities are for the financial statements and for the systems of internal control that produce the financial information. How do you know they have actually carried out their responsibilities?

RA3-2 Financial Statement Dates

Companies normally issue their annual financial statements within weeks of year end.

Instructions

(a) Identify the top five Canadian companies (by revenue) in the following industries. (*Hint*: Review the stock listings in a newspaper's financial pages to help find the largest companies.)

1. Banking

2. Insurance

3. Real estate

4. Gas and electrical utilities

(b) For each company, identify its year-end date and the date that the financial statements were finalized (look at the auditor's report). Go to SEDAR to find the statements.

(c) What is the likely reason that the banks have a different year end than the other companies?

(d) How many days does it take for the companies to produce the statements after their fiscal year ends? Look at the average time period for each industry. Within each industry, how close are the issue dates among companies? Comment on your findings.

(e) The ethical accountant has just finalized her company's financial statements, which indicate that net income will be less than analysts' expectations by several cents per share. The CEO has suggested that the company delay releasing its financial statements by a week because he is about to cash some stock options, and does not want any bad news to affect share price. Discuss.

Ethics

RA3-3 Enterprise Resource Planning (ERP)

ERP software systems include bookkeeping systems as well as systems to monitor and manage human resource functions, quality control functions, and many other aspects of business. The software runs off a centralized database that services all company departments and functions.

Instructions

Research and write a one- to two-page summary that gives details about what ERPs are and why they have gained so much attention. Why do companies find them so useful? What are the pros and cons of these systems? (*Hint*: Search "enterprise resource planning" on the Internet.)

RA3-4 Extensible Business Reporting Language

Extensible business reporting language (XBRL) has been under development and promotion for many years. Because of its potential for effective and efficient analysis of financial and other reports, XBRL has received support from many jurisdictions around the world, including in Britain, the Netherlands, Australia, and the United States.

Instructions

Prepare a one- to two-page report on how the XBRL system works. What are the system's benefits, and what are its limitations? Provide an update as to what extent its use is now required, specifically in the United States. Compare this with the Canadian situation. Use sources such as the international XBRL site (www.xbrl.org) and the Canadian site (www.XBRL.ca).

ENDNOTES

1. Most companies use accounting software systems instead of manual systems. The software allows the data to be entered into a database and various reports can then be generated, such as journals, trial balances, ledgers, and financial statements.

2. Accumulated Other Comprehensive Income (AOCI) would also be part of the expanded basic equation if the company had Fair Value-OCI Investments (or other items affecting Other Comprehensive Income and Accumulated Other Comprehensive Income). If the AOCI balance represented accumulated gains, it would be added in the equation, similar to retained earnings. If AOCI represented accumulated losses, it would be subtracted.

3. The transition to electronic bookkeeping systems and databases has dramatically changed the way bookkeeping is carried out. Much of the terminology and visual layout of the reports has been retained, however.

4. Other, less common adjustments, such as revaluation of property, plant, and equipment at the end of an accounting period, are discussed in later chapters.

5. Fair Value-OCI investments are not permitted under ASPE. All fair value investments would typically be treated as FV-NI Investments under ASPE. See Chapter 9 for a full discussion of accounting for investments.

6. Accumulated Other Comprehensive Income is a statement of financial position (SFP) account that is the total of all past charges and credits to OCI to the SFP date. It is similar to the Retained Earnings account.

7. Corporations are incorporated under a government act such as the Canada Business Corporations Act. The main reason for incorporation is to limit the liability for the owners if the corporation gets sued or goes bankrupt. When companies are incorporated, shares are issued to owners and the company becomes a separate legal entity (that is, it is distinct from its owners).

8. These techniques are discussed in IFRS 13.62 and the related appendix to IFRS 13 in the context of fair value measurements. IFRS 13 mentions a third approach that may be used to measure fair value: the cost approach. We will discuss the cost approach later in this chapter.

9. The rate of interest on Government of Canada bonds is published and freely available. It may be used in present value calculations as the risk-free rate.

10. These two approaches are discussed in IFRS 13 Appendix B in the context of fair value measurement and also in ASPE 3063 Appendix A in the context of impairment.

11. Although, as we shall see in subsequent chapters, in some cases, such as in non–arm's-length transactions, interest is not always charged or paid.

12. Business mathematics and business finance textbooks traditionally state simple interest as I (interest) $= P$ (principal) $\times R$ (rate) $\times T$ (time).

REPORTING FINANCIAL PERFORMANCE

**REFERENCE TO THE
CPA COMPETENCY MAP** **LEARNING OBJECTIVES**

After studying this chapter, you should be able to:

1.1.2, 1.2.1, 1.2.2, 1.2.3, 1.4.2, 1.4.4, 1.4.5, 2.3.1, 2.3.2, 2.3.3, 4.3.5, 5.1.1, 5.5.1	**1.** Understand how firms create value and manage performance.
1.1.1, 1.2.1, 1.2.2	**2.** Understand how users use information about performance to make decisions.
1.2.1, 1.2.2, 5.1.1	**3.** Understand the concept of and be able to assess the quality of earnings/information.
1.2.1, 1.2.2	**4.** Understand the differing perspectives on how to measure income.
1.2.1, 1.2.2, 1.3.1, 1.4.1	**5.** Measure and report results of discontinued operations.
1.2.1, 1.2.2, 1.3.1, 1.3.2	**6.** Measure income and prepare the income statement and the statement of comprehensive income using various formats.
1.2.1, 1.2.2, 1.3.1, 1.3.2	**7.** Prepare the statement of retained earnings and the statement of changes in equity.
1.2.1, 1.2.2, 1.3.2, 1.4.2, 1.4.4, 1.4.5, 5.4.2	**8.** Understand how disclosures and analysis help users of financial statements assess performance.
1.1.4	**9.** Identify differences in accounting between IFRS and ASPE and potential changes.

After studying Appendix 4A, you should be able to:

1.2.1, 1.2.2	**10.** Explain the differences between the cash basis of accounting and the accrual basis of accounting.

MAKING MONEY OUT OF THIN AIR

HOW CAN A business make money in the accommodations industry without actually owning any rooms? Airbnb does just that, by charging homeowners a fee to rent out lodging booked on its website. Since the site launched in 2008, Airbnb has had more than 1.2 million listings offering travellers a chance to stay in everything from an old railway car to a castle, in more than 34,000 cities in over 190 countries. This makes Airbnb the largest accommodations provider on the planet and a leader in the "sharing economy" that includes sites like the Uber car-sharing service.

The company, founded by two roommates who rented out their San Francisco living room floor to strangers to help pay their rent, charges homeowners between 6% and 12% of the amount of money that the listers get from their guests. It's free for homeowners to list their properties, and free for travellers to book directly with the homeowners. Spaces listed on Airbnb can cost as little as one-sixth the price of a hotel room in the same locations.

AFP Photo/Martin Bureau

Airbnb incurs considerable costs in running its website, including using professional photographers to snap pictures of the prime listings. It also spends large amounts on marketing, legal fees (the business model sometimes runs afoul of local zoning, tax, and other laws), and a 24/7 customer service hotline. Airbnb also now offers homeowners insurance in case some guests cause damage, which the company says happens extremely rarely. While it's a privately held company, Airbnb has raised more than U.S. $794 million in several rounds of venture capital fundraising.

To get venture capital funding, Airbnb would have had to show potential investors its financial statements and convince them that its business model of making money without any physical substance would work. It could have pointed to a high-growth year such as 2010, when its weekly revenue doubled every week. By 2013, it had more than $250 million in revenue. Without owning any properties, except for office space in various countries,

Airbnb's tangible asset line on its balance sheet would likely be fairly small.

Even without making its financial statements publicly available, Airbnb has shown the business world that it can create lasting value. Among other accolades, it was named the 2014 Company of the Year by the prestigious *Inc.* magazine. *Forbes* magazine said Airbnb was valued at U.S. $10 billion in 2014 by private equity sources when it underwent that round of venture capital funding.

Sources: Burt Helm, "Airbnb Is Inc.'s 2014 Company of the Year," *Inc.* magazine, November 25, 2014; Austin Carr, "Inside Airbnb's Grand Hotel Plans," *Fast Company*, March 17, 2014; Alex Konrad and Ryan Mac, "Airbnb Cofounders to Become First Sharing Economy Billionaires as Company Nears $10 Billion Valuation," *Forbes*, March 20, 2014; Airbnb corporate website, www.airbnb.com.

PREVIEW OF CHAPTER 4

The way items are reported in the statement of income/comprehensive income can affect how useful the statement is to users. Although the net income number (the bottom line) is a key focal point for many users, the other elements in the income statement have significant information value as well. This chapter examines the many different types of revenues, expenses, gains, and losses that are represented in the income statement and related information.

The chapter is organized as follows:

REPORTING FINANCIAL PERFORMANCE					
Performance	**The Statement of Income and the Statement of Comprehensive Income**	**The Statement of Retained Earnings and the Statement of Changes in Equity**	**Disclosure and Analysis**	**IFRS/ASPE Comparison**	**Appendix 4A— Cash Basis versus Accrual Basis Earnings**
▪ Business models and industries ▪ Communicating information about performance ▪ Quality of earnings/information	▪ Measurement ▪ Discontinued operations ▪ Presentation	▪ Presentation of the statement of retained earnings ▪ Presentation of the statement of changes in equity	▪ Disclosures ▪ Analysis ▪ Non-GAAP measures ▪ Other key measures	▪ A comparison of IFRS and ASPE ▪ Looking ahead	▪ Differences between cash and accrual bases ▪ Conversion from cash basis to accrual basis ▪ Theoretical weaknesses of the cash basis

PERFORMANCE

The **income statement**, also called the **statement of income/earnings** or **statement of comprehensive income**, is the report that measures the success of a company's operations for a specific time period. It is a key statement.

All income statements are not the same, however. This is partly due to underlying differences in business models and/or industries, and partly because of how this information is communicated. We will look at business models and industries first.

Business Models and Industries

Objective 1
Understand how firms create value and manage performance.

The basic **business model** consists of getting cash, investing it in resources, and then using these resources to generate profits. This model can be broken down into three distinct types of activities:

1. **Financing:** Obtaining cash funding, often by borrowing, issuing shares, or (in established companies) retaining profits. Financing activities also involve the repayment of debt and/or repurchase of shares.

2. **Investing:** Using the funding to buy assets and invest in people. Investing activities also include divestitures.

3. **Operating:** Using the assets to earn profits.

In performing these three types of activities, companies are exposed to different levels of **risk** and are given different **opportunities**. Some industries are riskier than others. Take, for instance, a small corner pizzeria, owned by a chef who makes fresh pizzas and sells them to the local neighbourhood, versus a big multinational chemical company that transports and sells chemicals. The biggest business risks the pizzeria has may be that the pizza ingredients are not fresh or that there are not sufficient cash flows. The multinational company faces many risks, including the risk of lawsuits due to pollution, the risk of fraud given the fact that many employees work for the company, the risk of workplace accidents, and many others.

FINANCIAL RISK MANAGEMENT
5.5.1
STRATEGY DEVLOPMENT
2.3.1, 2.3.2, 2.3.3

Managing risks takes money. There is an area of study devoted to this called **risk management**. It involves identifying risks, deciding if and how to manage risks, and monitoring risks. Companies can use various techniques to manage risks, such as educating their employees, buying insurance, and installing safety equipment. This all costs money, however. So the riskier the business, the more decisions need to be made about how to manage the risks, keeping in mind that the decisions made will affect profits. The market demands a greater return when there is greater risk. This is referred to as the **risk/return trade-off**.[1]

On the opportunities side, some industries have greater opportunities. Consider the potential for companies where there are emerging markets or technologies. Companies must make decisions about which opportunities to take and when. Value creation is central in any business model. It refers to the act of finding an optimal balance between managing risks and taking the right opportunities such that the firm's net assets and potential are maximized. Well-run companies develop strategies that will allow them to react to the best opportunities in order to maximize shareholder value and maintain risks at an acceptable level.

Illustration 4-1 presents an overview of the business model.

Different industries have different business models, and within industries different companies have different business models. Consider the two statements of income in Illustration 4-2. Partial statements have been presented to illustrate the differing business models. **Walmart Stores Inc.** is in the retail business. It buys large quantities of inventory in bulk wholesale and then sells them at the retail level through its stores at a markup. That is how it creates value for its investors. **Vermilion Energy Inc.** is in the business of exploration, development, acquisition, and production of crude oil and

UNDERLYING CONCEPT

The concept of representational faithfulness requires the financial statements to reflect the economic reality of running a business, including how it creates and sustains value.

Illustration 4-1

An Overview of the Business Model

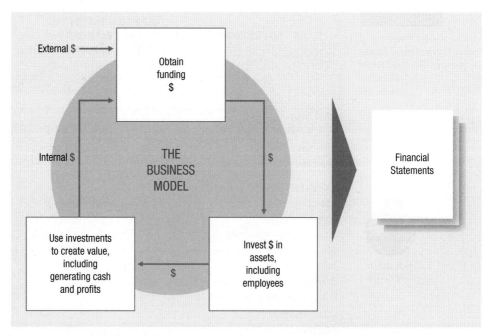

natural gas. Oil and gas that it sells are discovered, usually after spending a significant amount of time, effort, and money to find and develop them. This is how Vermilion creates value for its shareholders.

Illustration 4-2

Consolidated Statements of Income/Comprehensive Income (partial)—Walmart versus Vermilion

REAL WORLD EMPHASIS

WALMART STORES INC.
Consolidated Statements of Income

	For the years ended January 31,		
(Amounts in millions, except per share data)	**2014**	**2013**	**2012**
Revenues:			
Net sales	**$473,076**	$465,604	$443,416
Membership and other income	**3,218**	3,047	3,093
Total revenues	**476,294**	468,651	446,509
Costs and expenses:			
Cost of sales	**358,069**	352,297	334,993
Operating, selling, general and administrative expenses	**91,353**	88,629	85,025
Operating income	**26,872**	27,725	26,491
Interest:			
Debt	**2,072**	1,977	2,034
Capital leases	**263**	272	286
Interest income	**(119)**	(186)	(161)
Interest, net	**2,216**	2,063	2,159
Income from continuing operations before income taxes	**24,656**	25,662	24,332
Provision for income taxes:			
Current	**8,619**	7,976	6,722
Deferred	**(514)**	(18)	1,202
Total provision for income taxes	**8,105**	7,958	7,924
Income from continuing operations	**16,551**	17,704	16,408

(continued)

VERMILION ENERGY INC. CONSOLIDATED STATEMENTS OF NET EARNINGS AND COMPREHENSIVE INCOME (THOUSANDS OF CANADIAN DOLLARS)			
		Year Ended	
	Note	December 31, 2014	December 31, 2013
REVENUE			
Petroleum and natural gas sales		1,419,628	1,273,835
Royalties		(108,000)	(67,936)
Petroleum and natural gas revenue		1,311,628	1,205,899
EXPENSES			
Operating	21	232,307	195,043
Transportation		42,361	28,924
Equity based compensation	11	67,802	60,845
(Gain) loss on derivative instruments	13	(64,083)	1,971
Interest expense		49,655	38,183
General and administration	21	61,727	49,910
Foreign exchange loss (gain)		18,420	(50,162)
Other expense		760	457
Accretion	7	23,913	24,565
Depletion and depreciation	5, 6	425,694	322,386
Impairment (recovery)	5	–	(47,400)
		858,556	624,722
EARNINGS BEFORE INCOME TAXES		453,072	581,177

Because of these different business models and industries, Vermilion's cost structure is different than Walmart's. We can see from the statements for Walmart that 75.7 cents out of every dollar of sales is for cost of goods sold ($358,069/$473,076). Its main cost relates to the inventory that it has sold. For Vermilion, the largest cost is depletion and depreciation, which account for 32.5 cents out of every dollar of net sales ($425,694/$1,311,628). Its main cost relates to the depletion of its wells and natural resource properties.

Now let's look at another retailer, **Macy's, Inc.** The partial statement of income for Macy's (in U.S. $) is shown in Illustration 4-3.

MACY'S INC. Consolidated Statement of Income (millions, except per share)					
	2014	2013	2012	2011	2010
Net sales	$ 28,105	$ 27,931	$ 27,686	$ 26,405	$ 25,003
Cost of sales	(16,863)	(16,725)	(16,538)	(15,738)	(14,824)
Gross margin	11,242	11,206	11,148	10,667	10,179
Selling, general and administrative expenses	(8,355)	(8,440)	(8,482)	(8,281)	(8,260)
Impairments, store closing and other costs and gain on sale of leases	(87)	(88)	(5)	25	(25)
Operating income	2,800	2,678	2,661	2,411	1,894
Interest expense	(395)	(390)	(425)	(447)	(513)
Premium on early retirement of debt	(17)	–	(137)	–	(66)
Interest income	2	2	3	4	5
Income before income taxes	2,390	2,290	2,102	1,968	1,320

Note that, even though Macy's is in the same industry as Walmart, its cost structure is a bit different. Only 60 cents out of every dollar goes toward cost of goods sold ($16,863/$28,105). What is the difference between Macy's and Walmart? The numbers are different primarily because of a different business strategy. Walmart prices its goods

STRATEGY DEVELOPMENT
2.3.1, 2.3.2, 2.3.3
AUDIT AND ASSURANCE
4.3.5

lower to attract more customers and get higher volumes of sales. It follows what is known as a **low-cost/high-volume strategy**. Macy's, on the other hand, is able to attract higher prices because it sells more unique and higher-end products. This is referred to as a **cost differentiation strategy**. The purpose of this discussion is not to teach you everything you need to know about different industries, business models, and strategies. Rather, the goal is to introduce you to these ideas and get you thinking about how the financial statements might best reflect these factors in the interest of transparency. It is important to think about the nature of the industry as well as the business model and strategy when preparing and using financial statements. The statements should tell users about the business.

Note that as an auditor, it is very important to have a good understanding of the business and industry in order to perform the audit (and determine whether the financial statements fairly present the entity's financial position and performance).

Communicating Information about Performance

Objective 2
Understand how users use information about performance to make decisions.

There are several ways in which the income statement helps financial statement users decide where to invest their resources and evaluate how well management is using a company's resources.

For example, investors and creditors can use the information in the income statement to:

1. **Evaluate the enterprise's past performance and profitability.** By examining revenues, expenses, gains, and losses, users can see how the company (and management) performed and compare the company's performance with that of its competitors. (Statement of Financial Position information is also useful in assessing profitability, such as by calculating return on assets. See Appendix 5A.)

2. **Provide a basis for predicting future performance.** Information about business risk and past performance can be used to determine important trends that, if they continue, provide information about future performance. However, success in the past does not necessarily mean the company will have success in the future.

3. **Help assess the risk of not achieving future net cash inflows.** Information on the various components of income—revenues, expenses, gains, and losses—highlights the relationships among them and can be used to assess the risk of not achieving a particular level of cash flows in the future. For example, segregating a company's recurring **operating** income (results from continuing operations) from nonrecurring income sources (discontinued operations) is useful because **operations are usually the primary way to generate revenues and cash**. Thus, results from continuing operations usually have greater significance for predicting future performance than do results from nonrecurring activities.

UNDERLYING CONCEPT

A useful statement of income has both feedback and predictive value, which helps investors, creditors, and other users make decisions about stewardship and resource allocation.

In summary, a well-prepared statement of income/comprehensive income provides feedback and predictive value, which helps stakeholders understand the business.

Quality of Earnings/Information

Objective 3
Understand the concept of and be able to assess the quality of earnings/information.

Not all information is created equal. Some information is high quality and some is poor quality. For instance, information that is complete and unbiased is better than incomplete and biased information. Financial statements can be of a higher or lower quality also. Some statements better represent the underlying business and industry than others and it is important to understand why. Let's look at some of the things that make a statement of income/comprehensive income less useful.

The statement of income/comprehensive income and other key financial statements are presented as a series of point estimates. For instance, in Illustration 4-3, the net sales for Macy's for the year ended in 2014 were presented as U.S. $28,105 million. It is important to understand that, even though the statements show elements such as net sales as point estimates, revenues, expenses, gains, and losses are rarely exact dollar values. Rather, they

UNDERLYING CONCEPT

The conceptual framework, as discussed in Chapter 2, identifies all of the qualitative characteristics of useful information, including relevance, representational faithfulness, comparability, verifiability, timeliness, and understandability.

FINANCIAL ANALYSIS AND PLANNING

5.1.1

ETHICS

represent a range of possible values. This is because the numbers included in financial statements are based on numerous assumptions.

By definition, accrual accounting requires **estimates** of such things as sales and expenses. The income statement includes a mix of **hard** numbers (which are easily measured with a reasonable level of certainty, such as cash sales) and **soft** numbers (which are more difficult to measure, such as provision for bad debt). With soft numbers, there is significant measurement uncertainty.

Specifically, the statement of income/comprehensive income has the following shortcomings:

1. **Items that cannot be measured reliably are not reported in the income statement.** Currently, companies are not allowed to include certain items in the determination of income even though these items arguably affect an entity's performance from one point in time to another. For example, contingent gains cannot be recorded in income, because there is uncertainty about whether the gains will ever be realized. Note that if items are material, in general, they should be disclosed in the notes.

2. **Income numbers are affected by the accounting methods that are used.** For example, one company may choose to depreciate or amortize its plant assets on an accelerated basis; another may choose straight-line amortization. Assuming all other factors are equal, the first company's income will be lower even though the two companies are essentially the same. The result is that we are comparing "apples and oranges." GAAP requires that information about accounting methods be disclosed.

3. **Income measurement involves the use of estimates.** For example, one company may estimate in good faith that an asset's useful life is 20 years while another company uses a 15-year estimate for the same type of asset. Similarly, some companies may make overly optimistic estimates of future warranty returns and bad debt writeoffs, which would result in lower expenses and higher income. As mentioned above, when there is significant measurement uncertainty, the resulting numbers that are captured in the financial statements are sometimes called "soft numbers." GAAP requires that, where there is significant measurement uncertainty, additional disclosures be made. We looked at measurement in Chapters 2 and 3 and this will be a constant focus throughout this textbook.

4. **Financial reporting bias.** Chapter 1 discussed the importance of ethics. Chapter 2 discussed how pressures on financial reporting can lead to financial engineering and fraud. Bias exists and it degrades the quality of the financial statements.

5. **GAAP.** Because the process of standard setting is political, GAAP is not always optimal. For instance, historically, most leases were not recorded on the statement of financial position. Similarly, certain pension surpluses and deficits were excluded as well. Although the standard setters are systematically working their way through the standards to fix issues such as these, care should be taken to look for items that may not be properly represented in the financial statements.

Let's look specifically at the concept of **quality of earnings**. Quality of earnings refers to how solid the earnings numbers are. The concept of quality of earnings is used by analysts and investors to assess how well the reported income reflects the underlying business and future potential. If the quality is assessed as low, then the numbers are discounted. If the quality is assessed as high, then the numbers are accepted as is. Users start with the statement of income/comprehensive income and supplement that information with the other statements, notes to the statements, and other facts that they know about the company (perhaps from company announcements, news reports, or information in the MD&A).

When analyzing the quality of earnings, two aspects are generally considered:

1. **Content**, which includes:
    (a) the **integrity of the information**, including whether it is unbiased and reflects the underlying business fundamentals, and
    (b) the **sustainability of the earnings**.

UNDERLYING CONCEPT

Higher-quality earnings have greater predictive value.

2. **Presentation**, which means the earnings are presented in a clear, concise manner that makes the information easy to use and understandable.

Since quality of earnings analysis is often done to assess future earnings potential, sustainability of income is important. Sustainability of income refers to whether the company is able to continue to generate or sustain these earnings in the future given its current business model, the industry, and the economy. This can be difficult to assess.

Note that well-prepared statements send a signal by attempting to segregate income that is recurring from income that is not. For instance, where a company has sold part of its operations, the income statement segregates earnings from the part of the business that has been sold.

The statements may reflect the nature and source of the income on a historical basis but they cannot and do not make any promises about the future. Even though the underlying business might be accurately and appropriately reflected in GAAP financial statements, the quality of the earnings might be judged to be low because the earnings are felt to be unsustainable.[2]

Higher-quality earnings provide higher-quality information and have a lower likelihood of potential misstatement. They are more representative of the underlying business and economic reality. The shares of companies with higher-quality earnings are valued higher in the capital markets, all other things being equal. Earnings that cannot be replicated and/or appear significantly biased are discounted by the markets.

Illustration 4-4 presents some attributes of high-quality earnings.

Illustration 4-4

Some Attributes of High-Quality Earnings

High-quality earnings have the following characteristics:

1. Content
   - **Unbiased**, as numbers are not manipulated, and **objectively determined**. Consider the need to estimate, the accounting choices, and the use of professional judgement.
   - **Reflect the economic reality** as all transactions and events are appropriately captured.
   - **Reflect primarily the earnings generated from ongoing core business activities** instead of earnings from one-time gains or losses.
   - **Closely correlate with cash flows from operations.** Earnings that convert to cash more quickly provide a better measure of real earnings because there is little or no uncertainty about whether they will be realized.
   - **Based on sound business strategy and business model.** Consider the riskiness of the business, business strategy, industry, and the economic and political environments. Identify the effect of these on earnings stability, volatility, and sustainability. Consider also the cost structure of the company, including fixed versus variable costs. (High fixed costs can make the company riskier in times of falling selling prices.)

2. Presentation
   - **Transparent,** as no attempt is made to disguise or mislead. It reflects the underlying business fundamentals.
   - **Understandable**

ETHICS

THEORY

Earnings management may be defined as the process of **targeting certain earnings levels** (whether current or future) or desired earnings trends and then **working backwards to determine what has to be done to ensure that these targets are met**. This can involve the selection of accounting and other company policies, the use of estimates, and even the execution of transactions. In many cases, earnings management is used to increase income in the current year by reducing income in future years. For example, companies may prematurely recognize sales before they are complete in order to boost earnings. Some companies may enter into transactions only so that the statements look better, and thus incur unnecessary transaction costs.

Earnings management can also be used to decrease current earnings in order to increase future income. Reserves may be established by using aggressive assumptions to estimate items such as sales returns, loan losses, and warranty returns. These reserves can then be reduced in the future to increase income. Earnings management activities have a negative effect on the quality of earnings. As long as there is full disclosure, an efficient market should see through these attempts to mask the underlying economic reality. Unfortunately, companies do not always disclose all important information and markets do not always operate efficiently.

Although many users do not believe that management intentionally misrepresents accounting results, there is concern that much of the information that companies distribute is too promotional and that troubled companies take great pains to present their results in the best light. Preparers of financial statements must strive to present information that is of the highest quality. Users of this information should assess the quality of earnings before making their decisions.

As mentioned at the beginning of the chapter, the main statement that gives information about performance is the statement of income/comprehensive income. The statement of retained earnings and the statement of changes in equity show the accumulated and retained income over time. We will first look at the statement of income/comprehensive income and then the statements of retained earnings and changes in equity.

THE STATEMENT OF INCOME AND THE STATEMENT OF COMPREHENSIVE INCOME

Measurement

Objective 4
Understand the differing perspectives on how to measure income.

UNDERLYING CONCEPT

The conceptual framework provides definitions for the elements revenues, expenses, gains, and losses in Chapter 2.

THEORY

The big question is how do we measure income? Is it **net income** or is it comprehensive income or is it something else, such as operating income? This is very important since many users focus on income and treat it as one of the most important numbers on the income statement, if not the most important. Earnings per share (EPS) numbers are generally based on net income.

Net income represents revenues and gains less expenses and losses from both continuing and discontinued operations. **Comprehensive income** is net income plus/minus other comprehensive income/loss. The concept of **operating income** is not defined by GAAP but is generally seen to be ongoing revenues less expenses. It represents a measure of regular income before any irregular items[3] such as gains/losses, discontinued operations, and other comprehensive income.

The concept of net income has been around for many years and therefore is well understood. ASPE currently uses this view of income.

More recently, the concept of comprehensive income has emerged in GAAP.[4] Essentially, this newer measure of income includes all changes in equity aside from shareholder transactions and is therefore more "comprehensive," as its name suggests. This notion of earnings is sometimes referred to as the **all-inclusive approach** to measuring income. IFRS generally supports this view of income.

Some users support a **current operating performance approach** to income reporting. They argue that the most useful income measures are the ones that reflect only regular and recurring revenue and expense elements; that is, normalized, sustainable earnings. Irregular items do not reflect an enterprise's future earning power since, by definition, they are irregular and atypical or nonrecurring. Operating income supporters believe that including one-time items such as writeoffs and restructuring charges reduces the income measure's basic **predictive value**.

In contrast, others warn that a focus on operating income potentially misses important information about a firm's performance. Any gain or loss that is experienced by the firm, whether it is directly or indirectly related to operations, contributes to the firm's long-term profitability. In other words, a gain or loss has **feedback value**. As a result, some non-operating items can be used to assess the riskiness of future earnings—and therefore they have **predictive value**. Furthermore, determining which items are (regular) **operating** items and which are **irregular** requires judgement and this could lead to differences in the treatment of irregular items and to possible manipulation of income measures.

Other comprehensive income (OCI) is made up of certain specific gains or losses including unrealized gains and losses on certain securities, certain foreign exchange gains or losses, and other gains and losses as defined by IFRS.[5] Some items are "recycled" or reclassified. This means that they are recognized first in OCI and then reclassified later to net income. For instance, under IAS 39 and IFRS 9, gains and losses on certain investments classified as fair value through other comprehensive income (FV-OCI) are first booked to OCI and then booked to net income later, when the investment is impaired or sold. We will examine this in Chapter 9. Some items—such as gains on revaluing property, plant, and equipment under the revaluation method—are not recycled. They are recognized once in OCI. We will revisit this in Chapter 10.

Illustration 4-5 shows some items included in OCI and notes how these are dealt with under ASPE. An asterisk (*) shows which items are recycled.

Illustration 4-5

How OCI Items Are Treated under IFRS and ASPE

Items Defined as OCI under IFRS	ASPE Treatment
Changes in revaluation surplus under the revaluation method for property, plant, and equipment	Revaluation method not allowed.
Gains and losses on remeasurement of defined benefit pension plans	Recognized in net income under the immediate recognition approach.
Gains and losses arising from translating the financial statements of certain foreign operations*	Recognized directly in equity.
Gains and losses on hedging instruments for certain hedges*	Hedging instruments are generally not recognized until maturity, and related gains and losses are generally recognized in net income when the hedged item is recognized in net income.
Gains and losses on remeasuring FV-OCI Investments**	FV-OCI Investment category not applicable. Investments either measured at cost/amortized cost or at FV-NI.
Changes in fair value of certain liabilities measured at fair value through profit or loss relating to the liability's credit risk under IFRS 9	Recognized in net income.

* Subsequently recycled to or reclassified as net income.

** May be recycled or not depending on the type of investment and whether IFRS 9 or IAS 39 is followed. We will examine this in greater detail in Chapter 9.

Other comprehensive income is closed out to a balance sheet account that is often referred to as **Accumulated Other Comprehensive Income**, which acts as a type of retained earnings account. Accumulated Other Comprehensive Income is an equity account on the balance sheet. We will come back to this item later in the chapter.

WHAT DO THE NUMBERS MEAN?

Having these multiple views of income may confuse the marketplace. For instance, should EPS be based on comprehensive income instead of net income? Why does IFRS use the comprehensive income concept but ASPE does not?

Analysts focus on EPS, which is based on net income. It raises the interesting question as to whether the analysts don't understand the concept of comprehensive income or whether they believe that the "real number" is net income. Some argue that OCI represents only unrealized gains and losses and this is why it should be segregated. When looking at the items included in OCI, they generally include unrealized gains and losses. However, there are many unrealized gains and losses that are included in net income. Consider for instance the revaluation of a U.S. dollar receivable or a provision for obsolete inventory. These unrealized gains and losses are booked to net income.

The idea of comprehensive income is a sound one because it takes an all-inclusive view of income, defining it as all changes in equity other than shareholder transactions. As reaffirmed by the current IASB project on the conceptual framework (Chapter 2), it looks as though the concept of OCI is here to stay, at least for a while.

Discontinued Operations

One of the most common types of irregular items relates to **discontinued operations**. Discontinued operations include **components of an enterprise** that have been **disposed of** (by sale, abandonment, or spinoff) or are classified as held for sale where:

1. they represent (or are part of a plan to dispose of) a major line of business or geographical area; or

2. they are a subsidiary acquired for resale.[6]

Discontinued operations are presented separately on the statement of income/comprehensive income and also on the statement of cash flows. They are shown net of tax.

Separate Component

The **component** must have operations, cash flows, and financial elements that are clearly distinguishable from the rest of the enterprise.[7] It must generate its own net cash flows (sometimes referred to as a cash-generating unit) and be operationally distinct. That is, it must operate as a separate unit with its own assets, liabilities, and cash flows.

Some examples of a component include a hotel, an apartment building, a division, a subsidiary, a restaurant, or a geographical area such as the European operations of a company. All of these examples would operate as a separate unit and would have cash flows that are specifically tied to the unit. For instance, a hotel would generate cash inflows from its guests and cash outflows relating to operating costs including things such as payroll and heat, light, and power.

In addition, a component must be a **major** line of business or a geographical area.

What does the word "major" mean and what is a separate line of business? In practice there is no bright-line test for determining whether something is considered to be major or not. It is a matter of judgement. In 2011, **ATS Automation Tooling Systems Inc.** identified itself as operating in two different business segments:

1. The ASG segment produced custom-engineered turnkey automated manufacturing and test systems.
2. The Solar segment was a turnkey solar project developer and manufacturer of photovoltaic products.

These two distinct segments would be considered separate lines of business because the

nature of the products and services produced and sold is different (with the Solar segment focusing on that sector of the industry). Being separate segments likely also meant that the facilities were separate and thus operationally and financially distinct. The Solar segment would be considered to be major because at the time it represented 30% of total assets, 48% of total liabilities, and 34% of revenues. This is a clear case of the operations being sufficiently big in order to be considered to be major. In practice, the threshold is often significantly lower. The determination may be made in terms of whether the presentation as discontinued operations would make a difference to decision-making. In other words, is it material? Materiality was discussed in Chapter 2.

Assets Held for Sale

If the component is not yet disposed of, an additional condition must be met before the transaction can be given a different presentation on the income statement. This condition is that the assets relating to the component must be considered to be **held for sale** by the company. Assets are considered to be held for sale when all of the following criteria are met:

- There is an **authorized plan** to sell.

- The asset is **available for immediate sale** in its current state.

- There is an **active program** to find a buyer.

- Sale is **probable** within one year.

- The asset is **reasonably priced** and actively marketed.

- **Changes** to the plan are **unlikely**.[8]

In summary, for accounting purposes, assets may be considered as held for sale when there is a **formal plan** to dispose of the component. This ensures that only assets or asset groups for which management has a detailed, approved plan for disposal get measured and presented as held for sale.

Note that assets that are held for sale might not (and do not need to) meet the definition of discontinued operations. Where this is the case, these assets, as noted below, would be measured and presented in the same way (similar to discontinued operations) on the statement of financial position, but any related gains or losses on remeasurement would be recorded as part of income from continuing operations on the statement of income/comprehensive income.[9] If the asset does not meet the definition of a discontinued operation, the writedown is treated like any other asset impairment charge on the statement of income/comprehensive income.

Measurement and Presentation

When an asset is held for sale, the asset is **remeasured** to the lower of its carrying value and fair value less its cost to sell.[10] Note that if the value of an asset that has been written down later increases, the gain can be recognized up to the amount of the original loss. Once an asset has been classified as held for sale, no further depreciation is recognized.

Assets and related liabilities that are classified as held for sale are **presented** separately in the balance sheet (if material) and retain their original classification as assets (or liabilities) that are current or noncurrent under ASPE.[11] Under IFRS, assets held for sale are generally classified as current assets (and any related liabilities are shown separately as current liabilities).[12] Assets and liabilities are not offset.

The results of discontinued operations are shown separately on the income statement, net of tax for both the current and prior periods.[13] The entity must show the amount of gain or loss on disposal as well as the earnings or loss from discontinued operations. This can be shown either in the income statement or the notes along with revenues, expenses, and pre-tax profit or loss. Comparative information is required for prior years on the income statement but not on the statement of financial position. In addition to the detail shown on the income statement, note disclosures including a description of the disposal are required. Finally, the net cash flows attributable to operating, investing, and financing activities would be shown separately in the statement of cash flows.

The example that follows illustrates accounting concepts related to discontinued operations.

On November 1, 2017, top management of DeGrootes Corporation approves a detailed plan to discontinue its electronics division (a major line of business) at December 31, 2017. The plan, among other things, identifies steps to find a buyer and includes a timeline for disposition, along with a calculation of the expected gain or loss on disposition. The business is available for sale immediately.

Because top management has approved the disposal and has stated in reasonable detail which assets are to be disposed of and how, a **formal plan** exists. The division is a separate business (being a division) that is therefore operationally distinct, with separate cash flows. Since it is a division, it will also have separate financial information and is thus a **business component**. Separate financial information is critical so that the gain or loss from discontinued operations can be properly **measured**. The company will have no continuing involvement in the electronics division after it is sold.

During the current year, the electronics division lost $300,000 (net of tax). DeGrootes estimates that it can sell the business at a loss of $500,000 (net of tax).

The information would be shown as follows on the current year's annual statement of income/comprehensive income (assuming $20 million of income before discontinued operations).

Income from continuing operations		$20,000,000
Discontinued operations		
Loss from operation of discontinued electronics division (net of tax)	$300,000	
Loss from disposal of electronics division (net of tax)	500,000	800,000
Net income		$19,200,000

The company could also show a single amount on the statement of income/comprehensive income ($800,000) and show the detail in the notes. DeGrootes would stop recording depreciation on the division's assets and, in the following year, would show any operating losses or profits and/or revised gain or loss on disposal as discontinued operations. Estimated future losses would not be included in the loss from operations since they would already be implied (and therefore included) in the fair value estimate of the assets held for sale or sold. The assets of the discontinued operations would be shown separately on the statement of financial position.

Illustration 4-6 shows how **Dominion Diamond Corporation**, a company that mines and markets rough diamonds, presented its discontinued operation in its 2014 statements. The consolidated balance sheets, consolidated statements of income, and consolidated statement of cash flows are supplemented by note 10 and are reproduced in Illustration 4-6. By the end of 2014, the assets had been disposed of and therefore did not show up on the 2014 consolidated balance sheet.

The company must follow IFRS and therefore the held-for-sale assets and liabilities are shown separately as both current assets and current liabilities in the 2013 statement. In addition, the company has chosen to show one line on the income statement and statement of cash flows with a detailed breakdown in note 10.

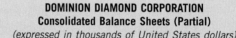

Illustration 4-6

Presentation of a Discontinued Operation—Dominion Diamond Corporation

REAL WORLD EMPHASIS

DOMINION DIAMOND CORPORATION
Consolidated Balance Sheets (Partial)
(expressed in thousands of United States dollars)

	January 31, 2014	January 31, 2013
ASSETS		
Current assets		
Cash and cash equivalents (note 5)	$ 224,778	$ 104,313
Accounts receivable (note 6)	20,879	3,705
Inventory and supplies (note 7)	440,853	115,627
Other current assets (note 8)	27,156	29,486
Assets held for sale (note 10)	–	718,804
	713,666	971,935
Property, plant and equipment (note 11)	1,469,557	727,489
Restricted cash (note 5, 9)	113,612	–
Other non-current assets (note 13)	4,737	6,937
Deferred income tax assets (note 16)	3,078	4,095
Total assets	$2,304,650	$1,710,456
LIABILITIES AND EQUITY		
Current liabilities		
Trade and other payables (note 14)	$ 103,653	$ 39,053
Employee benefit plans (note 15)	3,643	2,634
Income taxes payable (note 16)	33,442	32,977
Current portion of interest-bearing loans and borrowings (note 21)	794	51,508
Liabilities held for sale (note 10)	–	484,252
	141,532	610,424
Interest-bearing loans and borrowings (note 21)	3,504	4,799
Deferred income tax liabilities (note 16)	242,563	181,427
Employee benefit plans (note 15)	14,120	3,499
Provisions (note 17)	430,968	79,055
Total liabilities	832,687	879,204

(continued)

DOMINION DIAMOND CORPORATION
Consolidated Statements of Income
(expressed in thousands of United States dollars, except per share amounts)

	2014	2013
Sales	$ 751,942	$ 345,411
Cost of sales	650,872	267,584
Gross margin	101,070	77,827
Selling, general and administrative expenses	49,425	30,156
Operating profit (note 19)	51,645	47,671
Finance expenses	(27,352)	(9,083)
Exploration costs	(14,550)	(1,801)
Finance and other income	3,153	780
Foreign exchange (loss) gain	(8,879)	493
Profit before income taxes from continuing operations	4,017	38,060
Income tax expense (note 16)	35,505	15,276
Net profit (loss) from continuing operations	(31,488)	22,784
Net profit from discontinued operations (note 10)	502,656	12,434
Net profit	$ 471,168	$ 35,218
Net profit (loss) from continuing operations attributable to		
Shareholders	$ (22,975)	$ 22,276
Non-controlling interest	(8,513)	508
Net profit (loss) attributable to		
Shareholders	$ 479,681	$ 34,710
Non-controlling interest	(8,513)	508
Earnings (loss) per share—continuing operations		
Basic	$ (0.27)	$ 0.26
Diluted	(0.27)	0.26
Earnings per share		
Basic	5.64	0.41
Diluted	5.59	0.41
Weighted average number of shares outstanding (note 20)	85,019,802	84,875,789

The accompanying notes are an integral part of these consolidated financial statements.

DOMINION DIAMOND CORPORATION
Consolidated Statements of Cash Flows
(expressed in thousands of United States dollars)

	2014	2013
Cash provided by (used in)		
Net profit (loss)	$ 471,168	$ 22,784
Depreciation and amortization	140,061	80,266
Deferred income tax recovery	(4,894)	(9,752)
Current income tax expense	40,399	25,028
Finance expenses	27,351	9,083
Stock-based compensation	2,646	2,623
Other non-cash items	11,092	(1,761)
Foreign exchange (gain) loss	10,166	(45)
Loss (gain) on disposition of assets	362	(330)
Change in non-cash operating working capital, excluding taxes and finance expenses	6,320	8,871
Cash provided by (used in) operating activities	704,671	136,767
Interest paid	(6,383)	(5,318)
Income and mining taxes paid	(29,354)	(15,987)
Cash provided by (used in) operating activities— continuing operations	668,934	115,462
Cash provided by (used in) operating activities— discontinued operations	(502,656)	(10,339)
Net cash from (used in) operating activities	166,278	105,123

(continued)

Note 10:
Assets Held for Sale (Discontinued Operations)
On March 26, 2013, the Company completed the sale of the Luxury Brand Segment to Swatch group.

The major classes of assets and liabilities of the discontinued operations were as follows at the date of disposal:

	March 26, 2013
Cash and cash equivalents	$ 25,914
Accounts receivable and other current assets	61,080
Inventory and supplies	403,157
Property, plant and equipment	76,700
Intangible assets, net	126,779
Other non-current assets	7,478
Deferred income tax assets	54,017
Trade and other payables	(96,246)
Income taxes payable	(2,465)
Interest-bearing loans and borrowings	(292,709)
Deferred income tax liabilities	(106,137)
Other long-term liabilities	(13,743)
Net assets	$ 243,825
Consideration received, satisfied in cash	$ 746,738
Cash and cash equivalents disposed of	(25,914)
Net cash inflow	$ 720,824

Results of the discontinued operations are presented separately as net profit from discontinued operations in the consolidated statements of income, and comparative periods have been adjusted accordingly.

	2014	2013
Sales	$ 63,799	$ 435,835
Cost of sales	(31,355)	(208,574)
Other expenses	(30,964)	(212,562)
Other income and foreign exchange gain (loss)	(1,551)	1,888
Net income tax (expense) recovery	(186)	(4,153)
Net profit (loss) from discontinued operations before gain	$ (257)	$ 12,434
Gain on sale	$502,913	$ –
Net profit from discontinued operations	$502,656	$ 12,434
Earnings per share—discontinued operations		
Basic	$ 5.91	$ 0.15
Diluted	5.85	0.15

UNDERLYING CONCEPT

The business model should be transparent. This means that the financial statements should reflect the way that the company earns income and creates shareholder value.

Presentation

There are many different ways to present performance information. Some involve formatting only and some involve signalling information about core ongoing operations versus peripheral or discontinued operations. Income can be further classified by customer, product line, nature, or function, or by operating and non-operating, continuing and discontinued, and regular and irregular categories. Recall that the objective of financial reporting is to communicate information to users about the company and give them the information that they need to make decisions. Items should not be offset except in very limited situations. For example, gains and losses should generally be shown separately and not as a net item.

We have already looked at discontinued operations and other comprehensive income as unique items. Next let's look at items that are reflected in continuing operations on the statement of income/comprehensive income. We will then look at different ways to present the whole statement of income/comprehensive income.

Ordinary versus Peripheral Activities

What is the difference between revenues/expenses and gains/losses? Should they be shown separately? The importance of properly presenting these elements should not be underestimated. For many decision-makers, the parts of a financial statement may be more useful than the whole. From a business perspective, a company must be able to generate positive net cash flows from its normal ongoing core (regular) business activities (revenues minus expenses) in order to survive and prosper.[14] Having income statement elements shown in some detail and in a format that shows the data from prior years allows decision-makers to better assess whether a company does indeed generate cash flows from its normal ongoing core business activities and whether it is getting better or worse at it.

The **distinction** between revenues and gains (and expenses and losses) depends to a great extent on how the enterprise's **ordinary** or **typical business activities** are defined. It is therefore critical to understand an enterprise's typical business activities. For example, when McDonald's sells a hamburger, the selling price is recorded as **revenue**. However, when McDonald's sells a deep fryer machine, any excess of the selling price over the book value would be recorded as a **gain**. This difference in treatment results because the hamburger sale is part of the company's regular operations but the deep fryer sale is not. Only when a manufacturer of deep fryers sells a fryer, therefore, would the sale proceeds be recorded as **revenue**.

Unusual gains and losses are items that by their nature are not typical of everyday business activities or do not occur frequently. They include such items as writedowns of inventories and gains and losses from fluctuations of foreign exchange. However, they are generally presented as part of normal, recurring revenues, expenses, gains, and losses (as part of income from continuing operations). If they are not material in amount, they are combined with other items in the income statement. If they are material, they are disclosed separately. This separate presentation allows for greater transparency because the users are able to see the cause of major gains and losses.

If the same types of gains/losses recur each year, then they are not really unusual and care must be taken to classify them with other gains and losses as normal transactions. Otherwise, it is misleading.

Basic Presentation Requirements

Companies are required to include all elements in the financial statements as long as they are measurable and probable. In addition, the following items are specifically required to be presented separately in the statement of income/comprehensive income. Judgement may be used to determine where additional items are best presented (that is, in the income statement or notes).[15]

Illustration 4-7 shows the basic items that need to be presented in the statements of income/comprehensive income under ASPE and IFRS.

UNDERLYING CONCEPT

Any items that are material and/or relevant to understanding the financial performance should also be presented separately under the full disclosure principle.

Illustration 4-7

Items Required in the Statement of Income/Comprehensive Income under GAAP

ASPE per Section 1520	IFRS per IAS 1
• Revenue	• Revenue
• Income from investments	• Finance costs
• Income tax expense (before discontinued operations)	• Share of profit/loss for investments accounted for using the equity method
• Income or loss before discontinued operations	• Tax expense
• Results of discontinued operations	• Results of discontinued operations
• Net income or loss	• Profit or loss
	• Other comprehensive income classified by nature showing which will be recycled and which will not
	• Share of other comprehensive income of investments accounted for using the equity method
	• Comprehensive income
	• Profit or loss and comprehensive income attributable to non-controlling interest and owners
	• Comprehensive income

Combined Statement of Income/Comprehensive Income

Under IFRS, the statement of comprehensive income is presented either:[16]

1. in a single combined statement including revenues, expenses, gains, losses, net income, other comprehensive income, and comprehensive income; or

2. in two separate statements showing the traditional income statement in one and a second statement beginning with net income and displaying the components of other comprehensive income, as well as comprehensive income.

ALTERNATIVE TERMINOLOGY

Note that a company is not required to use the terms "Other comprehensive income" or "Comprehensive income" under IFRS. Other terminology may be used including identifying the specific items included, for example, revaluation adjustment on property, plant, and equipment.

By providing information on the components of comprehensive income, the company communicates information about all changes in net assets. With this information, users will be better able to understand the quality of the company's earnings. This information should help users predict the amounts, timing, and uncertainty of future cash flows.

A separate statement of comprehensive income is shown for Dominion Diamond Corporation in Illustration 4-8. Note the statement of income was shown in Illustration 4-6 (including discontinued operations). This statement starts off with net profit as presented on the statement of income. Recall from Illustration 4-5 that OCI items must be grouped and presented based on whether they will be recycled (reclassified to net income) or not. Note also that the comprehensive income attributable to shareholders is shown separately from that for non-controlling interests, as required by IFRS. This split was also presented for net profit as shown in Illustration 4-6.

Illustration 4-8

Separate Consolidated Statements of Comprehensive Income— Dominion Diamond Corporation

REAL WORLD EMPHASIS

DOMINION DIAMOND CORPORATION Consolidated Statements of Comprehensive Income (expressed in thousands of United States dollars)		
	2014	**2013**
Net profit	**$471,168**	$35,218
Other comprehensive income		
Items that may be reclassified to profit		
Net loss on translation of net foreign operations (net of tax of nil)	**(12,228)**	(2,883)
Items that will not be reclassified to profit		
Actuarial gain (loss) on employee benefit plans (net of tax of $1.5 million for the year ended January 31, 2014; 2013 – $0.1 million)	**3,424**	(846)
Other comprehensive loss, net of tax	**(8,804)**	(3,729)
Total comprehensive income	**$462,364**	$31,489
Comprehensive income (loss) from continuing operations	**$ (29,686)**	$22,778
Comprehensive income from discontinued operations	**492,050**	8,711
Comprehensive income (loss) attributable to Shareholders	**$470,877**	$30,981
Non-controlling interest	**(8,513)**	508

The accompanying notes are an integral part of these consolidated financial statements.

A combined income statement format is shown in Illustration 4-9 for **TELUS Corporation**, a Canadian company whose shares list on the TSX and NYSE.

Illustration 4-9

Combined Consolidated Statements of Income and Other Comprehensive Income—TELUS Corporation

REAL WORLD EMPHASIS

TELUS Consolidated statements of income and other comprehensive income			
Years ended December 31 (millions except per share amounts)	Note	2014	2013
OPERATING REVENUES			
Service		$11,108	$10,601
Equipment		819	735
Revenues arising from contracts with customers		11,927	11,336
Other operating income	6	75	68
		12,002	11,404
OPERATING EXPENSES			
Goods and services purchased		5,299	4,962
Employee benefits expense	7	2,487	2,424
Depreciation	16	1,423	1,380
Amortization of intangible assets	17(a)	411	423
		9,620	9,189
OPERATING INCOME		2,382	2,215
Financing costs	8	456	447
INCOME BEFORE INCOME TAXES		1,926	1,768
Income taxes	9	501	474
NET INCOME		1,425	1,294
OTHER COMPREHENSIVE INCOME	10		
Items that may subsequently be reclassified to income			
Change in unrealized fair value of derivatives designated as cash flow hedges		1	–
Foreign currency translation adjustment arising from translating financial statements of foreign operations		10	4
Change in unrealized fair value of available-for-sale financial assets		(4)	(13)
		7	(9)
Item never subsequently reclassified to income			
Employee defined benefit plan re-measurements		(445)	998
COMPREHENSIVE INCOME		$ 987	$ 2,283
NET INCOME PER EQUITY SHARE	11		
Basic		$ 2.31	$ 2.02
Diluted		$ 2.31	$ 2.01
TOTAL WEIGHTED AVERAGE EQUITY SHARES OUTSTANDING			
Basic		616	640
Diluted		618	643

The accompanying notes are an integral part of these consolidated financial statements.

By convention, income statements may be presented using one of a number of formats, including what are referred to as the single-step, multiple-step, and condensed formats. These are not GAAP-required formats. Companies choose which format that they think best presents the performance information. In addition, expenses may be grouped in different ways, perhaps emphasizing activities or functions (such as selling, production, research, and development) versus the nature of the expense (payroll, depreciation, and so on). We will discuss these formats next.

Single-Step Income Statements

In reporting revenues, gains, expenses, and losses, a format known as the **single-step income statement** is often used. In the single-step statement, only two main groupings are used: **revenues** and **expenses**. Expenses and losses are deducted from revenues and gains to arrive at net income. The expression "single-step" comes from the single subtraction that is needed to arrive at net income before discontinued operations. Frequently, income tax is reported separately as the last item before net income before discontinued operations to indicate its relationship to income before income tax.

Illustration 4-10 shows the single-step income statement of **DiagnoCure Inc.**, a biotech company. Note that DiagnoCure does not have any other comprehensive income numbers and so net income is equal to comprehensive income.

Illustration 4-10

Single-Step Consolidated Statements of Operations and Comprehensive Loss— DiagnoCure Inc.

REAL WORLD EMPHASIS

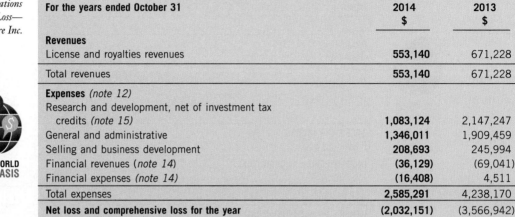

DIAGNOCURE INC. Consolidated Statements of Operations and Comprehensive Loss		
For the years ended October 31	2014 $	2013 $
Revenues		
License and royalties revenues	**553,140**	671,228
Total revenues	**553,140**	671,228
Expenses *(note 12)*		
Research and development, net of investment tax credits *(note 15)*	**1,083,124**	2,147,247
General and administrative	**1,346,011**	1,909,459
Selling and business development	**208,693**	245,994
Financial revenues *(note 14)*	**(36,129)**	(69,041)
Financial expenses *(note 14)*	**(16,408)**	4,511
Total expenses	**2,585,291**	4,238,170
Net loss and comprehensive loss for the year	**(2,032,151)**	(3,566,942)

See accompanying notes to the consolidated financial statements

The single-step form of income statement is widely used in financial reporting in smaller private companies. The **multiple-step** form described below is used almost exclusively by public companies.

The main advantages of the single-step format are that the **presentation is simple** and **no one type of revenue or expense item is implied to have priority over any other**. Potential classification problems are thus eliminated. The main disadvantage of the single-step format is oversimplification and less detail.

Multiple-Step Income Statements

Some users argue that **presenting other important revenue and expense data separately** makes the income statement more informative and more useful. For instance, additional information is communicated if there is separation between the company's operating and non-operating activities such as **other revenues and gains** and **other expenses and losses**. These other categories include interest revenue and expense, gains or losses from sales of miscellaneous items, and dividends received.

A **multiple-step income statement** separates **operating** transactions from **non-operating** transactions and **matches** costs and expenses with related revenues. It also highlights certain intermediate components of income that are used to calculate ratios for assessing the enterprise's performance (that is, gross profit/margin).

To illustrate, **Cameco Corporation's** multiple-step income statement is presented in Illustration 4-11. Note that the prior year's statements have been revised. This is to reflect a discontinued operation that was identified in 2014. In this statement, there are three main subtotals that are presented that deal with operating activities: cost of sales, gross profit, and earnings from operations.

The disclosure of revenue relating to the cost of products and services normally sold is useful because trends in revenue from continuing operations (typical business activities) should be easier to identify, understand, and analyze. Similarly, the reporting of gross profit provides a useful number for evaluating performance and assessing future earnings. A study of the trend in gross profits may show **how successfully a company**

Illustration 4-11

Multiple-Step Consolidated Statements of Earnings—Cameco Corporation

REAL WORLD EMPHASIS

CAMECO CORPORATION Consolidated Statements of Earnings			
			(Revised–note 6)
For the years ended December 31	Note	2014	2013
($Cdn thousands, except per share amounts)			
Revenue from products and services		$2,397,532	$2,438,723
Cost of products and services sold		1,420,768	1,549,238
Depreciation and amortization		338,983	282,756
Cost of sales		1,759,751	1,831,994
Gross profit		637,781	606,729
Administration		176,385	184,976
Impairment charges	10, 12, 13	326,693	70,159
Exploration		46,565	72,833
Research and development		5,044	7,302
Loss on disposal of assets	10	44,762	6,766
Earnings from operations		38,332	264,693
Finance costs	21	(77,122)	(62,121)
Losses on derivatives	28	(121,160)	(61,970)
Finance income		7,402	6,967
Share of loss from equity-accounted investees	13	(17,141)	(14,107)
Other income (expense)	22	50,591	(18,326)
Earnings (loss) before income taxes		(119,098)	115,136
Income tax recovery	23	(175,268)	(117,230)
Net earnings from continuing operations		56,170	232,366
Net earnings from discontinued operation	6	127,243	85,321
Net earnings		**$183,413**	**$317,687**
Net earnings (loss) attributable to:			
Equity holders		$185,234	$318,495
Non-controlling interest		(1,821)	(808)
Net earnings		**$183,413**	**$317,687**
Earnings per common share attributable to equity holders			
Continuing operations		0.15	0.59
Discontinued operation		0.32	0.22
Total basic earnings per share	24	**$0.47**	**$0.81**
Continuing operations		0.15	0.59
Discontinued operation		0.32	0.22
Total diluted earnings per share	24	**$0.47**	**$0.81**

See accompanying notes to consolidated financial statements.

UNDERLYING CONCEPT

This disclosure helps users recognize that incidental or irregular activities are unlikely to continue at the same level (in other words, it enhances predictive value).

uses its resources (prices paid for inventory, costs accumulated, wastage). It may also be a basis for **understanding how profit margins have changed** as a result of competitive pressure (which may limit the prices that the company is able to charge for its products and services). Gross profit percentage is a very important ratio in the retail business, for instance, and is regularly tracked by industry analysts, investors, and competitors.

Disclosing income from operations **highlights the difference between regular and irregular or incidental activities**. Disclosure of operating earnings may help in comparing different companies and assessing their operating efficiencies. Income/losses from discontinued operations are by definition **nonrecurring** and therefore have **little predictive value**. They do, however, give **feedback value** on past decisions made by management. Net income that consists mainly of net income from continuing operations would be viewed as **higher quality**.

When a multiple-step income statement is used, some or all of the following sections or subsections may be presented:

INCOME STATEMENT SECTIONS

1. *Continuing Operations*
  (a) **Operating** Section. A report of the **revenues and expenses** of the company's principal operations.
      i. **Sales or Revenue** Section. A subsection presenting sales, discounts, allowances, returns, and other related information. Its purpose is to arrive at the net amount of sales revenue.
      ii. **Cost of Goods Sold** Section. A subsection that shows the cost of goods that were sold to produce the sales.
      iii. **Selling Expenses.** A subsection that lists expenses resulting from the company's efforts to make sales.
      iv. **Administrative or General Expenses.** A subsection reporting expenses for general administration.
  (b) **Non-Operating** Section. A report of revenues and expenses resulting from the company's secondary or auxiliary activities. In addition, special gains and losses that are infrequent and/or unusual are normally reported in this section. Generally these items break down into two main subsections:
      i. **Other Revenues and Gains.** A list of the revenues earned or gains incurred from non-operating transactions, and generally net of related expenses.
      ii. **Other Expenses and Losses.** A list of the expenses or losses incurred from non-operating transactions, and generally net of any related income.
  (c) **Income Tax.** A short section reporting income taxes on income from continuing operations.
2. *Discontinued Operations*. Material gains or losses resulting from the disposition of a part of the business (net of taxes).
3. *Other Comprehensive Income*. Other gains/losses that are not required by primary sources of GAAP to be included in net income. This section includes all other changes in equity that do not relate to shareholder transactions (net of taxes).

UNDERLYING CONCEPT

This contributes to understandability because it reduces "information overload."

UNDERLYING CONCEPT

This is an example of a trade-off between understandability and full disclosure.

Although the **content** of the operating section is generally the same, the **presentation** or organization of the material does not need to be as described above. Sometimes the expenses are grouped by nature instead of function. This is discussed below.

Usually, financial statements that are provided to external users have **less detail** than internal management reports. The latter tend to have more expense categories, and they are usually grouped along lines of responsibility. This detail allows top management to judge staff performance.

Condensed Financial Statements

In some cases, it is impossible to present all the desired expense detail in a single income statement of convenient size. This problem is solved by including only the totals of expense groups in the statement of income and preparing **supplementary schedules** of expenses to support the totals. With this format, the income statement itself may be reduced to a few lines on a single page. In such instances, readers who want to study all the reported data on operations must give their attention to the supporting schedules.

Illustration 4-12 shows the statement of comprehensive income for **Brick Brewing Company Limited**. Note the high level of aggregation and also the numerous references to notes, which give more detail. An example of a supporting schedule, cross-referenced as Note 10 and detailing finance costs, is shown in Illustration 4-13.

Deciding **how much detail** to include in the income statement is always a problem. On the one hand, a simple, summarized statement allows a reader to quickly discover important factors. On the other hand, disclosure of the results of all activities provides users with detailed relevant information. Earlier, we looked at the basic presentation requirements under GAAP. As long as these requirements are met, there is a significant amount of flexibility in how to present the information.

REAL WORLD EMPHASIS

	Notes	January 31, 2013	January 31, 2012
BRICK BREWING COMPANY LIMITED			
STATEMENTS OF COMPREHENSIVE INCOME			
Years ended January 31, 2013 and 2012			
Net revenue	7	$35,769,967	$34,077,705
Cost of sales	8	26,674,244	26,091,149
Gross profit		9,095,723	7,986,556
Selling, marketing and administration expenses	8	6,971,418	6,078,003
Other expenses	8, 9	397,693	492,142
Finance costs	10	636,579	743,823
Income before tax		1,090,033	672,588
Income tax expense	11	361,000	16,000
Net income		729,033	656,588
Total comprehensive income for the year		$ 729,033	$ 656,588
Basic earnings per share	18	$ 0.03	$ 0.02
Diluted earnings per share	18	$ 0.02	$ 0.02

The accompanying notes are an integral part of these financial statements

Illustration 4-13

Sample Supporting Schedule— Brick Brewing Company Limited

10. FINANCE COSTS

The Company's finance costs consist of the following amounts:

	January 31, 2013	January 31, 2012
Interest on long-term debt and promissory note	$490,384	$547,667
Interest on finance leases	173	757
Interest on bank indebtedness	126,270	98,067
Other interest expense	55,651	8,177
Unwinding of discount on provisions	11,697	10,990
Fair value adjustments on financial instruments	(47,596)	78,165
	$636,579	$743,823

Presentation of Expenses: Nature versus Function

Whether the single-step or multiple-step method is used, consideration should be given to providing additional details about expenses. This helps ensure transparency. IFRS requires an entity to present an analysis of expenses based on either nature or function, as follows:

1. **Nature** refers to the type of expense (such as depreciation, purchases of materials, transport costs, and employee benefits). This method tends to be more straightforward since no allocation of costs is required between functions.

2. **Function** refers to business function or activity. Most businesses are structured around activities. For instance, a manufacturing business will have a production function, a selling function, and a head office function that supports the other two functions. Therefore, a statement that shows expenses by function for the manufacturing business would group costs by production, selling, and administration. These might be presented as cost of sales (production), distribution costs (selling), and administrative costs (administration). This method requires more judgement since costs such as payroll and amortization are allocated between functions. At a minimum, this method requires that cost of sales be presented separately from other costs. This presentation gives more insight into the various phases of operations (such as production and distribution).

Regardless of how the entity classifies the expenses (nature or function), it is encouraged to present the analysis in the statement of income/comprehensive income under IFRS; however, it may be presented elsewhere. Because information about the nature of expense is useful for predicting cash flows, additional information, including amortization, depreciation, and employee benefits expenses, must also be disclosed under IFRS when the income statement presents expenses by function.

Although ASPE does not mandate that companies present according to nature or function, an entity may choose to make such disclosures if it feels that the information is decision relevant.

Which method is better? That depends on the nature of the business and industry. For instance, as noted earlier, it is useful in the retail and manufacturing industries to focus on cost of sales and gross profit. Gross profit margins give important information about pricing and costs. Therefore, manufacturing and retail companies may wish to present costs by function. Similarly, entities that are heavily involved in research and development may wish to present costs by function to highlight this. Since research and development costs may be largely composed of payroll costs, they would otherwise be lumped with payroll or salary expenses if the expenses were presented by nature and not by function. Many public companies use a combination of both approaches or group the majority of expenses by function.

Recall the (condensed) statements of comprehensive income shown for Brick Brewing Company Limited above. Those statements are presented primarily by function. Since the company derives most of its revenues by creating and selling a product, it makes sense to group and present the expenses by these activities. The statement shows cost of sales (production function) and selling, marketing, and administration expenses (selling and head office functions). Additional disclosures are shown in the accompanying notes to the Brick Brewing Company Limited financial statements (as required under IFRS), which show the expenses by nature (Illustration 4-14).

Illustration 4-14

Additional Disclosures Required under IFRS Where Expenses Are Presented Primarily by Function—Brick Brewing Company Limited

REAL WORLD
EMPHASIS

8. EXPENSES BY NATURE

Expenses relating to depreciation, amortization, impairment and personnel expenses are included within the following line items on the statements of comprehensive income:

	January 31, 2013	January 31, 2012
Depreciation and impairment of property, plant and equipment		
Cost of sales	$2,198,224	$2,007,695
Other expenses	334,705	320,612
Amortization and impairment of intangible assets		
Other expenses	37,667	37,667
Salaries, benefits and other personnel-related expenses		
Cost of sales	6,554,347	6,024,301
Selling, marketing and administrative expenses	2,825,251	2,245,850
Other expenses	5,651	89,975

Illustration 4-15 shows the consolidated income statements for **Torstar Corporation.** The company show its expenses mostly by nature. The publishing industry is transitioning from primarily print to on-line business models so this statement reflects this. You can see that the most significant expenses are salaries and benefits as well as other operating costs (presumably including such things as heat, light, and power). The restructuring cost involves payments to employees.

Illustration 4-15

Consolidated Statement of Income—Torstar Corporation; Classified Primarily by Nature

REAL WORLD
EMPHASIS

TORSTAR CORPORATION
Consolidated Statement of Income
(Thousands of Canadian Dollars except per share amounts)

	Year ended December 31	
	2014	2013 Restated*
Operating revenue	$858,134	$935,773
Salaries and benefits	(361,544)	(388,985)
Other operating costs	(404,520)	(438,999)
Amortization and depreciation (notes 9 and 10)	(30,674)	(32,228)
Restructuring and other charges (note 17)	(22,646)	(33,170)
Impairment of assets (note 12)	(82,935)	(77,094)
Operating loss	(44,185)	(34,703)
Interest and financing costs (note 15(c))	(4,253)	(16,060)
Foreign exchange	(7,656)	(1,186)
Loss from joint ventures (note 7)	(9,152)	(3,733)

(continued)

Illustration 4-15

Consolidated Statement of Income—Torstar Corporation; Classified Primarily by Nature (continued)

Income of associated businesses (note 8)	**194**	2,345
Other income (expense) (note 23)	**3,754**	491
	(61,298)	(52,846)
Income and other taxes recovery (expense) (note 14)	**11,700**	(5,200)
Net loss from continuing operations	**(49,598)**	(58,046)
Gain on sale and income from discontinued operations (note 24)	**222,662**	30,633
Net income (loss)	**$173,064**	($27,413)
Attributable to:		
Equity shareholders	**$172,685**	($27,984)
Minority interests	**$379**	$571
Net income (loss) attributable to equity shareholders per Class A (voting) and Class B (non-voting) share (note 20(c)):		
Basic:		
From continuing operations	**($0.62)**	($0.73)
From discontinued operations	**$2.78**	$0.38
	$2.16	($0.35)
Diluted:		
From continuing operations	**($0.62)**	($0.73)
From discontinued operations	**$2.77**	$0.38
	$2.15	($0.35)
Net income (loss)	**$173,064**	($27,413)
Other comprehensive income (loss) that are or may be reclassified subsequently to net income (loss):		
Unrealized foreign currency translation adjustment (no income tax effect)	**(14)**	42
Unrealized foreign currency translation adjustment for associated businesses (no income tax efffect) (note 8)	**125**	24
Net movement on available-for-sale financial assets (no income tax effect)		6
Net movement on cash flow hedges		2,893
Income tax effect		(700)
Realized loss on cash flow hedges transferred to net income	**4,125**	
Income tax effect	**(1,096)**	
Unrealized loss on hedge of net investment (no income tax effect)		(5,496)
Realized loss on hedge of net investment transferred to net income (no income tax effect)	**5,520**	
	8,660	(3,231)
Other comprehensive income (loss) that will not be reclassified to net income (loss) in subsequent periods:		
Actuarial gain (loss) on employee benefits (note 19)	**(83,596)**	166,410
Income tax effect	**21,400**	(42,200)
Actuarial gain (loss) on employee benefits for associated businesses (no income tax effect) (note 8)	**(365)**	1,512
	(62,561)	125,722
Other comprehensive income (loss) from continuing operations, net of tax	**($53,901)**	$122,491
Other comprehensive income (loss) from discontinued operations	**(9,133)**	22,863
Income tax effect	**2,158**	(4,800)
Other comprehensive income (loss) from discontinued operations, net of tax (note 24)	**($6,975)**	$18,063
Total other comprehensive income (loss), net of tax	**($60,876)**	$140,554
Comprehensive income, net of tax	**$112,188**	$113,141
Attributable to:		
Equity shareholders	**$111,809**	$112,570
Minority interests	**$379**	$571

(see accompanying notes)

*The 2013 comparative amounts have been restated to reflect the classification of Harlequin into discontinued operations.

As mentioned earlier, most companies use some sort of combination of the nature and function presentations. While most items on the Torstar statement, for instance, are presented by nature, the restructuring charge could include many things, such as salaries, severance costs, or lease costs.

Intraperiod Tax Allocation

As previously noted, certain irregular items are shown on the income statement net of tax, which is a more informative disclosure to statement users. This procedure of allocating tax balances within a period is called **intraperiod tax allocation**. Intraperiod tax allocation relates the income tax expense or benefit of the fiscal period to the underlying income statement items and events that are being taxed. Intraperiod tax allocation is used for the following items: (1) income from continuing operations, (2) discontinued operations, and (3) other comprehensive income. Companies pay taxes at the federal and provincial level in Canada and rates are dictated by the Canada Revenue Agency.[17]

In applying the concept of intraperiod tax allocation, assume that Schindler Corp. has income before income tax and discontinued operations of $250,000 and a gain from the sale of one of its operations of $100,000. If the income tax rate is assumed to be 25%, the information in Illustration 4-16 is presented on the income statement.

Income before income tax and discontinued operations	$250,000
Income tax	62,500
Income before discontinued operations	187,500
Gain from sale of discontinued operations net of applicable taxes ($25,000)	75,000
Net income	$262,500

The income tax of $62,500 ($250,000 × 25%) that is attributed to income before income tax and discontinued operations is determined from the revenue and expense transactions related to this income. In this income tax calculation, the tax consequences of items excluded from the determination of income before income tax and discontinued operations are not considered. The "gain from sale of discontinued operation" then shows a separate tax effect of $25,000.

IFRS allows a company to present items included as other comprehensive income either net of tax or before tax with one amount shown for taxes related to all items. The amount of tax may be shown on the face of the statement or in the notes.

Earnings per Share

Typically, the results of a company's operations are summed up in one important figure: net income. As if this simplification were not enough, the financial world has widely accepted an even more distilled and compact figure as its most significant business indicator: **earnings per share (EPS)**. Many users focus primarily on the earnings per share number (rightly or wrongly) as a key indicator of the company's performance. While the earnings per share number yields significant information, it does not tell the whole story. This undue emphasis on earnings per share makes it a very sensitive number for companies. Note further that, when comprehensive income is presented, it begs the questions as to why EPS is not based on this more "comprehensive" measurement of income.

The calculation of earnings per share is usually straightforward. The calculation is:

$$\frac{\text{Net income} - \text{preferred dividends} = \text{income available to common shareholders}}{\text{Weighted average number of common shares outstanding}}$$

To illustrate, assume that Lancer Inc. reports net income of $350,000 and declares and pays preferred dividends of $50,000 for the year. The weighted average number of common shares outstanding during the year is 100,000 shares. Earnings per share is $3.00, as calculated in Illustration 4-17.

$$\frac{\text{Net Income} - \text{Preferred Dividends}}{\text{Weighted Average Number of Common Shares Outstanding}} = \text{Earnings per Share (EPS)}$$

$$= \frac{\$350,000 - \$50,000}{100,000}$$

$$= \$3.00$$

Note that the EPS figure measures the number of dollars earned by each common share, not the dollar amount paid to shareholders in the form of dividends.

"Net income per share" or "earnings per share" is a ratio that commonly appears in prospectuses, proxy material, and annual reports to shareholders. It is also highlighted in the financial press, by statistical services like Standard & Poor's, and by Bay Street securities analysts. Because of its importance, public companies are required to disclose earnings per share on the face of their income statement. In addition, a company that reports a discontinued operation must report earnings per share for income before discontinued operations as well as per share amounts for discontinued operations either on the face of the income statement or in the notes to the financial statements.[18] Throughout the chapter, we have included numerous sample income statements that include EPS. Earnings per share information related to comprehensive income is not required.

Many corporations have simple capital structures that include only common shares. For these companies, a presentation such as earnings per common share is appropriate on the income statement. In many instances, however, companies' earnings per share are subject to dilution (reduction) in the future because existing contingencies allow future issues of additional common shares. These corporations would present both basic EPS and fully diluted EPS.[19]

In summary, the simplicity and availability of figures for per share earnings mean that they are used widely. Because of the excessive importance that the public—even the well-informed public—attaches to earnings per share, this information should be made as meaningful as possible. Note that this area is of lesser relevance to private entities because most have shares that are closely held. Therefore, companies following ASPE are not required to include EPS.

THE STATEMENT OF RETAINED EARNINGS AND THE STATEMENT OF CHANGES IN EQUITY

Objective 7
Prepare the statement of retained earnings and the statement of changes in equity.

Net income is closed out to retained earnings at the end of the period. Retained earnings show the company's accumulated earnings (or deficit in the case of losses). Under ASPE, the **statement of retained earnings** shows this accumulated income (or deficit) as well as how much has been paid out as dividends.

Recall that OCI only exists under IFRS and that OCI is closed out to accumulated other comprehensive income (AOCI). Therefore, under IFRS we need an expanded statement that shows the changes in retained earnings and AOCI. Under IFRS, instead of a statement of retained earnings, we use a **statement of changes in equity** and show all changes in all equity accounts including retained earnings and AOCI.

Presentation of the Statement of Retained Earnings

Retained earnings are affected by many variables and can be presented in many different ways. Net income increases retained earnings and a net loss decreases retained earnings. Both cash and share dividends decrease retained earnings. Retroactively applied changes in accounting principles and corrections of errors may either increase or decrease retained earnings. Information on retained earnings, including the changes it has undergone, can be shown in different ways. For example, companies following ASPE usually prepare a separate retained earnings statement, as shown in Illustration 4-18.

Illustration 4-18
Retained Earnings Statement

STATEMENT OF RETAINED EARNINGS For the Year Ended December 31, 2017		
Balance, January 1, as reported		$1,050,000
Correction for understatement of net income in prior period (inventory error) (net of taxes of $12,000)		50,000
Balance, January 1, as adjusted		1,100,000
Add: Net income		360,000
		1,460,000
Less: Cash dividends	$100,000	
Less: Stock dividends	200,000	300,000
Balance, December 31		$1,160,000

The reconciliation of the beginning to the ending balance in retained earnings provides information about why net assets increased or decreased during the year. The association of dividend distributions with net income for the period indicates what management is doing with earnings: it may be putting part or all of the earnings back into the business, distributing all current income, or distributing current income plus the accumulated earnings of prior years. Note that the retained earnings statement may be combined with the income statement by adding it to the bottom of the income statement.

Changes in accounting occur frequently in practice, because important events or conditions may be in dispute or uncertain at the statement date. One type of accounting change occurs when a different accounting principle is adopted to replace the one previously used. **Changes in accounting principle** would include, for example, a change in the method of inventory pricing from FIFO to average cost. Accounting principle changes are allowed only if they are required by a primary source of GAAP or if they result in reliable and more relevant information. Under ASPE, there are some exceptions to this principle. For instance, where ASPE allows a choice of accounting policies such as accounting for income taxes, significant influence investment, or development costs, an accounting policy change may be made without having to prove that the new policy is reliable and more relevant. This is because, in principle, ASPE is meant to be more flexible and adaptable.

Changes in accounting principle are generally recognized through **retrospective restatement**, which involves determining the effect of the policy change on the income of prior periods that are affected. The financial statements for all prior periods that are presented for comparative purposes should be restated except when the effect cannot be determined reasonably. If all comparative years are not disclosed, a cumulative amount would instead be calculated and adjusted through the opening retained earnings amount.

To illustrate, Gaubert Inc. decided in March 2017 to change from the FIFO method of valuing inventory to the weighted average method. If prices are rising, cost of sales would be higher and ending inventory lower for the preceding period.

Illustration 4-19 shows what should be presented in the 2017 financial statements.

UNDERLYING CONCEPT

The retrospective application ensures consistency.

ASPE

Illustration 4-19		
Retained earnings, January 1, 2017, as previously reported		$120,000
Cumulative effect on prior years of retrospective application of new inventory costing method (net of $4,000 tax)		14,000
Adjusted balance of retained earnings, January 1, 2017		$106,000

Presentation of a Change in Accounting Principle

The journal entry would be:

A = L + SE
−14,000   −14,000

Cash flows: No effect

Income Tax Receivable	9,000	
Retained Earnings	14,000	
Inventory		23,000

The example in the illustration assumes that no comparative data for prior years are shown. A note describing the change and its impact would also be required. Another type of change is a change in accounting estimate that is accounted for prospectively with no catch-up adjustment. We will revisit accounting changes in Chapter 21.

Presentation of the Statement of Changes in Equity

IFRS

The statement of changes in equity reports the changes in each shareholders' equity account and in total shareholders' equity during the year, including comprehensive income. The statement of shareholders' equity is often **prepared in columnar form** with columns for each account and for total shareholders' equity. This is a required statement under IFRS.

The following must be presented in the statement:

1. Total comprehensive income (showing amounts attributable to owners and non-controlling interests)

2. For each component of equity: effects of retrospective application

3. For each component of equity: a reconciliation between the carrying amounts at the beginning and end of the period, including profit or loss, OCI, and transactions with owners.

The entity may disclose an analysis of OCI by item either in the statement or in the notes.

A statement of changes in equity for **Cameco Corporation** is shown in Illustration 4-20. Comparative information would also be disclosed although it is not included in the illustration. Note that Cameco has chosen to present the analysis of OCI by item in this statement.

Illustration 4-20

Presentation of Consolidated Statements of Changes in Equity—Cameco Corporation

| | | | | Attributable to equity holders | | | | | |
| **CAMECO CORPORATION** CONSOLIDATED STATEMENTS OF CHANGES IN EQUITY | | | | | | | | | |
($Cdn thousands)	Share capital	Contributed surplus	Retained earnings	Foreign currency translation	Cash flow hedges	Available-for-sale assets	Total	Non-controlling interest	Total equity
Balance at January 1, 2014	$1,854,671	$186,382	$3,314,049	$ (7,165)	$300	$ 28	$5,348,265	$1,129	$5,349,394
Net earnings	–	–	185,234	–	–	–	185,234	(1,821)	183,413
Other comprehensive income	–	–	(7,952)	58,832	(300)	(611)	49,969	58	50,027
Total comprehensive income for the year	–	–	177,282	58,832	(300)	(611)	235,203	(1,763)	233,440
Share-based compensation	–	15,808	–	–	–	–	15,808	–	15,808
Share options exercised	7,975	(5,375)	–	–	–	–	2,600	–	2,600
Dividends	–	–	(158,232)	–	–	–	(158,232)	–	(158,232)
Transactions with owners—contributed equity	–	–	–	–	–	–	–	794	794
Balance at December 31, 2014	$1,862,646	$196,815	$3,333,099	$51,667	$ –	$ (583)	$5,443,644	$ 160	$5,443,804

See accompanying notes to consolidated financial statements.

REAL WORLD EMPHASIS

The shareholders' equity section of the balance sheet of Cameco is shown in Illustration 4-21.

Illustration 4-21

Presentation of Shareholders' Equity in the Consolidated Statements of Financial Position—Cameco Corporation

Shareholders' equity		
Share capital	1,862,646	1,854,671
Contributed surplus	196,815	186,382
Retained earnings	3,333,099	3,314,049
Other components of equity	51,084	(6,837)
Total shareholders' equity attributable to equity holders	5,443,644	5,348,265
Non-controlling interest	160	1,129
Total shareholders' equity	5,443,804	5,349,394
Total liabilities and shareholders' equity	$8,472,667	$8,039,317

Note that the company has chosen to present the account "Accumulated Other Comprehensive Income" as "Other Components of Equity." This is fine since IFRS does not mandate the use of specific headings for these items.

DISCLOSURE AND ANALYSIS

Disclosures

Objective 8
Understand how disclosures and analysis help users of financial statements assess performance.

In addition to disclosures on the face of the financial statements, the notes to the financial statements are a great source of background and explanatory information. The notes supplement the main statements. They should be presented in a systematic manner and cross-referenced to the main financial statements. The notes should include the following:

1. Accounting policies;

2. Sources of estimation uncertainty;

3. Information about the capital of the company (including how the company manages its capital and any changes);

4. Information including dividends, the legal form of the entity, its country of incorporation, description of business name of the parent company, and information required under the full disclosure principle including the basis of preparation where the financial statements were not prepared on a going concern basis.

Analysis

As noted earlier, **financial analysts and investors** assess quality of earnings and factor it into their resource allocation decisions.

Some attributes of high-quality earnings were expressed in Illustration 4-4. To assess the quality of earnings, you must look at the whole set of financial statements, including the notes. In addition, the MD&A provides valuable insights into the nature of the business and industry and what is happening. Newspaper articles and analysts' reports are also good sources of information. When analyzing the health of a company and its quality of earnings, look for and analyze the following:

• **Accounting policies**—aggressive accounting policies, soft numbers

• **Notes to financial statements**—unrecognized liabilities and asset overstatement

• **Measurement uncertainty**—how hard/soft are the numbers? How risky is the business?

• **Financial statements** as a whole—complexity of presentation or language (which may obscure the company's performance or financial position)

• **Income statement**—percentage of net income derived from ongoing operations, to see whether the company can produce profits mainly from its core business

• **Cash flow statement**—cash from operating activities versus net income, to get a sense of whether net income is backed by cash or not

• **Statement of financial position**—to see how the company is financed and what the revenue-generating assets are

• **Other**—environmental factors such as the industry and economy. How is the company doing compared with its competitors? How is it positioning itself to take advantage of opportunities and manage risk? Where is the industry going? Are current earnings likely to be repeated in the future?

Non-GAAP Measures

Companies often try to help users assess the results of operations and their financial position by providing modified GAAP information such as **non-GAAP earnings**. Non-GAAP earnings start with GAAP net income and add back or deduct nonrecurring or non-operating items to arrive at an adjusted net income number. Non-GAAP earnings are not bad as such. If the calculation of the non-GAAP earnings is **clearly disclosed and explained**, and is also reconciled to net income, it hopefully adds value to the decision-making process. The danger with these numbers is that there are no standards to ensure that the calculation is **consistently** prepared and **comparable** between companies.

The OSC has issued a Staff Notice on these disclosures.[20] Its concern is that the additional information presented may mislead people. The OSC has therefore set out certain principles.

The Staff Notice states that, specifically, an issuer should do the following:

1. State explicitly that the non-GAAP financial measure does not have any standardized meaning prescribed by the issuer's GAAP and is therefore unlikely to be comparable to similar measures presented by other issuers.

2. Present, with equal or greater prominence to that of the non-GAAP financial measure, the most directly comparable measure calculated in accordance with the issuer's GAAP and presented in its financial statements.

3. Explain why the non-GAAP financial measure provides useful information to investors and the additional purposes, if any, for which management uses the non-GAAP financial measure.

4. Provide a clear quantitative reconciliation from the non-GAAP financial measure to the most directly comparable measure calculated in accordance with the issuer's GAAP and presented in its financial statements. The issuer should reference the reconciliation when the non-GAAP financial measure first appears in the document, or in the case of content on a website, in a manner that meets this objective (for example, by providing a link to the reconciliation).

5. Explain any changes in the composition of the non-GAAP financial measure when compared with previously disclosed measures.

REAL WORLD EMPHASIS

In staff's view, non-GAAP financial measures generally should not describe adjustments as non-recurring, infrequent, or unusual, when a similar loss or gain is reasonably likely to occur within the next two years or has occurred during the prior two years.

It is interesting to see how the OSC has defined the term "unusual items" in the Staff Notice—that is, if an item is reasonably likely to occur in the next two years, it is recurring.

WHAT DO THE NUMBERS MEAN?

In a review of 50 companies in 2013, the OSC found deficiencies in 86% of the companies' disclosures. According to the report (OSC Staff Notice 52-722), the OSC looked at the following:

- where non-GAAP financial measures or additional GAAP measures were reported,
- calculations of non-GAAP financial measures or additional GAAP measures,

- presentations of non-GAAP financial measures or additional GAAP measures, and
- disclosure of non-GAAP financial measures or additional GAAP measures.

The OSC continues to monitor the use of non-GAAP measures.

Other Key Measures

Chapters 5 (Appendix 5A) and 23 cover financial statement analysis in a bit more detail but it is worthwhile to note a couple of common ratios here that are based on earnings. We have already looked at how to calculate EPS and will come back to this in Chapter 17.

The other key ratio mentioned in Appendix 5A is the price earnings ratio. This is a very common ratio and it (or a variant of the ratio) is often used in the valuation of shares and/or companies. The ratio as presented in Appendix 5A is as follows:

$$\frac{\text{Market price per share}}{\text{EPS}}$$

For instance, if the shares are currently trading at $120 and EPS is $10, the price earnings ratio would be 12. This means that investors are willing to pay $12 for every dollar of earnings.

VALUATION
5.4.2

Conversely, for every dollar earned by the company, if we multiply that dollar by 12 then we should get the share value. When we present the analysis in this way, it is sometimes referred to as an **earnings multiple**. Analysts track and compare earnings multiples between companies and industries. There are many other ways to calculate multiples and they can be based on book values, market values, cash flows, or some variant of income. The above is a very simplistic overview of how earnings multiples are calculated and it is meant only as a very high-level introduction to show how important the EPS number can be when valuing companies. Multiples and price earnings ratios are generally covered in greater detail in finance texts.

IFRS/ASPE COMPARISON

Objective 9
Identify differences in accounting between IFRS and ASPE and potential changes.

A Comparison of IFRS and ASPE

Illustration 4-22 sets out the major differences between GAAP for private entities and international accounting standards for publicly accountable enterprises.

Illustration 4-22

IFRS and ASPE Comparison Chart

	IFRS—IAS 1, 8, and IFRS 5	Accounting Standards for Private Enterprises (ASPE)—*CPA Canada Handbook*, Part II, Sections 1400, 1506, 1520, 1521, 3251, and 3475	References to related illustrations and select brief exercises
Required presentation on face of income statement	As noted earlier in the chapter, IFRS mandates a list of required items that must be presented.	As noted earlier in the chapter, ASPE mandates a list of required items that must be presented.	Illustration 4-7
Guidance on how to classify expenses (nature versus function)	IFRS requires that the entity present an analysis of expenses based on either their nature or function.	There is no guidance on how or when to present expenses according to their nature or function. Entities are free, however, to present their income statements in a manner that is most transparent as long as they adhere to the required disclosures noted above.	Illustrations 4-12, 4-14, and 4-15
Discontinued operations	Held-for-sale assets and liabilities are reclassified as current assets/liabilities.	Held-for-sale assets and liabilities are classified as current or non-current depending on the nature of the assets/liabilities unless the assets have been sold prior to the completion of the financial statements.	Illustration 4-6 BE4-11

(continued)

Other comprehensive income/comprehensive income	Certain items must be classified as either comprehensive income or net income. In addition, entities must prepare a statement of comprehensive income.	Not recognized. Transactions are either booked through net income or directly to a separate component of shareholders' equity (such as certain foreign currency gains/losses).	Illustration 4-5 BE4-8
Earnings per share	Basic and diluted EPS must be presented in the statements.	Not mentioned since many private entities have closely held shareholdings by definition.	Illustrations 4-6, 4-9, 4-11, 4-12, 4-15, and 4-17
Statement of retained earnings versus statement of changes in shareholders' equity	The statement of changes in equity is a required statement.	The statement of retained earnings is one of the core financial statements. There is no requirement to present a statement of changes in shareholders' equity, although changes in shareholders' equity accounts must be disclosed.	Illustrations 4-18, 4-19, and 4-20
Accounting changes	For all accounting policy changes, new policy must be reliable and more relevant.	Certain accounting policy choice changes do not have to meet the "must be reliable and more relevant" test.	

Looking Ahead

The IASB has been working on its performance reporting project since September 2001. In October 2001, the FASB also began to work on a similar project. There was concern that the two projects were diverging in focus, and so, in April 2004, the IASB and FASB decided to work together to come up with a joint, converged standard. In March 2006, the name of the project was changed to financial statement presentation. At the time of printing, that broader project was on hold. The IASB was in discussions on financial performance reporting and was in the research project stage. As mentioned in Chapter 2, the IASB issued an Exposure Draft (ED) on the Conceptual Framework in May 2015. The ED proposes to relabel the statement of comprehensive income as the statement of financial performance.

SUMMARY OF LEARNING OBJECTIVES

1 Understand how firms create value and manage performance.

A business is based on a basic model of obtaining financing, investing in assets, and using those assets to generate profits. Different industries have different business models. Even within an industry, different businesses may have different strategies for generating revenues. Some businesses and industries are riskier than others. Companies must decide how and whether to manage these risks. Managing risks costs money, which reduces profits. Capital markets demand greater returns for riskier businesses.

2 Understand how users use information about performance to make decisions.

Users use information about performance to evaluate past performance and profitability and to provide a basis for predicting future performance. They also use the information to help assess risk and uncertainty regarding future cash flows.

3 Understand the concept of and be able to assess the quality of earnings/information.

The concept of quality of earnings is used by analysts and investors to assess how well the reported income reflects the underlying business and future potential. When assessing quality of earnings, users must consider all information about a company. High-quality earnings have various attributes, as noted in Illustration 4-4. Where the information is biased, this degrades the quality.

4 Understand the differing perspectives on how to measure income.

There are various ways to measure income, including operating income, net income, and comprehensive income. IFRS recognizes the concept of comprehensive income but this is not included under ASPE. Other comprehensive income consists of a set list of items identified under IFRS essentially dealing with certain unrealized gains/losses. Under IFRS, some of these items are recycled (reclassified) to net income and some are not.

5 Measure and report results of discontinued operations.

The gain or loss on disposal of a business component involves the sum of: (1) the income or loss from operations to the financial statement date, and (2) the gain or loss on the disposal of the business component. These items are reported net of tax among the irregular items in the income statement. Related assets are identified on the balance sheet where material. Under IFRS, non-current assets are reclassified to current assets.

6 Measure income and prepare the income statement and the statement of comprehensive income using various formats.

There are many ways to present the income statement and the statement of comprehensive income. GAAP lays out certain minimum requirements, but beyond that, a company has some leeway to present the information as it wishes. The goal is to ensure that the statements present information about performance in a transparent manner, including presenting items such that the users can see which are ordinary versus peripheral activities.

IFRS allows the statement of comprehensive income to be presented in a combined statement or two separate statements.

By convention, companies use what is known as a single-step method or a multiple-step method (or a variation of the two).

IFRS requires entities to provide information about either the nature or function of expenses. When information is presented using function, additional disclosures should be made regarding the breakdown of the nature of expenses as the latter has good cash flow predictive value. The entity should choose the method that best reflects the nature of the business and industry.

7 Prepare the statement of retained earnings and the statement of changes in equity.

The retained earnings statement should disclose net income (loss), dividends, prior period adjustments, and transfers to and from retained earnings (appropriations). This statement is required under ASPE.

The statement of changes in equity is a required statement under IFRS and takes the place of the statement of changes in retained earnings. It shows all changes in all equity accounts, including accumulated other comprehensive income.

8 Understand how disclosures and analysis help users of financial statements assess performance.

Disclosures include notes and supplementary information. They provide background and explanatory information necessary to understand the business. Investors and analysts use quality of earnings analysis to help determine a company's value.

9 Identify differences in accounting between IFRS and ASPE and potential changes.

The chart in Illustration 4-22 outlines the major differences. The IASB was in the research project stages regarding financial performance reporting.

KEY TERMS

all-inclusive approach, p. 156
business component, p. 159
business model, p. 150
changes in accounting principle, p. 174
comprehensive income, p. 156
current operating performance approach, p. 156
discontinued operations, p. 158
earnings management, p. 155
earnings multiple, p. 178

earnings per share (EPS), p. 172
function, p. 169
held for sale, p. 158
income statement, p. 150
intraperiod tax allocation, p. 172
multiple-step income statement, p. 166
nature, p. 169
net income, p. 156
non-GAAP earnings, p. 177
operating income, p. 156

other comprehensive income (OCI), p. 157
quality of earnings, p. 154
risk management, p. 150
risk/return trade-off, p. 150
single-step income statement, p. 165
statement of changes in equity, p. 173
statement of comprehensive income, p. 150
statement of income/earnings, p. 150
statement of retained earnings, p. 173

APPENDIX 4A

CASH BASIS VERSUS ACCRUAL BASIS EARNINGS

Differences Between Cash and Accrual Bases

Objective 10

Explain the differences between the cash basis of accounting and the accrual basis of accounting.

Most companies use the **accrual basis** of accounting: they recognize revenue when it is earned and recognize expenses in the period when they are incurred, which means that the time when cash is received or paid is not a factor in recognizing the transaction. Some small enterprises and the average individual taxpayer, however, use a strict or modified cash basis approach. Under the **strict cash basis**, revenue is recorded only when the cash is received, and expenses are recorded only when the cash is paid. Income is determined based on the actual collection of revenues and payment of expenses, and the revenue recognition and matching principles are ignored. Consequently, cash basis financial statements do not conform with generally accepted accounting principles.

To illustrate and contrast accrual basis accounting and cash basis accounting, assume that Quality Contractor signs an agreement to build a garage for $22,000. In January, Quality Contractor begins construction, incurs costs of $18,000 on credit, and by the end of January delivers a finished garage to the buyer. In February, Quality Contractor collects $22,000 cash from the customer. In March, Quality pays the $18,000 that is owed to the creditors. Illustrations 4A-1 and 4A-2 show the net income for each month under cash basis accounting and accrual basis accounting, respectively.

Illustration 4A-1

Income Statement—Cash Basis

QUALITY CONTRACTOR				
Income Statement Cash Basis				
For the Month of				
	January	February	March	Total
Cash receipts	$-0-	$22,000	$ -0-	$22,000
Cash payments	-0-	-0-	18,000	18,000
Net income (loss)	$-0-	$22,000	$(18,000)	$ 4,000

Illustration 4A-2

Income Statement—Accrual Basis

QUALITY CONTRACTOR				
Income Statement Accrual Basis				
For the Month of				
	January	February	March	Total
Revenues	$22,000	$-0-	$-0-	$22,000
Expenses	18,000	-0-	-0-	18,000
Net income (loss)	$ 4,000	$-0-	$-0-	$ 4,000

For the three months combined, total net income is the same under both cash basis accounting and accrual basis accounting; the difference is in the timing of net income. The balance sheet is also affected by the basis of accounting. For instance, if cash basis accounting were used, Quality Contractor's balance sheets at each month end would appear as in Illustration 4A-3.

QUALITY CONTRACTOR Balance Sheets Cash Basis As at			
	Jan. 31	Feb. 28	Mar. 31
Assets			
Cash	$–0–	$22,000	$4,000
Total assets	$–0–	$22,000	$4,000
Liabilities and Owners' Equity			
Owners' equity	$–0–	$22,000	$4,000
Total liabilities and owners' equity	$–0–	$22,000	$4,000

Illustration 4A-4 shows what Quality Contractor's balance sheets at each month end would look like if accrual basis accounting were used.

QUALITY CONTRACTOR Balance Sheets Accrual Basis As at			
	Jan. 31	Feb. 28	Mar. 31
Assets			
Cash	$ –0–	$22,000	$4,000
Accounts receivable	22,000	–0–	–0–
Total assets	$22,000	$22,000	$4,000
Liabilities and Owners' Equity			
Accounts payable	$18,000	$18,000	$ –0–
Owners' equity	4,000	4,000	4,000
Total liabilities and owners' equity	$22,000	$22,000	$4,000

An analysis of the preceding income statements and balance sheets shows the following ways in which cash basis accounting is inconsistent with basic accounting theory:

1. The cash basis understates revenues and assets from the construction and delivery of the garage in January. It ignores the $22,000 of accounts receivable, which is a near-term future cash inflow.

2. The cash basis understates the expenses incurred with the construction of the garage and the liability outstanding at the end of January. It ignores the $18,000 of accounts payable, which is a near-term future cash outflow.

3. The cash basis understates owners' equity in January by not recognizing the revenues and the asset until February, and it overstates owners' equity in February by not recognizing the expenses and liability until March.

In short, cash basis accounting violates the theory underlying the elements of financial statements.

The **modified cash basis**, a mixture of cash basis and accrual basis, is the method often followed by professional services firms (doctors, lawyers, accountants, consultants) and by retail, real estate, and agricultural operations. It is the pure cash basis of accounting with modifications that have substantial support, such as capitalizing and amortizing plant assets or recording inventory.[21]

Conversion from Cash Basis to Accrual Basis

Fairly often, a cash basis or a modified cash basis set of financial statements needs to be converted to the accrual basis so it can be presented to investors and creditors. To illustrate this conversion, assume that Dr. Diane Windsor keeps her accounting records on a cash basis. In the year 2017, Dr. Windsor received $300,000 from her dental patients and paid $170,000 for operating expenses, resulting in an excess of cash receipts over disbursements of \$130,000 (\$300,000 – \$170,000). At January 1 and December 31, 2017, she has the accounts receivable, unearned service revenue, accrued liabilities, and prepaid expenses shown in Illustration 4A-5.

Illustration 4A-5

Excerpt from General Ledger

	Jan. 1, 2017	Dec. 31, 2017
Accounts receivable	\$12,000	\$9,000
Unearned revenue	–0–	4,000
Accrued liabilities	2,000	5,500
Prepaid expenses	1,800	2,700

Service Revenue Calculation

To convert the amount of cash received from patients to service revenue on an accrual basis, changes in accounts receivable and unearned revenue during the year must be considered. Accounts receivable at the beginning of the year represent revenues earned last year that are collected this year. Ending accounts receivable indicate revenues earned this year that are not yet collected. Therefore, beginning accounts receivable are subtracted and ending accounts receivable added to arrive at revenue on an accrual basis, as shown in Illustration 4A-6.

Illustration 4A-6

Conversion of Cash Receipts to Revenue—Accounts Receivable

Cash receipts from customers	(– Beginning accounts receivable) (+ Ending accounts receivable)	=	Revenue on an accrual basis

Using similar analysis, beginning unearned service revenue represents cash received last year for revenues earned this year. Ending unearned service revenue results from collections this year that will be recognized as revenue next year. Therefore, beginning unearned service revenue is added and ending unearned service revenue is subtracted to arrive at revenue on an accrual basis, as shown in Illustration 4A-7.

Illustration 4A-7

Conversion of Cash Receipts to Revenue—Unearned Service Revenue

Cash receipts from customers	(+ Beginning unearned revenue) (– Ending unearned revenue)	=	Revenue on an accrual basis

Cash collected from customers, therefore, is converted to service revenue on an accrual basis, as Illustration 4A-8 shows.

Illustration 4A-8

Conversion of Cash Receipts to Service Revenue

Cash receipts from customers		\$300,000
Beginning accounts receivable	\$(12,000)	
Ending accounts receivable	9,000	
Beginning unearned revenue	–0–	
Ending unearned revenue	(4,000)	(7,000)
Service revenue (accrual)		\$293,000

Operating Expense Calculation

To convert cash paid for operating expenses during the year to operating expenses on an accrual basis, you must consider changes in prepaid expenses and accrued liabilities during the year. Beginning prepaid expenses should be recognized as expenses this year. (The cash payment occurred last year.) Therefore, the beginning prepaid expenses balance is added to cash paid for operating expenses to arrive at operating expense on an accrual basis.

Conversely, ending prepaid expenses result from cash payments made this year for expenses to be reported next year. (The expense recognition is deferred to a future period.) As a result, ending prepaid expenses are deducted from cash paid for expenses, as shown in Illustration 4A-9.

Illustration 4A-9	Cash paid for operating expenses
Conversion of Cash Payments to Expenses—Prepaid Expenses	(+ Beginning prepaid expenses) (− Ending prepaid expenses) = Expenses on an accrual basis

Using similar analysis, beginning accrued liabilities result from expenses recognized last year that require cash payments this year. Ending accrued liabilities relate to expenses recognized this year that have not been paid. Beginning accrued liabilities, therefore, are deducted and ending accrued liabilities are added to cash paid for expenses to arrive at expenses on an accrual basis, as shown in Illustration 4A-10.

Illustration 4A-10	Cash paid for operating expenses
Conversion of Cash Payments to Expenses—Accrued Liabilities	(− Beginning accrued liabilities) (+ Ending accrued liabilities) = Expenses on an accrual basis

For Dr. Diane Windsor, therefore, cash paid for operating expenses is converted to operating expenses on an accrual basis as in Illustration 4A-11.

Illustration 4A-11

Conversion of Cash Paid to Operating Expenses

Cash paid for operating expenses		$170,000
Beginning prepaid expenses	$ 1,800	
Ending prepaid expenses	(2,700)	
Beginning accrued liabilities	(2,000)	
Ending accrued liabilities	5,500	2,600
Operating expenses (accrual)		$172,600

Illustration 4A-12 shows how this entire conversion can be presented in a work sheet.

Illustration 4A-12

Conversion of Statement of Cash Receipts and Disbursements to Income Statement

DIANE WINDSOR, D.D.S.
Conversion of Income Statement Data from Cash Basis to Accrual Basis
For the Year 2017

	Cash Basis	Adjustments Add	Adjustments Deduct	Accrual Basis
Collections from customers	$300,000			
− Accounts receivable, Jan. 1			$12,000	
+ Accounts receivable, Dec. 31		$9,000		
+ Unearned revenue, Jan. 1		−		
− Unearned revenue, Dec. 31			4,000	
Service revenue				$293,000
Disbursement for expenses	170,000			
+ Prepaid expenses, Jan. 1		1,800		
− Prepaid expenses, Dec. 31			2,700	
− Accrued liabilities, Jan. 1			2,000	
+ Accrued liabilities, Dec. 31		5,500		
Operating expenses				172,600
Excess of cash collections over disbursements—cash basis	$130,000			
Net income—accrual basis				$120,400

Using this approach, collections and disbursements on a cash basis are adjusted to revenue and expenses on an accrual basis to arrive at accrued net income. In any conversion from the cash basis to the accrual basis, depreciation or amortization expense is an expense in arriving at net income on an accrual basis.

UNDERLYING CONCEPT

Accrual-based net income is a good predictor of future cash flows.

Theoretical Weaknesses of the Cash Basis

The cash basis does report exactly when cash is received and when cash is disbursed. To many people, that information represents something solid, something concrete. Isn't cash what it's all about? Does it make sense to invent something, design it, produce it, market it, and sell it, if you aren't going to get cash for it in the end? If so, then what is the merit of accrual accounting?

Today's economy is based more on credit than cash. And the accrual basis, not the cash basis, recognizes all aspects of credit. Investors, creditors, and other decision-makers seek timely information about an enterprise's future cash flows. Accrual basis accounting provides this information by reporting the cash inflows and outflows associated with earnings activities as soon as these cash flows can be estimated with an acceptable degree of certainty. Receivables and payables are forecasters of future cash inflows and outflows. In other words, accrual basis accounting aids in predicting future cash flows by reporting transactions and other events with cash consequences at the time the transactions and events occur, rather than when the cash is received and paid.

SUMMARY OF LEARNING OBJECTIVE FOR APPENDIX 4A

10 Explain the differences between the cash basis of accounting and the accrual basis of accounting.

Accrual basis accounting provides information about cash inflows and outflows associated with earnings activities as soon as these cash flows can be estimated with an acceptable degree of certainty. That is, accrual basis accounting aids in predicting future cash flows by reporting transactions and events with cash consequences at the time the transactions and events occur, rather than when the cash is received and paid. The cash basis focuses on when the cash is received or dispersed, and therefore it is not the best predictor of future cash flows if the company has irregular cash flow patterns.

KEY TERMS

accrual basis, p. 181   modified cash basis, p. 182   strict cash basis, p. 181

Note: All assignment material with an asterisk (*) relates to the appendix to the chapter.

Completion of this end-of-chapter material will help develop CPA enabling competencies (such as ethics and professionalism, problem-solving and decision-making and communication) and technical competencies. We have highlighted selected items with an integration icon and material in *WileyPLUS* has been linked to the competencies. All cases emphasize integration, especially of the enabling competencies. The brief exercises, exercises and problems generally emphasize problem-solving and decision-making.

Brief Exercises

(LO 1) BE 4-1 Sunmart Inc. is a discount retailer with 1,000 stores located across North America. Sunmart purchases bulk quantities of groceries and household goods, and then sells the goods directly to retail customers at a markup. Pharmedical Inc. is a pharmaceutical company that develops medications to prevent and treat diseases. Pharmedical develops, produces, and markets medications for purchase by patients of health care professionals and customers of retail pharmacies and stores. Referring to each company's business model, which company would have (a) a higher gross profit percentage, (b) a higher selling expense as a percentage of sales, (c) a higher research and development expense as a percentage of sales, and (d) higher net income?

(LO 1, 2) BE 4-2 Obtain the auditor's reports for **TELUS Corporation**. Identify and read the opinion paragraph. Explain why it is important for auditors to understand the business model and business environment (including the nature of the industry) before they can render an audit opinion. (*Hint:* Refer back to the discussion and sample audit report in chapter 2.)

AUDIT

(LO 1,2) BE4-3 What is the purpose of a financial audit? (*Hint:* Search "financial audit" on Wikipedia.)

(LO 2, 3) BE4-4 Several of Kimper Corporation's major customers experienced cash flow problems in 2017, mainly due to their increasing labour and production costs in 2016 and 2017. As a result, Kimper's accounts receivable turnover ratio (net sales revenue/average trade receivables [net]) decreased significantly in 2017. However, Kimper believes that its customers' cash flow problems are temporary. In estimating uncollectible accounts receivable as at December 31, 2017, Kimper decreased the estimated percentage of its outstanding accounts receivable that will become uncollectible (a lower percentage was applied in 2017 than was applied in the previous five years). Kimper's bad debt expense as a percentage of sales for the year ended December 31, 2017, was lower than the percentage reported in the previous five years, and no additional note disclosure regarding potentially higher risk of uncollectible accounts was reported. Based only on the information above, (a) evaluate the quality of information provided by Kimper and (b) indicate whether the earnings reported by Kimper will be discounted in the capital markets.

(LO 3) BE4-5 Environmental Corporation specializes in the production and sale of ecofriendly packaging. In 2017, Environmental reported net income (earnings) in excess of analyst expectations. This included a significant gain on sale of investments in the year and lower depreciation expense due to the company's change from the declining-balance method (used by competitors) to the straight-line method for depreciating its equipment. Answer the following questions based only on the information provided. (a) From the perspective of an investor, does Environmental have high-quality earnings? (b) Will the earnings reported by Environmental be discounted in the capital markets?

(LO 3) BE4-6 Cyan Corporation is a manufacturer of paints and specialty coatings. In March 2017, Beck Inc. filed a lawsuit against Cyan Corporation for alleged patent infringement, claiming $1.1 million in damages. Cyan's lawyer disputed the claim, but in December 2017, Cyan's lawyer informed management that Cyan will likely lose the dispute and have to pay between $900,000 and $1.1 million. Dissatisfied with this estimate and its potential impact on 2017 net income, Cyan's management sought a second legal opinion in December 2017. The lawyer who provided the second opinion suggested that Cyan will likely have to pay between $400,000 and $600,000. In its financial statements for the year ended December 31, 2017, Cyan recorded a provision for a loss on the lawsuit and a liability in the amount of $500,000. Answer the following questions based only on the information provided. (a) Does Cyan have high-quality earnings? (b) Will the earnings reported by Cyan be discounted in the capital markets?

(LO 4) BE4-7 On January 1, 2017, Twist Corp. had cash and common shares of $60,000. At that date, the company had no other asset, liability, or shareholders' equity balances. On January 2, 2017, Twist paid $40,000 cash for equity securities that it designated as fair value through other comprehensive income (FV-OCI) investments. During the year, Twist received non-taxable cash dividends of $18,000 and had an unrealized holding gain of $25,000 (net of tax) on these securities. Determine the following amounts for 2017: (a) net income, (b) other comprehensive income, (c) comprehensive income, and (d) accumulated other comprehensive income (as at the end of 2017).

(LO 4, 9) BE4-8 Delray Inc. follows IFRS and has the following amounts for the year ended December 31, 2017: gain on sale of FV-NI investments (before tax), $15,000; loss from operation of discontinued division (net of tax), $42,000; income from operations (before tax), $220,000; unrealized holding gain-OCI (net of tax), $12,000; income tax on income from continuing operations, $63,000; loss from disposal of discontinued division (net of tax), $75,000. The unrealized holding gain-OCI relates to investments that are not quoted in an active market. (a) Calculate income from continuing operations. (b) Calculate net income. (c) Calculate other comprehensive income. (d) Calculate comprehensive income. (e) How would your answers to parts (a) to (d) be different if Delray followed ASPE?

(LO 5) BE4-9 Billy's Burgers (BB) is a franchisor that operates several corporate-owned restaurants as well as several franchised restaurants. The franchisees pay 3% of their sales revenues to BB in return for advertising and support. During the year, BB sold its corporate-owned stores to a franchisee. BB continues to monitor quality in its franchised operations and franchisees must buy all products from it. The corporate-owned stores are not considered a separate major line of business. Would the sale qualify for discontinued operations treatment?

(LO 5) BE4-10 Argon Noble Limited has approved a formal plan to sell its head office tower to an outside party. A detailed plan has been approved by the board of directors. The building is on the books at $50 million (net book value). The estimated selling price is $49 million. The company will continue to use the building until the construction of the new head office is complete. Construction has not yet started on the new building, but the company has begun to look for a buyer. (a) Should Argon Noble present its existing head office tower as held for sale? (b) Assume it is now two years later and construction of the new building is complete. The company has moved into the new building. How would the old building be presented on the income statement and balance sheet under both ASPE and IFRS? The book value of the old building is now $45 million and the fair value is $42 million.

(LO 5, 9) BE4-11 Mega Inc.'s manufacturing division lost $100,000 (net of tax) for the year ended December 31, 2017, and Mega estimates that it can sell the division at a loss of $200,000 (net of tax). The division qualifies for treatment as a discontinued operation. (a) Explain how the discontinued operation would be measured and presented on the income statement and balance sheet under ASPE. (b) Explain how your answer to part (a) would be different if Mega prepared financial statements in accordance with IFRS.

(LO 6, 8) BE4-12 Sierra Corporation had net sales revenue of $5,850,000 and investment revenue of $227,000 for the year ended December 31, 2017. Other items pertaining to 2017 were as follows:

Cost of merchandise sold	$4,610,000
Salaries and wages	368,000
Advertising and promotion	126,000
Entertainment	78,000
Selling expenses	572,000
Salaries and wages	300,000
Rent	101,000
Utilities	44,000
Administrative expenses	445,000
Increase in value of company reputation	74,000
Unrealized gain on value of patents	36,000
Interest expense	160,000
Income tax expense	84,000

Sierra has 100,000 common shares outstanding throughout the year. Prepare a single-step income statement showing expenses by nature. Include calculation of EPS.

(LO 6, 8) BE4-13 Use the information in BE4-12 to prepare a multiple-step income statement for Sierra Corporation, showing expenses by function.

(LO 6, 8) BE4-14 The Blue Collar Corporation had income from continuing operations of $12.6 million in 2017. During 2017, it disposed of its restaurant division at an after-tax loss of $89,000. Before the disposal, the division operated at a loss of $315,000 (net of tax) in 2017. Blue Collar also had an unrealized gain-OCI of $43,000 (net of tax) related to its FV-OCI investments. Blue Collar had 10 million common shares outstanding during 2017. Prepare a partial statement of comprehensive income for Blue Collar, beginning with income from continuing operations. Include calculation of EPS.

(LO 6, 8) BE4-15 The Big and Rich Corporation had income from operations before tax for 2017 of $4.4 million. In addition, it suffered an unusual and infrequent loss of $1,060,000 from a tornado. Of this amount, $300,000 was insured. In addition, the company realized a loss from the sale of a building amounting to $150,000. The corporation's tax rate is 30%. Prepare a partial income statement for Big and Rich, beginning with income from operations. The corporation had 2 million common shares outstanding during 2017. Include calculation of EPS.

(LO 7) BE4-16 Parfait Limited reports the following for 2017: sales revenue, $900,000; cost of sales, $750,000; operating expenses, $100,000; and unrealized gain on FV-OCI investments, $60,000. The company had January 1, 2017 balances as follows: common shares, $600,000; accumulated other comprehensive income, $250,000; and retained earnings, $900,000. The company did not issue any shares during 2017. On December 15, 2017, the board of directors declared a $300,000 dividend payable on January 31, 2018. Prepare a statement of changes in equity. Ignore income tax.

(LO 7) BE4-17 Global Corporation prepares financial statements in accordance with ASPE. At January 1, 2017, the company had retained earnings of $1,038,000. In 2017, net income was $335,000, and cash dividends of $70,000 were declared and paid. Prepare a 2017 statement of retained earnings for Global Corporation.

(LO 7) BE4-18 Use the information in BE4-17 to prepare a statement of retained earnings for Global Corporation, assuming that in 2017, Global discovered that it had overstated 2014 depreciation by $40,000 (net of tax).

(LO 8) BE4-19 Neon Limited had 40,000 common shares on January 1, 2017. On April 1, 8,000 shares were repurchased. On August 31, 12,000 shares were issued. Calculate the number of shares outstanding at December 31, 2017, and the weighted average number of shares for 2017.

(LO 8) BE4-20 In 2017, I & T Corporation reported net income of $8.6 million, and declared and paid preferred share dividends of $3.2 million. During 2017, I & T had a weighted average of 900,000 common shares outstanding. Calculate I & T's 2017 earnings per share.

(LO 10) *BE4-21 In 2017, Renato Corp. had cash receipts from customers of $152,000 and cash payments for operating expenses of $97,000. At January 1, 2017, accounts receivable were $13,000 and total prepaid expenses were $17,500. At December 31, 2017, accounts receivable were $18,600 and total prepaid expenses were $23,200. Calculate (a) total service revenue and (b) total operating expenses.

Exercises

(LO 4) E4-1   (Comprehensive Income) Reach Out Card Company Limited reported the following for 2017: net sales revenue, $1.2 million; cost of goods sold, $750,000; selling and administrative expenses, $320,000; gain on disposal of building, $250,000; and unrealized gain-OCI (related to FV-OCI investments with gains/losses recycled), $18,000.

Instructions

Prepare a statement of comprehensive income. Ignore income tax and EPS. Assume investments are accounted for as FV-OCI investments, with gains/losses recycled through net income.

(LO 4, 9) E4-2   (Comprehensive Income) Pike Corporation, a clothing retailer, had income from operations (before tax) of $375,000, and recorded the following before-tax gains/(losses) for the year ended December 31, 2017:

Gain on sale of equipment	27,000
Unrealized (loss)/gain on FV-NI investments	(54,000)
(Loss)/gain on disposal of building	(68,000)
Gain on sale of FV-NI investments	33,000

Pike also had the following account balances as at January 1, 2017:

Retained earnings	$410,000
Accumulated other comprehensive income (this was due to a revaluation surplus on land)	74,000
Accumulated other comprehensive income (this was due to gains on FV-OCI investments)	55,000

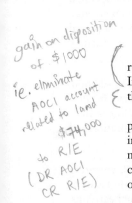

As at January 1, 2017, Pike had one piece of land that it accounted for using the revaluation model. It was most recently revalued to fair value on December 31, 2016, when its carrying amount was adjusted to fair value of $215,000. In January 2017, the piece of land was sold for proceeds of $216,000. In applying the revaluation model, Pike maintains the balance in the Revaluation Surplus (OCI) account until the asset is retired or disposed of.

In 2012, Pike purchased a portfolio of investments that the company intended to hold for longer-term strategic purposes, and classified the portfolio of investments as fair value through other comprehensive income (FV-OCI). The investments in the portfolio are traded in an active market. Pike records unrealized gains and losses on these investments as OCI, and then books these gains and losses to net income when they are impaired or sold. The portfolio's carrying amount on December 31, 2016, was $110,000. The entire portfolio was sold in November 2017 for proceeds of $126,000.

Pike's income tax expense for 2017 was $99,000. Pike prepares financial statements in accordance with IFRS.

Instructions

(a) Calculate net income for the year ended December 31, 2017.

(b) Calculate retained earnings as at December 31, 2017.

(c) Explain the change in accumulated other comprehensive income in 2017.

(d) Calculate net income for the year ended December 31, 2017, and retained earnings as at December 31, 2017, if Pike prepares financial statements in accordance with ASPE. Assume that under ASPE, Pike's retained earnings at January 1, 2017, would be $465,000, and that Pike's income tax expense would not change.

(LO 5, 9) E4-3   (Discontinued Operations) Assume that Elrond Inc. decided to sell DemandTV Ltd., a subsidiary, on September 30, 2017. There is a formal plan to dispose of the business component, and the sale qualifies for discontinued operations treatment. Pertinent data on the operations of the TV subsidiary are as follows: loss from operations from beginning of year to September 30, $1.9 million (net of tax); loss from operations from September 30 to end of 2017, $700,000 (net of tax); estimated loss on sale of net assets to December 31, 2017 (net of tax), $150,000. The year end is December 31. Elrond prepares financial statements in accordance with IFRS.

Instructions

(a) What is the net income/loss from discontinued operations reported in 2017?

(b) Prepare the discontinued operations section of the income statement for the year ended 2017.

(c) If the amount reported in 2017 as a gain or loss from disposal of the subsidiary becomes materially incorrect, when and how is the correction reported, if at all?

(d) How would the discontinued operation be presented on the balance sheet?

(e) How would your answer to part (d) be different if Elrond prepared financial statements in accordance with ASPE?

(LO 5, 9) E4-4 (Discontinued Operations) On October 5, 2017, Diamond in the Rough Recruiting Group Inc.'s board of directors decided to dispose of the Blue Division. A formal plan was approved. Diamond derives approximately 75% of its income from its human resources management practice. The Blue Division gets contracts to perform human resources management on an outsourced basis. The board decided to dispose of the division because of unfavourable operating results.

Net income for Diamond was $91,000 for the fiscal year ended December 31, 2017 (after a charge for tax at 30% and after a writedown for the Blue assets). Income from operations of the Blue Division accounted for $4,200 (after tax) of this amount.

Because of the unfavourable results and the extreme competition, the board believes that it cannot sell the business intact. Its final decision is to auction off the office equipment. The equipment is the division's only asset and has a carrying value of $25,000 at October 5, 2017. The board believes that proceeds from the sale will be approximately $5,000 after the auction expenses. Currently, the estimated fair value of the equipment is $8,000. The Blue Division qualifies for treatment as a discontinued operation. Diamond prepares financial statements in accordance with ASPE.

Instructions

(a) Prepare a partial income statement for Diamond in the Rough Recruiting Group and the appropriate footnote that relates to the Blue Division for 2017. The income statement should begin with income from continuing operations before income tax.

(b) Explain how the assets would be valued and presented on the balance sheet.

(c) Explain how the assets would be valued and presented on the balance sheet if Diamond prepared financial statements in accordance with IFRS.

DIGGING DEEPER

(d) From the perspective of an investor, comment on Diamond's quality of earnings if Diamond presented the Blue Division as a discontinued operation, but did not have a formal plan in place to dispose of the division.

(LO 6) E4-5 (Calculation of Net Income) The following are all changes in the account balances of Chili Lime Ltd. during the current year, except for Retained Earnings:

	Increase (Decrease)		Increase (Decrease)
Cash	$ 76,000	Accounts payable	$(64,000)
Accounts receivable (net)	59,000	Unearned revenue	18,000
Inventory	140,000	Bonds payable	69,000
Investments in FV-NI securities	(23,000)	Common shares	105,000
		Contributed surplus	63,000

Instructions

Calculate the net income for the current year, assuming that there were no entries in the Retained Earnings account except for net income and a dividend declaration of $16,000, which was paid in the current year.

(LO 6) E4-6 (Calculation of Net Income) Videohound Video Company, a sole proprietorship, had the following information for 2017:

Cash balance, January 1	$ 23,000	Total assets, December 31	$101,000
Accounts receivable, January 1	19,000	Cash balance, December 31	20,000
Collections from customers		Accounts receivable,	
during year	200,000	December 31	36,000
Capital account balance,		Merchandise taken for personal	
January 1	38,000	use	11,000
Total assets, January 1	75,000	Total liabilities, December 31	41,000
Cash investment by sole			
proprietor, July 1	5,000		

Instructions

Calculate the net income for 2017.

(LO 6) E4-7 (Income Statement Items) Certain account balances follow for Vincenti Products Corp.:

Rent revenue	$ 8,500	Sales discounts	$ 17,800
Interest expense	2,700	Selling expenses	79,400
Beginning retained earnings	114,400	Sales revenue	490,000
Ending retained earnings	74,000	Income tax expense	100
Dividend revenue	91,000	Cost of goods sold	384,400
Sales returns and allowances	22,400	Administrative expenses	82,500

Instructions

Based on the balances, calculate the following:

(a) Total net revenue,

(b) Net income or loss

(c) Dividends declared during the current year

(LO 6) E4-8 (Multiple-Step and Single-Step—Periodic Inventory Method) Income statement information for Flett Tire Repair Corporation for the year 2017 follows:

General and administrative expenses:		Freight-in	$ 14,000
Salaries and wages expense	$ 39,000	Purchase discounts	10,000
Depreciation expense—building	28,500	Dividend revenue	20,000
Office supplies expense	9,500	Inventory (beginning)	120,000
Inventory (ending)	137,000	Sales returns and allowances	15,000
Loss—other (due to flood damage)	50,000	Service expenses:	
Gain on the sale of equipment	5,500	Salaries and wages	71,000
Purchases	600,000	Depreciation expense—	
Sales revenue	930,000	garage equipment	18,000
Interest expense	9,000	Garage supplies expense	9,000

The effective tax rate on all income is 25%, and Flett applies ASPE.

Instructions

(a) Prepare a multiple-step income statement for 2017, showing expenses by function.

(b) Prepare a single-step income statement for 2017, showing expenses by nature.

(c) Discuss the merits of the two income statements, compared with each other.

(LO 6) E4-9 (Combined Single-Step) The following information was taken from the records of Biscay Inc. for the year 2017:

Gain—other (due to expropriation)	$300,000	Cash dividends declared	$ 220,000
Loss from operation of discontinued		Retained earnings, January 1, 2017	1,900,000
Rochelle Division	240,000	Cost of goods sold	2,680,000
Administrative expenses	750,000	Selling expenses	950,000
Rent revenue	130,000	Sales revenue	6,000,000
Loss—other (due to flood)	190,000		

The following additional information was also available: income tax applicable to income from continuing operations, $465,000; income tax recovery applicable to loss from operation of discontinued Rochelle Division, $60,000.

The company has elected to adopt ASPE.

Instructions

(a) Prepare a single-step income statement for 2017, showing expenses by function.

(b) Prepare a combined single-step income and retained earnings statement.

(LO 6, 7, 9) E4-10 (Multiple-Step Statement, Statement of Comprehensive Income, and Statement of Changes in Equity)
The following is information for Gottlieb Corp. for the year ended December 31, 2017:

Net sales revenue	$1,300,000	Loss on inventory due to decline in net	
Unrealized gain on FV-OCI		realizable value (NRV)	$ 80,000
investments	42,000	Loss on sale of equipment	35,000
Interest income	7,000	Depreciation expense related to buildings	
Cost of goods sold	780,000	omitted by mistake in 2016	55,000
Selling expenses	65,000	Retained earnings at December 31, 2016	980,000
Administrative expenses	48,000	Loss—other (due to expropriation of land)	60,000
Dividend revenue	20,000	Dividends declared	45,000

The effective tax rate is 25% on all items. Gottlieb prepares financial statements in accordance with IFRS. The FV-OCI investments trade on the stock exchange. Gains/losses on FV-OCI investments are recycled through net income.

Instructions

(a) Prepare a multiple-step statement of comprehensive income for 2017, showing expenses by function. Ignore calculation of EPS.

(b) Prepare the retained earnings section of the statement of changes in equity for 2017.

(c) Prepare the journal entry to record the depreciation expense omitted by mistake in 2016.

(d) How should Gottlieb account for the unrealized gain on FV-OCI investments if it prepares financial statements in accordance with ASPE? How would Gottlieb's retained earnings balance at December 31, 2016, be different if financial statements in all previous years had been prepared in accordance with ASPE?

(LO 6) E4-11 (Single-Step Income Statement) The financial records of Geneva Inc. were destroyed by fire at the end of 2017. Fortunately, the controller had kept the following statistical data related to the income statement:

1. The beginning merchandise inventory was $84,000 and it decreased by 20% during the current year.

2. Sales discounts amounted to $15,000.

3. There were 15,000 common shares outstanding for the entire year.

4. Interest expense was $20,000.

5. The income tax rate was 25%.

6. Cost of goods sold amounted to $420,000.

7. Administrative expenses were 20% of cost of goods sold but only 4% of gross sales.

8. Selling expenses were four fifths of cost of goods sold.

Instructions

Based on the available data, prepare a single-step income statement for the year ended December 31, 2017, including calculation of EPS. Expenses should be shown by function.

(LO 6, 8) E4-12 (Multiple-Step and Single-Step) Two accountants, Yuan Tsui and Sergio Aragon, are arguing about the merits of presenting an income statement in the multiple-step versus the single-step format. The discussion involves the following 2017 information for P. Bride Company (in thousands):

Administrative expenses		Selling expenses	
Officers' salaries	$ 4,900	Delivery	$ 2,690
Depreciation of office furniture and		Sales commissions	7,980
equipment	3,960	Depreciation of sales equipment	6,480
Cost of goods sold	60,570	Sales revenue	96,500
Rental revenue	17,230	Interest expense	1,860

Common shares outstanding for 2017 total 30,550. Income tax for the year was $9,070.

Instructions

(a) Prepare an income statement for the year ended December 31, 2017, using the multiple-step format. Include calculation of EPS.

(b) Prepare an income statement for the year ended December 31, 2017, using the single-step format. Include calculation of EPS.

DIGGING
DEEPER

(c) From the perspective of an investor who is interested in information about operating versus non-operating items and the various areas of the company's operations, which format is preferred? Explain why.

(LO 6) **E4-13** **(Multiple-Step and Unusual Items)** The following balances were taken from the books of Quality Fabrication Limited on December 31, 2017:

Interest income	$ 70,000	Accumulated depreciation—equipment	$ 32,000
Cash	40,000	Accumulated depreciation—buildings	23,000
Sales revenue	1,120,000	Notes receivable	125,000
Accounts receivable	122,000	Selling expenses	160,000
Prepaid insurance	16,000	Accounts payable	140,000
Sales returns and allowances	118,000	Bonds payable	81,000
Allowance for doubtful accounts	6,000	Administrative expenses	80,000
Sales discounts	40,000	Accrued liabilities	16,000
Land	80,000	Interest expense	50,000
Equipment	160,000	Notes payable	80,000
Building	115,000	Loss—other (due to storm damage)	124,000
Cost of goods sold	504,000	Depreciation expense	50,000

Assume the total effective tax rate on all items is 25%.

Instructions

Prepare a multiple-step income statement showing expenses by function. Assume that 150,000 common shares were outstanding during the year. Include calculation of EPS.

(LO 6) **E4-14** **(Condensed Income Statement—Periodic Inventory Method)** The following are selected ledger accounts of Holland Rose Corporation at December 31, 2017:

Cash	$ 185,000	Entertainment expense	$ 69,000
Inventory (as at Jan. 1, 2017)	535,000	Office expense	33,000
Sales revenue	4,275,000	Insurance expense	24,000
Unearned revenue	117,000	Advertising expense	54,000
Purchases	2,786,000	Freight-out	93,000
Sales discounts	34,000	Depreciation of office equipment	48,000
Purchase discounts	27,000	Depreciation of sales equipment	36,000
Salaries and wages (sales)	284,000	Telephone and Internet expense (sales)	17,000
Salaries and wages (administrative)	346,000	Utilities expense (administrative)	32,000
Purchase returns and allowances	15,000	Miscellaneous expense	8,000
Sales returns and allowances	79,000	Rental revenue	240,000
Freight-in	72,000	Loss on disposal of equipment	70,000
Accounts receivable	142,500	Interest expense	176,000
Sales commission expense	83,000	Common shares	900,000

Holland's effective tax rate on all items is 25%. A physical inventory indicates that the ending inventory is $686,000. The number of common shares outstanding is 90,000.

Instructions

Prepare a multi-step 2017 income statement for Holland Rose Corporation, showing expenses by function. Include calculation of EPS.

(LO 7) **E4-15** **(Statement of Retained Earnings)** Eddie Zambrano Corporation, a private company, began operations on January 1, 2014. During its first three years of operations, Zambrano reported net income and declared dividends as follows:

	Net income	Dividends declared
2014	$ 40,000	$　–0–
2015	125,000	50,000
2016	160,000	50,000

The following information is for 2017:

Income before income tax	$240,000
Prior period adjustment: understatement of 2015 depreciation expense (before tax)	25,000
Cumulative increase in prior years' income from change in inventory method (before tax)	35,000
Dividends declared (of this amount, $25,000 will be paid on January 15, 2018)	100,000
Effective tax rate	40%

Instructions

(a) Prepare a 2017 statement of retained earnings for Eddie Zambrano Corporation. The company follows ASPE.

(b) Assume Eddie Zambrano Corporation restricted retained earnings in the amount of $70,000 on December 31, 2017. After this action, what would Zambrano report as total retained earnings in its December 31, 2017, balance sheet?

(LO 7) E4-16 (Comprehensive Income) Rainy Day Umbrella Corporation had the following balances at December 31, 2016 (all amounts in thousands): preferred shares, $3,375; common shares, $8,903; contributed surplus, $3,744; retained earnings, $23,040; and accumulated other comprehensive income, $2,568.

During the year ended December 31, 2017, the company earned net income of $7,320,000, generated an unrealized holding gain on FV-OCI investments of $585,000, sold common shares of $285,000, and paid out dividends of $30,000 and $20,000 to preferred and common shareholders, respectively.

Instructions

Prepare a statement of changes in equity for the year ended December 31, 2017, as well as the shareholders' equity section of the Rainy Day Umbrella Corporation balance sheet as at December 31, 2017. Gains/losses on FV-OCI investments are recycled through net income.

(LO 8) E4-17 (Earnings per Share) The shareholders' equity section of Cadmium Corporation as at December 31, 2017, follows:

8% cumulative preferred shares, 100,000 shares authorized,	
80,000 shares outstanding	$ 4,500,000
Common shares, 10 million shares authorized and issued	10,000,000
Contributed surplus	10,500,000
	25,000,000
Retained earnings	177,000,000
	$202,000,000

Net income of $24 million for 2017 reflects a total effective tax rate of 25%. Included in the net income figure is a loss of $15 million (before tax) relating to the operations of a business segment that is to be discontinued.

Instructions

Calculate earnings per share information as it should appear in the financial statements of Cadmium Corporation for the year ended December 31, 2017.

(LO 8) E4-18 (Earnings per Share) At December 31, 2017, Tres Hombres Corporation had the following shares outstanding:

10% cumulative preferred shares, 107,500 shares outstanding	$10,750,000
Common shares, 4,000,000 shares outstanding	20,000,000

During 2017, the corporation's only share transaction was the issuance of 400,000 common shares on April 1. During 2017, the following also occurred:

Income from continuing operations before tax	$23,650,000
Discontinued operations (loss before tax)	3,225,000
Preferred dividends declared	1,075,000
Common dividends declared	2,200,000
Effective tax rate	30%

Instructions

Calculate earnings per share information as it should appear in the financial statements of Tres Hombres Corporation for the year ended December 31, 2017.

(LO 10) *E4-19 (Cash and Accrual Basis) Canviar Corp. maintains its financial records using the cash basis of accounting. As it would like to secure a long-term loan from its bank, the company asks you, as an independent CPA, to convert its cash basis income statement information to the accrual basis. You are provided with the following summarized data for 2015, 2016, and 2017:

	2015	2016	2017
Cash receipts from sales:			
On 2015 sales	$320,000	$160,000	$ 30,000
On 2016 sales	–0–	355,000	90,000
On 2017 sales	–0–	–0–	408,000
Cash payments for expenses:			
On 2015 expenses	185,000	67,000	25,000
On 2016 expenses	40,000ª	135,000	55,000
On 2017 expenses	–0–	45,000ᵇ	218,000

ªPrepayments of 2016 expense
ᵇPrepayments of 2017 expense

Instructions

Using the information above, prepare abbreviated income statements for the years 2015 and 2016, using:

(a) The cash basis of accounting,

(b) The accrual basis of accounting.

Problems

P4-1 In recent years, Grace Inc. has reported steadily increasing income. The company reported income of $20,000 in 2014, $25,000 in 2015, and $30,000 in 2016. Several market analysts have recommended that investors buy Grace Inc. shares because they expect the steady growth in income to continue. Grace is approaching the end of its 2017 fiscal **ETHICS** year, and it looks to be a good year once again. However, it has not yet recorded warranty expense.

Based on prior experience, this year's warranty expense should be around $5,000, but some members of top management have approached the controller to suggest that a larger, more conservative warranty expense should be recorded this year. Income before warranty expense is $43,000. Specifically, by recording an $8,000 warranty accrual this year, Grace could report an income increase for this year and still be in a position to cover its warranty costs in future years.

Instructions

DIGGING DEEPER

(a) What is earnings management?

(b) What would be the effect of the proposed accounting in 2017? In 2018?

(c) What is the appropriate accounting in this situation?

(d) Discuss the effect of the proposed accounting on a potential investor's decision to invest in the company.

P4-2 On November 1, 2016, Campbell Corporation management decided to discontinue operation of its Rocketeer Division and approved a formal plan to dispose of the division. Campbell is a successful corporation with earnings of $150 million or more before tax for each of the past five years. The Rocketeer Division, a major part of Campbell's operations, is being discontinued because it has not contributed to this profitable performance.

The division's main assets are the land, building, and equipment used to manufacture engine components. The land, building, and equipment had a net book value of $42 million on November 1, 2016.

Campbell's management has entered into negotiations for a cash sale of the division for $36 million (net of costs to sell). The sale date and final disposal date of the division is expected to be July 1, 2017. Campbell Corporation has a fiscal year ending May 31. The results of operations for the Rocketeer Division for the 2016–17 fiscal year and the estimated results for June 2017 are presented below. The before-tax losses after October 31, 2016, are calculated without depreciation on the building and equipment.

Period	Before-Tax Loss
June 1, 2016, to October 31, 2016	$(2,500,000)
November 1, 2016, to May 31, 2017	(1,600,000)
June 1 to 30, 2017 (estimated)	(300,000)

The Rocketeer Division will be accounted for as a discontinued operation on Campbell's financial statements for the year ended May 31, 2017. Campbell's tax rate is 25% on operating income and all gains and losses. Campbell prepares financial statements in accordance with IFRS.

Instructions

(a) Explain how the Rocketeer Division's assets would be reported on Campbell Corporation's balance sheet as at May 31, 2017.

(b) Explain how the discontinued operations and pending sale of the Rocketeer Division would be reported on Campbell Corporation's income statement for the year ended May 31, 2017.

(c) On July 5, 2017, Campbell Corporation disposes of the division's assets at an adjusted price of $40 million. Explain how the discontinued operations and sale of the Rocketeer Division would be reported on Campbell Corporation's income statement for the year ended May 31, 2018. Assume the June 2017 operating loss is the same as estimated.

**DIGGING
DEEPER**

(d) Assume that Campbell Corporation management was debating whether the sale of the Rocketeer Division qualified for discontinued operations accounting treatment under IFRS. List specific factors or arguments that management would use to suggest that the Rocketeer Division should be treated as a discontinued operation. Why might management have a particular preference about which treatment is given? From an external user's perspective, what relevance does the presentation of the discontinued operation have when interpreting the financial results?

P4-3   Information for 2017 follows for Rolling Thunder Corp.:

Retained earnings, January 1, 2017	$ 1,980,000
Sales revenue	36,500,000
Cost of goods sold	28,500,000
Interest income	170,000
Selling and administrative expenses	4,700,000
Unrealized gain on FV-OCI investments (gains/losses recycled)	320,000
Loss on impairment of goodwill (not tax-deductible)	520,000
Income tax on continuing operations for 2017 (assume this is correct)	797,500
Assessment for additional income tax for 2015 (normal, recurring)	500,000
Gain on sale of FV-NI investments (normal, recurring)	110,000
Loss—other (due to flood damage)	390,000
Loss from disposal of discontinued division (net of tax of $87,500)	262,500
Loss from operation of discontinued division (net of tax of $55,000)	165,000
Dividends declared on common shares	250,000
Dividends declared on preferred shares	70,000

Rolling Thunder decided to discontinue its entire wholesale division (a major line of business) and to keep its manufacturing division. On September 15, it sold the wholesale division to Dylane Corp. During 2017, there were 800,000 common shares outstanding all year. Rolling Thunder's tax rate is 25% on operating income and all gains and losses (use this rate where the tax provisions are not given). Rolling Thunder prepares financial statements in accordance with IFRS.

Instructions

Prepare a multiple-step statement of comprehensive income showing expenses by function. Include calculation of EPS.

P4-4   Wavecrest Inc. reported income from continuing operations before tax of $1,790,000 during 2017. Additional transactions occurring in 2017 but not included in the $1,790,000 are as follows:

1. The corporation experienced an insured flood loss of $80,000 during the year.

2. At the beginning of 2015, the corporation purchased a machine for $54,000 (residual value of $9,000) that has a useful life of six years. The bookkeeper used straight-line depreciation for 2015, 2016, and 2017, but failed to deduct the residual value in calculating the depreciable amount.

3. The sale of FV-NI investments resulted in a loss of $107,000.

4. When its president died, the corporation gained $100,000 from an insurance policy. The cash surrender value of this policy had been carried on the books as an investment in the amount of $46,000 (the gain is non-taxable).

5. The corporation disposed of its recreational division at a loss of $115,000 before tax. Assume that this transaction meets the criteria for accounting treatment as discontinued operations.

6. The corporation decided to change its method of inventory pricing from average cost to the FIFO method. The effect of this change on prior years is to increase 2015 income by $60,000 and decrease 2016 income by $20,000 before taxes. The FIFO method has been used for 2017.

Instructions

(a) Prepare an income statement for the year 2017, starting with income from continuing operations before income tax. Calculate earnings per share as required under IFRS. There were 80,000 common shares outstanding during the year. (Assume a tax rate of 30% on all items, unless they are noted as being non-taxable.)

(b) Assume that beginning retained earnings for 2017 is $2,540,000 and that dividends of $175,000 were declared during the year. Prepare the retained earnings portion of the statement of changes in equity for 2017.

**DIGGING
DEEPER**

(c) Discuss how proper classification and disclosure of items on the income statement help users in making their investment and credit decisions.

P4-5   The trial balance follows for Thompson Corporation at December 31, 2017:

THOMPSON CORPORATION
Trial Balance
December 31, 2017

	Debits	Credits
Purchase discounts		$ 10,000
Cash	$ 189,700	
Accounts receivable	105,000	
Rent revenue		18,000
Retained earnings		160,000
Salaries and wages payable		18,000
Sales revenue		1,100,000
Notes receivable	110,000	
Accounts payable		49,000
Accumulated depreciation—equipment		28,000
Sales discounts	14,500	
Sales returns and allowances	17,500	
Notes payable		70,000
Selling expenses	232,000	
Administrative expenses	99,000	
Common shares		300,000
Income tax expense	53,900	
Dividends	45,000	
Allowance for doubtful accounts		5,000
Supplies	14,000	
Freight-in	20,000	
Land	70,000	
Equipment	140,000	
Bonds payable		100,000
Gain on sale of land		30,000
Accumulated depreciation—building		19,600
Inventory	89,000	
Buildings	98,000	
Purchases	610,000	
Totals	$1,907,600	$1,907,600

A physical count of inventory on December 31 showed that there was $64,000 of inventory on hand.

Instructions

Prepare a single-step income statement and a statement of retained earnings, assuming that Thompson is a private company that prepares financial statements in accordance with ASPE. Assume that the only changes in retained earnings during the current year were from net income and dividends.

P4-6   Hamza Khan, vice-president of finance for Dani Ipo Corp., has recently been asked to conduct a seminar for the company's division controllers. He would discuss the proper accounting for items that are large but do not typify normal business transactions (due to either the nature or the frequency of the transaction). Khan prepares the situations that follow to use as examples in the discussion. He understands that accounting standards mandate separate presentation of certain items, that these standards change over time, and that different standards may have different requirements. He has decided to focus on general principles.

1. An earthquake destroys one of the oil refineries owned by a large multinational oil company. Earthquakes are rare in this location.

2. A publicly held company has incurred a substantial loss in the unsuccessful registration of a bond issue. The company accesses capital markets very frequently.

3. A large portion of a farmer's crops is destroyed by a hailstorm. Severe damage from hailstorms is rare in this area.

4. A large diversified company sells a block of shares from its portfolio of investments. The shares are currently treated as FV-OCI investments (with gains/losses recycled).

5. A company sells a block of common shares of a publicly traded company. The block of shares, which represents less than 10% of the publicly held company, is the only share investment that the company has ever owned. The shares are accounted for as FV-OCI investments (with gains/losses recycled).

6. A company that operates a chain of warehouses sells the extra land surrounding one of its warehouses. When the company buys property for a new warehouse, it usually buys more land than it needs for the warehouse because it expects the land to increase in value. Twice during the past five years, the company has sold excess land.

7. A textile manufacturer with only one plant moves to another location and incurs relocation costs of $725,000. Prior to the move, the company had been in the same location for 100 years.

8. A company experiences a material loss in the repurchase of a large bond issue that has been outstanding for three years. The company regularly repurchases bonds of this type.

9. A railroad experiences an unusual flood loss to part of its track system. Flood losses normally occur every three or four years. How would this be different if the company were to insure itself against this loss?

10. A machine tool company sells the only land it owns. The land was acquired 10 years ago for future expansion, but shortly after the purchase, the company abandoned all plans for expansion and decided to keep the land as an investment that would appreciate in value.

Instructions

For each situation, determine whether the item should be treated as unusual. Explain the reasons for your position. Assume that the company follows IFRS.

P4-7 The following financial statement was prepared by employees of Intellisys Corporation:

INTELLISYS CORPORATION
Income Statement
Year Ended December 31, 2017

Sales revenue	
Gross sales revenue, including sales taxes	$1,044,300
Less: Sales returns, and allowances	56,200
Net sales revenue	988,100
Dividend revenue, interest income, and purchase discounts	30,250
Recoveries of accounts written off in prior years	13,850
Total revenues	1,032,200
Operating expenses	
Cost of goods sold	465,900
Salaries and wages expense	60,500
Rent	19,100
Freight-in and freight-out	3,400
Bad debt expense	24,000
Appropriation of retained earnings for possible inventory losses	3,800
Total operating expenses	576,700
Income before unusual items	455,500
Unusual items	
Loss on discontinued styles (Note 1)	37,000
Loss on sale of FV-NI investments (Note 2)	39,050
Loss on sale of warehouse (Note 3)	86,350
Tax assessments for 2016 and 2015 (Note 4)	34,500
Total unusual items	196,900
Net income	$ 258,600
Net income per common share	$ 2.30

Note 1: New styles and rapidly changing consumer preferences resulted in a $37,000 loss on the disposal of discontinued styles and related accessories.

Note 2: The corporation sold an investment in trading securities at a loss of $39,050. The corporation normally sells securities of this type.

Note 3: The corporation sold one of its warehouses at an $86,350 loss (net of taxes).

Note 4: The corporation was charged $34,500 for additional income taxes resulting from a settlement in 2017. Of this amount, $17,000 was for 2016, and the balance was for 2015. This type of litigation recurs frequently at Intellisys Corporation.

Instructions

Identify and discuss the weaknesses in classification and disclosure in the single-step income statement above. You should explain why these treatments are weaknesses and what the proper presentation of the items would be in accordance with recent professional pronouncements.

P4-8 The following account balances were included in the trial balance of Reid Corporation at June 30, 2017:

Sales revenue	$1,928,500	Telephone and Internet expense (office)	$ 2,820
Sales discounts	31,150	Salaries and wages (office)	7,320
Cost of goods sold	1,071,770	Supplies expense (sales)	4,850
Salaries and wages (sales)	56,260	Maintenance and repairs expense (office)	9,130
Sales commission expense	97,600	Depreciation understatement due to error—	
Advertising expense (sales)	28,930	2015 (net of tax)	17,700
Freight-out	21,400	Miscellaneous expense (office)	6,000
Entertainment expense (sales)	14,820	Sales returns and allowances	62,300
Telephone and Internet expense (sales)	9,030	Dividend revenue	38,000
Depreciation of sales equipment	4,980	Interest expense	18,000
Maintenance and repairs expense (sales)	6,200	Income tax	133,000
Miscellaneous expenses (sales)	4,715	Dividends declared on preferred shares	9,000
Supplies expense (office)	3,450	Dividends declared on common shares	32,000
Depreciation of office furniture and equipment	7,250		

During 2017, Reid incurred production salary and wage costs of $710,000, consumed raw materials and other production supplies of $474,670, and had an increase in work-in-process and finished goods inventories of $112,900. The Retained Earnings account had a balance of $292,000 at June 30, 2017, before closing. There are 180,000 common shares outstanding. Assume Reid has elected to adopt IFRS. (*Hint:* Production payroll and materials costs reduced by the increase in ending work-in-process and finished goods inventories = the cost of goods sold.)

Instructions

(a) Prepare an income statement for the year ended June 30, 2017, using the multiple-step format and showing expenses by function.

(b) Prepare the retained earnings portion of the statement of changes in equity for the year ended June 30, 2017.

(c) Prepare an income statement for the year ended June 30, 2017, using the single-step format and showing expenses by nature.

P4-9 A combined single-step income and statement of retained earnings for California Tanning Salon Corp. follows for 2017 (amounts in thousands):

Net sales revenue		$640,000
Operating expenses		
Cost of goods sold		500,000
Selling, general, and administrative expenses		66,000
Other, net		17,000
		583,000
Income before income tax		57,000
Income tax		19,400
Net income		37,600
Retained earnings at beginning of period, as previously reported	141,000	
Adjustment required for correction of error	(7,000)	
Retained earnings at beginning of period, as restated		134,000
Dividends on common shares		(12,200)
Retained earnings at end of period		$159,400

Additional facts are as follows:

1. Selling, general, and administrative expenses for 2017 included a usual but infrequently occurring charge of $10.5 million for a loss on inventory due to decline in NRV.

2. Other, net for 2017 included the results of an identified component of the business that management had determined would be eliminated from the future operations of the business ($9 million). If the decision had not been made to discontinue the operation, income tax for 2017 would have been $22.4 million instead of $19.4 million. The component has one asset, a piece of equipment with a carrying value of $3.2 million, which is included on the company's balance sheet under property, plant, and equipment (and is equal to the fair value).

3. "Adjustment required for correction of an error" resulted from a change in estimate as the useful life of certain assets was reduced to eight years and a catch-up adjustment was made.

4. The company disclosed earnings per common share for net income in the notes to the financial statements. The company has elected to adopt ASPE.

Instructions

(a) Discuss the appropriate presentation of the facts in the California Tanning Salon Corp. income statement and statement of retained earnings, and discuss the theory that supports the presentation.

(b) Prepare a revised combined statement of income and retained earnings for California Tanning Salon Corp.

P4-10 A combined statement of income and retained earnings for DC 5 Ltd. for the year ended December 31, 2017, follows. (As a private company, DC 5 has elected to follow ASPE.) Also presented are three unrelated situations involving accounting changes and the classification of certain items as ordinary or unusual. Each situation is based on the combined statement of income and retained earnings of DC 5 Ltd.

DC 5 LTD.
Combined Statement of Income and Retained Earnings
For the Year Ended December 31, 2017

Sales revenue	$7,300,000
Cost of goods sold	3,700,000
Gross profit	3,600,000
Selling, general, and administrative expenses	2,300,000
Income before income tax	1,300,000
Income tax	390,000
Income before unusual item	910,000
Loss from tornado (net of taxes)	630,000
Net income	280,000
Retained earnings, January 1	1,250,000
Retained earnings, December 31	$1,530,000

Situation 1. In late 2017, the company discontinued its apparel fabric division. The loss on the sale of this discontinued division amounted to $790,000. This amount was included as part of selling, general, and administrative expenses. Before its disposal, the division reported the following for 2017: sales revenue of $1.5 million; cost of goods sold of $750,000; and selling, general, and administrative expenses of $580,000.

Situation 2. At the end of 2017, the company's management decided that the estimated loss rate on uncollectible accounts receivable was too low. The loss rate used for the years 2016 and 2017 was 1.2% of total sales revenue, and owing to an increase in the writeoff of uncollectible accounts, the rate was raised to 2.6% of total sales revenue. The amount recorded in Bad Debt Expense under the heading Selling, General, and Administrative Expenses for 2017 was $87,600 and for 2016 it was $95,700.

Situation 3. On January 1, 2015, the company acquired machinery at a cost of $640,000. The company adopted the declining-balance method of depreciation at a rate of 30% for this machinery, and had been recording depreciation over an estimated life of 10 years, with no residual value. At the beginning of 2017, a decision was made to adopt the straight-line method of depreciation for this machinery. Depreciation for 2017, based on the straight-line method, was included in selling, general, and administrative expenses. (*Hint:* A change in depreciation method is considered a change in estimate, not a change in accounting policy.)

Instructions

For each of the three unrelated situations, prepare a revised combined statement of income and retained earnings for DC 5 Ltd. The company has a 30% income tax rate.

P4-11 Zephyr Corporation began operations on January 1, 2014. Recently the corporation has had several unusual accounting problems related to the presentation of its income statement for financial reporting purposes. The company follows ASPE.

You are the CPA for Zephyr and have been asked to examine the following data:

ZEPHYR CORPORATION
Income Statement
For the Year Ended December 31, 2017

Sales revenue	$9,500,000
Cost of goods sold	5,900,000
Gross profit	3,600,000
Selling and administrative expense	1,300,000
Income before income tax	2,300,000
Income tax (30%)	690,000
Net income	$1,610,000

This additional information was also provided:

1. The controller mentioned that the corporation has had difficulty collecting certain receivables. For this reason, the bad debt accrual was increased from 1% to 2% of sales revenue. The controller estimates that, if this rate had been used in past periods, an additional $83,000 worth of expense would have been charged. The bad debt expense for the current period was calculated using the new rate and is part of selling and administrative expense.

2. There were 400,000 common shares outstanding at the end of 2017. No additional shares were purchased or sold in 2017.

3. The following items were not included in the income statement:

- Inventory in the amount of $112,000 was obsolete.

- The company announced plans to dispose of a recognized segment. For 2017, the segment had a loss, net of tax, of $162,000.

4. Retained earnings as at January 1, 2017, were $2.8 million. Cash dividends of $700,000 were paid in 2017.

5. In January 2017, Zephyr changed its method of accounting for plant assets from the straight-line method to the diminishing-balance method. The controller has prepared a schedule that shows what the depreciation expense would have been in previous periods if the diminishing-balance method had been used.

	Depreciation Expense under Straight-Line	Depreciation Expense under Diminishing-Balance	Difference
2014	$ 75,000	$150,000	$ 75,000
2015	75,000	112,500	37,500
2016	75,000	84,375	9,375
	$225,000	$346,875	$121,875

6. In 2017, Zephyr discovered that in 2016 it had failed to record $20,000 as an expense for sales commissions. The sales commissions for 2016 were included in the 2017 expenses.

Instructions

(a) Prepare the income statement for Zephyr Corporation. Do not prepare notes to the financial statements. The effective tax rate for past years was 30%. (*Hint:* A change in depreciation method is considered a change in estimate, not a change in accounting policy.)

DIGGING DEEPER

(b) Prepare a combined statement of net income and retained earnings.

(c) From the perspective of the reader of the financial statements, what is the purpose of intraperiod tax allocation for the statements of income and retained earnings?

P4-12 Joe Schreiner, controller for On Time Clock Company Inc., recently prepared the company's income statement and statement of changes in equity for 2017. Schreiner believes that the statements are a fair presentation of the company's financial progress during the current period, but he also admits that he has not examined any recent professional pronouncements on accounting.

ON TIME CLOCK COMPANY INC.
Income Statement
For the Year Ended December 31, 2017

Sales revenues			$377,852
Less: Sales returns and allowances			16,320
Net sales revenue			361,532
Cost of goods sold:			
Inventory, January 1, 2017		$ 50,235	
Purchases	$192,143		
Less: Purchase discounts	3,142	189,001	
Cost of goods available for sale		239,236	
Inventory, December 31, 2017		41,124	
Cost of goods sold			198,112
Gross profit			163,420
Selling expenses		41,850	
Administrative expenses		32,142	73,992
Income before income tax			89,428
Other revenues and gains			
Unrealized gain on FV-OCI investments			36,000
Dividend revenue			40,000
			165,428
Income tax			56,900
Net income			$108,528

ON TIME CLOCK COMPANY INC.
Excerpt from Statement of Changes in Equity
For the Year Ended December 31, 2017

Retained earnings, January 1, 2017			$216,000
Add:			
Net income for 2017	$108,528		
Gain on sale of long-term investments	31,400	$139,928	
Deduct:			
Loss on expropriation	13,000		
Correction of mathematical error (net of tax)	17,186	(30,186)	109,742
Retained earnings, December 31, 2017			$325,742

Instructions

(a) Assume that On Time Clock Company follows IFRS. Assume that investments are accounted for as FV-OCI investments with gains/losses recycled through net income. Prepare a statement of comprehensive income showing expenses by function. Ignore calculation of EPS.

(b) Prepare the retained earnings and accumulated other comprehensive income portion of the statement of changes in equity. Assume an opening balance of $120,000 in accumulated other comprehensive income.

P4-13 Faldo Corp. is a public company and has 100,000 common shares outstanding. In 2017, the company reported income from continuing operations before income tax of $2,710,000. Additional transactions not considered in the $2,710,000 are as follows:

1. In 2017, Faldo Corp. sold equipment for $140,000. The machine had originally cost $80,000 and had accumulated depreciation to date of $36,000. The gain or loss is considered ordinary.

2. The company discontinued operations of one of its subsidiaries during the current year at a loss of $290,000 before tax. Assume that this transaction meets the criteria for discontinued operations. The loss on operation of the discontinued subsidiary was $90,000 before tax. The loss from disposal of the subsidiary was $200,000 before tax.

3. The sum of $520,000 was received as a result of a lawsuit for a breached 2014 contract. Before the decision, legal counsel was uncertain about the outcome of the suit and had not established a receivable.

4. In 2017, the company reviewed its accounts receivable and determined that $54,000 of accounts receivable that had been carried for years appeared unlikely to be collected. No allowance for doubtful accounts was previously set up.

5. An internal audit discovered that amortization of intangible assets was understated by $35,000 (net of tax) in a prior period. The amount was charged against retained earnings.

Instructions

Analyze the above information and prepare an income statement for the year 2017, starting with income from continuing operations before income tax. Calculate earnings per share as it should be shown on the face of the income statement. (Assume a total effective tax rate of 25% on all items, unless otherwise indicated.)

P4-14 Amos Corporation was incorporated and began business on January 1, 2017. It has been successful and now requires a bank loan for additional working capital to finance an expansion. The bank has requested an audited income statement for the year 2017 using IFRS. The accountant for Amos Corporation provides you with the following income statement, which Amos plans to submit to the bank:

AMOS CORPORATION
Income Statement

Sales revenue		$850,000
Dividend revenue		32,300
Gain on recovery of insurance proceeds from earthquake loss (unusual)		27,300
Unrealized holding gain on FV-OCI investments		5,000
		914,600
Less:		
Selling expenses	$100,100	
Cost of goods sold	510,000	
Advertising expense	13,700	
Loss on inventory due to decline in NRV	34,000	
Loss on discontinued operations	48,600	
Administrative expenses	73,400	779,800
Income before income tax		134,800
Income tax		33,700
Net income		$101,100

Amos had 100,000 common shares outstanding during the year. Gains/losses on FV-OCI investments are recycled through net income.

Instructions

(a) Indicate the deficiencies in the income statement as it currently is. Assume that the corporation prepares a single-step income statement.

(b) Prepare a revised single-step statement of comprehensive income.

P4-15 The equity accounts of Good Karma Corp. as at January 1, 2017, were as follows:

Retained earnings, January 1, 2017	$257,600
Common shares	600,000
Preferred shares	250,000
Contributed surplus	300,000
Accumulated other comprehensive income	525,000

During 2017, the following transactions took place:

Adjustment to correct error in prior years (gain net of tax)	$ 48,000
Unrealized gains on FV-OCI investments (net of tax)	82,000
Dividends:	
Common shares	120,000
Preferred shares	62,000
Issue of equity:	
Common shares	300,000
Preferred shares	5,000
Net income	325,000

Instructions

Prepare a statement of changes in equity for the year ended December 31, 2017. The company follows IFRS. Assume that investments are accounted for as FV-OCI investments, with gains/losses recycled through net income.

P4-16 The following is from a recent income statement for Graben Inc. (a public company):

Sales revenue	$21,924,000,000
Costs and expenses	20,773,000,000
Income from operations	1,151,000,000
Other income	22,000,000
Interest and debt expense	(130,000,000)
Earnings before income tax	1,043,000,000
Income tax	(287,000,000)
Net income	$ 756,000,000

It includes only five separate numbers, two subtotals, and the net earnings figure.

Instructions

(a) Indicate the deficiencies in the income statement.

(b) What recommendations would you make to the company to improve the usefulness of its income statement?

(c) Why do some businesses provide only a minimal disclosure of financial statement elements on their income statement?

*P4-17 On January 1, 2017, Caroline Lampron and Jenni Meno formed a computer sales and service enterprise in Montreal by investing $90,000 cash. The new company, Razorback Sales and Service, has the following transactions in January:

1. Paid $6,000 in advance for three months' rent of office, showroom, and repair space.

2. Purchased 40 personal computers at a cost of $1,500 each, six graphics computers at a cost of $3,000 each, and 25 printers at a cost of $450 each, paying cash on delivery.

3. Sales, repair, and office employees earned $12,600 in salaries during January, of which $3,000 was still payable at the end of January.

4. Sold 30 personal computers for $2,550 each, four graphics computers for $4,500 each, and 15 printers for $750 each. Of the sales amounts, $75,000 was received in cash in January and $30,750 was sold on a deferred payment plan.

5. Other operating expenses of $8,400 were incurred and paid for during January; $2,000 of incurred expenses were payable at January 31.

Instructions

(a) Using the transaction data above, prepare (1) a cash basis income statement and (2) an accrual basis income statement for the month of January.

(b) Using the transaction data above, prepare (1) a cash basis balance sheet and (2) an accrual basis balance sheet as at January 31, 2017.

(c) Identify the items in the cash basis financial statements that make cash basis accounting inconsistent with the theory underlying the elements of financial statements.

*P4-18 Dr. Emma Armstrong, M.D., maintains the accounting records of the Blood Sugar Clinic on a cash basis. During 2017, Dr. Armstrong collected $146,000 in revenues and paid $55,470 in expenses. At January 1, 2017, and December 31, 2017, she had accounts receivable, unearned revenue, accrued liabilities, and prepaid expenses as follows (all long-lived assets are rented):

	January 1	December 31
Accounts receivable	$9,250	$16,100
Unearned revenue	2,840	1,620
Accrued liabilities	3,435	2,200
Prepaid expenses	2,000	1,775

PROFESSIONALISM AND COMMUNICATION

Instructions

Last week, Dr. Armstrong asked you, her CPA, to help her determine her income on the accrual basis. Write a letter to her explaining what you did to calculate net income on the accrual basis. Be sure to state net income on the accrual basis and to include a schedule of your calculations.

ENABLING COMPETENCIES

Case

Refer to the Case Primer on the Student Website and in *WileyPLUS* to help you answer this case.

CA4-1 As a reviewer for the Ontario Securities Commission, you are in the process of reviewing the financial statements of public companies. The following items have come to your attention:

1. A merchandising company overstated its ending inventory two years ago by a material amount. Inventory for all other periods is correctly calculated.

2. An automobile dealer sells for $137,000 an extremely rare 1930 S-type Invicta, which it purchased for $21,000 10 years ago. The Invicta is the only such display item that the dealer owns.

3. During the current year, a drilling company extended the estimated useful life of certain drilling equipment from 9 to 15 years. As a result, amortization for the current year was materially lowered.

4. A retail outlet changed its calculation for bad debt expense from 1% to 0.5% of sales because of changes in its clientele.

5. A mining company sells a large foreign subsidiary that does uranium mining, although the company continues to mine uranium in other countries.

PROFESSIONALISM AND COMMUNICATION

6. A steel company changes from straight-line depreciation to accelerated amortization in accounting for its plant assets, stating that the expected pattern of consumption of the future economic benefits has changed.

7. A construction company, at great expense to itself, prepares a major proposal for a government loan. The loan is not approved.

8. A water pump manufacturer has had large losses resulting from a strike by its employees early in the year.

9. Amortization for a prior period was incorrectly understated by $950,000. The error was discovered in the current year.

10. A large sheep rancher suffered a major loss because the provincial government required that all sheep in the province be killed to halt the spread of a rare disease. Such a situation has not occurred in the province for 20 years.

11. A food distributor that sells wholesale to supermarket chains and to fast-food restaurants (two major classes of customers) decides to discontinue the division that sells to one of the two classes of customers.

Instructions

Discuss the financial reporting issues.

Integrated Cases

ENABLING COMPETENCIES

ETHICS

(*Hint:* If there are issues here that are new, use the conceptual framework to help you support your analysis with solid reasoning.)

IC4-1 Snow Spray Corp. (SSC) recently filed for bankruptcy protection. The company manufactures downhill skis and reports under ASPE. With the increased popularity of such alternative winter sports as snowboarding and tubing, sales of skis are sagging. The company has decided to start a new line of products that focuses on the growing industry surrounding snowboarding and tubing. At present, however, the company needs interim financing to pay suppliers and its payroll. It also needs a significant amount of cash so that it can reposition itself in the marketplace. Management is planning to go to the bank with draft financial statements to discuss additional financing. The company's year end is December 31, 2016, and it is now January 15, 2017. Current interest rates for loans are 5%, but because it is in bankruptcy protection, SSC feels that it will likely have to pay at least 15% on any loan. There is concern that the bank will turn the company down.

At a recent management meeting, the company decided to convert its ski manufacturing facilities into snowboard manufacturing facilities. It will no longer produce skis. Management is unsure if the company will be able to recover the cost of the ski inventory. Although the conversion will result in significant expenditures, the company feels that this is justified if SSC wants to remain a viable business. The shift in strategic positioning will not result in any layoffs, as most employees will work in the retrofitted plant. The remaining employees will be trained in the new business.

The conversion to snowboard manufacturing facilities would not require selling the ski manufacturing machines, as these machines can be used to produce snowboards. The company estimates the results and cash flows from its operation of selling skis to be a $20-million loss.

On December 15, 2016, the company entered into an agreement with Cashco Ltd. to sell its entire inventory in ski bindings to Cashco. Under the terms of the deal, Cashco paid $10 million cash for the inventory (its regular selling price at the time). The cost to SSC of this inventory was $6 million and so a profit of $4 million was booked pre-tax. In a separate deal, SSC agreed to buy back the inventory in January for $10,125,000.

Before filing for bankruptcy protection, the company was able to buy a large shipment of snow tubes wholesale for a bargain price of $7 million from a supplier that was in financial trouble. The value of the inventory is approximately $10 million. The inventory was sitting in the SSC manufacturing facility taking up a lot of space. Because the manufacturing facility was being renovated, SSC reached an agreement with its leading competitor, Alpine Gear Ltd. (AGL). According to the contract, AGL agreed to purchase the snow tubes from SSC for $8 million, and SSC shipped the inventory on December 31 to arrive on January 5. The inventory was shipped f.o.b. shipping point. SSC normally reimburses its customers if the inventory is damaged in transit. SSC has a tentative verbal agreement that it will repurchase the snow tubes that AGL does not sell by the time the renovations are complete (in approximately six months). The buyback price will include an additional amount that will cover storage and insurance costs.

Instructions

Adopt the role of Rachel Glover—the company controller—and discuss the financial reporting issues related to the preparation of the financial statements for the year ended December 31, 2016

IC4-2 Brave Maven Inc. (BMI) operates in challenging economic times. It currently manufactures trucks and equipment used for construction, as well as off-road automobiles and automotive parts. During the year, net losses from off-road automobiles and parts totalled $1 million (net of tax). Future losses are expected to increase by an additional $1 million. BMI's management team is contemplating selling off this unprofitable business segment. In December, BMI's board of directors authorized a sale transaction.

Management would also like to expand the production of trucks and construction equipment. BMI's lenders are not willing to provide additional financing, so BMI will need to explore equity financing. Management is preparing the necessary documentation for an initial public offering.

The carrying value of the facility and equipment used to manufacture the automobiles and parts is $2 million. Two years ago, some modifications were made to the equipment. The equipment is now specialized for use by BMI, which would have to spend $500,000 to disassemble the previous modifications in order to sell the equipment. By year end, management had already hired a contractor to begin disassembling the equipment.

BMI has been in sale negotiations with one of its automotive parts suppliers interested in expanding its own automotive parts business. Negotiations are expected to continue, but the two companies are not able to agree on a price. The supplier has indicated it would only be willing to pay up to 90% of the asking price, as it would have to make its own modifications to the equipment first. The purchase would only go ahead if BMI completed the disassembly of the equipment's existing modifications and the supplier's engineer subsequently inspected and approved the equipment. Management feels that 90% of the asking price is just under what it would be willing to sell the assets at.

BMI is also in a dispute with one of its suppliers of truck parts. In order to get a discounted price, BMI had to commit to purchasing $500,000 of spare parts each year for three years. BMI recently upgraded its safety standards and consequently made modifications to its construction trucks in the current year. As a result, management did not accept delivery of the spare parts for the current year. There is a provision in the contract that stipulates an annual penalty of $250,000 for failure to take delivery. One more year remains in the contract. BMI's lawyers are reviewing the contract. They have suggested that BMI may qualify for exemption from the penalty for not taking delivery because its refusal resulted from a change in the safety specification for the part and not because of a

AUDIT

change in sales demand. The supplier is willing to modify its spare parts to conform to BMI's new safety standard.

Just before year end, management purchased an additional building. BMI plans to use 50% of the building and move the current sales team to the new location. It does not plan to use the other 50% as part of its current operations. BMI's real estate agent looked at the property and believes the part of the building that BMI will not occupy can be sold and leased separately. Management

does not want BMI to use fair value as its basis for measurement because it is concerned that changes in fair value will create too much volatility in the income statement. This may lower the price that BMI shares sell at in the future public offering.

Instructions

It is now two months after year end. Assume the role of BMI's auditor and discuss the financial reporting issues.

RESEARCH AND ANALYSIS

REAL WORLD EMPHASIS

RA4-1 Maple Leaf Foods Inc.

Locate the audited annual financial statements (including the accompanying notes) of **Maple Leaf Foods Inc. (Maple Leaf)** for its year ended December 31, 2014 (www.sedar.com).

Instructions

Refer to the statements and notes to answer the following questions.

(a) What type of income statement format does the company use: single- or multiple-step? Comment.

(b) What business(es) is the company in during 2014? (*Hint*: Look at Note 1 to the financial statements.)

(c) How are these businesses reflected in Maple Leaf's balance sheet and income statement?

(d) Is the income statement presented by function or nature? Why?

(e) Explain what makes up any reported amount for discontinued operations for the year ended December 31, 2014. Why is it important to disclose this information separately from other results for the year?

(f) What is included in other comprehensive income and what is the total of comprehensive income for the current year? How much of this income or loss is attributable to the shareholders of the parent and to the non-controlling shareholders?

(g) How has the EPS been calculated? How many EPS figures are presented and why? Where is the EPS disclosed?

REAL WORLD EMPHASIS

RA4-2 Royal Bank of Canada

Obtain the 2014 annual report for the **Royal Bank of Canada** from the company's website or from SEDAR (www.sedar.com). Note that financial reporting for Canadian banks is also constrained by the *Bank Act* and monitored by the Office of the Superintendent of Financial Institutions.

Instructions

(a) Revenues and expenses arise primarily from ordinary business activities. What are the bank's ordinary (core) business activities? What normal expenses must the bank incur in order to generate core revenues?

(b) How are the core business activities and other income and expenses reflected in the bank's statement of income?

(c) Calculate the percentage of the various revenue and income streams to total revenue and income. Discuss the trends from year to year. In other words, are these revenue and income streams increasing as a percentage of the total revenue and income or decreasing? What are the main sources of the revenue and income?

(d) Describe the types of transactions that are included in the statement of changes in equity.

REAL WORLD EMPHASIS

RA4-3 Brookfield Office Properties Inc. and Mainstreet Equity Corp.

Use the annual reports and/or the audited annual financial statements of **Brookfield Office Properties Inc.** for the year ended December 31, 2014, and of **Mainstreet Equity Corp.** for the year ended September 30, 2014, to answer the following questions. These reports are available on SEDAR (www.sedar.com) or the companies' websites.

Instructions

(a) Look at the Management Discussion and Analysis and the annual report in general. What business are both companies in?

(b) What type of income statement format(s) do these two companies use? Identify any differences in income statement format between the two companies. Are their income statements presented by function or by nature?

(c) What are the main sources of revenues for both companies? Are these increasing or decreasing?

(d) Is the nature of each business reflected in its balance sheet? (*Hint:* What is the main asset and what percentage of total assets does this asset account for?)

(e) What types of items are included in other comprehensive income for each company?

RA4-4   Canadian Securities Administrators

REAL WORLD EMPHASIS

The Canadian Securities Administrators (CSA), an umbrella group of Canadian provincial securities commissions, accumulates and publishes all documents that public companies are required to file under securities law. This database may be accessed from the sedar website (www.sedar.com).

Instructions

Visit the CSA website and find the company documents and financial reports for **Bank of Montreal** and **Royal Bank of Canada**. Company financial statements and other information can also be accessed through the company websites (www.bmo.com and www.rbcroyalbank.com). Answer the following questions:

(a) What types of company documents can be found here that provide useful information for investors who are making investment decisions?

(b) Locate the annual information form. Explain the nature of the information that it contains. As a financial statement analyst, is this information useful to you? Why or why not?

(c) Who is the auditor of each bank?

(d) Which stock exchange(s) does each bank trade on?

(e) Go to the company websites directly. Look under Investor Relations. What type of information is on these websites and how is it different from what is found on the CSA website? Should these websites contain the same information as the CSA website?

RA4-5   Quality of Earnings Assessment

REAL WORLD EMPHASIS

Quality of earnings analysis is a very important tool in assessing the value of a company and its shares. The chapter presents a framework for evaluating quality of earnings.

Instructions

Do an Internet search on the topic and write a critical essay discussing the usefulness of the quality of earnings assessment.

FINANCE

RA4-6   BCE Inc.

REAL WORLD EMPHASIS

An excerpt from Section 10.2 of the Management Discussion and Analysis in the 2014 annual report of **BCE Inc.** is shown below. The excerpt shows summarized financial information, including calculations of earnings before interest, tax, depreciation, and amortization (EBITDA), and adjusted net earnings—both non-GAAP earnings measures. The company provides information on these calculations, which is also shown.

Instructions

Read the excerpts below. Discuss the pros and cons of management's decision to report additional earnings numbers outside of the traditional audited financial statements. In the case of this company, in your opinion, do you think that this presentation provides good, useful information?

10.2   Non-GAAP financial measures ...

This section describes the non-GAAP financial measures ... we use in this MD&A to explain our financial results. It also provides reconciliations of the non-GAAP financial measures to the most comparable IFRS financial measures.

Adjusted EBITDA and Adjusted EBITDA margin

Beginning with Q2 2014, we reference Adjusted EBITDA and Adjusted EBITDA margin as non-GAAP financial measures. These terms replace the previously referenced non-GAAP financial measures EBITDA and EBITDA margin. Our definitions of Adjusted EBITDA and Adjusted EBITDA margin are unchanged from our former definition of EBITDA and EBITDA margin, respectively. Accordingly, this change in terminology has no impact on our reported financial results for prior periods.

The terms Adjusted EBITDA . . . do not have any standardized meaning under IFRS. Therefore, . . . are unlikely to be comparable to similar measures presented by other issuers.

We use Adjusted EBITDA . . . to evaluate the performance of our businesses as it reflects their ongoing profitability. We believe that certain investors and analysts use Adjusted EBITDA to measure a company's ability to

service debt and to meet other payment obligations or as a common measurement to value companies in the telecommunications industry. We believe that certain investors and analysts also use Adjusted EBITDA . . . to evaluate the performance of our businesses. Adjusted EBITDA is also one component in the determination of short-term incentive compensation for all management employees.

Adjusted EBITDA has no directly comparable IFRS financial measure. Alternatively, the following table provides a reconciliation of net earnings to Adjusted EBITDA.

	2014	2103
Net earnings	2,718	2,388
Severance, acquisition and other costs	216	406
Depreciation	2,880	2,734
Amortization	572	646
Finance costs		
Interest expense	929	931
Interest on post-employment benefit obligations	101	150
Other (income) expense	(42)	6
Income taxes	929	828
Adjusted EBITDA	8,303	8,089

Adjusted net earnings and Adjusted EPS

The terms Adjusted net earnings and Adjusted EPS do not have any standardized meaning under IFRS. Therefore, they are unlikely to be comparable to similar measures presented by other issuers.

We define Adjusted net earnings as net earnings attributable to common shareholders before severance, acquisition and other costs, net (gains) losses on investments, and early debt redemption costs. We define Adjusted EPS as Adjusted net earnings per BCE common share.

We use Adjusted net earnings and Adjusted EPS, and we believe that certain investors and analysts use these measures, among other ones, to assess the performance of our businesses without the effects of severance, acquisition and other costs, net (gains) losses on investments, and early debt redemption costs, net of tax and NCI. We exclude these items because they affect the comparability of our financial results and could potentially distort the analysis of trends in business performance. Excluding these items does not imply they are non-recurring.

The most comparable IFRS financial measures are net earnings attributable to common shareholders and EPS. The following table is a reconciliation of net earnings attributable to common shareholders and EPS to Adjusted net earnings on a consolidated basis and per BCE common share (Adjusted EPS), respectively.

	2014		2013	
	TOTAL	PER SHARE	TOTAL	PER SHARE
Net earnings attributable to common shareholders	2,363	2.98	1,975	2.55
Severance, acquisition and other costs	148	0.18	299	0.38
Net (gains) losses on investments	(8)	(0.01)	7	0.01
Early debt redemption costs	21	0.03	36	0.05
Adjusted net earnings	2,524	3.18	2,317	2.99

ENDNOTES

[1] For instance, if a risky company borrows from the bank, it will be charged a higher interest rate than a less risky company.

[2] In assessing whether earnings are sustainable, a strategic analysis of the company's positioning within the industry should be performed, as well as an assessment of the business model's viability. This is beyond the scope of this course.

[3] The term "irregular" is used for transactions and other events that come from developments that are outside the normal business operations.

[4] In actuality, this concept has its roots in **capital maintenance theory**, which says that as long as capital is maintained from year to year, the rest is assumed to be income. Capital may be defined as financial (in terms of amount of dollars invested in the business) or physical (earnings potential of the income-generating assets).

[5] These items will be discussed in greater detail in subsequent chapters.

[6] *CPA Canada Handbook—Accounting*, Part II, Section 3475.03(e) and IFRS 5.32.

[7] *CPA Canada Handbook—Accounting*, Part II, Section 3475.03(e) and IFRS 5.31.

[8] *CPA Canada Handbook—Accounting*, Part II, Section 3475.08 and IFRS 5.7 and .8.

[9] The term "income from continuing operations" is a financial statement subtotal often used. Its use is not mandated nor required by GAAP but companies use it where there are discontinued operations.

[10] *CPA Canada Handbook—Accounting*, Part II, Section 3475.13 and IFRS 5.15.

[11] *CPA Canada Handbook—Accounting*, Part II, Section 3475.33-.35. These assets and liabilities would be classified as current only if they have been sold before the financial statements are complete and if the proceeds are expected to be received within the year.

[12] IFRS 5.3 and .8.

[13] IFRS 5.33, .34, .41, 42, and *CPA Canada Handbook—Accounting*, Part II, Section 3475.30 and .36.

[14] In addition, these cash flows must be sufficient to cover other things such as cost of capital.

[15] *CPA Canada Handbook—Accounting*, Part II, Section 1520.04 and IAS 1.97–.105. ASPE notes that where these items may be set out "more readily" in the notes or in a schedule, this should be noted on the income statement.

[16] IAS 1.81A and B.

[17] Corporate tax rates in Canada have been declining over the past several years. As a general note, the federal rate is 15% and the provincial rate averages about 10%, for a total of 25%.

[18] IAS 33.68.

[19] Earnings per share will be covered in significant detail in Chapter 17.

[20] OSC Staff Notice 52-306.

[21] A cash or modified cash basis might be used in the following situations:

1. A company that is primarily interested in cash flows (for example, a group of physicians that distributes cash-basis earnings for salaries and bonuses)

2. A company that has a limited number of financial statement users (a small, closely held company with little or no debt)

3. A company that has operations that are relatively straightforward (small amounts of inventory, long-term assets, or long-term debt)

CHAPTER 5

FINANCIAL POSITION AND CASH FLOWS

REFERENCE TO THE CPA COMPETENCY MAP | LEARNING OBJECTIVES

After studying this chapter, you should be able to:

1.1.1, 1.4.2, 1.4.4, 5.1.1	**1.** Understand the statement of financial position and statement of cash flows from a business perspective.
1.1.1, 1.3.1	**2.** Identify the uses and limitations of a statement of financial position.
1.1.1, 1.2.1, 1.2.2, 1.2.3, 1.3.1, 1.4.2	**3.** Identify the major classifications of a statement of financial position.
1.3.1, 1.4.2, 1.4.5, 2.3.1	**4.** Prepare a classified statement of financial position.
1.3.1, 1.3.2, 1.4.1, 1.4.2	**5.** Identify statement of financial position information that requires supplemental disclosure.
1.1.1, 1.3.1, 1.3.2	**6.** Identify major disclosure techniques for the statement of financial position.
1.1.1, 1.2.1, 1.2.2, 1.3.1, 1.4.3	**7.** Indicate the purpose and identify the content of the statement of cash flows.
1.3.1, 1.3.2, 1.4.2, 5.2.1	**8.** Prepare a statement of cash flows using the indirect method.
1.1.1, 1.3.1, 1.4.2, 1.4.3, 5.1.1, 5.2.1	**9.** Understand the usefulness of the statement of cash flows.
1.1.4	**10.** Identify differences in accounting between IFRS and ASPE.
1.1.2, 1.1.4	**11.** Identify the significant changes planned by the IASB regarding financial statement presentation.

After studying Appendix 5A, you should be able to:

1.4.2, 1.4.4, 1.4.5, 5.1.1	**12.** Identify the major types of financial ratios and what they measure.

TOWARD BETTER DISCLOSURE

AS YOU'VE SEEN in previous chapters, solid financial reporting underpins the capital marketplace. Investors, creditors, and other stakeholders need assurance that publicly traded companies are presenting an accurate and transparent picture of their financial information.

One way to increase this assurance is by the Canadian Securities Administrators (CSA), the umbrella group of provincial securities regulators, reviewing a sample of the financial statements issued by public companies (called "issuers") to check their compliance with disclosure requirements. The CSA examines company financial statements (such as the statement of financial position), management discussion and analysis reports, and other regulatory disclosure documents.

Getty Images/DNY59

For the 2014 fiscal year, the CSA did a full review of 221 issuers and a partial review of 770 issuers (focusing on particular issues). The CSA found that in 76% of the reviews, the filer was required to take action to improve their disclosure, or in the most extreme instances was referred to enforcement, ceased trading, or was placed on the default list (which could require them to refile their financial statements). The deficiencies the CSA found regarding financial statement measurement and disclosure included a lack of information regarding: whether the company was a going concern; explanations of accounting policies used; sources of estimation uncertainty; and fair value measurement.

The CSA singled out some areas of IFRS requirements where it said "many issuers could improve compliance." One was revenue recognition. "IAS 18 Revenue . . . defines revenue as income that arises in the course of ordinary activities of an entity, and sets out a framework for recognizing revenue." The CSA noted that "One of the key determinations that needs to be made when recording revenue, is whether the issuer is acting as principal or agent. When an agency relationship exists an issuer collects amounts on behalf of a third party rather than on their own behalf. Therefore, in agency relationships the issuer can only recognize the fee, commission or mark-up that will be paid to the issuer as revenue."

The CSA found companies that did not sufficiently disclose how they determined who was principal or agent, and how they recognized revenue. "Examples have been noted whereby an issuer recognized revenue as either principal or agent but their disclosure documents . . . contradicted or did not support the accounting treatment. We expect issuers to provide sufficient disclosure of their accounting policies and judgements applied in determining those policies." The CSA gave an example of an issuer that noted that subcontracting revenues were generated by subcontractors who own and operate their own vehicles, which suggests an agency relationship. However, the company recognized the subcontracting revenue as revenue from a principal, and the CSA "questioned the issuer's rationale" for doing so.

Sources: Canadian Securities Administrators, "CSA Staff Notice 51-341 – Continuous Disclosure Review Program Activities for the Fiscal Year Ended March 31, 2014," Canadian Securities Administrators website, www.csa-acvm.ca.

PREVIEW OF CHAPTER 5

The statement of financial position and statement of cash flows complement the income statement, offering information about the company's financial position and how the firm generates and uses cash. This chapter examines the many different types of assets, liabilities, and shareholders' equity items that affect the statement of financial position and the statement of cash flows.

The chapter is organized as follows:

FINANCIAL POSITION AND CASH FLOWS				
Usefulness from a Business Perspective	**Statement of Financial Position**	**Statement of Cash Flows**	**IFRS/ASPE Comparison**	**Appendix 5A— Ratio Analysis: A Reference**
▪ Analyzing a statement of financial position ▪ Assessing earnings quality ▪ Assessing the creditworthiness of companies	▪ Usefulness and limitations of the statement of financial position ▪ Classification in the statement of financial position ▪ Preparation of the classified statement of financial position (balance sheet) ▪ Additional information reported ▪ Techniques of disclosure	▪ Purpose, content, and format of a statement of cash flows ▪ Preparation of the statement of cash flows ▪ Usefulness of the statement of cash flows ▪ Perspectives	▪ A comparison of IFRS and ASPE ▪ Looking ahead	▪ Business risks ▪ Financial ratios

Usefulness of the Statements of Financial Position and Cash Flows from a Business Perspective

Objective 1
Understand the
statement of financial
position and statement
of cash flows from a
business perspective.

It is important to understand how the users of financial statements use the statement of financial position and the statement of cash flows. For example, what might potential investors in a company focus on when analyzing a statement of financial position? What aspects of the statement of cash flows do financial analysts focus on when they are assessing earnings quality? How do creditors use financial statements to assess the creditworthiness of companies that have requested a loan? We will answer these questions below.

Analyzing a Statement of Financial Position

The statement of financial position (SFP) provides information about a company's liquidity and solvency in order to assess the risk of investing (or increasing the investment) in the company. In addition, the SFP provides details about the company's financial structure, such as whether it is financed primarily by debt or equity. If a company is heavily indebted, it may not be able to make the most of opportunities that occur as the economy improves. On the other hand, as discussed later in this chapter, companies with more financial flexibility are typically better able to survive economic downturns and to take advantage of opportunities to invest and expand. Investors can use the SFP and related notes to the financial statements to assess companies' financial flexibility and their risk of business failure.

Assessing Earnings Quality

ETHICS

It is important to understand how financial analysts and other users of the statement of cash flows use it to assess earnings quality. One concern of financial statement users is that company insiders might manipulate information to make earnings look better or worse than they are, for strategic reasons. For example, if managers are trying to increase their bonus or prevent the company from violating the terms of a loan, they may be tempted to artificially increase earnings. They could do this by reducing the allowance for doubtful accounts or reducing the provision for inventory obsolescence. Likewise, managers might try to lower earnings in a year when they have missed their bonuses, so that they can more easily increase earnings and their bonuses the next year. Analyzing the statement of cash flows is often done to assess earnings quality. For example, if net income is significantly higher than cash flows from operations, this is a sign of poor earnings quality that may require further analysis. Similarly, if a company relies on the issuance of shares or other financing activities to offset repeated negative cash flows from operations, the financial statement users should be concerned.

THEORY

Assessing the Creditworthiness of Companies

Creditors often rely on the SFP to assess a company's liquidity and its ability to service debt. Similarly, a review of a company's long-term debt and shareholders' equity section helps to determine its solvency level. For example, when a company has a high debt to total assets ratio, it is at higher risk of bankruptcy. Companies that use a higher proportion of debt are typically at higher risk and require higher cash flow from operations to ensure that they are able to make interest and principal payments as they come due. We discuss the preparation and use of the SFP and statement of cash flows in more detail below.

STATEMENT OF FINANCIAL POSITION

Usefulness and Limitations of the Statement of Financial Position

Objective 2
Identify the uses and limitations of a statement of financial position.

The **statement of financial position**, often referred to as the **balance sheet** (under ASPE), reports a business enterprise's assets, liabilities, and shareholders' equity at a specific date. This financial statement provides information about the nature and amounts of investment in enterprise resources, obligations to creditors, and the owners' equity (net resources). It therefore helps in predicting the amounts, timing, and uncertainty of future cash flows.

Usefulness

By providing information about assets, liabilities, and shareholders' equity, the SFP becomes a basis for calculating rates of return on invested assets and for evaluating the enterprise's capital structure. Information in the SFP is also used to assess business risk and future cash flows.[1] In this regard, the **SFP is useful for analyzing a company's liquidity, solvency**, and **financial flexibility**, as described below. It also helps in analyzing profitability (even though this is not the main focus of the statement).

FINANCIAL ANALYSIS AND PLANNING
5.1.1

    Liquidity depends on the amount of time that is expected to pass until an asset is realized (converted into cash) or until a liability has to be paid. Does the company have enough cash on hand and cash coming in to cover its short-term liabilities? Certain ratios help assess overall liquidity, including the **current ratio**, **quick or acid test ratio**, and **current cash debt coverage ratio**. The liquidity of certain assets, such as receivables and inventory, is assessed through **activity** or **turnover ratios**.[2] These ratios look at how fast the receivables or inventories are being collected or sold. Creditors are interested in **short-term** liquidity ratios, because these ratios indicate whether the enterprise will have the resources to pay its current and maturing obligations. Similarly, shareholders assess liquidity to evaluate the possibility of future cash dividends or the buyback of shares. In general, the greater the liquidity, the lower the risk of enterprise or business failure.[3]

    Solvency reflects an **enterprise's ability to pay its debts and related interest**. For example, when a company carries a high level of long-term debt compared with its assets, it is at higher risk for insolvency than a similar company with less long-term debt. Companies with higher debt are riskier because more of their assets will be required to meet these fixed obligations (such as interest and principal payments). Certain ratios help assess solvency. These are often called **coverage ratios** because they refer to a company's ability to cover its interest and long-term debt payments.

    Liquidity and solvency affect an entity's **financial flexibility**, which measures the **"ability of an enterprise to take effective actions to alter the amounts and timing of cash flows so it can respond to unexpected needs and opportunities."**[4] For example, a company may become so loaded with debt—so financially inflexible—that its cash sources to finance expansion or to pay off maturing debt are limited or non-existent. An enterprise with a high degree of financial flexibility is better able to survive bad times, to recover from unexpected setbacks, and to take advantage of profitable and unexpected investment opportunities. Generally, the greater the financial flexibility, the lower the risk of enterprise or business failure.

WHAT DO THE NUMBERS MEAN?

REAL WORLD EMPHASIS

Eastman Kodak Company is a technology company that focuses on digital imaging and printing for businesses. Kodak reported assets of U.S. $5.1 billion and debt of U.S. $6.8 billion in its Chapter 11 (bankruptcy) documents filed in New York in 2012. The company had failed to adapt from its strengths in areas such as traditional film and the Instamatic camera. At the time it entered into bankruptcy protection, Kodak had made a push into inkjet printers and commercial digital printers, but the new products did not generate enough demand to make up for a business model based on traditional film. The company had developed the first digital camera in 1975 but shelved it due to worries that it would threaten the more profitable film business.[5]

By September 2013, Kodak emerged from bankruptcy protection, with a plan to focus more on printing equipment and related services for businesses. By the third quarter of 2014, Kodak had earnings per share from continuing operations of $0.67 (offset partially by a loss on discontinued operations of $0.28). It also had net assets of U.S. $527 million. However, the company still faces significant business risks. For example, it was still generating negative cash flow from operations in late 2013 and acknowledged in its third-quarter SEC filings that "Our ability to generate positive operating cash flows will be necessary for us to continue to operate our business" and that the success of new products would depend on factors such as properly identifying customer needs, innovating, commercializing new technology on a timely basis, controlling product quality in manufacturing, and pricing products and services competitively.[6] Liquidity risk is an ongoing concern for the company given the nature of the industry. These risks are examined further below as part of our discussion of the SFP and the calculation of free cash flow.

Limitations

Because the income statement and the SFP are interrelated, it is not surprising that the SFP has many of the same limitations as the income statement. Here are some of the major limitations of the SFP:

UNDERLYING CONCEPT

"Soft" numbers are less reliable than "hard" numbers and have less predictive value because they are likely to change.

1. Many assets and liabilities are stated at their historical cost. As a result, the information that is reported in the SFP has higher reliability but it can be criticized as being less relevant than the current fair value would be. We discussed the use of historical cost and other valuation methods in Chapters 2 and 3. As noted there, as a general trend, we are moving toward greater use of fair value, specifically for things such as investments and biological assets.

2. Judgements and estimates are used in determining many of the items reported in the SFP. Recall the issues we identified in Chapter 4 when discussing income statement limitations. As we stated there, the financial statements include many "soft" numbers; that is, numbers that are significantly uncertain.

3. The SFP necessarily **leaves out many items** that are of relevance to the business but cannot be recorded objectively.[7] These may be either assets or liabilities. Recall again our discussion from Chapter 4. Because liquidity and solvency ratios worsen when liabilities are recognized, a company may be biased against including liabilities in the financial statements. Knowing this, analysts habitually look for and capitalize many liabilities that may be "off–balance sheet" before they calculate key liquidity and solvency ratios.[8] For example, when reviewing a company, analysts consider off–balance sheet liabilities such as certain types of leases. The information that is disclosed in the notes to the financial statements and the analyst's knowledge of the business and industry become critical in this context, because they make it possible to identify and measure off–balance sheet items that often represent additional risk to the company.

Classification in the Statement of Financial Position

SFP accounts are **classified** (like the income statement) so that **similar items are grouped together** to arrive at significant subtotals. The material is also arranged so that important relationships are shown.

As is true of the income statement, the SFP's parts and subsections can be more informative than the whole. Individual items should be separately reported and classified in enough detail so that users can assess the amounts, timing, and uncertainty of future cash flows, and evaluate the company's liquidity and financial flexibility, profitability, and risk.

Classification in financial statements helps analysts and other financial statement users by **grouping items with similar characteristics** and **separating items with different characteristics**. In this regard, the SFP provides additional information. Recall that many users use the information in financial statements to assess risk, including the company's financial flexibility, as noted earlier. Consider how the following groupings of assets and liabilities provide additional insight:

1. Assets that are of a different type or that have a different **function** in the company's activities should be reported as separate items. For example, merchandise inventories should be reported separately from property, plant, and equipment. Inventory will be sold and property, plant, and equipment will be used. In this way, investors can see how fast inventory is turning over or being sold.

2. Liabilities with **different implications for the enterprise's financial flexibility** should be reported as separate items. For example, long-term liabilities should be reported separately from current liabilities, and debt should be separate from equity.

3. Assets and liabilities with different **general liquidity characteristics** should be reported as separate items. For example, cash should be reported separately from accounts receivable, and property held for use is reported separately from that held for sale.

4. Certain assets, liabilities, and equity instruments have **attributes that allow them to be measured or valued more easily**. Reporting these separately takes advantage of this characteristic. Monetary assets, and liabilities and financial instruments are two such groupings. We will discuss each separately below.

Monetary versus Non-monetary Assets and Liabilities

UNDERLYING CONCEPT

With non-monetary assets, historical cost is often a more reliable measure where market values are not available.

Monetary assets represent either money itself **or claims to future cash flows that are fixed or determinable in amount and timing.**[9] Because of these characteristics, they are said to be easier to measure, and they generally are. In addition, their carrying values (which approximate net realizable value) are more representative of economic reality because they normally are close to the amount of cash that the company will receive in the future. Examples are accounts and notes receivable. Likewise, liabilities that require **future cash outflows that are fixed or determinable in amount and timing** are also considered to be monetary and thus easier to measure.[10] Accounts and notes payable and long-term debt are examples. In contrast, other assets—such as inventory; property, plant, and equipment; certain investments; and intangibles—are **non-monetary assets** because their value in terms of a monetary unit such as dollars is not fixed. There is therefore additional measurement uncertainty. These assets are frequently recorded at their historical cost (or amortized cost), which often does not reflect the economic value to the firm.

Financial Instruments

LAW

Financial instruments are contracts between two or more parties that create a financial asset for one party and a financial liability or equity instrument for the other. They are often marketable or tradable, and therefore easy to measure.[11] Many financial instruments are also monetary assets or liabilities. Financial assets include the following:

- **Cash**

- **Contractual rights to receive cash or another financial instrument**

- **Equity instruments of other companies**[12]

Contractual rights to **receive** cash or other financial instruments are assets, whereas contractual obligations to **pay** are liabilities. Cash, accounts receivable, and all payables are examples of financial instruments. These instruments are all monetary. Shares are also financial instruments. Current accounting standards on financial instruments require fair value accounting for certain types of financial instruments, including certain types of investments, especially where market values are readily available. This is due to the fact that fair value (often market value) is quite easy to obtain and represents an objective view of the measurement of the instrument. In addition, IFRS and ASPE generally allow an entity to choose to value financial instruments at fair value as an accounting policy choice (with gains and losses booked through net income). This is referred to as the **fair value** option. Financial instruments should not be offset against each other on the SFP except under limited circumstances. We discuss the accounting and reporting of financial instruments more extensively in Chapters 7, 9, 13, 14, 15, and 16. Derivatives, a more complex type of financial instrument, will be covered in Chapter 16. Most monetary assets and liabilities are financial instruments.

The three general classes of items that are included in the SFP are assets, liabilities, and equity. They are defined below.

ELEMENTS OF THE STATEMENT OF FINANCIAL POSITION

1. *Assets.* **Economic resources** controlled by an entity as a result of past transactions or events that are expected to result in future economic benefits.

2. *Liabilities.* **Present obligations that arise from past transactions or events.**

3. *Equity/Net assets.* The **residual interest** in an entity's assets that remains after deducting its liabilities. In a business enterprise, equity is the ownership interest.

SIGNIFICANT CHANGE

These are based on the definitions from Chapter 2 and the conceptual framework, but as discussed in the Looking Ahead section of this chapter, there have been proposed changes to these definitions. Illustration 5-1 shows a standard format for presenting the SFP for many companies.

Illustration 5-1

Statement of Financial Position Classifications

Assets	Liabilities and Shareholders' Equity
Current assets	Current liabilities
Long-term investments	Long-term debt
Property, plant, and equipment	Shareholders' equity
Intangible assets	Capital shares
Other assets	Contributed surplus
	Retained earnings
	Accumulated other comprehensive income/ other surplus

Although the SFP can be classified or presented in other ways, in actual practice the major subdivisions noted in Illustration 5-1 are closely followed, with exceptions in certain industries. When the SFP is for a proprietorship or partnership, the classifications in the owners' equity section are presented a little differently, as we will show later in the chapter. In addition, some companies following IFRS, such as **British Airways plc**, choose to invert the order of items in their SFP. It lists non-current assets first and current assets last. Similarly, it lists shareholders' equity first, followed by non-current liabilities, and then current liabilities.

These standard classifications make it easier to calculate important ratios, such as the current ratio for assessing liquidity and debt to equity ratios for assessing solvency. Because total assets are broken down into categories, users can easily calculate which assets are more significant than others and how these relationships change over time.[13] This gives insight into management's strategy and stewardship. Illustration 5-2 shows a classified SFP for **Air Canada**.

Illustration 5-2

Classified SFP—Excerpt from Air Canada's December 31, 2014 Financial Statements

REAL WORLD EMPHASIS

CONSOLIDATED STATEMENT OF FINANCIAL POSITION			
CANADIAN DOLLARS IN MILLIONS		DECEMBER 31, 2014	DECEMBER 31, 2013
ASSETS			
CURRENT			
Cash and cash equivalents	Note 2P	$ 661	$ 750
Short-term investments	Note 2Q	1,614	1,458
Total cash, cash equivalents and short-term investments		2,275	2,208
Restricted cash	Note 2R	89	92
Accounts receivable		656	589
Aircraft fuel inventory		72	71
Spare parts and supplies inventory	Note 2S	91	65
Prepaid expenses and other current assets		295	263
Total current assets		3,478	3,288
Property and equipment	Note 4	5,998	5,073
Intangible assets	Note 5	305	304
Goodwill	Note 6	311	311
Deposits and other assets	Note 7	556	494
TOTAL ASSETS		$10,648	$ 9,470
LIABILITIES			
CURRENT			
Accounts payable and accrued liabilities		$ 1,259	$ 1,129
Advance ticket sales		1,794	1,687
Current portion of long-term debt and finance leases	Note 8	484	374
Total current liabilities		3,537	3,190
Long-term debt and finance leases	Note 8	4,732	3,959
Pension and other benefit liabilities	Note 9	2,403	2,687
Maintenance provisions	Note 10	796	656
Other long-term liabilities	Note 11	313	375
TOTAL LIABILITIES		$11,781	$10,867
EQUITY			
SHAREHOLDERS' EQUITY			
Share capital	Note 13	835	827
Contributed surplus		77	80
Deficit		(2,113)	(2,367)
Total shareholders' equity		(1,201)	(1,460)
NON-CONTROLLING INTERESTS		68	63
TOTAL EQUITY		(1,133)	(1,397)
TOTAL LIABILITIES AND EQUITY		$10,648	$ 9,470

The accompanying notes are an integral part of the consolidated financial statements.

Note that the total shareholders' equity position improved in 2014, with total shareholders' equity (in millions) ending the year at –$1,133 versus –$1,397 at the end of 2013. Just a few years earlier, Air Canada was in a significantly worse equity position, with shareholders' equity of –$4,085 at the end of 2011.

Air Canada's improved equity position is partly due to passenger revenue increasing by over 7%, passenger load increasing to 83.4%, and comprehensive income of $272 million. The most dramatic improvement in equity actually occurred in 2013, when Air Canada recorded a $1,908-million improvement in equity as a result of "remeasurements on employee benefit liabilities." The change in pension-related liabilities included the impact of factors such as an increase in the discount rates used to value the liabilities, a 13.8% return on pension plan assets, and past service payments made during the year.

Preparation of the Classified Statement of Financial Position (Balance Sheet)

Current Assets

Objective 4
Prepare a classified statement of financial position.

Current assets include cash and other assets that will ordinarily be realized within one year from the date of the SFP or within the normal operating cycle if the cycle is longer than a year.[14] The operating cycle is the average time between the acquisition of assets for processing and the realization of cash or cash equivalents. Cash is realized through sales of the product that is created from the materials and supplies. The cycle begins with cash and then moves through inventory, production, and receivables, and back to cash. When there are several operating cycles within one year, the one-year period is used. If the operating cycle is more than one year, the longer period is used. Illustration 5-3 shows the operating cycle for manufacturing companies.

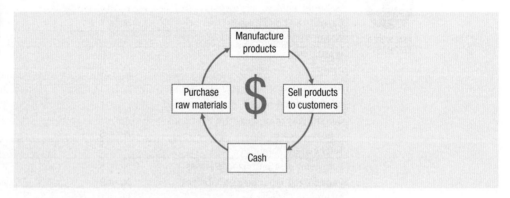

Illustration 5-3

The Business Operating Cycle for Manufacturing Companies

UNDERLYING CONCEPT

Grouping these similar items together reduces the amount of redundant information on the SFP and therefore makes the information easier to understand.

For most industries, current assets are generally segregated and presented in the SFP in order according to their liquidity.[15] The five major items that are found in the current assets section are cash, short-term investments (including derivatives), receivables, inventories, and prepayments. These items are valued as follows:

1. Cash: at its stated value

2. Investments: at cost/amortized cost or fair value

3. Accounts receivable: at the estimated amount that is collectible

4. Inventories: generally at the lower of cost and net realizable value

5. Prepaid items: at cost

Cash

Cash is often grouped with other cash-like liquid assets and reported as **cash and cash equivalents**. Cash and cash equivalents are defined as **cash, demand deposits**, and **short-term, highly liquid investments that are readily convertible into known amounts of cash and have an insignificant risk of changing in value**.[16] Illustration 5-4 details the cash and cash equivalents for Canadian-based retailer **Canadian Tire**.

Illustration 5-4

Consolidated Balance Sheet Presentation of Cash and Cash Equivalents—Excerpt from Canadian Tire Corporation' January 3, 2015 Financial Statements

REAL WORLD EMPHASIS

Cash and Cash Equivalents

Cash and cash equivalents are defined as cash plus highly liquid and rated certificates of deposit or commercial paper with an original term to maturity of three months or less.

Any restrictions on the general availability of cash or any commitments regarding how it is likely to be used must be disclosed and may affect whether the items are presented as current.

How much cash should a company hold? In general, a company needs enough liquid assets, including cash, to be able to settle its current liabilities in a timely manner; however, it must also ensure that its assets do not sit idle. Cash itself is generally non–interest-bearing and so does not contribute to net income. Too much cash can make a company a more likely target for a takeover bid if it is publicly traded.

Short-Term Investments

Investments in debt and equity securities are presented separately and valued at cost/amortized cost or fair value. Those measured at cost are written down when impaired. Companies that have excess cash often have significant amounts of short-term investments. While deciding what to do with the money, they will temporarily invest it to generate some profits (instead of letting the funds sit idle as non–interest-bearing cash). In addition, the way a company does business can result in higher levels of investments. For instance, the business models of insurance companies, pension funds, and banks result in significant amounts of temporary as well as long-term investments. Insurance companies collect premiums up front and invest the money so that they have funds available to pay out future claims that arise under the insurance policies. Pension plans likewise collect money up front (through pension contributions from individuals) and invest it for future payout when the contributors retire. Money is like a bank's inventory. The bank must decide how much of it should be invested and in which investments. Investment banks often trade short-term investments to maximize profits and manage risks.

Receivables

REAL WORLD EMPHASIS

Accounts receivable should be segregated to show **ordinary trade accounts**, amounts owing by **related parties**, and other **unusual items** of a substantial amount. Anticipated losses due to uncollectibles should be accrued. The amount and nature of any nontrade receivables and any receivables that have been designated or pledged as collateral should be disclosed. Accounts receivable are valued at their net realizable value. Illustration 5-5 shows how **IBI Group Inc.**, a Canadian architecture, engineering, and technology company, reported its financial instruments, including receivables, in Note 6 to its financial statements.

Statement of Financial Position Presentation of Financial Assets—Excerpt from IBI Group Inc.'s December 31, 2014 Financial Statements (from Note 6(c) in thousands of Canadian dollars)

(c) Financial assets and liabilities

The carrying amount of the Company's financial instruments as at December 31, 2014 are as follows:

	Financial assets and liabilities at FVTPL*	Loans and receivables	Other financial liabilities	Total
Financial assets				
Cash	$10,342	$ –	$ –	$ 10,342
Accounts receivable	–	106,451		106,451
Total	$10,342	$106,451	$ –	$116,793
Financial liabilities				
Accounts payable and accrued liabilities	$ –	$ –	$ 57,449	$ 57,449
Deferred share plan liability	391	–	–	391
Due to related parties	–	–	10,000	10,000
Vendor notes payable	–	–	5,013	5,013
Consent fee notes payable	–	–	2,631	2,631
Credit facilities	–	–	73,423	73,423
Convertible debentures	–	–	98,437	98,437
Total	$ 391	$ –	$246,953	$247,344

*Fair value through profit or loss

WHAT DO THE NUMBERS MEAN?

IBI Group Inc. ("Intelligence Buildings Infrastructure") is a planning, architecture, engineering, and technology firm that is based in Canada and operates globally. It focuses on areas such as designing sustainable buildings and efficient infrastructure, and working with governments to create sustainable (and "livable") public spaces. For the year ended December 31, 2014, the company had revenues of $298 million, but recorded a loss of just over $3 million due largely to income from continuing operations of approximately $6 million, offset by a loss on discontinued operations of $9 million. However, the company has shown signs of recovery from many of the challenges it faced during 2013, when it recorded a net loss of $223 million. For example, in 2013 it incurred significant impairment of goodwill and intangible assets ($174 million), and a major writedown of accounts receivable ($13 million) due to uncertainty related to collection of older amounts receivable. It also had a major writedown ($35 million) of work-in-process inventory (which, for this type of firm, relates mainly to time and materials charged to projects in excess of the amounts that can be billed to customers). The company took steps in 2014 to improve its financial performance by eliminating dividends and distributions, and improving financial reporting to better monitor regional offices and performance. Cost management initiatives and divesting of operations not in line with its growth strategies were planned for 2015.[17]

Inventories

"Inventories are assets:

1. **held for sale in the ordinary course of business,**

2. **in the process of production for such sale, or**

3. **in the form of materials or supplies to be consumed in the production process or in the rendering of service."**[18]

REAL WORLD EMPHASIS

Inventories are valued at the lower of cost and net realizable value, with cost being determined using a **cost formula,** such as first-in, first-out (FIFO), weighted average cost, or specific identification (where items are not ordinarily interchangeable). It is important to disclose these details because this information helps users understand the amount of judgement that was used in measuring this asset. For a manufacturer, the stage of the inventories' completion is also indicated (raw materials, work in process, and finished goods). Illustration 5-6 shows the breakdown of **BlackBerry Ltd.'s** inventory.

5. INVENTORIES

(In millions of U.S. dollars)	2014	2013
Raw materials	$ 51	$271
Work in process	156	278
Finished goods	37	54
	$244	$603

WHAT DO THE NUMBERS MEAN?

STRATEGY DEVELOPMENT 2.3.1

BlackBerry also discloses the following in its significant accounting policy note:

Inventories

Raw materials, work in process and finished goods are stated at the lower of cost or market value. Cost includes the cost of materials plus direct labour applied to the product and the applicable share of manufacturing overhead. Cost is determined on a first-in-first-out basis. Market is generally considered to be replacement cost; however, market is not permitted to exceed the ceiling (net realizable value) or be less than the floor (net realizable value less a normal markup). Net realizable value is defined as the estimated selling price in the ordinary course of business, less reasonably predictable costs of completion and disposal.

The year-end balance in inventory is not the only factor in assessing the impact of inventory on firm value—net realizable value is also very important. BlackBerry introduced its new generation of smart phones in early 2013, with the launch of the Z10 phone. The phone did not catch on with consumers to the extent the company had hoped and BlackBerry had to write off over $900 million of Z10 inventory during the second quarter of its 2014 fiscal year. In total, BlackBerry's 2014 inventory charges included a writedown of $1.6 billion and a charge against income for inventory commitments of $782 million. Since then, the company has restructured its business, introducing the BlackBerry Passport and Classic phones in 2014 and 2015, and reducing its inventory risk by outsourcing much of its production to Foxconn in a five-year strategic partnership to jointly develop and manufacture new devices.[19]

Which types of companies are likely to have significant inventory? Companies that sell and manufacture goods will normally carry inventory (as compared with companies that offer services only). How much inventory is enough or, conversely, how much inventory is too much? Companies must have at least enough inventory to meet customer demands. On the other hand, inventory ties up significant amounts of cash flows, creates storage costs, and subjects the company to risk of theft, obsolescence, and so on. Many companies operate on a just-in-time philosophy, meaning that they streamline their production and supply channels so that they can order the raw materials and produce the product in a very short time. Car manufacturers often follow this philosophy, thus freeing up working capital and reducing the need for storing inventory.

Prepaid Expenses

Prepaid expenses included in current assets are **expenditures already made for benefits (usually services) that will be received within one year or the operating cycle**, whichever is longer. These items are current assets because cash does not need to be used for them again in the current year or operating cycle as they have already been paid for. A common example is the payment in advance for an insurance policy. It is classified as a prepaid expense at the time of the expenditure because the payment occurs before the coverage benefit is received. Prepaid expenses are reported at the amount of the unexpired or unconsumed cost. Other common prepaid expenses include rent, advertising, property taxes, and office or operating supplies.

Companies sometimes include insurance and other prepayments for two or three years in current assets even though part of the advance payment applies to periods beyond one year or the current operating cycle. This is done by convention even though it is inconsistent with the definition of current assets.

Non-current Investments

Non-current investments normally consist of one of the types shown in Illustration 5-7.

Illustration 5-7

Types of Non-current Investments

TYPES OF NON-CURRENT INVESTMENTS	MEASUREMENT
Debt Securities	
Held to maturity	Amortized cost
Equity Securities	
Investments in associates (significant influence investments)	Equity method
Subsidiaries	Consolidated
Non-consolidated subsidiaries	Fair value or at cost
Where no influence or control	Fair value or at cost
Other	
Sinking funds, tangible assets held as investments, other	Generally at cost

Long-term investments are usually presented on the SFP just below current assets in a separate section called "Investments." Many securities that are properly shown among long-term investments are, in fact, readily marketable. They are not included as current assets unless management intends to convert them to cash in the short term; that is, within a year or the operating cycle, whichever is longer.

Management may be holding some of these investments for strategic reasons (such as for significant influence investments or non-consolidated subsidiaries). Investments that are held for strategic reasons are generally held for longer periods of time and are consolidated (subsidiaries) or accounted for using the equity method (significant influence investments in associates). We will examine this in greater detail in Chapter 9.

Long-term investments carried at other than fair value must be written down when impaired.

Property, Plant, and Equipment

Property, plant, and equipment are tangible capital assets—that is, properties of a durable nature—that are **used in ongoing business operations to generate income**. These assets consist of physical or tangible property, such as land, buildings, machinery, furniture, tools, and wasting resources (for example, timberland and minerals). They are generally carried at their cost or amortized cost. With the exception of land, most assets are either depreciable (such as buildings) or depletable (such as timberland or oil reserves). IFRS allows an option to carry them at fair value using a revaluation or fair value method. Like all other assets, property, plant, and equipment are written down when impaired.

REAL WORLD EMPHASIS

TWC Enterprises Limited (owners of ClubLink golf clubs) has significant capital assets. In fact, in 2014, property, plant, and equipment and intangible assets represented 89.4% of the corporation's total assets. This is not surprising as the company is one of Canada's largest golf club developers and operators. The bulk of these assets are in land (golf courses) and buildings and land improvements. Illustration 5-8 shows the detailed breakdown of these assets, as presented in Note 6 to TWC's financial statements.

WHAT DO THE NUMBERS MEAN?

Note that in the investing activities section of its statement of cash flows, TWC further segregates its spending into **operating** and **development** expenditures. This helps users understand which expenditures are made to maintain existing operations and which ones will be to expand operations, and are therefore enhancing the company's growth potential. The basis of measuring the property, plant, and equipment; any liens (creditor claims) against the properties; and accumulated depreciation should be disclosed, usually in notes to the statements. Under IFRS, a reconciliation is provided, reconciling the capital assets from the beginning to end of the period, showing items such as additions, disposals, impairment, and depreciation (IAS 16.73).

Aside from companies in the golf club business, those based in real estate, manufacturing, resources, or pharmaceuticals also have large amounts of capital assets on their statements of financial position. These types of companies are often referred to as being **capital-intensive** since they require large amounts of capital to invest in their long-term revenue-generating assets.

PROPERTY, PLANT AND EQUIPMENT

Property, plant and equipment consist of the following:

(thousands of Canadian dollars)	Land	Building and Land Improvements	Docks	Bunkers, Cart Paths and Irrigation	Rolling Stocks and Equipment	Total
Cost						
At January 1, 2013	$295,373	$189,853	$59,747	$ 99,445	$126,239	**$770,657**
Additions	589	2,906	1,835	1,902	8,366	**15,598**
Business combinations (Note 3)	1,135	1,178	–	1,037	160	**3,510**
Disposals	–	(1,913)	–	(747)	(2,126)	**(4,786)**
Foreign exchange difference	1,554	2,657	4,210	496	3,991	**12,908**
At December 31, 2013	298,651	194,681	65,792	102,133	136,630	**797,887**
Additions	1,315	1,390	248	1,525	7,527	**12,005**
Business combinations (Note 3)	5,577	1,350	–	1,417	656	**9,000**
Disposals	(874)	(1,216)	–	(1,937)	(1,440)	**(5,467)**
Foreign exchange difference	2,346	3,999	5,984	767	5,865	**18,961**
At December 31, 2014	$307,015	$200,204	$72,024	$103,905	$149,238	**$832,386**
Accumulated Depreciation						
At January 1, 2013	$ –	$ 58,054	$ 9,781	$ 47,768	$ 66,820	**$182,423**
Depreciation	–	5,653	3,485	5,401	8,162	**22,701**
Disposals	–	(1,424)	–	(556)	(2,106)	**(4,086)**
Foreign exchange difference	–	548	785	85	1,301	**2,719**
At December 31, 2013	–	62,831	14,051	52,698	74,177	**203,757**
Depreciation	–	5,982	3,848	5,714	8,261	**23,783**
Disposals	–	(306)	–	(1,335)	–	**(1,641)**
Foreign exchange difference	–	848	1,467	138	2,052	**4,527**
At December 31, 2014	$ –	$ 69,355	$19,366	$ 57,215	$ 84,490	**$230,426**
Net book value at December 31, 2013	$298,651	$131,850	$51,741	$ 49,435	$ 62,453	**$594,130**
Net book value at December 31, 2014	$307,015	$130,849	$52,658	$ 46,690	$ 64,748	**$601,960**

On December 16, 2014, TWC and a land developer have entered into a joint venture agreement to develop the Highland Gate Golf Club property into residential development. In order to effect the joint venture arrangement, TWC sold a 50% interest in the Highland Gate Golf Club including land, buildings, intangibles and goodwill for proceeds of $3,750,000.

As part of the joint venture arrangement, TWC and the developer share joint control of the Highland Gate land as TWC has a direct interest of 50% of the land. Given TWC has direct interest in the land, this structure meets the definition of joint operation under IFRS 11, Joint Arrangement ("IFRS 11"), and accordingly TWC is required to recognize its proportionate interest in the land as presented above.

Certain property, plant and equipment have been assigned as collateral for borrowings (note 10).

As at December 31, 2014, ClubLink had equipment under finance lease with a net book value of $8,823,000 (2013 – $7,859,000).

Illustration 5-8

SFP Presentation of Property, Plant, and Equipment—Excerpt from TWC Enterprises Limited's December 31, 2014 Financial Statements

Intangible Assets

Intangible assets are capital assets that have no physical substance and usually have a higher degree of uncertainty about their future benefits. They include patents, copyrights, franchises, goodwill, trademarks, trade names, and secret processes. These intangibles are initially recorded at cost and are divided into two groups for accounting purposes:

- those with finite lives, and
- those with indefinite lives.

Those with finite lives are amortized to expense over their useful lives. Those with indefinite lives are not amortized. Both are tested for impairment.

Intangibles can amount to significant economic resources, yet financial analysts often ignore them. This is because their **valuation and measurement are difficult**. Many intangible assets, especially those that are **internally generated** (such as internally generated goodwill), are never recognized at all on the SFP.

As Illustration 5-9 shows, a significant portion of **Valeant Pharmaceuticals International's** total assets (after the company merged with **Biovail Corporation**) is composed of goodwill and intangibles.

Illustration 5-9

Balance Sheet Presentation of Goodwill and Intangible Assets—Excerpt from Valeant Pharmaceuticals International Inc.'s Financial Statements (amounts in U.S. $ millions)

REAL WORLD EMPHASIS

	At December 31	
	2014	2013
ASSETS		
Current assets		
Cash and cash equivalents	$ 322.6	$ 600.3
Trade receivable, net	2,075.8	1,676.4
Inventories, net	950.6	883.0
Prepaid expenses and other current assets	641.9	343.4
Assets held for sale	8.9	15.9
Deferred income taxes, net	193.3	366.9
Total current assets	4,193.1	3,885.9
Property, plant and equipment, net	1,310.5	1,234.2
Intangible assets, net	11,255.9	12,848.2
Goodwill	9,346.4	9,752.1
Deferred tax assets, net	54.0	54.9
Other long-term assets, net	193.1	195.5
	$26,353.0	$27,970.8

WHAT DO THE NUMBERS MEAN?

A further look at the detail behind the amount for intangibles shows that Valeant's intangibles include product brands and product rights for several pharmaceutical products. It makes sense that the company would have a large amount of money invested in intangibles because Valeant is in the business of developing pharmaceutical products. The drugs are patented by the company and become main revenue generators. However, the true value of **internally generated** patents is generally not reflected in the SFP. Instead, it is most often the **purchased** rights to drugs that show up as intangible assets because the value of these rights is measured through their acquisition.

Other Assets

The items included in the **other assets** section vary widely in practice. Some of the items that are commonly included (if they are not included anywhere else) are non-current receivables, intangible assets, assets in special funds, deferred income tax assets, land held for speculation, and advances to subsidiaries. The company should be careful to disclose these assets in enough detail for users to get a better idea of their nature.

Alternative Terminology

Deferred income taxes under IFRS are referred to as *future income taxes* under ASPE.

Deferred income tax assets (called **future income tax assets** under ASPE) represent the taxes that may be avoided or saved due to deductions that a company may take when it prepares its **future** tax returns. These accounts are mainly a result of temporary differences between what has been recognized in the accounts as revenues and expenses under GAAP and what has been recognized on the tax return under the provisions of the Income Tax Act. We will discuss deferred (or future) income taxes in greater detail in Chapter 18.

Current Liabilities

Current liabilities are the **obligations that are due within one year from the date of the SFP or within the operating cycle, where this is longer**.[20] This concept includes:

1. Payables resulting from the acquisition of goods and services: trade accounts payable, wages payable, taxes payable

2. Collections received in advance for the delivery of goods or the performance of services, such as unearned rent revenue or unearned subscriptions revenue

3. Other liabilities whose liquidation will take place within the operating cycle, such as the portion of long-term bonds to be paid in the current period, or short-term obligations arising from a purchase of equipment

4. Short-term financing that is payable on demand (such as a bank overdraft)

5. Derivative financial instruments

At times, a liability that is payable within the year may not be included in the current liabilities section. This may occur either when the debt will be refinanced through another long-term issue, or when the debt is retired out of non-current assets.[21] This approach is justified because the liquidation of the liability does not result from the use of current assets or the creation of other current liabilities.

Current liabilities are not reported in any consistent order. The items that are most commonly listed first are bank indebtedness, accounts payable, or accrued liabilities. Those that are most commonly listed last are income taxes payable, current maturities of long-term debt, or other current liabilities. Any secured liability—for example, notes payable that have shares held as collateral for them—is fully described in the notes so that the assets providing the security can be identified.

The excess of total current assets over total current liabilities is referred to as working capital (sometimes called "net working capital"). Working capital is thus the net amount of a company's relatively liquid resources. That is, it is the liquidity buffer (or cushion) that is available to meet the operating cycle's financial demands. Working capital, as an amount, is rarely disclosed on the SFP, but it is calculated by bankers and other creditors as an indicator of a company's short-run liquidity. To determine the availability of working capital to meet current obligations, however, one must analyze the current assets' composition and their nearness to cash.

Long-Term Debt and Liabilities

Long-term liabilities are **obligations that are not reasonably expected to be liquidated within the normal operating cycle but instead are payable at some later date**. Bonds payable, notes payable, some deferred (future) income tax liabilities, lease obligations, and pension obligations are the most common examples. The terms of long-term liability agreements (including the maturity date or dates, interest rates, nature of the obligation, and any security pledged to support the debt) are frequently described in notes to the financial statements. Long-term liabilities that mature within the current operating cycle are generally classified as current liabilities.

Generally, long-term liabilities are of three types:

1. Obligations arising from **specific financing situations**, such as the issuance of bonds, long-term lease obligations, and long-term notes payable

2. Obligations arising from **ordinary enterprise operations**, such as pension obligations, deferred income tax liabilities, and deferred or unearned revenues

UNDERLYING CONCEPT

3. Obligations that **depend on the occurrence or non-occurrence of one or more future events to confirm the amount payable,** the payee, or the date payable, such as service or product warranties (and other contingencies (ASPE) or provisions (IFRS) that are not due within one year or operating cycle; these will be discussed further in Chapter 13)

Information about covenants and restrictions gives insight into the entity's financial flexibility and is therefore disclosed in respect of the full disclosure principle.

It is desirable to report any premium or discount as an addition to, or subtraction from, the bonds payable. Generally, extensive supplementary disclosure is also needed for bonds and notes payable, because most long-term debt is subject to various covenants and restrictions in order to protect lenders.[22] **Deferred income tax liabilities (future income tax liabilities)** are future amounts that are expected to be owed by the company to the government for income taxes. Deferred or unearned revenues are often treated as liabilities because a service or product is owed to the customer (performance obligation). They may be classified as long-term or current.

The excerpt from **Empire Company Limited** in Illustration 5-10 is an example of the liabilities section of the balance sheet. It also shows the treatment of shareholders' equity by Empire, which is discussed next in the Owners' Equity section of this chapter. The company owns Sobeys Inc. food stores.

REAL WORLD EMPHASIS

Illustration 5-10

Balance Sheet Presentation of Liabilities and Shareholders' Equity—Excerpt from Empire Company Limited's 2014 Balance Sheet (in millions of dollars)

Liabilities		
Current	**May 3, 2014**	May 4, 2013[1]
Bank indebtedness *(Note 14)*	$ –	$ 6.0
Accounts payable and accrued liabilities	**2,246.0**	1,765.8
Income taxes payable	**21.0**	75.2
Provisions *(Note 15)*	**82.4**	30.6
Long-term debt due within one year *(Note 16)*	**218.0**	47.6
	2,567.4	1,925.2
Provisions *(Note 15)*	**140.7**	52.9
Long-term debt *(Note 16)*	**3,279.9**	915.9
Other long-term liabilities *(Note 17)*	**389.2**	309.7
Deferred tax liabilities *(Note 13)*	**119.3**	180.6
	6,496.5	3,384.3
Shareholders' Equity		
Capital stock *(Note 19)*	**2,108.6**	319.3
Contributed surplus	**5.0**	6.7
Retained earnings	**3,585.9**	3,406.9
Accumulated other comprehensive income (loss)	**1.0**	(8.1)
	5,700.5	3,724.8
Non-controlling interest	**41.0**	31.3
	$12,238.0	$7,140.4

[1] Certain fiscal 2013 amounts have been restated (see Note 3(aa)(i)).

Note that the company's long-term debt mainly consists of notes payable and credit facilities. Details of the long-term debt are provided in Note 16 of Empire's financial statements. For example, the notes have interest rates that range between 3.5% and 7.2%, with maturity dates that extend as far as 2040!

Owners' Equity

LAW

The **owners' equity** (shareholders' equity) section is one of the most difficult sections to prepare and understand. This is due to the complexity of capital share agreements and the various restrictions on residual equity that are imposed by corporation laws, liability agreements, and boards of directors. As shown for Empire Company Limited in Illustration 5-10, the section is usually divided into four parts:

1. **Capital shares,** which represents the exchange value of shares that have been issued

2. **Contributed surplus,** which may include items such as amounts related to the repurchase of shares at an amount lower than the original purchase price

3. **Retained earnings,** which includes undistributed earnings, and is sometimes referred to as "earned surplus"

4. **Accumulated other comprehensive income,** which may include unrealized gains and losses on certain investments; certain gains or losses from hedging activities; gains or losses on revalued property, plant, and equipment; and other. This is not required to be called "accumulated other comprehensive income."

REAL WORLD EMPHASIS

The major disclosure requirements for capital shares (or stock) are their authorized, issued, and outstanding amounts. Contributed surplus is usually presented as one amount. Retained earnings, also presented as one amount, is positive if the company has undistributed accumulated profits. Otherwise, it will be a negative number and labelled "deficit." Any capital shares that have been reacquired by the company (treasury stock) are shown as a reduction of shareholders' equity.[23] The large increase in capital stock by Empire relates to the acquisition of Canada Safeway, which included 200 full-service stores, 190 in-store pharmacies, together with 63 fuel stations, 10 liquor stores, and distribution and manufacturing facilities. These are located primarily in Western Canada.

A corporation's ownership or shareholders' equity accounts are quite different from the equivalent accounts in a partnership or proprietorship. Partners' permanent capital accounts and the balances in their temporary accounts (drawings accounts) are shown separately. Proprietorships ordinarily use a single capital account that handles all of the owner's equity transactions.

Illustration 5-11 presents the shareholders' equity section from **Talisman Energy Inc.**

Illustration 5-11

Balance Sheet Presentation of Shareholders' Equity—Excerpt from Talisman Energy Inc.'s December 31, 2013 Balance Sheet (in U.S. $ millions)

SHAREHOLDERS' EQUITY	2013	2012
Common shares (note 21)	1,723	1,639
Preferred shares (note 21)	191	191
Contributed surplus	135	121
Retained earnings	5,695	7,148
Accumulated other comprehensive income (note 22)	811	811
	8,555	9,910

REAL WORLD EMPHASIS

Note that the company has chosen to show the details on the number of shares issued and authorized in the notes to the financial statements. Common shares are also referred to as "ordinary shares" under IFRS. Talisman Energy was acquired by Spain's Repsol SA in a U.S. $8.3-billion deal in the fourth quarter of 2014.[24]

Statement of Financial Position Format

One method of presenting a classified SFP is to list assets, by section, on the left side and liabilities and shareholders' equity, by section, on the right side. The main disadvantage of this format is that it requires two facing pages. To avoid the use of facing pages, another format, shown in Illustration 5-12, lists liabilities and shareholders' equity directly below assets on the same page.

Illustration 5-12

Classified SFP

SCIENTIFIC INNOVATION PRODUCTS, INC.
Statement of Financial Position
December 31, 2017

Assets
Current assets

Cash		$ 42,485
Investments—trading		28,250
Accounts receivable	$165,824	
Less: Allowance for doubtful accounts	1,850	163,974
Notes receivable		23,000
Inventory (at lower of average cost and NRV)		489,713
Supplies on hand		9,780
Prepaid expenses		16,252

(continued)

Illustration 5-12

Classified SFP (continued)

SCIENTIFIC INNOVATION PRODUCTS, INC.
Statement of Financial Position
December 31, 2017

Total current assets			$ 773,454
Long-term investments			87,500
Property, plant, and equipment			
Land (at cost)		125,000	
Buildings (at cost)	975,800		
Less: Accumulated depreciation	341,200	634,600	
Total property, plant, and equipment			759,600
Intangible assets, net of accumulated amortization			80,000
Goodwill			20,000
Total assets			$1,720,554
Liabilities and Shareholders' Equity			
Current liabilities			
Accounts payable		$247,532	
Accrued interest		500	
Income taxes payable		62,520	
Accrued salaries, wages, and other liabilities		9,500	
Deposits received from customers		420	
Total current liabilities			$ 320,472
Long-term debt			
(Twenty-year 12% debentures, due January 1, 2022)			500,000
Total liabilities			820,472
Shareholders' equity			
Paid in on capital shares			
Preferred (7%, cumulative—authorized, issued, and outstanding, 30,000 shares)	$300,000		
Common (authorized, 500,000 shares; issued and outstanding, 400,000 shares)	400,000		
Contributed surplus	37,500	737,500	
Retained earnings	102,333		
Accumulated other comprehensive income	60,249	162,582	
Total shareholders' equity			900,082
Total liabilities and shareholders' equity			$1,720,554

Additional Information Reported

Objective 5
Identify statement of financial position information that requires supplemental disclosure.

SUPPLEMENTAL STATEMENT OF FINANCIAL POSITION
DISCLOSURE INFORMATION

1. **Contingencies and provisions.** Material events that have an uncertain outcome.
2. **Accounting policies.** Explanations of the valuation methods that are used or the basic assumptions that are made for inventory valuations, amortization methods, investments in subsidiaries, and so on.
3. **Contractual situations.** Explanations of certain restrictions or covenants that are attached to specific assets or, more likely, to liabilities.
4. **Additional detail.** Expanded details on specific SFP line items.
5. **Subsequent events.** Events that happened after the SFP data were compiled.

Contingencies and Provisions

A **contingency** is an **existing situation in which there is uncertainty about whether a gain or loss will occur and that will finally be resolved when one or more future events occur or fail to occur** under ASPE. In short, contingencies are material (or potentially material) events that have an uncertain future. An example of a gain contingency is unsettled company litigation against another party. Typical loss contingencies relate to litigation against the company, environmental issues, or possible tax assessments. IFRS uses different terminology. For example, if a company is sued and it is more likely than not that it will lose the lawsuit, the estimated loss would be set up as a "provision" under IFRS (rather than as a contingent liability). A **provision** is a **liability that has an uncertain timing or amount** under IFRS.[25]

In general terms, a liability is recognized when it is probable or likely and measurable under both IFRS and ASPE. Additional note disclosures are required. Under IFRS, probable is defined as more likely than not whereas under ASPE the threshold for recognition is higher, requiring a high chance of occurrence. **Contingent gains** are not recognized under IFRS or ASPE, but are **disclosed** where an inflow of economic benefits is seen as probable.[26] The accounting and reporting requirements for provisions and contingencies are examined fully in Chapter 13.

Accounting Policies

Accounting standards recommend disclosure for all significant accounting principles and methods that management has chosen from among alternatives or that are peculiar to a particular industry. For instance, inventories can be calculated under different cost formulas (such as weighted average and FIFO); plant and equipment can be amortized under several accepted methods of cost allocation (such as diminishing balance and straight-line); and investments can be carried at different amounts (such as cost or fair value). Users of financial statements who are more informed know of these possibilities and examine the statements closely to determine the methods that are used and their impact on net income and key ratios.

Companies are also required to disclose information about their use of estimates in preparing the financial statements when the related measurement uncertainty is material.[27] The disclosure of significant accounting principles and methods and of risks and uncertainties is particularly useful when this information is given as one of the first notes or when it is presented in a separate summary that precedes the notes to the financial statements.

Contractual Situations

UNDERLYING CONCEPT

The basis for including additional information is the full disclosure principle; that is, the information needs to be important enough to influence the decisions of an informed user.

ETHICS

In addition to contingencies and different valuation methods, contractual obligations should also be disclosed in the notes to the financial statements when they are significant.[28] It is mandatory, for example, that the essential provisions of guarantees, lease contracts, pension obligations, and stock option plans be clearly stated in the notes. The analyst who examines a set of financial statements wants to know not only the liability amounts but also how the different contractual provisions (that is, the terms and conditions) are affecting the company now, and will affect it in the future.

Commitments that oblige a company to maintain a certain amount of working capital, limit its payment of dividends, restrict its use of assets, or require it to maintain certain financial ratios must all be disclosed if they are material. Considerable judgement is needed to determine whether leaving out such information is misleading. The principle in this situation is, "When in doubt, disclose." It is better to disclose a little too much information than not enough.

The accountant's judgement should include ethical considerations, because the way of disclosing the accounting principles, methods, and other items that have important effects on the enterprise may reflect the interests of a particular stakeholder in subtle ways that are at the expense of other stakeholders. A reader, for example, may benefit from having certain information highlighted in comprehensive notes, whereas the company—not wanting to emphasize that information—may prefer to provide limited (rather than comprehensive) information in its notes.

Additional Detail

For many SFP items, further detail is disclosed to make them clearer. This has already been discussed under the various headings of the SFP: assets, liabilities, and equity.

Subsequent Events

Several weeks or months may pass after the end of the year before the financial statements are issued. This time is used to count and price inventory, reconcile subsidiary ledgers with controlling accounts, prepare necessary adjusting entries, ensure that all transactions for the period have been entered, and obtain an audit of the financial statements.

During this period, important transactions and events may occur that materially affect the company's financial position or operating situation. These events are known as **subsequent events**.[29] Notes to the financial statements should explain any significant financial events that occur after (subsequent to) the formal date of the SFP but before the financial statements have been issued.

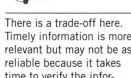

UNDERLYING CONCEPT

There is a trade-off here. Timely information is more relevant but may not be as reliable because it takes time to verify the information to ensure that it is complete and accurate.

Subsequent events fall into two types:

1. Events that provide further evidence of **conditions that existed** at the date of the SFP

2. Events that indicate **conditions that occurred after** the financial statement date

In the first type, the financial statements must be adjusted for the events reflecting conditions that existed at the date of the SFP. In the second type, the events reflecting conditions that occurred after the financial statements date must be disclosed in notes if the condition causes a significant change to assets or liabilities, and/or it will have a significant impact on future operations. We will cover these issues in further detail in Chapter 23.

Techniques of Disclosure

Objective 6

Identify major disclosure techniques for the statement of financial position.

The additional information that is reported should be disclosed as completely and as understandably as possible. The following methods of disclosing pertinent information are available: explanations in parentheses, notes, cross-references and contra items, and supporting schedules, as we will explain next.

Parenthetical Explanations

Additional information is often provided by explanations in parentheses that follow the item. For example, shareholders' equity may be shown as it is in Illustration 5-12 in the financial statements of Scientific Innovation Products.

Using parentheses makes it possible to disclose relevant additional SFP information that adds clarity and completeness. It has an advantage over a note because it brings the additional information into the body of the statement where it is less likely to be missed. Of course, lengthy parenthetical explanations that might distract the reader from the SFP information must be used carefully.

Notes

Notes are used if additional explanations cannot be shown conveniently as parenthetical explanations or to reduce the amount of detail on the face of the statement. For example, the details for property, plant, and equipment of Air Canada are shown in Note 4 to its financial statements rather than on the face of the statement. As Illustration 5-13 shows, including this level of detail on the face of the SFP would make it more difficult to read and to focus on the main groupings of assets.

REAL WORLD EMPHASIS

The notes should present all essential facts as completely and concisely as possible. Loose wording can mislead readers instead of helping them. Notes should add to the total information that is made available in the financial statements, not raise unanswered questions or contradict other parts of the statements. For example, the property and equipment note for Air Canada provides users with additional information about changes in the major classifications of property and equipment items during the year. The full Air Canada Note 4 also provides further details of flight equipment, leased equipment, and other items of property and equipment that are not reproduced here.

Illustration 5-13

Notes Disclosure—Excerpt from Notes to Air Canada's Financial Statements (in millions of dollars)

4. PROPERTY AND EQUIPMENT

	AIRCRAFT AND FLIGHT EQUIPMENT	BUILDINGS AND LEASEHOLD IMPROVEMENTS	GROUND AND OTHER EQUIPMENT	PURCHASE DEPOSITS AND ASSETS UNDER DEVELOPMENT	TOTAL
YEAR ENDED DECEMBER 31, 2014					
At January 1, 2014	$4,208	$ 352	$ 157	$ 356	$ 5,073
Additions	1,011	6	36	468	1,521
Reclassifications	259	76	2	(337)	–
Disposals	(94)	–	–	–	(94)
Depreciation	(440)	(35)	(27)	–	(502)
At December 31, 2014	$4,944	$ 399	$ 168	$487	$5,998
AT DECEMBER 31, 2014					
Cost	$7,264	$ 742	$ 397	$487	$8,890
Accumulated depreciation	(2,320)	(343)	(229)	–	(2,892)
	$4,944	$ 399	$ 168	$487	$5,998

During 2014, the Corporation took delivery of six Boeing 787 aircraft and one Boeing 777 aircraft. In 2014, the Corporation disposed of two A340-500 aircraft and repaid the financing related to these aircraft. No gain or loss was recorded on the disposition.

As at December 31, 2014, property and equipment included finance leased assets including 17 aircraft (2013 – 18) with a net book value of $145 (2013 – $150) and facilities with a net book value of $42 (2013 – $45).

Included in aircraft and flight equipment are 28 aircraft and 5 spare engines (2013 – 32 aircraft and six spare engines) which are leased to Sky Regional, Jazz (Note 16) and third parties with a cost of $361 (2013 – $481) less accumulated depreciation of $118 (2013 – $124) including accumulated impairment losses of $19 related to the fleet of A340-300 aircraft (2013 – $26) for a net book value of $243 (2013 – $357). Depreciation expense for 2014 for this aircraft and flight equipment amounted to $22 (2013 – $38).

Interest capitalized during 2014 amounted to $30 at an interest rate of 5.29% (2013 – $46 at an interest rate of 8.36%) and is included in Purchase deposits and assets under development in the table above.

Certain property and equipment are pledged as collateral as further described under the applicable debt instrument in Note 8.

Cross-References and Contra Items

When there is a direct relationship between an asset and a liability, this can be cross-referenced on the SFP. For example, a company with a sinking fund, used to set aside funds to redeem a bond payable, might deposit cash with a trust company for eventual redemption of the bond issue. This might be shown as follows among the current assets section of an SFP dated as at December 31, 2017:

Cash on deposit with sinking fund trustee for redemption of bonds payable—see Current liabilities	$800,000

In the same SFP, in the current liabilities section, would be the amount of bonds payable to be redeemed within one year:

Bonds payable to be redeemed in 2018—see Current assets	$2,300,000

This cross-reference points out that $2.3 million of bonds payable are to be redeemed currently, and thus far only $800,000 in cash has been set aside for the redemption. This means, therefore, that the additional cash will need to come from unrestricted cash, from sales of investments, from profits, or from some other source. The same information can be shown in parentheses if this technique is preferred.

Another common procedure is to establish contra or adjunct accounts. A **contra account** on an SFP is an item that reduces an asset, liability, or owners' equity account.

Examples include Accumulated Depreciation and Allowance for Doubtful Accounts. Contra accounts provide some flexibility in presenting the financial information. Use of the Accumulated Depreciation account, for example, allows a statement reader to see the asset's original cost and its amortization to date.

An **adjunct account**, on the other hand, increases an asset, liability, or owners' equity account. An example is Premium on Bonds Payable, which, when added to the Bonds Payable account, describes the enterprise's total bond liability.

Supporting Schedules

Often a separate schedule is needed to present more detailed information about certain assets or liabilities because the SFP provides only a single summary item.

Terminology

Account titles in the general ledger often use terms that are not the most helpful ones for an SFP. Account titles are often brief and may include technical terms that are understood only by accountants. Statements of financial position, meanwhile, are examined by many people who are not familiar with the technical vocabulary of accounting. Thus, statements of financial position should contain descriptions that will be generally understood and are less likely to be misinterpreted.

STATEMENT OF CASH FLOWS

Alternative Terminology

In 2007 the IASB changed the name of the cash flow statement to the statement of cash flows (see IAS 7). It is still known as the cash flow statement under ASPE (see CPA Canada Handbook Section 1540).

The SFP, the income statement, and the statement of changes in shareholders' equity each present information about an enterprise's cash flows during a period, but they do this to a limited extent and in a fragmented manner. For instance, comparative statements of financial position might provide an indication of what new assets have been acquired or disposed of and what liabilities have been incurred or liquidated. The income statement presents information about the resources provided by operations, but not the details of the cash that has been provided. The statement of changes in shareholders' equity shows the amount of dividends declared. None of these statements presents a detailed summary of all the cash inflows and outflows, or the sources and uses of cash during the period. To satisfy this need, the **statement of cash flows** (also called the cash flow statement) is required.[30]

The statement's value is that it helps users evaluate liquidity, solvency, and financial flexibility, as previously defined. The material in Chapter 5 is introductory as it reviews the statement of cash flows' existence and usefulness, the mechanics of calculating cash flows from operations, and preparing the statement using the indirect method. Note that Chapter 22 deals with the preparation and content of the statement of cash flows in greater detail.

Purpose, Content, and Format of a Statement of Cash Flows

Objective 7
Indicate the purpose and identify the content of the statement of cash flows.

The main purpose of a statement of cash flows is to allow users to **assess the enterprise's capacity to generate cash and cash equivalents and to enable users to compare the operating performance and cash flows of different entities.**[31]

Reporting the sources, uses, and net increase or decrease in cash helps investors, creditors, and others know what is happening to a company's most liquid resource. Because most people maintain their chequebook and prepare their tax return on a cash basis, they can relate to and understand the statement of cash flows because it shows the causes and effects of cash inflows and outflows and the net increase or decrease in cash. The statement of cash flows helps answer the following simple but important questions:

1. Where did cash come from during the period?

2. What was cash used for during the period?

3. What was the change in the cash balance during the period?

Cash receipts and cash payments during a period are classified in the statement of cash flows into three different activities: **operating**, **investing**, and **financing** activities. These are the main types of activities that companies engage in. These classifications are defined as follows:

1. **Operating activities** are the enterprise's main revenue-producing activities and all other activities that are not related to investing or financing.

2. **Investing activities** are the acquisitions and disposals of long-term assets and other investments that are not included in cash equivalents.

3. **Financing activities** are activities that result in changes in the size and composition of the enterprise's borrowings and equity capital.[32]

With cash flows classified into each of these categories, the statement of cash flows has assumed the basic format shown in Illustration 5-14.

Illustration 5-14

Basic Format of Statement of Cash Flows

Statement of Cash Flows	
Cash flows from operating activities	$XXX
Cash flows from investing activities	XXX
Cash flows from financing activities	XXX
Net increase (decrease) in cash	XXX
Cash at beginning of year	XXX
Cash at end of year	$XXX

Illustration 5-15 shows examples of cash inflows and outflows by activity when using the indirect method.

Illustration 5-15

Cash Inflows and Outflows

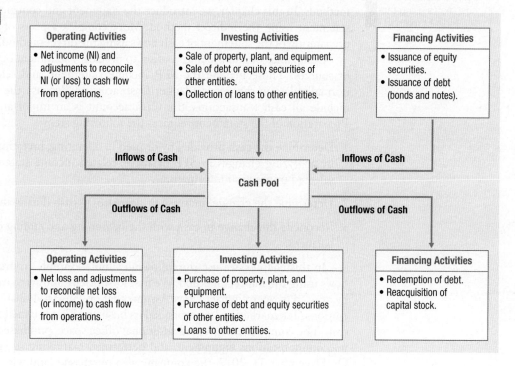

The following excerpt from the statement of cash flows of the **2014 fiscal year annual report** for **Loblaw Companies Limited** highlights the operating activities section of the statement. This example provides a summary of typical adjustments found in the reconciliation of net earnings to cash flows from operations.

REAL WORLD
EMPHASIS

Consolidated Statements of Cash Flow For the years ended January 3, 2015 and December 28, 2013 (millions of Canadian dollars)	2014	2013
Operating Activities		
Net earnings	$ 53	$ 627
Income taxes (note 7)	25	226
Net interest expense and other financing charges (note 6)	584	468
Depreciation and amortization	1,472	824
Income taxes paid	(293)	(272)
Interest received	29	49
Settlement of equity forward contracts (note 30)	—	(16)
Settlement of cross currency swaps (note 30)	—	94
Change in credit card receivables	(92)	(233)
Change in non-cash working capital	(321)	(224)
Fixed assets and other related impairments (recoveries)	16	(32)
Loss (gain) on disposal of assets	3	(1)
Recognition of fair value increment on inventory sold (note 12)	798	—
Change related to inventory measurement and other conversion differences (note 12)	190	—
Gain on defined benefit plan amendments (note 27)	—	(51)
Other	105	32
Cash Flows from Operating Activities	**2,569**	**1,491**

Preparation of the Statement of Cash Flows

Objective 8
Prepare a statement of cash flows using the indirect method.

Companies can prepare their statements of cash flows by using either the direct or indirect method. Only the operating activities section of the statement differs between the two methods. In this chapter, we introduce the statement and concentrate on preparing a basic statement using the indirect method. More complex aspects of the statement, including preparation of the statement of cash flows using the direct method, are covered in Volume 2.

Companies obtain the information to prepare a statement of cash flows from a variety of sources. These include the SFP, income statement, and selected transaction data—normally data in the general ledger Cash account. Because the statement is intended to include all cash transactions, the Cash account is an important source of information. Preparation of the statement requires the following steps:

1. Determine the cash provided by or used in operating, investing, and financing activities by analyzing changes in SFP balances, related income statement balances, and other selected transaction information.

2. Determine the change (increase or decrease) in cash during the period.

3. Reconcile the change in cash with the beginning and ending cash and cash equivalents balances.

In this chapter, we use the following simple example to prepare a statement of cash flows using the indirect method. We first look briefly at how to calculate the cash provided by or used in operating activities. Assume that on January 1, 2017, in its second year of operations, Telemarketing Inc. expanded its business. First it issued 50,000 shares for $50,000 cash. The company then rented additional office space, purchased additional furniture and telecommunications equipment, and performed marketing services throughout the year. On December 31, 2017, the company also purchased land with a fair value of $150,000, which was financed partially by the issuance of bonds. Finally, it paid cash dividends of $15,000 during the year. Illustration 5-16 shows the company's comparative statements of financial position at the beginning and end of 2017.

Illustration 5-16

Comparative Statements of Financial Position for Telemarketing Inc.

TELEMARKETING INC.
Statements of Financial Position

Assets	Dec. 31, 2017	Dec. 31, 2016	Increase/Decrease
Cash	$ 61,000	$ 30,000	$ 31,000 increase
Accounts receivable	86,000	45,000	41,000 increase
Land	150,000	–0–	150,000 increase
Property, plant, and equipment, net	300,000	200,000	100,000 increase
Total	$597,000	$275,000	
Liabilities and Shareholders' Equity			
Accounts payable	$ 62,000	$ 50,000	12,000 increase
Bonds payable	200,000	–0–	200,000 increase
Common shares	180,000	130,000	50,000 increase
Retained earnings	155,000	95,000	60,000 increase
Total	$597,000	$275,000	

Illustration 5-17 shows the company's income statement.

Illustration 5-17

Income Statement Data for Telemarketing Inc.

TELEMARKETING INC.
Income Statement
For the Year Ended December 31, 2017

Revenues	$250,000
Operating expenses	120,000
Depreciation expense	30,000
Income before income tax	100,000
Income tax	25,000
Net income	$ 75,000

Additional information:
Dividends of $15,000 were paid during the year. The bonds were issued on December 31, 2017, to help finance the acquisition of the land. Specifically, $100,000 worth of the land was acquired in exchange for $100,000 of bonds, with the remainder of the bonds being issued for cash.

Cash provided by operating activities is the excess of cash receipts over cash payments for operating activities. Companies determine this amount by converting net income on an accrual basis to a cash basis. To do this, they add to or deduct from net income those items in the income statement that do not affect cash, such as depreciation expense and noncash gains or losses. They then adjust net income for the items that are affected by changes in current asset or liability account balances. For example, increases in accounts receivable between years would reflect the fact that more sales remain uncollected at the end of the current year compared with the prior year. Similarly, a decrease in accounts payable would suggest that the current year's purchases have been paid off more quickly than similar purchases in the prior year. Determination of cash provided by (or used for) operating activities requires that a company analyze not only the current year's income statement but also the comparative SFP and selected transaction data (especially items affecting the Cash account). This analysis is important since, for instance, credit sales from last year that are collected this year (and were previously recorded as accounts receivable) will increase cash.

TREASURY MANAGEMENT
5.2.1

Analysis of Telemarketing Inc.'s comparative statements of financial position reveals two items that will affect the calculation of net cash provided by operating activities:

1. The increase in accounts receivable is a noncash increase of $41,000 in revenues from uncollected credit sales. This amount would have been included in net income as sales revenue and so must be deducted in arriving at cash from operations. In short, the company has to reduce cash flow from operations by $41,000, as it has fewer cash resources available to it due to a higher accounts receivable balance in 2017.

2. The increase in accounts payable is a noncash increase of $12,000 in expenses accrued but not yet paid. This amount would have been deducted in arriving at net income but, since these expenses did not require a cash outlay, they will be added back in arriving at cash from operations. The company has conserved some of its cash resources by not paying off its accounts payable as quickly in 2017 as it did in 2016.

A review of the income statement indicates that depreciation expense totalling $30,000 was deducted in arriving at net income. Because depreciation is a noncash item that has been deducted as an expense, it must be added back to net income to arrive at cash from operations. In addition, to obtain cash from operations, Telemarketing Inc. deducts from net income the increase in accounts receivable ($41,000) and it adds back to net income the increase in accounts payable ($12,000), as discussed above. Note that, since there were no sales of property, plant, and equipment during the year, there is no need to adjust for noncash gains or losses. As a result of these adjustments, the company determines that cash provided by operations amounted to $76,000, as calculated in Illustration 5-18.

Net income		$75,000
Adjustments to reconcile net income to net cash provided by operating activities:		
Depreciation expense	$ 30,000	
Increase in accounts receivable	(41,000)	
Increase in accounts payable	12,000	1,000
Net cash provided by operating activities		$76,000

Illustration 5-18

Calculation of Net Cash Provided by Operations

Telemarketing Inc.'s only investing activities were the land and property, plant, and equipment purchases. From the analysis of changes in SFP balances, we can see that land increased by $150,000. However, other available information states that $100,000 of the land purchased was paid for via an exchange for bonds. Since this is a noncash exchange, $100,000 of the increase in land (and the related $100,000 noncash increase in bonds payable) is not included on the statement of cash flows. Details of the exchange would be disclosed via a note to the financial statements. The remaining increase to land ($50,000) was cash-based and must be disclosed on the statement of cash flows.

There is also an increase to (net) property, plant, and equipment (PPE) of $100,000 on the SFP that requires further analysis. Since PPE is shown on a net basis on the SFP, it is net of related accumulated depreciation. From our analysis of operating activities and the income statement, we know that depreciation expense was $30,000 for the year. So the increase in PPE must have been $130,000 prior to the recording of depreciation expense ($130,000 − 30,000 = $100,000 [net] increase to PPE). The purchase of PPE of $130,000 is shown as part of investing activities.

Telemarketing Inc. has three financing activities:

1. the increase of $50,000 in common shares resulting from the issuance of these shares,

2. the cash portion of the increase in bonds payable as discussed above, and

3. the payment of $15,000 in cash dividends. (Dividends charged to retained earnings are a financing activity under ASPE, but could be shown as financing or operating under IFRS. Illustration 5-24 provides further discussion.)

Illustration 5-19 presents Telemarketing Inc.'s statement of cash flows for 2017.

The increase in cash of $31,000 that is reported in the statement of cash flows agrees with the increase in cash that was calculated from the comparative statements of financial position. Note that, in addition to the exchange of bonds payable for land, other examples of a company's activities not involving cash would include the conversion of bonds to shares, an issuance of debt in exchange for assets, and other non-monetary exchanges. These activities should not be included in the body of the statement of cash flows but should be disclosed elsewhere in the financial statements.

Illustration 5-19

Statement of Cash Flows

Cash flows from operating activities		
Net income		$ 75,000
Adjustments to reconcile net income to net cash		
provided by operating activities:		
Depreciation expense	$ 30,000	
Increase in accounts receivable	(41,000)	
Increase in accounts payable	12,000	1,000
Net cash provided by operating activities		76,000
Cash flows from investing activities		
Purchase of land	(50,000)	
Purchase of property, plant, and equipment	(130,000)	
Net cash used by investing activities		(180,000)
Cash flows from financing activities		
Issuance of common shares	50,000	
Issuance of bonds payable	100,000	
Payment of cash dividends	(15,000)	
Net cash provided by financing activities		135,000
Net increase in cash		31,000
Cash at beginning of year		30,000
Cash at end of year		$ 61,000

Note: During 2017, the company issued $100,000 of bonds payable in exchange for land.

Note that the net cash provided by operating activities section begins with net income and reconciles to cash. This presentation is called the indirect method of presenting cash flows from operating activities. Another option is the direct method. The direct method normally presents the following information in the operating activities portion of the statement:

- Cash received from customers

- Cash paid to suppliers and employees

- Interest paid or received

- Taxes paid

- Other

The investing and financing activities sections of the statement remain the same in both methods.

Under IFRS and ASPE, either method is acceptable, although standard setters prefer the direct method. See Chapter 22 for a more detailed discussion.

Usefulness of the Statement of Cash Flows

Objective 9
Understand the usefulness of the statement of cash flows.

Although net income provides a long-term measure of a company's success or failure, cash is a company's lifeblood. Without cash, a company will not survive. For small and newly developing companies, cash flow is often the single most important element of survival. Even medium and large companies indicate that controlling cash flow is a major concern.

Creditors examine the statement of cash flows carefully because they are concerned about being paid. They will usually start by assessing **net cash provided by operating activities.** What if there is a high amount of net cash provided by operating activities? This indicates that a company was able to generate enough cash internally from operations in the most recent period to pay its bills without further borrowing. Conversely, a low or negative amount of net cash provided by operating activities indicates that a company did not generate enough cash internally from its operations and, therefore, may have had to borrow or issue equity securities to acquire additional cash.

Just because a company was able to generate cash flows from operating activities in the most recent period, however, does not mean that it will be able to do so again in future periods. Consequently, creditors look for answers to the following questions in the company's statement of cash flows:

- How successful is the company in generating net cash provided by operating activities?

- What are the trends in net cash flow provided by operating activities over time?

- What are the major reasons for the positive or negative net cash provided by operating activities?

- Are the cash flows sustainable or renewable? In other words, are they expected to be repeated over time?

You should recognize that companies can fail even though they are profitable. The difference between net income and net cash provided by operating activities can be substantial. Why? One of the main reasons for the difference between a positive net income and negative net cash provided by operating activities is major increases in receivables and/or inventory. To illustrate, assume that in its first year of operations, Hinchcliff Inc. reported net income of $80,000. Its net cash provided by operating activities, however, was a negative $95,000, as shown in Illustration 5-20.

Illustration 5-20

Negative Net Cash Provided by Operating Activities

Net income		$ 80,000
Adjustments to reconcile net income to net cash		
provided by operating activities:		
Increase in receivables	$ (75,000)	
Increase in inventory	(100,000)	(175,000)
Net cash provided by operating activities		$ (95,000)

Note that the negative net cash provided by operating activities occurred for Hinchcliff even though it reported a positive net income. The company could easily experience a "cash crunch" because it has tied up its cash in receivables and inventory. If problems in collecting receivables occur or inventory is slow-moving or becomes obsolete, the company's creditors may have difficulty collecting on their loans.

Companies that are expanding often experience this type of "cash crunch" because they must buy increasing inventory amounts to meet increasing sales demands. This means that the cash outflow to purchase the inventory occurs before the cash inflow from the customer for sale of that product. This is often referred to as a "lead-lag" factor. The cash outflow leads (occurs first) and the cash inflow from sales lags (occurs later). The lead-lag factor requires the company to use up any excess cash that it has on hand or to borrow more funds. Refer back to Illustration 5-3 on the business operating cycle.

As mentioned earlier in the chapter, you can assess a company's financial flexibility by using information from the financial statements. The statement of cash flows is especially good for providing this type of information.

Financial Liquidity

One ratio that is used to assess liquidity is the **current cash debt coverage ratio**. It indicates whether the company can pay off its current liabilities for the year from its operations. The formula for this ratio is shown in Illustration 5-21.

Illustration 5-21

Formula for Current Cash Debt Coverage Ratio

Net Cash Provided by Operating Activities	÷	Average Current Liabilities	=	Current Cash Debt Coverage Ratio

**TREASURY
MANAGEMENT**
5.2.1

The higher this ratio, the less likely a company will have liquidity problems. For example, a ratio of at least 1:1 is good because it indicates that the company can meet all of its current obligations from internally generated cash flow. To compare this ratio with a benchmark number, it can be compared with the ratios for similar companies in the industry (or with the ratios of prior years for the company itself).

Financial Flexibility

A more long-run measure that provides information on financial flexibility is the **cash debt coverage ratio.** This ratio indicates a company's ability to repay its liabilities from net cash provided by operating activities without having to liquidate the assets that it uses in its operations. Illustration 5-22 presents the formula for this ratio.

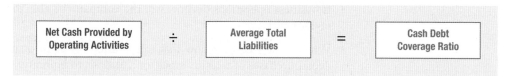

| Illustration 5-22 |
Formula for Cash Debt Coverage Ratio

The higher this ratio, the less likely a company will experience difficulty in meeting its obligations as they come due. As a result, this ratio signals whether the company can pay its debts and survive if external sources of funds become limited or too expensive.

Perspectives

Cash Flow Patterns

Refer to Illustration 5-19 showing the full statement of cash flows for Telemarketing Inc. The statement of cash flows can yield some interesting results when users look at the various patterns between cash inflows and outflows for the following subtotals on the statement: operating, investing, and financing cash flows. For instance, Telemarketing Inc. has positive cash flows (cash inflows; "+") from operating activities of $76,000, negative cash flows (cash outflows; "−") from investing activities of $180,000, and positive cash flows (cash inflows; "+") from financing activities of $135,000. Together these numbers thus yield a "+" "−" "+" pattern.

**FINANCIAL
ANALYSIS AND
PLANNING**
5.1.1

Interpreting this, the company is getting its cash from operations (which is a very good sign) and also from the issuance of common shares and long-term debt. It is investing this cash to expand the business. The fact that the company is able to raise funds in the capital markets by issuing shares indicates that the capital markets have faith in the company's ability to prosper. As the company expands, it may be able to move to having the bulk of the money used to finance purchases of capital assets being generated from operations. This would mean that the company would not have to increase its solvency risk by issuing debt or further dilute its shareholders' equity by issuing more shares. Telemarketing Inc. appears to be a successful company that's expanding.

Companies that generate cash from investing activities may be selling off long-term assets. This pattern generally goes with a company that is downsizing or restructuring. If the assets that are being disposed of are not needed, then it makes sense to free up the capital that is tied up. Similarly, if the assets being disposed of relate to operations that are not profitable, disposal reflects a good management decision. However, if the company **must** sell off core income-producing assets to generate cash, then it may be sacrificing future profitability and revenue-producing potential. This is obviously undesirable. Thus, cash flow patterns can reveal significant information.

Free Cash Flow

A more sophisticated way to examine a company's financial flexibility is to develop a **free cash flow** analysis. This analysis starts with net cash provided by operating activities and ends with free cash flow, which is calculated as follows:

Net cash provided by operating activities – Capital expenditures and
dividends = Free cash flow.[33]

Free cash flow is the amount of discretionary cash flow that a company has for purchasing additional investments, retiring its debt, purchasing treasury stock, or simply adding to its liquidity. This measure indicates a company's level of financial flexibility. A free cash flow analysis can answer questions such as these:

- Is the company able to pay its dividends without the help of external financing?

- If business operations decline, will the company be able to maintain its needed capital investment?

- What is the free cash flow that can be used for additional investments, retirement of debt, purchases of treasury stock, or additions to liquidity?

Illustration 5-23 shows a free cash flow analysis for Nestor Corporation.

Illustration 5-23

Free Cash Flow Analysis

NESTOR CORPORATION Free Cash Flow Analysis	
Net cash provided by operating activities	$411,750
Less: Capital expenditures	(252,500)
Dividends	(19,800)
Free cash flow	$139,450

FINANCIAL ANALYSIS AND PLANNING
5.1.1

This analysis shows that Nestor has positive, and substantial, net cash provided by operating activities of $411,750. Nestor reports on its statement of cash flows that it purchased equipment of $182,500 and land of $70,000 for total capital spending of $252,500. This amount is subtracted from net cash provided by operating activities because, without continued efforts to maintain and expand its facilities, it is unlikely that Nestor can continue to maintain its competitive position. Capital spending is deducted first on the analysis above to indicate it is generally the least discretionary expenditure that a company makes. Dividends are then deducted to arrive at free cash flow.

Nestor has more than enough cash flow to meet its dividend payment and therefore has satisfactory financial flexibility. Nestor used its free cash flow to redeem bonds and add to its liquidity. If it finds additional investments that are profitable, it can increase its spending without putting its dividend or basic capital spending in jeopardy. Companies that have strong financial flexibility can take advantage of profitable investments even in tough times. In addition, strong financial flexibility frees companies from worry about survival in poor economic times. In fact, those with strong financial flexibility often do better in poor economic times because they can take advantage of opportunities that other companies cannot.

In 2011, Air Canada found itself under pressure with respect to its free cash flow, due in part to payments required for its registered pension plans. Although Air Canada's cash, cash equivalents, and short-term investments totalled almost $2.3 billion as at June 30, 2011, in the second quarter of 2011, free cash flow of $241 million decreased by $56 million from the second quarter of 2010.[34] The drop in free cash flow was largely attributed to pension contributions in 2011. Air Canada had been able to avoid making past contributions to its pension plans for several years based on the terms of the Air Canada 2009 Pension Regulations, which had been passed by the federal government in 2009. However, these payments resumed in 2011.[35] Overall, the legislation provided funding relief in two parts: a moratorium on special payments until December 31, 2010, and a set schedule of payments

REAL WORLD EMPHASIS

for 2011, 2012, and 2013. The funding relief appears to have worked out well, because Air Canada's pension deficit on its domestic pension plans of $3.7 million in 2013 turned into a small surplus at the start of 2014. The turnaround related to a strong return on investments (almost 14% in 2013), a change in discount rate estimate for its pension obligations, and a $225-million contribution made toward its pension solvency deficit.[36]

Caution

As more and more complex financial instruments are created, more presentation issues arise for financial statement preparers. Many instruments have attributes of both debt and equity. This is significant for analysts because a misclassification will affect key ratios. Note disclosure of the details of the instruments helps analysts and other users in assessing a company's liquidity and solvency. We will discuss this issue further in subsequent chapters on liabilities and equities.

IFRS/ASPE COMPARISON

A Comparison of IFRS and ASPE

Objective 10
Identify differences in accounting between IFRS and ASPE.

The differences between the IFRS and ASPE sets of standards in how assets, liabilities, and shareholders' equity are accounted for and presented on the SFP and how cash activity is reported on the statement of cash flows are set out in Illustration 5-24.

Illustration 5-24

IFRS and ASPE Comparison Chart

	IFRS—IAS 1, 7, and 40	Accounting Standards for Private Enterprises (ASPE)—*CPA Canada Handbook*, Part II, Sections 1400, 1510, 1521, 1540, and 3251	References to related illustrations and select brief exercises
Specific items to be presented in the balance sheet/SFP	The following items are required to be presented under IFRS: • Investment property • Biological assets • Provisions	For the most part, IFRS and ASPE require essentially the same items to be presented.	Illustration 10-8 Illustration 8-26 Illustration 8-27 Illustration 8-28
Current versus non-current liabilities	If no unconditional right to defer payment of financial liability beyond one year as at the balance sheet date, must show as current (including situations where the company has refinanced the debt after the balance sheet date but before issue).	If company has refinanced debt by the issue date of the financial statements, may present as non-current.	BE5-8 and BE5-9
Statement of cash flows (cash flow statement)	Certain preferred shares acquired within a short period of maturity date may be classified as cash and cash equivalents. IFRS allows flexibility in how to treat interest and dividends (may be classified as operating, investing, or financing activities).	Equity investments are excluded from cash and cash equivalents. Interest and dividends included in net income are treated as operating activities and those booked through retained earnings are treated as financing activities.	BE5-15
Cash flow per share information	No prohibition on disclosure of this number.	Prohibited—may not be disclosed	BE5-17
Disclosure of date financial statements authorized for issue	Must disclose date that the financial statements were authorized for issue.	No requirement to disclose.	

Looking Ahead

Objective 11
Identify the significant
changes planned by
the IASB regarding
financial statement
presentation.

As noted in Chapter 4, the IASB and FASB are working on financial statement presentation as a major project. The idea is to present the main financial statements so as to highlight major business and financing activities. In July 2010, the IASB published a "staff draft" of an Exposure Draft on financial statement presentation. On March 1, 2011, IASB staff presented the results and findings of its outreach activities. However, the project was then paused as the IASB and FASB decided to conduct more outreach activities before issuing an Exposure Draft on financial statement presentation, which could ultimately result in the replacement of IAS 1 and IAS 7.

The IASB issued an Exposure Draft (ED) in May 2015 entitled "Conceptual Framework for Financial Reporting" that included proposed changes to the definitions of assets and liabilities. The ED defines an asset as "a present economic resource controlled by the entity as a result of past events" where "an economic resource is a right that has the potential to produce economic benefits." The ED then provides additional details regarding the definition as it relates to "rights," "economic benefits," and "control." Similarly, the ED defines a liability as "a present obligation of the entity to transfer an economic resource as a result of past events" and goes on to clarify aspects of the proposed definition. As discussed in Chapter 2, it is hoped that the revised conceptual framework will be released in 2016. For most assets and liabilities, applying the new definitions would yield the same accounting results as the current definitions.

In June 2014, the IASB issued an ED called the "Disclosure Initiative—Proposed Amendments to IAS 7." Rather than replacing IAS 7 *Statement of Cash Flows*, the ED proposes amendments that would provide additional information to financial statement users about financing activities (other than those that relate to equity items). If the ED is adopted, companies would be required to provide a reconciliation of items such as long-term borrowings and leases: disclosing the opening balances, cash flow–related changes, noncash changes, and reconciling to the closing balances of these financing-related items. In addition, the ED would require additional disclosures to help users understand the liquidity position of companies. These disclosures would include items such as restrictions on the use of cash and cash equivalents that might arise when repatriating foreign cash and cash equivalents. (For example, the repatriation of foreign cash equivalents might trigger tax liabilities that could affect the liquidity of the balances being repatriated.)[37]

SUMMARY OF LEARNING OBJECTIVES

1 Understand the statement of financial position and statement of cash flows from a business perspective.

It is important to understand how users of financial statements use the SFP and the statement of cash flows. For example, potential investors in a company may use the SFP to analyze a company's liquidity and solvency in order to assess the risk of investing. In addition, the SFP provides details about the company's financial structure. Users may use a company's statement of cash flows to assess its earnings quality and obtain information about its operating, investing, and financing activities.

2 Identify the uses and limitations of a statement of financial position.

The SFP provides information about the nature and amounts of investments in enterprise resources, obligations to creditors, and the owners' equity in net resources. The SFP contributes to financial reporting by providing a basis for (1) calculating rates of return, (2) evaluating the

enterprise's capital structure, and (3) assessing the enterprise's liquidity, solvency, and financial flexibility. The limitations of an SFP are as follows: (1) The SFP often does not reflect current value, because accountants have adopted a historical cost basis in valuing and reporting many assets and liabilities. (2) Judgements and estimates must be used in preparing an SFP. (3) The SFP leaves out many items that are of financial value to the business but cannot be recorded objectively, such as its human resources, customer base, and reputation.

3 Identify the major classifications of a statement of financial position.

The SFP's general elements are assets, liabilities, and equity. The major classifications within the SFP on the asset side are current assets; investments; property, plant, and equipment; intangible assets; and other assets. The major classifications of liabilities are current and long-term liabilities. In a corporation, owners' equity is generally classified as shares, contributed surplus, retained earnings, and accumulated other comprehensive income.

4 Prepare a classified statement of financial position.

The most common format lists liabilities and shareholders' equity directly below assets on the same page.

5 Identify statement of financial position information that requires supplemental disclosure.

Five types of information are normally supplemental to account titles and amounts presented in the SFP. (1) Contingencies: Material events that have an uncertain outcome. (2) Accounting policies: Explanations of the valuation methods that are used or the basic assumptions that are made for inventory valuation, amortization methods, investments in subsidiaries, and so on. (3) Contractual situations: Explanations of certain restrictions or covenants that are attached to specific assets or, more likely, to liabilities. (4) Additional information: Clarification by giving more detail about the composition of SFP items. (5) Subsequent events: Events that happen after the date of the SFP.

6 Identify major disclosure techniques for the statement of financial position.

There are four methods of disclosing pertinent information in the SFP: (1) Parenthetical explanations: Additional information or description is often provided by giving explanations in parentheses that follow the item. (2) Notes: Notes are used if additional explanations or descriptions cannot be shown conveniently as parenthetical explanations. (3) Cross-reference and contra items: A direct relationship between an asset and a liability is cross-referenced on the SFP. (4) Supporting schedules: Often a separate schedule is needed to present more detailed information about certain assets or liabilities because the SFP provides just a single summary item.

7 Indicate the purpose and identify the content of the statement of cash flows.

The main purpose of a statement of cash flows is to provide relevant information about an enterprise's cash receipts and cash payments during a period. Reporting the sources, uses, and net increase or decrease in cash lets investors, creditors, and others know what is happening to a company's most liquid resource. Cash receipts and cash payments during a period are classified in the statement of cash flows into three different activities: (1) Operating activities: Involve the cash effects of transactions that enter into the determination of net income. (2) Investing activities: Include making and collecting loans and acquiring and disposing of investments (both debt and equity) and property, plant, and equipment.

(3) Financing activities: Involve liability and owners' equity items and include (a) obtaining capital from owners and providing them with a return on their investment and (b) borrowing money from creditors and repaying the amounts borrowed.

8 Prepare a statement of cash flows using the indirect method.

This involves determining cash flows from operations by starting with net income and adjusting it for noncash activities, such as changes in accounts receivable (and other current asset/liability) balances, depreciation, and gains/losses. It is important to look carefully at prior year operating activities that might affect cash this year, such as cash collected this year from last year's credit sales and cash spent this year for last year's accrued expenses. The cash flows from investing and financing activities can then be determined by analyzing changes in SFP accounts and the cash account.

9 Understand the usefulness of the statement of cash flows.

Creditors examine the statement of cash flows carefully because they are concerned about being repaid. The amount of net cash flow provided by operating activities in relation to the company's liabilities is helpful in making this assessment. In addition, measures such as a free cash flow analysis provide creditors and shareholders with a better picture of the company's financial flexibility.

10 Identify differences in accounting between IFRS and ASPE.

Illustration 5-24 outlines the major differences in how both sets of standards account for and present items on the SFP and statement of cash flows. Both sets of standards largely require that the same SFP elements be presented. In addition, IFRS requires presentation of biological assets, investment properties, and provisions. The statement of cash flow presentation requirements are similar.

11 Identify the significant changes planned by the IASB regarding financial statement presentation.

The IASB has been planning to change the way financial statements are presented by issuing a new standard on financial statement presentation. However, the project was paused in 2011 "until the IASB concludes its ongoing deliberations about its future work plan." In June 2014, the IASB issued a more targeted Exposure Draft called the "Disclosure Initiative—Proposed Amendments to IAS 7." It proposes amendments to provide additional information to financial statement users about financing activities (other than those that relate to equity items).

KEY TERMS

adjunct account, p. 230	current assets, p. 216	financial flexibility, p. 211
cash and cash equivalents, p. 217	current cash debt coverage ratio, p. 236	financial instruments, p. 213
cash debt coverage ratio, p. 237	current liabilities, p. 222	financing activities, p. 231
contingency, p. 226	deferred income tax assets, p. 222	free cash flow, p. 238
contra account, p. 229	deferred income tax liabilities, p. 223	future income tax assets, p. 222

future income tax liabilities, p. 223
intangible assets, p. 221
investing activities, p. 231
liquidity, p. 211
long-term liabilities, p. 223
monetary assets, p. 213
non-current investments, p. 220

non-monetary assets, p. 213
operating activities, p. 231
other assets, p. 222
owners' equity, p. 224
prepaid expenses, p. 219
property, plant, and equipment, p. 220
provision, p. 227

solvency, p. 211
statement of cash flows, p. 230
statement of financial position, p. 211
subsequent events, p. 228
working capital, p. 223

APPENDIX 5A

RATIO ANALYSIS: A REFERENCE

Business Risks

Objective 12
Identify the major types of financial ratios and what they measure.

Companies expose themselves to many risks in doing business. Strategically, the goal is to identify these risks and then manage them in order to take advantage of opportunities and maximize shareholder value. How do users know whether a company is managing its risks in a way that will create the most shareholder value? Illustration 5A-1 shows the business model that we originally introduced in Chapter 4. Now risks have been added to the model, along with the key management personnel responsible for managing the risks.[38]

Illustration 5A-1

The Business Model and Various Related Risks That a Company Must Manage

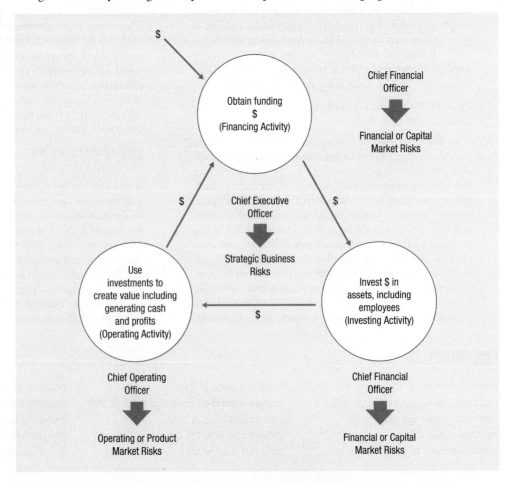

Financial or capital market risks are related to financing and investing activities. For example, when a company borrows funds, it might increase its solvency and liquidity risk. **Operating or product market risks** are related to operating activities. For instance, when it manufactures a drug, there is a risk that a company might not be able to produce quality products on time or successfully target the appropriate market for sale of the drug.

Information about risks is useful and much of this information is included in the annual report, both within the financial statements and in other parts. The financial statements give **information** about financing, investing, and operating activities and therefore provide indirect feedback on how related risks are being managed and how this in turn affects performance. A solvent company that constantly generates cash from operations has a solid business model where risks and opportunities are well managed to create value. Companies usually disclose explicit information about risks and risk management policies in the Management Discussion and Analysis section of the annual report.

Financial Ratios

Ratio analysis helps in assessing operating and financial risks by **expressing the relationship between selected financial statement data.** Qualitative information from financial statements is gathered by **examining relationships** between items on the statements and **identifying trends** in these relationships. Relationships are often expressed in terms of a percentage, a rate, or a simple proportion.

To illustrate, in its January 3, 2015 financial statements, **Loblaw Companies Limited** had current assets of $9,405 million and current liabilities of $6,395 million. The following relationship is determined by dividing current assets by current liabilities. The alternative means of expression are:

Percentage: Current assets are 147% of current liabilities.

Rate: Current assets are 1.47 times as great as current liabilities.

Proportion: The relationship of current assets to current liabilities is 1.47:1.

REAL WORLD EMPHASIS

For analyzing financial statements, ratios are generally classified into four types, as follows:

FINANCIAL ANALYSIS AND PLANNING
5.1.1

MAJOR TYPES OF RATIOS

Liquidity ratios. Measure the enterprise's short-term ability to pay its maturing obligations.

Activity ratios. Measure how effectively the enterprise is using its assets. Activity ratios also measure how liquid certain assets like inventory and receivables are; in other words, how fast the asset's value is realized by the company.

Profitability ratios. Measure financial performance and shareholder value creation for a specific time period.

Coverage or solvency ratios. Measure the degree of protection for long-term creditors and investors or a company's ability to meet its long-term obligations.

In Chapter 4, we briefly discussed profitability ratios, while in this chapter, we touched on liquidity, activity, and coverage ratios. Throughout the remainder of the textbook, we provide ratios to help you understand and interpret the information presented within the context of each subject area. The on-line resources available with this text look at the area of financial statement analysis, of which ratio analysis is one part. Illustration 5A-2 presents some common, basic ratios that will be used throughout the text. In practice, there are many other ratios that provide useful information and are therefore also used.

The key to a refined, information-rich analysis is having a good **understanding of the business, business risks, and industry** before calculating and interpreting any ratios. Specialized industries focus on different ratios depending on the critical success factors in their business. As discussed throughout the chapter, different companies and businesses would be expected to have different types of assets and capital structures. Furthermore, they would be expected to have different types of costs, revenue streams, and business models.

RATIO	FORMULA	WHAT IT MEASURES
I. Liquidity		
1. Current ratio	$\dfrac{\text{Current assets}}{\text{Current liabilities}}$	Short-term debt-paying ability
2. Quick or acid-test ratio	$\dfrac{\text{Cash, marketable securities, and receivables (net)}}{\text{Current liabilities}}$	Immediate short-term liquidity
3. Current cash debt coverage ratio	$\dfrac{\text{Net cash provided by operating activities}}{\text{Average current liabilities (net)}}$	Company's ability to pay off its current liabilities in a specific year from its operations
II. Activity		
4. Receivables turnover	$\dfrac{\text{Net sales}}{\text{Average trade receivables}}$	Liquidity of receivables
5. Inventory turnover	$\dfrac{\text{Cost of goods sold}}{\text{Average inventory}}$	Liquidity of inventory
6. Asset turnover	$\dfrac{\text{Net sales}}{\text{Average total assets}}$	How efficiently assets are used to generate sales
III. Profitability		
7. Profit margin on sales	$\dfrac{\text{Net income}}{\text{Net sales}}$	Net income generated by each dollar of sales
8. Rate of return on assets	$\dfrac{\text{Net income}}{\text{Average total assets}}$	Overall profitability of assets
9. Rate of return on common share equity	$\dfrac{\text{Net income minus preferred dividends}}{\text{Average common shareholders' equity}}$	Profitability of owners' investment
10. Earnings per share	$\dfrac{\text{Net income minus preferred dividends}}{\text{Weighted average shares outstanding}}$	Net income earned on each common share
11. Price earnings ratio	$\dfrac{\text{Market price of shares}}{\text{Earnings per share}}$	Ratio of the market price per share to earnings per share
12. Payout ratio	$\dfrac{\text{Cash dividends}}{\text{Net income}}$	Percentage of earnings distributed as cash dividends
IV. Coverage		
13. Debt to total assets	$\dfrac{\text{Total debt}}{\text{Total assets}}$	Percentage of total assets provided by creditors
14. Times interest earned	$\dfrac{\text{Income before interest changes and taxes}}{\text{Interest charges}}$	Ability to meet interest payments as they come due
15. Cash debt coverage ratio	$\dfrac{\text{Net cash provided by operating activities}}{\text{Average total liabilities}}$	Company's ability to repay its total liabilities in a specific year from its operations
16. Book value per share	$\dfrac{\text{Common shareholders' equity}}{\text{Number of common shares outstanding at SFP date}}$	Amount each share would receive if the company were liquidated at the amounts reported on the statement of financial position

Illustration 5A-2

A Summary of Financial Ratios

Success in the retail industry, for instance, comes from the ability to set prices and target customers in a way that gets maximum market penetration. Also critical is the ability to minimize inventory shrinkage (because there is a high risk of theft) and keep inventory moving so that it does not become obsolete or out of fashion. A company's ability to achieve this, or its failure to do so, is reflected in the gross profit margin (a ratio). This is calculated by dividing gross profit by revenues. Companies must achieve a gross profit that is high enough to cover other costs. A stable gross profit margin is a positive sign that management is dealing with all of the above issues.

Once ratios are calculated, they must then be examined and the information interpreted. Examining ratios by themselves provides very little insight. Instead, the **ratios must be compared with or benchmarked against similar ratios, perhaps for the same company from prior periods or, alternatively, for similar companies in the same industry.**

When benchmarking is done against industry numbers, it may be necessary to create industry benchmarks if they are not available. To do this, select several companies that have a similar business model and are in the same industry. Companies that are the same size are better comparators.

Note that average amounts may be approximated by taking opening and closing balances and dividing by two.

SUMMARY OF LEARNING OBJECTIVE FOR APPENDIX 5A

12 Identify the major types of financial ratios and what they measure.

Ratios express the mathematical relationship between one quantity and another, in terms of a percentage, a rate, or a proportion. Liquidity ratios measure the short-term ability to pay maturing obligations. Activity ratios measure how effectively assets are being used. Profitability ratios measure an enterprise's success or failure. Coverage ratios measure the degree of protection for long-term creditors and investors.

KEY TERMS

activity ratios, p. 243	liquidity ratios, p. 243	ratio analysis, p. 243
coverage ratios, p. 243	profitability ratios, p. 243	solvency ratios, p. 243

Note: Completion of this end-of-chapter material will help develop CPA enabling competencies (such as ethics and professionalism, problem-solving and decision-making and communication) and technical competencies. We have highlighted selected items with an integration icon and material in *WileyPLUS* has been linked to the competencies. All cases emphasize integration, especially of the enabling competencies. The brief exercises, exercises and problems generally emphasize problem-solving and decision-making.

All questions relating to the Statement of Cash Flows assume usage of the indirect method, unless the question states differently. The direct method is covered in Volume 2, Chapter 22.

All assignment material with an asterisk (*) relates to the appendix to this chapter.

Brief Exercises

(LO 1) BE5-1 Wong Corporation is a popular clothing retailer with 15 stores located across Canada. After five consecutive years of increasing sales, Wong would like to expand operations by adding 10 stores within the next three years. To help fund the expansion, Wong is seeking a loan from its bank. As Wong's bank manager, discuss the usefulness of (a) the statement of financial position and (b) the statement of cash flows, in evaluating Wong's operations.

(LO 1) BE5-2 Gator Printers Inc. is an on-line retailer of printing services, reaching thousands of customers across North America every year. The company was founded 15 years ago as a university campus copy shop and has reported consistent year-over-year sales growth every year since, with a fast-growing base of individual customers, as well as large corporate accounts. Two years ago, the company issued shares to the general public through a highly publicized and successful initial public offering. Gator is currently considering expanding to South America, and issuing bonds to fund the expansion. Identify the users of Gator Printers' statement of cash flows and how they are likely to use the statement.

(LO 2) BE5-3 One of the weaknesses or limitations of the statement of financial position is that it leaves out financial statement elements if they cannot be objectively recorded. Name three examples of items that are omitted because of this limitation.

(LO 3) BE5-4 Kahnert Corporation's adjusted trial balance contained the following asset accounts at December 31, 2017: Cash $3,000; Treasury Bills (with original maturity of three months) $4,000; Land $60,000; Intangible Assets—Patents $12,500; Accounts Receivable $90,000; Prepaid Insurance $5,200; Inventory $40,000; Allowance for Doubtful Accounts $4,000; FV-NI (Fair Value—Net Income) Investments $11,000. Prepare the current assets section of the statement of financial position, listing the accounts in proper sequence. Identify which items are monetary.

(LO 3) BE5-5 The following accounts are in Tan Limited's December 31, 2017 trial balance: Prepaid Rent $1,600; Fair Value—OCI Investments $62,000; Unearned Revenue $7,000; Land Held for Speculation $119,000; and Goodwill $45,000. Prepare the long-term investments section of the statement of financial position. Identify which items are financial instruments.

(LO 3) BE5-6 Lowell Corp.'s December 31, 2017 trial balance includes the following accounts: Inventory $120,000; Buildings $207,000; Accumulated Depreciation—Equipment $19,000; Equipment $190,000; Land Held for Speculation $46,000; Accumulated Depreciation—Buildings $45,000; Land $71,000; Equipment Under Lease $229,000; and Accumulated Depreciation—Leased Equipment $103,000. Prepare the property, plant, and equipment section of the statement of financial position.

(LO 3) BE5-7 Pine Corporation's adjusted trial balance contained the following asset accounts at December 31, 2017: Prepaid Rent $22,000; Goodwill $50,000; Franchise Fees Receivable $2,000; Intangible Assets—Franchises $47,000; Intangible Assets—Patents $33,000; and Intangible Assets—Trademarks $10,000. Prepare the intangible assets section of the statement of financial position.

(LO 3) BE5-8 Included in Cellin Limited's December 31, 2017 trial balance are the following accounts: Accounts Payable $251,000; Obligations under Lease $175,000; Unearned Revenue $141,000; Bonds Payable $480,000 (due Oct. 31, 2029); Salaries and Wages Payable $127,000; Interest Payable $42,000; Income Tax Payable $9,000; and Notes Payable $97,000 (due on March 31, 2018). On January 31, 2018, Cellin finalized refinancing of the notes payable with a new note payable due on March 31, 2019. The financial statements were issued on February 28, 2018.

(a) Prepare the current liabilities section of the statement of financial position if Cellin prepares financial statements in accordance with IFRS, and identify which items are monetary.

(b) Explain how your answer to part (a) would be different if Cellin prepares financial statements in accordance with ASPE.

(LO 3) BE5-9 Use the information presented in BE5-8 for Cellin Limited to prepare the non-current liabilities section of the statement of financial position in accordance with (a) IFRS and (b) ASPE.

(LO 3) BE5-10 Southern Corporation's adjusted trial balance contained the following accounts at December 31, 2017: Retained Earnings $120,000; Common Shares $700,000; Bonds Payable $100,000; Contributed Surplus $200,000; Preferred Shares $50,000; Goodwill $55,000; and Accumulated Other Comprehensive Income (Loss) ($150,000). Prepare the shareholders' equity section of the statement of financial position.

(LO 7) BE5-11 What is the purpose of the statement of cash flows? How does it differ from a statement of financial position and an income statement?

(LO 8) BE5-12 Agnu Inc. shows on its statement of financial position its investments accounted for as FV-OCI investments. At its year end of May 31, 2015, the balance in the FV-OCI Investments account was $96,000 and at its year end of May 31, 2016, the balance was $120,000. Agnu's statement of comprehensive income for the year ended May 31, 2016, shows an unrealized loss from fair value adjustment on FV-OCI investments of $23,000. There were no sales of FV-OCI investments during the year, only purchases. Determine the necessary caption(s) and amount(s) that should appear on Agnu's statement of cash flows prepared using the indirect method and determine if the entry(ies) appear under the operating, investing, or financing section(s) of the statement.

(LO 8) BE5-13 Newvo Ltd. shows on its statement of financial position a patent. At its year end of October 31, 2015, the caption read Patent (net) $66,000 and at its year end of October 31, 2016, the caption read Patent (net) $40,000. Newvo's recorded amortization on the patent in the amount of $6,000 for the 2016 fiscal year and the remaining change in the account were as a result of recording an impairment loss for the year ended May 31, 2016. There were no purchases or sales of patents during the year. Determine the necessary caption(s) and amount(s) that should appear on Newvo's statement of cash flow, using the indirect method. Be clear regarding where the item(s) would appear on the statement (i.e., the operating, investing, or financing section(s)).

(LO 8) BE5-14 Healey Corporation's statement of financial position as at December 31, 2017, showed the following amounts: Cash $100; Accounts Receivable $600; Land $1,000; Accounts Payable $300; Bonds Payable $500; Common Shares $400; and Retained Earnings $500. Healey's statement of financial position as at December 31, 2016, showed the following amounts: Cash $150; Accounts Receivable $450; Land $800; Accounts Payable $700; Common Shares $400; and Retained Earnings $300. Assume that no dividends were declared or paid in 2017. Calculate the net cash provided (used) by operating activities for the year ended December 31, 2017, using the indirect method.

(LO 8) BE5-15 Ames Company reported 2017 net income of $151,000. During 2017, accounts receivable increased by $15,000 and accounts payable increased by $9,000. Depreciation expense was $44,000. Prepare the cash flows from operating activities section of the statement of cash flows using the indirect method.

(LO 8) BE5-16 Miller Ltd. engaged in the following cash transactions during 2017:

Sale of land and building	$176,000
Repurchase of company's own shares	25,000
Purchase of land	44,000
Payment of cash dividend	58,000
Purchase of equipment	35,000
Issuance of common shares	140,000
Retirement of bonds payable	200,000

Miller prepares financial statements in accordance with ASPE. Calculate the net cash provided (used) by investing activities.

(LO 8) **BE5-17** Use the information from BE5-16 for Miller Ltd. (a) Calculate the net cash provided (used) by financing activities, under ASPE. (b) Explain how your answer to part (a) would be different if Miller prepares financial statements in accordance with IFRS, if Miller's policy is to treat dividends paid as operating activities.

FINANCE

(LO 9, 10, 12) ***BE5-18** Use the information from BE5-16 for Miller Ltd. Determine Miller's free cash flow, assuming that it reported net cash provided by operating activities of $400,000.

(LO 8, 9, 12) ***BE5-19** Midwest Co. reported the following items in the most recent year:

Net income	$40,000
Dividends paid	5,000
Increase in accounts receivable	10,000
Increase in accounts payable	7,000
Purchase of equipment	8,000
Depreciation expense	4,000
Issue of notes payable for cash	20,000

(a) Calculate net cash provided (used) by operating activities, the net change in cash during the year, and free cash flow. Dividends paid are treated as financing activities. Midwest uses the indirect method for its Statement of Cash Flows.

(b) Assuming Midwest had 100,000 common shares outstanding for the entire year, calculate cash flow per share to be included in the financial statements if Midwest follows IFRS and chooses to disclose the ratio.

FINANCE

(c) How would your answer to part (b) change if Midwest follows ASPE?

(LO 12) ***BE5-20** Melbourne Inc. reported a current ratio of 1.5:1 in the current year, which is higher than last year's current ratio of 1.3:1. It also reported an acid-test ratio of 1:1, which is higher than last year's acid-test ratio of 0.6:1. Is Melbourne's liquidity improving or deteriorating? Explain.

FINANCE

Exercises

(LO 3) **E5-1** **(Statement of Financial Position Classifications)** Several statement of financial position accounts of Greenspoon Inc. follow:

1. FV-OCI Investments
2. Common Shares
3. Dividends Payable
4. Accumulated Depreciation—Equipment
5. Construction in Process (Warehouse)
6. Petty Cash
7. Interest Payable
8. Deficit
9. FV-NI Investments
10. Income Tax Payable
11. Unearned Subscriptions Revenue
12. Work-in-Process Inventory—Direct Materials
13. Salaries and Wages Payable
14. Unearned Revenue
15. Litigation Liability

Instructions

For each account, indicate the proper statement of financial position classification. In the case of items that could be classified in more than one category, indicate the additional information that would be required to determine the proper classification. (Refer to Illustration 5-1 as a guideline.) Also identify which items are monetary and which are financial instruments (or both).

(LO 3) **E5-2** **(Classification of Statement of Financial Position Accounts)** The classifications on Chesapeake Limited's statement of financial position are as follows:

1. Current assets
2. Long-term investments
3. Property, plant, and equipment
4. Intangible assets
5. Other assets
6. Current liabilities
7. Non-current liabilities
8. Capital shares
9. Contributed surplus
10. Retained earnings
11. Accumulated other comprehensive income

Instructions

Indicate by number where each of the following accounts would be classified:

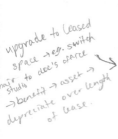

upgrade to leased space → eg. switch hair to doc's office studio → benefit → asset → depreciate over length of lease.

(a) Preferred Shares ⑧

(b) Franchises ④

(c) Salaries and Wages Payable ⑥

(d) Accounts Payable ⑥

(e) Leasehold Improvements ③ *Prop, plant, equipment.*

(f) FV-NI Investments ①

(g) Current Portion of Long-Term Debt ⑥

(h) Obligations under Lease (portion due next year) ⑥

(i) Allowance for Doubtful Accounts ①

(j) Accounts Receivable ①

(k) Bonds Payable (maturing in two years) ⑦

(l) Notes Payable (due next year) ⑥

(m) Supplies ① *Inventory*

(n) Mortgage Payable (principal portion only-mortgage due in 5 years) ⑦

(o) Land ③

(p) Bond Sinking Fund Investment   *→ setting against $ to pay back bond → invest it in meantime → long term investment* ②

(q) Inventory ①

(r) Prepaid Insurance ①

(s) Bonds Payable (maturing next year) ⑥

(t) Income Tax Payable ⑥

(u) Unrealized Gain or Loss—OCI ⑪ *AOCI*

(v) Deficit ⑩ *R/E*

(LO 3) E5-3 (Classification of Statement of Financial Position Accounts) Plato Inc. prepares financial statements in accordance with IFRS and uses the following headings on its statement of financial position:

1. Current assets
2. Long-term investments
3. Property, plant, and equipment
4. Intangible assets
5. Other assets
6. Current liabilities

7. Long-term liabilities
8. Capital shares
9. Contributed surplus
10. Retained earnings
11. Accumulated other comprehensive income

Instructions

Indicate by number how each of the following should usually be classified. If an item need not be reported at all on the statement of financial position, use the letter X. Also indicate whether an item is monetary and/or represents a financial instrument.

(a) Prepaid insurance

(b) Investment in associate

(c) Unearned subscriptions revenue (portion earned next year)

(d) Advances to suppliers

(e) Unearned rent revenue (portion to be earned in two years)

(f) Intangible assets—copyrights

(g) Petty cash

(h) HST payable

(i) Accrued interest on notes receivable

(j) Twenty-year issue of bonds payable that will mature within the next year (no sinking funds exist, and refinancing is not planned)

(k) Machinery retired from use and reclassified as held for sale

(l) Fully depreciated machine still in use

(m) Investment in bonds that will be held until maturity in two years

(n) Accrued interest on bonds payable

(o) Salaries that the company budget shows will be paid to employees within the next year

(p) Accumulated depreciation related to equipment

(q) Accumulated unrealized gains on securities accounted for under the fair value—OCI model

(r) Bank demand loan

(s) Land held for speculation

(LO 3, 4, 12) **E5-4** **(Preparation of Corrected Statement of Financial Position)** Bruno Corp. has decided to expand its operations. The bookkeeper recently completed the following statement of financial position in order to obtain additional funds for expansion:

BRUNO CORP.
Statement of Financial Position
For the Year Ended December 31, 2017

Current assets	
Cash (net of bank overdraft of $30,000)	$260,000
Accounts receivable (net)	340,000
Inventory at the lower of cost and net realizable value	401,000
FV-NI investments (at cost—fair value $120,000)	140,000
Property, plant, and equipment	
Building (net)	570,000
Equipment (net)	160,000
Land held for future use	175,000
Intangible assets	
Goodwill	80,000
Investment in bonds to be held until maturity, at amortized cost	90,000
Prepaid expenses	12,000
Current liabilities	
Accounts payable	195,000
Notes payable (due next year)	125,000
Pension obligation	82,000
Rent payable	49,000
Long-term liabilities	
Bonds payable	553,000
Shareholders' equity	
Common shares, unlimited authorized, 290,000 issued	290,000
Contributed surplus	180,000
Retained earnings	734,000 ?

(Handwritten annotations throughout: "Assets"; "@ diff. bank so can't net"; "290,000"; "Less ADA (17,000) 357,000"; "record investments @ FV 120,000"; "Less Accum. deprec. $160,000 → 730,000"; "Less Accum. deprec. $105,000 → 265,000"; "—unrealized loss 20,000"; "Bank overdraft 30,000"; "total CL"; "total liabilities"; "add in total current assets in CA"; "under own heading long-term investments"; "total assets"; "buy shares back @ Ter rate"; "(TA−TL − C/S − Cont. Surplus) → plug to make B/S balance"; "Total Liabilities & Shareholders' Equity"; "total debt / total assets = 0.4 − 0.6")

Instructions

(a) Prepare a revised statement of financial position using the available information. Assume that the bank overdraft relates to a bank account held at a different bank from the account with the cash balance. Assume that the accumulated depreciation balance for the buildings is $160,000 and that the accumulated depreciation balance for the equipment is $105,000. The allowance for doubtful accounts has a balance of $17,000. The pension obligation is considered a long-term liability.

DIGGING DEEPER

***(b)** What effect, if any, does the classification of the bank overdraft have on the working capital and current ratio of Bruno Corp.? What is the likely reason why the bank overdraft was given that particular classification?

(LO 3, 4, 12) **E5-5** **(Correction of Statement of Financial Position)** The bookkeeper for Garfield Corp. has prepared the following statement of financial position as at July 31, 2017:

GARFIELD CORP.
Statement of Financial Position
As at July 31, 2017

Cash	$ 69,000	Notes and accounts payable	$ 44,000
Accounts receivable (net)	40,500	Long-term liabilities	75,000
Inventory	60,000	Shareholders' equity	155,500
Equipment (net)	84,000		$274,500
Patents (net)	21,000		
	$274,500		

The following additional information is provided:

1. Cash includes $1,200 in a petty cash fund and $12,000 in a bond sinking fund.

2. The net accounts receivable balance is composed of the following three items: (a) accounts receivable debit balances $52,000; (b) accounts receivable credit balances $8,000; (c) allowance for doubtful accounts $3,500.

3. Inventory costing $5,300 was shipped out on consignment on July 31, 2017. The ending inventory balance does not include the consigned goods. Receivables of $5,300 were recognized on these consigned goods.

4. Equipment had a cost of $112,000 and an accumulated depreciation balance of $28,000.

5. Income tax payable of $9,000 was accrued on July 31. Garfield Corp., however, had set up a cash fund to meet this obligation. This cash fund was not included in the cash balance, but was offset against the income tax payable account.

6. Long-term liabilities are bonds payable issued at par, due in 2022.

7. Shareholders' equity is made up of two account balances: Common Shares of $105,000 and Retained Earnings of $50,500.

Instructions

DIGGING DEEPER

(a) Use the information available to prepare a corrected classified statement of financial position as at July 31, 2017. (Adjust the account balances based on the additional information.)

*(b) What effect, if any, does the treatment of the credit balances in accounts receivable of $8,000 have on the working capital and current ratio of Garfield Corp.? What is likely the reason that the credit balances in accounts receivable were given that particular classification? What is likely the cause of the credit balances in accounts receivable?

(LO 4) E5-6   (Preparation of Classified Statement of Financial Position) Assume that Lee Inc. has the following accounts at the end of the current year:

1. Common Shares
2. Raw Materials Inventory
3. FV-OCI Investments
4. Unearned Rent Revenue
5. Work-in-Process Inventory
6. Intangible Assets—Copyrights
7. Buildings
8. Notes Receivable (due in three months)
9. Cash (includes Restricted Cash—see item 12)
10. Salaries and Wages Payable
11. Accumulated Depreciation—Buildings

12. Restricted Cash (for plant expansion)
13. Land Held for Future Plant Site
14. Allowance for Doubtful Accounts
15. Retained Earnings
16. Unearned Subscriptions Revenue (earned in the next year)
17. Accounts Receivable—Officers (due in one year)
18. Finished Goods Inventory
19. Accounts Receivable
20. Bonds Payable (due in four years)
21. Accounts Payable
22. Goodwill

Instructions

Prepare a classified statement of financial position in good form (no monetary amounts are necessary).

(LO 4) E5-7   (Current versus Long-Term Liabilities) Samson Corporation is preparing its December 31, 2017 statement of financial position. The following items may be reported as either current or long-term liabilities:

1. On December 15, 2017, Samson declared a cash dividend of $1.50 per common share to shareholders of record on December 31. The dividend is payable on January 15, 2018. Samson has issued one million common shares.

2. Also, on December 31, Samson declared a 10% stock dividend to shareholders of record on January 15, 2018. The dividend will be distributed on January 31, 2018. Samson's common shares have a market value of $54 per share.

3. At December 31, bonds payable of $100 million is outstanding. The bonds pay 7% interest every September 30 and mature in instalments of $25 million every September 30, beginning on September 30, 2018.

4. At December 31, 2016, customer advances were $12 million. During 2017, Samson collected $40 million in customer advances, and advances of $25 million were earned.

5. At December 31, 2017, Samson has an operating line of credit with a balance of $3.5 million outstanding. For several years now, Samson has successfully met all the conditions of this bank loan. If Samson defaults on any of the loan conditions in any way, the bank has the right to demand payment of the loan.

6. Samson is contingently liable for a bank loan in the amount of $10 million of its associated company, DD Ross Ltd. Samson has guaranteed the bank that should DD Ross default on the loan or any outstanding interest payable, Samson will have to pay any and all outstanding balances. DD Ross Ltd. is in excellent financial position and shows no signs of defaulting on the terms of the bank loan.

Instructions

DIGGING DEEPER

(a) For each item above, indicate the dollar amounts to be reported as a current liability and as a long-term liability, if any.

(b) Referring to the definition of a liability (discussed in Chapter 2), explain the accounting treatment of item 4 above.

(c) Can you think of a reason why Samson would be willing to guarantee the bank loan of its associate, DD Ross Ltd.? What possible benefit could this burden bring Samson?

(LO 4) E5-8 (Preparation of Statement of Financial Position) The trial balance of Zhang Ltd. at December 31, 2017, follows:

	Debits	Credits
Cash	$ 205,000	
Sales revenue		$ 8,010,000
FV-NI investments (at fair value)	153,000	
Cost of goods sold	4,800,000	
Bond investment at amortized cost	299,000	
FV-OCI investments (fair value $345,000)	277,000	
Notes payable (due in six months)		98,000
Accounts payable		545,000
Selling expenses	1,860,000	
Investment income or loss*		13,000
Land	260,000	
Buildings	1,040,000	
Commission payable		136,000
Accrued liabilities		96,000
Accounts receivable	515,000	
Accumulated depreciation—buildings		152,000
Allowance for doubtful accounts		25,000
Administrative expenses	900,000	
Interest expense	211,000	
Inventory	687,000	
Gain on sale of land		60,000
Correction of prior year error	40,000	
Notes payable (due in five years)		900,000
Equipment	600,000	
Bonds payable (due in three years)		1,000,000
Accumulated depreciation—equipment		60,000
Intangible assets—franchises (net)	160,000	
Common shares		809,000
Intangible assets—patents (net)	195,000	
Retained earnings		218,000
Accumulated other comprehensive income		80,000
Totals	$12,202,000	$12,202,000

* The investment income or loss relates to the FV-NI investments.

Instructions

(a) Prepare a classified statement of financial position as at December 31, 2017. Ignore income taxes.

DIGGING DEEPER **(b)** Is there any situation where it would make more sense to have a statement of financial position that is not classified?

(LO 4, 5) E5-9 (Current Liabilities) Lujie Xie is the controller of Lincoln Corporation and is responsible for the preparation of the year-end financial statements on December 31, 2017. Lincoln prepares financial statements in accordance with ASPE. The following transactions occurred during the year:

1. On December 20, 2017, an employee filed a legal action against Lincoln for $100,000 for wrongful dismissal. Management believes the action to be frivolous and without merit. This opinion is shared by the corporate lawyer involved in the matter. The likelihood of payment to the employee is remote.

2. Bonuses to key employees based on net income for 2017 are estimated to be $150,000.

3. On December 1, 2017, the company borrowed $900,000 at 5% per year. Interest is paid quarterly.

4. Credit sales for the year amounted to $10 million. Lincoln's expense provision for doubtful accounts is estimated to be 2% of credit sales.

5. On December 15, 2017, the company declared a $2.00 per common share dividend on the 40,000 common shares outstanding, to be paid on January 5, 2018.

6. During the year, customer advances of $160,000 were received; $50,000 of this amount was earned by December 31, 2017.

7. Late in December, 2017, Lincoln received a notice of assessment for its 2016 income tax filing. The Canada Revenue Agency disallowed a deduction claimed by Lincoln and an additional $6,000 of income taxes are owing and will be paid in early January 2018.

Instructions

For each item above, indicate the dollar amount to be reported as a current liability. If a liability is not reported, explain why.

(LO 4, 5, 6) **E5-10** **(Current Assets Section of Statement of Financial Position)** Selected accounts follow of Aramis Limited at December 31, 2017:

Finished Goods Inventory	$152,000	Cost of Goods Sold	$2,100,000
Unearned Revenue	90,000	Notes Receivable	40,000
Bank Overdraft	8,000	Accounts Receivable	161,000
Equipment	253,000	Raw Materials Inventory	187,000
Work-in-Process Inventory	34,000	Supplies Expense	60,000
Cash	50,000	Allowance for Doubtful Accounts	12,000
FV-NI Investments	31,000	Intangible Assets—Trade Names	18,000
Interest Payable	36,000	Contributed Surplus	16,000
Restricted Cash (for Plant Expansion)	50,000	Common Shares	272,000

The following additional information is available:

1. Inventory is valued at the lower of cost and net realizable value using FIFO.

2. Equipment is recorded at cost. Accumulated depreciation, calculated on a straight-line basis, is $50,600.

3. The fair value—net income investments have a fair value of $29,000.

4. The notes receivable are due April 30, 2018, with interest receivable every April 30. The notes bear interest at 6%. (*Hint*: Accrue interest due on December 31, 2017.)

5. The allowance for doubtful accounts applies to the accounts receivable. Accounts receivable of $50,000 are pledged as collateral on a bank loan.

6. Intangible Assets—Trade Names are reported net of accumulated amortization of $14,000.

7. The bank overdraft is at the same bank as the amount reported above under Cash.

Instructions

(a) Prepare the current assets section of Aramis Limited's statement of financial position as at December 31, 2017, with appropriate disclosures.

(b) Outline the other ways or methods that can be used to disclose the details that are required for the financial statement elements in part (a).

(LO 4, 8) **E5-11** **(Preparation of Statement of Financial Position)** Uddin Corp.'s statement of financial position at the end of 2016 included the following items:

Current assets	$1,105,000	Current liabilities	$1,020,000
Land	30,000	Bonds payable	1,100,000
Building	1,120,000	Common shares	180,000
Equipment	320,000	Retained earnings	174,000
Accumulated depreciation—building	(130,000)	Total	$2,474,000
Accumulated depreciation—equipment	(11,000)		
Intangible assets—patents	40,000		
Total	$2,474,000		

The following information is available for the 2017 fiscal year:

1. Net income was $391,000.

2. Equipment (cost of $20,000 and accumulated depreciation of $8,000) was sold for $10,000.

3. Depreciation expense was $4,000 on the building and $9,000 on equipment.

4. Patent amortization expense was $3,000.

5. Current assets other than cash increased by $29,000. Current liabilities increased by $13,000.

6. An addition to the building was completed at a cost of $31,000.

7. A fair value—OCI investment in shares was purchased for $20,500 on the last day of the year. This was the first such investment made by Uddin in its history.

8. Bonds payable of $75,000 were issued at par.

9. Cash dividends of $180,000 were declared and paid. Dividends paid are treated as financing activities.

Uddin prepares financial statements in accordance with IFRS.

Instructions

(a) Prepare a statement of financial position (SFP) as at December 31, 2017. (*Hint:* You will need to adjust ("plug") the December 31, 2017 amount of current assets to ensure the SFP balances.)

(b) Prepare a statement of cash flows for the year ended December 31, 2017 using the indirect method.

(LO 4, 12) E5-12 **(Current Assets and Current Liabilities)** The current assets and current liabilities sections of the statement of financial position of Agincourt Corp. are as follows:

AGINCOURT CORP.
Statement of Financial Position (partial)
December 31, 2017

Cash		$ 40,000	Accounts payable	$ 61,000
Accounts receivable	$89,000		Notes payable	67,000
Allowance for doubtful accounts	7,000	82,000		$128,000
Inventory		171,000		
Prepaid expenses		9,000		
		$302,000		

The following errors have been discovered in the corporation's accounting:

1. January 2018 cash disbursements that were entered as at December 2017 included payments of accounts payable in the amount of $35,000, on which a cash discount of 2% was taken.

2. The inventory balance is based on an inventory count that included $27,000 of merchandise that was received at December 31 but with no purchase invoices received or entered. Of this amount, $10,000 was received on consignment; the remainder was purchased f.o.b. destination, terms 2/10, n/30.

3. Sales for the first four days in January 2018 in the amount of $30,000 were entered in the sales book as at December 31, 2017. Of these, $21,500 were sales on account and the remainder were cash sales.

4. Cash, not including cash sales, collected in January 2018 and entered as at December 31, 2017, totalled $35,324. Of this amount, $23,324 was received on account after cash discounts of 2% had been deducted; the remainder was proceeds on a bank loan (the amount owed to the bank for January 2018 was included as part of Notes Payable account).

Instructions

(a) Adjust (correct) the statement of financial position's current assets and current liabilities sections. (Assume that both accounts receivable and accounts payable are recorded gross.)

*(b) Calculate the current ratio before and after the corrections prepared in part (a). Did the changes improve or worsen this ratio?

(c) Calculate the net effect of your adjustments on Agincourt Corp.'s retained earnings balance.

(d) Assume that in February 2018, Agincourt approaches its bank for another bank loan, based on its corrected statement of financial position as at December 31, 2017. Also assume that the terms of the new bank loan would require that Agincourt maintain a current ratio of 1.5. As Agincourt's bank manager, discuss the importance of recording the adjustments above and correcting the statement of financial position as at December 31, 2017.

(e) If the adjustments had not been reflected in the statement of financial position provided to the bank manager, do you think the bank manager would have suspected that the financial statements were incorrect? If so, how would the manager have suspected this misstatement to be the case?

(LO 5) E5-13 **(Supplemental Disclosures)** It is February 2018 and Janix Corporation is preparing to issue financial statements for the year ended December 31, 2017. To prepare financial statements and related disclosures that are faithfully representative, Janix is reviewing the following events in 2017 and 2018:

1. In August 2017, Maddux Incorporated filed a lawsuit against Janix for alleged patent infringement, claiming $1.8 million in damages. In the opinion of Janix's management and legal counsel, it is not likely that damages will be awarded to Maddux.

2. In January 2018, there was a significant decline in the fair value of Janix's FV-NI (fair value—net income) investments, resulting in an unrealized holding loss of $720,000.

3. In January 2018, a customer filed a lawsuit against Janix for alleged breach of contract related to services provided in 2017. The customer is seeking damages of $950,000. Janix's legal counsel believes that Janix will likely lose the lawsuit and have to pay between $850,000 and $950,000.

4. In August 2017, Janix signed a contract to purchase 200,000 inventory units in August 2018 for a price of $12 per unit. According to the supplier's price list at December 31, 2017, the price per inventory unit had decreased to $10 per unit.

5. At December 31, 2017, Janix has a $1.1-million demand loan outstanding. The terms of the demand loan restrict Janix's payment of dividends to $2 per common share.

6. On January 31, 2018, Janix issued 100,000 new common shares, raising $2 million in new capital.

7. On January 28, 2018, management settled a dispute with the union of its factory workers. A strike had started on November 14, 2017. A portion of the settlement involved a lump sum payment to each worker in lieu of a retroactive adjustment in pay rate dating back to the beginning of the strike.

Janix prepares financial statements in accordance with IFRS.

Instructions

For each item above, indicate whether the event relates to a provision, contingency, commitment, or subsequent event, and explain the appropriate accounting treatment. If no adjustment or disclosure is required, explain why.

(LO 6, 8, 9) **E5-14   (Prepare Statement of Cash Flows)** A comparative statement of financial position for Carmichael Industries Inc. follows:

CARMICHAEL INDUSTRIES INC.
Statement of Financial Position
December 31, 2017

	December 31	
Assets	2017	2016
Cash	$ 21,000	$ 34,000
Accounts receivable	104,000	54,000
Inventory	220,000	189,000
Land	71,000	110,000
Equipment	260,000	200,000
Accumulated depreciation—equipment	(69,000)	(42,000)
Total	$607,000	$545,000
Liabilities and Shareholders' Equity		
Accounts payable	$ 52,000	$ 59,000
Bonds payable	150,000	200,000
Common shares	214,000	164,000
Retained earnings	191,000	122,000
Total	$607,000	$545,000

Additional information:

1. Net income for the fiscal year ending December 31, 2017, was $129,000.

2. Cash dividends of $60,000 were declared and paid. Dividends paid are treated as financing activities.

3. Bonds payable amounting to $50,000 were retired through issuance of common shares.

4. Land was sold at a gain of $5,000.

5. No equipment was sold during the year.

Instructions

(a) Prepare a statement of cash flows using the indirect method.

(b) Comment in general on the results reported in the statement of cash flows.

(LO 7) **E5-15   (Statement of Cash Flows—Classifications)** The major classifications of activities reported in the statement of cash flows are operating, investing, and financing. For this question, assume the following:

Instructions

Assume that the statement of cash flows is being prepared in accordance with ASPE using the indirect method. Classify each of the transactions in the lettered list that follows as:

1. Operating activity
2. Investing activity
3. Financing activity
4. Not reported as a cash flow

Transactions

(a) Issuance of common shares

(b) Purchase of land and building

(c) Redemption of bonds

(d) Proceeds on sale of equipment

(e) Depreciation of machinery

(f) Amortization of patent

(g) Issuance of bonds for plant assets

(h) Payment of cash dividends

(i) Exchange of furniture for office equipment

(j) Loss on sale of equipment

(k) Increase in accounts receivable during year

(l) Decrease in accounts payable during year

(m) Payment of interest

(n) Receipt of dividend revenue

(LO 8) E5-16   (Prepare Partial Statement of Cash Flows—Operating Activities) The statement of income of Kneale Transport Inc. for the year ended December 31, 2017, reported the following condensed information:

KNEALE TRANSPORT INC.
Statement of Income
Year Ended December 31, 2017

Service revenue		$545,000
Operating expenses		370,000
Income from operations		175,000
Other revenues and expenses		
Gain on sale of equipment	$25,000	
Interest expense	10,000	15,000
Income before income taxes		190,000
Income tax expense		42,000
Net income		$148,000

Kneale's statement of financial position included the following comparative data at December 31:

	2017	2016
Accounts receivable	$50,000	$60,000
Prepaid insurance	8,000	5,000
Accounts payable	30,000	41,000
Interest payable	2,000	750
Income tax payable	8,000	4,500
Unearned revenue	10,000	14,000

Additional information:

Operating expenses include $70,000 in depreciation expense. The company follows IFRS. Assume that interest is treated as an operating activity for purposes of the statement of cash flows.

Instructions

DIGGING DEEPER

(a) Prepare the operating activities section of the statement of cash flows for the year ended December 31, 2017, using the indirect method.

(b) From the perspective of an external user of Kneale Transport's financial statements, discuss the usefulness of the statement of cash flows prepared using either the indirect or the direct method.

(LO 8, 9) E5-17   (Prepare Statement of Cash Flows) The comparative statement of financial position of Dropafix Inc. as at June 30, 2017, and a statement of comprehensive income for the 2017 fiscal year follow:

DROPAFIX INC.
Statement of Financial Position
June 30, 2017

		June 30	
		2017	2016
Assets			
Cash	−18,000	$ 20,000	$ 38,000
Accounts receivable	+12,000	86,000	74,000
Inventory	+1,000	103,000	102,000
Prepaid expenses	−4,000	2,000	6,000
Fair Value—OCI Investments		47,000	45,000
Equipment	+14,000	173,000	159,000
Accumulated depreciation—equipment		(35,000)	(25,000)
Total		$396,000	$399,000
Liabilities and Shareholders' Equity			
Accounts payable	+15,000	$115,000	$100,000
Income taxes payable	−1,000	2,000	3,000
Dividends payable	+5,000	5,000	0
Long-term notes payable	−35,000	84,000	119,000
Common shares	+7,000	31,000	24,000
Retained earnings	+4,000	148,000	144,000
Accumulated other comprehensive income		11,000	9,000
Total		$396,000	$399,000

(handwritten annotations: "long term" pointing to Fair Value—OCI Investments; next to Equipment: "14000 / −8000 (exchange for non cash) / = $6000")

DROPAFIX INC.
Statement of Comprehensive Income
For the Year Ended June 30, 2017

Net sales	$323,000
Cost of goods sold	175,000
Gross profit	148,000
Operating expenses	120,000
Income from operations	28,000
Interest expense	9,000
Income before income taxes	19,000
Income taxes	6,000
Net income	13,000
Other comprehensive income	
Unrealized gain on FV-OCI investments	2,000
Comprehensive income	$ 15,000

Additional information:

1. Dropafix follows IFRS. Assume that interest is treated as an operating activity for purposes of the statement of cash flows.

2. Operating expenses include $10,000 in depreciation expense.

3. There were no disposals of equipment during the year.

4. Common shares were issued for cash.

5. During the year, Dropafix acquired $8,000 of equipment in exchange for long-term notes payable.

Instructions

(a) Prepare the statement of cash flows for Dropafix for the year ended June 30, 2014, using the indirect method along with any necessary note disclosure.

(b) From the perspective of a creditor holding several of the long-term notes in substantial amounts owed by Dropafix, how do you view the cash management demonstrated by Dropafix?

DIGGING DEEPER

(LO 8, 9) E5-18   (Prepare Statement of Cash Flows) The comparative statement of financial position of Sensify Corporation as at December 31, 2017, follows:

SENSIFY CORPORATION
Statement of Financial Position
December 31

	December 31	
Assets	2017	2016
Cash	$ 53,000	$ 13,000
Accounts receivable	91,000	88,000
Equipment	27,000	22,000
Less: Accumulated depreciation	(10,000)	(11,000)
Total	$161,000	$112,000
Liabilities and Shareholders' Equity		
Accounts payable	$ 20,000	$ 15,000
Common shares	100,000	80,000
Retained earnings	41,000	17,000
Total	$161,000	$112,000

Net income of $37,000 was reported and dividends of $13,000 were declared and paid in 2017. New equipment was purchased, and equipment with a carrying value of $5,000 (cost of $12,000 and accumulated depreciation of $7,000) was sold for $8,000.

Instructions

Prepare a statement of cash flows using the indirect method for cash flows from operating activities. Assume that Sensify prepares financial statements in accordance with ASPE.

(LO 12) ***E5-19** **(Analysis)** Use the information in E5-18 for Sensify Corporation.

Instructions

(a) Calculate the current ratio and debt to total assets ratio as at December 31, 2016 and 2017. Calculate the free cash flow for December 31, 2017.

FINANCE

(b) Based on the analysis in (a), comment on the company's liquidity and financial flexibility.

(LO 12) ***E5-20** **(Analysis)** Use the information in E5-14 for Carmichael Industries.

Instructions

(a) Calculate the current and acid test ratios for 2016 and 2017.

(b) Calculate Carmichael's current cash debt coverage ratio for 2017.

FINANCE

(c) Based on the analyses in (a) and (b), comment on Carmichael's liquidity and financial flexibility.

(d) Calculate Carmichael's payout ratio. Is the ratio too high? What would be a reasonable payout ratio?

(LO 12) ***E5-21** **(Analysis)** Use the information in E5-17 for Dropafix Inc.

Instructions

(a) Calculate the current and acid test ratios for 2016 and 2017.

(b) Calculate Dropafix's current cash debt coverage ratio for 2017.

FINANCE

(c) Calculate Dropafix's cash debt coverage ratio for 2017.

(d) Calculate Dropafix's times interest earned ratio for 2017.

(e) Based on the analyses in (a) through (d), comment on Dropafix's liquidity, financial flexibility, and ability to repay current and all liabilities from its operations and ability to meet interest payments as they come due.

DIGGING DEEPER

(f) Looking at the statement of income, the statement of financial position, and the statement of cash flows, provide one recommendation that could improve Dropafix's liquidity, financial flexibility, and ability to repay current and all liabilities from its operations.

Problems

P5-1 A list of accounts follows:

Accounts Receivable	Pension Obligation, non-current
Land	Bonds Payable—due in four years
Salaries and Wages Payable	Prepaid Rent
Land Held for Future Plant Site	Buildings
Accumulated Depreciation—Buildings	Purchase Returns and Allowances
Loss on Investments	Cash
Accumulated Depreciation—Equipment	Purchases
Notes Payable (due in six months)	Restricted Cash
Accumulated Other Comprehensive Income	Notes Receivable (due in five years)
Intangible Assets—Patents (net of accumulated amortization)	Commission Expense
	Retained Earnings
Advances to Employees	Common Shares
Advertising Expense	Sales Revenue
Petty Cash	Intangible Assets—Copyrights (net of accumulated amortization)
Allowance for Doubtful Accounts	
Preferred Shares	Sales Discounts
Fair Value—OCI Investments	Dividends Payable
Equipment	Selling Expenses
Income Tax Payable	Inventory
Gain on Sale of Equipment	Unearned Subscriptions Revenue
FV-NI (Fair Value—Net Income) Investments	Unrealized Holding Gain or Loss—OCI
Interest Receivable	

Instructions

Prepare a classified statement of financial position in good form, without specific amounts.

P5-2 Statement of financial position items for Montoya Inc. follow for the current year, 2017:

Goodwill	$ 125,000	Accumulated depreciation—equipment	$ 292,000
Payroll taxes payable	177,591	Inventory	239,800
Bonds payable due 2021	285,000	Rent payable	45,000
Discount on bonds payable	15,000	Income tax payable	98,362
Cash	360,000	Rent payable (long-term)	480,000
Land	480,000	Common shares (20,000 shares issued)	200,000
Notes receivable	445,700	Preferred shares (15,000 shares issued)	150,000
Notes payable	265,000	Prepaid expenses	87,920
Accounts payable	490,000	Equipment	1,470,000
Retained earnings	?	FV-NI investments	121,000
Income tax receivable	97,630	Accumulated depreciation—buildings	270,200
Notes payable (due in five years)	1,600,000	Buildings	1,640,000

Instructions

(a) Prepare a classified statement of financial position in good form. The numbers of authorized shares are as follows: unlimited common and 20,000 preferred. Assume that income tax accounts, notes receivable, and notes payable are short-term, unless stated otherwise, and that the fair value—net income investments are stated at fair value.

(b) What additional disclosures would you expect to provide for the rental obligation?

P5-3 The trial balance of Eastwood Inc. and other related information for the year 2017 follows:

EASTWOOD INC.
Trial Balance
December 31, 2017

	Debits	Credits
Cash	$ 41,000	
Accounts receivable	163,500	
Allowance for doubtful accounts		$ 8,700
Prepaid insurance	5,900	
Inventory	208,500	
Fair value—OCI investments	339,000	
Land	85,000	
Construction in progress	124,000	
Intangible assets—patents	36,000	
Equipment	400,000	
Accumulated depreciation—equipment		240,000
Accounts payable		148,000
Accrued liabilities		49,200
Notes payable		94,000
Bonds payable		180,000
Common shares		500,000
Accumulated other comprehensive income		45,000
Retained earnings		138,000
	$1,402,900	$1,402,900

Additional information:

1. The inventory has a net realizable value of $212,000. The FIFO method of inventory valuation is used.

2. The fair value—OCI investments' fair value is $378,000.

3. The amount of the Construction in Process account represents the costs to date on a building in the process of construction. (The company is renting factory space while waiting for the new building to be completed.) The land that the building is being constructed on cost $85,000, as shown in the trial balance.

4. The company purchased the patents at a cost of $40,000 and the patents are being amortized on a straight-line basis.

5. The bonds payable have a face value of $200,000, bear interest at 7% payable every December 31, and are due January 1, 2029.

6. Of the remaining $20,000 unamortized discount on bonds payable (face value $200,000 less carrying amount $180,000), $2,000 will be amortized in 2018.

7. The notes payable represent bank loans that are secured by fair value—OCI investments carried at $120,000. These bank loans are due in 2018.

8. For common shares, an unlimited number are authorized and 500,000 are issued and outstanding.

Instructions

(a) Prepare a statement of financial position as at December 31, 2017, ensuring that all important information is fully disclosed.

(b) From the perspective of a potential creditor, discuss the importance of proper classification of Eastwood's Construction in Progress account.

P5-4   The statement of financial position of Delacosta Corporation as at December 31, 2017, is as follows:

DELACOSTA CORPORATION
Statement of Financial Position
December 31, 2017

Assets

Goodwill (Note 1)	$ 70,000
Buildings (Note 2)	1,640,000
Inventory	312,100
Investments—trading (Note 3)	100,000
Land	950,000
Accounts receivable	170,000
Investments in shares (fair value through OCI) (Note 4)	87,000
Cash	175,900
Assets allocated to trustee for plant expansion	
Cash	120,000
Treasury notes, at cost and fair value	138,000
	$3,763,000

Equities

Notes payable (Note 4)	$ 600,000
Common shares, unlimited authorized, 500,000 issued	730,000
Retained earnings	958,000
Accounts payable	420,000
Appreciation capital (Note 2)	570,000
Income tax payable	75,000
Reserve for depreciation of building	410,000
	$3,763,000

Note 1: Goodwill in the amount of $70,000 was recognized because the company believed that the carrying amount of assets was not an accurate representation of the company's fair value. The gain of $70,000 was credited to Retained Earnings.

Note 2: Buildings are stated at cost, except for one building that was recorded at its appraised value as management determined the building to be worth more than originally paid at acquisition. The excess of the appraisal value over cost was $570,000. Depreciation has been recorded based on cost.

Note 3: Investments—trading are fair value through net income investments and have a fair value of $75,000. Investments in shares (fair value through OCI) have a fair value of $200,000. Both investments are currently recorded at cost.

Note 4: Notes payable are long-term except for the current instalment due of $100,000.

Instructions

(a) Prepare a corrected classified statement of financial position in good form. The notes above are for information only. Assume that you have decided not to use the revaluation model for property, plant, and equipment.

(b) From the perspective of a user of Delacosta's statement of financial position, discuss the importance of proper accounting for goodwill.

P5-5   Lydia Trottier has prepared baked goods for sale since 1998. She started a baking business in her home and has been operating in a rented building with a storefront since 2003. Trottier incorporated the business as MLT Inc. on January 1, 2017, with an initial share issue of 1,000 common shares for $2,500. Lydia Trottier is the principal shareholder of MLT Inc.

Sales have increased by 30% annually since operations began at the present location, and additional equipment is needed for the continued growth that is expected. Trottier wants to purchase some additional baking equipment and to finance the equipment through a long-term note from a commercial bank. Fidelity Bank & Trust has asked Trottier to submit a statement of income for MLT Inc. for the first five months of 2017 and a statement of financial position as at May 31, 2017.

Trottier assembled the following information from the corporation's cash basis records to use in preparing the financial statements that the bank wants to see:

1. The bank statement showed the following 2017 deposits through May 31:

Sale of common shares	$ 2,500
Cash sales	22,770
Rebates from purchases	130
Collections on credit sales	5,320
Bank loan proceeds	2,880
	$33,600

2. The following amounts were disbursed through May 31, 2017:

Baking materials	$14,400
Rent	1,800
Salaries and wages	5,500
Maintenance	110
Utilities	4,000
Insurance premium	1,920
Display cases and equipment	3,600
Principal and interest payment on bank loan	298
Advertising	424
	$32,052

3. Unpaid invoices at May 31, 2017, were as follows:

Baking materials	$256
Utilities	270
	$526

4. Accounts receivable records showed uncollected sales of $4,336 at May 31, 2017.

5. Baking materials costing $2,075 were on hand at May 31, 2017. There were no materials in process or finished goods on hand at that date. No materials were on hand or in process and no finished goods were on hand at January 1, 2017.

6. The note for the three-year bank loan is dated January 1, 2017, and states a simple interest rate of 8%. The loan requires quarterly payments on April 1, July 1, October 1, and January 1. Each payment is to consist of equal principal payments [$2,880 ÷ (3 × 4) = $240] plus accrued interest since the last payment.

7. Lydia Trottier receives a salary of $750 on the last day of each month. The other employees have been paid through May 25, 2017, and are due an additional $270 on May 31, 2017.

8. New display cases and equipment costing $3,600 were purchased on January 2, 2017, and have an estimated useful life of five years with no residual value. These are the only fixed assets that are currently used in the business. Straight-line depreciation is used for book purposes.

9. Rent was paid for six months in advance on January 2, 2017.

10. A one-year insurance policy was purchased on January 2, 2017.

11. MLT Inc. is subject to an income tax rate of 20%. No tax instalments have been paid.

FINANCE

12. Payments and collections from the unincorporated business through December 31, 2016, were not included in the corporation's records, and no cash was transferred from the unincorporated business to the corporation.

Instructions

(a) Using the accrual basis of accounting, prepare a statement of income for the five months ended May 31, 2017.

(b) Using the accrual basis, prepare a statement of financial position as at May 31, 2017.

**DIGGING
DEEPER**

*(c) Assume the role of a bank manager at Fidelity Bank & Trust. Based only on MLT's current ratio as a measure of liquidity, and times interest earned ratio as a measure of MLT's ability to pay interest, would you recommend extending a long-term note for financing of MLT's purchase of additional baking equipment?

P5-6 In an examination of Garganta Limited as at December 31, 2017, you have learned about the following situations. No entries have been made in the accounting records for these items.

1. The corporation erected its present factory building in 2001. Depreciation was calculated using the straight-line method, based on an estimated life of 35 years. Early in 2017, the board of directors conducted a careful survey and estimated that the factory building had a remaining useful life of 25 years as at January 1, 2017.

2. An additional assessment of 2016 corporate income taxes was levied and paid in 2017.

3. When calculating the accrual for officers' salaries at December 31, 2017, it was discovered that the accrual for officers' salaries for December 31, 2016, had been overstated.

4. On December 15, 2017, Garganta Limited declared a common shares dividend of $1 per share on its issued common shares outstanding, payable February 1, 2018, to the common shareholders of record on December 31, 2017.

5. Garganta Limited, which is on a calendar-year basis, changed its inventory cost formula as at January 1, 2017. The inventory for December 31, 2016, was costed by the weighted average method, and the inventory for December 31, 2017, was costed by the FIFO method.

6. On January 15, 2018, Garganta's warehouse containing raw materials was damaged by a flash flood.

7. During December 2017, the former president retired and a new president was appointed.

8. Garganta suffered a loss from a former employee stealing cash from a deposit of cash sales in the first quarter of the year. The amount has been a reconciling item on the bank reconciliation ever since the theft. Garganta has not yet made any journal entry.

Instructions

Describe fully how each item above should be reported in the financial statements of Garganta Limited for the year 2017.

P5-7   Aero Inc. had the following statement of financial position at the end of operations for 2016:

AERO INC.
Statement of Financial Position
December 31, 2016

Cash	$ 20,000	Accounts payable	$ 30,000
Accounts receivable	21,200	Bonds payable	41,000
FV-NI investments	32,000	Common shares	100,000
Equipment (net)	81,000	Retained earnings	23,200
Land	40,000		
	$194,200		$194,200

During 2017, the following occurred:

1. Aero liquidated its FV-NI investments portfolio at a loss of $5,000.

2. A parcel of land was purchased for $38,000.

3. An additional $30,000 worth of common shares was issued.

4. Dividends totalling $10,000 were declared and paid to shareholders.

5. Net income for 2017 was $35,000, including $12,000 in depreciation expense.

6. Land was purchased through the issuance of $30,000 in additional bonds.

7. At December 31, 2017, Cash was $70,200; Accounts Receivable was $42,000; and Accounts Payable was $40,000.

Instructions

(a) Prepare the statement of financial position as it would appear at December 31, 2017.

(b) Prepare a statement of cash flows for the year ended December 31, 2017 using the indirect method. Assume dividends paid are treated as financing activities.

FINANCE

*(c) Calculate the current and acid test ratios for 2016 and 2017.

*(d) Calculate Aero's free cash flow and the current cash debt coverage ratio for 2017.

(e) What is the cash flow pattern? Discuss the sources and uses of cash.

DIGGING DEEPER

(f) Use the analysis of Aero to illustrate how information in the statement of financial position and statement of cash flows helps the user of the financial statements.

P5-8   Jia Inc. applies ASPE and had the following statement of financial position at the end of operations for 2016:

JIA INC.
Statement of Financial Position
December 31, 2016

Cash	$ 50,500	Accounts payable	$ 93,000
Accounts receivable	90,000	Long-term debt	85,000
Inventory	82,000	Common shares	100,000
Machinery (net)	125,000	Retained earnings	89,500
Trademarks	20,000		
	$367,500		$367,500

During 2017, the following occurred:

1. Jia Inc. sold some of its trademarks. The trademarks had an unlimited useful life and a cost of $10,000. They were sold for proceeds of $20,000.

2. Machinery was purchased in exchange for long-term debt of $40,000.

3. Long-term debt in the amount of $15,000 were retired before maturity by paying $15,000 cash.

4. An additional $12,000 in common shares was issued.

5. Dividends totalling $14,000 were declared and paid to shareholders.

6. Net income for 2017 was $44,000 after allowing for depreciation of $19,000.

7. Machinery with a carrying value of $18,000 was sold for a gain of $7,000.

8. At December 31, 2017, Cash was $68,500; Accounts Receivable was $111,000; Accounts Payable was $83,000 and inventory increased to $107,000.

FINANCE

Instructions

(a) Prepare a statement of cash flows for the year ended December 31, 2017 using the indirect method.

(b) Prepare the statement of financial position as it would appear at December 31, 2017.

(c) How might the statement of cash flows help the user of the financial statements?

*(d) Calculate the following ratios:

   1. Free cash flow

   2. Current cash debt coverage ratio

   3. Cash debt coverage ratio

DIGGING DEEPER

(e) What is Jia's cash flow pattern? Discuss any areas of concern.

P5-9   The statement of financial position of Sargent Corporation follows for the current year, 2017:

SARGENT CORPORATION
Statement of Financial Position
December 31, 2017

Current assets	$ 485,000	Current liabilities	$ 380,000
Investments	640,000	Long-term liabilities	960,000
Property, plant, and equipment	1,720,000	Shareholders' equity	1,770,000
Intangible assets	265,000		$3,110,000
	$3,110,000		

The following additional information is available:

1. The Current Assets section includes the following: cash $150,000; accounts receivable $170,000, less $10,000 allowance for doubtful accounts; inventory $180,000; and unearned revenue $5,000. The cash balance is composed of $190,000, less a bank overdraft of $40,000 (at a separate financial institution). Inventory is stated at the lower of FIFO cost and net realizable value.

2. The Investments section includes the following: note receivable from a related company, due in 2023, $40,000; fair value—net income investments in shares, $80,000 (fair value $80,000); fair value—OCI investments in shares, $125,000 (fair value $155,000); bond sinking fund $250,000; and patents $115,000, net of accumulated amortization.

3. Property, Plant, and Equipment includes buildings $1,040,000, less accumulated depreciation $360,000; equipment $450,000, less accumulated depreciation $180,000; land $500,000; and land held for future use $270,000.

4. Intangible Assets include the following: franchise, net of accumulated amortization $165,000; and goodwill $100,000.

5. Current Liabilities include the following: accounts payable $140,000; notes payable, short-term $80,000, long-term $120,000; and income tax payable $40,000.

6. Long-term Liabilities are composed solely of 7% bonds payable issued at a discount, due in 2025.

7. Shareholders' Equity has 70,000 preferred shares (200,000 authorized), which were issued for $450,000, and 100,000 common shares (unlimited number authorized), which were issued at an average price of $10 per share. In addition, the corporation has retained earnings of $290,000 and accumulated other comprehensive income of $30,000.

Instructions

(a) Prepare a statement of financial position in good form (adjust the amounts in each statement of financial position classification based on the additional information).

(b) What makes the condensed format of the original statement of financial position inadequate in terms of the amount of detail that needs to be disclosed under IFRS and ASPE?

DIGGING DEEPER

P5-10 The statement of financial position of Manion Corporation follows (in thousands):

MANION CORPORATION
Statement of Financial Position
December 31, 2017

Assets		
Current assets		
Cash	$26,000	
Investments—trading (fair value through net income)	18,000	
Accounts receivable	25,000	
Inventory	20,000	
Supplies	4,000	
Investment in subsidiary company	20,000	$113,000
Investments		
Investments in shares		25,000
Property, plant, and equipment		
Buildings and land	91,000	
Less: Reserve for depreciation	31,000	60,000
Other assets		
Investment in bonds to be held to maturity (at cost)		19,000
		$217,000
Liabilities and equity		
Current liabilities		
Accounts payable	$22,000	
Reserve for income taxes	15,000	
Customer accounts with credit balances	1	$ 37,001
Long-term liabilities		
Bonds payable		62,000
Total liabilities		99,001
Shareholders' equity		
Common shares issued	85,000	
Earned surplus and other accumulated surplus	24,999	
Cash dividends declared	8,000	117,999
		$217,000

Instructions

Evaluate the statement of financial position. Briefly describe the proper treatment of any item that you find incorrect. Assume the company follows IFRS.

P5-11 A comparative statement of financial position for Spencer Corporation follows:

SPENCER CORPORATION
Statement of Financial Position

	December 31	
Assets	2017	2016
Cash	$ 65,000	$ 29,000
Accounts receivable	87,000	59,000
Inventory	133,000	81,000
Investments in shares (fair value through OCI)	63,000	84,000
Land	65,000	103,000
Equipment	390,000	430,000
Accumulated depreciation—equipment	(117,000)	(86,000)
Goodwill	124,000	173,000
Total	$810,000	$873,000
Liabilities and Shareholders' Equity		
Accounts payable	$ 12,000	$ 51,000
Dividends payable	15,000	32,000
Notes payable	220,000	335,000
Common shares	265,000	125,000
Retained earnings	288,000	284,000
Accumulated other comprehensive income	10,000	46,000
Total	$810,000	$873,000

Additional information:

1. Net income for the fiscal year ending December 31, 2017, was $19,000.

2. In March 2017, a plot of land was purchased for future construction of a plant site. In November 2017, a different plot of land with original cost of $86,000 was sold for proceeds of $95,000.

3. In April 2017, notes payable amounting to $140,000 were retired through the issuance of common shares. In December 2017, notes payable amounting to $25,000 were issued for cash.

4. Fair value—OCI investments were purchased in July 2017 for a cost of $15,000. By December 31, 2017, the fair value of Spencer's portfolio of fair value—OCI investments decreased to $63,000. No fair value—OCI investments were sold in the year.

5. On December 31, 2017, equipment with an original cost of $40,000 and accumulated depreciation to date of $12,000 was sold for proceeds of $21,000. No equipment was purchased in the year.

6. Dividends on common shares of $32,000 and $15,000 were declared in December 2016 and December 2017, respectively. The 2016 dividend was paid in January 2017 and the 2017 dividend was paid in January 2018. Dividends paid are treated as financing activities.

7. Goodwill impairment loss was recorded in the year to reflect a decrease in the recoverable amount of goodwill. No goodwill was purchased or sold in the year.

DIGGING DEEPER

Instructions

(a) Prepare a statement of cash flows using the indirect method for cash flows from operating activities.

(b) From the perspective of a shareholder, comment in general on the results reported in the statement of cash flows.

ENABLING COMPETENCIES

Cases

REAL WORLD EMPHASIS

Refer to the Case Primer on the Student Website and in *WileyPLUS* to help you answer these cases.

CA5-1 In the late 1990s, **CIBC** helped **Enron Corporation** structure 34 "loans" that appeared in the financial statements as cash proceeds from sales of assets. Enron subsequently went bankrupt in 2001 and left many unhappy investors and creditors with billions of dollars lost. In December 2003, CIBC settled four regulatory investigations with the U.S. Securities and Exchange Commission, U.S. Federal Reserve, U.S. Justice Department, and Canadian Office of the Superintendent of Financial Institutions. The settlement, which amounted to U.S. $80 million, was then one of the largest regulatory penalties against a Canadian bank. The regulatory authorities felt that CIBC had aided Enron in boosting its earnings and hiding debt. CIBC set aside a $109-million reserve in early 2003 in preparation for this settlement. No additional reserves were set aside.

As part of the settlement, CIBC agreed to get rid of its structured financing line of business (where all of these "loans" were created). Bank management noted that the decision to get rid of the structured financing business would reduce annual earnings by 10 cents a share. The bank had previously reported annual earnings of $5.21 per share. In addition, the bank had to accept the appointment of an outside monitor whose role, among other things, would be to review the bank's compliance with the settlement. Strategically, the bank

had already reduced its emphasis on corporate lending (having suffered heavy losses in 2002) in favour of an increased focus on earnings from branch banking operations.

At the end of 2003, CIBC was still owed $213 million by Enron. There were many additional Enron-related lawsuits pending against the bank, but the bank announced that the lawsuits were without merit. The bank had insurance against many of these claims and noted that it planned to vigorously defend itself.

In 2005, the bank settled a lawsuit with institutional investors, paying $2.4 billion, again setting a standard for the size of the settlement. Then in 2009, the Canada Revenue Agency (CRA) challenged the bank regarding the tax deductibility of the payment.

In note 20 of CIBC's annual financial statements for the year ending October 31, 2014, relating to the subject of income taxes, the outstanding issue is updated. CIBC mentions that the Tax Court of Canada trial on the deductibility of the Enron payments is scheduled to commence in October 2015. As well, CIBC mentions that, should it successfully defend its tax filing position in its entirety, the bank would recognize an additional accounting tax benefit of $214 million and taxable refund interest of approximately $207 million. Should CIBC fail to defend its position in its entirety, the bank would incur an additional tax expense of approximately $866 million and non-deductible interest of approximately $124 million.

Instructions

Discuss any financial reporting issues relating to CIBC's 2003 and 2014 financial statements. Use the conceptual framework noted in Chapter 2 for the analysis.

ETHICS

CA5-2 Hastings Inc. (HI) is a manufacturer that produces stainless steel car parts. It began as a family business several years ago and all shares are owned by the Hastings family. The company's main assets are its manufacturing facility and surrounding land. The property was purchased many years ago and the carrying value reflects only a fraction of the asset's cost.

The company currently follows ASPE and is wondering what the impact would be of switching to IFRS. Several of the Hastings family members would like to take the company public in the next five to 10 years.

Because of the recent dip in the economy, the company has suffered losses over the past three years. However, as the economy has recently begun picking up, management is confident that this year will be a profitable one.

ENABLING COMPETENCIES

Instructions

Adopt the role of the company's auditors and discuss any financial reporting issues. Use the conceptual framework noted in Chapter 2 for the analysis.

Integrated Case

ETHICS AND AUDITING

(*Hint:* If there are issues here that are new, use the conceptual framework to help you support your analysis with solid reasoning.)

IC5-1 Franklin Drug Ltd. (FDL) is a global public company that researches, develops, markets, and sells prescription drugs. Revenues and net income are down this year, partly because one of the company's competitors, Balogun Drug Inc. (BDI), has created and is selling generic versions of two of FDL's best-selling drugs. The drugs, known as FD1 and FD2, are still protected by patents that will not expire for another three years. Normally, when a drug is patented, other drug companies are not legally allowed to sell generic versions of the drug. This practice of patenting new drugs allows the companies that develop the drugs enough time to recover their large investment in research and development.

In recent years, however, generic drug companies have become more aggressive in producing and selling generic copies of drugs before patents expire. FDL refers to this practice as "launching the generic products at risk" because, legally, the competitors are not allowed to sell them while the patent is still in force. Currently, FDL has about $2 million in development costs capitalized on the balance sheet. It has launched a lawsuit against BDI, ordering it to cease and desist selling the generic drugs. These types of lawsuits are usually long and very expensive. By the time the lawsuit is settled one way or the other, the patents will have expired. So far, legal costs incurred for the lawsuit are $300,000.

During the year, the patent on a third drug, FD3, expired and several competitor drug companies began actively marketing generic replacements. FDL still has $500,000 worth of FD3 development costs on the balance sheet. Although the increased competition may result in this asset being impaired, FDL feels that it can hold its market share based on FD3's past success in treating patients. So far, sales of FD3 have declined only 3%, but there remains considerable price pressure on the drug. On the other hand, the company's share price has declined significantly because of the uncertainty surrounding future sales. Company management is not happy with the drop in share price, because a significant portion of their remuneration is based on stock options.

The company gives volume rebates to some of its larger customers. Under the terms of the sales agreements, the more purchases that a customer makes in a certain time frame, the larger the rebate percentage is on these purchases. The length of the time frame varies. Three large contracts are currently outstanding at year end with new customers. The time frames on these contracts extend beyond year end. FDL must estimate the volume rebates by considering what the total sales will be under these contracts. The company always bases this estimate on past experience.

FDL had a distribution centre in South America. Late in the year, FDL was approached by a competitor to buy the distribution centre. FDL accepted the offer and is confident the price obtained is generous. FDL has not yet arrived at an analysis of what the corresponding effect of the sale will be on its global operations, along with the impairment of remaining assets whose values are affected by the sale and will require impairment writedowns.

It is now early January and the auditors are coming in for an audit planning meeting.

Instructions

In preparation for the meeting, you, as audit senior on the job, have done some preliminary research on the company. Write a memo that outlines the potential financial reporting issues.

RESEARCH AND ANALYSIS

RA5-1 Brookfield Asset Management Inc.

REAL WORLD EMPHASIS

The financial statements of **Brookfield Asset Management Inc.** for its year ended December 31, 2014, appear at the end of this book.

Instructions

(a) What alternative formats could the company have used for its balance sheet? Which format did it adopt?

(b) Identify the various techniques of disclosure that the company could have used to present additional financial information that is pertinent. Which techniques does it use in its financial statements?

(c) Which presentation method does the company use for its statement of cash flows (direct or indirect method)? What were the company's cash flows from its operating, investing, and financing activities for the year ended December 31, 2014? What was the trend in net cash provided by operating activities over the year ended December 31, 2014? Is the cash generated from operating activities significantly different from net earnings in both 2013 and 2014? Suggest why this might happen.

(d) Calculate the company's (1) current cash debt coverage ratio, (2) cash debt coverage ratio, and (3) free cash flow for the years ended December 31, 2014 and 2013. What do these ratios indicate about the company's financial condition?

RA5-2 Bombardier Inc.

REAL WORLD EMPHASIS

The financial statements for **Bombardier Inc.** for the year ended December 31, 2014, can be found on the company's website or from SEDAR (www.sedar.com).

Instructions

(a) What form of presentation does the company use in preparing its balance sheet?

(b) Calculate the ratios identified in Appendix 5A for both years that are presented in the financial statements. Make note of any ratios that cannot be reported and provide the reason why.

(c) Comment on the company's liquidity, solvency, activity, and profitability.

(d) Review the cash flow patterns on the statements of cash flows. Comment on the basic sources of the company's cash and where it is spent.

(e) Perform a "vertical analysis" of the assets. (Calculate each asset as a percentage of total assets.) Comment on the results of your analysis. How have the assets changed from year to year?

RA5-3 Maple Leaf Foods Inc.

REAL WORLD EMPHASIS

The audited annual financial statements of **Maple Leaf Foods Inc.** for the year ended December 31, 2014, can be found on the company's website or from SEDAR (www.sedar.com).

Instructions

(a) Calculate the liquidity and coverage (solvency) ratios identified in Appendix 5A for both years that are presented in the financial statements. Make note of any ratios that cannot be reported and provide the reason why.

(b) Comment on the company's financial flexibility.

(c) Review the cash flow patterns on the statements of cash flows and comment on the basic sources of the company's cash and where it is spent.

(d) Perform a "horizontal analysis" for the components of working capital. (Calculate each financial statement item for the current year as a percentage of the amount reported for a specific prior year.) Comment on any change in the company's liquidity.

RA5-4 Goldcorp Inc.

REAL WORLD EMPHASIS

Obtain the 2001 and 2014 annual reports of **Goldcorp Inc.** from SEDAR (www.sedar.com). Read the annual report material leading up to the financial statement section and answer the following questions:

(a) Explain how the company's business changed in the thirteen years from 2001 to 2014. What significant events occurred in 2014?

(b) Prepare a horizontal analysis of key elements of the financial statements from 2001 to 2014. (Calculate each financial statement item for the current year as a percentage of the amount reported for a specific prior year.) Include revenue, operating earnings (loss), current assets, current liabilities, working capital, net earnings (loss) from continuing operations, and shareholders' equity. Include also the ratios of operating income (loss) to revenue, the current ratio, and the return on shareholders' equity.

(c) What was the effect on key ratios of the event(s) identified in part (a)? Include in your answer as well the total cost to produce an ounce of gold and the average selling price of gold. (This information can be found in the Management Discussion and Analysis part of the annual report.)

RA5-5 Quebecor Inc. and Thomson Reuters Corporation

The financial statements of **Quebecor Inc.** and **Thomson Reuters Corporation** for their fiscal years ended December 31, 2014, can be found on SEDAR (www.sedar.com) or the companies' websites.

Instructions

(a) What business is Quebecor Inc. in? Is Thomson Reuters Corporation a good benchmark for comparing against? Explain.

(b) Identify three other companies that might be used for comparisons.

(c) Calculate industry averages for these five companies for their current ratio and debt to total assets ratio.

(d) Based on this very brief analysis, which company, Quebecor and Thomson Reuters, is in a better position in terms of liquidity and solvency? How do these companies compare with the other three companies?

(e) Review the statements of cash flows for Quebecor and Thomson Reuters for 2013 and 2014. Summarize the cash flow patterns for each company.

(f) Comment on these cash flow patterns, noting changes over the two-year period.

RA5-6 IASB's Disclosure Initiative—Proposed Amendments to IAS 7

In December 2014, the IASB issued an Exposure Draft (ED) called *Disclosure Initiative: Proposed Amendments to IAS 7* concerning potential improvements to the statement of cash flows. The first proposed recommendation's purpose is to improve the information provided to users about companies' financing activities, excluding equity financing. It would require entities to provide a reconciliation of the opening and closing balances of amounts reported on the statement of financial position that would involve financing activities (excluding those dealing with equity items). The effect will be to provide improved information useful in understanding an entity's debt and changes in debt during the period.

Instructions

(a) Obtain access to the December 2014 exposure draft on the IASB website, and to the financial statements of **Brookfield Office Properties Inc.** for its year ended December 31, 2014, from SEDAR (www.sedar.com). Relate the information on the statement of financial position and the corresponding financial statement notes 14, 15, and 30 with the entries on the statement of cash flows for the largest element of debt for Brookfield Office Properties—its commercial property debt. Attempt to prepare a reconciliation, as suggested by the exposure draft, using the current disclosure that has been provided.

(b) If your reconciliation does not balance, suggest a likely source of any difference. Comment on the usefulness of the reconciliation you have prepared in part (a).

(c) Where else in the current financial statement disclosure is the user provided with a reconciliation of the beginning and ending balances of elements in the statement of financial position?

RA5-7 Auditor's Letter

The partner in charge of the Spencer Corporation audit comes by your desk and leaves a letter he has started to the CEO and a copy of the statement of cash flows for the year ended December 31, 2017. Because he must leave on an emergency, he asks you to finish the letter by explaining (1) the difference between the net income and cash flow amounts, (2) the importance of operating cash flow, (3) the sustainable source(s) of cash flow, and (4) possible suggestions to improve the cash position. Spencer is a small corporation that relies on its auditor for financial statement preparation.

Cash flows from operating activities		
Net income		$ 100,000
Adjustments to reconcile net income to net cash provided by operating activities:		
Depreciation expense	$ 11,000	
Loss on sale of fixed assets	5,000	
Increase in accounts receivable (net)	(40,000)	
Increase in inventory	(35,000)	
Decrease in accounts payable	(41,000)	(100,000)
Net cash provided by operating activities		–0–
Cash flows from investing activities		
Sale of plant assets	25,000	
Purchase of equipment	(100,000)	
Purchase of land	(200,000)	
Net cash used by investing activities		(275,000)
Cash flows from financing activities		
Payment of dividends	(10,000)	
Redemption of bonds	(100,000)	
Net cash used by financing activities		(110,000)
Net decrease in cash		(385,000)
Cash balance, January 1, 2017		400,000
Cash balance, December 31, 2017		$ 15,000

Date

James Spencer III, CEO

James Spencer Corporation

125 Bay Street

Toronto, ON

Dear Mr. Spencer:

I have good news and bad news about the financial statements for the year ended December 31, 2017. The good news is that net income of $100,000 is close to what we predicted in the strategic plan last year, indicating strong performance this year. The bad news is that the cash balance is seriously low. Enclosed is the Statement of Cash Flows, which best illustrates how both of these situations occurred at the same time . . .

Instructions

Complete the letter to the CEO, including the four elements that the partner asked for.

RA5-8   A Moral Dilemma

ETHICS

The ethical accountant for Khouri Industries, is trying to decide how to present property, plant, and equipment in the notes to the balance sheet. She realizes that the statement of cash flows will show that the company made a significant investment in purchasing new equipment this year, but overall she knows the company's plant assets are rather old. She feels that she can disclose one amount for the title "Property, plant, and equipment, net of depreciation," and the result will be a low figure. However, it will not disclose the assets' age. If she chooses to show the cost less accumulated depreciation, the assets' age will be visible. She proposes the following:

Property, plant, and equipment, net of depreciation	$10,000,000
rather than	
Property, plant, and equipment	$50,000,000
Less: Accumulated depreciation	(40,000,000)
Net book value	$10,000,000

Instructions

Discuss the financial reporting issues, including any ethical issues.

ENDNOTES

[1] Risk means the unpredictability of the enterprise's future events, transactions, circumstances, and results.

[2] The formulas for these ratios and other ratios are summarized in Appendix 5A.

[3] Liquidity measures are important inputs to bankruptcy prediction models, such as those developed by Altman and others. See G. White, A. Sondhi, and D. Fried, *The Analysis of Financial Statements* (New York: John Wiley & Sons, 2003), Chapter 18.

[4] "Reporting Income, Cash Flows, and Financial Position of Business Enterprises," Proposed Statement of Financial Accounting Concepts (Stamford, Conn.: FASB, 1981), par. 25.

[5] D. McCarty and B. Jinks, "Kodak Files for Bankruptcy as Digital Era Spells End to Film," Bloomberg News, January 2, 2012.

[6] See Eastman Kodak Co. Form 10Q (quarterly report filed November 4, 2014, for the period ended September 30, 2014).

[7] Several of these omitted items (such as internally generated goodwill and certain commitments) are discussed in later chapters.

[8] While the term "capitalize" is often used in the context of recording costs as assets, it is sometimes used differently: in the context here, it means recognizing the liabilities on the SFP for the purpose of performing financial statement analysis.

[9] *CPA Canada Handbook—Accounting*, Part II, Section 3831.05.

[10] *CPA Canada Handbook—Accounting*, Part II, Section 3831.05.

[11] See *CPA Canada Handbook—Accounting*, Part II, Section 3856.05 for the definition of a financial instrument. Markets often exist or can be created for these instruments because of their nature and measurability. Liabilities are included because they represent the other side of an asset contract; for example, accounts payable to one company represent accounts receivable to another.

[12] See *CPA Canada Handbook—Accounting*, Part II, Section 3856.05, IAS 32.11, IAS 39.9, and IFRS 9 Appendix A for more complete definitions.

[13] This type of comparison is done by performing a **vertical analysis**, which calculates the percentage that a specific asset represents when divided by total assets. This number may then be compared with the same percentage from past years. The latter comparison is generally called **horizontal** or **trend analysis.** Horizontal and vertical analyses are discussed further in Chapter 23 and on the Student Website under Financial Statement Analysis.

[14] *CPA Canada Handbook—Accounting*, Part II, Section 1510.03 and IAS 1.66.

[15] The real estate industry is an example of an industry that does not follow this approach. This is because the industry feels that a more meaningful presentation results when the most important assets are presented first. In most real estate development companies, the most important and largest asset is investment properties. This asset includes hotels, shopping centres, leased buildings, and so on that generate revenue or profits for the company. Brookfield Office Properties Inc. records this asset first on its balance sheet. On the liabilities side, the corresponding debt related to the properties is recorded. For Brookfield, this asset represented over 80% of total assets in 2014. Many real estate companies follow specialized industry accounting principles (REALpac *IFRS Handbook* and REALpac *ASPE Handbook*) as published by the Real Property Association of Canada or REALpac (www.realpac.ca).

[16] *CPA Canada Handbook—Accounting*, Part II, Section 1540.06 and IAS 7.6. Copyright © International Financial Reporting Standards Foundation. All rights reserved. Reproduced by John Wiley & Sons Canada, Ltd with the permission of the International Financial Reporting Standards Foundation®. Reproduction and use rights are strictly limited. No permission granted to third parties to reproduce or distribute.

[17] IBI Group 2013 and 2014 annual reports (www.ibigroup.com).

[18] *CPA Canada Handbook—Accounting*, Part II, Section 3031.07 and IAS 2.6. Copyright © International Financial Reporting Standards Foundation. All rights reserved. Reproduced by John Wiley & Sons Canada, Ltd with the permission of the International Financial Reporting Standards Foundation®. Reproduction and use rights are strictly limited. No permission granted to third parties to reproduce or distribute.

[19] See BlackBerry Limited March 1, 2014 financial statements; H. Miller, "BlackBerry Enlists Foxconn to Make Phones as Sales Plunge," Bloomberg News, December 23, 2013; and R. Miller, "BlackBerry Lose Nearly $1 Billion from Unsold Z10 Inventory Write-Down," eTeknix.com, www.eteknix.com/blackberry-lose-nearly-1-billion-unsold-z10-inventory-write/, accessed January 8, 2015.

[20] *CPA Canada Handbook—Accounting*, Part II, Section 1510.08 and IAS 1.69.

[21] In Chapter 13, there is a more detailed discussion of debt refinancing.

[22] The rights and privileges of the various securities that are outstanding (both debt and equity) are usually explained in the notes to the financial statements. Examples of information that should be disclosed are dividend and liquidation preferences, participation rights, call prices and dates, conversion or exercise prices or rates and pertinent dates, sinking fund requirements, unusual voting rights, and significant terms of contracts to issue additional shares.

[23] In Canada, under the Canada Business Corporations Act, shares that are reacquired must be cancelled. However, some provincial jurisdictions and other countries (such as the United States) still allow treasury shares to exist.

[24] J. Jones, "Talisman Energy Acquired by Repsol in $8.3-billion Deal," *The Globe and Mail*, December 15, 2014.

[25] *CPA Canada Handbook—Accounting*, Part II, Section 3290.05. The IFRS definition differs somewhat (see IAS 37.10). In short, under IFRS, provisions are required for situations such as lawsuits where it is more likely than not that a present obligation exists. (These are considered liabilities under IFRS, not contingencies.) However, provisions are not required for loss contingencies for items like lawsuits where it is more likely than not that no obligation exists at the date of the financial statements. These are "possible obligations" whose existence will only be confirmed by uncertain future events. The differences in the definitions are examined in more detail in Chapter 13.

[26] IAS 37.27 to IAS 37.35 and *CPA Canada Handbook*, Part II, Section 3290.08 to 3290.24.

[27] *CPA Canada Handbook—Accounting*, Part II, Section 1508 discusses measurement uncertainty, as do various other sections.

[28] See *CPA Canada Handbook—Accounting*, Part II, Section 3280 ("Contractual Obligations") and various other sections.

[29] IAS 10 and *CPA Canada Handbook—Accounting*, Part II, Section 3820.

[30] According to the *CPA Canada Handbook—Accounting*, Part II, Section 1540.03 (and IAS 7.1), the cash flow statement (statement of cash flows) should be presented as an integral part of the financial statements.

[31] *CPA Canada Handbook—Accounting*, Part II, Section 1540.01 and IAS 7.4. Copyright © International Financial Reporting Standards Foundation. All rights reserved. Reproduced by John Wiley & Sons Canada, Ltd with the permission of the International Financial Reporting Standards Foundation®. Reproduction and use rights are strictly limited. No permission granted to third parties to reproduce or distribute.

[32] *CPA Canada Handbook—Accounting*, Part II, Section 1540.06 and IAS 7.6. Copyright © International Financial Reporting Standards Foundation. All rights reserved. Reproduced by John Wiley & Sons Canada, Ltd with the permission of the International Financial Reporting Standards Foundation®. Reproduction and use rights are strictly limited. No permission granted to third parties to reproduce or distribute.

[33] In determining free cash flow, some companies do not subtract dividends, because they believe these expenditures are discretionary.

[34] "Air Canada Reports Second Quarter 2011 Results: Operating Income Improvement of $26 Million to $73 Million," company news release, August 4, 2011.

[35] Air Canada Pension Plan Funding Regulations, 2009, available at www.gazette.gc.ca/rp-pr/p2/2009/2009-08-05/html/sor-dors211-eng.html.

[36] The Canadian Press, "Air Canada $3.7B Pension Deficit Eliminated," CBC News on-line, January 22, 2014.

[37] For further details on the "staff draft" on financial statement presentation, see the related page on the IASB website at www.ifrs.org, and for details of the disclosure initiative Exposure Draft, see www.ifrs.org/Current-Projects/IASB-Projects/Amendments-to-IAS-1/ED-March-2014/Documents/ED-Disclosure-Initiative-Amendments-IAS-1-March-2014.pdf.

[38] This is a brief overview only. It is meant to link risk with the business model and with the use of financial statements in communicating information about risk management. A thorough review of risk models and risk management is beyond the scope of this text.

Cumulative Coverage and Task-Based Simulation: Chapters 3 to 5

Templates to complete this task-based simulation are available in WileyPLUS and on the instructor website.

Erskine Consulting Ltd. has been in business for several years, providing software consulting to its customers on an annual contract or special assignment basis. All work is done over the Internet, although some travel is occasionally required for meeting with customers to negotiate contracts and renewals of contracts, as well as resolving possible disputes in invoicing for their services. Erskine operates out of rented premises and has a modest investment in equipment that is used by the consulting team. Erskine is a private company that follows ASPE and that has a calendar year end.

At the end of each year, Erskine obtains the services of an accountant to complete the annual accounting cycle of the business and prepare any year-end adjusting of journal entries, financial statements, and corporate tax returns.

Upon arrival in early 2018, the accountant was given an unadjusted trial balance and obtained the following additional information to complete his work.

ERSKINE CONSULTING LTD.
Unadjusted Trial Balance
December 31, 2017

Account	Debit	Credit
Petty cash	$ 600	
Cash	18,500	
Accounts receivable	44,700	
Allowance for doubtful accounts		1,800
Interest receivable	0	
Prepaid insurance	4,000	
Supplies	2,000	
FV-NI investments	20,000	
Notes receivable	25,000	
Equipment	94,000	
Accumulated depreciation—equipment		36,000
Goodwill	22,000	
Bank loans		18,000
Accounts payable		7,950
Salaries and wages payable		0
Accrued liabilities		0
Unearned revenue		4,200
Litigation liability		0
Income tax payable	30,000	
Common shares		36,000
Retained earnings		59,800
Dividends	26,000	
Service revenue		242,768
Interest revenue		1,042
Unrealized gain or loss—FV-NI		0
Gain on disposal of equipment		300
Depreciation expense	0	
Office expense	4,100	
Travel expense	6,700	
Insurance expense	900	
Interest expense	1,300	
Utilities expense	750	
Rent expense	54,000	
Salaries and wages expense	49,510	
Supplies expense	0	
Bad debt expense	0	
Telephone and Internet expense	3,200	
Repairs and maintenance expense	600	
Litigation expense	0	
Income tax expense	0	
	$407,860	$407,860

Additional information:

1. Management has been going over the list of accounts receivable for possible accounts that are not collectible. One account for $700 must be written off. In the past, 5% of the balance of all accounts receivable has been the basis of an estimate for the required balance in the allowance for doubtful accounts. Management feels that this estimate should be followed for 2017.

2. After doing a count of supplies on hand, management determined that $400 of supplies remained unused at December 31, 2017.

3. The account balance in Prepaid Insurance of $4,000 represents the annual cost of the renewal of all of Erskine's insurance policies that expire in one year. The policies' coverage started April 1, 2017.

4. FV-NI Investments are long-term investments. The fair value of the portfolio of investments was $22,500 at December 31, 2017.

5. In January 2017, some old equipment was sold for proceeds of $300 cash. The entry made when depositing the cash was debit Cash, credit Gain on Disposal of Equipment. The original cost of the equipment was $4,300 and the accumulated depreciation was $4,200.

6. The depreciation expense for the remaining equipment was calculated to be $7,200 for the 2017 fiscal year.

7. The notes receivable from customers are due October 31, 2020, and bear interest at 5%, with interest paid semi-annually. The last interest collected related to the notes was for the six months ended October 31, 2017.

8. Bank loans are demand bank loans for working capital needs and vary in amount as the needs arise. The bank advised that the interest charge for December 2017 that will go though on the January 2018 bank statement is in the amount of $200.

9. Unpaid salaries and wages at December 31, 2017, totalled $790. These will be paid as part of the first payroll of 2018.

10. After some analysis, management informs the accountant that the Unearned Revenue account should have a balance of $1,000.

11. Erskine was sued by one of its former clients for $50,000 for giving bad advice and instructions. Upon discussion with legal counsel, it has been agreed that it will likely take $5,000 to settle this dispute out of court. No entry has yet been recorded.

12. The accountant is told that a sublet lease arrangement for some excess office space has been negotiated and signed. It will provide Erskine with rent revenue starting on February 1, 2018, at a rate of $400 per month.

13. Erskine has been making income tax instalments as required by the Canada Revenue Agency. All instalment payments have been debited to the Income Taxes Payable account.

14. After recording all of the necessary adjustments and posting to the general ledger, management drafted a new trial balance to arrive at the income before income taxes. Using this result, the accountant prepared the tax returns, and determined that a tax rate of 28% needed to be applied to the income before income tax amount. The necessary adjusting entry for taxes has not yet been recorded.

Instructions

(a) Prepare all necessary adjusting and correcting entries required based on the information given, up to item 13.

(b) Post the journal entries in adjustment columns and arrive at an adjusted trial balance. Enter the journal entries in the following worksheet format:

Account	Unadjusted Trial Balance		Adjustments		Adjusted Trial Balance	
	Debit	Credit	Debit	Credit	Debit	Credit

(c) Using the adjusted trial balance columns of your worksheet, calculate the amount of income before income taxes. Use the information provided in item 14 to record income tax expense for the year.

(d) Prepare a single-step statement of income, a statement of retained earnings, and a statement of financial position for 2017.

(e) Calculate the current ratio and the payout ratio.

REFERENCE TO THE CPA COMPETENCY MAP	LEARNING OBJECTIVES
	After studying this chapter, you should be able to:
1.1.1, 1.2.1, 1.2.2, 1.2.3, 1.4.5	**1.** Understand the economics and legalities of selling transactions from a business perspective.
1.2.1, 1.2.2	**2.** Identify the five steps in the revenue recognition process.
1.2.1, 1.2.2	**3.** Identify the contract with customers.
1.2.1, 1.2.2	**4.** Identify the separate performance obligations in the contract.
1.1.2, 1.2.1, 1.2.2, 1.2.3	**5.** Determine the transaction price.
1.1.2, 1.2.1, 1.2.2	**6.** Allocate the transaction price to the separate performance obligations.
1.2.1, 1.2.2	**7.** Understand how to recognize revenue when the company satisfies its performance obligation.
1.2.1, 1.2.2	**8.** Analyze and determine whether a company has earned revenues under the earnings approach.
1.2.1, 1.2.2, 1.2.3	**9.** Identify other revenue recognition issues.
1.2.1, 1.2.2, 1.3.1, 1.3.2	**10.** Describe presentation and disclosure regarding revenue.
1.1.4	**11.** Identify differences in accounting between IFRS and ASPE and potential changes.
	After studying Appendix 6A, you should be able to:
1.2.1, 1.2.2, 1.3.1	**12.** Apply the percentage-of-completion method for long-term contracts.
1.2.1, 1.2.2	**13.** Apply the completed-contract method for long-term contracts.

THE ACTUAL ACCOUNTING FOR VIRTUAL GAMING

TODAY'S DIGITAL ECONOMY presents some interesting accounting challenges. For example, how does a company that produces on-line games recognize revenue—when the gamer pays for access or when they actually play? When to recognize revenue has been a challenge for California-based Zynga Inc., maker of such popular on-line games as FarmVille, Mafia Wars, and Words With Friends.

Zynga's business model is to sell "virtual" services—access to its games through on-line social media or mobile apps. It makes money in two ways: from consumers and from advertisers. While basic access to its on-line games through social media such as Facebook is free, players who want to add features, such as moving up to the next level of play, need to pay for them. Facebook collects these fees and then remits a portion to Zynga. The other way Zynga earns revenues is from advertisers whose ads and products appear in the games. (Some product placements can cost up to $750,000 per game.)

How does Zynga recognize revenue from players? Within its games, players can buy virtual goods with Facebook local

Getty Images/Justin Sullivan

currency payments or other means, such as a credit card, PayPal, or Google Wallet. "We recognize revenue when all of the following conditions are satisfied: there is persuasive evidence of an arrangement; the service has been provided to the player; the collection of our fees is reasonably assured; and the amount of fees to be paid by the player is fixed or determinable," the company said in its 2014 annual report.

But how does Zynga determine when the service has been provided to the customer and revenue should therefore be recognized? The company divides virtual goods into two kinds: consumable or durable. Consumable virtual goods are those that can be consumed by a specific player action, such as goods that can be used immediately and disappear from the playing board. Zynga recognizes revenue from consumable virtual goods as they are consumed, which usually happens within a month of being purchased. Durable virtual goods are those that the player can access over an extended period of time. Recognizing this revenue requires some estimation. "We recognize revenue from the sale of durable virtual goods ratably over the estimated average playing period of paying players for the applicable game, which represents our best estimate of the average life of durable virtual goods," the annual report states.

Recognizing revenue from advertisers is much simpler than recognizing revenue from players. Zynga recognizes advertising revenue "as advertisements are delivered to customers as long as evidence of the arrangement exists (executed contract), the price is fixed or determinable, and we have assessed collectability as reasonably assured," according to its annual report.

Though the popularity of Zynga's games comes and goes, the revenue continues to flow: in 2014, the company reported $690.4 million in revenue.

Sources: Brandon Gaille, "Zynga Business Model and Growth Strategy," The Blog Millionaire, www.brandongaille.com, February 23, 2015; Zynga Inc. 2014 annual report; Zynga Inc. corporate website, https://zynga.com.

PREVIEW OF CHAPTER 6

As indicated in the opening story, the issue of when revenue should be recognized is complex. The many methods of marketing products and services make it difficult to develop guidelines that will apply to all situations. This chapter provides you with general guidelines used in most business transactions. The content and organization of the chapter are as follows.

REVENUE RECOGNITION					
Understanding the Nature of Sales Transactions from a Business Perspective	**Recognition and Measurement**	**Other Revenue Recognition Issues**	**Presentation and Disclosure**	**IFRS/ASPE Comparison**	**Appendix 6A — Long-Term Contracts**
■ Economics of sales transactions ■ Legalities of sales transactions ■ Information for decision-making	■ Asset-liability approach ■ Five-step revenue recognition process—example ■ Identifying the contract with customers ■ Identifying separate performance obligations ■ Determining the transaction price ■ Allocating the transaction price to separate performance obligations ■ Recognizing revenue when (or as) each performance obligation is satisfied ■ Summary of the five-step revenue recognition process ■ Earnings approach	■ Right of return ■ Repurchase agreements ■ Bill-and-hold arrangements ■ Principal-agent relationships ■ Consignments ■ Warranties ■ Non-refundable upfront fees ■ Summary of other revenue recognition issues	■ Presentation ■ Disclosure	■ A comparison of IFRS and ASPE ■ Looking ahead	■ Percentage-of-completion method ■ Completed-contract method ■ Losses on long-term contracts

UNDERSTANDING THE NATURE OF SALES TRANSACTIONS FROM A BUSINESS PERSPECTIVE

Objective 1

Understand the economics and legalities of selling transactions from a business perspective.

Much of the complexity of accounting for revenues comes from the way sales transactions are structured. It is critical to understand from a **business perspective** what is being given up in the transaction and what is being received. Business people are not necessarily accountants, yet they generally understand how to price their products and services in order to make a profit and what they need to do to make a sale. In most selling transactions, an entity gives up one asset (for instance, inventory) in exchange for another (for instance, cash). The process of capturing this information for financial reporting purposes involves deciding when to recognize the transaction (on both the statement of financial position and income statement) and how to measure and present it. Accountants must therefore understand the business an entity is engaged in, in order to account for transactions properly.[1]

Let's go a little deeper and examine the economics and the legalities of sales transactions.

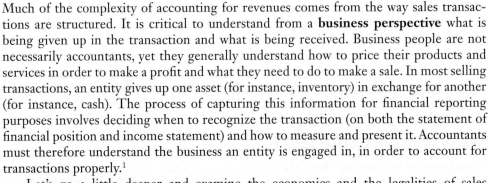

UNDERLYING CONCEPT

Users of financial statements must be able to see the economics and legalities underlying the business and business transactions when looking at the financial statements.

Economics of Sales Transactions

Certain economic attributes underlie most sales transactions. We will discuss some of these below and explain why these attributes matter for accounting purposes.

Fundamentals of Understanding Sales Transactions

Before we can account for a sales transaction, we need to ask some basic questions. Are we selling goods, services, or both? What is the physical nature of the transaction?

Selling transactions involves an entity transferring goods or services to its customers. The goods or services are often referred to as deliverables. It is important to focus on whether goods or services (or both) are being transferred.

ECONOMICS

Why Does This Matter for Accounting Purposes?

Sales of goods and of services are different.

Goods are tangible assets. As a result, there is a definite point in time when control over the goods or the item being sold passes to the buyer. Control of an asset means that the entity has access to the benefits provided by the asset where others do not. This normally coincides with the transfer of risks and rewards as indicated by **possession** and **legal title**. Normally this would be a point in time but it may span several periods, such as in a construction contract.

Services are not tangible assets and therefore the concepts of possession and legal title are irrelevant. Service contracts may be completed in one period but often span more than one period. Therefore, there is the added complexity of how much, if any, revenue is earned in any given period. Many contracts involve both goods and services (referred to as **multiple deliverables** or **bundled sales**), and this complicates the accounting when the goods and services are sold together as a bundle for one price. This is because possession and legal title to goods might pass before, after, or during the time when the services are rendered. Example 1 looks at a bundled sale.

> **EXAMPLE 1**
>
> A manufacturing company sells cameras and provides a warranty for a total of $100. Under the terms of the warranty, the company promises to fix the camera if it breaks over the next year. Thus, the company has contracted to provide not only the camera (goods) but also a service (under the warranty). The value of the camera is estimated at $80 and the warranty at $20. The company also sells warranties separately.

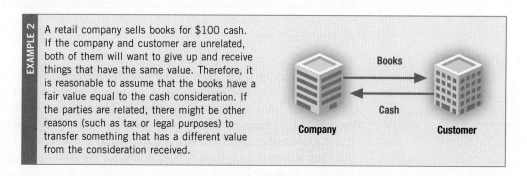

Understanding what the company is selling will help to determine when to recognize revenues. Care should be taken to identify the terms of the transaction, whether it is documented in one or more agreements or not at all. When products and services are sold and priced together as one package, as in Example 1, this creates complexities when determining how much revenue to recognize and when. How much should be attributed to the sale of the camera and how much to the warranty service? Obligations to deliver something in the future can increase measurement uncertainty because we do not always know what will happen in the future.

Reciprocal Nature

Next, we need to ask regarding a sales transaction: What is being received?

Most business transactions are **reciprocal**; that is, the entity gives something up and receives something in return. In addition to assessing what we are giving up, we should determine what we are getting back. **Consideration** is what the entity receives in return for the provision of goods or services. Is the consideration cash or cash-like or is it another good or service?

Why Does This Matter for Accounting Purposes?

If we assume that the transactions are at **arm's length**—that is, they are between unrelated parties—then we may assume that the value of what is given up usually approximates the value of what is received in the transaction. Unless otherwise noted, we will generally assume that transactions are at arm's length and reciprocal. Example 2 illustrates this.

> **EXAMPLE 2**
>
> A retail company sells books for $100 cash. If the company and customer are unrelated, both of them will want to give up and receive things that have the same value. Therefore, it is reasonable to assume that the books have a fair value equal to the cash consideration. If the parties are related, there might be other reasons (such as tax or legal purposes) to transfer something that has a different value from the consideration received.

Sales agreements normally specify what is being given up and what is being acquired as follows:

- **Acquired:** Consideration or rights to the consideration. The amount, nature, and timing of what the customer agrees to pay are normally agreed upon.

- **Given up:** Goods/services (now or in the future). Details regarding delivery (quantities, nature of goods/services, timing, shipping terms) are agreed upon.

Recognizing and focusing on the reciprocal and arm's-length nature of transactions, as well as the detailed agreement between the customer and vendor, allows us to better capture and measure the economics of transactions in the financial statements. Just as obligations to deliver in the future create measurement uncertainty, so do rights to receive consideration in the future. For instance, if the entity sells on credit, there is a risk that the customer will not pay. (This is known as **credit risk**.)

Consideration that is nonmonetary[2] (as with **barter** transactions) presents greater challenges for accounting purposes. **Barter** or **nonmonetary transactions** are transactions where few or no monetary assets are received as consideration when goods or services are sold. For instance, a computer manufacturing company might sell a computer, but instead of receiving cash as consideration, the company might receive another type of asset, such as office furniture. From a business perspective, is this still a sale? How should it be measured?

Generally, a barter transaction is seen as a sale if the transaction has **commercial substance**. What does "commercial substance" mean? It means that the transaction is a **bona fide**—or legitimate—purchase and sale and that the entity has entered into the transaction for business purposes, exchanging one type of asset or service for a different type of asset or service. After the transaction, the entity will be in a different position and its future cash flows are expected to change significantly as a result of the transaction in terms of timing, amount, and/or riskiness.

When a reciprocal transaction occurs, the entity's risk profile changes. For instance, in Example 3 below, before the sale, the company did not know how much it would eventually sell the gold for[3] or how much it would realize on the sale. The risk that the price of an asset will change is referred to as a **price risk**. Once the sale occurs, the company gets rid of the price risk of the gold.

UNDERLYING
CONCEPT

The representational faithfulness concept supports full disclosure of risks and changes in risk, as they affect the entity's ability to generate future cash flows.

EXAMPLE 3

A resource company sells gold bars (which it has mined and refined) to its customers in exchange for electricity. It uses the electricity immediately in its production operations. The transaction has commercial substance, because the company no longer has the price risk associated with the gold. It also has the use of the electricity.

Gold →
← Electricity

Company   Customer

Sometimes, it is common in the industry for companies to swap inventory in order to facilitate a sale. For instance, oil Company A may ask oil Company B to ship oil to A's customer, who might be geographically located close to B. In this way, A's customer receives the oil faster. A would then repay B with the oil at a later date. B would not treat this as a sale as it is not a bona fide sale to B. After the transaction is complete, it is in exactly the same situation as before; that is, it has oil. We will discuss nonmonetary transactions further in Chapter 10.

Concessionary Terms

Another question to ask regarding a sales transaction is: Are the terms of sale normal or is this a special deal?

In some cases, one party is in a better bargaining position than the other. This might occur, for instance, where supply exceeds demand. In this case, the buyer in the transaction may be able to negotiate a better deal than normal because there are many sellers who want to sell their products but there are few buyers. **Concessionary terms** are terms negotiated by a party to the contract that are more favourable than normal.

Examples of concessionary terms are as follows:

The selling price is deeply discounted.

The seller agrees to a more **lenient return or payment policy** (including paying in instalments over an extended term or using consignment sales).

The seller loosens its **credit policy**.

The seller transfers legal title but allows the customer to take delivery at a later date (sometimes referred to as "**bill and hold**").

The goods are shipped subject to **customer acceptance conditions**. Extended trial periods are an example.

The seller agrees to provide **ongoing or additional services** beyond the main goods/ services agreed to in order to make the sale. This might include, for example, installation of an asset, ongoing servicing, or continuing fees, such as in a franchise agreement.

The **seller continues to have some involvement**, including a guarantee of resale (or permission to return) or guarantee of profit.

Why Does This Matter for Accounting Purposes?

Care must be taken to identify concessionary (or abnormal) terms in any deal because they may complicate the accounting. Concessionary terms are terms that are more lenient than usual and are meant to induce sales.

Concessionary or abnormal terms may create additional obligations or may reflect the fact that the risks and rewards or control has not yet passed to the customer. These situations must be carefully analyzed because they create additional recognition and measurement uncertainty. They may even indicate that no sale has taken place at all.

The question we should ask is whether the selling terms are normal business practices for the company or are special or unusual in some way. There is a fine line between what is normal and what is abnormal. In order to do this analysis properly, we must obtain an understanding of normal business practices. (We can do this by looking at standard documentation of selling transactions, such as contracts and/or a history of past transactions.)

Illustration 6-1 helps differentiate between normal selling terms and abnormal concessionary terms. The normal selling terms are examples of the standard terms that many companies use.

Illustration 6-1

Normal versus Concessionary Terms

	Examples of Normal Selling Terms	Examples of Concessionary Selling Terms
Selling price	Selling price reflects a normal profit margin for the company for that product.	Selling price is deeply discounted.
Payment terms	Sell for cash or on credit. If credit, payment is usually expected within 30 to 60 days.	Any terms that are more lenient than this; for example, • selling on credit where the buyer does not have to pay for 90 days or more, or • instalment sales where these are not normal industry practice.
Extension of credit	Sell to customers that are creditworthy.	Sell to customers that are riskier than the existing customer base.
Shipping terms	Ship when ordered and ready to ship.	Ship at a later date; for example, the entity may hold the inventory in its warehouse for an extended period.
Other terms	Once shipped and legal title passes, no continuing involvement except for normal rights of return and/or standard warranties.	Extended right of return/warranty period, cash flow guarantee on future rental of building sold, profit guarantees on future resale, or buyback provisions.

Example 4 illustrates a contract with concessionary terms.

EXAMPLE 4

A merchandising company sells inventory to a customer for $100 cash. Legal title passes when the cash is paid (a few days before year end). The merchandise is stored in the warehouse for a few days until after year end. Is this a sale at year end or not? It is not clear. Normally, delivery to the customer would accompany the sales order and payment. However, the merchandising company is agreeing to a non-standard selling term (that is, to store the goods) in order to make the sale more attractive. This might mean revenue cannot be recognized until it is delivered to the customer or that the company is selling both the inventory and a storage service.

WHAT DO THE NUMBERS MEAN?

One last thought on the topic of normal business practices. Note that many companies continue to change their product mix and selling terms in an effort to provide maximum value to customers and shareholders. This is a completely normal part of evolving the business and dealing with changes that may be happening in the industry. For instance, a company that usually sells a product to ensure a certain profit margin may sell the product at a deep discount in order to achieve market penetration and get customers using the product.

BlackBerry Limited (then called Research In Motion) did this in 2011 with its BlackBerry PlayBook tablet. Hoping to get customers using the PlayBook instead of the very popular iPad, RIM offered the PlayBook at a deeply discounted price of $199. This was about $300 less than the original suggested retail price. The company hoped that by getting a significant number of

REAL WORLD EMPHASIS

PlayBooks into the hands of users, it would encourage software developers to create new applications. In this case, the selling price was well received by the market and the sales were recognized as revenues since all revenue recognition criteria were met and there were bona fide business reasons for changing the selling terms. Because of the deep discount, however, the company took an inventory writedown of $485 million in the third quarter of 2011 related to the PlayBooks.

Sources: Jared Newman, "BlackBerry PlayBook: $199 Yet Again," *PCWorld*, February 2, 2012; "Research In Motion Announces Third Quarter Provision Related to PlayBook Inventory and Confirms Commitment to Tablet Market; Provides Update to Q3 and Fiscal 2012 Guidance," company news release, December 2, 2011; Matt Hartley, "RIM Offering Discounted PlayBooks at Several Retailers," *Financial Post*, September 26, 2011.

Legalities of Sales Transactions

LAW AND ECONOMICS

Companies operate within environments governed by law, including contract law, common law, and securities law. Laws exist to protect the rights of individuals and legal entities. It is important to understand the legal environment because rights and obligations often arise from the operation of the law. In this section, we explore the legalities of sales transactions and what each item means for accounting purposes.

Contract Law

UNDERLYING CONCEPT

Any promise that is enforceable under law and any obligation that is imposed by law should be included in the statements under the full disclosure and transparency principles assuming that they are material.

When an entity sells something, both the entity and the customer enter into a contract. A contract with customers is an agreement that creates enforceable obligations and establishes the terms of the deal.[4] The contract may be written or verbal or may be evidenced by, for instance, a cash register receipt. The important thing is that two parties have promised to exchange assets and this creates a contract. There is a promissor (the seller), a promissee (the customer), and an agreement. Thus, the act of entering into a sales agreement creates legal rights and obligations.

In addition, the contract establishes the point in time when **legal title** (entitlement and ownership under law) passes. When the customer takes physical **possession** of the goods straight away, legal title would normally pass at this point. If the goods are shipped, the point at which legal title passes is often indicated by the shipping terms as follows:

FOB shipping point: title passes at the point of shipment.

FOB destination: title passes when the asset is delivered to the customer.

Why Does This Matter for Accounting Purposes?

As noted above, if the entity has promised to provide goods and/or services now or in the future, the contract binds it and can be enforced. It creates contractual rights and obligations that may meet the definition of assets and liabilities. The contract also establishes the substantive terms of the deal, which need to be analyzed when determining if revenue has been earned (including when legal title has passed). If, for instance, the contract stipulates that customers must sign invoices as evidence that they are satisfied with the goods, it may mean that no revenue may be recognized until this is done.

Constructive Obligation

Performance obligations may arise even if not stated in a contract. In many cases, an entity may have an implicit obligation even if it is not explicitly noted in a selling contract. This is referred to as a **constructive obligation**. A constructive obligation is an obligation that is created through past practice or by signalling something to potential customers. Constructive obligations are often enforceable under common or other law. Example 5 illustrates the concept of a constructive obligation.

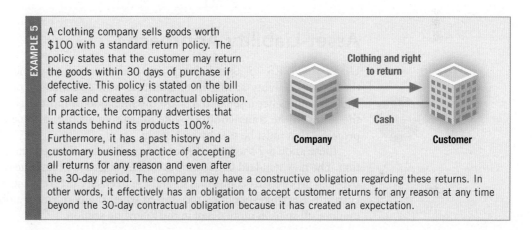

EXAMPLE 5

A clothing company sells goods worth $100 with a standard return policy. The policy states that the customer may return the goods within 30 days of purchase if defective. This policy is stated on the bill of sale and creates a contractual obligation. In practice, the company advertises that it stands behind its products 100%. Furthermore, it has a past history and a customary business practice of accepting all returns for any reason and even after the 30-day period. The company may have a constructive obligation regarding these returns. In other words, it effectively has an obligation to accept customer returns for any reason at any time beyond the 30-day contractual obligation because it has created an expectation.

Why Does This Matter for Accounting Purposes?

Any enforceable promise that results from the sale (whether implicit or explicit) may create a performance obligation that needs to be recognized in the statement of financial position. This includes both contractual and other promises.

Information for Decision-Making

ETHICS

A trend analysis showing changes in revenues from year to year is a very common form of analysis. Due to the sensitivity and high profile of the revenues number on the income statement, there is a lot of pressure to report biased revenue numbers. Biased reporting is possible under both a principles-based accounting standards system (because there is less specific guidance) and a rules-based accounting standards system (by finding loopholes in the rules). Revenue is a key number used to judge management's job performance and they are a signal in the marketplace of sustainable growth potential. The value of firms in certain industries, such as Internet companies, is often based on revenues, since many of these firms do not generate profits in their early years.

THEORY

Revenue recognition is one of the main areas of misrepresentation in financial statements. It is often difficult to spot such misrepresentations, because the note disclosures may be very general. It is therefore important to carefully understand the company's underlying business and business model and to ensure that any changes in the business model are reflected appropriately in the statements. Care should also be taken to ensure that large and unusual transactions are entered into for bona fide business reasons (for example, to add value for the shareholders) rather than to make the company's performance look better than it really is.

RECOGNITION AND MEASUREMENT

There are two approaches to recognizing revenues: (1) the asset-liability approach (sometimes called the contract-based approach) and (2) the earnings approach.

The new IFRS standard, *IFRS 15 Revenue from Contracts with Customers*, adopts an **asset-liability approach** as the basis for revenue recognition. The asset-liability approach recognizes and measures revenue based on changes in assets and liabilities. The earnings approach recognizes and measures revenue based on whether it has been earned. We will discuss this approach in greater detail later in this section. The IASB decided that focusing on (a) the recognition and measurement of assets and liabilities and (b) changes in those assets or liabilities over the life of the contract brings more discipline to the measurement of revenue than the "earned and realized" criteria in prior IFRS standards. Note that ASPE still follows the **earnings approach**.

Asset-Liability Approach

Under the IFRS 15 asset-liability approach, companies account for revenue based on the asset or liability arising from contracts with customers. Companies analyze contracts with customers because contracts are the lifeblood of most businesses. Contracts indicate the terms of the transaction, provide measurement of the consideration, and specify the promises that must be met by each party.

Illustration 6-2 shows the key concepts related to this new standard on revenue recognition. The new standard first identifies the key objective of revenue recognition, followed by a five-step process that companies should use to ensure that revenue is measured and reported correctly. Revenue should be recognized when the performance obligation is satisfied. We examine all steps in more detail in the following section.

Illustration 6-2
Key Concepts of Revenue Recognition*

> **KEY OBJECTIVE**
>
> Recognize revenue to depict the transfer of goods or services to customers in an amount that reflects the consideration that the company receives, or expects to receive, in exchange for these goods or services.
>
> **FIVE-STEP PROCESS FOR REVENUE RECOGNITION**
>
> 1. Identify the contract with customers.
> 2. Identify the separate performance obligations in the contract.
> 3. Determine the transaction price.
> 4. Allocate the transaction price to the separate performance obligations.
> 5. Recognize revenue when each performance obligation is satisfied.
>
> **REVENUE RECOGNITION PRINCIPLE**
>
> Recognize revenue in the accounting period when the performance obligation is satisfied.

Five-Step Revenue Recognition Process—Example

Let's use a hypothetical example to illustrate the five steps in the revenue recognition process. Assume that Boeing Corporation signs a contract to sell airplanes to WestJet for $100 million. Illustration 6-3 shows the five steps that Boeing would follow to recognize revenue.

Illustration 6-3

Five Steps of Revenue Recognition

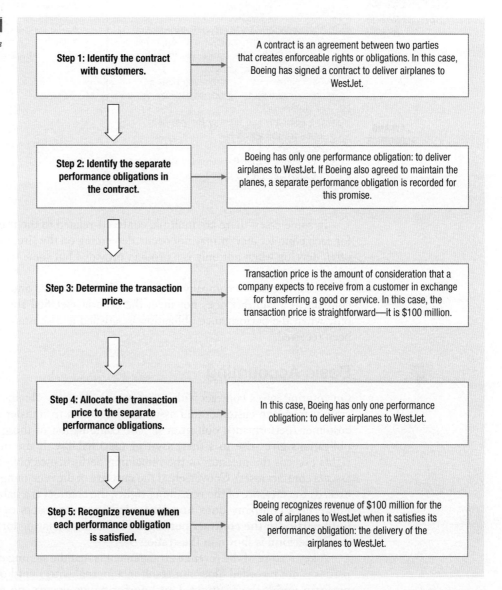

Step 1: Identify the contract with customers.	A contract is an agreement between two parties that creates enforceable rights or obligations. In this case, Boeing has signed a contract to deliver airplanes to WestJet.
Step 2: Identify the separate performance obligations in the contract.	Boeing has only one performance obligation: to deliver airplanes to WestJet. If Boeing also agreed to maintain the planes, a separate performance obligation is recorded for this promise.
Step 3: Determine the transaction price.	Transaction price is the amount of consideration that a company expects to receive from a customer in exchange for transferring a good or service. In this case, the transaction price is straightforward—it is $100 million.
Step 4: Allocate the transaction price to the separate performance obligations.	In this case, Boeing has only one performance obligation: to deliver airplanes to WestJet.
Step 5: Recognize revenue when each performance obligation is satisfied.	Boeing recognizes revenue of $100 million for the sale of airplanes to WestJet when it satisfies its performance obligation: the delivery of the airplanes to WestJet.

Illustration 6-3 highlights the five-step process used to recognize revenue. Step 5 is when Boeing recognizes revenue related to the sale of the airplanes to WestJet. At this point, Boeing delivers the airplanes to WestJet and satisfies its performance obligation. The performance obligation is settled when a change in **control** from Boeing to WestJet occurs. WestJet now controls the assets because it has the ability to direct the use of and obtain substantially all the remaining benefits from the airplanes. Control also includes WestJet's ability to prevent other companies from directing the use of, or receiving the benefits from, the airplanes.[5] In the following sections, we provide an expanded discussion of this five-step process.

Identifying the Contract with Customers—Step 1

A **contract** is an agreement between two or more parties that creates enforceable rights or obligations. Contracts can be written, oral, or implied from customary business practice. A company applies the revenue guidance to a contract according to the criteria summarized in Illustration 6-4.

Illustration 6-4

Contract Criteria for Revenue Guidance

LAW AND ECONOMICS

Apply IFRS 15 to Contract If:	Disregard IFRS 15 If:
• The contract has commercial substance. • The parties to the contract have approved the contract and are committed to perform their respective obligations. • The company can identify each party's rights regarding the goods or services to be transferred. • The company can identify the payment terms for the goods and services to be transferred. • It is probable that the company will collect the consideration to which it will be entitled.[6]	• The contract is wholly unperformed, and • Each party can unilaterally terminate the contract without compensation.

In some cases, there are multiple contracts related to the transaction, and accounting for each contract may or may not occur, depending on the circumstances. These situations often develop when not only is a product provided but some type of service is performed as well.

In some cases, a company should combine contracts and account for them as one contract. If a contract does not meet the criteria specified above, revenue is recognized only when the performance obligation is satisfied and substantially all consideration has been received.[7]

Basic Accounting

On entering into a contract with a customer, a company obtains rights to receive consideration from the customer and assumes obligations to transfer goods or services to the customer (performance obligations). The combination of those rights and performance obligations gives rise to a (net) asset or (net) liability. If the measure of the remaining rights exceeds the measure of the remaining performance obligations, the contract is an asset (a contract asset). Conversely, if the measure of the remaining performance obligations exceeds the measure of the remaining rights, the contract is a liability (a contract liability). However, **a company does not recognize contract assets or liabilities until one or both parties to the contract perform.** The basic accounting for a contract in which both parties perform is shown in Illustration 6-5.

A key feature of the revenue arrangement is that the signing of the contract by the two parties is not recorded (does not result in a journal entry) until one or both of the parties **perform under the contract. Until performance occurs, no net asset or net liability occurs.**

Illustration 6-5

Basic Revenue Transaction

CONTRACTS AND RECOGNITION

Facts: On March 1, 2017, Margo Company enters into a contract to transfer a product to Soon Yoon on July 31, 2017. The contract is structured such that Soon Yoon is required to pay the full contract price of $5,000 on August 31, 2017. The cost of goods transferred is $3,000. Margo delivers the product to Soon Yoon on July 31, 2017.

Question: What journal entries should Margo Company make regarding this contract in 2017?

(continued)

Illustration 6-5

Basic Revenue Transaction
(continued)

A = L + SE
+2,000   +2,000

Cash flows: No effect

A = L + SE
0

Cash flows: ↑5,000 inflow

Solution: No entry is required on March 1, 2017, because neither party has performed on the contract. On July 31, 2017, Margo delivers the product and therefore should recognize revenue on that date because it satisfies its performance obligation by delivering the product to Soon Yoon. There is now an unconditional right to receive the payment (and therefore an Account Receivable).

The journal entry to record the sale and related cost of goods sold is as follows.

July 31, 2017

Accounts Receivable	5,000	
Sales Revenue		5,000
Costs of Goods Sold	3,000	
Inventory		3,000

After receiving payment on August 31, 2017, Margo makes the following entry.

August 31, 2017

Cash	5,000	
Accounts Receivable		5,000

Contract Modifications

Companies sometimes change the contract terms while the contract is ongoing. This is called a **contract modification**. When a contract modification occurs, companies determine whether a new contract (and performance obligations) results or whether it is a modification of the existing contract.

A company accounts for a contract modification as a new contract if **both** of the following conditions are satisfied:

1. The promised **goods or services are distinct**. (We will look at this in more detail in the next section.)

2. The price increases by an amount of consideration that reflects the stand-alone selling price of the promised goods or services (that is, the price for which the entity could sell the goods or services).

For example, Crandall Co. has a contract to sell 100 products to a customer for $10,000 ($100 per product) at various times over a six-month period. After 60 products have been delivered, Crandall modifies the contract by promising to deliver 20 more products for an additional $1,900, or $95 per product (which is the stand-alone selling price of the products at the time of the contract modification). Crandall regularly sells the products separately. In this situation, the contract modification for the additional 20 products is, in effect, a **new and separate contract** because it meets both of the conditions above. It does not affect the accounting for the original contract.

Given a new contract, Crandall recognizes an additional $4,000 [(100 units − 60 units) × $100] related to the original contract terms and $1,900 (20 units × $95) related to the new products. Total revenue after the modification is therefore $5,900 ($4,000 + $1,900). Accounting for modifications of existing contracts that are not treated as if they are new contracts is beyond the scope of this book.[8]

Identifying Separate Performance Obligations—Step 2

Objective 4
Identify the separate performance obligations in the contract.

A **performance obligation** is a promise in a contract to provide a product or service to a customer. This promise may be explicit, implicit, or possibly based on customary business practice. To determine whether a performance obligation exists, **the company must provide a distinct product or service** (or a series of distinct products or services that are substantially the same). A good or service is distinct if the customer can benefit from it.[9] Illustration 6-6 summarizes some classic situations when revenue is recognized as a result of providing a distinct product or service, therefore satisfying a performance obligation.

The accounting for the transactions in Illustration 6-6 is straightforward because only one performance obligation exists. However, many revenue arrangements may have

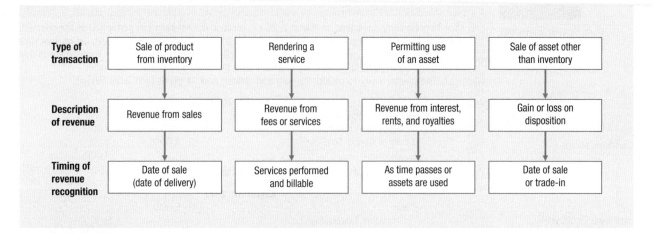

Illustration 6-6

Revenue Recognition Situations

more than one performance obligation. To determine whether a company has to account for multiple performance obligations, it evaluates a second condition. That is, it assesses **whether the product is distinct within the contract**.[10] In other words, if the performance obligation is not highly dependent on, or interrelated with, other promises in the contract, then each performance obligation should be accounted for separately. Conversely, if each of these services is interdependent and interrelated, these services are combined and reported as one performance obligation.

To illustrate, assume that General Motors sells an automobile to Marquart Auto Dealers at a price that includes six months of telematics services such as navigation and remote diagnostics. These telematics services are regularly sold on a stand-alone basis by General Motors for a monthly fee. After the six-month period, the consumer can renew these services on a fee basis with General Motors. In this case, two performance obligations exist: one related to providing the automobile and the other related to the telematics services. **The two are distinct (they can be sold separately) and are not interdependent.**

Illustration 6-7 provides additional case examples of issues related to identifying performance obligations.

Illustration 6-7

Identifying Performance Obligations

Case 1: Single Performance Obligation

SoftTech Inc. licenses customer-relationship software to Lopez Company. In addition to providing the software itself, SoftTech promises to perform consulting services, extensively customizing the software to Lopez's information technology environment, for a total consideration of $600,000. In this case, SoftTech is providing a significant service by integrating the goods and services (the licence and the consulting service) into one combined item for which Lopez has contracted. In addition, the software is significantly customized by SoftTech in accordance with specifications negotiated by Lopez. As a result, **the licence and the consulting services are distinct but interdependent, and therefore should be accounted for as one performance obligation.**

Case 2: Separate Performance Obligation

Chen Computer Inc. manufactures and sells computers that include a warranty to make good on any defect in its computers for 120 days. (This is often referred to as an assurance warranty.) In addition, Chen sells separately an extended warranty, which provides protection from defects for three years beyond the 120 days. (This is often referred to as a service warranty.) In this case, two performance obligations exist: one related to the sale of the computer and the assurance warranty, and the other to the extended warranty (service warranty). In this case, **the sale of the computer and related assurance warranty are one performance obligation because they are interdependent and interrelated with each other. However, the extended warranty is separately sold and is not interdependent.**

When a customer purchases goods or services, sometimes, a company will grant the customer an option to acquire future items (for free or at a discount). Examples include loyalty points and coupons. These rights are treated as separate performance obligations as long as the option gives the customer what is known as a "material right" (that it would not otherwise have been entitled to). In these cases, the customer is in effect paying in advance for future goods or services and the transaction price must be allocated between the goods or services currently purchased and the goods or services to be purchased in the future under the option. These are two distinct performance obligations. The revenue relating to the option is deferred.

For instance, many airline companies offer points to their customers based on the amount and distance travelled on purchased flight tickets. These points transfer to the customer a right to travel for free or at a discount in future (that is, less than the fair value of the flight). The revenue would be recognized when the future goods or services are transferred to the customer.

One final note regarding these distinct performance obligations. Even when they are part of larger long-term contracts, they are accounted for as separate obligations. If they are treated as part of a larger long-term performance obligation, the revenue may be recognized over time in certain situations. For instance, some contracts may involve a promise to transfer a series of distinct goods or services that are substantially the same like 10 km units of a highway. We will look at this in more depth later in the chapter and again when we discuss construction contracts in Appendix 6A.

Determining the Transaction Price—Step 3

Objective 5
Determine the transaction price.

The **transaction price** is the amount of consideration that a company expects to receive from a customer in exchange for transferring goods and services. The transaction price in a contract is often easily determined because the customer agrees to pay a fixed amount of cash to the company over a short period of time. In other contracts, companies must consider the following factors:

- Variable consideration
- Time value of money
- Noncash consideration
- Consideration paid or payable to the customer

Variable Consideration

In some cases, the price of a good or service is dependent on future events. These future events might include discounts, rebates, credits, performance bonuses, or royalties. In these cases, the company estimates the amount of variable consideration it will receive from the contract to determine the amount of revenue to recognize. Companies use either the **expected value**, which is a probability-weighted amount, or the **most likely amount** in a range of possible amounts to estimate variable consideration. Companies choose between these two methods based on which approach better predicts the amount of consideration to which a company is entitled. Illustration 6-8 highlights the issues to be considered in selecting the appropriate method.

Illustration 6-8
Estimating Variable Consideration

Expected Value: Probability-weighted amount in a range of possible consideration amounts.	**Most Likely Amount:** The single most likely amount in a range of possible consideration outcomes.
• May be appropriate if a company has a large number of contracts with similar characteristics. (An example follows in Illustration 6-9.) • Can be based on a limited number of discrete outcomes and probabilities.	• May be appropriate if the contract has only two possible outcomes. (For instance, a bonus will be paid if the goods are delivered early but it will not be paid if the goods are not delivered early.)

Illustration 6-9 provides an application of the two estimation methods.

Illustration 6-9

*Transaction Price—Variable
Consideration*

ESTIMATING VARIABLE CONSIDERATION

Facts: Peabody Construction Company enters into a contract with a customer to build a warehouse for $100,000, with a performance bonus of $50,000 that will be paid based on the timing of completion. The amount of the performance bonus decreases by 10% per week for every week beyond the agreed-upon completion date. The contract requirements are similar to contracts that Peabody has performed previously, and management believes that such experience is predictive for this contract. Management estimates that there is a 60% probability that the contract will be completed by the agreed-upon completion date, a 30% probability that it will be completed one week late, and a 10% probability that it will be completed two weeks late.

Question: How should Peabody account for this revenue arrangement?

Solution: The transaction price should include management's estimate of the amount of consideration to which Peabody will be entitled. Management has concluded that the **probability-weighted method** is the most predictive approach for estimating the variable consideration in this situation:

60% chance of $150,000 [$100,000 + ($50,000 × 1.0)] =	$ 90,000
30% chance of $145,000 [$100,000 + ($50,000 × .90)] =	43,500
10% chance of $140,000 [$100,000 + ($50,000 × .80)] =	14,000
	$147,500

Thus, the total transaction price is $147,500, based on the probability-weighted estimate. Management should update its estimate at each reporting date. Using a most likely outcome approach may be more predictive if a performance bonus is binary (Peabody either will or will not earn the performance bonus), such that Peabody earns either $50,000 for completion on the agreed-upon date or nothing for completion after the agreed-upon date. In this scenario, if management believes that Peabody will meet the deadline and estimates the consideration using the **most likely outcome**, the total transaction price would be $150,000 (the outcome with 60% probability).

A word of caution—a company only **allocates variable consideration if it is reasonably assured that it will be entitled to that amount.** Companies therefore may recognize variable consideration only if (1) they have experience with similar contracts and are able to estimate the cumulative amount of revenue, and (2) based on experience, it is highly probable that there will not be a significant reversal of revenue previously recognized.[11] If these criteria are not met, revenue recognition is constrained.

Illustration 6-10 provides an example of how the revenue constraint works.

Time Value of Money

**UNDERLYING
CONCEPT**

Refer back to Chapters 2 and 3 for a discussion on measurement and the time value of money.

Timing of payment to the company sometimes does not match the transfer of the goods or services to the customer. In most situations, companies receive consideration after the product is provided or the service performed. In essence, the company provides financing for the customer.

Companies account for the time value of money if the contract **involves a significant financing component.** When a sales transaction involves a significant financing component (that is, interest is accrued on consideration to be paid over time), the amount of revenue is determined by discounting the payments. The discount rate reflects the credit risk associated with the sales contract and the customer. For instance, the discount rate would be higher for a customer who has a higher credit risk.[12] Alternatively, you would calculate the interest rate needed to equate the discounted amount of payments to the cash consideration that a customer would pay for the item at the time of sale.

The company will report the effects of the financing as either interest expense or interest revenue. Illustration 6-11 provides an example of a financing transaction.

Illustration 6-10

Transaction Price—Revenue Constraint

REVENUE CONSTRAINT

Facts: On January 1, Shera Company enters into a contract with Hornung Inc. to perform asset-management services for one year. Shera receives a quarterly management fee based on a percentage of Hornung's assets under management at the end of each quarter. In addition, Shera receives a performance-based incentive fee of 20% of the fund's return in excess based on an observable index at the end of the year.

Shera accounts for the contract as a single performance obligation to perform investment-management services for one year because the services are interdependent and interrelated. To recognize revenue for satisfying the performance obligation over time, Shera selects an output method of measuring progress toward complete satisfaction of the performance obligation. Shera has had a number of these types of contracts with customers in the past.

Question: At what point should Shera recognize the management fee and the performance-based incentive fee related to Hornung?

Solution: Shera should record the management fee each quarter as it manages the fund over the year. However, Shera should not record the incentive fee until the end of the year. Although Shera has experience with similar contracts, that experience is not predictive of the outcome of the current contract because the amount of consideration is highly susceptible to volatility in the market. In addition, the incentive fee has a large number and high variability of possible consideration amounts. Thus, revenue related to the incentive fee is constrained (not recognized) until the incentive fee is known at the end of the year.

Illustration 6-11

Transaction Price—Extended Payment Terms

EXTENDED PAYMENT TERMS

Facts: On July 1, 2017, SEK Company sold goods to Grant Company for $900,000 in exchange for a four-year, zero-interest-bearing note with a face amount of $1,416,163. The goods have an inventory cost on SEK's books of $590,000 and the fair value is $900,000.

Questions: (a) How much revenue should SEK Company record on July 1, 2017? (b) How much revenue should it report related to this transaction on December 31, 2017?

Solution:
(a) SEK should record revenue of $900,000 on July 1, 2017, which is the fair value of the inventory in this case.
(b) SEK is also financing this purchase and records interest income on the note over the four-year period. Since no other information is available, the interest rate is imputed and is determined to be 12%. The 12% is the rate that discounts the final payment of $1,416,163 to the fair value of the goods ($900,000). SEK records interest revenue of $54,000 (12% × ½ × $900,000) at December 31, 2017.

The entry to record SEK's sale to Grant Company is as follows.

July 1, 2017

Notes Receivable	900,000	
Sales Revenue		900,000

The related entry to record the cost of goods sold is as follows.

July 1, 2017

Cost of Goods Sold	590,000	
Inventory		590,000

SEK makes the following entry to record interest revenue at the end of the year.

December 31, 2017

Notes Receivable	54,000	
Interest Income (12% × ½ × $900,000)		54,000

A = L + SE
+310,000   +310,000

Cash flows: No effect

A = L + SE
+54,000   +54,000

Cash flows: No effect

As a practical expedient, companies are not required to reflect the time value of money to determine the transaction price if the time period for payment is less than a year.[13]

Noncash Consideration

Companies sometimes receive consideration in the form of goods, services, or other non-cash consideration. When these situations occur, **companies generally recognize revenue on the basis of the fair value of what is received**. For example, assume that Raeylinn Company receives common stock of Monroe Company in payment for consulting services. In that case, Raeylinn Company recognizes revenue in the amount of the fair value of the common stock received. If Raeylinn cannot determine this amount, then it should estimate the selling price of the services performed and recognize this amount as revenue.

Customers sometimes contribute goods or services, such as equipment or labour, to help fulfill the contract. This consideration should be treated as noncash consideration as long as control passes to the company.[14]

Consideration Paid or Payable to Customers

Companies often make payments to their customers as part of a revenue arrangement. Consideration paid or payable may include discounts, volume rebates, or coupons. In general, these elements reduce the consideration received and the revenue to be recognized. In certain situations, these amounts may be treated as assets or expenses. For instance, where the company is reimbursing the customer for shared advertising costs, the amounts paid would be treated as an expense.[15] Illustration 6-12 provides an example of consideration paid to a customer.

Illustration 6-12

Transaction Price—Volume Discount

VOLUME DISCOUNT

Facts: Sansung Company offers its customers a 3% volume discount if they purchase at least $2 million of its products during the calendar year. On March 31, 2017, Sansung has made sales of $700,000 to Arctic Co. In the previous two years, Sansung sold over $3 million to Arctic in the period from April 1 to December 31.

Question: How much revenue should Sansung recognize for the first three months of 2017?

Solution: In this case, Sansung should reduce its revenue by $21,000 ($700,000 × 3%) because it is probable that it will provide this rebate. Revenue is therefore $679,000 ($700,000 − $21,000). To not recognize this volume discount overstates Sansung's revenue for the first three months of 2017. In other words, the appropriate revenue is $679,000, not $700,000.

Given these facts, Sansung makes the following entry on March 31, 2017, to recognize revenue.

Accounts Receivable	679,000	
Sales Revenue		679,000

Assuming that Sansung's customer **meets the discount threshold**, Sansung makes the following entry.

Cash	679,000	
Accounts Receivable		679,000

If Sansung's customer **fails to meet the discount threshold**, Sansung makes the following entry upon payment.

Cash	700,000	
Accounts Receivable		679,000
Sales Discounts Forfeited		21,000

As indicated in Chapter 7, Sales Discounts Forfeited is reported in the "Other revenues and gains" section of the income statement.

A = L + SE
+679,000   +679,000

Cash flows: ↑679,000 inflow

A = L + SE
+21,000   +21,000

Cash flows: ↑700,000 inflow

In many cases, companies provide cash discounts to customers for a short period of time. (This is often referred to as prompt settlement discounts.) For example, assume that terms are payment due in 60 days, but if payment is made within five days, a 2% discount is given (referred to as 2/5, net 60). These prompt settlement discounts should reduce revenues, if material. In most cases, companies record the revenue at full price (gross) and record a sales discount if payment is made within the discount period.

Allocating the Transaction Price to Separate Performance Obligations—Step 4

Objective **6**
Allocate the transaction price to the separate performance obligations.

Companies often have to allocate the transaction price to more than one performance obligation in a contract. If an allocation is needed, the transaction price allocated to the various performance obligations is based on their relative fair values. The best measure of fair value is what the company could sell the good or service for on a stand-alone basis, referred to as the **stand-alone selling price**. If this information is not available, companies should use their best estimate of what the good or service might sell for as a stand-alone unit. Illustration 6-13 summarizes the approaches that companies may follow (in preferred order of use).[16] All information that is reasonably available should be used (such as market conditions and type of customer) and maximum use should be made of observable information.

Illustration 6-13

Transaction Price—Allocation

UNDERLYING CONCEPT

Refer back to Chapters 2 and 3 for a discussion on fair value measurement

Allocation Approach	Implementation
Adjusted market assessment approach	Estimate the price that customers purchasing the goods or services will pay. The company might also look at competitor prices for similar goods or services.
Expected cost plus a margin	Forecast expected costs and add a reasonable profit margin.
Residual approach	Use where the selling price is highly variable or uncertain. Estimate the standalone selling price by starting with the total price for the contract and deducting the observable selling prices of other items being sold.[17]

Illustrations 6-14 and 6-15 are examples of the measurement issues involved in allocating the transaction price.

Illustration 6-14

Allocation—Multiple Performance Obligations

MULTIPLE PERFORMANCE OBLIGATIONS—EXAMPLE 1

Facts: Lonnie Company enters into a contract to build, run, and maintain a highly complex piece of electronic equipment for five years, starting upon delivery of the equipment. There is a fixed fee for each of the build, run, and maintenance deliverables. Any progress payments made are non-refundable. All the deliverables have a stand-alone value. There is verifiable evidence of the selling price for the building and maintenance but not for running the equipment. It is determined that the transaction price must be allocated to the three performance obligations: building, running, and maintaining the equipment.

> *Question:* What procedure should Lonnie Company use to allocate the transaction price to the three performance obligations?

Solution: The performance obligations relate to building the equipment, running the equipment, and maintaining the equipment. As indicated, Lonnie can determine the stand-alone values for the equipment and the maintenance agreements. The company then can make a best estimate of the selling price for running the equipment, using the adjusted market assessment approach or expected cost plus a margin approach. Lonnie next applies the relative fair value method at the inception of the transaction to determine the proper allocation to each performance obligation. Once the allocation is performed, Lonnie recognizes revenue independently for each performance obligation using regular revenue recognition criteria.

If, on the other hand, Lonnie is unable to estimate the stand-alone selling price for running the equipment because such an estimate is highly variable or uncertain, Lonnie may use a residual approach. In this case, Lonnie uses the fair value from the total transaction price to arrive at a residual value for running the equipment.

Illustration 6-15

Multiple Performance Obligations—Product, Installation, and Service

MULTIPLE PERFORMANCE OBLIGATIONS—EXAMPLE 2

Facts: Handler Company is an experienced manufacturer of construction equipment. Handler's products range from small to large pieces of automated equipment, to complex systems containing numerous components. Unit selling prices range from $600,000 to $4 million and are quoted inclusive of installation and training. The installation process does not involve changes to the features of the equipment and does not require proprietary information about the equipment in order for the installed equipment to perform to specifications. Handler has the following arrangement with Chai Company.

- Chai purchases equipment from Handler for $2 million and chooses Handler to do the installation. Handler charges $2.0 million for the equipment whether it does the installation or not. (Some companies do the installation themselves because they prefer their own employees to do the work or because of relationships with other customers.) The price of the installation service if sold separately is estimated to have a fair value of $20,000.
- The fair value of the training sessions is estimated at $50,000. Other companies could also perform these training services but Chai chooses to use Chandler for its training so it does not have to pay extra to another company.
- Chai is obligated to pay Handler the $2 million upon the delivery and installation of the equipment.
- Handler delivers the equipment and completes the installation on November 1, 2017. (In other words, transfer of control is complete.) Training related to the equipment starts once the installation is completed and lasts for one year. The equipment has a useful life of 10 years.

Questions: (a) What are the performance obligations for purposes of accounting for the sale of the equipment? (b) If there is more than one performance obligation, how should the payment of $2 million be allocated to various components?

Solution:
(a) The equipment, installation, and training are distinct and not interdependent because the equipment, installation, and training are three separate products or services. Each of these items has a stand-alone selling price.
(b) The total revenue of $2 million should be allocated to the three components based on their relative fair values. In this case, the fair value of the equipment should be considered to be $2 million, the installation fee is $20,000, and the training is $50,000. The total fair value to consider is $2,070,000 ($2,000,000 + $20,000 + $50,000). The allocation is as follows.

Equipment	$1,932,367 [($2,000,000 ÷ $2,070,000) × $2,000,000]
Installation	$19,324 [($20,000 ÷ $2,070,000) × $2,000,000]
Training	$48,309 [($50,000 ÷ $2,070,000) × $2,000,000]

Handler makes the following entry on November 1, 2017, to record both sales revenue and service revenue on the installation, as well as the unearned service revenue.

November 1, 2017

Cash	2,000,000	
Service Revenue—Installation		19,324
Unearned Revenue		48,309
Sales Revenue		1,932,367

Assuming the cost of the equipment is $1.5 million, the entry to record cost of goods sold is as follows.

November 1, 2017

Cost of Goods Sold	1,500,000	
Inventory		1,500,000

As indicated by these entries, Handler recognizes revenue from the sale of the equipment once the installation is completed on November 1, 2017. In addition, it recognizes revenue for the installation fee because these services have been performed.

Handler recognizes the training revenues on a straight-line basis starting on November 1, 2017, or $4,026 ($48,309 ÷ 12) per month for one year (unless a more appropriate method such as the percentage-of-completion method is warranted). The journal entry to recognize the training revenue for two months in 2017 is as follows.

December 31, 2017

Unearned Revenue	8,052	
Service Revenue—Training ($4,026 × 2)		8,052

Therefore, Handler recognizes revenue for the year ended December 31, 2017 in the amount of $1,959,743 ($1,932,367 + $19,324 + $8,052). Handler makes the following journal entry to recognize the training revenue in 2018, assuming adjusting entries are made at year end.

December 31, 2018

Unearned Revenue	40,257	
Service Revenue—Training ($48,309 − $8,052)		40,257

A = L + SE
+500,000 +48,309 +451,691

Cash flows: ↑2,000,000 inflow

A = L + SE
−8,052 +8,052

Cash flows: No effect

When a company sells a bundle of goods or services, the selling price of the bundle may be less than the sum of the individual stand-alone prices due to a specific service or product. In this case, the company should allocate the discount to the service or product that is causing the discount and not to the entire bundle. Illustration 6-16 indicates this.

Illustration 6-16

Allocating Transaction Price with a Discount

DISCOUNTED TRANSACTION PRICE

Facts: Manitoba Joe's Golf Shop provides the following information related to three items that are often sold as a package. The company often sells the putter and irons as a separate bundle for $525.

Item	Stand-Alone Selling Price	Price when Bundled
(a) Lessons (per session)	$100	(b) + (c) $525
(b) Custom irons	$525	
(c) Putter	$125	
Total	$750	(a) + (b) + (c) $625

Question: How should the discount be allocated to the elements of the revenue arrangement?

Solution: As indicated, the stand-alone price for the lesson, custom irons, and putter is $750, but the bundled price for all three is $625. In this case, the discount applies to the performance obligations related to providing the custom irons and putter. As a result, Manitoba Joe's allocates the discount solely to the custom irons and putter, and not to the lessons, as follows.

	Allocated Amounts
Lessons	$100
Custom irons and putter	525
Total	$625

Recognizing Revenue When (or as) Each Performance Obligation Is Satisfied—Step 5

Objective 7

Understand how to recognize revenue when the company satisfies its performance obligation.

A company satisfies its performance obligation when the customer obtains control of the good or service. As indicated earlier, the concept of change in control is the deciding factor in determining when a performance obligation is satisfied. The customer controls the product or service when it has the ability to direct the use of and obtain substantially all the remaining benefits from the asset or service. Control also includes the customer's ability to prevent other companies from directing the use of, or receiving the benefits from, the asset or service.[18] Illustration 6-17 summarizes some indicators that the customer has obtained control.[19]

Illustration 6-17

Change in Control Indicators

1. The company has a right to payment for the asset.
2. The company has transferred legal title to the asset.
3. The company has transferred physical possession of the asset.
4. The customer has significant risks and rewards of ownership.
5. The customer has accepted the asset.

Companies satisfy performance obligations either at a point in time or over a period of time. According to IFRS 15.35 companies recognize revenue over a period of time only if one or more of the following criteria are met:

1. The customer receives and consumes the benefits as the seller performs.

2. The customer controls the asset as it is created or enhanced. (For example, a builder constructs a building on a customer's property.)

3. The company does not have an alternative use for the asset created or enhanced. (For example, an aircraft manufacturer builds specialty jets to a customer's specifications and the company has an enforceable right to payment.)

Illustration 6-18 provides an example of the point in time when revenue should be recognized.

Illustration 6-18

Satisfying a Performance Obligation

TIMING OF REVENUE RECOGNITION

Facts: Gomez Software Company enters into a contract with Hurly Company to develop and install customer relationship management (CRM) software. Progress payments are made upon completion of each stage of the contract. If the contract is terminated, then the partly completed CRM software passes to Hurly Company. Gomez Software is prohibited from redirecting the software to another customer.

Question: At what point should Gomez Software Company recognize revenue related to its contract with Hurly Company?

Solution: Gomez Software creates an asset with no alternative use because it is prohibited from redirecting the software to another customer. In addition, Gomez Software is entitled to payments for performance to date and expects to complete the project. Therefore, Gomez Software concludes that the contract meets the criteria for recognizing revenue over time.

A company recognizes revenue from a performance obligation over time by measuring the progress toward completion. The method selected for measuring progress should depict the transfer of control from the company to the customer. Companies use various methods to determine the extent of progress toward completion. The most common are the cost-to-cost and units-of-delivery methods. The objective of all these methods is to measure the extent of progress in terms of costs, units, or value added. Companies identify the various measures (such as costs incurred, labour hours worked, tonnes produced, or floors completed) and classify them as input or output measures.

Input measures (such as costs incurred and labour hours worked) are efforts devoted to a contract. Output measures (with units of delivery measured as tonnes produced, floors of a building completed, kilometres of a highway completed, and so on) track results. Neither is universally applicable to all long-term projects. Their use requires the exercise of judgement and careful tailoring to the circumstances.

The most popular input measure used to determine the progress toward completion is the cost-to-cost basis. Under this basis, a company measures the percentage of completion by comparing costs incurred to date with the most recent estimate of the total costs required to complete the contract. We discuss the percentage-of-completion method more fully in Appendix 6A, which examines the accounting for long-term contracts.

Summary of the Five-Step Revenue Recognition Process

Illustration 6-19 provides a summary of the five-step revenue recognition process.

Step in Process	Description	Implementation
1. Identify the contract with customers.	A contract is an agreement that creates enforceable rights or obligations.	A company applies the revenue guidance to contracts with customers and must determine if new performance obligations are created by a contract modification.
2. Identify the separate performance obligations in the contract.	A performance obligation is a promise in a contract to provide a product or service to a customer. A performance obligation exists if the customer can benefit from the good or service on its own or together with other readily available resources.	A contract may be composed of multiple performance obligations. The accounting for multiple performance obligations is based on evaluation of whether the product or service is distinct within the contract. If each of the goods or services is distinct, but is interdependent and interrelated, these goods and services are combined and reported as one performance obligation.
3. Determine the transaction price.	The transaction price is the amount of consideration that a company expects to receive from a customer in exchange for transferring goods and services.	In determining the transaction price, companies must consider the following factors: (1) variable consideration, (2) time value of money, (3) noncash consideration, and (4) consideration paid or payable to the customer.
4. Allocate the transaction price to the separate performance obligations.	If more than one performance obligation exists, allocate the transaction price based on relative fair values.	The best measure of fair value is what the good or service could be sold for on a stand-alone basis (the stand-alone selling price). Estimates of stand-alone selling price can be based on (1) adjusted market assessment, (2) expected cost plus a margin approach, or (3) a residual approach.
5. Recognize revenue when each performance obligation is satisfied.	A company satisfies its performance obligation when the customer obtains control of the good or service.	Companies satisfy performance obligations either at a point in time or over a period of time. Companies recognize revenue over a period of time if (1) the customer controls the asset as it is created or (2) the company does not have an alternative use for the asset.

Illustration 6-19

Summary of the Five-Step Revenue Recognition Process

Earnings Approach

Objective 8

Analyze and determine whether a company has earned revenues under the earnings approach.

ASPE uses the earnings approach. Under the earnings approach, revenues for **sale of goods** and related costs are recognized when all the following conditions are met:[20]

1. The **risks and rewards** of ownership are transferred to the customer.

2. The vendor has **no continuing involvement in, nor effective control over**, the goods sold.

3. Costs and revenues can be **measured reliably**.

4. **Collectibility** is probable.[21]

If the company cannot measure the transaction, then either there is too much uncertainty surrounding the transaction (for instance, where there are abnormal concessionary terms), or the company has not completed all that it has to do to earn the revenues.

---

*Illustration based on IFRS 15.IN7. Copyright © International Financial Reporting Standards Foundation. All rights reserved. Reproduced by John Wiley & Sons Canada, Ltd with the permission of the International Financial Reporting Standards Foundation®. Reproduction and use rights are strictly limited. No permission granted to third parties to reproduce or distribute.

What does the company do to create valuable products or services that customers will pay for? How does it add value? **Earnings process** refers to the actions that a company takes to add value. It is an important part of the business model because it focuses on operating activities. The earnings process is unique to each company and each industry. Different industries add value in different ways. For example, companies that sell goods that they manufacture have vastly differing earnings processes than those that sell goods that they buy wholesale and sell retail. In addition, companies that are in the biotechnology business have models that are different from real estate companies. For this reason, it is important to begin with an understanding of the earnings process.

Selling Goods

When an entity sells goods, there is often one main act or **critical event** in the earnings process that signals **substantial completion or performance**. At this point, although some uncertainty remains, its level is acceptable and revenues can be recognized under accrual accounting. In businesses that sell goods, substantial completion normally occurs at the **point of delivery**. This is generally when the risks and rewards of ownership (including legal title and possession) pass. If the earnings process has a critical event, it is often referred to as a **discrete earnings process**.

As an example, **Magnotta Winery Corporation** makes wine (among other products). Its business involves the steps shown in Illustration 6-20.

<table>
<tr><td>**Illustration 6-20**

Magnotta Winery's Earnings Process</td><td>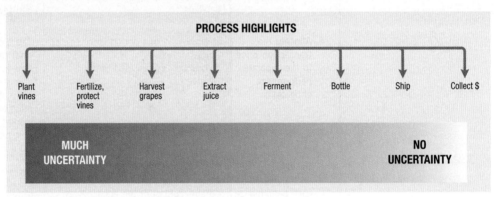</td></tr>
</table>

Magnotta must perform all of the acts in the illustration in order to make a profit from the sale of its wine. The entity starts with cash, invests it in producing inventory, sells the inventory at a price that is higher than its cost, and collects cash. At the early points of the earnings process, there is significant uncertainty about how much product will be produced and its quality. What if the vines get diseased? What if temperatures are too low or it rains too much? What if there is no market for the product? Moving along the earnings process timeline (from left to right), the conditions creating the uncertainty resolve themselves. At the far right-hand side of the earnings process, once the product is shipped and paid for, all uncertainty is eliminated about the creation of the product itself, the measurability of both its costs and revenues, and the collectibility of those revenues.

The concept of **risks and rewards (benefits) of ownership** is a core concept in the earnings approach to revenue recognition. It helps to establish ownership and to indicate when ownership passes from one party to another. As a general rule, the entity that has the risks and rewards treats the goods as an asset.[22]

Illustration 6-21 presents some of the risks and rewards associated with the sale of wine at Magnotta.

Illustration 6-21

Risks and Rewards of Ownership—Case of Wine

Risks	Rewards
— Wine will age poorly and therefore decline in value — Wine will be stolen/vandalized — Wine will be stored improperly	— Wine will age well and appreciate in value — Wine can be consumed by owner or buyer — Wine inventory may be used as collateral for bank loan — Wine may be sold for cash

Risks and rewards of ownership of wine

Magnotta → Customers

Cash (no credit risk) or promise to pay (credit risk)

In determining who has the risks and rewards of ownership and, therefore, whether a sale has occurred at the point of delivery, it is important to look at who has **possession** of the goods and who has **legal title**. The risks and rewards usually stem from these two factors. For example, Magnotta is not entitled to sell inventory or pledge it as collateral (that is, to reap the rewards) unless it has legal title to it. Legal title and possession expose Magnotta to risk of loss.

The principle is quite general and, therefore, there are a wide range of practical applications. Different companies interpret these principles in different ways.[23] We will discuss inventory more fully in Chapter 8.

What about recognizing income before possession and legal title to goods pass to a customer? Is there ever a situation whereby revenue might be recognized before this critical event? In some cases, revenue may be recognized even before there is a specific customer. Examples of such situations can be found in the forestry and agricultural industries when some products have assured prices and ready markets. Revenue is recognized over time as the assets mature. The critical event is the appreciation in value of the asset.[24]

Selling Services

The focus is different when determining the earnings process for services. When services are provided, the focus is on **performance of the service**. An example of an earnings process for a service that is a discrete earnings process is a maintenance inspection on a car. The service is offered on the spot and is completed in a very short time. The critical event is when the mechanic hands over the inspected car and the bill. As mentioned earlier, long-term contracts are more challenging to account for and will be covered in Appendix 6A.

OTHER REVENUE RECOGNITION ISSUES

Objective 9
Identify other revenue recognition issues.

There are several other situations where revenue recognition issues arise. In this section, we illustrate the **revenue recognition principle** and the concept of control for the following situations. This next section is based on IFRS 15. ASPE has little specific guidance in these areas, but is otherwise generally consistent with the following material.

- Right of return
- Repurchase agreements
- Bill and hold
- Principal-agent relationships
- Consignments
- Warranties
- Non-refundable upfront fees

Right of Return

Sales with rights of return have long been a challenge in the area of revenue recognition. For example, assume that Hogland Glass Works transfers control of hurricane glass to Henlo Builders. Hogland grants Henlo the **right of return** for the product for various reasons (for example, dissatisfaction with the product) and the right to receive any combination of the following.

1. A refund.

2. A credit.

3. An alternative product in exchange.

Hogland should recognize all of the following.

(a) Revenue (considering the products expected to be returned).

(b) A refund liability.

(c) An asset (and corresponding adjustment to cost of sales) for its right to recover glass from Henlo on settling the refund liability.

An example of a return situation is presented in Illustration 6-22.[25]

Illustration 6-22

Recognition—Right of Return

RIGHT OF RETURN

Facts: Venden Company sells 100 products for $100 each to Amaya Inc. for cash. Venden allows Amaya to return any unused product within 30 days and receive a full refund. The cost of each product is $60. To determine the transaction price, Venden decides that the approach that is most predictive of the amount of consideration to which it will be entitled is the most likely amount. Using the most likely amount, Venden estimates that:

1. Three products will be returned.
2. The costs of recovering the products will be immaterial.
3. The returned products are expected to be resold at a profit.

Question: How should Venden record this sale?

Solution: Upon transfer of control of the products, Venden recognizes (a) revenue of $9,700 ($100 × 97 products expected not to be returned), (b) a refund liability for $300 ($100 refund × 3 products expected to be returned), and (c) an asset of $180 ($60 × 3 products) for its right to recover products from customers on settling the refund liability. Hence, the amount recognized in cost of sales for 97 products is $5,820 ($60 × 97).

Venden records the sale as follows.

Cash	10,000	
Sales Revenue		9,700
Refund Liability		300

Venden also records the related cost of goods sold with the following entry.

Cost of Goods Sold	5,820	
Estimated Inventory Returns	180	
Inventory		6,000

When a return occurs, Venden should reduce the Refund Liability and Estimated Inventory Returns accounts. In addition, Venden recognizes the returned inventory in a Returned Inventory account as shown in the following entries for the return of two products.

Refund Liability (2 × $100)	200	
Accounts Payable		200
Returned Inventory (2 × $60)	120	
Estimated Inventory Returns		120

A   =   L   +   SE
+4,180   +300   +3,880

Cash flows: ↑10,000 inflow

A   =   L   +   SE
0   0

Cash flows: No effect

Companies record the returned asset in a separate account from inventory to provide transparency. The carrying value of the returned asset is subject to impairment testing, separate from the inventory. If a company is unable to estimate the level of returns with any reliability, it should not report any revenue until the returns become predictive. Under ASPE, Sales Revenues would generally be recorded at the full amount with a sales returns and allowance amount being shown as a contra account. The Refund Liability account has historically not been used. The journal entry would be as follows:

Cash	10,000	
Sales Revenues		10,000
Sales Returns and Allowances	300	
Allowance for Sales Returns and Allowances		300

We will discuss this further in Chapter 7.

Repurchase Agreements

In some cases, companies enter into **repurchase agreements**, which allow them to transfer an asset to a customer but have an obligation or right to repurchase the asset at a later date. In these situations, the question is whether the company sold the asset. Generally, companies report these transactions as a financing (borrowing). That is, if the company has an obligation or right to repurchase the asset for an amount **greater than or equal to its selling price**, then the transaction is a financing transaction by the company. Illustration 6-23 examines the issues related to a repurchase agreement.

Illustration 6-23

Recognition—Repurchase Agreement

REPURCHASE AGREEMENT

Facts: Morgan Inc., an equipment dealer, sells equipment on January 1, 2017, to Lane Company for $100,000. It agrees to repurchase this equipment from Lane Company on December 31, 2018, for a price of $121,000.

Question: Should Morgan Inc. record a sale for this transaction?

Solution: For a sale and repurchase agreement, the terms of the agreement need to be analyzed to determine whether Morgan Inc. has transferred control to the customer, Lane Company. As indicated earlier, control of an asset refers to the ability to direct the use of and obtain substantially all the benefits from the asset. Control also includes the ability to prevent other companies from directing the use of and receiving the benefit from a good or service. In this case, Morgan Inc. continues to have control of the asset. Therefore, this agreement is a financing transaction and not a sale. Thus, the asset is not removed from the books of Morgan Inc.

Assuming that an interest rate of 10% is imputed from the agreement, Morgan Inc. makes the following entries to record this agreement. Morgan Inc. records the financing on January 1, 2017 as follows.

January 1, 2017

Cash	100,000	
Contract Liability		100,000

Morgan Inc. records interest on December 21, 2017, as follows.

December 31, 2017

Interest Expense	10,000	
Contract Liability		
($100,000 × 10%)		10,000

Morgan Inc. records interest and retirement of its liability to Lane Company as follows.

December 31, 2017

Interest Expense	11,000	
Contract Liability		
($110,000 × 10%)		11,000
Contract Liability	121,000	
Cash ($100,000 + $10,000 + $11,000)		121,000

A = L + SE
+100,000   +100,000

Cash flows: ↑100,000 inflow

A = L + SE
−121,000 −100,000 −21,000

Cash flows: ↓121,000 outflow

Investors in **Lucent Technologies** were negatively affected when Lucent violated one of the fundamental criteria for revenue recognition. In this particular case, Lucent agreed to take back shipped inventory from its distributors if the distributors were unable to sell the items to their customers.

In essence, Lucent was "stuffing the distribution or sales channel." By booking sales when goods were shipped, even though the company most likely would get them back, Lucent was able to report continued sales growth. However, Lucent investors got a nasty surprise when distributors returned those goods and Lucent had to restate its financial results. The restatement erased $679 million in revenues, turning an operating profit into a loss. In response to this bad news, Lucent's share price declined $1.31 per share, or 8.5%. Lucent is not alone in this practice. **Sunbeam** got caught stuffing the sales channel with barbecue grills and other outdoor items, which contributed to its troubles when it was forced to restate its earnings.

Investors can be tipped off to potential channel stuffing by carefully reviewing a company's revenue recognition policy for generous return policies or use of cash incentives to encourage distributors to buy products and by watching inventory and receivables levels. When sales increase along with receivables, that's one sign that customers are not paying for goods shipped on credit. And growing inventory levels are an indicator that customers have all the goods they need. Both scenarios suggest a higher likelihood of goods being returned and revenues and income being restated. So remember, no take-backs!

Sources: S. Young, "Lucent Slashes First Quarter Outlook, Erases Revenue from Latest Quarter," *Wall Street Journal Online* (December 22, 2000); Tracey Byrnes, "Too Many Thin Mints: Spotting the Practice of Channel Stuffing," *Wall Street Journal Online* (February 7, 2002); and H. Weitzman, "Monsanto to Restate Results After SEC Probe," *Financial Times* (October 5, 2011).

Bill-and-Hold Arrangements

A **bill-and-hold arrangement** is a contract under which an entity bills a customer for a product but the entity retains physical possession of the product until it is transferred to the customer at a point in the future. Bill-and-hold sales result when the buyer is not yet ready to take delivery but does take title and accepts billing. For example, a customer may request that a company enter into such an arrangement because of (1) lack of available space for the product, (2) delays in its production schedule, or (3) more than sufficient inventory in its distribution channel. Illustration 6-24 provides an example of a bill-and-hold arrangement.

Illustration 6-24

Recognition—Bill and Hold

BILL AND HOLD

Facts: Butler Company sells $450,000 (cost $280,000) of fireplaces on March 1, 2017, to a local coffee shop, Baristo, which is planning to expand its locations around the city. Under the agreement, Baristo asks Butler to retain these fireplaces in its warehouses until the new coffee shops that will house the fireplaces are ready. Title passes to Baristo at the time the agreement is signed.

Question: When should Butler recognize the revenue from this bill-and-hold arrangement?

Solution: When to recognize revenue in a bill-and-hold arrangement depends on the circumstances. Butler determines when it has satisfied its performance obligation to transfer a product by evaluating when Baristo obtains control of that product. For Baristo to have obtained control of a product in a bill-and-hold arrangement, all of the following criteria should be met (IFRS 15.B81):

(a) The reason to hold the inventory must be substantive.
(b) The product must be identified separately and belong to Baristo.
(c) The product must be ready to ship.
(d) Butler cannot use the product nor sell it to another customer.

In this case, it appears that the above criteria were met, and therefore revenue recognition should be permitted at the time the contract is signed. Butler has transferred control to Baristo; that is, Butler has a right to payment for the fireplaces and legal title has transferred.

Butler makes the following entry to record the bill-and-hold sale and related cost of goods sold.

March 1, 2017

Accounts Receivable	450,000	
Sales Revenue		450,000
Cost of Goods Sold	280,000	
Inventory		280,000

A = L + SE
+170,000   +170,000

Cash flows: No effect

Principal-Agent Relationships

In a **principal-agent relationship**, the principal's performance obligation is to provide goods or perform services for a customer. The agent's performance obligation is to arrange for the principal to provide these goods or services to a customer. Examples of principal-agent relationships are as follows.

- Preferred Travel Company (agent) facilitates the booking of cruise excursions by finding customers for Regency Cruise Company (principal).

- Pricey Limited (agent) facilitates the sale of various services such as car rentals at Hero Limited (principal).

In these types of situations, amounts collected on behalf of the principal are not revenue of the agent. Instead, revenue for the agent is the amount of the commission it receives (usually a percentage of the total sale price). Illustration 6-25 provides an example of the issues related to principal-agent relationships.

Illustration 6-25

Recognition—Principal-Agent Relationship

PRINCIPAL-AGENT RELATIONSHIP

Facts: Fly-Away Travel sells airplane tickets for British Airways (BA) to various customers.

Questions: (a) What are the performance obligations in this situation? (b) How should revenue be recognized for both the principal and agent?

Solution:
(a) The principal in this case is BA and the agent is Fly-Away Travel. Because BA has the performance obligation to provide air transportation to the customer, it is the principal. Fly-Away Travel facilitates the sale of the airline ticket to the customer in exchange for a fee or commission. Its performance obligation is to arrange for BA to provide air transportation to the customer.
(b) Although Fly-Away collects the full airfare from the customer, it then remits this amount to BA less the commission. Fly-Away therefore should not record the full amount of the fare as revenue on its books; to do so overstates revenue. Its revenue is the commission, not the full price. Control of performing the air transportation is with BA, not Fly-Away Travel.

Some might argue that there is no harm in letting Fly-Away record revenue for the full price of the ticket and then charging the cost of the ticket against the revenue. (This is often referred to as the **gross method** of recognizing revenue.) Others note that this approach overstates the agent's revenue and is misleading. The revenue received is the commission for providing the travel services, not the full fare price. (This is often referred to as the **net approach**.) The accounting profession believes that the net approach is the correct method for recognizing revenue in a principal-agent relationship. As a result, the IASB has developed specific criteria to determine when a principal-agent relationship exists.[26] An important feature in deciding whether Fly-Away is acting as an agent is whether the amount it earns is predetermined, being either a fixed fee per transaction or a stated percentage of the amount billed to the customer.

WHAT DO THE NUMBERS MEAN?

REAL WORLD EMPHASIS

Many corporate executives obsess over the bottom line—net income. However, analysts on the outside look at the big picture, which includes examining both the top line—revenues—and the important subtotals in the income statement, such as gross profit. Recently, the top line is causing some concern, with nearly all companies in the S&P 500 reporting a 2% decline in the bottom line and a 1% decline in the top line. This is troubling because it was the first decline in revenues since North America crawled out of the recession following the financial crisis. **McDonald's** gave an ominous preview—it saw its first monthly sales decline in nine years. And sales in the United States, rather than foreign markets, led to the drop.

What about income subtotals like gross margin? These metrics too have been under pressure. There is a concern that struggling companies may manipulate numbers to mask the impact of gross margin declines on the bottom line. In fact, the U.S. drugstore chain **Rite Aid** prepares an income statement that omits the gross margin subtotal. That is not surprising when you consider that Rite Aid's gross margin steadily declined from 28% in 2010 to 26% in 2012. Rite Aid has used a number of suspect accounting adjustments related to tax allowances and inventory gains to offset its weak gross margin.

Or, consider the classic case of **Priceline.com**, the company made famous by William Shatner's ads about "naming your own price" for airline tickets and hotel rooms. In one quarter, Priceline reported that it earned $152 million in revenues. But that included the full amount customers paid for tickets, hotel rooms, and rental cars. Traditional travel agencies call that amount "gross bookings," not revenues. And, much like regular travel agencies, Priceline keeps only a small portion of gross bookings—namely, the spread between the customers' accepted bids and the price it paid for the merchandise. The rest, which Priceline calls "product costs," it pays to the airlines and hotels that supply the tickets and rooms.

However, Priceline's product costs came to $143 million, leaving Priceline just $18 million of what it calls "gross profit" and what most other companies would call revenues. And that's before all of Priceline's other costs, like advertising and salaries, which netted out to a loss of $102 million. The difference isn't academic. Priceline shares traded at about 23 times its reported revenues but a mind-boggling 214 times its "gross profit." This and other aggressive recognition practices explain the stricter revenue recognition guidance, indicating that, if a company performs as an agent or broker without assuming the risks and rewards of ownership of the goods, the company should report sales on a net (fee) basis.

Sources: Jeremy Kahn, "Presto Chango! Sales Are Huge," *Fortune* (March 20, 2000), p. 44; A. Catanach and E. Ketz, "RITE AID: Is Management Selling Drugs or Using Them?" *Grumpy Old Accountants* (August 22, 2011); S. Jakab, "Weak Revenue Is New Worry for Investors," *Wall Street Journal* (November 25, 2012).

Consignments

A common principal-agent relationship involves consignments. In these cases, manufacturers (or wholesalers) deliver goods but retain title to the goods until they are sold. This specialized method of marketing certain types of products makes use of an agreement known as a **consignment**. Under this arrangement, the **consignor** (manufacturer or wholesaler) ships merchandise to the **consignee** (dealer), who is to act as an agent for the consignor in selling the merchandise. Both consignor and consignee are interested in selling—the consignor to make a profit or develop a market, the consignee to make a commission on the sale.

The consignee accepts the merchandise and agrees to exercise due diligence in caring for and selling it. The consignee remits to the consignor cash received from customers, after deducting a sales commission and any chargeable expenses. In consignment sales, the consignor uses a modified version of the point-of-sale basis of revenue recognition. That is, the consignor recognizes revenue only after receiving notification of the sale and the cash remittance from the consignee.

The consignor carries the merchandise as inventory throughout the consignment, separately classified as Inventory (consignments). **The consignee does not record the merchandise as an asset on its books.** Upon sale of the merchandise, the consignee has **a liability for the net amount due the consignor**. The consignor periodically receives from the consignee a report called **account sales** that shows the merchandise received, merchandise sold, expenses chargeable to the consignment, and the cash remitted. Revenue is then recognized by the consignor. Analysis of a consignment arrangement is provided in Illustration 6-26.

Under the consignment arrangement, the consignor accepts the risk that the merchandise might not sell and relieves the consignee of the need to commit part of its working capital to inventory. Consignors use a variety of systems and account titles to record consignments, but they all share the common goal of postponing the recognition of revenue until it is known that a sale to a third party has occurred. **Consignees only recognize revenue associated with commissions.**

Warranties

Companies often provide one of two types of **warranties** to customers:

1. Warranties that the product **meets agreed-upon specifications in the contract at the time the product is sold**. This type of warranty is included in the sales price of a company's product and is often referred to as an **assurance-type warranty**.

Illustration 6-26

*Recognition—Sales on
Consignment*

SALES ON CONSIGNMENT

Facts: Nelba Manufacturing Co. ships merchandise costing $36,000 on consignment to Best Value Stores. Nelba pays $3,750 of freight costs, and Best Value pays $2,250 for local advertising costs that are reimbursable from Nelba. By the end of the period, Best Value has sold two-thirds of the consigned merchandise for $40,000 cash. Best Value notifies Nelba of the sales, retains a 10% commission, and remits the cash due to Nelba.

Question: What are the journal entries that the consignor (Nelba) and the consignee (Best Value) make to record this transaction?

Solution:

NELBA MFG. CO. (Consignor)		BEST VALUE STORES (Consignee)	
Shipment of consigned merchandise			
Inventory on Consignment	36,000	No entry (record memo of merchandise	
Finished Goods Inventory	36,000	received).	
Payment of freight costs by consignor			
Inventory on Consignment	3,750	No entry	
Cash	3,750		
Payment of advertising by consignee			
No entry until notified.		Accounts Receivable	2,250
		Cash	2,250
Sales of consigned merchandise			
No entry until notified.		Cash	40,000
		Accounts Payable	40,000
Notification of sales and expenses and remittance of amount due			
Cash	33,750	Accounts Payable	40,000
Advertising Expense	2,250	Accounts Receivable	2,250
Commission Expense	4,000	Revenue from	
Revenue from		Consignment Sales	4,000
Consignment Sales	40,000	Cash	33,750
Adjustment of inventory on consignment for cost of sales			
Cost of Goods Sold	26,500	No entry.	
Inventory on Consignment	26,500		
[2/3 ($36,000 + $3,750) = $26,500]			

2. Warranties that provide an **additional service beyond the assurance-type warranty**. This warranty is not included in the sales price of the product and is referred to as a **service-type warranty**. As a consequence, it is recorded as a separate performance obligation.

Companies do not record a separate performance obligation for assurance-type warranties. This type of warranty is nothing more than a quality guarantee that the good or service is free from defects at the point of sale. These types of obligations should be expensed in the period when the goods are provided or services performed (in other words, at the point of sale). In addition, the company should record a warranty liability. The estimated amount of the liability includes all the costs that the company will incur after sale due to the correction of defects or deficiencies required under the warranty provisions.

In addition, companies sometimes provide customers with an option to purchase a warranty separately. In most cases, these extended warranties provide the customer with a service beyond fixing defects that existed at the time of sale. For example, when you purchase a TV, you are entitled to the company's warranty. You will also undoubtedly be offered an extended warranty on the product at an additional cost. These service-type warranties represent a **separate service and are an additional performance obligation**. As a result, companies should allocate a portion of the transaction price to this performance obligation. The company recognizes revenue in the period that the service-type warranty is in effect. Illustration 6-27 presents an example of both an assurance-type and a service-type warranty.

Illustration 6-27

Recognition—Performance Obligations and Warranties

WARRANTIES

Facts: Maverick Company sold 1,000 Rollomatics during 2017 at a total price of $6 million, with a warranty guarantee that the product was free from any defects. The cost of Rollomatics sold is $4 million. The term of the assurance warranty is two years, with an estimated cost of $30,000. In addition, Maverick sold extended warranties related to 400 Rollomatics for three years beyond the two-year period for $12,000.

Question: What are the journal entries that Maverick Company should make in 2017 related to the sale and the related warranties?

Solution: To record the revenue and liabilities related to the warranties:

Cash ($6,000,000 + $12,000)	6,012,000	
Warranty Expense	30,000	
Warranty Liability		30,000
Unearned Warranty Revenue		12,000
Sales Revenue		6,000,000

To reduce inventory and recognize cost of goods sold:

Cost of Goods Sold	4,000,000	
Inventory		4,000,000

$$A = L + SE$$
$$+2,012,000 \quad +42,000 \quad +1,970,000$$

Cash flows: ↑6,012,000 inflow

Maverick Company reduces the Warranty Liability account over the first two years as the actual warranty costs are incurred. The company also recognizes revenue related to the service-type warranty over the three-year period that extends beyond the assurance warranty period (two years). In most cases, the unearned warranty revenue is recognized on a straight-line basis. The costs associated with the service-type warranty are expensed as incurred.

Non-refundable Upfront Fees

Companies sometimes receive payments (**upfront fees**) from customers before they deliver a product or perform a service. Upfront payments generally relate to the initiation, activation, or setup of a good or service to be provided or performed in the future. In most cases, these upfront payments are non-refundable. Examples include fees paid for membership in a health club or buying club, and activation fees for phone, Internet, or cable. Zynga, in our opening feature story, accepts some advance payments that are non-refundable from customers using its on-line games.

Companies must determine whether these non-refundable advance payments are for products or services in the current period. In most situations, these payments are for future delivery of products and services and should therefore not be recorded as revenue at the time of payment. In some cases, the upfront fee is seen as similar to a renewal option for future products and services at a reduced price. An example would be a health club, where once the initiation fee is paid, no additional fee is necessary upon renewal. Illustration 6-28 provides an example of an upfront fee payment.

Summary of Other Revenue Recognition Issues

Illustration 6-29 provides a summary of the additional issues related to transfer of control and revenue recognition.

Illustration 6-28

Transaction Price—Upfront Fee Considerations

UPFRONT FEE CONSIDERATIONS

Facts: Erica Felise signs a one-year contract with Bigelow Health Club. The terms of the contract are that Erica is required to pay a non-refundable initiation fee of $200 and an annual membership fee of $50 per month. Bigelow determines that its customers, on average, renew their annual membership twice before terminating their membership.

Question: What is the amount of revenue Bigelow Health Club should recognize in the first year?

Solution: In this case, the membership fee arrangement may be viewed as a single performance obligation. (Similar services are provided in all periods and the customers use the services as they are provided.) Bigelow determines the total transaction price to be $2,000—the upfront fee of $200 and the three years of monthly fees of $1,800 ($50 × 36)—and allocates it over the three years. In this case, Bigelow would report revenue of $55.56 ($50 + $200/36) each month for three years.

Illustration 6-29

Summary—Other Revenue Recognition Issues

Issue	Description	Implementation
Right of return	Return of product by customer (such as due to dissatisfaction with the product) in exchange for refunds, a credit against amounts owed or that will be owed, and/or another product in exchange.	Seller may recognize (a) an adjustment to revenue for the product expected to be returned, (b) a refund liability, and (c) an asset for the right to recover the product under IFRS. Under ASPE a sales allowance account is used.
Repurchase agreements	Seller has an obligation or right to repurchase the asset at a later date.	Generally, if the company has an obligation to repurchase the asset for an amount greater than its selling price, then the transaction is a financing transaction.
Bill and hold	Results when the buyer is not yet ready to take delivery but takes title and accepts billing.	Revenue is recognized depending on when the customer obtains control of that product.
Principal-agent	Arrangement in which the principal's performance obligation is to provide goods or perform services for a customer. The agent's performance obligation is to arrange for the principal to provide these goods or services to a customer.	Amounts collected on behalf of the principal are not revenue of the agent. Instead, revenue for the agent is the amount of the commission it receives. The principal recognizes revenue when the goods or services are sold to a third-party customer.
Consignments	A principal-agent relationship in which the consignor (manufacturer or wholesaler) ships merchandise to the consignee (dealer), who is to act as an agent for the consignor in selling the merchandise.	The consignor recognizes revenue only after receiving notification of the sale and the cash remittance from the consignee. (Consignor carries the merchandise as inventory throughout the consignment.) The consignee records commission revenue (usually some percentage of the selling price).
Warranties	Warranties can be assurance-type (product meets agreed-upon specifications) or service-type (provides additional service beyond the assurance-type warranty).	A separate performance obligation is not recorded for assurance-type warranties (considered part of the product). Service-type warranties are recorded as separate performance obligation. Companies should allocate a portion of the transaction price to service type-warranties, when present.
Non-refundable upfront fees	Upfront payments generally relate to initiation, activation, or setup activities for a good or service to be delivered in the future.	The upfront payment should be allocated over the periods benefited.

PRESENTATION AND DISCLOSURE

Presentation

Objective 10
Describe presentation and disclosure regarding revenue.

When General Mills delivers cereal to a Loblaw Companies Limited store (satisfying its performance obligation), it has a right to consideration from Loblaw and therefore has a contract asset. If, on the other hand, Loblaw performs first, by prepaying for this cereal, General Mills has a contract liability. Companies must present these contract assets and contract liabilities on their balance sheets.

Contract Assets and Liabilities

Contract assets are of two types:

1. unconditional rights to receive consideration; for instance, where the company has satisfied its performance obligation with a customer or the amounts due to the company are non-refundable; or

2. conditional rights to receive consideration; for instance, where the company has not satisfied the performance obligation or has satisfied one performance obligation but must satisfy another performance obligation in the contract before it is entitled to the consideration.

Companies should report unconditional rights to receive consideration as a receivable on the balance sheet. Conditional rights on the balance sheet should be reported separately as contract assets. Illustration 6-30 provides an example of the accounting and reporting for a contract asset.[27]

Illustration 6-30

Contract Asset Recognition and Presentation

CONTRACT ASSET

Facts: On January 1, 2017, Finn Company enters into a contract to transfer Product A and Product B to Obermine Co. for $100,000. The contract specifies that payment of Product A will not occur until Product B is also delivered. In other words, payment will not occur until both Product A and Product B are transferred to Obermine. Finn determines that stand-alone prices are $30,000 for Product A and $70,000 for Product B. Finn delivers Product A to Obermine on February 1, 2017. On March 1, 2017, Finn delivers Product B to Obermine.

Question: What journal entries should Finn Company make in regard to this contract in 2017?

Solution: No entry is required on January 1, 2017, because neither party has performed on the contract. On February 1, 2017, Finn records the following entry.

February 1, 2017

Contract Asset	30,000	
Sales Revenue		30,000

$A = L + SE$
$+30,000 \quad +30,000$

Cash flows: No effect

On February 1, Finn has satisfied its performance obligation and therefore reports revenue of $30,000. However, it does not record an account receivable at this point because it does not have an unconditional right to receive the $100,000 unless it also transfers Product B to Obermine. In other words, a contract asset occurs generally when a company must satisfy another performance obligation before it is entitled to bill the customer. When Finn transfers Product B on March 1, 2017, it makes the following entry.

March 1, 2017

Accounts Receivable	100,000	
Contract Asset		30,000
Sales Revenue		70,000

$A = L + SE$
$+70,000 \quad +70,000$

Cash flows: No effect

As indicated above, a **contract liability** is a company's obligation to transfer goods or services to a customer for which the company has received consideration from the customer. Illustration 6-31 provides an example of the recognition and presentation of a contract liability.

Illustration 6-31

Contract Liability Recognition and Presentation

CONTRACT LIABILITY

Facts: On March 1, 2017, Henly Company enters into a contract to transfer a product to Propel Inc. on July 31, 2017. Propel agrees to pay the full price of $10,000 in advance on April 15, 2017. Henly delivers the product on July 31, 2017. The cost of the product is $7,500.

Question: What journal entries are required in 2017?

Solution: No entry is required on March 1, 2017, because neither party has performed on the contract. On receiving the cash on April 5, 2017, Henly records the following entry.

April 15, 2017

Cash	10,000	
Unearned Sales Revenue		10,000

July 31, 2017

Unearned Sales Revenue	10,000	
Sales Revenue		10,000

In addition, Henly records cost of goods sold as follows.

Cost of Goods Sold	7,500	
Inventory		7,500

A = L + SE
+10,000 +10,000
Cash flows: ↑10,000 inflow

A = L + SE
−7,500 −10,000 +2,500
Cash flows: No effect

Companies are not required to use the terms "contract assets" and "contract liabilities" on the balance sheet. For example, contract liabilities are performance obligations and therefore more descriptive titles (as noted earlier)—such as unearned service revenue, unearned sales revenue, repurchase liability, and return liability—may be used where appropriate. For contract assets, it is important that financial statement users can differentiate between unconditional and conditional rights through appropriate account presentation.

Costs to Obtain and/or Fulfill a Contract

Companies recognize an asset for the incremental costs if these costs are incurred to obtain or fulfill a contract with a customer. In other words, incremental costs are those that a company would not incur if the contract had not been obtained (such as selling commissions). Additional examples are as follows.

(a) Direct labour, direct materials, and allocation of costs that relate directly to the contract (for example, costs of contract management and supervision, insurance, and depreciation of tools and equipment).

(b) Costs that generate or enhance resources of the company that will be used in satisfying performance obligations in the future (for example, intangible design or engineering costs that will continue to give rise to benefits in the future).

Other costs that are expensed as incurred include general and administrative costs (unless those costs are explicitly chargeable to the customer under the contract) as well as costs of wasted materials, labour, or other resources to fulfill the contract that were not reflected in the price of the contract. That is, **companies only capitalize costs that are direct, incremental, and recoverable** (assuming that the contract period is more than one year). Illustration 6-32 provides an example of costs capitalized to fulfill a contract.[28]

Illustration 6-32

Recognition—Contract Costs

CONTRACT COSTS

Facts: Rock Integrators enters into a contract to operate Dello Company's information technology data centre for five years. Rock Integrators incurs selling commission costs of $10,000 to obtain the contract. Before performing the services, Rock Integrators designs and builds a technology platform that interfaces with Dello's systems. That platform is not transferred to Dello. Dello promises to pay a fixed fee of $20,000 per month. Rock Integrators incurs the following costs: design services for the platform $40,000, hardware for the platform $120,000, software $90,000, and migration and testing of data centre $100,000.

Question: What are Rock Integrators' costs for fulfilling the contract to Dello Company?

Solution: The $10,000 selling commission costs related to obtaining the contract are recognized as an asset. The design services, the hardware, and the software are also capitalized (as property, plant, and equipment, and intangible assets). The migration and testing costs may also be capitalized since they are direct, incremental, and recoverable.

As a practical expedient, a company recognizes the incremental costs of obtaining a contract as an expense when incurred if the amortization period of the asset that the company otherwise would have recognized is one year or less.

Collectibility

As indicated earlier, if it is probable that the transaction price will not be collected, this is an indication that the parties are not committed to their obligations. As a result, one of the criteria for the existence of a contract is not met and therefore revenue is not recognized.

Any time a company sells a product or performs a service on account, a possible collectibility issue occurs. **Collectibility** refers to a customer's credit risk; that is, the risk that a customer will be unable to pay the amount of consideration in accordance with the contract. Under the revenue guidance, as long as a contract exists (it is probable that the customer will pay), the amount recognized as revenue is not adjusted for customer credit risk.

Thus, companies report the revenue gross (without consideration of credit risk) and then present an allowance for any impairment due to bad debts (recognized initially and subsequently in accordance with the respective bad debt guidance). An impairment related to bad debts is reported as an operating expense in the income statement.

Disclosure

The disclosure requirements for revenue recognition are designed to help financial statement users understand the nature, amount, timing, and uncertainty of revenue and cash flows arising from contracts with customers. To achieve that objective, companies disclose qualitative and quantitative information about all of the following:

- *Contracts with customers.* These disclosures include the disaggregation of revenue, presentation of opening and closing balances in contract assets and contract liabilities, and significant information related to their performance obligations.

- *Significant judgements.* These disclosures include judgements and changes in these judgements that affect the determination of the transaction price, the allocation of the transaction price, and the determination of the timing of revenue.

- *Assets recognized from costs incurred to fulfill a contract.* These disclosures include the closing balances of assets recognized to obtain or fulfill a contract, the amount of amortization recognized, and the method used for amortization.

To implement these requirements and meet the disclosure objectives, companies provide a range of disclosures, as summarized in Illustration 6-33.[29]

Disclosure Type	Requirements
Disaggregation of revenue	Disclose disaggregated revenue information in categories that depict how the nature, amount, timing, and uncertainty of revenue and cash flows are affected by economic factors. Reconcile disaggregated revenue to revenue for reportable segments.
Reconciliation of contract balances	Disclose opening and closing balances of contract assets (such as unbilled receivables) and liabilities (such as deferred revenue) and provide a qualitative description of significant changes in these amounts. Disclose the amount of revenue recognized in the current period relating to performance obligations satisfied in a prior period (such as from contracts with variable consideration). Disclose the opening and closing balances of trade receivables if not presented elsewhere.
Remaining performance obligations	Disclose the amount of the transaction price allocated to performance obligations of any remaining performance obligations not subject to significant revenue reversal. Provide a narrative discussion of potential additional revenue in constrained arrangements.
Costs to obtain or fulfill contracts	Disclose the closing balances of capitalized costs to obtain and fulfill a contract and the amount of amortization in the period. Disclose the method used to determine amortization for each reporting period.
Other qualitative disclosures	Disclose significant judgements and changes in judgements that affect the amount and timing of revenue from contracts with customers. Disclose how management determines the minimum amount of revenue not subject to the variable consideration constraint.

Illustration 6-33
Revenue Disclosures

ASPE disclosure requirements include accounting policy and major revenue categories (only).

IFRS/ASPE COMPARISON

A Comparison of IFRS and ASPE

Objective 11
Identify differences in accounting between IFRS and ASPE and potential changes.

Illustration 6-34 presents a comparison of IFRS and ASPE related to revenue recognition.

Illustration 6-34
IFRS and ASPE Comparison Chart

	IFRS 15	**Accounting Standards for Private Enterprises (ASPE)—*CPA Canada Handbook*, Part II, Section 3400**	**References related to journal illustrations and select brief exercises**
Recognition	Contract-based approach consists of five steps: 1. Identify contract. 2. Identify separate performance obligations (must be distinct and separately identifiable from other obligations in the contract). 3. Determine transaction price (expected consideration). 4. Allocate transaction price to each performance obligation on the basis of stand-alone value. 5. Recognize revenue when performance obligation is satisfied (when control passes).	Earnings approach requires recognition when performance is achieved (risks and rewards have passed and services are rendered and measurable) and collectible.	NA

(continued)

Illustration 6-34

IFRS and ASPE Comparison Chart (continued)

	IFRS 15	Accounting Standards for Private Enterprises (ASPE)—*CPA Canada Handbook*, Part II, Section 3400	References related to journal illustrations and select brief exercises
	Recognize revenue for each distinct performance obligation at a point in time or over time.	Percentage-of-completion and completed-contract methods allowed for long-term contracts. See Appendix 6A.	Illustrations 6A-5 and 6A-10; BE6-28, BE6-29, and BE6-30
	Recognize revenue over time only if one of the following is met: (1) the customer receives and consumes the benefit over time, (2) the customer controls the asset being created, or (3) the asset does not have any alternate use and the company has an enforceable right to payment.		
	If providing goods and services together, must consider if performance obligations are interrelated. (If they are, treat as one performance obligation.)		
	Percentage-of-completion method is acceptable. See Appendix 6A.		
	May recognize revenue equal to cost if outcome is not determinable (zero-profit method). See Appendix 6A.		
	Assurance-type warranties are accrued as costs/liabilities and service-type warranties are treated as separate performance obligations (if sold separately).	Warranty costs have historically been accrued as costs/obligations when revenues recognized. More recently, these may have been accounted for as bundled sales (unearned revenues).	N/A In practice, the two standards are very similar.
Measurement	Transaction price is the amount that the entity expects to receive.	At transaction or consideration price, which is generally assumed to be fair value.	Illustrations 6-8 and 6-11; BE6-6, BE6-8, BE6-9, and BE6-10
	Greater emphasis is placed on using measurement models to quantify risk/uncertainty.	Where payment is received over time, ASPE notes that the amount should be discounted using a prevailing market rate.	
	Guidance is provided as to how to calculate discount rate where the sale is financed. If the term is less than one year, there is no need to separate out the financing component.		
	Where variable consideration exists, revenue is recognized only if it is highly probable that a future reversal will not occur.		

(continued)

IAS 41 deals with biological assets. It still stands because the proposed standard does not cover these areas.	Accounting for biological assets is not explicitly discussed.	Illustration 8-26 (Chapter 8)
The transaction price for transactions with multiple elements is allocated using relative fair value (although may estimate where not available and may use residual method to estimate). Specific guidance is given.	The transaction price for transactions with multiple elements is allocated using relative fair value or residual value method (choice).	Illustration 6-13
Where a right of return exists, a refund liability is recognized.	Where a right of return exists, sales returns and allowances are recognized as contra accounts to Revenues and Accounts Receivable.	

Looking Ahead

At the time of writing this chapter, the IASB had agreed to push back the mandatory adoption date for IFRS 15 to periods beginning on or after January 1, 2018. Earlier adoption is permitted. It will be interesting to see whether the IFRS 15 guidance is incorporated into ASPE in future. Given that ASPE guidance is fairly general and high level, and IFRS 15 provides a fair bit of insight as to the nature of different revenue contracts, these insights may find their way into ASPE informally, even if the wording of the standard is not changed.

SUMMARY OF LEARNING OBJECTIVES

1 Understand the economics and legalities of selling transactions from a business perspective.

It is critical to understand a transaction from a business perspective before attempting to account for it. The analysis should begin with what is being sold to the customer (goods or services) and also note the nature and amount of the consideration. When one party is in a better bargaining position than the other, it may be able to negotiate concessions such as more lenient payment terms. These concessions complicate the accounting because they introduce measurement uncertainty in many cases.

Selling transactions are based on contractual arrangements between a buyer and a seller. Contracts create rights and obligations under law that must be considered when accounting for the transactions. In addition to contractual law, rights and obligations may exist under other forms of the law, such as common law or contract law. These should also be considered.

2 Identify the five steps in the revenue recognition process.

The five steps in the revenue recognition process are (1) identify the contract with customers, (2) identify the separate performance obligations in the contract, (3) determine the transaction price, (4) allocate the transaction price to the separate performance obligations, and (5) recognize revenue when each performance obligation is satisfied.

3 Identify the contract with customers.

A contract is an agreement that creates enforceable rights or obligations. A company applies the revenue guidance to contracts with customers and must determine if new performance obligations are created by a contract modification.

4 Identify the separate performance obligations in the contract.

A performance obligation is a promise in a contract to provide a product or service to a customer. A contract may be composed of multiple performance obligations. The accounting for multiple performance obligations is based on evaluation of whether the product or service is distinct within the contract. If each of the goods or services is distinct, but they are interdependent and interrelated, these goods and services are combined and reported as one performance obligation.

5 Determine the transaction price.

The transaction price is the amount of consideration that a company expects to receive from a customer in exchange for transferring goods and services. In determining the transaction price, companies must consider the following factors: (1) variable consideration, (2) time value of money, (3) noncash consideration, and (4) consideration paid or payable to a customer.

6 Allocate the transaction price to the separate performance obligations.

If more than one performance obligation exists in a contract, allocate the transaction price based on relative fair values. The best measure of fair value is what the good or service could be sold for on a stand-alone basis (stand-alone selling price). Estimates of stand-alone selling price can be based on (1) adjusted market assessment, (2) expected cost plus a margin approach, or (3) a residual approach.

7   Understand how to recognize revenue when the company satisfies its performance obligation.

A company satisfies its performance obligation when the customer obtains control of the good or service. Companies satisfy performance obligations either at a point in time or over a period of time. Companies recognize revenue over a period of time if (1) the customer controls the asset as it is created or the company does not have an alternative use for the asset, and (2) the company has a right to payment.

8   Analyze and determine whether a company has earned revenues under the earnings approach.

Under ASPE, the revenues are earned when the risks and rewards of ownership are passed or when the company has done what it said it would do to be entitled to the revenues. Where sales of goods are involved, legal title and possession provide evidence of this. The accounting is more complex when the contract is a long-term contract and when it involves both goods and services.

9   Identify other revenue recognition issues.

Refer to Illustration 6-29 for a summary of the accounting for (1) right of return, (2) repurchase agreements,

(3) bill-and-hold sales, (4) principal-agent relationships, (5) consignments, (6) warranties, and (7) non-refundable upfront fees.

10   Describe presentation and disclosure regarding revenue.

Under the asset-liability approach, to recognize revenue, companies present contract assets and contract liabilities on their balance sheets (net). Contract assets are rights to receive consideration. A contract liability is a company's obligation to transfer goods or services to a customer for which the company has received consideration from the customer. Companies may also report assets associated with fulfillment costs and contract acquisition costs related to a revenue arrangement. Companies disclose qualitative and quantitative information about (1) contracts with customers with disaggregation of revenue, presentation of opening and closing balances in contract assets and contract liabilities, and significant information related to their performance obligations; (2) significant judgements that affect the determination of the transaction price, the allocation of the transaction price, and the determination of the timing of revenue; and (3) assets recognized from costs incurred to fulfill a contract.

11   Identify differences in accounting between IFRS and ASPE and potential changes.

The main differences are identified in the chart in Illustration 6-34.

KEY TERMS

arm's length, p. 275
asset-liability approach, p. 280
assurance-type warranty, p. 300
barter transactions, p. 276
bill-and-hold arrangement, p. 298
bundled sales, p. 274
collectibility, p. 306
commercial substance, p. 276
consignee, p. 300
consignment, p. 300
consignor, p. 300
constructive obligation, p. 279

contract, p. 282
contract assets, p. 304
contract liability, p. 305
contract modification, p. 283
control, p. 281
credit risk, p. 276
earnings approach, p. 280
FOB destination, p. 278
FOB shipping point, p. 278
legal title, p. 278
multiple deliverables, p. 274
nonmonetary transactions, p. 276

performance obligation, p. 283
possession, p. 278
price risk, p. 276
principal-agent relationship, p. 298
repurchase agreements, p. 296
revenue recognition principle, p. 295
right of return, p. 295
service-type warranty, p. 301
transaction price, p. 285
upfront fees, p. 302
warranties, p. 300

APPENDIX 6A

LONG-TERM CONTRACTS

Objective 12
Apply the percentage-of-completion method for long-term contracts.

For the most part, companies recognize revenue at a point in time because that is when the control over the goods and services passes and the performance obligation is satisfied. Accounting for long-term contracts poses some challenges, however, because they have some unique features. Not only are they longer term (often spanning several reporting periods) but they often include unique contract terms, such as granting the ability to send progress billings. This right to bill helps the company finance the project. Examples of long-term contracts are construction-type contracts, development of military and commercial aircraft, weapons delivery systems, and space exploration hardware.

We view some long-term contracts as a series of distinct performance obligations and therefore revenue is recognized over time as each performance obligation is satisfied (at various points in time throughout the life of the contract). When the project consists of separable units, such as a group of buildings or kilometres of roadway, the contract may provide for delivery over time as each stage is complete. In that case, the seller would bill the buyer and transfer title at stated stages of completion, such as the completion of each building unit or every 10 km of road. Revenue is recognized at each stage.

As noted earlier in the chapter, under IFRS 15.35 a company satisfies a performance obligation and recognizes revenue over time **only if** at least one of the following criteria is met and the company is able to estimate progress toward completion:

1. The customer receives and consumes the benefit as the seller performs;

2. The customer controls the asset; or

3. The company does not have an alternate use for the asset and has a right to payment for its performance.[30]

If one of these criteria is not met, then revenue is recognized at a point in time. ASPE criteria are more general, requiring that revenue should reflect the work accomplished. This is not necessarily different but could result in differences in accounting in practice.

Percentage-of-Completion Method

Alternative Terminology

For construction contracts, Contract Assets may be referred to as "Construction in Process" and Contract Liabilities as "Billings." We will use the terms Contract Asset/Liability, since the amount is reported on a net basis and is more transparent in that it shows the net contract position.

If one of the criteria is met, and **if the company can reasonably estimate its progress toward satisfaction of the performance obligations, then the company recognizes revenue over time.** That is, it recognizes revenues and gross profits each period based upon the progress of the construction—referred to as the **percentage-of-completion method.** The company accumulates construction costs and progress billings in separate accounts that represent contractual rights and obligations (Contract Asset/Liability, and Accounts Receivable). To defer recognition of these items until completion of the entire contract is to misrepresent the efforts (costs) and accomplishments (revenues) of the accounting periods during the contract.

The rationale for using percentage-of-completion accounting is that under most of these contracts, the buyer and seller have enforceable rights. The buyer has the legal right to require specific performance on the contract. The seller has the right to require progress payments that provide evidence of the buyer's ownership interest. As a result, a continuous sale occurs as the work progresses. Companies should recognize revenue according to that progression.

Under IFRS, if one of the criteria is met but an estimate cannot be made, then the company records recoverable revenues equal to costs until the uncertainty is resolved. This is known as the **zero-profit method.** Under ASPE, the entity would use the **completed-contract method** as a default method and recognize revenues only at the end of the contract. We will discuss this further later in this Appendix.

In order to apply the percentage-of-completion method, a company must have some basis or standard for measuring the progress toward completion at particular interim dates.

Measuring the Progress Toward Completion

Companies use various methods to determine the **extent of progress toward completion.** The most common are the cost-to-cost and units-of-delivery methods.

As indicated in the chapter, the objective of all these methods is to measure the extent of progress in terms of costs, units, or value added. Companies identify the various measures (costs incurred, labour hours worked, tonnes produced, floors completed, and so on) and classify them as input or output measures. **Input measures** (costs incurred, labour hours worked) are efforts devoted to a contract. **Output measures** (with units of delivery measured as tonnes produced, floors of a building completed, kilometres of a highway completed) track results. Neither measure is universally applicable to all long-term projects. Their use requires the exercise of judgement and careful tailoring to the circumstances.

Both input and output measures have certain disadvantages. The input measure is based on an established relationship between a unit of input and productivity. If inefficiencies cause the productivity relationship to change, inaccurate measurements result. Another potential problem is front-end loading, in which significant upfront costs result in higher estimates of completion. To avoid this problem, companies should disregard some early-stage construction costs—for example, costs of uninstalled materials or costs of subcontracts not yet performed—if they do not relate to contract performance.

Similarly, output measures can produce inaccurate results if the units used are not comparable in time, effort, or cost to complete. For example, using floors (storeys) completed can be deceiving. Completing the first floor of an eight-storey building may require more than one-eighth the total cost because of the substructure and foundation construction.

The most popular input measure used to determine the progress toward completion is the **cost-to-cost basis**. Under this basis, a company like CGI, the Montreal-based information technology consulting company, could measure the percentage of completion by comparing costs incurred to date with the most recent estimate of the total costs required to complete the contract. Illustration 6A-1 shows the formula for the cost-to-cost basis.

Illustration 6A-1	
Formula for Percentage-of-Completion, Cost-to-Cost Basis	$$\frac{\text{Costs incurred to date}}{\text{Most recent estimate of total costs}} = \text{Percent complete}$$

Once CGI knows the percentage that costs incurred represent of total estimated costs, it would apply that percentage to the total revenue or the estimated total gross profit on the contract. The resulting amount is the revenue or the gross profit to be recognized to date. Illustration 6A-2 shows this calculation.

Illustration 6A-2	
Formula for Total Revenue (or Gross Profit) to Be Recognized to Date	$$\begin{array}{c}\text{Percent} \\ \text{complete}\end{array} \times \begin{array}{c}\text{Estimated} \\ \text{total revenue} \\ \text{(or gross profit)}\end{array} = \begin{array}{c}\text{Revenue (or gross} \\ \text{profit) to be} \\ \text{recognized to date}\end{array}$$

To find the amounts of revenue and gross profit recognized each period, CGI would subtract total revenue or gross profit recognized in prior periods, as shown in Illustration 6A-3.

Illustration 6A-3	
Formula for Amount of Current-Period Revenue (or Gross Profit), Cost-to-Cost Basis	$$\begin{array}{c}\text{Revenue (or gross} \\ \text{profit) to be} \\ \text{recognized to date}\end{array} - \begin{array}{c}\text{Revenue (or gross} \\ \text{profit) recognized} \\ \text{in prior periods}\end{array} = \begin{array}{c}\text{Current-period} \\ \text{revenue} \\ \text{(or gross profit)}\end{array}$$

Because **the cost-to-cost method is widely used** (without excluding other bases for measuring progress toward completion), we have adopted it in our examples.

Example of Percentage-of-Completion Method—Cost-to-Cost Basis

To illustrate the percentage-of-completion method, assume that Hardhat Construction Company has a non-cancellable contract to construct a $4.5-million bridge at an estimated cost of $4 million. The contract is to start in July 2017, and the bridge is to be completed in October 2019. The following data pertain to the construction period. (Note that by the end of 2018, Hardhat has revised the estimated total cost from $4,000,000 to $4,050,000.) Assume that progress billings are non-refundable.

	2017	2018	2019
Costs to date	$1,000,000	$2,916,000	$4,050,000
Estimated costs to complete	3,000,000	1,134,000	–
Progress billings during the year	900,000	2,400,000	1,200,000
Cash collected during the year	750,000	1,750,000	2,000,000

Hardhat would calculate the percentage complete as shown in Illustration 6A-4.

Illustration 6A-4

Application of Percentage-of-Completion Method, Cost-to-Cost Basis

	2017	2018	2019
Contract price	$4,500,000	$4,500,000	$4,500,000
Less estimated cost:			
Costs to date	1,000,000	2,916,000	4,050,000
Estimated costs to complete	3,000,000	1,134,000	–
Estimated total costs	4,000,000	4,050,000	4,050,000
Estimated total gross profit	$ 500,000	$ 450,000	$ 450,000
Percent complete	25%	72%	100%
	$\left(\dfrac{\$1,000,000}{\$4,000,000}\right)$	$\left(\dfrac{\$2,916,000}{\$4,050,000}\right)$	$\left(\dfrac{\$4,050,000}{\$4,050,000}\right)$

On the basis of the data above, Hardhat would make the following entries to record (1) the costs of construction, (2) progress billings, (3) collections, and (4) revenues and costs. These entries appear as summaries of the many transactions that would be entered individually as they occur during the year. Note that the amount of billings represents consideration that is unconditional because the contract is non-cancellable and the billings non-refundable. It is therefore recorded as Accounts Receivable. The entries are shown in Illustration 6A-5.

Illustration 6A-5

Journal Entries—Percentage-of-Completion Method, Cost-to-Cost Basis

	2017		2018		2019	
To record cost of construction						
Contract Asset/Liability	$1,000,000		$1,916,000		$1,134,000	
Materials, Payables, Cash, and so on		$1,000,000		$1,916,000		$1,134,000
To record progress billings						
Accounts Receivable	$900,000		$2,400,000		$1,200,000	
Contract Asset/Liability		$900,000		$2,400,000		$1,200,000
The debit represents an unconditional right to receive consideration because the billings are non-refundable and the contract non-cancellable. The credit represents unearned revenue.						
To record collections						
Cash	$750,000		$1,750,000		$2,000,000	
Accounts Receivable		$750,000		$1,750,000		$2,000,000
To record revenues						
Contract Asset/Liability	$1,125,000		$2,115,000		$1,260,000	
Revenue from Long-Term Contracts		$1,125,000		$2,115,000		$1,260,000
To record construction expense						
Construction Expenses	$1,000,000		$1,916,000		$1,134,000	
Contract Asset/Liability		$1,000,000		$1,916,000		$1,134,000

In this example, the costs incurred to date are a measure of the extent of progress toward completion. To determine this, Hardhat evaluates the costs incurred to date as a proportion of the estimated total costs to be incurred on the project. The estimated revenues that Hardhat will recognize for each year are calculated as shown in Illustration 6A-6.

Illustration 6A-6

Percentage-of-Completion Revenue, Costs, and Gross Profit by Year

	To Date	Recognized in Prior Years	Recognized in Current Year
2017			
Revenues ($4,500,000 × 25%)	$1,125,000		$1,125,000
Costs	1,000,000		1,000,000
Gross profit	$ 125,000		$ 125,000
2018			
Revenues ($4,500,000 × 72%)	$3,240,000	$1,125,000	$2,115,000
Costs	2,916,000	1,000,000	1,916,000
Gross profit	$ 324,000	$ 125,000	$ 199,000
2019			
Revenues ($4,500,000 × 100%)	$4,500,000	$3,240,000	$1,260,000
Costs	4,050,000	2,916,000	1,134,000
Gross profit	$ 450,000	$ 324,000	$ 126,000

Recall that the Hardhat Construction Company example contained a **change in estimated costs**: In the second year, 2018, it increased the estimated total costs from $4,000,000 to $4,050,000. The change in estimate is accounted for in a **cumulative catch-up manner**. This is done by first adjusting the percent completed to the new estimate of total costs. Next, Hardhat deducts the amount of revenues recognized in prior periods from revenues calculated for progress to date. That is, it accounts for the change in estimate in the period of change. That way, the statement of financial position at the end of the period of change and the accounting in subsequent periods are as they would have been if the revised estimate had been the original estimate.

Financial Statement Presentation— Percentage-of-Completion

During the life of the contract, Hardhat reports the contract asset/liability **as current** (assuming the related revenues will be earned in the following year). Accounts receivable are reported as current assuming they will be received within the following year. In general, the Contract Asset/Liability position is shown net on the Statement of Financial Position.

Using data from the bridge example, Hardhat Construction Company would report the status and results of its long-term construction activities under the percentage-of-completion method as shown in Illustration 6A-7.

Illustration 6A-7

Financial Statement Presentation—Percentage-of-Completion Method (2017)

HARDHAT CONSTRUCTION COMPANY	
Income Statement	2017
Revenue from long-term contracts	$1,125,000
Construction expenses	1,000,000
Gross profit	$ 125,000
Balance Sheet (12/31)	2017
Current assets	
Accounts receivable ($900,000 − $750,000)	$ 150,000
Contract asset (net)	$ 225,000*
*($1,000,000 − $900,000 + $1,125,000 − $1,000,000)	

In 2018, its financial statement presentation is as shown in Illustration 6A-8.

Illustration 6A-8

*Financial Statement
Presentation—Percentage-of-
Completion Method (2018)*

HARDHAT CONSTRUCTION COMPANY	
Income Statement	2018
Revenue from long-term contracts	$2,115,000
Construction expenses	1,916,000
Gross profit	$ 199,000
Balance Sheet (12/31)	2018
Current assets	
Accounts receivable ($150,000 + $2,400,000 – $1,750,000)	$ 800,000
Current liabilities	
Contract liability (net)	$ 60,000
($225,000 + $1,916,000 – $2,400,000 + $2,115,000 – $1,916,000)	

In 2019, Hardhat's financial statements only include an income statement because the bridge project was completed and settled. This is shown in Illustration 6A-9.

Illustration 6A-9

*Financial Statement
Presentation—Percentage-of-
Completion Method (2019)*

HARDHAT CONSTRUCTION COMPANY	
Income Statement	2019
Revenue from long-term contracts	$1,260,000
Construction expenses	1,134,000
Gross profit	$ 126,000

As noted earlier, where the outcome of the contract is not determinable and IFRS is a constraint, recoverable amounts equal to cost would be recognized under the zero-profit method. Therefore in 2017 in the example above—only revenues of $1,000,000 would be recognized. The other entries would remain the same. IFRS 15 requires fairly extensive note disclosures.

Completed-Contract Method

Objective 13
Apply the completed-contract method for long-term contracts.

Under ASPE and the completed-contract method, companies recognize revenue and gross profit when the contract is completed. Companies accumulate costs of long-term contracts in process, but they make no interim charges or credits to income statement accounts for revenues, costs, or gross profit. The completed contract method is used where performance consists of a single act or the company is unable to estimate progress toward completion.

The principal advantage of the completed-contract method is that reported revenue reflects final results rather than **estimates** of unperformed work. Its major disadvantage is that it does not reflect current performance when the period of a contract extends into more than one accounting period. Although operations may be fairly uniform during the period of the contract, the company will not report revenue until the year of completion, creating a distortion of earnings.

Under the completed-contract method, the company would make the same **annual entries** to record costs of construction, progress billings, and collections from customers as those illustrated under the percentage-of-completion method. The significant difference is that the company **would not make entries to recognize revenue and construction expenses**.

For example, under the completed-contract method for the bridge project illustrated on the preceding pages, Hardhat Construction Company would make the following entries in 2019 to recognize revenue and costs and to close out the inventory and billing accounts. As noted earlier—sometimes the Construction in Process account is used instead of Contract Asset/Liability.

A = L + SE
+450,000   +450,000

Cash flows: No effect

Contract Asset/Liability	450,000	
Construction Expense	4,050,000	
Revenue from Long-Term Contracts		4,500,000

Illustration 6A-10 compares the amount of gross profit that Hardhat Construction Company would recognize for the bridge project under the two revenue recognition methods.

Illustration 6A-10

Comparison of Gross Profit Recognized under Different Methods

	Percentage-of-Completion	Completed-Contract
2017	$125,000	$ 0
2018	199,000	0
2019	126,000	450,000

Losses on Long-Term Contracts

Two types of losses can occur under long-term contracts:

1. **Loss in current period on a profitable contract:** This condition occurs when there is a significant increase in the estimated total contract costs during construction but the increase does not eliminate all profit on the contract. Under the percentage-of-completion method only, the increase in the estimated cost requires an adjustment in the current period for the excess gross profit that was recognized on the project in prior periods. This adjustment is recorded as a loss in the current period because it is a change in accounting estimate (discussed in Chapter 21).

2. **Loss on an unprofitable contract:** Cost estimates at the end of the current period may indicate that a loss will result once the contract is completed. Under both the percentage-of-completion and completed-contract methods, the entire loss that is expected on the contract must be recognized in the current period.

Loss in Current Period

To illustrate a loss in the current period on a contract that is expected to be profitable upon completion, assume that on December 31, 2018, Hardhat estimates the costs to complete the bridge contract at $1,468,962 instead of $1,134,000. Assuming all other data are the same as before, Hardhat would calculate the percent complete and recognize the loss as shown in Illustration 6A-11. Compare these calculations with those for 2018 in Illustration 6A-4. The percent complete has dropped from 72% to 66½% due to the increase in estimated future costs to complete the contract.

Illustration 6A-11

Calculation of Recognizable Loss, 2018—Loss in Current Period

Cost to date (12/31/18)	$2,916,000
Estimated costs to complete (revised)	1,468,962
Estimated total costs	$4,384,962
Percent complete ($2,916,000 ÷ $4,384,962)	66½%
Revenue recognized in 2018	
($4,500,000 × 66½%) − $1,125,000	$1,867,500
Costs incurred in 2018	1,916,000
Loss recognized in 2018	$ 48,500

The loss of $48,500 in 2018 is a cumulative adjustment of the gross profit that was recognized on the contract in 2017. Instead of restating the prior period, the new estimation is absorbed entirely in the current period. In this illustration, the adjustment was large enough to result in recognition of a loss.

Hardhat would record the loss in 2018 as follows:

A = L + SE
−48,500   −48,500

Cash flows: No effect

Construction Expense	1,916,000	
Contract Asset/Liability		48,500
Revenue from Long-Term Contracts		1,867,500

The loss of $48,500 will be reported on the 2018 income statement as the difference between the reported revenues of $1,867,500 and the costs of $1,916,000.[31] Under the completed-contract method, no loss is recognized in 2018, because the contract is still expected to result in a profit that will be recognized in the year of completion.

Loss on an Unprofitable Contract

Where a contract becomes onerous (that is, the total estimated costs associated with the contract exceed the total revenues), the entity would recognize an overall loss. Any prior profits would be reversed and additional losses recognized.

SUMMARY OF LEARNING OBJECTIVES FOR APPENDIX 6A

12 Apply the percentage-of-completion method for long-term contracts.

To apply the percentage-of-completion method to long-term contracts, a company must have some basis for measuring the progress toward completion at particular interim dates. One of the most popular input measures used to determine the progress toward completion is the cost-to-cost basis. Using this basis, a company measures the percentage of completion by comparing costs incurred to date with the most recent estimate of the total costs to complete the contract. The company applies that percentage to the total revenue or the estimated total gross profit on the contract, to arrive at the amount of revenue or gross profit to be recognized to date.

13 Apply the completed-contract method for long-term contracts.

Under this ASPE method, companies recognize revenue and gross profit only when the company completes the contract. The company accumulates costs of long-term contracts in process and current billings. It makes no interim charges or credits to income statement accounts for revenues, costs, and gross profit. The annual journal entries to record costs of construction, progress billings, and collections from customers would be identical to those for the percentage-of-completion method—with the significant exclusion of the recognition of revenue and gross profit.

KEY TERMS

completed-contract method p. 311	input measures p. 312	percentage-of-completion method p. 311
cost-to-cost basis p. 312	output measures p. 312	zero-profit method p. 311

Note: All assignment material with an asterisk (*) relates to the appendix to the chapter.

Completion of this end-of-chapter material will help develop CPA enabling competencies (such as ethics and professionalism, problem-solving and decision-making and communication) and technical competencies. We have highlighted selected items with an integration icon and material in *WileyPLUS* has been linked to the competencies. All cases emphasize integration, especially of the enabling competencies. The brief exercises, exercises and problems generally emphasize problem-solving and decision-making.

Brief Exercises

(LO 1) BE6-1 Explain the basic economics of what is being received and what is being given up in each of the following business transactions.

ECONOMICS

(a) A company sells packaging material to another company. The terms of sale require full payment upon delivery.

(b) A company sells packaging material to another company. The terms of sale require payment over one year with interest.

(c) A law firm provides legal services to an accounting firm. In lieu of payment, the accounting firm provides accounting services to the law firm.

(d) A company sells telecommunications equipment for a set fee that includes delivery, installation, a 60-day trial period, a three-year maintenance package (often sold separately), and a one-year manufacturer's warranty (often sold separately). Payment will be received over one year without interest.

(LO 1) BE6-2 Explain the rights and obligations created in the following transactions.

(a) A manufacturer sells goods with terms f.o.b. shipping point.

(b) A manufacturer sells goods with terms f.o.b. destination point.

LEGAL

(c) A manufacturer sells goods with terms f.o.b. shipping point, but routinely replaces products lost or damaged during shipping.

(LO 1, 8) BE6-3 XYZ Company has manufactured a new product that will be marketed and sold during the current year. To encourage distributors to carry the product, XYZ will not require payment until the distributor receives the final payment from its customers. This is not a normal business practice for XYZ Company. Should XYZ record revenue of the new product upon delivery to its distributors under the earnings approach? Why or why not?

(LO 3, 10) BE6-4 On May 10, 2017, Cosmo Co. enters into a contract to deliver a product to Greig Inc. on June 15, 2017. Greig agrees to pay the full price of $2,000 on July 15, 2017. The cost of goods is $1,300. Cosmo delivers the product to Greig on June 15, 2017, and receives payment on July 15, 2017. Prepare the journal entries for Cosmo related to this contract.

(LO 4) BE6-5 Ellicott Construction enters into a contract to design and build a hospital. Ellicott is responsible for the overall management of the project and identifies various goods and services to be provided, including engineering, site clearance, foundation, procurement, construction of the structure, piping and wiring, installation of equipment, and finishing. Under IFRS, does Ellicott have a single performance obligation to the customer in this revenue arrangement? Explain.

(LO 5) BE6-6 Gardi Inc. sold a unit of inventory to a buyer for $1,000 payable in one year. Gardi estimates that the interest rate for a similar financing arrangement would be 8%. The unit of inventory normally sells for $900. Assuming that the company recognizes an interest component, calculate the discount rate to be applied in calculating the cash selling price of the unit of inventory. Gardi prepares financial statements in accordance with IFRS.

(LO 5) BE6-7 Massey Ltd., an equipment manufacturer, sold and delivered a piece of equipment to a buyer for $100,000, with 50% payable in one year and the remaining 50% payable in two years from the date of sale. Massey estimates that the interest rate for a similar financing arrangement would be 12%. Calculate the amount of revenue that Massey should recognize on the date of sale.

(LO 5) BE6-8 Nair Corp. enters into a contract with a customer to build an apartment building for $1,000,000. The customer hopes to rent apartments at the beginning of the school year and offers a performance bonus of $150,000 to be paid if the building is ready for rental beginning August 1, 2017. The bonus is reduced by $50,000 each week that completion is delayed. Nair commonly includes these completion bonuses in its contracts and, based on prior experience, estimates the following completion outcomes:

Completed by	Probability
August 1, 2017	70%
August 8, 2017	20
August 15, 2017	5
After August 15, 2017	5

Determine the transaction price for this contract under IFRS.

(LO 5) BE6-9 Referring to the revenue arrangement in BE6-8, determine the transaction price for this contract, assuming (a) Nair is only able to estimate whether the building can be completed by August 1, 2017, or not (Nair estimates that there is a 70% chance that the building will be completed by August 1, 2017); and (b) Nair has limited information with which to develop a reliable estimate of completion by the August 1, 2017 deadline.

(LO 5) BE6-10 On January 2, 2017, Adani Inc. sells goods to Geo Company in exchange for a zero-interest-bearing note with a face value of $11,000, with payment due in 12 months. The fair value of the goods at the date of sale is $10,000 (cost $6,000). Assume that the company chooses to reflect the interest component. Prepare the journal entry to record this transaction on January 2, 2017. How much total revenue should be recognized in 2017?

(LO 5) **BE6-11** On March 1, 2017, Parnevik Company sold goods to Goosen Inc. for $660,000 in exchange for a five-year, zero-interest-bearing note in the face amount of $1,062,937. The goods have an inventory cost on Parnevik's books of $400,000. Prepare the journal entries for Parnevik on (a) March 1, 2017, and (b) December 31, 2017.

(LO 5) **BE6-12** Manual Company sells goods to Nolan Company during 2017. It offers Nolan the following rebates based on total sales to Nolan. If total sales to Nolan are 10,000 units, it will grant a rebate of 2%. If it sells up to 20,000 units, it will grant a rebate of 4%. It if sells up to 30,000 units, it will grant a rebate of 6%. In the first quarter of the year, Manual sells 11,000 units to Nolan at a sales price of $110,000. Based on past experience, Manual has sold over 40,000 units to Nolan, and these sales normally take place in the third quarter of the year. Prepare the journal entry that Manual should make to record the sale of the 11,000 units in the first quarter of the year. Manual follows IFRS.

(LO 6) **BE6-13** Telephone Sellers Inc. sells prepaid telephone cards to customers. Telephone Sellers then pays the telecommunications company, TeleExpress, for the actual use of its telephone lines related to the prepaid telephone cards. Assume that Telephone Sellers sells $4,000 of prepaid cards in January 2017. It then pays TeleExpress based on usage, which turns out to be 50% in February, 30% in March, and 20% in April. The total payment by Telephone Sellers for TeleExpress lines over the three months is $3,000. Indicate how much income Telephone Sellers should recognize in January, February, March, and April under IFRS.

(LO 7) **BE6-14** Mauer Company follows IFRS and licenses consumer-relationship software to Hedges Inc. for three years. In addition to providing the software, Mauer promises to provide consulting services over the life of the licence to maintain operability within Hedges' computer system. The total transaction price is $200,000. Based on stand-alone values, Mauer estimates the consulting services have a value of $75,000 and the software licence has a value of $125,000. Upon installation of the software on July 1, 2017, Hedges pays $100,000; the contract balance is due on December 31, 2017. Identify the performance obligations and the revenue in 2017, assuming (a) the performance obligations are interdependent, and (b) the performance obligations are not interdependent.

(LO 5, 7, 10) **BE6-15** Geraths Windows manufactures and sells custom storm windows for three-season porches. Geraths also provides installation service for the windows. The installation process does not involve changes in the windows, so this service can be performed by other vendors. Geraths enters into the following non-cancellable contract on July 1, 2017, with a local homeowner. The customer purchases windows for a price of $2,400 and chooses Geraths to do the installation. Geraths charges the same price for the windows regardless of whether it does the installation or not. The price of the installation service is estimated to have a fair value of $600. The customer pays Geraths $2,000 (which equals the fair value of the windows, which have a cost of $1,100) upon delivery and the remaining balance upon installation of the windows. The windows are delivered on September 1, 2017, Gerath completes installation on October 15, 2017, and the customer pays the balance due. Prepare the journal entries for Geraths in 2017. (Assume IFRS is a constraint and round amounts to nearest dollar.)

(LO 5, 7, 10) **BE6-16** Refer to the revenue arrangement in BE6-15. Repeat the requirements, assuming (a) Geraths estimates the stand-alone value of the installation based on an estimated cost of $400 plus a margin of 20% on cost, and (b) given the uncertainty of finding skilled labour, Geraths is unable to develop a reliable estimate for the fair value of the installation. (Round to the nearest dollar.)

(LO 2, 8) **BE6-17** What is the earnings process under ASPE for each of the following scenarios?

    (a) A manufacturer makes and sells farm equipment. The customer picks up the equipment upon purchase. In addition, there is a one-year warranty that will be honoured by another company.

    (b) A company sells books on-line and ships to the customer. Payment is made via credit cards and the company does not accept any product returns.

    (c) A company provides cable television services for residential customers. The customer signs a three-year contract. The wiring was already in place from the prior homeowner.

(LO 8) **BE6-18** For each of the scenarios noted in BE6-17, when would revenue be recognized under the earnings approach?

(LO 9) **BE6-19** On August 15, 2017, Japan Ideas consigned 500 electronic play systems, costing $100 each, to YoYo Toys Company. The cost of shipping the play systems amounted to $1,250 and was paid by Japan Ideas. On December 31, 2017, an account sales summary was received from the consignee, reporting that 420 play systems had been sold for $160 each. Remittance was made by the consignee for the amount due, after deducting a 20% commission. Calculate the following at December 31, 2017.

    (a) The inventory value of the units unsold in the hands of the consignee.

    (b) The profit for the consignor for the units sold.

    (c) The amount of cash that will be remitted by the consignee.

(LO 9) BE6-20 On July 10, 2017, Amodt Music sold CDs to retailers on account for a selling price of $700,000 (cost $560,000). Amodt grants the right to return CDs that do not sell in three months following delivery. Past experience indicates that the normal return rate is 15%. By October 11, 2017, retailers returned CDs to Amodt and were granted credits of $78,000. Prepare Amodt's journal entries to record (a) the sale on July 10, 2017, and (b) the $78,000 of actual returns on October 10, 2017. The company follows IFRS.

(LO 9) BE6-21 Kristin Company sells 300 units of its products for $20 each to Logan Inc. for cash. Kristin allows Logan to return any unused product within 30 days and receive a full refund. The cost of each product is $12. To determine the transaction price, Kristin decides that the approach that is most predictive of the amount of consideration to which it will be entitled is the probability-weighted amount. Using the probability-weighted amount, Kristin estimates that (1) 10 products will be returned, and (2) the returned products are expected to be resold at a profit. Prepare the journal entry for Kristin at the time of the sale to Logan. The company follows IFRS.

(LO 9) BE6-22 On June 1, 2017, Mills Company sells $200,000 of shelving units to a local retailer, ShopBarb, which is planning to expand its stores in the area. Under the agreement, ShopBarb asks Mills to retain the shelving units at its factory until the new stores are ready for installation. Title passes to ShopBarb at the time the agreement is signed. The shelving units are delivered to the stores on September 1, 2017, and ShopBarb pays in full. Prepare the journal entries for this bill-and-hold arrangement (assuming that conditions for recognizing the sale have been met) for Mills on June 1 and September 1, 2017. The cost of the shelving units to Mills is $110,000.

(LO 9) BE6-23 Travel Inc. sells tickets for a Caribbean cruise on ShipAway Cruise Lines to Carmel Company employees. The total cruise package price to Carmel Company employees is $70,000. Travel Inc. receives a commission of 6% of the total price. Travel Inc. therefore remits $65,800 to ShipAway. Prepare the journal entry to record the remittance and revenue recognized by Travel Inc. on this transaction.

(LO 9) BE6-24 Jansen Corporation shipped $20,000 of merchandise on consignment to Gooch Company. Jansen paid freight costs of $2,000. Gooch Company paid $500 for local advertising, which is reimbursable from Jansen. By year end, 60% of the merchandise had been sold for $21,500. Gooch notified Jansen, retained a 10% commission, and remitted the cash due to Jansen. Prepare Jansen's journal entry when cash is received.

(LO 9) BE6-25 Talarczyk Company sold 10,000 Super Spreaders on July 1, 2017, at a total price of $1,000,000, with a warranty guarantee that the product was free of any defects. The cost of the spreaders sold is $550,000. The assurance warranties extend for a two-year period and are estimated to cost $40,000. Talarczyk also sold extended warranties (service-type warranties) related to 2,000 spreaders for two years beyond the two-year period for $12,000. Prepare the journal entries that Talarczyk should make in 2017 related to the sale and the related warranties.

(LO 9, 10) BE6-26 On May 1, 2017, Mount Company enters into a contract to transfer a product to Eric Company on September 30, 2017. It is agreed that Eric will pay the full price of $25,000 in advance on June 15, 2017. Eric pays on June 15, 2017, and Mount delivers the product on September 30, 2017. Prepare the journal entries required for Mount in 2017.

(LO 9) BE6-27 Nate Beggs signs a one-year contract with BlueBox Video. The terms of the contract are that Nate is required to pay a non-refundable initiation fee of $100. After the first year, membership can be renewed by paying an annual membership fee of $5 per month. BlueBox determines that its customers, on average, renew their annual membership three times after the first year before terminating their membership. What amount of revenue should BlueBox recognize in its first year? The company follows IFRS.

(LO 10, 12) *BE6-28 Turner Inc. began work on a $7,000,000 non-cancellable contract in 2017 to construct an office building. During 2017, Turner Inc. incurred costs of $1,700,000, billed its customers for $1,200,000 (non-refundable), and collected $960,000. At December 31, 2017, the estimated future costs to complete the project total $3,300,000. Prepare Turner's 2017 journal entries using the percentage-of-completion method.

(LO 10, 13) *BE6-29 Guillen Inc. began work on a $7,000,000 non-cancellable contract in 2017 to construct an office building. Guillen uses the completed-contract method under ASPE. At December 31, 2017, the balances in certain accounts were Contract Asset $1,715,000; Accounts Receivable $240,000; and Contract Liability $1,000,000. Indicate how these accounts would be reported in Guillen's December 31, 2017 balance sheet.

LO 10, 12, 13 *BE6-30 During 2017, Darwin Corporation started a construction job with a contract price of $4.2 million. Darwin ran into severe technical difficulties during construction but managed to complete the job in 2019. The contract is non-cancellable. Under the terms of the contract, Darwin sends billings as revenues are earned. Billings are non-refundable. The following information is available:

	2017	2018	2019
Costs incurred to date	$ 600,000	$2,100,000	$4,100,000
Estimated costs to complete	3,150,000	2,100,000	-0-

Instructions

(a) Calculate the amount of gross profit that should be recognized each year under the percentage-of-completion method.

(b) Prepare the journal entries for 2018 to recognize the revenue from the contract, assuming the percentage-of-completion method is used. Explain the treatment of losses under the percentage-of-completion method.

(c) Calculate the amount of gross profit or loss that should be recognized each year under the completed-contract method. Explain the treatment of losses under the completed-contract method.

Exercises

ECONOMICS

(LO 1) E6-1 (Economics of the Transaction—Various Consumer Industries) The following are independent situations that require professional judgement for determining when to recognize revenue from the transactions.

1. Costco sells you a one-year membership with a single, one-time upfront payment. This non-refundable fee is paid at the time of signing the contract, and entitles you to shop at Costco for one year.

2. DOT Home and Patio sells you patio furniture on a "no money down, no interest, and no payments for one year" promotional deal. The furniture is delivered to your home the same day.

3. The Toronto Blue Jays sell season tickets on-line to games in the Rogers Centre. Fans can purchase the tickets at any time, although the season does not officially begin until April 1. The season runs from April 1 through October each year. Payment is due in full at the time of purchase.

4. CIBC lends you money in August. The loan and interest are repayable in full in two years.

5. Students pre-register for fall classes at Seneca College in August. The fall term runs from September to December.

6. Sears sells you a sweater. In August, you place the order using Sears' on-line catalogue. The sweater is shipped and arrives in September and you charge it to your Sears credit card. In October, you receive the Sears credit card statement and pay the amount due.

7. In March, Hometown Appliances sells a washing machine with an extended warranty plan for five years. The washing machine will not be delivered to the customer until June. Payment is due upon delivery. The extended warranty plans are normally sold separately.

8. Premier Health Clubs sells you a membership with an initiation fee (which covers a medical assessment) and an ongoing monthly fee. The initiation fee is payable at the time of the medical assessment and approximates the cost of the medical assessment.

Instructions

For each scenario, identify what is being "sold": goods, services, or a combination.

(LO 5) E6-2 (Sales with Discounts) Jupiter Company sells goods to Danone Inc. on account on January 1, 2017. The goods have a sales price of $610,000 (cost $500,000). The terms of the sale are net 30. If Danone pays within five days, it receives a cash discount of $10,000. Past history indicates the cash discount will be taken.

Instructions

(a) Prepare the journal entries for Jupiter for January 1, 2017.

(b) Prepare the journal entries for Jupiter for January 31, 2017, assuming Danone does not make payment until January 31, 2017.

(LO 5) E6-3 (Transaction Price) Presented below are three revenue recognition situations.

(a) Grupo sells goods to MTN for $1,000,000, payment due at delivery.

(b) Grupo sells goods on account to Grifols for $800,000, payment due in 30 days.

(c) Grupo sells goods to Magnus for $500,000, payment due in two instalments: the first instalment payable in 18 months, and the second payment due 6 months later. The present value of the future payments is $464,000.

Instructions

Indicate the transaction price for each of these transactions and when revenue will be recognized.

(LO 5) E6-4 (Variable Consideration) Blair Biotech enters into a licensing agreement with Pang Pharmaceutical for a drug under development. Blair will receive a payment of $10,000 if the drug receives regulatory approval. Based on prior experience with the drug-approval process, Blair determines it is 90% likely that the drug will gain approval, with a 10% chance of denial.

Instructions

(a) Determine the transaction price of the arrangement for Blair Biotech.

(b) Assuming that regulatory approval was granted on December 20, 2017, and that Blair received the payment from Pang on January 15, 2018, prepare the journal entries for Blair.

(LO 5) E6-5 (Trailing Commission) Aaron's Agency sells an insurance policy offered by Capital Insurance Company for a commission of $100. In addition, Aaron will receive a further commission of $10 each year for as long as the policyholder does not cancel the policy. After selling the policy, Aaron does not have any remaining performance obligations. Based on its significant experience with these types of policies, Aaron estimates that policyholders on average renew the policy for 4.5 years. It has no evidence to suggest that previous policyholder behaviour will change.

Instructions

(a) Determine the transaction price of the arrangement for Aaron, assuming 100 policies are sold.

(b) Prepare the journal entries, assuming that the 100 policies are sold in January 2017 and that Aaron receives commissions from Capital.

(LO 5) E6-6 (Sales with Discounts) On June 3, 2017, Hunt Company sold to Ann Mount merchandise having a sales price of $8,000 (cost $5,600) with terms of 2/10, n/60, f.o.b. shipping point. Hunt estimates that merchandise with a sales value of $800 will be returned. An invoice totalling $120, terms n/30, was received by Mount on June 8 from Olympic Transport Service for the freight cost. Upon receipt of the goods, on June 5, Mount notified Hunt that $300 of merchandise contained flaws. The same day, Hunt issued a credit memo covering the defective merchandise and asked that it be returned at Hunt's expense. Hunt estimated the returned items to have a fair value of $120. The freight on the returned merchandise was $24, paid by Hunt on June 7. On June 12, the company received a cheque for the balance due from Mount.

Instructions

(a) Prepare journal entries for Hunt Company to record all the events noted above, assuming sales and receivables are entered at gross selling price.

(b) Prepare the journal entry, assuming that Ann Mount did not remit payment until August 5.

(LO 5) E6-7 (Sales with Discounts) Taylor Marina has 300 available slips that rent for $800 per season. Payments must be made in full by the start of the boating season, April 1, 2018. The boating season ends October 31, and the marina has a December 31 year-end. Slips for future seasons may be reserved if paid for by December 31, 2018. Under a new policy, if payment for 2019 season slips is made by December 31, 2018, a 5% discount is allowed. If payment for 2020 season slips is made by December 31, 2018, renters get a 20% discount (this promotion will hopefully provide cash flow for major dock repairs).

On December 31, 2017, all 300 slips for the 2018 season were rented at full price. On December 31, 2018, 200 slips were reserved and paid for the 2019 boating season, and 60 slips were reserved and paid for the 2020 boating season.

FINANCE

Instructions

(a) Prepare the appropriate journal entries for December 31, 2017, and December 31, 2018.

DIGGING
DEEPER

(b) Assume the marina operator is unsophisticated in business. Explain the managerial significance of the above accounting to this person.

(LO 6) E6-8 (Allocate Transaction Price) Sanchez Co. enters into a contact to sell Product A and Product B on January 2, 2017, for an upfront cash payment of $150,000. Product A will be delivered in two years (January 2, 2019) and Product B will be delivered in five years (January 2, 2022). Sanchez Co. allocates the $150,000 to Products A and B on a relative stand-alone selling price basis as follows.

	Stand-Alone Selling Prices	Percent Allocated	Allocated Amounts
Product A	$ 40,000	25%	$ 37,500
Product B	120,000	75%	112,500
	$160,000		$150,000

Sanchez Co. uses an interest rate of 6%, which is its incremental borrowing rate.

Instructions

(a) Prepare the journal entries necessary on January 2, 2017, and December 31, 2017.

(b) Prepare the journal entries necessary on December 31, 2018.

(c) Prepare the journal entries necessary on January 2, 2019.

(LO 6) E6-9 (Allocate Transaction Price) Shaw Company sells goods that cost $300,000 to Ricard Company for $410,000 on January 2, 2017. The sales price includes an installation fee, which is valued at $40,000. The fair value of the goods is $370,000. The installation is considered a separate performance obligation and is expected to take six months to complete.

Instructions

(a) Prepare the journal entries (if any) to record the sale on January 2, 2017.

(b) Shaw prepares an income statement for the first quarter of 2017, ending on March 31, 2017 (installation was completed on June 18, 2017). How much revenue should Shaw recognize related to its sale to Ricard?

(LO 6) E6-10 (Allocate Transaction Price) Crankshaft Company manufactures equipment. Crankshaft's products range from simple automated machinery to complex systems containing numerous components. Unit selling prices range from $200,000 to $1,500,000, and are quoted inclusive of installation. The installation process does not involve changes to the features of the equipment to perform to specifications. Crankshaft has the following arrangement with Winkerbean Inc.

- Winkerbean purchases equipment from Crankshaft for a price of $1,000,000 and contracts with Crankshaft to install the equipment. Crankshaft charges the same price for the equipment irrespective of whether it does the installation or not. Using market data, Crankshaft determines that the installation service is estimated to have a fair value of $50,000. The cost of the equipment is $600,000.

- Winkerbean is obligated to pay Crankshaft the $1,000,000 upon delivery and installation of the equipment.

Crankshaft delivers the equipment on June 1, 2017, and completes the installation of the equipment on September 30, 2017. The equipment has a useful life of 10 years. Assume that the equipment and the installation are two distinct performance obligations that should be accounted for separately.

Instructions

(a) How should the transaction price of $1,000,000 be allocated among the service obligations?

(b) Prepare the journal entries for Crankshaft for this revenue arrangement in 2017, assuming Crankshaft receives payment when installation is completed.

↳ equipment useless until installed

	Sept. 30	Cash	1,000,000	
		Sales revenue		952,381
		Service revenue - Installation		47,619
		COGS	600,000	
		Inventory		600,000

(LO 6) E6-11 (Allocate Transaction Price) Refer to the revenue arrangement in E6-10.

Instructions

Repeat requirements (a) and (b), assuming Crankshaft does not have market data with which to determine the stand-alone selling price of the installation services. As a result, an expected cost plus margin approach is used. The cost of installation is $36,000; Crankshaft prices these services with a 25% margin relative to cost.

(LO 6) E6-12 (Allocate Transaction Price) Appliance Centre is an experienced home appliance dealer. Appliance Centre also offers a number of services together with the home appliances that it sells. Assume that Appliance Centre sells ovens on a stand-alone basis. Appliance Centre also sells installation services and maintenance services for ovens. However, Appliance Centre does not offer installation or maintenance services to customers who buy ovens from other vendors. Pricing for ovens is as follows.

Oven only	$ 800
Oven with installation service	850
Oven with maintenance services	975
Oven with installation and maintenance services	1,000

In each instance in which maintenance services are provided, service is separately priced within the arrangement at $175. Additionally, the incremental amount charged by Appliance Centre for installation approximates the amount charged by independent third parties. Ovens are sold subject to a general right of return.

Instructions

(a) Assume that a customer purchases an oven with both installation and maintenance services for $1,000. Based on its experience, Appliance Centre believes that it is probable that the installation of the equipment will be performed satisfactorily to the consumer. Assume that the maintenance services are priced separately. Identify the separate performance obligations related to the Appliance Centre revenue arrangement.

(b) Indicate the amount of revenue that should be allocated to the oven, the installation, and to the maintenance contract.

(LO 6, 10) E6-13 (Existence of a Contract) On January 1, 2017, Gordon Co. enters into a contract to sell a customer a wiring base and a shelving unit that sits on the base in exchange for $3,000. The contract requires delivery of the base first but states that payment for the base will not be made until the shelving unit is delivered. Gordon identifies two performance obligations and allocates $1,200 of the transaction price to the wiring base and the remainder to the shelving unit. The cost of the wiring base is $700; the shelves have a cost of $320.

Instructions

(a) Prepare the journal entry on January 1, 2017, for Gordon.

(b) Prepare the journal entry on February 5, 2017, for Gordon when the wiring base is delivered to the customer.

(c) Prepare the journal entry on February 25, 2017, for Gordon when the shelving unit is delivered to the customer and Gordon receives full payment.

(LO 6, 9, 10) **E6-14** **(Existence of a Contract)** On May 1, 2017, Richardson Inc. entered into a contract to deliver one of its specialty mowers to Kickapoo Landscaping Co. The contract requires Kickapoo to pay the contract price of $900 in advance on May 15, 2017. Kickapoo pays Richardson on May 15, 2017, and Richardson delivers the mower (with a cost of $565) on May 31, 2017.

Instructions

(a) Prepare the journal entry on May 1, 2017, for Richardson.

(b) Prepare the journal entry on May 15, 2017, for Richardson.

(c) Prepare the journal entry on May 31, 2017, for Richardson.

(LO 7, 9) **E6-15** **(Sales with Returns)** Organic Growth Company is presently testing a number of new agricultural seeds that it has recently harvested. To stimulate interest, it has decided to grant five of its largest customers the unconditional right to return these products if not fully satisfied. The right of return extends for four months. Organic Growth sells these seeds on account for $1,500,000 (cost $800,000) on April 2, 2017. Customers are required to pay the full amount due by June 15, 2017. The company follows IFRS.

Instructions

(a) Prepare the journal entry for Organic Growth at April 2, 2017, assuming Organic Growth estimates returns of 20% based on prior experience.

(b) Assume that one customer returns the seeds on June 1, 2017. Prepare the journal entry to record this transaction, assuming this customer purchased $100,000 of seeds from Organic Growth.

(c) Briefly describe the accounting for these sales if Organic Growth is unable to reliably estimate returns.

(LO 7, 9) **E6-16** **(Sales with Returns)** Uddin Publishing Co. publishes college textbooks that are sold to bookstores on the following terms. Each title has a fixed wholesale price, terms f.o.b. shipping point, and payment is due 60 days after shipment. The retailer may return a maximum of 30% of an order at the retailer's expense. Sales are made only to retailers who have good credit ratings. Past experience indicates that the normal return rate is 12% and the average collection period is 72 days. The company follows IFRS.

Instructions

(a) Identify the revenue recognition criteria that Uddin could employ concerning textbook sales.

(b) Briefly discuss the reasoning for your answers in (a).

(c) On July 1, 2017, Uddin shipped books invoiced at $15,000,000 (cost $12,000,000). Prepare the journal entry to record this transaction.

(d) On October 3, 2017, $1.5 million of the invoiced July sales were returned according to the return policy, and the remaining $13.5 million was paid. Prepare the journal entries for the return and payment.

(LO 7, 9) **E6-17** **(Sales with Repurchase)** Cramer Corp. sells idle machinery to Enyart Company on July 1, 2017, for $40,000. Cramer agrees to repurchase this equipment from Enyart on June 30, 2018, for a price of $42,400 (an imputed interest rate of 6%).

Instructions

(a) Prepare the journal entry for Cramer for the transfer of the asset to Enyart on July 1, 2017.

(b) Prepare any other necessary journal entries for Cramer in 2017.

(c) Prepare the journal entry for Cramer when the machinery is repurchased on June 30, 2018.

(LO 7, 9) **E6-18** **(Repurchase Agreement)** Zagat Inc. enters into an agreement on March 1, 2017, to sell Werner Metal Company aluminum ingots in two months (receiving cash of $200,000 on this date). As part of this agreement, Zagat also agrees to repurchase the ingots in 60 days at the original sales price of $200,000 plus 2%. (Because Zagat has an unconditional obligation to repurchase the ingots at an amount greater than the original sales price, the transaction is treated as a financing.)

Instructions

(a) Prepare the journal entry necessary on March 1, 2017.

(b) Prepare the journal entry for the repurchase of the ingots on May 1, 2017.

(LO 8) **E6-19** **(Revenue Recognition under Earnings Approach—Various Consumer Industries)**

Instructions

(a) Explain the principles and criteria for revenue recognition under the earnings approach.

(b) For each scenario noted in E6-1, discuss when revenue should be recognized under the earnings approach. Provide the journal entries that would be recorded to recognize the revenue under the earnings approach.

(LO 8) **E6-20** **(Transactions with Customer Acceptance Provisions under Earnings Approach)** Consider the following unrelated situations:

1. Book of the Week Limited sends books out to potential customers on a trial basis. If the customers do not like the books, they can return them at no cost.

2. Sea Clothing Company Inc. has a return policy that allows customers to return merchandise in good order for a full refund within 30 days of purchase.

3. Shivani Inc. sells machinery to manufacturers. Customers have the right to inspect the equipment upon delivery and may return it if certain customer-specific requirements for size and weight are not met.

Instructions

(a) Explain the implications of customer acceptance provisions for revenue transactions.

(b) Indicate the point at which these transactions may be recognized as sales under the earnings approach.

**DIGGING
DEEPER**

(c) Using the information provided in scenario 2, assume Sea Clothing Company Inc. advertises that "customer satisfaction is guaranteed," and assume the role of a customer of Sea Clothing Company. Has the company's advertised statement created an expectation that returns will be accepted at any time, perhaps even beyond the thirty-day refund period? Discuss the implications of this expectation for Sea Clothing Company's books, if any.

(LO 9) **E6-21** **(Bill and Hold)** Wood-Mode Company is involved in the design, manufacture, and installation of various types of wood products for large construction projects. Wood-Mode recently completed a large contract for Stadium Inc., which consisted of building 35 different types of concession counters for a new soccer arena under construction. The terms of the contract are that, upon completion of the counters, Stadium would pay $2,000,000. Unfortunately, due to the depressed economy, the completion of the new soccer arena is now delayed. Stadium has therefore asked Wood-Mode to hold the counters for two months at its manufacturing plant until the arena is completed. Stadium acknowledges in writing that it ordered the counters and that it now has ownership. The time that Wood-Mode Company must hold the counters is totally dependent on when the arena is completed. Because Wood-Mode has not received additional progress payments for the arena due to the delay, Stadium has provided a deposit of $300,000.

Instructions

(a) Explain this type of revenue recognition transaction.

(b) What factors should be considered in determining when to recognize revenue in this transaction?

(c) Prepare the journal entry(ies) that Wood-Mode should make, assuming it signed a valid sales contract to sell the counters and received the $300,000 deposit at the time.

(LO 9) **E6-22** **(Consignment Sales)** On May 31, 2017, Eisler Company consigned 80 freezers, costing $500 each, to Remmers Company. The cost of shipping the freezers amounted to $740 and was paid by Eisler Company. On December 30, 2017, a report was received from the consignee, indicating that 40 freezers had been sold for $750 each. Remittance was made by the consignee for the amount due after deducting a commission of 6%, advertising of $200, and total installation costs of $320 on the freezers sold.

Instructions

(a) Calculate the inventory value of the units unsold in the hands of the consignee.

(b) Calculate the profit for the consignor for the units sold.

(c) Calculate the amount of cash that will be remitted by the consignee.

(LO 9) **E6-23** **(Warranty Arrangement)** On December 31, 2017, Grando Company sells production equipment to Fargo Inc. for $50,000. Grando includes a one-year assurance warranty service with the sale of all its equipment. The customer receives and pays for the equipment on December 31, 2017. Grando estimates the prices to be $48,800 for the equipment and $1,200 for the cost of warranty.

Instructions

(a) Prepare the journal entry to record this transaction on December 31, 2017.

(b) Repeat the requirements for (a), assuming that, in addition to the assurance warranty, Grando sold an extended warranty (service-type warranty) for an additional two years (2019–2020) for $800.

(LO 9) E6-24   (Warranties) Celic Inc. manufactures and sells computers that include an assurance-type warranty for 90 days. Celic offers an optional extended coverage plan under which it will repair or replace any defective part for three years from the expiration of the assurance-type warranty. Because the optional extended coverage plan is sold separately, Celic determines that the three years of the extended coverage represent a separate performance obligation. The total transaction price for the sale of a computer and the extended warranty is $3,600 on October 1, 2017, and Celic determines the stand-alone selling price of each is $3,200 and $400, respectively. Further, Celic estimates, based on historical experience, it will incur $200 in costs to repair defects that arise within the 90-day coverage period for the assurance-type warranty. The cost of the equipment is $1,440.

Instructions

(a) Prepare the journal entry (or entries) to record the sale of the computer, cost of goods sold, and liabilities related to the warranties.

(b) Briefly describe the accounting for the service-type warranty after the 90-day assurance-type warranty period.

(LO 10) E6-25   (Contract Costs) Rex's Reclaimers entered into a contract with Dan's Demolition to manage the processing of recycled materials on Dan's various demolition projects. Services for the three-year contract include collecting, sorting, and transporting reclaimed materials to recycling centres or contractors who will reuse them. Rex's incurs selling commission costs of $2,000 to obtain the contract. Before performing the services, Rex's also designs and builds specialty receptacles and loading equipment that interface with Dan's demolition equipment, at a cost of $27,000. These receptacles and equipment are retained by Rex's. Dan's promises to pay a fixed fee of $12,000 per year, payable every six months, for the services under the contract. Rex's incurs the following costs: design services for the receptacles to interface with Dan's equipment $3,000, loading equipment controllers $6,000, and special testing and health and safety inspection fees $2,000 (some of Dan's projects are on government property).

Instructions

(a) Determine the costs that should be capitalized as part of Rex's revenue arrangement with Dan's Demolition.

(b) Rex's also expects to incur general and administrative costs related to this contract, as well as costs of wasted materials and labour that likely cannot be factored into the contract price. Can these costs be capitalized? Explain.

(LO 10) E6-26   (Contract Costs, Collectibility) Refer to the information in E6-25.

Instructions

(a) Does the accounting for capitalized costs change if the contract is for one year rather than three years? Explain.

(b) Dan's Demolition is a start-up company; as a result, there is more than insignificant uncertainty about Dan's ability to make the six-month payments on time. Does this uncertainty affect the amount of revenue to be recognized under the contract? Explain.

DIGGING DEEPER

LO 11, *E6-27   (Recognition of a Profit on Long-Term Contracts) During 2017, Nilsen Company started a construction
12, 13) job with a contract price of $1,600,000. The job was completed in 2019. The following information is available. The contract is non-cancellable.

	2017	2018	2019
Costs incurred to date	$400,000	$825,000	$1,070,000
Estimated costs to complete	600,000	275,000	–0–
Billings to date (non-refundable)	300,000	900,000	1,600,000
Collections to date	270,000	810,000	1,425,000

Instructions

(a) Calculate the amount of gross profit to be recognized each year, assuming the percentage-of-completion method is used.

(b) Prepare all necessary journal entries for 2018.

(c) Calculate the amount of gross profit to be recognized each year, assuming the completed-contract method is used.

(LO 12) *E6-28   (Gross Profit on Uncompleted Contract) On April 1, 2017, Dougherty Inc. entered into a cost plus fixed fee non-cancellable contract to construct an electric generator for Altom Corporation. At the contract date, Dougherty estimated that it would take two years to complete the project at a cost of $2,000,000. The fixed fee stipulated in the contract was $450,000. Dougherty appropriately accounts for this contract under the percentage-of-completion method. During 2017, Dougherty incurred costs of $800,000 related to this project. The estimated cost at December 31, 2017, to complete the contract is $1,200,000. Altom was billed $600,000 under the contract. The billings are non-refundable.

Instructions

Prepare a schedule to calculate the amount of gross profit to be recognized by Dougherty under the contract for the year ended December 31, 2017. Show supporting calculations in good form.

(Adapted from AICPA.)

(LO 11, 12) ***E6-29** **(Recognition of Revenue on Long-Term Contract and Entries)** Hamilton Construction Company uses the percentage-of-completion method of accounting. In 2017, Hamilton began work under a non-cancellable contract #E2-D2, which provided for a contract price of $2,200,000. Other details follow:

	2017	2018
Costs incurred during the year	$640,000	$1,425,000
Estimated costs to complete, as at December 31	960,000	–0–
Billings during the year (non-refundable)	420,000	1,680,000
Collections during the year	350,000	1,500,000

Instructions

(a) How much revenue should be recognized in 2017? In 2018?

(b) Assuming the same facts as those above except that Hamilton uses the completed-contract method of accounting, how much revenue should be recognized in 2018?

(c) Prepare a complete set of journal entries for 2017 (using the percentage-of-completion method).

(LO 11, 12, 13) ***E6-30** **(Recognition of Profit and Balance Sheet Amounts for Long-Term Contracts)** Yanmei Construction Company began operations on January 1, 2017. During the year, Yanmei Construction Company entered into a non-cancellable contract with Lundquist Corp. to construct a manufacturing facility. At that time, Yanmei estimated that it would take five years to complete the facility at a total cost of $4,500,000. The total contract price for construction of the facility is $6,000,000. During the year, Yanmei incurred $1,185,800 in construction costs related to the construction project. The estimated cost to complete the contract is $4,204,200. Lundquist Corp. was billed and paid 25% of the contract price. The billings are non-refundable.

Instructions

Prepare schedules to calculate the amount of gross profit to be recognized for the year ended December 31, 2017, and the amount to be shown as contract assets or liabilities at December 31, 2017, under each of the following methods. Show supporting calculations in good form.

(a) Completed-contract method.

(b) Percentage-of-completion method.

(Adapted from AICPA.)

Problems

P6-1 BBQ Master Company sells total outdoor barbecue solutions, providing gas and charcoal barbecues, accessories, and installation services for custom patio barbecue stations.

Instructions

Respond to the requirements related to the following independent revenue arrangements for BBQ Master products and services. Assume that BBQ Master follows IFRS.

(a) BBQ Master offers contract BM205, which comprises a free-standing gas barbecue for small patio use plus installation to a customer's gas line for a total price of $800. On a stand-alone basis, the barbecue sells for $700 (cost $425), and BBQ Master estimates that the fair value of the installation service (based on cost-plus estimation) is $150. BBQ Master signed 10 BM205 contracts on April 20, 2017, and customers paid the contract price in cash. The barbecues were delivered and installed on May 15, 2017. Prepare journal entries for BBQ Master for BM205 in April and May 2017.

(b) The province of Ontario is planning major renovations in its parks during 2017 and enters into a contract with BBQ Master to purchase 400 durable, easy maintenance, standard charcoal barbecues during 2017. The barbecues are priced at $200 each (with a cost of $160 each), and BBQ Master provides a 6% volume discount if Ontario purchases at least 300 grills during 2017. BBQ Master delivers and receives payment for 280 barbecues on April 17, 2017. Based on prior experience with province of Ontario renovation projects, the delivery of this many barbecues makes it certain that Ontario will meet the discount threshold. Prepare the journal entries for BBQ Master for barbecues sold on April 17, 2017.

(c) BBQ Master sells its specialty combination gas/wood-fired barbecues to local restaurants. Each barbecue is sold for $1,000 (cost $550) on credit with terms 3/30, net/90. Prepare the journal entries for the sale of 20 barbecues on September 1, 2017, and upon payment, assuming the customer paid on (1) September 25, 2017, and (2) October 15, 2017. Assume the company records sales net and therefore the account receivable is recorded at 97% of the selling price.

(d) On October 1, 2017, BBQ Master sold one if its super deluxe combination gas/charcoal barbecues to a local builder. The builder plans to install it in one of its "Parade of Homes" houses. BBQ Master accepted a three-year, zero-interest-bearing note with a face amount of $5,324. The barbecue has an inventory cost of $2,700. An interest rate of 10% is an appropriate market rate of interest for this customer. Prepare the journal entries on October 1, 2017, and December 31, 2017.

P6-2   Economy Appliance Co. manufactures low-price, no-frills appliances that are in great demand for rental units. Pricing and cost information on Economy's main products are as follows.

Item	Stand-Alone Selling Price (Cost)
Refrigerator	$500 ($260)
Range	$560 ($275)
Stackable washer/dryer unit	$700 ($400)

Customers can contract a purchase either individually at the stated prices or for a three-item bundle with a price of $1,800. The bundle price includes delivery and installation. Economy provides delivery and installation as a stand-alone service for any of its products for a price of $100. The company follows IFRS.

Instructions

Respond to the requirements related to the following independent revenue arrangements for Economy Appliance Co.

(a) On June 1, 2017, Economy sold 100 washer/dryer units without installation to Laplante Rentals for $70,000. Laplante is a newer customer and is unsure of how this product will work in its older rental units. Economy offers a 60-day return privilege and estimates, based on prior experience with sales of this product, that 4% of the units will be returned. Prepare the journal entries for the sale and related cost of goods sold on June 1, 2017.

(b) YellowCard Property Managers operates upscale student apartment buildings. On May 1, 2017, Economy signs a contract with YellowCard for 300 appliance bundles to be delivered and installed in one of its new buildings. YellowCard pays 20% cash at contract signing and will pay the balance upon delivery and installation no later than August 1, 2017. Prepare journal entries for Economy on (1) May 1, 2017, and (2) August 1, 2017, when all appliances are delivered and installed.

DIGGING DEEPER

(c) Refer to the arrangement in part (b). It would help YellowCard secure lease agreements with students if the delivery and installation of the appliance bundles can be completed by July 1, 2017. YellowCard offers a 10% bonus payment if Economy can complete delivery and installation by July 1, 2017. Economy estimates its chances of meeting the bonus deadline to be 60%, based on a number of prior contracts of similar scale. Repeat the requirement for part (b), given this bonus provision. Assume installation is completed by July 1, 2017.

(d) Epic Rentals would like to take advantage of the bundle price for its 400-unit project; on February 1, 2017, Economy signs a contract with Epic for delivery and installation of 400 bundles. Under the agreement, Economy will hold the appliance bundles in its warehouses until the new rental units are ready for installation. Epic pays 10% cash at contract signing. On April 1, 2017, Economy completes manufacture of the appliances in the Epic bundle order and places them in the warehouse. Economy and Epic have documented the warehouse arrangement and identified the units designated for Epic. The units are ready to ship, and Economy may not sell these units to other customers. Prepare journal entries for Economy on (1) February 1, 2017, and (2) April 1, 2017.

P6-3   Van Hatten Consolidated has three operating divisions: DeMent Publishing Division, Ankiel Security Division, and Depp Advisory Division. Each division maintains its own accounting system but follows IFRS.

DeMent Publishing Division

The DeMent Publishing Division sells large volumes of novels to a few book distributors, which in turn sell to several national chains of bookstores. DeMent allows distributors to return up to 30% of sales, and the distributors give the same terms to bookstores. While returns from individual titles fluctuate greatly, the returns from distributors have averaged 20% in each of the past five years. A total of $7,000,000 of paperback novel sales were made to distributors during fiscal 2017. On November 30, 2017 (the end of the fiscal year), $1,500,000 of fiscal 2017 sales were still subject to return privileges over the next six months. The remaining $5,500,000 of fiscal 2017 sales had actual returns of 21%. Sales from fiscal 2016 totalling $2,000,000 were collected in fiscal 2017 less 18% returns. This division records revenue according to the revenue recognition method when the right of return exists.

Ankiel Security Division

The Ankiel Security Division works through manufacturers' agents in various cities. Orders for alarm systems and down payments are forwarded from agents, and the division ships the goods f.o.b. factory directly to the customers (usually police departments and security guard companies). Customers are billed directly for the balance due plus actual shipping costs. The company received orders for $6,000,000 of goods during the fiscal year ended November 30, 2017. Down payments of $600,000 were received, and $5,200,000 of goods were billed and shipped. Actual freight costs of $100,000 were also billed. Commissions of 10% on product price are paid to manufacturing agents after goods are shipped to customers. Such goods are covered by the warranty for 90 days after shipment, and warranty returns have been about 1% of sales. Revenue is recognized at the point of sale by this division.

Depp Advisory Division

The Depp Advisory Division provides asset management services. This division grew out of Van Hatten's own treasury and asset management operations, which several of its customers asked to have access to. On January 1, 2017, Depp entered into a contract with Scutaro Co. to perform asset management services for one year. Depp receives a quarterly management fee of 0.25% on Scutaro's assets under management at the end of each quarter. In addition, Depp receives a performance-based incentive fee of 20% of the fund's annual return in excess of the return on the S&P 500 index at the end of the year. At the end of the first quarter of 2017, Depp was managing $2,400,000 of Scutaro assets. The annualized return on the portfolio was 6.2% (the S&P 500 index had an annualized return of 5.7%).

Instructions

(a) For each division's revenue arrangements, identify the separate performance obligations, briefly explain allocation of the transaction process to each performance obligation, and indicate when the performance obligations are satisfied.

(b) Calculate the revenue to be recognized in fiscal year 2017 for each of the three operating divisions of Van Hatten in accordance with generally accepted accounting principles.

P6-4   Presented below are three independent revenue arrangements for Colbert Company. The company follows IFRS.

Instructions

Respond to the requirements related to each revenue arrangement.

(a) Colbert sells 3-D printer systems. Recently, Colbert provided a special promotion of zero-interest financing for two years on any new 3-D printer system. Assume that Colbert sells Lyle Cartright a 3-D system, receiving a $5,000 zero-interest-bearing note on January 1, 2017. The cost of the 3-D printer system is $4,000. Colbert imputes a 6% interest rate on this zero-interest note transaction. Prepare the journal entry to record the sale on January 1, 2017, and calculate the total amount of revenue to be recognized in 2017.

(b) Colbert sells 20 nonrefundable $100 gift cards for 3-D printer plastic on March 1, 2017. The plastic has a stand-alone selling price of $100 (cost $80). The gift card expiration date is June 30, 2017. Colbert estimates that customers will not redeem 10% of these gift cards. The pattern of redemption is as follows.

	Cumulative Redemption Rate to Date
March 31	50%
April 30	80%
June 30	85%

Prepare the 2017 journal entries related to the gift cards at March 1, March 31, April 30, and June 30.

(c) Colbert sells 3-D printers along with a number of retail items. The package price and stand-alone selling prices of each item are as follows. The printer and stand are often sold as a bundle with the bundling discount noted below.

Item	Stand-Alone Selling Price	Price When Bundled	Bundling Discount
3-D printer (cost $4,000)	$5,000	$4,500	$500
Custom stand (cost $200)	450	450	–0–
Special 3-D plastic (cost $135)	175	175	–0–
Total for bundle	$5,625	$5,125	$500

Due to the timing of the delivery—the plastic is delivered six months after the printer is delivered to the customer— Colbert chooses to account for two performance obligations: (1) the printer and stand, and (2) the plastic. Prepare the journal entries for Colbert on (a) March 1, 2017, when Colbert receives $51,250 for the sale of 10 printer bundles, and (b) September 1, 2017, when the plastic is delivered to customers.

P6-5   Ritt Ranch & Farm is a distributor of ranch and farm equipment. Its products include small tools, power equipment for trench-digging and fencing, grain dryers, and barn winches. Most products are sold direct via its company catalogue and Internet site. However, given some of its specialty products, select farm implement stores carry Ritt's products. Pricing and cost information on three of Ritt's most popular products are as follows.

Item	Stand-Alone Selling Price (Cost)	
Mini-trencher	$ 3,600	($2,000)
Power fence hole auger	1,200	($800)
Grain/Hay dryer	14,000	($11,000)

Instructions

Respond to the requirements related to the following independent revenue arrangements for Ritt Ranch & Farm. IFRS is a constraint.

(a) On January 1, 2017, Ritt sells augers to Mills Farm & Fleet for $48,000. Mills signs a six-month note at an annual interest rate of 12%. Ritt allows Mills to return any auger that it cannot use within 60 days and receive a full refund. Based on prior experience, Ritt estimates that 5% of units sold to customers like Mills will be returned (using the most likely outcome approach). Ritt's costs to recover the products will be immaterial, and the returned augers are expected to be resold at a profit. Prepare the journal entry for Ritt on January 1, 2017.

(b) On August 10, 2017, Ritt sells 16 mini-trenchers to a farm co-op in western Canada. Ritt provides a 4% volume discount on the mini-trenchers if the co-op has a 15% increase in purchases from Ritt compared to the prior year. Given the slowdown in the farm economy, sales to the co-op have been flat, and it is highly uncertain that the benchmark will be met. Prepare the journal entry for Ritt on August 10, 2017.

(c) Ritt sells three grain/hay dryers to a local farmer at a total contract price of $45,200. In addition to the dryers, Ritt provides installation, which has a stand-alone sales value of $1,000 per unit installed. The contract payment also includes a $1,200 maintenance plan for the dryers for three years after installation. Ritt signs the contract on June 20, 2017, and receives a 20% down payment from the farmer. The dryers are delivered and installed on October 1, 2017, and full payment is made to Ritt. Prepare the journal entries for Ritt in 2017 related to this arrangement as well as any adjusting journal entries at its December year end.

(d) On April 25, 2017, Ritt ships 100 augers to Farm Depot, a farm supply dealer in Alberta , on consignment. By June 30, 2017, Farm Depot has sold 60 of the consigned augers at the listed price of $1,200 per unit. Farm Depot notifies Ritt of the sales, retains a 10% commission, and remits the cash due to Ritt. Prepare the journal entries for Ritt and Farm Depot for the consignment arrangement.

P6-6   Martz Inc. has a customer loyalty program that rewards a customer with one customer loyalty point for every $100 of purchases. Each point is redeemable for a $3 discount on any future purchases. On July 2, 2017, customers purchase products for $300,000 (with a cost of $171,000) and earn 3,000 points redeemable for future purchases. Martz expects 2,500 points to be redeemed (based on its past experience, which is predictive of the amount of consideration to which it will be entitled). Martz estimates a stand-alone selling price of $2.50 per point (or $7,500 total) on the basis of the likelihood of redemption. The points provide a material right to customers that they would not receive without entering into a contract. As a result, Martz concludes that the points are a separate performance obligation.

Instructions

(a) Determine the transaction price for the product and the customer loyalty points.

(b) Prepare the journal entries to record the sale of the product and related points on July 2, 2017.

(c) At the end of the first reporting period (July 31, 2017), 1,000 loyalty points are redeemed. Martz continues to expect 2,500 loyalty points to be redeemed in total. Determine the amount of loyalty point revenue to be recognized at July 31, 2017. Prepare the journal entry for cash sales on July 31, 2017, assuming the points were applied to cash sales of $75,000 with a cost of $39,000.

P6-7   Tablet Tailors sells tablet PCs combined with Internet service (Tablet Bundle A) that permits the tablet to connect to the Internet anywhere (that is, set up a Wi-Fi hot spot). The price for the tablet and a four-year Internet connection service contract is $500. The stand-alone selling price of the tablet is $250 (cost to Tablet Tailors $175). Tablet Tailors sells the Internet access service independently for an upfront payment of $100, plus $72 payments at the beginning of years 2 to 4 of the contract. With an imputed interest rate of 8%, the stand-alone value of the service is $286. On January 2, 2017, Tablet Tailors signed 100 contracts, receiving a total of $31,445 in cash (full payment of $500 each in cash, less the upfront fee for Internet service, less the present value of the note for the future service plan payments), delivered the tablets, and started service for 100 tablet packages.

Instructions

(a) Prepare any journal entries to record this revenue arrangement on January 2, 2017.

(b) Prepare any journal entries to record this revenue arrangement on December 31, 2018.

(c) Prepare any journal entries to record this revenue arrangement on December 31, 2019.

(d) Prepare the requirements for part (a), assuming that Tablet Tailors has no reliable data with which to estimate the stand-alone selling price for the Internet service.

P6-8 Hale Hardware takes pride in being the "shop around the corner" that can compete with the big-box home improvement stores by providing good service from knowledgeable sales associates (many of whom are retired local handymen). Hale has developed the following two revenue arrangements to enhance its relationships with customers and increase its bottom line.

1. Hale sells a specialty portable winch that is popular with many of the local customers for use at their lake homes (putting docks in and out, launching boats, and so on). The Hale winch is a standard-manufacture winch that Hale modifies so the winch can be used for a variety of tasks. Hale sold 70 of these winches during 2017 at a total price of $21,000, with a warranty guarantee that the product was free of any defects. The cost of winches sold is $16,000. The assurance warranties extend for a three-year period with an estimated cost of $2,100. In addition, Hale sold extended warranties related to 29 Hale winches for two years beyond the three-year period for $400 each.

2. To bolster its already strong customer base, Hale implemented a customer loyalty program that rewards a customer with one loyalty point for every $10 of purchases on a select group of Hale products. Each point is redeemable for a $1 discount on any purchases of Hale merchandise in the following two years. During 2017, customers purchased select group products for $100,000 (all products are sold to provide a 45% gross profit) and earned 10,000 points redeemable for future purchases. The stand-alone selling price of the purchased products is $100,000. Based on prior experience with incentive programs like this, Hale expects 9,500 points to be redeemed related to these sales (Hale appropriately uses this experience to estimate the value of future consideration related to bonus points).

Instructions

(a) Identify the separate performance obligations in the Hale warranty and bonus point programs, and briefly explain the point in time when the performance obligations are satisfied.

(b) Prepare the journal entries for Hale related to the sales of Hale winches with warranties.

(c) Prepare the journal entries for the bonus point sales for Hale in 2017.

*P6-9 (Recognition of Profit on Long-Term Contract) Shanahan Construction Company has entered into a non-cancellable contract beginning January 1, 2017, to build a parking complex. It has been estimated that the complex will cost $600,000 and will take three years to construct. The complex will be billed to the purchasing company at $900,000. The following data pertain to the construction period.

	2017	2018	2019
Costs to date	$270,000	$450,000	$610,000
Estimated costs to complete	330,000	150,000	–0–
Progress billings to date (non-refundable)	270,000	550,000	900,000
Cash collected to date	240,000	500,000	900,000

Instructions

(a) Using the percentage-of-completion method, calculate the estimated gross profit that would be recognized during each year of the construction period.

(b) Using the completed-contract method, calculate the estimated gross profit that would be recognized during each year of the construction period.

ENABLING COMPETENCIES

Cases

Refer to the Case Primer on the Student Website and in *WileyPLUS* to help you answer these cases.

CA6-1 *BudgetVacations* is a monthly magazine that has been on the market for 18 months. It is owned by a private company and has a circulation of 1.4 million copies. The company is thinking of going public to raise funds for expansion. However, currently, negotiations are under way to obtain a bank loan in order to update its facilities. It is producing close to its capacity and expects to grow at an average of 20% per year over the next three years.

After reviewing the financial statements of *BudgetVacations*, Grace Hall, the bank loan officer, said that a loan could only be offered to *BudgetVacations* if it could increase its current ratio and decrease its debt-to-equity ratio

to a specified level. Thomas Zang, the marketing manager of *BudgetVacations*, has devised a plan to meet these requirements. Zang indicates that an advertising campaign can be used to immediately increase circulation. The potential customers would be contacted after *BudgetVacations* purchases another magazine's mailing list. The campaign would include:

1. An offer to subscribe to *BudgetVacations* at three-quarters of the normal price.

2. A special offer to all new customers to receive the most current world atlas whenever requested at a guaranteed price of $2.00.

3. An unconditional guarantee of a full refund for any subscriber who is dissatisfied with the magazine.

Although the offer of a full refund is risky, Zang claims that few people will ask for a refund after receiving half of their subscription issues. Zang notes that other magazine companies have tried this sales promotion technique and experienced great success. Their average cancellation rate was 25%. On average, each company increased its initial circulation threefold and in the long run increased circulation to twice the level that it was before the promotion. In addition, 60% of the new subscribers are expected to take advantage of the atlas premium. Zang feels confident that the increased subscriptions from the advertising campaign will increase the current ratio and decrease the debt-to-equity ratio.

In addition to the above, Zang has just signed a large deal with a newly opened store to take delivery of the current edition of the magazine. The new customer has asked that the magazines be held by *BudgetVacations* for a couple of weeks.

Instructions

Assume the role of the controller and discuss the financial reporting issues that *BudgetVacations* faces.

CA6-2   Rouge Valley Golf and Health Club (RVGH) is a public company that operates eight clubs in a large city and offers one-year memberships. Membership provides members with access to golf and the fitness centre including fitness classes. The members may use any of the eight facilities but must reserve golf time and pay a separate fee before using one of the golf courses. As an incentive, RVGH advertised that any customers who are not satisfied for any reason can receive a refund of the remaining portion of their unused membership fees. Membership fees are due at the beginning of the individual membership period; however, customers are given the option of financing the membership fee over the membership period at an interest rate of 8%.

In the past, some customers have said they would like to take only the regularly scheduled aerobic classes and not pay for the full membership. During the current fiscal year, RVGH began selling coupon books for aerobic classes only to accommodate these customers. Each book is dated and contains 50 coupons that may be redeemed for any regularly scheduled aerobics class over a one-year period. After the one-year period, unused coupons are no longer valid.

During 2017, RVGH expanded into the health equipment market by purchasing a local company that manufactures elliptical machines. These machines are used in RVGH's facilities and are sold through the clubs and mail-order catalogues. Customers must make a 20% down payment when placing an equipment order. Delivery is in 60 to 90 days after an order is placed. The machines are sold with a one-year unconditional guarantee against defaults. Based on experience, RVGH expects the costs of repairing machines under guarantee to be 4% of sales.

RVGH is in the process of preparing financial statements as at May 1, 2017, the end of its fiscal year. Jaymie Hogan, corporate controller, expressed concern over the company's performance for the year and decided to review the preliminary financial statements prepared by Karen Browning, RVGH's assistant controller, for the company's bankers. After reviewing the statements, Browning proposed that the following changes be reflected in the May 31, 2017 published financial statements.

1. Membership revenue should be recognized when the membership fee is collected.

2. Revenue from the coupon books should be recognized when the books are sold.

3. Down payments on equipment purchases and expenses associated with the guarantee on the elliptical machines should be recognized when they are paid.

Browning told Hogan that the proposed changes are not in accordance with IFRS, but Hogan insisted that the changes be made. Browning believes Hogan wants to manipulate income to delay any potential financial problems and increase her year-end bonus. At this point, Browning is unsure what action to take.

ETHICS   **Instructions**

Discuss the financial reporting issues and how any ethical issues should be handled. If RVGH decided that it wanted to become a private company, describe how the financial reporting issues should be handled.

ENABLING COMPETENCIES   # Integrated Cases

(*Hint:* If there are issues that are new, use the conceptual framework to help support your analysis with solid reasoning.)

IC6-1   Standford Pharmaceuticals Inc. (SP) researches, develops, and produces over-the-counter drugs. During the year, it acquired 100% of the net assets of Jenstar Drugs Limited (JDL) for $200 million.

The fair value of the identifiable assets at the time of the purchase was $150 million (which included $120 million for patents). The plan is to sell the patents to a third party at the end of seven years, even though the remaining legal life of the patents at that time will be five years. SP already has a commitment from a specific third party that has agreed to pay $50 million for the patents (in seven years).

In January, in an unrelated deal, the company acquired a trademark that has a remaining legal life of three years. The trademark is renewable every 10 years at little cost. SP is unsure if it will renew the trademark or not.

Because of the two acquisitions, SP was short of cash and entered into an arrangement with Dev Drugs Corporation (DDC) whereby DDC paid $30 million to SP upfront when the contract was signed. Under the terms, the money is to be used to develop drugs and new distribution channels, and SP has already spent a considerable portion of this money. SP agreed that it will pay DDC 2% of the revenues from the subsequent sale of the drugs (which are now close to the point of commercial production).

Because of the cash shortage, the company entered into negotiations with its bank to increase its line of credit. The bank is concerned about the company's liquidity. SP's top management has graciously agreed to take stock options instead of any bonuses or pay raises for the next two years in order to reduce cash flow constraints.

AUDITING

It is now year end and SP is preparing its financial statements. It is concerned because one of its major

competitors has just come out with several new drugs that will compete directly with the drugs that JDL sells. Management is worried that this may erode the market for JDL's products. In fact, SP is considering selling JDL and has contacted a consultant to find a buyer.

Joe Song, the controller, is preparing for a planning meeting with SP's auditors. The auditors are analyzing SP's draft financial statements to identify critical and high-risk areas. The draft financial statements show the company is barely breaking even. The CFO has commented that the company's share price is likely to "take a tumble," since the company has always been profitable in past years and its competitors seem to be doing well. Song is also considering the latest news from SP's lawyers—apparently, the company is being sued in a class-action lawsuit (by a significant number of people) for an illness that was allegedly caused by one of SP's main pharmaceutical products. The claim is for an amount equal to revenues from last year. At this point, the lawyers are concerned that the case against SP may be successful and they are trying to estimate the potential loss to the company.

Instructions

Adopt the role of the auditor and prepare an analysis of all financial reporting issues that SP is facing.

IC6-2 Shannonrock Racing Inc. (SR) is a promoter and sponsor of motor-sport activities. It is privately owned. The owner is looking to expand and has approached the local bank who has agreed to accept financial statements prepared in accordance with ASPE. The company owns two racetracks where it hosts races (including those sponsored by NASCAR— the National Association for Stock Car Auto Racing) and operates a driving school. In between races, it rents the facilities out.

SR operates like a club. An upfront fee is charged, which gives the individual the right to belong to the club for his or her lifetime. SR owns a fleet of high-performance stock cars that members may "adopt." All members adopt a car, as this is a main reason for joining the club. Under the adoption agreement, individuals pay a monthly fee for access to the stock car and the rights to race the car on the racetracks for a certain number of hours a week (including unlimited gas). Individuals must get insurance in order to adopt a car, but this is provided by SR, which has a master insurance plan. Race-car driving is risky and insurance premiums are very high (as is the injury and mortality rate). The master insurance plan is negotiated by SR with an outside insurance company and covers all club members. The monthly fee covers the insurance. Adoptions are annual and individuals often switch cars each year. The company just completed a membership drive and has signed 100 new members at $20,000 each. This amount has been paid upfront and received prior to year end. It is non-refundable. In order to become a member, individuals have to prove that they are capable of driving race cars safely. To this end, all

members must take a two-week racing course and qualify for the company's stringent insurance program. All new members had completed the requirements by year end.

Last year, oil and gas prices began to skyrocket. Given that the company uses a lot of oil and gas in its business, Ted Rocket (the president and CEO of the company) decided to strategically diversify the company's operations into the oil and gas sector. Ted hired two additional traders to deal with this part of the business. At first, they were entering into advance gas purchase commitments to secure a steady supply of gas at a fixed price. However, the traders soon found that they were able to create profits by trading in the gas contracts. As a matter of fact, half of the company's net income for the current year came from trading gains. As part of their activities, the traders have purchased shares in three oil and gas companies. They have not decided whether they will keep these shares for the longer term. It really depends on the markets. Ted is currently in discussions with the traders as to what their job is supposed to be. Even though he likes the profits, he is not convinced that he likes the additional risk that this activity is exposing the company to. The company has a major shareholder who has declared that SR should only be in the business of racing cars and nothing else.

The company is being sued by the surrounding community for alleged pollution from the racing activities. Apparently, the racing cars produce a fair amount of airborne toxins, which settle in the surrounding area. Unknown to SR, the nearby city had passed a bylaw stating that companies must clean up any pollution that they are responsible for. SR's lawyers have argued on a preliminary basis that the alleged pollution in the surrounding area is due to the nearby superhighway and airport and that it is not possible to prove that SR is the cause of the pollution. Even if it were found to be responsible for a small fraction of it, it would be very difficult to determine just what that fraction is. The lawyers are therefore denying that SR has any responsibility with respect to cleanup. The lawyers for the surrounding community have asked for the financial statements of SR to determine whether the company is profiting at their expense.

Instructions

Assume the role of the controller and discuss the financial reporting issues.

IC6-3 Towers Inc. (TI) is a leader in delivering communications technology that powers global commerce and secures the world's most critical information. Its shares trade on the Canadian and U.S. national stock exchanges. The company had been experiencing unprecedented growth, but then, in 2015, industry demand for the company's services and products declined dramatically due to an industry realignment, an economic downturn, and a tightening in global capital and product markets. By the end of 2017, the industry stabilized and the company began to enter a turnaround period after significant downsizing.

In 2017, employee morale was very low because of all the downsizing. Many employees were being actively recruited away from TI. Management decided to set up bonus programs for employees who stayed to see the company through the difficult times and back to profitability. Under one plan, every employee would receive a bonus in the first quarter that the company achieved enough profit to cover the bonus costs. In order to help achieve profitability, the CFO met with the managers of his divisions and established profitability targets and what he referred to as "roadmaps" that showed how these targets could be achieved. The roadmaps included statements that the profits could only be achieved through the release from the statement of financial position of excess provisions (that is, provisions for obsolete inventory and bad debts). The provisions had been over-provided for in earlier years in an effort to "manage" profits.

In 2018, the company came under scrutiny from the securities regulators. The government notified it of a criminal investigation into alleged accounting irregularities. In addition, there were several class-action lawsuits outstanding against the company by shareholders alleging that TI had provided misleading information to them in the financial statements for 2016 and 2017. Once news of this was released, credit-rating agencies significantly downgraded their ratings of TI's securities. As a result of this negative activity, the company had not released its financial statements for 2018 and was now in breach of stock exchange requirements to file financial statements. Although the stock exchanges had not done so, they now had the power to delist TI's shares.

The controller of TI must now finalize the financial statements and has come across the following information.

1. During the year, the company signed contracts to sell optical products, which include software. Before year end, the company shipped out what it called an "interim product solution"—in other words, the optical product ordered by the company was not yet ready in its final form so the company shipped a beta or draft version of it. This interim product would be followed shortly by the final version. Revenues were recognized upon shipment of the interim product solution, as it was felt that the final version just needed minor refinements. The customers generally paid more than half of what was owed under the contract when they received the interim product solution. It was rare for customers to back out of this type of contract for any reason.

2. In 2017, TI had purchased a subsidiary of DEF Inc. and agreed to pay additional future consideration for the purchase (the consideration would take the form of additional TI shares). The additional consideration was a function of the profitability of the subsidiary. The more profitable the subsidiary, the more shares that TI would issue as consideration. Given that TI's shares are highly volatile, TI and DEF agreed that the number of shares to be issued should be based on the average price per share in the three months prior to the future issuance date of the shares. So far, the subsidiary has been performing above expectations.

3. By the end of 2018, TI was still restructuring to streamline its core operations and activities. Part of the restructuring included abandoning its voice-over-fibre operations. The operations would be closed down in early 2019, and this would involve workforce reductions and abandonment of plant and equipment.

Instructions

Adopt the role of controller and analyze the financial reporting issues.

RESEARCH AND ANALYSIS

RA6-1 Brookfield Asset Management Inc.

Brookfield Asset Management's financial statements can be found at the end of this book.

Instructions

Refer to the company's financial statements and accompanying notes to answer these questions.

(a) What business is Brookfield Asset Management in?

(b) What were the company's gross revenues for the fiscal years 2014 and 2013? What is the percentage change? Why has the company seen this result?

(c) Based on your findings in (b), comment on the company's net income/loss over the period.

(d) Review the notes to the financial statements to determine the company's revenue recognition policies. Identify the major policies, considering the nature of the business and the industry.

RA6-2 BCE Inc. and TELUS Corporation

Access the financial statements of both **BCE Inc.** and **TELUS Corporation** for their years ended December 31, 2014, from either the companies' websites or SEDAR (www.sedar.com).

Instructions

Using the financial statements for BCE Inc. and TELUS, answer the following.

(a) What types of revenue does BCE have and when are they recognized?

(b) What types of revenue does TELUS have and when are they recognized?

(c) Are there any examples of when either company would report revenue on a net basis? What factors does the company consider?

(d) Explain the types of contracts where the companies have multiple deliverables. How does each company allocate the revenues on these types of contracts?

(e) TELUS has a unique accounting policy for dealing with revenues in non-high-cost serving areas. Review the accounting policy note as well as Note 6 for details. Explain the business reason for the transaction and comment on the appropriateness of the accounting.

(f) Do you find one company's disclosure on revenue recognition better than the other's? Comment.

(g) Does either company address IFRS 15 *Revenue from Contracts with Customers*, issued in 2014 but with a 2017 effective date? Comment. (Note that the mandatory adoption date is now 2018).

RA6-3 AIRBUS GROUP NV

Airbus Group NV, previously known as **European Aeronautic Defence and Space Company** or **EADS NV**, is incorporated in the Netherlands and its shares are traded in France, Germany, and Spain. Access the financial statements of **Airbus Group NV** for its year ended December 31, 2014, from the company's website (www.airbus-group.com).

Instructions

Answer the following questions with respect to Airbus Group NV.

(a) What business is Airbus Group in?

(b) Explain how the revenue related to the construction contracts is recorded. How does the company determine when revenue should be recognized on these contracts?

(c) What are the balance sheet amounts related to this revenue recognition? What was the aggregated amount of costs and profits recognized to December 31, 2014? What was the gross amount due from customers and due to customers at December 31, 2014? What do these amounts represent? (*Hint*: See Note 19.)

RA6-4 The Procter & Gamble Company

Access the financial statements of **The Procter & Gamble Company** for its year ended June 30, 2014, from the company's website (www.pginvestor.com).

Instructions

Refer to P&G's financial statements and the accompanying notes to answer the following questions.

(a) What business is P&G in?

(b) What were P&G's net sales for its year ended June 30, 2014?

(c) What was the percentage of increase or decrease in P&G's net sales from 2013 to 2014? From 2012 to 2013? From 2012 to 2014?

(d) What is the source of P&G's revenues? How does P&G decide on the timing of revenue recognition, and how does the company define its net sales?

(e) What are trade promotions and how does P&G account for them? Does the accounting conform to accrual accounting concepts? Explain.

RA6-5   The Coca-Cola Company and PepsiCo.

REAL WORLD EMPHASIS

Coca-Cola Company and **PepsiCo** are two of the best known companies worldwide. Their 2014 financial statements can be found in the investor information sections of their company websites: www.coca-colacompany.com/investor and http://origin-www.pepsico.com/investors.

Instructions

Go to the company websites and use information found there as part of their annual reports to answer the following questions related to Coca-Cola Company and PepsiCo.

(a) What were Coca-Cola's and PepsiCo's net revenues (sales) for the year 2014? Which company increased its revenue more (dollars and percentage) from 2013 to 2014?

(b) Are the revenue recognition policies of Coca-Cola and PepsiCo similar? Explain.

(c) In which foreign countries (geographical areas) did Coca-Cola and PepsiCo earn significant revenues in 2014? Compare the amounts of foreign revenues to U.S. revenues for both Coca-Cola and PepsiCo.

ENDNOTES

[1] Recall that we presented a view of the business model in Chapters 4 and 5.

[2] Monetary consideration includes anything that is cash or measured in terms of cash, such as a receivable. Nonmonetary consideration includes other types of assets such as other inventory or fixed assets.

[3] Where the asset being sold is a commodity, prices fluctuate because they are based on supply and demand.

[4] IFRS 15.IN7.

[5] IFRS 15.33. Copyright © International Financial Reporting Standards Foundation. All rights reserved. Reproduced by John Wiley & Sons Canada, Ltd with the permission of the International Financial Reporting Standards Foundation®. Reproduction and use rights are strictly limited. No permission granted to third parties to reproduce or distribute.

[6] The FASB introduced this criterion (which acts like a collectibility threshold) because the Board concluded that the assessment of a customer's credit risk was an important part of determining whether a contract is valid. Under step 5 of the 5-step revenue recognition guidance, collectibility is not a consideration for determining whether revenue is recognized. However, collectibility may be a consideration in assessing whether parties to the contract are committed to perform. In determining whether it is probable that a company will collect the amount of consideration to which it is entitled, the company assesses both the customer's ability and intent to pay as amounts become due (IFRS 15.9).

[7] IFRS 15.15.

[8] Essentially, the company must decide which of the following treatments is acceptable: (1) termination of the existing contract and creation of a new contract (prospective basis), (2) revision of the existing contract and adjustment of revenue on a cumulative catch-up basis, or (3) a combination of the first two options.

[9] IFRS 15.27.

[10] IFRS 15.27.

[11] According to IFRS 15.57, conditions such as any of the following would indicate that the revenue is constrained (or not recognized):

1. The amount of consideration varies based on factors such as volatility in a market or weather conditions which are outside the control of the company.

2. The uncertainty will not be resolved for a long period of time.

3. The company's experience with similar contracts is limited.

4. There are a large number and broad range of possible amounts.

[12] IFRS 15.64.

[13] IFRS 15.63.

[14] IFRS 15.69.

[15] IFRS 15.70/.71.

[16] IFRS 15.79. Copyright © International Financial Reporting Standards Foundation. All rights reserved. Reproduced by John Wiley & Sons Canada, Ltd with the permission of the International Financial Reporting Standards Foundation®. Reproduction and use rights are strictly limited. No permission granted to third parties to reproduce or distribute.

[17] A selling price is highly variable when a company sells the same good or service for different amounts. A selling price may be uncertain when a company has not yet established a selling price (IFRS 15.79). Copyright © International Financial Reporting Standards Foundation. All rights reserved. Reproduced by John Wiley & Sons Canada, Ltd with the permission of the International Financial Reporting Standards Foundation®. Reproduction and use rights are strictly limited. No permission granted to third parties to reproduce or distribute.

[18] IFRS 15.33. Copyright © International Financial Reporting Standards Foundation. All rights reserved. Reproduced by John Wiley & Sons Canada, Ltd with the permission of the International Financial Reporting Standards Foundation®. Reproduction and use rights are strictly limited. No permission granted to third parties to reproduce or distribute.

[19] IFRS 15.38. Copyright © International Financial Reporting Standards Foundation. All rights reserved. Reproduced by John Wiley & Sons Canada, Ltd with the permission of the International Financial Reporting Standards Foundation®. Reproduction and use rights are strictly limited. No permission granted to third parties to reproduce or distribute.

[20] Recognition is the process of including an item in the financial statements. Recognition is not the same as realization, although the terms are sometimes used interchangeably in accounting literature and practice.

21 *CPA Canada Handbook*, Part II, Section 3400.04. Note that the predecessor standards to IFRS 15 (IAS 11 and 18) generally followed the earnings approach.

22 In order to recognize an asset on the balance sheet, a company must prove that it has control over substantially all of the risks and rewards of ownership. If these have been passed on to another party, a disposition has occurred.

23 Because of this, and in part also because of the increased profile of revenue recognition issues with securities commissions, companies are required to disclose the revenue recognition method in the notes to their financial statements.

24 IAS 41 deals with biological assets such as beef cattle. It requires that these assets be measured at fair value less estimated point-of-sale-costs. We will discuss this topic in greater detail in Chapter 8.

25 Adapted from IFRS 15 Illustrative Example 22 and taking into account guidance in IFRS 15.B20 and B21. Copyright © International Financial Reporting Standards Foundation. All rights reserved. Reproduced by John Wiley & Sons Canada, Ltd with the permission of the International Financial Reporting Standards Foundation®. Reproduction and use rights are strictly limited. No permission granted to third parties to reproduce or distribute.

26 Indicators that the company is an agent (and should recognize revenue in the net amount) include the following: (a) the other party is primarily responsible for fulfilling the contract; (b) the company does not have risks associated with the inventory (c) the company does not have the ability to set selling prices (d) the company's receives commission; and (e) the company does not have customer credit risk for the amount receivable (IFRS 15.B37). Copyright © International Financial Reporting Standards Foundation. All rights reserved. Reproduced by John Wiley & Sons Canada, Ltd with the permission of the International Financial Reporting Standards Foundation®. Reproduction and use rights are strictly

limited. No permission granted to third parties to reproduce or distribute.

27 Adapted from IFRS 15 Illustrative Example 39. Copyright © International Financial Reporting Standards Foundation. All rights reserved. Reproduced by John Wiley & Sons Canada, Ltd with the permission of the International Financial Reporting Standards Foundation®. Reproduction and use rights are strictly limited. No permission granted to third parties to reproduce or distribute.

28 Adapted from IFRS 15 Illustrative Example 37. Copyright © International Financial Reporting Standards Foundation. All rights reserved. Reproduced by John Wiley & Sons Canada, Ltd with the permission of the International Financial Reporting Standards Foundation®. Reproduction and use rights are strictly limited. No permission granted to third parties to reproduce or distribute.

29 See *PricewaterhouseCoopers Dataline* 2013–2014.

30 According to IFRS 15.37, the company must be entitled to an amount that would compensate the company for performance completed to date (even if the customer can terminate the contract for reasons other than the company's failure to perform as promised). Copyright © International Financial Reporting Standards Foundation. All rights reserved. Reproduced by John Wiley & Sons Canada, Ltd with the permission of the International Financial Reporting Standards Foundation®. Reproduction and use rights are strictly limited. No permission granted to third parties to reproduce or distribute.

31 In 2019, Hardhat will recognize the remaining 33½% of the revenue ($1,507,500), with costs of $1,468,962 as expected, and report a gross profit of $38,538. The total gross profit over the three years of the contract would be $115,038 [$125,000 (2017) − $48,500 (2018) + $38,538 (2019)], which is the difference between the total contract revenue of $4,500,000 and the total contract costs of $4,384,962.

CASH AND RECEIVABLES

REFERENCE TO THE CPA COMPETENCY MAP	LEARNING OBJECTIVES

After studying this chapter, you should be able to:

1.1.1, 1.4.5, 2.4.1, 5.2.1　**1.** Understand cash and accounts receivable from a business perspective.

1.2.1, 1.2.2　**2.** Define financial assets, and identify items that are considered cash and cash equivalents and how they are reported.

1.2.1, 1.2.2　**3.** Define receivables and identify the different types of receivables from an accounting perspective.

1.1.2, 1.2.1, 1.2.2, 1.2.3, 5.2.1　**4.** Account for and explain the accounting issues related to the recognition and measurement of accounts receivable.

1.2.1, 1.2.2, 1.2.3　**5.** Account for and explain the accounting issues related to the impairment in value of accounts receivable.

1.2.1, 1.2.2, 1.2.3　**6.** Account for and explain the accounting issues related to the recognition and measurement of short-term notes and loans receivable.

1.2.1, 1.2.2, 1.2.3　**7.** Account for and explain the accounting issues related to the recognition and measurement of long-term notes and loans receivable.

1.2.1, 1.2.2, 1.2.3, 1.2.4, 5.2.3　**8.** Account for and explain the basic accounting issues related to the derecognition of receivables.

1.2.1, 1.2.2, 1.2.3, 1.2.4, 1.3.2, 1.4.1, 1.4.2, 1.4.4, 5.1.1, 5.2.1　**9.** Explain how receivables and loans are reported and analyzed.

1.1.4　**10.** Identify differences in accounting between IFRS and accounting standards for private enterprises (ASPE), and what changes are expected in the near future.

After studying Appendix 7A, you should be able to:

1.2.1, 1.2.2, 1.2.3, 1.2.4, 3.1.1, 3.1.2, 4.1.1, 4.1.2　**11.** Explain common techniques for controlling cash.

LAST CALL FOR CUSTOMER PAYMENTS

INTERNET AND PHONE BILLS are ones that most Canadians pay in full every month. But what happens when customers fall behind in their accounts?

One of Canada's top communications companies, Rogers Communications, has accounts receivable in the hundreds of millions every month, from both residential and business customers. Its revenues, which were $12.9 billion in 2014, include fees for home and business telephone, cellular, high-speed Internet, television, and magazines, along with advertising revenues from businesses that advertise on its TV channels (such as Sportsnet), radio stations, and publishing ventures (such as *Maclean's* magazine).

©Getty Images/Sean Russell

Some of Rogers' billing terms are regulated by the federal Canadian Radio-television and Telecommunications Commission (CRTC). The company bills monthly for services in advance, and payments are due within about three weeks of the billing date. Late payment charges begin to accrue at 30 days from the billing date. Most companies intend late payment charges to be punitive, to encourage customers to pay on time. Rogers charges 2% per month for overdue accounts. "We use various internal controls, such as credit checks, deposits on account and billing in advance, to mitigate credit risk," Rogers says in its annual report.

If a customer's bill does not get paid on time, companies such as Rogers will start making calls, sending reminder notices, and perhaps negotiating new payment terms. If there is still no payment, telecom companies will typically suspend the account for 21 days, then reconnect for one day, and contact the client again. If there is still no payment, it will permanently disconnect the customer. The company then would send final notices to the client, and finally the bill goes to a collection agency. "We monitor and take appropriate action to suspend services when customers have fully used their approved credit limits or violated established payment terms," Rogers says in its annual report.

As at December 31, 2014, Rogers reported accounts receivable of $1.6 billion, which increased mainly due to "customer receivables as a result of increased NHL advertising revenue and timing of collections." While having significant accounts receivable can be a credit risk, many companies, including Rogers, capitalize on their accounts receivable. In 2013, Rogers announced that it would, for the first time, sell part of its accounts receivable to an unnamed financial institution, borrowing against the expected revenue to raise money, a strategy known as securitization. In 2014, Rogers received funding of $192 million, net of repayments, under its accounts receivable securitization program.

Sources: Barry Critchley, "Rogers Communications Enters the World of Securitizing Accounts Receivables, Makes an Initial $400-Million Draw," *Financial Post,* March 18, 2013; Rogers Communications 2014 annual report; "Rogers Terms of Service, Acceptable Use Policy and Privacy Policy," 2015.

PREVIEW OF CHAPTER 7

As our opening story implies, estimating the collectibility of accounts receivable has important implications for accurate reporting of operating profits, net income, and assets. In this chapter, we discuss cash and receivables—two assets that are important to companies as diverse as giant **Rogers** and small owner-operated private operations. The chapter is organized as follows:

CASH AND RECEIVABLES					
Understanding Cash and Accounts Receivable	**Cash Recognition and Measurement**	**Receivables— Recognition and Measurement**	**Presentation, Disclosure, and Analysis of Receivables**	**IFRS/ASPE Comparison**	**Appendix 7A— Cash Controls**
▪ How do companies manage and control cash? ▪ What types of companies have extensive accounts receivable? ▪ What are the types of accounts receivable? ▪ How do companies manage accounts receivable?	▪ What is cash? ▪ Reporting cash ▪ Summary of cash-related items	▪ Definition and types ▪ Recognition and measurement of accounts receivable ▪ Impairment of accounts receivable ▪ Recognition and measurement of short-term notes and loans receivable ▪ Recognition and measurement of long-term notes and loans receivable ▪ Derecognition of receivables	▪ Presentation and disclosure ▪ Analysis	▪ A comparison of IFRS and ASPE ▪ Looking ahead	▪ Management and control of cash ▪ Using bank accounts ▪ The imprest petty cash system ▪ Physical protection of cash balances ▪ Reconciliation of bank balances

Understanding Cash and Accounts Receivable

It is important to understand the business of the company when considering issues relating to cash and accounts receivable. We need to ask ourselves questions such as the following.

- How do companies manage and control cash?

- What types of companies are more likely to carry significant accounts receivable balances?

- What are the different types of accounts receivable?

- What aspects of accounts receivable must be managed and how do companies do this?

We will address these questions below.

How Do Companies Manage and Control Cash?

**TREASURY MANAGEMENT
5.2.1**

Cash management and control is a key issue for many companies, including retailers that have significant cash sales. Businesses rely on cash flow budgets to help anticipate cash needs and minimize borrowing requirements. Generally, companies with surplus cash try to minimize "idle" cash by putting extra cash resources into short-term deposits. Banks and other financial institutions take this to the extreme with very short-term borrowing and lending in the overnight money market, where borrowed funds plus interest must be repaid at the start of the next business day. For companies without surplus cash, management must still carefully manage its cash resources to minimize any bank loans and other borrowings. The control of cash includes implementing internal control over physical custody of cash on hand and preparation of regular bank reconciliations. Control of cash is so important that we devote an entire appendix to it at the end of this chapter, where we discuss it in much more detail.

What Types of Companies Have Extensive Accounts Receivable?

**REAL WORLD
EMPHASIS**

As a general rule, manufacturers and wholesalers often have a significant amount of accounts receivable. For instance, **Magna International Inc.**, a large Canadian automobile supplier, reported accounts receivable of U.S. $5,635 million (or over 50% of current assets) at the end of 2014. This was Magna's largest current asset and it reflected an increase of 7.4% from 2013 to 2014. An increase in accounts receivable might be cause for concern for some companies, when it indicates an inability to collect receivables on a timely basis. However, Magna also showed a significant 5.2% increase in sales that year. Magna adopted U.S. generally accepted accounting principles in 2011, and uses the U.S. dollar as its functional currency. Therefore, its Canadian accounts receivable are translated into U.S. dollars on its balance sheet.

On the other hand, retailers such as **Hudson's Bay Company (HBC)** often have relatively low accounts receivable. This is due to customers' use of major credit cards (like Visa) and debit cards for payments. For example, at the end of the 2013–2014 fiscal year, HBC had trade and other receivables of only $137.2 million (or approximately 6% of current assets). Of that $137.2-million balance, the company reported that 70.3% of its receivables were other receivables, which were mainly sundry receivables from vendors. This likely makes monitoring of collection issues less difficult.

What Are the Types of Accounts Receivable?

**REAL WORLD
EMPHASIS**

Manufacturers and wholesalers have accounts receivable relating to their sales transactions, as discussed in Chapter 6. Let's look for instance at **Suncor Energy**, a major Canadian integrated energy company with operations including oil sands development, retail operations (such as products marketed under the PetroCanada brand), and wholesale operations. Suncor had accounts receivable of $4,275 million at the end of 2014 (or 10.7% of revenues, down from 13.3% at the end of 2013). These receivables represented one of Suncor's largest current assets each year. Large accounts receivable balances are typical in the oil and gas industry, in part due to extended payment terms, which can stretch from 30 to 60 days.

For most companies, typical accounts-receivable-related categories include trade receivables, loans receivable, and nontrade receivables (including items like interest receivable, amounts due from officers, and advances to employees). However, there are more complicated items sometimes included in accounts receivable. For example, Suncor enters into arrangements that allow the offsetting of derivative financial instruments and accounts receivable as part of its accounts receivable balance. Suncor's derivatives include swaps related to Suncor's fixed rate debt. The fair value of derivative contracts recorded as part of accounts receivable totalled $211 million at the end of 2014 ($225 million at the end of 2013). Interest rate swaps generally involve one party that was making payments based on a fixed interest rate, and another that was making payments based on a floating rate, agreeing to swap or exchange their payment streams. Swaps are discussed in more detail in Chapter 16, as part of Complex Financial Instruments.

How Do Companies Manage Accounts Receivable?

**STRATEGY IMPLEMENTATION
2.4.1
TREASURY MANAGEMENT
5.2.1**

For many reasons, it is important for management to carefully consider how to manage and control its accounts receivable balances. Of course, accounts receivable are directly related to sales. If the sales department is overly aggressive with its credit policy, it could result in significant increases in bad debts and uncollectible accounts. Companies will typically assess the creditworthiness of new customers and grant them a credit limit accordingly. Established customers' track records and payment history will also affect how credit limits change over time.

Receivables management can be a delicate balancing act. If credit policies are too "tight," or restrictive, potential sales could be lost to competitors. On the other hand, if the credit policy is too "loose," or flexible, an aggressive sales team might enter into contracts with higher-risk customers, resulting in collectibility difficulties. Some companies offer discounts to encourage faster payment of outstanding balances. These discounts are popular with customers, because the savings from early payment are much better than the interest that could be earned on short-term investments. However, the costs to the company offering the discount must also be considered.

Companies also need to monitor outstanding accounts receivable balances. An important tool for management to monitor outstanding accounts receivable is to conduct an aged accounts receivable analysis, discussed in the section "Impairment of Accounts Receivable" later in this chapter. Companies that do not regularly assess and follow up on overdue accounts receivable may find that some of their customers take advantage of the situation. In particular, customers that are facing cash flow difficulties may be influenced regarding which companies they pay first by the number of phone calls and follow-up letters they receive from collection departments. (After all, it is easier to "oil the squeaky wheel" than to listen to it!). Discussions with tardy customers may result in a schedule of payments that is beneficial to both the seller and customer.

Companies should therefore monitor accounts receivable levels carefully to:

- minimize the stress on working capital and related bank debt, and also

- encourage prompt payment from their customers.

WHAT DO THE NUMBERS MEAN?

As noted above, companies should monitor their accounts receivable balances carefully and may want to take a variety of actions to speed up collections. For example, **Bell Aliant**, one of North America's largest land-line communications and Internet service providers, uses late payment charges and follow-up letters to help encourage prompt payment. It only uses a collection agency as a last resort in the collection process! The opening story to this chapter provides details of how Rogers encourages payment of its overdue accounts.

Other companies may sell accounts receivable to factors to convert the receivables into cash more quickly, rather than waiting for customers to pay. These services tend to be used more by small and medium-sized businesses that may not have the cash resources to wait for payment (or the credit history to allow them to obtain a bank loan at a better interest rate). Alternatively, larger companies may rely on securitization of pools of accounts receivable, where the receivables are grouped together and turned into securities for sale to investors. We discuss the use of factors and asset-backed securities by large companies to raise funds and improve cash flow in more detail as part of the subsection "Sales of Receivables" later in this chapter.

CASH RECOGNITION AND MEASUREMENT

Objective 2
Define financial assets, and identify items that are considered cash and cash equivalents and how they are reported.

We now begin our detailed study of statement of financial position accounts and the recognition and measurement concepts that apply to the different categories of assets, liabilities, and shareholders' equity. The first assets we cover are highly liquid, and they are considered financial assets. A **financial asset** is any asset that is:

(i) cash;

(ii) a contractual right to receive cash or another financial asset from another party;

(iii) a contractual right to exchange financial instruments with another party under conditions that are potentially favourable to the entity; or

(iv) an equity instrument of another entity.[1]

Financial assets are covered in several chapters of this text. Chapter 7 deals with cash and cash equivalents, and with accounts, notes, and loans receivable. Chapter 9 covers other major categories of financial assets—mainly investments in the debt and equity instruments of other companies. The financial assets in these two chapters fit parts (i), (ii), and (iv) of the definition above. Chapter 3 highlights the profession's recent move away from the long-standing transactions-based historical cost model toward one that relies more on fair values. Chapter 3 includes a discussion of what fair value is and how it is measured. We will cover the more complex instruments that fit part (iii) of the definition above, such as derivatives, along with financial liabilities and equity, in Chapter 16 of Volume 2.

What Is Cash?

Cash is the most liquid asset and is the standard medium of exchange and the basis for measuring and accounting for all other items. It meets the definition of a financial asset, and is generally classified as a current asset.

Cash consists of coins, currency, and other available funds that are on deposit at a bank. Negotiable instruments such as money orders, certified cheques, cashier's cheques, and bank drafts are also viewed as cash. Although a company's bank may have a legal right to demand advance notice before it allows a withdrawal from a savings account, banks rarely ask for this notice. Therefore, savings accounts are also usually classified as cash.

It is more appropriate to classify money-market funds, certificates of deposit, and similar types of deposits and "short-term paper" that allow investors to earn interest as

cash equivalents (defined in the section "Reporting cash" below) or **short-term investments** than as cash. The reason is that there are usually restrictions, or penalties, on these securities if they are converted to cash before maturity. Money-market funds that give chequing account privileges, however, are usually classified as cash.

Certain items present classification problems: for example, postdated cheques from customers and IOUs are treated as receivables. It is proper to treat travel advances granted to employees as receivables if the advances are to be collected from the employees or deducted from their salaries. Otherwise, it is more appropriate to classify the travel advance as a prepaid expense. Postage stamps on hand are classified as part of office supplies inventory or as a prepaid expense. Petty cash funds and change funds are included in current assets as cash because these funds are used to meet current operating expenses and to liquidate current liabilities.

Reporting Cash

Although the reporting of cash is fairly straightforward, there are some issues that need special attention. They concern the reporting of:

- Restricted cash

- Cash in foreign currencies

- Bank overdrafts

- Cash equivalents

Restricted Cash

Petty cash (see Appendix 7A) and special payroll and dividend bank accounts are examples of cash that has been set aside for a particular purpose. In most situations, these balances are not material and therefore are not segregated from cash when it is reported in the financial statements. When an amount is material, restricted cash is segregated from regular cash for reporting purposes. The **restricted cash** is separately disclosed and reported in the current assets section or is classified separately in the long-term assets section, depending on the date of availability or of the expected disbursement.[2] In general, cash should not be classified in current assets if there are restrictions that prevent it from being used for current purposes, unless the restricted cash offsets a current liability. Cash that is classified in the long-term section has often been set aside for investment or financing purposes, such as for a plant expansion, long-term debt retirement, or as collateral for a long-term loan.

Some lending institutions require customers who borrow money from them to keep minimum cash balances in their chequing or savings accounts. These minimum balances are called **compensating balances**. They are defined as the portion of any demand deposit (or any time deposit or certificate of deposit) that a corporation keeps as support for its existing or maturing obligations with a lending institution.[3] By requiring a compensating balance, the bank gets an effective interest rate on its loan that is higher than the stated rate because it can use the restricted amount that must remain on deposit. In the United States, where banks more often require compensating balances, the accounting practice is to report in current assets any legally restricted deposits that are held as compensating balances against short-term borrowing arrangements.

To ensure that investors are not misled about the amount of cash that is available to meet recurring obligations, legally restricted balances have to be reported separately in current assets or non-current assets, as appropriate. In practice, many companies report this through note disclosure.

LAW

Cash in Foreign Currencies

Many companies have bank accounts in other countries, especially if they have recurring transactions in that country's currency. The foreign currency is translated into Canadian dollars at the exchange rate on the date of the statement of financial position. In situations where there is no restriction on the transfer of those funds to the Canadian company, they are included as cash in current assets. If there are restrictions on the flow of capital out of a country, the cash is reported as restricted. The classification of the cash as current or non-current is based on the circumstances. In extreme cases, restrictions may be so severe that the foreign balances do not even qualify for recognition as assets.

Bank Overdrafts

Bank overdrafts occur when cheques are written for more than the amount in the bank account. Overdrafts are reported in the current liabilities section, and companies sometimes do this by adding the amount to what is reported as accounts payable. If the overdraft amount is material, it should be disclosed separately either on the face of the statement of financial position or in the related notes.

In general, bank overdrafts should not be offset against the Cash account. A major exception is when there is available cash in another account at the same bank as the overdraft. Offsetting in this case is appropriate.

Cash Equivalents

Cash is often reported with the asset category called cash equivalents. **Cash equivalents** are defined as "short-term, highly liquid investments that are readily convertible to known amounts of cash and which are subject to an insignificant risk of changes in value."[4] Companies usually hold cash equivalents to meet upcoming cash requirements. Generally, only investments with **maturities of three months or less** when acquired qualify under the definition of cash equivalents. Equity investments are excluded from the ASPE definition of cash equivalents. However, IFRS allows preferred shares that are acquired close to their maturity date to qualify. Examples of cash equivalents are investments in treasury bills, commercial paper, and money-market funds.

In some circumstances, bank overdrafts may be deducted when the amount of cash and cash equivalents is being determined. Overdrafts may be considered part of cash and cash equivalents if:

- they are part of the firm's cash management activities,

- they are repayable on demand, and

- the bank balance fluctuates often between a positive and negative balance.

Because some companies report investments that qualify as cash equivalents in other categories of current assets, such as short-term or trading investments, it is important for entities to disclose their reporting policy in a note to the financial statements. Investments that are classified as cash equivalents are held to be sold in the very short term. These are generally reported at fair value. Their fair values at acquisition plus accrued interest to the date of the statement of financial position often approximate fair value at the date of the statement of financial position.

Illustration 7-1 shows the information that British Columbia–incorporated **Thompson Creek Metals Company (TCM)** reports in its financial statements for the year ended December 31, 2014 (in millions of U.S. dollars). TCM is a copper and gold producer and owns and operates a U.S.-based metallurgical facility.

REAL WORLD EMPHASIS

Illustration 7-1

Reporting of Cash and Cash Equivalents—Thompson Creek Metals Company

ASSETS	2014	2013
Current assets:		
Cash and cash equivalents	$265.6	$233.9
Restricted cash	5.7	5.7

TCM also has Restricted Cash that is a current asset.

2. Significant Accounting Policies

Cash and Cash Equivalents and Restricted Cash

   Cash is comprised of cash deposits held at banks. Cash equivalents are financial instruments issued or guaranteed by major financial institutions and governments that have an original maturity date of less than 90 days. Cash equivalents are stated at cost, which approximates market value. Restricted cash is primarily comprised of amounts withheld related to certain construction contracts and amounts to fund TCM's deferred compensation program.

Summary of Cash-Related Items

Cash and cash equivalents include currency and most negotiable instruments. If the item cannot be converted to coin or currency on short notice, it is classified separately as an investment, receivable, or prepaid expense. Cash that is not available for paying liabilities that are currently maturing is classified in the long-term assets section. The chart below summarizes the classification of cash-related items. Appendix 7A provides further details on the control of cash.

Classification of Cash, Cash Equivalents, and Noncash Items		
Item	**Classification**	**Comment**
Cash	Cash	Report as cash. If restricted, identify and report separately as a current or non-current asset.
Petty cash	Cash	Report as cash.
Short-term paper	Cash equivalents	Classify as cash equivalents if investments have a maturity of three months or less when acquired.
Short-term paper	Short-term investments	Classify as short-term investments if investments have a maturity of over 3 months to 12 months when acquired.
Postdated cheques and IOUs	Receivables	Classify as receivables if they are considered to be collectible.
Travel advances	Receivables or prepaid expenses	Classify as receivables or prepaid expenses if they are collectible from employees or to be spent on travel in the future, respectively.
Postage on hand (as stamps or in postage meters)	Prepaid expenses	Alternatively, these may be classified as office supplies inventory.
Bank overdrafts	Current liability	If there is a right of offset, report as a reduction of cash.
Compensating balances	Classified separately as a deposit that is maintained as a compensating balance	Classify as current asset in the statement of financial position. Disclose details of the arrangement.

RECEIVABLES—RECOGNITION AND MEASUREMENT

We now turn to the second financial asset that is important to companies: receivables.

Definition and Types

Objective 3
Define receivables and
identify the different
types of receivables
from an accounting
perspective.

In general, receivables are claims that a company has against customers and others, usually for specific cash receipts in the future. As we saw in the introduction to this chapter, when the claim is a **contractual** right to receive cash or other financial assets from another party, the receivable is a financial asset. On a classified statement of financial position, receivables are either current (short-term) or non-current (long-term). Current receivables are expected to be realized (converted to cash) within a year or during the current operating cycle, whichever is longer. All other receivables are classified as non-current.

These financial assets are generally referred to in a more specific way as loans or receivables, with loans being a type of receivable.[5] **Loans and receivables** result from one party delivering cash (or other assets or services) to a borrower in exchange for a promise to repay the amount on a specified date or dates, or on demand, along with interest to compensate for the time value of money and the risk of non-payment. They are not usually acquired to be held as a cash equivalent or temporary investment of excess cash. Investments in government debt, corporate bonds, convertible debt, commercial paper, and other securities, while similar, are not loans and receivables. They are traded in an active market, while loans and receivables are not.

Trade receivables are amounts owed by customers to whom the company has sold goods or services as part of its normal business operations; that is, they are amounts that result from operating transactions. They can be either open accounts receivable or notes receivable. Open accounts receivable are short-term extensions of credit that are based on a purchaser's **verbal** promise to pay for goods and services that have been sold. They are normally collectible within 30 to 60 days, but credit terms may be longer—or shorter—depending on the industry. **Notes receivable** are **written** promises to pay a certain amount of money on a specified future date. They may arise from sales of goods and services, or from other transactions.

As the term "loan" suggests, **loans receivable** are created when one party advances cash or other assets to a borrower and receives a promise to be repaid later. Loans tend to result from financing transactions by borrowers and investing transactions by lenders. When there is a written document that gives the terms and conditions of the loan receivable, the loan is then also called a note receivable.

Nontrade receivables are created by a variety of transactions and can be written promises either to pay cash or to deliver other assets. Examples of nontrade receivables include the following:

- Advances to officers and employees, or to subsidiaries or other companies

- Amounts owing from a purchaser on the sale of capital assets or investments where delayed payment terms have been agreed on

- Amounts receivable from the government for income taxes paid in excess of the amount owed, GST/HST payments recoverable, investment tax credits, or other tax rebates receivable

- Dividends and interest receivable

- Claims against insurance companies for losses the company has suffered; against trucking companies or railways for damaged or lost goods; against creditors for returned, damaged, or lost goods; or against customers for returnable items (crates, containers, etc.)

REAL WORLD EMPHASIS

Because of their special nature, nontrade receivables are generally classified and reported as separate items in the statement of financial position or in a note that is cross-referenced to the statement. Illustration 7-2 shows the balance sheet and separate reporting of the cash and cash equivalents and receivables on the financial statements of Nova Scotia–based **Empire Company Limited** for its year ended May 3, 2014.

Illustration 7-2

Receivables Reporting—Empire Company Limited

CONSOLIDATED BALANCE SHEETS

(in millions)	May 3, 2014	May 4, 2013
Assets		
Current		
Cash and cash equivalents	$429.3	$455.2
Receivables	460.5	381.7
Income taxes receivable	39.7	33.8
Loans and other receivables (Note 5)	46.4	66.2
Loans and other receivables (Note 5)	52.5	53.8

Note 5 Loans and Other Receivables

	May 3, 2014	May 4, 2013
Loans receivable	$ 61.8	$ 60.3
Notes receivable and other	37.1	59.7
	98.9	120.0
Less amount due within one year	46.4	66.2
	$ 52.5	$ 53.8

Loans receivable represent long-term financing by Empire to certain retail associates. These loans are primarily secured by inventory, fixtures, and equipment; bear various interest rates; and have repayment terms of up to 10 years. The carrying amount of the loans receivable approximates fair value based on the variable interest rates charged on the loans and the operating relationship of the associates with the company.

Note that the following discussion of **accounts and notes receivable** assumes that they are short-term trade receivables, and that the discussion of **loans receivable** is based on long-term nontrade loans or notes. In addition, it is assumed that they all are financial assets. The basic accounting issues are discussed in the following sections: **recognition and measurement**, **impairment**, and **derecognition**.

Recognition and Measurement of Accounts Receivable

Objective 4
Account for and explain the accounting issues related to the recognition and measurement of accounts receivable.

The general accounting standards for the recognition and initial measurement of accounts receivable are as follows:

- Recognize an account receivable when the entity becomes a party to the contractual provisions of the financial instrument.

- Measure the receivable initially at its fair value.[6]

- After initial recognition, measure receivables at amortized cost.

The entity becomes a party to the contractual provisions of the financial instrument only when it has a legal claim to receive cash or other financial assets. While a commitment to sell goods or services to a customer might be made when a customer's order is received, there is usually no legal claim until one of the parties to the contract has performed under the agreement. Therefore, the timing of recognition of accounts receivable is intertwined with the recognition of revenue, which was discussed in Chapter 6. Typically, when the sale is recognized, either cash is received (realized) or an account receivable is recognized if there is an unconditional right to receive consideration (that is, where the company has satisfied its performance obligation or the amounts due are non-refundable). As discussed in Chapter 6, where there is a conditional right to receive consideration, a contract asset would be recorded rather than accounts receivable.

Recognizing receivables initially at their fair value is not as straightforward as it might seem. This is because fair value may not be the same as the exchange price that the parties agree on. The **exchange price**, **the amount due** from the customer or borrower, is generally indicated on a business document, usually an invoice. Two factors can make measuring the fair value of short-term receivables more complicated: (1) the availability of discounts (trade and cash discounts) and (2) the length of time between the sale and the payment due date (the interest element).

Trade Discounts

Customers are often quoted prices based on list or catalogue prices that may have trade or quantity discounts. **Trade discounts** are used to avoid frequent changes in catalogues, to quote different prices for different quantities purchased, or to hide the true invoice price from competitors.

Trade discounts are commonly quoted in percentages. For example, if your textbook has a list price of $90 and the publisher sells it to college and university bookstores for list less a 30% trade discount, the receivable recorded by the publisher is $63 per textbook. The normal practice is simply to deduct the trade discount from the list price and recognize the net amount as the receivable and revenue.

Cash Discounts (Sales Discounts)

TREASURY MANAGEMENT
5.2.1

Cash discounts or **sales discounts** are offered to encourage fast payment. They are expressed in specific terms. For example, 2/10, n/30 means there is a 2% discount if the invoice is paid within 10 days and that the gross amount is due in 30 days. Meanwhile, 2/10 E.O.M., n/30 E.O.M. means there is a 2% discount if the invoice is paid before the 10th day of the following month, with full payment due by the 30th of the following month. (E.O.M. stands for "end of month.")

Companies that buy goods or services but fail to take sales discounts are usually not using their money as effectively as they could. An enterprise that receives a 1% reduction in the sales price for paying within 10 days when the total payment is due within 30 days is basically earning 18.25% interest (1.0% divided by 20/365) because of the discount—or, more technically, it is at least avoiding that rate of interest implicit in the undiscounted invoice price. For this reason, companies usually take the discount unless their cash is severely limited.[7]

In theory, the receivable and the associated sale should both be recognized at the net amount or fair value; that is, the expected future cash flows. Under this **net method** approach, sales to customers who pay within the discount period are reported at the cash price. For customers who pay after the discount period expires, the company separately records these amounts in the Sales Discounts Forfeited account, similar to interest income earned.

However, the most commonly used method of recording short-term receivables and related sales is to **record the gross amounts of the receivable and sale. That is, the amounts are recorded at the full amount assuming no discount will be taken.** Under this **gross method** approach, sales discounts are recognized in the accounts only when payment is received within the discount period. Sales discounts are then shown in the income statement as a deduction from sales to arrive at net sales.

The entries in Illustration 7-3 show the difference between the gross and net methods.

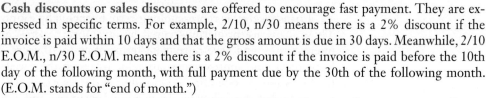

Illustration 7-3	Gross Method		Net Method	
Entries under Gross and Net Methods of Recording Cash (Sales) Discounts	**Sales of $10,000, terms 2/10, n/30:**			
	Accounts Receivable 10,000		Accounts Receivable 9,800	
	Sales Revenue	10,000	Sales Revenue	9,800
	Payment on $4,000 of sales received within discount period:			
	Cash 3,920		Cash 3,920	
	Sales Discounts 80		Accounts Receivable	3,920
	Accounts Receivable	4,000		

(continued)

Payment on $6,000 of sales received after discount period:

Cash	6,000		Accounts Receivable	120*	
Accounts Receivable		6,000	Sales Discounts Forfeited		120
			Cash	6,000	
			Accounts Receivable		6,000*
			*One net entry could be made:		
			Cash	6,000	
			Accounts Receivable		5,880
			Sales Discounts Forfeited		120

If the **gross method** is used, proper asset valuation requires that a reasonable estimate be made of discounts that are expected to be taken after the date of the statement of financial position and that the amount be recorded if it is material. Allowance for Sales Discounts, a **contra account** to Accounts Receivable on the statement of financial position, is credited for such amounts and the Sales Discounts account on the income statement is increased (debited). If the **net method** is used, the receivables are already at their realizable value so no further adjustment is needed. The Sales Discounts Forfeited account is recognized as an item of "Other revenue" on the income statement.

Although the net method is theoretically preferred, it is rarely used. This is because it requires more bookkeeping for the additional adjusting entries after the discount period has passed. The gross method, together with the added requirement to estimate and record discounts that are expected to be taken after the date of the statement of financial position, results in the same impact on the statement of financial position and income statement as long as "sales discounts forfeited" are not material.

Sales Returns and Allowances

To properly measure **sales revenues** and **receivables** for sales with a right of return, under IFRS a Refund Liability account is credited, as discussed in Chapter 6. Under ASPE, allowance accounts are normally used. Probable sales returns and price reductions are estimated and deducted as contra accounts against sales on the income statement and accounts receivable on the statement of financial position. This results in net sales and the net estimated amount of accounts receivable being properly reported on the financial statements.

This procedure is followed so that Sales Revenue is not overstated. Under IFRS, Sales Revenue is debited. Under ASPE, the sales returns or price allowances (called **sales returns and allowances**) are reported in the same period as the sales that they relate to. If this adjustment is not made, however, the amount of mismatched returns and allowances is usually not material as long as the items are handled consistently from year to year. The situation changes when a company completes a few special orders for large amounts near the end of its accounting period. In this case, sales returns and allowances should be anticipated and recognized in the period of the sale to avoid distorting the current period's income statement. There are some companies that by their nature have significant returns and therefore usually have an allowance for sales returns.

As an example, assume that Astro Corporation estimates that approximately 5% of its $1 million of trade receivables outstanding will be returned or some adjustment will be made to the sales price. Leaving out a $50,000 charge could have a material effect on net income for the period. The entries to show the expected Refund Liability (IFRS) and Allowance for Sales Returns and Allowances (ASPE) are:

A = L + SE
-50,000   -50,000

Cash flows: No effect

IFRS			ASPE		
Sales Revenue	50,000		Sales Returns and Allowances	50,000	
Refund Liability		50,000	Allowance for Sales Returns and Allowances		50,000

The account Sales Returns and Allowances is reported as a deduction from Sales Revenue in the income statement so the net effect on sales revenue is the same under IFRS and ASPE. Allowance for Sales Returns and Allowances is an asset valuation account (contra asset) that is deducted from total accounts receivable. It is similar to the Allowance for Doubtful Accounts discussed below. In contrast, the Refund Liability account would be a current liability under IFRS.

Nonrecognition of Interest Element

UNDERLYING CONCEPT

Ideally, receivables should be measured initially at their fair value, represented by their present value; that is, the amount of cash that would be required at the date of the sale to satisfy the outstanding claim. As mentioned in the previous section, this is equivalent to the discounted value of the cash that will be received in the future. When a company has to wait for the cash receipts, the receivable's face amount is not a precise measure of its fair value.

To illustrate, assume that a company makes a sale on account for $1,000. The applicable annual interest rate is 12%, and cash is to be received at the end of four months. The receivable's present value is not $1,000 but $961.56 ($1,000 × 0.96156, Table A-2 $n = 1, i = 4\%$).[8] In other words, $1,000 to be received in four months is equivalent to $961.56 received today.

In theory, the discounted amount of $961.56 is the fair value of the receivable and sales revenue, and any additional amount received after the sale is interest revenue. **In practice, accountants generally ignore this for accounts receivable because the discount amount is not usually material when compared with the net income for the period.**

ASPE and IFRS both support measuring financial assets at the **present value of the cash that is expected to be received.** However, both allow net realizable value to approximate the present value for short-term trade receivables because the effect of the time value of money is immaterial.

Materiality means that an amount in question would make a difference to a decision-maker. Standard setters believe that interest and present value concepts do not need to be strictly applied if omitting them results in financial statements that are not materially different.

Measurement of Accounts Receivable after Acquisition

Accounts receivable are measured in subsequent accounting periods at amortized cost. Where there is no interest element recognized, as discussed above, there is nothing to amortize, so amortized cost and cost are the same thing. For notes and loans receivable that have an interest component, the asset's carrying amount is amortized as described later in this chapter.

Impairment of Accounts Receivable

Objective 5

Account for and explain the accounting issues related to the impairment in value of accounts receivable.

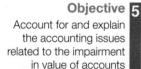

SIGNIFICANT CHANGE

The goal in valuing accounts receivable on the statement of financial position is to report them at no more than the benefits they will ultimately provide to the entity. Because of this, in addition to reductions for expected returns, allowances, or cash discounts that will be granted, all receivables have to be assessed for indications of uncollectibility or impairment. Impaired trade receivables are usually referred to as **bad debts** or **uncollectible accounts.** Under ASPE, loans and receivables are impaired if there has been a "significant adverse change" in either the expected timing of the future cash flows or in the amount expected to be repaid this is consistent with the use of a triggering event (under an incurred loss impairment model). This topic is discussed in detail in Chapter 9. Under IFRS 9, for accounts receivable without a significant financing component, the loss allowance is to be based on "lifetime expected credit losses." This is defined as expected credit losses resulting from all possible default events over the life of the accounts receivable, consistent with the expected loss impairment model discussed in Chapter 9.

Estimating Uncollectible Trade Accounts Receivable

As one accountant so aptly noted, the credit manager's idea of heaven would probably be a place where everyone (eventually) paid his or her debts.[9] With the exception of some segments in the retail sector, the usual method of conducting business is through extending credit to customers. This means that most companies are exposed to varying levels of **credit risk:** the likelihood of loss because of the failure of the other party to fully pay the amount owed. Except for cash sales, it is possible that the full amount of any sale will never be collected. Many companies set their credit policies to allow for a certain percentage of uncollectible accounts. In fact, some companies feel that if the control over sales is too "tight," it may indicate that sales are being lost because credit policies are too strict.

The **accounting issue**, therefore, is ensuring that a reasonable estimate is made of the amount of the accounts receivable that is unlikely to be collected. An allowance for this amount is then deducted from the receivables reported on the statement of financial position. If there are only a few relatively large accounts, an analysis of each separate account can be made, but most companies have large numbers of similar accounts with smaller balances in each. How does management obtain an unbiased estimate of how much may be uncollectible? The estimate should be based on reasonable and supportable information that is readily available at the year-end date about past events, current conditions, and expected future economic conditions (as required by IFRS 9).

The single most important indicator used to identify expected credit losses for accounts receivable is the age of the accounts; that is, how long the amounts owed have been outstanding, especially beyond their due dates. Other factors that are considered include the company's past loss experience and current economic conditions. Accounts are also analyzed by grouping those with similar credit risk characteristics—perhaps by geographic location or type of industry. If one area of the country is experiencing high unemployment and depressed economic conditions, this may affect the ability of debtors in that area to pay their accounts. Or a particular industry, such as forestry or real estate, may be going through a low in the business cycle with a higher than usual incidence of tight cash, or receivership or bankruptcy.

One common method used by most companies to estimate how much of their total accounts receivable is probably uncollectible is the **aging method**. This approach allows a company to use its past experience to estimate the percentage of its outstanding receivables that will become uncollectible, without identifying specific accounts. This is referred to as the **percentage-of-receivables approach**. Its objective is to report receivables on the statement of financial position at their **net realizable value**—the net amount expected to be received in cash. The percentage that is used in this approach may be a combined rate that reflects an overall estimate of the uncollectible receivables. A better approach is to set up an **aging schedule**, which is more sensitive to the actual status of the accounts receivable. This approach determines the age of each account receivable and uses a **provision matrix** to apply a different percentage estimated to be uncollectible to each of the various age categories, based on historical observed default rates. At each reporting date, these default rates in the provision matrix are updated to take into account matters such as changes in economic conditions. Aging schedules are often used because they show which accounts need special attention by highlighting how long various accounts receivable have been outstanding. The schedule of Wilson & Co. in Illustration 7-4 is an example.

Illustration 7-4

Accounts Receivable Aging Schedule, Wilson & Co.

WILSON & CO.
Aging Schedule

Name of Customer	Balance Dec. 31	Age (number of days accounts are outstanding)			
		Under 60 days	61–90 days	91–120 days	Over 120 days
Atlantic Stainless Steel Corp	$ 9,800	$ 7,000	$ 2,800		
Brockville Steel Company	34,000	34,000			
Cambridge Sheet & Tube Co.	4,500				$ 4,500
Eastern Iron Works Ltd.	7,200	6,000		$ 1,200	
Other individual customers	491,500	413,000	15,200	12,800	50,500
	$547,000	$460,000	$18,000	$14,000	$55,000

Summary

Age	Amount	Percentage Estimated to Be Uncollectible	Estimate of Uncollectible Accounts
Under 60 days old	$460,000	4%	$18,400
61–90 days old	18,000	15%	2,700
91–120 days old	14,000	20%	2,800
Over 120 days	55,000	25%	13,750
Year-end balance of Allowance for Doubtful Accounts should equal this amount			$37,650

Allowance Method

This analysis indicates that Wilson & Co. expects to receive $547,000 less $37,650, or $509,350 net cash receipts from the December 31 amounts owed. That is, $509,350 is the accounts receivable's estimated net realizable value. The **allowance method** is used to account for this estimate of impairment. On Wilson & Co.'s December 31 statement of financial position, a contra account, Allowance for Doubtful Accounts (or Allowance for Uncollectible Accounts) of $37,650, is reported, as shown in Illustration 7-5. A contra account is used because the Accounts Receivable account is supported by a subsidiary ledger of each customer's balance owing and management does not know yet which specific accounts will result in non-collection and bad debt losses.

<table>
<tr><td></td><td colspan="2" align="center">Illustration 7-5</td></tr>
</table>

Accounts Receivable on the Statement of Financial Position, Wilson & Co.

WILSON & CO. STATEMENT OF FINANCIAL POSITION
December 31

Current assets	
Accounts receivable	$547,000
Less: Allowance for doubtful accounts	37,650
	$509,350

The ending balance in the allowance account should be $37,650. The appropriate entry, therefore, depends on what the balance is in the account before making the adjusting entry. Assume this is Wilson's first year of operations and that there is **no previous balance in the allowance account before this adjustment.** In this case, the entry to record the impairment for the current year is:

A	=	L	+	SE
−37,650				−37,650

Cash flows: No effect

Bad Debt Expense	37,650	
Allowance for Doubtful Accounts		37,650

To change the illustration slightly, assume that **the allowance account already has a credit balance of $18,800 before adjustment**. In this case, the amount to be added to the account is $18,850 ($37,650 − $18,800). This will bring the balance in the allowance account to $37,650. The following entry is made:

A	=	L	+	SE
−18,850				−18,850

Cash flows: No effect

Bad Debt Expense	18,850	
Allowance for Doubtful Accounts		18,850

If instead the **balance in the allowance account before adjustment is a debit balance of $200**, then the amount to bring the allowance account to the correct credit balance of $37,650 is $37,850 ($37,650 desired credit balance + elimination of the $200 debit balance). When using the allowance procedure, the balance that is already in the allowance account before the adjusting entry is made **cannot be ignored**; it has to be considered to calculate the amount needed for the adjustment.

Bad Debt Expense and the Allowance Account

So far, we have focused on the balance in Allowance for Doubtful Accounts. This is because our current accounting model emphasizes ensuring good measurements of assets and liabilities. The model assumes that if assets and liabilities are measured properly, the related revenues and expenses will be as well. Let's turn now to bad debt expense.

The allowance method reports receivables at their estimated realizable value and recognizes bad debt losses as an expense in the same accounting period as when the sales on account are made. The allowance method accomplishes two things: a proper carrying amount for receivables on the statement of financial position, and the resulting matching of expenses and revenues in the same period. Using the allowance method, companies typically follow one of two accounting procedures, both of which result in the same ending balances in the Allowance and Bad Debt Expense accounts.

1. **Allowance procedure only:** At the end of every month, management carries out an analysis of the Accounts Receivable balances and assesses the estimated uncollectible accounts. An accounting entry is prepared, as illustrated above for Wilson & Co., adjusting the Allowance for Doubtful Accounts to its correct balance. The Bad Debt Expense account is debited or credited as necessary and at the end of the fiscal year, the total of all the entries to the expense account during the year is the bad debt expense for the year. The balance in the allowance account is an appropriate amount because all entries are based on an analysis of the receivables.

UNDERLYING CONCEPT

The percentage-of-sales approach is a good illustration of using the matching concept, which relates expenses to revenues earned. The final adjustment based on the net realizable value of the receivables, however, supports the primacy of asset measurement in the model.

2. **Mix of procedures:** At the end of every month, management estimates the company's **bad debt expense** for that month. This estimate is based on a percentage of the sales reported, and is therefore called the **percentage-of-sales approach**. If there is a fairly stable relationship between previous years' credit sales and bad debts, then that relationship can be turned into a percentage and used to estimate any period's bad debt expense. Because the amount of sales is known, this is a **fast and simple way** to estimate the expense each period. Each month, Bad Debt Expense is debited and Allowance for Doubtful Accounts is credited.

At the end of the fiscal year, however, when financial statements are issued, management still has to assess the year-end receivables to ensure that the balance in the allowance account is appropriate. If necessary, an adjustment is then made to the allowance account to bring it to the necessary balance, with the offsetting debit or credit made to Bad Debt Expense.

As an example, assume that every month Dockrill Corp. estimates from past experience that about 2% of net credit sales will become uncollectible. If Dockrill Corp. has net credit sales of $400,000 in 2017, the entries made through the year to record bad debt expense in 2017 can be summarized in one entry as follows:

A = L + SE
−8,000   −8,000

Cash flows: No effect

| Bad Debt Expense (2% × $400,000) | 8,000 | |
| Allowance for Doubtful Accounts | | 8,000 |

At year end, management prepares an analysis of receivables and estimates that $9,900 will not be collectible. Therefore, the balance in the allowance account **after adjustment** must be a credit of $9,900. The correct adjusting entry depends on the balance in the Allowance account before the adjustment is made. The allowance is a statement of financial position account and therefore would have had an opening balance, and entries to record increases and accounts written off (as explained below) would also have been made to the account during the current year.

Assuming the balance in Allowance for Doubtful Accounts before adjustment is a $7,500 credit, then the following adjusting entry is needed:

A = L + SE
−2,400   −2,400

Cash flows: No effect

| Bad Debt Expense | 2,400 | |
| Allowance for Doubtful Accounts ($9,900 − $7,500 = $2,400) | | 2,400 |

Either approach can be used. Many companies use the percentage-of-sales method for internal reporting through the year because of its ease of use. For their external financial statements, they make an adjustment at year end based on the collectibility of receivable balances at the date of the statement of financial position.

Accounts Written Off and the Allowance Account

Accounts Receivable Written Off.   Under the allowance method, after all efforts have been made to collect a **specific account** and it is determined to be uncollectible, its balance is removed from Accounts Receivable and the Allowance for Doubtful Accounts is reduced. For example, assuming the account of Brown Ltd. of $550 is considered uncollectible, the write off entry is as follows:

A = L + SE
0

Cash flows: No effect

| Allowance for Doubtful Accounts | 550 | |
| Accounts Receivable | | 550 |

Note that there is no effect on the income statement **from writing off an account**, nor should there be. This is because the associated bad debt expense was **previously** recognized as an estimate **in the period of the sale**. There is also no effect on the net amount of the receivables because Accounts Receivable and its contra account are **both** reduced by equal amounts.

Collection of an Account Previously Written Off.   If a collection is made on a receivable that was previously written off, the procedure is to first re-establish the receivable by reversing the write off entry, and **then** recognize the cash inflow as a regular receipt on account. To illustrate, assume that Brown Ltd. eventually remits $300, and indicates that this is all that will be paid. The entries to record this transaction are as follows:

A = L + SE
0

Cash flows: No effect

Accounts Receivable	300	
Allowance for Doubtful Accounts		300
(To reinstate the account written off and now determined to be collectible)		

A = L + SE
0

Cash flows: ↑ 300 inflow

Cash	300	
Accounts Receivable		300
(To record the receipt of cash on account from Brown Ltd.)		

Effects on Accounts

Illustration 7-6 summarizes the transactions and events that affect the accounts related to accounts receivable.

Illustration 7-6

Effects on Related Accounts

Accounts Receivable		Allowance for Doubtful Accounts	
Opening balance			Opening balance
1. Credit sales	2. Cash received on account		3. Bad debt expense recognized
5. Reinstatement of accounts previously written off	4. Accounts written off	4. Accounts written off	5. Reinstatement of accounts previously written off
		6. Year-end adjustment to reduce balance in allowance account	7. Year-end adjustment to increase balance in allowance account

Bad Debt Expense		Sales	
3. Bad debt expense recognized			1. Credit sales
7. Year-end adjustment to increase balance in allowance account	6. Year-end adjustment to reduce balance in allowance account		

The ending balance of the Accounts Receivable account represents the total of all amounts owed to the company at the date of the statement of financial position, except those accounts written off, of course. This amount is backed up by a subsidiary ledger of the individual customers and the amount owed by each. The ending balance of the allowance account represents management's estimate of the total accounts receivable that will not be collected. When reported together, the net amount is the estimated net realizable value of the total amount owed.

REAL WORLD EMPHASIS

The allowance for doubtful accounts as a percentage of receivables varies considerably, depending on the industry and recent economic conditions. **Stantec Inc.**, a professional engineering services firm, for example, reported an allowance for doubtful accounts of $18.2 million (4.3% of its trade receivables at December 31, 2014, down considerably from the 5.1% reported in 2013). Meanwhile, **Potash Corporation of Saskatchewan Inc.**, an integrated fertilizer and related industrial and feed products company, reported a provision for impairment of 1% of its trade accounts receivable in its 2014 annual report.

WHAT DO THE NUMBERS MEAN?

In its 2014 Annual Report, **Canadian Tire Corporation**'s results for its Financial Services subsidiaries are influenced in large part by growth in "gross average accounts receivable" (GAAR), which drives interest revenue. The key indicators of performance in the Financial Services segment are the size, profitability, and quality of the total managed portfolio of receivables. Growth in the total managed portfolio of receivables is measured by growth in the average number of accounts and growth in the average account balance. A key profitability measure the company tracks is the return on the average total managed portfolio (also referred to as "return on receivables," which the company reported as being 7.4% for 2014). This is calculated by dividing income before tax and gains/losses on disposal of property and equipment by GAAR over a 12-month period. The quality of the portfolio is reflected in the allowance for credit losses,

the aging of the portfolio, and the allowance rate (which the company reports as having increased by 2.3% in 2014).

A continuity schedule from Canadian Tire's 2014 Annual Report shows changes in its **allowance for credit losses** (below). As the continuity schedule indicates, the change in the allowance relates primarily to an increase in the net impairments for credit of $12.7 million (4.8%) offset by an increase in write offs of $32.3 million. The overall increase in the amount set aside for "Impairment for credit losses, net of recoveries" reflects the fact that "Loans receivable" on Canadian Tire's Consolidated Balance Sheets increased by 7.3% (from $4,569.7 million to $4,905.5 million) while "Trade and other receivables" increased by $121.7 million (up 16% from 2013 to 2014). Similarly, increases in the amounts past due totalled $36.4 million (9.9%) for the year (see below).

Allowance for Credit Losses

The Company's allowances for receivables are maintained at levels that are considered adequate to provide for future credit losses. A continuity of the Company's allowances for loans receivable[†] is as follows:

Allowance for credit losses continuity schedule:

(C$ in millions)	2014	2013
Balance, beginning of year	$ 121.4	$ 110.7
Impairment for credit losses, net of recoveries	279.7	267.0
Recoveries	59.8	59.1
Write-offs	(347.7)	(315.4)
Balance, end of year	$ 113.2	$ 121.4

[†]Loans include credit card loans, personal loans and line of credit loans. No allowances for credit losses have been made with respect to Franchise Trust and FGL sports loans receivable (where FGL Sports Ltd. includes Sport Chek, Sports Experts and similar retail businesses).

The Company's aging of the trade and other receivables and loans receivable that are past due, but not impaired is as follows:

(C$ in millions)	2014			2013		
	1-90 days	> 90 days	Total	0-90 days	> 90 days	Total
Loans receivable[‡]	$342.9	$60.4	$403.3	$308.9	$58.0	$366.9

[‡]No past due loans for Franchise Trust and FGL Sports.

A loan is considered past due when the counterparty has not made a payment by the contractual due date. Credit card and line of credit loan balances are written off when a payment is 180 days in arrears. Line of credit loans are considered impaired when a payment is over 90 days in arrears and are written off when a payment is 180 days in arrears. Personal loans are considered impaired when a payment is over 90 days in arrears and are written off when a payment is 365 days in arrears. No collateral is held against loans receivable, except for loans to Dealers (as discussed elsewhere in the annual report).

Direct Write Off Method

Some cash-based businesses, such as corner grocery stores, do not extend credit often and therefore have very few credit transactions and small accounts receivable balances. For such businesses, **where the effect of not applying the allowance method is highly immaterial**, the simpler **direct write off method** is sometimes used. No estimates are made in advance and no allowance account is used. Instead, when an account is determined to be uncollectible, the specific account receivable is written off, with the debit recognized as bad debt expense:

A = L + SE
−$$ 0 −$$

Cash flows: No effect

| Bad Debt Expense | $$ | |
| Accounts Receivable | | $$ |

If amounts are later collected on an account that was previously written off, a notation is made in the customer's record. The amount collected is recognized through entries to Cash and a revenue account entitled Uncollectible Amounts Recovered.

A = L + SE
+$$ 0 +$$

Cash flows: ↑ $$ inflow

| Cash | $$ | |
| Uncollectible Amounts Recovered | | $$ |

Recognition and Measurement of Short-Term Notes and Loans Receivable

Objective 6
Account for and explain the accounting issues related to the recognition and measurement of short-term notes and loans receivable.

A note receivable is similar to an account receivable, with one difference: the note is supported by a formal **promissory note**, which is a **written** promise to pay a specific sum of money at a specific future date. This makes a note receivable a negotiable instrument.

The note is signed by a **maker** in favour of a designated **payee** who can then legally and readily sell or transfer the note to others. **Notes always contain an interest element** because of the time value of money, but they may be classified as interest-bearing or non–interest-bearing. **Interest-bearing notes** have a stated rate of interest that is payable in addition to the face value of the note. **Zero-interest-bearing notes** (or **non–interest-bearing notes**) also include interest, but the rate is equal to the difference between the amount that was borrowed (the proceeds) and the higher face amount that will be paid back. The rate may not be stated explicitly.

Companies often accept notes receivable from customers who need to extend the payment period of an outstanding account receivable. Notes are also sometimes required from high-risk or new customers. In addition, they are often used in loans to employees and subsidiaries and in sales of property, plant, and equipment. In some industries (such as the pleasure and sport boat industry), almost all credit sales are supported by notes. Most notes, however, are created by lending transactions. The basic issues in accounting for notes receivable are the same as those for accounts receivable: recognition, measurement, impairment, and disposition. This section discusses only the recognition and measurement of **short-term** notes or loans. Longer-term instruments are covered in the next section.

To illustrate the accounting for notes or loans receivable, assume that on March 14, 2017, Prime Corporation agreed to allow its customer, Gouneau Ltd., to substitute a six-month note for the account receivable of $1,000 that Gouneau was unable to pay when it came due for payment. This means that Gouneau is basically borrowing $1,000 from Prime for six months. It was agreed that the note would bear interest at a rate of 6%. Prime's entries to record the substitution and payment of the note are as follows:

A = L + SE
0

Cash flows: No effect

March 14, 2017		
Notes Receivable	1,000	
Accounts Receivable		1,000

<table>
<tr><td colspan="3" align="center">**September 14, 2017**</td></tr>
<tr><td>Cash</td><td align="right">1,030</td><td></td></tr>
<tr><td>   Notes Receivable</td><td></td><td align="right">1,000</td></tr>
<tr><td>   Interest Income</td><td></td><td align="right">30*</td></tr>
<tr><td colspan="3">*$1,000 × .06 × $^{6}/_{12}$</td></tr>
</table>

A = L + SE
+30   +30
Cash flows: ↑ 1,030 inflow

Alternatively, a note could be accepted in exchange for lending money to an employee or subsidiary company; for example, in a **non–interest-bearing note** situation. In this case, the interest is the difference between the amount of cash that is borrowed and the face or maturity value of the note receivable. Assume that the president of Ajar Ltd. borrowed money from the company on February 23, 2017, and signed a promissory note for $5,000 repayable in nine months' time. Assume an interest rate of 8% is appropriate for this type of loan. Instead of borrowing $5,000 and repaying this amount with 8% interest added at the maturity date, the president receives only $4,717 on February 23. The $283 difference between the $4,717 borrowed and the $5,000 repaid represents interest for the nine-month period that the note is outstanding: $4,717 × 8% × $^{9}/_{12}$ = $283. Ajar's entries are as follows:[10]

<table>
<tr><td colspan="3" align="center">**February 23, 2017**</td></tr>
<tr><td>Notes Receivable</td><td align="right">4,717</td><td></td></tr>
<tr><td>   Cash</td><td></td><td align="right">4,717</td></tr>
<tr><td colspan="3" align="center">**November 23, 2017**</td></tr>
<tr><td>Cash</td><td align="right">5,000</td><td></td></tr>
<tr><td>   Notes Receivable</td><td></td><td align="right">4,717</td></tr>
<tr><td>   Interest Income</td><td></td><td align="right">283*</td></tr>
<tr><td colspan="3">*4,717 × .08 × $^{9}/_{12}$</td></tr>
</table>

A = L + SE
0
Cash flows: ↓ 4,717 outflow

A = L + SE
+283   +283
Cash flows: ↑ 5,000 inflow

In both examples provided, if financial statements are prepared while the note receivable is still outstanding, interest is accrued to the date of the statement of financial position.

Recognition and Measurement of Long-Term Notes and Loans Receivable

Objective 7
Account for and explain the accounting issues related to the recognition and measurement of long-term notes and loans receivable.

Since some form of **promissory note** is often the proof that a loan exists, the above explanation of notes receivable applies equally well to loans receivable. The examples of loans receivable that are illustrated below assume that a note is the basis for each transaction. What changes as we move from short-term to long-term notes and loans is the length of time to maturity and the importance of interest in measuring and accounting for the financial asset.

The accounting standards for the recognition and measurement of loans receivable are the same as those identified above for accounts receivable.

- Recognize a loan receivable when the entity becomes a party to the contractual provisions of the financial instrument.

- When recognized initially, measure the loan receivable at its fair value.

- After initial recognition, measure loans receivable at amortized cost.

- Recognize bad debt losses on the loans receivable when they are deemed to be impaired.[11]

The **fair value** of a note or loan receivable is measured as **the present value of the cash amounts that are expected to be collected in the future, with the amounts discounted at the market rate of interest that is appropriate for a loan with similar**

credit risk and other characteristics. When the interest stated on an interest-bearing note is the same as the effective (market) rate of interest, the note's fair value is equal to its **face value.** (The **stated interest rate,** also referred to as the **face rate** or the **coupon rate,** is the rate that is part of the note contract. The **effective interest rate,** also referred to as the **market rate** or the **yield rate,** is the rate that is used in the market to determine the note's value; that is, the discount rate that is used to determine its present value.) When the stated rate is not the same as the market rate, the note's **fair value** (its **present value**) is different from the note's **face value.** The difference between the price for the note now and its maturity value—resulting in either a discount or a premium—is then amortized over the note's life, affecting the amount of interest income that is reported. Under **IFRS,** the **effective interest method of amortization** is required, while under **ASPE,** the **amortization method is not specified.** The effective interest method is illustrated further below in the subsection "Notes Issued at Other than Face Value."

Transaction costs that are incurred in acquiring a loan or note receivable, such as commissions, can be treated in one of two ways:

1. They can be recognized as an expense when they are incurred.

2. They can be added to the fair value of the instrument, which then increases the original amount that is recognized as its "cost" at acquisition. In this case, the transaction costs are an adjustment to the discount or premium that will be amortized over the life of the loan, requiring the effective rate of interest to be recalculated under IFRS (and ASPE when the effective interest method of amortization is used).

Both ASPE and IFRS agree that transaction costs associated with financial assets that are carried at amortized cost should be accounted for as explained in the second treatment above.

Under ASPE, loans and receivables are accounted for at amortized cost. **Amortized cost** is the amount that was recognized when the instrument was acquired, reduced by any principal payments received, and adjusted for the amortization of any discount or premium, if appropriate, and writedowns for impairment. Under IFRS, the same accounting applies provided the note or loan has basic loan features and is managed on a contractual yield basis.[12] **Basic loan features** means that the instrument has contractual terms that result in cash flows that are payments of principal and interest. Management on a **contractual yield basis** refers to a company's business model of holding the instruments for their principal and interest flows. Let's see how this works.

Notes Issued at Face Value

To illustrate an interest-bearing note issued at face value, assume that Bigelow Corp. lends Scandinavian Imports $10,000 in exchange for a $10,000, three-year note bearing interest at 10% payable annually. The market rate of interest for a note of similar risk is also 10%. The first step is always to identify the amounts and timing of the cash flows. For our example, the following diagram shows both the interest and principal cash flows:

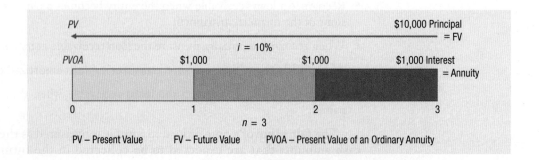

The note's present value and exchange price is calculated in Illustration 7-7.

Illustration 7-7

Present Value of Note—Stated and Market Rates the Same

Face value of the note	$10,000
Present value of the lump sum principal:	
$10,000 (PV*$_{3, 10\%}$) = $10,000 (0.75132) (Table A-2) $7,513	
Present value of the ordinary interest annuity:	
$1,000 (PVOA$_{3, 10\%}$) = $1,000 (2.48685) (Table A-4) 2,487	
Present value of the note	10,000
Difference	$ –0–

*Present value (PV) factors found in Tables A-2, A-4 and A-5

In this case, the note's fair value, present value, and face value are the same ($10,000) **because the effective and stated interest rates are the same**. Bigelow Corp. records its acquisition of the note as follows:

A = L + SE
0

Cash flows: ↓ 10,000 outflow

Notes Receivable	10,000	
Cash		10,000

Bigelow Corp. later recognizes the interest earned each year ($10,000 × 0.10) as follows:

A = L + SE
+1,000   0   +1,000

Cash flows: ↑ 1,000 inflow

Cash	1,000	
Interest Income		1,000

Notes Issued at Other than Face Value

Not all notes are issued at market rates of interest. Sometimes companies issue non–interest-bearing notes or notes with interest rates below market rates to encourage sales or to facilitate intercompany transactions.

Zero-Interest-Bearing Notes

If a zero-interest-bearing note is received in exchange for cash, its present value is usually the cash paid to the issuer. Because both the note's future amount and present value are known, the interest rate can be calculated; in other words, it is implied. The **implicit interest rate** is the rate that equates the cash paid with the amounts receivable in the future. The difference between the future (face) amount and the present value (cash paid) is a discount and this amount is amortized to interest income over the life of the note. In most cases, the implicit interest rate is the market rate. This is because the transaction is usually carried out between two parties who are at arm's length and acting in their own best interests.[13]

To illustrate, assume Jeremiah Company receives a three-year, $10,000 zero-interest-bearing note, and the present value is known to be $7,721.80. The implicit rate of interest of 9% (assumed to approximate the market rate) can be calculated as shown in Illustration 7-8.

Illustration 7-8

Determination of Implicit Interest Rate

PV of note	=	PV of future cash flows
PV of note	=	Maturity value of note × PVF$_{3, ?\%}$ (Table A-2)
$7,721.80	=	$10,000 × PVF$_{3, ?\%}$
PVF$_{3, ?\%}$	=	$\dfrac{\$7,721.80}{\$10,000}$
PVF$_{3, ?\%}$	=	0.77218
Per table A-2: Where n	=	3 and PVF = 0.77218, i = 9%
		[Note: PVF = present value factor.]

Thus, the implicit rate that makes the total cash to be received at maturity ($10,000) equal to the present value of the future cash flows ($7,721.80) is 9%. Note that if any two of the three variables of the equation on the second line in Illustration 7-8 are known, the third variable can be determined. For example, if the note's maturity value **(face value)** and **present value factor (*i* and *n*)** are known, the note's **present value** can be calculated.

The time diagram for the single cash flow of Jeremiah's note is as follows:

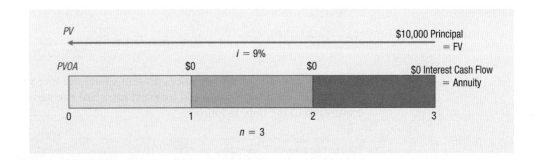

The entry to record the transaction is:

A = L + SE
0

Cash flows: ↓ 7,721.80 outflow

Notes Receivable	7,721.80	
Cash		7,721.80

Effective Interest Method of Amortization.   Under IFRS, and as applied by many private enterprises, the discount (that is, the $2,278.20 difference between the $7,721.80 provided as a loan and the $10,000 that will be repaid) is amortized each year using the **effective interest method** to recognize the interest income. This method requires that the effective interest or yield rate be calculated at the time when the investment is made. This rate is then later used to calculate interest income by applying it to the carrying amount (book value) of the investment for each interest period. The note's carrying amount changes as it is increased by the amount of discount amortized. **Thus, the net carrying amount is always equal to the present value of the note's remaining cash flows (principal and interest payments) discounted at the market rate at acquisition.** Jeremiah's three-year discount amortization and interest income schedule is shown in Illustration 7-9.

Illustration 7-9

Discount Amortization Schedule—Effective Interest Method

SCHEDULE OF NOTE DISCOUNT AMORTIZATION
Effective Interest Method
0% Note Discounted at 9%

	Cash Received	Interest Income	Discount Amortized	Carrying Amount of Note
Date of issue				$ 7,721.80
End of year 1	$–0–	$ 694.96[a]	$ 694.96[b]	8,416.76[c]
End of year 2	–0–	757.51	757.51	9,174.27
End of year 3	–0–	825.73[d]	825.73	10,000.00
	$–0–	$2,278.20	$2,278.20	

[a]$7,721.80 × 0.09 = $694.96
[b]$694.96 – 0 = $694.96
[c]$7,721.80 + $694.96 = $8,416.76 or $10,000 – ($2,278.20 – $694.96) = $8,416.76
[d]Includes $0.05 adjustment for rounding

Interest income at the end of the first year using the effective interest method is recorded as follows:

A = L + SE		
+694.96		+694.96

Cash flows: No effect

Notes Receivable	694.96	
Interest Income ($7,721.80 × 9%)		694.96

Note that the amount of the total discount, $2,278.20 in this case, represents the interest income on the note over the three years. Rather than recognize it as interest income on a straight-line basis over this period, it is recognized in increasing amounts based on the balance of the loan and previous interest earned that is still outstanding. This can be seen in Illustration 7-9. When the note comes due at the end of Year 3, the Notes Receivable account will have a balance of $10,000.00. Therefore, Jeremiah Company makes the following entry:

A = L + SE		
0		

Cash flows: ↑ 10,000 inflow

Cash	10,000	
Notes Receivable		10,000

Straight-Line Method of Amortization. Some private entities that follow ASPE prefer to use the **straight-line method** of amortizing discounts and premiums because of its simplicity. For example, in the Jeremiah Company example above, the total discount of $2,278.20 is amortized over the three-year period in equal amounts each year. Therefore, the annual amortization is $2,278.20 ÷ 3 or $759.40 each year. The entry to record the annual interest for years 1 and 2 under the straight-line method is compared with the effective interest method below:

Straight-line

A = L + SE		
+759.40		+759.40

Cash flows: No effect

	Effective interest		Straight-line	
Notes Receivable (Year 1)	694.96		759.40	
Interest Income		694.96		759.40
Notes Receivable (Year 2)	757.51		759.40	
Interest Income		757.51		759.40

At the end of Year 3, the Notes Receivable's balance is $10,000 and the same entry is made to record the receipt of the cash.

While easier to apply, the results of using straight-line amortization do not reflect the economic reality of a loan. That is, in Year 3 Jeremiah should be reporting more interest income than in Year 1 because of the interest that also accrues on the accumulating and unpaid interest for Years 1 and 2. Under the straight-line method, equal amounts of income are reported each period.

UNDERLYING CONCEPT

Using a simpler method that gives similar results to the effective interest method is an application of the materiality concept.

Interest-Bearing Notes

A note's stated rate and its effective rate are often different, as they were in the zero-interest-bearing case above. To illustrate a different situation, assume that Morgan Corp. makes a loan to Marie Co. and receives in exchange a $10,000, three-year note bearing interest at 10% annually. The market rate of interest for a note of similar risk is 12%. The time diagram for all cash flows is as follows:

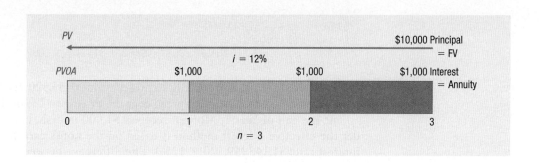

Note that the **interest cash flows are dictated by the stated rate** (10%) but that **all cash flows are discounted at the market rate** (12%) in determining the note's present value. The present value ($9,520) of the two streams of cash is calculated in Illustration 7-10.[14]

Illustration 7-10

*Calculation of Present Value—
Effective Rate Different from
Stated Rate*

Face value of the note		$10,000
Present value of the principal:		
$10,000 (PVF*₃, ₁₂%,) = $10,000 (0.71178)	$7,118	
Present value of the interest:		
$1,000 (PVFOA**₃, ₁₂%) = $1,000 (2.40183)	2,402	
Present value of the note		9,520
Difference		$ 480

*Present value factor
**Present value factor of an ordinary annuity

Because the effective interest rate or market interest rate (12%) is higher than the rate that the note actually pays (10%), you would expect the note's present value (also its fair value) to be less than its face value. That is, the note would be exchanged at a **discount**. This makes intuitive sense. If you were to invest in a note that promises 10% when you could get 12% elsewhere in the market at the same level of risk, you would not be willing to pay face value for the 10% note.

Morgan would record the receipt of the note in exchange for cash equal to its fair value as follows:

A = L + SE
0

Cash flows: ↓ 9,520 outflow

Notes Receivable	9,520	
Cash		9,520

Over the term of the note, Morgan will receive $1,000 interest each year (a rate of 10%) and at maturity get $480 more than the cash originally loaned. This $480 (the discount) effectively increases the return on the investment from 10% to 12%. It is amortized each period and the amount of interest income that is recognized is greater than the $1,000 received each year. Morgan's three-year discount amortization and interest income schedule using the effective interest method is shown in Illustration 7-11.

Illustration 7-11

*Discount Amortization
Schedule—Effective Interest
Method*

SCHEDULE OF NOTE DISCOUNT AMORTIZATION
Effective Interest Method
10% Note Discounted at 12%

	Cash Received	Interest Income	Discount Amortized	Carrying Amount of Note
Date of issue				$ 9,520
End of year 1	$1,000ª	$1,142ᵇ	$142ᶜ	9,662ᵈ
End of year 2	1,000	1,159	159	9,821
End of year 3	1,000	1,179	179	10,000
	$3,000	$3,480	$480	

ª$10,000 × 10% = $1,000
ᵇ$9,520 × 12% = $1,142
ᶜ$1,142 − $1,000 = $142
ᵈ$9,520 + $142 = $9,662 or $10,000 − ($480 − $142) = $9,662

On the date of issue, the note has a present value of $9,520. Its unamortized discount—the interest income that will be spread over the three-year life of the note—is $480.

At the end of Year 1, Morgan receives $1,000 in cash, but the interest income under the effective interest method is based on the note's carrying amount and effective interest rate: $1,142 ($9,520 × 12%). The difference between $1,000 and $1,142 is the discount to be amortized, $142, and it is amortized directly to the Notes Receivable account.

The note's carrying amount has now been increased to $9,662 ($9,520 + $142). This process is repeated until the end of Year 3.

Under the **straight-line method**, allowed only under ASPE, the initial discount of $480 is amortized at a rate of $480 ÷ 3 = $160 each year with the following entry. The same entry is made each year. Morgan would record the annual interest received at the end of the first year as follows:

Effective interest

A = L + SE
+1,142   +1,142

Cash flows: ↑ 1,000 inflow

	Effective interest		Straight-line	
Cash	1,000		1,000	
Notes Receivable	142		160	
Interest Income		1,142		1,160

When the stated rate is higher than the effective interest rate, the note's fair value (its present value) is more than its face value and the note is exchanged at a **premium**. The premium on a note receivable is recognized by recording the note receivable at its higher initial present value. The excess is amortized over the life of the note by crediting Notes Receivable and reducing (debiting) the amount of interest income that is recognized.

Notes Received for Property, Goods, or Services

When property, goods, or services are sold and a long-term note is received as the consideration instead of cash or a short-term receivable, there may be an issue in determining the selling price. If an appropriate market rate of interest is known for the note, or for a note of similar risk, there is no problem. The sale amount is the present value of the cash flows promised by the note, discounted at the market rate of interest. Remember that **if the stated rate and market rate are the same, the note's face value and fair value are also the same.** It is when the two rates are different that the note's fair value has to be calculated by discounting the cash flows at the market rate. What if we don't know what the market rate is? In this case, we can use one of two approaches.

1. We can use the fair value of the property, goods, or services that are given up as an estimate of the fair value of the note received. In this case, because we would have an estimate of the note's present value, the actual cash flow amounts, and the timing of the cash flows, we can calculate the market or yield interest rate. We need this in order to apply the effective interest method.

2. An appropriate interest rate can be imputed. **Imputation** is the process of determining an appropriate interest rate. The resulting rate is called an **imputed interest rate**. The objective for calculating the appropriate interest rate is to approximate the rate that would have been agreed on if an independent borrower and lender had negotiated a similar transaction. The choice of a rate is affected by the prevailing rates for similar instruments of issuers with similar credit ratings. It is also affected by such factors as restrictive covenants, collateral, the payment schedule, and the existing prime interest rate.

To illustrate, assume that Oasis Corp. sold land in exchange for a five-year note that has a maturity value of $35,247 and no stated interest rate. The property originally cost Oasis $14,000. What are the proceeds on disposal of the land? In other words, what selling price should be recognized in this transaction?

Situation 1: Assume that the market rate of interest of 12% is known. In this case, the proceeds from the sale are equal to the present value of the note, which we calculate (below) to be $20,000. This is a non–interest-bearing note, so the only cash flow is the $35,247 received in five periods' time: $35,247 × .56743 (Table A-2) = $20,000. The entry to record the sale is:

Notes Receivable	20,000	
Land		14,000
Gain on Sale of Land ($20,000 − $14,000)		6,000

A = L + SE
+6,000   +6,000

Cash flows: No effect

Situation 2: Assume that the market rate of interest is unknown, but the land has been appraised recently for $20,000 and the future cash flow amount is known to be $35,247. In this case, the property's fair value determines the amount of the proceeds and the note's fair value. The entry is the same as in Situation 1. To amortize the discount using the effective interest method, however, we must determine the implicit interest rate. We do this by finding the interest rate that makes the present value of the future cash flow amount of $35,247 equal to its present value of $20,000. The procedure is as follows. First we calculate the present value factor: $20,000 ÷ $35,247 = .567424. Table A-2 then identifies the interest rate for five periods and a factor of .56743 as 12%.

Situation 3: Assume that neither the market rate nor the land's fair value is known. In this case, a market rate must be imputed and then used to determine the note's present value. It will also be used to recognize the effective interest income over the five years and amortize the discount. If a 12% rate is estimated based on prevailing interest rates for companies similar to the one purchasing the land, and the future cash flow amount is $35,247, then the entry will be the same as in Situation 1. If a different rate results, the note receivable and the gain on sale will both be different as well.

Fair Value Not Equal to Cash Consideration

Accountants need to be alert when recognizing and measuring loans receivable. Sometimes, the cash that is exchanged when the loan is made may not be the same as the fair value of the loan. In this situation, the substance of the transaction has to be determined and accounted for. Imagine a situation where a company advances $20,000 to an officer of the company, charges no interest on the advance, and makes it repayable in four years. Assuming a market rate of 6%, the fair value of the loan receivable is $15,842 ($20,000 × .79209, the PV factor for $n = 4$ and $i = 6$). Although the loan's fair value is $15,842, the company officer actually received $20,000. This $4,158 difference must then be recognized and accounted for according to its nature. In this case, it is likely for additional compensation. It is required to be recognized immediately as an expense unless it qualifies to be reported as an asset. The entry to record this transaction is as follows:

Notes Receivable	15,842	
Salaries and Wages Expense	4,158	
Cash		20,000

A = L + SE
−4,158   −4,158

Cash flows: ↓ 20,000 outflow

Derecognition of Receivables

Objective 8
Account for and explain the basic accounting issues related to the derecognition of receivables.

In the normal course of events, accounts and notes receivable are collected when they are due and then removed from the books, or **derecognized**. However, as credit sales and receivables have grown in size and significance, this normal course of events has evolved. **In order to receive cash more quickly from receivables, owners now often transfer accounts or loans receivable to another company for cash.**

There are various reasons for this early transfer. First, for competitive reasons, providing sales financing for customers is almost mandatory in many industries. In the sale of durable goods, such as automobiles, trucks, industrial and farm equipment, computers, and appliances, a large majority of sales are on an instalment contract basis. This means that the seller is financing the purchase by allowing the buyer to pay for it over time, usually in equal periodic payments or instalments. Many major companies in these and other

industries have created wholly owned subsidiaries that specialize in receivables financing. For example, Canadian Tire Financial Services segment incorporated a federally regulated bank, **Canadian Tire Bank**. This wholly owned subsidiary manages and finances Canadian Tire's MasterCard and retail credit card and personal loan portfolios, as well as other finance-related products.

Second, the **holder** may sell receivables because money is tight and access to normal credit is not available or is far too expensive, or because the holder wants to accelerate its cash inflows. A firm may have to sell its receivables, instead of borrowing, to avoid violating the terms of its current borrowing agreements. In addition, the billing and collecting of receivables is often time-consuming and costly. Credit card companies, such as MasterCard and Visa, and other finance companies take over the collection process. They provide merchants with immediate cash in exchange for a fee to cover their collection and bad debt costs. There are also **purchasers** of receivables who buy the receivables to obtain the legal protection of ownership rights that are given to a purchaser of assets, instead of the lesser rights that an unsecured creditor like Visa or MasterCard has. In addition, banks and other lending institutions may be forced to purchase receivables because of legal lending limits. That is, they may not be allowed to make any additional loans but still are able to buy receivables and charge a fee for this service.

Receivables can be used to generate immediate cash for a company in two ways. Often referred to as **asset-backed financing**, these ways are:

1. secured borrowings and

2. sales of receivables

Secured Borrowings

Like many other assets, receivables are often used as collateral in borrowing transactions. A creditor may require that the debtor assign or pledge receivables as security for a loan, but leave the receivables under the control of the borrowing company. The note or loan payable, a liability, is reported on the statement of financial position. If it is not paid when it is due, the creditor has the right to convert the collateral to cash; that is, to collect the receivables. Canadian banks commonly use receivables as collateral under lending agreements.

A company accounts for the collateralized assets in a **secured borrowing in the same way as it did before the borrowing**, and it accounts for the liability according to accounting policies for similar liabilities. The debtor thus recognizes interest expense on the borrowed amount, and may have to pay an additional finance charge, which is expensed. Each month, the proceeds from collecting accounts receivable are used to retire the loan obligation. Details of the secured borrowing are disclosed in the company's financial statements.

Sales of Receivables

The selling of receivables has increased significantly in recent years. One common type is a sale to a factor. **Factors** are financial intermediaries, such as finance companies, that buy receivables from businesses for a fee and then collect the amounts owed directly from the customers. **Factoring receivables** was traditionally associated with the garment trade in Montreal, but it is now common in other industries as well, such as furniture, consumer electronics, and automotive aftermarkets. Illustration 7-12 shows a factoring arrangement.

It is common today for larger companies to **transfer receivables** through a process known as **securitization**. Securitization is the process by which interests in financial assets are sold to a third party. It is the transformation of financial assets such as loans and receivables into securities, which are then referred to as **asset-backed securities**. The process takes a pool of assets that produces interest and principal payments, such as credit card receivables, mortgage receivables, or car loan receivables, and issues debt and equity interests

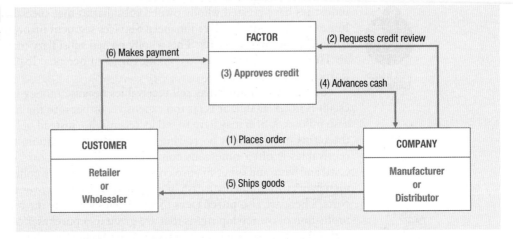

Illustration 7-12

Basic Procedures in Factoring

in these pools. The resulting securities are backed by pools of assets. Almost every asset that has a payment stream (that is, it produces payments) and has a long-term payment history is a candidate for securitization.

REAL WORLD EMPHASIS

For example, Canadian Tire Corporation, Limited's 2014 annual report indicates that, instead of owning all of its receivables throughout the collection period, it sells interests in its customer credit card loans receivable to **Glacier Credit Card Trust** ("Glacier"). Glacier was formed to handle receivables portfolios and is financed by the issue of debt securities to third-party investors. By this process, the receivables are transformed into securities being held by a **special purpose entity (SPE)**, the trust.

The arrangements that are made in a securitization transaction differ from company to company. Canadian Tire, for example, sells pools of these receivables for cash and retains interest in some components of the receivables. The components it gets back typically include the right to the interest portion of the receivables (but not the principal), a subordinated interest in the accounts sold, and a securitization reserve along with a servicing liability. Canadian Tire continues to service the receivables; that is, it manages the accounts, including the responsibility to collect the amounts due. Canadian Tire securitized $500 million of credit card receivables through Glacier in 2014.

WHAT DO THE NUMBERS MEAN?

What is the motivation for this type of transaction? Basically, it is a financing transaction that gives companies a more attractive way to raise funds than by issuing a corporate bond or note. The credit risk for a bond or note issued by a company is higher than the credit risk of a special purpose entity that holds the company's receivables. For example, **Sears Canada Inc.**'s annual report several years ago reported a credit rating of AAA and R-1 (High) **for its trust securitized debt issues and commercial paper**, respectively, which are the highest possible ratings for these debt classifications. Compare these with the BBB and BBB (High) ratings at the same time for Sears's **senior unsecured debt**. The higher credit rating is due to the fact that receivables transferred to an SPE are often credit enhanced[15] and the cash flows to the SPE are much more predictable than the cash flows to the operating company because there are no operating risks for an SPE. When the risk is less, the cost of financing is also less. The net result is that the company that transfers its receivables gets access to lower-cost financing that it can then use to pay off debt that has a higher interest rate.

UNDERLYING CONCEPT

The complexity involved and the relative uncertainty of some of the measurements require more transparency of information, resulting in increased amounts of disclosure.

The differences between factoring and securitization are as follows. **Factoring** usually involves a sale to only one company, fees are relatively high, the quality of the receivables may be lower, and the seller does not usually service the receivables afterward. In a **securitization**, many investors are involved, margins are tight, the receivables are generally of higher quality, and the seller usually continues to service the receivables. When the company making the transfer continues to be involved in some way with the transferred assets, and measurement of the underlying transaction amounts involves some uncertainty, many disclosures are required in the financial statements.

Underlying Principles

Before identifying the criteria that need to exist for a transaction to be treated as a sale, it is important to understand two basic concepts that underlie the decisions of standard setters.

1. The first concept, which is the focus under IFRS, is that an entity (the transferor) should derecognize the financial asset from its financial statements only when it transfers substantially all of the risks and rewards of ownership of that financial asset. (However, the transferor would recognize separately as assets or liabilities any rights and obligations created or retained in the transfer.)

2. Where it cannot be determined whether the risks and rewards have been transferred, then IFRS considers the second concept: control. When assessing control, if the transferee can sell the entire asset to an unrelated party, and can make that decision on its own and without imposing further restrictions on the transfer, then the transferor has not retained control. If the transferor has not retained control, it would derecognize the financial asset (and recognize separately as assets or liabilities any rights and obligations created or retained in the transfer). If the transferee cannot sell the entire asset to an unrelated party or cannot make the decision to sell an asset on its own without any further restrictions, then the transferor has retained control. If the transferor has retained control, it will continue to recognize the financial asset.

Accounting standards governing the derecognition of financial assets differ somewhat between ASPE and IFRS. For example, as discussed above, the initial focus under IFRS is the first concept of whether the risks and rewards have been transferred. The focus under ASPE is the second concept of whether the entity retains control of the financial assets. In many cases, change in control and transfer of the risks and rewards occur at the same time. (See, for example, BCE Inc. in Illustration 7-17 later in this chapter.) However, the treatment under IFRS and ASPE often differs. For example, under IFRS, Canadian Tire Corporation, Limited noted in its 2011 annual report that "Since 1995, the Company has securitized credit card receivables … Under previous GAAP, the Company recorded a gain/loss on sale and derecognized the credit card receivables. Under IFRS, an entity may not derecognize an asset when it maintains the majority of the risks and rewards associated with the asset. Therefore, the securitization transactions no longer qualify for derecognition under IFRS and the Company must recognize the receivables in the Consolidated Balance Sheets. Accordingly, the gain/loss on the sale of the receivables was reversed."[16]

REAL WORLD EMPHASIS

The following discussion illustrates the key concepts involved, with some illustrative examples that would apply under ASPE and IFRS.

Criteria for Treatment as a Sale

Not long ago, it was common for companies to account for many transactions as sales of receivables, even when they had a major continuing interest in and control over the transferred receivables. Doing this resulted in derecognizing accounts receivable (that is, removing them from the statement of financial position), reporting no additional debt but often recording a gain on sale. The major challenge for accounting standards is to identify when a transfer of receivables qualifies for **being treated as a sale** (derecognition), and when it is merely a **secured borrowing**. Most managers would prefer to have the transaction treated as a sale for accounting purposes because this results in not having to record additional debt on the statement of financial position.

In general, standard setters have concluded that the receivable or component parts of the receivable should be derecognized when the risks and rewards have been transferred (IFRS) or when control over the accounts receivable has been surrendered (ASPE). This is problematic in situations when the company "selling" the receivables has a continuing involvement in the asset. Currently there are disagreements as to how to interpret and apply the control criteria and the retention of partial interests. The accounting issues are important because of a company's ability to remove significant assets from the statement of financial position, and not report liabilities when substantial risks have been retained.

The discussion below illustrates standards set out in IFRS 9. The following conditions are used to indicate whether the receivables have actually been transferred by an entity, supporting treatment as a sale. The entity transfers a financial asset, such as accounts receivable, if the entity:

1. transfers the contractual rights to receive cash flows from the accounts receivable; or

2. retains the contractual rights to receive cash flows from the accounts receivable, but has a contractual obligation to pay the cash flows to one or more recipients. Three additional conditions also must be met:

    (a) The entity has no obligation to pay amounts to the eventual recipient unless it collects equivalent amounts from the original receivable.

    (b) The entity is prohibited by the terms of the transfer contract from selling or pledging the original asset other than as security to the eventual recipients for the obligation to pay them cash flows.

    (c) The entity has an obligation to remit any cash flows it collects on behalf of the eventual recipients without material delay.

Accounting for transfers of receivables under ASPE also focuses on whether a company has retained or given up control of the receivables. Under ASPE, if all three conditions set out in Illustration 7-13 do not apply, the transferring company records the transfer as a secured borrowing. **Only when all three conditions are satisfied** is control over the assets assumed to be given up, and the transaction accounted for as a sale. If accounting for the transaction as a sale is appropriate but there is continuing involvement, the specific asset components retained need to be identified, as well as any liability components that were assumed. This approach is shown in a decision tree format in Illustration 7-13.

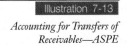

Accounting for Transfers of Receivables—ASPE

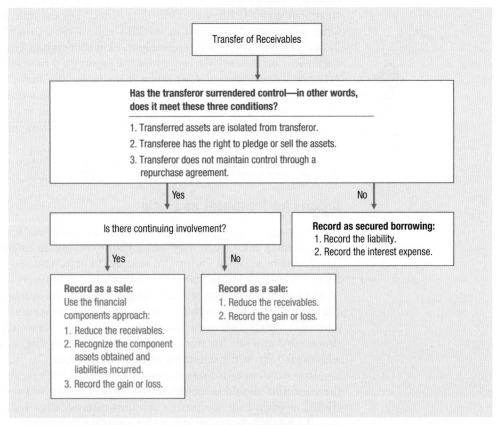

These transactions become more complex because of specialized contracts with different terms and conditions between companies, the securitization of receivables, and special purpose entities. The illustrations that follow are somewhat simplified to make the basic process of accounting for such transactions easier to follow.

Sale with No Continuing Involvement by Transferor

The most straightforward transaction is when the receivables are sold outright to another unrelated party, such as a factor, and they are sold without recourse. In this situation, it is apparent that the risks and rewards have been transferred to the other party (the factor). This is because the company is no longer exposed to risk associated with variability in the amounts and timing of cash flows from the factored/transferred accounts receivable.

When receivables are sold **without recourse**, the purchaser assumes the risk of collection and absorbs any credit losses.[17] Such a transfer is an outright sale of the receivables, both in form (the title is transferred) and substance (control is transferred). In nonrecourse transactions, as in any sale of assets, Cash is debited for the proceeds. Accounts Receivable is credited for the receivables' face value. The difference, reduced by any provision for probable adjustments (such as discounts, returns, and allowances), is recognized in the account Gain or Loss on the Sale of Receivables. When appropriate, the seller uses a Due from Factor account (reported as a receivable) to account for the proceeds that are retained by a factor in order to cover probable sales discounts, sales returns, and sales allowances.

To illustrate, Crest Textiles Ltd. factors $500,000 of accounts receivable with Commercial Factors, Inc. on a **without recourse** basis. The receivables records are transferred to Commercial Factors, which takes over full responsibility for the collections. Commercial Factors assesses a finance charge of 3% of the amount of accounts receivable and withholds an initial amount equal to 5% of the accounts receivable for returns and allowances. Illustration 7-14 shows the journal entries for both Crest Textiles and Commercial Factors for this receivables transfer without recourse.

Illustration 7-14

Entries for Sale of Receivables without Recourse

Crest Textiles Ltd.			Commercial Factors, Inc.		
Cash	460,000		Accounts Receivable	500,000	
Due from Factor	25,000[a]		Due to Crest Textiles		25,000
Loss on Sale of Receivables	15,000[b]		Finance Revenue		15,000
Accounts Receivable		500,000	Cash		460,000
[a](5% × $500,000)					
[b](3% × $500,000)					

To recognize the outright sale of the receivables, Crest Textiles records a loss of $15,000. The factor's net income will be the difference between the financing revenue of $15,000 and the amount of any uncollectible receivables. The accounting treatment for a transfer of receivables without recourse would be the same under IFRS and ASPE, assuming that the risks and rewards have been transferred and that control has also been transferred.

Sale with Continuing Involvement by Transferor— Recourse Component Retained

If receivables are sold **with recourse**, the seller or transferor guarantees payment to the purchaser if the customer fails to pay. In this situation, under IFRS, if the risks and rewards have not been transferred to the factor company, then the transaction would not be treated as a sale (and the secured borrowing treatment discussed earlier could be applied). However, under ASPE, the accounting treatment would be based on the decision tree set out in Illustration 7-13. Specifically, a **financial components approach** is used to record this type of transaction because the seller has a continuing involvement with the receivable. Each party to the sale recognizes the components (assets and liabilities) that it controls after the sale and derecognizes the assets and liabilities that were sold or extinguished.

To illustrate, assume the same information as in Illustration 7-14 for Crest Textiles and Commercial Factors except that the receivables are sold **with recourse**. Crest Textiles estimates that the recourse obligation (a liability) has a fair value of $6,000. This is the company's estimate of the cost of its agreement in the contract to pay the amount of any receivables that debtors fail to pay. To determine the loss on the sale of Crest Textiles' receivables, the net proceeds from the sale are calculated and compared with the carrying amount of the assets that were sold, as shown in Illustration 7-15. Net proceeds are cash or other assets received in a sale less any liabilities incurred.

Illustration 7-15		
Calculation of Net Proceeds and Loss on Sale		

Calculation of net proceeds:		
Cash received (an asset)	$460,000	
Due from factor (an asset)	25,000	$485,000
Less: Recourse obligation (a liability)		6,000
Net proceeds		$479,000
Calculation of loss on sale:		
Carrying amount of receivables		$500,000
Net proceeds		479,000
Loss on sale of receivables		$ 21,000

Illustration 7-16 shows the journal entries for both Crest Textiles and Commercial Factors for the receivables sold with a recourse component being retained.

Illustration 7-16		
Entries for Sale of Receivables with Recourse Component Retained		

Crest Textiles Ltd.			**Commercial Factors, Inc.**		
Cash	460,000		Accounts Receivable	500,000	
Due from Factor	25,000		Due to Crest Textiles		25,000
Loss on Sale of Receivables	21,000		Finance Revenue		15,000
Accounts Receivable		500,000	Cash		460,000
Recourse Liability		6,000			

In this case, Crest Textiles recognizes a loss of $21,000. In addition, it records a liability of $6,000 to indicate the probable payment to Commercial Factors for uncollectible receivables. If all the receivables are collected, Crest Textiles would eliminate its recourse liability and increase income. Commercial Factors' net income is the financing revenue of $15,000 because it will have no bad debts related to these receivables.

What about servicing? Often, the transferor in a securitization will retain the responsibility for servicing the receivables. This usually includes collecting the principal and interest, monitoring slow-paying accounts, and remitting cash to those who hold **beneficial interests** in the receivables. It may also include other specified services. If the transferor receives no reimbursement for these activities or receives less than the estimated cost of carrying them out, a **servicing liability component** is recorded. This decreases the net proceeds on disposal. Alternatively, a **servicing asset component** is recognized if the benefits of servicing (such as servicing fees under contract or late charges recovered from customers) are greater than the estimated cost.

Most of the complications associated with the accounting for the disposition of accounts receivable are related to situations when the transferor continues to have some involvement with those assets.

Disclosure

Transparency requires significant disclosures for securitized receivables that are accounted for as sales. The goal is to inform readers about the fair value measurements and key assumptions that were used, the characteristics of the securitizations, cash flows between the special purpose entity and the transferor, and the balances and risk of servicing the assets and liabilities. Illustration 7-17 in the next section of the chapter gives an example of the main securitization disclosures made by BCE Inc. for its year ended December 31, 2014.

PRESENTATION, DISCLOSURE, AND ANALYSIS OF RECEIVABLES

Presentation and Disclosure

When financial statements are prepared, the presentation of and disclosures related to receivables have to be addressed. The objective is to allow users to evaluate:

- the significance of these financial assets to the entity's financial position and performance and

- the nature and extent of the associated risks

Aside from providing information about the accounting policies applied, entities are required to present the following data associated with loans and receivables, with more information required under IFRS than ASPE:

1. The segregation and separate reporting of ordinary trade accounts, amounts owing by related parties, prepayments, and other significant amounts

2. An indication of the amounts and, where practicable, the maturity dates of accounts with a maturity of more than one year

3. Separate reporting of receivables that are current assets from those that are non-current

4. Separate reporting of any impaired balances, and the amount of any allowance for credit losses with, under IFRS, a reconciliation of the changes in the allowance account during the accounting period

5. Disclosure on the income statement of the amounts of interest income, impairment losses, and any reversals associated with such losses

Major disclosures are also required about the securitization or transfers of receivables, whether derecognized or not. Users are particularly interested in the risks to which the entity is exposed in general, and as a result of such transactions. Credit risk is the major concern associated with loans and receivables. Therefore, under IFRS, extensive qualitative and quantitative information is required about the entity's situation, as is fair value information about loans and receivables, except for short-term trade accounts. Far less information about risk exposures and fair values is required under ASPE.

REAL WORLD EMPHASIS

Extensive excerpts from the December 31, 2014 statement of financial position of the well-known Canadian communications company **BCE Inc.**, along with the notes cross-referenced to its statement of financial position, are presented in Illustration 7-17. These disclosures are based on IFRS.

Illustration 7-17

BCE Inc. Disclosures of Receivables and Loans

Consolidated Statements of Financial Position

AT DECEMBER 31 (in $ millions)	NOTE	2014	2013
ASSETS			
Current assets			
Cash		142	220
Cash equivalents		424	115
Trade and other receivables	12	3,069	3,043
Inventory	13	333	383
Prepaid expenses		379	415
Assets held for sale	4	3	719
Other current assets		198	175
Total current assets		4,548	5,070
Other non-current assets	17	875	698

(continued)

Illustration 7-17

*BCE Inc. Disclosures of
Receivables and Loans (continued)*

NOTE 2: SIGNIFICANT ACCOUNTING POLICIES/Extracts

Cash Equivalents

Cash equivalents are comprised of highly liquid investments with original maturities of three months or less from the date of purchase.

Securitization of Trade Receivables

Proceeds on the securitization of trade receivables are recognized as collateralized borrowing as we do not transfer control and substantially all of the risks and rewards of ownership to another entity.

NOTE 12: TRADE AND OTHER RECEIVABLES

AT DECEMBER 31	2014	2013
Trade receivables	3,068	3,074
Allowance for doubtful accounts	(69)	(79)
Allowance for revenue adjustments	(86)	(90)
Current tax receivable	87	36
Other accounts receivable	69	102
Total trade and other receivables	3,069	3,043

NOTE 17: OTHER NON-CURRENT ASSETS

AT DECEMBER 31	NOTE	2014	2013
Net assets of post-employee benefit plans	22	151	136
AFS publicly-traded and privately-held securities	24	107	91
Long-term notes and other receivables		47	45
Derivative assets		269	199
Other		301	227
Total other non-current assets		875	698

NOTE 24: FINANCIAL AND CAPITAL MANAGEMENT/Extracts

FINANCIAL MANAGEMENT

Management's objectives are to protect BCE and its subsidiaries on a consolidated basis against material economic exposures and variability of results against various financial risks that include credit risk, liquidity risk, interest rate risk and equity price risk.

DERIVATIVES

We use derivative instruments to manage our exposure to foreign currency risk, interest rate risk and changes in the price of BCE common shares under our share-based payment plans.

The following derivative instruments were outstanding during 2014 and/or 2013:

- foreign currency forward contracts and options that manage the foreign currency risk of certain purchase commitments
- interest rate swaps that hedge interest rate risk on a portion of our long-term debt
- forward contracts on BCE common shares that mitigate the cash flow exposure related to share-based payment plans
- cross-currency basis swaps that hedge foreign currency risk on a portion of our long-term debt due within one year
- interest rate locks on future debt issuances

CREDIT RISK

We are exposed to credit risk from operating activities and certain financing activities, the maximum exposure of which is represented by the carrying amounts reported on the statements of financial position.

We are exposed to credit risk if counterparties to our trade receivables and derivative instruments are unable to meet their obligations. The concentration of credit risk from our customers is minimized because we have a large and diverse customer base. We regularly monitor our credit risk and credit exposure. There was minimal credit risk relating to derivative instruments at December 31, 2014 and 2013. We deal with institutions that have strong credit ratings and as such we expect that they will be able to meet their obligations. We regularly monitor our credit risk and credit exposure.

The following table provides the change in allowance for doubtful accounts for trade accounts receivable.

AT DECEMBER 31	2014	2013
Balance, beginning of the year	(79)	(97)
Additions	(101)	(123)
Use	111	145
Acquisition through business combinations	–	(4)
Balance, end of the year	(69)	(79)

(continued)

In many instances, trade receivables are written off directly to bad debt expense if the account has not been collected after a predetermined period of time.

The following table provides further details on trade receivables not impaired.

At December 31	**2014**	2013
Trade receivables not past due	**2,267**	2,274
Trade receivables past due and not impaired		
Under 60 days	**317**	325
60 to 120 days	**352**	365
Over 120 days	**63**	31
Trade receivables, net of allowance for doubtful accounts	**2,999**	2,995

Analysis

TREASURY MANAGEMENT
5.2.1

Analysts often calculate financial ratios to evaluate the liquidity of a company's accounts receivable. To assess the receivables' liquidity, the **receivables turnover ratio** is used. This ratio measures the number of times, on average, that receivables are collected during the period. The ratio is calculated by dividing net sales by average receivables (net) outstanding during the year. Theoretically, the numerator should include only credit sales, but this information is often not available. As long as the relative amounts of credit and cash sales stay fairly constant, the trend indicated by the ratio will still be valid. Average receivables outstanding can be calculated from the beginning and ending balances of net trade receivables unless seasonal factors are significant. If significant, as they often are for many retail enterprises, using an average of the year's opening balance and the amounts at the end of each quarter will be more representative.

REAL WORLD EMPHASIS

To illustrate, we use the 2014 accounts of **Canadian Utilities Limited**, a Canadian-based company in the power generation, transmission, and distribution business. Canadian Utilities reported 2014 revenue of $3,600 million and accounts receivable balances at December 31, 2013 and 2014, of $477 million and $485 million, respectively. Its accounts receivable turnover ratio is calculated in Illustration 7-18.

Illustration 7-18

Calculation of Accounts Receivable Turnover

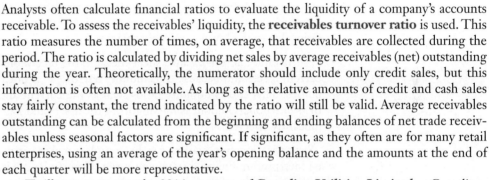

$$\text{Accounts Receivable Turnover} = \frac{\text{Net Sales/Revenue}}{\text{Average Trade Receivables (net)}}$$
$$= \frac{\$3,600}{(\$477 + \$485)/2}$$
$$= 7.5 \text{ times, or every } 48.7 \text{ days}$$
$$(365/7.5 = 48.7)$$

UNDERLYING CONCEPT

Providing information that will help users assess an enterprise's current liquidity and potential future cash flows is one of the main objectives of accounting.

THEORY

The results give information about the quality of the receivables. They also give an idea of how successfully the firm collects its outstanding receivables, particularly when compared with prior periods, industry standards, the company's credit terms, or internal targets. Management would also prepare an aging schedule to determine how long specific receivables have been outstanding. It is possible that a satisfactory receivables turnover may have resulted because certain receivables were collected quickly although others have been outstanding for a relatively long time. An aging schedule would reveal such patterns.

Because the estimated expense for uncollectible accounts is subject to judgement, there is always some concern that companies can use this judgement to manage earnings. By overestimating the amount of uncollectible loans in a good earnings year, a bank, for example, can "save for a rainy day." In future less profitable periods, the bank will then be able to reduce its overly conservative allowance for its loan loss account and increase earnings as a result.[18] Remember, though, that reversals of such impairment losses should be based on specific events and circumstances occurring after the original bad debt loss was recognized.

Further analysis is often carried out on changes in the basic related accounts. Ordinarily, sales, accounts receivable, and the allowance for doubtful accounts should all move

FINANCIAL ANALYSIS
AND PLANNING
5.1.1

in the same direction. Higher sales should generate more receivables and an increased allowance. If sales have increased as well as receivables, but the allowance has not increased proportionately, the reader should be alert to the possibility of earnings management. If the allowance grows faster than receivables, particularly when sales have not increased, this could indicate deterioration in credit quality. Alternatively, perhaps the company has built up its allowance account so that there is a cushion for poorer-performing years ahead. The answers are not always obvious, but this type of analysis can identify concerns.

With the increased practice of selling receivables through securitization transactions, especially where a company retains servicing (such as collection) responsibilities, the financial ratios have to be calculated and interpreted carefully. Consider the following:

- It is not appropriate to directly compare the turnover ratio of a company that securitizes or factors its receivables with the ratio of another company that does not. This financing comes at a cost, but should provide cash flow for other value-adding purposes. Therefore, each company's situation has to be analyzed separately.

- Growth in a company's sales and growth in its receivables generally go hand in hand, but will not for a company involved in selling its receivables. Any company that begins such a program in the year should notice a significant change in the key accounts receivable ratios due to the lower receivable balances.

- Securitization is "off–balance sheet" because the receivables sold are removed from the current assets and because the amount "borrowed" is not reported in a company's liabilities. This affects liquidity ratios such as the current and quick ratios. Even though the same dollar amount is missing from the assets and liabilities, the ratios can be significantly affected.

Securitization transactions can be complex, making it necessary to be very cautious when interpreting financial statement ratios. Companies are increasingly required by regulators to provide a full discussion in the management discussion and analysis of critical issues like liquidity, especially if the company depends on such off–balance sheet financing arrangements.

Objective 10

Identify differences in accounting between IFRS and accounting standards for private enterprises (ASPE), and what changes are expected in the near future.

IFRS/ASPE COMPARISON

A Comparison of IFRS and ASPE

From an intermediate accounting perspective, the general approaches explained in the chapter are expected to continue, although the standards may evolve to have more specific application guidance. ASPE is designed to eliminate much of the complexity in pre-2011 financial instrument standards, and IFRS has a similar goal.

Illustration 7-19 presents the more important differences that are expected to continue.

Illustration 7-19

IFRS and ASPE Comparison Chart

	IAS 1, 32, 39 and IFRS 7, 9	Accounting Standards for Private Enterprises (ASPE)—*CPA Canada Handbook*, Part II, Sections 1510 and 3856	References to Related Illustrations and Select Brief Exercises
Cash and cash equivalents	IFRS allows preferred shares that are acquired close to their maturity date to qualify as a cash equivalent.	Cash equivalents are non-equity, short-term, highly liquid investments that are readily convertible to known amounts of cash with a negligible risk of change in value.	BE7-3

(continued)

Receivables: Recognition and measurement	The effective interest method is required for recognizing interest income and amortizing discounts and premiums.	The standard does not require use of the effective interest method of recognizing interest income and amortizing any discounts or premiums; therefore, either the straight-line method or the effective interest method may be used.	Illustrations 7-9 to 7-11 and related examples BE7-15 and BE7-16
Impairment	Impairment of financial assets such as long-term notes receivable is assessed on a continuous basis using the expected loss model. (See Chapter 9 for details.)	Impairment of financial assets, such as long-term notes receivable, is assessed when there is a significant adverse change in expected future cash flows. Trigger events indicating impairment are evaluated using the incurred loss model. (See Chapter 9 for details.)	Illustration 9-18
Derecognition	To determine whether a financial asset should be derecognized, IFRS first considers whether the risks and rewards of ownership have been transferred.	To determine whether a financial asset should be derecognized, ASPE considers whether control of receivables has been retained or given up.	Illustrations 7-13 and 7-14. More detailed analysis is beyond the scope of this text. BE7-18 and BE7-19
Disclosures	Detailed quantitative and qualitative disclosures are required about the receivables, interest income, related risks, and sensitivity analysis linked to the measurements made. IFRS has detailed disclosure requirements for transferred financial assets that are either partly or entirely derecognized.	Basic disclosures are required related to the significance of receivables to the entity's financial position and financial performance, and the financial risks to which it is exposed.	Not applicable

Looking Ahead

IFRS

The IASB has been working, along with the FASB, to simplify aspects of the accounting for and reporting of financial instruments. The IASB and FASB have also been working toward a new model for impairments. In July 2014, the IASB finalized IFRS 9, including a requirement for a forward-looking impairment model. Expected credit losses are to be based on reasonable and supportable information available without undue cost, including historical, current, and forecast information. The issues relating to impairment are discussed further in Chapter 9.

In July 2014, the IASB amended IFRS 9 to require application of the new standard for annual periods beginning on or after January 1, 2018.

ASPE

While most requirements set out under ASPE are not likely to change in the short term, one area that is open to change is that of the derecognition (transfer) of receivables. The Accounting Standards Board (AcSB) has indicated that changes may be made to ASPE after the International Accounting Standards Board (IASB) and Financial Accounting Standards Board (FASB) develop final standards on derecognition of financial assets, and these are now complete. Also, as discussed earlier in this chapter, the IASB has finalized its proposed changes regarding impairment. Although the AcSB issued a "Request for Information" in November 2014 as part of its post-implementation review of Section 3856, changes in ASPE are unlikely in the near term.

SUMMARY OF LEARNING OBJECTIVES

1 Understand cash and accounts receivable from a business perspective.

Companies often have a significant amount of accounts receivable, which require time and effort to manage and control. Companies strive to ensure that their collection policy is restrictive enough to minimize large losses in the form of uncollectible accounts receivable, while not being so restrictive that it interferes with the ability to attract new customers. Typical accounts receivable–related categories include trade receivables, loans receivable, and non-trade receivables (including items like interest receivable, amounts due from officers, and advances to employees).

2 Define financial assets, and identify items that are considered cash and cash equivalents and how they are reported.

Financial assets are a major type of asset, defined as cash, a contractual right to receive cash or another financial asset, an equity holding in another company, or a contractual right to exchange financial instruments under potentially favourable conditions. To be reported as cash, an asset must be readily available to pay current obligations and not have any contractual restrictions that would limit how it can be used in satisfying debts. Cash consists of coins, currency, and available funds on deposit at a bank. Negotiable instruments such as money orders, certified cheques, cashier's cheques, personal cheques, and bank drafts are also viewed as cash. Savings accounts are usually classified as cash. Cash equivalents include highly liquid short-term investments (that is, those maturing three months or less from the date of purchase) that can be exchanged for known amounts of cash and have an insignificant chance of changing in value. Examples include treasury bills, commercial paper, and money-market funds. In certain circumstances, temporary bank overdrafts may be deducted in determining the balance of cash and cash equivalents.

Cash is reported as a current asset in the statement of financial position, with foreign currency balances reported at their Canadian dollar equivalent at the date of the statement of financial position. The reporting of other related items is as follows: (1) Restricted cash: Legally restricted deposits that are held as compensating balances against short-term borrowing are stated separately in current assets. Restricted deposits held against long-term borrowing arrangements are separately classified in non-current assets either in investments or other assets. (2) Bank overdrafts: These are reported in the current liabilities section and may sometimes be added to the amount reported as accounts payable. (3) Cash equivalents: This item is often reported together with cash as "cash and cash equivalents."

3 Define receivables and identify the different types of receivables from an accounting perspective.

Receivables are claims held against customers and others for money, goods, or services. Most receivables are financial assets. The receivables are described in the following

ways: (1) current or non-current; (2) trade or nontrade; and (3) accounts receivable or notes or loans receivable.

4 Account for and explain the accounting issues related to the recognition and measurement of accounts receivable.

The entity becomes a party to the contractual provisions of the accounts receivable financial instrument only when it has a legal claim to receive cash or other financial assets. Therefore the timing of recognition of accounts receivable is intertwined with the timing of recognition of revenue, as was discussed in Chapter 6. For example, under ASPE, allowance accounts are normally used for sales with a right of return. Under IFRS, a Refund Liability account is credited for estimated returns.

Two issues that may complicate the measurement of accounts receivable are (1) the availability of discounts (trade and cash discounts) and (2) the length of time between the sale and the payment due dates (the interest element). Ideally, receivables should be measured initially at their fair value, which is their present value (discounted value of the cash to be received in the future). Receivables that are created by normal business transactions and are due in the short term are excluded from present value requirements.

5 Account for and explain the accounting issues related to the impairment in value of accounts receivable.

Short-term receivables are reported at their net realizable value—the net amount that is expected to be received in cash, which is not necessarily the amount that is legally receivable. Determining net realizable value requires estimating uncollectible receivables and any future returns or allowances and discounts that are expected to be taken. The adjustments to the asset account also affect the income statement amounts of bad debt expense, sales returns and allowances, and sales discounts. The assessment of impairment usually takes into account an aged accounts receivable report, with higher percentages of uncollectible accounts applied using a provision matrix for older amounts outstanding. Under IFRS 9, impairment represents "expected credit losses resulting from all possible default events" (consistent with the expected loss model). Under ASPE, receivables are impaired if there has been a "significant adverse change" (or a triggering event, consistent with the incurred loss model).

6 Account for and explain the accounting issues related to the recognition and measurement of short-term notes and loans receivable.

The accounting issues related to short-term notes receivable are similar to those of accounts receivable. However, because notes always contain an interest element, interest income must be properly recognized. Notes receivable either bear interest on the face amount (interest-bearing) or have an interest element that is the difference between the amount lent and the maturity value (non–interest-bearing).

7 Account for and explain the accounting issues related to the recognition and measurement of long-term notes and loans receivable.

Long-term notes and loans receivable are recognized initially at their fair value (the present value of the future cash flows) and subsequently at their amortized cost. Transaction costs are capitalized. This requires amortizing any discount if the item was issued at less than its face value, or any premium if it was issued for an amount greater than its face value, using the effective interest method. The straight-line method may be used under ASPE. Amortization of the premium (or discount) results in a reduction of (or increase in) interest income below (or above) the cash amount received.

8 Account for and explain the basic accounting issues related to the derecognition of receivables.

To accelerate the receipt of cash from receivables, the owner may transfer the receivables to another entity for cash. The transfer of receivables to a third party for cash may be done in one of two ways: (1) Secured borrowing: the creditor requires the debtor to designate or pledge receivables as security for the loan. (2) Sale (factoring or securitization) of receivables: factors are finance companies or banks that buy receivables from businesses and then collect the remittances directly from the customers. Securitization is the transfer of receivables to a special purpose entity that is mainly financed by highly rated debt instruments. In many cases, transferors have some continuing involvement with the receivables they sell. For the transfer to be recorded as a sale, IFRS focuses on whether the risks and rewards of ownership have been transferred to the transferee. ASPE focuses on whether the transferor has surrendered control and has continued involvement with the receivables.

9 Explain how receivables and loans are reported and analyzed.

Disclosure of receivables requires that (1) valuation accounts be appropriately offset against receivables, (2) the receivables be appropriately classified as current or non-current, and (3) pledged or designated receivables be identified. As financial instruments, specific disclosures are required for receivables so that users can determine their significance to the company's financial position and performance and can assess the nature and extent of associated risks and how these risks are managed and measured. Private entities require less disclosure than those reporting under IFRS. Receivables are analyzed in terms of their turnover and age (number of days outstanding), and in terms of relative changes in the related sales, receivables, and allowance accounts.

10 Identify differences in accounting between IFRS and accounting standards for private enterprises (ASPE), and what changes are expected in the near future.

The two sets of standards are very similar, with minor differences relating to what is included in cash equivalents. ASPE does not require use of the effective interest method, whereas IFRS does require it for financial asset investments that are not held for trading purposes. Impairment provisions represent an issue that was recently resolved under IFRS. However, changes to the IFRS impairment model under IFRS 9 have led to additional differences between IFRS and ASPE which are examined in Chapter 9.

KEY TERMS

aging method, p. 351
aging schedule, p. 351
allowance method, p. 352
amortized cost, p. 358
asset-backed financing, p. 365
asset-backed securities, p. 365
bad debts, p. 350
bank overdrafts, p. 344
basic loan features, p. 358
beneficial interest, p. 370
cash, p. 342
cash discounts, p. 348
cash equivalents, p. 344
compensating balances, p. 343
contra account, p. 349
contractual yield basis, p. 358
coupon rate, p. 358
credit risk, p. 350
derecognized, p. 364
direct write off method, p. 356

discount, p. 362
effective interest method, p. 360
effective interest rate, p. 358
face rate, p. 358
face value, p. 358
factoring receivables, p. 365
fair value, p. 357
financial asset, p. 342
financial components approach, p. 369
implicit interest rate, p. 359
imputed interest rate, p. 363
interest-bearing notes, p. 356
loans and receivables, p. 346
loans receivable, p. 346
market rate, p. 358
net realizable value, p. 351
non–interest-bearing notes, p. 356
nontrade receivables, p. 346
notes receivable, p. 346
percentage-of-receivables approach, p. 351

percentage-of-sales approach, p. 353
premium, p. 363
promissory note, p. 356
provision matrix, p. 351
receivables turnover ratio, p. 373
restricted cash, p. 343
sales discounts, p. 348
sales returns and allowances, p. 349
secured borrowing, p. 367
securitization, p. 365
servicing asset component, p. 370
servicing liability component, p. 370
stated interest rate, p. 358
straight-line method, p. 361
trade discounts, p. 348
trade receivables, p. 346
with recourse, p. 369
without recourse, p. 369
yield rate, p. 358
zero-interest-bearing notes, p. 356

APPENDIX 7A

CASH CONTROLS

Management and Control of Cash

Of all assets, cash is at the greatest risk of being diverted or used improperly. Management must overcome two problems in accounting for cash transactions:

1. It must establish proper controls to ensure that no unauthorized transactions are entered into by officers, employees, or others.

2. It must ensure that the information that is needed in order to properly manage cash on hand and cash transactions is made available.

Yet even with sophisticated control devices, errors can and do happen. *The Wall Street Journal* once ran a story entitled "A $7.8 Million Error Has a Happy Ending for a Horrified Bank," which described how **Manufacturers Hanover Trust Co.** mailed about $7.8 million too much in cash dividends to its shareholders. As the headline suggests, most of the money was eventually returned.

To safeguard cash and ensure the accuracy of the accounting records for this asset, companies need effective **internal control** over cash. There are new challenges to maintaining control over liquid assets as more and more transactions are done with the swipe of a debit or credit card or through unregulated electronic payment services like PayPal. Canadians are among the highest users of debit and credit cards in the world. The shift from hard cash to digital cash brings new challenges for the internal control systems that are designed to control this asset. The purpose of this appendix is to identify some of the basic controls related to cash.

**MANAGEMENT REPORTING
NEEDS AND SYSTEMS**
3.1.1, 3.1.2

Using Bank Accounts

Even with the increased use of electronic banking, a company may use different banks in different locations and different types of bank accounts. For large companies that operate in multiple locations, the location of bank accounts can be important. Having collection accounts in strategic locations can speed up the flow of cash into the company by shortening the time between a customer's payment mailing and the company's use of the cash. Multiple collection centres are generally used to reduce the size of a company's **collection float**. The collection float is the difference between the amount on deposit according to the company's records and the amount of collected cash according to the bank record.

The **general chequing account** is the main bank account in most companies and often the only bank account in small businesses. Cash is deposited in and disbursed from this account as all transactions are cycled through it. Deposits from and disbursements to all other bank accounts are made through the general chequing account. Traditionally companies also used **imprest bank accounts** for some disbursements such as payroll or dividend payments. Direct deposit is now much more common for these types of payments.[19]

Lockbox accounts are often used by large companies with multiple locations to make collections in cities where most of their customer billing occurs. The company rents a local post office box and authorizes a local bank to pick up the remittances mailed to that box number. The bank empties the box each day and immediately credits the company's account for collections. The greatest advantage of a lockbox is that it accelerates the availability of collected cash. Generally, in a lockbox arrangement, the bank makes a copy of each cheque for record-keeping purposes and provides the company with a deposit slip, a list of collections, and any customer correspondence. If the control over cash is improved and if the income generated from accelerating the receipt of funds is more than what the lockbox system costs, it is considered worthwhile to use it.

Companies continue to increase their use of systems that electronically transfer funds from customers and to suppliers. While these advances will make many of the controls in a paper cheque–based system obsolete, companies will still always need to improve the effectiveness of the controls that are part of their information and processing systems.

The Imprest Petty Cash System

Almost every company finds it necessary to pay small amounts for a great many things, such as taxi fares, minor office supplies, and other miscellaneous expenses. It is usually impractical to require that such disbursements be made by cheque, but some control over them is important. A simple method of obtaining reasonable control, while following the rule of disbursement by cheque, is the **petty cash** system, particularly an imprest system.

This is how the system works.

1. Someone is designated as the petty cash custodian and given a small amount of currency from which to make small payments. The transfer of funds from the bank account to petty cash is recorded as follows, assuming a $300 transfer:

A = L + SE
0

Cash flows: No effect

Petty Cash	300	
Cash		300

2. As payments are made out of this fund, the petty cash custodian gets signed receipts from each individual who receives cash from the fund. If possible, evidence of the disbursement should be attached to the petty cash receipt. Petty cash transactions are not recorded in the accounts until the fund is reimbursed, and they are recorded by someone other than the petty cash custodian.

3. When the cash in the fund runs low, the custodian presents to the controller or accounts payable cashier a request for reimbursement that is supported by the petty cash receipts and other disbursement evidence. In exchange for these, the custodian receives a company cheque to replenish the fund. At this point, transactions are recorded in the accounting system based on the petty cash receipts. For example:

A = L + SE
−173   −173

Cash flows: ↓ 173 outflow

Office Expense	42	
Postage Expense	53	
Entertainment Expense	76	
Cash Over and Short	2	
Cash		173

4. If it is decided that the fund's balance is too high, an adjustment may be made and the surplus amount is then deposited back into the bank account. The following adjustment is made to record the reduction in the fund balance from $300 to $250:

A = L + SE
0

Cash flows: No effect

Cash	50	
Petty Cash		50

Note that **only** entries to increase or decrease the size of the fund are made **to the Petty Cash account**.

A **Cash Over and Short** account is used when the cash in the petty cash fund plus the dollar amount of the receipts does not add up to the imprest petty cash amount. When this occurs, it is usually due to an error, such as a failure to provide correct change, overpayment of an expense, or a lost receipt. If cash is short (in other words, the sum of the receipts and cash in the fund is less than the imprest amount), the shortage is debited to the Cash Over and Short account. If there is more cash than there should be, the overage is credited to Cash Over and Short. Cash over and short is typically left open until the end of the year, when it is closed and generally shown on the income statement as part of "other expense or revenue."

Unless a reimbursement has just been made, there are usually expense items in the fund. This means that, if accurate financial statements are wanted, the fund needs to be reimbursed at the end of each accounting period in addition to when it is nearly empty.

Under an **imprest system**, the petty cash custodian is responsible at all times for the amount of the fund on hand, whether the amount is in cash or signed receipts. These receipts are the evidence that the disbursing officer needs in order to issue a reimbursement cheque. Two additional procedures are followed to obtain more complete control over the petty cash fund.

1. Surprise counts of the fund are made from time to time by a superior of the petty cash custodian to determine that the fund is being accounted for satisfactorily.

2. Petty cash receipts are cancelled or mutilated after they have been submitted for reimbursement so that they cannot be used again.

Physical Protection of Cash Balances

It is not only cash receipts and cash disbursements that need to be safeguarded through internal control measures. Cash on hand and in banks must also be protected. Because receipts become cash on hand and disbursements are made from the cash in banks, adequate control of receipts and disbursements is part of protecting cash balances. Certain other procedures, therefore, are also carried out.

The physical protection of cash is such an elementary necessity that it requires little discussion. Every effort should be made to minimize the cash on hand in the office. A petty cash fund, the current day's receipts, and perhaps funds for making change should be the only funds on hand at any time. As much as possible, these funds should be kept in a vault, safe, or locked cash drawer. Each day's receipts should be transmitted intact to the bank as soon as is practical. Intact means that the total receipts are accounted for together and no part of the amount is used for other purposes. This leaves a clear trail from the receipts activity to the bank.

Every company has a record of cash received and disbursed, and the cash balance. Because of the many cash transactions, however, errors or omissions can occur in keeping this record. It is therefore necessary to periodically prove the balance shown in the general ledger. Cash that is actually present in the office—petty cash, funds kept for making change, and undeposited receipts—can be counted and compared with the company records. Cash on deposit is not available for count so it is proved by preparing a bank reconciliation, which is a reconciliation of the company's record and the bank's record of the company's cash.

Reconciliation of Bank Balances

At the end of each calendar month, the bank sends each customer a bank statement (a copy of the bank's account with the customer), together with the customer's cheques that were paid by the bank during the month or a list of the company's payments that have been presented to and cleared by the bank during the month.[20] Less and less hard copy is being returned as banks provide companies with electronic access to this information. If no errors were made by the bank or the customer, if all deposits made and all cheques drawn by the customer reached the bank within the same month, and if no unusual transactions occurred that affected either the company's or the bank's record of cash, the balance of cash reported by the bank to the customer will be the same as the balance in the customer's own records. This rarely occurs, because of one or more of the following:

RECONCILING ITEMS

1. **Deposits in transit:** End-of-month deposits of cash that are recorded on the depositor's books in one month are received and recorded by the bank in the following month.

2. **Outstanding cheques:** Cheques written by the depositor are recorded when they are written but may not be recorded by (or "clear") the bank until the next month.

3. **Bank charges:** Charges are recorded by the bank against the depositor's balance for such items as bank services, printing cheques, **not-sufficient-funds (NSF)** cheques, and safe-deposit box rentals. The depositor may not be aware of these charges until the bank statement is received.

4. **Bank credits:** Collections or deposits by the bank for the depositor's benefit may not be known to the depositor until the bank statement is received. These are reconciling items as long as they have not yet been recorded on the company's records. Examples are note collections for the depositor, interest earned on interest-bearing accounts, and direct deposits by customers and others.

5. **Bank or depositor errors:** Errors by either the bank or the depositor cause the bank balance to disagree with the depositor's book balance.

For these reasons, differences between the depositor's record of cash and the bank's record are usual and expected. The two records therefore need to be reconciled to determine the reasons for the differences between the two amounts.

A **bank reconciliation** is a schedule that explains any differences between the bank's and the company's records of cash. If the difference results only from transactions not yet recorded by the bank, the company's record of cash is considered correct. But if some part of the difference is due to other items, the bank's records or the company's records must be adjusted. The bank reconciliation helps to safeguard cash by ensuring the accuracy of the accounting records. Timely bank reconciliations are needed to provide effective internal control, and to detect errors and possible misappropriations of cash. Bank reconciliations are typically reviewed by senior accounting personnel and company auditors to ensure that the control is operating effectively.

Two forms of bank reconciliation can be prepared. One form reconciles from the bank statement balance to the book balance or vice versa. The other form reconciles both the bank balance and the book balance to a correct cash balance. This latter form is more popular. A sample of this form and its common reconciling items is shown in Illustration 7A-1.

INTERNAL CONTROL
4.1.1, 4.1.2

Illustration 7A-1

*Bank Reconciliation
Form and Content*

Balance per bank statement (end of period)		$$$
Add: Deposits in transit	$$	
Undeposited receipts (cash on hand)	$$	
Bank errors that understate the bank statement balance	$$	$$
		$$$
Deduct: Outstanding cheques	$$	
Bank errors that overstate the bank statement balance	$$	$$
Correct cash balance		$$$
Balance per company's books (end of period)		$$$
Add: Bank credits and collections not yet recorded in the books	$$	
Book errors that understate the book balance	$$	$$
		$$$
Deduct: Bank charges not yet recorded in the books	$$	
Book errors that overstate the book balance	$$	$$
Correct cash balance		$$$

This form of reconciliation has two sections: (1) the "Balance per bank statement" and (2) the "Balance per company's books." Both sections end with the same correct cash balance. The correct cash balance is the amount that the books must be adjusted to and is the amount reported on the statement of financial position. **Adjusting journal entries are prepared for all the addition and deduction items that appear in the "Balance per company's books" section**, and the bank should be notified immediately about any errors that it has made.

To illustrate, Nugget Mining Company's books show a cash balance at the Ottawa National Bank on November 30, 2017, of $20,502. The bank statement covering the month of November shows an ending balance of $22,190. An examination of Nugget's accounting records and the November bank statement identified the following reconciling items.

1. A deposit of $3,680 was taken to the bank late on November 30 but does not appear on the November bank statement.

2. Cheques written in November but not charged to (deducted from) the November bank statement are:

Cheque	#7327	$ 150
	#7348	4,820
	#7349	31

3. Nugget has not yet recorded the $600 of interest collected by the bank on November 20 on Sequoia Co. bonds held by the bank for Nugget.

4. Bank service charges of $18 are not yet recorded on Nugget's books.

5. A $220 cheque for Nugget from a customer was returned with the bank statement and marked "NSF." The bank, having originally recognized this as part of one of Nugget's deposits, now deducted this bad cheque as a disbursement from Nugget's account.

6. Nugget discovered that cheque #7322, written in November for $131 in payment of an account payable, had been incorrectly recorded in its books as $311.

7. A cheque written on Nugent Oil Co.'s account for $175 had been incorrectly charged to Nugget Mining and was included with the bank statement.

Illustration 7A-2 shows the reconciliation of the bank and book balances to the correct cash balance of $21,044.

Illustration 7A-2	
Sample Bank Reconciliation	

NUGGET MINING COMPANY
Bank Reconciliation
Ottawa National Bank, November 30, 2017

Balance per bank statement, November 30/17			$22,190
Add: Deposit in transit	(1)	$3,680	
Bank error—bank incorrectly charged cheque to account	(7)	175	3,855
			26,045
Deduct: Outstanding cheques	(2)		5,001
Correct cash balance, November 30/17			$21,044
Balance per books, November 30/17			$20,502
Add: Interest collected by the bank	(3)	$ 600	
Error in recording cheque #7322	(6)	180	780
			21,282
Deduct: Bank service charges	(4)	18	
NSF cheque returned	(5)	220	238
Correct cash balance, November 30/17			$21,044

The journal entries to adjust and correct Nugget Mining's books in early December 2017 are taken from the items in the "Balance per books" section and are as follows:

Cash	600	
Interest Income		600
(To record interest on Sequoia Co. bonds, collected by bank)		
Cash	180	
Accounts Payable		180
(To correct error in recording amount of cheque #7322)		
Office Expense—Bank Charges	18	
Cash		18
(To record bank service charges for November)		
Accounts Receivable	220	
Cash		220
(To record customer's cheque returned NSF)		

A = L + SE
+762 +180 +582

Cash flows: ↑ 542 inflow

Alternatively, one summary entry could be made with a net $542 debit to Cash, which is the difference between the balance before adjustment of $20,502 and the correct balance of $21,044. When the entries are posted, Nugget's cash account will have a balance of $21,044. Nugget should return the Nugent Oil Co. cheque to Ottawa National Bank, informing the bank of the error.

SUMMARY OF LEARNING OBJECTIVE FOR APPENDIX 7A

11 Explain common techniques for controlling cash.

The common techniques that are used to control cash are as follows: (1) Using bank accounts: A company can vary the number and location of banks and the types of accounts to meet its control objectives. (2) The imprest petty cash system: It may be impractical to require small amounts of various expenses to be paid by cheque, yet some control over them is important. (3) Physical protection of cash balances: Adequate control of receipts and disbursements is part of protecting cash balances. Every effort should be made to minimize the cash on hand in the office. (4) Reconciliation of bank balances: Cash on deposit is not available for counting and is proved by preparing a bank reconciliation.

KEY TERMS

bank reconciliation, p. 381

deposits in transit, p. 381

imprest system, p. 380

not-sufficient-funds (NSF) cheques, p. 381

outstanding cheques, p. 381

petty cash, p. 379

Note: All assignment material with an asterisk (*) relates to the appendix to the chapter.

Completion of this end-of-chapter material will help develop CPA enabling competencies (such as ethics and professionalism, problem-solving and decision-making and communication) and technical competencies. We have highlighted selected items with an integration icon and material in *WileyPLUS* has been linked to the competencies. All cases emphasize integration, especially of the enabling competencies. The brief exercises, exercises and problems generally emphasize problem-solving and decision-making.

Brief Exercises

(LO 1) BE7-1 Creative Corporation is a manufacturer of children's toys. Creative has significant debt outstanding that has been used to purchase equipment and inventory used in its manufacturing process. Creative has positive cash from operating activities during the holiday season (November and December), but negative cash from operating activities during the months preceding the holiday season. Meanwhile, Technology Inc. is a mature, successful software development company with no debt outstanding and very few non-current assets. Which company requires a higher amount of cash on hand? Discuss, in general terms, how much cash each firm should have on hand for effective cash management.

FINANCE

(LO 1) BE7-2 Topaz Inc. has accounts receivable terms of 2/10, n/30. In the past, 50% of Topaz's customers have taken advantage of the discount and paid within 10 days of the invoice date, and the remaining 50% of customers have paid in full within 30 days of the invoice date. However, due to an economic recession this year, 30% of customers have paid within 10 days, 60% of customers have paid within 30 days, and the remaining 10% of customers have paid within 40 days. What steps might Topaz consider to speed up collection of its accounts receivable?

(LO 2) BE7-3 Stowe Enterprises owns the following assets at December 31, 2017:

Cash in bank savings account	56,200	Chequing account balance	46,300
Cash on hand	14,800	Postdated cheque from Yu Co.	450
Cash refund due (overpayment of income taxes)	21,400	Cash in a foreign bank (CAD equivalent)	90,000
Preferred shares acquired shortly before their		Debt instrument with a maturity date of	
fixed maturity date	15,500	three months from the date acquired	12,000

If Stowe follows ASPE, what amount should be reported as cash and cash equivalents? Explain how your answer would differ if Stowe followed IFRS.

(LO 3) BE7-4 Staj Co., a clothing manufacturer, is preparing its statement of financial position at December 31, 2017. For each of the following amounts as at December 31, 2017, indicate whether the amount is (a) current or non-current; and (b) a trade receivable, a nontrade receivable, or not a receivable. If the amount is not a receivable, indicate its correct statement of financial position classification.

1. Cheque received from a customer for $1,200, dated January 1, 2018
2. Bank overdraft balance of $50,000
3. Income taxes recoverable of $14,000
4. $10,300 owing from a customer (now 10 days overdue), exchanged for a two-year note bearing interest at 8% payable annually
5. Staj sold a piece of machinery to Marus Company this past year. As part of the sale transaction, $20,000 is owing from Marus, due to be received on January 31, 2019

(LO 4) BE7-5 Boyko Company received an order from Lister Inc. on May 15, 2017, valued at $3,800. Boyko shipped the goods to Lister on May 31, 2017, with terms f.o.b. shipping point, and credit terms 2/10, n/30. Assuming Boyko uses the gross method of recording sales, prepare the required journal entries for Boyko on May 15, 2017, and May 31, 2017 (if any).

(LO 4) BE7-6 Melon Company made sales of $40,000 with terms 1/10, n/30. Within the discount period, it received a cash payment on $35,000 of the sales from customers. After the discount period, it received $5,000 in payments from customers. Assuming Melon uses the gross method of recording sales, prepare journal entries for the above transactions.

(LO 4) BE7-7 Use the information for Melon Company in BE7-6, but assume instead that Melon uses the net method of recording sales. Prepare the journal entries for the transactions.

(LO 4) BE7-8 Yoshi Corp. uses the gross method to record sales made on credit. On June 1, the company made sales of $110,000 with terms 1/15, n/45. On June 12, Yoshi received full payment for the June 1 sale. Prepare the required journal entries for Yoshi Corp.

(LO 4) BE7-9 Use the information from BE7-8, assuming Yoshi Corp. uses the net method to account for cash discounts. Prepare the required journal entries for Yoshi Corp.

(LO 5) BE7-10 Battle Tank Limited had net sales in 2017 of $2.3 million. At December 31, 2017, before adjusting entries, the balances in selected accounts were as follows: Accounts Receivable $350,000 debit; Allowance for Doubtful Accounts $4,600 credit. Assuming Battle Tank has examined the aging of the accounts receivable and has determined the Allowance for Doubtful Accounts should have a balance of $42,000, prepare the December 31, 2017 journal entry to record the adjustment to Allowance for Doubtful Accounts.

(LO 5) BE7-11 Use the information for Battle Tank Limited in BE7-10 and assume instead that the unadjusted balance in Allowance for Doubtful Accounts is a debit balance of $3,000. Based on this, prepare the December 31, 2017 journal entry to record the adjustment to Allowance for Doubtful Accounts.

(LO 6) BE7-12 Emil Family Importers sold goods to Acme Decorators for $20,000 on November 1, 2017, accepting Acme's $20,000, six-month, 6% note. (a) Prepare Emil's November 1 entry, December 31 annual adjusting entry, and May 1 entry for the collection of the note and interest. (b) Assume instead that Emil uses reversing entries. Prepare any appropriate reversing entry at January 1, 2018, and the May 1, 2018 entry for the collection of the note and interest.

(LO 6) BE7-13 Aero Acrobats lent $47,573 to Afterburner Limited, accepting Afterburner's $49,000, three-month, zero-interest-bearing note. The implied interest is approximately 12%. Prepare Aero's journal entries for the initial transaction and the collection of $49,000 at maturity.

(LO 7) **BE7-14** Lin Du Corp. lent $30,053 to Prefax Ltd., accepting Prefax's $40,000, three-year, zero-interest-bearing note. The implied interest is 10%. (a) Prepare Lin Du's journal entries for the initial transaction, recognition of interest each year assuming use of the effective interest method, and the collection of $40,000 at maturity. (b) Use time value of money tables, a financial calculator, or Excel functions to prove that the note will yield 10%.

(LO 7) **BE7-15** Aitocs Inc. sold used equipment with a cost of $15,000 and a carrying amount of $2,500 to Disc Corp. in exchange for a $5,000, three-year non–interest-bearing note receivable. Although no interest was specified, the market rate for a loan of that risk would be 9%. Assume that Aitocs follows IFRS. Prepare the entries to record (a) the sale of Aitocs' equipment and receipt of the note, (b) the recognition of interest each year, and (c) the collection of the note at maturity.

(LO 7) **BE7-16** Use the information for Aitocs Inc. in BE7-15 and assume instead that Aitocs follows ASPE. Prepare the entries to record (a) the sale of Aitocs' equipment and receipt of the note, (b) the recognition of interest each year if Aitocs uses the straight-line method, and (c) the collection of the note at maturity.

(LO 8) **BE7-17** On October 1, 2017, Alpha Inc. assigns $3 million of its accounts receivable to Alberta Provincial Bank as collateral for a $2.6-million loan evidenced by a note. The bank's charges are as follows: a finance charge of 4% of the assigned receivables and an interest charge of 10% on the loan. Prepare the October 1 journal entries for both Alpha and Alberta Provincial Bank.

(LO 8) **BE7-18** Landstalker Enterprises sold $750,000 of accounts receivable to Leander Factors, Inc. on a without recourse basis under IFRS, as the risks and rewards have been transferred to Leander. The transaction meets the criteria for a sale, and no asset or liability components of the receivables are retained by Landstalker. Leander Factors assesses a finance charge of 4% of the amount of accounts receivable and retains an amount equal to 5% of accounts receivable. Prepare journal entries for both Landstalker and Leander.

(LO 8) **BE7-19** Use the information for Landstalker Enterprises in BE7-18 and assume instead that the receivables are sold with recourse. Prepare the journal entry for Landstalker to record the sale, assuming the recourse obligation has a fair value of $9,000 and that Landstalker follows ASPE.

(LO 8) **BE7-20** Keyser Woodcrafters sells $600,000 of receivables with a fair value of $620,000 to Keyser Trust in a securitization transaction that meets the criteria for a sale. Keyser Woodcrafters receives full fair value for the receivables and agrees to continue to service them, estimating that the fair value of this service liability component is $26,000. Prepare the journal entry for Keyser Woodcrafters to record the sale.

(LO 9) **BE7-21** The financial statements of winery **Andrew Peller Limited** reported net sales of $297,824 thousand for its year ended March 31, 2014. Accounts receivable were $22,693 thousand at March 31, 2014, and $25,484 thousand at March 31, 2013. Calculate the company's accounts receivable turnover ratio and the average collection period for accounts receivable in days.

FINANCE

(LO 9) **BE7-22** The financial statements of **BCE Inc.** reported net sales of $21,042 million for its year ended December 31, 2014, and $20,400 million for its year ended December 31, 2013. Accounts receivable (net) were $2,999 million at December 31, 2014, $2,995 million at December 31, 2013, and $2,978 million at December 31, 2012. Calculate the company's accounts receivable turnover ratio for 2013. Did it improve in 2014?

FINANCE

(LO 11) ***BE7-23** Genesis Ltd. designated Alexa Kidd as petty cash custodian and established a petty cash fund of $400. The fund is reimbursed when the cash in the fund is at $57. Petty cash receipts indicate that funds were disbursed for $174 of office supplies and $167 of freight charges on inventory purchases. Genesis uses a perpetual inventory system. Prepare journal entries for the establishment of the fund and the reimbursement.

(LO 11) ***BE7-24** Use the information in BE7-23. Assume that Genesis decides (a) to increase the size of the petty cash fund to $600 immediately after the reimbursement, and (b) to reduce the size of the petty cash to $250 immediately after the reimbursement. Prepare the entries that are necessary to record the (a) and (b) transactions.

(LO 11) ***BE7-25** Jaguar Corporation is preparing a bank reconciliation and has identified the following potential reconciling items. For each item, indicate if it is (a) added to the balance per bank statement, (b) deducted from the balance per bank statement, (c) added to the balance per books, (d) deducted from the balance per books, or (e) not needed for the reconciliation.

1. Deposit in transit of $5,500
2. Previous month's outstanding cheque for $298 cleared the bank in the current month
3. Interest credited to Jaguar's account of $31
4. Bank service charges of $20
5. Outstanding deposit from previous month of $876 shown by bank as deposit of current month
6. Outstanding cheques of $7,422
7. NSF cheque returned of $260, and related service charge of $20

(LO 11) ***BE7-26** Use the information for Jaguar Corporation in BE7-25. Prepare any entries that are necessary to make Jaguar's accounting records correct and complete.

Exercises

(LO 2)   E7-1   (Determining Cash Balance) The controller for Fashion Co. is trying to determine the amount of cash to report on the December 31, 2017 statement of financial position. The following information is provided:

[handwritten margin notes: +600,000 +900,000]

1. A commercial savings account with $600,000 and a commercial chequing account balance of $900,000 are held at First National Bank. There is also a bank overdraft of $35,000 in a chequing account at the Royal Scotia Bank. No other accounts are held at the Royal Scotia Bank. *→ liability*

[handwritten margin notes: disclosure (possible restriction)]

2. Fashion has agreed to maintain a cash balance of $100,000 at all times in its chequing account at First National Bank to ensure that credit is available in the future.

[handwritten margin notes: +5,000,000]

3. Fashion has a $5-million investment in a Commercial Bank of Montreal money-market mutual fund. This fund has chequing account privileges. *(ie. readily accessible)*

[handwritten margin notes: not cash, prepaid expense]

4. There are travel advances of $18,000 for executive travel for the first quarter of next year. (Employees will complete expense reports after they travel.)

[handwritten margin notes: separate restricted cash account]

5. A separate cash fund in the amount of $1.5 million is restricted for the retirement of long-term debt.

[handwritten margin notes: +3,000]

6. There is a petty cash fund of $3,000.

[handwritten margin notes: employee advance / A/R]

7. A $1,900 IOU from Marianne Koch, a company officer, will be withheld from her salary in January 2018.

[handwritten margin notes: +11,000]

8. There are 20 cash floats for retail operation cash registers: 8 at $475, and 12 at $600.

[handwritten margin notes: not cash, temp. investment (maturity >90days)]

9. The company has two certificates of deposit, each for $500,000. These certificates of deposit each had a maturity of 120 days when they were acquired. One was purchased on October 15 and the other on December 27. *(type of investment)*

[handwritten margin notes: post-dated cheque → worthless until can be cashed]

10. Fashion has received a cheque dated January 12, 2018, in the amount of $25,000 from a customer owing funds at December 31. It has also received a cheque dated January 8, 2018, in the amount of $11,500 from a customer as an advance on an order that was placed on December 29 and will be delivered February 1, 2018.

[handwritten margin notes: either cash OR temp investment]

11. Fashion holds $2.1 million of commercial paper of Rocco Leone Co., which is due in 60 days.

[handwritten margin notes: +7,700]

12. Currency and coin on hand amounted to $7,700.

[handwritten margin notes: FV-NI Investment]

13. Fashion acquired 1,000 shares of Sortel for $3.90 per share in late November and is holding them for trading. The shares are still on hand at year end and have a fair value of $4.10 per share on December 31, 2017.

Instructions

[handwritten: $6,521,700 →]

(a) Calculate the amount of cash to be reported on Fashion's statement of financial position at December 31, 2017.

(b) Indicate the proper way to report items that are not reported as cash on the December 31, 2017 statement of financial position.

(c) Referring to item 2 above, why would First National Bank require Fashion to maintain a cash balance of $100,000 at all times in its chequing account?

DIGGING DEEPER

(d) From the perspective of a potential lender to Fashion, discuss the importance of proper reporting of item 5.

(LO 2)   E7-2   (Determining Cash Balance) Several independent situations follow. *[handwritten: ✓ not prepaid b/c no expense (A/R)]*

1. Chequing account balance $625,000; certificate of deposit $1.1 million; cash advance to subsidiary $980,000; utility deposit paid to gas company $180. *[handwritten: (cash) (temp. investment)]*

2. Chequing account balance $500,000; overdraft in special chequing account at same bank as normal chequing account $17,000; cash held in bond sinking fund $200,000; petty cash fund $300; cash on hand $1,350. *[handwritten: (cash) (A/R) (-cash) → restricted cash to pay back maturity of bond.]*

3. Chequing account balance $540,000; postdated cheque from customer $11,000; cash restricted to maintain compensating balance requirement $100,000; certified cheque from customer $9,800; postage stamps on hand $620.

4. Chequing account balance at bank $57,000; money-market balance at mutual fund (has chequing privileges) $38,000; NSF cheque received from customer $800.

5. Chequing account balance $700,000; cash restricted for future plant expansion $500,000; short-term (60-day) treasury bills $180,000; cash advance received from customer $900 (not included in chequing account balance); cash advance of $7,000 to company executive, payable on demand; refundable deposit of $26,000 paid to federal government to guarantee performance on construction contract.

Instructions

For each situation above, determine the amount that should be reported as cash. If items are not reported as cash, explain why.

(LO 3, 9) E7-3 (Financial Statement Presentation of Receivables) LeBlanc Inc. shows a balance of $519,289 in the Accounts Receivable account on December 31, 2017. The balance consists of the following:

Instalment accounts due in 2018	$ 91,000
Instalment accounts due after 2018	80,000
Overpayments to creditors	12,640
Due from regular customers, of which $40,000 represents	
accounts pledged as security for a bank loan	165,000
Advances to employees	69,649
Advance to subsidiary company (made in 2012)	101,000
	$519,289

Instructions

Show how the information above should be presented on the statement of financial position of LeBlanc Inc. at December 31, 2017.

(LO 4, 11) *E7-4 (Determining Ending Accounts Receivable) Your accounts receivable clerk, Mitra Adams, to whom you pay a salary of $1,500 per month, has just purchased a new Cadillac. You have decided to test the accuracy of the accounts receivable balance of $86,500 shown in the general ledger.

The following information is available for your first year in business:

1. Collections from customers are $198,000.

2. Merchandise purchased totalled $320,000.

3. Ending merchandise inventory is $99,000.

4. Goods are marked to sell at 40% above cost.

Instructions

(a) Estimate the ending balance of accounts receivable from customers that should appear in the ledger and any apparent shortages. Assume that all sales are made on account.

INTERNAL CONTROLS

(b) Discuss cash controls that can be implemented to prevent theft in this situation. Also discuss a cash control that can be implemented to detect any differences between the company's records of cash collected and cash actually received by the company.

(LO 4) E7-5 (Recording Sales Transactions) Information from Salini Computers Ltd. follows:

July	1	Sold $82,000 of computers to Robertson Corp., terms 2/15, n/30.
	5	Robertson Corp. returned for full credit one computer with an invoice price of $6,200.
	10	Salini received payment from Robertson for the full amount owed from the July transactions.
	17	Sold $160,000 in computers and peripherals to Nawaz Store, terms 2/10, n/30.
	26	Nawaz Store paid Salini for half of its July purchases.
Aug.	30	Nawaz Store paid Salini for the remaining half of its July purchases.

Instructions

(a) Prepare the entries for Salini Computers Ltd., assuming the gross method is used to record sales and cash discounts. Salini follows ASPE.

(b) Prepare the entries for Salini Computers Ltd., assuming the net method is used to record sales and cash discounts.

(LO 4) E7-6 (Recording Sales Gross and Net) On June 3, Arnold Limited sold to Chester Arthur merchandise having a sale price of $3,000 with terms 3/10, n/60, f.o.b. shipping point. A $90 invoice, terms n/30, was received by Chester on June 8 from John Booth Transport Service for the freight cost. When it received the goods on June 5, Chester notified Arnold that $500 of the merchandise contained flaws that rendered it worthless; the same day, Arnold Limited issued a credit memo covering the worthless merchandise and asked that it be returned to them at their expense. The freight on the returned merchandise was $25, which Arnold paid on June 7. On June 12, the company received a cheque for the balance due from Chester Arthur.

Instructions

(a) Prepare journal entries on Arnold Limited's books assuming that:

1. Sales and receivables are entered at gross selling price.

2. Sales and receivables are entered net of cash discounts.

(b) Prepare the journal entry under assumption 2, if Chester Arthur did not pay until July 29.

(c) From Chester Arthur's perspective, calculate the implied annual interest rate on accounts receivable not paid to Arnold within the discount period. Chester Arthur has a line of credit facility with its bank at 10%.

(LO 4, 5, 8) E7-7 (Journalizing Various Receivable Transactions) Information on Janut Corp., which reports under ASPE, follows:

July	1	Janut Corp. sold to Harding Ltd. merchandise having a sales price of $9,000, terms 3/10, n/60. Janut records its sales and receivables net.
	3	Harding Ltd. returned defective merchandise having a sales price of $700.
	5	Accounts receivable of $19,000 (gross) are factored with Jackson Credit Corp. without recourse at a financing charge of 9%. Cash is received for the proceeds and collections are handled by the finance company. (These accounts were subject to a 2% discount and were all past the discount period.)
	9	Specific accounts receivable of $15,000 (gross) are pledged to Landon Credit Corp. as security for a loan of $11,000 at a finance charge of 3% of the loan amount plus 9% interest on the outstanding balance. Janut will continue to make the collections. All the accounts receivable pledged are past the discount period and were originally subject to a 2% discount.
Dec.	29	Harding Ltd. notifies Janut that it is bankrupt and will be able to pay only 10% of its account. Give the entry to write off the uncollectible balance using the allowance method. (*Note*: First record the increase in the receivable on July 11 when the discount period passed.)

Instructions

(a) Prepare all necessary journal entries on Janut Corp.'s books.

(b) Would your treatment of the July 5 transaction change if Janut reported under IFRS? If yes, how?

(c) What if the receivables factored on July 5 were with recourse? Would your answer change if Janut reported under IFRS or ASPE?

(LO 5) E7-8 (Recording Bad Debts) At the end of 2017, Perez Corporation has accounts receivable of $2.5 million and an allowance for doubtful accounts of $120,000. On January 16, 2018, Perez determined that its $20,000 receivable from Morganfield Ltd. will not be collected, and management has authorized its write off. On January 31, 2018, Perez received notification that the company will be receiving $0.10 for every $1.00 of accounts receivable relating to McKinley Ltd. The company had previously written off 100% of the amount due from McKinley ($60,000).

Instructions

(a) Prepare the journal entry for Perez Corporation to write off the Morganfield receivable and any journal entry necessary to reflect the notice regarding McKinley Ltd.

(b) What is the estimated net realizable value of Perez's accounts receivable before and after the entries in part (a)? What is the book value of Perez's accounts receivable before and after the entries in part (a)?

(LO 5) E7-9 (Calculating Bad Debts) At January 1, 2017, the credit balance of Andy Corp.'s Allowance for Doubtful Accounts was $400,000. During 2017, the bad debt expense entry was based on a percentage of net credit sales. Net sales for 2017 were $80 million, of which 90% were on account. Based on the information available at the time, the 2017 bad debt expense was estimated to be 0.8% of net credit sales. During 2017, uncollectible receivables amounting to $500,000 were written off against the allowance for doubtful accounts. The company has estimated that at December 31, 2017, based on a review of the aged accounts receivable, the allowance for doubtful accounts would be properly measured at $525,000.

Instructions

Prepare a schedule calculating the balance in Andy Corp.'s Allowance for Doubtful Accounts at December 31, 2017. Prepare any necessary journal entry at year end to adjust the allowance for doubtful accounts to the required balance.

(LO 5) E7-10 (Reporting Bad Debts) The chief accountant for Dickinson Corporation provides you with the following list of accounts receivable that were written off in the current year:

Date	Customer	Amount
Mar. 31	Eli Masters Ltd.	$ 7,700
June 30	Crane Associates	6,800
Sept. 30	Annie Lowell's Dress Shop	12,000
Dec. 31	Vahik Uzerian	6,830

Dickinson Corporation follows the policy of debiting Bad Debt Expense as accounts are written off. The chief accountant maintains that this procedure is appropriate for financial statement purposes.

All of Dickinson Corporation's sales are on a 30-day credit basis, and the accounts written off all related to current year sales. Sales for the year total $3.2 million, and your research suggests that bad debt losses approximate 2% of sales.

Instructions

(a) Do you agree with Dickinson Corporation's policy on recognizing bad debt expense? Why?

(b) By what amount would net income differ if bad debt expense was calculated using the allowance method and percentage-of-sales approach?

(c) Under what conditions is using the direct write off method justified?

(LO 5) E7-11 (Calculating Bad Debts and Preparing Journal Entries) The trial balance before adjustment of Chloe Inc., which follows ASPE, shows the following balances:

[handwritten: ie. wrote off more than you accounted for]

	Dr.	Cr.
Accounts receivable	$105,000	
Allowance for doubtful accounts	1,950	
Sales revenue (all on credit)		$684,000
Sales returns and allowances	30,000	

Instructions

(a) Give the entry for bad debt expense for the current year assuming:

1. The allowance should be 4% of gross accounts receivable.   *[handwritten: (105,000 × 0.04 = 4,200) → 4,200 + 1,950 = 6,150] [current (DR) CR]*

2. Historical records indicate that, based on accounts receivable aging, the following percentages will not be collected: *[handwritten: to ADA]*

	Balance	Percentage Estimated to Be Uncollectible	
0–30 days outstanding	$36,000	1%	*= 360*
31–60 days outstanding	48,000	5%	*= 2400*
61–90 days outstanding	12,200	12%	*= 1464*
Over 90 days outstanding	8,800	18%	*= 1584*

[handwritten: $5808 total in ADA] [5808 + 1950 = $7758 CR to ADA] [CR to ADA]

3. Allowance for Doubtful Accounts is $1,950 but it is a credit balance and the allowance should be 4% of gross accounts receivable.   *[handwritten: 4200 – 1950 = CR $2250 to ADA]*

DIGGING DEEPER

4. Allowance for Doubtful Accounts is $1,950 but it is a credit balance and historical records indicate that the same percentages in part 2. are to be used to determine the Allowance for Doubtful Accounts.   *[handwritten: CR 5808 – 1950 = $3858 to ADA]*

(b) From the perspective of an independent reviewer of Chloe's trial balance, comment on the unadjusted debit balance in Chloe's allowance for doubtful accounts at year end.   *[handwritten: → a lot of write offs during last year (more than expected ADA)]*

(c) Assume Chloe reports under IFRS and has adopted IFRS 9. What should Chloe's approach be for determining its Allowance for Doubtful Accounts when considering "lifetime expected credit losses"? What is meant by this concept? Would a percentage-of-sales approach be appropriate for determining the Allowance for Doubtful Accounts under IFRS 9? Why or why not? How would Chloe's approach to accounting for sales returns differ under IFRS?

(LO 5) E7-12 (Bad Debts—Aging) Lenai Co. has the following account among its trade receivables:

Hopkins Co.

1/1	Balance forward	$ 850	1/28	Cash (#1710)	1,100
1/20	Invoice #1710	1,100	4/2	Cash (#2116)	1,350
3/14	Invoice #2116	1,350	4/10	Cash (1/1 Balance)	155
4/12	Invoice #2412	2,110	4/30	Cash (#2412)	1,000
9/5	Invoice #3614	490	9/20	Cash (#3614 and part of #2412)	790
10/17	Invoice #4912	860	10/31	Cash (#4912)	860
11/18	Invoice #5681	2,000	12/1	Cash (#5681)	1,250
12/20	Invoice #6347	800	12/29	Cash (#6347)	800

Instructions

Age the Hopkins Co. account at December 31 and specify any items that may need particular attention at year end.

(LO 6) E7-13 (Interest-Bearing and Non–Interest-Bearing Notes) Little Corp. was experiencing cash flow problems and was unable to pay its $105,000 account payable to Big Corp. when it fell due on September 30, 2017. Big agreed to substitute a one-year note for the open account. The following two options were presented to Little by Big Corp.:

Option 1: A one-year note for $105,000 due September 30, 2018. Interest at a rate of 8% would be payable at maturity.

Option 2: A one-year non–interest-bearing note for $113,400. The implied rate of interest is 8%.

Assume that Big Corp. has a December 31 year end.

Instructions

DIGGING DEEPER

(a) Assuming Little Corp. chooses Option 1, prepare the entries required on Big Corp.'s books on September 30, 2017, December 31, 2017, and September 30, 2018.

(b) Assuming Little Corp. chooses Option 2, prepare the entries required on Big Corp.'s books on September 30, 2017, December 31, 2017, and September 30, 2018.

(c) Compare the amount of interest income earned by Big Corp. in 2017 and 2018 under both options. Comment briefly.

(d) From management's perspective, does one option provide better liquidity for Big at December 31, 2017? Does one option provide better cash flows than the other?

FINANCE

(LO 6) E7-14 (Non–Interest-Bearing Note) On September 1, 2017, Myo Inc. sold goods to Khin Corporation, a new customer. Before shipping the goods, Myo's credit and collections department conducted a procedural credit check and determined that Khin is a high-credit-risk customer. As a result, Myo did not provide Khin with open credit by recording the sale as an account receivable. Instead, Myo required Khin to provide a non–interest-bearing promissory note for $35,000 face value, to be repaid in one year. Khin has a credit rating that requires it to pay 12% interest on borrowed funds. Myo pays 10% interest on a loan recently obtained from its local bank. Myo has a December 31 year end.

Instructions

(a) Prepare the entries required on Myo's books to record the sale, annual adjusting entry, and collection of the full face value of the note.

(b) Assume that on the note's maturity date, Khin informs Myo that it is having cash flow problems and can only pay Myo 80% of the note's face value. After extensive discussions with Khin's management, Myo's credit and collections department considers the remaining balance of the note uncollectible. Prepare the entry required on Myo's books on the note's maturity date.

(c) What else could Myo have done to decrease collection risk related to the sale to Khin?

(LO 7) E7-15 (Notes Receivable with Zero and Unrealistic Interest Rates) On July 1, 2017, Agincourt Inc. made two sales:

1. It sold excess land in exchange for a four-year, non–interest-bearing promissory note in the face amount of $1,101,460. The land's carrying value is $590,000.

2. It rendered services in exchange for an eight-year promissory note having a face value of $400,000. Interest at a rate of 3% is payable annually.

The customers in the above transactions have credit ratings that require them to borrow money at 12% interest. Agincourt recently had to pay 8% interest for money it borrowed from British National Bank.

3. On July 1, 2017, Agincourt also agreed to accept an instalment note from one of its customers in partial settlement of accounts receivable that were overdue. The note calls for four equal payments of $20,000, including the principal and interest due, on the anniversary of the note. The implied interest rate on this note is 10%.

Instructions

DIGGING DEEPER

(a) Prepare the journal entries to record the three notes receivable transactions of Agincourt Inc. on July 1, 2017.

(b) Prepare an effective-interest amortization table for the instalment note obtained in partial collection of accounts receivable. From Agincourt's perspective, what are the advantages of an instalment note compared with a non–interest-bearing note?

(LO 7, 9) E7-16 (Notes Receivable with Zero Interest Rate) By December 31, 2017, Clearing Corp. had performed a significant amount of environmental consulting services for Rank Ltd. Rank was short of cash, and Clearing agreed to accept a $200,000, non–interest-bearing note due December 31, 2019, as payment in full. Rank is a bit of a credit risk and typically borrows funds at a rate of 12%. Clearing is much more creditworthy and has various lines of credit at 9%. Clearing Corp. reports under IFRS.

Instructions

(a) Prepare the journal entry to record the transaction on December 31, 2017, for Clearing Corp.

(b) Assuming Clearing's fiscal year end is December 31, prepare the journal entry required at December 31, 2018.

(c) Assuming Clearing's fiscal year end is December 31, prepare the journal entry required at December 31, 2019.

(d) What are the amount and classification of the note on Clearing Corp.'s statement of financial position as at December 31, 2018?

(e) Assume instead that Clearing reports under ASPE and uses the straight-line method to amortize the discount on the note. What would the interest income be relating to the note for 2018 and 2019?

(f) If an appropriate market rate of interest for the note receivable is not known, how should the transaction be valued and recorded on December 31, 2017?

(LO 8) E7-17   (Assigning Accounts Receivable) On April 1, 2017, Ibrahim Corporation assigns $400,000 of its accounts receivable to First National Bank as collateral for a $200,000 loan that is due July 1, 2017. The assignment agreement calls for Ibrahim to continue to collect the receivables. First National Bank assesses a finance charge of 3% of the accounts receivable, and interest on the loan is 10%, a realistic rate for a note of this type.

Instructions

(a) Prepare the April 1, 2017 journal entry for Ibrahim Corporation.

(b) Prepare the journal entry for Ibrahim's collection of $350,000 of the accounts receivable during the period April 1 to June 30, 2017.

(c) On July 1, 2017, Ibrahim paid First National Bank the entire amount that was due on the loan.

(LO 8) E7-18   (Journalizing Various Receivables Transactions) The trial balance before adjustment for Bassel Company shows the following balances.

	Dr.	Cr.
Accounts receivable	$82,000	
Allowance for doubtful accounts	1,750	
Sales revenue		$430,000

The following cases are independent:

1. To obtain cash, Bassel factors without recourse $20,000 of receivables with Anila Finance. The finance charge is 10% of the amount factored.

2. To obtain a one-year loan of $55,000, Bassel assigns $65,000 of specific accounts receivable to Ruddin Financial. The finance charge is 8% of the loan; the cash is received.

3. The company wants to maintain the Allowance for Doubtful Accounts at 5% of gross accounts receivable.

4. The company wishes to increase the allowance account by $1\frac{1}{2}$% of sales.

Instructions

Using the data above, prepare the journal entries to record each of the above cases.

(LO 8, 9) E7-19   (Transfer of Receivables with Recourse) Chessman Corporation factors $600,000 of accounts receivable with Liquidity Financing, Inc. on a with recourse basis. Liquidity Financing will collect the receivables. The receivable records are transferred to Liquidity Financing on August 15, 2017. Liquidity Financing assesses a finance charge of 2.5% of the amount of accounts receivable and also reserves an amount equal to 5.25% of accounts receivable to cover probable adjustments. Chessman prepares financial statements under ASPE.

Instructions

(a) According to ASPE, what conditions must be met for a transfer of receivables to be accounted for as a sale?

(b) Assume the conditions from part (a) are met. Prepare the journal entry on August 15, 2017, for Chessman to record the sale of receivables, assuming the recourse obligation has a fair value of $6,000.

FINANCE

(c) What effect will the factoring of receivables have on calculating the accounts receivable turnover for Chessman? Comment briefly.

(d) Assume that Chessman is a private enterprise and prepares financial statements under IFRS. What conditions must be met for the transfer of receivables to be accounted for as a sale?

(LO 8, 9) E7-20   (Transfer of Receivables with Servicing Retained) Lute Retail Ltd. follows ASPE. It transfers $355,000 of its accounts receivable to an independent trust in a securitization transaction on July 11, 2017, receiving 96% of the receivables balance as proceeds. Lute will continue to manage the customer accounts, including their collection. Lute estimates this obligation has a liability value of $12,500. In addition, the agreement includes a recourse provision with an estimated value of $9,900. The transaction is to be recorded as a sale.

FINANCE

Instructions

(a) Prepare the journal entry on July 11, 2017, for Lute Retail Ltd. to record the securitization of the receivables.

(b) What effect will the securitization of receivables have on Lute Retail Ltd.'s accounts receivable turnover? Comment briefly.

(handwritten note, left margin, top): cash sales not relevant to receivables turnover.

(c) Would the treatment of the transaction change if Lute Retail followed IFRS? Compare how ASPE and IFRS differ in how you determine if the receivables should be derecognized.

(handwritten note, left margin): net sales / avg. trade receivables

(LO 9) E7-21 (Analysis of Receivables) Information follows for Patuanak Company:

1. The beginning-of-the-year Accounts Receivable balance was $25,000.

2. Net sales for the year were $410,000. (Credit sales were $200,000 of the total sales.) Patuanak does not offer cash discounts.

3. Collections on accounts receivable during the year were $140,000.

(handwritten, left margin, calculations):
$= \frac{200,000}{25,000 + 200,000 - 140,000}$
$= \frac{200,000}{85,000 \rightarrow avg!!}$
$\frac{200,000}{\left(\frac{25,000 + 85,000}{2}\right)}$ beg + end ÷2
$= \frac{200,000}{55,000}$
$= 3.63$
$\hookrightarrow \frac{365}{3.63} = 100$ days

(handwritten, right of problem 3):
Cash   210,000
AR   200,000
    Sales Revenue   410,000

Instructions

(a) Prepare summary journal entries to record the items noted above.

(b) Calculate Patuanak Company's accounts receivable turnover ratio for the year. How old is the average receivable?

FINANCE **(c)** Use the turnover ratio calculated in part (b) to analyze Patuanak Company's liquidity. The turnover ratio last year was 4.85.

(handwritten): $\frac{365}{4.85} = 75$ days vs. 100 days this year $\Rightarrow$ getting worse. (Ter ratio better b/c results in ↓ collection period)

(LO 9) E7-22 (Receivables Turnover) The **Becker Milk Company Limited**, a real estate and investment management company, reports the following information in its financial statements for the years ended April 30, 2014, 2013, and 2102:

REAL WORLD EMPHASIS

Accounts receivable, net of allowance for doubtful accounts	April 30, 2014	$ 62,389
	April 30, 2013	120,504
	April 30, 2012	103,613
Revenue, year ended	April 30, 2014	3,887,131
	April 30, 2013	4,017,858
	April 30, 2012	4,051,440

Note 8: Revenue and Economic Dependence
For the year ended April 30, 2014, the Company's largest single tenant, Alimentation Couche-Tard Inc., accounted for 83% (2013 - 86%) of rental revenue.

FINANCE

Instructions

(a) Calculate the accounts receivable turnover and days sales outstanding (or average collection period of accounts receivable in days) for the two most recent years provided.

(b) Comment on your results.

DIGGING DEEPER **(c)** Why do you think the company provided the information in Note 8?

(LO 11) *E7-23 (Petty Cash) Kali Corp. established a petty cash fund early in 2017 to increase the efficiency of accounting for small cash transactions and to improve control over many of the small expenditures it makes. The company decided to set up the imprest fund at $500 and a cheque was issued for this amount and given to the petty cash custodian.

During January, the petty cash custodian made the following disbursements and placed a receipt for each in the cash box provided.

Tim Hortons coffee order for a management meeting	$ 28.62
Office supplies purchased	49.50
Courier charges paid	25.00
Travel advance to employee	150.00
Card, wrapping paper for gift for employee in hospital	19.40

The petty cash was replenished on January 22 when the amount of cash in the fund was $225.15. In June, after six months' experience with the fund, management decided to increase the imprest fund to $700.

Instructions

(a) Prepare the journal entries to establish the petty cash fund, to reimburse it on January 22, and to increase the fund in June.

(b) Describe where the petty cash will be reported on Kali Corp.'s financial statements.

(c) Explain briefly why many companies have a policy of reimbursing the petty cash fund on each balance sheet date.

(LO 11) *E7-24 (Bank Reconciliation and Adjusting Entries) Ling Corp. deposits all receipts intact and makes all payments by cheque. The following information is available from the cash records:

April 30 Bank Reconciliation	
Balance per bank	$ 7,120
Add: Deposits in transit	1,540
Deduct: Outstanding cheques	(2,000)
Balance per books	$ 6,660

Month of May Results

	Per Bank	Per Books
Balance on May 31	$8,760	$9,370
May deposits	5,000	5,810
May cheques	4,000	3,100
May note collected (not included in May deposits)	1,000	—
May bank service charge	25	—
May NSF cheque from a customer, returned by the bank (recorded by the bank as a charge)	335	—

Instructions

(a) Keeping in mind the time lag between deposits and cheques being recorded in the books and when they are recorded by the bank, determine the amount of outstanding deposits and outstanding cheques at May 31.

(b) Prepare a May 31 bank reconciliation showing balance per bank statement and balance per books and correct cash balance.

(c) Prepare the journal entry or entries to correct the Cash account at May 31.

(LO 11) **E7-25* **(Bank Reconciliation and Adjusting Entries)** Eli Corp. has just received its August 31, 2017 bank statement, which is summarized as follows:

Provincial Bank of Manitoba	Disbursements	Receipts	Balance
Balance, August 1			$ 9,369
Deposits during August		$32,200	41,569
Note collected for depositor, including $40 interest		1,040	42,609
Cheques cleared during August	$34,500		8,109
Bank service charges	20		8,089
Balance, August 31			8,089

The general ledger Cash account contained the following entries for the month of August:

Cash			
Balance, August 1	10,050	Disbursements in August	34,903
Receipts during August	35,000		

Deposits in transit at August 31 are $3,800, and cheques outstanding at August 31 total $1,050. Cash currently on hand at August 31 is $310 and there were postdated cheques from customers (for September 1) in the amount of $540. The bookkeeper improperly entered one cheque in the books at $146.50. The cheque was actually written for $164.50 for supplies (expense) and cleared the bank during the month of August.

Instructions

(a) Prepare a bank reconciliation dated August 31, 2017, proceeding to a correct balance.

(b) Prepare any entries that are needed to make the books correct and complete.

INTERNAL CONTROLS (c) What amount of cash should be reported on the August 31 statement of financial position?

Problems

P7-1 Dev Equipment Corp. usually closes its books on December 31, but at the end of 2017 it held its cash book open so that a more favourable statement of financial position could be prepared for credit purposes. Cash receipts and disbursements for the first 10 days of January were recorded as December transactions. The company uses the gross method to record cash discounts and a periodic inventory system.

The following information is given:

1. January cash receipts recorded in the December cash book totalled $38,900. Of that amount, $25,300 was for cash sales and $13,600 was for collections on 2017 accounts receivable for which cash discounts of $630 were given.

2. January cash disbursements that were recorded in the December cheque register were for payments relating to $24,850 of accounts payable on which discounts of $520 were taken.

3. The general ledger has not been closed for 2017.

4. The amount shown as inventory was determined by a physical count on December 31, 2017.

Instructions

(a) Prepare any entries that you consider necessary to correct Dev Equipment Corp.'s accounts at December 31.

(b) To what extent was Dev Equipment Corp. able to show a more favourable statement of financial position at December 31 by holding its cash book open? (Use ratio analysis.) Assume that the statement of financial position that was prepared by the company showed the following amounts prior to any required adjustments:

	Debit	Credit
Cash	$39,000	
Accounts receivable	42,000	
Inventory	67,000	
Accounts payable		$45,000
Accrued liabilities		14,200

ETHICS

(c) Discuss the ethical implications of holding the cash book open and showing a more favourable statement of financial position.

P7-2 A series of unrelated situations follow:

1. Atlantic Inc.'s unadjusted trial balance at December 31, 2017, included the following accounts (accounted for using ASPE):

	Debit	Credit
Allowance for doubtful accounts	$ 8,000	
Sales revenue		$1,980,000
Sales returns and allowances	60,000	
Sales discounts	4,400	

2. An analysis and aging of Central Corp.'s accounts receivable at December 31, 2017, disclosed the following:

Amounts estimated to be uncollectible	$ 160,000
Accounts receivable	1,790,000
Allowance for doubtful accounts (per books)	125,000

3. Western Co. provides for doubtful accounts based on 4.5% of credit sales. The following data are available for 2017:

Credit sales during 2017	$3,200,000
Allowance for doubtful accounts 1/1/17	37,000
Collection of accounts written off in prior years	
(customer credit was re-established)	18,000
Customer accounts written off as uncollectible during 2017	36,000

4. At the end of its first year of operations, on December 31, 2017, Pacific Inc. reported the following information:

Accounts receivable, net of allowance for doubtful accounts	$950,000
Customer accounts written off as uncollectible during 2017	24,000
Bad debt expense for 2017	92,000

5. The following accounts were taken from Northern Inc.'s unadjusted trial balance at December 31, 2017:

	Debit	Credit
Sales revenue (all on credit)		$950,000
Sales discounts	$ 21,400	
Allowance for doubtful accounts	34,000	
Accounts receivable	610,000	

Instructions

(a) For situation 1, Atlantic estimates its bad debt expense to be 1.5% of net sales. Determine its bad debt expense for 2017.

(b) For situation 2, what is the net realizable value of Central Corp.'s receivables at December 31, 2017?

(c) For situation 3, what is the balance in Allowance for Doubtful Accounts at December 31, 2017?

(d) For situation 4, what is the balance in Accounts Receivable at December 31, 2017, before subtracting the allowance for doubtful accounts?

(e) For situation 5, if doubtful accounts are 7% of accounts receivable, what is the bad debt expense amount to be reported for 2017?

P7-3   Fortini Corporation had record sales in 2017. It began 2017 with an Accounts Receivable balance of $475,000 and an Allowance for Doubtful Accounts of $33,000. Fortini recognized credit sales during the year of $6,675,000 and made monthly adjusting entries equal to 0.5% of each month's credit sales to recognize bad debt expense. Also during the year, the company wrote off $35,500 of accounts that were deemed to be uncollectible, although one customer whose $4,000 account had been written off surprised management by paying the amount in full in late September. Including this surprise receipt, $6,568,500 cash was collected on account in 2017.

In preparation for the audited year-end financial statements, the controller prepared the following aged listing of the receivables at December 31, 2017:

Days Account Outstanding	Amount	Probability of Collection
Less than 16 days	$270,000	97%
Between 16 and 30 days	117,000	92%
Between 31 and 45 days	80,000	80%
Between 46 and 60 days	38,000	70%
Between 61 and 75 days	20,000	50%
Over 75 days	25,000	0%
	$550,000	

Instructions

(a) Reconcile the 2017 opening balance in Accounts Receivable to the $550,000 ending balance on the controller's aged listing.

(b) Prepare an analysis of the aged accounts receivable using a provision matrix. Based on your analysis, prepare the adjusting entry to bring the Allowance for Doubtful Accounts to its proper balance at year end.

(c) Show how accounts receivable would be presented on the December 31, 2017 statement of financial position.

(d) What is the dollar effect of the year-end bad debt adjustment on the before-tax income?

P7-4   From its first day of operations to December 31, 2017, Campbell Corporation provided for uncollectible accounts receivable under the allowance method: entries for bad debt expense were made monthly based on 2.5% of credit sales, bad debts that were written off were charged to the allowance account, recoveries of bad debts previously written off were credited to the allowance account, and no year-end adjustments were made to the allowance account. Campbell's usual credit terms were net 30 days, and remain unchanged.

The balance in Allowance for Doubtful Accounts was $184,000 at January 1, 2017. During 2017, credit sales totalled $9.4 million, interim entries for bad debt expense were based on 2.5% of credit sales, $95,000 of bad debts were written off, and recoveries of accounts previously written off amounted to $15,000. Campbell upgraded its computer facility in November 2017, and an aging of accounts receivable was prepared for the first time as at December 31, 2017. A summary of the aging analysis follows:

Classification by Month of Sale	Balance in Each Category	Estimated % Uncollectible
November–December 2017	$1,080,000	8.0%
July–October 2017	650,000	12.5%
January–June 2017	420,000	20.0%
Before January 1, 2017	150,000	60.0%
	$2,300,000	

Based on a review of how collectible the accounts really are in the "Before January 1, 2017" aging category, additional receivables totalling $69,000 were written off as at December 31, 2017. The 60% uncollectible estimate therefore only applies to the remaining $81,000 in the category. Finally, beginning with the year ended December 31, 2017, Campbell adopted a new accounting method for estimating the allowance for doubtful accounts: it now uses the amount indicated by the year-end aging analysis of accounts receivable which provides its best estimate of "expected credit losses resulting from all possible default events."

Instructions

(a) Prepare a schedule that analyzes the changes in Allowance for Doubtful Accounts for the year ended December 31, 2017. Show supporting calculations by preparing a provision matrix in good form. (*Hint:* In calculating the allowance amount at December 31, 2017, subtract the $69,000 write off of receivables.)

(b) Prepare the journal entry for the year-end adjustment to the Allowance for Doubtful Accounts balance as at December 31, 2017.

(AICPA adapted)

P7-5 The following information relates to Shea Inc.'s accounts receivable for the 2017 fiscal year:

1. An aging schedule of the accounts receivable as at December 31, 2017, is as follows:

Age	Net Debit Balance	% to Be Applied after Write off Is Made
Under 60 days	$172,342	1%
61–90 days	136,490	3%
91–120 days	39,924*	7%
Over 120 days	23,644	$4,200 definitely
	$372,400	uncollectible; 20% of remainder is estimated uncollectible

*The $2,740 write off of receivables (see item 4 below) is related to the 91–120-day category.

2. The Accounts Receivable control account has a debit balance of $372,400 on December 31, 2017.

3. Two entries were made in the Bad Debt Expense account during the year: (1) a debit on December 31 for the amount credited to Allowance for Doubtful Accounts, and (2) a credit for $2,740 on November 3, 2017, and a debit to Allowance for Doubtful Accounts because of a bankruptcy.

4. Allowance for Doubtful Accounts is as follows for 2017:

	Allowance for Doubtful Accounts			
11/3	Uncollectible accounts written off 2,740	1/1	Beginning balance	8,750
		12/31	5% of $372,400	18,620

5. There is a credit balance in Accounts Receivable (61–90 days) of $4,840, which represents an advance on a sales contract.

Instructions

Assuming that the books have not been closed for 2017, make the necessary correcting entries.

P7-6 The statement of financial position of Alice Inc. at December 31, 2016, includes the following:

Notes receivable	$300,000	
Accounts receivable	282,100	
Less: Allowance for doubtful accounts	(47,300)	$534,800

Transactions in 2017 include the following:

1. Accounts receivable of $146,000 were collected. This amount includes gross accounts of $50,000 on which 2% sales discounts were allowed.

2. An additional $16,700 was received in payment of an account that was written off in 2017.

3. Customer accounts of $39,500 were written off during the year.

4. At year end, Allowance for Doubtful Accounts was estimated to need a balance of $52,000. This estimate is based on an analysis of aged accounts receivable.

Instructions

Prepare all necessary journal entries for Alice Inc. to reflect the information above.

(AICPA adapted)

P7-7 On October 1, 2017, Healy Farm Equipment Corp. sold a harvesting machine to Homestead Industries. Instead of a cash payment, Homestead Industries gave Healy Farm Equipment a $150,000, two-year, 10% note; 10% is a realistic rate for a note of this type. The note required interest to be paid annually on October 1, beginning October 1, 2018. Healy Farm Equipment's financial statements are prepared on a calendar-year basis.

Instructions

(a) Assuming that no reversing entries are used and that Homestead Industries fulfills all the terms of the note, prepare the necessary journal entries for Healy Farm Equipment Corp. for the entire term of the note.

(b) Repeat the journal entries under the assumption that Healy Farm Equipment Corp. uses reversing entries.

P7-8 On December 31, 2017, Zhang Ltd. rendered services to Beggy Corp. at an agreed price of $91,844.10. In payment, Zhang accepted $36,000 cash and agreed to receive the balance in four equal instalments of $18,000 that are due each December 31. An interest rate of 11% is applicable.

Instructions

(a) Calculate the value of the note receivable at December 31, 2017, and prepare an effective-interest amortization table for the note.

(b) Prepare the entries recorded by Zhang Ltd. for the sale and for the receipts including interest on the following dates:

1. December 31, 2017	**4.** December 31, 2020
2. December 31, 2018	**5.** December 31, 2021
3. December 31, 2019	

DIGGING DEEPER

(c) From Zhang Ltd.'s perspective, what are the advantages of an instalment note compared with a non–interest-bearing note?

P7-9 Desrosiers Ltd. had the following long-term receivable account balances at December 31, 2016:

Notes receivable	$1,800,000
Notes receivable—Employees	400,000

Transactions during 2017 and other information relating to Desrosiers' long-term receivables were as follows:

1. The $1.8-million note receivable is dated May 1, 2016, bears interest at 9%, and represents the balance of the consideration received from the sale of Desrosiers' electronics division to New York Company. Principal payments of $600,000 plus appropriate interest are due on May 1, 2017, 2018, and 2019. The first principal and interest payment was made on May 1, 2017. Collection of the note instalments is reasonably assured.

2. The $400,000 note receivable is dated December 31, 2016, bears interest at 8%, and is due on December 31, 2019. The note is due from Marcia Cumby, president of Desrosiers Ltd., and is secured by 10,000 Desrosiers common shares. Interest is payable annually on December 31, and the interest payment was made on December 31, 2017. The quoted market price of Desrosiers' common shares was $45 per share on December 31, 2017.

3. On April 1, 2017, Desrosiers sold a patent to Pinot Company in exchange for a $200,000 non–interest-bearing note due on April 1, 2019. There was no established exchange price for the patent, and the note had no ready market. The prevailing rate of interest for a note of this type at April 1, 2017, was 12%. The present value of $1 for two periods at 12% is 0.79719 (use this factor). The patent had a carrying amount of $40,000 at January 1, 2017, and the amortization for the year ended December 31, 2017 would have been $8,000. The collection of the note receivable from Pinot is reasonably assured.

4. On July 1, 2017, Desrosiers sold a parcel of land to Four Winds Inc. for $200,000 under an instalment sale contract. Four Winds made a $60,000 cash down payment on July 1, 2017, and signed a four-year, 11% note for the $140,000 balance. The equal annual payments of principal and interest on the note will be $45,125, payable on July 1, 2018, through July 1, 2021. The land could have been sold at an established cash price of $200,000. The cost of the land to Desrosiers was $150,000. Collection of the instalments on the note is reasonably assured.

5. On August 1, 2017, Desrosiers agreed to allow its customer, Saini Inc., to substitute a six-month note for accounts receivable of $200,000 it owed. The note bears interest at 6% and principal and interest are due on the maturity date of the note.

Instructions

(a) For each note:

1. Describe the relevant cash flows in terms of amount and timing.

2. Determine the amount of interest income that should be reported in 2017.

3. Determine the portion of the note and any interest that should be reported in current assets at December 31, 2017.

4. Determine the portion of the note that should be reported as a long-term investment at December 31, 2017.

(b) Prepare the long-term receivables section of Desrosiers' statement of financial position at December 31, 2017.

(c) Prepare a schedule showing the current portion of the long-term receivables and accrued interest receivable that would appear in Desrosiers' statement of financial position at December 31, 2017.

(d) Determine the total interest income from the long-term receivables that would appear on Desrosiers' income statement for the year ended December 31, 2017.

P7-10   Logo Limited follows ASPE. It manufactures sweatshirts for sale to athletic-wear retailers. The following summary information was available for Logo for the year ended December 31, 2016:

Cash	$20,000
Accounts receivable	40,000
Inventory	85,000
Accounts payable	65,000
Accrued liabilities	15,000

Part 1

During 2017, Logo had the following transactions:

1. Total sales were $465,000. Of the total sales amount, $215,000 was on a credit basis.

2. On June 30, a $50,000 account receivable of a major customer was settled, with Logo accepting a $50,000, one-year, 11% note, with the interest payable at maturity.

3. Logo collected $160,000 on accounts receivable during the year.

4. At December 31, 2017, Cash had a balance of $15,000, Inventory had a balance of $80,000, Accounts Payable was $70,000, and Accrued Liabilities was $16,000.

Instructions

(a) Prepare summary journal entries to record the items noted above.

(b) Calculate the current ratio and the receivables turnover ratio for Logo at December 31, 2017. Use these measures to assess Logo's liquidity. The receivables turnover ratio last year was 4.75.

FINANCE

Part 2

Now assume that at year end 2017, Logo enters into the following transactions related to the company's receivables:

1. Logo sells the note receivable to Prairie Bank for $50,000 cash plus accrued interest. Given the creditworthiness of Logo's customer, the bank accepts the note without recourse and assesses a finance charge of 3.5%. Prairie Bank will collect the note directly from the customer.

2. Logo factors some accounts receivable at the end of the year. Accounts totalling $40,000 are transferred to Primary Factors, Inc., with recourse. Primary Factors retains 6% of the balances and assesses a finance charge of 4% on the transfer. Primary Factors will collect the receivables from Logo's customers. The fair value of the recourse obligation is $4,000.

Instructions

(c) Prepare the journal entry to record the transfer of the note receivable to Prairie Bank.

(d) Prepare the journal entry to record the sale of receivables to Primary Factors.

(e) Calculate the current ratio and the receivables turnover ratio for Logo at December 31, 2017. Use these measures to assess Logo's liquidity. The receivables turnover ratio last year was 4.75.

(f) Discuss how the ratio analysis in part (e) would be affected if Logo had transferred the receivables in secured borrowing transactions.

(g) From Prairie Bank's perspective, what is the total effect on its net income as a result of purchasing the note receivable without recourse?

DIGGING DEEPER

(h) From Primary Factors' perspective, what is the total effect on its net income as a result of purchasing the accounts receivable with recourse?

P7-11   In 2017, Ibran Corp. required additional cash for its business. Management decided to use accounts receivable to raise the additional cash and has asked you to determine the income statement effects of the following transactions:

1. On July 1, 2017, Ibran assigned $600,000 of accounts receivable to Provincial Finance Corporation as security for a loan. Ibran received an advance from Provincial Finance of 90% of the assigned accounts receivable less a commission of 3% on the advance. Before December 31, 2017, Ibran collected $220,000 on the assigned accounts receivable, and remitted $232,720 to Provincial Finance. Of the latter amount, $12,720 was interest on the advance from Provincial Finance.

2. On December 1, 2017, Ibran sold $300,000 of accounts receivable to Wunsch Corp. for $275,000. The receivables were sold outright on a without recourse basis and Ibran has no continuing interest in the receivables.

3. On December 31, 2017, an advance of $120,000 was received from First Bank by pledging $160,000 of Ibran's accounts receivable. Ibran's first payment to First Bank is due on January 30, 2018.

Instructions

(a) Prepare a schedule showing the income statement effects of these transactions for the year ended December 31, 2017.

(b) Considering the three different methods Ibran used to obtain financing above, why might a company choose one method over the other?

FINANCE

P7-12   The Cormier Corporation sells office equipment and supplies to many organizations in the city and surrounding area on contract terms of 2/10, n/30. In the past, over 75% of the credit customers have taken advantage of the discount by paying within 10 days of the invoice date. However, the number of customers taking the full 30 days to pay has increased within the last year. It now appears that fewer than 60% of the customers are taking the discount. Bad debts as a percentage of gross credit sales have risen from the 1.5% of past years to about 4% in the current year.

The controller responded to a request for more information on the deterioration in collections of accounts receivable by preparing the following report:

FINANCE

THE CORMIER CORPORATION
Finance Committee Report—Accounts Receivable Collections
May 31, 2017

The fact that some credit accounts will prove uncollectible is normal. Annual bad debt write offs have been 1.5% of gross credit sales over the past five years. During the last fiscal year, this percentage increased to slightly less than 4%. The current Accounts Receivable balance is $1.6 million. The condition of this balance in terms of age and probability of collection is as follows:

Proportion of Total (%)	Age Categories	Probability of Collection (%)
68	not yet due	99
15	less than 30 days past due	96.5
8	30 to 60 days past due	95
5	61 to 120 days past due	91
2.50	121 to 180 days past due	70
1.50	more than 180 days past due	20

Allowance for Doubtful Accounts had a credit balance of $43,300 on June 1, 2016. The Cormier Corporation has provided for a monthly bad debt expense accrual during the current fiscal year based on the assumption that 4% of gross credit sales will be uncollectible. Total gross credit sales for the 2016–17 fiscal year amounted to $4 million. Write offs of bad accounts during the year totalled $145,000.

Instructions

(a) Prepare an accounts receivable aging schedule (provision matrix) for the Cormier Corporation using the age categories identified in the controller's report to the finance committee. Show (1) the amount of accounts receivable outstanding for each age category and in total, and (2) the estimated amount that is uncollectible for each category and in total.

(b) Calculate the amount of the year-end adjustment that is needed to bring Allowance for Doubtful Accounts to the balance indicated by the aging analysis. Then prepare the necessary journal entry to adjust the accounting records.

(c) Assuming that the economy is currently in recession, with tight credit and high interest rates:

1. Identify steps that the Cormier Corporation might consider to improve the accounts receivable situation.

2. Evaluate each step you identify in terms of the risks and costs that it involves. Assume that Cormier follows IFRS.

P7-13   The Patchwork Corporation manufactures sweaters for sale to athletic-wear retailers. The following information was available on Patchwork for the years ended December 31, 2016 and 2017:

	12/31/16	12/31/17
Cash	$ 20,000	$ 15,000
Accounts receivable	90,000	?
Allowance for doubtful accounts	8,500	?
Inventory	85,000	80,000
Current liabilities	80,000	86,000
Total credit sales	600,000	550,000
Collections on accounts receivable	440,000	500,000

During 2017, Patchwork had the following transactions:

1. On June 1, 2017, sales of $80,000 to a major customer were settled, with Patchwork accepting an $80,000, one-year note bearing 7% interest that is payable at maturity. The $80,000 is not included in the total credit sales amount above.

2. Patchwork factors some accounts receivable at the end of the year. Accounts totalling $60,000 are transferred to Primary Factors Inc., with recourse. Primary Factors retains 5% of the balances, and will receive the collections directly from Patchwork's customers. Patchwork is assessed a finance charge of 6% on this transfer. The fair value of the recourse obligation is $7,000.

3. Patchwork wrote off $3,200 of accounts receivable during 2017.

4. Based on the latest available information, the 2017 allowance for doubtful accounts should have a balance of $12,000 at December 31, 2017.

Additional information:

Included in the cash balance at December 31, 2017, are the following: a chequing account with a balance of $9,600, postage stamps of $100, petty cash of $300, coins and currency on hand of $3,000, and postdated cheques from customers of $2,000. Patchwork is a private company that follows ASPE.

Instructions

(a) Prepare the journal entry for the sale to the customer from June 1.

(b) Prepare the journal entry for the factoring of the accounts receivable to Primary Factors Inc.

(c) Based on the above transactions and additional information, determine the balances of Accounts Receivable and Bad Debt Expense at December 31, 2017.

(d) Prepare the current assets section of Patchwork's statement of financial position at December 31, 2017.

FINANCE

(e) Calculate the current ratios for Patchwork for 2016 and 2017.

(f) Calculate the receivables turnover ratio for Patchwork for 2017. Patchwork's receivables turnover ratio for 2016 was 3.8 times.

(g) Comment on Patchwork's liquidity and ability to collect accounts receivable. Comment also on the improvement or deterioration of the current and accounts receivable turnover ratios.

DIGGING DEEPER

(h) Discuss the effect on the current and accounts receivable turnover ratios if Patchwork had decided to assign $40,000 of accounts receivable instead of factoring them to Primary Factors Inc. Recalculate the ratios to support your conclusions.

*P7-14 Joseph Kiuvik is reviewing the cash accounting for Connolly Corporation, a local mailing service. Kiuvik's review will focus on the petty cash account and the bank reconciliation for the month ended May 31, 2017. He has collected the following information from Connolly's bookkeeper:

Petty Cash

1. The petty cash fund was established on May 10, 2017, in the amount of $400.

2. Expenditures from the fund as at May 31, 2017, were supported by approved receipts for the following:

Postage expense	$63.00
Envelopes and other supplies	25.00
In-house business lunch provided	99.50
Donation to local charity	35.00
Shipping charges, for goods to customers	48.50
Newspaper advertising	22.80
Taxi for sales manager to attend meeting downtown	18.75
Freight paid on incoming purchases	37.70

3. On May 31, 2017, the petty cash fund was replenished and increased to $500; currency and coin in the fund at that time totalled $47.10.

SCOTIA IMPERIAL BANK
Bank Statement

	Disbursements	Receipts	Balance
Balance, May 1, 2017			$9,019
Deposits		$28,000	
Note payment, direct from customer (interest of $30)		930	
Cheques cleared during May	$31,100		
Bank service charges	37		
Balance, May 31, 2017			6,812

Connolly's general ledger Cash account had a balance of $9,300 on May 1. During the month, the company deposited $31,000 in the bank and wrote cheques in payment of accounts payable and the payroll for $31,685. Deposits in transit at the end of the month are determined to be $3,000, cash still on hand with the company cashier is $246 (besides petty cash), and cheques outstanding at May 31 total $550. Connolly uses a periodic inventory system.

Instructions

(a) Prepare the journal entries to record the transactions related to the petty cash fund for May.

(b) Prepare a bank reconciliation dated May 31, 2017, proceeding to a correct balance, and prepare the journal entries to make the books correct and complete.

(c) What amount of cash should be reported in the May 31, 2017 statement of financial position?

*P7-15 The cash account of Villa Corp. shows a ledger balance of $3,969.85 on June 30, 2017. The bank statement as at that date indicates a balance of $4,150. When the statement was compared with the cash records, the following facts were determined:

1. There were bank service charges for June of $25.00.

2. A bank memo stated that Bao Dai's note for $900 and interest of $36 had been collected on June 29, and the bank had made a charge of $5.50 on the collection. (No entry had been made on Villa's books when Bao Dai's note was sent to the bank for collection.)

3. Receipts for June 30 of $2,890 were not deposited until July 2.

4. Cheques outstanding on June 30 totalled $2,136.05.

5. On June 29, the bank had charged Villa Corp.'s account for a customer's uncollectible cheque amounting to $453.20.

6. A customer's cheque for $90 had been entered as $60 in the cash receipts journal by Villa Corp. on June 15.

7. Cheque no. 742 in the amount of $491 had been entered in the cashbook as $419, and cheque no. 747 in the amount of $58.20 had been entered as $582. Both cheques were issued to pay for purchases of equipment.

8. In May 2017, the bank had charged a $27.50 Wella Corp. cheque against the Villa Corp. account. The June bank statement indicated that the bank had reversed this charge and corrected its error.

Instructions

(a) Prepare a bank reconciliation dated June 30, 2017, proceeding to a correct cash balance.

(b) Prepare any entries that are needed to make the books correct and complete.

*P7-16 Information related to Bonzai Books Ltd. is as follows: balance per books at October 31, $41,847.85; November receipts, $173,528.91; November disbursements, $166,193.54; balance per bank statement at November 30, $56,270.20. The following cheques were outstanding at November 30:

#1224	$1,635.29	#1232	$3,625.15
#1230	2,468.30	#1233	482.17

Included with the November bank statement and not recorded by the company were a bank debit memo for $31.40 covering bank charges for the month, a debit memo for $572.13 for a customer's cheque returned and marked NSF, and a credit memo for $1,400 representing bond interest collected by the bank in the name of Bonzai Books Ltd. Cash on hand at November 30 that had been recorded and was not yet deposited amounted to $1,920.40.

Instructions

(a) Prepare a bank reconciliation proceeding to the correct balance at November 30 for Bonzai Books Ltd.

(b) Prepare any journal entries that are needed to adjust the Cash account at November 30.

*P7-17 Information follows for Quartz Industries Ltd.:

QUARTZ INDUSTRIES LTD.
Bank Reconciliation
May 31, 2017

Balance per bank statement		$30,928.46
Less: Outstanding cheques		
No. 6124	$2,125.00	
No. 6138	932.65	
No. 6139	960.57	
No. 6140	1,420.00	5,438.22
		25,490.24
Add deposit in transit		4,710.56
Balance per books (correct balance)		$30,200.80

CHEQUE REGISTER—JUNE

Date		Payee	No.	Invoice Amount	Discount	Cash
June	1	Bren Mfg.	6141	$ 237.50		$ 237.50
	1	Stempy Mfg.	6142	915.00	$ 9.15	905.85
	8	Regent Co., Inc.	6143	122.90	2.45	120.45
	9	Bren Mfg.	6144	306.40		306.40
	10	Petty Cash	6145	89.93		89.93
	17	Pretty Babies Photo	6146	706.00	14.12	691.88
	22	Hey Dude Publishing	6147	447.50		447.50
	23	Payroll Account	6148	4,130.00		4,130.00
	25	Dragon Tools, Inc.	6149	390.75	3.91	386.84
	28	Be Smart Construction	6151	2,250.00		2,250.00
	29	M M T, Inc.	6152	750.00		750.00
	30	Lasso Co.	6153	400.00	8.00	392.00
				$10,745.98	$37.63	$10,708.35

PROVINCIAL BANK
Bank Statement
General Chequing Account of Quartz Industries—June 2017

Date		Debits			Credits	Balance
						$30,928.46
June	1	$2,125.00	$ 237.50	$ 905.85	$4,710.56	32,370.67
	12	932.65	120.45		1,507.06	32,824.63
	23	1,420.00	447.50	306.40	1,458.55	32,109.28
	26	4,130.00	11.05			27,968.23
	30	89.93	2,250.00	1,050.00	4,157.48	28,735.78

Additional information:

- One June 26 transaction was for bank service charges.
- One June 30 transaction was a bank debit memo for $1,050.00 for a customer's cheque returned and marked NSF (included with the June bank statement).
- Cash received on June 30 and put in the bank's night deposit box on the evening of June 30 was recorded by the bank in the general chequing account on July 3 for the amount of $4,607.96.

INTERNAL CONTROL

Instructions

(a) Prepare a bank reconciliation to the correct balance as at June 30, 2017, for Quartz Industries.

(b) Discuss the importance of the bank reconciliation to control cash.

ENABLING COMPETENCIES

Cases

Refer to the Case Primer to help you answer these cases.

CA7-1 Hanley Limited manufactures camera equipment. The company plans to list its shares on the Venture Exchange. To do so, it must meet all of the following initial listing requirements (among others):

1. Net tangible assets must be at least $500,000.

2. Pre-tax earnings must be $50,000.

3. The company must have adequate working capital.

ETHICS AND FINANCE

Hanley has experienced significant growth in sales and is having difficulty estimating its bad debt expense. During the year, the sales team has been extending credit more aggressively in order to increase their commission compensation. Under the percentage-of-receivables approach using past percentages, the estimate is $50,000. Hanley has performed an aging and estimates the bad debts at $57,000. Finally, using a percentage of sales, the expense is estimated at $67,000. Before booking the allowance, net tangible assets are approximately $550,000. The controller decides to accrue $50,000, which results in pre-tax earnings of $60,000.

Instructions

Adopt the role of the Venture Exchange staff and decide whether the company meets the financial aspects of the initial requirements for listing on the Venture Exchange.

CA7-2   TELUS Corporation is one of Canada's largest telecommunications companies and provides both products and services. Its shares are traded on the Toronto and New York stock exchanges, and its credit facilities contain certain covenants relating to the amount of debt the company is allowed to hold.

The following are selected excerpts from the 2014 audited financial statements:

REAL WORLD EMPHASIS

Note 1(p) – Sales of trade receivables – SUMMARY OF SIGNIFICANT ACCOUNTING POLICIES

Sales of trade receivables in securitization transactions are recognized as collateralized short term borrowings and thus do not result in our de-recognition of the trade receivables sold.

Note 19 - SHORT-TERM BORROWINGS

On July 26, 2002, one of our subsidiaries TELUS Communications Inc. (see Note 24(a)) entered into an agreement with an arm's-length securitization trust associated with a major Schedule I bank under which it is able to sell an interest in certain of its trade receivables up to a maximum of $500 million (2013 – $500 million). This revolving-period securitization agreement was renewed in 2014, its current term ends December 31, 2016, and it requires minimum cash proceeds from monthly sales of interests in certain trade receivables of

$100 million; the term of the agreement in place at December 31, 2013, ended August 1, 2014, and minimum proceeds from monthly sales were $400 million. TELUS Communications Inc. is required to maintain at least a BB (2013 – BBB (low)) credit rating by Dominion Bond Rating Service or the securitization trust may require the sale program to be wound down prior to the end of the term.

When we sell our trade receivables, we retain reserve accounts, which are retained interests in the securitized trade receivables, and servicing rights. As at December 31, 2014, we had sold to the trust (but continued to recognize) trade receivables of $113 million (2013 – $458 million). Short-term borrowings of $100 million (2013 – $400 million) are comprised of amounts loaned to us by the arm's-length securitization trust pursuant to the sale of trade receivables.

The balance of short-term borrowings (if any) comprised amounts drawn on our bilateral bank facilities.

Instructions

Assume the role of a private company in the same business as TELUS that is considering going public. Discuss the differing accounting treatment regarding the securitization transactions under IFRS and ASPE.

ENABLING COMPETENCIES

Integrated Cases

(*Hint:* If there are issues here that are new, use the conceptual framework to help you support your analysis with solid reasoning.)

IC7-1 Fritz's Furniture (FF) is a mid-sized owner-operated business that was started 25 years ago by Fred Fritz. The retail furniture business is cyclical, with business dropping off in times of economic downturn, as is the case currently. In order to encourage sales, the store offers its own credit cards to good customers. FF has run into a bit of a cash crunch and is planning to go to the bank to obtain an increase in its line of credit in order to replenish and expand the furniture stock. At present, the line of credit is limited to 70% of the credit card receivables and inventory. The receivables and inventory have been pledged as security for the loan.

Fred has identified two possible sources of the cash shortage: outstanding credit card receivables and a buildup in old inventory. He has come up with two strategies to deal with the problem:

1. Credit card receivables: For the existing receivables, Fred has found the company Factors Inc., which will buy the receivables for 93% of their face value. The two companies are currently negotiating the terms of the deal. So far, FF has agreed to transfer legal title to the receivables to Factors Inc., and FF will maintain and collect the receivables. The one term that is still being discussed is whether Factors Inc. will have any recourse to FF if the amounts become uncollectible.

2. Excess inventory: A new sales promotion has been advertised in the newspaper for the past two months. Under the terms of the promotion, customers do not pay anything up front and will be able to take the furniture home and begin payments the following year. Response to the advertisement has been very good and a significant amount of inventory has been moved to date, leaving room for new inventory once the bank financing comes through.

Instructions

Assume the role of FF's bookkeeper and advise Fred about the impact of the strategies on the company's financial reporting. The company follows ASPE.

IC7-2 Bowearth Limited (BL) is in the lumber business. The company sells pulp and paper products as well as timber and lumber. It has over 500,000 hectares of timberland that it either owns or leases. The company's shares trade on the public stock exchange. Net income for the past few years has been positive and increasing, and it has averaged approximately $1 million over the past five years. This year, however, due to various factors, the company is expecting to just break even.

During the year, BL announced an exclusive licensing agreement with Lindor Inc. (LI), an unrelated company. Under the terms of the agreement, BL will have exclusive sales and distribution rights for LI's technology and products. In return, it will pay LI royalties. The technology and products target the pulp and paper industry. During the first five years of the agreement, royalty payments that BL must pay to LI are 3% of sales in the first year, 2% in the second, and 1% thereafter. A minimum royalty of $500,000 must be paid regardless of the level of sales. LI has been in business many years and the technology is proven and in great demand. It is therefore very likely that BL will have to pay.

The U.S. government has recently levied anti-dumping fees of 8% on all softwood lumber shipped to the United States. Anti-dumping fees are levied on foreign imports that a government thinks are being sold below fair market value. The U.S. government has also imposed countervailing duties of 20% on Canadian lumber. Countervailing duties are meant to counteract imported goods that are subsidized by their home countries. The amounts must be paid by the company to the U.S. government in order to continue to sell in the United States. The Canadian government has challenged the right of the U.S. government to charge these duties and has appealed to the World Trade Organization. Canada feels that, under the North American Free Trade Agreement (NAFTA), such charges cannot be legally levied. In the meantime, BL has been accruing and setting the amounts aside in cash deposits with the bank just in case the appeal is unsuccessful. The amounts accrued and set aside to date are approximately $3 million. The U.S. government is continuing to allow the company to ship lumber as long as the cash is set aside in the bank. To date, the appeal process is going well and the

Canadian government feels that the duties will at least be reduced significantly, if not completely eliminated. There are rumours that the duties may be cancelled next year.

In addition, BL is currently being sued by a former major shareholder, who alleges BL provided misleading financial statements. The lawsuit alleges that net income was materially misstated. The case has not yet gone to court. BL feels that the case is not very strong but has nonetheless fired the president, William Chesiuk, to be on the safe side. As a result, BL is also being sued for wrongful dismissal by its former president. Chesiuk is suing for a lost bonus of $300,000 as well as lost future income in the amount of $10 million. BL is investigating the claim of overstated net income and, to date, has not found anything that indicates a material misstatement.

BL's controller, Youssef Haddad, is unsure of how to book all of the above in the financial statements (or if he even should). He has a meeting with the bank next week to discuss increasing the company's line of credit. He is hopeful that once the ruling comes down from the World Trade Organization, the increased line of credit will not be needed. In the meantime, the bank has signalled that it will be looking at the company's liquidity very closely. The auditors will also be coming in to review the statements in the next month.

Instructions

Adopt the role of Youssef Haddad and discuss the financial reporting issues.

IC7-3 Creative Choice Corporation (CC) is a publicly traded company that has been providing traditional mortgage loans for the past 10 years. In an effort to grow its business, it has decided to build another five banking service locations across the country. The expected cost of construction is around $10 million. The company contracted to build the new banks requires a $2-million retainer upfront before it begins construction.

To accelerate cash flow, CC pooled outstanding mortgage loans for a value of $2 million and transferred them to a newly created special purpose entity (the trust). The trust in turn has sold mortgage-backed securities to third-party investors for cash. CC will continue to service and manage the mortgage receivables sold, including collecting the principal and interest payments from customers and remitting cash to the trust for payment to investors. An annual fee of $25,000 will be earned by CC for servicing and collecting the mortgage receivables. The fee will be paid as a reduction of the returns earned on the securities.

As part of the agreement, CC is still responsible to pay the full payment to investors even when a customer defaults on a mortgage payment. This recourse obligation, or the liability that CC may be at risk of incurring as a result of any mortgage payments not collected, has an estimated fair value of 2% of the mortgage receivables at year end, based on CC's historical payment defaults. The majority of pooled mortgage receivables sold have adjustable rates after five years, meaning the interest rate charged on the mortgage may increase if there is an overall increase in interest rates.

At the beginning of the year, CC loaned $133,500 to a smaller independent bank in exchange for a two-year, $150,000 non–interest-bearing note. The note's present value is $133,500. CC has recorded the note receivable at $150,000. No interest has been recorded in relation to the note receivable.

In the last quarter, customer mortgage defaults have increased by 1 percentage point over the 2% historical rate. With a 1-percentage-point increase in market interest rates chargeable on the mortgage expected over the next quarter, CC expects an another increase of 1-percentage point in the default rate next quarter.

An excerpt of the note for the mortgage receivables is provided below.

Mortgage loans (pooled and sold)	$ 2,000,000
Mortgage loans, net of allowance	45,700,000
Mortgage servicing asset	0
Accrued interest receivable	15,000

CC uses credit lines from a larger independent bank to finance the majority of its mortgage lending practice. Given the recent changes in economic conditions, the bank has been monitoring CC's liquidity. As such, CC is subject to certain covenants, including a debt to equity ratio of no more than 2 to 1. Prior to pooling the mortgage receivables, CC's debt to equity ratio was 1.8 to 1. The majority of mortgage loans that remain on the balance sheet have also been pledged as collateral to the bank.

Instructions

It is now the week after month end and you are reviewing the current-year results. Assume the role of the controller and discuss the financial reporting issues. Provide journal entries when appropriate.

RESEARCH AND ANALYSIS

RA7-1 Maple Leaf Foods Inc.

REAL WORLD EMPHASIS

Access the annual financial statements for **Maple Leaf Foods Inc.** for the year ended December 31, 2014. These statements are available from the company's website or from SEDAR (www.sedar.com).

Instructions

(a) Explain the securitization that the company is involved in (see Notes 5 and 28). What are the amounts involved and how does the company account for the securitized receivables?

(b) Calculate the accounts receivable turnover for 2014 and 2013 and the average age of the accounts receivable at December 31, 2014 and 2013. Comment on your results. For the calculation of turnover and average age, use the closing balance of accounts receivable rather than an average in the formula.

(c) Calculate the percentage growth in sales and accounts receivable in 2014 and 2013. Comment on your results.

(d) Recalculate your ratios and percentages taking into account the amounts of accounts receivable securitized as indicated in Note 28. Did the securitizations have an effect on your assessment of the company? Explain. Should securitizations be taken into account in the calculations in parts (b) and (c) above, or not taken into account at all?

RA7-2 Impairment Testing

IFRS provides guidance on impairment testing—in particular, what is supportable evidence of impairment of loans and receivables.

Instructions

Read IFRS 9, 5.5 "Impairment" and reference as appropriate IFRS 9's Appendix A "Defined Terms" to answer the following questions.

(a) When is a financial asset tested for impairment?

(b) How does IFRS 9 define "lifetime expected credit losses"?

(c) What requirements exist regarding reviewing forward-looking information to assess credit risk?

RA7-3 Canadian Tire Corporation, Limited

REAL WORLD EMPHASIS

Canadian Tire Corporation, Limited is one of Canada's best-known retailers. The company operates 493 "hard-goods" retail stores through associate dealers, 383 corporate and franchise stores under its subsidiary Mark's Work Wearhouse, 297 independently operated gasoline sites, and 436 FGL Sports retail stores (operating under banners including Sport Chek, Sports Experts, and Atmosphere). It offers financial services through its branded credit cards and now provides personal loans and a variety of insurance and warranty products.

Instructions

Access the financial statements of Canadian Tire Corporation, Limited for its year ended January 3, 2015, either on the company's website or the SEDAR website (www.sedar.com). Refer to these financial statements and their accompanying notes to answer the following questions.

(a) How does Canadian Tire define cash and cash equivalents on its statement of financial position? What is included in the cash and cash equivalents balance at January 3, 2015 (referred to as "2014")?

(b) What criteria does the company use to determine what short-term investments to include in this category?

(c) Review the financial statements and notes and identify the assets reported by Canadian Tire that qualify as loans and receivables. Does the company disclose the amount of its allowance for doubtful accounts? What was the amount of impairment for credit losses for the year? How does the company determine its allowance for impairment? Be specific. What were the amounts for the write offs, recoveries, and impairment for credit losses for the year?

(d) When is a loan impaired? How is an impaired loan valued by Canadian Tire? Be specific.

(e) Accounting standards require companies to disclose information about their exposure to credit risk. What is credit risk? What does Canadian Tire report? What is your assessment of its exposure to credit risk?

(f) Canadian Tire uses its accounts receivable to generate cash before the receivables are due via securitization. Briefly describe the forms of "securitization" activities that the company uses. Does Canadian Tire have a continuing relationship with the accounts?

RA7-4 Auditor's Report

AUDIT

Soon after beginning the year-end audit work on March 10 for the 2017 year end at Arkin Corp., the auditor has the following conversation with the controller:

Controller: The year ending March 31, 2017, should be our most profitable in history and, because of this, the board of directors has just awarded the officers generous bonuses.

Auditor: I thought profits were down this year in the industry, at least according to your latest interim report.

Controller: Well, they were down, but 10 days ago we closed a deal that will give us a substantial increase for the year.

Auditor: Oh, what was it?

Controller: Well, you remember a few years ago our former president bought shares of Hi-Tek Enterprises Ltd. because he had those grandiose ideas about becoming a conglomerate? They cost us $3 million, which is the current carrying amount. On March 1, 2017, we sold the shares to Campbell Inc., an unrelated party, for $4 million. So, we'll have a gain of $686,000, which results from $1 million pre-tax minus a commission of $20,000 for legal fees and taxes at 30%. This should increase our net income for the year to $5.2 million, compared with last year's $4.8 million. The transaction fees were higher than normal due to the setting up of the note receivable. As far as I know, we'll be the only company in the industry to register an increase in net income this year. That should help the market value of our shares!

Auditor: Do you expect to receive the $4 million in cash by March 31, your fiscal year end?

Controller: No. Although Campbell Inc. is an excellent company, they're a little tight for cash because of their rapid growth. We have a $4-million non–interest-bearing note with $400,000 due each year for the next 10 years, which Campbell signed. The first payment is due March 1 of next year and future payments are due on the same date every year thereafter.

Auditor: Why is the note non–interest-bearing? I thought the market rate of interest was closer to 8%.

Controller: Because that's what everybody agreed to. Since we don't have any interest-bearing debt, the funds invested in the note don't cost us anything, and we weren't getting any dividends on the Hi-Tek shares.

Instructions

(a) Prepare the auditor's written report to the controller on (1) how this transaction should be accounted for, and (2) how any corrections that are necessary will affect the reported results for the current year ending March 31. Assume that the company reports under IFRS. Make assumptions where required.

(b) Make the appropriate journal entries at March 1 and March 31, 2017, relating to the transaction and corrections in part (a).

(c) What is the revised net income for the company for the year ending March 31?

(d) What changes would be necessary if the company reported under ASPE? (Assume that Arkin records the investment in Hi-Tek as an FV-NI investment under both IFRS and ASPE, and that in all prior years, fair value equalled cost.)

RA7-5   Loblaw Companies Limited and Empire Company Limited

Instructions

From SEDAR (www.sedar.com), or the company websites, access the financial statements of **Loblaw Companies Limited** for its year ended January 3, 2015, and of **Empire Company Limited** for its year ended May 3, 2014. Review the financial statements and answer the following questions.

(a) What businesses are the companies in?

(b) Compare how the two companies report cash and cash equivalents on the statement of financial position. What is included in the cash and cash equivalents of each and what are the amounts of these? Is any restricted cash reported by either company?

(c) What types of receivables do Loblaw and Empire have and what was the reported amount for each? How does each type of receivable arise? Which types are similar or different between the companies? How are the loans and receivables reported?

(d) Explain the type of credit risk that the companies have and how this risk is managed. What was the allowance for doubtful accounts at the end of the year? What percentages of the accounts receivable were past due? How was the allowance for doubtful accounts determined for each company? How does the company test for impairment? What was the bad debt expense for the year? Is the allowance adequate?

(e) Does either company dispose of receivables before their due date to generate cash? Comment on how this is done and what the company has retained.

(f) Can an accounts receivable turnover ratio be determined for either company? Why or why not?

RA7-6   An Ethical Dilemma

Rudolph Corp. is a subsidiary of Huntley Corp. and follows IFRS. The ethical accountant, working as Rudolph's controller, believes that the yearly charge for doubtful accounts for Rudolph should be 2% of net credit sales. The president, nervous that the parent company might expect the subsidiary to sustain its 10% growth rate, suggests that the controller increase the charge for doubtful accounts to 3% yearly. The supervisor thinks that the lower net income, which reflects a 6% growth rate, will be a more sustainable rate for Rudolph.

Instructions

(a) Should the controller be concerned with Rudolph Corp.'s growth rate in estimating the allowance? Explain.

(b) Does the president's request pose an ethical dilemma for the controller? Why or why not?

ENDNOTES

[1] Based on *CPA Canada Handbook*, Part II, Section 3856 *Financial Instruments*. The IFRS definition in IAS 32 introduces additional complexity beyond the scope of this text related to when the entity enters into a contract that will be settled with its own shares. ASPE excludes from its definition the entity's costs of rights to reacquire its own equity instruments.

[2] Under IFRS, if current and non-current asset classifications are not used on the balance sheet, separate disclosure is required of the amounts to be recovered within 12 months and more than 12 months after the balance sheet date.

[3] *Accounting Series Release No. 148*, "Amendments to Regulations S-X and Related Interpretations and Guidelines Regarding the Disclosure of Compensating Balances and Short-Term Borrowing Arrangements," Securities and Exchange Commission, November 13, 1973.

[4] *CPA Canada Handbook–Accounting*, Part II, Section 1540.06(b) and IAS 7.6. Copyright © IFRS Foundation. All rights reserved. Reproduced by Wiley Canada with the permission of the IFRS Foundation®. Reproduction and use rights are strictly limited. No permission granted to third parties to reproduce or distribute.

[5] Some receivables are not financial assets. They are excluded when the claim does not result from a contractual commitment, such as income taxes receivable, which result from government legislation, or when the claim is not for cash or another financial asset.

[6] Receivables that are created by related party transactions may be an exception. Chapter 23 discusses the issues underlying related party transactions.

[7] Note that 18.25% is the stated annual rate. If the compounded, or effective, rate of interest is required, the following formula is used: Rate $= [1/(1 - .01)]^{365/(30-10)} - 1$. This results in an effective annual rate of 20.13%. See David B. Vicknair, "The Effective Annual Rate on Cash Discounts: A Clarification," *Journal of Accounting Education* 18 (2000), pp. 55–62.

[8] Present and future value tables are provided immediately following Chapter 12.

[9] William J. Vatter, *Managerial Accounting* (Englewood Cliffs, N.J.: Prentice-Hall, 1950), p. 60.

[10] Alternatively, the entries could initially recognize the note's maturity value in Notes Receivable and the discount in Discount on Notes Receivable, a contra account to Notes Receivable:

Feb. 23 Notes Receivable	5,000	
Cash		4,717
Discount on Notes Receivable		283
Nov. 23 Cash	5,000	
Notes Receivable		5,000
Discount on Notes Receivable	283	
Interest Income		283

[11] Possible impairment is assessed on a continuous basis under IFRS 9 using the expected loss impairment model. Under ASPE, companies look for evidence of impairment when there has been a significant adverse change in expected future cash flows, based on a trigger event. Impairment of long-term loans is discussed in Chapter 9 along with the impairment of other financial asset investments, and is not repeated in Chapter 7.

[12] IFRS also allows loans and receivables to be measured at fair value if certain criteria are met (either FV-OCI or FV-NI). ASPE provides the option to measure at FV-NI. These are explained in more detail in Chapter 9.

[13] There may be situations when the implicit interest rate is not the market rate; that is, when the fair value of the loan differs from the cash consideration. This circumstance is dealt with later in this chapter.

[14] Be alert to the fact that "n" equals the number of interest periods, **not one year**, and that "i" is the interest rate **for the period defined by** *n*. If interest were paid semi-annually in this example, *n* would be 6, not 3, and *i* would be 6%, not 12%, and these would be used to discount both the maturity amount **and** the interest flows. The interest cash flow used in the present value calculation would be $500, not $1,000.

[15] Credit enhancements include guaranteeing payment through recourse to the company selling the receivables or third-party guarantee provisions, the use of cash reserve accounts, or over-collateralization (providing security with a greater fair value than the amount that is at risk).

[16] In 2009, the IASB fast-tracked a replacement standard for IAS 39 *Financial Instruments—Recognition and Measurement*. This included the adoption of IFRS 9 to reduce the number of classifications and accounting methods for financial assets. In June 2010, the IASB decided to retain the existing requirements from IAS 39 for the derecognition of financial assets and financial liabilities, while improving related disclosure requirements. (The original requirements for derecognition were carried forward from IAS 39 to IFRS 9 in October 2010.) For further discussion of the status of expected changes to IFRS, see Learning Objective 10 in this chapter.

[17] Recourse is defined as "the right of a transferee of receivables to receive payment from the transferor of those receivables for failure of debtors to pay when due, the effects of prepayments, or adjustments resulting from defects in the eligibility of the transferred receivables" (*CPA Canada Handbook*, Part II, Section 3856 *Financial Instruments*, Appendix B, Transfers of Receivables).

[18] Recall from the earnings management discussion in Chapter 4 that increasing or decreasing income through management manipulation reduces the quality of financial reports.

[19] Imprest bank accounts are used to make a specific amount of cash available for a limited purpose. The account acts as a clearing account for a large volume of cheques or for a specific type of cheque. The specific and intended amount to be cleared through the imprest account, such as for a payroll, is deposited by transferring that amount from the general chequing account or other source. In addition to payroll and dividend cheques, imprest bank accounts are sometimes used for disbursing commissions, bonuses, confidential expenses (such as officers' salaries), and travel expenses, although increasingly these payments are being made in electronic form.

[20] Use of paper cheques continues to be a popular means of payment in Canada. However, easy access to desktop publishing software and hardware has created new opportunities for cheque fraud in the form of duplicate, altered, or forged cheques. At the same time, new fraud-fighting technologies, such as ultraviolet imaging, high-capacity bar codes, and biometrics, are being developed. These technologies convert paper documents into document files that are processed electronically, thereby reducing the risk of fraud.

**REFERENCE TO THE
CPA COMPETENCY MAP**   **LEARNING OBJECTIVES**

After studying this chapter, you should be able to:

1.1.1, 1.1.2, 1.2.1, 1.2.2, 1.4.5, 3.3.1	**1.** Understand inventory from a business perspective.
1.2.1, 1.2.2	**2.** Define inventory from an accounting perspective.
1.2.1, 1.2.2, 3.3.1, 3.3.2, 4.3.6	**3.** Identify which inventory items should be included in ending inventory.
1.2.1, 1.2.2, 5.1.1	**4.** Identify the effects of inventory errors on the financial statements and adjust for them.
1.2.1, 1.2.2, 3.3.1	**5.** Determine the components of inventory cost.
1.1.3, 1.2.1, 1.2.2	**6.** Distinguish between perpetual and periodic inventory systems and account for them.
1.2.1, 1.2.2	**7.** Identify and apply GAAP cost formula options and indicate when each cost formula is appropriate.
1.2.1, 1.2.2	**8.** Explain why inventory is measured at the lower of cost and net realizable value, and apply the lower of cost and net realizable value standard.
1.2.1, 1.2.2, 1.2.3	**9.** Identify inventories that are or may be valued at amounts other than the lower of cost and net realizable value.
1.2.1, 1.2.2	**10.** Apply the gross profit method of estimating inventory.
1.2.1, 1.2.2, 1.3.2, 1.4.2	**11.** Identify how inventory should be presented and the type of inventory disclosures required by IFRS and ASPE.
1.4.1, 1.4.2, 1.4.4, 5.1.1	**12.** Explain how inventory analysis provides useful information and apply ratio analysis to inventory.
1.1.4	**13.** Identify differences in accounting between IFRS and ASPE, and what changes are expected in the near future.

After studying Appendix 8A, you should be able to:

1.2.1, 1.2.2	**14.** Apply the retail method of estimating inventory.

After studying Appendix 8B, you should be able to:

1.2.1, 1.2.2, 1.2.3, 1.2.4	**15.** Identify other primary sources of GAAP for inventory.

SIGNALLING BETTER INVENTORY TRACKING

TECHNOLOGIES SUCH AS bar code scanners at checkouts and electronic security tags have drastically changed retail operations in the last three decades. Now, more retailers are using radio-frequency identification (RFID), which involves putting special tags on merchandise with antennas and computer chips that track their movement through radio signals.

RFID began as a way to speed up inventory counting, which retailers typically only do once or twice a year because it's so labour-intensive. Because at least two people must be present to count inventory, it's also expensive, costing some large department stores millions of dollars every year. Inventory was usually counted just for accounting purposes, so companies could assign a value to what they had on hand at year end.

© istockphoto.com/Clerkenwell Images

RFID makes it easier for retailers to switch to a perpetual inventory system, since the tags can keep a constant count of items. It's also transforming inventory cost formulas, helping stores move to a specific identification method for goods that typically had to be valued based on their average cost. An RFID tag allows a retailer to see exactly how much each item cost and how much it sold for.

RFID goes far beyond its initial use as an accounting tool. Whereas traditional inventory counting can be less than 50% accurate, RFID can increase inventory accuracy to over 95%, which significantly reduces stockouts (what happens when an item runs out of stock). It's estimated that retailers typically lose about 4% of their sales each year to stockouts. To help reduce stockouts, the U.S. department stores Saks Fifth Avenue and Lord & Taylor, owned by Canada's Hudson's Bay Company, use RFID to ensure the correct shoes are always on the sales floor. RFID also reduces the carrying costs of having too much inventory. RFID helps retailers locate products on shelves, in the backroom, and in warehouses.

What's next for RFID? More manufacturers are tagging their items so retailers won't have to. The technology will extend to canned food as the metal tins become antennas to transmit signals. RFID will therefore help improve food safety and quality. And retailers are using RFID data to learn more about consumers' buying habits to enhance their shopping experience and boost sales. A Canadian company, Moxie Retail, recently piloted a test at an unnamed Toronto supermarket that temporarily tracked customers' movements through the store via RFID tags on shopping carts. As a result, the store rearranged some displays to make some products more visible and accessible.

Sources: Will Roche, "4 Clear Business Benefits of RFID," Retail Info Systems News, www.risnews.edgl.com, June 30, 2014; Mary Catherine O'Connor, "Can RFID Save Brick-and-Mortar Retailers After All?", *Fortune*, April 16, 2014; Claire Swedberg, "Saks' RFID Deployment Ensures Thousands of Shoes Are on Display," *RFID Journal*, September 18, 2013; Claire Swedberg, "Temporary RFID System Tracks Flow of Shoppers," *RFID Journal*, April 15, 2013.

PREVIEW OF CHAPTER 8

This chapter introduces the issues related to the recognition, measurement, and reporting of inventory on the statement of financial position and income statement. Appendix 8A explains how to determine inventory cost using the retail inventory method. Accounting for long-term construction and other contracts, a closely related topic, was examined in Chapter 6.

The chapter is organized as follows:

INVENTORY						
Understanding Inventory	**Recognition**	**Measurement**	**Presentation, Disclosure, and Analysis**	**IFRS/ASPE Comparison**	**Appendix 8A—The Retail Inventory Method of Estimating Inventory Cost**	**Appendix 8B—Accounting Guidance for Specific Inventory**
▪ What types of companies have inventory? ▪ Inventory categories ▪ Inventory planning and control ▪ Information for decision-making	▪ Accounting definition of inventory ▪ Physical goods included in inventory ▪ Inventory errors	▪ Costs included in inventory ▪ Inventory accounting systems ▪ Cost formulas ▪ Lower of cost and net realizable value ▪ Exceptions to lower of cost and net realizable value model ▪ Estimating inventory	▪ Presentation and disclosure of inventories ▪ Analysis	▪ Comparison of IFRS and ASPE ▪ Looking ahead	▪ Retail method terminology ▪ Retail inventory method with markups and markdowns—conventional method ▪ Special items ▪ Evaluation of retail inventory method	

UNDERSTANDING INVENTORY

It is important to understand the business of the company before thinking about issues relating to inventory. What types of companies carry significant amounts of inventory? What are the different types of inventory? What aspects of inventory must be managed and how is this done? Finally, what information do financial statement users need? We will answer these questions below.

What Types of Companies Have Inventory?

As a general rule, companies in industries such as manufacturing, retail, and wholesale often have a significant amount of inventories. For instance, **Airbus Group N.V.** manufactures commercial aircraft, civil and military helicopters, commercial space launch vehicles, missiles, military aircraft, satellites, defence systems, and defence electronics. Inventories make up approximately 26% of its total assets. **The Jean Coutu Group (PJC) Inc.** is one of the leading pharmacy chains in Canada. The company operates primarily through its franchised outlets and inventories make up approximately 17% of its total assets.

Some companies, such as **Toyota Motor Corporation**, follow a strategy of producing inventories on a "just-in-time" basis. This means they wait until a customer orders a product and then they arrange with other companies to actually manufacture the product. Thus their inventories are only about 4.6% of total assets.

Inventory Categories

Retailers and wholesalers have inventory that is ready for sale. For instance, **Sears Canada Inc.**, a major Canadian retailer of consumer products, reported just over $641 million of inventory at the end of 2014. This accounted for 36% of total assets. Like other **merchandising concerns**, Sears purchases most of its merchandise in a form that is ready for sale, and unsold units left on hand at each reporting date are usually referred to as merchandise inventory.

Manufacturing companies, on the other hand, have inventories in various states of completion. **Potash Corporation of Saskatchewan Inc.**, one of Canada's most profitable companies, is an integrated fertilizer and related industrial and feed products company. It is a manufacturer. At December 31, 2014, Potash Corporation reported inventories amounting to 33% of its current assets. Although the products that manufacturers produce can be quite different, they normally have three types of inventory accounts: Raw Materials, Work in Process, and Finished Goods. Amounts for goods and materials that are on hand but have not yet gone into production are reported as raw materials inventory. Raw materials include the wood to make a baseball bat, for example, or the steel to make a car. These materials can be traced directly to the end product. At any point in a continuous production process, some units are not completely processed. The cost of the raw material on which production has started but is not yet complete, plus the direct labour cost applied specifically to this material and its applicable share of manufacturing overhead costs, make up the work-in-process inventory. The costs associated with the completed but still unsold units on hand are reported as finished goods inventory.

Inventory Planning and Control

How much and what types of inventories should be on hand? How does a company control inventories so that it can maximize profits? For many reasons, management is vitally interested in inventory planning and control.

Inventory management is a double-edged sword. On the one hand, management wants to have a wide variety and sufficient quantities on hand so that customers have the greatest selection and always find what they want in stock. On the other hand, such a policy may result in excessive carrying costs (for example, in investment, storage, insurance, taxes, obsolescence, risk of theft, and damage). The higher the levels of inventories held, the higher the costs of looking after them. For instance, most companies that sell in retail markets have a significant risk of theft and so must incur costs to reduce this risk, such as insurance and theft deterrent equipment. Low inventory levels generally have lower carrying costs, but this may lead to running out of specific products, lost sales, and unhappy customers.

Inefficient purchasing procedures, faulty manufacturing techniques, or inadequate sales efforts may leave management with excessive and unusable inventories. All of this reduces profits.

Companies must therefore monitor inventory levels carefully to:

- minimize carrying costs, and

- meet customer demands.

Whether a company manufactures or merchandises goods, it needs an accurate accounting system with up-to-date records.

WHAT DO THE NUMBERS MEAN?

REAL WORLD EMPHASIS

As noted above, companies must monitor the quantity and quality of inventories on hand. **Eli Lilly and Company** actually goes one step further and also monitors inventory levels of its wholesale customers for significant products that it supplies. The company develops, manufactures, and distributes drugs, primarily through wholesalers or major retail chains. According to the company's annual report, Eli Lilly's management tries to keep wholesaler inventory levels at an average of one month's supply. They monitor unusual wholesaler buying patterns to determine the impact on future sales and demand for product. The company notes that the production processes are complex and highly regulated, varying from product to product. Unusual demand could result in an interruption of supply, which is undesirable. It could also signal potential problems with a drug (if there is a significant decrease in demand, for instance).

Information for Decision-Making

Just as management is interested in monitoring and controlling inventory, users of financial statements such as creditors and investors are also interested in this information. While management has access to all types of inventory-related information that is generated by internal management information systems, external users of financial statements often look to the statements as a significant source of information. Therefore, they also want to know how management is controlling and managing its inventory in order to maximize profits. Information about inventory must therefore be presented so that it is transparent regarding the nature of the business. The **existence** of various types of inventory that the company owns must be clearly represented and information as to **how this inventory has been measured** must also be disclosed. The rest of the chapter will look at how inventory is accounted for, including how it is recognized, measured, presented, and disclosed in the statements.

Because the goods that are sold or used during an accounting period almost never correspond exactly with the goods that were bought or produced during that period, the physical inventory of items either increases or decreases. In addition, the cost of the number of items could be higher or lower at the end of the period than at the beginning. The cost of all the goods that are available for sale or use has to be allocated between the goods that were sold or used and those that are still on hand. The **cost of goods available for sale or use** is calculated as follows:

Cost of goods on hand at the beginning of the period + Cost of goods acquired or produced during the period = Cost of goods available for sale or use

The **cost of goods sold** is calculated as follows:

Cost of goods available for sale during the period – Cost of goods on hand at the
end of the period = Cost of goods sold

The calculation of cost of goods sold is shown in Illustration 8-1.

Illustration 8-1

Calculation of Cost of Goods Sold

Beginning inventory, Jan. 1	$100,000
Cost of goods acquired or produced during the year	800,000
Total cost of goods available for sale	**900,000**
Ending inventory, Dec. 31	200,000
Cost of goods sold during the year	**$700,000**

Calculating the cost of ending inventory takes several steps. It can be a complex process that requires answers to each of the following questions:

1. **Which physical goods should be included as part of inventory?** Who owns inventory still in transit at the statement of financial position date, or inventory on consignment? What about inventory under special sales agreements?

2. **What costs should be included as part of inventory cost?** Consider purchase discounts and vendor rebates, product versus period costs, capacity considerations in allocating overhead, and standard costs.

3. **What cost formula should be used?** Consider specific identification, average cost, or first-in, first-out (FIFO).

Determining the final value that should be reported on the statement of financial position requires answering one additional question:

4. **Has there been an impairment in value of any of the inventory items?** Inventory cannot be reported on the statement of financial position at more than the net cash amount that is expected to be recovered from its sale or use.

We will now explore these and other basic issues one at a time.

RECOGNITION

Objective 2
Define inventory from an
accounting perspective.

Which items should be recognized as inventory in the financial statements and at what point should they be recognized? In order to make this decision, we need a common understanding of what inventory is.

Inventory comes in many forms. Here are just a few examples of items of inventory:

- securities held by an investment dealer

- land and other property held by developers for resale

- unbilled employee and partner time spent on client files in a law office or professional accounting practice

- grain in silos

- salmon in a fish farming operation

Some of these are not covered by the basic accounting standards for inventories: *CPA Canada Handbook, Part II*, Section 3031 under ASPE or IAS 2 under IFRS. These standards exclude some inventories entirely, and exclude others from only the measurement requirements of the standards.

In general, inventories of financial instruments, biological assets and agricultural products, mineral products, and inventories held by producers of agricultural and forest producers and by commodity broker-traders may have special requirements. Appendix 8B summarizes the accounting guidance for these forms of inventory.

Accounting Definition of Inventory

For accounting purposes, **inventories** are defined as:

"assets

(a) held for sale in the ordinary course of business;

(b) in the process of production for such sale; or

(c) in the form of materials or supplies to be consumed in the production process or in the rendering of services."[1]

Recall the definition of an asset as previously discussed in Chapter 2. As assets, inventories represent a **future benefit**, which the entity has **control over or access to**. The inventory purchase is the **transaction** that gives rise to the recognition of an inventory asset.

An inventory purchase is the opposite side of a sales transaction. The diagram here was taken from Chapter 6 and was used there to illustrate a basic sale of wine transaction.

Just as accountants recognize a sale when the risks and rewards of ownership are passed to the purchaser (when control passes), the purchaser can use the same "risks and rewards" test to determine when the inventory should be recognized. Once the risks and rewards pass, the inventory meets the definition of an asset for the purchaser. (That is, it is no longer an asset for the vendor.) Recall Illustration 6-21 from Chapter 6, which lists the risk and rewards of ownership for wine. This has been reproduced below in Illustration 8-2.

Illustration 8-2

Risks and Rewards of Wine Inventory

Risks	Rewards
— Wine will age poorly and therefore decline in value	— Wine will age well and appreciate in value
— Wine will be stolen/vandalized	— Wine can be consumed by owner or buyer
— Wine will be stored improperly	— Wine inventory may be used as collateral for bank loan
	— Wine may be sold for cash

Objective 3

Identify which inventory items should be included in ending inventory.

UNDERLYING CONCEPT

It is important to look at the terms of the transaction to identify when legal title passes. If there is some doubt about whether or not title has passed, in coming to a conclusion, the accountant considers other evidence, such as the sales agreement's intent, past transactions, the policies of the parties involved, and industry practices.

Physical Goods Included in Inventory

When substantially all risks and rewards of ownership and therefore control have passed to the purchaser, inventory is recognized. Legal title and possession help make this determination. Usually purchased goods would be included as inventory when legal title passes. In practice, however, acquisitions are often recorded when the goods are received (possession) because it may be difficult for the buyer to identify the exact time when the legal title passes to the buyer for every purchase. At the point when the goods are received, the entity has control over and access to the future benefits. As a general rule, legal title has often passed by then as well.

Both legal title and possession are important factors because they give rise to risks and rewards and signal the passing of control. For instance, possession allows the owner to use the inventory and legal title allows the owner to sell the inventory or pledge it to obtain a loan. It is important to use professional judgement to decide when the inventory should be recognized as an asset, because legal title and possession do not always pass to the purchaser at the same time. Let's analyze some specific transactions in a little more detail.

Goods in Transit

LAW

Sometimes purchased goods are in transit—that is, not yet received—at the end of a fiscal period. Although the company does not yet have possession, we may look to the legal title to determine whether the goods should be recognized as inventory. The legal title is determined by the shipping terms that have been agreed upon between the buyer and the seller. If the goods are shipped **f.o.b. shipping point**, the legal title passes to the buyer when the seller delivers the goods to the common carrier (transporter), who then acts as an agent for the buyer. (The abbreviation "f.o.b." stands for "free on board.") If the goods are shipped **f.o.b. destination**, legal title passes when the goods reach the destination. "Shipping point" and "destination" are often indicated by naming a specific location; for example, f.o.b. Regina.[2] Once legal title passes, it is argued that the purchaser has the risks of ownership. For instance, if something happened to the inventory while in transit for goods shipped f.o.b. shipping point, it would be the purchaser's loss.

Goods in transit at the end of a fiscal period that were sent f.o.b. shipping point are recorded by the buyer as purchases of the period and should be included in ending inventory. If these purchases are not recognized, the result is **understated** inventories and accounts payable in the statement of financial position and **understated** purchases and ending inventories when calculating the cost of goods sold for the income statement.

The accountant normally prepares a purchase **cut-off schedule** for the end of each period to ensure that goods received from suppliers around the end of the year are recorded in the appropriate period. Cut-off procedures can be extensive and include the following controls:

- Curtailing and controlling the receipt and shipment of goods around the time of the count

- Marking freight and shipping documents as "before" or "after" the inventory count

- Ensuring that receiving reports on goods received before the count are linked to invoices that are also recorded in the same period

**AUDIT AND
ASSURANCE
4.3.6**

Because goods that are bought f.o.b. shipping point may still be in transit when a period ends, the cut-off schedule is not completed until a few days after the period's end. This gives time for goods in transit at year end to be received. Auditors often verify the cut-off procedures during their audit to ensure the existence and completeness of the inventory reported in the financial statements.

Consigned Goods

**UNDERLYING
CONCEPT**

Accounting for the sale of consigned goods was covered in Chapter 6. In terms of accounting for inventory, it is important to recognize that goods out on consignment remain the consignor's property. They are included in the consignor's inventory at their purchase price or production cost plus the cost of handling and shipping the goods to the consignee. In this case, even though possession rests with the consignee, legal title is held by the consignor. The consignor essentially has the risks and rewards of ownership. For instance, if the inventory becomes obsolete while held by the consignee, it is the consignor that suffers the loss. When the consignee sells the **consigned goods**, the revenue, less a selling commission and expenses incurred in accomplishing the sale, is remitted to the consignor.

Occasionally, the inventory out on consignment is shown as a separate item or there are additional disclosures in the notes, but unless the amount is large, there is little need for this. For the consignee, no entry is made to adjust its Inventory account for the goods it received, because the goods remain the consignor's property. In addition, the consignee should be extremely careful not to include any consigned goods in its inventory count.

Even though some transactions are not called consignment sales, they may be consignment sales in substance. Therefore, the terms of the agreement should be examined carefully because consignment accounting may have to be used.

Recognizing revenue when inventory is "parked" violates the revenue recognition principle. This principle requires that the earnings process be substantially completed, with the risks and rewards of ownership transferred to the purchaser. In addition, the economic substance of this transaction is that it is a financing transaction.

Sales with Buyback Agreements

Sometimes an enterprise uses its inventory to obtain financing without reporting either the liability or the inventory on its statement of financial position. This type of transaction—often referred to as a product financing arrangement—usually involves a transfer of the inventory with either a real or implied "buyback" agreement. Under the terms of these types of arrangements, the purchaser agrees to buy the inventory and then sell it back later to the same supplier. These are sometimes called "parking transactions" because the seller simply "parks" the inventory on another company's statement of financial position for a short period of time, agreeing to repurchase it in the future. **If the risks and rewards of ownership and therefore control have not been transferred, the inventory should remain on the seller's books**.

EXAMPLE 1

Company A needs $1,000 of financing but is unable to borrow funds from traditional sources (such as the bank) because the bank believes the loan would be too risky. The company therefore enters into an agreement with Company B to obtain the funds. A's inventory is used to support the value of the loan and legal title is transferred to B. At the same time, both parties agree to transfer the same inventory back to A at the end of 30 days for $1,010.

Note that the risks and rewards and therefore control have not transferred in this example when you look at the two transactions as one (even though the legal title and possession are transferred in the first part of the transaction). To illustrate, if the value of the inventory declines over the 30-day period, Company A still has to pay $1,010 to buy it back. Company A therefore retains the risk that the inventory will decline in value. (This is sometimes referred to as **price risk**.)

Upfront

Inventory
$1,000

Company A   Company B

In 30 days

$1,010
Inventory

Company A   Company B

We looked at this issue in Chapter 6 from the perspective of revenue recognition. (See the section "repurchase agreements" in Chapter 6.)

Sales with High Rates of Return

There are often formal or informal agreements in such industries as book and magazine publishing, music, toys, and sporting goods that allow a buyer to return inventory for a full or partial refund. Essentially, the vendor retains the risks and rewards for those items expected to be returned. This does not necessarily prevent the vendor from recognizing a sale nor the purchaser from recognizing the inventory as an asset. **If a reasonable prediction of the returns can be established**, then the goods may be considered sold by the vendor and **the expected value of the sale is recorded as revenues.**

Conversely, if the returns are unpredictable, the sale is not recognized and the goods are not removed from the Inventory account. Note disclosure would be important in this case.

Sales with Delayed Payment Terms

Because the risk of loss due to uncollectible accounts is higher in delayed payment sales than in other sales transactions, the seller often retains legal title to the merchandise until all payments have been received. Should the inventory be considered sold, even though legal title has not passed? If all other revenue recognition criteria are met, then the answer is yes—the sale is recorded and the goods are removed from the seller's inventory.

Purchase Commitments

In many lines of business, it is common for a company to agree to buy inventory weeks, months, or even years in advance. Such arrangements may be made based on either estimated or firm sales commitments from the company's customers. Generally, title to the merchandise or materials described in these **purchase commitments** does not pass to the buyer until delivery. Indeed, when the commitment is made, the goods may exist only as natural resources or, in the case of commodities, as unplanted seed, or in the case of a product, as work in process.

Ordinary orders, where the prices are determined at the time of shipment and **the buyer or seller can still cancel the order**, do not represent either an asset or a liability to the buyer. They are therefore not recorded in the books or reported in the financial statements.

Even with formal, **non-cancellable purchase contracts**, no asset or liability is recognized on the date when the contract takes effect, because it is an **executory contract**. In other words, neither party has performed (or fulfilled) its part of the contract. However, if the amounts are abnormal in relation to the entity's normal business operations or financial position, the contract details should be disclosed in the notes to the buyer's financial statements.

If the unavoidable costs of completing the contract are higher than the benefits expected from receiving contracted goods or services, a loss provision is recognized according to IAS 37 *Provisions, Contingent Liabilities, and Contingent Assets*. This is known as an **onerous contract**. Although ASPE has no similar requirement, Canadian practice has historically been to recognize the loss and liability as well. Under ASPE, if the loss is likely and measurable, the loss would be recognized.

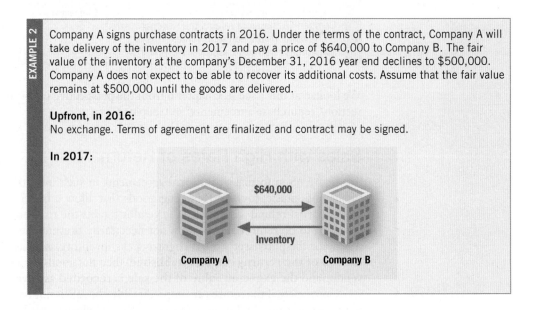

EXAMPLE 2

Company A signs purchase contracts in 2016. Under the terms of the contract, Company A will take delivery of the inventory in 2017 and pay a price of $640,000 to Company B. The fair value of the inventory at the company's December 31, 2016 year end declines to $500,000. Company A does not expect to be able to recover its additional costs. Assume that the fair value remains at $500,000 until the goods are delivered.

Upfront, in 2016:
No exchange. Terms of agreement are finalized and contract may be signed.

In 2017:

$640,000

Inventory

Company A   Company B

The following entry is made on December 31, 2016:

A	=	L	+	SE
		+140,000		−140,000

Cash flows: No effect

Loss on Purchase Contracts	140,000	
Liability for Onerous Contracts		140,000

When the goods are delivered in 2017, the entry is:

A = L + SE
+500,000   +500,000

Cash flows: No effect

Inventory	500,000	
Liability for Onerous Contracts	140,000	
Accounts Payable		640,000

If the price has partially or fully recovered before the inventory is received, the Liability for Onerous Contracts amount is reduced. A resulting gain (Recovery of Loss) is then reported in the period of the price increase for the amount of the partial or full recovery. This accounting treatment is very similar to recognizing an impairment in inventory value by recording inventories at the lower of cost and net realizable value.

Accounting for purchase commitments (indeed, for all commitments) is unsettled and controversial. Some argue that these contracts should be reported as assets and liabilities when the contract is signed; others believe that recognition at the delivery date is more appropriate. As work proceeds on the IFRS conceptual framework, this debate is likely to be resolved.[3]

UNDERLYING CONCEPT

Reporting the loss reflects the risks associated with locking into the contract at a fixed price in advance. However, reporting the decline in market price is debatable because no asset is recorded and the accrued liability on purchase contracts is not a present obligation. If the fair value changes again, the value might recover before the purchase takes place. This area demonstrates the need for good definitions of assets and liabilities.

Summary of When to Recognize Inventory Based on Change in Control and Risks and Rewards

Illustration 8-3 summarizes various purchase transactions in terms of the risks and rewards/change in control test and inventory recognition. Note that, in cases where the legal title is held by one party and the other party has possession, increased judgement is required to determine whether risks and rewards of ownership have passed. Even where the same party has legal title and possession, care should be taken to analyze the underlying substance of the transaction.

Illustration 8-3

Determining When to Recognize Inventory Based on Change in Control and Risks and Rewards

Transaction	Who has legal title?	Who has possession?	Have control/ substantially all risks and rewards passed?	Who recognizes inventory?
Goods in transit shipped f.o.b. shipping point	Purchaser	Shipping company	Yes	Purchaser
Consignment sale	Consignor	Consignee	No	Consignor
Sale with buyback (same goods, fixed buyback price that includes a charge for carrying costs)	Purchaser	Purchaser	No (where it is essentially a financing transaction)	Vendor
Sales with high rates of return where returns estimable	Purchaser	Purchaser	Yes	Purchaser
Sales with delayed payment terms where vendor retains title until consideration collected (bad debts are estimable)	Vendor	Purchaser	Yes	Purchaser
Purchase commitments (non-cancellable)	Vendor (assuming the inventory exists)	Vendor (assuming the inventory exists)	No, but may have to accrue losses if onerous contract	Vendor (assuming the inventory exists)

COST MANAGEMENT

3.3.1, 3.3.2

Flow of Costs

As Illustration 8-4 shows, the flow of costs for merchandising and manufacturing companies is different. The **cost of goods manufactured** referred to in Illustration 8-4 represents the product costs of goods that are completed and transferred to Finished Goods

Inventory. You are probably familiar with a statement of cost of goods manufactured that summarizes all the product costs incurred during the period that resulted in finished goods. (You may want to refer to a managerial accounting text for an example.) A cost of goods manufactured statement is far more detailed than information found in published financial statements. Note that **the cost of goods manufactured during the year is similar to the cost of goods purchased in a merchandising company**. Each is the source of the cost of goods available for sale in the period.

Illustration 8-4

Flow of Costs through Manufacturing and Merchandising Companies

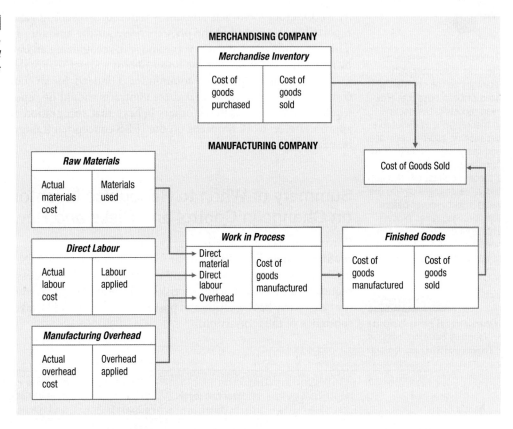

Before we move on to the next section, it is important to look at changing business models and how they might affect which assets are included in inventory on the statement of financial position. Consider **Indigo Books & Music Inc.** Indigo is the largest book retailer in Canada and operates under the names of Chapters, Indigo, Coles, SmithBooks, as well as others. In 2009, the company launched a new business called Shortcovers. Shortcovers provided on-line access to books and other print materials. In December 2009, Indigo transferred the net assets of Shortcovers to a newly created company called Kobo Inc. Indigo described 2010 as a "tipping point," a year when reading digitally went mainstream. Indigo now had two quite differing business segments: one selling hard copy books and one selling on-line access to books.

While we would generally agree that the hard copy books are inventory to Indigo, what about the e-books? In essence, Indigo is in the business of selling books, whether hard copies or e-books, so shouldn't they both appear as inventory on the balance sheet? Not necessarily. Selling access

to an e-book represents a very different business model than selling an actual hard copy of a book. With paper books, the company has to purchase the books, merchandise them, and hopefully sell them. One might argue that it has control of the inventory. In other words, if a book sells, the company profits, but if it does not sell, unless it can be returned to the publisher, the company suffers a loss. With an e-book, all the company needs is an agreement that allows it to sell or distribute access to the e-books. For this, the company likely earns some sort of percentage of the revenues. This relationship is more of an agency relationship: the company is acting as a selling agent and essentially earning a commission.

In November 2011, Indigo announced that it had entered a deal to sell Kobo to Rakuten Inc., a large Japanese e-commerce company. Indigo still sells Kobo e-reader devices as well as e-books. The following excerpt from the 2015 financial statements shows that revenues from e-reading make up just 2% of total revenues. Revenues from printed material continue to be the most significant.

WHAT DO THE NUMBERS MEAN?

REAL WORLD EMPHASIS

15. SUPPLEMENTARY OPERATING INFORMATION

Supplemental product line revenue information:

	52-week period ended March 28, 2015	52-week period ended March 29, 2014
Print [1]	583,492	587,618
General merchandise [2]	270,675	230,063
eReading [3]	18,148	24,633
Other [4]	23,061	25,353
Total	895,376	867,668

1 Includes books, calendars, magazines, newspapers, and shipping revenue.
2 Includes lifestyle, paper, toys, music, DVDs, electronics, and shipping revenue.
3 Includes eReaders, eReader accessories, Kobo revenue share, and shipping revenue.
4 Includes cafés, irewards, gift card breakage, Plum breakage, and corporate sales.

Sources: Sunny Freeman, The Canadian Press, "Indigo Books and Music Sells Kobo Ereader to Rakuten in US$315 Million Deal," *Canadian Business*, November 8, 2011; "Indigo Spins off Shortcovers to Launch Kobo," company news release, December 15, 2009; Indigo Books & Music Inc. 2015 annual report.

Inventory Errors

Objective 4

Identify the effects of inventory errors on the financial statements and adjust for them.

Items that have been incorrectly included or excluded in determining the ending inventory amount create errors in both the income statement and the statement of financial position. Decisions that are based on financial statement amounts affected by such errors (such as bonuses paid to management based on net income) would therefore be in error and comparability would also be impaired. Let's look at two cases and the effects on the financial statements.

Ending Inventory Misstated

What would happen if the beginning inventory and purchases are recorded correctly, but some items are omitted from ending inventory by mistake? For example, what if items were in the warehouse but were missed in the physical count, or they were out on consignment? The effects of this error on the financial statements at the end of the period are shown in Illustration 8-5.

Illustration 8-5

Financial Statement Effects of Understated Ending Inventory

Statement of Financial Position		Income Statement	
Inventory	Understated	Cost of goods sold	Overstated
Retained earnings	Understated	Net income	Understated
Working capital (current assets less current liabilities)	Understated		
Current ratio (current assets divided by current liabilities)	Understated		

FINANCIAL ANALYSIS AND PLANNING
5.1.1

Working capital and the current ratio are understated because a portion of the ending inventory is omitted. Net income is understated because cost of goods sold is overstated. This could affect decisions made by investors and lenders.

To illustrate the effect on net income over a two-year period, assume that the 2017 ending inventory of Wei Ltd. is understated by $10,000 and that all other items are stated correctly. The effect of this error is an understatement of net income in the current year and an overstatement of net income in the following year. The error affects the following year because the beginning inventory of that year is understated, which causes net income to be overstated. Both net income figures are misstated, but the total for the two years is correct because the two errors will be counterbalanced (or offset), as shown in Illustration 8-6.

WEI LTD.

	Incorrect Recording		Correct Recording	
	2017	2018	2017	2018
Revenues	$100,000	$100,000	$100,000	$100,000
Cost of goods sold				
Beginning inventory	25,000	20,000	25,000	30,000
Purchased or produced	45,000	60,000	45,000	60,000
Goods available for sale	70,000	80,000	70,000	90,000
Less: Ending inventory*	20,000	40,000	30,000	40,000
Cost of goods sold	50,000	40,000	40,000	50,000
Gross profit	50,000	60,000	60,000	50,000
Administrative and selling expenses	40,000	40,000	40,000	40,000
Net income	$ 10,000	$ 20,000	$ 20,000	$ 10,000

Total income
for two years = $30,000

Total income
for two years = $30,000

*Ending inventory understated by $10,000 in 2017; correct amount is $30,000.

If the error is discovered in 2017 just before the books are closed, the correcting entry in 2017 would be:

A = L + SE
+10,000   +10,000
Cash flows: No effect

Inventory	10,000	
Cost of Goods Sold		10,000

If the error is not discovered until 2018, after the books are closed for 2017, the correcting entry in 2018 would be:

A = L + SE
+10,000   +10,000
Cash flows: No effect

Inventory	10,000	
Retained Earnings		10,000

If the error is discovered after the books for 2018 are closed, **no entry is required because the error is self-correcting over the two-year period.** The inventory on the statement of financial position at the end of 2018 is correct, as is the total amount of retained earnings. **However, whenever comparative financial statements are prepared that include 2017 or 2018, the inventory and net income for those years are restated and reported at the correct figures.**

If ending inventory is **overstated** at the end of 2017, the reverse effect occurs. Inventory, working capital, current ratio, and net income are overstated and cost of goods sold is understated in 2017. The error's effect on net income will be counterbalanced in the next year, but both years' net income figures are incorrect, which distorts any analysis of trends in earnings and ratios.

Purchases and Inventory Misstated

Suppose that certain goods that the company owns are **not recorded as a purchase** and are **not counted in ending inventory.** Illustration 8-7 shows the effect on the financial statements, assuming this is a purchase on account.

Statement of Financial Position		Income Statement	
Inventory	Understated	Purchases	Understated
Retained earnings	No effect	Ending inventory	Understated
Accounts payable	Understated	Cost of goods sold	No effect
Working capital	No effect	Net income	No effect
Current ratio	Overstated		

Omitting both the purchase of goods and the inventory results in understated inventory and accounts payable on the statement of financial position, and understated purchases and ending inventory on the income statement. **Net income for the period is not affected by omitting such goods, because purchases and ending inventory are both understated by the same amount. That is, the error offsets itself in cost of goods sold.**[4] Total working capital is unchanged, but the current ratio is overstated (assuming it was greater than 1 to 1) because equal amounts were omitted from inventory and accounts payable.

To illustrate the effect on the current ratio, assume that a company understates its accounts payable and ending inventory by $40,000. The understated and correct data are shown in Illustration 8-8.

Illustration 8-8

Effects of Purchases and Ending Inventory Errors

Purchases and Ending Inventory Understated		Purchases and Ending Inventory Correct	
Current assets	$120,000	Current assets	$160,000
Current liabilities	$ 40,000	Current liabilities	$ 80,000
Current ratio	3 to 1	Current ratio	2 to 1

The correct current ratio is 2 to 1 rather than 3 to 1. Thus, understating accounts payable and ending inventory can lead to a "window dressing" of the current ratio. In other words, it can appear better than it really is.

If purchases (on account) and ending inventory are both overstated, then the effects on the statement of financial position are exactly the reverse. That is, inventory and accounts payable are overstated, and the current ratio is understated, even though the dollar amount of working capital is not affected. Cost of goods sold and net income are also unaffected because the errors offset each other. The preceding examples show some of the errors that can occur and their consequences, but there are many other types of possible errors. These include:

- not recording a purchase but counting the new inventory,

- not recording a sale in the current period although the items have been delivered,

- omitting the adjusting entry to update the account Allowance for Sales Returns and Allowances in situations where the sales are known to have a high rate of return, and

- failing to adjust inventory to the lower of cost and net realizable value.

ETHICS

Determining correct amounts for purchases, sales, and inventory in the correct accounting period is a critical step in preparing reliable financial statements. We only have to read the financial press to learn how misstating inventory can generate high income numbers. For example, in the past some Canadian farm equipment manufacturers treated deliveries to dealers as company sales (which reduced their inventory), even though sales to the ultimate consumer did not occur as quickly as the deliveries to the dealers. The result was a significantly inflated reported income for the manufacturers.

When an error from a prior period is corrected, it is accounted for retroactively as an adjustment to retained earnings. Full disclosure requires a description of the error and a statement of the effect on the current and prior-period financial statements.

MEASUREMENT

Costs Included in Inventory

Objective 5
Determine the components of inventory cost.

After deciding what items are to be included in the ending inventory, the next step in accounting for inventory is to determine its cost. As mentioned previously, inventories—like other non-financial assets—are generally recognized initially on the basis of cost. How is cost determined, and what should be included in "cost"?

**COST
MANAGEMENT**
3.3.1

Both IFRS and ASPE indicate that inventory cost is made up of "all costs of purchase, costs of conversion and other costs incurred in bringing the inventories to their present location and condition."[5] This includes transportation and handling costs and other direct costs of acquisition, such as non-recoverable taxes and duties.

Purchase Discounts

Suppliers often offer cash discounts to purchasers for prompt payment. There are two alternate methods to account for the purchases and discounts: the gross method and the net method. Under the **gross method**, both the purchases and payables are recorded at **the gross amount of the invoice**, and any **purchase discounts** that are later taken **are credited to a Purchase Discounts** account. This account is reported as a contra account to Purchases, as a reduction in the cost of the period's purchases.

The alternative approach, called the **net method**, records the purchases and accounts payable initially at an amount net of the cash discounts. If the account payable is paid within the discount period, the cash payment is exactly equal to the amount originally set up in the payable account. **If the account payable is paid after the discount period** is over, the discount that is lost is recorded in a **Purchase Discounts Lost account.** Recording the loss allows the company to assign responsibility for the loss to a specific employee. This treatment is considered more theoretically appropriate because it (1) provides a correct reporting of the asset cost and related liability,[6] and (2) makes it possible to measure the inefficiency of financial management if the discount is not taken.

Assume Company A purchases goods for $10,000 with terms 2/10, net 30. Company A pays for $4,000 of this amount within the discount period and the rest after the discount period. Illustration 8-9 illustrates the difference between the gross and net methods.

Illustration 8-9

Entries Under Gross and Net Methods

Gross Method			Net Method		
Purchase cost of $10,000, terms 2/10, net 30:					
Purchases	10,000		Purchases	9,800	
Accounts Payable		10,000	Accounts Payable		9,800
Invoices of $4,000 are paid within discount period:					
Accounts Payable	4,000		Accounts Payable	3,920	
Purchase Discounts		80	Cash		3,920
Cash		3,920			
Invoices of $6,000 are paid after discount period:					
Accounts Payable	6,000		Accounts Payable	5,880	
Cash		6,000	Purchase Discounts Lost	120	
			Cash		6,000

**UNDERLYING
CONCEPT**

Not using the net method because of difficulties that may result is an example of applying the cost/benefit constraint.

Under the gross method, purchase discounts are deducted from purchases in determining cost of goods sold. If the net method is used, purchase discounts not taken are considered a financial expense and are reported in the income statement's Other Expenses section. Many believe that the difficulty of using the more complicated net method outweighs its benefits. This may explain why the less theoretically correct, but simpler, gross method is so popular.

Vendor Rebates

Assume that Johnston Corp., with a June 30 year end, has been purchasing more and more inventory from Roster Limited in recent years. Roster offers its customers a special **vendor rebate** of $0.10 per unit on each unit purchased, if the customer buys more than 100,000 units in the calendar year (from January 1 to December 31). This year, for the first time, Johnston management expects to exceed the 100,000-unit volume. It has purchased 60,000 units in the first six months of the current year and its forecast purchases for the next six months are over 50,000 units. Should Johnston recognize the anticipated rebate in its current year ended June 30? If so, how much should be recognized, and how does this affect the financial statements?

UNDERLYING CONCEPT

Revenues and expenses are defined in terms of changes in assets and liabilities. Therefore, if an asset does not exist or cannot be recognized in this situation, an expense recovery cannot be recognized either.

Cash rebates are generally a reduction of the purchase cost of inventory. If the "rebate receivable" meets both the definition of an asset and its recognition criteria, the rebate is recognized before it is received. In general:

- If the rebate is discretionary on the part of the supplier, no rebate is recognized until it is paid or the supplier becomes obligated to make a payment.

- If the rebate is **probable** and the amount can be **reasonably estimated**, the asset recognition criteria are met and the receivable can be recorded.[7] In this case, it is recognized as a reduction in the cost of purchases for the period. The amount receivable is allocated between the goods remaining in inventory, and the goods sold.

- The amount of the receivable recognized is based on the proportion of the total rebate that is expected relative to the transactions to date.

Johnston will recognize the rebate in the entry that follows for its current year ended June 30 if:

- the rebate offered by Roster Limited is not discretionary,

- it is probable that Johnston will purchase 110,000 units by December 31, and

- management is able to make a reasonable estimate of the total rebate for the calendar year.

The entry assumes only 5,000 units are still on hand at year end.

A = L + SE
+5,500   +5,500

Cash flows: No effect

Rebate Receivable	6,000	
Inventory (5,000 units)		500
Cost of Goods Sold (55,000 units)		5,500

110,000 units × $0.10 = $11,000; 60,000/110,000 × $11,000 = $6,000
or 60,000 units × $0.10 = $6,000

Illustration 8-10 provides an excerpt from the financial statement notes for **OfficeMax Incorporated**.

Illustration 8-10

Note on Vendor Rebates—Excerpt from OfficeMax Financial Statements

REAL WORLD EMPHASIS

Vendor Rebates and Allowances

We participate in volume purchase rebate programs, some of which provide for tiered rebates based on defined levels of purchase volume. We also participate in programs that enable us to receive additional vendor subsidies by promoting the sale of vendor products. Vendor rebates and allowances are accrued as earned. Rebates and allowances received as a result of attaining defined purchase levels are accrued over the incentive period based on the terms of the vendor arrangement and estimates of qualifying purchases during the rebate program period. These estimates are reviewed on a quarterly basis and adjusted for changes in anticipated product sales and expected purchase levels. Vendor rebates and allowances earned are recorded as a reduction in the cost of merchandise inventories and are included in operations (as a reduction of cost of goods sold) in the period the related product is sold.

Illustration 8-11 provides an excerpt from the financial statement notes for **Canadian Tire Corporation, Limited**. Note that the rebate may be recorded as a reduction of selling, general, and administrative costs.

Illustration 8-11

Note on Vendor Rebates—Excerpt from Canadian Tire Financial Statements

Vendor rebates

The Company records cash consideration received from vendors as a reduction in the price of vendors' products and recognizes it as a reduction to the cost of related inventory or, if the related inventory has been sold, to the cost of producing revenue. Certain exceptions apply where the cash consideration received is either a reimbursement of incremental selling costs incurred by the Company or a payment for assets or services delivered to the vendor, in which case the cost is reflected as a reduction in selling, general and administrative expenses.

The Company recognizes rebates that are at the vendor's discretion when the vendor either pays the rebates or agrees to pay them and payment is considered probable and is reasonably estimable.

Product Costs

Product costs are costs that "attach" to inventory and are recorded in the inventory account. That is, they are capitalized. These costs are directly connected with bringing goods to the buyer's place of business and converting them to a saleable condition. They include freight charges on goods purchased, other direct costs of acquisition, and labour and other production costs that are incurred in processing the goods up to the time they are ready for sale. Under IFRS, product costs also include any eventual decommissioning or restoration costs incurred as a result of production, even though the related expenditures may not be incurred until far into the future. Under ASPE, such costs are generally added to the cost of the related property, plant, and equipment. Such **asset retirement costs** are discussed more fully in Chapters 10 and 13.

How should taxes be accounted for? Taxes that cannot be recovered from the government by the purchaser, such as some provincial sales taxes that are paid on goods that are purchased for resale or manufacturing purposes, are a cost of inventory. Taxes that can be recovered from the government, such as the federal Goods and Services Tax and the Harmonized Sales Tax charged in many provinces, are not included as part of the inventory's cost. Chapter 13 discusses these types of taxes in more detail.

Conversion costs include direct labour and an allocation of the fixed and variable production overhead costs that are incurred in processing direct materials into finished goods. The allocation of fixed production costs is based on the company's **normal production capacity**.[8] In this way, costs of idle capacity or low production levels do not end up in inventory, but instead are charged to expense as they are incurred. However, if production levels are abnormally high, the fixed costs are spread out over the larger number of units that are produced so that inventory is not measured at an amount higher than its cost. Actual production levels can be used if they are close to normal levels. Actual levels are also used to charge variable costs to production.

It is theoretically correct to allocate a share of any buying costs to inventory, or expenses of a purchasing department, insurance costs in transit, or other costs that are incurred in handling the goods before they are ready for sale. This is because such costs are incurred to bring the inventories "to their present location and condition." However, on a cost/benefit basis, these items are not ordinarily included in inventory cost.

Borrowing Costs

If interest costs are incurred to finance activities that help bring inventories to a condition and place ready for sale, they are considered by many to be as much a cost of the asset as materials, labour, and overhead.[9] Under IFRS, interest costs incurred for an inventory item that takes an extended period of time to produce or manufacture are considered **product costs**. However, if the financing relates to inventories that are manufactured or produced in large quantities and on a repetitive basis, companies can choose whether to capitalize them or not.[10] Under ASPE, the only requirement is that, **if interest is capitalized**, this policy and the amount that is capitalized in the current period must be **disclosed**.

Standard Costs

A company that uses a **standard cost system** predetermines the unit costs for material, labour, and manufacturing overhead. Usually the standard costs are based on the costs that should be incurred per unit of finished goods when the plant is operating at normal levels of efficiency and capacity. When actual costs are not the same as the standard costs, the differences are recorded in variance accounts that management can examine and follow up on by taking appropriate action to achieve greater control over costs. For financial statement purposes, **reporting inventories at standard cost is acceptable only as long as the results approximate actual cost**. Unallocated overheads are **expensed** as they are incurred.

Cost of Service Providers' Work in Process

Companies that provide services rather than manufacture products may accumulate significant costs of work-in-process inventories. These, too, are measured at their production costs. For service providers, the major "production" costs are for service personnel and overhead costs associated with this "direct labour." Supervisory costs and other overheads are allocated using the same principles as for manufactured products.

Costs Excluded from Inventory

Some costs are closely related to acquiring and converting a product, but they are not considered to be product costs. An example is storage costs, unless they are necessary because the product must be held before the next stage of production, such as in wine production. Other examples are abnormal spoilage or wastage of materials, labour, or other production costs; and interest costs when inventories that are ready for use or sale are purchased on delayed payment terms.

Selling expenses and, under ordinary circumstances, **general and administrative expenses** are not considered directly related to the acquisition or conversion of goods and, therefore, are not considered a part of inventory. Such costs are **period costs**. Why are these costs not considered part of inventory? Selling expenses are generally more directly related to the cost of goods sold than to the unsold inventory. In most cases, these costs are so unrelated or indirectly related to the actual production process that any allocation would be completely arbitrary.

"Basket" Purchases and Joint Product Costs

A special problem occurs when a group of units with different characteristics is purchased at a single lump-sum price, in what is called a **basket purchase**. Assume that Woodland Developers purchases land for $1 million and it can be subdivided into 400 lots. These lots are of different sizes and shapes but can be roughly sorted into three groups, graded A, B, and C. The purchase cost of $1 million must be allocated among the lots so that the cost of the lots that are later sold (cost of goods sold) and those remaining on hand (ending inventory) can be calculated.

It is inappropriate to use the average lot cost of $2,500 (the total cost of $1 million divided by the 400 lots) because the lots vary in size, shape, and attractiveness. When this kind of situation occurs—and it is not at all unusual—the most reasonable practice is to allocate the total cost among the various units **based on their relative sales value**. For our example, the cost allocation is shown in Illustration 8-12.

		Number of Lots	Sales Price per Lot	Total Sales Value	Relative Sales Value	Total Cost	Cost Allocated to Lots	Cost per Lot
Illustration 8-12	Lots							
Allocation of Costs, Using Relative Sales Value	A	100	$10,000	$1,000,000	100/250	$1,000,000	$ 400,000	$4,000
	B	100	6,000	600,000	60/250	1,000,000	240,000	2,400
	C	200	4,500	900,000	90/250	1,000,000	360,000	1,800
				$2,500,000			$1,000,000	

This method, the **relative sales value method**, is rational, can be applied consistently, and is commonly used whenever there is a **joint cost** that needs to be allocated. In Chapter 6, this was referred to as the relative fair value method. Other examples where amounts are allocated using sales or fair values include when two or more products are produced at the same time and the costs for each product cannot be distinguished. The petroleum industry uses this technique to value (at cost) the many products and by-products obtained from a barrel of crude oil, as does the food processing industry, where different cuts of meat of varying value are "split off" from one animal carcass. When the value of a by-product is relatively minor, it is often measured at its net realizable value and deducted from the cost of the major product.

Inventory Accounting Systems

Objective 6
Distinguish between perpetual and periodic inventory systems and account for them.

Technology has played an important role in the development of inventory systems. As mentioned in the opening story, radio-frequency identification data communications systems for warehouses, for example, have helped companies increase the accuracy of their inventory information and the efficiency of their inventory management.

Management is well aware that the level of inventory can materially affect the amount of current assets, total assets, net income, and, therefore, retained earnings. These amounts, or totals that include them, are used to calculate ratios that allow users to evaluate management's performance (for use in calculation of bonuses) and adherence to debt restrictions (for calculation of the debt to total assets ratio or dividend payout ratio).

For these and other reasons, companies are very interested in having an inventory accounting system that gives accurate, up-to-date information. One of two systems is commonly used for maintaining accurate inventory records: a perpetual system or a periodic system.

Perpetual System

A **perpetual inventory system** continuously tracks changes in the Inventory account. This means that the cost of all purchases and the cost of the items sold (or issued out of inventory) are recorded directly in the Inventory account as the purchases and sales occur. The accounting features of a perpetual inventory system are as follows.

1. Purchases of merchandise for resale or raw materials for production are debited to Inventory rather than to Purchases.

2. Freight-in is debited and purchase returns and allowances and purchase discounts are credited to Inventory instead of being accounted for in separate accounts.

3. The cost of the items sold is recognized at the time of each sale by debiting Cost of Goods Sold and crediting Inventory.

4. Inventory is a control account that is supported by a subsidiary ledger of individual inventory records. The subsidiary records show the quantity and cost of each type of inventory on hand.

The perpetual inventory system provides a continuous record of the balances in both the Inventory account and the Cost of Goods Sold account. In a computerized record-keeping system, changes in these accounts can be recorded almost instantaneously. The popularity and affordability of computerized accounting software have made the perpetual system cost-effective for many kinds of businesses. It is now common for most retail stores, big or small, to use optical scanners at the cash register that record reductions in inventory as it is sold as part of the store's perpetual inventory system.

WHAT DO THE NUMBERS MEAN?

REAL WORLD EMPHASIS

In 2014, **Loblaw Companies Limited** completed the conversion of its information technology system to a perpetual inventory system, which allowed it to better estimate the value of the inventory. An excerpt from the notes to the company's financial statements is presented below.

As at the end of 2014, with the upgrade of its information technology ("IT") infrastructure, the Company had completed the conversion of substantially all of its corporate grocery stores to the new systems. The implementation of a perpetual inventory system, combined with visibility to integrated costing information provided by the new IT systems, enabled the Company to estimate the cost of inventory using a more precise system-generated average cost. As a result of the conversion, the Company recognized a $190 million charge to cost of merchandise inventories sold and a corresponding reduction in inventory, representing the estimate of the difference between the measurement of the cost of corporate grocery store inventory using a system generated weighted average cost compared to the retail inventory method and other conversion differences associated with the implementation of a perpetual inventory system.

Periodic System

In a **periodic inventory system**, the quantity of inventory on hand is determined, as the name implies, only **periodically**. Each acquisition of inventory during the accounting period is recorded by a debit to the Purchases account. The total in the Purchases account at the end of the accounting period is added to the cost of the inventory on hand at the beginning of the period to determine the total cost of the goods available for sale during the period. The cost of ending inventory is subtracted from the cost of goods available for sale to calculate the cost of goods sold.

Note that under a periodic inventory system, the **cost of goods sold** is a **residual amount that depends on first calculating the cost of the ending inventory**. The cost of the ending inventory can be determined by physically counting and costing it. This process is referred to as "taking a physical inventory." Companies that use the periodic system take a physical inventory at least once a year.

Comparing Perpetual and Periodic Systems

To illustrate the difference between a perpetual and a periodic system, assume that Fesmire Limited had the following balances and transactions during the current year:

Beginning inventory	100 units at $ 6 = $ 600
Purchases	900 units at $ 6 = $5,400
Defective units returned to the supplier	50 units at $ 6 = $ 300
Sales	600 units at $12 = $7,200
Ending inventory	350 units at $ 6 = $2,100

The entries to record these transactions during the current year are shown in Illustration 8-13.

Illustration 8-13

Comparative Entries—Perpetual Versus Periodic

Perpetual Inventory System			Periodic Inventory System		
1. Beginning Inventory, 100 units at $6:					
The Inventory account shows the inventory on hand at $600.			The Inventory account shows the inventory on hand at $600.		
2. Purchase 900 units at $6:					
Inventory	5,400		Purchases	5,400	
Accounts Payable		5,400	Accounts Payable		5,400
3. Return 50 defective units:					
Accounts Payable	300		Accounts Payable	300	
Inventory		300	Purchase Returns		
			and Allowances		300
4. Sale of 600 units at $12:					
Accounts Receivable	7,200		Accounts Receivable	7,200	
Sales Revenue		7,200	Sales Revenue		7,200
Cost of Goods Sold					
(600 at $6)	3,600				
Inventory		3,600	(No entry)		
5. End-of-period entries for inventory accounts, 350 units at $6 = $2,100:					
No entry necessary.			Purchase Returns		
The account, Inventory, shows the ending			and Allowances	300	
balance of $2,100			Inventory ($2,100 – $600)	1,500	
($600 + $5,400 – $300 – $3,600).			Cost of Goods Sold	3,600	
			Purchases		5,400

When a **perpetual inventory system** is used and there is a difference between the perpetual inventory record and the physical inventory count, a separate entry is needed to adjust the perpetual Inventory account. To illustrate, assume that at the end of the reporting period, the perpetual Inventory account reported a balance of $4,000, but a physical count indicated $3,800 was actually on hand. The adjusting entry is:

A	=	L	+	SE	
–200				–200	

Cash flows: No effect

Inventory Over and Short	200	
Inventory		200

The overage or shortage may be due to normal and expected shrinkage, breakage, shoplifting, or record-keeping errors, and is usually recognized as an adjustment of Cost of Goods Sold. Alternatively, the Loss on Inventory account is sometimes reported in the "Other revenues and gains" or "Other expenses and losses" section of the income statement. When this is done, the gross profit percentage is not affected by the costs of shrinkage, breakage, and theft.

In a **periodic inventory system**, there is no separate account to track these inventory losses. This is because there is no up-to-date inventory account that can be compared with the physical count. The amount of any inventory overage or shortage is therefore included in cost of goods sold.

Supplementary System—Quantities Only

In a perfect world, companies would like a continuous record of inventory levels, their cost, and the cost of goods sold. However, even with advances in technology, it may not be cost-effective to have a complete perpetual inventory system that keeps track of both inventory quantities and their cost. Because management needs current information about inventory levels to avoid stockouts and overpurchasing, to respond to customer queries, and to help prepare monthly or quarterly financial data, many companies use a **quantities only system**. This system provides detailed inventory records of increases and decreases **in quantities only**—not dollar amounts. This memorandum record is not part of the double-entry accounting system; therefore, the company would need to use a periodic system in its main accounts.

Whether a company maintains a perpetual inventory in quantities and dollars, in quantities only, or no perpetual inventory record at all, it usually takes a physical inventory once a year. No matter what type of inventory records are used or how well controlled the procedures for recording purchases and requisitions are, the dangers of loss and error are always present. Waste, breakage, theft, improper data entry, failure to prepare or record requisitions, and similar possibilities may cause the inventory records to be different from the actual inventory on hand. Therefore, all companies need periodic verification of the inventory records by actual count, weight, or measurement, with the **counts compared with the detailed records**. The **records are then corrected** so that they agree with the quantities actually on hand.

As far as possible, the physical inventory should be taken near the end of a company's fiscal year so that correct inventory quantities are used in preparing annual accounting reports and statements. Because this is not always possible, physical inventories that are taken within two or three months of the year end are considered satisfactory as long as the **internal controls** indicate that the detailed inventory records are maintained with a fair degree of accuracy.[11]

Objective **7**

Identify and apply GAAP cost formula options and indicate when each cost formula is appropriate.

Cost Formulas

Two main issues have now been addressed in determining inventory cost: which inventory items to include, and which costs to include in, or exclude from, the product's cost. The next issue is this: if inventories need to be priced at cost and many purchases have been made at **different unit costs, which of the various cost prices should be assigned to Inventory** on the statement of financial position and **which costs should be charged to Cost of Goods Sold** on the income statement?

Conceptually, **identifying the specific costs** of the actual items sold and those unsold seems ideal, but doing this is often too expensive or simply impossible to achieve. Consequently, companies must choose another acceptable inventory cost formula. A **cost formula** is a method of assigning inventory costs incurred during the accounting period to inventory that is still on hand at the end of the period (ending inventory) and to inventory that was sold during the period (cost of goods sold).

Illustration 8-14 provides data to use in the discussion of the cost formula choice. The data summarize the inventory-related activities of Call-Mart Inc. for the month of March. Note that the company experienced increasing unit costs for its purchases throughout the month.

Illustration 8-14

Data Used to Illustrate Inventory Calculation—Cost Formula Choice

	CALL-MART INC.		
Date	Purchases	Sold or Issued	Balance
Mar. 1	(beginning inventory)		
	500 @ $3.80		500 units
Mar. 2	1,500 @ $4.00		2,000 units
Mar. 15	6,000 @ $4.40		8,000 units
Mar. 19		4,000	4,000 units
Mar. 30	2,000 @ $4.75		6,000 units
	10,000	4,000	

From this information, we see that there were 10,000 units available for sale, made up of 500 units in opening inventory and 9,500 units purchased during the month. Of the 10,000 available, 4,000 were sold, leaving 6,000 units in ending inventory.

The **cost of goods available for sale** is calculated as follows:

500 units @ $3.80 =	$ 1,900
1,500 units @ $4.00 =	6,000
6,000 units @ $4.40 =	26,400
2,000 units @ $4.75 =	9,500
10,000 units	$43,800

Having this information, the question now is: **which price or prices should be assigned to the 6,000 units still in inventory and which to the 4,000 units sold?** The answer depends on which cost formula is chosen.

Both IFRS and ASPE recognize three acceptable cost methods:

1. Specific identification

2. Weighted average cost

3. First-in, first-out (FIFO)

Specific Identification

When using the **specific identification** cost formula, each item that is sold and each item in inventory needs to be identified. The costs of the specific items that are sold are included in the cost of goods sold, and the costs of the specific items on hand are included in the ending inventory. This method is appropriate and required for goods that are not ordinarily interchangeable, and for goods and services that are produced and segregated for specific projects. It is used most often in situations involving a relatively small number of items that are costly and easily distinguishable by such things as their physical characteristics, serial numbers, or special markings. In the retail trade, this includes some types of jewellery, fur coats, automobiles, and furniture. In manufacturing, it includes special orders and many products manufactured under a job cost system.

To illustrate this method, assume that Call-Mart Inc.'s inventory items are distinguishable and that the 6,000 units of ending inventory consist of 100 units from the opening inventory, 900 from the March 2 purchase, 3,000 from the March 15 purchase, and 2,000 from the March 30 purchase. The ending inventory and cost of goods sold are calculated as shown in Illustration 8-15.

<table>
<tr><td>**Units from**</td><td>**No. of Units**</td><td>**Unit Cost**</td><td>**Total Cost**</td></tr>
<tr><td>Beginning inventory</td><td>100</td><td>$3.80</td><td>$ 380</td></tr>
<tr><td>March 2 purchase</td><td>900</td><td>4.00</td><td>3,600</td></tr>
<tr><td>March 15 purchase</td><td>3,000</td><td>4.40</td><td>13,200</td></tr>
<tr><td>March 30 purchase</td><td>2,000</td><td>4.75</td><td>9,500</td></tr>
<tr><td>**Ending inventory**</td><td>**6,000**</td><td></td><td>**$26,680**</td></tr>
<tr><td></td><td></td><td></td><td></td></tr>
<tr><td>Cost of goods available for sale
(beginning inventory + purchases)</td><td>$43,800</td><td></td><td></td></tr>
<tr><td>Deduct: Ending inventory</td><td>26,680</td><td></td><td></td></tr>
<tr><td>**Cost of goods sold**</td><td>**$17,120**</td><td></td><td></td></tr>
</table>

Illustration 8-15

Specific Identification Cost Formula

Conceptually, this method appears ideal because actual costs are matched against actual revenue, and ending inventory items are reported at their specific cost. In fact, the requirement that this method **only be used for goods that are not ordinarily interchangeable** is an attempt to make sure this benefit is achieved and to prevent management from manipulating the amount of net income.

Consider what might happen if businesses were allowed to use this method more generally. Assume, for instance, that a wholesaler purchases identical plywood early in the year at three different prices. When the plywood is sold, the wholesaler can choose either the lowest or the highest price to charge to expense simply by choosing which plywood is delivered to the customer. This means that a manager can manipulate net income simply by delivering to the customer the higher- or lower-priced item, depending on whether lower or higher reported income is wanted for the period.

Another problem with the broader use of the specific identification cost formula is that allocating certain costs can become arbitrary when the inventory items are interchangeable. In many circumstances, **it is difficult to directly relate shipping charges, storage costs, discounts, and other blanket charges to a specific inventory item.** The only option, then, is to allocate these costs somewhat arbitrarily, which eliminates some of the benefits offered by the specific identification method.[12]

Weighted Average Cost

As its name implies, an average cost method prices inventory items based on the average cost of the goods that are available for sale during the period. The **weighted average cost formula** takes into account that the volume of goods acquired at each price is different. Assuming that Call-Mart Inc. uses a periodic inventory method, the ending inventory and cost of goods sold are calculated as indicated in Illustration 8-16.

Note that the beginning inventory units and cost are both included in calculating the average cost per unit.

Another weighted-average cost method uses the **moving-average cost formula**. This method is used with **perpetual** inventory records that are **kept in both units and dollars**. Use of the moving-average cost formula for full perpetual records is shown in Illustration 8-17.

Illustration 8-16

Weighted Average Cost Formula—Periodic Inventory

	Date	No. of Units	Unit Cost	Total Cost
Inventory	Mar. 1	500	$3.80	$ 1,900
Purchases	Mar. 2	1,500	4.00	6,000
Purchases	Mar. 15	6,000	4.40	26,400
Purchases	Mar. 30	2,000	4.75	9,500
Total goods available		10,000		$43,800

Weighted average cost per unit $\dfrac{\$43,800}{10,000} = \$4.38$

Ending inventory in units 6,000
Cost of ending inventory **6,000 × $4.38 = $26,280**

Cost of goods available for sale $43,800
Deduct ending inventory 26,280

Cost of goods sold $17,520 (= 4,000 × $4.38)

Illustration 8-17

Moving-Average Cost Formula— Full Perpetual Inventory

Date	Purchased		Sold or Issued		Balance*	
Mar. 1	Beginning inventory				(500 @ $3.80)	$ 1,900
Mar. 2	(1,500 @ $4.00)	$ 6,000			(2,000 @ $3.95)	7,900
Mar. 15	(6,000 @ $4.40)	26,400			(8,000 @ $4.2875)	34,300
Mar. 19			(4,000 @ $4.2875)			
				$17,150	(4,000 @ $4.2875)	17,150
Mar. 30	(2,000 @ $4.75)	9,500			(6,000 @ $4.4417)	26,650

*Calculation of moving-average cost per unit:
After March 2 purchase

= Cost of units available / Units available

= [$1,900 + (1,500 × $4.00)] / (500 + 1,500)

= ($1,900 + $6,000) / 2,000

= $7,900 / 2,000

= $3.95

After March 15 purchase

= [$7,900 + (6,000 × $4.40)] / (2,000 + 6,000)

= ($7,900 + $26,400) / 8,000

= $34,300 / 8,000

= $4.2875

After March 30 purchase

= [$17,150 + (2,000 × $4.75)] / (4,000 + 2,000)

= ($17,150 + 9,500) / 6,000

= $26,650 / 6,000

= $4.4417

In this method, a **new average unit cost is calculated each time** a purchase is made. This is **because the cost of goods sold at the updated average cost has to be recognized at the time of the next sale.** On March 15, after 6,000 units are purchased for $26,400, 8,000 units with a total cost of $34,300 ($7,900 plus $26,400) are on hand. The average unit cost is $34,300 divided by 8,000, or $4.2875. This unit cost is used in costing withdrawals of inventory until another purchase is made, when a new average unit cost is calculated. Accordingly, the cost of each of the 4,000 units withdrawn on March 19 is shown at $4.2875, which makes a total cost of goods sold of $17,150. On March 30, following the purchase of 2,000 units for $9,500, the total inventory cost of the 6,000 units is $26,650. The new unit cost is now $4.4417.

Justification for using the average cost method is that the costs it assigns to inventory and cost of goods sold closely follow the actual physical flow of many inventories that are interchangeable. While it is impossible to measure the specific physical flow of inventory, it is reasonable to cost items based on an average price. There are also practical reasons that support this method. It is simple to apply, objective, and not very open to income manipulation. This argument is particularly persuasive when the inventory involved is relatively homogeneous in nature. In terms of achieving financial statement objectives, an average cost method results in an average of costs being used to determine both the cost of goods sold in the income statement and ending inventory in the statement of financial position.

First-In, First-Out (FIFO)

The **first-in, first-out (FIFO) cost formula** assigns costs based on the assumption that goods are used in the order in which they are purchased. In other words, it assumes that **the first items purchased are the first ones used** (in a manufacturing concern) **or sold** (in a merchandising concern). The inventory remaining, therefore, must come from the most recent purchases.

To illustrate, assume that Call-Mart Inc. uses a periodic inventory system, where the inventory cost is calculated only at the end of the month. **The ending inventory's cost** for the 6,000 units remaining is calculated by taking the **cost of the most recent purchase and working back until all units in the ending inventory are accounted for.** The ending inventory and cost of goods sold are calculated as shown in Illustration 8-18.

Illustration 8-18
FIFO Cost Formula—
Periodic Inventory

Date	No. of Units	Unit Cost	Total Cost
Mar. 30	2,000	$4.75	$ 9,500
Mar. 15	4,000	4.40	17,600
Ending inventory	6,000		$27,100
Cost of goods available for sale	$43,800		
Deduct: Ending inventory	27,100		
Cost of goods sold	$16,700		

If a full perpetual inventory system **in quantities and dollars** is used, a cost figure is attached to each withdrawal from inventory when the units are withdrawn and sold. In the example, the cost of the 4,000 units removed on March 19 is made up first from the items in the beginning inventory, then the items purchased on March 2, and finally some from the March 15 purchases. The inventory recorded under FIFO and **a perpetual system** for Call-Mart Inc. is shown in Illustration 8-19, which also results in an ending inventory of $27,100 and a cost of goods sold of $16,700.

Illustration 8-19
FIFO Cost Formula—
Perpetual Inventory

Date	Purchased	Sold or Issued	Balance	
Mar. 1	Beginning inventory		500 @ $3.80	$ 1,900
Mar. 2	(1,500 @ $4.00) $ 6,000		500 @ 3.80 / 1,500 @ 4.00	7,900
Mar. 15	(6,000 @ $4.40) 26,400		500 @ 3.80 / 1,500 @ 4.00 / 6,000 @ 4.40	34,300
Mar. 19		500 @ $3.80 / 1,500 @ 4.00 / 2,000 @ 4.40 = **$16,700**	4,000 @ 4.40	17,600
Mar. 30	(2,000 @ $4.75) 9,500		4,000 @ 4.40 / 2,000 @ 4.75	**27,100**

Notice that in these two FIFO examples, the cost of goods sold and ending inventory are the same. **In all cases where FIFO is used, the inventory and cost of goods sold are the same at the end of the period whether a perpetual or periodic system is used.** This is true because the same costs will always be first in and, therefore, first out, whether cost of goods sold is calculated as goods are sold throughout the accounting period (the perpetual system) or based on what remains at the end of the accounting period (the periodic system).

One objective of FIFO is to roughly follow the actual physical flow of goods. When the physical flow of goods really is first-in, first-out, the FIFO method approximates the use of specific identification. At the same time, it does not permit manipulation of income because the enterprise is not free to choose a certain cost to be charged to expense.

Another advantage of the FIFO method is that the ending inventory is close to its current cost. Because the costs of the first goods in are transferred to cost of goods sold, the ending inventory is made up of the cost of the most recent purchases. This approach generally provides a cost that is close to the replacement cost for inventory on the statement of financial position, particularly when the inventory turnover is rapid or price changes have not occurred since the most recent purchases.

The FIFO method's basic disadvantage is that current costs are not matched against current revenues on the income statement. The oldest costs are charged against current revenue, which can lead to distortions in gross profit and net income when prices are changing rapidly.

Choice of Cost Formula

The inventory standards limit the ability of preparers to choose a cost formula. Specific identification is required when inventory is made up of goods that are not ordinarily interchangeable, and when goods and services are produced and segregated for specific projects. Otherwise, the choice is between an average cost method and FIFO. The choice is further restricted by the requirement that companies apply the same inventory cost formula to all inventories of a similar nature and use.

The overriding objectives that underlie the inventory standards and guide management are as follows.

1. Choose an approach that corresponds as closely as possible to the physical flow of goods.

2. Report an inventory cost on the statement of financial position that is representative of the inventory's recent cost.

3. Use the same method for all inventory assets that have similar economic characteristics for the entity.

UNDERLYING CONCEPT

Applying the standards results in statement of financial position and income statement amounts that faithfully represent the asset's cost and the cost of the inventory that was sold, respectively. Consistently applying the same formula also improves the comparability of the financial statements.

These requirements are consistent with standard setters' emphasis on an asset and liability approach to the accounting model, as explained in Chapter 2. That is, assets and liabilities are the fundamental building blocks whose definition and measurement underlie the amounts and timing of revenues and expenses.

Income taxes are also a consideration. Methods that permit a lower ending inventory valuation result in lower income and reduced cash outflows for taxes. Compared with the FIFO cost formula, an average cost formula results in recent costs being reflected more in the cost of goods sold and older costs in ending inventory. In a period of rising prices, there may be tax advantages to the average cost formula.

If companies were permitted to switch from one inventory costing method to another, this would adversely affect the comparability of financial statements. Therefore, companies choose the costing formula that is most suitable to their particular circumstances and, once selected, apply it consistently from then on. If conditions indicate that another accounting policy would result in a reliable and more relevant presentation in the financial statements, a change may be made. Such a change is unusual, but is accounted for retroactively and its effect should be clearly disclosed in the financial statements.

Last-In, First-Out (LIFO)

The **last-in, first-out (LIFO) cost formula** is no longer permitted under ASPE and IFRS. LIFO assigns costs based on the assumption that the cost of the most recent purchase is the first cost to be charged to cost of goods sold. The cost assigned to the inventory remaining therefore comes from the earliest acquisitions (those that are "first-in, still-here") and is made up of the oldest costs.

This method is no longer permitted under Canadian standards for the following reasons.

1. In almost all situations, LIFO does not represent the actual flow of costs.

2. The statement of financial position cost of ending inventory is not a fair representation of the recent cost of inventories on hand.

3. Use of LIFO can result in serious distortions of reported income, especially when old inventory costs are expensed in the period. This happens when old, low-cost inventory gets charged to cost of goods sold due to a reduction in base inventory levels.

Because the Canada Revenue Agency has never allowed companies to use LIFO to calculate their income for tax purposes, this method was not widely used in Canada. However, it is permitted under U.S. GAAP, and allowed for tax purposes there if a company also uses the method for financial reporting purposes. Canadian public companies that are listed on a U.S. stock exchange as well as a Canadian exchange are permitted to prepare their financial statements under U.S. GAAP, so it is likely that LIFO-based inventories will continue to be seen in Canada for a while yet.

Lower of Cost and Net Realizable Value

Rationale for Lower of Cost and Net Realizable Value (LC&NRV)

So far in the chapter, we have learned how to calculate the cost of ending inventory at the statement of financial position date, determining:

1. the goods to include in ending inventory,

2. the costs to capitalize in inventory cost, and

3. the cost formulas available to allocate costs to ending inventory.

The last step in applying this cost-based model is to decide whether cost is appropriate for reporting inventory on the statement of financial position.

A departure from reporting inventory at cost makes sense if the value of inventory to the entity falls below its cost. This reduction in value may be due to the inventory itself (if, for example, the goods are obsolete or damaged), a reduction in selling prices, or an increase in the costs to complete and dispose of the inventory. **Cost is not appropriate if the asset's value (its ability to generate net cash flows) is now less than its carrying amount.** Inventories therefore are valued at the **lower of cost and net realizable value**.

This departure from cost is justified for two main reasons. First, readers presume that **current assets can be converted into at least as much cash as the amount reported on the statement of financial position.** Second, **a loss of utility should be deducted from (matched with) revenues in the period in which the loss occurs,** not in the period when the inventory is sold.

For many years, inventory was valued in the cost-based system at the lower of cost and market (LCM), and there were a variety of alternative definitions of "market." The term **market** in LCM valuation could mean replacement cost, net realizable value, or net realizable value less a normal profit margin. Under U.S. GAAP, all these terms are still incorporated in a rule that is applied to calculate market and therefore to measure inventory on the statement of financial position.

The option of choosing a meaning of "market" has been eliminated in Canada and under IFRS. The phrase **lower of cost and market** is no longer part of GAAP in Canada, and market is now strictly defined as **net realizable value (NRV)**: the estimated selling price less the estimated costs to complete and sell the goods. Why has there been such support for this concept of market?

The use of a "replacement cost" definition of market is based on the assumption that a decline in an item's replacement cost results in a decline in its selling price. While replacement cost may be appropriate in a few specific circumstances, it is not reasonable to assume that prices will fall in the same proportion as input costs fall, or that they will fall below inventory cost, or that such market conditions exist for all products. Also, the use of a "net realizable value less a normal profit margin" definition of market value has the effect of arbitrarily shifting profits from one period to another. In effect, a very large writedown may be taken in the year the inventory's value drops, so that a normal profit can be reported in the period in which it is later sold.

If inventory is written down only to its net realizable value, a lower loss is recognized in the current period and, if the estimates are correct, the company breaks even on the sale of the item. Although the net result is the same when you add the two periods together, there is little justification for the arbitrary shifting of profit into a future period as happens when the NRV is further reduced by the profit margin. Therefore, ASPE and IFRS both require the use of NRV as "market."

What Is Net Realizable Value?

Net realizable value is an estimate. Unlike inventory cost, which usually remains at a determined value, net realizable value changes over time for a variety of reasons, including the following.

- Inventory may deteriorate or become obsolete with time.

- Selling prices fluctuate with changes in supply and demand.

- Substitute products become available.

- Input costs to complete and sell, liquidate, or otherwise dispose of the product vary with conditions and the specific markets that the inventory is sold into.

Estimates of NRV are based on the best evidence available at and shortly after the statement of financial position date. The objective is to determine the most likely (net) realizable value of the product on hand at the end of the accounting period given the specific circumstances of the particular entity. A new assessment is required at each statement of financial position date. If economic circumstances change and the estimate of the net realizable value changes from the previous estimate, the revised amount is used in determining the lower of cost and NRV at the end of the next period.

Application of Lower of Cost and Net Realizable Value

The **lower of cost and net realizable value (LC&NRV) standard** requires that inventory be valued at cost unless NRV is lower than cost, in which case the inventory is valued at NRV. To apply this:

1. Determine the cost.

2. Calculate the net realizable value.

3. Compare the two.

4. Use the lower value to measure inventory for the statement of financial position.

To demonstrate, consider the information in Illustration 8-20 for the inventory of Regner Foods Limited.

Illustration 8-20				
Applying the Lower of Cost and NRV	**Food**	**Cost**	**Net Realizable Value**	**LC&NRV**
	Spinach	$ 80,000	$120,000	$ 80,000
	Carrots	100,000	100,000	100,000
	Cut beans	50,000	40,000	40,000
	Peas	90,000	72,000	72,000
	Mixed vegetables	95,000	92,000	92,000
	Final inventory value at LC&NRV			$384,000

To establish the LC&NRV of each item of inventory, compare the net realizable value in the NRV column of Illustration 8-20 with cost. The lower of the two values is then chosen. Cost is the lower amount for spinach; net realizable value is lower for cut beans, peas, and mixed vegetables; and cost and NRV are identical for carrots. The inventory amount reported on Regner Foods' statement of financial position is therefore $384,000.

This analysis is usually applied only to losses in value that occur in the normal course of business from such causes as style changes, a shift in demand, or regular shop wear. Damaged or deteriorated goods are reduced directly to net realizable value. If the amount is significant, such goods may be carried in separate inventory accounts.

In Illustration 8-20 for Regner Foods, we assumed that the lower of cost and net realizable value rule is applied to each separate item of food. Indeed, **the accounting standards specify that the comparison is usually applied on an item-by-item basis**. However, the standards recognize that it may be appropriate in some circumstances to group similar or related items and then compare their cost and NRV as a group. Grouping inventory for this purpose may be appropriate, for example, for inventory items relating to the same product line in the following situations:

1. They are closely related in terms of their end use.

2. They are produced and marketed in the same geographical area.

3. They cannot be evaluated separately from other items in the product line in a practical or reasonable way.[13]

Grouping all finished goods inventory, all products within a geographic area, or all inventory that is specific to an industry, is **not** considered appropriate.

The extent to which inventory items are grouped and their subtotals of cost and net realizable value are compared can affect the amount of inventory that is reported on the statement of financial position. To illustrate, assume that Regner Foods separates its food products into "frozen" and "canned" categories.

As indicated in Illustration 8-21, if the lower of cost and NRV rule is applied to the **subtotals** of these groups, the valuation of inventory is $394,000. If it is applied to individual items, it is $384,000. The reason for the difference is that individual realizable values lower than cost are offset against realizable values higher than cost when categories are used. For example, the lower NRVs for cut beans, peas, and mixed vegetables are partially offset by the higher NRV for spinach. **The item-by-item approach** is always the more conservative method (that is, lower asset cost) because net realizable values above cost are never included in the calculations.[14]

			Lower of Cost and NRV by:	
	Cost	NRV	Individual Items	Related Products
Frozen				
Spinach	$ 80,000	$120,000	$ 80,000	
Carrots	100,000	100,000	100,000	
Cut beans	50,000	40,000	40,000	
Total frozen	230,000	260,000		$230,000
Canned				
Peas	90,000	72,000	72,000	
Mixed vegetables	95,000	92,000	92,000	
Total canned	185,000	164,000		164,000
Total			$384,000	$394,000

Illustration 8-21

Grouping Inventory Categories

Recording the Lower of Cost and Net Realizable Value

Two different methods are used for **recording** inventory at the lower market amount. The **direct method** records the NRV of the inventory directly in the Inventory account at the reporting date if the amount is lower than cost. No loss is reported separately in the income statement because the loss is buried in cost of goods sold. The other method does not change the Inventory account itself. Instead it keeps the Inventory account at cost and establishes a separate contra asset account to Inventory on the statement of financial position. (This is very similar to Accounts Receivable and the Allowance for Doubtful Accounts.) A loss account is recognized in the income statement to record the write-off. This second approach is referred to as the **indirect method** or **allowance method**.

The following data are the basis for Illustrations 8-22 and 8-23, which show the entries under both methods:

Inventory	At Cost	At NRV
Beginning of the period	$65,000	$65,000
End of the period	82,000	70,000

The entries in Illustration 8-22 assume the use of a **periodic** inventory system. Those in Illustration 8-23 assume a **perpetual** inventory system.

<table>
<tr><td>Illustration 8-22

Accounting for the Reduction of Inventory to NRV—Periodic Inventory System</td><td colspan="2">**Ending Inventory Recorded at NRV (Direct Method)**</td><td colspan="2">**Ending Inventory Recorded at Cost and Reduced to NRV Using an Allowance**</td></tr>
<tr><td></td><td colspan="2">**To transfer out beginning inventory balance:**</td><td colspan="2"></td></tr>
<tr><td></td><td>Cost of Goods Sold</td><td>65,000</td><td>Cost of Goods Sold</td><td>65,000</td></tr>
<tr><td></td><td> Inventory</td><td>65,000</td><td> Inventory</td><td>65,000</td></tr>
<tr><td></td><td colspan="2">**To record ending inventory:**</td><td colspan="2"></td></tr>
<tr><td></td><td>Inventory</td><td>70,000</td><td>Inventory</td><td>82,000</td></tr>
<tr><td></td><td> Cost of Goods Sold</td><td>70,000</td><td> Cost of Goods Sold</td><td>82,000</td></tr>
<tr><td></td><td colspan="2">**To write down inventory to lower NRV:**</td><td colspan="2"></td></tr>
<tr><td></td><td> No entry</td><td></td><td>Loss on Inventory Due to
  Decline in NRV*</td><td>12,000</td></tr>
<tr><td></td><td></td><td></td><td> Allowance to Reduce
    Inventory to NRV</td><td>12,000</td></tr>
<tr><td></td><td colspan="4">*A debit to Cost of Goods Sold is also acceptable. In either case, the debit would be presented as part of cost of goods sold.</td></tr>
</table>

<table>
<tr><td>Illustration 8-23

Accounting for the Reduction of Inventory to NRV—Perpetual Inventory System</td><td colspan="2">**Direct Method**</td><td colspan="2">**Indirect or Allowance Method**</td></tr>
<tr><td></td><td colspan="2">**To reduce inventory from cost to NRV:**</td><td colspan="2"></td></tr>
<tr><td></td><td>Cost of Goods Sold</td><td>12,000</td><td>Loss on Inventory Due to</td><td></td></tr>
<tr><td></td><td> Inventory</td><td>12,000</td><td> Decline in NRV*</td><td>12,000</td></tr>
<tr><td></td><td></td><td></td><td> Allowance to Reduce
    Inventory to NRV</td><td>12,000</td></tr>
<tr><td></td><td colspan="4">*A debit to Cost of Goods Sold is also acceptable. In either case, the debit would be presented as part of cost of goods sold.</td></tr>
</table>

The advantage of identifying the loss due to the decline in net realizable value separately is that it may be reported separately. It thus clearly discloses the loss resulting from the market decline in inventory prices instead of burying it in the cost of goods sold. The advantage of using an allowance account is that inventory cost numbers are retained in both the Inventory control and subsidiary ledger accounts.

Although using an allowance account makes it possible to disclose the inventory at cost and at the lower of cost and NRV on the statement of financial position, it raises the problem of how to dispose of the new account balance in the following period. If the particular merchandise is still on hand, the allowance account should be retained. Otherwise, beginning inventory and cost of goods available for sale will be overstated. But **if the goods have been sold,** then the account should be closed. A new allowance account balance is then established for any decline in inventory value that exists at the end of the next accounting period.

Many accountants leave the allowance account on the books and merely adjust its balance at the next reporting date to agree with the difference between cost and

the lower of cost and NRV at that time. If prices are falling, a loss is recorded. If prices are rising, a loss recorded in prior years is recovered and a gain (which is not really a gain, but **a recovery of a previously recognized loss**) is recorded, as shown in Illustration 8-24. The recovery amount is ordinarily recognized as a reduction in the cost of goods sold.

Illustration 8-24

Effect on Net Income of Adjustments to the Allowance Account

Date	Inventory at Cost	Inventory at NRV	Amount Required in Allowance Account	Allowance Account before Adjustment	Adjustment of Allowance Account Balance	Effect on Net Income
Dec. 31/16	$188,000	$176,000	$12,000 cr.	$ –0–	$12,000 increase	Loss
Dec. 31/17	194,000	187,000	7,000 cr.	12,000 cr.	5,000 decrease	Gain
Dec. 31/18	173,000	174,000	–0–	7,000 cr.	7,000 decrease	Gain
Dec. 31/19	182,000	180,000	2,000 cr.	–0–	2,000 increase	Loss

Any net "gain" can be thought of as the excess of the credit effect of closing the beginning allowance balance over the debit effect of setting up the current year-end allowance account. Recovering the loss up to the original cost is permitted, **but it may not exceed the original cost.** That is, the Allowance account cannot have a debit balance.

Evaluation of the Lower of Cost and Net Realizable Value Rule

Measuring inventories at the LC&NRV has some conceptual and practical deficiencies. Recognizing net realizable values only when they are lower than cost is an inconsistent treatment that can lead to distortions in reported income. The accounting values that are reported are not neutral and unbiased measures of income and net assets. Also, because NRV is an estimate, company management has the opportunity to over- or underestimate realizable values, depending on the results it would like to report for the period. Others feel that any accounting method that arbitrarily transfers income from one period to another reduces the quality of earnings.

On the other hand, many financial statement users appreciate the lower of cost and net realizable value requirement because they know that inventory and income are not overstated. Supporters contend that accounting measurement has not reached a level of sophistication that enables us to provide acceptably reliable (that is, verifiable) fair values for inventory above cost.

Exceptions to Lower of Cost and Net Realizable Value Model

Inventories Measured at Net Realizable Value

Objective 9
Identify inventories that are or may be valued at amounts other than the lower of cost and net realizable value.

For most companies and in most situations, inventory is reported at the lower of cost and net realizable value. Some critics believe that inventory should always be valued at its **net realizable value** because that is the net amount that will be collected in cash from the inventory in the future. In certain restricted circumstances, it is possible to record inventory at its net realizable value even if that amount is above cost. The following criteria have to be met to value inventory above cost and for revenue to be recognized before the point of sale:

1. The sale is assured or there is an active market for the product and minimal risk of failure to sell.

2. The costs of disposal can be estimated.

In certain industries, items such as agricultural produce, forest products, and mineral products inventories may be accounted for at net realizable value in accordance with well-established industry practices.

Measurement at net realizable value may also be used when cost figures are too difficult to obtain. In some cases, minor marketable by-products are produced where the costs are indistinguishable. Instead of the company attempting a costly exercise of arbitrary cost allocation, the by-products are measured at the selling price of the by-product less any costs to bring them to market.

Inventories Measured at Fair Value Less Costs to Sell

Inventories of Commodity Broker-Traders and Similar Entities

Another exception to the lower of cost and net realizable value measurement standard is the inventory of commodity broker-traders and entities with similar business models that measure their inventories at **fair value less costs to sell**.[15] This inventory consists of such items as grain and livestock futures contracts. Changes in the fair value less costs to sell the inventory items are recognized in net income in the period of the change.

Glencore PLC, with operations in grain handling, agri-products, and agri-food processing, among others, reports such a policy in the notes to its 2014 financial statements. The note is shown in Illustration 8-25. Recall from Chapter 3 that, when measuring fair value, the inputs to the measurement are classified as levels 1, 2, or 3, with level 1 being the highest quality input and level 3 being the lowest quality input. The asset is then classified as a level 1, 2, or 3 asset based on the level of inputs used to measure fair value.

REAL WORLD EMPHASIS

REAL WORLD EMPHASIS

Illustration 8-25

Inventory Valued at Net Realizable Value—Glencore PLC

12. INVENTORIES

US$ million	**2014**	2013
Production inventories	4,938	6,108
Marketing inventories	19,498	16,645
Total	**24,436**	22,753

Production inventories consist of materials, spare parts and work in process. Marketing inventories are saleable commodities held primarily by the marketing entities as well as finished goods and certain other readily saleable materials held by the industrial assets. Marketing inventories of $16,297 million (2013: $12,997 million) are carried at fair value less costs of disposal.

Fair value of inventories is a Level 2 fair value measurement (see note 28) using observable market prices obtained from exchanges, traded reference indices or market survey services adjusted for relevant location and quality differentials. There are no significant unobservable inputs in the fair value measurement of marketing inventories.

Biological Assets and Agricultural Produce at Point of Harvest

There is often confusion about what is a biological asset, agricultural produce, and a product that results from processing after harvest. Recall the opening story to Chapter 2 on plant-bearer assets, which discussed recent changes to the international standard covering agricultural assets, IAS 41 *Agriculture*.

Illustration 8-26 contains excerpts of examples from IAS 41 *Agriculture to* help clarify what is included as each type of asset.

Illustration 8-26

Examples of Agricultural Activity Assets

Biological assets	Agricultural produce	Products that are the result of processing after harvest
Sheep	Wool	Yarn, carpet
Trees in a timber plantation	Felled trees	Logs, lumber
Dairy cattle	Milk	Cheese
Pigs	Carcass	Sausage, cured hams
Cotton plants	Harvested cotton	Thread, clothing
Sugarcane	Harvested cane	Sugar
Tobacco plants	Picked leaves	Cured tobacco
Tea bushes	Picked leaves	Tea

(continued)

Illustration 8-26

*Examples of Agricultural
Activity Assets
(continued)*

Biological assets	Agricultural produce	Products that are the result of processing after harvest
Grapevines	Picked grapes	Wine
Fruit trees	Picked fruit	Processed fruit
Oil palms	Picked fruit	Palm oil
Rubber trees	Harvested latex	Rubber products

Some plants, for example, tea bushes, grapevines, oil palms, and rubber trees, usually meet the definition of a bearer plant and are within the scope of IAS 16. However, the produce growing on bearer plants, for example, tea leaves, grapes, oil palm fruit, and latex, is within the scope of IAS 41.

ASPE. Inventories of biological assets (living plants and animals) and products of the entity's biological assets (agricultural produce) at the point of harvest are excluded from the **measurement** requirements of ASPE for inventories if they are accounted for at NRV in accordance with well-established industry practices, as noted earlier. However, these inventories must follow the accounting requirements relating to **expense recognition** and **disclosure**. Otherwise, Section 3031 applies in full.

A review of the financial statements of many Canadian companies with such assets indicates that they tend to follow a lower of cost and net realizable value approach for the inventory. This is reasonable considering that this valuation corresponds closely to the **primary source of GAAP** for similar assets.

There is no guidance for biological assets such as the grapevines or olive trees themselves (that is, those assets that produce the inventory over a long period of time). They may be treated as property, plant, and equipment for accounting purposes.

IFRS. Under IFRS, accounting for biological assets and agricultural produce at the point of harvest is covered in a separate standard: IAS 41 *Agriculture*. Similar to ASPE, those inventories that are measured at NRV in accordance with well-established industry practices do not fall under IAS 2 for measurement purposes.

Biological assets are measured at fair value less costs to sell under IAS 41. Note that plants used to grow produce including tea bushes, grapevines and rubber trees are called "bearer plants." Because they produce saleable products such as tea or grapes each season, they are treated like property, plant, and equipment under IFRS. As such, they are accounted for using the cost or the revaluation method. We will cover these two methods in Chapters 10 and 11.

Otherwise, for all other agricultural produce at the point of harvest, such as grapes or picked fruit, the "fair value less costs to sell" measure is deemed to be the inventory's "cost" for purposes of subsequent accounting (and further processing, if applicable) under IAS 2 *Inventories*.

Basic entries to account for this measurement model are set out in Illustration 8-27.[16] Assume that the enterprise is a farm that raises sheep for their wool. The sheep are biological assets, lambs born into the existing flock are biological assets, and the wool is an agricultural product.

Note that the costs to raise or produce the lambs may be capitalized to the Biological Assets account.[17] If these costs are capitalized as an accounting policy choice, direct costs would be included, whereas more general costs would be expensed. In this manner, when revalued to fair value less cost to sell, the unrealized gain for instance will be net of the direct costs. The account Biological Assets, representing the fair value less selling costs of the sheep, seems to have some of the characteristics of both inventory and plant and equipment assets. However, biological assets are classified as neither. They require separate disclosure on the statement of financial position.

Let's see how a real-world company accounts for biological assets. **Nutreco N.V.** is a private company with operations in 30 countries. The company was taken private in 2015. Nutreco is in the animal nutrition and fish feed business. Illustration 8-28 is taken from the notes to the 2014 financial statements, issued when it was a public company.

While revaluing the assets, unrealized gains/losses are generated. Once sold, the gains/losses become realized. This is an important distinction and should be disclosed under the full disclosure principle.

Illustration 8-27

*Accounting for Inventories at
Fair Value Less Costs to Sell
(IFRS Versus ASPE)*

	IFRS		ASPE*	
To record the birth of a lamb (fair value $500):				
Biological Assets	500		NA	
Unrealized Gain or Loss		500		
To record general farm expenditures of $200:				
Expenses	200		200	
Cash/Accounts Payable		200		200
To record an increase in value of lambs and other sheep of $700:				
Biological Assets	700			
Unrealized Gain or Loss		700	NA	
To record the wool inventory produced from the sheep (valued at $100):				
Inventory	100			
Biological Assets		100	NA	
To record the immediate sale of wool produced for $100:				
Cash/Accounts Receivable	100		100	
Inventory		100		
Unrealized Gain or Loss	100			
Realized Gain or Loss		100		100

*ASPE does not offer any guidance. Therefore, as long as the accounting policy choice is supportable under the conceptual framework, companies following ASPE might use the same accounting as IFRS or perhaps use historical cost as a default. The above-noted accounting uses historical cost and recognizes gains/profits when realized (that is, when the wool is sold). The flock would have to be tested for impairment. In other words, how long will the sheep produce wool? Older sheep might not have the same value as younger sheep. Some interesting questions arise. If one animal dies, should we write off part of the flock? Alternatively, given that the flock is likely replenishing itself because new lambs are born as old animals die, is there a need to write anything down? There are no easy answers here and first principles must be applied as well as professional judgement. Care would also be taken to determine how significant the amounts are. If animals die, the company would have to write the balance down to recoverable or net realizable value if this was below cost. New sheep would not necessarily be recorded since they were not purchased; however, all costs directly attributable to getting the sheep ready to produce could be capitalized. Finally, it may be argued that direct costs of maintaining the sheep could also be capitalized. If this were done, we would have to be careful to set a limit on the total carrying value. In addition, if this were the case, we would likely have to recognize some costs when sold.

Illustration 8-28

*Note Disclosure of Biological
Assets—Nutreco N.V.*

**REAL WORLD
EMPHASIS**

19 Biological assets

(€ × million)	2014	2013
Balance at 1 January	**152.6**	**165.0**
Expenses capitalised	619.4	673.5
Decrease due to sales	−290.7	−331.4
Decrease due to harvest	−323.8	−353.4
Change in fair value	−0.9	−0.6
Effect of movement in foreign exchange rates	0.2	−0.5
Balance at 31 December	**156.8**	**152.6**

At balance sheet date, Nutreco has biological assets in Spain, Canada and the Netherlands related to poultry livestock, pig livestock, turkey livestock, hatching eggs and a small amount of animals for research purposes.

The table below shows the biological assets per relevant country and applied valuation method:

(€ × million)	Spain	Canada	The Netherlands	Total
Fair value less costs to sell	125.2	3.3	0.1	128.6
At cost less accumulated depreciation and impairment losses	26.9	1.3	–	28.2
Carrying amount at 31 December 2014	**152.1**	**4.6**	**0.1**	**156.8**

As you can see in the Nutreco note, expenses are capitalized. Note further that some of their biological assets are carried at cost less depreciation and impairment losses. This is because of an inability to reliably measure fair values.

Estimating Inventory

The Need for Estimates

Recall that the basic purpose of taking a physical inventory is to verify the accuracy of the perpetual inventory records or, if there are no perpetual records, to arrive at an inventory amount. Sometimes, taking a physical inventory is impractical or impossible. In such cases, estimation methods are used to approximate inventory on hand. One such method is called the gross profit, or gross margin, method. This method is used in situations where (1) only an estimate of inventory is needed (for example, preparing interim reports or testing the reasonableness of the cost calculated by some other method), or where (2) inventory has been destroyed by fire or some other catastrophe. It may also be used to provide a rough check on the accuracy of a physical inventory count. For example, the estimated amount is compared with the physical count amount to see if they are reasonably close; if they are not, the reason for the difference is investigated.

Another method that is widely used with retail inventories is the retail inventory method. Like the gross profit method, it depends on establishing a relationship between selling (retail) prices and cost. Appendix 8A discusses the retail inventory method in detail.

Applying the Gross Profit Method

The **gross profit method** is based on three premises:

1. The beginning inventory plus purchases equals the **cost of goods available for sale**.

2. Goods not included in cost of goods sold must be on hand **in ending inventory**.

3. When an estimate of cost of goods sold is deducted from the cost of goods available for sale, the result is an estimate of ending inventory.

To illustrate, assume that a company has a beginning inventory of $60,000 and purchases of $200,000, both at cost. Sales at selling price amount to $280,000. The gross profit on the selling price is 30%. Illustration 8-29 walks you through the gross profit method of estimating ending inventory.[18]

Beginning inventory (at cost)		$ 60,000
Purchases (at cost)		200,000
Goods available for sale (at cost)		260,000
Sales (at selling price)	$280,000	
Less: Gross profit (30% of $280,000)	84,000	
Sales at cost = Estimated cost of goods sold		196,000
Estimated inventory (at cost)		$ 64,000

Note that the estimated cost of goods sold could also have been calculated directly as 70% of sales; that is, 100% less 30%. **The cost of goods sold percentage is always the complement of the gross profit percentage.** That is, the cost of goods sold percentage plus the gross profit percentage add up to 100%.

All the information needed to estimate the inventory at cost, except for the gross profit percentage, is available in the current period's accounting records. The gross profit percentage is determined by reviewing company policies and the records of prior periods. The percentage is adjusted if the prior periods are not considered representative of the current period.

Alternative Terminology

The terms "gross profit percentage," "gross margin percentage," "rate of gross profit," and "rate of gross margin" mean the same thing: they all reflect the relationship of gross profit to the selling price. The terms "percentage markup" or "rate of markup" are used to describe the relationship of gross profit to cost. It is important to understand the difference.

Gross Profit Percentage Versus Markup on Cost

In most situations, the **gross profit percentage** is used and it is the gross profit as a percentage of the selling price. The previous illustration, for example, used a 30% gross profit on sales. Gross profit on selling price is the common method for quoting the profit for several reasons.

1. Most goods are stated on a retail basis, not a cost basis.

2. A profit quoted on the selling price is lower than one based on cost, and this lower rate gives a favourable impression to the consumer.

3. The gross profit based on selling price can never exceed 100%.

In the previous example, the percentage was given to you. But how was that figure derived? To see how a gross profit percentage is calculated, assume that an article cost $15.00 and sells for $20.00, a gross profit of $5.00. This markup of $5.00 is one quarter or 25% of the selling (or retail) price but is one third or 33⅓% of cost (see Illustration 8-30).

Illustration 8-30

Gross Profit Percentage Versus Percentage of Markup on Cost

$$\frac{\text{Gross profit}}{\text{Selling price}} = \frac{\$5.00}{\$20.00} = 25\% \text{ of selling price} \qquad \frac{\text{Gross profit}}{\text{Cost}} = \frac{\$5.00}{\$15.00} = 33\frac{1}{3}\% \text{ of cost}$$

Although gross profit is based on sales, you should understand the relationship between this ratio and the percentage of **markup on cost**.

For example, assume that you were told that the **markup on cost** for a specific item is 25%. What, then, is the **gross profit on selling price?** To find the answer, assume that the item's selling price is $1.00. In this case, the following formula applies:

$$
\begin{aligned}
\text{Cost} + \text{Gross profit} &= \text{Selling price} \\
C + .25C &= \$1.00 \\
1.25C &= \$1.00 \\
C &= \$0.80
\end{aligned}
$$

The amount of gross profit is $0.20 ($1.00 − $0.80), and the rate of gross profit on selling price is 20% ($0.20/$1.00).

Alternatively, assume that you know that the **gross profit on selling price** is 20%. What is the **markup on cost?** To find the answer, again assume that the selling price is $1.00. The same formula can be used:

$$
\begin{aligned}
\text{Cost} + \text{Gross profit} &= \text{Selling price} \\
C + .20 (\$1.00) &= \$1.00 \\
C + \$0.20 &= \$1.00 \\
C &= \$0.80
\end{aligned}
$$

Here, as in the example above, the amount of the markup or gross profit is $0.20 ($1.00 − $0.80), and the percentage markup on cost is 25% ($0.20/$0.80). Retailers use the formulas in Illustration 8-31 to express these relationships.

Illustration 8-31

Formulas Relating to Gross Profit

1. $\text{Percent gross profit on selling price} = \dfrac{\text{Percent markup on cost}}{100\% + \text{Percent markup on cost}}$

2. $\text{Percent markup on cost} = \dfrac{\text{Percent gross profit on selling price}}{100\% - \text{Percent gross profit on selling price}}$

Using the Results

What are the disadvantages of using the gross profit method? There are several.

1. The gross profit method **provides an estimate** only.

2. The gross profit method uses **past percentages** in determining the markup. Although the future may repeat the past, a current rate is usually more appropriate. Whenever fluctuations in the rate of profit occur, the percentage must be adjusted appropriately.

3. **It may be inappropriate to apply a single gross profit rate.** Often, a store or department handles merchandise with very different rates of gross profit. In these situations, the gross profit method may have to be applied by type of merchandise, or by combining merchandise with similar profit margins.

Because the result is only an estimate, the gross profit method is **not normally acceptable for financial reporting purposes.** A physical inventory is needed as an additional verification that the inventory indicated in the records is actually on hand. Nevertheless, the gross profit method is used to estimate ending inventory for **interim** (monthly and quarterly) **reporting** and for **insurance purposes** (such as fire losses). Note that the results of applying the gross profit method will reflect the inventory method that is used (specific identification, FIFO, or average cost) because this method is based on historical records.

PRESENTATION, DISCLOSURE, AND ANALYSIS

Presentation and Disclosure of Inventories

Objective 11

Identify how inventory should be presented and the type of inventory disclosures required by IFRS and ASPE.

Sometimes there is a fine line between what is considered to be inventory and what is better classified as property, plant, and equipment. Minor spare parts and servicing equipment, for example, are usually classified as inventory. Major spare parts and standby equipment, on the other hand, are recognized as capital assets if they are expected to provide benefits beyond the current accounting period. The classification issue often requires the exercise of professional judgement. In addition, as previously mentioned in this chapter, certain biological assets referred to as bearer plants are classified as property, plant, and equipment.

Inventories are one of the most significant assets of manufacturing and merchandising companies, and of many service enterprises. For this reason, companies are required to disclose additional information about these resources.

Some disclosures are similar to the ones required for other statement of financial position items:

- the choice of accounting policies adopted to measure the inventory;

- the carrying amount of the inventory in total and by classification (such as supplies, material, work in process, and finished goods);

- the amount of inventories recognized as an expense in the period, including unabsorbed and abnormal amounts of production overheads; and

- the carrying amount of inventory pledged as collateral for liabilities.

The amount of inventory recognized as an expense is usually reported according to its function—as cost of goods sold. However, a company that chooses to present its expenses according to the nature of its costs instead of by function would present expenses for raw materials and consumables used, labour costs, and other expenses along with the change in inventories for the period.

Additional disclosures are required for inventories **under IFRS**. These include the carrying amount of inventory carried at fair value less costs to sell, and details about inventory writedowns and reversals of writedowns, such as information about what led to the reversal of any writedowns. Considerable information is required in addition for biological assets and agricultural produce at the point of harvest, such as a reconciliation of opening to ending account balances.

Note also that IAS 1 requires the disclosure of any judgements used in applying accounting policies as well as sources of estimation uncertainty in measuring financial statement elements.

REAL WORLD EMPHASIS

The excerpts in Illustration 8-32 are taken from the 2014 financial statements of Sears Canada Inc. The excerpts illustrate the company's disclosure of its accounting policy choices for determining inventory cost, including the cost formula used, the basis of valuation on the statement of financial position, the carrying value of major categories making up the total inventory, and the cost of goods sold. In addition, the company reports its accounting policy for vendor rebates.

The Sears Canada Inc. disclosures exceed those now required under ASPE, and meet the requirements for disclosures under IFRS.

Illustration 8-32

Inventory Disclosures from Notes to the 2014 Financial Statements—Sears Canada Inc.

REAL WORLD EMPHASIS

2. Significant accounting policies

2.7 Inventories

Inventories are measured at the lower of cost and net realizable value. Cost is determined using the weighted average cost method, based on individual items. The cost is comprised of the purchase price, plus the costs incurred in bringing the inventory to its present location and condition. Net realizable value is the estimated selling price in the ordinary course of business less the estimated costs to sell. Rebates and allowances received from vendors are recognized as a reduction to the cost of inventory, unless the rebates clearly relate to the reimbursement of specific expenses. A provision for shrinkage and obsolescence is calculated based on historical experience. All inventories consist of finished goods.

4. Critical accounting judgments and key sources of estimation uncertainty

In the application of the Company's accounting policies, management is required to make judgments, estimates and assumptions with regards to the carrying amounts of assets and liabilities that are not readily apparent from other sources. The estimates and underlying assumptions are based on historical experience and other factors that are considered to be relevant. Actual results may differ from these estimates. The estimates and underlying assumptions are reviewed on an ongoing basis. Revisions to accounting estimates are recognized in the period in which the estimate is revised if the revision affects only that period, or in the period of the revision and future periods, if the revision affects both current and future periods.

The following are the critical judgments that management has made in the process of applying the Company's accounting policies, key assumptions concerning the future and other key sources of estimation uncertainty that have the potential to materially impact the carrying amounts of assets and liabilities.

4.2 Inventory

4.2.1 Obsolescence, valuation and inventory stock losses

Inventory is written down to reflect future losses on the disposition of obsolete merchandise. Future losses are estimated based on historical trends that vary depending on the type of inventory.

An adjustment is made each period to value inventory at the lower of cost and net realizable value. This adjustment is estimated based on historical trends that vary depending on the type of inventory.

Inventory is adjusted to reflect estimated inventory stock losses incurred in the year based on recent historical inventory count data.

4.2.2 Vendor rebates

Inventory is adjusted to reflect vendor rebates received or receivable based on vendor agreements. This adjustment is estimated based on historical data and current vendor agreements.

4.2.3 Freight

Inbound freight incurred to bring inventory to its present location is estimated each reporting period and is included in the cost of inventory. This estimate is based on historical freight costs incurred.

Changes in estimates may result in changes to "Inventories" on the Consolidated Statements of Financial Position and a charge or credit to "Cost of goods and services sold" in the Consolidated Statements of Net (Loss) Earnings and Comprehensive (Loss) Income. For additional information, see Note 7.

7. Inventories

The amount of inventory recognized as an expense during Fiscal 2014 was $2,111.4 million (2013: $2,344.3 million), which includes $106.0 million (2013: $90.7 million) of inventory write-downs. These expenses are included in "Cost of goods and services sold" in the Consolidated Statements of Net (Loss) Earnings and Comprehensive (Loss) Income. Reversals of prior period inventory write-downs for Fiscal 2014 were $4.0 million (2013: $4.9 million).

Inventory is pledged as collateral under the Company's revolving credit facility (see Note 17).

Analysis

Objective 12

Explain how inventory analysis provides useful information and apply ratio analysis to inventory.

Financial ratios can be used to help management make decisions about how much and what types of inventory to carry and to help investors assess management's performance in terms of controlling inventory to maximize profits. Common ratios that are used to evaluate inventory levels are the inventory turnover and a related measure: average days to sell (or average age of) the inventory.

The **inventory turnover ratio** measures the number of times on average that the inventory was sold during the period. This ratio helps to measure the liquidity of the investment in inventory because the faster the turnover, the sooner the company generates cash inflows from this asset. A manager may use past turnover experience to determine how long the inventory now in stock will take to be sold. This ratio is calculated by dividing the cost of goods sold by the average inventory on hand during the period.

Average inventory can be calculated from the beginning and ending inventory balances.* For example, Sears Canada Inc. reported beginning inventory of $774.6 million, ending inventory of $641.4 million, and cost of goods sold of $2,308 million for its 2014 fiscal year. The calculation of Sears's 2014 inventory turnover is shown in Illustration 8-33.

Illustration 8-33
Inventory Turnover Ratio

FINANCIAL ANALYSIS AND PLANNING
5.1.1

$$\text{Inventory Turnover} = \frac{\text{Cost of Goods Sold}}{\text{Average Inventory}}$$

$$= \frac{\$2,308.0}{(\$641.4 + \$774.6) \div 2}$$

$$= 3.3 \text{ times}$$

A closely related ratio is the **average days to sell inventory**, which represents the average age of the inventory on hand or the number of days it takes to sell inventory after it is acquired. For example, if Sears's inventory turns over 3.3 times per year, that means it takes, on average, 365 days divided by 3.3 or approximately 111 days to sell its investment in inventory.

Is this a good turnover ratio? If the company sells fresh fruit and vegetables, you would know that this is not a good number. However, for other products, it is not as easy to come to a firm conclusion. For example, Sears sells a wide range of household goods and fashion items so you might expect that it would move its inventory out faster than only every three to four months. Each industry has its norms, however, so the industry average is one standard that the company's ratio can be compared against. Because the choice of inventory cost formula may affect the inventory reported on the statement of financial position and the cost of goods sold, these differences make adjustments necessary in any intercompany comparisons. This is true not only for turnover ratios but for any analysis that includes inventory: the amount of working capital, the working capital ratio, and the gross profit percentage, for example. Internally, company management compares these numbers with its goals and objectives for the year.

There is no absolute standard of comparison for most ratios, but generally speaking, companies that are able to keep their inventory at lower levels with higher turnovers than those of their competitors, and still satisfy customer needs, are the most successful.

IFRS/ASPE COMPARISON

A Comparison of IFRS and ASPE

Objective 13
Identify differences in accounting between IFRS and ASPE, and what changes are expected in the near future.

The *CPA Canada Handbook*, Part II, Section 3031 *Inventories* is converged with IAS 2 *Inventories*. Therefore, there are few differences in the recognition and measurement standards for most inventories. The most significant difference is that there is a separate international standard (IAS 41) covering biological assets and agricultural produce at the point of harvest, and these assets are not specifically covered by ASPE. Illustration 8-34 identifies the differences between IFRS and ASPE.

---

*Some seasonal variation is common in most companies. Fiscal year ends are usually chosen at a low activity point in the year's operations, which means that inventories in the annual financial statements are at their lowest levels in the year. Management can make adjustments to use the average monthly inventory level. External users, however, are limited to using the average between the opening and closing annual inventory balances. Public companies are required to issue quarterly reports, so external users can base the average on four inventory amounts through the year.

	IFRS—IAS 2, 11, 23, and 41	**Accounting Standards for Private Enterprises (ASPE)—*CPA Canada Handbook*, Part II, Sections 3031 and 3850**	**References to Illustrations and Select Brief Exercises**
Scope	IAS 41 provides standards for biological assets and agricultural produce at the point of harvest.	There is no primary source of GAAP covering biological assets and agricultural produce at the point of harvest.	Illustration 8-27 BE8-19, BE8-20 and BE8-21
Measurement	Asset retirement and decommissioning costs arising from production activities are added to the cost of the inventory.	Asset retirement and decommissioning costs arising from production activities are added to the carrying amount of the property, plant, and equipment asset.	Discussed in further detail in Chapter 10.
	Interest costs directly attributable to the acquisition, construction, or production of qualifying inventory are capitalized. Such costs may be expensed for inventory measured at fair value and for qualifying inventory produced in large quantities on a repetitive basis.	Companies may choose a policy of capitalizing interest or a policy of expensing the costs. No guidance is provided on what is a qualifying asset.	BE8-13
	A liability and loss are required to be recognized for onerous contracts if the unavoidable costs exceed the benefits from receiving the contracted goods or services.	No guidance is provided for onerous contractual obligations such as may occur with purchase commitments.	Illustration 8-3 and subsequent discussion.
	Biological assets and agricultural produce at the point of harvest are measured at fair value less costs to sell. At harvest, this becomes the inventory's deemed cost, and subsequently it is accounted for at the lower of cost and NRV unless it is accounted for at NRV in accordance with well-established practices in industry (and is therefore not covered by IAS 2). Bearer plants are accounted for under IAS 16. Once the biological assets are harvested from the bearer plants, the harvest becomes inventory and is accounted for as noted above (either under IAS 2 or at NRV).	No guidance is provided for measuring biological assets and agricultural produce prior to and at the point of harvest. After harvest, its carrying amount becomes the inventory's deemed cost, and subsequently it is accounted for at the lower of (the deemed) cost and net realizable value (NRV) unless it is accounted for at NRV in accordance with well-established practices in industry (and it is therefore not covered by Section 3031).	Illustration 8-27 BE8-19, BE8-20 and BE8-21
Presentation and disclosure	Additional disclosures are required, particularly about writedowns and any reversals as well as critical judgements and sources of estimation uncertainty. In addition, significant information is required about biological assets and agricultural produce.	Limited disclosures are required.	

Illustration 8-34

IFRS and ASPE Comparison Chart

Looking Ahead

No major changes were expected in the general inventory standards in the near future.

SUMMARY OF LEARNING OBJECTIVES

1 Understand inventory from a business perspective.

It is important to understand the nature of the various types of businesses that have significant inventory as well as the different types of inventory. Retailers, manufacturers, and wholesalers generally carry significant amounts of inventory. However, different companies have different business models. For example, some manufacturers follow a just-in-time strategy and carry very little inventory on hand. Only one inventory account, Merchandise Inventory, appears in the financial statements of a merchandising concern. A manufacturer normally has three inventory accounts: Raw Materials, Work in Process, and Finished Goods. There may also be an inventory account for factory or manufacturing supplies. Management must manage inventory levels in order to ensure sufficient choice and quantities to meet customer needs yet keep costs to a minimum. The financial statements need to provide information about all of this.

2 Define inventory from an accounting perspective.

Differing companies have different types of inventories including such things as securities, land for development, work in progress, and grain. For accounting purposes, inventory is defined as an asset that is held for sale in the ordinary course of business or for the production of such inventory (including raw materials, work in process, and supplies). Special guidance and/or industry practice exists for inventories of financial instruments, biological assets, agricultural products, mineral products, inventories held by producers of agricultural and forest products, and inventories held by commodity broker-traders.

3 Identify which inventory items should be included in ending inventory.

Inventory is included on the statement of financial position of the entity that has substantially all of the risks and rewards of ownership, which is generally the company that has possession and legal title to the goods. Professional judgement must be used to determine whether substantially all of the risks and rewards have passed. For instance, consigned goods remain the property of the consignor. Purchase commitments are generally not recognized unless onerous.

4 Identify the effects of inventory errors on the financial statements and adjust for them.

If the ending inventory is misstated, (1) the inventory, retained earnings, working capital, and current ratio in the statement of financial position will be incorrect; and (2) the cost of goods sold and net income in the income statement will be incorrect. If purchases and inventory are misstated, (1) the inventory, accounts payable, and current ratio will be incorrect; and (2) purchases and ending inventory will be incorrect.

5 Determine the components of inventory cost.

Inventory costs include all costs of purchase, conversion, and other costs incurred in bringing the inventories to the present location and condition necessary for sale. Such charges include freight charges on goods purchased, other direct costs of acquisition, and labour and other direct production costs incurred in processing the goods up to the time of sale. Manufacturing overhead costs are allocated to inventory based on the normal capacity of the production facilities. Interest and asset retirement costs may be included as part of the cost of inventory in some circumstances.

6 Distinguish between perpetual and periodic inventory systems and account for them.

Under a perpetual inventory system, a continuous record of changes in inventory is maintained in the Inventory account. That is, all purchases into and transfers of goods out of the account are recorded directly in the Inventory account as they occur. No such record is kept under a periodic inventory system. Under the periodic system, year-end inventory is determined by a physical count, and the amount of ending inventory and cost of goods sold is based on this count. Even under the perpetual system, an annual count is needed to test the accuracy of the records.

7 Identify and apply GAAP cost formula options and indicate when each cost formula is appropriate.

The specific identification method is used to assign costs for items of inventory that are not ordinarily interchangeable or that are produced for specific projects. The weighted-average or first-in, first-out cost formula is used to assign costs to other types of inventory. All inventory items that have a similar nature and use to the entity apply the same cost formula.

8 Explain why inventory is measured at the lower of cost and net realizable value, and apply the lower of cost and net realizable value standard.

Current assets should not be reported on the statement of financial position at a higher amount than the net cash that is expected to be generated from their use or sale. When this amount is less than "cost," inventory is written down and the loss in value is recognized in the same period as the decline. Net realizable value is the estimated selling price in the ordinary course of business reduced by the expected costs to complete and sell the goods. Ordinarily, each item's cost and NRV are compared and the lower value is chosen. However, items that are related to each other and have similar purposes, that are produced and marketed in the same geographical area, and that cannot be evaluated separately from other items may be grouped and the lower of the group's cost and net realizable value is chosen.

9 Identify inventories that are or may be valued at amounts other than the lower of cost and net realizable value.

Inventories of financial instruments, biological assets related to agricultural activity, agricultural produce at the point of harvest and after harvest, inventories held by producers of agricultural and forest products, mineral products, and inventories of commodity broker-traders all may be accounted for at other than the lower of cost and net realizable value.

10 Apply the gross profit method of estimating inventory.

Ending inventory is determined by deducting an estimate of cost of goods sold from the actual cost of goods available for sale. Cost of goods sold is estimated by multiplying net sales by the percentage of cost of goods sold to sales. This percentage is derived from the gross profit percent: 100% − gross profit percentage = cost of goods sold percentage.

11 Identify how inventory should be presented and the type of inventory disclosures required by IFRS and ASPE.

ASPE requires disclosure of how cost is determined, inventory that is pledged as security, the amount charged to the income statement as expense in the period, and the inventories' carrying value by category. Additional information is required by IFRS, including details about inventory impairment writedowns and any recoveries, the circumstances responsible for these, and the carrying amounts and reconciliations of items measured at NRV or fair value. Biological assets must be presented separately on the statement of financial position under IFRS. In general, cost of sales is presented on the income statement under both IFRS and ASPE unless expenses are grouped by nature.

12 Explain how inventory analysis provides useful information and apply ratio analysis to inventory.

Common ratios that are used in the management and evaluation of inventory levels are the inventory turnover and a related measure, average days to sell the inventory, often called the average age of inventory. This is useful information because excessive investment in inventory is expensive to carry, yet too little inventory results in lost sales and dissatisfied customers.

13 Identify differences in accounting between IFRS and ASPE, and what changes are expected in the near future.

IFRS and ASPE are substantially harmonized. IFRS has specific guidance on the measurement of biological assets, the capitalization of borrowing costs on qualifying assets, and onerous contracts. Asset retirement obligations may be treated differently under IFRS. No major changes are expected in the near future.

KEY TERMS

allowance method, p. 437
asset retirement costs, p. 424
average days to sell inventory, p. 446
basket purchase, p. 425
consigned goods, p. 414
conversion costs, p. 424
cost formula, p. 429
cost of goods available for sale
    or use, p. 411
cost of goods manufactured, p. 417
cost of goods sold, p. 412
current ratio, p. 421
cut-off schedule, p. 414
direct method, p. 436
executory contract, p. 416
finished goods inventory, p. 410
first-in, first-out (FIFO) cost formula,
    p. 432
f.o.b. (free on board) destination,
    p. 414

f.o.b. (free on board) shipping point,
    p. 414
gross method, p. 422
gross profit method, p. 442
gross profit percentage, p. 443
indirect method, p. 437
inventories, p. 413
inventory turnover ratio, p. 446
joint cost, p. 425
last-in, first-out (LIFO) cost formula,
    p. 433
lower of cost and market, p. 434
lower of cost and net realizable value,
    p. 434
lower of cost and net realizable value
    (LC&NRV) standard, p. 435
market, p. 434
markup on cost, p. 443
merchandise inventory, p. 410
moving-average cost formula, p. 430

net method, p. 422
net realizable value (NRV), p. 434
normal production capacity, p. 424
onerous contract, p. 416
period costs, p. 425
periodic inventory system, p. 427
perpetual inventory system, p. 426
price risk, p. 415
product costs, p. 424
purchase commitments, p. 416
purchase discounts, p. 422
quantities only system, p. 428
raw materials inventory, p. 410
relative sales value method, p. 425
specific identification, p. 429
standard cost system, p. 424
vendor rebate, p. 422
weighted average cost formula, p. 430
work-in-process inventory, p. 410

APPENDIX 8A

THE RETAIL INVENTORY METHOD OF ESTIMATING INVENTORY COST

Objective 14
Apply the retail method of estimating inventory.

Accounting for inventory in a retail operation presents several challenges. Some retailers can use the specific identification method to value their inventories. As explained in the chapter, this approach makes sense when individual inventory units are significant, such as automobiles, pianos, or fur coats. However, imagine attempting to use such an approach at Hudson's Bay or Sears—high-volume retailers that have many different types of merchandise at relatively low unit costs! It would be difficult to determine the cost of each sale, to enter cost codes on the tickets, to change the codes to reflect declines in value of the merchandise, to allocate costs such as transportation, and so on. An alternative is to estimate inventory cost when necessary by taking a physical inventory at retail prices. Also, to avoid misstating the inventory, especially in retail operations where losses due to shoplifting and breakage are common, periodic inventory counts are made at retail prices and are then converted to cost. Differences between the records and the physical count require an adjustment to make the records agree with the count.

In most retail businesses, there is an observable pattern between cost and selling prices. Retail prices can be converted to cost simply by multiplying them by the cost-to-retail ratio. This method, called the **retail inventory method**, **requires that the following information be available**:

1. **the total cost and retail value of the goods purchased,**
2. **the total cost and retail value of the goods available for sale, and**
3. **the sales for the period.**

REAL WORLD EMPHASIS

Here is how it works. The sales for the period are deducted from the retail value of the goods available for sale. The result is an estimate of the ending inventory at retail (selling prices). The ratio of cost to retail for all goods is calculated by dividing the total goods available for sale at cost by the total goods available for sale at retail. The ending inventory valued at selling prices is then converted to the ending inventory at cost by applying the **cost-to-retail ratio**. Use of the retail inventory method is very common. For example, the **North West Company Inc.**, a retailer with its roots in Northern and Western Canada, reports using the retail inventory method in determining inventory cost. North West Company's note disclosure of its policy for the year ended January 31, 2015 is shown in Illustration 8A-1.

Illustration 8A-1

Example of Retail Inventory Method Note—North West Company Inc.

(D) Inventories Inventories are valued at the lower of cost and net realizable value. The cost of warehouse inventories is determined using the weighted-average cost method. The cost of retail inventories is determined primarily using the retail method of accounting for general merchandise inventories and the cost method of accounting for food inventories on a first-in, first-out basis. Cost includes the cost to purchase goods net of vendor allowances plus other costs incurred in bringing inventories to their present location and condition. Net realizable value is estimated based on the amount at which inventories are expected to be sold, taking into consideration fluctuations in retail prices due to obsolescence, damage or seasonality.

Inventories are written down to net realizable value if net realizable value declines below carrying amount. When circumstances that previously caused inventories to be written down below cost no longer exist or when there is clear evidence of an increase in selling price, the amount of the write-down previously recorded is reversed.

An example of how the retail inventory method works is shown in Illustration 8A-2.

	Cost	Retail
Beginning inventory	$14,000	$ 20,000
Purchases	63,000	90,000
Goods available for sale	$77,000	110,000
Deduct: Sales		85,000
Ending inventory, at retail		$ 25,000
Ratio of cost to retail ($77,000 ÷ $110,000)		70%
Ending inventory at cost (70% of $25,000)		$ 17,500

The retail method is approved by various retail associations and the accounting profession under both ASPE and IFRS. It is also allowed by the Canada Revenue Agency. **One advantage of the retail inventory method is that the inventory balance can be approximated without a physical count.** This makes the method particularly useful when preparing interim reports. Insurance adjusters use this approach to estimate losses from fire, flood, or other types of casualty.

This method also **acts as a control device** because any deviations from a physical count at year end have to be explained. In addition, the retail method **speeds up the physical inventory count at year end.** The crew taking the inventory only needs to record the retail price of each item, which is often done using a scanner. There is no need to determine each item's invoice cost, thus saving time and expense.

Retail Method Terminology

The amounts shown in the Retail column of Illustration 8A-2 represent the original retail or selling prices (cost plus an original markup or mark-on), assuming no price changes.

Sales prices, however, are often marked up or down from the original sales price. For retailers, the term **markup** means an increase in the price above the original sales price. **Markup cancellations** are decreases in merchandise prices that had been marked up above the original retail price. Markup cancellations cannot be greater than markups. **Net markups** refer to markups less markup cancellations.

Markdowns are reductions in price below the original selling price. They are a common phenomenon and occur because of a decline in general price levels, special sales, soiled or damaged goods, overstocking, and competition. **Markdown cancellations** occur when the markdowns are later offset by increases in the prices of goods that had been marked down, such as after a one-day sale. A markdown cancellation cannot exceed the original markdown. Markdowns less markdown cancellations are known as **net markdowns.**

To illustrate these different concepts, assume that Designer Clothing Store recently purchased 100 dress shirts from a supplier. The cost for these shirts was $1,500, or $15 a shirt. Designer Clothing established the selling price on these shirts at $30 each. The manager noted that the shirts were selling quickly, so she added $5 to the price of each shirt. This markup made the price too high for customers and sales lagged. The manager then responded by reducing the price to $32. To this point, there has been a **markup of $5** and a **markup cancellation of $3** on the original selling price of a shirt. When the major marketing season ended, the manager set the price of the remaining shirts at $23. This price change constitutes a **markup cancellation of $2** and a **$7 markdown.** If the shirts are later priced at $24, a **markdown cancellation of $1** occurs.

Retail Inventory Method with Markups and Markdowns—Conventional Method

To determine the ending inventory figures, a decision must be made on the treatment of markups, markup cancellations, markdowns, and markdown cancellations **when calculating the ratio of cost to retail.**

To illustrate the different possibilities, consider the data for In-Fashion Stores Inc., shown in Illustration 8A-3. In-Fashion's ending inventory at cost can be calculated under two different cost-to-retail ratios.

Ratio A: Reflects a cost percentage that includes net markups but excludes net markdowns.

Ratio B: Reflects a cost ratio that incorporates both net markups and net markdowns.

Illustration 8A-3

Retail Inventory Method with Markups and Markdowns— In-Fashion Stores Inc.

Information in Records

	Cost	Retail
Beginning inventory	$ 500	$ 1,000
Purchases (net)	20,000	35,000
Markups		3,000
Markup cancellations		1,000
Markdowns		2,500
Markdown cancellations		2,000
Sales (net)		25,000

Retail Inventory Method

	Cost		Retail
Beginning inventory	$ 500		$ 1,000
Purchases (net)	20,000		35,000
Merchandise available for sale	20,500		36,000
Add:			
Markups		$ 3,000	
Less: Markup cancellations		(1,000)	
Net markups			2,000
	20,500		38,000

Cost-to-retail ratio $\dfrac{\$20,500}{\$38,000} = 53.9\%$ ———————————————————————— (A)

	Cost		Retail
Deduct:			
Markdowns		2,500	
Less: Markdown cancellations		(2,000)	
Net markdowns			500
	$20,500		37,500

Cost-to-retail ratio $\dfrac{\$20,500}{\$37,500} = 54.7\%$ ———————————————————————— (B)

			Retail
Deduct: Sales (net)			25,000
Ending inventory at retail			$12,500

The calculations to determine the cost of ending inventory for In-Fashion Stores are therefore:

> Ending inventory at retail × Cost ratio = Ending inventory, at cost
> Under **(A)**: $12,500 × 53.9% = $6,737.50
> Under **(B)**: $12,500 × 54.7% = $6,837.50

Which percentage should be used to calculate ending inventory? The answer depends on whether you are trying to determine inventory "cost" or a more conservative lower of cost and market figure.

The **conventional retail inventory method** uses the cost-to-retail ratio **that includes net markups but excludes net markdowns,** as shown in the calculation of ratio A.

It is designed to approximate **the lower of average cost and market**, with market being defined **as net realizable value less a normal profit margin.** To understand why net markups but not net markdowns are included in the cost-to-retail ratio, we must understand how a retail outlet operates. When a company has a net markup on an item, this normally indicates that the item's market value has increased. On the other hand, if the item has a net markdown, this means that the item's utility has declined. Therefore, to approximate the lower of cost and market, net markdowns are considered a current loss and are not included in calculating the cost-to-retail ratio. **This makes the denominator a larger number and the ratio a lower percentage.** With a lower cost-to-retail ratio, the result approximates a lower of cost and market amount.

To make this clearer, assume two different items were purchased for $5 each, and the original sales price was established at $10 each. One item was then marked down to a selling price of $2. Assuming no sales for the period, if markdowns are included in the cost-to-retail ratio (**ratio B** above), the ending inventory is calculated as shown in Illustration 8A-4.

Illustration 8A-4			

Retail Inventory Method Including Markdowns— Cost Method

Markdowns Included in Cost-to-Retail Ratio

	Cost	Retail
Purchases	$10.00	$20.00
Deduct: Markdowns		8.00
Ending inventory, at retail		$12.00
Cost-to-retail ratio $\dfrac{\$10.00}{\$12.00} = 83.3\%$		
Ending inventory at average cost ($12.00 × .833) =		$10.00

This approach results in ending inventory at the average cost of the two items on hand without considering the loss on the one item.

If markdowns are excluded from the ratio (**ratio A** above), the result is ending inventory at the lower of average cost and market. The calculation is shown in Illustration 8A-5.

Illustration 8A-5			

Retail Inventory Method Excluding Markdowns— Conventional Method (LCM)

Markdowns Not Included in Cost-to-Retail Ratio

	Cost	Retail
Purchases	$10.00	$20.00
Cost-to-retail ratio $\dfrac{\$10.00}{\$20.00} = 50\%$		
Deduct: Markdowns		8.00
Ending inventory, at retail		$12.00
Ending inventory at lower of average cost and market ($12 × .50) =		$6.00

The $6 inventory valuation includes two inventory items: one inventoried at $5 (its cost) and the other at $1 (its NRV less a normal profit margin of 50%). For the item with the market decline, the price was reduced from $10 to $2 and the cost was reduced from $5 to $1. Therefore, to approximate the lower of average cost and market, the cost-to-retail ratio is established by dividing the cost of goods available by the sum of the original retail price of these goods plus the net markups; the **net markdowns are excluded** from the ratio.

Many possible cost-to-retail ratios could be calculated. The schedule below summarizes how including or excluding various items in the cost-to-retail ratio relates to specific inventory valuation methods. Note that net purchases are always included in the ratio:

Beginning Inventory	Net Markups	Net Markdowns	Inventory Cost Formula and Valuation Method Approximated
Include	Include	Include	Average cost
Include	Include	Exclude	Lower of average cost and market (conventional method)
Exclude	Include	Include	FIFO cost
Exclude	Include	Exclude	Lower of FIFO cost and market

Using the FIFO cost formula, the estimated ending inventory (and its cost) will, by definition, come from the purchases of the current period. **Therefore, the opening inventory, at cost and retail, is excluded in determining the cost ratio.** The retail price of the opening inventory is then added to determine the total selling price of goods available for the period.

CPA Canada Handbook, Part II, Section 3031 and IAS 2 are clear that, for purposes of determining inventory **cost**, markdowns below the original sales price are included in calculating the ratio. This means that a separate adjustment has to be made to get a **lower of cost and NRV** valuation. Why not just exclude the markdowns from the cost-to-retail ratio? As mentioned above, this results in a lower of cost and market value where market represents NRV less a normal profit margin. This concept of market is not permitted by either ASPE or IFRS.

Special Items

The retail inventory method becomes more complicated when such items as freight-in, purchase returns and allowances, and purchase discounts are involved. In the retail method, we treat such items as follows:

- **Freight costs** are treated as a part of the purchase cost.

- **Purchase returns** are ordinarily considered a reduction of the cost price and retail price.

- **Purchase allowances** are considered a reduction of the purchase cost column only unless normal selling prices are adjusted because of the allowance.

- **Purchase discounts** are usually considered a reduction of the purchase cost only.

In short, the treatment for the items affecting the cost column of the retail inventory approach follows the calculation of cost of goods available for sale.

Note also that it is considered proper to treat **sales returns and allowances** as adjustments to gross sales. **Sales discounts to customers**, however, are not recognized when sales are recorded gross. If the Sales Discount account were adjusted in such a situation, the ending inventory figure at retail would be overvalued.

In addition, a number of special items require careful analysis.

- **Transfers-in** from another department are reported in the same way as purchases from an outside enterprise.

- **Normal shortages** (breakage, damage, theft, shrinkage) are deducted in the retail column because these goods are no longer available for sale. These costs are reflected in the selling price because a certain amount of shortage is considered normal in a retail enterprise. As a result, this amount is not considered in calculating the cost-to-retail percentage. Rather, it is shown as a deduction, similar to sales, to arrive at ending inventory at retail.

- **Abnormal shortages** are deducted from both the cost and retail columns before calculating the cost-to-retail ratio and are reported as a special inventory amount or as a loss. To do otherwise distorts the cost-to-retail ratio and overstates ending inventory.

- **Employee discounts** (given to employees to encourage loyalty, better performance, and so on) are deducted from the retail column in the same way as sales. These discounts should not be considered in the cost-to-retail percentage because they do not reflect an overall change in the selling price.

Illustration 8A-6 shows some of these concepts in more detail, using the conventional retail inventory method to determine the ending inventory at the lower of average cost and market.

Illustration 8A-6

Conventional Retail Inventory Method—Special Items Included

	Cost	Retail
Beginning inventory	$ 1,000	$ 1,800
Purchases	30,000	60,000
Freight-in	600	–0–
Purchase returns	(1,500)	(3,000)
Totals	30,100	58,800
Net markups		9,000
Abnormal shrinkage	(1,200)	(2,000)
Totals	$28,900	65,800
Deduct:		
Net markdowns		1,400
Sales	$36,000	
Sales returns	(900)	35,100
Employee discounts		800
Normal shrinkage		1,300
Ending inventory at retail		$27,200

Cost-to-retail ratio $\dfrac{\$28,900}{\$65,800} = 43.9\%$

Ending inventory, lower of average cost and market (43.9% × $27,200) = $11,940.80

Evaluation of Retail Inventory Method

The retail inventory method of calculating inventory is used for these reasons:

1. To permit the calculation of net income without a physical count of inventory

2. As a control measure in determining inventory shortages

3. To control quantities of merchandise on hand

4. As a source of information for insurance and tax purposes

One characteristic of the retail inventory method is that it **has an averaging effect for varying rates of gross profit**. When it is used in a business where rates of gross profit vary among departments, the method should be refined by calculating inventory separately by departments or by classes of merchandise with similar rates of gross profit. This method's reliability rests on the assumption that the mix of inventory items is similar to the mix in the total goods available for sale.

SUMMARY OF LEARNING OBJECTIVE FOR APPENDIX 8A

14 Apply the retail method of estimating inventory.

The retail inventory method is based on converting the retail price of ending inventory by a cost-to-retail percentage, which is derived from information in the accounting and supplementary records. To use this method, records must be kept of the costs and retail prices for beginning inventory, net purchases, and abnormal spoilage, as well as the retail amount of net markups, net markdowns, and net sales. Which items go into the numerator and denominator of the cost-to-retail ratio depends on the type of inventory valuation estimate that is wanted.

KEY TERMS

conventional retail inventory method, p. 452

cost-to-retail ratio, p. 450

markdown, p. 451

markdown cancellations, p. 451

markup, p. 451

markup cancellations, p. 451

net markdowns, p. 451

net markups, p. 451

retail inventory method, p. 450

APPENDIX 8B

ACCOUNTING GUIDANCE FOR SPECIFIC INVENTORY

Objective 15

Identify other primary sources of GAAP for inventory.

Illustration 8B-1 summarizes the primary sources of GAAP for most types of inventory.

Illustration 8B-1

Inventory—Primary Sources of GAAP

Form of Inventory	ASPE Source of Guidance	IFRS Source of Guidance
Most inventories apply a lower of cost and net realizable value model	*CPA Canada Handbook–Accounting*, Part II, Section 3031 *Inventories*	IAS 2 *Inventories*
Excluded from Section 3031 and IAS 2 but Covered by Other Primary Sources of GAAP		
Financial instruments	*CPA Canada Handbook–Accounting*, Part II, Section 3856 *Financial Instruments*	IAS 32 *Financial Instruments: Presentation*, and IFRS 9 *Financial Instruments*
Biological assets related to agricultural activity, and agricultural produce at the point of harvest	See below	IAS 41 *Agriculture*
Industry-Specific Exclusions, from Only the Measurement Provisions of Section 3031 and IAS 2 (disclosure requirements still apply)		
Inventory held by producers of agricultural and forest products, agricultural produce after harvest, and minerals and mineral products	Excluded from the measurement provisions of Section 3031 if measured at net realizable value in accordance with established industry practice; otherwise, apply Section 3031	Excluded from the measurement provisions of IAS 2 if measured at net realizable value in accordance with established industry practice; otherwise, apply IAS 2
Inventory held by commodity broker-traders	Excluded from the measurement provisions of Section 3031 if measured at fair value less costs to sell; otherwise, apply Section 3031	Excluded from the measurement provisions of IAS 2 if measured at fair value less costs to sell; otherwise, apply IAS 2
Biological assets and harvested agricultural produce	Excluded from the measurement provisions of Section 3031. Not covered by any specific primary source of GAAP.	See above

Note: All assignment material with an asterisk (*) relates to the appendices to the chapter.

Completion of this end-of-chapter material will help develop CPA enabling competencies (such as ethics and professionalism, problem-solving and decision-making and communication) and technical competencies. We have highlighted selected items with an integration icon and material in *WileyPLUS* has been linked to the competencies. All cases emphasize integration, especially of the enabling competencies. The brief exercises, exercises and problems generally emphasize problem-solving and decision-making.

Brief Exercises

(LO 1) BE8-1 **Walmart** uses a just-in-time inventory system to reduce its costs, allowing it to sell goods to its customers at lower prices. What are the benefits of a good inventory management system? What are the risks associated with a very tight inventory control system? How does a good just-in-time inventory system impact key ratios?

(LO 1, 13) BE8-2 Indicate whether the following would be considered inventory for a public company like **Ford Motor Corporation**. If so, indicate the inventory category to which that item would belong.

MANAGEMENT CONTROL

    (a) Engines purchased to make the Ford F-150

    (b) Nuts and bolts purchased to attach the engine to the car body

    (c) Spare parts purchased for the manufacturing equipment

    (d) Standby equipment in case a machine breaks down

    (e) Wages paid to assembly-line employees

    (f) Rent for a manufacturing facility

    (g) Wages paid to a supervisor

    (h) Ford F-150 ready to be shipped to the dealer

    (i) Manufacturing plant

How would your responses change if the manufacturer followed ASPE?

(LO 2) BE8-3 Betadyne Corp. is a public company that manufactures and sells medical equipment. What kind of information would be useful for users of the company's financial statements?

(LO 2) BE8-4 Highfliers Inc. is a public company that purchases airplanes for sale to others. However, until the airplanes are sold, the company charters and services them. What is the proper way to report these airplanes in the company's financial statements?

(LO 2) BE8-5 Which of the following would be included in inventory? For any amount not included in inventory, explain where the amount would be recorded.

    (a) Raw materials costs of leather to a manufacturer of leather furniture

    (b) The cost of cans of corn held on the shelves of a grocery store

    (c) The cost of a truck in the process of being manufactured by an automobile manufacturer

    (d) The cost of land being held for development to a property developer

    (e) The cost of a van being used as a courtesy vehicle to an automobile service centre

    (f) The costs of construction for a home being built for a specific customer to a builder

    (g) The cost of soap and paper towels for the washrooms of a restaurant

(LO 3) BE8-6 Saving Energy Inc. is a company that wants to buy coal deposits but does not want the financing for the purchase to be reported on its financial statements. The company therefore establishes a trust to acquire the coal deposits. The company agrees to buy the coal over a certain period of time at specified prices. The trust is able to finance the coal purchase and then pay off the loan when it is paid by the company for the minerals. How should this transaction be reported?

(LO 3) BE8-7 Able Limited is a company that is involved in the wholesaling and retailing of automobile tires for foreign cars. Most of the inventory is imported, and it is valued on the company's records at the actual inventory cost plus freight-in.

    (a) At year end, the warehousing costs are pro-rated over cost of goods sold and ending inventory. Are warehousing costs considered a product cost or a period cost?

    (b) A certain portion of Able Limited's inventory consists of obsolete items. Should obsolete items that are not currently consumed in the production of goods or services to be available for sale be classified as part of inventory?

(LO 3) BE8-8 Tansley Ltd. took a physical inventory count on December 31 and determined that goods costing $4,000 were on hand. This amount included $1,000 of goods held on consignment for Woods Corporation. Not included in the physical count were $800 of goods purchased from Timmons Corporation, f.o.b. shipping point, and $400 of goods sold to Myers Ltd. for $600, f.o.b. destination. Both the Timmons purchase and the Myers sale were in transit at year end. What amount should Tansley report as its December 31 inventory?

(LO 3, 6) BE8-9   Global Ltd. had beginning inventory of 50 units that cost $100 each. During September, the company purchased 200 units on account at $100 each, returned 6 units for credit, and sold 150 units at $200 each.

(a) Journalize the September transactions, assuming that Global Ltd. uses a perpetual inventory system.

(b) Journalize the September transactions, assuming that Global Ltd. uses a periodic inventory system.

(c) Assume that Global Ltd. uses a periodic system and prepares financial statements at the end of each month. An inventory count determines that there are 94 units of inventory remaining at September 30. Prepare the necessary adjusting entry at September 30.

(LO 3, 5, 13) BE8-10   Best Corp., a public company using IFRS, signed a long-term non-cancellable purchase commitment with a major supplier to purchase raw materials at an annual cost of $1 million. At December 31, 2016, the raw materials to be purchased in 2017 have a market price of $950,000.

(a) Prepare any necessary December 31, 2016 entry.

(b) In 2017, Best receives the raw materials and pays the required $1 million. The raw materials now have a market value of $920,000. Prepare the entry to record the purchase.

(c) Explain how the accounting treatment under (a) compares with the accounting treatment for private companies under ASPE.

(LO 4) BE8-11   Angus Enterprises Ltd. reported cost of goods sold for 2017 of $2.5 million and retained earnings of $4.0 million at December 31, 2017. Angus later discovered that its ending inventories at December 31, 2016 and 2017, were overstated by $150,000 and $50,000, respectively. Determine the correct amounts for 2017 cost of goods sold and December 31, 2017 retained earnings.

(LO 5) BE8-12   Gamers' World buys 1,000 computer game CDs from a distributor that is discontinuing those games. The purchase price for the lot is $7,500. Gamers' World will group the CDs into three price categories for resale, as follows:

Group	Number of CDs	Price per CD
1	100	$ 5
2	800	10
3	100	15

Determine the cost per CD for each group, using the relative sales value method.

(LO 5) BE8-13   Sunny Valley Limited produces wine. Certain vintage wines take more than one year to age. The company has borrowed funds to cover the costs of this aging process. The company meets the interest capitalization criteria under IFRS. Capitalizable interest under IFRS is $1,000.

(a) Prepare the journal entry to record the $1,000 interest under IFRS.

(b) Show the possible journal entries under ASPE.

(c) Discuss the accounting treatment under IFRS for the grapevines used to grow grapes that are eventually used for wine production.

(d) Discuss the accounting treatment under ASPE for the grapevines used to grow grapes that are eventually used for wine production.

(LO 5) BE8-14   Doors Unlimited Ltd. purchases units of wood frames that have manufacturer's rebates from Traders Inc. The rebate requires Doors Unlimited to purchase a minimum number of units in a calendar year. The initial unit cost of each wood frame is $2.50 before any rebate. If more than 3,500 units are purchased, the rebate is $0.25 per unit for all units purchased beyond the base amount of 3,500 units. Doors Unlimited Ltd. has a June 30 fiscal year end. By June 30, 2017, Doors Unlimited had purchased 3,000 wood frames for the six-month period from January 1, 2017, to June 30, 2017. Doors Unlimited estimates that an additional 3,000 wood frames will be purchased from July 1, 2017, to December 31, 2017. Doors Unlimited's management is very confident that this estimate will be confirmed by future purchases from Traders.

(a) Explain the conceptual principles involved in determining if an accrual should be made for the volume rebate from Traders. Under what circumstances would an accrual not be permissible?

(b) Calculate the amount of any rebate that Doors Unlimited should accrue at June 30, 2017, assuming the rebate cannot be cancelled by Traders.

(c) Calculate the unit cost that Doors Unlimited should use in the costing of wood frames, using the perpetual inventory system. (Round to four decimal places.)

(LO 6, 7) BE8-15   Canali Corporation uses a perpetual inventory system. On November 19, the company sold 600 units. The following additional information is available:

	Units	Unit Cost	Total Cost
Nov. 1 inventory	250	$12	$ 3,000
Nov. 15 purchase	400	14	5,600
Nov. 23 purchase	350	15	5,250
	1,000		$13,850

Calculate the November 30 inventory and the November cost of goods sold, using

(a) the moving-average cost formula, and

(b) the FIFO cost formula.

(LO 6, 8) **BE8-16** Bluebell Enterprises Ltd.'s records reported an inventory cost of $55,600 and a net realizable value of $54,000 at December 31, 2015. At December 31, 2016, the records indicated a cost of $68,700 and a net realizable value of $61,625. All opening inventory had been sold during the year.

(a) Assuming that Bluebell Enterprises uses a perpetual inventory system, prepare the necessary December 31, 2016 entry under (1) the direct method and (2) the indirect method.

(b) Assume that at December 31, 2017, the records indicate inventory with a cost of $60,000 and a net realizable value of $60,900. Prepare the necessary December 31, 2017 entry under (1) the direct method and (2) the indirect method. Explain why a "gain" is reported under the indirect method of accounting.

(LO 7) **BE8-17** More & More Limited uses a periodic inventory system. On June 24, the company sold 600 units. The following additional information is available:

	Units	Unit Cost	Total Cost
June 1 inventory	200	$12	$ 2,400
June 15 purchase	400	14	5,600
June 23 purchase	400	15	6,000
	1,000		$14,000

(a) Calculate the June 30 inventory and the June cost of goods sold, using the weighted average cost formula.

(b) Calculate the June 30 inventory and the June cost of goods sold, using the FIFO formula.

(c) Assume that 200 units sold on June 24 had a unit cost of $12; 300 had a unit cost of $14; and the remaining 100 units had a unit cost of $15. Calculate the June 30 inventory and the June cost of goods sold, using the specific identification method.

(LO 8, 13) **BE8-18** Antimatter Corporation has the following four items in its ending inventory:

Item	Cost	Estimated Selling Price	Estimated Disposal Costs
Neutrinos	$1,820	$2,100	$100
Ocillinos	5,000	4,900	100
Electrons	4,290	4,625	200
Protons	3,200	4,210	100

(a) Assume that Antimatter is a public company using IFRS. Determine the total value of ending inventory, using the lower of cost and net realizable value model applied on an individual item basis.

(b) Would there be any difference in accounting if Antimatter were a private entity using ASPE?

(LO 9) **BE8-19** Consider a large dairy farming company that reports under IFRS. Beyond manufacturing, farm property, and equipment, the farm's main assets are the dairy cows and the milk that they produce. Describe how these assets may be presented on the financial statements. Additionally, discuss the accounting treatments of the following events:

(a) A new dairy cow is bought by the farm

(b) A cow owned by the farm loses its ability to produce milk

How would this differ if the farm reported under ASPE? Comment on which standard you believe provides better presentation of the assets, and why.

(LO 9, 13) **BE8-20** Farmer Brown Industries Inc. is in the business of producing organic foods for sale to restaurants and in local markets. The company uses IFRS and has a June 30 fiscal year end.

As an experiment, the company has decided to attempt raising organic free-range chickens. On May 1, 2017, Farmer Brown purchased 100 new hatchlings for cash at a total cost of $1,000. The company incurred feed and labour costs of $150 per month to look after the chicks. Their (acceptable) accounting policy is to capitalize these costs.

On June 30, the company estimated that the chickens would mature in mid-October. At year end they had a fair value of $1,800 and the company would have to transport the chickens to their customers at an average cost of $3 per chicken.

On October 30, all 100 chickens had matured and the company sold and shipped 50 of the chickens to one of its key customers for $30 per chicken. Transportation costs were $3 per chicken, as expected.

(a) Prepare the journal entries to record the inventory activity relating to the chickens for the month of May.

(b) Prepare the journal entries to record the inventory activity relating to the chickens for the month of June, including any year-end adjustments required under IAS 41.

(c) How would the result be different if the company used ASPE?

(LO 9, 13) BE8-21

(a) Briefly explain the criteria that have to be met for inventory to be recorded at an amount greater than cost.

(b) Briefly explain the accounting for the following inventory items under ASPE:

1. Sheep

2. Wool

3. Carpet

(c) Briefly explain the accounting for the items in (b) under IFRS.

(d) Briefly explain the treatment of a bearer plant under IFRS.

(LO 10) BE8-22 Oil Tankers Inc.'s April 30 inventory was destroyed by the explosion of an underground oil tank. January 1 inventory was $250,000 and purchases for January through April totalled $620,000. Sales for the same period were $1 million. Oil Tankers' normal gross profit percentage is 30%. Using the gross profit method, estimate the amount of Oil Tankers' April 30 inventory that was destroyed.

(LO 10, 13) BE8-23 Loza Corp. purchases inventory costing $4,000 on July 11 on terms 3/10, n/30, and pays the invoice in full on July 15.

(a) Prepare the required entries to record the two transactions, assuming Loza uses (1) the gross method of recording purchases, and (2) the net method of recording purchases. Assume the periodic method is used.

(b) Journalize the two transactions under (1) the gross method and (2) the net method, assuming the invoice was paid on July 31 instead of July 15.

(c) Assuming that Loza is a private company reporting under ASPE, can interest costs incurred to finance inventory be added to the cost of the inventory?

(d) Assuming that Loza is a public company following IFRS, under what circumstances can interest costs incurred to finance inventory be added to the cost of the inventory?

(LO 11) BE8-24 IFRS requires greater disclosure for inventory than ASPE. List the additional requirements and explain what benefit each one might provide for the users of the financial statements. List some items that would specifically contribute to estimation uncertainty as it relates to inventory and how this would impact disclosure requirements.

(LO 12) BE8-25 Delicious Foods Inc. reported inventory of $5,706 million at the end of its 2017 fiscal year and $5,310 million at the end of its 2016 fiscal year. It reported cost of goods sold of $35,350 million for the fiscal year 2017 and net sales of $54,365 million for fiscal year 2017. Calculate the company's inventory turnover and the average days to sell inventory for the fiscal year 2017.

(LO 14) *BE8-26 Lang Inc. had beginning inventory of $22,000 at cost and $30,000 at retail. Net purchases were $157,500 at cost and $215,000 at retail. Net markups were $10,000, net markdowns were $7,000, and sales were $184,500. Calculate the ending inventory at cost using the conventional retail method. Round the cost-to-retail percentage to one decimal place.

(LO 15) *BE8-27 What are the primary sources of GAAP relating to inventory

(a) under IFRS?

(b) under ASPE?

(LO 15) *BE8-28 There are many forms of inventory that are not covered under the basic accounting standards for inventory: *CPA Handbook*, Part II, Section 3031 (ASPE) and IAS 2 for IFRS. For each of the following forms of inventory, briefly explain how the inventory would be reported and where guidance would be found under ASPE and IFRS. Explain the impact on the balance sheet and the income statements that would result.

(a) Unbilled work in progress for a legal firm (that is, employee and partner time spent on client work not yet billed)

(b) Milk from dairy cattle

(c) Sheep that are kept for wool production

(d) Construction contracts in progress

(e) Nickel resources not yet mined

Exercises

(LO 1, 5, 6) **E8-1** **(Purchases Recorded—Gross Method and Net Method)** Transactions follow for Cassio Limited:

March 10	Purchased goods billed at $40,000, terms 3/10, n/60.	
11	Purchased goods billed at $25,000, terms 1/15, n/30.	
19	Paid invoice of March 10.	
24	Purchased goods billed at $10,000, terms 3/10, n/30.	

Instructions

(a) Prepare general journal entries for the transactions above, assuming that purchases are to be recorded at net amounts after cash discounts and that discounts lost are to be treated as a financial expense. Assume a periodic inventory system.

(b) Assuming there are no purchase or payment transactions other than the ones mentioned above, prepare the adjusting entry required on March 31 if financial statements are to be prepared as at that date.

(c) Prepare general journal entries for the transactions above, assuming that purchases are to be recorded using the gross method. Assume a periodic inventory system.

(d) Indicate whether there are entries required at March 31 in addition to those in (c) if financial statements are to be prepared. Explain.

MANAGEMENT CONTROL

(e) Which method would provide the general manager of Cassio with better information for managing the business?

(LO 3, 4) **E8-2** **(Inventoriable Costs—Perpetual)** The Ogale Equipment Corporation maintains a general ledger account for each class of inventory, debiting the individual accounts for increases during the period and crediting them for decreases. The transactions that follow are for the Raw Materials inventory account, which is debited for materials purchased and credited for materials requisitioned for use.

1. An invoice for $8,100, terms f.o.b. destination, was received and entered on January 2, 2018. The receiving report shows that the materials were received on December 28, 2017.

2. Materials costing $7,300 were returned to the supplier on December 29, 2017, on f.o.b. shipping point terms. The returns were entered into Ogale's general ledger on December 28, even though the returned items did not arrive at the vendor's office until January 6, 2018.

3. Materials costing $28,000, shipped f.o.b. destination, were not entered by December 31, 2017, because they were in a railroad car on the company's siding on that date and had not been unloaded.

4. An invoice for $7,500, terms f.o.b. shipping point, was received and entered on December 30, 2017. The receiving report shows that the materials were received on January 4, 2018, and the bill of lading shows that they were shipped on January 2, 2018.

5. Materials costing $19,800 were received on December 30, 2017. No entry was made for them as at that date, because they were ordered with a specified delivery date of no earlier than January 10, 2018.

6. Materials costing $20,000 were received on December 29, 2017. The supplier's warehouse was full and the supplier asked Ogale to hold these items on its behalf and has also insured these items for the period that Ogale will be holding them. The purchase terms indicate that the supplier will purchase these items back from Ogale in early January 2018 at $20,000 plus storage fees.

7. Materials costing $5,500 were received on December 20, 2017, on consignment from P. Perry Company.

DIGGING DEEPER

Instructions

(a) Prepare any correcting journal entries that are required at December 31, 2017, assuming that the books have not been closed. Also indicate which entries must be reversed after closing so that the next period's accounts will be correct.

ETHICS (b) Are there any ethical concerns raised by these transactions? How should Ogale deal with this situation?

(LO 3, 4) **E8-3** **(Inventoriable Costs—Error Adjustments)** Jaeco Corporation asks you to review its December 31, 2017 inventory values and prepare the necessary adjustments to the books. The following information is given to you:

1. Jaeco uses the periodic method of recording inventory. A physical count reveals $234,890 of inventory on hand at December 31, 2017, although the books have not yet been adjusted to reflect the ending inventory.

2. Not included in the physical count of inventory is $10,420 of merchandise purchased on December 15 from Shamsi. This merchandise was shipped f.o.b. shipping point on December 29 and arrived in January. The invoice arrived and was recorded on December 31.

3. Included in inventory is merchandise sold to Sage on December 30, f.o.b. destination. This merchandise was shipped after it was counted. The invoice was prepared and recorded as a sale on account for $12,800 on December 31. The merchandise cost $7,350, and Sage received it on January 3.

4. Included in the count of inventory was merchandise received from Dutton on December 31 with an invoice price of $15,630. The merchandise was shipped f.o.b. destination. The invoice, which has not yet arrived, has not been recorded.

5. Not included in inventory is $8,540 of merchandise purchased from Growler Industries. This merchandise was received on December 31, after the inventory had been counted. The invoice was received and recorded on December 30.

6. Included in inventory was $10,438 of inventory held by Jaeco on consignment from Jackel Industries.

7. Included in inventory is merchandise sold to Kemp, f.o.b. shipping point. This merchandise was shipped after it was counted, on December 31. The invoice was prepared and recorded as a sale for $18,900 on December 31. The cost of this merchandise was $11,520, and Kemp received the merchandise on January 5.

8. Excluded from inventory was a carton labelled "Please accept for credit." This carton contained merchandise costing $1,500, which had been sold to a customer for $2,600. No entry had been made to the books to record the return, but none of the returned merchandise seemed damaged.

9. Jaeco sold $12,500 of inventory to Simply Corp. on December 15, 2017. These items were shipped f.o.b. shipping point. The terms of sale indicate that Simply Corp. will be permitted to return an unlimited amount until May 15, 2018. Jaeco has never provided unlimited returns in the past and is not able to estimate the amount of any potential returns that Simply may make.

Instructions

(a) Determine the proper inventory balance for Jaeco Corporation at December 31, 2017.

(b) Prepare any adjusting/correcting entries necessary at December 31, 2017. Assume the books have not been closed.

(LO 3, 4, 5, 13) **E8-4 (Inventoriable Costs)** The following is a list of items that may or may not be reported as inventory in J Soukas Corp.'s December 31 balance sheet:

1. Goods out on consignment at another company's store Inv

2. Goods sold on an instalment basis Not Inv (Purchaser has control)

3. Goods purchased f.o.b. shipping point that are in transit at December 31 Inv

4. Goods purchased f.o.b. destination that are in transit at December 31 Not Inv (not ours until arrives @ our dock)

5. Goods sold to another company, with Soukas having signed an agreement to repurchase the goods at a set price that covers all costs related to the inventory Inv (have to take it back so can't recognize revenue)

6. Goods sold where large returns are predictable Not Inv

7. Goods sold f.o.b. shipping point that are in transit at December 31 Not Inv (became theirs as soon as left)

8. Freight charges on goods purchased Inv

9. Freight charges on goods sold Not Inv (simply sale cost)

10. Factory labour costs incurred on goods that are still unsold Inv (needed to get goods ready for sale)

11. Interest costs incurred for inventories that are routinely manufactured in large quantities Not Inv (doesn't take long time)

12. Costs incurred to advertise goods held for resale Not Inv (not necessary to prepare for sale)

13. Materials on hand and not yet placed into production by a manufacturing firm

14. Office supplies

15. Raw materials on which a manufacturing firm has started production, but which are not completely processed

16. Factory supplies

17. Goods held on consignment from another company

18. Goods held on consignment by another company

19. Costs identified with units completed by a manufacturing firm, but not yet sold

20. Goods sold f.o.b. destination that are in transit at December 31

21. Temporary investments in shares and bonds that will be resold in the near future

22. Costs of uncleared land to be developed by a property development company

23. Cost of normal waste or spoilage of raw materials during production

24. Cost of waste and spoilage experienced above normal levels—that is, abnormal levels of waste of raw materials

25. Costs to store excess materials inventory for a manufacturer

26. Costs to store wine as it ages for a wine producer

27. Decommissioning costs incurred as a part of the extraction of minerals

Instructions

(a) Assuming that ASPE is followed, indicate which of these items would typically be reported as inventory in the financial statements. If an item should not be reported as inventory, indicate how it should be reported in the financial statements.

(b) How would your response to (a) change under IFRS?

(LO 3, 5, 13) **E8-5** **(Inventoriable Costs)** In an annual audit of Solaro Company Limited, you find that a physical inventory count on December 31, 2017, showed merchandise of $441,000. You also discover that the following items were excluded from the $441,000:

1. Merchandise of $61,000 is held by Solaro on consignment from BonBon Corporation.

2. Merchandise costing $33,000 was shipped by Solaro f.o.b. destination to XYZ Ltd. on December 31, 2017. This merchandise was accepted by XYZ on January 6, 2018.

3. Merchandise costing $46,000 was shipped f.o.b. shipping point to ABC Company on December 29, 2017. This merchandise was received by ABC on January 10, 2018.

4. Merchandise costing $73,000 was shipped f.o.b. destination from Wholesaler Inc. to Solaro on December 30, 2017. Solaro received the items on January 3, 2018.

5. Merchandise costing $51,000 was shipped by Distributor Ltd. f.o.b. shipping point on December 30, 2017, and received at Solaro's office on January 2, 2018.

6. Solaro had excess inventory and incurred an additional $1,500 in storage costs due to delayed shipment in transaction (3) above.

7. Solaro incurred $2,000 for interest expense on inventory it purchased through delayed payment plans in fiscal 2017.

Instructions

(a) Based on the information provided above, calculate the amount of inventory that should appear on Solaro's December 31, 2017 balance sheet.

(b) Under what circumstances can a private company reporting under ASPE capitalize interest costs incurred to finance inventory?

(c) Under what circumstances can a public company reporting under IFRS capitalize interest costs incurred to finance inventory?

(d) Explain some audit procedures that the auditor would perform to satisfy the financial statement assertion for cut-off for inventory transactions and events.

AUDIT

(LO 3, 8) **E8-6** **(Cost Allocation and Lower of Cost and NRV)** During 2017, Buildit Furniture Limited purchased a railway-car load of wicker chairs. The manufacturer of the chairs sold them to Buildit for a lump sum of $59,850, because it was discontinuing manufacturing operations and wanted to dispose of its entire stock. Three types of chairs are included in the carload. The three types and the estimated selling price for each are as follows:

Type	Number of Chairs	Estimated Selling Price per Chair
Lounge chairs	400	$95
Straight chairs	700	55
Armchairs	300	85

Buildit estimates that the costs to sell this inventory would amount to $2 per chair. During 2017, Buildit sells 350 lounge chairs, 210 armchairs, and 120 straight chairs, all at the same prices as estimated. At December 31, 2017, the remaining chairs were put on sale: the lounge chairs at 25% off the regular price, the armchairs at 30% off, and the straight chairs at 40% off. All were expected to be sold at these prices.

Instructions

(a) Rounding percentages to one decimal place and all other amounts to two decimal places, what is the total cost of the chairs remaining in inventory at the end of 2017, using the relative sales value method?

(b) What is the net realizable value of the chairs remaining in inventory?

(c) What is the appropriate inventory value to be reported on the December 31, 2017 statement of financial position, assuming the lower of cost and NRV is applied on an individual item basis?

(LO 3, 13) E8-7 (Purchase Commitments) At December 31, 2017, Igor Ltd. has outstanding non-cancellable purchase commitments for 32,500 litres of raw material at $2.00 per litre. The material will be used in Igor's manufacturing process, and the company prices its raw materials inventory at cost or NRV, whichever is lower.

Instructions

(a) Explain the accounting treatment for purchase commitments under ASPE and IFRS.

(b) Assuming that the market price as at December 31, 2017, is $2.25 per litre, how would this commitment be treated in the accounts and statements? Explain.

(c) Assuming that the market price as at December 31, 2017, is $1.80 per litre instead of $2.25, how would you treat this commitment in the accounts and statements?

(d) Prepare the entry for January 15, 2018, when the entire shipment is received, assuming that the situation in (c) existed at December 31, 2017, and that the market price in January 2018 is $1.80 per litre. Explain your treatment.

(e) Why would users of the financial statements want to see disclosure about purchase commitments? Is it ever ethical
ETHICS   for a company to decide not to disclose this information?

(LO 4) E8-8 (Inventory Errors—Periodic) Salamander Limited makes the following errors during the current year. Each error is an independent case.

1. Ending inventory is overstated by $1,020, but purchases are recorded correctly.

2. Both ending inventory and a purchase on account are understated by the same amount. (Assume this purchase of $1,500 was recorded in the following year.)

3. Ending inventory is correct, but a purchase on account was not recorded. (Assume this purchase of $850 was recorded in the following year.)

Instructions
Indicate the effect of each error on working capital, current ratio (assume that the current ratio is greater than 1),
FINANCE   retained earnings, and net income for the current year and the following year.

(LO 4) E8-9 (Inventory Errors) Eureka Limited has a calendar-year accounting period. The following errors were discovered in 2017.

1. The December 31, 2015 merchandise inventory had been understated by $51,000.

2. Merchandise purchased on account in 2016 was recorded on the books for the first time in February 2017, when the original invoice for the correct amount of $2,400 arrived. The merchandise had arrived on December 28, 2016, and was included in the December 31, 2016 merchandise inventory. The invoice arrived late because of a mix-up by the wholesaler.

3. Inventory, valued at $1,000, held on consignment by Eureka was included in the December 31, 2016 count.

Instructions

(a) Calculate the effect of each error on the 2016 net income.

(b) Calculate the effect, if any, that each error had on the related December 31, 2016 statement of financial position items.

(LO 4) E8-10 (Inventory Errors) The net income per books of Russell Industries Limited was determined without any knowledge of the following errors. The 2012 year was Russell's first year in business. No dividends have been declared or paid.

Year	Net Income per Books	Error in Ending Inventory	
2012	$50,000	Overstated	$ 5,000
2013	52,000	Overstated	9,000
2014	54,000	Understated	11,000
2015	56,000	No error	
2016	58,000	Understated	2,000
2017	60,000	Overstated	10,000

Instructions

(a) Prepare a work sheet to show the adjusted net income figure for each of the six years after taking the inventory corrections into account.

(b) Prepare a schedule that indicates both the original retained earnings balance reported at the end of each year and the corrected amount.

(c) Consider the trends in the increase in income from 2012 to 2017 as originally reported and as revised after the corrections. Would you suspect that the income is being manipulated by adjusting the ending balance in the inventory account?

ETHICS

(LO 4, 8, 12, 13) **E8-11** **(Lower of Cost and Net Realizable Value—Effect of Error)** Iqbal Corporation uses the lower of FIFO cost and net realizable value method on an individual item basis, applying the direct method. The inventory at December 31, 2016, included product AG. Relevant per-unit data for product AG follow:

Estimated selling price	$50
Cost	45
Replacement cost	51
Estimated selling expense	19
Normal profit	14

There were 1,000 units of product AG on hand at December 31, 2016. Product AG was incorrectly valued at $35 per unit for reporting purposes. All 1,000 units were sold in 2017.

Instructions

Assume that Iqbal follows ASPE and answer the following questions.

(a) Was net income for 2016 overstated or understated? By how much? (Ignore income tax aspects.)

(b) Was net income for 2017 overstated or understated? By how much?

(c) Indicate whether the current ratio, inventory turnover ratio, and debt to total assets ratio would be overstated, understated, or not affected for the years ended December 31, 2016, and December 31, 2017. Explain briefly.

FINANCE (d) Assume that management did not discover the error in inventory until after the end of the fiscal year but before the closing entries were made and the financial statements were released. Should the adjustment be recorded? How would the error be treated if it were discovered after the financial statements were released?

(e) How would your responses above change if Iqbal followed IFRS?

(LO 4, 10) **E8-12** **(Gross Profit Method)** Linsang Corporation's retail store and warehouse closed for an entire weekend while the year-end inventory was counted. When the count was finished, the controller gathered all the count books and information from the clerical staff, completed the ending inventory calculations, and prepared the following partial income statement for the general manager for Monday morning:

Sales		$2,750,000
Beginning inventory	$ 650,000	
Purchases	1,550,000	
Total goods available for sale	2,200,000	
Less ending inventory	650,000	
Cost of goods sold		1,550,000
Gross profit		$1,200,000

The general manager called the controller into her office after quickly reviewing the preliminary statements. "You've made an error in the inventory," she stated. "My pricing all year has been carefully controlled to provide a gross profit of 35%, and I know the sales are correct."

Instructions

(a) How much should the ending inventory have been?

(b) If the controller's ending inventory amount was due to an error, suggest where the error might have occurred.

(LO 5) **E8-13** **(Relative Sales Value Method)** In fiscal 2017, Ivanjoh Realty Corporation purchased unimproved land for $55,000. The land was improved and subdivided into building lots at an additional cost of $34,460. These building lots were all the same size but, because of differences in location, were offered for sale at different prices, as follows:

Group	Number of Lots	Price per Lot
1	9	$3,500
2	15	4,500
3	17	2,400

Operating expenses that were allocated to this project totalled $18,200 for the year. At year end, there were also unsold lots remaining, as follows:

Group 1	5 lots
Group 2	7 lots
Group 3	2 lots

Instructions

Determine the year-end inventory and net income of Ivanjoh Realty Corporation. Round all amounts to the nearest dollar. Ignore income taxes.

(LO 6) E8-14 (Determining Merchandise Amounts—Periodic) Two or more items are omitted in each of the following tabulations of income statement data. Fill in the amounts that are missing.

	2015	2016	2017
Sales	$290,000	$_____	$410,000
Sales returns	6,000	13,000	_____
Net sales	_____	347,000	_____
Beginning inventory	20,000	32,000	_____
Ending inventory	_____	_____	_____
Purchases	_____	260,000	298,000
Purchase returns and allowances	5,000	8,000	10,000
Transportation-in	8,000	9,000	12,000
Cost of goods sold	238,000	_____	303,000
Gross profit on sales	46,000	91,000	97,000

(LO 6, 7) E8-15 (Periodic Versus Perpetual Entries) Ruggers Corporation sells one product, with information for July as follows:

July	1	Inventory	100 units at $15.00 each
	4	Sale	80 units at $18.00 each
	11	Purchase	150 units at $16.50 each
	13	Sale	120 units at $18.75 each
	20	Purchase	160 units at $17.00 each
	27	Sale	100 units at $20.00 each

Ruggers uses the FIFO cost formula. All purchases and sales are on account.

Instructions

(a) Assume Ruggers uses a periodic system. Prepare all necessary journal entries, including the end-of-month adjusting entry to record cost of goods sold. A physical count indicates that the ending inventory for July is 110 units.

(b) Calculate gross profit using the periodic system.

(c) Assume Ruggers uses the periodic system, and a count on July 31 reports only 102 units in ending inventory. How would your entries in (a) change, if at all? Explain briefly.

(d) Assume Ruggers uses a perpetual system. Prepare all July journal entries.

(e) Calculate gross profit using the perpetual system.

(f) Assume Ruggers uses the perpetual system, and a count on July 31 reports only 102 units in ending inventory. How would your entries in (d) change, if at all? Explain briefly.

(LO 6, 7) E8-16 (FIFO and Weighted Average) Aquino Corporation is a multi-product firm. The following information concerns one of its products, the Trinton:

Date	Transaction	Quantity	Price/Cost
Jan. 1	Beginning inventory	1,000	$12
Feb. 4	Purchase	2,000	18
Feb. 20	Sale	2,500	30
Apr. 2	Purchase	3,000	23
Nov. 4	Sale	2,000	33

Instructions

Calculate cost of goods sold, assuming Aquino uses:

(a) A periodic inventory system and FIFO cost formula

(b) A periodic inventory system and weighted average cost formula

(c) A perpetual inventory system and moving-average cost formula

(LO 6, 7) E8-17 (Alternative Inventory Methods) Schonfeld Corporation began operations on December 1, 2016. The only inventory transaction in 2016 was the purchase of inventory on December 10, 2016, at a cost of $20 per unit. None of this inventory was sold in 2016. Relevant information for fiscal 2017 is as follows:

Ending inventory units:		
Dec. 31, 2016		100
Dec. 31, 2017, by purchase date		
—Dec. 2, 2017	100	
—July 20, 2017	30	130

During 2017, the following purchases and sales were made:

Purchases			Sales	
Mar. 15	300 units at $24		Apr. 10	200
July 20	300 units at $25		Aug. 20	300
Sept. 40	200 units at $28		Nov. 18	170
Dec. 2	100 units at $30		Dec. 12	200

The company uses the periodic inventory method.

Instructions

Determine ending inventory under (1) specific identification, (2) FIFO, and (3) weighted average cost.

(LO 6, 7, 12) E8-18 (Calculate FIFO, Weighted Average Cost—Periodic) The following information is for the inventory of mini-kettles at Funnell Company Limited for the month of May:

Date	Transaction	Units In	Unit Cost	Total	Units Sold	Unit Price	Total
May 1	Balance	100	$4.10	$ 410			
6	Purchase	800	4.20	3,360			
7	Sale				300	$7.00	$ 2,100
10	Sale				300	7.30	2,190
12	Purchase	400	4.50	1,800			
15	Sale				200	7.40	1,480
18	Purchase	300	4.60	1,380			
22	Sale				400	7.40	2,960
25	Purchase	500	4.58	2,290			
30	Sale				200	7.50	1,500
Totals		2,100		$9,240	1,400		$10,230

Instructions

(a) Assuming that the periodic inventory method is used, calculate the inventory cost at May 31 under each of the following cost flow formulas:
1. FIFO
2. Weighted average (round the weighted average unit cost to the nearest one tenth of one cent)

FINANCE (b) Which method will yield the higher current ratio or gross profit?

(LO 6, 7) E8-19 (Calculate FIFO, Moving-Average Cost—Perpetual) Information is presented in E8-18 on the inventory of mini-kettles at Funnell Company Limited for the month of May.

Instructions

(a) Assuming that the perpetual inventory method is used, calculate the inventory cost at May 31 under each of the following cost flow formulas:
1. FIFO
2. Moving-average (round all unit costs to the nearest one-tenth of one cent)

(b) Indicate where the inventory costs that were calculated in this exercise are different from the ones in E8-18 and explain the possible reasons why.

(LO 6, 8, 12) E8-20 (Lower of Cost and Net Realizable Value, Periodic Method—Journal Entries) As a result of its annual inventory count, Tarweed Corp. determined its ending inventory at cost and at lower of cost and net realizable value at December 31, 2016, and December 31, 2017. This information is as follows:

	Cost	Lower of Cost and NRV
Dec. 31, 2016	$321,000	$283,250
Dec. 31, 2017	385,000	351,250

Instructions

(a) Prepare the journal entries required at December 31, 2016 and 2017, assuming that the inventory is recorded directly at the lower of cost and net realizable value and a periodic inventory system is used. Assume that cost was lower than NRV at December 31, 2015.

(b) Prepare the journal entries required at December 31, 2016 and 2017, assuming that the inventory is recorded at cost and an allowance account is adjusted at each year end under a periodic system.

(c) Which of the two methods above provides the higher net income in each year?

(LO 8) E8-21   (Lower of Cost and Net Realizable Value) The inventory of 3T Company on December 31, 2017, consists of the following items.

Part No.	Quantity	Cost per Unit	NRV
110	600	$ 90	$100
111	1,000	60	52
112	500	80	76
113	200	170	180
120	400	205	208
121*	1,600	16	.20
122	300	240	235

*Part No. 121 is obsolete and has a realizable value of $0.20 each as scrap.

Instructions

(a) Determine the inventory as at December 31, 2017, by the lower of cost and net realizable value method, applying this method directly to each item.

(b) Determine the inventory as at December 31, 2017, by the lower of cost and net realizable value method, applying the method to the total of the inventory.

(LO 8) E8-22   (Lower of Cost and NRV Valuation Account) The following information is for Takin Enterprises Ltd.:

	Jan. 31	Feb. 28	Mar. 31	Apr. 30
Inventory at cost	$25,000	$25,100	$29,000	$23,000
Inventory at the lower of cost and net realizable value	24,500	17,600	22,600	17,300
Purchases for the month		20,000	24,000	26,500
Sales for the month		29,000	35,000	40,000

Instructions

(a) Using the above information, prepare monthly income statements (as far as the data permit) in columnar form for February, March, and April. Show the inventory in the statement at cost; show the gain or loss due to fluctuations in NRV separately. Takin uses the indirect or allowance method.

(b) Prepare the journal entry that is needed to establish the valuation account at January 31 and the entries to adjust it at the end of each month after that.

(LO 9, 13) E8-23   (Biological Inventory Assets) Nicholas's Christmas Tree Farm Ltd. grows pine, fir, and spruce trees. The farm cuts and sells trees during the Christmas season and exports most of the trees to the United States. The remaining trees are sold to local tree-lot operators.

It normally takes 12 years for a tree to grow to a suitable size, and the average selling price of a tree is $24. The biggest costs to the business are pest control, fertilizer, and pruning trees over the 12-year period. These costs average $12 per tree (assume these are incurred evenly over the 12-year growing cycle).

Instructions

(a) How should this inventory be recorded under ASPE?

(b) How should the costs of pest control, fertilizer, and pruning be recognized under IFRS?

(c) Assume that the fair value of each tree at the end of 2017 is $8 and the opening value was $5. Prepare the journal entries if the costs are *capitalized* each year.

(d) Assume that the fair value of each tree at the end of 2017 is $8 and the opening value was $5. Prepare the journal entries if the costs are *expensed* each year.

(LO 10) E8-24 **(Gross Profit Method)** Milan Company Limited uses the gross profit method to estimate inventory for monthly reports. Information follows for the month of May:

Inventory, May 1	$360,000	Sales	$1,200,000
Purchases	700,000	Sales returns	70,000
Freight-in	50,000	Purchase discounts	12,000

Instructions

(a) Calculate the estimated inventory at May 31, assuming that the gross profit is 25% of sales.

(b) Calculate the estimated inventory at May 31, assuming that the markup on cost is 25%. Round the gross profit percentage to two decimal places.

(LO 12) E8-25 **(Analysis of Inventories)** The financial statements of Trifolium Corporation for fiscal 2015 to fiscal 2017 are as follows (in thousands):

	Fiscal 2017	Fiscal 2016	Fiscal 2015
Inventory	$ 291,497	$ 319,445	$ 302,207
Sales	1,346,758	1,331,009	1,263,955
Gross margin	483,519	478,401	451,592
Net income	29,325	47,451	35,217

Instructions

(a) Calculate Trifolium's (1) inventory turnover and (2) average days to sell inventory for each of the two years ending in 2017 and 2016.

(b) Calculate Trifolium's gross profit percentage and percentage markup on cost for each fiscal year.

FINANCE **(c)** Is the growth in inventory levels over the last year consistent with the increase in sales? Explain your answer.

(LO 12) E8-26 **(Ratios)** Partial information follows for a Canadian manufacturing company:

	Year 10	Year 9	Year 8	Year 7
Sales	$401,244	$_____	$344,759	
Cost of goods sold	_____	286,350	263,979	
Gross margin	95,086	87,957	_____	
Ending inventory	34,511	_____	34,750	36,750
Gross profit percentage	_____	23.5%	_____	
Inventory turnover	_____	8.19 times	_____	
Days sales in inventory	_____	44.57 days	_____	

Instructions

FINANCE **(a)** Enter the missing amounts where indicated for years 8, 9, and 10 in the above schedule.

MANAGEMENT **(b)** Comment on the profitability and inventory management trends, and suggest possible reasons for these results.
CONTROL

(LO 14) ***E8-27** **(Retail Inventory Method)** The records of Sudbury Menswear report the following data for the month of September:

Sales	$118,500	Purchases (at cost)	$ 59,500
Sales returns	2,500	Purchases (at sales price)	112,600
Additional markups	10,500	Purchase returns (at cost)	2,500
Markup cancellations	1,500	Purchase returns (at sales price)	3,500
Markdowns	9,300	Beginning inventory (at cost)	32,000
Markdown cancellations	2,800	Beginning inventory (at sales price)	48,500
Freight on purchases	3,600		

Instructions

(a) Estimate the ending inventory using the conventional retail inventory method.

(b) Assuming that a physical count of the inventory determined that the actual ending inventory at retail prices at the end of September was $42,000, estimate the loss due to shrinkage and theft.

(c) Identify four reasons why the estimate of inventory may be different from the actual inventory at cost.

(LO 15) *E8-28   (Primary Sources of GAAP) There are a few primary sources of GAAP for inventory under both ASPE and IFRS. List the sources of guidance in the table below.

Type of Inventory	Primary Guidance under ASPE	Primary Guidance under IFRS
Equipment manufactured		
Financial derivatives held by a financial institution		
Biological assets at the point of harvest		
Harvested agricultural produce		

Problems

P8-1   The following independent situations relate to inventory accounting:

1. Kessel Co. purchased goods with a list price of $175,000 and a trade discount of 20% based on the quantity purchased, with terms 2/10, net 30.

2. Sanderson Company's inventory of $1.1 million at December 31, 2017, was based on a physical count of goods priced at cost and before any year-end adjustments relating to the following items:
   (a) Goods shipped f.o.b. shipping point on December 24, 2017, from a vendor at an invoice cost of $69,000 to Sanderson Company, received on January 4, 2018.
   (b) Goods worth $29,000 and included in the physical count, billed to Makee Corp., f.o.b. shipping point, on December 31, 2017. The carrier picked up these goods on January 3, 2018.
   (c) Goods shipped f.o.b. destination received by Sanderson on January 5, 2018. The invoiced amount was $77,000.
   (d) Goods shipped f.o.b. destination and received by Sanderson on December 25, 2017, that are on consignment. The value of the goods is $83,500 and they have not been included in the physical inventory count.

3. Howe Corp. had 1,500 units on hand of part 54169 on May 1, 2017, with a cost of $21 per unit. Howe uses a periodic inventory system. Purchases of part 54169 during May were as follows:

	Units	Unit Cost
May 9	2,000	$22.00
17	3,500	23.00
26	1,000	24.00

A physical count on May 31, 2017, shows 2,000 units of part 54169 on hand.

4. Grossman Ltd., a retail store chain, had the following information in its general ledger for the year 2017:

Merchandise purchased for resale	$909,400
Interest on notes payable to vendors for the purchase of inventory	8,700
Purchase returns	16,500
Freight-in	22,000
Freight-out	17,100
Cash discounts on purchases	6,800
Storage costs incurred when warehouse became full	8,300

Instructions

Answer the following questions for the situations above and explain your answer in each case:

(a) For situation 1, how much should Kessel Co. record as the purchase cost of these goods on the date of purchase, assuming the company uses (i) the gross method and (ii) the net method?

(b) For situation 2, what should Sanderson Company report as its inventory amount on its 2017 balance sheet?

(c) For situation 3, using the FIFO method, what is the inventory cost of part 54169 at May 31, 2017? Using the weighted average cost formula, what is the inventory cost?

(d) For situation 4, assume that Grossman Ltd. is a private company reporting under ASPE. What is Grossman's inventoriable cost for 2017? Explain any items that are excluded.

(e) How would your answer to part (d) differ if Grossman used IFRS? Which of these standards provides the most useful information to users: ASPE or IFRS? Why?

P8-2 On February 1, 2017, Akeson Ltd. began selling electric scooters that it purchased exclusively from Ionone Motors Inc. Ionone Motors offers vendor rebates based on the volume of annual sales to its customers, and calculates and pays the rebates at its fiscal year end, December 31. Akeson has a September fiscal year end and uses a perpetual inventory system. The rebate offer that Akeson received is for a $75 rebate on each scooter that is purchased in excess of 150 units in the calendar year, ending December 31. An additional rebate of $30 is given for all units purchased in excess of 175 units in the same year. By September 30, 2017, Akeson had purchased 190 units from Ionone Motors and had sold all but 35. Although it only made its first purchase on February 1, 2017, Akeson expects to purchase a total of 250 electric scooters from Ionone Motors by December 31, 2017. Before arriving at the estimate of 250 electric scooters, Akeson's management looked carefully at trends in purchases by its competitors and the strong market for sales of electric scooters in the coming months; sales are especially strong among environmentally conscious customers in suburban areas. Management is very confident the 250 electric scooters will be purchased by December 31, 2017.

Instructions

Assuming that Akeson follows the reporting requirements under ASPE, answer the following questions.

(a) Based on the conceptual framework, discuss the reasoning that Akeson should use in how it treats the rebate that it expects to receive from Ionone Motors.

(b) Would your opinion change if the rebate that is expected from Ionone Motors had been discretionary?

(c) Discuss some of the factors that management should consider in arriving at a reasonable estimate of its amount of purchases to December 31, 2017.

(d) Calculate the amount of any accrued rebate to be recorded by Akeson at September 30, 2017, assuming that the rebate is not discretionary and that management has a high degree of confidence in its estimate of the amount of purchases that will occur by December 31, 2017.

(e) Record the accruals that are necessary at Akeson's fiscal year end of September 30, 2017.

(f) How would your response change if Akeson followed the reporting requirements of IFRS?

P8-3 Ianthe Limited, a manufacturer of small tools, provided the following information from its accounting records for the year ended December 31, 2017:

Inventory at December 31, 2017 (based on physical count of goods in Ianthe's plant, at cost, on December 31, 2017)	$1,720,000
Accounts payable at December 31, 2017	1,300,000
Total current assets	2,680,000
Total current liabilities	1,550,000
Net sales (sales less sales returns)	8,550,000

Additional information:

1. Included in the physical count were tools billed to a customer f.o.b. shipping point on December 31, 2017. These tools had a cost of $37,000 and were billed at $57,000. The shipment was on Ianthe's loading dock waiting to be picked up by the common carrier.

2. Goods were in transit from a vendor to Ianthe on December 31, 2017. The invoice was for $51,000, and the goods were shipped f.o.b. shipping point on December 29, 2017. Ianthe will sell these items in 2018 for $87,500. These were excluded from the inventory count.

3. Work-in-process inventory costing $38,000 was sent to an outside processor for plating on December 30, 2017. This was excluded from the inventory count.

4. Tools that were returned by customers and awaiting inspection in the returned goods area on December 31, 2017, were not included in the physical count. On January 8, 2018, these tools, costing $38,000, were inspected and returned to inventory. Credit memos totalling $48,000 were issued to the customers on the same date.

5. Tools shipped to a customer f.o.b. destination on December 26, 2017, were in transit at December 31, 2017, and had a cost of $21,000. When it was notified that the customer received the goods on January 2, 2018, Ianthe issued a sales invoice for $42,000. These were excluded from the inventory count.

6. Goods with an invoice cost of $27,000 that were received from a vendor at 5:00 p.m. on December 31, 2017, were recorded on a receiving report dated January 2, 2018. The goods were not included in the physical count, but the invoice was included in accounts payable at December 31, 2017.

7. Goods that were received from a vendor on December 26, 2017, were included in the physical count. However, the vendor invoice of $56,000 for these goods was not included in accounts payable at December 31, 2017, because the accounts payable copy of the receiving report was lost.

8. On January 3, 2018, a monthly freight bill in the amount of $7,000 was received. The bill specifically related to merchandise purchased in December 2017, and half of this merchandise was still in the inventory at December 31, 2017. The freight charges were not included in either the inventory account or accounts payable at December 31, 2017.

Instructions

(a) Using the format shown below, prepare a schedule of adjustments to the initial amounts in Ianthe's accounting records as at December 31, 2017. Show separately the effect, if any, of each of the eight transactions on the December 31, 2017 amounts. If the transaction has no effect on the initial amount that is shown, write "NONE."

DIGGING
DEEPER

	Inventory	Accounts Payable	Net Sales
Initial amounts	$1,720,000	$1,300,000	$8,550,000
Adjustments—increase (decrease)			
Total adjustments			
Adjusted amounts	$	$	$

FINANCE

(b) After you arrive at the adjusted balance for part (a) above, determine if the following ratios have improved or if they have deteriorated:
1. Working capital
2. Current ratio
3. Gross profit
4. Profit margin

(Adapted from AICPA.)

P8-4 Halm Skidoos Limited, a private company that began operations in 2014, always values its inventories at their current net realizable value. The company uses ASPE. Its annual inventory figure is arrived at by taking a physical count and then pricing each item in the physical inventory at current resale prices. The condensed income statements for the company's past four years are as follows:

	2014	2015	2016	2017
Sales	$850,000	$880,000	$950,000	$990,000
Cost of goods sold	560,000	590,000	630,000	650,000
Gross profit	290,000	290,000	320,000	340,000
Operating expenses	190,000	180,000	200,000	210,000
Income before taxes	$100,000	$110,000	$120,000	$130,000

Instructions

(a) Comment on the procedures that Halm uses for valuing inventories.

(b) Prepare corrected condensed income statements using an acceptable method of inventory valuation, assuming that the inventory at cost and as determined by the corporation (using net realizable value) at the end of each of the four years is as follows:

Year	At Cost	Net Realizable Value
2014	$150,000	$160,000
2015	147,000	160,000
2016	178,000	170,000
2017	175,000	189,000

FINANCE

(c) Compare the trend in income for the four years using the corporation's approach to valuing ending inventory and using a method that is acceptable under GAAP.

(d) Calculate the cumulative effect of the difference in the valuation of inventory on the ending balance of retained earnings from 2014 through 2017.

(e) Comment on the differences that you observe after making the corrections to the inventory valuation over the four years.

P8-5 Some of the transactions of Collins Corp. during August follow. Collins uses the periodic inventory method.

Aug. 10	Purchased merchandise on account, $12,000, terms 2/10, n/30.
13	Returned $1,200 of the purchase of August 10 and received a credit on account.
15	Purchased merchandise on account, $16,000, terms 1/10, n/60.
25	Purchased merchandise on account, $20,000, terms 2/10, n/30.
28	Paid the invoice of August 15 in full.

Instructions

(a) Assuming that purchases are recorded at gross amounts and that discounts are to be recorded when taken:
   1. Prepare general journal entries to record the transactions.
   2. Describe how the various items would be shown in the financial statements.

(b) Assuming that purchases are recorded at net amounts and that discounts lost are treated as financial expenses:
   1. Prepare general journal entries to enter the transactions.
   2. Prepare the adjusting entry that is necessary on August 31 if financial statements are prepared at that time.
   3. Describe how the various items would be shown in the financial statements.

(c) Which method results in a higher reported gross profit ratio? Explain.

(d) Which of the two methods do you prefer and why?

P8-6   Lupulin Limited stocks a variety of sports equipment for sale to institutions. The following stock record card for basketballs was taken from the records at the December 31, 2017 year end:

Date	Invoice Number	Terms	Units Received	Unit Invoice Cost	Gross Invoice Amount
Jan. 1	balance	Net 30	100	$20.00	$2,000.00
15	10624	Net 30	60	20.00	1,200.00
Mar. 15	11437	1/5, net 30	65	16.00	1,040.00
June 20	21332	1/10, net 30	90	15.00	1,350.00
Sept. 12	27644	1/10, net 30	84	12.00	1,008.00
Nov. 24	31269	1/10, net 30	76	11.00	836.00
	Totals		475		$7,434.00

A physical inventory on December 31, 2017, reveals that 100 basketballs are in stock. The bookkeeper informs you that all the discounts were taken. Assume that Lupulin Limited uses a periodic inventory system and records purchases at their invoice price less discounts. During 2017, the average sales price per basketball was $22.25.

Instructions

(a) Calculate the December 31, 2017 inventory using the FIFO formula.

(b) Calculate the December 31, 2017 inventory using the weighted average cost formula. (Round unit costs to the nearest cent.)

(c) Prepare income statements for the year ended December 31, 2017, as far as the "gross profit" line under each of the FIFO and weighted average methods, and calculate the gross profit rate for each. Explain the difference in the gross profit under the two methods.

(d) If the selling prices for the basketballs that were sold follow the same pattern as their wholesale prices from the supplier, might this have an effect on the inventory cost that is reported on the December 31, 2017 balance sheet? (*Hint:* Review your answers to parts [a] to [c].)

DIGGING DEEPER

P8-7   The summary financial statements of Langford Landscaping Ltd. on December 31, 2017, are as follows:

LANDFORD LANDSCAPING LTD.
Balance Sheet, December 31, 2017
Assets

Cash	$ 5,000
Accounts and notes receivable	39,000
Inventory	79,000
Property, plant, and equipment (net)	125,000
	$248,000

Liabilities and Shareholders' Equity

Accounts and notes payable	$ 75,000
Long-term debt	62,000
Common shares	60,000
Retained earnings	51,000
	$248,000

The following errors were made by the inexperienced accountant on December 31, 2016, and were not corrected.

1. The inventory was overstated by $13,000.

2. A prepaid expense of $2,400 was omitted. (It was fully expensed in 2016.)

3. Accrued revenue of $2,500 was omitted. (It was recognized when cash was received in 2017.)

4. A supplier's invoice for $1,700 for purchases made in 2016 was not recorded until 2017.

On December 31, 2017, there were further errors:

5. The inventory was understated by $17,000.

6. A prepaid expense of $750 was omitted.

7. Accrued December 2017 salaries of $1,800 were not recognized.

8. Unearned income of $2,300 was recorded in the 2017 revenue.

9. In addition, it was determined that $20,000 of the accounts payable were long-term, and that a $500 dividend was reported as dividend expense and deducted in calculating net income.

The net income reported on the books for 2017 was $53,000.

Instructions

(a) Calculate the working capital, current ratio, and debt to equity ratio for Langford Landscaping Ltd. based on the original balance sheet information provided above.

(b) Calculate the corrected net income for 2017.

(c) Prepare a corrected balance sheet at December 31, 2017.

FINANCE

(d) Using the corrected data, recalculate the ratios in part (a). Explain the resulting differences in the ratios as a result of the use of the corrected data.

P8-8 Astro Languet established Languet Products Co. as a sole proprietorship on January 5, 2017. At the company's year end of December 31, 2017, the accounts had the following balances (in thousands):

Current assets, excluding inventory	$ 10
Other assets	107
Current liabilities	30
Long-term bank loan	50
Owner's investment (excluding income)	40
Purchases during year	
Jan. 2: 5,000 @ $11	55
June 30: 8,000 @ $12	96
Dec. 10: 6,000 @ $16	96
	247
Sales	284
Other expenses	40

A count of ending inventory on December 31, 2017, showed there were 4,000 units on hand.

Astro is now preparing financial statements for the year. He is aware that inventory may be costed using the FIFO or weighted average cost formula. He is unsure of which one to use and asks for your assistance. In discussions with Astro, you learn the following.

1. Suppliers to Languet Products provide goods at regular prices as long as Languet Products' current ratio is at least 2 to 1. If this ratio is lower, the suppliers increase their price by 10% in order to compensate for what they consider to be a substantial credit risk.

2. The terms of the long-term bank loan include the bank's ability to demand immediate repayment of the loan if the debt to total assets ratio is greater than 45%.

3. Astro thinks that, for the company to be a success, the rate of return on total assets should be at least 30%.

4. Astro has an agreement with the company's only employee that, for each full percentage point above a 25% rate of return on total assets, she will be given an additional one day off with pay in the following year.

ETHICS
FINANCE

Instructions

(a) Prepare an income statement and a year-end balance sheet, assuming the company applies:
1. The FIFO cost formula
2. The weighted average cost formula

(b) Recalculate the key ratios given each formula in (a).

(c) Discuss the impact of using each formula on the key ratios.

(d) Which method do you recommend? Explain briefly.

DIGGING
DEEPER

(e) Considering the choice of inventory cost formulas that are available, do the ratios noted above adequately measure the financial performance of Languet Products from the perspective of the users?

P8-9 Milford Company determined its ending inventory at cost and at lower of cost and net realizable value at December 31, 2015, 2016, and 2017, as follows:

	Cost	Lower of Cost and Net Realizable Value
Dec. 31, 2015	$60,000	$60,000
Dec. 31, 2016	79,000	74,500
Dec. 31, 2017	78,800	69,000

Instructions

(a) Prepare the journal entries that are required at December 31, 2016 and 2017, assuming that a periodic inventory system and the direct method of adjusting to NRV are used.

(b) Prepare the journal entries that are required at December 31, 2016 and 2017, assuming that a periodic inventory system is used, with inventory recorded at cost and reduced to NRV through the use of an allowance account.

P8-10 Reena Corp. lost most of its inventory in a fire in December, just before the year-end physical inventory was taken. The corporation's books disclosed the following:

Beginning inventory	$440,000	Sales	$1,350,000
Purchases for the year	850,000	Sales returns	50,000
Purchase returns	55,000	Gross margin on sales	40%

Merchandise with a selling price of $42,000 remained undamaged after the fire. Damaged merchandise with an original selling price of $30,000 had a net realizable value of $10,600.

Instructions

(a) Calculate the amount lost because of the fire, assuming that the corporation had no insurance coverage.

(b) Prepare the journal entry to record the loss and account for the damaged inventory in a separate Damaged Inventory account. In the same entry, record cost of goods sold for the year ended December 31.

(c) How would the loss be classified on the income statement of Reena Corp.?

(d) While the gross profit percentage has averaged 40% over the past five years, it has been as high as 42% and as low as 37.5%. Given this information, should a range of possible loss amounts be provided instead of a single figure? Explain.

DIGGING
DEEPER

P8-11 Sier Specialty Corp., a division of FH Inc., manufactures three models of bicycle gearshift components that are sold to bicycle manufacturers, retailers, and catalogue outlets. Since beginning operations in 1969, Sier has used normal absorption costing and has assumed a first-in, first-out cost flow in its perpetual inventory system. Except for overhead, manufacturing costs are accumulated using actual costs. Overhead is applied to production using predetermined overhead rates. The balances of the inventory accounts at the end of Sier's fiscal year, September 30, 2017, follow. The inventories are stated at cost before any year-end adjustments.

Finished goods	$757,000
Work in process	192,500
Raw materials	300,000
Factory supplies	69,000

The following information relates to Sier's inventory and operations:

1. The finished goods inventory consists of these items:

	Cost	Net realizable value
Down tube shifter		
Standard model	$ 97,500	$ 67,000
Click adjustment model	94,500	87,000
Deluxe model	108,000	110,000
Total down tube shifters	300,000	264,000
Bar end shifter		
Standard model	133,000	120,050
Click adjustment model	79,000	108,150
Total bar end shifters	212,000	228,200
Head tube shifter		
Standard model	128,000	103,650
Click adjustment model	117,000	145,300
Total head tube shifters	245,000	248,950
Total finished goods	$757,000	$741,150

2. Half of the finished goods inventory of head tube shifters is at catalogue outlets on consignment.

3. Three-quarters of the finished goods inventory of bar end shifters has been pledged as collateral for a bank loan.

4. Half of the raw materials balance is for derailleurs acquired at a contracted price that is 20% above the current market price. The net realizable value of the rest of the raw materials is $135,500.

5. The total net realizable value of the work-in-process inventory is $105,500.

6. Included in the cost of factory supplies are obsolete items with a historical cost of $4,200. The net realizable value of the remaining factory supplies is $65,900.

7. Sier applies the lower of cost and net realizable value method to each of the three types of shifters in finished goods inventory. For each of the other three inventory accounts, Sier applies the lower of cost and net realizable value method to the total of each inventory account.

8. Consider all of the amounts presented above as being material amounts in relation to Sier's financial statements as a whole.

Instructions

(a) Assuming that ASPE is followed, prepare the inventory section of Sier's statement of financial position as at September 30, 2017, including any required note(s).

(b) Regardless of your answer to (a), assume that the net realizable value of Sier's inventories is less than cost. Explain how this decline would be presented in Sier's income statement for the fiscal year ended September 30, 2017, under ASPE.

(c) Assume that Sier has a firm purchase commitment for the same type of derailleur that is included in the raw materials inventory as at September 30, 2017, and that the purchase commitment is at a contracted price that is 15% higher than the current market price. These derailleurs are to be delivered to Sier after September 30, 2017. Discuss the impact, if any, that this purchase commitment would have on Sier's financial statements prepared for the fiscal year ended September 30, 2017, under ASPE.

(d) How would your response to (c) change under IFRS?

(e) Explain and compare the disclosure requirements under ASPE and IFRS.

P8-12 The Eserine Wood Corporation manufactures desks. Most of the company's desks are standard models that are sold at catalogue prices. At December 31, 2017, the following finished desks appear in the company's inventory:

Finished Desks	Type A	Type B	Type C	Type D
2017 catalogue selling price	$460	$490	$890	$1,040
FIFO cost per inventory list, Dec. 31, 2017	410	450	830	960
Estimated current cost to manufacture (at Dec. 31, 2017, and early 2018)	460	440	790	1,000
Sales commissions and estimated other costs of disposal	40	65	95	130
2018 catalogue selling price	575	650	780	1,420
Quantity on hand	15	117	113	110

The 2017 catalogue was in effect through November 2017, and the 2018 catalogue is effective as of December 1, 2017. All catalogue prices are net of the usual discounts. Generally, the company tries to obtain a 20% gross margin on the selling price and it has usually been successful in achieving this.

Instructions

(a) Assume that the company has adopted a lower of FIFO cost and net realizable value approach for the valuation of inventories and applies it on an individual inventory item basis. At what total inventory value will the desks appear on the company's December 31, 2017 balance sheet?

(b) Explain the rationale for using the lower of cost and net realizable rule for inventories.

(c) Explain the impact if inventory was valued at lower of cost and net realizable value on a total basis.

*P8-13 The records for the Clothing Department of Danny's Discount Store are summarized below for the month of January.

Inventory, January 1: at retail $25,000; at cost $17,000

Purchases in January: at retail $137,000; at cost $82,500

Freight-in: $7,000 Purchase returns: at retail $3,000; at cost $2,300

Transfers in from suburban branch: at retail $13,000; at cost $9,200

Net markups: $8,000

Net markdowns: $4,000

Inventory losses due to normal breakage, and so on: at retail $400

Sales revenue at retail: $95,000

Sales returns: $2,400

Instructions

(a) Calculate the inventory for this department as at January 31, at retail prices.

(b) Calculate the ending inventory using the lower of cost and net realizable value method

*P8-14 The records for the Clothing Department of Ji-Woon's Department Store are summarized as follows for the month of January:

1. Inventory, January 1: at retail, $28,000; at cost, $18,000

2. Purchases in January: at retail, $147,000; at cost, $110,000

3. Freight-in: $6,000

4. Purchase returns: at retail, $3,500; at cost, $2,700

5. Purchase allowances: $2,200

6. Transfers in from suburban branch: at retail, $13,000; at cost, $9,200

7. Net markups: $8,000

8. Net markdowns: $4,000

9. Inventory losses due to normal breakage, and so on: at retail, $400

10. Sales at retail: $121,000

11. Sales returns: $2,400

Instructions

(a) Estimate the inventory for this department as at January 31 at (1) retail and (2) the lower of average cost and market. Round the cost-to-retail ratio to two decimal places.

(b) Assume that a physical inventory count taken at retail prices after the close of business on January 31 indicated an inventory amount that is $450 less than what was estimated in (a), part (1). What could have caused this discrepancy?

P8-15 Some of the information found on a detailed inventory card for Soave Stationery Ltd. for May is as follows:

Date	Received No. of Units	Received Unit Cost	Issued No. of Units	Balance No. of Units
May 1 (opening balance)	1,150	$2.90		1,150
2	1,050	3.00		2,200
7			700	1,500
10	600	3.20		2,100
13			500	1,600
18	1,000	3.30	300	2,300
20			1,100	1,200
23	1,300	3.40		2,500
26			800	1,700
28	1,500	3.60		3,200
31			1,300	1,900

Instructions

(a) From the above data, calculate the ending inventory based on each of the following cost formulas. Assume that perpetual inventory records are kept in units only and average cost is calculated monthly at each month end. Carry unit costs to the nearest cent and ending inventory to the nearest dollar.

1. First-in, first-out (FIFO)
2. Weighted average cost

(b) Based on your results in part (a), and assuming that the average selling price per unit during May was $7.25, prepare partial income statements up to the "gross profit on sales" line. Calculate the gross profit percentage under each inventory cost formula. Comment on your results.

(c) Assume the perpetual inventory record is kept in dollars, and costs are calculated at the time of each withdrawal. Recalculate the amounts under this revised assumption, carrying average unit costs to four decimal places. Would the ending inventory amounts under each of the two cost formulas above be the same? Explain.

P8-16 Hull Company's record of transactions concerning part X for the month of April was as follows.

	Purchases			Sales	
April	1 (balance on hand)	100 @ $5.00	April	5	300
	4	400 @ 5.10		12	200
	11	300 @ 5.30		27	800
	18	200 @ 5.35		28	150
	26	600 @ 5.60			
	30	200 @ 5.80			

(a) Calculate the inventory at April 30 on each of the following bases. Assume that perpetual inventory records are kept in units only. Carry unit costs to the nearest cent.

1. First-in, first-out (FIFO)
2. Average cost

(b) If the perpetual inventory record is kept in dollars, and costs are calculated at the time of each withdrawal, what amount would be shown as ending inventory in (1) and (2) above? (Carry average unit costs to four decimal places.)

Cases

Refer to the Case Primer on the Student Website and in *WileyPLUS* to help you answer these cases.

CA8-1 Tobacco Group Inc. (TGI) is in the consumer packaged goods industry. Its shares are widely held and key shareholders include several very large pension funds.

In the current year, 59% of the net revenues and 61% of operating income came from tobacco product sales. Because of the health risks related to the use of tobacco products, the industry is increasingly regulated by government and the company is implicated in substantial tobacco-related litigation.

During the past three years, the company entered into agreements with the government to settle asserted and unasserted health-care recovery costs and other claims. The agreements, known as the Government Settlement Agreements, call for payments by the domestic tobacco industry into a fund in the following amounts:

Current year	$10.9 billion
Following four years	$8 billion each year
Thereafter	$9 billion each year

The fund will be used to settle claims and aid tobacco growers. Each company's share of these payments is based on its market share, and TGI records its portion of the settlement costs as cost of goods sold upon shipment. These amounts may increase based on several factors, including inflation and industry volume. In the past three years, the company has accrued costs of more than $5 billion each year.

Another significant lawsuit, the class action, is still in process. Last year, the jury returned a verdict assessing punitive damages against various defendants, and TGI was responsible for $74 billion. The company is contesting this and the lawsuit continues. As a result of preliminary judicial stipulations, the company has placed $500 million in a separate interest-bearing escrow account. This money will be kept by the court and distributed to the plaintiffs regardless of the outcome of the trial. The company also placed $1.2 billion in another escrow account, and this amount will be returned to the company if it wins the case.

Instructions

Assume the role of a financial analyst and discuss the related financial reporting issues. Specifically, note alternative accounting treatments for each issue and recommend how each issue should be treated in the financial statements.

CA8-2   Findit Gold Inc. (FGI) was created in 2008 and is 25% owned by Findit Mining Corporation (FMC). FGI's shares trade on the local exchange and its objective is to become a substantial low-cost mineral producer in developing countries. FMC provided substantial financial support to FGI when FGI was in the exploration stage.

Over the most recent five-year period, FGI carried its gold bullion inventory at net realizable value and recognized revenues on the gold produced (net of refining and selling costs) at net realizable value, when the minerals were produced. Gold is a commodity that trades actively and whose price fluctuates according to supply and demand.

Instructions

Assume the role of the controller of FMC and assess the financial reporting policies relating to inventory valuation and revenue recognition.

CA8-3   Lots Lumber Limited is a private company that operates in the forestry sector and owns timber lots. The company produces specialty lumber and sells to distributors and retailers. Currently, Lots uses ASPE when preparing its financial statements. It has an October 31 year end. The company has a management bonus plan, which is based on net earnings and gross profits.

In the past, the company estimated decommissioning costs related to its sawmill facility and recorded them as a liability, with an offsetting increase to the cost of the plant. Since the production period can be fairly long, including the curing and special treatments applied to the lumber, the company has had to borrow to finance the production process. Lots' borrowings are primarily from a private investor, who has set two key requirements in the loan agreement. The agreement requires Lots to maintain a certain debt to equity ratio and to submit audited financial statements prepared using GAAP. The audited financial statements are due within 60 days of the year-end date. Historically, the company has expensed this interest for borrowings from the private investor.

The company has a purchase commitment to buy a minimum amount of specialty resins used to treat the lumber. This is a five-year contract at a fixed price. At the time the contract was signed, Lots was very excited about it, but now, early in the fourth year of the contract, the company has realized that it will not need the volumes that it committed to buy, because it has developed a new technique that is cheaper and that uses a different solution to treat the wood. In fact, it looks as though the company will have to pay for items that will not be required. Lots is trying to decide whether to break the contract or remain with the contract and just pay for the items but not take delivery. There are two years remaining on the contract.

Instructions

Lots Lumber Limited has just hired you as its new controller. It is trying to decide whether to adopt IFRS or continue to report under ASPE. Provide the president with a report that details the impact of reporting under IFRS on the company's financial results, management bonus plan, and debt covenant, giving consideration to the issues indicated above.

FINANCE

ENABLING COMPETENCIES # Integrated Case

(*Hint:* If there are issues here that are new, use the conceptual framework to help you support your analysis with solid reasoning.)

IC8-1   Grappa Grapes Inc. (GGI) grows grapes and produces sparkling wines. The company is located in a very old area of town with easy access to fertile farmland that is excellent for growing grapes. It is owned by the Grappa family. The company has been in operation for 100 years and a large part of its success lies in the excellent vineyards and unique process for producing vintage wines. About every three years, new farmland is purchased from land owners adjacent to the original farm. New vines are planted on the newly purchased land. Generally, it takes about another three years for the vines to produce quality grapes for wine-making.

The winery sits at the edge of a range of hills that are composed of chalk. GGI has dug "caves" into the side of the hills at a significant cost and the chalk caves provide the perfect temperature and humidity for the maturing wines. All of the vintage wines are produced, aged, and stored in these chalk caves. People come from all over the country to visit the "caves." As a matter of fact, 25% of the company's revenues are from winery tours.

The company has had three years where it has managed to produce vintage wines. Vintage wines are of higher quality and sell for a higher price. In addition, they contribute to the prestige of the winery. Because of this success,

GGI has started to sell wine "futures." Under the terms of the contract, large wholesalers pay GGI up front and agree to take delivery of a certain number of bottles in two years at 20% off the predetermined future price. A market for trading these contracts now exists for the buyers of the futures.

During the year, in anticipation of increasing costs, the company placed a purchase order for a significant number of oak barrels from France. The barrels are used to age the wines. Because of the declining value of the dollar during a current economic recession and the demand for wines in general over the past year, the value of the barrels has actually declined to below the price locked into under the purchase commitments. The supplier is confident that this is only a temporary decline in value and that the price of the barrels will increase within the next couple of months. GGI may get out of the purchase commitment either by taking delivery of the barrels at the agreed-upon price or by settling net in cash for the difference between the agreed-upon price and the market price (times the number of barrels ordered).

The year has been a very rainy one and some of the very old chalk caves have begun to leak and deteriorate. One of the caves holding a large number of vintage wines collapsed. It is unclear whether the wine is salvageable. The company's insurance will not cover the expected loss, although GGI has hired its lawyers to challenge this, as it feels that the insurance company should cover the loss.

GGI has decided to follow GAAP for the current year's financial statements, as it is planning to go to the bank for a loan. The company's bookkeeper has prepared the draft comparative financial statements for the years ended March 2017 and 2016, but has not dealt with the special issues identified above. GGI's comparative draft financial statements are presented below.

GRAPPA GRAPES INC.
Balance Sheet
December 31, 2017
(in thousands of Canadian dollars)

Assets

	March 31, 2017	March 31, 2016
Cash	$ 87	$ 44
Accounts and notes receivable	3,900	3,256
Inventory	17,453	16,112
Prepaid expense	137	124
Property, plant and equipment (net)	15,890	14,389
	$37,467	$33,925

Liabilities and Shareholders' Equity

	March 31, 2017	March 31, 2016
Accounts payable and accrued liabilities	$ 5,009	$ 4,678
Unearned revenue	3,208	3,320
Income taxes payable	3	2
Current portion of long-term debt	490	490
Long-term debt	4,520	5,010
Common shares	100	100
Retained earnings	24,137	20,325
	$37,467	$33,925

GRAPPA GRAPES INC.
Income Statement
For the years ended March 31
(in thousands of Canadian dollars)

	2017	2016
Sales	$43,303	$41,039
Cost of goods sold	26,329	24,956
Amortization of plant and equipment used in production	754	686
Gross profit	16,220	15,397
Selling and administration	10,143	9,461
Amortization of plant and equipment used in selling and administration	441	410
Interest	352	385
Operating earnings	5,284	5,141
Other expenses	21	15
Earnings before income taxes	5,263	5,126
Income taxes	1,412	1,314
Net earnings for the year	3,851	3,812

Instructions

Assume the role of the controller and analyze the financial reporting issues.

RESEARCH AND FINANCIAL ANALYSIS

RA8-1 Brookfield Asset Management Inc.

Brookfield Asset Management Inc. (Brookfield), as described in Note 1 to its financial statements, is a "global alternative asset management company" that "owns and operates assets with a focus on property, renewable energy, infrastructure and private equity." Brookfield's financial statements for its annual period ended December 31, 2014, are at the end of this book.

Instructions

(a) How much inventory does Brookfield have at December 31, 2014, and at December 31, 2013? Identify the types of inventory that the company reports on its December 31, 2014 balance sheet. What do you know about these assets, since they are included in the inventory category?

(b) How much inventory was recognized as an expense in the year? What comments, if any, can you make about the inventory held at the end of the reporting period?

(c) Describe the accounting policies for inventory. Is there any additional information you would like to know?

RA8-2 Stora Enso Oyj

Stora Enso Oyj described its business in its annual report as the "global rethinker of the biomaterials, paper, packaging and wood products industry."

Instructions

Access the financial statements in the financial report of Stora Enso Oyj for its year ended December 31, 2014, from the company's website. With reference to the financial statements, answer the following questions.

(a) Describe the accounting policies that the company uses for reporting inventories. What types of expenses are included in costs? Is interest included in inventory costs?

(b) What different components make up Stora's inventory and what is the percentage of each of the total for December 31, 2014 and 2013? Which items represent a high percentage of the inventory? How has this changed over the years? Is there any cause for concern? What was the amount reported on the income statement related to inventory items? Is it possible to calculate the days in inventory ratio?

(c) Does the company use the allowance method or the direct method to record writedowns to the inventory? What was the writedown amount during 2014? Were there any amounts reversed during the year?

(d) How are the inventories of standing trees measured and reported? What types of assumptions are needed to determine the reported amount of these assets? Where are these assets located? How much was harvested this year? What other changes occurred in 2014 in the company's biological assets? What are the effects on earnings for the current year and previous year?

(e) Is this inventory-related disclosure useful to the reader? Is there any other information you would like to have?

RA8-3 Canadian Tire Corporation, Limited

Refer to the 2014 annual report of **Canadian Tire Corporation, Limited**, available at SEDAR (www.sedar.com) or the company's website (www.canadiantire.ca). Note that the company provides a 10-year financial review at the end of its annual report. This summary gives relevant comparative information that is useful for determining trends and predicting the company's future results and position.

Instructions

Prepare three graphs covering the 2010–2014 period. (Express all amounts for the first two graphs in $ millions.) The first graph is for net earnings from continuing operations over this five-year period, the second for working capital, and the third for the current ratio. Based on the graphs, predict the values you might expect for the next fiscal period.

RA8-4 Andrew Peller Limited

Access the annual financial statements of **Andrew Peller Limited** for the year ended March 31, 2015, on SEDAR (www.sedar.com) or the company's website (www.andrewpeller.com).

Instructions

Refer to these financial statements and the accompanying notes to answer the following questions.

(a) How significant are the inventories relative to total current assets? What categories of inventory does Andrew Peller Limited report?

(b) Identify all the accounting policies that are the basis for the inventory values reported on the March 31, 2015 balance sheet.

(c) Which category of inventory represents the highest percentage? Is this what you would expect?

(d) What was the amount recognized in expense related to inventory for the years ended March 31, 2015 and 2014? Were there any writedowns of inventory or reversals of writedowns for these two years?

(e) What was Andrew Peller's inventory turnover ratio for the year ended March 31, 2015? What is the average age of the inventory? Comment briefly.

(f) Compare the gross profit ratios for the two most recent years that are reported. Comment briefly on why there might be changes from year to year.

(g) If Andrew Peller Limited was a private enterprise that followed ASPE, how would the company have accounted for its vineyard and grape assets? What would be the likely impact on the balance sheet? On the income statement?

(h) In 2014, the IASB released amendments to IAS 16 *Property, Plant, and Equipment,* and to IAS 41 *Biological Assets.* The amendments relate to bearer plants such as grapevines. What do the amendments require, when are they effective, and what effect does Peller indicate the change will have on its financial statements?

RA8-5   Loblaw Companies Limited and Empire Company Limited

Instructions

From SEDAR (www.sedar.com) or the company websites, access the financial statements of **Loblaw Companies Limited** for its year ended January 3, 2015, and **Empire Company Limited** for its year ended May 2, 2015. Review the financial statements and answer the following questions.

(a) Describe the businesses that Loblaw and Empire operate in.

(b) What is the amount of inventory reported by Loblaw at January 3, 2015, and by Empire at May 2, 2015? What percent of total assets is invested in inventory by each company? How does this compare with the previous year?

(c) Identify the inventory policies for each company that support the inventory values reported on their respective balance sheets. Comment on whether any aspects of inventory valuation might be open to significant estimation.

(d) How much did each company report for inventory expenses in the current and previous year? What was the writedown (and reversal of writedowns) related to inventories for the current and previous year for each company?

(e) What are vendor rebates and allowances? How do the companies account for these? Is this the appropriate treatment? How might the amount recognized change if proposed changes in the conceptual framework are adopted?

(f) Calculate and compare the inventory turnover ratios and days to sell inventory for the two companies for the most current year.

(g) Comment on the results of your calculations in (f) above. Would any differences identified in any of the earlier analyses above help explain differences in the ratios between the two companies? What might be some reasons for the differences between the two companies?

RA8-6   Research: Manufacturing Inventory

Identify a company in your local community that develops a product through some form of manufacturing process. Consider a farming operation, bakery, cement supplier, or other company that converts or assembles inputs to develop a different product.

Instructions

Write a report on the company's inventory and its conversion process. (*Suggestions:* Visit the manufacturing site, view a video of the operation, or speak to company management.) Identify what types of costs are incurred in the manufacturing process. Determine which costs are included in inventory cost in the accounting records, and explain why some may be treated as period costs. Does the company use a periodic or a perpetual system? What cost formula does the company use? How does the company determine NRV, or does it?

ENDNOTES

¹ *CPA Canada Handbook–Accounting,* Part II, Section 3031.07 and IAS 2.6. Copyright © IFRS Foundation. All rights reserved. Reproduced by John Wiley & Sons Canada, Ltd. with the permission of the IFRS Foundation®. Reproduction and use rights are strictly limited. No permission granted to third parties to reproduce or distribute.

² Terms other than "f.o.b. shipping point" or "f.o.b. destination" (for example, "CIF" for "cost, insurance, freight") are often used to identify when legal title passes. The f.o.b. terms are used in this text to reflect that an agreement on when title passes must be reached between the buyer and seller in the purchase–sale contract. In a particular situation, the terms of the sales contract are examined to determine when the risks and rewards of ownership pass from the seller to the buyer.

³ Purchase commitments sometimes have the characteristics of derivatives. Derivatives are generally recognized and valued at fair value on an ongoing basis. Should purchase commitments be accounted for as derivatives? We will revisit this topic in Chapter 16.

⁴ To correct the error in the same year before the books are closed, and assuming inventories are adjusted before the closing entries, the following entries are needed, depending on whether the periodic or perpetual method is used. We will come back to these two methods later in the chapter.

Periodic Method		Perpetual Method	
Purchases	$x	Inventory	$x
Accounts Payable	$x	Accounts Payable	$x
Inventory	$x		
Cost of Goods Sold	$x		

⁵ *CPA Canada Handbook,* Part II, Section 3031.11 and IAS 2.10. Copyright © IFRS Foundation. All rights reserved. Reproduced by John Wiley & Sons Canada, Ltd. with the permission of the IFRS Foundation®. Reproduction and use rights are strictly limited. No permission granted to third parties to reproduce or distribute.

6 Both *CPA Canada Handbook*, Part II, Section 3031 and IAS 2 indicate that trade discounts are deducted in determining the costs of purchase. They also indicate that, to the extent the purchase arrangement contains a financing element, the amount paid in excess of the amount payable under normal credit terms is recognized as interest expense over the period when the payable is outstanding.

7 As indicated in Chapter 2, as work progresses on a revised conceptual framework, it is likely that the "probable" criterion of the asset definition will be removed. Instead, probability will be taken into account in the measurement of the asset.

8 Normal capacity is "the production expected to be achieved on average over a number of periods or seasons under normal circumstances, taking into account the loss of capacity resulting from planned maintenance" (*CPA Canada Handbook*, Part II, Section 3031.14 and IAS 2.13). Copyright IFRS Foundation. All rights reserved. Reproduced by John Wiley & Sons Canada, Ltd. with the permission of the IFRS Foundation®. Reproduction and use rights are strictly limited. No permission granted to third parties to reproduce or distribute.

9 The reporting rules on interest capitalization have their greatest impact in accounting for property, plant, and equipment and, therefore, are discussed in detail in Chapter 10.

10 IAS 23.7 and 8 as well as IAS 23.4. This option also exists for qualifying inventory items measured at fair value, such as biological assets.

11 In recent years, some companies have developed methods of determining inventories, including statistical sampling, that are sufficiently reliable to make an annual count of each item of inventory unnecessary.

12 *CPA Canada Handbook*, Part II, Section 3031.28 and IAS 2.29. Copyright IFRS Foundation. All rights reserved. Reproduced by Wiley Canada with the permission of the IFRS Foundation®. Reproduction and use rights are strictly limited. No permission granted to third parties to reproduce or distribute.

13 The Canada Revenue Agency requires that, in determining the lower of cost and NRV, the comparison should be made separately and individually in respect of each item in the inventory (or each usual class of items if specific items are not readily distinguishable). Comparing total cost and total market is only permitted when the cost of the specific items (using specific identification, FIFO, or average cost) is not known and only an average cost is available (*CRA Interpretation Bulletin*—473R, December 21, 1998, on "Inventory Valuation," par. 3).

14 While fair value less costs to sell appears to be the same as net realizable value (selling price less costs to sell), it is different. NRV is an entity-specific value, whereas fair values reflect a market-based valuation.

15 The entries to account for inventories carried at net realizable value are similar to those for assets carried at fair value less costs to sell. The changes in NRV are recognized in the Inventory account and in income in the period the NRV changes.

16 The IASB issued an amendment to IAS 41 in June 2014 effective for years beginning on or after January 1, 2016. Essentially, the amendment treats bearer plants like property, plant, and equipment; however, animals are still accounted for under IAS 41.

17 IAS 41.B61 notes that the standard does not deal with how to account for expenditures related to biological assets. Therefore, there is a choice to capitalize or expense. In addition, there is judgement involved in determining which costs should be capitalized if this option is used. Inventory accounting would generally support direct costs and a reasonable allocation of overhead.

18 An alternative approach to estimating inventory using the gross profit percentage, considered by some to be less complicated than the method in Illustration 8-29, uses the standard income statement format as follows (assume the same data as in Illustration 8-29):

Sales		$280,000		$280,000
Cost of goods sold				
Beginning inventory	$ 60,000		$ 60,000	
Purchases	200,000		200,000	
Goods available for sale	260,000		260,000	
Ending inventory	(3) ?		(3) 64,000 Est.	
Cost of goods sold		(2) ?		(2) 196,000 Est.
Gross profit on sales (30%)		(1) ?		(1) $84,000 Est.

Calculate the unknowns as follows: first the gross profit amount, then cost of goods sold, and then the ending inventory.

(1) $280,000 × 30\% = \$84,000$ (gross profit on sales)

(2) $280,000 - \$84,000 = \$196,000$ (cost of goods sold)

(3) $260,000 - \$196,000 = \$64,000$ (ending inventory)

REFERENCE TO THE CPA COMPETENCY MAP	LEARNING OBJECTIVES
	After studying this chapter, you should be able to:
1.1.1, 1.1.2, 1.2.1, 1.4.5, 5.2.2	**1.** Understand the nature of investments, including which types of companies have significant investments.
1.2.1, 1.2.2, 5.2.2	**2.** Explain and apply the cost/amortized cost model of accounting for investments.
1.2.1, 1.2.2, 1.2.3	**3.** Explain and apply the fair value through net income model of accounting for investments.
1.1.2, 1.2.1, 1.2.2, 1.2.3	**4.** Explain and apply the fair value through other comprehensive income model of accounting for investments.
1.2.1, 1.2.2, 1.2.3, 2.3.1	**5.** Explain and apply the incurred loss, expected loss, and fair value loss impairment models.
1.2.1, 1.2.2, 1.2.3	**6.** Explain the concept of significant influence and apply the equity method.
1.2.1, 1.2.2, 1.2.3	**7.** Explain the concept of control and when consolidation is appropriate.
1.2.1, 1.2.2, 1.2.3, 1.3.2, 1.4.1, 1.4.2, 1.4.4, 1.4.5, 5.1.1, 5.2.2	**8.** Explain how investments are presented and disclosed in the financial statements, noting how this facilitates analysis.
1.1.4	**9.** Identify differences in accounting between IFRS and ASPE, and what changes are expected in the near future.

MINIMIZING RISK, MAXIMIZING RETURNS

SOME OF THE biggest investors in the world aren't billionaires or even corporations. They're institutional investors, such as pension plans, which invest money on behalf of large groups of people. In the case of pension plans, they invest contributions made by employers and employees to fund their retirement. The stakes are high, as pension plans often need billions of dollars to pay member benefits. The plans' investment strategies have to pay off in the long term.

One of the largest institutional investors in Canada is OMERS, the Ontario Municipal Employees Retirement System. It provides pension benefits on behalf of about 1,000 employers across Ontario. Its more than 450,000 members include working and retired employees from municipalities, non-teaching staff of school boards, and utilities, among others. At the end of 2014, OMERS had $76.9 billion in pension obligations—money that it will eventually owe members—but only $72.0 billion in net assets. The difference is called a funding shortfall.

OMERS is trying to get higher returns on its investments so that it can wipe out its funding shortfall between 2021 and 2025. But it has to minimize risk while achieving higher returns.

GettyImages/Peter Dazeley

To do this, OMERS has been changing the proportion of assets in public markets (such as publicly traded stocks) versus private markets (such as investments in private companies). Over several years, it's been moving from roughly an 80/20 public-private split to a goal of about 50/50. "The shift in asset mix policy reflected the concerns of [employers] that the Pension Plan was over exposed to volatile stock markets," OMERS says in a strategy document. "Stock market shocks have occurred more frequently since 2002 with declines by 10% or more on five occasions, including the 33% meltdown due to the 2008 global credit crisis. Large stock market surprises to the upside were less frequent. The first priority of a prudent pension plan investor is to preserve capital, recognizing that a 33% decline on $1 billion in a single year would require a 50% return to get back to $1 billion."

Part of OMERS' investment in private assets is its own company, Oxford Properties, which owns, develops, and manages real estate in cities such as Toronto, New York, and London. These properties, including office towers, hotels, and shopping malls, produce rental income from long-term tenants. OMERS has another arm, Borealis Infrastructure, that invests in large infrastructure projects such as Bruce Power, Canada's largest nuclear power generation facility, and a natural gas transmission facility in the Czech Republic.

By diversifying its asset mix, OMERS is keeping some investments for long-term income, and others to be bought and sold for short-term gains.

Sources: John Tilak and Euan Rocha, "Canada's OMERS Posts Solid 2014 Results, Targets Asset Mix Shift," Reuters, February 27, 2015; "Managing Risk to Earn More Consistent Long-Term Returns: Background Paper on OMERS Investment Strategies," OMERS, February 2014; OMERS 2014 annual report.

PREVIEW OF CHAPTER 9

This chapter focuses on the different types of financial asset investments in equity and debt instruments, and the various models used to account for them. The nature of the investments and the company's business model help determine how the investments are accounted for and reported. This chapter covers a variety of investments, from those held for short-term profit-taking to those held for longer term strategic purposes. We covered accounting for investments in loans and receivables, also financial assets, in Chapter 7. We will cover accounting for investments in nonmonetary assets such as land and investment properties in Chapter 10.

The problems with the historical cost model have been recognized for a long time, especially in accounting for financial instruments. Because of this, accounting for such instruments has been on the agendas of standard-setting bodies around the world for many years. Standard setters have put accounting standards in place that require many of these assets to be accounted for at fair value. However, financial reporting under these standards has its problems. Because only some of the instruments are recognized at fair value, the standards are unnecessarily complicated. While many of the problems are related to more complex issues, accounting for ordinary investments in other companies' debt and equity instruments continues to be controversial.

The IASB has issued comprehensive guidance on how to measure fair values, as we discussed in Chapters 2 and 3, as well as a new standard dealing with investments (IFRS 9). The mandatory implementation date for IFRS 9 was pushed back to 2018. This was to allow companies time to assess the impact of this standard. Until then, IAS 39 deals with accounting for investments unless companies make a decision to adopt IFRS 9 early. Once the current version of IFRS 9 is fully implemented, IAS 39 will disappear except for some additional guidance on hedging. Because the area is in transition, this chapter focuses on the basics, including the measurement of investments and recognition of income. It also focuses on the IFRS 9 accounting as well as the guidance provided under ASPE.

INVESTMENTS				
Understanding Investments	**Measurement**	**Strategic Investments**	**Presentation, Disclosure, and Analysis**	**IFRS/ASPE Comparison**
▪ Types of investments ▪ Types of companies that have investments ▪ Information for decision-making	▪ Cost/amortized cost model ▪ Fair value through net income (FV-NI) model ▪ Fair value through Other Comprehensive Income (FV-OCI) model ▪ Impairment models	▪ Investments in associates ▪ Investments in subsidiaries	▪ Presentation and disclosure ▪ Analysis	▪ A comparison of IFRS and ASPE ▪ Looking ahead

UNDERSTANDING INVESTMENTS

Types of Investments

As a general rule, companies hold investments for one of two reasons:

1. to have the capital appreciate, or

2. to earn dividends and/or income.

Various types of investments can provide a return for either or both of these reasons. There are two main types of investments: debt instruments and equity instruments.

Companies that invest in **debt instruments** of another entity are creditors of the issuing company. Debt instruments include **debt securities**, whose prices are normally quoted in an active market, such as investments in government and corporate bonds, convertible debt, and commercial paper. Debt instruments generally have contractual requirements regarding repayment of principal and payment of interest. The rights depend on the specific debt instrument. As shown in the transaction box, when a company invests in debt instruments, it usually pays cash upfront and receives the rights to receive interest and the return of principal at a later date.

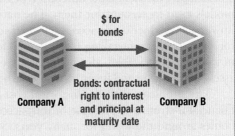

Company A buys bonds from Company B. The bonds carry with them contractual rights to annual interest and repayment of principal in 10 years. Bonds may also be purchased through intermediaries.

$ for bonds

Company A

Bonds: contractual right to interest and principal at maturity date

Company B

LAW AND TREASURY MANAGEMENT
5.2.2

Equity instruments, on the other hand, represent ownership interests. Typical examples are common, preferred, or other capital stock or shares. They also include rights to acquire or dispose of ownership interests at an agreed-upon or determinable price, such as warrants, rights, and call or put options. An equity instrument is any contract that is evidence of a residual interest in the assets of an entity after deducting all of its liabilities. Equity instruments generally do not have a maturity date and pay dividends (instead of interest). The holder of the share is entitled to certain rights depending on the nature of the instrument. As shown in the transaction box, when a company purchases equity instruments, it pays cash upfront and receives various rights, which may include rights to dividends, voting rights, and rights to residual assets upon liquidation.

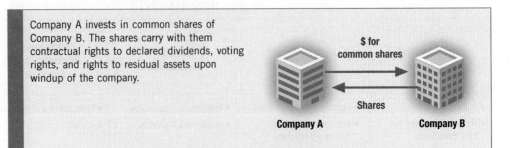

Company A invests in common shares of Company B. The shares carry with them contractual rights to declared dividends, voting rights, and rights to residual assets upon windup of the company.

$ for common shares

Company A

Shares

Company B

This chapter will deal with investments in equity and debt instruments, both temporary and long-term. Chapter 16 will discuss the more complex financial instruments such as stock options and other derivatives.

Types of Companies That Have Investments

Before looking at how to account for investments, we address the **different motivations that companies have for investing** in debt and equity instruments issued by other companies. One motivation is **the returns provided by investments** through interest, dividends, or capital appreciation (an increase in the underlying value of the investment). Note that some types of investments provide guaranteed returns (such as term deposits), while others are riskier (such as investments in shares of other companies). Managers may invest for **short-term returns** or **longer-term returns**, depending on their business and whether, and when, they need the cash for other purposes.

Another reason for investing in equity instruments such as common shares has more to do with **corporate strategy** than returns. Companies may invest in common shares of other companies because they want to have a special relationship with a supplier or customer, such as being able to access certain distribution channels or a supply of raw materials. Other investments are made so that the **investor** can exercise its rights to influence or control the operations of the other company, the **investee**. The intent with these strategic investments is usually to establish a long-term operating relationship between the two entities.

Not all companies invest in other companies. It depends on the nature of the business model and the industry that they operate in. Examples of companies that carry significant amounts of investments in financial instruments include financial institutions such as banks, pension funds, and insurance companies. Banks add value by investing other people's money and earning a return that is higher than their cost of capital. Their expertise lies in understanding how and when to buy and sell shares and debt instruments in order to maximize profits. They often buy and sell investments over the short term for profit (referred to as **trading**). Pension plans, such as **OMERS** in our feature story, collect money from employees and pay out funds as pensions when the employees retire. In order to maximize the payout on retirement, pension plans generally invest the money in the interim and try to maximize the value of the investments. Illustration 9-1 shows the significance of investments in

REAL WORLD EMPHASIS

Illustration 9-1

Excerpt from the Financial Statements of the Royal Bank of Canada

Consolidated Balance Sheets		
	As at	
(Millions of Canadian dollars)	**October 31 2014**	October 31 2013
Assets		
Cash and due from banks	$ 17,421	$ 15,550
Interest-bearing deposits with banks	8,399	9,039
Securities (Note 4)		
Trading	151,380	144,023
Available-for-sale	47,768	38,687
	199,148	182,710
Assets purchased under reverse repurchase agreements and securities borrowed	135,580	117,517
Loans (Note 5)		
Retail	334,987	320,627
Wholesale	102,236	90,182
	437,223	410,809
Allowance for loan losses (Note 5)	(1,994)	(1,959)
	435,229	408,850
Segregated fund net assets (Note 16)	675	513
Other		
Customers' liability under acceptances	11,462	9,953
Derivatives (Note 8)	87,402	74,822
Premises and equipment, net (Note 9)	2,684	2,636
Goodwill (Note 10)	8,647	8,332
Other intangibles (Note 10)	2,775	2,777
Investments in joint ventures and associates (Note 12)	295	247
Employee benefit assets (Note 17)	138	161
Other assets (Note 13)	30,695	26,638
	144,098	125,566
Total assets	$940,550	$859,745

securities for the **Royal Bank of Canada**. Investments in securities represent just over 21% of total assets, with their trading portfolio accounting for most of the investments.

Illustration 9-2 is an excerpt from the financial statements of **Canada Life Financial Corporation**, an insurance company. Note that insurance companies sell coverage against risk of loss. They charge their customers insurance premiums upfront in return for assuming the risk of loss. If an insured loss occurs in future, they have to pay out a settlement to the insured party. In the meantime, they invest the premiums in order to maximize their value. Investments in bonds and stocks represent 32.6% of the total assets of Canada Life. In addition, the segregated funds are primarily investments in stocks and bonds, so when we adjust for this, the percentage is actually approximately 79.4%.

REAL WORLD EMPHASIS

Illustration 9-2

Excerpt from the Financial Statements of Canada Life Financial Corporation

CONSOLIDATED BALANCE SHEETS
(in Canadian $ millions)

	December 31	
	2014	2013
Assets		
Cash and cash equivalents (note 4)	$ 1,545	$ 1,793
Bonds (note 5)	55,226	48,522
Mortgage loans (note 5)	6,822	6,120
Stocks (note 5)	2,412	2,565
Investment properties (note 5)	3,286	2,985
Loans to policyholders	906	885
	70,197	62,870
Funds held by ceding insurers (note 6)	11,823	10,566
Goodwill (note 11)	675	691
Intangible assets (note 11)	289	312
Derivative financial instruments (note 31)	326	342
Owner occupied properties (note 12)	215	205
Fixed assets (note 12)	54	57
Reinsurance assets (note 15)	8,408	7,805
Premiums in course of collection, accounts, and interest receivable	1,354	1,382
Other assets (note 13)	1,144	1,109
Current income taxes (note 29)	15	15
Deferred tax assets (note 29)	226	52
Investments on account of segregated fund policyholders (note 14)	82,083	76,326
Total assets	**$176,809**	**$161,732**

Note the diversity in presentation in these two illustrations. Sometimes the investments are labelled for the nature of the instruments, such as bonds or stocks, and sometimes they are labelled with accounting labels, such as **available for sale** or **held for trading**.[1] Many companies use different labels, so it is important to recognize which items represent investments.

A quick look at the level of investments in other industries, such as the airline, resort, and retail industries, shows that very few, if any, investments are generally reported on the statement of financial position. Examples include Air Canada, ClubLink, Sobeys, and Indigo Books & Music. Why don't they have significant amounts of investments? This is a good question. The answer lies in the fact that these companies' business models do not require investments to be held. Excess cash is normally used to reinvest in the business, pay down loans, or pay dividends. These companies make their income in other ways, such as selling airline tickets, golf club memberships, groceries, and books.

Information for Decision-Making

Because the nature and risk of various investments are different, it is useful to provide this information in the financial statements. It is also important to show how significant the investments are, including how much income is being earned (both realized and unrealized). In order to be transparent, financial reporting should therefore present this information, either in the notes or on the face of the statement of financial position. For this reason, disclosure and presentation requirements for investments are significant.

MEASUREMENT

UNDERLYING CONCEPT

Any information that assists users with decision-making is important. As we will see later, ASPE and IFRS mandate numerous specific disclosures regarding investments. Care must be taken to ensure that all relevant information is disclosed under the full disclosure principle.

How investments are accounted for can depend on **the type of instrument, management's intent**, company **strategy**, and the **ability to reliably measure the investment's fair value**.

The next section of this chapter explains the accounting models generally applied in accounting for straightforward investments in other companies' debt and equity instruments—situations where the investment does not result in the investor having significant influence or control over the other company. After these models are explained, the chapter turns to investments where the investor can exercise significant influence over or control the strategic decisions of the investee company. For these investments, the investor's ownership interest is usually large enough to give the investor a substantial voice at the investee's boardroom table in decisions about the entity's operations, investments, and financing. This, in turn, affects how these investments are accounted for and reported.

Accounting for investments usually requires them to be recognized and measured initially at their fair value at acquisition. Recall that Chapters 2 and 3 discuss what is meant by fair value and identify various ways that fair value can be measured. Chapters 2 and 3 also indicate that some methods of measuring fair value are preferred over others, with prices in an active market being the best evidence of the value we are trying to capture. We saw in previous chapters that unless there is evidence to the contrary, the price paid to acquire an asset is usually considered to be its fair value.

The price of a **debt** instrument is quoted as a percentage of its par or face value. For example, if a $25,000 face value bond is priced at 99, this means that its fair value is 99% of $25,000, or $24,750. If it is priced at 103.5, it will sell for 103.5% of $25,000, or $25,875. **Shares** that are traded on a stock exchange are usually quoted at the market price per share in dollars and cents.

Investments in shares may be acquired **on margin**. This means that the investor pays only part of the purchase price to acquire the shares. The rest is financed by the broker. Since the shares legally belong to the investor, the asset is recorded at the full share price and a liability to the broker for the amount that was financed is also recognized.

TREASURY MANAGEMENT
5.2.2

If financial assets are measured initially at their fair value, how should **transaction costs** that are directly related to the acquisition—such as fees, commissions, or transfer taxes—be accounted for?[2] The obvious choices are either (1) to expense these amounts immediately or (2) to add them to the cost of the assets acquired. The answer is—it depends.[3] It is logical to capitalize the transaction costs associated with any investment that is accounted for using a cost-based model because transaction costs are a necessary cost of acquiring the asset. Alternatively, for assets accounted for using a fair value model, it makes more sense to expense the transaction costs because the fair value of an asset is its market price. Regardless of how transaction costs are accounted for at acquisition, they are **not included** in the fair value amount at later statement of financial position dates.

When a financial instrument is measured at fair value after acquisition, changes in its fair value carrying amount are called **unrealized holding gains or losses**. The change in value is unrealized because it has not been converted to cash or a claim to cash—the asset is still held by the entity. Such gains and losses are only **realized** when the asset is disposed of. Unrealized holding gains and losses may be separately identified from realized gains and losses on the financial statements.[4]

With this brief introduction of basics, let's turn to the specific accounting models for a variety of investments in debt and equity securities. This next section of the chapter identifies and explains three major models of accounting for investments:

1. Cost/amortized cost model

IFRS

2. Fair value through net income model (FV-NI)

3. Fair value through other comprehensive income model (FV-OCI)

These models are summarized in Illustration 9-3.

Illustration 9-3

Application of Accounting Models

	Cost/Amortized Cost Model	Fair Value through Net Income Model (FV-NI)	Fair Value through OCI Model (FV-OCI)
At acquisition, measure at:	Cost (equal to fair value + transaction costs)	Fair value	Fair value (transactions costs tend to be added at acquisition)
At each reporting date, measure at:	Cost or amortized cost	Fair value	Fair value
Report unrealized holding gains and losses (changes in fair value):	N/A	In net income	In OCI
Report realized holding gains and losses:	In net income	In net income	Transfer total realized gains/losses to net income (recycling) or directly to retained earnings (no recycling)

Note that there are only two choices when it comes to measuring these types of investments: (1) cost/amortized cost and (2) fair value. Note further that, where fair value is used, the unrealized gains and losses are booked either to net income or to OCI. It is easier to think about how to account for investments using this simple framework rather than focusing on the labels and various definitions that the different standard setters use for investments. The equity method is another method that will be looked at later in the chapter.

Cost/Amortized Cost Model

Objective 2

Explain and apply the cost/amortized cost model of accounting for investments.

The accounting standards do not always differentiate between the cost and the amortized cost models, referring to them both as amortized cost. The amortized cost model applies only to investments in debt instruments and long-term notes and loans receivable, while the cost model may be applied to investments in equity instruments (shares) of other companies. Regardless, they are both cost-based methods.

Investments in Shares of Other Entities

Alternative Terminology

Investments in debt securities accounted for under the amortized cost method are sometimes referred to as **held to maturity investments**.

Application of the **cost model** to the investment one company makes in another entity's shares is straightforward:

1. Recognize the cost of the investment at the fair value of the shares acquired (or the fair value of what was given up to acquire them, if more reliable). Add to this any direct transaction costs (such as commissions) incurred to acquire the shares.

2. Unless impaired, report the investment at its cost at each statement of financial position date.

3. Recognize dividend income when the entity has established its right to receive the dividend.

4. When the shares are disposed of, derecognize them and report a gain or loss on disposal in net income. The gain or loss is the difference between the investment's carrying amount and the net proceeds on disposal.

To illustrate, assume that Kiwan Corp. (KC) purchases 1,000 shares of Hirj Co. at $4.25 per share on March 8, 2017. A 1.5% commission is charged on the transaction. On December 15, 2017, Hirj Co. directors declare a dividend of $0.10 per share to shareholders of record on December 31, 2017, payable on January 15, 2018. On July 11, 2018, KC sells

800 of the Hirj Co. shares for $5.08 per share and pays a 1.5% commission on the sale. KC has a December 31 year end. KC's entries to record these transactions and events are as follows:

March 8, 2017

A = L + SE	Other Investments 4,314
0 0 0	Cash 4,314
Cash flows: ↓ 4,314 outflow	(1,000 × $4.25) + (1,000 × $4.25 × .015)

December 31, 2017

A = L + SE	Dividend Receivable 100
+100 +100	Dividend Revenue 100
Cash flows: No effect	(1,000 × $0.10)

January 15, 2018

A = L + SE	Cash 100
0 0 0	Dividend Receivable 100
Cash flows: ↑ 100 inflow	

July 11, 2018

A = L + SE	Cash 4,003
+552 +552	Other Investments 3,451
Cash flows: ↑ 4,003 inflow	Gain on Sale of Investments 552
	(800 × $5.08) − (800 × $5.08 × .015) = $4,003
	$4,314 × 800/1,000 = $3,451
	$4,003 − $3,451 = $552

When shares of a company have been purchased at various times and at various costs and only a portion of the holdings is sold, it logical to use an average carrying value for the disposal. This is specifically required under ASPE.

Investments in Debt Instruments of Other Entities

When the cost model is applied to an investment in debt instruments (and long-term notes and loans receivable), it is referred to as the **amortized cost model**. This is because any difference between the acquisition cost recognized and the face value of the security is amortized over the period to maturity.[5] Amortized cost is the amount recognized at acquisition minus principal repayments, where applicable, plus or minus the cumulative amortization of any discount or premium; that is, amortization of the difference between the initial amount recognized and the maturity value. Impairment charges, discussed later in the chapter, also reduce the amortized cost. The following statements describe this method.

1. Recognize the cost of the investment at the fair value of the debt instrument acquired (or the fair value of what was given up to acquire it, if a more reliable measure). Add to this any direct transaction costs, such as commissions, incurred to acquire the investment.

2. Unless impaired, report the investment at its amortized cost as well as any outstanding interest receivable at each statement of financial position date.

3. Recognize interest income as it is earned, amortizing any discount or premium at the same time by adjusting the carrying amount of the investment.

4. When the investment is disposed of, first record the accrued interest and discount or premium amortization up to date. Derecognize the investment, reporting any gain or loss on disposal in net income. The gain or loss is the difference between the proceeds received for the security and the investment's amortized cost at the date of disposal.

TREASURY MANAGEMENT
5.2.2

Accounting for investments in debt securities using the amortized cost method should be familiar to you. The procedures are the same as accounting for long-term notes and loans receivable, and you may find it useful to review this section of Chapter 7 before continuing. One complication is added in this chapter: the acquisition and disposal of investments between interest payment dates.

Income under the Amortized Cost Model

Income from debt investments is usually in the form of interest. It can be received in one of two ways, depending on whether the investment is interest-bearing or non–interest-bearing. If it is **interest-bearing**, the party holding the investment on the interest payment date receives all the interest since the last interest payment date. Because debt securities can be bought and sold throughout the year, practice has developed for the purchaser to pay the seller an amount equal to the accrued interest since the last interest payment date. This interest is paid to the seller over and above the agreed-upon exchange price for the investment. If the instrument is **non–interest-bearing**, the price of the bond or other instrument is equal to its present value at the date of the transaction.

The total income from this type of investment is the net cash flow over the time that the investment is held. In the case of investments that are held until they mature, the total income is the difference between the principal amount that is received at maturity plus all periodic interest that is received, and the amount paid to acquire the investment including the accrued interest. Because the decision to acquire and hold the investment is usually based on its yield on the date when it is purchased, the yield rate is also the most appropriate rate to measure periodic income over the term that the investment is held.

To illustrate, assume that on January 1, 2017, Robinson Limited pays $92,278 to purchase $100,000 of Chan Corporation 8% bonds.[6] Robinson accounts for this investment at amortized cost. The bonds mature on January 1, 2022, and interest is payable each July 1 and January 1. The lower-than-face-value purchase price of $92,278 provides an effective interest rate of 10%. This is a combination of the 8% interest received in cash each year and the benefit of the $7,722 discount on the bond ($100,000 – $92,278). Note that the bond is acquired on an interest payment date and there is therefore no accrued interest for Robinson to pay on January 1. Assume Robinson Limited has an August 31 year end.

Cash principal received on maturity of bond	$100,000
Add cash interest to be received: ($100,000 × 0.08)/2 × 10 payments	40,000
Less cash paid to acquire the bond	(92,278)
Less cash paid for accrued interest when purchased	–0–
Total income to be recognized	$ 47,722

Because Robinson decided to purchase the bond based on its yield, the amount of income that is recognized each period should ideally reflect the yield rate. The **effective interest method**, required under IFRS unless the investment is held for trading purposes, results in recognizing interest income at a constant yield rate on the investment each period. We explained the straight-line method of recognizing interest and amortizing the discount or premium, permitted under ASPE, in Chapter 7 and briefly review it again below. Note that ASPE does not specify a method and so either the effective interest method or straight-line method would be acceptable.

Illustration 9-4 shows the application of the effective interest method to Robinson's investment in the Chan bonds. The original discount is fully amortized by the date the bond matures.

Illustration 9-4

Schedule of Interest Income and Bond Discount Amortization— Effective Interest Method

	8% Bonds Purchased to Yield 10%			
Date	Cash Received	Interest Income	Bond Discount Amortization	Amortized Cost of Bonds
1/1/17				$ 92,278
7/1/17	$ 4,000ᵃ	$ 4,614ᵇ	$ 614ᶜ	92,892ᵈ
1/1/18	4,000	4,645	645	93,537
7/1/18	4,000	4,677	677	94,214
1/1/19	4,000	4,711	711	94,925
7/1/19	4,000	4,746	746	95,671
1/1/20	4,000	4,783	783	96,454
7/1/20	4,000	4,823	823	97,277
1/1/21	4,000	4,864	864	98,141
7/1/21	4,000	4,907	907	99,048
1/1/22	4,000	4,952	952	100,000
	$40,000	$47,722	$7,722	

ᵃ $4,000 = 100,000 × 0.08 × 6/12
ᵇ $4,614 = $92,278 × 0.10 × 6/12
ᶜ $614 = $4,614 − $4,000
ᵈ $92,892 = $92,278 + $614

The entry to record the purchase of the investment is:

A = L + SE
0   0   0

Cash flows: ↓ 92,278 outflow

Jan 1/14	Bond Investment at Amortized Cost	92,278	
	Cash		92,278

In practice, and as illustrated, **the discount or premium on a bond investment is not usually recognized and reported separately**.

If Robinson Limited follows ASPE, it may decide to use **straight-line amortization** instead of the effective interest method. If so, the original discount of $7,722 ($100,000 − $92,278) is amortized to interest income in equal amounts from the date of acquisition to maturity, a period of 60 months. For each month of interest income recognized, 1/60 of $7,722 or $128.70 of discount is amortized. Under this approach, a constant **amount** of interest income is recognized each period instead of a constant **rate** of interest. All the other entries that involve interest income and the carrying amount of the investment will be affected in the same way when the straight-line method is used.

The journal entry to record the receipt of the first semi-annual interest payment on July 1, 2017, is:

IFRS
A = L + SE
+4,614   +4,614

Cash flows: ↑ 4,000 inflow

ASPE
A = L + SE
+4,772   +4,772

Cash flows: ↑ 4,000 inflow

IFRS: effective interest method (allowed under ASPE as well)			**ASPE: may use straight-line method since no specific method is mandated**		
July 1/17			July 1/17		
Cash	4,000		Cash	4,000	
Bond Investment at Amortized Cost	614		Bond Investment at Amortized Cost (6 × $128.70)	772	
Interest Income		4,614	Interest Income		4,772

At its year end on August 31, 2017, Robinson recognizes the interest income that has accrued since July 1 and amortizes the discount for the two-month period:

IFRS
A = L + SE
+1,548   +1,548

Cash flows: No effect

ASPE
A = L + SE
+1,590   +1,590

Cash flows: No effect

IFRS: effective interest method (allowed under ASPE as well)			ASPE: may use straight-line method since no specific method is mandated		
August 31/17			August 31/17		
Interest Receivable	1,333		Interest Receivable	1,333	
($4,000 × 2/6)					
Bond Investment at			Bond Investment at		
Amortized Cost	215		Amortized Cost	257	
($645 × 2/6)			(2 × $128.70)		
Interest Income		1,548	Interest Income		1,590
($4,645 × 2/6)					

When the interest payment is received on January 1, 2018, the following entry is made, assuming that Robinson does not use reversing entries:

IFRS
A = L + SE
+3,097   +3,097

Cash flows: ↑ 4,000 inflow

ASPE
A = L + SE
+3,182   +3,182

Cash flows: ↑ 4,000 inflow

IFRS: effective interest method (allowed under ASPE as well)			ASPE: may use straight-line method since no specific method is mandated		
January 1/18			January 1/18		
Cash	4,000		Cash	4,000	
Bond Investment at			Bond Investment at		
Amortized Cost	430		Amortized Cost	515	
($645 × 4/6)			(4 × $128.70)		
Interest Receivable		1,333	Interest Receivable		1,333
Interest Income		3,097	Interest Income		3,182
($4,645 × 4/6)					

Sale of Investments

Assume that Robinson Limited sells its investment in the Chan Corporation bonds on November 1, 2021, at 99.75% plus accrued interest. Remember that interest receivable of $1,333 (2/6 × $4,000) and discount amortization of $317 (2/6 × $952) were recognized at the company's August 31, 2021 year end. The following entry is then made on November 1, 2021, to accrue an additional two months' interest (September and October), to amortize the discount from September 1 to November 1, and to bring the investment to its correct carrying amount at the date of disposal. The discount amortization for this two-month period is $317 (2/6 × $952). Assume the effective interest method is used.

A = L + SE
+1,650   +1,650

Cash flows: No effect

Nov. 1/21	Interest Receivable (2/6 × $4,000)	1,333	
	Bond Investment at Amortized Cost	317	
	Interest Income (2/6 × $4,952)		1,650

The calculation of the realized gain on the sale is explained in Illustration 9-5.

Illustration 9-5

Calculation of Gain on Sale of Bonds

Selling price of bonds ($100,000 × .9975)		$99,750
Less: Carrying amount of bonds on November 1, 2021:		
Amortized cost, July 1, 2021 (see amortization schedule)	$99,048	
Add: Discount amortized for the period July 1, 2021, to November 1, 2021 ($317 to August 31 + $317 from September 1 to November 1)	634	99,682
Gain on sale of bonds		$ 68

The entry to record the sale of the bonds is:

Nov. 1/21	Cash	102,416	
	Interest Receivable		2,666
	Bond Investment at Amortized Cost		99,682
	Gain on Sale of Investments		68

The credit to Interest Receivable is for the four months of accrued interest from July 1 to November 1, all of which the purchaser pays in cash to Robinson. The debit to Cash is made up of the selling price of the bonds, $99,750, plus the four months of accrued interest, $2,666. The credit to the Bond Investment at Amortized Cost account is the bonds' carrying amount on the sale date, and the credit to Gain on Sale of Investments is the excess of the selling price over the bonds' carrying amount.

Fair Value through Net Income (FV-NI) Model

The **fair value through net income (FV-NI)** model is required for many financial assets and liabilities, including many investments in other entities' debt and equity securities. When investments to be accounted for at FV-NI are acquired, they are recognized at their fair value. Consistent with measurement at fair value, transaction costs incurred in acquiring such assets are expensed as incurred. The name of the method—fair value through net income—is very descriptive of how the accounting works! The carrying amount of each FV-NI investment is adjusted to its current fair value at each reporting date. All resulting holding gains and losses are reported in net income along with any dividends or interest income earned.

As explained for investments carried at amortized cost, the total income on the investment is the net cash flow from the investment: the gain or loss on the instrument itself plus any interest or dividend return. Accounting for income on an investment is the art of allocating the total income to specific accounting periods.

For FV-NI investments, periodic income is a combination of the change in an investment's carrying amount plus the interest or dividend income that has been received or is receivable for the period. For FV-NI investments in general, and especially those that are held for trading purposes—that is, they are held to sell in the near term or to generate a profit from short-term fluctuations in price—it may not be important to report interest and dividend income separately from the holding gains or losses. Under IFRS, both types of income may be accounted for and reported together because this tends to mirror how such investments are managed.[7] ASPE requires separate reporting of interest income and net gains or losses recognized on financial instruments. Note that many companies may wish to report dividends and interest separately for tax purposes and because the financial statements provide the basis for the tax returns, it may be worthwhile to show these items separately in the financial statements as well. Let's look at an example showing both separate and combined reporting of the income.

The reporting entity may need or want to keep track of holding gains and losses separately from interest and dividend income whether it is required or for additional transparency and decision-making. Accounting for dividend income separately from holding gains and losses is straightforward.

- When a dividend is received (or receivable), it is recognized as Dividend Revenue.

- When the investment is adjusted to its fair value at each reporting date, the change in value is recognized in a separate account, such as Unrealized Gain or Loss.

It is now easier for the entity to report the dividend income separately from the fair value changes because the information has been captured in two different accounts.

Recognizing interest income under the effective interest method (or even the straight-line method) separately requires more complex entries than described above. This is because **any**

discount or premium must be amortized before the change in fair value is recognized. Amortizing the discount or premium changes the investment's carrying amount. Therefore, the subsequent adjustment to bring the investment to its new fair value has to take this interest adjustment into account. Two sets of information have to be kept to make this work: (1) a schedule of the investment's amortized cost, for purposes of interest income calculations; and (2) information on its fair value, in order to report the asset at the appropriate amount.

The bookkeeping can be handled in at least two different ways.

1. One method keeps the investment in the accounts at its amortized cost and uses a separate valuation allowance account to bring it to its fair value at each statement of financial position date.

2. Alternatively, the investment account itself is maintained at fair value and the necessary amortized cost information is kept in records that are supplementary to the accounts.

In this chapter, for purposes of explanation, the second approach is used. The authors prefer this method because it emphasizes the use of fair value measurement rather than an adjusted cost-based measure. In short, the entries are as follows.

- Recognize interest income in an account such as Interest Income as it is earned, adjusting the investment's book value by the amount of any discount or premium amortization.

- When the investment is adjusted to its current fair value at each reporting date, the change in value is recognized in a separate account such as Unrealized Gain or Loss—FV-NI.

The following illustrates the accounting for an investment in a debt instrument at FV-NI using the effective interest method. Assume that a company purchases $100,000, 10%, five-year bonds of Graff Corporation on January 1, 2017, with interest payable on July 1 and January 1. The bond sells for $108,111, resulting in a bond premium of $8,111 and an effective interest rate of 8%. The entry to record the purchase of the bonds is:

A	=	L	+	SE
0		0		0

Cash flows: ↓ 108,111 outflow

| Jan. 1/17 | FV-NI Investments | 108,111 | |
| | Cash | | 108,111 |

Illustration 9-6 shows the effect that the premium amortization has on the interest income that is reported each period. The process is identical to the amortization of debt investments explained earlier in this chapter, except this situation involves a premium instead of a discount.

Illustration 9-6

Schedule of Interest Income and Bond Premium Amortization— Effective Interest Method

10% BONDS PURCHASED TO YIELD 8%

Date	Cash Received	Interest Income	Bond Premium Amortization	Amortized Cost of Bonds
1/1/17				$108,111
7/1/17	$ 5,000[a]	$ 4,324[b]	$ 676[c]	107,435[d]
1/1/18	5,000	4,297	703	106,732
7/1/18	5,000	4,269	731	106,001
1/1/19	5,000	4,240	760	105,241
7/1/19	5,000	4,210	790	104,451
1/1/20	5,000	4,178	822	103,629
7/1/20	5,000	4,145	855	102,774
1/1/21	5,000	4,111	889	101,885
7/1/21	5,000	4,075	925	100,960
1/1/22	5,000	4,040	960	100,000
	$50,000	$41,889	$8,111	

[a] $5,000 = $100,000 × 0.10 × 6/12
[b] $4,324 = $108,111 × 0.08 × 6/12
[c] $676 = $5,000 − $4,324
[d] $107,435 = $108,111 − $676

The entries to record interest income on the first interest date and at the December 31 year end are:

IFRS
A	=	L	+	SE
+5,000				+5,000

Cash flows: ↑ 5,000 inflow

ASPE
A	=	L	+	SE
+4,324				+4,324

Cash flows: ↑ 5,000 inflow

IFRS: no requirement to report interest separately under FV-NI			ASPE: requirement to report interest separately (including amortization of premiums and discounts)		
July 1/17			July 1/17		
Cash	5,000		Cash	5,000	
Investment Income or Loss		5,000	FV-NI Investments		676
			Interest Income		4,324

IFRS
A	=	L	+	SE
+5,000				+5,000

Cash flows: No effect

ASPE
A	=	L	+	SE
+4,297				+4,297

Cash flows: No effect

IFRS: no requirement to report interest separately under FV-NI			ASPE: requirement to report interest separately (including amortization of premiums and discounts)		
December 31/17			December 31/17		
Interest Receivable	5,000		Interest Receivable	5,000	
Investment Income or Loss		5,000	FV-NI Investments		703
			Interest Income		4,297

Assume that at December 31, 2017, the fair value of the Graff Corporation bonds is $105,000. Their carrying amount at this time is $106,732 (assuming that we have amortized the premium) and the adjustment needed to bring the Investment account to fair value is $1,732:

Original cost and carrying amount of bonds		$108,111
Entries made to Investment in Graff Corp. Bonds account during year when recognizing interest income:		
July 1, 2017	$676 credit	
Dec. 31, 2017	703 credit	(1,379)
Carrying amount before fair value adjustment		106,732
Fair value, December 31, 2017		105,000
Fair value adjustment needed		$ 1,732 credit

If we had not amortized the premium, the carrying amount would still be $108,111 and the adjustment amount would be $108,111 − $105,000 = $3,111. The entry to adjust the investment to its fair value at December 31, 2017, is:

IFRS
A	=	L	+	SE
−3,111				−3,111

Cash flows: No effect

ASPE
A	=	L	+	SE
−1,732				−1,732

Cash flows: No effect

IFRS: no requirement to report interest separately under FV-NI			ASPE: requirement to report interest separately (including amortization of premiums and discounts)		
December 31/17			December 31/17		
Investment Income or Loss	3,111		Unrealized Gain or Loss	1,732	
FV-NI Investments		3,111	FV-NI Investments		1,732

The impact on net income is the same under both methods noted above. However, it is presented differently, with ASPE showing interest (including the bond amortization) separately.

For a **non–interest-bearing debt investment** that is held for short-term trading, the investment income that is earned is the difference between the instrument's purchase price and its maturity value or the proceeds on its disposal. Treasury bills, for example, are usually traded in non–interest-bearing form. Assume that Investor Inc. pays $19,231 on March 15 for a $20,000 six-month treasury bill that matures on September 15. The investment, purchased to yield an 8% return, is designated as an FV-NI investment. Illustration 9-7 shows how to account for the investment income, assuming that interest income is not reported separately.

Illustration 9-7

*Income on a Non–Interest-
Bearing Debt Instrument
Accounted for at FV-NI, Interest
Income Not Reported Separately*

Mar. 15	FV-NI Investments	19,231	
	Cash		19,231
	(To record purchase of a $20,000, six-month treasury bill)		
Sept. 15	Cash	20,000	
	FV-NI Investments		19,231
	Investment Income or Loss		769
	(To record the proceeds on maturity of a $20,000 treasury bill)		

Note that the investment income, which consists entirely of interest in this case, is equal to an 8% yield on the amount paid for the investment: $19,231 × 8% × 6/12 = $769. If Investor Inc. needed cash prior to September 15 and sold the investment before maturity, the investment income reported is the difference between its carrying amount and the proceeds on disposal.

Investments in **equity securities** that are held for short-term trading profits may pay dividends. If the company does not report interest income separately, it is unlikely that it would report dividend income separately, either. Because the holder of the shares on the date of record is entitled to the dividend and this date is generally a few weeks before the dividend is paid, a dividend receivable and the related income may be recognized before the cash is received. As an FV-NI investment, the shares are remeasured to their fair value at each statement of financial position date with the change in fair value also recognized in the Investment Income or Loss account. When the investment is sold, its carrying amount is removed from the investment account and investment income is recognized.

To demonstrate the accounting for a portfolio of temporary investments accounted for at FV-NI with no separate reporting of interest and dividend income, assume that on December 31, 2017, Western Publishing Corporation provides the information shown in Illustration 9-8 about its investments portfolio. Assume that all investments were acquired in 2017. The investments were recorded at their fair value at acquisition in an account entitled FV-NI Investments, and this value is their **carrying amount** on the books before any adjustment.

Alternative Terminology

The terms 'temporary investments' and 'held-for-trading' investments are often used interchangeably.

FV-NI INVESTMENTS PORTFOLIO
December 31, 2017

Investments	Carrying Amount	Fair Value
Burlington Corp. shares	$ 43,860	$ 51,500
Genesta Corp. 8% bonds	184,230	175,200
Warner Ltd. shares	86,360	91,500
Total portfolio	$314,450	$318,200

Adjustment needed to the portfolio to bring it to fair value at December 31, 2017:
$318,200 − $314,450 = $3,750 debit

At December 31, an adjusting entry is made to bring the investments portfolio to its year-end fair value and to record the holding gain. This entry assumes that Western Publishing has one control account in its general ledger for the entire portfolio. It would be equally correct to make a separate entry for each of the three different investments.

A = L + SE	Dec. 31/17	FV-NI Investments	3,750	
+3,750 +3,750		Investment Income or Loss		3,750

Cash flows: No effect

The Investment Income or Loss account is included in net income on the income statement, and the fair values of the investments at December 31, 2017, now become the carrying amounts on the books. With a fair value measurement approach, the original cost or fair value at acquisition is not relevant.[8]

Now assume that the Genesta Corp. bonds are sold for $174,000 on February 4, 2018—their interest payment date—and that 1,000 shares of Next Ltd. are acquired for their fair value of $49,990 on September 21, 2018. The entries to record the February 4 and September 21 transactions follow. Note that the bonds' carrying amount before the sale is $175,200, their fair value at the last statement of financial position date.

A = L + SE	Feb. 4/18	Cash	174,000	
−1,200 −1,200		Investment Income or Loss	1,200	
		FV-NI Investments		175,200

Cash flows: ↑ 174,000 inflow

A = L + SE	Sept. 21/18	FV-NI Investments	49,990	
0 0 0		Cash		49,990

Cash flows: ↓ 49,990 outflow

Because the gains and losses on FV-NI investments are reported in net income, the distinction between the portions that are realized and unrealized is blurred. This is not usually an issue, however, particularly for trading securities that are acquired for short-term profit-taking.

Illustration 9-9 indicates the carrying amounts and fair values of the investments port-folio at December 31, 2018. As Western Publishing prepares financial statements only once a year, the carrying amounts of the Burlington Corp. and Warner Ltd. shares that are still on hand are the fair values reported at December 31, 2018. The carrying amount of the Next Ltd. shares acquired during the year is their fair value at acquisition.

Illustration 9-9		
Fair Value Adjustment—FV-NI Investments Portfolio, December 31, 2018		

FV-NI INVESTMENTS PORTFOLIO
December 31, 2018

Investments	Carrying Amount	Fair Value
Burlington Corp. shares	$ 51,500	$ 50,500
Warner Ltd. shares	91,500	90,100
Next Ltd. shares	49,990	50,600
Total portfolio	$192,990	$191,200

Adjustment needed to bring the portfolio to fair value at December 31, 2018:
$192,990 − $191,200 = $1,790 credit

At December 31, an adjusting entry is made to bring the investments to their year-end fair values.

A = L + SE	Dec. 31/18	Investment Income or Loss	1,790	
−1,790 −1,790		FV-NI Investments		1,790

Cash flows: No effect

The investment loss is included in the 2018 income statement, added to the loss recognized on February 4.

Fair Value through Other Comprehensive Income (FV-OCI) Model

Alternative Terminology

FV-OCI is sometimes referred to as *available for sale*.

We explained the concept of other comprehensive income in Chapter 4. It is an income statement account and is closed out to an account called Accumulated Other Comprehensive Income.[9]

Illustration 9-10 shows how these financial statement categories are related.

Illustration 9-10

A Review of How Net Income, Other Comprehensive Income, and Accumulated Other Comprehensive Income Are Related

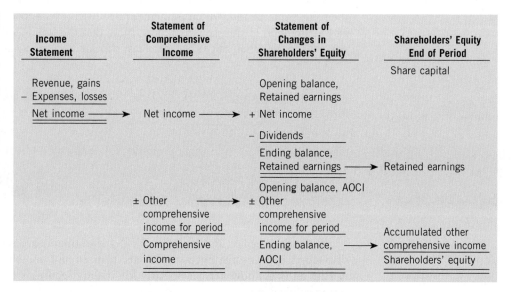

Investments accounted for at **fair value through other comprehensive income (FV-OCI)** are recognized at acquisition at their fair value. However, unlike the FV-NI model, the transaction costs tend to be added to the carrying amount of the investment. When the investment is adjusted to its fair value at the first reporting date, the transaction costs automatically end up as part of the holding gain or loss recognized in OCI at that time.

At each reporting date, the carrying amount of each FV-OCI investment is remeasured and adjusted to its current fair value. As the name of the model implies, the changes in fair value—the holding gains and losses—are recognized in other comprehensive income net of income tax.[10]

There are two different versions of the FV-OCI model. The difference between them relates to how they treat the holding gains and losses once they are realized. The two methods are as follows:

1. FV-OCI with recycling, and

2. FV-OCI without recycling.

Under the **FV-OCI model with recycling**, when the investments are disposed of and converted to cash or a claim to cash, the previously unrealized holding gains or losses to the date of disposal are transferred or "recycled" into net income.[11] Under the **FV-OCI model without recycling**, the realized gains and losses do not get recycled through net income but are transferred directly into retained earnings. Aside from this, both versions of the FV-OCI model are the same.

Investments in Shares of Other Entities

The accounting differs for FV-OCI investments depending on whether the investments are equity or debt instruments. Let's look at equity securities first.

Income from FV-OCI Investments (Shares)

UNDERLYING CONCEPT

Recycling supports the continued use of net income as the main performance measure, while not recycling supports the concept that comprehensive income is the appropriate measure of performance.

IFRS 9 requires FV-OCI (with no recycling) for investments in shares. Since the focus of this chapter is on IFRS 9, the examples adopt this approach. Dividend income from these investments is reported directly in net income. Remeasurement gains and losses are recorded in OCI. Let's look at an example of FV-OCI accounting for investments in shares of another entity.

Assume that on November 3, 2016, Manitoba Corporation purchases common shares of three companies, with the investments to be accounted for at FV-OCI. The purchases are as follows:

	Fair value and cost at acquisition
Nova Industries Ltd.	$259,700
Columbia Soup Corp.	317,500
St. Boniface Pulp Ltd.	141,350
Total cost	$718,550

The purchase of the investments is recorded as follows:

```
A   =   L   +   SE
0       0       0
Cash flows: ↓ 718,550 outflow
```

Nov. 3/16	FV-OCI Investments	718,550	
	Cash		718,550

Above we have used one control account for all three investments. Alternatively, Manitoba Corporation could use separate investment accounts to track each investment separately. On December 6, 2016, the company receives a cash dividend of $4,200 on its investment in the common shares of Columbia Soup. The cash dividend is recorded through net income as follows:

```
A     =   L   +   SE
+4,200            +4,200
Cash flows: ↑ 4,200 inflow
```

Dec. 6/16	Cash	4,200	
	Dividend Revenue		4,200

Illustration 9-11 indicates the carrying amounts (and cost), fair values, and unrealized gains and losses at December 31, 2016, for Manitoba's FV-OCI investments.

Illustration 9-11

Schedule of Investments and Holding Gains/Losses—FV-OCI Investments (Shares) Portfolio (2016)

FV-OCI INVESTMENTS (SHARES) PORTFOLIO
December 31, 2016

Investments	Carrying Amount	Fair Value	Holding Gain (Loss) for Period
Nova Industries Ltd.	$259,700	$275,000	$ 15,300
Columbia Soup Corp.	317,500	304,000	(13,500)
St. Boniface Pulp Ltd.	141,350	104,000	(37,350)
Total of portfolio	$718,550	$683,000	$(35,550)

For Manitoba's portfolio, the gross holding gains are $15,300, and the gross holding losses are $50,850 ($13,500 + $37,350), resulting in a net unrealized loss of $35,550. The portfolio's fair value is $35,550 less than its carrying amount (and cost, in this first accounting period). The unrealized gains and losses are recorded in a Holding Gain or Loss account and are reported as part of OCI. The carrying amount of the investments is adjusted in the following entry to their fair value at the statement of financial position date. Note that, even though there is a loss (and perhaps an impairment), the loss is booked through OCI.

<table>
<tr><td>A = L + SE
−35,550   −35,550
Cash flows: No effect</td><td>Dec. 31/16
  Unrealized Gain or Loss—OCI
    FV-OCI Investments</td><td>35,550

</td><td>
35,550</td></tr>
</table>

Sale of FV-OCI Investments (Shares)

We carry on our example to show how to account for the sale of FV-OCI investments in shares. Now assume that Manitoba sells all of its Nova Industries Ltd. common shares on January 23, 2017, receiving proceeds of $287,220. This is $12,220 more than the current carrying amount of the Investment in Nova Industries in the accounts.

While it is possible to record this event using different combinations of entries, the following series of three entries clearly accomplishes what is needed:

(a) The **first entry** adjusts the investment's carrying amount to its fair value at the date of disposal and captures the holding gain up to that date in OCI.

(b) The **second entry** removes the investment's carrying amount from the asset account and records the proceeds on disposal.

(c) The **third entry** is a **reclassification adjustment** that transfers the holding gain that is now realized out of OCI and into retained earnings (FV-OCI without recycling under IFRS 9).

<table>
<tr><td>Jan. 23/17</td><td>(a) FV-OCI Investments
    Unrealized Gain or Loss—OCI
    ($287,220 − $275,000)</td><td>12,220

</td><td>
12,220</td></tr>
<tr><td></td><td>(b) Cash
    FV-OCI Investments
    ($275,000 + $12,220)</td><td>287,220

</td><td>
287,220</td></tr>
<tr><td></td><td>(c) Unrealized Gain or Loss—OCI
    Retained Earnings
    ($287,220 − $259,700) or ($15,300 + $12,220)</td><td>27,520

</td><td>
27,520</td></tr>
</table>

The amount transferred to Retained Earnings is the difference between the investment's original cost and the proceeds on disposal ($287,220 − $259,700). It is also the sum of all prior entries to OCI for the Nova Industries shares: a $15,300 gain on December 31, 2016, and a $12,220 gain on January 23, 2017, for a total of $27,520. All that remains in Accumulated Other Comprehensive Income now is the unrealized net holding gains/losses on the remaining investments.

To continue with this example, assume that the information in Illustration 9-12 is provided for Manitoba's FV-OCI portfolio at December 31, 2017.

Illustration 9-12

Calculation of Holding Gain/ Loss for Period—FV-OCI Equity Investments Portfolio (2017)

FV-OCI INVESTMENTS PORTFOLIO (Shares)
December 31, 2017

Investments	Cost	Carrying Amount	Fair Value	Holding Gain (Loss) for Period
Columbia Soup Corp.	$317,500	$304,000	$362,550	$58,550
St. Boniface Pulp Ltd.	141,350	104,000	139,050	35,050
Total of portfolio	$458,850	$408,000	$501,600	$93,600

The entry to bring the investments to their fair value at December 31, 2017 is:

<table>
<tr><td>A = L + SE
+93,600   +93,600
Cash flows: No effect</td><td>Dec. 31/17
  FV-OCI Investments
    Unrealized Gain or Loss—OCI</td><td>93,600

</td><td>
93,600</td></tr>
</table>

Investments in Debt Instruments of Other Entities

Now let's look at debt instruments. There is an added complexity when dealing with debt instruments. Under IFRS 9, interest income, amortization of premiums/discounts, and impairment losses are recognized directly in net income. In addition, remeasurement gains and losses recognized through OCI are subsequently recycled when the investment is disposed of. Therefore, the FV-OCI (with recycling) approach is followed under IFRS 9 for debt instruments.

The following example illustrates this. Let's continue with the Graff Corporation example from Illustration 9-6. The numbers in the following journal entries come from that illustration.

The buyer records the purchase of the bond in the FV-OCI Investments account as follows:

A = L + SE
0   0   0
Cash flows: ↓ 108,111 outflow

| Jan. 1/17 | FV-OCI Investments | 108,111 | |
| | Cash | | 108,111 |

SIGNIFICANT CHANGE

Income from FV-OCI Investments (Debt Instruments)

The entry to record the interest income on July 1, 2017, is as follows:

A = L + SE
4,324 0   4,324
Cash flows: ↑ 5,000 inflow

July 1/17	Cash	5,000	
	FV-OCI Investments		676
	Interest Income		4,324

The entry to record interest receivable at December 31, 2017, is noted below:

A = L + SE
4,297 0   4,297
Cash flows: No effect

Dec. 31/17	Interest Receivable	5,000	
	FV-OCI Investments		703
	Interest Income		4,297

So far, the accounting is straightforward. It generally follows the same accounting as for the amortized cost method. Now we will look at how to account for the remeasurement to fair value. Assume that at year end (December 31, 2017), the fair value of the bonds is $105,000 and the carrying value is $106,732. Note that the carrying value is calculated as $108,111 – $676 – $703 and is shown in Illustration 9-6. There is an unrealized holding loss of $1,732 ($106,732 – $105,000). Graff reports this loss through OCI and makes the following entry:

A = L + SE
−1,732 0   −1,732
Cash flows: No effect

| Unrealized Gain or Loss—OCI | 1,732 | |
| FV-OCI Investments | | 1,732 |

At each reporting date, the company remeasures the bonds at fair value and records the gain or loss through OCI as noted above. In the journal entry above, we are assuming that there is no impairment. We will look at impairments below.

To illustrate the accounting for a portfolio of debt securities, assume that Robinson Limited has two debt securities classified as FV-OCI. For the Chan bonds, assume the amortization table noted in Illustration 9-4. Assume further that the Anacomp bonds were purchased at par value and therefore there are no premiums or discounts.

Illustration 9-13 identifies amortized cost, fair value, and the amount of unrealized gain or loss.

Illustration 9-13

Calculation of the Unrealized Gain or Loss on Remeasurement of FV-OCI Debt Securities— December 31, 2017

FV-OCI INVESTMENT PORTFOLIO (Debt Securities) December 31, 2017			
Investments	Amortized Cost	Fair Value	Unrealized Gain (Loss)
Chan Corporation 8% bonds	$ 93,537	$103,600	$ 10,063
Anacomp Corporation 10% bonds	200,000	180,400	(19,600)
Total of portfolio	$293,537	$284,000	(9,537)
Previous fair value adjustment balance			–0–
Fair value adjustment—Cr.			$ (9,537)

The fair value of Robinson's portfolio totals $284,000. The gross unrealized gains are $10,063, and the gross unrealized losses are $19,600. The fair value of the portfolio is lower than the amortized cost. Therefore, an adjusting entry is needed to record the remeasurement to fair value. Once again, we assume that there is no impairment. The entry is shown below.

A = L + SE
−9,537   0   −9,537
Cash flows: No effect

Unrealized Gain or Loss—OCI	9,537	
FV-OCI Investments		9,537

Sale of FV-OCI Investments (Debt Instruments)

If a company sells its FV-OCI debt securities before maturity, it must derecognize the investments. To illustrate, assume that Robinson Corporation sold the Chan bonds (from Illustration 9-13) on July 1, 2018, for $90,000, at which time they had an amortized cost of $94,214 as noted in Illustration 9-4 (after adjusting for discount amortization of $677).

The three journal entries that we used to record the sale of the FV-OCI Investments in shares will be used.

1. First we revalue the investment to fair value.

2. Then we recognize the sale.

3. Then we reclassify (recycle) the accumulated unrealized loss from OCI to net income. Robinson records the following entries:

July 1/18	(a) Unrealized Gain or Loss—OCI	14,277	
	FV-OCI Investments		14,277
	[$103,600 + $677 (amortization of discount to July 1) − $90,000]		
	(b) Cash	90,000	
	FV-OCI Investments		90,000
	(c) Loss on Sale of Investments	4,214	
	Unrealized Gain or Loss—OCI		4,214
	($10,063 gain minus $14,277 loss)		

After adjusting for the sale of the Chan bonds, the balance in the Unrealized Gain or Loss—OCI account is $9,537 + $14,277 − $4,214 = $19,600. As shown in Illustration 9-13, this represents the unrealized loss on the Anacomp Corporation bonds as at December 31, 2017.

Robinson prepares the following schedule on December 31, 2018 (as noted in Illustration 9-14), when the fair value of the remaining bonds is $195,000. There was no other activity in the investment portfolio between July 1 and December 31, 2018.

Illustration 9-14

Calculation of the Unrealized Gain or Loss on Remeasurement of FV-OCI Debt Securities— December 31, 2018

FV-OCI INVESTMENTS PORTFOLIO (Debt Securities)
December 31, 2018

Investments	Amortized Cost	Fair Value	Unrealized Gain (Loss)
Anacomp Corporation 10% bonds	$200,000	$195,000	($5,000)
Total portfolio	$200,000	$195,000	($5,000)

We need one more entry to adjust the carrying value of the remaining bonds to fair value. The entry is as follows:

A = L + SE
+14,600   0   +14,600
Cash flows: No effect

FV-OCI Investments	14,600	
Unrealized Gain or Loss - OCI		14,600
($19,600 − $5,000)		

Now that the three common methods of accounting for financial instruments have been explained and illustrated, how does a company decide which method is accepted under accounting standards for a particular investment? The correct answer is, "It depends on when you are asking." **Illustration 9-15 summarizes how the three measurement models are used by IFRS and ASPE. We have included a summary for IAS 39 because this is permitted until January 1, 2018 (or until a company adopts IFRS 9).**

Illustration 9-15

Classification of Investments Under IFRS and ASPE (Where No Significant Influence or Control)

Measurement models	ASPE (in effect since 2011)	IFRS 9 (effective 2018 but may adopt early)	IAS 39 (currently in effect)
Cost/amortized cost	All investments except those that are equity instruments quoted in an active market, derivatives, or where the company elects to use FV-NI (see below).	Debt investments that are managed on a contractual yield basis where the business model requires the entity to hold the investments to maturity (and collect principal and interest).	Debt investments where the company has the ability and intent to hold the debt instrument to maturity. These investments are sometimes referred to as "held to maturity" in financial statements. Equity investments where fair value is not estimable.
FV-NI (sometimes referred to as fair value through profit or loss)	Equity investments that are quoted in an active market and derivatives. Companies may make an accounting policy choice and elect to account for investments using FV-NI (fair value option).	Equity instruments not accounted for under FV-OCI model. Debt instruments that do not meet the criteria for the amortized cost or FV-OCI models. Derivatives. May elect to account for investments under this model (fair value option) as long as certain conditions are met (for example, to avoid an accounting mismatch where an item is hedged and gains and losses on the hedge might not offset).	Debt and equity investments (including derivatives) that are held for short-term profit-taking and are bought and sold on a regular basis. These investments are sometimes referred to as held for trading. May elect to account for investments using FV-NI (fair value option) as long as certain conditions are met.
FV-OCI	N/A	Certain equity investments (where no significant influence or control and not trading investments). The entity must make an election to classify these investments here.	Debt and equity investments that are not **held to maturity** or **held for trading**.

(continued)

		For equity investments, no recycling but dividend income recognized in net income unless it is deemed to be a return of capital. Debt investments where the company's business model is to **either** manage on a contractual yield basis **or** sell the securities. For debt instruments, discounts, premiums, interest income, and impairment losses are recognized in net income. Unrealized gains and losses are recycled to net income when the security is sold.[12]	These investments are sometimes referred to as available for sale investments. Use recycling where there is objective evidence of impairment or investments are sold.
Notes	Interest must be disclosed or presented separately.	Interest must be disclosed or presented separately if FV-NI model not used.	Interest must be disclosed or presented separately if FV-NI model not used.
Reclassifications between categories	Not addressed specifically.	Not permitted unless change in business model.	Reclassifications permitted in very limited situations.

Illustration 9-16 shows a decision tree that helps to determine the classification and measurement of financial assets under IFRS 9. IFRS requires that you look at the company's business model for each type of investment; i.e., is the business model such that the investments are held for the longer term to collect principal and interest payments or for sale or both?

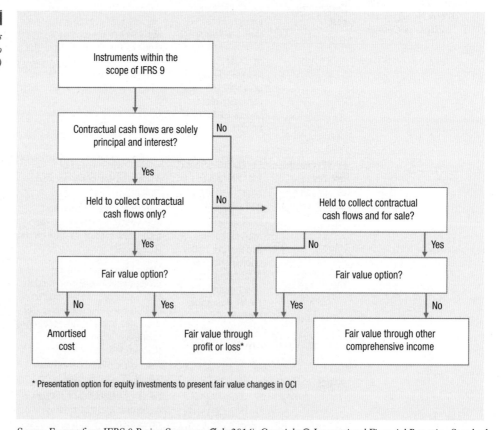

* Presentation option for equity investments to present fair value changes in OCI

Impairment Models

Objective 5
Explain and apply the incurred loss, expected loss, and fair value loss impairment models.

Financial asset investments are reviewed for possible impairment for the same reasons that non-financial assets are: the statement of financial position (SFP) value for any asset cannot be more than the expected benefits the asset can bring to the organization. Since financial assets measured at fair value are already measured at their current fair value amount, it is usually only those measured at cost or amortized cost that need a method of accounting for impairment (unless impairment losses are required to be recycled).

Both IFRS and ASPE require that entities adjust for impairment at least at each reporting date. To the extent possible, this review is carried out at the level of individual assets. However, sometimes the information is not available on a timely basis to do this for each specific asset, so investments with similar characteristics are grouped. Even if assets are assessed for impairment on an individual basis, they should also be assessed for impairment as a group where they share similar risk characteristics. For instance, a portfolio of loans to a certain industry that is experiencing an economic downturn should be assessed as a group as well as individually. If an instrument, or portfolio of instruments, is determined to be impaired, the amount of the impairment loss is calculated and recognized. There are differences of opinion, however, on how such a loss should be determined and reported. Three different impairment models are explained next: an incurred loss model, an expected loss model, and a full fair value model. We will then summarize which models are used under IFRS and ASPE and when.

Incurred Loss Model

Under the **incurred loss impairment model**, investments are recognized as impaired when there is no longer reasonable assurance that the future cash flows associated with them will either be collected in their entirety or when due. Entities look for objective evidence that there has been a significant adverse change in the period in the expected amount of future cash flows, or in the timing of those cash flows.[13] These events are called **trigger events or loss events**. Examples of situations that might indicate impairment include the fact that the entity that issued the debt or equity instrument:

- is experiencing significant financial difficulties,

- has defaulted on, or is late making, interest or principal payments,

- is likely to undergo a major financial reorganization or enter bankruptcy, or

- is in a market that is experiencing significant negative economic change.[14]

ASPE

If such evidence exists, the next step is to measure the investment's estimated realizable amounts. This is calculated as the highest of the following:

1. present value of the revised amounts and timing of the future cash flows, discounted at the current market rate, or

2. the amount realized if the asset were sold, or

3. the amount realized if the entity called the loan and took any collateral that it had rights to.

The **impairment loss** is the difference between this amount and the instrument's carrying amount.

After the impairment is recorded, interest income is recognized based on the revised cash flow estimates and the **discount rate that was used to determine the present value of those flows**. Any further change in the investment's realizable value related to an event occurring after the original impairment is recognized as an adjustment of the impairment loss. The change could result from a further decline in value (an increased loss) or a recovery of the previous estimated impairment loss.

This impairment method is described as an **incurred loss impairment model** because it captures only credit losses that were triggered by events that occurred by the SFP date. Let's look at an example.

Assume a company purchased an investment in AB Ltd. bonds for $100,000 at par value at the beginning of the year. The bonds pay interest on December 31 each year.

The bond is carried at amortized cost. AB Ltd. is experiencing financial difficulties. The company determines that the existence of financial difficulties provides objective evidence of impairment and represents a triggering or loss event. The company follows ASPE.

The present value of the discounted revised cash flows is $70,000 using the current market interest rate. The journal entry is as follows:

A   =   L   +   SE
−30,000   0   −30,000
Cash flows: No effect

Loss on Impairment	30,000	
Bond Investment at Amortized Cost		30,000
($100,000 − $70,000)		

Expected Loss Model

Under an **expected loss impairment model**, estimates of future cash flows used to determine the present value of the investment are made on a **continuous basis** and do not rely on a triggering event to occur. These revised expected cash flows are generally discounted at the same effective interest rate used when the instrument was **first acquired**, therefore retaining a cost-based measurement.[15] Estimates of impairment losses are based on reasonably available information that is obtainable without undue cost or effort. Under this approach, almost all financial assets will need to be assessed to determine if there might be expected losses.

SIGNIFICANT CHANGE

The company must record any impairment loss by the first reporting date and must assess whether the credit risk on an investment has increased significantly since the investment was first recognized. As a general rule, there is a significant increase in credit risk when principal or interest payments are more than 30 days past due (unless the entity has evidence to the contrary).[16] Credit risk may also have increased significantly even before the debtor defaults on payments. Factors to consider include decreased sales, profit, or cash flows, worsening economy, breach of covenants, and risk of default.[17]

If the company determines that the credit risk has not significantly increased, then it considers the 12-month expected credit losses. This approach looks at the possibility of defaults within the 12-month period (and the present value of any losses due to defaults over the 12-month period, probability weighted).

If the company decides that the default risk on the investment has increased significantly, then the company must look at lifetime expected credit losses.[18] This means that it would consider all possible default events over the life of the instrument. So if the instrument was a 10-year bond, then the company would consider possible default events over the 10-year life of the bond (and the present value of these cash shortfalls over the life, probability weighted).

Illustration 9-17 contains a decision tree summarizing this approach.

Illustration 9-17

Decision Tree of the Expected Loss Model for Impairment

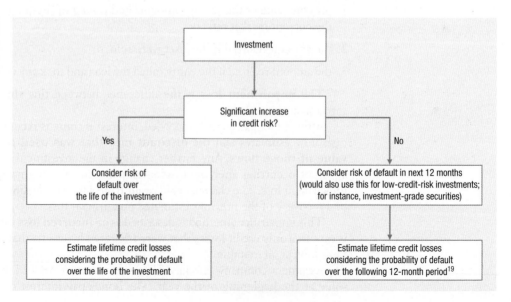

For instance, in a situation where there is no significant increase in the risk of default (such as if the credit risk is low), an entity might feel that the probability of default within the next 12 months is zero and therefore no impairment loss would be recognized. Conversely, if there is a significant increase in the risk of default, the entity would have to consider the probability of default over the life of the investment, which would generally be higher.

IFRS notes that there are three stages of impairment, as follows:[†]

Stage 1	Stage 2	Stage 3
- There is no significant increase in expected credit losses. - Use a 12-month time frame to assess the probability of default. - Calculate interest income on the investment's gross carrying amount.	- There is a significant increase in expected credit losses. - Use the investment lifetime to assess the probability of default. - Calculate interest income on the investment's gross carrying amount.	- The asset is a credit-impaired investment (for instance, the company is in financial difficulty, a default in payment has occurred, or bankruptcy is probable).* - Use the investment lifetime to assess the probability of default. - Calculate interest on the investment's net carrying amount
*Note that this would generally be when an impairment loss is first recognized under the incurred loss model.		

As a practical expedient, IFRS 9 allows the use of lifetime expected credit losses for trade receivables, contract assets, and lease receivables.[20]

When measuring the amount of the impairment under either scenario (that is, lifetime or 12-month expected credit losses), the company must consider the following:

1. an unbiased and probability-weighted amount,

2. the time value of money (as mentioned earlier, this is usually the effective rate of interest as determined when the company first made the investment), and

3. information that is reasonable and supportable (that is, it is available without undue effort or cost).[21]

The impairment loss is measured as the difference between the asset's gross carrying amount and the present value of the expected cash flows discounted at the original effective interest rate. Probabilities are factored in.[22]

Let's look at an example. Jay Corporation purchases a 5% bond at par value for $100,000. Interest is paid annually. The bond is carried at amortized cost. Because the bond is issued at par, there is no amortization of discount or premium. Jay determines that there has not been a significant increase in the credit risk. Upon detailed analysis, Jay estimates that there is a slight chance that it might not collect 25% of the face value of the bond. In addition, Jay estimates that there is a .5% probability of default within the next 12 months. The loss allowance is calculated based on the 12-month expected credit losses, as follows:

$$.005 \times .25 \times \$100,000 = \$125$$

The journal entry is as follows:

A = L + SE		
−125 0 −125		
Cash flows: No effect		

Loss on Impairment	125	
Bond Investment at Amortized Cost		125

Recall that the face value of the bond ($100,000) represents the present value of the principal and interest payments. Therefore, the impairment loss is calculated as a percentage of that present value number and the time value is already considered.[23]

[†]Based on information from IFRS 9 Project Summary, July 2014.

We could also do this calculation as follows:

$$.005 \times .25 \times [(\$100,000 + \$5,000)/1.05]$$

Let's look at another example relating to a debt instrument accounted for using FV-OCI.[24] Assume Sandal Inc. purchases a debt instrument for $10,000. Assume that this is the fair value. At the following reporting date, the fair value of the instrument is $9,000. Half of this is due to changes in market interest rates. Assume that there has not been a significant increase in credit risk and therefore the entity will measure the expected losses using a 12-month time frame. Assume that this is estimated at $500. How will this be recorded in the books of Sandal? The journal entry follows.

A   =   L   +   SE
−1,000   0   −1,000
Cash flows: No effect

Loss on Impairment	500	
Unrealized Gain or Loss—OCI	500	
FV-OCI Investments		1,000

The part of the loss relating to changes in market interest rates is booked through OCI. It is not considered to be an impairment. It arises solely due to changes in the market and is nothing to do with whether the debt instrument is potentially in default. The other half, however, is considered to be an impairment and must be booked through net income, as discussed earlier. In this case, because the investment is measured at fair value, the time value of money is already considered.

Because the impairment loss under the expected loss model reflects both incurred losses to date and future expected credit losses, it results in earlier recognition of such losses in net income. This model is more difficult to apply, especially in continually estimating the amounts of the expected future cash flows. In addition, this model is only relevant for investments at cost/amortized cost and FV-OCI debt investments. There is no need to worry about FV-NI investments because they are continually revalued to fair value with all gains and losses booked to net income. There is no need to worry about FV-OCI equity investments, either, because they are also continually revalued to fair value. In addition, all gains and losses are booked to OCI with no recycling. This means that impairment losses are not separately assessed or recycled through net income.

UNDERLYING CONCEPT

The expected loss model provides more objective information because the assessment of a trigger or loss event can be very subjective. This may be offset by the fact that it is not easy to measure the expected loss.

Fair Value Loss Model

Under the **fair value loss impairment model**, the impairment loss is the difference between the asset's fair value and its current carrying amount, assuming the fair value is less than the carrying amount. Fair value is calculated using all current information, including revised cash flows, current interest rates, and market values. Refer back to Chapters 2 and 3 for a discussion regarding calculating fair values. For investments valued using FV-NI, there is no need to do a separate impairment test. This is because the FV-NI model requires that all changes in fair value be recognized in net income, whether they are gains or losses.

Illustration 9-18 summarizes the various impairment models under ASPE and IFRS.

Illustration 9-18

Summary of Impairment Models

Impairment Models	ASPE	IFRS 9	IAS 39
Incurred loss	Used for all investments measured at cost/amortized cost. Reduce carrying value to the higher of the discounted cash flow (DCF; discounted using the market interest rate) and net realizable value (either through sale or by exercising the entity's rights to collateral).	N/A	Used for all investments measured using cost/amortized cost. Reduce carrying value to DCF (discounted using historic interest rate for debt instruments and market interest rate for equity instruments measured at cost). May use an allowance account or reduce carrying value directly. Used for FV-OCI investments where a loss/trigger event has occurred.

(continued)

	May use an allowance account or reduce carrying value directly. Impairment losses may be reversed.		Reduce carrying value to fair value and book loss through net income. Impairment losses may be reversed for debt instruments only.
Expected loss	N/A	Used for all investments carried at cost/amortized cost as well as debt investments carried at FV-OCI. Must determine whether the credit risk has significantly increased. If not, use a 12-month time frame for assessing defaults. Otherwise, consider defaults over the lifetime of the investment. Must consider a probability-weighted range of outcomes and the time value of money. Information shall be available, reasonable, and supportable.	N/A
Fair value	Used for equity investments (where active market) and derivatives. No need to do a separate impairment test because the assets are continually revalued to fair value with gains and losses booked to net income.	Used for all investments that are accounted for as FV-NI and equity investments accounted for at FV-OCI. No need to do a separate impairment test because the assets are continually revalued to fair value under the FV-NI model with gains and losses booked to net income. Impairment losses on equity investments accounted for at FV-OCI are not recycled to net income so impairment testing is not done.	Used for all investments that are accounted for as FV-NI. No need to do a separate impairment test because the assets are continually revalued to fair value with gains and losses booked to net income.

Illustration 9-18

Summary of Impairment Models (continued)

STRATEGIC INVESTMENTS

STRATEGY DEVELOPMENT
2.3.1

Accounting for investments in the common shares of another corporation after acquisition depends mostly on the relationship that exists between the investor and the investee. Relationships are classified by the level of influence that is exercised by the investor and this, in turn, is generally related to the degree of share ownership. In other words, more shares usually mean more influence. When the investment is made for strategic purposes, management usually wants to influence or control the investee's policies. Therefore, the investor is more likely to acquire a higher percentage of the outstanding voting shares.

The levels of influence and types of investment are summarized in Illustration 9-19 with reference to the percentage of ownership. Note that the percentages given are guidelines only.

Illustration 9-19

*Levels of Influence and
Types of Investment*

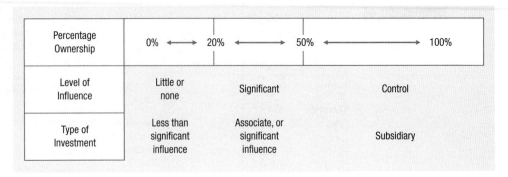

Investments in Associates

Objective 6
Explain the concept of
significant influence and
apply the equity method.

The accounting standards and reporting for equity investments depend on the level of influence that dictates what type of investment a particular holding is.[25] The first part of this chapter covered how to account for investments where the investor is not able to exercise significant influence, let alone control of the investee company. Although some of those investments could have been made for strategic purposes, it was assumed earlier in the chapter that the required level of **significant influence** was not reached.

Significant Influence

When an investor has an interest of less than 20%, **it is presumed that the investor has little or no influence over the investee**. This may not be the case, however. For example, a 16% interest may allow an investor to significantly influence decisions if the remaining shares are widely held. Alternatively, ownership of 30% of a company's shares may not give an investor company any influence at all if a 70% majority shareholder does not permit any.

Although an equity interest of less than 50% of an investee corporation does not give an investor **legal control**, it might give an investor significant influence over the investee's strategic policies. To provide guidance, the IASB defines significant influence as "the power to participate in the financial and operating policy decisions" of an entity, but not control over those policies.[26] This is similar to the ASPE concept, and both indicate that an ability to exercise influence at a significant level over another company's operating, investing, and financing activities may be indicated in several ways. Examples include the following: representation on the board of directors, participation in policy-making processes, material inter-company transactions, interchange of managerial personnel, or provision of technical information.[27] Under IFRS the term **associate** refers to the entity that the investor has significant influence over, provided it is neither a subsidiary nor a **joint venture**.

To ensure that the significant influence criterion is applied in a reasonably consistent manner, the standard setters concluded that an investment (direct or indirect) of 20% or more of the voting shares of another company should lead to a presumption that, unless there is evidence to the contrary, an investor can exercise significant influence over an investee. With less than a 20% voting interest, the assumption is that the investor cannot exercise the required degree of influence, unless the ability to influence is clearly shown. If the investor holds potential voting rights that can be exercised or converted currently, these also should be considered in deciding whether or not it has the power to exercise significant influence.

As indicated above, the extent of influence dictates the type of investment, and this, in turn, dictates the appropriate method of accounting. For investments in associates, **IFRS** requires the investor to use the equity method of accounting.[28] **ASPE** allows investors to choose the equity method or the cost method in accounting for this type of investment, but the investor must choose one method for all "significant influence" investments. However, if the associate's shares are quoted in an active market, the cost method cannot be used. Instead, the fair value approach, with gains and losses being recognized in income, can be chosen. We explained both the cost and FV-NI models earlier in this chapter, so we turn next to how the equity method works.

Equity Method Basics

Under the **equity method,** the investment is initially recorded at the cost of the acquired shares. After this, its carrying amount is adjusted each period for the investor's proportionate share of the changes in the investee's net assets. The equity method sounds complex at first, but it is basically **the accrual basis of accounting applied to investment income.**

The investor recognizes its share of investment income as the investee earns income by debiting the Investment account and crediting Investment Income. When cash is received from the investment (that is, the investee pays a dividend on the shares), this converts part of an asset that has already been recognized—the Investment—to cash. Therefore, Cash is debited and the Investment account is credited.

As indicated, the Investment account under the equity method changes to mirror the increases and decreases in the investee's book value:

- **When the associate's net assets increase** because it earns income, **the investor increases the carrying amount of its investment** for its proportionate share of the associate's increase in net assets and also **reports its share of the associate's income as investment income.**

- **When the associate's net assets decrease** because the company pays a dividend, **the investor recognizes the cash received and decreases the carrying amount of the investment** by its share of the decrease in the associate's net assets.

To illustrate the basics of the equity method, assume that Maxi Corp. purchases a 20% interest in Mini Corp. and has the ability to exercise significant influence over Mini's financial and operating policies. The entries are shown in Illustration 9-20. Note the effects on the Investment account and on the income statement.

Alternative Terminology

Under ASPE, investments in associates are often called *significant influence investments.*

Illustration 9-20

Application of Equity Method Basics (in $000's)

	IFRS/ASPE Equity Method ($000)		ASPE FV-NI (may use where traded in an active market) ($000)		ASPE Cost Model (may use except where shares are traded in an active market) ($000)	
On January 2, 2016, Maxi Corp. acquires 48,000 shares (20% of Mini Corp. common shares) at a cost of $10 a share.	Investment in Associate 480 Cash	480	FV-NI Investments 480 Cash	480	Other Investments 480 Cash	480
For the year 2016, Mini Corp. reports net income of $200,000; Maxi Corp.'s share is 20%, or $40,000.	Investment in Associate 40 Investment Income or Loss*	40	N/A		N/A	
At December 31, 2016, the 48,000 shares of Mini Corp. have a fair value of $12 a share, or $576,000.	N/A		FV-NI Investments 96 Unrealized Gain or Loss	96	N/A	
On January 28, 2017, Mini Corp. announces and pays a cash dividend of $100,000; Maxi Corp. receives 20%, or $20,000.	Cash 20 Investment in Associate	20	Cash 20 Investment Income or Loss	20	Cash 20 Investment Income or Loss	20
For the year 2017, Mini Corp. reports a net loss of $50,000; Maxi Corp.'s share is 20%, or $10,000.	Investment Income or Loss* 10 Investment in Associate	10	N/A		N/A	
At December 31, 2017, the 48,000 Mini Corp. shares have a fair value of $11 a share, or $528,000. The investment value is not considered impaired.	N/A		Unrealized Gain or Loss 48 FV-NI Investments	48	N/A	

*This entry is sometimes referred to as the **equity pickup**, because the investor is picking up its share of income or loss under the equity method. Another commonly used account title is Equity in Earnings of Associate Company.

Under the equity method, **the accrual basis of accounting** is applied. Maxi Corp. therefore reports investment income as Mini Corp. earns income. Revenue recognition is permitted before receiving a dividend, because of the degree of influence that the investor has over the investee's decisions, including dividend decisions. If the investee company suffers a loss, as Mini Corp. did in 2017, the investor accrues its share of the loss and reduces the carrying amount of its investment.

One of the benefits of this method is that the investor's income statement reports the economics of the situation: if the associate performs well, the investor's income statement reflects positive investment income. If the associate incurs losses, the investor's income statement reflects its share of the loss. In addition, when the equity method is used, the investor cannot manipulate its own income by influencing the timing of a dividend from the associate.

Expanded Illustration of the Equity Method

There are two more complexities in applying the equity method:[29]

1. Differences between what was originally paid for the investment and the investor's share of the associate's book value need to be identified and accounted for according to the reason for the extra payment.

2. The major classifications of the income reported by the associate are retained and reported in the same way on the investor's income statement.

The first item requires an understanding of what the cost of the investment represents. It is unusual for the investor to pay an amount for the investment that is exactly equal to its share of the other company's book value. The excess payment (usually it is extra) could be due to several reasons, such as the following:

• There may be unrecorded assets.

• There may be assets whose fair value is greater than the carrying amount on the associate's books, or liabilities whose fair value is less than book value.

• There may be intangibles, such as goodwill, that the associate has but that are not recognized in its books.

Any payment in excess of (or less than) the investor's share of book value is part of the cost of the investment, and after acquisition, it has to be accounted for appropriately.
If the difference is caused by long-lived assets with fair values that are greater than book value, the amount above the asset's book value must be amortized. If it relates to inventory with a fair value in excess of its carrying amount on the associate's books, it will be recognized as an increased expense as the inventory is sold. There may also be assets with fair values that are lower than book value or liabilities with present values higher than book value. **None of these differences are recorded on the associate's books, but they are captured as part of the purchase cost of the investment**, so it is the investment account itself and the investment income or loss that need to be adjusted over time.

Because the equity method recognizes and reports the investor's share of the associate's income, **the type of income that is reported should remain the same**. That is, the portion that is the investor's share of the associate's discontinued operations is reported separately from the investor's share of income before discontinued operations. The same principle applies to the investor's portion of the associate's other comprehensive income, changes in accounting policy reported in retained earnings, and capital charges. The investor reports its share of all of these in the appropriate place in its financial statements.

To illustrate, assume that on January 1, 2017, Investor Company purchases 250,000 of Investee Company's 1 million outstanding common shares for $8.5 million. Investor has therefore acquired a 25% interest in Investee. The book value (net assets) of Investee Company on this date is $30 million and Investor's proportionate share is 25% of this, or $7.5 million. Investor Company therefore has paid $1 million in excess of its share of the book value ($8,500,000 − $7,500,000).

Why did Investor pay $1 million more than its share of Investee's book value? Assume that part of the reason is because Investee's depreciable assets **are undervalued on the books** by $2.4 million. This explains $600,000 ($2,400,000 × 25%) of the excess, because Investor would only pay more in proportion to its ownership interest. Investor Company estimates the remaining life of the depreciable assets to be eight years, so the $600,000 excess payment included in the Investment account will have to be amortized over this period.

The remaining $400,000 is unexplained and therefore is determined to be unrecorded goodwill. Investor will have to assess the carrying amount of the balance of the Investment account each year to determine whether there has been any impairment in its value. This purchase is analyzed in Illustration 9-21.

<table>
<tr><td>**Illustration 9-21**

Analysis of Acquisition of Associate Company</td><td>Cost of 25% investment in Investee Co. shares</td><td>$8,500,000</td></tr>
<tr><td></td><td>25% of book value of Investee Co. represented by investment
  25% × $30,000,000</td><td>7,500,000</td></tr>
<tr><td></td><td>Payment in excess of share of book value</td><td>1,000,000</td></tr>
<tr><td></td><td>Fair value allocation to depreciable assets
  25% × $2,400,000</td><td>600,000</td></tr>
<tr><td></td><td>Unexplained excess assumed to be goodwill</td><td>$ 400,000</td></tr>
<tr><td></td><td>Annual amortization of excess payment for capital assets
  $600,000/8-year life</td><td>$ 75,000</td></tr>
</table>

Investee Company later reports net income of $2.8 million for its 2017 fiscal year, including a loss on discontinued operations of $400,000. **Income before discontinued operations**, therefore, is $3.2 million. Dividends of $1.4 million are declared and paid by Investee Company on December 31, 2017. To record these transactions and events, Investor Company makes the following 2017 entries.

A = L + SE
0   0   0
Cash flows: ↓ 8,500,000 outflow

Jan. 1/17	Investment in Associate	8,500,000	
	Cash		8,500,000
	(To record the acquisition of 25% of Investee Co.)		

A = L + SE
0   0   0
Cash flows: ↑ 350,000 inflow

Dec. 31/17	Cash	350,000	
	Investment in Associate		350,000
	(To record the dividend from Investee Co. [$1,400,000 × 0.25])		

On December 31, Investor Company recognizes its 25% share of Investee Company's net income. Because its associate's income includes both continuing and discontinued operation components, 25% of each amount is reported separately by Investor Company. The account Investment in Associate is increased by 25% of the increase in Investee's net assets from earning net income (25% × $2,800,000). Furthermore, Investor Company paid more than book value for Investee Company's net assets and a portion of the excess amount relates to assets that are depreciable. The "extra cost" of the depreciable assets to Investor has not been recognized on the associate's books, nor has the additional depreciation. As a result, the investment income needs to be adjusted for this additional expense.

A = L + SE
+700,000 0 +700,000
Cash flows: No effect

Dec. 31/17	Investment in Associate	700,000	
	Loss on Discontinued Operations	100,000	
	Investment Income or Loss		800,000
	(To record the investment income from Investee Co.		
	[Investee Co. income × 0.25])		

A = L + SE
−75,000   −75,000
Cash flows: No effect

Dec. 31/17	Investment Income or Loss	75,000	
	Investment in Associate		75,000
	(Amortization of fair value difference, depreciable assets)		

Illustration 9-22 shows the calculation of the investment in Investee Company that is presented on Investor Company's December 31, 2017 SFP.

Illustration 9-22

Calculation of Investment Carrying Amount

Acquisition cost, January 1, 2017	$8,500,000
Add: 25% of increase in Investee's net assets from earning net income	700,000
Less: 25% of decrease in Investee's net assets from declaration/payment of dividend	(350,000)
Less: Amortization of fair value difference related to capital assets	(75,000)
Investment in Investee Co., December 31, 2017, at equity	$8,775,000

Impairment in Value, Equity Method

Under both **IFRS** and **ASPE**, an investment that results in significant influence is assessed at each statement of financial position date to determine if there are any indications that the investment may be impaired (objective evidence of a loss event). If there are, its carrying amount is compared with the investment's **recoverable amount**: the higher of its value in use and fair value less costs to sell, both of which are discounted cash flow concepts. If the carrying amount is more than the investment's recoverable amount, an impairment loss equal to the difference is recognized in net income and the investment is written down directly. This loss may be reversed if future events indicate that the recoverable amount has improved.

Disposal of Investment in Associate

When the investment in the associate is sold, the statement of financial position Investment in Associate account and the Investment Income or Loss account are first brought up to date as at the date of sale. This involves adjusting these accounts for the investor's share of the associate's earnings and changes in book value since the last reporting date. Then the investment's carrying value is removed from the accounts and the difference between this and the proceeds on disposal is recognized in income as a gain or loss.

Continuing with the example in Illustrations 9-20 and 9-21, assume that Investor Company sells its investment in Investee Company on January 2, 2018, for $9 million. Because the accounts are already up to date in this case, the entry to record the sale is:

A = L + SE
+225,000   +225,000
Cash flows: ↑ 9,000,000 inflow

Cash	9,000,000	
Investment in Associate		8,775,000
Gain on Sale of Investments		225,000

Summary of Accounting Standards for Associates

The equity method is also known as "one-line consolidation" and is applied in ways that are related to how consolidation principles are applied. In fact, the equity method "investment income" is the same amount that is needed to increase or decrease the investor's income to the amount that would be reported if the investor had consolidated the results of the investee with those of the investor, with possible exceptions related to goodwill and investment impairment. Given this similarity, other complexities that result from such investments are left for an advanced accounting course that covers inter-corporate investments.

Illustration 9-23 summarizes the accounting for investments in the equity instruments of companies in which the investor has significant influence.

	IFRS	ASPE		
Measurement after recognition	Equity method	Equity method is used for all or the cost method is used for all. If shares are quoted in an active market, cannot use cost method. May use FV-NI where traded in an active market.		
		Equity method	**Cost method**	**FV-NI model**
Unrealized holding gains/losses	Not recognized	Not recognized	Not recognized	Recognized in net income
Investment income	Percentage of associate's income, adjusted for differences between cost and share of book value and inter-company profits	Percentage of associate's income, adjusted for differences between cost and share of book value and inter-company profits	Dividends received or receivable	Dividends received or receivable
Impairment, when assessment indicates possibility	Loss = carrying amount less recoverable amount (higher of value in use and fair value less costs to sell)	Loss = carrying amount less recoverable amount (higher of value in use and fair value less costs to sell)	Loss = carrying amount less recoverable amount (higher of DCF and NRV; essentially the same as the value in use and fair value less costs to sell)	N/A
Impairment reversal	Permitted	Permitted	Permitted	N/A

Illustration 9-23

Accounting for Associates

Investments in Subsidiaries

Objective 7
Explain the concept of control and when consolidation is appropriate.

When one corporation acquires control of another entity, the investor corporation is referred to as the **parent** and the investee corporation as the **subsidiary**. Control is assumed when the investor owns 50% or more of the voting shares of another company. This is because it holds a majority of the votes at the board of directors' meetings of the investee company, and therefore, the investor's management controls all the subsidiary's net assets and operations.

Standard setters have wrestled for many years with the best way to explain what **control** really is. They acknowledge that sometimes an entity with less than 50% of the voting shares can have control, while an entity with more than 50% sometimes may not have control. According to **ASPE**, control is the continuing power to determine the strategic operating, financing, and investing policies of another entity without the co-operation of others. Under **IFRS**, a new definition has been put forward that allows control to extend to a broader range of investments. This definition indicates that an investor controls another if it has the power to direct the activities of the other entity to generate returns, either positive or negative, for the investor. Similar to previous descriptions, the "power to direct the activities of another" means that an investor can determine the other entity's strategic operating and financing policies. The differences in the definitions are subtle but real, and they will become more apparent in an advanced accounting course that deals with inter-corporate investments.

An investment in the common shares of a subsidiary is presented as a long-term investment on the separate financial statements of the parent, usually accounted for by either the equity or cost method. When preparing **IFRS** statements, however, an investor with subsidiaries is required to present consolidated financial statements for the group of companies under its control. In other words, the investor **eliminates the investment account** and instead **reports all the assets and liabilities of the subsidiary on a line-by-line basis**. Under **ASPE**, this is a **permitted**, but **not required**, option. A parent company can choose to:

1. consolidate all its subsidiaries, or

2. present all of its subsidiaries under either the equity method or cost model.

The same choice is applied to all subsidiaries, although investments in shares that are quoted in an active market are not permitted to be accounted for using the cost model. They may instead be measured and reported at FV-NI. You can see here the similarities between ASPE for associates and subsidiary companies. Separate reporting on the balance sheet is required for subsidiaries accounted for using the equity method and for those using the cost method. The income statement also reports the income from each group of subsidiaries accounted for on a different basis.

Because we have already covered the cost, equity, and FV-NI methods and models, the emphasis now is on understanding **consolidation**. In place of the one-line long-term investment in subsidiary, the parent reports 100% of each of the assets and liabilities over which it has control. Instead of reporting investment income on the income statement, 100% of each of the revenues and expenses reported by the subsidiary is reported on a line-by-line basis with those of the parent company. That is, the parent presents **consolidated financial statements**. This method of reporting an investment in a controlled company is much more informative to the parent company's shareholders than a single-line statement of financial position and a single-line income statement account.

The requirement to include 100% of the assets and liabilities and 100% of the revenues, expenses, gains, and losses under the parent's control even when the ownership is less than 100% leads to the recognition of unique statement of financial position and income statement accounts. These **noncontrolling interest** accounts (sometimes referred to as **minority interest**) represent the portion of the net assets **not** owned and the portion of the entity's consolidated net income that does **not** accrue to the parent company's shareholders. These claims to net assets and net income are **equity claims** because they represent the interests of the noncontrolling **shareholders** of the subsidiary companies.

Consolidated financial statements disregard the distinction between separate legal entities and treat the parent and subsidiary corporations as an economic unit—an **economic entity**. After acquisition, this means that all inter-company balances and unrealized inter-company gains and losses are eliminated for reporting purposes. An entity cannot report sales or make a profit selling to itself. The preparation of consolidated financial statements is discussed in detail in advanced financial accounting.

The rules for consolidation seem very straightforward: If a company owns more than 50% of another company, it generally should be consolidated. If it owns less than 50%, it generally is not consolidated. However, with complex modern business relationships, standard setters realize that this test is too artificial, and that determining who really has control is often based on factors other than share ownership. This topic is covered in advanced accounting courses.

UNDERLYING CONCEPT

The consolidation of the financial results of different companies follows the economic entity assumption. It disregards the legal boundaries between entities. The key objective is to provide useful information to financial statement users about all the resources under the control of parent company management.

PRESENTATION, DISCLOSURE, AND ANALYSIS

Objective 8
Explain how investments are presented and disclosed in the financial statements, noting how this facilitates analysis.

Where should a company report investments on its statement of financial position? What types of disclosures are necessary for transparency? Finally, what information is important for users when analyzing financial statements? We will answer these questions in this section of the chapter.

Presentation and Disclosure

First, let's take a look at presentation and disclosure issues. For purposes of this discussion, investments are subdivided into two groups: those where the investor has no significant influence or control and those where the investor has significant influence.

Investments without Significant Influence or Control

Should investments that the investor cannot exercise significant influence over or control be reported as current or long-term assets? The requirements for presentation of an investment as a current asset are the same as for other assets. In general, those classified as current are continuously turning over or affecting working capital. As indicated in Chapter 5, **IFRS** specifies that, if an investment has any one of the following characteristics, it is classified as current:

- It is expected to be sold or otherwise realized within the entity's normal operating cycle or within 12 months from the statement of financial position date.

- It is held primarily for trading purposes.
- It is a cash equivalent.

Under **ASPE**, the conditions are similar: an investment is classified as a current asset only if it is usually realizable within 12 months from the balance sheet date (or normal operating cycle, if longer) and it can be converted to cash relatively quickly.

This means that debt and equity investments measured at cost or amortized cost and those at FV-NI could be either current or long-term assets, depending on the specific situation. Debt instruments are likely to be classified as current only if they are held to be traded, or expected to mature or be sold, within the following year. Equity instruments will be current only if they are marketable and are expected to be converted to cash that can be used for current purposes. Under the revised IFRS 9, investments carried at FV-OCI are most likely non-current assets: they are held for longer-term strategic purposes, and not for current trading.

The **objective of the disclosures** required for financial assets that are investments in debt and equity instruments is generally the same under both ASPE and IFRS: to provide information that allows users to assess the following:

- how significant these financial assets are to an entity's financial position and performance,
- the nature and extent of risks that the entity faces as a result of these assets, and
- how the entity manages these risks.

TREASURY MANAGEMENT 5.2.2

The specific standards are the best source of the many required disclosures for financial asset investments. The following section is meant to provide you with an understanding of the **types of information** that are required to be made available to users of the financial statements. Understanding the goal of the disclosures is helpful in determining and even predicting what information is reported.

- To help readers understand the significance of these investments to the statement of financial position, companies disclose the following:
  - the **carrying amount of investments** in instruments carried at amortized cost, cost, FV-NI (noting those where the fair value option was taken), and FV-OCI (noting those that were designated as such as an accounting policy choice and why this choice was made); and
  - the carrying amount of any impaired investments (including defaults and breaches) and related allowances for impairment, by type (method of accounting for the assets), which is also separately reported, as well as any reclassifications and collateral underlying the investments.
- To enable readers to relate the **income statement effects** to the investments on the statement of financial position, companies disclose the following:
  - net gains or losses recognized (by method of accounting),
  - total interest income (under IFRS, include only interest income calculated using the effective interest method for financial assets except for those at FV-NI), and
  - gains/losses on derecognition including reasons for derecognizing.
- IFRS requires significant amounts of fair value information including valuation techniques and inputs for those investments measured using fair value and those measured using level 3 inputs.
- For each type of **financial risk** that results from the investments, disclose what the risk exposures are, how they arise, any changes over the accounting period, and information about any concentrations of risk such as those that arise from significant investments in particular industries or foreign currency. IFRS requires additional information, such as how risks are managed, credit risk by classification of instrument, past due and impaired investments, and sensitivity analyses for each type of market risk to which the entity is exposed.[30]
- For impaired assets, IFRS requires disclosures of the following:
  - impairment losses and reversals,
  - interest on impaired investment,

- the basis for expected credit loss calculations,
- how these losses are measured, and
- how the company assesses changes in credit risks.

IFRS also requires reconciliation between opening balances in the impairment allowance and closing balances.

Refer back to Illustration 9-2, which shows the balance sheet of Canada Life. Illustration 9-24 provides additional excerpts from the financial statements, including the statement of earnings, additional details regarding what is included as investments, and information about how fair valued is assessed. The bulk of the investments are in bonds and are carried at fair value using either FV-NI (fair value through profit or loss) or FV-OCI (available for sale). You can see from the statement of earnings the significance of the income from investments, which make up 51% of total income. Note that the company has split out the investments designated as fair value through profit or loss (FVTPL) and presents both carrying value and fair value. The actual disclosures are significantly greater than we have presented here and it would be worthwhile for you to read through the full set of disclosures in the financial statements by accessing the annual report on the company's website.

REAL WORLD EMPHASIS

Illustration 9-24

Excerpts from the Statement of Earnings and Selected Notes—Canada Life Financial Corporation

CONSOLIDATED STATEMENTS OF EARNINGS
(in Canadian $ millions except per share amounts)

	For the years ended December 31	
Income	**2014**	2013
Premium income		
Gross premiums written	$ 12,394	$11,911
Ceded premiums	(5,748)	(6,428)
Total net premiums	6,646	5,483
Net investment income (note 5)		
Regular net investment income	2,990	2,999
Changes in fair value through profit or loss	5,374	(2,018)
Total net investment income	8,364	981
Fee and other income	1,305	951
	16,315	7,415

5. Portfolio Investments

(a) Carrying values and estimated fair values of portfolio investments are as follows:

	2014		2013	
	Carrying Value	Fair Value	Carrying Value	Fair Value
Bonds				
Designated fair value through profit or loss [1]	$ 43,757	$ 43,757	$ 38,925	$ 38,925
Classified fair value through profit or loss [1]	32	32	21	21
Available-for-sale	5,619	5,619	4,217	4,217
Loans and receivables	5,818	6,585	5,359	5,777
	55,226	55,993	48,522	48,940
Mortgage loans				
Residential	1,627	1,791	1,526	1,571
Non-residential	5,195	5,897	4,594	4,647
	6,822	7,688	6,120	6,218
Stocks				
Designated fair value through profit or loss [1]	2,090	2,090	2,216	2,216
Available-for-sale	3	3	2	2
Available-for-sale, at cost [2]	125	N/A	121	N/A
Equity method	194	194	226	226
	2,412	2,287	2,565	2,444
Investment properties	3,286	3,286	2,985	2,985
Total	$ 67,746	$ 69,254	$ 60,192	$ 60,587

(continued)

Illustration 9-24

Excerpts from the Statement of Earnings and Selected Notes—Canada Life Financial Corporation (continued)

2.Basis of Presentation and Summary of Accounting Policies (cont'd)

The significant accounting policies are as follows:

(a) Portfolio Investments

Portfolio investments include bonds, mortgage loans, stocks, and investment properties. Portfolio investments are classified as fair value through profit or loss, available-for-sale, held-to-maturity, loans and receivables or as non-financial instruments based on management's intention relating to the purpose and nature of the instrument or characteristics of the investment. The Company currently has not classified any investments as held-to-maturity.

Investments in bonds and stocks normally actively traded on a public market are either designated or classified as fair value through profit or loss or classified as available-for-sale on a trade date basis. A financial asset is designated as fair value through profit or loss on initial recognition if it eliminates or significantly reduces an accounting mismatch. Changes in the fair value of financial assets designated as fair value through profit or loss are generally offset by changes in insurance contract liabilities, since the measurement of insurance contract liabilities is determined with reference to the assets supporting the liabilities. A financial asset is classified as fair value through profit or loss on initial recognition if it is part of a portfolio that is actively traded for the purpose of earning investment income. Fair value through profit or loss investments are recognized at fair value on the Consolidated Balance Sheets with realized and unrealized gains and losses reported in the Consolidated Statements of Earnings. Available-for-sale investments are recognized at fair value on the Consolidated Balance Sheets with unrealized gains and losses recorded in other comprehensive income. Realized gains and losses are reclassified from other comprehensive income and recorded in the Consolidated Statements of Earnings when the available-for-sale investment is sold. Interest income earned on both fair value through profit or loss and available-for-sale bonds is recorded as net investment income in the Consolidated Statements of Earnings.

Investments in equity instruments where a fair value cannot be measured reliably are classified as available-for-sale, carried at cost and fair value disclosure is not applicable. Investments in stocks for which the Company exerts significant influence over but does not control are accounted for using the equity method of accounting. Investments in stocks include the Company's investment in Allianz Ireland, an unlisted general insurance company operating in Ireland, over which the Company exerts significant influence but does not control. The investment is accounted for using the equity method of accounting.

Investments in mortgages and bonds not normally actively traded on a public market are classified as loans and receivables and are carried at amortized cost net of any allowance for credit losses. Interest income earned and realized gains and losses on the sale of investments classified as loans and receivables are recorded in the Consolidated Statements of Earnings and included in net investment income.

Investment properties are real estate held to earn rental income or for capital appreciation. Investment properties are initially measured at cost and subsequently carried at fair value on the Consolidated Balance Sheets. All changes in fair value are recorded as net investment income in the Consolidated Statements of Earnings. Fair values for investment properties are determined using independent qualified appraisal services and include management adjustments for material changes in property cash flows, capital expenditures or general market conditions in the interim period between appraisals. Properties held to earn rental income or for capital appreciation that have an insignificant portion that is owner occupied or where there is no intent to occupy on a long-term basis are classified as investment properties. Properties that do not meet these criteria are classified as owner occupied properties. Property that is leased that would otherwise be classified as investment property if owned by the Company is also included within investment properties.

Selected excerpts from notes to the financial statements:

Fair Value Measurement

Financial instrument carrying values necessarily reflect the prevailing market liquidity and the liquidity premiums embedded within the market pricing methods the Company relies upon.

The following is a description of the methodologies used to value instruments carried at fair value:

Bonds—Fair Value Through Profit or Loss and Available for Sale

Fair values for bonds classified as fair value through profit or loss or available for sale are determined with reference to quoted market bid prices primarily provided by third party independent pricing sources. Where prices are not quoted in a normally active market, fair values are determined by valuation models. The Company maximizes the use of observable inputs and minimizes the use of unobservable inputs when measuring fair value. The Company obtains quoted prices in active markets, when available, for identical assets at the balance sheet date to measure bonds at fair value in its fair value through profit or loss and available for sale portfolios.

The Company estimates the fair value of bonds not traded in active markets by referring to actively traded securities with similar attributes, dealer quotations, matrix pricing methodology, discounted cash flow analyses and/or internal valuation models. This methodology considers such

(continued)

factors as the issuer's industry, the security's rating, term, coupon rate and position in the capital structure of the issuer, as well as, yield curves, credit curves, prepayment rates and other relevant factors. For bonds that are not traded in active markets, valuations are adjusted to reflect illiquidity, and such adjustments generally are based on available market evidence. In the absence of such evidence, management's best estimate is used.

Stocks—Fair Value Through Profit or Loss and Available for Sale

Fair values for public stocks are generally determined by the last bid price for the security from the exchange where it is principally traded. Fair values for stocks for which there is no active market are determined by discounting expected future cash flows. The Company maximizes the use of observable inputs and minimizes the use of unobservable inputs when measuring fair value. The Company obtains quoted prices in active markets, when available, for identical assets at the balance sheet date to measure stocks at fair value in its fair value through profit or loss and available-for-sale portfolios.

Mortgages and Bonds—Loans and Receivables

For disclosure purposes only, fair value for bonds and mortgages classified as loans and receivables are determined by discounting expected future cash flows using current market rates. Valuation inputs typically include benchmark yields and risk-adjusted spreads based on current lending activities and market activity.

Investment Properties

Fair values for investment properties are determined using independent qualified appraisal services and include management adjustments for material changes in property cash flows, capital expenditures or general market conditions in the interim period between appraisals. The determination of the fair value of investment property requires the use of estimates including future cash flows (such as future leasing assumptions, rental rates, capital and operating expenditures) and discount, revisionary and overall capitalization rates applicable to the asset based on current market conditions. Investment property under construction is valued at fair value if such values can be reliably determined otherwise they are recorded at cost.

Impairment

Investments are reviewed regularly on an individual basis to determine impairment status. The Company considers various factors in the impairment evaluation process, including, but not limited to, the financial condition of the issuer, specific adverse conditions affecting an industry or region, decline in fair value not related to interest rates, bankruptcy or defaults and delinquency in payments of interest or principal.

Investments are deemed to be impaired when there is no longer reasonable assurance of timely collection of the full amount of the principal and interest due. The market value of an investment is not a definitive indicator of impairment, as it may be significantly influenced by other factors including the remaining term to maturity and liquidity of the asset. However market price must be taken into consideration when evaluating impairment.

For impaired mortgages and bonds classified as loans and receivables, provisions are established or write-offs made to adjust the carrying value to the net realizable amount. Wherever possible the fair value of collateral underlying the loans or observable market price is used to establish net realizable value. For impaired available for sale bonds, recorded at fair value, the accumulated loss recorded in accumulated other comprehensive income (AOCI) is reclassified to net investment income. Impairments on available for sale debt instruments are reversed if there is objective evidence that a permanent recovery has occurred. All gains and losses on bonds classified or designated as fair value through profit or loss are already recorded in income, therefore a reduction due to impairment of these assets will be recorded in income. As well, when determined to be impaired, interest is no longer accrued and previous interest accruals are reversed.

Fair value movement on the assets supporting insurance contract liabilities is a major factor in the movement of insurance contract liabilities. Changes in the fair value of bonds designated or classified as fair value through profit or loss that support insurance and investment contract liabilities are largely offset by corresponding changes in the fair value of liabilities except when the bond has been deemed impaired.

Securities Lending

The Company engages in securities lending through securities custodians as lending agents. Loaned securities are not derecognized, and continue to be reported within investment assets, as the Company retains substantial risks and rewards and economic benefits related to the loaned securities.

8. Fair Value Measurement

The Company's assets and liabilities recorded at fair value have been categorized based upon the following fair value hierarchy:

Level 1: Fair value measurements utilize observable, quoted prices (unadjusted) in active markets for identical assets or liabilities that the Company has the ability to access. Assets and liabilities utilizing level 1 inputs include actively exchange traded equity securities, exchange traded futures, and mutual and segregated funds which have available prices in an active market with no redemption restrictions.

(continued)

Illustration 9-24

Excerpts from the Statement of Earnings and Selected Notes—Canada Life Financial Corporation (continued)

Level 2: Fair value measurements utilize inputs other than quoted prices included in Level 1 that are observable for the asset or liability, either directly or indirectly. Level 2 inputs include quoted prices for similar assets and liabilities in active markets, and inputs other than quoted prices that are observable for the asset or liability, such as interest rates and yield curves that are observable at commonly quoted intervals. The fair values for some Level 2 securities were obtained from a pricing service. The pricing service inputs include, but are not limited to, benchmark yields, reported trades, broker/dealer quotes, issuer spreads, two-sided markets, benchmark securities, offers and reference data. Level 2 assets and liabilities include those priced using a matrix which is based on credit quality and average life, government and agency securities, restricted stock, some private bonds and equities, most investment-grade and high-yield corporate bonds, most asset-backed securities, most over-the-counter derivatives, and mortgage loans. Investment contracts that are measured at fair value through profit or loss are mostly included in the Level 2 category.

Level 3: Fair value measurements utilize one or more significant inputs that are not based on observable market inputs and include situations where there is little, if any, market activity for the asset or liability. The values of the majority of Level 3 securities were obtained from single broker quotes, internal pricing models, or external appraisers. Assets and liabilities utilizing Level 3 inputs generally include certain bonds, certain asset-backed securities, some private equities, investments in mutual and segregated funds where there are redemption restrictions, certain over-the-counter derivatives, and investment properties.

Investments in Associates

As a general rule, the significance of an investment to the investor's financial position and performance generally determines how much disclosure is required. Investments in associates are classified as non-current assets (unless they are held for sale), and income from these significantly influenced companies is reported as income before discontinued operations, discontinued operations, or other comprehensive income, according to its nature in the associate's financial statements. Management reports the following for associates accounted for using the equity method:

1. separate disclosure of the investment category on the statement of financial position or in the notes to the financial statements, and the method of accounting used;

2. the fair value of any of these investments that has a price quoted in an active market;

3. separate disclosure of the income from investments that are accounted for using the equity method; and

4. information about associates' year ends that are different from the investors' year end.

Under **IFRS**, additional information is required, such as summarized financial information about the associates' assets, liabilities, revenue, and net income, and any relevant contingent liabilities that may affect the investor. Under **ASPE**, the information required to be provided is a list of any significant investments, including a description of the investment, the names, carrying amounts, and percentage ownership held. Because private enterprises are allowed to use methods other than the equity method, they are also required to separately report the carrying amount of investments in companies subject to significant influence accounted for at cost, as well as the amount of investment income reported from these investments.

Analysis

FINANCIAL ANALYSIS
5.1.1

To effectively analyze a company's performance and position, it is essential to understand the accounting and reporting for the entity's investments. Some of the key aspects that analysts watch for include the following:

1. separation of investment results from operating results (although where the management of investments is a key part of operations, such as for financial institutions, this is not as relevant);

2. the relationship between the investment asset and related returns (income);

3. information that is lost in the process of consolidation; and

4. risks related to the investments and how they are managed.

Because the income statement reports on management's performance in operating the company's assets, it is important to separate the results of active operating income from the investment returns, where management's role is often more passive. As gains or losses on sales of investments or special dividends can obscure a company's operating performance, these must be separately identified and assessed.

Accounting standards require disclosures that make it possible for a reader to relate the investment category on the SFP to the investment income reported on the income statement, and to the holding gains and losses in other comprehensive income.

Understanding the effects of the accounting methods that are used for different categories of investments is a key requirement for the analyst. If an entity has significant investments in companies that are accounted for by the equity method, for example, the analyst needs to be aware that some information is not available because the one-line investment account hides the debt and risk characteristics of the investee company that the entity is exposed to.

Consolidation of subsidiary companies also presents problems. While the financial statements reflect the combined operations of the economic entity, important information is lost through aggregating the parent's results with those of its subsidiaries. This is why segmented information, discussed in Chapter 23, has to be separately reported in the notes. Analysts also watch for major acquisitions during the current or previous year. The statement of financial position contains all the assets of the subsidiary, but the income statement includes only the income earned by the subsidiary after it was acquired by the parent. Any analysis that looks at relationships between income and assets has to adjust for major acquisitions in the period(s) being examined.

IFRS/ASPE COMPARISON

Objective **9**

Identify differences in accounting between IFRS and ASPE, and what changes are expected in the near future.

As indicated earlier, accounting for financial assets in general is in the midst of change.

A Comparison of IFRS and ASPE

Illustration 9-25 sets out the major differences between IFRS and ASPE concerning accounting for investments.

Illustration 9-25

IFRS and ASPE Comparison Chart

	IAS 1, 27, 28, IFRS 3, 7, 9, and 13 (IFRS 9 requires mandatory adoption in 2018 but may adopt early)	Accounting Standards for Private Enterprises (ASPE)— *CPA Canada Handbook*, Part II, Sections 1582, 1601, 1602, 3051, and 3856	References to Related Illustrations and Select Brief Exercises
Investments— no significant influence or control: Measurement models	Permits three measurement models: 1. amortized cost (for debt instruments where the business model requires holding to maturity), 2. FV-OCI with no recycling (for certain equity instruments only) and FV-OCI for debt securities with recycling where the business model includes both holding to maturity and holding for sale (depending on the security and the circumstances), and 3. FV-NI for everything else.	Permits only two measurement models: 1. FV-NI (for equity investments that trade in an active market, derivatives, and those accounted for under the fair value option), and 2. cost/amortized cost (everything else).	Illustration 9-15 BE9-14

(continued)

Fair value option	FV-NI can be designated on initial recognition if it reduces or eliminates an accounting mismatch.	FV-NI can be designated on initial recognition.	N/A
Interest and dividend income	Use effective interest method when interest income is required to be reported separately; all interest and dividends to net income except for those at FV-OCI where dividends that are a return of investment are recognized in OCI. Where using FV-NI, may show investment income combined (no need to show interest separately).	Use either straight-line or effective interest method when applicable; all interest and dividends to net income. Must show interest separately.	Illustrations 9-4 and 9-6 and related journal entries BE9-4, BE9-5, and BE9-6
Realized gains and losses	Recognize in net income, except for those equity investments accounted for at FV-OCI (no recycling).	Recognize in net income.	Illustration 9-11 and subsequent journal entries
Reclassifications	No reclassification is permitted between measurement models unless there is a rare occurrence of a change in the entity's business model.	FV option designation is irrevocable; otherwise this issue is not addressed.	N/A
Impairment	Use expected loss model for cost/amortized cost and debt securities accounted for at FV-OCI. May reverse impairment losses.	Use the incurred loss model with a market discount rate to measure revised discounted cash flow (DCF); reversals are permitted if due to a specific subsequent event. New carrying value is higher of DCF and NRV through sale or by exercising right to collateral.	Illustrations 9-17 and 9-18 BE9-16 and BE9-17
Investments—in associates/ significant influence: Method of accounting	Requires the equity method.	Allows an accounting policy choice of the equity method or the cost method. If shares are quoted in an active market, cannot use cost model; may use FV-NI.	Illustrations 9-20 and 9-23 BE9-20 and BE9-21
Investments—in subsidiaries: Control	Definition expands the meaning of control. Emphasis is on the power to direct another entity's activities to generate returns for the investor.	Has a narrower definition of control that relies more strongly on holding more than 50% of the voting interests in another entity.	N/A
Method of reporting	Use consolidation.	Allows an accounting policy choice of consolidation or presenting all subsidiaries using the equity method or the cost method. If shares are quoted in an active market, cannot use cost model; may use FV-NI.	N/A (covered in advanced accounting courses)
Disclosures	Requires more extensive disclosures.	Uses the same financial reporting objectives as IFRS, but more limited disclosures are required.	BE9-24

Illustration 9-25

IFRS and ASPE Comparison Chart (continued)

Looking Ahead

At the time of writing, the IASB had recently issued a new standard, IFRS 9, which is effective in 2018. This chapter encompasses the content of this new standard.

SUMMARY OF LEARNING OBJECTIVES

1 Understand the nature of investments, including which types of companies have significant investments.

This chapter deals with investments in basic debt and equity instruments of other companies. Debt instruments such as bonds generally carry contractual rights to receive principal and interest payments. Equity instruments such as shares may carry contractual rights to receive dividends (depending on the type of share) and may also carry voting rights and/or rights to receive residual assets upon windup of a company. Care must be taken to determine exactly what rights the investments entitle the holder to because this will help determine the accounting. Not all companies carry significant investments. It depends on the business model. Examples of types of companies that generally carry significant investments are financial institutions, insurance companies, and pension funds.

2 Explain and apply the cost/amortized cost model of accounting for investments.

At acquisition, the cost of the investment is recognized as its fair value plus transaction costs. If the investment is a debt instrument, any premium or discount is amortized to interest income. Holding gains are recognized only when realized, as are holding losses, unless the investment is impaired. The investment is reported at its cost or amortized cost as either a current asset or a long-term investment, depending on its maturity and management's intention to hold it. ASPE uses this model for most investments excluding equity investments where an active market exists for trading the shares and derivatives. IFRS 9 uses this model for debt instruments where the entity's business model is to hold the investments to maturity.

3 Explain and apply the fair value through net income model of accounting for investments.

At acquisition, the investment is recognized at its fair value, with transaction costs being expensed. At each reporting date, the investment is revalued to its current fair value, with holding gains and losses recognized in net income. Dividend and interest income is also recognized in net income. If the investment is not held for trading purposes, any interest income is reported separately and is adjusted for discount or premium amortization. If held for trading or other current purposes, the investment is reported as a current asset. ASPE uses this for equity instruments where there is an active market and derivatives. IFRS 9 uses this model for all investments not accounted for under the cost/amortized cost model or the FV-OCI model. ASPE and IFRS both allow any

investment to be accounted for using FV-NI under the fair value option.

4 Explain and apply the fair value through other comprehensive income model of accounting for investments.

At acquisition, the investment is recognized at fair value plus transaction costs. At each reporting date, the investment is revalued to its current fair value, with the holding gains or losses reported in other comprehensive income. On disposal, the accumulated holding gains or losses are either recycled to net income (debt securities) or transferred directly to retained earnings (equity securities). Investments are reported as current or long-term assets, depending on marketability and management intent. ASPE does not allow this method. IFRS 9 allows this method for certain equity investments and debt securities where the business model is achieved by both holding to maturity and selling (depending on the investment and circumstances).

5 Explain and apply the incurred loss, expected loss, and fair value loss impairment models.

The three impairment loss models differ in the timing of the recognition of impairment losses and the discount rate used. Under the incurred loss approach, a triggering event is required before a loss is recognized and measured, and the revised cash flows are discounted using either the historical or a current market rate. Under the expected loss approach, no triggering event is required, and revised cash flows and impairment losses are determined on a continual basis. The discount rate is the historical/original rate. Using the fair value loss model, the asset is written down to fair value taking into account market information (refer back to Chapters 2 and 3). ASPE uses the incurred loss model for all cost/amortized cost investments, although the post-impairment carrying values are measured differently. IFRS 9 uses the expected loss model for all cost/amortized cost investments as well as FV-OCI debt securities. Under IFRS 9, impairment losses on FV-OCI equity investments are not recognized in net income. Where the FV-NI model is used, there is no need to specifically assess impairment because the investment is continually revalued to fair value and any gains or losses are booked to income.

6 Explain the concept of significant influence and apply the equity method.

Significant influence is the ability to have an effect on strategic decisions made by an investee's board of directors, but not enough to control those decisions. The equity method, sometimes referred to as one-line consolidation, is used because income is recognized by the investor as it is earned. The investor's income statement will reflect the performance of the investee company. Under this method, the investment account is adjusted for all changes in the investee's book value and for the amortization of any purchase discrepancy. IFRS requires use of the equity method for its associates (investees a company can significantly influence). ASPE provides a policy choice: either the equity method or the cost method, except that associates with a quoted price in an active market cannot be accounted for at cost. Instead, the FV-NI model can be used.

7 Explain the concept of control and when consolidation is appropriate.

Control relates to the ability to direct the strategic decisions of another entity and to generate returns for your own benefit or loss. When one company controls another, it controls all the net assets of that entity and is responsible for all its revenues and expenses. Therefore, all of the subsidiary's assets and liabilities, and revenues and expenses, are reported by the parent investor on a line-by-line basis in consolidated financial statements. The interests of the noncontrolling shareholders in the subsidiary company are reported separately as noncontrolling interest. Under IFRS, all subsidiaries are consolidated. ASPE, on the other hand, allows consolidation or a choice of the equity or cost method. Investments in companies with shares traded in an active market cannot be reported using the cost method, but may use FV-NI.

8 Explain how investments are presented and disclosed in the financial statements, noting how this facilitates analysis.

The objectives of disclosure are to provide information so users can assess the significance of the financial asset investments to the entity's financial position and performance, the extent of risks to which the company is exposed as a result, and how those risks are managed. As a result, the investments are identified on the statement of financial position according to how they are classified for accounting purposes, with the income statement reporting information on the returns by method of classification. Extensive disclosure is required, particularly under IFRS, on the entity's risk exposures and how it manages those risks.

9 Identify differences in accounting between IFRS and ASPE, and what changes are expected in the near future.

The differences are noted in Illustrations 9-15, 9-17, 9-18, 9-20 and 9-23. There are significant differences because there are two standards currently in effect under IFRS (IAS 39 and IFRS 9) and because the standards are currently in transition.

KEY TERMS

amortized cost model, p. 491	expected loss impairment model, p. 508	joint venture, p. 512
associate, p. 512	fair value loss impairment model, p. 510	minority interest, p. 518
available for sale investments, p. 488	fair value option, p. 505	noncontrolling interest, p. 518
consolidation, p. 518	fair value through net income	on margin, p. 489
control, p. 517	(FV-NI), p. 495	realized, p. 489
cost model, p. 490	fair value through other comprehensive	significant influence, p. 512
debt instruments, p. 486	income (FV-OCI), p. 500	straight-line amortization, p. 493
debt securities, p. 486	fair value through profit or loss	subsidiary, p. 517
effective interest method, p. 492	(FVTPL), p. 495	trading, p. 487
equity instruments, p. 486	held for trading investments, p. 488	transaction costs, p. 489
equity method, p. 513	held to maturity investments, p. 490	unrealized holding gains or
equity pickup, p. 513	incurred loss impairment model, p. 507	losses, p. 489

Note: Completion of this end-of-chapter material will help develop CPA enabling competencies (such as ethics and professionalism, problem-solving and decision-making and communication) and technical competencies. We have highlighted selected items with an integration icon and material in *WileyPLUS* has been linked to the competencies. All cases emphasize integration, especially of the enabling competencies. The brief exercises, exercises and problems generally emphasize problem-solving and decision-making.

Brief Exercises

FINANCE

(LO 1) BE9-1 Bali Corp. has $10,000 in surplus funds to invest and is considering investing in either Company A or Company B. Company A promises to return the $10,000 original amount invested in three years' time and pay a 2% annual return on the principal amount. Company B does not promise to repay the original amount invested, but indicates that it is likely that the $10,000 investment will be worth more than $10,000 if Company B is profitable. Whether Bali will receive an annual return on the investment depends on Company B's cash flows and whether Company B's board of directors votes to distribute the cash.

(a) Identify whether the potential investments are investments in debt or in equity securities.

(b) Explain how you determined your answer.

(LO 1) **BE9-2**   Jax Taylor has the financial statements of an old established university, a manufacturing company, an insurance company, a real estate developer, a major retail enterprise, and a pension plan.

(a) Identify the organizations whose statements of financial position are most likely to report a significant proportion of investments.

FINANCE   (b) For those identified, what types of investments would you expect to find?

(LO 2) **BE9-3**   Eastwind Corporation purchased 400 common shares of Ditch Inc. for $13,200 on February 21. Eastwind paid a 1% commission on the share purchase and, because the shares were not publicly traded, decided to account for them using the cost/amortized cost method. On June 30, Ditch declared and paid a cash dividend of $1.50 per share. Prepare Eastwind Corporation's journal entries to record (a) the purchase of the investment, (b) the dividends received, and (c) the sale of the Ditch Inc. shares in early January the following year for $15,100 less a 1% commission paid on the sale.

(LO 2) **BE9-4**   Beta Corp. invested in a three-year, $100 face value 8% bond, paying $95.03. At this price, the bond will yield a 10% return. Interest is payable annually.

(a) Prepare a bond discount amortization table for Beta Corp., assuming Beta uses the effective interest method required by IFRS.

(b) Prepare journal entries to record the initial investment, receipt of interest, and recognition of interest income in each of the three years, and the maturity of the bond at the end of the third year.

(c) Assuming Beta Corp. applies ASPE and has chosen to use the straight-line method of amortization, determine the amount of discount that is amortized each year.

(d) Under the assumption in (c), prepare journal entries to record the initial investment receipt of interest, and recognition of interest income in each of the three years, and the maturity of the bond at the end of the third year.

(e) Compare the total interest income under the two methods over the three-year period.

(LO 2) **BE9-5**   Gamma Corp. invested in a three-year, $100 face value 6% bond, paying $105.55. At this price, the bond will yield a 4% return. Interest is payable annually.

(a) Prepare a bond premium amortization table for Gamma Corp., assuming Gamma uses the effective interest method required by IFRS.

(b) Prepare journal entries to record the initial investment, receipt of interest, and recognition of interest income in each of the three years, and the maturity of the bond at the end of the third year.

(c) Assuming Gamma Corp. applies ASPE and has chosen to use the straight-line method of amortization, determine the amount of premium that is amortized each year.

(d) Under the assumption in (c), prepare journal entries to record the initial investment, receipt of interest, and recognition of interest income in each of the three years, and the maturity of the bond at the end of the third year.

(e) Compare the total interest income under the two methods over the three-year period.

(LO 2) **BE9-6**   Carras Corporation purchased $60,000 of five-year, 6% bonds of Hu Inc. for $55,133 to yield an 8% return, and classified the purchase as an amortized cost method investment. The bonds pay interest semi-annually.

(a) Assuming Carras Corporation applies IFRS, prepare its journal entries for the purchase of the investment and the receipt of semi-annual interest and discount amortization for the first two interest payments that will be received. Round amounts to the nearest dollar.

(b) Assuming Carras applies ASPE and has chosen the straight-line method of discount amortization, prepare the same three entries requested in part (a), rounding amounts to the nearest dollar.

(LO 2) **BE9-7**   On September 1, Louisa Ltd. purchased $80,000 of five-year, 9% bonds for $74,086, resulting in an effective (yield) rate of 11%. The bonds pay interest each March 1 and September 1. Louisa Ltd. applies ASPE, accounts for the investment under the amortized cost approach using the effective interest accounting policy, and has a December 31 year end. The following March 1, after receiving the semi-annual interest on the bonds, Louisa sells the bonds for $75,100. Rounding amounts to the nearest dollar, prepare Louisa's journal entries for (a) the purchase of the investment, (b) any adjusting entry(ies) needed at December 31, (c) the receipt of interest on March 1, and (d) the sale of the bond investment on March 1.

(LO 3) **BE9-8**   Abdul Corporation purchased 400 common shares of Sigma Inc. for trading purposes for $13,200 on September 8 and accounted for the investment under ASPE at FV-NI. In December, Sigma declared and paid a cash dividend of $1.75 per share. At year end, December 31, Sigma shares were selling for $35.50 per share. In late January, Abdul sold the Sigma shares for $34.95 per share. Prepare Abdul Corporation's journal entries to record (a) the purchase of the investment, (b) the dividends received, (c) the fair value adjustment at December 31, and (d) the January sale of the investment.

(LO 3) BE9-9 On October 1, Qilan Ltd. purchased 7% bonds with a face value of $1,000 for trading purposes, accounting for the investment at FV-NI. The bonds were priced at 1.044 to yield Qilan 6%, and pay interest annually each October 1. Qilan has a December 31 year end, and at this date, the bonds' fair value was $1,055. Assuming Qilan applies IFRS and follows a policy of not reporting interest income separately from other investment income, prepare Qilan's journal entries for (a) the purchase of the investment, (b) the December 31 interest accrual, and (c) the year-end fair value adjustment. Assuming Qilan applies ASPE, uses the effective interest method, and follows a policy of reporting interest income separately, prepare Qilan's journal entries for (d) the December 31 interest accrual, and (e) the year-end fair value adjustment. Round amounts to two decimal places.

(LO 3) BE9-10 On March 31, Ramesh Corp. invests in a $1,000, 6% bond to be held for short-term trading purposes, and accounts for this investment using the FV-NI method. The bond's fair value when acquired was $970, but an additional $10 was paid (and debited to Interest Receivable) representing the interest accrued since the annual interest payment date of February 1. Ramesh applies IFRS, does not report interest separately from other investment income, and prepares financial statements each December 31. The fair value of the bond on December 31 is $963 and on February 1, when Ramesh sells the bond, it is $961. Prepare journal entries to record (a) the purchase of the bond, (b) any December 31 adjustments needed, (c) the receipt of interest on February 1, and (d) the sale of the bond on February 1. Ramesh Corp. does not use reversing entries.

(LO 4) BE9-11 Alaska Corporation purchased 300 common shares of Burke Inc. for $23,400 and accounted for them using FV-OCI. During the year, Burke paid a cash dividend of $3.25 per share. At year end, Burke shares had a fair value of $74.50 per share. Prepare Alaska's journal entries to record (a) the purchase of the investment, (b) the dividends received, and (c) the fair value adjustment.

(LO 4) BE9-12 Early in its 2017 fiscal year (December 31 yearend), Hayes Company purchased 10,000 shares of Kenyon Corporation common shares for $26.18 per share, plus $1,800 in brokerage commissions. These securities were accounted for at FV-OCI (with no recycling), and transaction costs are capitalized. In September, Kenyon declared and paid a dividend of $1.02 per share, and on December 31, 2017, the fair value of these shares was $271,500. On April 13, 2018, Hayes sold all the Kenyon shares at a price of $28.10 each, incurring $1,925 in brokerage commissions on the sale. Prepare the entries to record (a) the purchase of the Kenyon shares, (b) the receipt of the dividend, (c) the fair value adjustment at December 31, 2017, and (d) all entries associated with the disposal of the investment on April 13, 2018. (*Hint*: In part [d], first bring the investment to its April 13 fair value net of the brokerage commission.)

(LO 4) BE9-13 The following information relates to Cortez Corp. for 2017: net income of $672,683; unrealized loss of 20,830 related to investments accounted for at FV-OCI during the year; and accumulated other comprehensive income of $37,273 on January 1, 2017. Determine (a) other comprehensive income for 2017, (b) comprehensive income for 2017, and (c) accumulated other comprehensive income at December 31, 2017.

(LO 2, 3, BE9-14 A review of the financial statements of private and publicly accountable enterprises may result in finding the
4, 9) following measurement approaches used for their non-strategic investments: (1) cost/amortized cost, (2) FV-NI (or FVTPL), (3) FV-OCI (with recycling), and (4) FV-OCI (without recycling). Indicate by number (1, 2, 3, or 4) which methods are permitted for enterprises applying (a) ASPE, and (b) IFRS 9.

(LO 5) BE9-15 The standard setters identify three approaches to accounting for the impairment of financial asset investments: an incurred loss model, an expected loss model, and a fair value model. Identify which models are required to be used by enterprises applying (a) ASPE, and (b) IFRS 9. If more than one model is used under each of (a) and (b), identify when each model would be applied.

(LO 5) BE9-16 Under the expected loss model, the entity must assess whether there has been a significant increase in credit risk. Explain what the impact is if the assessment results in a yes answer or a no answer.

(LO 5) BE9-17 Assume that Gush Inc. invests in a bond for $55,000. The bond was purchased at par and is accounted for using amortized cost. At year end, management has determined that there is no significant increase in credit risk, but that there is a 1% chance that the company will not collect 20% of the face value of the bond (which also represents the present value of the bond) in the next 12 months. The expected loss model is used. Prepare the required year-end journal entries.

(LO 5) BE9-18 Assume the same information as in BE9-17. Assume also that management feels that there has been a significant increase in the credit risk and that there is a 5% chance that the company will not collect 50% of the face value of the bond over its life. The expected loss model is used. Prepare the required journal entries.

(LO 5) BE9-19 Ramirez Company has an investment in 6%, 10-year bonds of Soto Company. The investment was originally purchased at par for $100 in 2016 and it is accounted for at amortized cost. Early in 2017, Ramirez recorded an impairment on the Soto investment due to Soto's financial distress. At that time, the present value of the cash flows discounted using the original effective interest rate was $90, and the present value of the cash flows using the then current market rate was $91. In 2018, Soto returned to profitability and the Soto investment was no longer considered impaired. Prepare the entries Ramirez would make in 2017 and 2018 under ASPE.

(LO 6) BE9-20 Poot Corporation purchased a 40% interest in Moss Inc. for $100. This investment gave Poot significant influence over Moss. During the year, Moss earned net income of $15 and paid dividends of $5. Assuming the purchase price was equal to 40% of Moss's net carrying amount when it was acquired, prepare Poot's journal entries related to this investment using the equity method. Poot applies IFRS.

(LO 6) BE9-21 Julip Corporation purchased a 25% interest in Krov Corporation on January 2, 2017, for $1,000. At that time, the carrying amount of Krov's net assets was $3,600. Any excess of the cost of the investment over Julip's share of Krov's carrying amount can be attributed to unrecorded intangibles with a useful life of 20 years. Krov declared and paid a dividend of $12 and reported net income of $60 for its year ended December 31, 2017. Prepare Julip's 2017 entries to record all transactions and events related to the investment in its associate. Assume that Julip is a publicly accountable enterprise that applies IFRS.

(LO 6) BE9-22 Use the information from BE9-21, except that Julip Corporation is a private enterprise that applies ASPE. Prepare Julip's 2017 entries to record all transactions and events related to its significant influence investment in Krov Corporation, assuming that (a) Krov's shares are traded in an active market, Julip applies the FV-NI approach, and the fair value of Julip's share of Krov Corp. at December 31, 2017, is $1,020; and that (b) Julip applies the cost method to account for its investment in Krov (the shares are not traded in an active market).

(LO 6, 7) BE9-23 Beckett Corp. is facing a decision as to whether to purchase 40% of Kyla Corp.'s shares for $1.6 million cash, giving Beckett significant influence over the investee company, or 60% of Kyla's shares for $2.4 million cash, making Kyla a subsidiary company. The book value of Kyla's net assets is $4 million (assets are $10 million and liabilities are $6 million). How will this investment affect Beckett's GAAP statement of financial position if Beckett acquires (a) a 40% interest and (b) a 60% interest, assuming Beckett applies IFRS? That is, for each of (a) and (b), indicate the immediate effect on Beckett's total assets, total liabilities, and shareholders' equity, assuming Beckett applies IFRS.

(LO 8) BE9-24 Both ASPE and IFRS require disclosures about an enterprise's investments that include the carrying amount of each type of investment by the accounting method used and the income, gains, or losses classified in a similar way. Identify the disclosure objective for financial assets that this information is intended to help meet.

Exercises

(LO 1, 2, 3, 4) E9-1 **(Investment Classifications)** Each of the following investments is independent of the others.

1. A bond that will mature in four years was bought one month ago when the price dropped. As soon as the value increases, which is expected next month, it will be sold.

2. Ten percent of the outstanding shares of Farm Corp. were purchased. The company is planning on eventually getting a total of 30% of the outstanding shares.

3. Ten-year bonds were purchased this year. The bonds mature on January 1 of next year.

4. Bonds that will mature in five years are purchased. The company would like to hold them until they mature, but money has been tight recently and the bonds may need to be sold.

5. A bond that matures in 10 years was purchased with money that the company had set aside for an expansion project that is planned for 10 years from now.

6. Preferred shares were purchased for their consistent dividend. The company is planning to hold the preferred shares for a long time.

7. Common shares of a distributor are purchased to meet a regulatory requirement for doing business in the distributor's region. The investment is expected to be held indefinitely.

Instructions

(a) Identify the best accounting model classification(s) for each of the investments described above under (i) ASPE, and (ii) IFRS 9. Note where there are choices or options. Assume that the criteria for the fair value option (FV-NI) under IFRS are not met.

(b) Assume that the controller of the company would like to use methods that create "less volatility in net income." Identify which methods create less volatility and explain why this is so.

(c) Discuss whether it is ethical to make a decision as to which method should be used based on the controller's wishes as explained in (b).

ETHICS

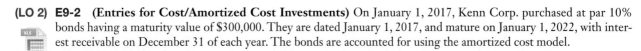

(LO 2) E9-2 (Entries for Cost/Amortized Cost Investments) On January 1, 2017, Kenn Corp. purchased at par 10% bonds having a maturity value of $300,000. They are dated January 1, 2017, and mature on January 1, 2022, with interest receivable on December 31 of each year. The bonds are accounted for using the amortized cost model.

Instructions

(a) Prepare the journal entry to record the bond purchase.

(b) Prepare the journal entry to record the interest received for 2017.

(c) Prepare the journal entry to record the interest received for 2018.

(d) Prepare the journal entry to record the redemption of the bond at maturity.

(LO 2) E9-3 (Entries for Cost/Amortized Cost Investments) On January 1, 2017, Mustafa Limited paid $537,907.40 for 12% bonds with a maturity value of $500,000. The bonds provide the bondholders with a 10% yield. They are dated January 1, 2017, and mature on January 1, 2022, with interest receivable on December 31 of each year. Mustafa accounts for the bonds using the amortized cost approach, applies ASPE using the effective interest method, and has a December 31 year end.

Instructions

(a) Prepare the journal entry to record the bond purchase.

(b) Prepare a bond amortization schedule, rounding to two decimal places.

(c) Prepare the journal entry to record interest received and interest income for 2017.

(d) Prepare the journal entry to record interest received and interest income for 2018.

(e) Prepare the journal entry to record the redemption of the bond at maturity.

(f) If Mustafa used the straight-line method of discount/premium amortization, prepare the journal entry to record interest received and interest income the company would make each year.

(g) Compare the total interest income reported over the five-year period under the effective interest method and the straight-line method. What can you conclude?

DIGGING DEEPER

(h) Why might a reader of the financial statements find the effective interest method more relevant than the straight-line method?

(LO 2) E9-4 (Cost/Amortized Cost Investments) On January 1, 2017, Phantom Corp. acquires $300,000 of Spider Products, Inc. 9% bonds at a price of $278,384. The interest is payable each December 31, and the bonds mature on December 31, 2019. The investment will provide Phantom Corp. with a 12% yield. Phantom Corp. applies IFRS and accounts for this investment using the amortized cost model.

Instructions

(a) Prepare a three-year bond amortization schedule, rounding to the nearest dollar.

(b) Prepare the journal entry to record interest received and interest income on December 31, 2018.

(c) Prepare the journal entries to record interest received and interest income on December 31, 2019, and the maturity of the bond.

(d) Prepare the entry for the disposal of the investment if Phantom had sold the bond on December 31, 2018, for $285,270 instead of holding it to maturity. Assume that 2018 interest received and interest income have already been recorded.

(LO 3) E9-5 (FV-NI Investment in Bonds) Refer to the information in E9-3, except assume that Mustafa hopes to make a gain on the bonds as interest rates are expected to fall. Mustafa accounts for the bonds at fair value with changes in value taken to net income, and separately recognizes and reports interest income. The fair value of the bonds at December 31 of each year end is as follows:

2017	$534,200	2020	$507,000
2018	$515,000	2021	$500,000
2019	$513,000		

Instructions

(a) Prepare the journal entry at the date of the bond purchase.

(b) Prepare the journal entries to record interest income and interest received and recognition of fair value at December 31, 2017, 2018, and 2019.

DIGGING DEEPER

(c) Did market interest rates fall as expected? Explain briefly.

(LO 2, 3) E9-6 (Amortized Cost and FV-NI Investments in Bonds Purchased between Interest Payment Dates) The following information relates to the debt investments of Wildcat Inc. during a recent year:

1. On February 1, the company purchased Gibbons Corp. 10% bonds with a face value of $300,000 at 100 plus accrued interest. Interest is payable on April 1 and October 1.

2. On April 1, semi-annual interest was received on the Gibbons bonds.

3. On June 15, Sampson Inc. 9% bonds were purchased. The $200,000 par-value bonds were purchased at 100 plus accrued interest. Interest dates are June 1 and December 1.

4. On August 31, Gibbons Corp. bonds with a par value of $60,000 purchased on February 1 were sold at 99 plus accrued interest.

5. On October 1, semi-annual interest was received on the remaining Gibbons Corp. bonds.

6. On December 1, semi-annual interest was received on the Sampson Inc. bonds.

7. On December 31, the fair values of the bonds purchased on February 1 and June 15 were 98.5 and 101, respectively.

Assume the investments are accounted for under the recognition and measurement requirements of IFRS 9 *Financial Instruments*.

FINANCE

DIGGING DEEPER

Instructions

(a) Prepare all journal entries that you consider necessary, including December 31 year-end entries, assuming these investments are accounted for at FV-NI and interest income is not reported separately from other related investment gains and losses.

(b) Assume instead that Wildcat manages these investments based on their yield to maturity. Prepare all journal entries that you consider necessary, including December 31 adjusting entries.

(c) Briefly explain what it means to manage an investment on the basis of yield to maturity, and why the recommended accounting method is reasonable in such a situation.

(LO 3) E9-7 (FV-NI Equity Investments) On December 31, 2016, Zurich Corp. provided you with the following pre-adjustment information regarding its portfolio of investments held for short-term profit-taking:

	December 31, 2016	
Investments	Carrying Amount	Fair Value
Moonstar Corp. shares	$20,000	$19,000
Bilby Corp. shares	10,000	9,000
Radius Ltd. shares	20,000	20,600
Total portfolio	$50,000	$48,600

During 2017, the Bilby Corp. shares were sold for $9,500. The fair values of the securities on December 31, 2017, were as follows: Moonstar Corp. shares $19,300 and Radius Ltd. shares $20,500. Dividends and other investment income and losses are all reported in one investment income account.

Instructions

(a) Prepare the adjusting journal entry needed on December 31, 2016.

(b) Prepare the journal entry to record the sale of the Bilby Corp. shares during 2017.

(c) Prepare the adjusting journal entry needed on December 31, 2017.

(LO 3) E9-8 (Investment in Debt Instruments Held for Trading Purposes, Accounted for Using FV-NI) NB Corp. purchased a $100,000 face-value bond of Myers Corp. on August 31, 2016, for $104,490 plus accrued interest. The bond pays interest annually each November 1 at a rate of 9%. On November 1, 2016, NB Corp. received the annual interest. On December 31, 2016, NB's year end, *The Globe and Mail* newspaper indicated a fair value for these bonds of 103.2. NB sold the bond on January 15, 2017, for $102,900 plus accrued interest. Assume NB Corp. follows IFRS and does not report interest income separately from gains and losses on these investments.

FINANCE

Instructions

(a) Prepare the journal entries to record the purchase of the bond, the receipt of interest, any adjustments required at year end, and the subsequent sale of the bond.

(b) How many months was the bond held for by NB Corp. in 2016? Based on this, how much of the income reported on this bond should be for interest received? Verify that your answer fits with the income that is reported.

(c) How would the accounting and reporting change if NB Corp. applied accounting standards for private enterprises? (Explain how interest and net gains or losses would be reported.)

(d) If this bond had been acquired to earn a return on excess funds, did the company meet its objective? If yes, how much return did NB Corp. earn while the bond was held? If not, why not?

(LO 3) E9-9 (FV-NI Equity Investment Entries) Activet Corporation, a Canadian-based international company that follows IFRS 9, has the following securities in its portfolio of investments acquired for trading purposes and accounted for using the FV-NI method on December 31, 2016:

Investments	Carrying Amount (before adjustment)	Fair Value
1,500 shares of David Jones Inc., common	$ 71,500	$ 69,000
5,000 shares of Hearn Corp., common	180,000	175,000
400 shares of Alessandro Inc., preferred	60,000	61,600
	$311,500	$305,600

In 2017, Activet completed the following securities transactions:

Mar. 1 Sold the 1,500 shares of David Jones Inc. common at $45 per share, less fees of $500.
Apr. 1 Bought 700 shares of Oberto Ltd. common at $75 per share, plus fees of $1,300.

Activet Corporation's portfolio of trading securities appeared as follows on December 31, 2017:

Investments	Original Cost	Fair Value
5,000 shares of Hearn Corp., common	$180,000	$175,000
700 shares of Oberto Ltd., common	52,500	50,400
400 shares of Alessandro Inc., preferred	60,000	58,000
	$292,500	$283,400

Instructions

Prepare the Activet Corporation general journal entries for the following, assuming the company does not recognize and report dividends and other components of investment gains and losses separately:

(a) The December 31, 2016 adjusting entry

(b) The sale of the David Jones Inc. shares

(c) The purchase of the Oberto Ltd. shares

(d) The December 31, 2017 adjusting entry

(LO 3, 4) E9-10 (Entries for FV-NI and FV-OCI Equity Investments) The following information is available about Kao Corp.'s investments at December 31, 2017. This is the first year Kao has purchased securities for investment purposes.

Securities	Cost	Fair Value
3,000 shares of Petra Corporation common shares	$40,000	$46,000
1,000 shares of Dugald Inc. preferred shares	25,000	22,000
	$65,000	$68,000

Assume that Kao Corp. follows IFRS and applies IFRS 9.

Instructions

(a) Prepare the adjusting entry(ies), if any, at December 31, 2017, assuming the investments are acquired for trading purposes and accounted for using the FV-NI model with no separate reporting of dividends and other types of FV-NI investment income and losses.

(b) Prepare the adjusting entry(ies), if any, at December 31, 2017, assuming the investments are accounted for using the FV-OCI model.

(c) Discuss how the amounts reported in the financial statements are affected by the choice of accounting method.

(LO 3, 4) E9-11 (Equity Investment Entries—FV-NI and FV-OCI) Arantxa Corporation made the following purchases of investments during 2017, the first year in which Arantxa invested in equity securities:

1. On January 15, purchased 9,000 shares of Nirmala Corp.'s common shares at $33.50 per share plus commission of $1,980.

2. On April 1, purchased 5,000 shares of Oxana Corp.'s common shares at $52.00 per share plus commission of $3,370.

3. On September 10, purchased 7,000 shares of WTA Corp.'s preferred shares at $26.50 per share plus commission of $2,910.

On May 20, 2017, Arantxa sold 3,000 of the Nirmala common shares at a market price of $35 per share less brokerage commissions of $2,850. The year-end fair values per share were as follows: Nirmala $30; Oxana $55; and WTA $28. The chief accountant of Arantxa tells you that Arantxa Corporation holds these investments with the intention of selling them in order to earn short-term profits from appreciation in their prices and accounts for them using the FV-NI model, with no separate reporting of dividends and other types of FV-NI investment income and losses.

Assume that Arantxa Corporation follows IFRS 9.

Instructions

(a) Prepare the journal entries to record the three investments.

(b) Prepare the journal entry(ies) for the sale of the 3,000 Nirmala shares on May 20.

(c) Prepare the adjusting entries needed on December 31, 2017.

(d) Repeat parts (a) to (c), assuming the investments are accounted for using FV-OCI with no recycling. Arantxa's policy is to capitalize transaction costs on the acquisition of FV-OCI investments and reduce the proceeds on disposal.

(LO 4) E9-12 (Debt Investment Entries—Amortized Cost) On January 1, 2016, Hi and Lois Company purchased 12% bonds having a maturity value of $300,000 for $322,744.72. The bonds provide the bondholders with a 10% yield. They are dated January 1, 2016, and mature January 1, 2021, with interest receivable December 31 of each year. Hi and Lois Company uses the effective interest method to allocate unamortized discount or premium. The bonds are classified as amortized cost investments.

Instructions

(a) Prepare the journal entry at the date of the bond purchase.

(b) Prepare a bond amortization schedule.

(c) Prepare the journal entry to record the interest received and the amortization for 2016.

(d) Prepare the journal entry to record the interest received and the amortization for 2017.

(LO 4) E9-13 (Debt Investment Entries—FV-OCI) Assume the same information as in E9-12, except that the bonds are carried at FV-OCI. The fair value of the bonds at December 31 of each year-end is as follows:

2016	$320,500	2017	$309,000

Instructions

(a) Prepare the journal entries to record the interest received and recognition of fair value for 2016.

(b) Prepare the journal entries to record the recognition of fair value for 2017 and assuming the sale of the investment for $307,200 on December 31, 2017.

(LO 4) E9-14 (FV-OCI Investment Entries and Financial Statement Presentation) At December 31, 2017, the equity investments of Wang Inc. that were accounted for using the FV-OCI model without recycling (application of IFRS 9) were as follows:

Investment	Cost and Carrying Amount	Fair Value	Unrealized Gain (Loss)
Ahn Inc.	$175,200	$150,000	$(25,200)
Burnham Corp.	121,500	140,600	19,100
Chi Ltd.	73,000	75,500	2,500
Total	$369,700	$366,100	$ (3,600)

Because of a change in relationship with Ahn Inc., Wang Inc. sold its investment in Ahn for $153,300 on January 20, 2018. No other investments were acquired or sold during 2018; however, a dividend of $1,300 was received from Burnham Corp. in June. At December 31, 2018, the fair values of Burnham and Chi shares were $153,750 and $72,600, respectively.

Instructions

(a) Prepare the entry to adjust the portfolio of investments to fair value at December 31, 2017.

(b) Prepare the presentation of all investment-related accounts on the statement of financial position at December 31, 2017.

(c) Indicate what accounts and amounts would be reported on the statement of comprehensive income for the year ended December 31, 2017, and where each would be reported.

(d) Prepare the journal entries for the 2018 sale of the investment in Ahn Inc. and for the dividend received from Burnham Corp.

(e) Prepare the journal entry required at December 31, 2018, to adjust the investments to fair value.

(LO 4) E9-15   (FV-OCI Investments—Entries) Niger Corp. provided you with the following information about its investment in Fahad Corp. shares purchased in May 2017 and accounted for using the FV-OCI method:

Cost	$39,900
Fair value, December 31, 2017	$41,750
Fair value, December 31, 2018	$32,200
Fair value, December 31, 2019	$36,400

Instructions

(a) Prepare the adjusting journal entries needed on December 31, 2017, 2018, and 2019.

(b) Determine the balance in accumulated other comprehensive income on the statement of financial position on each of December 31, 2017, 2018, and 2019.

(c) Assume that Niger sold its investment in Fahad Corp. on February 13, 2020, for $38,000. Prepare the journal entry(ies) needed on this date, assuming no recycling.

(LO 2, 3, 4, 8, 9) E9-16   (Entry and Financial Statement Comparison of Cost, FV-NI, and FV-OCI Approaches) In early 2017, for the first time, HTSM Corp. invested in the common shares of another Canadian company. It acquired 5,000 shares of Toronto Stock Exchange–traded Bayscape Ltd. at a cost of $68,750. Bayscape is projected to reach a value of $15.50 per share by the end of 2017 and $17.00 by the end of 2018, and has consistently paid an annual dividend of $0.90 per share. HTSM is also a Canadian public corporation with a December 31 year end.

The controller of HTSM is uncertain about which accounting method to use. The company is interested in establishing a closer relationship with Bayscape, but if that fails, HTSM considers the investment a good opportunity to make a gain on its sale in the future. The controller has been advised that the investment could be accounted for at cost or at fair value. If at fair value, a decision would have to be made about whether to put the changes in fair value through net income or other comprehensive income. As one step in making a decision, the controller would like to know what the effect would be on total assets and net income in each of 2017 and 2018 if the predictions about Bayscape's share prices and dividends are correct. Assume there would be no recycling of realized investment gains and losses.

Instructions

(a) Prepare and complete a table with a column for each of the three accounting alternatives indicated and rows for journal entries to recognize each of the following: (1) the 2017 dividend, (2) any December 31, 2017 adjustments, (3) the 2018 dividend, and (4) any December 31, 2018 adjustments.

(b) Based on the table in (a), prepare a summary comparison of each accounting method, indicating the effect of applying each of the three accounting methods on: (1) total assets at December 31, 2017, (2) 2017 net income, (3) total assets at December 31, 2018, and (4) 2018 net income.

(c) Determine the effect on net income for the year ended December 31, 2019, under each of the accounting method options, assuming the investment in Bayscape was sold in early 2019 for $17.00 per share.

(d) Identify the accounting policy choices that would be available to the controller if HTSM applied ASPE instead of IFRS 9, and when each would be appropriate.

(e) Which method, if any, would result in higher income being reported earlier on (assuming IFRS 9)? Would it be considered unethical for HTSM to choose that method?

ETHICS

(LO 5) E9-17   (Impairment of Debt Investment and Subsequent Recovery in Value) Tsui Corporation owns corporate bonds at December 31, 2017, accounted for using the amortized cost model. These bonds have a par value of $800,000 and an amortized cost of $788,000. After an impairment review was triggered, Tsui determined that the discounted impaired cash flows are $737,500 using the current market rate of interest, but are $734,000 using the market rate when the bonds were first acquired. The company follows a policy of directly reducing the carrying amount of any impaired assets. For simplicity purposes, assume that no impairment loss had been recorded earlier.

Instructions

(a) Assuming Tsui Corporation is a private enterprise that applies ASPE, prepare any necessary journal entry(ies) related to (1) the impairment at December 31, 2017, and (2) a December 31, 2018 fair value of $760,000 and an adjusted carrying amount at that date of $741,500.

(b) Assuming that Tsui Corporation applies IFRS 9 and that there has been a significant increase in credit risk, prepare any necessary journal entry(ies) related to (1) the impairment at December 31, 2017, and (2) a December 31, 2018 fair value of $760,000 and an adjusted carrying amount at that date of $741,500. Assume that the discounted cash flow numbers provided reflect the lifetime expected risk of default.

(c) Assume that Tsui is a private enterprise under the situation described in part (a) and that the company uses a valuation allowance instead of directly reducing the carrying amount of the investment. Prepare the entries required in part (a) for (1) the impairment and (2) the subsequent increase in fair value.

(d) In practice, which method would recognize losses earlier—the incurred loss model or the expected loss model? Explain briefly.

(LO 2, 3, 5) **E9-18 (Impairment of FV-NI Investment and Subsequent Recovery in Value)** On January 1, 2015, Mamood Ltd. paid $322,744.44 for 12% bonds of Variation Ltd. with a maturity value of $300,000. The bonds provide the bondholders with a 10% yield. They are dated January 1, 2015, mature on January 1, 2021, and pay interest each December 31. Mamood acquired the bond investment as part of its portfolio of trading securities. It accounts for the bonds at FV-NI and reports interest income separately from other investment gains and losses. At December 31, 2015, Mamood's year end, the bonds had a fair value of $320,700. Mamood applies IFRS 9.

DIGGING DEEPER

During 2016, the economic outlook related to Variation Ltd.'s primary business took a major downturn, so that Variation's debt was downgraded. By the end of 2016, the bonds were priced at 85.5, and at December 31, 2017, they were selling in the market at 87. Conditions reversed in 2018 and the outlook for Variation Ltd. significantly improved, leaving their bonds with a fair value of 99.5 at December 31, 2018.

Instructions

(a) Prepare the entries to record Mamood's purchase of the bonds on January 1, 2015, the recognition of interest income and interest received on December 31, 2015, and the fair value adjustment required at December 31, 2015.

(b) Prepare all entries required for 2016, including recognition of the impairment in value if necessary, and for 2017.

(c) Prepare all entries required for 2018, including recognition of the recovery of the impairment in value, if necessary.

(d) Identify the impairment loss model applied in this situation. If Mamood had accounted for this investment at amortized cost, identify and briefly describe the impairment model the company would have used if Mamood applied (1) IFRS 9, and (2) ASPE.

(LO 2, 3, 4, 5) **E9-19 (Investment in Shares, Impairment, and Subsequent Recovery)** Weekly Corp., a December 31 year-end company that applies IFRS, acquired an investment of 1,000 shares of Credence Corp. in mid-2013 for $29,850. Between significant volatility in the markets and in the business prospects of Credence Corp., the accounting for this investment presented a challenge to Weekly. Toward the end of 2017, Credence discontinued the small annual dividend of $0.50 per share that it had been paying and announced that a major patent responsible for 50% of its income had lost most of its value due to a technological improvement by a competitor.

Situation 1: Credence Corp. is a publicly traded company on the Toronto Stock Exchange, and Weekly has opted to account for its investment at FV-NI. By the end of 2016, the price of Credence shares had fallen to $26.50 per share from $29.00 the previous year, and by the end of 2017 they were trading at $11.10.

Situation 2: Credence Corp. is a private enterprise owned by a group of 20 investors and is a supplier of materials to Weekly. Weekly purchased the shares to cement the relationship between the two companies and has opted to account for its investment at FV-OCI. In late 2016, Weekly was beginning to worry about its investment and determined that its value had probably fallen marginally to an estimated fair value of approximately $26,000 from $27,000 the previous year. In 2017, Weekly was more concerned and, at year end, carried out a thorough analysis of the present value of the likely cash flows to be derived from this investment and estimated an amount of $12,400.

Weekly Corp. adjusts the carrying amount of its investments directly when recognizing an impairment loss, and each type of investment income is accounted for and reported separately.

Instructions

(a) For each situation, identify the impairment model that Weekly should apply, assuming it applies IFRS 9.

(b) Assuming Weekly applies IFRS 9, prepare the appropriate journal entries at December 31, 2016, and December 31, 2017, under each situation presented.

(c) Assuming Weekly is a private company that applies ASPE, prepare the appropriate journal entries at December 31, 2016, and December 31, 2017, under situation 1.

(LO 2, 3, 6) **E9-20 (Accounting Methods with and without Significant Influence under ASPE)** Holmes, Inc. purchased 30% of Nadal Corporation's 30,000 outstanding common shares at a cost of $15 per share on January 3, 2017. The purchase price of $15 per share was based solely on the book value of Nadal's net assets. On September 21, Nadal declared and paid a cash dividend of $39,000. On December 31, Holmes's year end, Nadal reported net income of $85,000 for the year. Nadal shares had a fair value of $14.75 per share at December 31. Holmes, Inc., a private Canadian corporation, applies ASPE.

Instructions

(a) Under the assumption that the 30% holding of Nadal does not give Holmes significant influence over Nadal, identify the possible accounting methods Holmes could use under ASPE to account for its investment. Prepare all required 2017 journal entries under each acceptable method.

(b) Under the assumption that the 30% holding of Nadal gives Holmes significant influence over Nadal, prepare all required 2017 journal entries, assuming Holmes uses the equity method of accounting.

(c) Indicate the other possible accounting methods, if any, that Holmes could have chosen under the assumption in (b).

(d) From the perspective of a financial analyst, why might the equity method be considered a more informative presentation when the investor has significant influence?

(LO 6) E9-21 (Equity Method) Fox Ltd. invested $1 million in Gloven Corp. early in the current year, receiving 25% of its outstanding shares. At the time of the purchase, Gloven Corp. had a carrying amount of $3.2 million. Gloven Corp. pays out 35% of its net income in dividends each year. Assume that Fox Ltd. applies IFRS and that the 25% holding of Gloven shares is sufficient to enable Fox to significantly influence the operating, investing, and financing decisions of Gloven.

Instructions

Use the information in the following T account for the investment in Gloven to answer the following questions:

Investment in Gloven Corp.

1,000,000	
110,000	
	38,500
	14,000

(a) How much was Fox Ltd.'s share of Gloven Corp.'s net income for the year?

(b) How much was Fox Ltd.'s share of Gloven Corp.'s dividends for the year?

(c) How much was Fox Ltd.'s annual depreciation of the excess payment for capital assets?

(d) What was Gloven Corp.'s total net income for the year?

(e) What were Gloven Corp.'s total dividends for the year?

(f) Assuming that depreciable assets had a remaining useful life of 10 years when Fox acquired its investment in Gloven, how much of the payment in excess of carrying amount was assigned to goodwill?

(LO 4, 6, 8) E9-22 (Fair Value-OCI and Equity Method Compared) Harnish Inc. acquired 25% of the outstanding common shares of Gregson Inc. on December 31, 2016. The purchase price was $1,250,000 for 62,500 shares, and is equal to 25% of Gregson's carrying amount. Gregson declared and paid a $0.75 per share cash dividend on June 15 and again on December 15, 2017. Gregson reported net income of $520,000 for 2017. The fair value of Gregson's shares was $21 per share at December 31, 2017. Harnish is a public company and applies IFRS.

Instructions

(a) Prepare the journal entries for Harnish for 2016 and 2017, assuming that Harnish cannot exercise significant influence over Gregson. The investment is accounted for using the FV-OCI model.

(b) Prepare the journal entries for Harnish for 2016 and 2017, assuming that Harnish can exercise significant influence over Gregson.

(c) What amount is reported for the investment in Gregson shares on the December 31, 2017 statement of financial position under each of these methods in (a) and (b), and where is the investment reported on this statement?

(d) What amount is reported on Harnish's statement of comprehensive income in 2017 under each of these methods, and where are the amounts reported?

(LO 3, 5, 6) E9-23 (Long-Term Equity Investments, Equity Method, and Impairment) On January 1, 2017, Rae Corporation purchased 30% of the common shares of Martz Limited for $196,000. Martz Limited shares are not traded in an active market. The carrying amount of Martz's net assets was $520,000 on that date. Any excess of the purchase cost over Rae's share of Martz's carrying amount is attributable to unrecorded intangibles with a 20-year life. During the year, Martz earned net income and comprehensive income of $75,000 and paid dividends of $15,000. The investment in Martz had a fair value of $201,000 at December 31, 2017. During 2018, Martz incurred a net loss and comprehensive loss of $80,000 and paid no dividends. At December 31, 2018, the fair value of the investment was $140,000 and the recoverable amount was $149,000. Assume that Rae follows IFRS.

Instructions

(a) Prepare all relevant journal entries related to Rae's investment in Martz for 2017 and 2018, assuming this is its only investment and Rae cannot exercise significant influence over Martz's policies. Rae accounts for this investment using the FV-NI model and separately records and reports each type of income (loss) separately. Illustrate how the statement of comprehensive income is affected in 2017 and 2018.

(b) Prepare all relevant journal entries related to Rae's investment in Martz for 2017 and 2018, assuming this is its only investment and Rae exercises significant influence over its associates' policies. Illustrate how the statement of comprehensive income is affected in 2017 and 2018. Briefly explain.

(c) How would your answer to part (b) be different if you were told that Martz's 2017 statement of comprehensive income included a loss from discontinued operations of $20,000 (net of tax)?

(LO 4, 6, 8) E9-24 (Proper Income Reporting) The following are two independent situations.

Situation 1: Lauren Inc. received dividends from its common share investments during the year ended December 31, 2017, as follows:

- A cash dividend of $12,250 is received from Peel Corporation. Lauren owns a 1.2% interest in Peel.

- A cash dividend of $68,000 is received from Vonna Corporation. Lauren owns a 30% interest in Vonna and a majority of Lauren's directors are also directors of Vonna Corporation.

- A cash dividend of $172,000 is received from Express Inc., a subsidiary of Lauren.

Situation 2: On April 11, 2017, Chad Corp. purchased as a long-term investment (accounted for using FV-OCI without recycling) 6,000 common shares of Roddy Ltd. for $76 per share, which represents a 2% interest. On December 31, 2017, the shares' market price was $81 per share. On March 3, 2018, Chad sold all 6,000 shares of Roddy for $94 per share.

Assume that all companies follow IFRS.

Instructions

(a) For situation 1, determine how much dividend income Lauren should report on its 2017 consolidated statement of comprehensive income.

(b) For situation 2, determine the amount of the gain or loss on disposal that should be included in Chad's net income in 2018 and in its other comprehensive income. The investment in Roddy Ltd. was Chad Corp.'s only investment.

(LO 5, 6, 8) E9-25 (Equity Method with Cost in Excess of Share of Carrying Amount, Impairment) On January 3, 2017, Mego Limited purchased 3,000 (30%) of the common shares of Sonja Corp. for $438,000. The following information is provided about the identifiable assets and liabilities of Sonja at the date of acquisition:

	Carrying Amount	Fair Value
Assets not subject to depreciation	$ 550,000	$ 550,000
Assets subject to depreciation (10 years remaining)	760,000	880,000
Total identifiable assets	1,310,000	1,430,000
Liabilities	110,000	110,000

During 2017, Sonja reported the following information on its statement of comprehensive income:

Income before discontinued operations	$200,000
Discontinued operations (net of tax)	(50,000)
Net income and comprehensive income	150,000
Dividends declared and paid by Sonja, November 15, 2017	110,000

Assume that the 30% interest is sufficient to make Sonja an associate of Mego, and that Mego is required to apply IFRS for its financial reporting. The fair value of Sonja's shares at December 31, 2017, is $147 per share.

Instructions

(a) Prepare the journal entry to record Mego's purchase of the Sonja shares on January 3, 2017. (*Hint:* Any unexplained payment represents unrecognized goodwill of Sonja.)

(b) Prepare all necessary journal entries associated with Mego's investment in Sonja for 2017. Depreciable assets are depreciated on a straight-line basis.

(c) Would any of your entries in (b) change if you were informed that Mego's long-term business prospects had deteriorated and that the most Mego could expect to recover in the future or to sell its investment in Sonja for at December 31, 2017, is $115 per share? If so, prepare the entry and explain briefly.

ETHICS

(d) A member of senior management has approached you, a CPA, CA, informing you that instead of the shares being worth $115 per share as in (c), the shares are worth $150 each. Senior management receives a bonus based on net income. He mentions that the assumptions about long-term business prospects are too pessimistic and are not reflective of the economic reality at Sonja. You feel pressure to appease management, given that your boss is a member of senior management. What should you do?

(LO 6, 8) E9-26 (ASPE, Significant Influence, Equity Method with Cost in Excess of Carrying Amount, Alternative Methods) In early January 2017, Chi Inc., a private enterprise that applies ASPE, purchased 40% of the common shares of Washi Corp. for $410,000. Chi was now able to exercise considerable influence in decisions made by Washi's management. Washi Corp.'s statement of financial position reported the following information at the date of acquisition:

Assets not subject to being amortized	$205,000
Assets subject to amortization (10 years average life remaining)	620,000
Liabilities	115,000

Additional information:

1. Both the carrying amount and fair value are the same for assets that are not subject to amortization and for liabilities.

2. The fair value of the assets subject to amortization is $750,000.

3. The company amortizes its capital assets on a straight-line basis.

4. Washi reported net income of $163,000 and declared and paid dividends of $112,000 in 2017.

Instructions

(a) Prepare the journal entry to record Chi's investment in Washi Corp. Assume that any unexplained payment is goodwill.

(b) Assuming Chi applies the equity method to account for its investment in Washi, prepare the journal entries to record Chi's equity in the net income and the receipt of dividends from Washi Corp. in 2017.

(c) Assume the same facts as above and in part (b), except that Washi's net income included a loss on discontinued operations of $38,000 (net of tax). Prepare the journal entries necessary to record Chi's equity in the net income of Washi for 2017.

(d) Assume that Chi is a publicly accountable enterprise that applies IFRS and therefore also applies the equity method to account for its associate. In addition to the information in parts (a) and (b), you are told that Washi also reports an unrealized gain of $45,000 on investments accounted for using FV-OCI. If Chi Inc. reports net income of $172,400 and an unrealized gain in OCI of $10,000 on its own financial statements before including the results of its investment in Washi, determine Chi Inc.'s net income, other comprehensive income, and comprehensive income reported on its 2017 statement of comprehensive income. Both Chi and Washi follow a policy of not reclassifying realized gains and losses on FV-OCI equity investments to net income.

Problems

P9-1 MacAskill Corp. has the following portfolio of securities acquired for trading purposes and accounted for using the FV-NI model at September 30, 2017, the end of the company's third quarter:

Investment	Cost	Fair Value
50,000 common shares of Yuen Inc.	$215,000	$200,000
3,500 preferred shares of Monty Ltd.	135,000	140,000
2,000 common shares of Oakwood Inc.	180,000	179,000

On October 8, 2017, the Yuen shares were sold for $4.30 per share. On November 16, 2017, 3,000 common shares of Patriot Corp. were purchased at $44.50 per share. MacAskill pays a 1% commission on purchases and sales of all securities. At the end of the fourth quarter, on December 31, 2017, the fair values of the shares held were as follows: Monty $106,000; Patriot $122,000; and Oakwood $203,000. MacAskill prepares financial statements every quarter. Assume MacAskill follows IFRS 9 and does not recognize dividends and other investment income accounts separately.

Instructions

(a) Prepare the journal entries to record the sale, purchase, and adjusting entries related to the portfolio for the fourth quarter of 2017.

(b) Indicate how and where the investments would be reported on the December 31, 2017 statement of financial position.

(c) Under what conditions might you recommend that the portfolio accounted for at FV-NI be reported somewhere other than where you indicated in part (b)?

P9-2   The following information relates to the 2017 debt and equity investment transactions of Wildcat Ltd., a publicly accountable Canadian corporation. All of the investments were acquired for trading purposes and accounted for using the FV-NI model, with all transaction costs being expensed. No investments were held at December 31, 2016, and the company prepares financial statements only annually, each December 31, following IFRS 9. Dividend and interest income are not recorded or reported separately from other investment income accounts.

1. On February 1, the company purchased Williams Corp. 12% bonds, with a par value of $500,000, at 106.5 plus accrued interest to yield 10%. Interest is payable April 1 and October 1.

2. On April 1, semi-annual interest was received on the Williams bonds.

3. On July 1, 9% bonds of Saint Inc. were purchased. These bonds, with a par value of $200,000, were purchased at 101 plus accrued interest to yield 8.5%. Interest dates are June 1 and December 1.

4. On August 12, 3,000 shares of Scotia Corp. were acquired at a cost of $59 per share. A 1% commission was paid.

5. On September 1, Williams Corp. bonds with a par value of $100,000 were sold at 104 plus accrued interest.

6. On September 28, a dividend of $0.50 per share was received on the Scotia Corp. shares.

7. On October 1, semi-annual interest was received on the remaining Williams Corp. bonds.

8. On December 1, semi-annual interest was received on the Saint Inc. bonds.

9. On December 28, a dividend of $0.52 per share was received on the Scotia Corp. shares.

10. On December 31, the following fair values were determined: Williams Corp. bonds 101.75; Saint Inc. bonds 97; and Scotia Corp. shares $60.50.

Instructions

(a) Prepare all 2017 journal entries necessary to properly account for the investment in the Williams Corp. bonds.

(b) Prepare all 2017 journal entries necessary to properly account for the investment in the Saint Inc. bonds.

(c) Prepare all 2017 journal entries necessary to properly account for the investment in the Scotia Corp. shares.

(d) Assume that there were trading investments on hand at December 31, 2016, accounted for using the FV-NI model, and that they consisted of shares with a cost of $400,000 and a fair value of $390,000. These non–dividend-paying shares were sold early in 2017 and their original cost was recovered exactly. What effect would this transaction have on 2017 net income?

(e) Assume that the interest income on the Saint Inc. bonds that were purchased on July 1, 2017, was separately tracked and reported. Prepare the entries that are required on July 1, December 1, and December 31, 2017, to account for this investment.

P9-3   The following amortization schedule is for Flagg Ltd.'s investment in Spangler Corp.'s $100,000, five-year bonds with a 7% interest rate and a 5% yield, which were purchased on December 31, 2016, for $108,660:

	Cash Received	Interest Income	Bond Premium Amortized	Amortized Cost of Bonds
Dec. 31, 2016				$108,660
Dec. 31, 2017	$7,000	$5,433	$1,567	107,093
Dec. 31, 2018	7,000	5,354	1,646	105,447
Dec. 31, 2019	7,000	5,272	1,728	103,719
Dec. 31, 2020	7,000	5,186	1,814	101,905
Dec. 31, 2021	7,000	5,095	1,905	100,000

The following schedule presents a comparison of the amortized cost and fair value of the bonds at year end:

	Dec. 31, 2017	Dec. 31, 2018	Dec. 31, 2019	Dec. 31, 2020	Dec. 31, 2021
Amortized cost	$107,093	$105,447	$103,719	$101,905	$100,000
Fair value	$106,500	$107,500	$105,650	$103,000	$100,000

Assume that Flagg Ltd. follows IFRS 9 and reports interest income separately from other investment income, except for trading investments accounted for at FV-NI.

Instructions

(a) Prepare the journal entry to record the purchase of these bonds on December 31, 2016, assuming the bonds are accounted for using the amortized cost model.

(b) Prepare the journal entry(ies) related to the bonds accounted for using the amortized cost model for 2017.

(c) Prepare the journal entry(ies) related to the bonds accounted for using the amortized cost model for 2019.

(d) Prepare the journal entry(ies) to record the purchase of these bonds, assuming they are held for trading purposes and accounted for using the FV-NI model.

(e) Prepare the journal entry(ies) related to the trading bonds accounted for using the FV-NI model for 2017.

(f) Prepare the journal entry(ies) related to the trading bonds accounted for using the FV-NI model for 2019.

DIGGING
DEEPER

(g) As a member of Flagg's management, suggest a reason why you might have a different policy related to the reporting of interest income (separately versus combined with other investment income) that depends on the accounting measurement method chosen.

P9-4 Pascale Corp. has the following securities (all purchased in 2017) in its investment portfolio on December 31, 2017: 2,500 Anderson Corp. common shares, which cost $48,750; 10,000 Munter Ltd. common shares, which cost $580,000; and 6,000 King Corp. preferred shares, which cost $255,000. Their fair values at the end of 2017 were as follows: Anderson Corp. $49,580; Munter Ltd. $569,500; and King Corp. $254,400.

In 2018, Pascale completed the following transactions:

1. On January 15, sold 2,500 Anderson common shares at $21 per share less fees of $2,150.

2. On April 17, purchased 1,000 Castle Ltd. common shares at $33.50 per share plus fees of $1,980.

The company adds transaction costs to the cost of acquired investments and deducts them from cash received on the sale of investments. On December 31, 2018, the fair values per share of the securities were as follows: Munter $61; King $40; and Castle $29. Pascale's accounting supervisor tells you that all these securities have fair values that can be readily determined, but the company is not likely to actively trade them. Management accounts for them using the FV-OCI method without recycling. Ignore income taxes.

Instructions

(a) Prepare the entries for the sale of the Anderson Corp. investment on January 15, 2018.

(b) Prepare the entry to record the Castle Ltd. share purchase on April 17, 2018.

FINANCE

(c) Calculate the unrealized gains or losses and prepare any required adjusting entry(ies) for Pascale Corp. on December 31, 2018.

(d) Indicate how all amounts will be reported on Pascale's statement of financial position and statement of comprehensive income, and the changes in the accumulated other comprehensive income portion of the statement of changes in shareholders' equity for 2018.

(e) Pascale Corp.'s shareholders carefully watch the company's reported earnings per share (EPS). If Pascale used an accounting policy of FV-OCI with recycling (as allowed under IAS 39) and the company had 10,000 shares outstanding, would this make the EPS any different than it would be with the policy indicated above (that is, without recycling)? If not, why not? If so, by what amount per share?

P9-5 Castlegar Ltd. had the following investment portfolio at January 1, 2017:

Investment	Quantity	Cost per Share	Fair Value at Dec. 31, 2016
Earl Corp.	1,000	$15.00	$11.50
Josie Corp.	900	20.00	16.50
Asher Corp.	500	9.00	7.20

During 2017, the following transactions took place:

1. On March 1, Josie Corp. paid a $2 per share dividend.

2. On April 30, Castlegar sold 300 shares of Asher Corp. for $10 per share.

3. On May 15, Castlegar purchased 200 more Earl Corp. shares at $16 per share.

4. At December 31, 2017, the shares had the following market prices per share: Earl Corp. $17; Josie Corp. $19; and Asher Corp. $8.

During 2018, the following transactions took place:

5. On February 1, Castlegar sold the remaining Asher Corp. shares for $7 per share.

6. On March 1, Josie Corp. paid a $2 per share dividend.

7. On December 21, Earl Corp. declared a cash dividend of $3 per share to be paid in the next month.

8. At December 31, 2018, the shares had the following market prices per share: Earl Corp. $19 and Josie Corp. $21.

Instructions

(a) Assuming that Castlegar Ltd. is a publicly accountable enterprise that applies IFRS 9 and accounts for its investment portfolio at FV-OCI (with no recycling), prepare journal entries to record all of the 2017 and 2018 transactions and year-end events.

(b) Prepare the relevant parts of Castlegar Ltd.'s 2018 and 2017 comparative statements of financial position, statements of comprehensive income, and statements of changes in shareholders' equity (accumulated other comprehensive income portion), where applicable, to show how the investments and related accounts are reported.

FINANCE

(c) Assume that Castlegar Ltd. is a private enterprise that applies ASPE and accounts for its investment portfolio at cost (that is, the securities do not have actively traded market prices). Determine the amount by which the company's 2017 net income and 2018 net income would differ from the amounts reported under the assumptions in parts (a) and (b). Explain your results.

DIGGING DEEPER

(d) Refer to your answers to parts (b) and (c). From an investor's perspective, what additional relevant information, if any, is provided in the financial statements under part (b) that would not be available in financial statements prepared under the method used in part (c)?

P9-6 On December 31, 2016, Nodd Corp. acquired an investment in GT Ltd. bonds with a nominal interest rate of 10% (received each December 31), and the controller produced the following bond amortization schedule based on an effective rate of approximately 15%. The bonds mature on December 31, 2019. The company prepares financial statements each December 31 following IFRS and has adopted the provisions of IFRS 9. Management is in the process of determining whether to hold these bonds for their future cash flows in order to repay debt that is also maturing at the end of 2019, or whether they will hold them for trading purposes.

	Dec. 31, 2016	Dec. 31, 2017	Dec. 31, 2018	Dec. 31, 2019
Amortized cost of GT Ltd. bonds	$487,214	$505,296	$526,090	$550,000
Fair value at each year end	487,214	499,000	523,000	550,000

Instructions

(Round amounts to the nearest dollar.)

(a) Assume that management determines these bonds will be held until the end of 2019, with the proceeds being used to retire maturing debt. Prepare all journal entries required at December 31, 2016, 2017, 2018, and 2019, including the recognition of interest income and the bonds' ultimate redemption.

(b) Assume that management determines the investment in the bonds is speculative in nature and will be held for trading purposes. Prepare all journal entries required at December 31, 2016, 2017, 2018, and 2019, including the receipt of interest each year and the bonds' ultimate redemption, if Nodd continues to hold the GT Ltd. bonds until maturity. Nodd will not recognize interest separately from other investment income.

P9-7 On January 1, 2017, Novotna Company purchased $400,000 worth of 8% bonds of Aguirre Co. for $369,114. The bonds were purchased to yield 10% interest. Interest is payable semi-annually, on July 1 and January 1. The bonds mature on January 1, 2022. Novotna Company uses the effective interest method to amortize the discount or premium. On January 1, 2019, to meet its liquidity needs, Novotna Company sold the bonds for $370,726, after receiving interest.

Instructions

(a) Prepare the journal entry to record the purchase of bonds on January 1. Assume that the bonds are classified as FV-OCI.

(b) Prepare the amortization schedule for the bonds.

(c) Prepare the journal entries to record the semi-annual interest on July 1, 2017, and December 31, 2017.

(d) Assuming the fair value of Aguirre bonds is $372,726 on December 31, 2018, prepare the necessary adjusting entry. (Assume that the fair value adjustment balance on January 1, 2018, is a debit of $3,375.)

(e) Prepare the journal entry to record the sale of the bonds on January 1, 2019.

P9-8 Presented below is information taken from a bond investment amortization schedule, with related fair values provided. These bonds are classified as FV-OCI.

	12/31/17	12/31/18	12/31/19
Amortized cost	$491,150	$519,442	$550,000
Fair value	$497,000	$509,000	$550,000

Instructions

(a) Were the bonds purchased at a discount or at a premium?

(b) Prepare the adjusting entry to record the bonds at fair value at December 31, 2017. The fair value adjustment account has a debit balance of $1,000 prior to adjustment.

(c) Prepare the adjusting entry to record the bonds at fair value at December 31, 2018.

P9-9 The following information relates to the debt securities investments of Wild Company:

1. On February 1, the company purchases 10% bonds of Gibbons Co. having a par value of $300,000 at 100 plus accrued interest. Interest is payable April 1 and October 1.

2. On April 1, semi-annual interest is received.

3. On July 1, 9% bonds of Sampson, Inc. are purchased. These bonds with a par value of $200,000 are purchased at 100 plus accrued interest. Interest dates are June 1 and December 1.

4. On October 1, semi-annual interest is received.

5. On December 1, semi-annual interest is received.

6. On December 31, the fair values of the bonds purchased on February 1 and July 1 are 95 and 93, respectively.

Instructions

(a) Prepare any journal entries you consider necessary, including year-end entries (December 31), assuming these are FV-OCI securities.

(b) If Wild Company classified these as cost/amortized cost, explain how the journal entries would differ from those in part (a).

P9-10 Octavio Corp. prepares financial statements annually on December 31, its fiscal year end. At December 31, 2017, the company has the account Investments in its general ledger, containing the following debits for investment purchases, and no credits:

Feb. 1, 2017	Chiang Corp. common shares, no par value, 200 shares	$ 37,400
Apr. 1	Government of Canada bonds, 6%, due April 1, 2027, interest payable April 1 and October 1, 100 bonds of $1,000 par value each	100,000
July 1	Monet Corp. 12% bonds, par $50,000, dated March 1, 2017, purchased at 108 plus accrued interest to yield 11%, interest payable annually on March 1, due on March 1, 2037	56,000
Nov. 1	$60,000, six-month non–interest-bearing note that matures on May 1, 2018, bought to yield 10%	57,143

The fair values of the individual securities on December 31, 2017, were:

Chiang Corp. common shares (active stock market price)	$ 33,800
Government of Canada bonds	105,900
Monet Corp. bonds	55,600
Note receivable	58,350

Instructions
(Round amounts to the nearest dollar.)

(a) Prepare the entries necessary to correct any errors in the Investments account, assuming that the Government of Canada bonds were being managed for their yield to maturity, and that the Monet bonds were acquired with the hope of gaining from falling interest rates. The Chiang Corp. shares were acquired with the hope of ensuring the supply of raw materials from this company in the future. Octavio has adopted the recognition and measurement standards of IFRS 9 and tracks interest income only for investments accounted for at cost/amortized cost.

(b) Prepare the entries required to record any accrued interest, amortization of any premium or discount, and recognition of fair values on December 31, 2017.

(c) During 2018, the following transactions took place:

1. The note was sold on February 1, 2018, for $59,600.

2. The Government of Canada bonds were sold on July 1, 2018, for $109,200 plus accrued interest. Prepare entries to record these transactions.

(d) Using the information from parts (a) and (b), assume that the note was not sold on February 1, 2018, but instead was held until it matured. Provide the proper entry to record the disposal of the note at maturity.

(e) Assume that Octavio Corp. is a private entity and applies ASPE. Identify which, if any, of your answers to parts (a) to (d) would change under this assumption. Explain briefly.

(f) Can Octavio management choose which standards to follow, or is it restricted by the type of company it is? Explain.

DIGGING
DEEPER

P9-11 Brooks Corp. is a medium-sized corporation that specializes in quarrying stone for building construction. The company has long dominated the market, and at one time had 70% market penetration. During prosperous years, the company's profits and conservative dividend policy resulted in funds becoming available for outside investment. Over the years, Brooks has had a policy of investing idle cash in equity instruments of other companies. In particular, Brooks has made periodic investments in the company's main supplier, Norton Industries Limited. Although Brooks currently owns 18% of the outstanding common shares of Norton, it does not yet have significant influence over the operations of this investee company. Brooks accounts for its investment in Norton using IFRS 9 and FV-OCI without recycling.

Yasmina Olynyk has recently joined Brooks as assistant controller, and her first assignment is to prepare the 2017 year-end adjusting entries. Olynyk has gathered the following information about Brooks's relevant investment accounts:

1. In 2017, Brooks acquired shares of Delaney Motors Corp. and Isha Electric Ltd. for short-term trading purposes. Brooks purchased 100,000 shares of Delaney Motors for $1.4 million, and the shares currently have a fair value of $1.6 million. Brooks's investment in Isha Electric has not been profitable: the company acquired 50,000 shares of Isha at $20 per share and they currently have a fair value of $720,000.

2. Before 2017, Brooks had invested $22.5 million in Norton Industries and, at December 31, 2016, the investment had a fair value of $21.5 million. While Brooks did not sell or purchase any Norton shares this year, Norton declared and paid a dividend totalling $2.4 million on all of its common shares, and reported 2017 net income of $13.8 million. Brooks's 18% ownership of Norton Industries has a December 31, 2017 fair value of $22,225,000.

Instructions

(a) Prepare the appropriate adjusting entries for Brooks as at December 31, 2017.

(b) For both categories of investments, describe how the results of the valuation adjustments made in (a) would appear in the body of and/or notes to Brooks's 2017 financial statements.

(c) Prepare the dividend and adjusting entries for the Norton investment, assuming that Brooks's 18% interest results in significant influence over Norton's activities.

(d) If Brooks Corp. were a private enterprise and followed ASPE, identify how your answers to parts (a), (b), and (c) would differ.

(e) Could an 18% ownership interest actually result in Brooks having significant influence? Could Brooks have a 45% ownership interest and yet not have significant influence? Explain your answers.

DIGGING
DEEPER

P9-12 Harper Corporation had the following portfolio of investments at December 31, 2017, that qualified and were accounted for using the FV-OCI method:

	Quantity	Percent Interest	Cost per Share	Fair Value per Share
Frank Inc.	2,000 shares	8%	$11	$16
Ellis Corp.	5,000 shares	14%	23	19
Mendota Ltd.	4,000 shares	2%	31	24

Early in 2018, Harper sold all the Frank Inc. shares for $17 per share, less a 1% commission on the sale. On December 31, 2018, Harper's portfolio consists of the following common shares:

	Quantity	Percent Interest	Cost	Fair Value per Share
Ellis Corp.	5,000 shares	14%	$23	$28
Mendota Ltd.	4,000 shares	2%	31	23
Kaptein Inc.	2,000 shares	1%	25	22

Assume that Harper reports net income of $158,300 for its year ended December 31, 2018, and that the company follows a policy of capitalizing transaction costs and of transferring realized gains and losses from accumulated other comprehensive income directly to retained earnings.

Instructions

(a) What should be reported on Harper's December 31, 2017 statement of financial position for this long-term portfolio?

(b) What should be reported on Harper's December 31, 2018 statement of financial position for these investments?

(c) What should be reported on Harper's 2018 statement of comprehensive income for the investments accounted for using the FV-OCI model? Prepare a partial 2018 statement of comprehensive income for Harper.

(d) Assuming that comparative financial statements for 2017 and 2018 are presented in 2018, draft the footnote that is necessary for full disclosure of Harper's transactions and investments.

(e) As a potential investor in Harper Corporation, explain what information the other comprehensive income portion of the statement of comprehensive income provides for you.

DIGGING
DEEPER

P9-13 Fellows Inc., a publicly traded manufacturing company in the technology industry, has a November 30 fiscal year end. The company grew rapidly in its first 10 years and made three public offerings over this period. During its rapid growth period, Fellows acquired common shares in Yukasato Inc. and Admin Importers.

In 2006, Fellows acquired 25% of Yukasato's common shares for $588,000 and accounts for this investment using the equity method. The book value of Yukasato's net assets at the date of purchase was $1.8 million. The excess of the purchase price over the book value of the net assets relates to assets that are subject to amortization. These assets have a remaining life of 20 years. For its fiscal year ended November 30, 2017, Yukasato Inc. reported net income of $250,000 and paid dividends of $100,000.

In 2008, Fellows acquired 10% of Admin Importers' common shares for $204,000 and accounts for this investment using the FV-OCI model.

Fellows also has a policy of investing idle cash in equity securities to generate short-term profits. The following data are for Fellows' trading investment portfolio:

TRADING INVESTMENTS (USING THE FV-NI MODEL)
at November 30, 2016

	Cost	Fair Value
Craxi Electric	$326,000	$314,000
Renoir Inc.	184,000	181,000
Seferis Inc.	95,000	98,500
Total	$605,000	$593,500

INVESTMENTS (USING THE FV-OCI MODEL)
at November 30, 2016

Admin Importers	$204,000	$198,000

TRADING INVESTMENTS (USING THE FV-NI MODEL)
at November 30, 2017

	Cost	Fair Value
Craxi Electric	$326,000	$323,000
Renoir Inc.	184,000	180,000
Mer Limited	105,000	108,000
Total	$615,000	$611,000

INVESTMENTS (USING THE FV-OCI MODEL)
at November 30, 2017

Admin Importers	$204,000	$205,000

On November 14, 2017, Ted Yan was hired by Fellows as assistant controller. His first assignment was to prepare the entries to record the November activity and the November 30, 2017 year-end adjusting entries for the current trading investments and the investment in common shares of Admin Importers. Using Fellows' ledger of investment transactions and the data given above, Yan proposed the following entries and submitted them to Julie O'Brien, controller, for review:

ENTRY 1 (NOVEMBER 8, 2017)

Cash	99,500	
FV-NI Investments		98,500
Investment Income or Loss		1,000
(To record the sale of Seferis Inc. shares for $99,500)		

ENTRY 2 (NOVEMBER 26, 2017)

FV-NI Investments	105,000	
Cash		105,000
(To record the purchase of Mer common shares for $102,200 plus brokerage fees of $2,800)		

ENTRY 3 (NOVEMBER 30, 2017)

Investment Income or Loss	3,000	
Allowance for Investment Impairment		3,000
(To recognize a loss equal to the excess of cost over fair value of equity securities)		

ENTRY 4 (NOVEMBER 30, 2017)

Cash	38,500	
Investment Income or Loss		38,500
(To record the following dividends received from investments:		
Yukasato Inc. $25,000; Admin Importers $9,000; and Craxi		
Electric $4,500)		

ENTRY 5 (NOVEMBER 30, 2017)

Investment in Associate	62,500	
Investment Income or Loss		62,500
(To record share of Yukasato Inc. income under the equity method,		
$250,000 × 0.25)		

Instructions

(a) The journal entries proposed by Ted Yan will establish the value of Fellows' equity investments to be reported on the company's external financial statements. Review each journal entry and indicate whether it is in accordance with the applicable accounting standards, assuming the company has adopted the recognition and measurement standards of IFRS 9 *Financial Instruments*. If an entry is incorrect, prepare the entry(ies) that should have been made.

(b) Because Fellows owns more than 20% of Yukasato Inc., Julie O'Brien has adopted the equity method to account for this investment. Under what circumstances would it be inappropriate to use the equity method to account for a 25% interest in the common shares of Yukasato Inc.? If the equity method is not appropriate in this case, what method would you recommend? Why?

**DIGGING
DEEPER**

(c) Are there any differences between the characteristics of trading investments accounted for using the FV-NI model and investments accounted for using the FV-OCI model in general? Explain. Are there any differences in the specific case of Fellows Inc.'s investments?

P9-14 On January 1, 2017, Melbourne Corporation, a public company, acquired 15,000 of the 50,000 outstanding common shares of Noah Corp. for $25 per share. The statement of financial position of Noah reported the following information at the date of the acquisition:

Assets not subject to depreciation	$290,000
Assets subject to depreciation	860,000
Liabilities	150,000

Additional information:

1. On the acquisition date, the fair value is the same as the carrying amount for the assets that are not subject to depreciation and for the liabilities.

2. On the acquisition date, the fair value of the assets that are subject to depreciation is $960,000. These assets had a remaining useful life of eight years at that time.

3. Noah reported 2017 net income of $100,000 and paid dividends of $5,000 in December 2017.

4. Noah's shares are not actively traded on the stock exchange, but Melbourne has determined that they have a fair value of $24 per share on December 31, 2017.

  Melbourne Corporation accounts for its FV-NI and FV-OCI investments under the provisions of IFRS 9.

Instructions

(a) Prepare the journal entries for Melbourne Corporation for 2017, assuming that Melbourne cannot exercise significant influence over Noah and accounts for the investment at FV-OCI.

(b) Prepare the journal entries for Melbourne Corporation for 2017, assuming that Melbourne can exercise significant influence over Noah's operations.

(c) How would your answers to parts (a) and (b) change if Melbourne had acquired the Noah shares on July 2 instead of January 1?

(d) Prepare the 2017 journal entries if Melbourne Corporation were a private company applying ASPE, clearly identifying the methods of accounting you have chosen.

(e) For your answers to (d), prepare a table of the investment amount reported on the statement of financial position and the amount reported on the income statement under each approach identified. As a shareholder of Melbourne Corporation, which method of accounting do you think provides better information? Explain briefly.

**DIGGING
DEEPER**

P9-15 On December 31, 2016, Acker Ltd. reported the following statement of financial position.

ACKER LTD.
Statement of Financial Position
As at December 31, 2016

Assets		Equity	
FV-OCI investments	$240,000	Contributed capital	$260,000
Cash	50,000	Accumulated other comprehensive income	30,000
Total	$290,000		$290,000

The accumulated other comprehensive income was related only to the company's non-traded equity investments. Some of these were sold in 2017 for cash, resulting in a gain of $30,000. The fair value of Acker Ltd.'s investments at December 31, 2017, was $185,000 and their cost was $140,000. No FV-OCI investments were purchased during 2017. Although Acker is a private company, it applies IFRS and does not recycle OCI gains and losses to net income when realized.

Acker Ltd. received dividend income of $5,000 (cash) during 2017 and realized a gain of $30,000 on the purchase and sale of FV-NI investments.

Instructions

Ignoring income taxes and assuming that all transactions during the year were for cash:

(a) Prepare the journal entry related to the sale of the FV-OCI investments in 2017.

(b) Prepare a statement of comprehensive income for 2017.

(c) Prepare a statement of financial position as at December 31, 2017.

DIGGING DEEPER

(d) Assume that Acker Ltd. applies ASPE and management had identified the equity investment as an FV-NI investment when it was first acquired. Identify and explain any differences in the opening balance sheet at December 31, 2016, the 2017 statement of net income, and the closing balance sheet at December 31, 2017, when the FV-NI method is used instead of the method used under the original IFRS assumption.

P9-16 Minute Corp., a Canadian public corporation, reported the following on its December 31, 2016 statement of financial position:

	$
Investment in Hysenaj Ltd. shares, at FV-NI: 6,400 shares, original cost of $251,540	316,300
Investment in Growthpen Corp. shares, at FV-OCI, without recycling:	
4,000 shares, original cost of $28,800	26,100
Investment in Metal Corp. bonds, at amortized cost:	
$500,000 face value, 6% bonds, due November 1, 2021, interest paid each May 1 and November 1 to yield 5% (See Note 1)	521,227
Interest receivable on Metal Corp. bonds	5,000
Shareholders' equity	
Accumulated other comprehensive income: unrealized loss on Growthpen Corp. shares	2,700

Additional information:

1. The bond amortization table used by Minute Corp. for this bond indicated the following for the November 1, 2016 interest received and interest income:

Date	Interest Received	Interest Income	Premium Amortization	Balance, Bond Carrying Amount
Nov. 1/16	15,000	13,095	1,905	521,878

Hint: On December 31, 2016, Minute's accountant pencilled in the following numbers below the November 1, 2016 line:

Date	Interest Received	Interest Income	Premium Amortization	Balance, Bond Carrying Amount
Dec. 31/16 adjustment	5,000	4,349	651	521,227

2. Minute Corp. follows the provisions of IFRS 9 for its FV-NI and FV-OCI investments, using the FV-NI method for investments acquired for trading purposes, and the FV-OCI method for investments that it intends to hold for their growth potential. For the FV-OCI investments, transaction costs are capitalized, and when gains and losses are realized, they are reclassified to retained earnings. Interest and dividends are not reported separately from other investment income for investments held for trading and accounted for at FV-NI.

The following transactions and events took place during the company's year ended December 31, 2017:

Jan.   2   Sold 1,000 Growthpen shares for $8.50 per share less a $300 commission. (*Hint:* Remember that only 25% of the holdings have been sold.)

Jan.   3   Purchased 3,600 of the 12,000 outstanding shares of Lloyd Corp. for $234,000. Minute Corp. and Lloyd Corp. managements have worked together on joint projects in the past and Lloyd often asks Minute management for advice on operational and financing issues that Lloyd faces. A review of Lloyd's financial statements on the date these shares were acquired indicated total assets of $1.4 million and total liabilities of $750,000. In addition, the company has an internally developed patent that has a fair value of $60,000 but is unrecorded in the accounts. The patent is likely to have value to Lloyd for another six years.

Mar. 18   Received a $1 per share dividend on Growthpen shares and a $3 per share dividend on Hysenaj shares.

May   1   Received the semi-annual interest on the Metal Corp. bonds.

June 30   Sold the Metal Corp. bonds for 102 plus accrued interest. (*Hint:* Start by making an entry to accrue the interest income on the bonds to June 30, then make an entry to record the cash received.)

Sept. 17   Sold all the shares of Hysenaj for $58 per share. Paid a 1% commission.

Oct. 15   Received a dividend of $1 per share on the Lloyd Corp. shares.

Dec. 31   Lloyd Corp. management reported that the company earned a net income of $48,000 for its year ended December 31, 2017.

Dec. 31   The fair values of the remaining investments are: Growthpen Corp. $7 per share; Lloyd Corp. $217,800.

Instructions

(a) Showing all calculations, prepare all required entries during 2017 and at December 31, 2017, if necessary, for the transactions and adjustments relating to the investments in the Hysenaj Ltd. shares, the Growthpen Corp. shares, the Metal Corp. bonds, and the Lloyd Corp. shares.

(b) Determine the December 31, 2017 balances in each asset account related to the investments and in accumulated other comprehensive income. Prepare a partial statement of financial position, indicating where and how each of the investments and AOCI would be reported.

FINANCE

(c) Determine the December 31, 2017 balances in each income and OCI account related to the investments. Assuming that Minute Corp. reports a net income of $1,422,600, including all revenue, expense, gain, and loss accounts that are correctly included in net income, prepare a statement of comprehensive income for Minute's year ended December 31, 2017.

(d) After Minute Corp.'s December 31, 2017 financial statements were released, the members of an investment club met to look at Minute as a possible investment. The club members were not familiar with the term "accumulated other comprehensive income" that they saw on the statement of financial position. Explain what the balance in this account represents, using terms the club members would understand.

DIGGING DEEPER

ENABLING COMPETENCIES

Cases

Refer to the Case Primer on the student website and in *WileyPLUS* to help you answer these cases.

CA9-1 Investment Company Limited (ICL) is a private company owned by 10 doctors. The company's objective is to manage the doctors' investment portfolios. It actually began as an investment club 10 years ago. At that time, each doctor invested equal amounts of cash and the group met every other week to determine where the money should be invested. Eventually, they decided to incorporate the company and each doctor now owns one-tenth of the voting shares. The company employs two managers who look after the business full-time and make the investment decisions with input from the owners. Earnings per year after taxes now average $1.5 million. During the year, the following transactions took place:

Investment A (IA): Purchased common shares of IA for $1 million. IA allows researchers to use expensive lab equipment (which is owned by the company) on a pay-per-use basis. These shares represent 15% of the total outstanding common shares of IA. Because of its percentage ownership, ICL is allowed to appoint one member of IA's board of directors. There are three directors on the board. One of the ICL owners has also been hired as a consultant to IA to advise on equipment acquisitions. The company is unsure of how long it will keep the shares. At least two of the ICL owners are interested in holding on to the investments for the longer term, as they use the services of IA. The fair value of the shares of IA is determined annually by a valuations expert.

Investment B (IB): Purchased preferred shares of IB representing 25% of the total outstanding shares. The shares will likely be resold within two months, although no decision has yet been made. The fair value of this investment is known.

Investment C (IC): Purchased 25% interest in voting common shares of IC for $1 million two years ago. The current carrying amount is $950,000, since the company has been in the drug development stage. IC develops drug delivery technology. In the past week, a major drug on which the company has spent large amounts (approximately $10 million) for research and development was declined by the Food and Drug Administration for sale in the United States. Most of the $10 million had previously been capitalized in the financial statements of IC. This is a significant blow to IC, as it had been projecting that 50% of its future revenues would come from this drug. IC does not produce financial statements until two months after ICL's year end.

Although the investments have been mainly in private companies so far, the doctors are thinking of revising their investment strategy and investing in more public companies. They feel that the stock market is poised for recovery, and are therefore planning to borrow some funds for investment. The accountant is currently reviewing the above transactions in preparation for a meeting with the bank. The company has never prepared GAAP statements before but is considering doing so. The company has not made a decision as to which GAAP to follow (IFRS or ASPE). If they adopt IFRS, they are planning to use IFRS 9.

Instructions

Adopt the role of the company's accountant and analyze the financial reporting issues.

FINANCE

CA9-2 Cando Communications (CC) is a public company that owns and operates 10 broadcast television stations and several specialty cable channels, 10 newspapers (including the *International Post*), and many other non-daily publications. It has a 57.6% economic interest in Australia TV (in Australia), and a 29.9% interest in Ulster TV (in Northern Ireland).

According to the notes to the annual financial statements, the company owns approximately 15% of the shares and all of the convertible and subordinated debentures of Australia TV. The convertible debentures are convertible into shares that would represent 50% of the company's total issued shares at the time of conversion. In total, including the debentures, the investment in Australia TV yields a distribution that is equivalent to 57.5% of all distributions paid by Australia TV. CC has a contractual right to be represented on the board of directors and has appointed three of the board's 12 members.

Although the company has made an attempt to influence the decisions made by Ulster TV management, it has been unsuccessful and does not have any representation on the board of directors.

Investments represent approximately $150 million (about 5% of total assets). Even though revenues were up by 15%, net income was only $8 million for the year end, down from $50 million the prior year. Assume that the company will adopt IFRS 9.

Instructions

Adopt the role of a financial analyst and analyze the financial reporting issues.

CA9-3 Impaired Investments Limited (IIL) is in the real estate industry. Last year, the company divested itself of some major investments in real estate and invested the funds in several instruments, as follows:

1. Investments in 5% bonds: currently carried at amortized cost

2. Investments in common shares (no significant influence or control and not held for trading)—Company A: currently carried at fair value, with gains and losses booked to income

3. Investments in common shares—Company B: currently carried at fair value, with gains and losses booked to other comprehensive income

During the current year, similar bonds available in the marketplace are yielding 6%. Although the company is not certain why this is the case, the controller feels it may be due to greater perceived risk associated with changes in the economy and specifically the real estate industry. The investment in Company A shares is significantly below cost at year end, according to current market prices (Company A's shares trade on a stock exchange). The investment in Company B shares is also below cost, but the controller feels that this is just a temporary decline and not necessarily an impairment. The shares of Company B also trade on a stock exchange.

IIL is currently a private entity but has recently considered going public, perhaps in the next five years, and plans to adopt IFRS this year. It will also adopt IFRS 9.

Instructions

Adopt the role of the controller and discuss the financial reporting issues related to the IIL financial statements.

Integrated Case

**ENABLING
COMPETENCIES**

FINANCE

IC9-1   EMI Inc. is a public company that operates numerous movie theatres in Canada. Historically, it operated as a trust and its business model consisted of distributing all of its earnings to shareholders through dividends. As a result of tax changes two years ago, it converted to a corporation and adopted a strategy of using its excess cash to invest in short-term and strategic investments. Some of EMI's investment transactions for 2017 are identified below.

In the last quarter of 2016, EMI purchased 40% of the outstanding voting shares of ABC. ABC is a movie distributor and has a contract with EMI whereby it pays management fees to EMI to have two of EMI's executives on its strategic committee. Also, as part of the investment, one member of EMI's board of directors is eligible to serve as a member of ABC's board of 12 executive members. Just before year end, EMI signed as a guarantor for ABC's newly issued debt, which it will use to build new movie theatres. EMI agreed to the arrangement, provided it could use ABC's existing movie theatres as future collateral. ABC is also a public company and, of the remaining 60% of outstanding shares, no individual shareholder holds more than 1%. EMI is unsure of how to treat this strategic investment.

At the beginning of the year, EMI invested some of its excess money in corporate bonds with a face value of $100,000, for $94,758. The bonds pay a 6% semi-annual interest rate and provide an effective interest rate of 8% over three years. The bonds mature on January 1, 2020. Management has purchased similar corporate bonds in the past for short-term profits and continues to do so with its existing bonds. However, at the annual board meeting, management had stated its intention to hold these particular corporate bonds as an investment for earning income. EMI has the ability to hold the investment to maturity. EMI is unsure of how to record the investment upon inception and the initial subsequent semi-annual interest payment.

EMI also invested funds into two stock portfolios, A and B. Management's intention for the investment is unclear; however, in the past, similar stock portfolios were purchased with the intention of holding only to generate a short-term gain. Portfolio A consists of a 5% ownership of shares in a publicly traded company, Masrani Corp., for a total investment of $25,000. Portfolio B consists of a 3% ownership in another private movie theatre, for a total investment of $15,000. Transaction costs for both portfolios were 2% of the purchase price. At year end, the fair value of portfolio A had dropped to $19,222. EMI is unsure of the method of measurement for each portfolio investment.

As EMI's shares are trading on the capital market, its financial information and filings are tracked by an equity analyst who produces quarterly analyst reports. These reports are used by shareholders and future investors as an independent review of EMI's results. It is now year end and management is preparing for a meeting with its equity analyst to review its accounting policies. The board of directors is expected to approve the financial statements after the meeting with the analyst.

An excerpt from EMI's 2017 financial statements is shown below.

Consolidated Balance Sheet
As at December 31, 2017
Assets
Current Assets

Cash and cash equivalents (Note 1)	$1,890,877
Accounts receivable	567,321
Inventory	36,455
Securities	
Bonds—FV-NI	
and held to maturity (Note 2)	756,210
Portfolio investments (FV-NI and cost)	
(Note 3)	899,321
Total Current Assets	4,150,184
Fixed assets	
Property, plant, and equipment	12,321,888
Accumulated depreciation	(3,490,211)
Net fixed assets	8,831,677
Long-term investments	21,999
Deferred tax assets	563,422
Total Assets	**$13,567,282**

Instructions

Assume the role of EMI's equity analyst and complete an analysis of EMI's required application of accounting policies for investments. Discuss any choices and differences between IFRS and ASPE for information purposes only, but assume that EMI has adopted IFRS 9.

RESEARCH AND ANALYSIS

REAL WORLD EMPHASIS

RA9-1 Brookfield Asset Management Inc.

Refer to the annual financial statements of **Brookfield Asset Management Inc.** for its fiscal year ended December 31, 2014, found at the end of the book.

Instructions

(a) Review Brookfield Asset Management Inc.'s balance sheet. Identify all financial investments that are reported, along with their carrying amounts and the method of accounting for each. You may need to read the notes to the financial statements to get the necessary details. Do you think these financial asset investments are significant to an assessment of the company? Comment.

(b) Does Brookfield Asset Management Inc. have any investments in subsidiary companies? Does it own 100% of all its subsidiaries? Can you tell this by looking at the balance sheet? At the income statement? What information is disclosed about these subsidiaries?

(c) Did Brookfield Asset Management acquire any companies during the year? If so, what type of information is provided about these acquisitions? Comment briefly on how such transactions might affect any analysis of the parent company for the year.

REAL WORLD EMPHASIS

RA9-2 Royal Bank of Canada

Refer to the 2014 financial statements and accompanying notes of **Royal Bank of Canada** (RBC) that are found on the company's website (www.royalbank.ca) or at www.sedar.com.

Instructions

(a) What percentage of RBC's total assets is held in investments (at October 31, 2014 and 2013)? Note that RBC also holds a significant loan portfolio. What is the business reason for holding loans versus securities? Comment on how the investments are classified and presented on the balance sheet.

(b) What percentage of total interest income comes from securities (2014 and 2013)? Are there any other lines on the income statement or in other comprehensive income (OCI) relating to the securities? What percentage of net income (include any relevant OCI items) relates to securities (2014 versus 2013)? Calculate an approximate return on the investments in securities. Comment on the return, while looking at the nature of the securities that are being invested in.

(c) Read the notes to the financial statements that relate to the securities. Indicate and briefly explain the valuation method(s) applied.

RA9-3 Research Issue—Structured or Variable Interest Entities

Structured entities or variable interest entities (VIEs) have long been on the agendas of the financial accounting standard-setting communities. Recently, however, standards have been updated to deal with the issues presented by such entities.

Instructions

Write a one- to two-page report on structured entities or VIEs. Your report should indicate what the major accounting issue was that needed resolution, how the IASB has dealt with it, and what the FASB and ASPE positions are on similar situations. Also, identify at least one company that has a structured entity and discuss how the investment is reported.

RA9-4 Potash Corporation of Saskatchewan

REAL WORLD EMPHASIS

Instructions

Gain access to the 2014 financial statements of **Potash Corporation of Saskatchewan** from the company's website (www.potashcorp.com) or www.sedar.com. The company, also known as PotashCorp, indicates prior to Note 1 to the financial statements that it has made changes to the structure and content of its financial statements since its 2013 Annual Integrated Report.

(a) What reason is given for the changes made in the structure and content of PotashCorp's financial statements? What are the major changes that have been made? Review several of the notes to the financial statements. What common features are presented in each note? What is your opinion of the changes?

(b) Note 2 provides information on the principles of consolidation that PotashCorp applies. What does the company mean by "control"? Does any judgement have to be applied in determining whether control over another entity exists? Explain briefly.

(c) Does PotashCorp apply IAS 39 or IFRS 9 in accounting and reporting its financial asset investment assets?

(d) Refer to Note 14 Investments. Identify, by name, the investee companies of PotashCorp. For each, identify the classification of investment, the percentage of voting rights held by PotashCorp, the method of accounting for the investee, its carrying amount, and its fair value.

(e) What additional information is provided in Note 14 about the investments accounted for using the equity method? Explain in general terms only why the income reported on the Statement of Income from associates and joint ventures differs from the $172 million of dividends received from them as reported in this note.

(f) Explain the impairment assessment policy for PotashCorp's available-for-sale investments discussed in Note 14. Include information about the event that triggered the impairment assessment in 2014.

RA9-5   Impairment Models

Write a short essay (one or two pages) describing the incurred loss model and the expected loss model of impairment. Summarize each model and compare the two models, indicating the potential benefits and drawbacks of each. Which model do you think provides the more transparent information for users?

RA9-6   Specific Disclosure Requirements

Discuss the three objectives of disclosure of financial instruments under ASPE and IFRS. In your discussion, explain how specific disclosure requirements meet these objectives.

ENDNOTES

[1] IAS 39 introduces the labels "held to maturity," "available for sale," and "held for trading." These are defined terms for investments under the standard. Although the standard notes that the labels do not need to be used, many companies do indeed use these labels. We will define these labels later in the chapter. Note that IFRS 9 does not use these labels.

[2] Brokerage commissions are usually incurred when buying and selling most securities. Commissions vary with the share value and the number of shares/units purchased, but they are often between 1% and 3% of the trade value for smaller trades. For larger trades, the commissions are often substantially lower as a percentage. Discount brokerages offer significant discounts even on smaller trades. Transactions involving mutual funds may have no commission attached to them (no-load funds) but a commission may be charged when the funds are redeemed (back-end commission).

[3] Companies also have a choice of when to recognize (and derecognize) the financial asset. This could be on the trade date, when the commitment is made to buy or sell, or on the settlement date, when the asset is delivered and title is transferred—usually a short time thereafter. When the period between these dates is the standard term for the instrument and the market—termed a **regular-way purchase or sale**—either trade-date or settlement-date accounting may be used. Canadian equities settle in three business days. The same policy is applied consistently to all purchases and sales that belong to the same category of financial asset and the policy that is chosen is disclosed. This chapter's illustrations assume that trade and settlement dates are the same.

[4] It is interesting to note how accounting for investments at fair value may have influenced the revenue and proposed lease standards. Accounting for financial instruments such as investments and derivatives reflects a contract-based approach, which is the approach adopted for revenues and currently under discussion for leases. In addition, the accounting standards for financial instruments have helped move our thinking forward regarding embracing fair value as opposed to historical cost for measurement purposes.

[5] If the instrument's "cost" and face value are the same, the method is applied in the same way as for an investment in shares except that interest income is recognized instead of dividend income.

[6] As previously indicated, the value is determined by the investment community and is equal to the present value (PV) of the cash inflows of principal and interest payments on the bond, discounted at the market rate. This is relatively straightforward if the bond is bought or sold on its issue date or on an interest payment due date. At other times, a bond's purchase price can be estimated as follows:

PV of cash flows on the immediately preceding
   interest payment date   = $x
Add the increase in PV to date of sale or purchase at yield rate:
   $x × annual yield rate × portion of year since
      interest payment date   = y
Deduct the cash interest earned since last interest payment date:
   Face value × annual stated rate × portion of year since
      last interest date   = (z)
Purchase price of a bond bought or sold between
   interest payment dates: x + y − z

[7] IFRS 7 *Financial Instruments: Disclosures* indicates in paragraph B5(e) that entities may disclose whether the net gains or losses on financial assets measured at fair value through profit or loss (FV-NI) and reported on the income statement include interest and dividend income. ASPE, on the other hand, requires separate reporting (*CPA Canada Handbook*, Part II, Section 3856.52).

[8] Certainly management's ability to earn a return and realize gains on the investments is relevant. In addition, the entity has to keep track in its files of the securities' original cost because only realized gains and losses are taxable or deductible for tax purposes.

[9] ASPE does not make use of OCI.

[10] Intraperiod tax allocation requires that the unrealized holding gains and losses be recognized in other comprehensive income, net of tax. This is explained more fully in Chapter 18. The illustrations that follow do not include the related taxes to simplify the examples.

[11] Under IAS 39, changes in fair value that represent an impairment loss were transferred out of OCI and into net income (recycled).

[12] Per IFRS 9.5.6.5 and 5.6.7, if an entity reclassifies an FV-OCI debt investment to amortized cost, it is transferred at fair value and any unrealized gain or loss recorded in OCI is removed from OCI and adjusted against the investment account. This means that the investment ends up being measured at the same amount that it would otherwise have been measured at if the investment had always been classified as an amortized cost investment. If the entity reclassifies an FV-OCI investment to FV-NI, any unrealized gain or loss recorded in OCI is reclassified to net income.

[13] ASPE 3856.17.

[14] ASPE 3856.A15.

[15] IFRS 9.B5.5.44.

[16] IFRS 9.5.5.11.

[17] IFRS 9 does not define the word "default." Instead, the standard allows companies to apply their own definition. The standard does note, however, that financial assets that are 90 days past due are in default unless the company can make a case to argue otherwise.

[18] Both definitions for 12-month and lifetime expected credit losses are defined in IFRS 9 – Appendix A.

[19] These calculations are fairly complex and generally beyond the scope of this text.

[20] IFRS 9.5.5.15.

[21] IFRS 9.5.5.17.

[22] IFRS 9.B5.5.33.

[23] IFRS 9 IE 8 (footnote 68).

[24] Based on IFRS 9 IE – Example 13.

[25] Joint ventures are another type of equity investment. Since they can be incorporated companies, they can issue shares. Joint ventures are characterized by joint control (versus unilateral control). This is usually shown through a contractual agreement that states that the venturers (investors) must share key decision-making.

[26] IAS 28 *Investments in Associates*, para. 3. Copyright © International Financial Reporting Standards Foundation. All rights reserved. Reproduced by John Wiley & Sons Canada, Ltd. with the permission of the International Financial Reporting Standards Foundation®. Reproduction and use rights are strictly limited. No permission granted to third parties to reproduce or distribute.

[27] *CPA Canada Handbook*, Part II, Section 3051.04.

[28] IAS 28 identifies some exceptions. These include investments in associates that are held for sale and those reported by a parent that is not required to prepare consolidated financial statements.

[29] A third aspect involves eliminating the effects of unrealized inter-company gains and losses. This issue and situations where investors pay less for the shares than their proportionate interest in the identifiable net assets of the associate (that is, "negative goodwill") are topics for an advanced accounting course.

[30] The types of risk that are associated with financial assets in general—credit, liquidity, and market risk—are discussed more fully in Chapter 16.

Cumulative Coverage and Task-Based Simulation: Chapters 6 to 9

Templates to complete this task-based simulation are available in WileyPLUS and on the instructor website.

Posh Hotels Ltd. (PHL) is a small boutique hotel that provides 38 suites that can be rented by the day, week, or month. Food service is available through room service as well. In addition, there are two suites that have been rented on a long-term basis to corporate tenants, who have access to their suite anytime throughout the year without making a reservation. The company has a December 31 year end, and you are preparing the year-end financial statements using ASPE.

The following issues require your consideration:

1. Cash
   - The hotel keeps a significant amount of euro currency on hand to meet the needs of its guests. At year end, there was €12,000 on hand. The year-end exchange rate was $1.35, and the average rate for the year was $1.42.
   - The bank statement balance at December 31 was $158,293. There were outstanding cheques of $52,375 and an outstanding deposit of $15,487. Bank charges per the bank statement were $65 for the month of December and have been recorded.

2. Accounts receivable and allowance for doubtful accounts
   - The hotel charges $150 per night for accommodation in one of the rental suites, and guests pay at the end of their stay, with daily revenue being accrued as it is earned. At December 31, the amount outstanding from short-term guests was $10,500. At year end, management expects to be unable to collect an amount equal to 5% of the outstanding receivables for this type of suite. During the year, sales amounted to $1,750,000, and the balance in Allowance for Doubtful Accounts at the end of the previous year was $15,000. During the year, $32,000 in accounts was written off.
   - The two corporate suites are rented for $45,000 per year. The payment for these longer-term rentals is due in advance each July 1 for the following 12 months. One of these corporate suites has been in use for part of the year, but the corporate tenant went bankrupt and was unable to pay the $45,000 fee. Hotel management had hoped the tenant would eventually be able to pay, and it allowed the company to use the suite until the end of October. Since then, the hotel has been in negotiations with the bankruptcy accountant and expects to eventually receive a settlement of $10,000. The balance will become uncollectible; no allowance for doubtful accounts has been recorded with respect to these suites as there have never been collection problems in the past.

3. Inventory
   - PHL follows a policy of FIFO costing, and values items at the lower of cost and market based on an individual item basis.

- The hotel has a standing weekly order at set prices with a local catering firm. If the food is not eaten before the next delivery is received, it is donated to the local women's shelter. This ensures that all meals are of appropriate quality for the hotel guests.

- On December 31, the following items were delivered:

Item	Unit Cost	Net Realizable Value
40 chicken dinners	$5	$12
35 beef dinners	$6	$15
75 frozen vegetable servings	$1	$2
75 units of fresh fruit	$1	$2
100 desserts	$3	$5

- The invoice for the food delivery on December 31 included an additional delivery charge of $0.10 per item, totalling $32.50.

- On December 31, an ice storm resulted in a loss of electricity to the hotel building. As a result, 20 chicken and 10 beef dinners thawed and were unusable.

- The hotel also maintains an inventory of white terry cloth bathrobes and towels that are available for sale to its clients. At December 31, the following information is available:

Product	Quantity	Cost/Unit	Selling Price/Unit
Bathrobes, assorted sizes	40	$49.50	$85.00
Towels, extra-large	25	$19.30	$18.00*
Towels, large	20	$15.00	$28.00

*The extra-large towels are no longer popular and management has decided to discontinue them. It offers the hotel staff a 20% commission for all extra-large towels they sell at the sale price of $18.00.

4. Investments

- On December 1, PHL purchased a $100,000, 90-day Canadian government treasury bill for $98,039 to yield 8%.

- During the year, PHL purchased 30% of the shares in Western Hotel Company, a company that owns a similar hotel property in a nearby city, for $5 million, a price corresponding to 30% of its book value. Subsequently, Western Hotel Company paid a dividend totalling $100,000 and earned income of $250,000. The fair value of the common shares as at December 31 was $5,100,000.

- PHL also purchased common shares of Dufort Corp. as a temporary investment for $48,000. At the end of the year, these shares had a fair value of $47,000, according to the December 31 closing price on the Toronto Stock Exchange. A dividend of $500 was received during the year.

Instructions

Part A: Cash and investments presentation

Determine whether each financial instrument should be presented in the cash and cash equivalents or investments section of the statement of financial position. Place an X in the appropriate column in the table below.

Financial Instrument	Cash and Cash Equivalents	Investments
Euro currency		
Bank account		
90-day Canadian government treasury bill		
Western Hotel Company common shares		
Dufort Corp. common shares		

Part B: Bank reconciliation

Prepare a bank reconciliation for PHL as at December 31 to determine the adjusted cash balance per the general ledger. Enter the description and amount of any adjustment in the table below.

	(Description)	($)
Cash per bank account:		
Add:		
Deduct:		
Adjusted cash per general ledger:		

Part C: Investment income

Calculate the carrying value as at December 31 and investment income for the year ended December 31 for each of the financial instruments listed below. Enter the total investment income in the appropriate space in the table below.

Financial instrument	Carrying Value ($)	Investment Income ($)
90-day Canadian government treasury bill Using: amortized cost		
Western Hotel Company common shares Using: equity method		
Western Hotel Company common shares Using: FV-OCI		
Dufort Corp. common shares Using: FV-NI		

Part D: Inventory carrying values

Calculate the carrying value of each inventory item as at December 31. Identify any inventory that requires a writedown. Enter the carrying value in the appropriate space in the table below. Place an X in the space for any inventory that requires a writedown.

	Carrying Value ($)	Writedown Required
Food:		
Chicken dinners		
Beef dinners		
Vegetable servings		
Fruit servings		
Desserts		
Bathrobes and towels:		
Bathrobes		
Towels, extra-large		
Towels, large		

Part E: Accounts receivable

Calculate the accounts receivable, allowance for doubtful accounts, and bad debt balances as at December 31. Enter the dollar amount for each item in the appropriate space in the table below.

	Amount as at December 31
Accounts receivable	
Allowance for doubtful accounts	
Bad debt expense	

PROPERTY, PLANT, AND EQUIPMENT: ACCOUNTING MODEL BASICS

REFERENCE TO THE CPA COMPETENCY MAP	LEARNING OBJECTIVES
	After studying this chapter, you should be able to:
1.1.1, 1.1.5, 1.2.1, 1.2.2, 1.2.3, 2.3.3	**1.** Identify the business importance and characteristics of property, plant, and equipment and explain the recognition criteria.
1.2.1, 1.2.2, 1.2.3	**2.** Identify the costs to include in the measurement of property, plant, and equipment at acquisition.
1.2.1, 1.2.2, 1.2.3	**3.** Determine asset cost when the transaction has delayed payment terms or is a lump-sum purchase, a nonmonetary exchange, or a contributed asset.
1.2.1, 1.2.2, 1.2.3	**4.** Identify the costs included in specific types of property, plant, and equipment.
1.1.2, 1.2.1, 1.2.2, 1.2.3, 1.2.4	**5.** Understand and apply the cost model, and the revaluation model using the asset adjustment method.
1.1.2, 1.2.1, 1.2.3, 1.2.4	**6.** Understand and apply the fair value model.
1.1.2, 1.2.1, 1.2.2, 1.3.2	**7.** Explain and apply the accounting treatment for costs incurred after acquisition.
1.1.4	**8.** Identify differences in accounting between IFRS and ASPE, and what changes are expected in the near future.

After studying Appendix 10A, you should be able to:

1.1.1, 1.1.2, 1.2.1, 1.2.3	**9.** Calculate the amount of borrowing costs to capitalize for qualifying assets.

After studying Appendix 10B, you should be able to:

1.1.2, 1.2.1, 1.2.3, 1.2.4	**10.** Understand and apply the revaluation model using the proportionate method.

MOVING TO FAIR VALUE

TORONTO, ON. — Toronto-based Brookfield Asset Management Inc. is a global alternative asset manager with over $200 billion in assets under management. The company has over a 100-year history of owning and operating assets with a focus on property, renewable power, infrastructure, and private equity in Canada and around the world.

With so much property, plant, and equipment (PP&E) under management, asset valuations are a critical component of Brookfield's business model. The company has always internally measured the fair value of its PP&E, so management would know how much Brookfield's assets were actually worth. But it reported these balances under its previous accounting framework, Canadian GAAP, using the historical cost method, which depreciated PP&E based on their actual cost, over a number of years. For example, "we have owned some of our power plants for over 50 years. Under Canadian GAAP, we had fully depreciated some of these assets and the amount of financing placed on the assets has increased to reflect their current value, resulting in a negative net asset value," said Derek Gorgi, Brookfield's Senior Vice President Finance.

Courtesy Brookfield Asset Management Inc.

IFRS, however, allows public companies to utilize the fair value method for PP&E. Partly because of this, Brookfield adopted IFRS in 2010, one year earlier than required. "We elected to use the fair value method because, in our perspective, it provides shareholders better information about the value of our assets," Mr. Gorgi said.

The move to IFRS and fair value for reporting for the company's PP&E had a material impact on Brookfield's financial statements. For example, when it accounted for its power assets at fair value, "we recognized approximately a $5-billion fair value adjustment to record these assets at their current values from increases in the value of the assets since acquisition and the fact that we had depreciated them," he said. All told, the move to fair value under IFRS from Canadian GAAP doubled the common equity reported on Brookfield's consolidated balance sheet the first year to $11.3 billion. Common equity has continued to increase since then to a total of $20.2 billion as at December 31, 2014.

While the company feels the move to IFRS was overall very positive, the international standards do present some challenges. For example, Brookfield's different asset classes are treated differently for valuation and recognition purposes. Its commercial (office and retail) properties are considered investment properties, and its timber assets are considered biological assets. Both of these asset classes are fair valued through net income; they are not depreciated. On the other hand, its power plants and infrastructure are considered to be PP&E. These assets are recorded at fair value (because the company elects to do so) annually via other comprehensive income but depreciated quarterly through net income. Furthermore, other asset classes are carried at historical cost. "Net income only includes certain of our asset revaluations, while others are recorded through other comprehensive income or not at all," Mr. Gorgi said.

PREVIEW OF CHAPTER 10

This chapter is the first of three chapters that explain the accounting, reporting, and disclosure requirements for an entity's investment in long-lived non-financial assets. Chapter 10 introduces investments in property, plant, and equipment assets and how they are accounted for at acquisition. It then sets out and explains three different accounting models that are used to measure such assets, and the accounting treatment for costs incurred after acquisition. This chapter, like those preceding it, finishes by summarizing significant differences between IFRS and ASPE requirements.

Chapter 11 continues the coverage of tangible long-lived assets by explaining how these assets are accounted for after acquisition (depreciation), when their capacity to generate future cash flows is reduced (impairment), and when they are disposed of (derecognition). That chapter also addresses significant presentation and disclosure requirements. Chapter 12 zeroes in on recognition and measurement issues related to intangible long-lived assets and goodwill.

The chapter is organized as follows:

PROPERTY, PLANT, AND EQUIPMENT: ACCOUNTING MODEL BASICS						
Definition and Recognition of Property, Plant, and Equipment	Cost Elements	Measurement of Cost	Measurement after Acquisition	IFRS/ASPE Comparison	Appendix 10A— Capitalization of Borrowing Costs	Appendix 10B— Revaluation: The Proportionate Method
▪ Property, plant, and equipment— business perspective ▪ Property, plant, and equipment— characteristics	▪ Self-constructed assets ▪ Borrowing costs ▪ Dismantling and restoration costs	▪ Determining asset cost when cash is not exchanged at acquisition ▪ Costs associated with specific assets	▪ Cost and revaluation models ▪ Fair value model ▪ Costs incurred after acquisition	▪ A comparison of IFRS and ASPE ▪ Looking ahead	▪ Qualifying assets ▪ Capitalization period ▪ Avoidable borrowing costs ▪ Disclosures	

DEFINITION AND RECOGNITION OF PROPERTY, PLANT, AND EQUIPMENT

Objective 1

Identify the business importance and characteristics of property, plant, and equipment and explain the recognition criteria.

Property, Plant, and Equipment—Business Perspective

Almost every enterprise, whatever its size or activity, invests in long-lived assets. Such long-lived assets include both those that are physical assets—property, plant, and equipment—and those that are not physical, such as patents. Long-lived assets are particularly important for manufacturers because these assets allow them to produce goods and/or provide services. Too much investment in long-lived assets results in costly overcapacity, and too little investment means lost opportunities for profits and future cash flows. Both situations lower the company's rate of return. To properly assess an enterprise's potential for future cash flows, users need:

1. a solid understanding of the enterprise's investment in long-term productive assets,

2. the extent to which this investment has changed in the period, and

3. the accounting policies applied to these assets.

It is not just companies, however, that need to focus on investment in long-lived assets. Local and municipal governments often have a significant stock of long-lived assets. These can include buildings, roads, public transit vehicles, fleets of trucks and other vehicles used for servicing parks and open spaces, and water and sewage infrastructure. The Public Sector Accounting Board of the Chartered Professional Accountants Canada (CPA Canada) has provided some guidance for municipalities and local governments as they struggle to maintain and revitalize their long-lived assets. They draw on the accounting requirements set out in the CPA Canada *Public Sector Accounting Handbook* and research reports on infrastructure in the public sector.[1] The federal government's Infrastructure Canada is helping to develop a long-term infrastructure plan for the federal government, provinces, territories, and municipalities.[2] While in this chapter, and the next two, we concentrate on accounting for long-lived assets by companies and the requirements of IFRS and ASPE, keep in mind that many of the issues faced by businesses also need to be considered by governments as they renew infrastructure over the next decade and beyond.

STRATEGY DEVELOPMENT

2.3.3

Property, Plant, and Equipment—Characteristics

Property, plant, and equipment (PP&E) include long-term resources such as office, factory, and warehouse buildings; investment property; equipment (machinery, furniture, tools); and mineral resource properties. PP&E is also commonly referred to as **tangible capital assets**, **plant assets**, or **fixed assets**.

Consistent with the terminology in IFRS, the term "depreciation" is used in this and other chapters to refer specifically to the amortization of property, plant, and equipment. We use "depletion" for the amortization of mineral resource properties, and "amortization" is used for intangibles. In addition, the term **amortization** may be used in a general sense to refer to the allocation of the cost of any long-lived asset to different accounting periods.

Let's begin by defining the types of assets dealt with in this chapter. **Property, plant, and equipment** are defined in both IAS 16 *Property, Plant, and Equipment* and in the standards that apply to private enterprises, *CPA Canada Handbook*, Part II, Section 3061, as assets that have the following characteristics:

1. **They are held for use in the production of goods and services, for rental to others, or for administrative purposes.** They are not intended for sale in the ordinary course of business.

2. **They are used over more than one accounting period** and are usually depreciated. Property, plant, and equipment provide services over many years. Through periodic depreciation charges, the cost of the investment in these assets, with the usual exception of land, is assigned to the periods that benefit from using them.

3. **They are tangible.** These assets have a physical existence or substance, which makes them different from goodwill and intangible assets such as patents.

At times there is a fine line between what is categorized as a capital asset and what is categorized as a supply inventory. Assume, for example, that a company has a substantial fleet of trucks (capital assets) and a variety of assets related to the trucks: spare tires, major motor parts, oil and grease, and truck cleaning equipment. What type of asset is each of these? The general approach is to include any items that have multiple uses and are regularly used and replaced within the accounting period as **inventory**. Major spare parts and standby or servicing equipment used only with a specific capital asset and useful for more than one period are classified as items of **property, plant, and equipment**.

What about agricultural assets, such as trees in an apple orchard, grapevines in a vineyard, or livestock held to produce milk, wool, or additional livestock? These **biological assets**—living plants and animals—have all the characteristics necessary to be items of PP&E. Entities with such assets apply the same accounting principles used for other items of property, plant, and equipment if they report under ASPE. However, companies applying IFRS are required to follow specific standards for biological assets and agricultural produce that are set out in IAS 41 *Agriculture*, and standards for bearer plants set out in IAS 16. We briefly describe these later in this chapter. We also discussed biological assets in Chapters 6 and 8, and in the opening story of Chapter 2.

Recognition Principle

Entities incur many costs, but how do they know which ones should be recognized as an item of PP&E? Assuming the resulting item meets the definition of property, plant, and equipment, accounting standards require that the following two recognition criteria be satisfied:

1. It is probable that the item's associated future economic benefits will flow to the entity.

2. Its cost can be measured reliably.

UNDERLYING CONCEPT

This recognition principle applies to costs incurred when an asset is first acquired and later when incurring costs to upgrade, replace, or service the asset.

If both are met, the item is **capitalized** (included in the asset's cost) and recognized as a PP&E asset. Some costs, such as those for government-imposed pollution reduction equipment, may not appear to generate any net future cash inflows (future economic benefits), but are still recognized as property, plant, and equipment. This is because these expenditures are necessary in order to obtain the economic benefits from related assets.

If costs are incurred but recognition criteria are **not met**, the costs are recognized as an expense, such as when repair and ongoing maintenance expenditures are made.

While the recognition principle is clear, the standards do not specify what level of asset should be recognized. This is referred to as a **unit of measure** issue. For example, if you buy or construct a building, what items should be recognized? Should it be one asset—"building"—or should each component be recognized as a separate asset, such as the foundation and frame, roof, windows, and elevators? Alternatively, can a number of smaller items, such as individual tools, be aggregated and recognized as a single asset?

The degree of **componentization** is left up to professional judgement. A primary consideration is the **significance of the individual parts** to the "whole" asset. On a cost-benefit basis, an entity would only separate out components that make up a relatively significant portion of the asset's total cost. As we will explain in the depreciation discussion in Chapter 11, other factors include whether items have **differing useful lives** and/or **different patterns of delivering economic benefits** to the company, making alternative depreciation methods appropriate. The significance of the items and the similarity of their life and use are also considerations in deciding whether to aggregate smaller items into a single larger asset component. While both IFRS and ASPE speak to the need to recognize components, the discussion and application under IFRS are more fully developed.

Once an item of property, plant, and equipment meets the definition and recognition criteria, it is recognized at its cost. This raises two issues that need to be addressed:

1. What elements of cost are capitalized?

2. How is cost measured?

We answer these questions in the next two sections.

COST ELEMENTS

In general, the **cost** of an item of property, plant, and equipment includes all expenditures needed to **acquire** the asset and bring it to its **location** and **ready it for use**. Once the item reaches this stage, no further costs are included in the asset's acquisition cost, and capitalization stops. More specifically, costs capitalized include the following:

- The item's purchase price net of trade discounts and rebates, plus any non-refundable purchase taxes (such as many provincial sales taxes) and duties.

- The expenditures necessary to bring the asset to its required location and condition to operate as management intended. These include employee costs needed to acquire or construct the asset; delivery and handling costs; site preparation, installation, and assembly costs; net material and labour costs incurred to ensure it is working properly; and professional fees.

- The estimate of the costs of obligations associated with the asset's eventual disposal. An example is some or all of the costs of the asset's decommissioning and site restoration.

Costs that are not capitalized as part of the PP&E asset include initial operating losses, the costs of training employees to use the asset, and costs associated with a reorganization of operations. Also excluded are administration and general overhead costs and the costs of opening a new facility, introducing a new product or service, and operating in a new location.

Although this general principle is the same under both IFRS and ASPE, it is applied somewhat differently under each and this may result in different outcomes. Consider a situation where a company, after clearing land and while waiting for construction to be completed, either incurs net costs or generates net income from using the property as a parking lot. Should these net costs or revenue be added to or deducted from the cost of the building, or should they be recognized immediately in net income? The answer depends on whether the company follows IFRS or ASPE, as shown in Illustration 10-1 below.

*Accounting for Temporary Use of
Land during Construction*

IFRS	ASPE
Capitalization of costs stops when the asset is in place and ready to be used as management intended, even if it has not begun to be used or is used at less than a desirable capacity level.	Capitalization of costs stops when an asset is substantially complete and ready for productive use as determined in advance by management in relation to factors such as reaching a given level of productive capacity, occupancy level, period of time, or other industry-specific consideration.
The principle of being a necessary cost to acquire and get in place and ready for use is strictly applied. The temporary use of land as a parking lot and its net cost or revenue is not necessary to develop the asset being constructed; therefore, it cannot be included in the asset cost. The net cost or net revenue is recognized in income when incurred or earned.	Any net revenue or expenses generated prior to substantial completion and readiness for use are included in the asset's cost. Therefore, the net parking lot cost or net revenue while the asset is being readied for use would be debited or credited to the asset account.
If the rent from parking lot spaces in the basement of the building was $1,000 while the rest of the building was being finished, the following journal entry would be recorded:	If the rent from parking lot spaces in the basement of the building was $1,000 while the rest of the building was being finished, the following journal entry would be recorded:

Cash	1,000		Cash	1,000	
Rent Revenue		1,000	Building		1,000

Three specific cost issues are more fully discussed in this chapter. They are (1) costs incurred when assets are constructed internally rather than purchased outright, (2) associated borrowing costs, and (3) site restoration or asset retirement costs.

Self-Constructed Assets

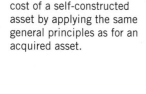

Often, companies construct their own assets. Even after deciding what components will be separately recognized, determining the cost of **self-constructed assets** such as machinery or buildings can be a challenge. Without a firm purchase or contract price, the company has to review numerous expenditures that were incurred to arrive at its cost.

The costs of materials and direct labour used in construction are not difficult to identify and measure; they can be traced directly to actual work orders and materials used in the constructed assets. However, allocating the indirect costs of manufacturing may create special problems. These indirect costs, called **overhead** or **burden**, include power, heat, light, insurance, property taxes on factory buildings and equipment, factory supervisory labour, depreciation of fixed assets, and supplies. Which of the following accounting choices is appropriate?

1. Assign a portion of all overhead to the construction project.

2. Assign no fixed overhead to the cost of the constructed asset.

Although the standards for manufactured inventories (see Chapter 8) require that a portion of all production overhead costs be applied to an inventory asset, the principle for PP&E assets is different. For these assets, only **directly attributable costs**—costs directly related to the specific activities involved in the construction process—are capitalized. Therefore, no fixed overhead is usually charged to the PP&E asset account.[3] Whether the entity also makes similar assets for resale or uniquely for its own purposes, care has to be taken to ensure that no abnormal amounts of wasted inputs and related excess costs were experienced. If so, these are expensed in the period.

Borrowing Costs

Entities often acquire or construct capital assets that take substantial time to get ready for their intended use. To finance any interim expenditures that have to be made, a company may have to increase its bank loans, otherwise borrow money, or use existing company funds that could be used for other purposes. Do the financing or borrowing costs that are incurred for this purpose meet the criteria to be capitalized as part of the asset's cost, or should they be expensed in the period incurred?

Not surprisingly, IAS 23 *Borrowing Costs* requires capitalization of **avoidable** borrowing costs that are directly attributable to the cost of acquiring, constructing, or producing qualifying assets that take a substantial period of time to get ready for use, such as manufacturing plants. These costs are therefore added to the cost of the PP&E asset. ASPE permits management to choose between a policy of capitalizing interest and expensing such costs.

Appendix 10A explains how **borrowing costs** are defined, how to determine which are **avoidable**, and how to determine the **amount to capitalize**.

Until Canadian publicly accountable entities adopted IFRS in 2011, they had a choice of whether to capitalize interest for qualifying assets or to report all interest as an expense in the income statement as incurred. Interest capitalization can have a substantial effect on the financial statements. For example, **TransAlta Corporation** capitalized $3.0 million of interest to property, plant, and equipment in 2014 under IFRS. Because it previously capitalized interest under prior Canadian GAAP, it did not have to change this accounting policy when it adopted IFRS. But what if TransAlta had previously expensed all interest? Earnings per share would have been $0.16 in 2014 if TransAlta had expensed its interest under prior Canadian GAAP, instead of $0.17 per share (a decrease of

$0.01 per share). However, in some years this policy could have a much more significant impact. For example, EPS would have been $0.14 lower in 2011 if TransAlta had not capitalized any of its interest.*

How can statement users determine the effect of interest capitalization on a company's bottom line? The amount of interest capitalized in the period has to be disclosed in the notes to the financial statements. For example, **Imperial Metals Corporation**, a British Columbia exploration, development, and mining company, reported $38.4 million of capitalized interest in 2014—an amount equal to 93.7% of the total interest expense and finance costs that would have been reported if no interest had been capitalized! The prior year's numbers were lower: only $9.6 million.

*This calculation is just for illustrative purposes. For example, the comparison ignores the impact of depreciation of capitalized interest costs on EPS.

Regardless, the policy chosen and amount capitalized are required to be disclosed. In 2014, **BCE Inc.** (one of Canada's leading communications companies) capitalized $33.0 million of its interest costs under IFRS (see excerpt below). It had also capitalized interest under Canadian GAAP prior to adopting IFRS.

BCE Inc. Annual Report 2014
NOTES TO CONSOLIDATED FINANCIAL STATEMENTS
NOTE 8
INTEREST EXPENSE

FOR THE YEAR ENDED DECEMBER 31	2014	2013
Interest expense on long-term debt	**(865)**	(850)
Interest expense on other debt	**(97)**	(97)
Capitalized interest	**33**	16
Total interest expense	**(929)**	(931)

Dismantling and Restoration Costs

In some industries, when a company acquires and uses its long-lived assets, it takes on obligations that need to be met when the assets are eventually retired. For example, a nuclear facility must be decommissioned at the end of its useful life, mine sites must be closed and dismantled and the property restored, and landfill sites have significant closure and post-closure costs associated with the end of their operations.

In order to be able to use the long-lived asset, companies often assume responsibility for the costs associated with dismantling the item, removing it, and restoring the site at the end of its useful life. These **asset retirement costs** meet the recognition criteria for capitalization and are added to the PP&E asset cost.

Once again, while this general principle underlies both IFRS and ASPE, it is applied differently under each, as shown in Illustration 10-2. The differences relate to the types of obligations and activities undertaken.

		IFRS	ASPE
	Category of obligations	Recognizes costs of both legal and constructive obligations, such as when an entity creates an expectation in others through its own actions that it will meet this obligation.	Recognizes costs associated with legal obligations only.
	Category of activities	Costs include only those related to the acquisition of the asset, not those related to the use of the asset in the production of goods or services (product costs).	Costs include both retirement obligations resulting from the acquisition of the asset and its subsequent use in producing inventory, such as the mining of coal.

Illustration 10-2

Asset Retirement Costs: IFRS versus ASPE

LAW

Under both IFRS and ASPE, the original cost estimates and any changes in them are capitalized in the asset account and a credit is made to an asset retirement or restoration liability. Because the actual expenditures will often not be incurred for a number of years, the obligation provision and the asset are both measured using the present value of the future costs. There is a fuller discussion of provisions and liability recognition and measurement issues in Chapters 2 and 13. For now, you should be aware that the cost of property, plant, and equipment in the mining and oil and gas industries will often include such a charge when the asset is acquired.

Measurement of Cost

Now that you have a better idea of what is included in "cost," the second step is to determine how it is measured. In general, **cost** is measured by the amount of cash or cash equivalents paid or the fair value of the other consideration given to acquire an asset when it is acquired.[4]

Determining Asset Cost when Cash Is Not Exchanged at Acquisition

Objective 3
Determine asset cost when the transaction has delayed payment terms or is a lump-sum purchase, a nonmonetary exchange, or a contributed asset.

Cost is the **cash cost** when an asset is recognized. This amount may not always be obvious. The paragraphs that follow discuss how several common issues are resolved when cash is not exchanged at the date of acquisition:

1. Cash discounts not taken

2. Deferred payment terms

3. Lump-sum purchases

4. Nonmonetary exchanges—share-based payments

5. Nonmonetary exchanges—asset exchanges

6. Contributed assets and government grants

Cash Discounts

When cash discounts for prompt payment are offered on purchases of plant assets, how should the discount be handled? If the discount is taken, it is definitely a reduction in the asset's purchase price. It is not recognized in a purchase discount account (see Chapter 8), because purchase discounts relate only to inventory purchases that are included in the cost of goods sold. What is not clear, however, is whether the asset's cost should be reduced even if the discount is not taken. There are two points of view on this matter.

Under one approach, the net-of-discount amount is considered the asset's cost, **regardless of whether the discount is taken or not**. The rationale for this view is that an asset's cost is its cash or cash equivalent price. The discount, if it is lost, is the cost of not paying at an earlier date and should be recognized according to its nature as a financing or interest expense. Under the **other approach**, supporters argue that the discount should not always be deducted from the asset's cost, because the terms may be unfavourable or because it might not be prudent for the company to take the discount. Both methods are used in practice. Recognition of the asset at its lower "cash cost" is preferred, at least on conceptual grounds.

Deferred Payment Terms

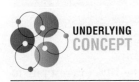

UNDERLYING CONCEPT

Use of present value is consistent with the IAS 16 definition of cost, which includes the fair value of other consideration given to acquire an asset at the time of its acquisition or construction.

Plant assets are often purchased on long-term credit arrangements through the use of notes, mortgages, bonds, or equipment obligations. The cost of an asset whose payment is deferred beyond normal credit terms is its **cash price equivalent**. Any difference between this fair value and the total payments made is recognized as **interest**. That is, the asset's cost is the **present value of the consideration** that is exchanged at the transaction date.

For example, equipment purchased today in exchange for a $10,000, non–interest-bearing note that is payable four years from now is not recorded at $10,000 because waiting four years without charging interest before payment far exceeds normal credit terms. Assuming the cash price is not known, the **present value of the note is the transaction's exchange price** and the asset's "cash cost." If 8% is an appropriate interest rate, the equipment is recognized at a cost of $7,350.30 [$10,000 × 0.73503; see Table A-2 for the present value of a single sum, PV = $10,000 $(PV_{4,8})$].

When no interest rate is stated, or if the specified rate is unreasonable, an appropriate interest rate is imputed. The objective is to approximate the interest rate that the buyer and seller would negotiate in a similar arm's-length borrowing transaction. Factors to consider in determining an appropriate interest rate are the borrower's credit rating, the note's amount and maturity date, and prevailing interest rates. If the acquired asset's cash exchange price can be determined, it is used as the basis for measuring the asset's cost and identifying the interest element.

To illustrate, assume that Sutter Corporation purchases a specially built robot spray painter for its production line. The company issues a $100,000, five-year, non–interest-bearing note to Wrigley Robotics Ltd. for the new equipment when the prevailing market interest rate for obligations of this nature is 10%. Sutter is to pay off the note in five $20,000 instalments made at the end of each year. Assume that the fair value of this specially built robot cannot readily be determined. Therefore, it has to be approximated by establishing the note's fair value (the present value of an ordinary annuity [PVOA]). This calculation and the entries at the purchase and payment dates are as follows:

A = L + SE
+75,816 +75,816

Cash flows: No effect

At date of purchase		
Equipment	75,816	
Notes Payable		75,816

Present value of note $= \$20,000 \ (PVOA_{5,\ 10\%})$
$= \$20,000 \ (3.79079) \ (Table\ A\text{-}4)$
$= \$75,816$

The $24,184 difference between the asset's cash cost of $75,816 and the $100,000 cash that is eventually payable ($20,000 × 5) is the discount or interest on the $75,816 amount borrowed.

A = L + SE
+7,582 −7,582

Cash flows: No effect

A = L + SE
−20,000 −20,000

Cash flows: ↓ 20,000 outflow

At end of first year		
Interest Expense	7,582	
Notes Payable		7,582
Notes Payable	20,000	
Cash		20,000

Interest expense for the first year under the effective interest method (as required by IFRS and allowed by ASPE) is $7,582 [($75,816) × 10%]. The entries at the end of the second year to record interest and to pay off a portion of the note are as follows:

A = L + SE
+6,340 −6,340

Cash flows: No effect

A = L + SE
−20,000 −20,000

Cash flows: ↓ 20,000 outflow

At end of second year		
Interest Expense	6,340	
Notes Payable		6,340
Notes Payable	20,000	
Cash		20,000

Interest expense in the second year is calculated by applying the 10% interest rate to the net book value of the outstanding Notes Payable. At the end of the first year, the Notes Payable account was reduced to $63,398 ($75,816 + $7,582 − $20,000) and this was the note's carrying amount throughout the second year. The second year's interest expense is $63,398 × 10%, or $6,340.

If interest is not taken into account in such deferred payment contracts, the asset would be recorded at an amount that is higher than its fair value. In addition, no interest expense would be reported in any of the periods involved.

Lump-Sum Purchases

UNDERLYING CONCEPT

This is the same approach that is applied to a basket purchase of inventory.

There is a special problem in determining the cost of specific capital assets when they are purchased together for a single **lump-sum price**. When this occurs, and it is not at all unusual, the practice is to allocate the total cost among the various assets based on their relative fair values. The assumption is that costs will vary in direct proportion to those values.

To determine the individual fair value of the parts making up the total purchase, any of the following might be used: an appraisal for insurance purposes, the assessed valuation for property taxes, estimates of replacement costs, or simply an independent appraisal by an engineer or other appraiser. Which approach is most appropriate will depend on the information available in the specific situation. When a property is acquired consisting of a building and the land it sits on, the relative property tax value of each is often used. Estimates of replacement cost or independent appraisal might be used to determine the relative values of the components making up the building acquired.

To illustrate, assume that a company decides to purchase several assets of a smaller company in the same business for a total price of $80,000. The assets purchased are as follows:

	Seller's Book Value	Asset Fair Value
Inventory	$30,000	$ 25,000
Land	20,000	25,000
Building	35,000	50,000
	$85,000	$100,000

The allocation of the $80,000 purchase price based on the relative fair values is shown as follows.

	Asset Cost
Inventory	$\dfrac{\$25,000}{\$100,000} \times \$80,000 = \$20,000$
Land	$\dfrac{\$25,000}{\$100,000} \times \$80,000 = \$20,000$
Building	$\dfrac{\$50,000}{\$100,000} \times \$80,000 = \underline{\$40,000}$
	$\underline{\$80,000}$

Note that the assets' carrying amounts on the seller's books are not representative of their fair values. **They are irrelevant.** Depending on the situation and the company's accounting policies, the $40,000 cost allocated to the building may have to be further broken down and allocated to more specific components of the building, such as the basic structure, the roof, and the windows. If so, once the relative fair value of each is determined, the process of allocation is carried out using the same approach that is explained above.

Nonmonetary Exchanges

Share-Based Payments

When property, plant, and equipment assets are acquired and the company issues its own shares in payment, the cost of the asset is based on either the fair value of the shares given up or the fair value of the assets acquired. But which should be used?

IFRS 2 *Share-based Payment* indicates that the fair value of the asset acquired should be used to measure its acquisition cost, and it presumes that this value can be determined except in rare cases.[5] If the asset's fair value cannot be determined reliably, then its fair value and cost are determined by using the fair value of the shares given in exchange. If the company shares are widely traded, their fair value should be a good indication of the current cash-equivalent price of the PP&E asset acquired.[6] ASPE is more flexible, indicating only that the more reliable of the fair value of the goods received or the equity instruments given up is the asset cost. Because private company shares are not widely traded, the acquired asset's fair value is more likely to be used.

To illustrate, assume that a hardware company decides to purchase land next to its current property in order to expand its carpeting and cabinet operation. Instead of paying cash for the land, it issues 5,000 no par value common shares to the seller. Assuming a recent appraisal valued the land at $62,000, the following entry is made:

| Land | 62,000 | |
| Common Shares | | 62,000 |

If no fair value can be reliably determined for the land, and assuming the company's shares have been recently traded with a fair market value of $12 per share, the land is assigned a cost equal to the estimated fair value of the shares, or 5,000 × $12 = $60,000.

Asset Exchanges

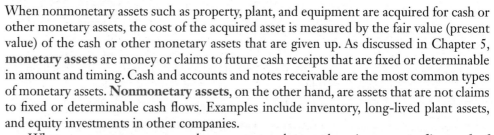

UNDERLYING CONCEPT

The FASB standard recommends that a nonmonetary exchange be considered monetary if 25% or more of the fair value of the consideration is monetary. There is no such threshold under ASPE or IFRS where the transaction's economic substance has to be assessed.

When nonmonetary assets such as property, plant, and equipment are acquired for cash or other monetary assets, the cost of the acquired asset is measured by the fair value (present value) of the cash or other monetary assets that are given up. As discussed in Chapter 5, **monetary assets** are money or claims to future cash receipts that are fixed or determinable in amount and timing. Cash and accounts and notes receivable are the most common types of monetary assets. **Nonmonetary assets**, on the other hand, are assets that are not claims to fixed or determinable cash flows. Examples include inventory, long-lived plant assets, and equity investments in other companies.

When nonmonetary assets such as property, plant, and equipment **are disposed of and the company receives monetary assets in exchange**, a gain or loss on disposal is recognized in income. The gain is recognized in income because it is realized—that is, it has been converted to cash or a claim to cash—and the entity's economic situation has clearly changed in terms of its future cash flows.

However, when an existing **nonmonetary asset is exchanged for a new nonmonetary asset such as an item of property, plant, and equipment**, the proper accounting is not necessarily obvious. There are two underlying issues:

1. What should be the cost of the nonmonetary asset acquired?

2. Should a gain or loss on disposal be recognized on the nonmonetary asset that was given up?

Some argue that the new asset's cost should be determined by its **fair value**, or by the fair value of the assets given up, and that a **gain or loss should be recognized** on the disposal of the old asset. Others believe that the cost of the new asset should be determined by the **carrying amount** of the assets given up, with **no gain or loss recognized**. Still others favour an approach that would **recognize losses** in all cases, but **defer gains** in special situations.

General Principle—The Fair Value Standard

International and Canadian standard setters have been in agreement for a number of years on the preferred answer to these choices. The general principle is that **nonmonetary transactions are accounted for on the same basis as monetary transactions**. Therefore, the cost of the PP&E asset acquired—by giving up a nonmonetary asset or a combination of monetary and nonmonetary assets—is determined by the fair value of the assets given up unless the fair value of the asset received can be more reliably measured. Any gains or losses that result are recognized in income.

Why is the accounting like this? Although cash or a claim to cash is not received or is relatively minor in nonmonetary exchanges, the earnings process related to the "old" asset is usually substantially complete. The specific values to the entity of the assets that are received generally are different from those of the assets that are given up. That is, the company's economic circumstances change as a result of the exchange.

The general standard that **nonmonetary exchanges are measured at fair value** is applied, therefore, **unless one of the following conditions is true**:

1. The transaction lacks commercial substance.

2. Fair values are not reliably measurable.

UNDERLYING CONCEPT

Under ASPE, a third condition is stated, but it could be interpreted as an example of a transaction that lacks commercial substance.

In these situations, as explained below, the exchange is recorded **at the carrying amount of the asset(s) given up, which is adjusted for the inclusion of any cash or other monetary assets.**

1. **Commercial substance.** When following the general standard, the entity:

   - derecognizes (takes out of the accounts) the carrying value of the asset(s) given up,

   - recognizes the fair value of the asset(s) received in exchange, and then

   - reports the difference as a gain (or loss) in net income.

Because the company's underlying economic situation has changed as a result of the transaction—in other words, the transaction has commercial or economic substance—income is permitted to be reported. However, if the company is in the same economic position after the exchange as it was before, then no gain or loss would be reported. This is because there is little or no justification for reporting increased asset values or income.[7]

What does **commercial substance** really mean? Simply, it means that there is a **significant change** in the company's expected future cash flows and therefore its value. The exchange transaction has commercial substance if:

   - the amount, timing, or risk of future cash flows associated with the asset(s) received is different from the configuration of cash flows for the asset(s) given up, or

   - the specific value of the part of the entity affected by the transaction has changed as a result. For example, a company may benefit from significant cost savings from economies of scale made possible by acquiring and using the asset.

   In either case, the change must be **significant relative to the fair values of the exchanged assets**. This often requires using professional judgement.

ETHICS

2. **Ability to measure fair values.** As might be expected, the exchange cannot be recorded at fair value if the fair value of neither the asset given up nor the asset received can be reliably measured. Also, this exception helps reduce the risk that entities can assign arbitrarily high values to assets exchanged as a way of engineering and reporting gains.

   An overriding caution: When an asset is acquired, **it cannot be recognized at more than its fair value**. In an exchange lacking commercial substance, the cost of the new asset is based on the carrying amount of the asset(s) given up. If the carrying amount of the asset(s) given up in the exchange is more than the fair value of the asset(s) received, the new asset has to be recorded at the lower fair value amount (the fair value of the asset received) and a loss would be recognized.

   Accounting for asset exchanges is summarized in Illustration 10-3. We follow this with examples to illustrate the appropriate entries.

Illustration 10-3

Accounting for Asset Exchanges

Does the exchange meet both criteria? In other words, does it have commercial substance, and can fair values can be reliably determined?

Yes	No
Apply the fair value standard:	Exception to the fair value standard:
Cost of asset(s) received = fair value of what is given up, or what is acquired, if more reliably measurable.	Cost of asset(s) received = carrying amount of asset(s) given up.
Difference between carrying amount and fair value of asset(s) given up is recognized in income as a gain or loss.	No gain is recognized. Loss is recognized if fair value of asset(s) acquired is less than the carrying amount of the asset(s) given up.

When assets are exchanged or traded in, the transaction often requires a payment or receipt of cash or some other monetary asset. When the transaction's monetary component—or **boot**, as it is sometimes called—is significant, there is less need to question whether the transaction has commercial substance. As the percentage gets smaller, the transaction becomes primarily a nonmonetary exchange and the need to evaluate whether or not the transaction has commercial substance increases.

Asset Exchange—Example 1

Assume that Information Processing, Inc. trades in its used machine for a new model. The machine given up has a book value of $8,000 (original cost of $12,000 less $4,000 accumulated depreciation) and a fair value of $6,000. It is traded for a new model that has a list price of $16,000. In negotiations with the seller, a trade-in allowance of $9,000 is finally agreed on for the used machine.

Note that the amount agreed on as a **trade-in allowance is not necessarily the used asset's fair value**. In many cases, such as with automobiles, the trade-in allowance is essentially used to change the new asset's selling price without reducing its list price.

The cash payment that is needed and the cost of the new machine are calculated in Illustration 10-4. Because the cash paid is significant relative to the fair value of the total consideration, the change in the configuration of the company's future cash flows justifies a conclusion that this transaction has commercial substance.

Illustration 10-4

Calculation of Cost of New Machine

Fair value of assets given up	
Amount of cash given up = list price less trade-in allowance	$16,000 − $9,000 = $ 7,000
Fair value of machine given up	6,000
Cost of new machine = fair value of assets given up	$13,000

The journal entry to record this transaction is:

Machinery (new)	13,000	
Accumulated Depreciation—Machinery (old)	4,000	
Loss on Disposal of Machinery	2,000	
Machinery (old)		12,000
Cash		7,000

The loss on the disposal of the used machine is verified in Illustration 10-5.

Illustration 10-5

Calculation of Loss on Disposal of Used Machine

Fair value of used machine	$6,000
Carrying amount of used machine	8,000
Loss on disposal of used machine	$2,000

Asset Exchange—Example 2

Cathay Corporation exchanges several used trucks plus cash for vacant land that might be used for a future plant site. The trucks have a combined carrying amount of $42,000 (cost of $64,000 less $22,000 of accumulated depreciation). Cathay's purchasing agent, who has had previous dealings in the second-hand market, indicates that the trucks have a fair value of $49,000. In addition to the trucks, Cathay pays $4,000 cash for the land.

This exchange has commercial substance because the pattern and timing of cash flows from the investment in land are very different from those of the trucks. In addition, fair values can be determined. Assuming that the land's fair value is not known, or its fair value is not as reliable as that of the trucks, the cost of the land is calculated as indicated in Illustration 10-6.

Illustration 10-6

Calculation of Land's Acquisition Cost

Cost of land = fair value of assets given up:	
Fair value of trucks exchanged	$49,000
Fair value of cash given up	4,000
Acquisition cost of the land	$53,000

The journal entry to record the exchange is:

A = L + SE
+7,000 +7,000

Cash flows: ↓ 4,000 outflow

Land	53,000	
Accumulated Depreciation—Trucks	22,000	
Trucks		64,000
Cash		4,000
Gain on Disposal of Trucks		7,000

The gain is the difference between the trucks' fair value of $49,000 and their carrying amount of $42,000. However, if the trucks' fair value was $39,000 instead of $49,000, the land's cost would be $43,000 ($39,000 + $4,000) and a loss on the exchange of $3,000 ($42,000 − $39,000) would be reported.

Asset Exchange—Example 3

Westco Limited owns a number of rental properties in Western Canada as well as a single property in Ontario. Management has decided to concentrate its business in the west and to dispose of its one property outside this area. Westco agrees to exchange its Ontario property for a similar commercial property outside Lethbridge, Alberta, owned by Eastco Limited, a company with most of its properties east of Manitoba. The two properties are almost identical in size, rentals, and operating costs. Eastco agrees to the exchange but requires a cash payment of $30,000 from Westco to equalize and complete the transaction. Illustration 10-7 sets out information about these two properties.

Illustration 10-7

Property Exchange—Westco and Eastco

	Westco Ltd. Property	Eastco Ltd. Property
Carrying amounts:		
Building	$520,000	$540,000
Accumulated depreciation	100,000	145,000
	$420,000	$395,000
Fair value	$615,000	$645,000
Cash paid	$ 30,000	
Cash received		$ 30,000

Assume an evaluation by both Westco and Eastco management indicates that there is an insignificant difference in the configuration of future cash flows and that commercial substance is not indicated. What entry would be made by each company to record this asset exchange? Remember that fair values are not recorded in this situation and that the cost of the assets acquired by each company is recognized at the carrying amount of the assets given up by each. Because the companies are recognizing amounts equal to the book value of what is given up, no gain or loss is recorded by either.

A = L + SE
0   0   0

Cash flows: ↓ 30,000 outflow

Westco Ltd. Entry		
Building (new)	450,000	
Accumulated Depreciation—Building (old)	100,000	
Building (old)		520,000
Cash		30,000

A = L + SE
0   0   0

Cash flows: ↑ 30,000 inflow

Eastco Ltd. Entry		
Building (new)	365,000	
Accumulated Depreciation (old)	145,000	
Cash	30,000	
Building (old)		540,000

Westco recognizes its new asset (the Lethbridge building) at the carrying amount of the assets given up. It gave up cash with a book value of $30,000 and a building with a book value of $420,000, for a total of $450,000. Eastco recognizes its new asset at the carrying amount of what it gave up, which is $395,000. Of this, $30,000 was cash received, leaving $365,000 to be recognized as the new building's cost. Because both companies remain in the same economic position after the exchange as before, there is no reason to recognize any change in asset values and related gain or loss on the exchange.

Remember to check whether the fair value of the asset acquired is less than the cost assigned to it. Assets cannot be recognized at more than their fair value, so the asset would have to be recorded at the lower fair value amount and a loss equal to the difference recognized.

Contributed Assets and Government Grants

Companies sometimes receive contributions of assets as donations, gifts, or government grants. Such contributions are referred to as **non-reciprocal transfers** because they are transfers of assets in one direction only—nothing is given in exchange. The grants may be in the form of assets such as land, buildings, or equipment, or cash to acquire such assets, or even the forgiveness of a debt. There are two important accounting issues for non-reciprocal transfers:

1. How should the asset be measured at acquisition?

2. What account should be credited?

When assets are acquired as a donation, a strict cost concept would dictate that the asset's acquisition cost is zero. A departure from the cost principle is justified, however. This is because the only costs that are incurred (legal fees and other relatively minor expenditures) do not form a reasonable basis of accounting for the assets received. To record nothing would ignore the economic reality of an increase in the entity's resources. Therefore, accounting standards generally require that **the asset's fair value be used to establish its "cost" on the books.**[8]

Having established the asset's acquisition cost, a further question remains about the credit entry in the transaction. Is it income, or is it contributed capital? Two general approaches have been used to record the credit in this type of transaction.

The **capital approach** considers donated assets as contributed capital financing and they are therefore accounted for with a credit directly to Contributed Surplus—Donated Capital. This approach is only appropriate, however, for a donation from an owner, and such donations are rare. The **income approach** reflects contributions in **net income** because the contribution is a non-owner source of the change in net assets.[9]

Accounting standards generally take the position that government assistance should be recognized in income, either as revenue or as a reduction of expense. If the contributed assets are expected to be used over several future periods, as in the case of a grant for a building or equipment, then the effect on income is spread out over the future periods that benefit from having received the grant. When assets or funds to acquire assets are received from federal, provincial, territorial, or municipal governments, GAAP requires that recipients defer and recognize the amount received over the periods when the related assets are used. This is accomplished in one of two ways:

1. by reducing the asset cost and therefore future depreciation by the amount of government assistance received (the **cost reduction method**); or

2. by recording the amount of assistance received as a deferred credit and amortizing it to revenue over the life of the related asset (the **deferral method**).

To illustrate the **cost reduction method**, assume that a company receives a grant of $225,000 from the federal government to upgrade its sewage treatment equipment. The entry to record the receipt of the grant under this method is as follows:

A = L + SE
0   0   0

Cash flows: ↑ 225,000 inflow

Cash	225,000	
Equipment		225,000

This results in the equipment being carried on the books **at cost less the related government assistance**. Assuming a 10-year life and straight-line depreciation, the annual depreciation expense for the equipment is reduced by $22,500 and net income therefore is increased by this amount each year.

Alternatively, the **deferral method** credits a deferred revenue account with the grant amount. This amount is then recognized in income each year **on the same basis that is used to amortize the underlying asset**. The entries to record the receipt of the grant and its amortization for the first year under the **deferral method** are as follows:

A = L + SE
+225,000 +225,000

Cash flows: ↑ 225,000 inflow

A = L + SE
0 -22,500 +22,500

Cash flows: No effect

Cash	225,000	
Deferred Revenue—Government Grants		225,000
Deferred Revenue—Government Grants	22,500	
Revenue—Government Grants		22,500

A weakness of the cost reduction method is that it reports assets at less than their fair value to the entity. This issue is resolved if the deferral method is used, but this method also has a weakness. The deferral method is not consistent with the conceptual framework because the Deferred Revenue account does not usually meet the definition of a liability.

Note that a donation **of land** by a government would be deferred and taken into income over future periods if the grant requires the company to fulfill certain obligations or conditions. If the requirement is to build and operate a manufacturing plant on the land over a specific period of time, then the grant is taken into income over the same period. Only when there is no way to associate the grant with future period costs is it taken directly into income when received.

Government grants that are awarded to a company **for incurring certain current expenditures**, such as those related to payroll, are recognized in income in the same period as the related expenses. If grants or donations that have been received have a condition attached to them that requires a future event to occur—such as being required to maintain a specified number of employees on the payroll—the contingency is reported in the notes to the financial statements.

Entities are required to provide extensive disclosure about the amounts, terms and conditions, and accounting treatment they use for government assistance they have received. Readers can then evaluate the effect of such assistance on the entity's financial position and performance.

Costs Associated with Specific Assets

Land

Land costs typically include (1) the purchase price; (2) closing costs, such as title to the land, legal fees, and recording fees; (3) costs incurred to condition the land for its intended use, such as grading, filling, draining, and clearing; (4) the costs of assuming any liens, such as taxes in arrears or mortgages or encumbrances on the property; and (5) any additional land improvements that have an indefinite life.

When land has been purchased to construct a building, all costs that are incurred up to the excavation for the new building are considered land costs. **Removal of old buildings, clearing, grading, and filling are considered land costs because these costs are necessary to get the land in condition and ready for its intended purpose.** Any proceeds that are obtained in the process of getting the land ready for its intended use—such as amounts received for salvaged materials from the demolition of an old building or the sale of timber that has been cleared—are treated as reductions in the land cost.

Special amounts assessed for local improvements—such as for roads, street lights, and sewers and drainage systems—are usually charged to the Land account because they are relatively permanent and are maintained and replaced by the local government. In addition, it is also proper to charge permanent improvements that are made by the owner, such as landscaping, to the Land account. Improvements with limited lives—such as private driveways, walks, fences, and parking lots—are recorded separately as Land Improvements so they can be amortized over their estimated lives.

Generally, land is considered part of property, plant, and equipment. If the major purpose of acquiring and holding land is for capital appreciation or rentals or an undetermined future use, it is classified as investment property, a special category of PP&E we discuss below. If the land is held by a real estate company for resale, or is held by land developers or subdivided, it is classified as inventory.

Buildings

One accounting issue relates to the cost of an old building that is on the site of a planned new building. Is the cost to remove the old building a cost of the land or of the new building? The standards indicate that, if land is purchased with an old building on it that will not be used, then the demolition cost less its salvage value is a cost of getting the land ready for its intended use. The costs relate to the land rather than to the new building.

On the other hand, if a company razes (tears down) an old building that it owns and previously used in order to construct a new building on the same land, the costs of the demolition net of any cost recoveries are expensed as disposal costs of the old building. This increases any loss on disposal of the old asset. The remaining book value of the old building is included in depreciation expense in its final year of use.

Under ASPE, an exception is made when a building is torn down to redevelop rental real estate. In this case, the remaining carrying amount of the building and the net costs of removing it can be capitalized as part of the redeveloped property, but only to the extent the costs can be recovered from the project in the future.

Leasehold Improvements

What is the proper accounting for capital expenditures that are made on property that is being leased or rented? Long-term leases ordinarily specify that any **leasehold improvements** revert to the lessor at the end of the lease. If the lessee constructs new buildings on leased land or reconstructs and improves existing buildings, the lessee has the right to use those facilities during the life of the lease, but they become the property of the lessor when the lease expires. The lessee charges the facilities' cost to a separate capital asset account, Lease-hold Improvements, and the cost is amortized as an operating expense over the remaining life of the lease or the useful life of the improvements, whichever is shorter.

Equipment

The term "equipment" in accounting includes delivery equipment, office equipment, machinery, furniture and fixtures, furnishings, factory equipment, and similar tangible capital assets. The cost of such assets includes the purchase price, freight and handling charges that are incurred, insurance on the equipment while it is in transit, the cost of special foundations if they are required, assembling and installation costs, testing (less net proceeds of items, such as samples produced and sold during testing), and costs of making any adjustments to the equipment to make it operate as intended. The asset's acquisition cost does not include Goods and Services Tax (GST), Harmonized Sales Tax (HST), or Quebec Sales Tax (QST) that is paid on the acquired assets as a recoverable tax eligible for an input tax credit.

Investment Property

Investment property, or rental real estate, is a separate category of PP&E that may be accounted for after acquisition in a special way by entities using IFRS. It is defined as property held to generate rentals and/or appreciate in value rather than to sell in the ordinary course of business or to use in production, administration, or supplying goods and services.[10] It includes property that is currently under construction for investment purposes as well.

Investment property is covered in international standards by IAS 40. This is different from owner-occupied property, which is covered by IAS 16 *Property, Plant, and Equipment*. Complexities arise when one property is used partly as an investment property and is partly owner-occupied. In general, if the two parts could be sold separately (or leased under a finance lease separately), then the two parts should be accounted for separately. Another problem arises when an owner provides a variety of services in connection with an investment property. If providing the services exposes the owner to the normal risks of running a business (as distinct from investment risk), the classification as an investment property may not be appropriate. Consider a situation where a company rents out office space to tenants and provides furnished units and secretarial support in addition to the space. Judgement is often needed to determine whether the services provided are such a significant component of the arrangement that the property is actually "owner-occupied" space and not investment property.[11]

The cost of investment property under IFRS and ASPE is determined following the same principles as used for PP&E. Also, if the property continues to be accounted for at cost, the components of the property are accounted for separately for purposes of depreciation.

Natural Resource Properties

Mineral resources, sometimes called "wasting assets," generally are minerals and oil and gas resources that do not regenerate. **Mineral resource properties** are capitalized costs associated with the acquired rights, and the exploration, evaluation, and development of these minerals. Unlike buildings and machinery, natural resource properties are consumed physically over the period of use and do not retain their original physical characteristics. Regardless, many of the accounting problems associated with these assets are similar to those for other capital assets.

How is the acquisition cost of a mineral resource property determined? For example, a company like **Petro-Canada** needs to spend large amounts to find oil and gas reserves, and projects often end in failure. Furthermore, there are long delays between the time it incurs costs and the time it obtains benefits from any extracted resources. The acquisition cost of natural resource property normally includes some costs from each of four stages: (1) acquisition of the property, (2) exploration for and evaluation of reserves, (3) development, and (4) decommissioning and site restoration. In general, the capitalized costs of acquisition, exploration, development, and restoration make up the **depletion base** of the natural resource. As its name implies, the depletion base is the amount that later will be amortized (through a depletion charge) and will form a significant portion of the cost of the mined or extracted inventory. Through depletion, the costs of the long-term mineral resource capital asset become part of the cost of the inventory that is produced—very similar to the direct materials cost of a manufactured product.

Two main methods of accounting for oil and gas properties are the full cost method and the successful efforts method. While IFRS 6 does not currently discuss these, the full cost method is covered under ASPE by Accounting Guideline 16 (AcG 16 *Oil and Gas Accounting—Full Cost*). Under the full cost accounting method, companies capitalize all of their exploration costs, even those representing "dry holes" that do not contain oil and gas reserves. Each time a company prepares its annual financial statements, it assesses the net capitalized costs to determine whether it is likely that the costs will be recovered in the future. Companies must determine the proper level of analysis when assessing the cost centres for possible impairment. This assessment is based on an estimate of the recoverable amount of oil and gas reserves (and, for example, the level of analysis of the amount of recoverable reserves could be based on a comparison of the costs capitalized compared to the total reserves in a province, a country, or an entire continent). AcG 16 recommends that recoverability be assessed by country, with only one cost centre for each country. An impairment loss is recognized if the carrying amount of the cost centre exceeds the sum of the undiscounted cash flows expected to arise from its use and eventual disposition (AcG 16.40). In contrast, under the successful efforts approach, companies initially capitalize exploration costs until the drilling activities for each oil field are complete. If the drilling activities are not successful and no proved reserves are found, the costs are written off to expense as a "dry hole." Alternatively, for successful efforts exploration activities that are likely to be commercially developed, the costs remain capitalized as an asset until production (and related amortization) begins. Later in this chapter, we provide an example of the accounting policy of a company that follows the successful efforts method (BP plc, in Illustration 10-14).

Accounting for natural resources is a specialized area, and it is only introduced here. Because of the complex nature of this industry, additional coverage is beyond the scope of an intermediate text. You should note, however, that many of the issues that need to be resolved are familiar ones: they involve bringing accounting practice into greater consistency with general standards for asset recognition and measurement, cost allocation, and impairment testing. Not surprisingly, these issues are complicated by the uncertainties caused by estimating the volume and fair values of reserves and resources. Differences between IFRS and ASPE exist.

Biological Assets

SIGNIFICANT CHANGE

Under ASPE, the general principles established for PP&E assets are also followed for biological assets. Under IFRS, however, separate standards are set out in IAS 16 *Property, Plant and Equipment* for bearer plants and IAS 41 *Agriculture* for other assets related to agricultural activity. Bearer plants include fruit trees, grapevines, and rubber trees. However, as discussed in Chapter 8, livestock such as sheep are considered biological assets (and the wool is an agricultural product). Biological assets are measured initially, and at every statement of financial position date, at **fair value less costs to sell**, with changes in value recognized in the income statement as gains or losses as the values change. The accounting is similar to the fair value model we explain later in this chapter. In the rare situation that no reliable fair value measure can be determined, the asset is measured at cost less accumulated depreciation and accumulated impairment losses. However, bearer plants are accounted for using the cost or revaluation methods, which are described later in this chapter.

MEASUREMENT AFTER ACQUISITION

After recognizing the cost of property, plant, or equipment assets at acquisition, companies may have a choice of how to account for them after this point. Three different models have been identified and are currently used: a **cost model (CM)**, a **revaluation model (RM)**, and a **fair value model (FVM)**. However, the GAAP choice of model depends on the type of asset and whether international or private enterprise standards are being applied. The features of the three models are summarized in Illustration 10-8.

Illustration 10-8

Accounting Model Choices

	ASPE			IFRS		
	CM	RM	FVM	CM	RM	FVM
Investment property	✓			✓		✓
Other property, plant, and equipment assets	✓			✓	✓	

UNDERLYING CONCEPT

Historical costs are **verifiable** and therefore are considered more reliable. On the other hand, they often do not **faithfully represent** the value of the asset to the business and therefore are considered a less reliable measure. This is an example of a qualitative characteristic trade-off.

For example, under IFRS, a company must choose whether to measure all of its **investment property** under the cost model or under the fair value model, with few exceptions. All **other items defined as PP&E** are separated into classes and a decision is made whether to apply the cost model or the revaluation model to each class. The same method must be used for **all assets in each class**. Common classes of assets include:

- Land
- Land and buildings
- Office equipment
- Motor vehicles

- Machinery
- Ships
- Aircraft
- Furniture and fixtures

Not surprisingly, the revaluation model can be applied only to assets whose fair value can be reliably measured. This method is used by relatively few companies but is included as an IFRS alternative. It tends to be used by companies that operate in countries with relatively high rates of inflation, making the revaluation measure more relevant than historical cost. This leaves the cost model as the most commonly used method under IFRS and the only one acceptable under ASPE. Let's now review how each of these models works.

Cost and Revaluation Models

Cost Model

Objective 5

Understand and apply the cost model, and the revaluation model using the asset adjustment method.

The **cost model (CM)** is by far the most widely used model to account for PP&E, and you are probably familiar with the basics of how it works from introductory accounting. This model measures property, plant, and equipment assets after acquisition **at their cost less accumulated depreciation and any accumulated impairment losses**. We provide details about depreciation and impairment in Chapter 11.

Revaluation Model

The choice of a **revaluation model (RM)** is new to most Canadian companies. Under this approach, property, plant, and equipment assets **whose fair value can be measured reliably** are carried after acquisition **at their fair value at the date of the revaluation less any subsequent accumulated depreciation and any subsequent impairment losses**. We will defer the discussion of depreciation and impairment under this model to Chapter 11.

A revaluation is not required at each reporting date but must be carried out often enough that the carrying amount reported is not materially different from the assets' fair value. Some assets need to be remeasured only every three to five years, but for assets whose values change rapidly, an annual revaluation may be needed. Between revaluation dates, **depreciation is taken** on the revalued amount.

What is **fair value**, and how do companies determine this value for their PP&E assets? Fair value is "the price that would be received to sell an asset or paid to transfer a liability in an orderly transaction between market participants at the measurement date."[12] Professional valuators use active market or market-related evidence to the greatest extent possible, but may have to revert to other methods if equipment, for example, is very specialized.[13]

UNDERLYING CONCEPT

IAS 29 sets out how companies reporting in the currency of a hyper-inflationary economy should restate their financial statements.

Before walking through an example of how the RM works, we need to resolve one issue. If you regularly revalue or change the asset's carrying amount, what do you do with the increases and decreases in the carrying amount? The changes are accounted for as follows.

If the asset's carrying amount is **increased (debited)**	If the asset's carrying amount is **decreased (credited)**
The amount is recorded as a credit to Revaluation Surplus (OCI), an equity account, unless the increase reverses a revaluation decrease previously recognized in income. If so, recognize the increase in income to the extent of the prior decrease.	The amount is recorded as a debit to Revaluation Surplus (OCI), an equity account, to the extent of any credit balance associated with that asset. This account cannot have a debit (that is, a negative) balance. Any remaining amount is recognized in income.

The amounts debited or credited to the Revaluation Surplus account are reported in the statement of comprehensive income as other comprehensive income (OCI) items. Over the life of the asset, the effect of the treatment described is that there is no **net increase** in net income from revaluing the asset.

When revaluing an asset, two methods of accounting for the balance in the Accumulated Depreciation account are permitted. The account (1) **may be adjusted proportionately**, or (2) under the **asset adjustment (or elimination) method**, its balance may be eliminated. The proportionate approach adjusts both the asset's carrying amount and its accumulated depreciation, so that the net balance is the fair value of the asset at the revaluation date.[14] The second method eliminates the balance in the Accumulated Depreciation account, writing it off against the asset itself. The asset is then adjusted to its new revalued amount. The second, and simpler, method is illustrated in the example that follows. For a similar example using the proportionate method, see Appendix 10B.

Revaluation Model Example

Convo Corp. (CC) purchases a building in early January 2013 and the cost of the basic structure of $100,000 is classified in an account called Buildings. CC accounts for this class of asset using the revaluation model, revalues the class every three years, and uses straight-line depreciation. The building structure is expected to have a useful life of 25 years with no residual value. CC has a December 31 fiscal year end. The asset's fair value at December 31, 2015, is $90,000 and at December 31, 2018, it is $75,000.

Illustration 10-9 walks us through the depreciation for the first three years and the revaluation entries needed at December 31, 2015, assuming the balance in the Accumulated Depreciation account is eliminated.

Illustration 10-9

Convo Corp. 2013 to 2015 and December 31, 2015 Adjustment

A   =   L   +   SE
−4,000   −4,000

Cash flows: No effect

Annual depreciation in each of 2013, 2014, and 2015:

Depreciation Expense	4,000	
Accumulated Depreciation—Buildings		4,000

$$\frac{\$100,000 - \$0}{25 \text{ years}} = \$4,000$$

December 31, 2015

	Before Revaluation	Adjustments	After Revaluation
Buildings	$100,000	$(12,000)	$90,000
		2,000	
Accumulated depreciation			
$4,000 × 3	(12,000)	12,000	–0–
Carrying amount	$ 88,000	$ 2,000	$90,000

A = L + SE
0   0   0

Cash flows: No effect

Entries, December 31, 2015:		
Accumulated Depreciation—Buildings	12,000	
Buildings		12,000
To eliminate the accumulated depreciation.		

A = L + SE
+2,000   0   +2,000

Cash flows: No effect

Buildings (90,000 – 88,000)	2,000	
Revaluation Surplus (OCI)		2,000
To adjust the Buildings account to fair value.		

Statement of financial position presentation, December 31, 2015:

Long-term assets:
Buildings	$90,000
Less accumulated depreciation	–0–
	$90,000
Shareholders' equity	
Revaluation surplus (OCI)	$ 2,000

We need to calculate a new depreciation rate because there has been a change in the asset's carrying amount. This calculation and the revaluation adjustment amounts on December 31, 2018, are provided in Illustration 10-10.

Illustration 10-10

Convo Corp. 2016 to 2018 and December 31, 2018 Adjustment

A = L + SE
–4,091   –4,091

Cash flows: No effect

Annual depreciation in each of 2016, 2017, and 2018:		
Depreciation Expense	**4,091**	
Accumulated Depreciation—Buildings		**4,091**

$$\frac{\$90,000 - \$0}{22 \text{ years}} = \$4,091$$

December 31, 2018

	Before Revaluation	Adjustments	After Revaluation
Buildings	$90,000	$(12,273)	$75,000
		(2,727)	
Accumulated depreciation			
$4,091 × 3	(12,273)	12,273	–0–
Carrying amount	$ 77,727	$ (2,727)	$75,000

A = L + SE
0   0   0

Cash flows: No effect

Entries, December 31, 2018:		
Accumulated Depreciation—Buildings	12,273	
Buildings		12,273
To eliminate the accumulated depreciation.		

A = L + SE
–2,727   –2,727

Cash flows: No effect

Revaluation Surplus (OCI)	2,000	
Revaluation Gain or Loss	727	
Buildings		2,727
To adjust the Buildings account to fair value.		

Statement of financial position presentation, December 31, 2018:

Long-term assets:
Building	$75,000
Less accumulated depreciation	–0–
	$75,000

Notice that the Revaluation Surplus (OCI) account can only be reduced to zero. The remaining loss in value is recognized in the income statement. Once again, the depreciation rate going forward has to be recalculated. The $75,000 carrying amount is now allocated over the remaining 19 years of useful life, so the new rate is $75,000/19 = $3,947 each year.

Revaluation Surplus Account

What happens to the Revaluation Surplus (OCI) account? A company has two choices. One option is to transfer amounts from the account directly into Retained Earnings every period. The amount transferred is the difference between the depreciation expense based on the revalued carrying amount and the expense based on the original cost. Alternatively, the balance in the Revaluation Surplus (OCI) could remain there until the asset is retired or disposed of. At that point, the balance would be transferred directly to Retained Earnings, without going through the income statement.

Notice that the amounts in the Revaluation Surplus (OCI) account are not "recycled" through net income as the asset is depreciated, impaired, or disposed of. The revaluation model, therefore, is closer to a current cost measurement approach, where holding gains and losses are equity adjustments, than to a true fair value model. In this example, Convo chose the alternative of not transferring any amounts to retained earnings until the building was sold.[15]

Illustration 10-11 provides the accounting entries assuming that Convo Corp. sells the building in the example above on **January 2, 2016**, for $93,000.

	Illustration 10-11
Revaluation Surplus Adjustment on Disposal of Asset	

A	= L +	SE
+3,000		+3,000

Cash flows: ↑ 93,000 Inflow

A	= L +	SE
0	0	0

Cash flows: No effect

Cash	93,000	
Buildings		90,000
Gain on Sale of Buildings		3,000
To record the proceeds on sale of the building.		

Revaluation Surplus (OCI)	2,000	
Retained Earnings		2,000
To transfer the Revaluation Surplus in OCI related to the building sold to Retained Earnings.		

Fair Value Model

Objective 6
Understand and apply the fair value model.

As indicated above, investment property is the only tangible capital asset that may be accounted for under the **fair value model (FVM)**. Under this approach, the investment property is recognized on the statement of financial position after acquisition at its fair value. Changes in its value are reported in net income in the period of the change, and no depreciation is recognized over the life of the asset. Once this method is chosen instead of the cost model, the property continues to be measured at fair value until it is disposed of, becomes owner-occupied, or is developed for sale in the ordinary course of business. The example that follows illustrates how the FV model is applied. Note that, although biological assets are measured at **fair value less costs to sell** instead of **fair value**, the example provided for investment property below is similar to the accounting for changes in value of biological assets.

WHAT DO THE NUMBERS MEAN?

REAL WORLD EMPHASIS

As discussed in the feature story at the start of this chapter, Brookfield Asset Management adopted the fair value model to account for its commercial properties when it moved from former Canadian GAAP to IFRS in 2010. This resulted in an increase of $2,640 million in equity for its opening consolidated balance sheet, relating to its commercial properties, when it adopted IFRS. Brookfield continues to use the fair value model for its investment properties. For the year ended December 31, 2014, its investment properties (including office, retail, multifamily, and industrial properties) had a fair value of $46,083 million (including fair value changes during the year of $3,266 million). For 2014, Brookfield recorded total fair value increases of $3,674 million relating primarily to its investment properties, but also due to items such as its investment in Canary Wharf in London, England, and its forest products investment. The changes in fair value were recorded in its consolidated statement of operations.

Fair Value Model Example

Erican Corp. (EC) acquired a small 10-store shopping mall in eastern Canada for $1 million on February 2, 2017. The mall qualifies as investment property under IAS 40 *Investment Property*. At this time, nine of the stores were leased with remaining lease terms of two to four years. In addition to the purchase price, EC had to pay a $40,000 property transfer fee and legal fees of $3,000, and the company decided to paint the empty store at a cost of $2,000 before advertising it for rent. The acquisition was financed by assuming a $730,000 mortgage from the previous owner, who also turned over $37,000 of tenant damage deposits. The remainder of the transaction was settled in cash. On December 31, 2017, the fair value of the shopping centre property was determined to be $1,040,000; on December 31, 2018, it was $1,028,000, and on December 31, 2019, it had risen to $1,100,000. EC has a December 31 year end and applies the fair value method to all its investment property.

The summary entry to record the acquisition of the property is as follows.

<table>
<tr><td colspan="3" align="center">February 2, 2017</td></tr>
<tr><td>Investment Property (1,000,000 + 40,000 + 3,000)</td><td align="right">1,043,000</td><td></td></tr>
<tr><td>Repairs and Maintenance Expense</td><td align="right">2,000</td><td></td></tr>
<tr><td>   Mortgage Payable</td><td></td><td align="right">730,000</td></tr>
<tr><td>   Tenant Deposits Liability</td><td></td><td align="right">37,000</td></tr>
<tr><td>   Cash</td><td></td><td align="right">278,000</td></tr>
</table>

A = L + SE
+765,000 +767,000 −2,000

Cash flows: ↓ 278,000 outflow

The acquisition cost includes the transfer and legal fees, while the incidental painting is a period expense. The mortgage and the tenant deposits are both liabilities and they reduce the amount of cash EC has to pay on the date of acquisition. Because the building is not being amortized, the land and the building may be reported together, as illustrated in the entry. On each December 31, the investment property is remeasured to its new fair value, with the following entries being made.

<table>
<tr><td colspan="3" align="center">December 31, 2017</td></tr>
<tr><td>Loss in Value of Investment Property</td><td align="right">3,000</td><td></td></tr>
<tr><td>   Investment Property</td><td></td><td align="right">3,000</td></tr>
<tr><td>   ($1,043,000 − $1,040,000)</td><td></td><td></td></tr>
<tr><td colspan="3" align="center">December 31, 2018</td></tr>
<tr><td>Loss in Value of Investment Property</td><td align="right">12,000</td><td></td></tr>
<tr><td>   Investment Property</td><td></td><td align="right">12,000</td></tr>
<tr><td>   ($1,040,000 − $1,028,000)</td><td></td><td></td></tr>
<tr><td colspan="3" align="center">December 31, 2019</td></tr>
<tr><td>Investment Property</td><td align="right">72,000</td><td></td></tr>
<tr><td>   Gain in Value of Investment Property</td><td></td><td align="right">72,000</td></tr>
<tr><td>   ($1,100,000 − $1,028,000)</td><td></td><td></td></tr>
</table>

A = L + SE
−3,000   −3,000
−12,000   −12,000
+72,000   +72,000

Cash flows: No effect

The gains and losses are recognized directly in income. They are not reported in other comprehensive income.

It is important to realize that the fair value of investment property must be **disclosed in the financial statements, even if the cost model is used**. Therefore, all companies with such properties need to develop appropriate methods to measure fair value.

Costs Incurred after Acquisition

Objective ⑦
Explain and apply the
accounting treatment
for costs incurred after
acquisition.

UNDERLYING CONCEPT

Applying the same principle both at acquisition and at a point after acquisition makes for more consistent accounting for similar events.

UNDERLYING CONCEPT

Expensing long-lived staplers, pencil sharpeners, and wastebaskets is an application of the materiality constraint.

After plant assets are installed and ready for use, additional costs are incurred for anything from ordinary servicing and repairs to periodic overhauls, significant additions, or replacement of components. The major problem is allocating these costs to the proper time periods. Is the cost expensed in the current period, or capitalized and recognized over the future periods benefiting?

Accounting standards take the position that the recognition criteria for these costs should be the same when an asset is acquired and subsequently. If future economic benefits are expected to result from an expenditure, then the cost is capitalized, assuming it can be measured reliably. For a cost after acquisition to be included as part of an asset's cost, the assumption is that there has been **an increase** in the future economic benefits, **not merely a restoration** of the asset to normal operating efficiency.

Day-to-day servicing costs and other maintenance-type expenditures do not meet the asset recognition criteria and are expensed in the period incurred. These costs tend to keep an asset in its proper working condition; they do not add significantly to the asset's future cash-generating ability.

It is not uncommon, however, for companies to expense costs below an arbitrary minimum amount even if they meet the capitalization criteria. For example, an entity may adopt a rule that expenditures below, say, $300 or $500 or even higher (depending on the size of the company) are always expensed. Although this treatment may not be correct conceptually, a cost-benefit assessment and materiality may justify it.

The distinction between a **capital expenditure** (an asset) and a **revenue expenditure** (an expense) is not always clear-cut, and **this accounting choice can have a significant effect on reported income**. If costs are capitalized as assets on the statement of financial position, the income statement is freed from immediate expense charges that would otherwise reduce the bottom line and earnings per share in that period.

WHAT DO THE NUMBERS MEAN?

REAL WORLD EMPHASIS

The "managing" of earnings has been behind many of the well-publicized accounting scandals. **WorldCom** executives accounted for billions of dollars of current operating costs as capital additions. **Adelphia Communications Corp.** aggressively deferred operating items as assets on its statement of financial position. Closer to home, **Livent** carried out similar actions in Canada. There is also the case of Toronto-based **Atlas Cold Storage Income Trust**, the second-largest cold storage firm in North America, which announced that expenditures of approximately $3.6 million were inappropriately recorded as additions to capital assets during the previous year. Atlas also adjusted the financial statements of another prior year for an additional $1.6 million of expenditures that had been recognized as assets. While management may set out intentionally to exaggerate profits and mislead investors, decisions are made daily where the distinction between whether an expenditure should be capitalized or expensed is not always clear-cut.

Generally, companies incur four major types of expenditures related to existing assets, as shown below.

MAJOR TYPES OF EXPENDITURES

Additions Increase or extension of existing assets.

Replacements, major overhauls, and inspections Substitution of a new part or component for an existing asset, and performing significant overhauls or inspections of assets, whether or not physical parts are replaced.

Rearrangement and reinstallation Movement of assets from one location to another.

Repairs Servicing expenditures that maintain assets in good operating condition.

Additions

Additions present no major accounting problems. By definition, any **addition to plant assets is capitalized** because a new asset has been acquired. Adding a wing to a hospital or an air conditioning system to an office, for example, increases the service potential of that facility. These costs are capitalized and then recognized as expenses in the future periods that benefit from the asset's use.

One problem that arises in this area is the accounting for any changes related to an existing structure as a result of the addition. Is the cost incurred to tear down an old wall to make room for an addition a cost of the addition or a disposal cost of the portion of the existing asset that is being eliminated? In theory, it is a disposal cost of a part of the existing asset. From a practical standpoint, however, if the wall is a minor portion of the cost of the original asset, most companies would keep the carrying amount of the old wall in the accounts and include the cost to tear down the wall in the cost of the addition.

Replacements, Major Overhauls, and Inspections

Replacements are substitutions of one asset or asset component for another, often resulting from a general policy to modernize or rehabilitate a building, piece of equipment, or interior of an aircraft, for example. Costs of **major overhauls**, reconditioning, or **inspections** are similar to replacements in that they recur and are often needed in order to permit continued use of an asset.

Costs such as those for the replacement of significant parts, or the periodic inspection, overhaul, or reconditioning of major assets, often meet the capitalization criteria. If so, they are, in effect, asset acquisitions. As such, the costs are capitalized and added to the asset's carrying amount. Because it is a replacement of something already incorporated in the asset's cost or of an item recognized as a separate component, the depreciated carrying amount of the original part or inspection is removed. If the original cost of the replaced part or previous overhaul is not known, it has to be estimated. The current cost of the part or overhaul can be used to help estimate the original cost of what is being replaced. Once the original cost is determined, it and the associated accumulated depreciation are both removed from the accounts.

Let's work through the examples described in Illustrations 10-12 and 10-13.

Illustration 10-12	**Situation 1—Asset Replacement** Ace Manufacturing Ltd. (AML) incurred $27,000 in costs for roofing work on its factory: $26,000 to replace the previous roof installed when the building was first built, and $1,000 to repair and replace a few shingles on the garage extension as a result of a recent storm. The factory building was constructed 15 years ago.
Asset Replacement	**Assumption (a):** The original roof was identified as a separate component of the building (Building—Roof) when it was constructed. It cost $16,000 and had been depreciated on a straight-line basis over its (estimated) 20-year life.
	Assumption (b): The original roof was not recognized as a separate component of the building and its original cost is not known. The building had been depreciated on a straight-line basis assuming a 40-year useful life. Construction costs in the area have doubled since the factory was completed 15 years ago.

In **Situation 1(a),** $26,000 of the roofing costs meets the capitalization criteria and $1,000 does not. The first entry below accounts for the $27,000 expenditure, and the second one removes the original roof's carrying amount and recognizes the associated loss.

A = L + SE	Repairs and Maintenance Expense	1,000	
−1,000 −1,000	Building—Roof (new)	26,000	
Cash flows: ↓ 27,000 outflow	Cash		27,000

A = L + SE		
-4,000 -4,000		
Cash flows: No effect		

Accumulated Depreciation—Roof (old)	12,000	
Loss on Disposal of Roof	4,000	
Building—Roof (old)		16,000
($16,000/20 years × 15 years = $12,000)		

Under **Situation 1(b)**, the exact cost and accumulated depreciation are not known, but can be estimated. If construction costs have doubled in the area since the building was acquired, a reasonable estimate of the roof's original cost might be 50% of $26,000, or $13,000. The first entry below records the $27,000 expenditure assuming the roof is not accounted for after replacement as a separate component. This is a reasonable decision if AML estimates that the new roof will not have to be replaced before the building's useful life is over. If the new roof has a useful life of only 15 years, however, then it should be recognized as a separate asset. The numbers in the second entry below are different than in 1(a) because the old roof was being depreciated over a 40-year life as part of the building.

A = L + SE		
-1,000 -1,000		
Cash flows: ↓ 27,000 outflow		

Repairs and Maintenance Expense	1,000	
Building	26,000	
Cash		27,000

A = L + SE		
-8,125 -8,125		
Cash flows: No effect		

Accumulated Depreciation	4,875	
Loss on Disposal of Roof	8,125	
Building		13,000
($13,000/40 years × 15 years = $4,875)		

Illustration 10-13
Overhaul Costs

Situation 2—Overhaul Beta Corp. (BC) maintains a fleet of specialized trucks. BC has an operating policy of taking its trucks out of service and giving them a significant overhaul after every 50,000 km of use. The overhaul is a requirement for maintaining the company's insurance coverage. When Truck #B14, acquired two years ago for $63,000, completed its first 50,000 km of service, it was taken off the road and given its first major overhaul. The overhaul cost BC $9,000. When Truck #B14's odometer reading was 92,100 km, the truck was experiencing difficulties and BC management decided to take it in for an early overhaul. This time, the servicing costs totalled $11,000. The useful life of a truck is assumed to be 300,000 km.

Assumption (a): When the truck was acquired, the cost of the benefits to be restored by the overhaul after 50,000 km was estimated to be $8,000, based on current overhaul costs. Therefore the truck was recognized at its cost of $63,000 − $8,000 = $55,000, and the overhaul service component was recognized separately at a cost of $8,000.

Assumption (b): No separate asset components were recognized initially for the truck, but one will be recognized separately when the first full overhaul is carried out.

In **Situation 2(a)**, the same approach is used for the overhaul as for the replacement of the roof in Situation 1(a). The first entry below records the $9,000 overhaul expenditure, and the second one removes the original overhaul component's cost and accumulated depreciation from the accounts. The third entry recognizes the asset cost of the overhaul at 92,100 km, and the fourth entry removes the cost of the first overhaul and its accumulated depreciation to the date of the second one. The first actual overhaul costs of $9,000 were being depreciated at a rate of $9,000 ÷ 50,000 = $0.18 per km. When the truck reached 92,100 km, it had travelled an additional 92,100 − 50,000 = 42,100 km.

First overhaul		
Truck Overhaul #B14 (1)	9,000	
Cash		9,000
Accumulated Depreciation (old)	8,000	
Truck Overhaul #B14 (old)		8,000
($8,000/50,000 km × 50,000 km = $8,000)		

A   =   L   +   SE
0   0   0
Cash flows: ↓ 9,000 outflow

A   =   L   +   SE
0   0   0
Cash flows: No effect

A   =   L   +   SE
0   0   0
Cash flows: ↓ 11,000 outflow

A   =   L   +   SE
−1,422   −1,422
Cash flows: No effect

Second overhaul		
Truck Overhaul #B14 (2)	11,000	
Cash		11,000
Accumulated Depreciation (1)	7,578	
Loss on Overhaul	1,422	
Truck Overhaul #B14 (1)		9,000
(42,100 km × $0.18/km = $7,578)		

Under **Situation 2(b)**, because no "overhaul" component was recognized separately when the truck was acquired, a representative cost and the carrying amount have to be determined for it at the time of the 50,000 km servicing. If truck service bay costs have increased 10% over the two-year period since the truck was acquired, this might imply an original cost of $9,000/1.10, or $8,182. The first entry below records the overhaul cost as a separate asset component and the second entry removes the appropriate amount from the truck's book value. We assumed that the cost of the truck, and therefore any unrecognized overhaul component, was being depreciated over the full useful life of the truck in this situation.

A   =   L   +   SE
0   0   0
Cash flows: ↓ 9,000 outflow

A   =   L   +   SE
−6,818   −6,818
Cash flows: No effect

First overhaul		
Truck Overhaul #B14 (1)	9,000	
Cash		9,000
Accumulated Depreciation	1,364	
Loss on Overhaul	6,818	
Trucks #B14 (1)		8,182
($8,182/300,000 km × 50,000 km = $1,364)		

Now recognized separately, the Truck Overhaul asset is depreciated over the next 50,000 km at a rate of $9,000/50,000 km, or $0.18 per km. When Truck #B14's odometer reads 92,100 km and it is taken out of service again, the depreciation accumulated on the overhaul service asset is $0.18 × 42,100 km, or $7,578. The two entries required for the second overhaul are exactly the same as under Situation 2(a) above. The first entry below recognizes the cost of the second overhaul and the second entry removes the old overhaul's carrying amount and recognizes a loss.

A   =   L   +   SE
0   0   0
Cash flows: ↓ 11,000 outflow

A   =   L   +   SE
−1,422   −1,422
Cash flows: No effect

Second overhaul		
Truck Overhaul #B14 (2)	11,000	
Cash		11,000
Accumulated Depreciation (1)	7,578	
Loss on Overhaul	1,422	
Truck Overhaul #B14 (1)		9,000
(42,100 km × $0.18/km = $7,578)		

When an entity uses the revaluation model or the fair value model, the basic principle for replacements and overhauls continues to apply. If the **revaluation model** is used, the cost of the "new" asset component, part, or overhaul is added to the asset's carrying amount, and the carrying amount of the replaced asset component or part is removed, with a gain or loss recognized on disposal. When the **fair value model** is applied to investment property, the property's fair value may already reflect the reduced value of the part to be replaced. This fact may not be known or it may be difficult to reasonably determine the carrying amount of the part being replaced. A practical solution, therefore, is to add the cost of the replacement part or overhaul to the asset and then reassess and adjust the asset to its fair value after the replacement.

Accounting for replacements and major overhauls or inspections, as illustrated in Situations 1 and 2 above, is required by IFRS, with the entries being a direct application of general PP&E principles. ASPE has not required such a strict application of general principles, although this may change.

For now, ASPE removes the net book value of a part and capitalizes the replacement only if the cost and accumulated depreciation of the old part are known. When the carrying amount cannot be determined, and when major overhauls or renovations are carried out, practice differs depending on the circumstances. If the asset's useful life is extended, the Accumulated Depreciation account is often debited, on the basis that the renewal is "recovering" part of the past depreciation. If the quantity or quality of the asset's service potential or productivity is increased, the cost of the improvement is usually capitalized as part of the asset's cost.

Rearrangement and Reinstallation

Rearrangement and reinstallation costs that are intended to benefit future periods are different from additions, replacements, and major overhauls. An example is the rearrangement and reinstallation of a group of machines to facilitate future production. If the original installation cost and the accumulated depreciation taken to date on it can be determined, the rearrangement and reinstallation cost could be handled as a replacement. These amounts, however, are rarely known and may be difficult to estimate. In this case, because the asset's cost at acquisition already includes installation costs, any additional costs incurred to rearrange or reinstall it are recognized as an expense of the current period.

If the amounts are material, ASPE may allow capitalization of such costs on the basis that the original cost of installation is not known, and is likely to have been depreciated to a significant extent.

UNDERLYING CONCEPT

This is an example of how the asset-liability approach to our accounting model works. If the cost is not an asset, it is an expense.

Repairs

Ordinary repairs are expenditures that are made to maintain plant assets in good operating condition. They are charged to an expense account in the period in which they are incurred, based on the argument that there is no increase in a PP&E asset. Replacing minor parts, the ongoing lubricating and adjusting of equipment, repainting, and cleaning are examples of maintenance charges that occur regularly and are treated as ordinary operating expenses.[16]

BP plc, an international integrated oil and gas giant, reported net property, plant, and equipment of U.S. $130,692 million on its December 31, 2014 statement of financial position. Illustration 10-14 includes excerpts from Note 1 to BP's financial statements that explain the acquisition costs of these assets. BP engages in oil and gas exploration and production activities, operates refineries and service stations, and provides a variety of petrochemical products. The company's financial statements are prepared under IFRS.

REAL WORLD EMPHASIS

Illustration 10-14

*Property, Plant, and Equipment
Accounting Policies—BP plc*

BP Annual Report and Accounts 2014

Notes on financial statements [excerpt]
1. Significant accounting policies

Oil and natural gas exploration, appraisal and development expenditure
Oil and natural gas exploration, appraisal and development expenditure is accounted for using the principles of the successful efforts method of accounting.

Exploration and appraisal expenditure
Geological and geophysical exploration costs are charged against income as incurred. Costs directly associated with an exploration well are initially capitalized as an intangible asset until the drilling of the well is complete and the results have been evaluated. These costs include employee remuneration, materials and fuel used, rig costs and payments made to contractors. If potentially commercial quantities of hydrocarbons are not found, the exploration well is written off as a dry hole. If hydrocarbons are found and, subject to further appraisal activity, are likely to be capable of commercial development, the costs continue to be carried as an asset.

Costs directly associated with appraisal activity, undertaken to determine the size, characteristics and commercial potential of a reservoir following the initial discovery of hydrocarbons, including the costs of appraisal wells where hydrocarbons were not found, are initially capitalized as an intangible asset. When proved reserves of oil and natural gas are determined and development is approved by management, the relevant expenditure is transferred to property, plant and equipment.

Development expenditure
Expenditure on the construction, installation and completion of infrastructure facilities such as platforms, pipelines and the drilling of development wells, including service and unsuccessful development or delineation wells, is capitalized within property, plant and equipment and is depreciated from the commencement of production as described below in the accounting policy for property, plant and equipment.

Property, plant and equipment
Property, plant and equipment is stated at cost, less accumulated depreciation and accumulated impairment losses. The initial cost of an asset comprises its purchase price or construction cost, any costs directly attributable to bringing the asset into the location and condition necessary for it to be capable of operating in the manner intended by management, the initial estimate of any decommissioning obligation, if any, and, for assets that necessarily take a substantial period of time to get ready for their intended use, finance costs. The purchase price or construction cost is the aggregate amount paid and the fair value of any other consideration given to acquire the asset. The capitalized value of a finance lease is also included within property, plant and equipment.

Expenditure on major maintenance refits or repairs comprises the cost of replacement assets or parts of assets, inspection costs and overhaul costs. Where an asset or part of an asset that was separately depreciated is replaced and it is probable that future economic benefits associated with the item will flow to the group, the expenditure is capitalized and the carrying amount of the replaced asset is derecognized. Inspection costs associated with major maintenance programmes are capitalized and amortized over the period to the next inspection. Overhaul costs for major maintenance programmes, and all other maintenance costs are expensed as incurred.

Objective **8**

Identify differences in accounting between IFRS and ASPE, and what changes are expected in the near future.

IFRS/ASPE Comparison

Comparison of IFRS and ASPE

Illustration 10-15 sets out the major differences between international accounting standards for publicly accountable enterprises and ASPE.

	IFRS—IAS 16, 20, 23, 37, and 40; IFRS 6	Accounting Standards for Private Enterprises (ASPE)—*CPA Canada Handbook,* Part II, Sections 3061, 3110, 3800, 3831, 3850, and AcG-16	References to related illustrations and select brief exercises
Scope	The costs of mineral rights and reserves, including oil, natural gas, and similar non-regenerative resources, are not covered specifically as PP&E in IAS 16. Only the costs of the exploration for and evaluation of mineral resources are addressed in IFRS 6.	The costs of mining and oil and gas properties are considered items of PP&E, with specific application guidance for the full cost method of accounting in the oil and gas industry covered in AcG-16.	N/A
	Investment property is considered an item of PP&E, but a separate IFRS—IAS 40—applies to it. Biological assets are accounted for by standards IAS 41 for agricultural assets and IAS 16 for bearer plants.	Investment property is considered an item of PP&E and Section 3061 applies.	BE10-20 Illustration 10-8 Illustration 8-27 (Chapter 8)
Recognition	Recognition criteria are incorporated in IAS 16 and used for costs both at and after initial recognition—same criteria, based on measurement reliability and probability that associated future economic benefits will flow to the entity.	Uses general recognition principle in Section 1000 based on measurability and probability of future economic benefits to be received. Less guidance is provided.	N/A
Components	Requires the parts of PP&E with relatively significant costs to be depreciated separately. There is no mention made of practicability. Practice under IAS 16 results in more componentization than under Section 3061.	Indicates that the costs of significant separable component parts are allocated to those parts when practicable, but practice has not been to carry this out to the same extent as required internationally.	BE10-2
Measurement at recognition	Initial measurement is at cost, but more detail is provided on how cost is measured.	Initial measurement is at cost.	BE10-9
	Net revenue or expense derived from an item of PP&E prior to its being in place and ready for use as intended is taken into income, on the basis that it was not needed to acquire the asset and bring it to its location and use.	Any net revenue or expense from using an item of PP&E prior to substantial completion and readiness for use is included in the asset's cost.	Illustration 10-1 BE10-3
	Capitalization of costs in the initial carrying amount stops when the item is in the location and condition necessary for it to be used as management intended, even if it has not begun to be used or is used at less than desired capacity. No initial operating losses or costs of relocation or reorganization of the asset(s) are capitalized.	Capitalization of costs at acquisition stops when the asset is substantially complete and ready for productive use, as predetermined by management with reference to productive capacity, occupancy level, passage of time, or other industry considerations. This is a more flexible approach than under IFRS.	BE10-4
	Borrowing costs directly attributable to the acquisition, construction, or development of qualifying assets are capitalized under IAS 23.	Interest costs directly attributable to the acquisition, construction, or development of items of PP&E may be capitalized if that is the accounting policy used by the entity.	Illustration 10A-6 BE10-25

(*continued*)

Illustration 10-15

IFRS versus ASPE Comparison

	The cost of legal and constructive obligations related to asset retirement is capitalized, measured under IAS 37 *Provisions, Contingent Liabilities, and Contingent Assets.* Increases in the cost of the obligation related to the production of inventory are specifically excluded.	Only the cost of legal obligations related to asset retirement is capitalized. Changes in the estimate of the cost are also capitalized in the asset.	Illustration 10-2 BE10-17
Measurement after recognition	All investment property is accounted for either under the cost model or fair value model. Each class of items of other PP&E is accounted for under the cost model or the revaluation model. Companies using the revaluation model have the choice of using the asset adjustment method or the proportionate method. Changes in fair value, above carrying amount under the cost model, are recorded via Revaluation Surplus (OCI). The cost model continues to be used to the greatest extent.	Only one model—the cost model—applies to all items of PP&E.	Illustrations 10-9, 10-10, 10-11, 10B-1, and 10B-2 BE10-18 and BE10-19
Costs incurred after acquisition	All expenditures that meet the recognition criteria for an item of PP&E are capitalized. Does not specifically refer to betterments, but does refer to replacement parts that meet the recognition criteria. These are capitalized and the replaced part's carrying amount is removed, whether originally recognized as a separate component or not. The carrying amount of the building being redeveloped would not be carried forward as part of the cost of the new asset. Major inspections or overhauls that allow the continued use of an asset are treated similarly to replacements.	Betterments are capitalized and costs that are incurred to maintain service potential are expensed. Increased service potential means increased physical output or service capacity, lower operating costs, an increase in useful life, or an increase in quality of output. For betterments and major replacements, if the cost of the previous part is known, its carrying amount is removed. If not, and depending on the circumstances, the asset account, its accumulated depreciation, or an expense could be charged with the cost. The redevelopment of rental real estate qualifies as a betterment, with the book value of the existing building included in the cost of the redeveloped property, if recoverable. Overhauls are not specifically addressed and are usually expensed when incurred.	BE10-22

Illustration 10-15

IFRS versus ASPE Comparison
(continued)

When Canadian publicly accountable entities applied IFRS for the first time, they were permitted to revalue items of PP&E to fair value at the transition date. This amount became the assets' deemed cost at that point. Many Canadian companies took advantage of this transition exemption, even though they were likely to apply the cost model going forward.

Looking Ahead

A project related to the IASB's research agenda is particularly important to many companies in Canada. It deals with the development of comprehensive accounting standards for the extractive industries, such as mining and oil and gas. The project's objective is to eventually issue a replacement standard for IFRS 6 *Exploration and Evaluation of Mineral Resources*. The project expects to cover all financial reporting issues associated with upstream extractive activities, reserves, and resources from the exploration for, discovery of, and extraction of minerals and oil and gas. The IASB issued a Discussion Paper on key issues in 2009. In October 2010, IASB staff presented to the board a summary of comments received on the Discussion Paper on extractive activities prepared for it by national standard setters from Australia, Canada, Norway, and South Africa. While the board planned to use the feedback on the Discussion Paper to help it decide whether to add the project to its active agenda, the project relating to extractive activities remained paused as of May 2015.

The IASB paused a project to update IAS 20 *Accounting for Government Grants and Disclosure of Government Assistance*. It eventually intends to update IAS 20 to improve the information provided to users of financial statements by "eliminating inconsistencies with the Framework, in particular the recognition of a deferred credit when the entity has no liability; and eliminating options that can reduce the comparability of financial statements and understate the assets controlled by an entity." However, the IASB decided to defer work on the project until further progress is made in related projects (such as work on IAS 37 *Provisions, Contingent Liabilities and Contingent Assets*).

IAS 16 was updated in June 2014 relating to accounting for *Agriculture: Bearer Plants*, effective for annual periods beginning on or after January 1, 2016. The new requirements state that bearer plants are to be accounted for similar to self-constructed property, plant, and equipment items that are not yet in the location and condition needed to operate in the way intended by management. We do not examine this area in detail in this chapter because it is quite specialized. However, Illustration 8-27 in Chapter 8, provides an overview of the accounting for biological assets under IAS 41.

SUMMARY OF LEARNING OBJECTIVES

1   Identify the business importance and characteristics of property, plant, and equipment assets and explain the recognition criteria.

Almost every enterprise invests in long-lived assets. These long-term items include both those that are physical assets—property, plant, and equipment—and those that are intangible. Long-lived assets are particularly important for manufacturing companies because they provide the company with the capacity or infrastructure to produce goods and/or provide services.

Property, plant, and equipment assets are tangible assets held for use in the production of goods and services, for rental to others, or for administrative purposes, and have a useful life of more than one accounting period. This type of asset provides an entity with its operating capacity and infrastructure, but also adds to fixed costs. For this reason, it is important that a company invest enough in PP&E to meet its potential, but not so much that it has to bear the related costs of overcapacity.

PP&E costs that provide probable future economic benefits to the entity and that can be measured reliably are recognized as assets. Asset components should be recognized separately to the extent their costs are significant and/or the related assets have different useful lives or patterns of depreciation.

2   Identify the costs to include in the measurement of property, plant, and equipment at acquisition.

Asset costs used when measuring PP&E include all necessary costs directly attributed to acquiring the asset, bringing it to its location, and making it ready for use. These include direct material, direct labour, and variable overhead costs for self-constructed PP&E assets, borrowing costs for those taking substantial time to get ready for use, and dismantling and restoration costs required as a result of the asset's acquisition. Once the asset is in place and ready for use, costs are no longer capitalized.

3   Determine asset cost when the transaction has delayed payment terms or is a lump-sum purchase, a nonmonetary exchange, or a contributed asset.

Cost means the asset's cash equivalent cost. When payment is deferred beyond normal credit terms, the excess paid over cash cost is interest. When a number of assets are acquired in a basket purchase, the cost is allocated based on the relative fair value of each. When PP&E assets are acquired and paid for by issuing the entity's shares, cost is usually determined as the fair value of the asset acquired. When acquired in an exchange of assets, cost is the fair value of the assets given up, unless the fair value of the assets received can be more reliably measured. However, if the transaction lacks commercial substance or fair values cannot be reliably determined, the assets acquired are measured at the book value of the assets given up. This amount cannot exceed the fair value of the assets acquired. Assets contributed to a company are measured at fair value and credited to Contributed Surplus if donated by a shareholder. This is rare. If contributed by government, the contribution is accounted for under the income approach whereby the amount credited flows through the income statement, usually as the asset is used by the entity.

4 Identify the costs included in specific types of property, plant, and equipment.

Land: Includes all expenditures made to acquire land and to make it ready for use. Land costs typically include the purchase price; closing costs, such as title to the land, legal fees, and registration fees; costs incurred to condition the land for its intended use, such as grading, filling, draining, and clearing; the assumption of any liens, mortgages, or encumbrances on the property; and any additional land improvements that have an indefinite life. **Buildings, including investment property:** Includes all expenditures related directly to their acquisition or construction. These costs include materials, labour, and direct overhead costs that are incurred during construction and professional fees and building permits. **Equipment:** Includes the purchase price, freight, and handling charges that are incurred; insurance on the equipment while it is in transit; the cost of special foundations if they are required; assembling and installation costs; and the costs incurred in calibrating the equipment so that it can be used as intended. **Mineral resource properties:** Four types of costs may be included in establishing the cost of mineral resource assets. These are (1) acquisition costs, (2) exploration and evaluation costs, (3) development costs, and (4) site restoration and asset retirement costs. Two main methods of accounting for oil and gas properties are the full cost method and the successful efforts method.

5 Understand and apply the cost model, and the revaluation model using the asset adjustment method.

The cost model is appropriate for all classes of PP&E, including investment property. Under this model, the assets are carried at cost less accumulated depreciation and any accumulated impairment losses.

Under IFRS, the revaluation model may be applied to any class of PP&E except investment property, provided fair value can be measured reliably. Under this model, the assets are carried at their fair value at the revaluation date less any subsequent accumulated depreciation and any subsequent accumulated impairment losses. While held, net increases in fair value are not reported in income, but are accumulated in a Revaluation Surplus (OCI) account in equity. Net losses are reported in income once the revaluation surplus has been eliminated. At the time of revaluation, under the asset adjustment method, the accumulated depreciation account is eliminated (written off against the asset itself). The asset is then adjusted to its new revalued amount.

6 Understand and apply the fair value model.

The fair value model can be applied only to investment property under IFRS, and the choice between cost and fair value must be made for all investment property reported. Under this model, all changes in fair value are recognized in net income. No depreciation is recognized.

7 Explain and apply the accounting treatment for costs incurred after acquisition.

Day-to-day servicing, repair, and maintenance costs, and costs of rearrangement and relocation, are expensed as incurred. PP&E expenditures that provide future economic benefits and whose costs can be reliably measured are capitalized. The cost of additions, replacements, and major overhauls and inspections are capitalized and the carrying amount of the replaced asset or the previous overhaul or inspection is removed from the accounts.

8 Identify differences in accounting between IFRS and ASPE, and what changes are expected in the near future.

In general, the accounting for PP&E assets is very similar under both IFRS and ASPE because the principles underlying both are very similar. However, under IFRS, practice remains closer to the principles identified. This is seen, for example, in accounting for components and major overhauls and inspections, incidental revenues and expenses before asset use, and borrowing costs. IFRS permits application of a revaluation model and a fair value model, neither of which is acceptable under ASPE. The IASB is researching activities related to the extractive industry with the objective of developing accounting standards to cover the exploration for, and the development and extraction of, minerals and oil and gas resources and assets.

KEY TERMS

additions, p. 581

asset retirement costs, p. 562

biological assets, p. 559

boot, p. 568

capital approach, p. 571

capital expenditure, p. 580

capitalized, p. 559

commercial substance, p. 567

cost, p. 560

cost model (CM), p. 574

cost reduction method, p. 571

deferral method, p. 571

depletion base, p. 574

fair value, p. 566

fair value model (FVM), p. 575

fixed assets, p. 558

income approach, p. 571

inspections, p. 581

investment property, p. 573

leasehold improvements, p. 572

lump-sum price, p. 565

major overhauls, p. 581

mineral resources, p. 573

mineral resource properties, p. 573

monetary assets, p. 566

nonmonetary assets, p. 566

non-reciprocal transfers, p. 570

ordinary repairs, p. 584

plant assets, p. 558

property, plant, and equipment, p. 558

rearrangement and reinstallation costs, p. 584

replacements, p. 581

revaluation model (RM), p. 574

revenue expenditure, p. 580

self-constructed assets, p. 561

tangible capital assets, p. 558

unit of measure, p. 559

APPENDIX 10A

CAPITALIZATION OF BORROWING COSTS

Objective 9
Calculate the amount of borrowing costs to capitalize for qualifying assets.

Chapter 10 introduces some of the issues for the capitalization of borrowing costs, underscoring the underlying principle that borrowing costs that are directly attributable to acquiring, producing, or constructing a qualifying asset are included as part of the cost of the asset. Other borrowing costs are expensed. This appendix continues the discussion in more detail and illustrates the recognition guidance in IAS 23 *Borrowing Costs*. Private enterprises that choose a policy of capitalizing interest costs for relevant PP&E assets are also likely to apply this guidance.

Borrowing costs are made up of interest and related costs that a company incurs related to the borrowing of funds. The cost of equity financing is specifically excluded. Interest and other costs include interest expense that results from applying the effective interest method, finance charges on finance leases, and exchange adjustments on foreign currency borrowings if they are viewed as adjustments to interest costs.

Four issues need to be considered in determining the amount of borrowing costs to be capitalized and how to report them:

1. Which assets qualify?

2. What is the capitalization period?

3. What are the avoidable borrowing costs—the amount eligible to capitalize?

4. What disclosures are needed?

Qualifying Assets

To qualify for inclusion in the cost of an asset, the borrowing costs must:

1. be directly attributable to acquiring, constructing, or producing a qualifying asset and

2. meet both recognition criteria—it is probable that associated future economic benefits will flow to the entity, and the cost can be measured reliably.

Qualifying assets must require **substantial time to get ready** for their intended use or sale. This may include inventories; items of property, plant, and equipment; investment properties; or intangible assets.

Borrowing costs for qualifying assets measured at fair value and inventories that are produced in large quantities on a repetitive basis **may be capitalized**, but it is not required.

Examples of assets that **do not qualify**, aside from financial assets, include (1) assets that are already in use or ready for their intended use when acquired; (2) those produced over a short period of time; and (3) assets not undergoing activities necessary to get them ready for use, such as land that is not being developed and assets that are not being used because of obsolescence, excess capacity, or needed repairs.

Capitalization Period

The **capitalization period** is the time over which interest must be capitalized. It **begins** on the **commencement date**, which is when **all three** of the following conditions are met:

1. Expenditures for the asset have been made.

2. Activities that are necessary to get the asset ready for its intended use or sale are in progress, including necessary pre-construction administrative and technical work.

3. Borrowing costs are being incurred.

Capitalization **ends** when substantially all the activities needed to prepare the asset for its intended use or sale are complete. This is usually when the physical activities associated with construction are finished, even if minor matters are still outstanding. If a project is finished in stages so that the parts completed can be used while activities continue on the remainder, capitalization stops on the parts that are substantially complete. If active development of a project is on hold, capitalization of the borrowing costs is **suspended**. Note that this does not refer to temporary delays needed as part of the development process.

Let's apply this to different situations associated with land. What if land was purchased with the intention of developing it for a particular use? If the land is purchased as a site for a structure (such as a plant site), the borrowing costs that are capitalized **during the construction period** are part of the cost of the plant, not of the land. Borrowing costs on the land while held and awaiting the start of construction are expensed. If land is being developed for sale as lots, the borrowing cost is part of the developed land's acquisition cost. However, borrowing costs involved in purchasing land that is held for speculation are not capitalized, because the asset is ready for its intended use.

Avoidable Borrowing Costs

To qualify for capitalization, the costs must be **directly attributable** to a project; in other words, they must be **avoidable borrowing costs**. When an entity borrows funds to finance a specific qualifying asset, the avoidable costs are the actual borrowing costs that would not have been incurred if the expenditures for the qualifying asset had not been made. These costs are reduced by the investment income earned on any temporary investment of these monies.

Avoidable costs are more difficult to calculate when a company's borrowings are not directly related to specific assets or projects. Some companies borrow funds using a variety of debt instruments to support their general financing requirements. In this case, the calculation is not as straightforward and professional judgement is often needed to determine which costs were avoidable.

In general, the following steps are taken to calculate the borrowing costs to capitalize:

1. Determine the expenditures on the qualifying asset.

2. Determine the avoidable borrowing costs on the asset-specific debt.

3. Determine the avoidable borrowing costs on the non–asset-specific debt.

4. Determine the borrowing costs to capitalize.

Step 1: Determine the Expenditures on the Qualifying Asset

The **expenditures on the qualifying asset** mean the **weighted-average accumulated expenditures**—the construction expenditures weighted by the amount of time (fraction of a year or accounting period) in which borrowing costs could be incurred. The expenditures include amounts paid for by cash or other asset or an interest-bearing liability, including previously capitalized borrowing costs. The expenditures are reduced by any progress payments received from a customer (in the case of construction of an inventory item) and by any grants received, such as from one or more levels of government.

To illustrate, assume a 17-month bridge construction project with current-year payments to the contractor of $240,000 on March 1, $480,000 on July 1, and $360,000 on November 1. The weighted-average accumulated expenditures for the year ended December 31 are calculated in Illustration 10A-1.

Illustration 10A-1

Calculation of Weighted-Average Accumulated Expenditures

Expenditures			Capitalization Period*		Weighted-Average Accumulated Expenditures
Date	Amount	×		=	
Mar. 1	$ 240,000		10/12		$200,000
July 1	480,000		6/12		240,000
Nov. 1	360,000		2/12		60,000
	$1,080,000				$500,000

*Months between the date of expenditure and the date when interest capitalization stops or year end arrives, whichever comes first (in this case, December 31)

The costs incurred are weighted by the amount of time that borrowing costs could have been incurred on each expenditure in the year. For the March 1 expenditure, 10 months of borrowing costs could be associated with the expenditure. For the expenditure on July 1, only 6 months of interest could have been incurred. For the November 1 expenditure, there would only be 2 months.

Step 2: Determine the Avoidable Borrowing Costs on the Asset-Specific Debt

In this example, there is no asset-specific borrowing and therefore, no asset-specific borrowing costs. If there were, remember that the borrowing costs on this debt would have to be reduced by the investment income on any temporary investment of the funds.

Step 3: Determine the Avoidable Borrowing Costs on the Non–Asset-Specific Debt

The next step entails (a) calculating an appropriate **capitalization rate** and (b) applying it to the weighted-average expenditures financed by general debt. The rate is a weighted-average borrowing rate on the general borrowings. Assume that the borrowings identified in Illustration 10A-2 were all outstanding for the full year.

Illustration 10A-2

Calculation of Capitalization Rate

	Principal	Borrowing costs[17]
12%, 2-year note	$ 600,000	$ 72,000
9%, 10-year bonds	2,000,000	180,000
7.5%, 20-year bonds	5,000,000	375,000
	$7,600,000	$627,000

Because each debt instrument was outstanding for the full year, each principal amount is already weighted by $12/12$. The interest also represents a full 12 months of borrowing costs. The weighted-average capitalization rate on the general-purpose debt is calculated as follows:

$$\frac{\text{Total borrowing costs}}{\text{Weighted-average principal outstanding}} = \frac{\$627,000}{\$7,600,000} = 8.25\%$$

The avoidable borrowing cost on non–asset-specific debt is the total weighted-average amount of accumulated expenditures (from step 1) reduced by the weighted-average expenditures financed by asset-specific debt from step 2, multiplied by the capitalization rate: ($500,000 − $0) × 8.25% = $41,250.

Step 4: Determine the Borrowing Costs to Capitalize

This step adds the eligible borrowing costs on asset-specific borrowings of $0 (step 2) and those on general borrowings of $41,250 (step 3) for a total of $41,250. This is the amount of cost to capitalize, unless the actual borrowing costs incurred in the year are less than this. The lower amount is used.

An example that incorporates both asset-specific and general borrowings is explained next.

Illustration

Assume that on November 1, 2016, Shalla Corporation contracted with Pfeifer Construction Co. Ltd. to have a building constructed for its own use for $1.4 million, on land costing $100,000. The land is acquired from the contractor and its purchase price is included in the first payment. Shalla made the following payments to the construction company during 2017:

January 1	March 1	May 1	December 31	Total
$210,000	$300,000	$540,000	$450,000	$1,500,000

Construction of the building began very early in January and it was completed and ready for occupancy on December 31, 2017. Shalla had the following debt outstanding at December 31, 2017:

Specific Construction Debt	
15%, 3-year note to finance construction of the building, dated December 31, 2016, with interest payable annually on December 31	$750,000
Other Debt	
10%, 5-year note payable, dated December 31, 2014, with interest payable annually on December 31	$550,000
12%, 10-year bonds issued December 31, 2010, with interest payable annually on December 31	$600,000

Step 1

Determine the expenditures on the qualifying asset. The weighted-average accumulated expenditures during 2017 are calculated in Illustration 10A-3.

Illustration 10A-3

Calculation of Weighted-Average Accumulated Expenditures

	Expenditures			Current Year Capitalization		Weighted-Average Accumulated
Date		Amount	×	Period	=	Expenditures
Jan. 1		$ 210,000		12/12		$210,000
Mar 1		300,000		10/12		250,000
May 1		540,000		8/12		360,000
Dec. 31		450,000		–0–		–0–
		$1,500,000				$820,000

Note that the expenditure made on December 31, the last day of the year, gets a zero weighting in the calculation. It will have no borrowing cost assigned to it.

Step 2

Determine the avoidable borrowing costs on the asset-specific debt. The asset-specific construction debt of $750,000 was outstanding for the full year and is therefore weighted for a full 12 months. Therefore, the avoidable borrowing cost on this debt is $750,000 × 15% = $112,500.

Step 3

Determine the avoidable borrowing costs on the non–asset-specific debt. Illustration 10A-4 shows the calculation of this borrowing cost. It is the weighted-average accumulated expenditures financed by general borrowings multiplied by the capitalization rate.

Illustration 10A-4

Calculation of Avoidable Borrowing Cost on General Debt

Total weighted-average accumulated expenditures	$820,000	
Less financed by specific construction loan	750,000	
Weighted-average accumulated expenditures financed by general borrowings	$ 70,000	
Capitalization rate calculation:	Principal	Borrowing Cost
10%, 5-year note: $550,000 × 12/12	$ 550,000	$ 55,000
12%, 10-year bonds: $600,000 × 12/12	600,000	72,000
	$1,150,000	$127,000

$$\text{Capitalization rate} = \frac{\text{Borrowing cost on general debt}}{\text{Weighted principal outstanding}} = \frac{\$127,000}{\$1,150,000} = 11.04\%$$

Avoidable borrowing cost on general debt: $70,000 × 11.04% = $7,728

Step 4

Determine the borrowing costs to capitalize. Use the lower of the total avoidable borrowing costs eligible for capitalization (result of 2 and 3 above) and the actual borrowing costs incurred. The calculations are shown in Illustration 10A-5.

Illustration 10A-5

Calculation of Total Avoidable and Actual Borrowing Costs

Avoidable costs on asset-specific debt		$112,500
Avoidable costs on general debt		7,728
Total avoidable borrowing costs		$120,228
Total actual borrowing costs for the period:		
Construction note	$750,000 × 0.15 =	$112,500
5-year note	$550,000 × 0.10 =	55,000
10-year bonds	$600,000 × 0.12 =	72,000
Actual borrowing costs		$239,500

The amount of borrowing costs capitalized, therefore, is $120,228.

The journal entries made by Shalla Company during 2017 are shown in Illustration 10A-6.

Jan. 1	Land	100,000	
	Buildings (or Construction in Process)	110,000	
	Cash		210,000
Mar. 1	Buildings	300,000	
	Cash		300,000
May 1	Buildings	540,000	
	Cash		540,000
Dec. 31	Buildings	450,000	
	Cash		450,000
Dec. 31	Buildings	120,228	
	Interest Expense		120,228

Illustration 10A-6

Journal Entries for Recording of Expenditures and Interest Costs

The capitalized borrowing costs of $120,228 are added to the building's acquisition cost and are amortized as part of its depreciation charge. In other words, under IFRS and ASPE, where it is the company's policy to capitalize interest costs, they will be recognized in expense over the useful life of the asset and not over the term of the debt. However, if under ASPE the company's policy is to expense all interest costs, the final journal entry above would not be recorded.

Disclosures

Only two disclosures are required for borrowing costs: the amount capitalized and the capitalization rate.

Illustration 10A-7 provides an example of BCE Inc.'s disclosures in its 2014 financial statements.

Illustration 10A-7

Disclosures Related to Borrowing Costs Capitalized

NOTE 8 INTEREST EXPENSE

FOR THE YEAR ENDED DECEMBER 31	2014	2013
Interest expense on long-term debt	(865)	(850)
Interest expense on other debt	(97)	(97)
Capitalized interest	33	16
Total interest expense	(929)	(931)

Interest expense on long-term debt includes interest on finance leases of $166 million and $174 million for 2014 and 2013, respectively.

Capitalized interest was calculated using an average rate of 4.49% and 5.03% for 2014 and 2013, respectively, which represents the weighted average interest rate on our outstanding long-term debt.

REAL WORLD EMPHASIS

SUMMARY OF LEARNING OBJECTIVE FOR APPENDIX 10A

9 Calculate the amount of borrowing costs to capitalize for qualifying assets.

The avoidable borrowing costs related to the financing of eligible expenditures on qualifying assets are capitalized

to the extent they are less than the total borrowing costs incurred in the period.

KEY TERMS

avoidable borrowing costs, p. 591
borrowing costs, p. 590
capitalization period, p. 590

capitalization rate, p. 592
qualifying assets, p. 590

weighted-average accumulated
   expenditures, p. 591

APPENDIX 10B

REVALUATION: THE PROPORTIONATE METHOD

Objective 10
Understand and apply the revaluation model using the proportionate method.

Like the asset adjustment method, when using the proportionate method, a revaluation should be carried out often enough to ensure the carrying amount reported does not become materially different from fair value. For this example, we will assume that the asset only needs to be remeasured every three years. Between revaluation dates, **depreciation is taken** on the revalued amount that has been increased proportionately. Specifically, on January 1, 2013, Convo Corporation acquires a building at a cost of $100,000. The building is expected to have a 25-year life and no residual value, resulting in depreciation of $4,000 per year for the first 3 years ($100,000/25 years = $4,000). The asset is accounted for using the proportionate revaluation method and revaluation is carried out every three years. On December 31, 2015, the fair value of the building is appraised at $90,000, and on December 31, 2018, its fair value is $75,000.

Similar to the asset adjustment method, the amounts debited or credited to the Revaluation Surplus account are reported in the statement of comprehensive income as other comprehensive income (OCI) items. Also, over the life of the asset, the effect of the treatment described is that there is no **net increase** in net income from revaluing the asset. However, when revaluing an asset, the account is adjusted proportionately.

Specifically, both the asset's carrying amount and its accumulated depreciation are adjusted (upwards if there has been an increase in fair value, or downwards for a decrease in fair value), so that the net balance is the fair value of the asset at the revaluation date. Illustration 10B-1 demonstrates the proportionate method for the building on December 31, 2015, when fair value was $90,000. The related journal entry records the differences for buildings and accumulated depreciation between the amounts before (and after) revaluation, with the overall increase being credited to revaluation surplus.

Illustration 10B-1		Before revaluation		Proportionate amount after revaluation
Proportionate Method: Illustration				
Buildings		$100,000	× 90/88	$102,273
Accumulated depreciation		12,000	× 90/88	12,273
Carrying amount		$ 88,000	× 90/88	$ 90,000

Proportionate Method: Illustration

A = L + SE	Buildings	2,273	
+2,000 +2,000	Accumulated Depreciation—Buildings		273
Cash flows: No effect	Revaluation Surplus (OCI)		2,000

Illustration 10B-2 demonstrates the calculations and journal entries for the 2016–2018 depreciation entries and the revaluation adjustment using the proportionate method for 2018 (where accumulated depreciation before revaluation is calculated as $12,273 + ($4,091 × 3) = $24,546). The second journal entry records the differences for Buildings and Accumulated Depreciation—Buildings similar to the entry in 2015. However, after the Revaluation Surplus (OCI) account is reduced to zero, the remaining loss is recognized in the income statement.

	Illustration 10B-2
Revaluation Model Using the Proportionate Method: Illustration	

Annual depreciation in each of 2016, 2017, and 2018:

Depreciation Expense	4,091	
Accumulated Depreciation—Buildings		4,091

$$\frac{(\$102{,}273 - \$12{,}273)}{22 \text{ years}} = \$4{,}091$$

A = L + SE
−4,091   −4,091

Cash flows: No effect

	Before revaluation		Proportionate amount after revaluation
Buildings	$102,273	× 75,000/77,727	$98,685
Accumulated depreciation	24,546	× 75,000/77,727	23,685
Carrying amount	$ 77,727	× 75,000/77,727	$75,000

A = L + SE
−2,727   −2,727

Cash flows: No effect

Accumulated Depreciation—Buildings	861	
Revaluation Surplus (OCI)	2,000	
Revaluation Gain or Loss	727	
Buildings		3,588

SUMMARY OF LEARNING OBJECTIVE FOR APPENDIX 10B

10 **Understand and apply the revaluation model using the proportionate method.**

The revaluation model may be applied using the proportionate method, provided fair value can be measured reliably. Similar to the asset adjustment method, the amounts debited or credited to the Revaluation Surplus (OCI) account are reported in the statement of comprehensive income as other comprehensive income (OCI) items. However, when revaluing an asset, the account is adjusted proportionately so that both the carrying amount of the asset and the accumulated depreciation are adjusted (upwards if there has been an increase in fair value, or downwards for a decrease in fair value). After adjustment, the net balance is the fair value of the asset at the revaluation date.

Note: Completion of this end-of-chapter material will help develop CPA enabling competencies (such as ethics and professionalism, problem-solving and decision-making and communication) and technical competencies. We have highlighted selected items with an integration icon and material in *WileyPLUS* has been linked to the competencies. All cases emphasize integration, especially of the enabling competencies. The brief exercises, exercises and problems generally emphasize problem-solving and decision-making.

All assignment material with an asterisk (*) relates to the appendices to the chapter.

Brief Exercises

(LO 1) BE10-1 Caruso Airlines Incorporated is a privately owned commercial airline servicing short-haul routes in Western Canada. Caruso has operated successfully and profitably for five years. It is now considering expanding its fleet of 10 aircraft by adding 15 new aircraft, in order to service its existing routes more efficiently. Caruso would pay for the expansion with a combination of internally generated funds and a new bank loan. Discuss the effects of Caruso's expansion on the company's (a) business and operations, (b) financial statements, and (c) rate of return on assets and asset turnover.

(LO 1) BE10-2 Playtime Corporation purchased a new piece of equipment for production of a new children's toy. According to market research tests, the toy is expected to be very popular among preschool-aged children. The equipment consists of the following significant and separable parts: injection unit (useful life of six years), clamping unit (useful life of six years), and electrical equipment (useful life of three years). The equipment also includes other parts (useful life of five years). Discuss (a) the recognition criteria for recording purchase of the equipment, (b) how the equipment purchase should be recorded if Playtime prepares financial statements in accordance with IFRS, and (c) how the equipment purchase should be recorded if Playtime prepares financial statements in accordance with ASPE.

(LO 2, 4, 8) BE10-3 Barnet Brothers Inc. purchased land and an old building with the intention of removing the old building and then constructing the company's new corporate headquarters on the land. The land and old building were purchased for $570,000. Closing costs were $6,000. The old building was removed at a cost of $48,000. After readying the land for its intended use, and while waiting for construction to begin, Barnet generated net revenue of $4,000 from using the land as a parking lot. Determine the amount to be recorded as the land cost, and the treatment of the net revenue of $4,000, if Barnet prepares financial statements in accordance with (a) IFRS and (b) ASPE.

(LO 2, 4, 8) BE10-4 Northern Utilities Corporation incurred the following costs in constructing a new maintenance building during the fiscal period:

(a) Direct labour costs incurred up to the point when the building is in a condition necessary for use as management intended, but before Northern begins operating in the building, $73,000

(b) Additional direct labour costs incurred before Northern begins operating in the building, $6,000

(c) Material purchased for the building, $82,500

(d) Interest on the loan to finance construction until completion, $2,300

(e) Allocation of variable plant overhead based on labour hours worked on the building, $29,000

(f) Architectural drawings for the building, $7,500

(g) Allocation of the president's salary, $54,000

What costs should be included in the cost of the new building if Northern prepares financial statements in accordance with IFRS? With ASPE? (Assume that, if there is no specific guidance from GAAP, Northern's management would consider a building ready for productive use when Northern begins operating in the building and would prefer not to capitalize interest costs directly attributable to the acquisition, construction, or development of property, plant, and equipment.)

(LO 3) BE10-5 Parolin Limited purchased equipment for an invoice price of $40,000, terms 2/10, n/30. (a) Record the purchase of the equipment and the subsequent payment, assuming the payment was made within the discount period. (b) Repeat (a), but assume the company's payment missed the discount period. (c) What would be a good policy or procedure to adopt for purchases of property, plant, and equipment where a discount is offered, and how would it work?

(LO 3) BE10-6 Chavez Corporation purchased a truck by issuing an $80,000, four-year, non–interest-bearing note to Equinox Inc. The market interest rate for obligations of this nature is 8%. Calculate the purchase price using any of the three methods (tables, financial calculator, or Excel). Prepare the journal entry to record the truck purchase.

(LO 3) BE10-7 Martin Corporation purchased a truck by issuing an $80,000, 8% note to Equinox Inc. Interest is payable annually and the note is payable in four years. Prepare the journal entry to record the truck purchase.

(LO 3) BE10-8 Hamm Inc. purchased land, a building, and equipment from Spamela Corporation for a cash payment of $406,000. The assets' estimated fair values are land $95,000, building $250,000, and equipment $110,000. At what amounts should each of the three assets be recorded?

(LO 3, 8) BE10-9 Wizard Corp., a private company, obtained land by issuing 2,000 of its common shares. The land was appraised at $85,000 by a reliable, independent valuator on the date of acquisition. Last year, Wizard sold 1,000 common shares at $41 per share. Prepare the journal entry to record the land acquisition (a) if Wizard elects to prepare financial statements in accordance with IFRS and (b) if Wizard prepares financial statements in accordance with ASPE.

(LO 3) BE10-10 Kongus Inc. traded a used truck (cost $23,000, accumulated depreciation $20,700) for another used truck with a fair value of $3,700. Kongus also paid $300 cash in the transaction. Prepare the journal entry to record the exchange, assuming the transaction lacks commercial substance.

(LO 3) BE10-11 Seymour Ltd. traded a used welding machine (cost $9,000, accumulated depreciation $2,000, fair value $3,000) for office equipment with an estimated fair value of $8,000. Seymour also paid $4,000 cash in the transaction. Prepare the journal entry to record the exchange. The equipment results in different cash flows for Seymour, compared with those the welding machine produced.

(LO 3) BE10-12 Spencer Ltd. traded a used truck (cost $30,000, accumulated depreciation $27,000, fair value $2,000) for a new truck with a fair value of $33,000. Spencer also made a cash payment of $31,000. Prepare Spencer's entry to record the exchange, and state any assumptions that you have made.

(LO 3) BE10-13 Use the information for Spencer Ltd. from BE10-12. The same used truck is being traded, but Spencer does not know the fair value of the new truck. Spencer did look up the value of its used truck and determined its fair value at the date of the trade is $2,000. The list price of the new truck is $36,000 and the trade-in allowance given on the trade was $5,000. If Spencer paid $31,000, what should be the amount used as the cost of the new truck? Prepare Spencer's entry to record the exchange.

(LO 3) BE10-14 In early January, Swanton Corp. purchased a building to house its manufacturing operations in Moose Jaw for $470,000. The company agreed to lease the land that the building stood on for $14,000 per year from the industrial park owner, and the municipality donated $140,000 to Swanton as an incentive to locate in the area and acquire the building. Prepare entries to record the cash that was exchanged in each of the transactions, assuming the cost reduction method is used.

(LO 3) BE10-15 Use the information for Swanton Corp. in BE10-14. Prepare the entries to record the three cash transactions, assuming the deferral method is used.

(LO 3) BE10-16 Dubois Inc. received equipment as a donation. The equipment has a fair value of $55,000. Prepare the journal entry to record the receipt of the equipment under each of the following assumptions:

(a) The equipment was donated by a shareholder.

(b) The equipment was donated by a retired employee.

(LO 4) BE10-17 Lowell Corporation acquires a gold mine at a cost of $400,000. Development costs that were incurred total $100,000, including $12,300 of depreciation on movable equipment to construct mine shafts. Based on construction to date, the legal obligation to restore the property after the mine is exhausted has a present value of $75,000. Lowell has publicly pledged an additional $20,000 (present value) for improved reclamation of the area surrounding the mine. Prepare the journal entries to record the cost of the natural resource if Lowell prepares financial statements in accordance with (a) IFRS and (b) ASPE. (*Hint:* Use a Mineral Resources account.)

(LO 5, 10) *BE10-18 Valued Assets Inc., a publicly listed company, has a building with an initial cost of $400,000. At December 31, 2017, the date of revaluation, accumulated depreciation amounted to $110,000. The fair value of the building, by comparing it with transactions involving similar assets, is assessed to be $330,000. Prepare the journal entries to revalue the plant under the revaluation model using (a) the asset adjustment method and (b) the proportionate method.

(LO 5, 10) *BE10-19 Use the information for Valued Assets Inc. from BE10-18. On January 5, 2018, Valued sold the building for $325,000 cash. Prepare the journal entries to record the sale of the building after having used (a) the cost model, (b) the revaluation model using the asset adjustment method, and (c) the revaluation model using the proportionate method.

(LO 6, 8) BE10-20 TrueNorth Investment Properties Inc. and its subsidiaries have provided you with a list of the properties they own:

(a) Land held by TrueNorth for undetermined future use

(b) A vacant building owned by TrueNorth and to be leased out under an operating lease

(c) Property held by a subsidiary of TrueNorth, a real estate firm, in the ordinary course of its business

(d) Property held by TrueNorth for use in the manufacturing of products

Advise TrueNorth and its subsidiaries as to the proper presentation and measurement options for the above properties under both IFRS and ASPE.

(LO 7) BE10-21 Identify whether the following costs should be treated as a capital expenditure or a revenue expenditure when they are incurred.

(a) $13,000 paid to rearrange and reinstall machinery

(b) $400 paid for a tune-up and oil change on a delivery truck

(c) $200,000 paid for an addition to a building

(d) $7,000 paid to replace a wooden floor with a concrete floor

(e) $4,000 paid for a major overhaul that extends the useful life of a truck

(f) $700,000 paid for relocating company headquarters

(g) $6,000 to replace 18 tires on a trailer

(LO 7) BE10-22 Shipper Inc. has acquired a large transport truck at a cost of $90,000 (with no breakdown of the component parts). The truck's estimated useful life is 10 years. At the end of the seventh year, the powertrain requires replacement. It is determined that it is not economical to put any more money or time into maintaining the old powertrain. The rest of the transport truck is in good working condition and is expected to last for the next 3 years. The cost of a new powertrain is $40,000. (a) Should the cost of the new powertrain be recognized as an asset or as an expense? (b) How should the transaction be measured and recorded if Shipper prepares financial statements in accordance with IFRS? (c) How should the transaction be measured and recorded if Shipper prepares financial statements in accordance with ASPE?

(LO 2, 9) *BE10-23 Brent Hill Company is constructing a building. Construction began on February 1 and was completed on December 31. Expenditures were $1.5 million on March 1, $1.2 million on June 1, and $3 million on December 31. Calculate Brent Hill's weighted-average accumulated expenditures that would be used for capitalization of borrowing costs.

(LO 2, 9) *BE10-24 Brent Hill Company (see BE10-23) borrowed $1 million on March 1 on a five-year, 12% note to help finance the building construction. In addition, the company had outstanding all year a $2-million, five-year, 13% note payable and a $3.5-million, four-year, 15% note payable. Calculate the appropriate capitalization rate on general borrowings that would be used for capitalization of borrowing costs.

(LO 2, 9) *BE10-25 Use the information for Brent Hill Company from BE10-23 and BE10-24. Calculate the company's avoidable borrowing costs assuming Brent Hill Company follows IFRS. How would your answer change if the company followed ASPE?

Exercises

(LO 1) E10-1 (Cost Elements and Asset Componentization) The following assets have been recognized as items of property, plant, and equipment:

1. Head office boardroom table and executive chairs

2. Landfill site

3. Escalator in shopping mall

4. Forklift vehicles in a manufacturing plant

5. Stand-alone training facility for pilot training, including a flight simulator and classrooms equipped with desks, whiteboards, and electronic instructional aids

6. Large passenger aircraft used in commercial flights

7. Medical office building

8. Computer equipment

Instructions

For each of the items listed:

(a) Identify what specific costs are likely to be included in the acquisition cost.

(b) Explain whether any components of this asset should be given separate recognition, and why.

(LO 2, 3) E10-2 (Purchase and Cost of Self-Constructed Assets) Wen Corp., a public company located in Manitoba, both purchases and constructs various pieces of machinery and equipment that it uses in its operations. The following items are for machinery that was purchased and a piece of equipment that was constructed during the 2017 fiscal year:

Machinery		
Cash paid for machinery, including sales tax of $7,000 and recoverable GST of $5,000	$112,000	107,000
Freight and insurance cost while in transit	2,000	2,000
Cost of moving machinery into place at factory	3,100	3,100
Wage cost for technicians to test machinery	4,000	4,000
Materials cost for testing	500	500
Insurance premium paid on the machinery for its first year of operation	1,500	—
Special plumbing fixtures required for new machinery	8,000	8,000
Repair cost on machinery incurred in first year of operations	1,300	—
Cash received from provincial government as incentive to purchase machinery	25,000	(25,000)
		$99,600
Equipment (Self-Constructed)		
Material and purchased parts (gross cost $200,000; failed to take 2% cash discount; the company uses the net method of recording purchases of material and parts)	$200,000	196,000
Imputed interest on funds used during construction (*Note:* The company has no borrowing costs but it has calculated imputed interest on its equity/share financing)	14,000	
Labour costs manufacturing the equipment	190,000	190,000
Overhead costs (fixed $20,000; variable $30,000)	50,000	30,000
Profit on self-construction	30,000	
Cost of installing equipment	4,400	4,400
		$420,000

Handwritten annotations: "not included", "operating cost", "(needed to be ready for use)", "operating cost", "gov't grant reduces cost", "$4000 discount lost (financing expense)", "only count variable", "not a real cost → $ save by making it themselves)", "what would it have cost if financed w debt instead of equity? opportunity cost"

Instructions

Prepare a schedule to (a) calculate the cost of the machinery and (b) calculate the cost of the equipment (show details of each item separately). (*Note:* If an item is not capitalized as a machinery or equipment cost, indicate how it should be reported.)

(LO 2, 3, 8) **E10-3** **(Entries for Asset Acquisition, Including Self-Construction)** The following are transactions related to Producers Limited:

1. The City of Piedmont gives the company five hectares of land as a plant site. This land's fair value is determined to be $92,000.

2. Producers issues 13,000 common shares in exchange for land and buildings. The property has been appraised at a fair value of $1,630,000, of which $407,000 has been allocated to land, $887,000 to the structure of the buildings, $220,000 to the building HVAC (heating, ventilation, air conditioning), and $116,000 to the interior coverings in the buildings (such as flooring). Producers' shares are not listed on any exchange, but a block of 100 shares was sold by a shareholder 12 months ago at $57 per share, and a block of 200 shares was sold by another shareholder 18 months ago at $33 per share.

3. No entry has been made to remove amounts for machinery constructed during the year that were charged to the accounts Inventory, Supplies, and Salaries and Wages Expense and should have been charged to plant asset accounts. The following information relates to the costs of the machinery that was constructed:

Construction materials on hand in opening inventory used	$23,000
Direct materials used in calibrating the equipment	625
Factory supplies used	980
Direct labour incurred	56,000
Additional variable overhead (over regular) caused by construction of machinery, excluding factory supplies used (charged to Inventory)	8,700
Fixed overhead rate applied to regular manufacturing operations	70% of direct labour cost
Lost revenue due to downtime during construction	45,000
Cost of similar machinery if it had been purchased from outside suppliers	125,000

Instructions

(a) Prepare journal entries on the books of Producers Limited to record these transactions. Assume that Producers Limited prepares financial statements in accordance with IFRS.

(b) Determine how your answer in (a) would change if Producers follows ASPE.

(LO 2, 3, 8) **E10-4** **(Treatment of Various Costs)** Farrey Supply Ltd. is a newly formed public corporation that incurred the following costs related to land, buildings, and machinery:

(L) Legal fees for title search		$ 520
(L) Property tax in arrears at property purchase date		4,500
(B) Architect's fees (old)		2,800
(L) Cash paid for land and dilapidated building on it		112,000
(L) Removal of old building	$20,000	
Less: Salvage	5,500	14,500
(B) Surveying before construction		370
(B) Interest on short-term loans during construction		7,400
(B) Excavation before construction for basement and foundation		19,000
(M) Machinery purchased (subject to 2% cash discount, which was not taken) $1300 discount lost = financing expense.		65,000 63,700
(M) Freight on machinery purchased		1,340
(M) Exchange on foreign currency purchase of machinery		1,200
Storage charges on machinery, made necessary because building was still under construction when machinery was delivered		2,180
(B) New building constructed (building construction took six months from date of purchase of land and old building)		485,000
(L) Assessment by city for drainage project		1,600
Fence surrounding the property for security		15,000
(M) Hauling charges for delivery of machinery from storage to new building		620
(M) Installation of machinery		2,000
(M) Customs duty on importing machinery		5,400
(B) Municipal grant to promote locating building in the municipality (reduction)		(8,000)

take hit for inefficiency → have to expense it

other → land improvements

Instructions   (L)   (B)   (M)

(a) Determine the amounts that should be included in the cost of land, buildings, and machinery. Indicate how any amounts that are not included in these accounts should be recorded.

(b) Assume that Farrey is not a public company, and that it prepares financial statements in accordance with ASPE. Would the solution provided in part (a) be affected?

(c) From the perspective of a potential investor, what are the financial statement effects of capitalizing borrowing costs related to qualifying assets?

(d) What effects, if any, will the recording of purchases to an incorrect account (land, building, machinery, or any other property, plant, and equipment asset) have on the financial statements? Provide an example.

(LO 2, 3, 9) ***E10-5** **(Asset Acquisition)** Hayes Industries Corp. purchased the following assets and also constructed a building. All this was done during the current year using a variety of financing alternatives.

Assets 1 and 2

These assets were purchased together for $100,000 cash. The following information was gathered:

Description	Initial Cost on Seller's Books	Depreciation to Date on Seller's Books	Book Value on Seller's Books	Appraised Value
Machinery	$100,000	$50,000	$50,000	$90,000
Office Equipment	60,000	10,000	50,000	30,000

Asset 3

This machine was acquired by making a $10,000 down payment and issuing a $30,000, two-year, zero-interest-bearing note. The note is to be paid off in two $15,000 instalments made at the end of the first and second years. It was determined that the asset could have been purchased outright for $35,000.

Asset 4

A truck was acquired by trading in an older truck that has the same value in use. The newer truck has options that will make it more comfortable for the driver; however, the company remains in the same economic position after the exchange as before. Facts concerning the trade-in are as follows:

Cost of truck traded	$85,000
Accumulated depreciation to date of sale	35,000
Fair market value of truck traded	60,000
Cash paid by Hayes	10,000
Fair market value of truck acquired	70,000

Asset 5

Office equipment was acquired by issuing 100 common shares. The shares are actively traded and had a closing market price a few days before the office equipment was acquired of $9.25 per share. Alternatively, the office equipment could have been purchased for a cash price of $900.

Construction of Building

A building was constructed on land that was purchased January 1 at a cost of $150,000. Construction began on February 1 and was completed November 1. The payments to the contractor were as follows:

Date	Payment
Feb. 1	$120,000
June 1	360,000
Sept. 1	480,000
Nov. 1	100,000

To finance construction of the building, a $600,000, 12% construction loan was taken out on February 1. At the beginning of the project, Hayes invested the portion of the construction loan that was not yet expended and earned investment income of $4,600. The loan was repaid on November 1 when the construction was completed. The firm had $200,000 of other outstanding debt during the year at a borrowing rate of 8% and a $350,000 loan payable outstanding at a borrowing rate of 6%.

Instructions

(a) Hayes uses a variety of alternatives to finance its acquisitions. Record the acquisition of each of these assets, assuming that Hayes prepares financial statements in accordance with IFRS.

(b) How might your answer to part (a) change regarding the "Construction of Building" item if the company followed ASPE instead of IFRS?

(c) What was the effective interest used in negotiating the note payable used to acquire the machinery in Asset 3? Use Excel or a financial calculator to arrive at your answer.

(LO 2, 4) E10-6   (Acquisition Costs of Equipment) Lavoie Corporation acquired new equipment at a cost of $100,000 plus 7% provincial sales tax and 5% GST. (GST is a recoverable tax.) The company paid $1,700 to transport the equipment to its plant. The site where the equipment was to be placed was not yet ready and Lavoie Corporation spent another $500 for one month's storage costs. When installed, $300 in labour and $200 in materials were used to adjust and calibrate the machine to the company's exact specifications. The units produced in the trial runs were subsequently sold to employees for $400. During the first two months of production, the equipment was used at only 50% of its capacity. Labour costs of $3,000 and material costs of $2,000 were incurred in this production, while the units sold generated $5,500 of sales. Lavoie paid an engineering consulting firm $11,000 for its services in recommending the specific equipment to purchase and for help during the calibration phase. Borrowing costs of $800 were incurred because of the one-month delay in installation.

Instructions

Determine the capitalized cost of the equipment and explain why the remainder of the costs have not been capitalized.

(LO 2, 4) E10-7   (Directly Attributable Costs) DAC Manufacturing Inc. is installing a new plant at its production facility. It has incurred these costs:

Cost of the manufacturing plant (cost per supplier's invoice plus non-recoverable taxes)	$2,500,000
Initial delivery and handling costs	200,000
Cost of site preparation	600,000
Consultants used for advice on the acquisition of the plant	100,000
Interest charges paid to supplier of plant for deferred credit	200,000
Estimated dismantling costs to be incurred after seven years	300,000
Operating losses before commercial production	400,000

Instructions

Determine which costs DAC Manufacturing Inc. can capitalize in accordance with IAS 16.

(LO 2, 4) E10-8   (Acquisition Costs of Realty) The following expenditures and receipts are related to land, land improvements, and buildings that were acquired for use in a business enterprise. The receipts are in parentheses.

1. Money borrowed to pay a building contractor (signed a note), ($275,000)

2. A payment for building construction from note proceeds, $275,000

3. The cost of landfill and clearing, $8,000

4. Delinquent real estate taxes on property, assumed by the purchaser, $7,000

5. A premium on a six-month insurance policy during construction, $6,000

6. Refund of one month's insurance premium because construction was completed early, ($1,000)

7. An architect's fee on a building, $22,000

8. The cost of real estate purchased as a plant site (land $200,000, building $50,000), $250,000

9. A fee paid to a real estate agency for finding the property, $9,000 relating to the land purchase (see 8)

10. The installation of fences around a property, $4,000

11. The cost of razing (demolishing) and removing the building on the plant site (see 8), $11,000

12. Proceeds from the salvage of the demolished building, ($5,000)

13. Interest paid during construction on money borrowed for construction, $13,000

14. The cost of parking lots and driveways, $19,000

15. The cost of trees that were planted (non-permanent in nature, to be replaced every 20 years), $14,000

16. Excavation costs for new building, $3,000

17. The recoverable GST on the excavation cost, $150

Instructions

Identify each item by number and list the items in columnar form, as shown below. Using the column headings that follow, write the number for each item in the first column and its amount under the column heading where it would be recorded. All receipt amounts should be reported in parentheses. For any amounts that should be entered in the Other Accounts column, also indicate the account title.

Item	Land	Land Improvements	Building	Other Accounts

(LO 2, 4) E10-9 (Acquisition Costs of Realty) Glesen Corp. purchased land with two old buildings on it as a factory site for $460,000. The property tax assessment (that is, assessed value) on this property was $350,000: $250,000 for the land and the rest for the buildings. It took six months to tear down the old buildings and construct the factory.

The company paid $50,000 to raze the old buildings and sold salvaged copper, lumber, and brick for $6,300. Legal fees of $1,850 were paid for title search and drawing up the purchase contract. Payment to an engineering firm was made for a land survey, $2,200, and for drawing the factory plans, $82,000. The land survey had to be made before final plans could be drawn. The liability insurance premium that was paid during construction was $900. The contractor's charge for construction was $3,640,000. The company paid the contractor in two instalments: $1,200,000 at the end of three months and $2,440,000 upon completion. The architects and engineers estimated the cost of the building to be 55% attributable to the structure, 35% attributable to the HVAC services (heating, ventilation, air conditioning), and the remainder attributable to the roof structure, as each of these elements is expected to have a different useful life. Interest costs of $170,000 were incurred to finance the construction.

Instructions

Determine the land and building costs as they should be recorded on the books of Glesen Corp. Assume that the land survey was for the building.

(LO 2, 4) E10-10 (Natural Resource—Copper) Copper Products Limited leases property on which copper has been discovered. The lease provides for an immediate payment of $472,000 to the lessor before drilling has begun and an annual rental of $55,000. In addition, the lessee is responsible for cleaning up the waste and debris from drilling and for the costs associated with reconditioning the land for farming when the mine is abandoned. It is estimated that the legal obligation related to cleanup and reconditioning has a present value of $46,000. Copper Products has publicly pledged an additional $30,000 (present value) to reclaim the area surrounding the mine. Copper Products prepares financial statements in accordance with IFRS.

Instructions

(a) Determine the amount that should be capitalized in the Mineral Resources asset account as a result of the lease agreement.

(b) Would the amount provided in part (a) differ if Copper Products prepared financial statements in accordance with ASPE?

FINANCE

(c) Prior to entering into the lease agreement, assume that Copper Products had total debt of $580,000 and total assets of $1,000,000. Also assume that the immediate payment of $472,000 was paid up front in cash. From the perspective of a creditor, discuss the effect of the lease agreement on Copper Products' debt to total assets ratio. Assume that Copper Products follows IFRS.

DIGGING DEEPER

(LO 3) E10-11 (Acquisition Costs of Trucks) Wu Inc. operates a retail computer store. To improve its delivery services to customers, the company purchased four new trucks on April 1, 2017. The terms of acquisition for each truck were as follows:

1. Truck #1 had a list price of $27,000 and was acquired for a cash payment of $23,900.

2. Truck #2 had a list price of $28,000 and was acquired for a down payment of $2,000 cash and a non–interest-bearing note with a face amount of $26,000. The note is due April 1, 2018. Wu would normally have to pay interest at a rate of 10% for such a borrowing, and the dealership has an incremental borrowing rate of 8%.

3. Truck #3 had a list price of $25,000. It was acquired in exchange for a computer system that Wu carries in inventory. The computer system cost $16,500 and is normally sold by Wu for $21,000. Wu uses a perpetual inventory system.

4. Truck #4 had a list price of $26,000. It was acquired in exchange for 1,000 common shares of Wu Inc. The common shares trade in an active market value at $23 per share.

Instructions

(a) Prepare the appropriate journal entries for Wu Inc. for the above transactions, assuming that Wu prepares financial statements in accordance with IFRS. If there is some uncertainty about the amount, give reasons for your choice. For Truck #2, calculate the purchase price using any of the three methods (tables, financial calculator, or Excel).

(b) Would the journal entries for transaction 4 provided in part (a) differ if Wu prepared financial statements in accordance with ASPE?

(LO 3) E10-12 (Correction of Improper Cost Entries) Plant acquisitions for selected companies are as follows:

1. Bella Industries Inc. acquired land, buildings, and equipment from a bankrupt company, Torres Co., for a lump-sum price of $700,000. At the time of purchase, Torres's assets had the following book and appraisal values:

	Book Value	Appraisal Value
Land	$200,000	$150,000
Buildings	250,000	350,000
Equipment	300,000	300,000

Bella Industries decided to take the lower of the two values for each asset it acquired. The following entry was made:

Land	150,000	
Buildings	250,000	
Equipment	300,000	
Cash		700,000

Bella Industries expects the building structure to last another 20 years; however, it expects that it will have to replace the roof in the next 5 years. Torres Co. indicated that, on initial construction of the building, the roof amounted to 20% of the cost of the building. In meetings with contractors, because of the unique design and materials required to replace the roof, the contractors stated that the roof structure is currently worth 15% of the value of the building purchase.

2. Hari Enterprises purchased store equipment by making a $2,000 cash down payment and signing a $23,000, one-year, 10% note payable. The purchase was recorded as follows:

Store Equipment	27,300	
Cash		2,000
Notes Payable		23,000
Interest Payable		2,300

3. Kim Company purchased office equipment for $20,000, terms 2/10, n/30. Because the company intended to take the discount, it made no entry until it paid for the acquisition. The entry was:

Office Equipment	20,000	
Cash		19,600
Purchase Discounts		400

4. Kaiser Inc. recently received land at zero cost from the Village of Chester as an inducement to locate its business in the village. The land's appraised value was $27,000. The company made no entry to record the land because it had no cost basis.

5. Zimmerman Company built a warehouse for $600,000. It could have contracted out and purchased the building for $740,000. The controller made the following entry:

Buildings	740,000	
Cash		600,000
Gain		140,000

Instructions

(a) Prepare the entry that should have been made at the date of each acquisition. Round to the nearest dollar.

(b) Prepare the correcting entry that is required in each case to correct the accounts. In other words, do not simply reverse the incorrect entry and replace it with the entry in part (a).

DIGGING DEEPER

(c) List the accounting principle, assumption, or constraint from the conceptual framework that has been violated in each case.

(LO 3) **E10-13 (Entries for Equipment Acquisitions)** Geddes Engineering Corporation purchased conveyor equipment with a list price of $50,000. Three independent cases that are related to the equipment follow. Assume that the equipment purchases are recorded gross.

1. Geddes paid cash for the equipment 25 days after the purchase, along with 5% GST (recoverable) and provincial sales tax of $3,500, both based on the purchase price. The vendor's credit terms were 1/10, n/30.

2. Geddes traded in equipment with a book value of $2,000 (initial cost $40,000), and paid $40,500 in cash one month after the purchase. The old equipment could have been sold for $8,000 at the date of trade, but was accepted for a trade-in allowance of $9,500 on the new equipment.

3. Geddes gave the vendor a $10,000 cash down payment and a 9% note payable with blended principal and interest payments of $20,000 each, due at the end of each of the next two years.

DIGGING DEEPER

Instructions

(a) Prepare the general journal entries that are required to record the acquisition and the subsequent payment, including any notes payable, in each of the three independent cases above. Round to the nearest dollar. For item 3, use a tables, financial calculator, or Excel.

(b) Compare the treatment of the cash discount in item 1 above with the accounting for purchase discounts for inventories using the net method in Chapter 8.

(LO 3) E10-14   (Entries for Acquisition of Assets) Information for Craig Ltd. follows:

1. On July 6, Craig acquired the plant assets of Desbury Company, which had discontinued operations. The property was appraised by a reliable, independent valuator on the date of acquisition as follows:

Land	$ 550,000
Building—structure	1,500,000
Building—HVAC	175,000
Machinery	725,000
Total	$2,950,000

Craig gave 18,000 of its common shares in exchange. The most recent sale of Craig's common shares took place last month, when 5,000 shares were sold for $170 per share.

2. Craig had the following cash expenses between July 6 and December 15, the date when it first occupied the building:

Renovations and refurbishments of building	$ 98,000
Construction of bases for machinery to be installed later	110,000
Driveways and parking lots	131,000
Remodelling of office space in building, including new partitions and walls	59,000
Special assessment by city on land	16,000

On December 20, Craig purchased machinery for $305,000, subject to a 2% cash discount, and paid freight on the machinery of $14,000. The machine was dropped while being placed in position, which resulted in paying the supplier for repairs costing $12,500. The company paid the supplier within the discount period, and records purchases of machinery using the net method.

Instructions

(a) Prepare the entries for these transactions on the books of Craig Ltd. Craig prepares financial statements in accordance with IFRS.

(b) Would the journal entries for item 1 provided in part (a) differ if Craig prepared financial statements in accordance with ASPE?

(c) Prepare the entry for the purchase and payment of the machinery in item 2, assuming the discount was not taken.

(LO 3) E10-15   (Purchase of Equipment with Non–Interest-Bearing Debt) Native Inc. decided to purchase equipment from Central Ontario Industries on January 2, 2017, to expand its production capacity to meet customers' demand for its product. Native issued a $900,000, five-year, non–interest-bearing note to Central Ontario for the new equipment when the prevailing market interest rate for obligations of this nature was 10%. The company will pay off the note in five $180,000 instalments due at the end of each year of the note's life.

Instructions

(Round to nearest dollar in all calculations.)

(a) Prepare the journal entry(ies) at the date of purchase. Calculate the purchase price using any of the three methods (tables, financial calculator, or Excel).

(b) Prepare the journal entry(ies) at the end of the first year to record the payment of principal and interest, assuming that the company uses the effective interest method.

(c) Prepare the journal entry(ies) at the end of the second year to record the payment of principal and interest.

(d) Assuming that the equipment has an eight-year life and no residual value, prepare the journal entry that is needed to record depreciation in the first year. (The straight-line method is used.)

(LO 3) †E10-16   (Purchase of Equipment with Debt) On September 1, 2017, Rupert Ltd. purchased equipment for $30,000 by signing a two-year note payable with a face value of $30,000 due on September 1, 2019. The going rate of interest for this level of risk was 8%. The company has a December 31 year end.

---

†This item was originally published by *Certified General Accountants Association of Canada* (CGA Canada), as an examination question. Adapted with permission of the Chartered Professional Accountants of Canada, Toronto, Canada. Any changes to the original material are the sole responsibility of the publisher and have not been reviewed or endorsed by the Chartered Professional Accountants of Canada.

Instructions

(a) Calculate the cost of the equipment, where necessary using any of the three methods (tables, financial calculator, or Excel), assuming the note is as follows:

1. An 8% interest-bearing note, with interest due each September 1.

2. A 2% interest-bearing note, with interest due each September 1.

3. A non–interest-bearing note.

(b) Record all journal entries from September 1, 2017, to September 1, 2019, for the three notes in (a). Ignore depreciation of the equipment.

(LO 3) E10-17 (Asset Exchange, Monetary Transaction) Cannon Ltd. purchased an electric wax melter on April 30, 2017, by trading in its old gas model and paying the balance in cash. The following data relate to the purchase:

List price of new melter	$15,800
Cash paid	10,000
Cost of old melter (five-year life, $700 residual value)	11,200
Accumulated depreciation on old melter (straight-line)	6,300
Market value of old melter in active secondary market	5,200

Instructions

Assuming that Cannon's fiscal year ends on December 31 and depreciation has been recorded through December 31, 2016, prepare the journal entry(ies) that are necessary to record this exchange. Give reasons for the accounting treatment you used.

(LO 3) E10-18 (Nonmonetary Exchange) Stacey Limited exchanged equipment that it uses in its manufacturing operations for similar equipment that is used in the operations of Chokar Limited. Stacey also paid Chokar $3,000 in cash. The following information pertains to the exchange:

	Stacey	Chokar
Equipment (cost)	$50,000	$55,000
Accumulated depreciation	31,250	22,000
Fair value of equipment	25,000	28,000

Instructions

(a) Prepare the journal entries to record the exchange on the books of both companies, assuming the exchange is determined to have commercial substance.

(b) Repeat part (a), assuming the exchange is determined not to have commercial substance.

DIGGING DEEPER

(c) List some of the factors that the accountant would need to consider in order to determine whether the transaction has commercial substance.

(LO 3) E10-19 (Nonmonetary Exchange) Carver Inc. recently replaced a piece of automatic equipment at a net price of $4,000, f.o.b. factory. The replacement was necessary because one of Carver's employees had accidentally backed his truck into Carver's original equipment and made it inoperable. Because of the accident, the equipment had no resale value to anyone and had to be scrapped. Carver's insurance policy provided for a replacement of its equipment and paid the price of the new equipment directly to the new equipment manufacturer, minus the deductible amount paid to the manufacturer by Carver. The $4,000 that Carver paid was the amount of the deductible that it has to pay on any single claim on its insurance policy. The new equipment represents the same value in use to Carver. The used equipment had originally cost $65,000. It had a book value of $45,000 at the time of the accident and a second-hand market value of $50,800 before the accident, based on recent transactions involving similar equipment. Freight and installation charges for the new equipment cost Carver an additional $1,100 cash.

Instructions

(a) Prepare the general journal entry to record the transaction to replace the equipment that was destroyed in the accident.

(b) Repeat part (a), but assume that the new equipment will result in significant savings to Carver, since the new equipment is more efficient and requires less staff time to operate.

(LO 3) E10-20 (Nonmonetary Exchange) Jamil Jonas is an accountant in public practice. Not long ago, Jamil struck a deal with his neighbour Ralph to prepare Ralph's business income tax and GST returns for 2017 in exchange for Ralph's services as a landscaper. Ralph provided labour and used his own equipment to perform landscaping services for Jamil's personal residence, for which he would normally charge $500. Jamil would usually charge $650 for the number of hours spent completing Ralph's returns but considers the transaction well worth it since he really dislikes doing his own landscaping.

Instructions

How would each party record this transaction? Prepare the journal entries for both Jamil's and Ralph's companies. Ignore any GST/HST that would apply in each transaction.

(LO 3) E10-21   (Government Assistance) Lightstone Equipment Ltd. wanted to expand into New Brunswick and was impressed by the provincial government's grant program for new industry. Once it was sure that it would qualify for the grant program, it purchased property in downtown Saint John on June 15, 2017. The property cost $235,000 and Lightstone spent the next two months gutting the building and reconstructing the two floors to meet the company's needs. The building has a useful life of 20 years and an estimated residual value of $65,000. In late August 2017, the company moved into the building and began operations. Additional information follows:

1. The property was assessed at $195,000, with $145,000 allocated to the land.

2. Architectural drawings and engineering fees related to the construction cost $18,000.

3. The company paid $17,000 to the contractor for gutting the building and $108,400 for construction. Lightstone expects that these improvements will last for the remainder of the life of the building.

4. The provincial government contributed $75,000 toward the building costs.

Instructions

(a) Assuming that the company uses the cost reduction method to account for government assistance, answer the following:

   1. What is the cost of the building on Lightstone Equipment's statement of financial position at August 31, 2017, its fiscal year end?

   2. What is the effect of this capital asset on the company's income statement for the company's year ended August 31, 2018?

(b) Assuming the company uses the deferral method to account for government assistance, answer the following:

   1. What is the cost of the building on Lightstone Equipment's statement of financial position at August 31, 2017?

   2. What is the effect of this capital asset on the company's income statement for the company's year ended August 31, 2018?

DIGGING DEEPER

(c) Compare the statement of financial position and income statement presentations for the two alternative treatments for government assistance for the fiscal year ended August 31, 2018.

(LO 4, 8) E10-22   (Biological Assets) On March 1 2017, Russell Winery Ltd. purchased a five-hectare commercial vineyard for $1,050,000. The total purchase price was based on appraised market values of the building, grapevines, and equipment ($580,000, $260,000, and $210,000, respectively). Russell Winery incurred the following cash expenditures between March 1 and June 30, the date of Russell Winery's first harvest from the grapevines:

Major repairs to sprayer equipment	$28,000
Grapevine fertilizer	7,000
Phase 1 construction of a new grape trellis system for the grapevines	31,000
Construction of a new custom wine cellar	62,000
Harvesting labour	36,000

The fair value of the grapevines was estimated to have increased to $295,000 by December 31, 2017, the company's fiscal year end, and any sale of vineyard assets would attract a 4% realtor commission. Russell Winery prepares financial statements in accordance with IFRS.

Instructions

(a) What is the carrying amount of the grapevines on the statement of financial position at December 31, 2017? If there are differing accounting treatments of the items involved, discuss the options.

(b) In 2018, Russell Winery incurs $17,000 in costs related to Phase 2 construction of the new grape trellis system for the grapevines, and the fair value of the grapevines increases to $330,000 by December 31, 2018. What is the carrying amount of the grapevines on the statement of financial position at December 31, 2018?

(c) Would the carrying amount of the grapevines provided in part (a) differ if Russell Winery prepared financial statements in accordance with ASPE?

(LO 5, 6) E10-23   (Measurement after Acquisition—Fair Value Model versus Cost Model) Plaza Holdings Inc., a publicly listed company in Canada, ventured into construction of a mega–shopping mall in Edmonton, which is rated as the largest shopping mall in North America. The company's board of directors, after much market research, decided that instead of selling the shopping mall to a local investor who had approached them several times with excellent offers that he steadily increased during the year of construction, the company would hold this property for the purposes of capital appreciation and earning rental income from mall tenants. Plaza Holdings retained the services of a real estate company to find and attract many important retailers to rent space in the shopping mall, and within months of completion at the end of 2017, the shopping mall was fully occupied.

According to the company's accounting department, the total construction cost of the shopping mall was $50 million. The company used an independent appraiser to determine the mall's fair value annually. According to the appraisal, the fair values of the shopping mall at December 31, 2017, and at each subsequent year end were:

2017	$50 million
2018	$60 million
2019	$63 million
2020	$58 million

The independent appraiser felt that the useful life of the shopping mall was 20 years and its residual value was $10 million.

Instructions

Describe the impact on the company's income statement and prepare the necessary journal entries for 2018, 2019, and 2020 if it decides to treat the shopping mall as an investment property under IAS 40:

(a) Using the fair value model.

(b) Using the cost model.

Note that the mall's rental income and expenses would be the same under both options, and thus can be omitted from the analysis for this exercise.

(LO 5, 6) E10-24 (Measurement after Acquisition—Fair Value Model) Nevine Corporation owns and manages a small 10-store shopping centre and classifies the shopping centre as an investment property. Nevine has a May 31 year end and initially recognized the property at its acquisition cost of $10.8 million on June 2, 2016. The acquisition cost consisted of the purchase price of $10 million, costs to survey and transfer the property of $500,000, and legal fees for the acquisition of the property of $300,000. Nevine determines that approximately 25% of the shopping centre's value is attributable to the land, with the remainder attributable to the building. The following fair values are determined:

Date	Fair Value
May 31, 2017	$10,500,000
May 31, 2018	$10,300,000
May 31, 2019	$11,000,000

Nevine expects the shopping centre building to have a 35-year useful life and a residual value of $1.1 million. Nevine uses the straight-line method for depreciation.

Instructions

(a) Assume that Nevine decides to apply the cost model. What journal entries, if any, are required each year, and how will the investment property be reported on each year-end statement of financial position?

(b) Assume that Nevine decides to apply the fair value model. Prepare the journal entries, if any, required at each year end. In addition, explain how the property would be reported if Nevine prepared a statement of financial position shortly after acquisition in 2016.

(LO 5, 10) *E10-25 (Measurement after Acquisition—Revaluation Model) A partial statement of financial position of Bluewater Ltd. on December 31, 2016, showed the following property, plant, and equipment assets accounted for under the cost model (accumulated depreciation includes depreciation for 2016):

Buildings	$350,000	
Less: accumulated depreciation	50,000	$300,000
Equipment	$120,000	
Less: accumulated depreciation	40,000	80,000

Bluewater uses straight-line depreciation for its building (remaining useful life of 20 years, no residual value) and for its equipment (remaining useful life of 8 years, no residual value). Bluewater applies IFRS and has decided to adopt the revaluation model for its building and equipment, effective December 31, 2016. On this date, an independent appraiser assessed the fair value of the building to be $275,000 and that of the equipment to be $90,000.

Instructions

(a) Prepare the necessary general journal entry(ies), if any, to revalue the building and the equipment as at December 31, 2016, using the asset adjustment method.

(b) Prepare the entries to record depreciation expense for the year ended December 31, 2017.

(c) Repeat parts (a) and (b) using the proportionate method to revalue the building and the equipment.

(LO 5, 10) ***E10-26** **(Measurement after Acquisition—Revaluation Model)** On January 1, 2017, Algo Ltd. acquires a building at a cost of $230,000. The building is expected to have a 20-year life and no residual value. The asset is accounted for under the revaluation model, using the asset adjustment method. Revaluations are carried out every three years. On December 31, 2019, the fair value of the building is appraised at $205,000, and on December 31, 2022, its fair value is $150,000. Algo Ltd. applies IFRS.

Instructions

(Round to the nearest dollar in all calculations.)

(a) Prepare the journal entry(ies) required on December 31, 2017.

(b) Prepare the journal entry(ies) required on December 31, 2018.

(c) Prepare the journal entry(ies) required on December 31, 2019.

(d) Prepare the journal entry(ies) required on December 31, 2020.

(e) Prepare the journal entry(ies) required on December 31, 2021.

(f) Prepare the journal entry(ies) required on December 31, 2022.

*(g) Prepare the journal entry required on December 31, 2019, and the journal entry required on December 31, 2022, to revalue the building, if Algo uses the proportionate method.

*(h) Prepare a continuity schedule showing the amounts recorded to the Buildings account and to the Accumulated Depreciation account, as well as indicating the carrying amount for each fiscal year from date of purchase to December 31, 2022, using (1) the asset adjustment method and (2) the proportionate method. Show the carrying amount under each method at the end of each fiscal year.

DIGGING DEEPER

(i) From the perspective of an investor in Algo, discuss the financial statement effects of using the revaluation model to determine the carrying amount of Algo's building.

(LO 7) **†E10-27** **(Analysis of Subsequent Expenditures)** On January 1, 2017, the accounting records of Sasseville Ltée included a debit balance of $15 million in the building account and of $12 million in the related accumulated depreciation account. The building was purchased in January 1977 for $15 million, and was estimated to have a 50-year useful life with no residual value. Sasseville uses the straight-line depreciation method for all of its property, plant, and equipment. During 2017, the following expenditures relating to the building were made:

1. The original roof of the building was removed and replaced with a new roof. The old roof cost $1 million. The new roof cost $2.5 million and is expected to have a 15-year useful life.

2. The ongoing frequent repairs on the building during the year cost $57,000.

3. The building's old heating system was replaced with a new one. The new HVAC cost $700,000 and is estimated to have a seven-year useful life and no residual value. The cost of the old HVAC is unknown, but is estimated to be $200,000 and fully depreciated.

4. A natural gas explosion caused $44,000 of uninsured damage to the building. This major repair did not change the estimated useful life of the building or its residual value.

Instructions

Prepare the journal entries to record the expenditures related to the building during 2017.

(LO 7) **E10-28** **(Analysis of Subsequent Expenditures)** The following transactions occurred during 2017. Assume that depreciation of 10% per year is charged on all machinery and 5% per year on buildings, on a straight-line basis, with no estimated residual value. Assume also that depreciation is charged for a full year on all fixed assets that are acquired during the year, and that no depreciation is charged on fixed assets that are disposed of during the year.

Jan. 30   A building that cost $132,000 in 2000 was torn down to make room for a new building structure. The wrecking contractor was paid $5,100 and was permitted to keep all materials salvaged.

Mar. 10   A new part costing $2,900 was purchased and added to a machine that was purchased in 2015 for $16,000. The new part replaces an original machine part, and does not extend the machine's useful life. The old part's cost was not separable from the original machine's cost.

Mar. 20   A gear broke on a machine that cost $9,000 in 2012, and the gear was replaced at a cost of $185. The replacement does not extend the machine's useful life.

May 18   A special base that was installed for a machine in 2011 when the machine was purchased had to be replaced at a cost of $5,500 because of defective workmanship on the original base. The cost of the machinery was $14,200 in 2011. The cost of the base was $3,500, and this amount was charged to the Machinery account in 2011.

June 23   One of the buildings was repainted at a cost of $6,900. It had not been painted since it was constructed in 2013.

---

†This item was originally published by *Certified General Accountants Association of Canada* (CGA Canada), as an examination question. Adapted with permission of the Chartered Professional Accountants of Canada, Toronto, Canada. Any changes to the original material are the sole responsibility of the publisher and have not been reviewed or endorsed by the Chartered Professional Accountants of Canada.

Instructions

(a) Prepare general journal entries for the transactions. (Round to nearest dollar.)

(b) Assume that the gear replacement purchased on March 20 extends the machine's useful life. How would your journal entry change?

(LO 7) **E10-29** **(Analysis of Subsequent Expenditures)** Plant assets often require expenditures subsequent to acquisition. It is important that they be accounted for properly. Any errors will affect both the statements of financial position and income statements for several years.

Instructions

For each of the following items, indicate whether the expenditure should be capitalized (C) or expensed (E) in the period when it was incurred:

(a) _____ A betterment

(b) _____ Replacement of a minor broken part on a machine

(c) _____ An expenditure that increases an existing asset's useful life

(d) _____ An expenditure that increases the efficiency and effectiveness of a productive asset but does not increase its residual value

(e) _____ An expenditure that increases the efficiency and effectiveness of a productive asset and its residual value

(f) _____ An expenditure that increases a productive asset's output quality

(g) _____ An overhaul to a machine that increases its fair market value and its production capacity by 30% without extending the machine's useful life

(h) _____ Ordinary repairs

(i) _____ A major overhaul

(j) _____ Interest on borrowing that is necessary to finance a major overhaul of machinery that extends its life

(k) _____ An expenditure that results in a 10%-per-year production cost saving

(l) _____ Costs of a major overhaul that brings the asset's condition back to "new," with no change in the estimated useful life

(LO 2, 9) ***E10-30** **(Capitalization of Borrowing Costs)** On December 31, 2016, Omega Inc., a public company, borrowed $3 million at 12% payable annually to finance the construction of a new building. In 2017, the company made the following expenditures related to this building structure (unless otherwise noted): March 1, $360,000; June 1, $600,000; July 1, $1.5 million (of which $400,000 was for the roof); December 1, $1.5 million (of which $700,000 was for the building HVAC).

Additional information follows:

1. Other debt outstanding:

$4-million, 10-year, 13% bond, dated December 31, 2010, with interest payable annually

$1.6-million, six-year, 10% note, dated December 31, 2014, with interest payable annually

2. The March 1, 2017 expenditure included land costs of $150,000.

3. Interest revenue earned in 2017 on the unused idle construction loan amounted to $49,000.

Instructions

(a) Determine the interest amount that could be capitalized in 2017 in relation to the building construction.

(b) Prepare the journal entry to record the capitalization of borrowing costs and the recognition of interest expense, if any, at December 31, 2017.

(LO 2, 9) ***E10-31** **(Capitalization of Borrowing Costs)** The following three situations involve the capitalization of borrowing costs for public companies following IFRS.

Situation 1

On January 1, 2017, Oksana Inc. signed a fixed-price contract to have Builder Associates construct a major head office facility at a cost of $4 million. It was estimated that it would take three years to complete the project. Also on January 1, 2017, to finance the construction cost, Oksana borrowed $4 million that is repayable in 10 annual instalments of $400,000, plus interest at the rate of 10%. During 2017, Oksana made deposit and progress payments totalling $1.5 million under the contract; the weighted-average amount of accumulated expenditures was $800,000 for the year. The excess amount of borrowed funds was invested in short-term securities, from which Oksana realized investment income of $25,000.

Situation 2

During 2017, Midori Ito Corporation constructed and manufactured certain assets and incurred the following borrowing costs in connection with these activities:

Borrowing Costs Incurred	
Warehouse constructed for Midori Ito's own use	$30,000
Special-order machine for sale to unrelated customer, produced according to customer's specifications	9,000
Inventories routinely manufactured, produced on a repetitive basis, that require many months to complete	8,000

Situation 3

Fleming, Inc. has a fiscal year ending April 30. On May 1, 2017, Fleming borrowed $10 million at 11% to finance construction of its own building. Repayments of the loan are to begin the month after the building's completion. During the year ended April 30, 2018, expenditures for the partially completed structure totalled $7 million. These expenditures were incurred evenly throughout the year. Interest that was earned on the part of the loan that was not expended amounted to $450,000 for the year.

Instructions

(a) For situation 1, what amount should Oksana report as capitalized borrowing costs at December 31, 2017?

(b) For situation 2, assuming the effect of capitalization of borrowing costs is material, what is the total amount of borrowing costs to be capitalized?

(c) For situation 3, how much should be shown as capitalized borrowing costs on Fleming's financial statements at April 30, 2018?

(Adapted from CPA.)

(LO 2, 9) *E10-32 (Capitalization of Borrowing Costs) In early February 2017, Huey Corp. began construction of an addition to its head office building that is expected to take 18 months to complete. The following 2017 expenditures relate to the addition:

Feb. 1	Payment #1 to contractor	$120,000
Mar. 1	Payment to architect	24,000
July 1	Payment #2 to contractor	60,000
Dec. 1	Payment #3 to contractor	180,000
Dec. 31	Asset carrying amount	$384,000

On February 1, Huey issued a $100,000, three-year note payable at a rate of 12% to finance most of the initial payment to the contractor. No other asset-specific debt was entered into. Details of other interest-bearing debt during the period are provided in the table below:

Other Debt Instruments Outstanding—2017	Principal Amount
9%, 15-year bonds, issued May 1, 2002, matured May 1, 2017	$300,000
7%, 10-year bonds, issued June 15, 2011	$500,000
6%, 12-year bonds, issued May 1, 2017	$300,000

Instructions

What amount of interest should be capitalized for the fiscal year ending December 31, 2017, according to IAS 23?

Problems

P10-1   Air Canada's December 31, 2014 Consolidated Statement of Financial Position lists property and equipment at $6 billion and total assets of $10.6 billion.

Air Canada's Note 4 to the financial statements titled Property and Equipment provides a schedule of the transactions that have occurred during the year in four major categories. One category is dedicated to Aircraft and Flight Equipment. Another category is titled Purchase Deposits and Assets under Development (PDAD). Under the latter category, sources of increases are additions and sources of decreases are reclassifications to Aircraft and Flight Equipment. No depreciation is recorded for this category of Property and Equipment. The balance in PDAD at December 31, 2014, was $487 million. In Note 4, more details are provided, including a statement that Aircraft and Flight Equipment includes spare engines. As well, the following is revealed: "Interest capitalized during 2014 amounted to $30 million at an interest rate of 5.29% and is included in PDAD." Although not specifically stated, the purchase deposits are likely for the future deliveries of aircraft and related equipment.

Air Canada's significant accounting policies are provided in Note 2 to the financial statements. Note 2S states that spare parts, other than rotables, are included in inventory. Rotables are components that can be repeatedly and economically restored to a fully serviceable condition. In the case of Air Canada, spare engines are rotables. Strict regulations require that engines be used a limited number of flight hours before they must be removed from the aircraft and completely overhauled regardless of their condition. This explains the need for spare engines that are ready for quick replacement, making the aircraft available at all times.

Instructions

(a) For each of the following, provide an argument as to why Air Canada has classified the item under Property and Equipment:

1. Capitalized interest

2. Spare engines

3. Purchase deposits

(b) Why does Air Canada not record depreciation on Purchase Deposits and Assets under Development?

(c) Discuss the rationale for not recording depreciation throughout the useful life of spare engines.

DIGGING DEEPER

(d) If Air Canada were not a public company following IFRS, and instead followed ASPE, would there be any difference in the way it would account for the three items discussed in part (a)?

P10-2 Adamski Corporation manufactures ballet shoes and is experiencing a period of sustained growth. In an effort to expand its production capacity to meet the increased demand for its product, the company recently made several acquisitions of plant and equipment. Tanya Mullinger, newly hired with the title Capital Asset Accountant, requested that Walter Kaster, Adamski's controller, review the following transactions:

Transaction 1

On June 1, 2017, Adamski purchased equipment from Venghaus Corporation. Adamski issued a $20,000, four-year, non–interest-bearing note to Venghaus for the new equipment. Adamski will pay off the note in four equal instalments due at the end of each of the next four years. At the transaction date, the prevailing market interest rate for obligations of this nature was 10%. Freight costs of $425 and installation costs of $500 were incurred in completing this transaction. The new equipment qualifies for a $2,000 government grant.

Transaction 2

On December 1, 2017, Adamski purchased several assets of Haukap Shoes Inc., a small shoe manufacturer whose owner was retiring. The purchase amounted to $210,000 and included the assets in the following list. Adamski engaged the services of Tennyson Appraisal Inc., an independent appraiser, to determine the assets' fair values, which are also provided.

	Haukap Book Value	Fair Value
Inventory	$ 60,000	$ 50,000
Land	40,000	80,000
Building	70,000	120,000
	$170,000	$250,000

During its fiscal year ended May 31, 2018, Adamski incurred $8,000 of interest expense in connection with the financing of these assets.

Transaction 3

On March 1, 2018, Adamski traded in four units of specialized equipment and paid an additional $25,000 cash for a technologically up-to-date machine that should do the same job as the other machines, but much more efficiently and profitably. The equipment that was traded in had a combined carrying amount of $35,000, as Adamski had recorded $45,000 of accumulated depreciation against these assets. Adamski's controller and the sales manager of the supplier company agreed that the new equipment had a fair value of $64,000.

Instructions

(a) Tangible capital assets such as land, buildings, and equipment receive special accounting treatment. Describe the major characteristics of these assets that differentiate them from other types of assets.

(b) For each of the three transactions described above, determine the value at which Adamski Corporation should record the acquired assets. Support your calculations with an explanation of the underlying rationale. For any measurement involving present value concepts, provide your calculations using any of the following: tables, Excel, or a financial calculator.

(c) The books of Adamski Corporation show the following additional transactions for the fiscal year ended May 31, 2018:

1. Acquisition of a building for speculative purposes

2. Purchase of a two-year insurance policy covering plant equipment

3. Purchase of the rights for the exclusive use of a process used in the manufacture of ballet shoes

For each of these transactions, indicate whether the asset should be classified as an item of property, plant, and equipment. If it should be, explain why. If it should not be, explain why not, and identify the proper classification.

(Adapted from CMA.)

P10-3 At December 31, 2016, certain accounts included in the property, plant, and equipment section of Golden Corporation's statement of financial position had the following balances:

Land	$310,000
Buildings—Structure	883,000
Leasehold Improvements	705,000
Equipment	845,000

During 2017, the following transactions occurred:

1. Land site No. 621 was acquired for $800,000 plus a fee of $7,000 to the real estate agent for finding the property. Costs of $33,500 were incurred to clear the land. In clearing the land, topsoil and gravel were recovered and sold for $11,000.

2. Land site No. 622, which had a building on it, was acquired for $560,000. The closing statement indicated that the land's assessed tax value was $309,000 and the building's value was $102,000. Shortly after acquisition, the building was demolished at a cost of $28,000. A new building was constructed for $340,000 plus the following costs:

Excavation fees	$38,000
Architectural design fees	15,000
Building permit fee	2,500
"Green roof" design and construction (to be retrofitted every seven years)	36,000
Imputed interest on funds used during construction (share financing)	8,500

The building, completed and occupied on September 30, 2017, is expected to have a 30-year useful life.

3. A third tract of land (No. 623) was acquired for $265,000 and was put on the market for resale.

4. During December 2017, costs of $89,000 were incurred to improve leased office space. The related lease will terminate on December 31, 2019, and is not expected to be renewed.

5. A group of new machines was purchased under a royalty agreement. The terms of the agreement require Golden Corporation to pay royalties based on the units of production for the machines. The machines' invoice price was $111,000, freight costs were $3,300, installation costs were $3,600, and royalty payments for 2017 were $15,300.

Instructions

(a) Prepare a detailed analysis of the changes in each of the following statement of financial position accounts for 2017: Land, Leasehold Improvements, Buildings—Structure, Buildings—Roof, and Equipment. Ignore the related Accumulated Depreciation accounts.

(b) List the items in the situation that were not used to determine the answer to part (a) above, and indicate where, or if, these items should be included in Golden's financial statements.

DIGGING
DEEPER

(c) Using the terminology from the conceptual framework in Chapter 2, explain why the items in part (b) were not included in the accounts Land, Leasehold Improvements, Buildings (the Structure and Roof accounts), and Equipment.

(Adapted from AICPA.)

P10-4 Webb Corporation prepares financial statements in accordance with IFRS. Selected accounts included in the property, plant, and equipment section of the company's statement of financial position at December 31, 2016, had the following balances:

Land	$ 300,000
Land Improvements	140,000
Buildings	1,100,000
Equipment	960,000

During 2017, the following transactions occurred:

1. A tract of land was acquired for $150,000 as a potential future building site.

2. A plant facility consisting of land and a building was acquired from Knorman Corp. for use in production in exchange for 20,000 of Webb's common shares. The most recent sale of Webb's common shares took place last month, when 4,000 of Webb's common shares sold for $57 per share. The plant facility was carried on Knorman's books at $110,000 for land and $320,000 for the building at the exchange date. At the exchange date, a reliable, independent valuator determined the fair value of the land and building to be $230,000 and $690,000, respectively.

3. Equipment was purchased for a total cost of $400,000. Additional costs incurred were as follows:

Freight and unloading	$13,000
Provincial sales taxes	28,000
GST (recoverable)	20,000
Installation	26,000

4. Expenditures totalling $95,000 were made for new parking lots, streets, and sidewalks at the corporation's various plant locations. These expenditures had an estimated useful life of 15 years.

5. A piece of equipment that cost $80,000 on January 1, 2009, was scrapped on June 30, 2017. Double-declining-balance depreciation had been recorded based on a 10-year life.

6. A piece of equipment was sold for $20,000 on July 1, 2017. Its original cost was $44,000 on January 1, 2014, and it was depreciated on the straight-line basis over an estimated useful life of seven years, assuming a residual value of $2,000.

Instructions

(a) Prepare a detailed analysis of the changes in each of the following statement of financial position accounts for 2017: Land, Land Improvements, Buildings, and Machinery and Equipment. (*Hint:* Ignore the related accumulated depreciation accounts.)

DIGGING DEEPER

(b) List the items in the transactions above that were not used to determine the answer to (a), and show the relevant amounts and supporting calculations in good form for each item. In addition, indicate where, or if, these items should be included in Webb's financial statements.

(c) How will the land in item 1 be accounted for when it is used as a building site?

(Adapted from AICPA.)

P10-5 Kiev Corp. was incorporated on January 2, 2017, but was unable to begin manufacturing activities until July 1, 2017, because new factory facilities were not completed until that date. The Land and Building account at December 31, 2017, contained the following entries and balance:

2017			
Jan.	31	Land and building	$166,000
Feb.	28	Cost of removal of building	9,800
May	1	Partial payment of new construction	60,000
	1	Legal fees paid	3,770
June	1	Second payment on new construction	40,000
	1	Insurance premium	2,280
	1	Special tax assessment	4,000
	30	General expenses	36,300
July	1	Final payment on new construction	10,000
	1	Payment for HVAC (furnace, air conditioning system)	30,000
Dec. 31		Asset write-up to market value	43,800
			405,950
	31	Depreciation for 2017 at 1%	4,060
	Account balance		$401,890

The following additional information needs to be considered:

1. To acquire land and a building, the company paid $110,400 cash and 800 of its $5 cumulative preferred shares. The fair value of each share was estimated at $98 per share; however, Kiev's shares are not actively traded. The land and building were assessed by an independent, reliable valuator to have a combined fair value of $166,000.

2. The costs for removing the building amounted to $9,800, and the demolition company kept all the salvaged building materials.

3. Legal fees covered the following:

Land title search before purchase	$1,300
Legal work in connection with construction contract	2,470
	$3,770

4. The insurance premium covered the building for a two-year term beginning May 1, 2017.

5. The special tax assessment by the municipality covered street improvements that are permanent in nature.

6. General expenses covered the following for the period from January 2, 2017, to June 30, 2017:

President's salary during construction	$32,100
Plant superintendent's wages covering supervision of new building	4,200
	$36,300

7. Because of a general increase in construction costs after entering into the building contract, the board of directors increased the building's value by $43,800. It believed that such an increase was justified to reflect the current market at the time when the building was completed. Retained Earnings was credited for this amount.

8. The estimated life of the building structure is 50 years. The depreciation for 2017 on the building structure was 1% of the asset value (1% of $405,950, or $4,060). The estimated useful life of the building services (heating system, plumbing, air conditioning) is 20 years. No depreciation has been recorded on the building services. Kiev expects no residual value at the end of the useful life of these assets.

Instructions

Prepare the entries to reallocate the proper balances into the Land, Buildings, and Accumulated Depreciation accounts at December 31, 2017.

(Adapted from AICPA.)

P10-6   On June 28, 2017, in relocating to a new town, Kerr Corp. purchased a property consisting of two hectares of land and an unused building for $225,000 plus property taxes in arrears of $4,500. The company paid a real estate broker a fee of $12,000 for finding the property and legal fees on the purchase transaction of $6,000. The closing statement indicated that the assessed values for property tax purposes were $175,000 for the land and $35,000 for the building. Shortly after acquisition, the building was demolished at a cost of $24,000.

Kerr Corp. then entered into a $1.3-million fixed-price contract with Maliseet Builders Inc. on August 1, 2017, for the construction of an office building on this site. The building was completed and occupied on April 29, 2018, as was a separate maintenance building that was constructed by Kerr's employees. Additional costs related to the property included:

Plans, specifications, and blueprints	$25,000
Architects' fees for design and supervision	82,000
Landscaping	42,000
Extras on contract for upgrading of windows	46,000
External signage on the property	23,000
Advertisements in newspaper and on television announcing opening of the building	10,600
Gala opening party for customers, suppliers, and friends of Kerr	18,800
Costs of internal direct labour and materials for maintenance building	67,000
Allocated variable plant overhead based on direct labour hours worked on maintenance building	10,000
Allocated cost of executive time spent on project	54,000
Interest costs on debt incurred to pay contractor's progress billings up to building completion	63,000
Interest costs on short-term loan to finance maintenance building costs	3,200

As an incentive for Kerr to locate and build in the town, the municipality agreed not to charge its normal building permit fees of approximately $36,000. This amount was included in the $1.3-million contract fee. The building and the maintenance building are estimated to have a 40-year life from their dates of completion and will be depreciated using the straight-line method with no residual value.

Kerr is a private company with an April 30 year end, and the company accountant is currently analyzing the new Buildings account that was set up to capture all the expenditures and credits explained above that relate to the property.

Instructions

(a) Prepare a schedule that identifies the costs that would be capitalized and included in the new Buildings account on the April 30, 2018 statement of financial position, assuming the accountant wants to comply with ASPE but tends to be very conservative in nature; in other words, she does not want to overstate income or assets. Briefly justify your calculations. How would your answer change if Kerr were to comply with IFRS?

(b) Prepare a schedule that identifies the costs that would be capitalized and included in the new Buildings account on the April 30, 2018 statement of financial position, assuming the accountant wants to comply with ASPE, but is aware that Kerr needs to report increased income to support a requested increase in its bank loan next month. Briefly justify your calculations.

(c) Comment on the difference in results for (a) and (b) above. Calculate the total expenses related to the building under both scenarios. What else should be considered in determining the amount to be capitalized?

P10-7   Vidi Corporation, a private enterprise, made the following purchases related to its property, plant, and equipment during its fiscal year ended December 31, 2017. The company uses the straight-line method of depreciation for all its capital assets.

1. In early January, Vidi issued 140,000 common shares in exchange for property consisting of land and a warehouse. On the date of acquisition, a reliable, independent appraiser estimated that the fair value of the land and warehouse was $600,000 and $300,000, respectively. The seller had advertised a price of $860,000 or best offer for the land and warehouse in a commercial retail magazine. Vidi paid a local real estate broker a finder's fee of $35,000. The most recent sale of Vidi's shares took place a month prior when 15,000 common shares were sold for $9 per share.

2. On March 31, the company acquired equipment on credit. The terms were a $7,000 cash down payment plus payments of $5,000 on March 31 for each of the next two years. The implicit interest rate was 12%. The equipment's list price was $17,000. Additional costs that were incurred to install the equipment included $1,000 to tear down and replace a wall and $1,500 to rearrange existing equipment to make room for the new equipment. An additional $500 was spent to repair the equipment after it was dropped during installation.

During the year, the following events also occurred:

3. A new motor was purchased for $50,000 for a large grinding machine (original cost of the machine, $350,000; accumulated depreciation at the replacement date, $100,000). The motor will not improve the quality or quantity of production; however, it will extend the grinding machine's useful life from the current 8 years to 10 years (ignore the IFRS requirement to estimate and remove the cost of the old motor).

4. The company purchased a small building in a nearby town for $125,000 to use as a display and sales location. The municipal tax assessment indicated that the property was assessed for $95,000, which consists of $68,000 for the building and $27,000 for the land. The building had been empty for six months and required considerable maintenance work before it could be used. The following costs were incurred in 2017 prior to the company moving into the building on September 30: former owner's unpaid property taxes on the property for the previous year, $900; current year's (2017) taxes, $1,000; reshingling of roof, $2,200; cost of hauling refuse out of the basement, $230; cost of spray-cleaning the outside walls and washing windows, $750; cost of painting inside walls, $3,170; and incremental fire and liability insurance for 15 months starting September 30, $940.

5. The company repaired the plumbing system in its factory for $35,000. The original plumbing costs were not known.

6. On June 30, the company replaced a freezer with a new one that cost $20,000 cash (fair value of $21,000 for the new freezer less trade-in value of the old freezer). The cost of the old freezer was $15,000. At the beginning of the year, the company had depreciated 60% of the old freezer; that is, 10% per year of use.

7. The company painted the factory exterior at a cost of $12,000.

Instructions

(a) Prepare the journal entries that are required to record the acquisitions and/or costs incurred in the above transactions. In the case of present value calculations, use any of the three methods (tables, financial calculator, or Excel).

(b) If there are alternative methods to account for any of the transactions, indicate what the alternatives are and your reason for choosing the method that you used.

P10-8 The production manager of Chesley Corporation wants to acquire a different brand of machine by exchanging the machine that it currently uses in operations for the brand of equipment that others in the industry are using. The brand being used by other companies is more comfortable for the operators because it has different attachments that allow the operators to adjust the controls for a variety of arm and hand positions. The production manager has received the following offers from other companies:

1. Secord Corp. offered to give Chesley a similar machine plus $23,000 in exchange for Chesley's machine.

2. Bateman Corp. offered a straight exchange for a similar machine with essentially the same value in use.

3. Shripad Corp. offered to exchange a similar machine with the same value in use, but wanted $8,000 cash in addition to Chesley's machine.

4. The production manager has also contacted Ansong Corporation, a dealer in machines. To obtain a new machine from Ansong, Chesley would have to pay $93,000 and also trade in its old machine.

Chesley's equipment has a cost of $160,000, a net book value of $110,000, and a fair value of $92,000. The following table shows the information needed to record the machine exchange between the companies:

	Secord	Bateman	Shripad	Ansong
Machine cost	$120,000	$147,000	$160,000	$130,000
Accumulated depreciation—machinery	45,000	71,000	75,000	–0–
Fair value	69,000	92,000	100,000	185,000

Instructions

(a) For each of the four independent situations, assume that Chesley accepts the offer. Prepare the journal entries to record the exchange on the books of each company. (Round to the nearest dollar.) When you need to make assumptions for the entries, state the assumptions so that you can justify the entries.

DIGGING DEEPER

(b) Suggest scenarios or situations where different entries would be appropriate. Prepare the entries for these situations.

P10-9 During the current year, Garrison Construction Ltd. traded in two relatively new small cranes (cranes no. 6RT and S79) for a larger crane that Garrison expects will be more useful for the particular contracts that the company has to fulfill over the next couple of years. The new crane is acquired from Pisani Manufacturing Inc., which has agreed to take the smaller equipment as trade-ins and also pay $17,500 cash to Garrison. The new crane cost Pisani $165,000 to manufacture and is classified as inventory. The following information is available:

	Garrison Const.	Pisani Mfg.
Cost of crane #6RT	$130,000	
Cost of crane #S79	120,000	
Accumulated depreciation, #6RT	15,000	
Accumulated depreciation, #S79	18,000	
Fair value, #6RT	128,000	
Fair value, #S79	87,500	
Fair value of new crane		$198,000
Cash paid		17,500
Cash received	17,500	

Instructions

(a) Assume that this exchange has commercial substance. Prepare the journal entries on the books of (1) Garrison Construction Ltd. and (2) Pisani Manufacturing Inc. Pisani uses a perpetual inventory system.

(b) Assume that this exchange lacks commercial substance. Prepare the journal entries on the books of (1) Garrison Construction and (2) Pisani Manufacturing. Pisani uses a perpetual inventory system.

(c) Assume that you have been asked to recommend whether it is more appropriate for the transaction to have commercial substance or not to have commercial substance. Develop arguments that you could present to the controllers of both Garrison Construction and Pisani Manufacturing to justify both alternatives. Which arguments are more persuasive?

DIGGING DEEPER

P10-10 On July 1, 2017, Lucas Ltd., a publicly listed company, acquired assets from Jared Ltd. On the transaction date, a reliable, independent valuator assessed the fair values of these assets as follows:

Manufacturing plant (building #1)	$400,000
Storage warehouse (building #2)	210,000
Machinery (in building #1)	75,000
Machinery (in building #2)	45,000

The buildings are owned by the company, and the land that the buildings are situated on is owned by the local municipality and is provided free of charge to the owner of the buildings as a stimulus to encourage local employment.

In exchange for the acquisition of these assets, Lucas issued 156,000 common shares. Lucas' shares are thinly traded, and in the most recent sale of Lucas' shares on the Toronto Stock Exchange, 1,000 shares were sold for $5 per share. At the time of acquisition, both buildings were considered to have an expected remaining useful life of 10 years, the machinery in building #1 was expected to have a remaining useful life of 3 years, and the machinery in building #2 was expected to have a useful life of 9 years. Lucas uses straight-line depreciation with no residual values.

At December 31, 2017, Lucas' fiscal year end, Lucas recorded the correct depreciation amounts for the six months that the assets were in use. An independent appraisal concluded that the assets had the following fair values:

Manufacturing plant (building #1)	$387,000
Storage warehouse (building #2)	178,000

At December 31, 2018, Lucas once again retained an independent appraiser and determined that the fair value of the assets was:

Manufacturing plant (building #1)	$340,000
Storage warehouse (building #2)	160,000

Instructions

(a) Prepare the journal entries required for 2017 and 2018, assuming that the buildings are accounted for under the revaluation model (using the asset adjustment method), and that the machinery is accounted for under the cost model.

(b) Assume that the asset revaluation surplus for the buildings was prepared based on a class-by-class basis rather than on an individual asset basis as required by IAS 16. Prepare the journal entries required for 2017 and 2018 that relate to the buildings. (Ignore the machinery accounts since they are accounted for using the cost model.)

(c) Comment on the effects on the 2017 income statement with respect to parts (a) and (b).

*P10-11   Camco Manufacturers Inc., a publicly listed company, has two machines that are accounted for under the revaluation model. Technology in Camco's industry is fast-changing, causing the fair value of each machine to change significantly approximately every two years. The following information is available:

	Machine #1	Machine #2
Acquisition date	Jan. 2, 2014	June 30, 2013
Original cost	$440,000	$540,000
Original estimate of useful life	8 years	12 years
Original estimate of residual value	–0–	–0–
Pattern of depreciation	Straight-line	Straight-line
Fair value at Dec. 31, 2015	310,000	440,000
Balance in Machinery account after proportionate method revaluation on Dec. 31, 2015	413,333	555,789
Balance in Accumulated Depreciation account after proportionate method revaluation on Dec. 31, 2015	103,333	115,789
Cumulative balance in (Revaluation Gain or Loss)/ Revaluation Surplus (OCI) at Jan. 1, 2017	(20,000)	12,500
Fair value at Dec. 31, 2017	230,000	328,000

Both machines were last revalued on December 31, 2015. Camco has a December 31 year end.

Instructions

(a) Prepare the journal entries required for 2017, using the asset adjustment method.

(b) Prepare the journal entries required for 2017, using the proportionate method.

(c) Prepare a continuity schedule showing for each machine the amounts recorded to the Machine account and to the Accumulated Depreciation account, as well as indicating the carrying amount for each fiscal year from date of purchase to December 31, 2017, using (1) the asset adjustment method and (2) the proportionate method. Show the carrying amount under each method at the end of each fiscal year.

(d) Comment on the effects on the 2017 statement of comprehensive income with respect to parts (a) and (b).

(e) Comment on the effects on the December 31, 2017 statement of financial position with respect to parts (a) and (b).

DIGGING DEEPER

(f) Would a potential investor prefer Camco to use the asset adjustment method or the proportionate method to apply the revaluation model?

P10-12   On March 1, 2017, Jessi Corp. acquired a 10-unit residential complex for $1,275,000, paid in cash. An independent appraiser determined that 75% of the total purchase price should be allocated to buildings, with the remainder allocated to land. On the date of acquisition, the estimated useful life of the building was 25 years, with estimated residual value of $325,000. Jessi estimates that straight-line depreciation would best reflect the pattern of benefits to be received from the building. Fair value of the complex, as assessed by an independent appraiser on each date, is as follows:

Date	Fair Value
December 31, 2017	$1,322,000
December 31, 2018	$1,255,000
December 31, 2019	$1,223,000

The complex qualifies as an investment property under IAS 40 *Investment Property*. Jessi has a December 31 year end.

Instructions

(a) Prepare the journal entries required for 2017, 2018, and 2019, assuming that Jessi applies the fair value model to all of its investment property.

(b) Prepare the journal entries required for 2017, 2018, and 2019, assuming that Jessi applies the cost model to all of its investment property.

(c) Comment on the effects on the 2017 statement of comprehensive income with respect to parts (a) and (b).

(d) Comment on the effects on the December 31, 2017 statement of financial position with respect to parts (a) and (b).

DIGGING DEEPER

(e) From the perspective of an investor in Jessi, discuss the financial statement effects of using the fair value model to determine the property's carrying amount.

P10-13   Donovan Resources Group has been in its plant facility for 15 years. Although the plant is quite functional, numerous repair costs are incurred to keep it in good working order. The book value of the company's plant is currently $800,000, calculated as follows:

Original cost	$1,200,000
Accumulated depreciation	400,000
	$ 800,000

During the current year, the following expenditures were made to the plant:

1. Because of increased demand for its product, the company increased its plant capacity by building a new addition at a cost of $270,000.

2. The entire plant was repainted at a cost of $23,000.

3. The roof was made of asbestos cement slate. For safety purposes, it was removed at a cost of $4,000 and replaced with a wood shingle roof at a cost of $61,000. The original roof's cost had been $40,000 and it was being depreciated over an expected life of 20 years.

4. The electrical system was completely updated at a cost of $22,000. The cost of the old electrical system was not known. It is estimated that the building's useful life will not change as a result of this updating.

5. A series of major repairs was made at a cost of $47,000, because parts of the wood structure were rotting. The cost of the old wood structure was not known. These extensive repairs are estimated to increase the building's useful life.

Instructions
Indicate how each of these transactions would be recorded in the accounting records.

*P10-14   Inglewood Landscaping Corp. began constructing a new plant on December 1, 2017. On this date, the company purchased a parcel of land for $184,000 cash. In addition, it paid $2,000 in surveying costs and $4,000 for title transfer fees. An old dwelling on the premises was immediately demolished at a cost of $3,000, with $1,000 being received from the sale of materials.

Architectural plans were also formalized on December 1, 2017, when the architect was paid $30,000. The necessary building permits costing $3,000 were obtained from the city and paid on December 1, 2017. The excavation work began during the first week in December and payments were made to the contractor as follows:

Date of Payment	Amount of Payment
Mar. 1	$240,000
May 1	360,000
July 1	60,000

The building was completed on July 1, 2018.

To finance the plant construction, Inglewood borrowed $600,000 from a bank on December 1, 2017. Inglewood had no other borrowings. The $600,000 was a 10-year loan bearing interest at 10%.

Instructions
(a) Calculate the balance in each of the following accounts at the year ends December 31, 2017, and December 31, 2018. Assume that Inglewood prepares financial statements in accordance with IFRS.

   1. Land

   2. Buildings

   3. Interest Expense

(b) Identify what the effects would be on Inglewood's financial statements for the years ending December 31, 2017 and 2018, if its policy were to expense all borrowing costs as they are incurred. Assume that Inglewood prepares financial statements in accordance with ASPE.

(c) Prepare a table showing the balance in the Buildings and Interest Expense accounts at the 2017 and 2018 fiscal years under IFRS and ASPE. Indicate the differences in the balances for each year. Do you believe the amounts of the differences are material to the statement of income and statement of financial position?

(d) Discuss the financial statement effects of capitalization of borrowing costs. Contrast the financial statement effects of capitalizing borrowing costs against the financial statement effects of paying for the construction with internally generated funds.

DIGGING DEEPER

*P10-15   Wordcrafters Inc. is a book distributor that had been operating in its original facility since 1988. The increase in certification programs and continuing education requirements in several professions has contributed to an annual growth rate of 15% for Wordcrafters since 2011. Wordcrafters' original facility became obsolete by early 2017 because of the increased sales volume and the fact that Wordcrafters now carries audio books and e-texts in addition to hard-copy books.

On June 1, 2017, Wordcrafters contracted with Favre Construction to have a new building constructed for $5 million on land owned by Wordcrafters. Wordcrafters made the following payments to Favre Construction:

Date	Amount
July 30, 2017	$1,200,000
Jan. 30, 2018	1,500,000
May 31, 2018	1,000,000
June 30, 2018	1,300,000
Total payments	$5,000,000

Construction was completed and the building was ready for occupancy on May 27, 2018. Wordcrafters had no new borrowings directly associated with the new building but had the following debt outstanding at May 31, 2018, the end of its fiscal year:

14½%, five-year note payable of $2 million, dated April 1, 2014, with interest payable annually on April 1

12%, 10-year bond issue of $3 million sold at par on June 30, 2010, with interest payable annually on June 30

The company is an international distributor and prepares financial statements in accordance with IFRS.

Instructions

(a) Calculate the weighted-average accumulated expenditures on Wordcrafters' new building during the capitalization period.

(b) Calculate the avoidable interest on Wordcrafters' new building.

(c) Wordcrafters Inc. capitalized some of its interest costs for the year ended May 31, 2018:

1. Identify the item(s) relating to interest costs that must be disclosed in Wordcrafters' financial statements.

2. Calculate the amount of the item(s) that must be disclosed.

(Adapted from CMA.)

ENABLING COMPETENCIES ## Case

Refer to the Case Primer on the student website and in *WileyPLUS* to help you with your answers for this case.

CA10-1 Real Estate Investment Trust (RE) was created to hold hotel properties. RE currently holds 15 luxury and first-class hotels in Europe. The entity is structured as an investment trust, which means that the trust does not pay income taxes because it distributes to unitholders taxable income from the assets that it holds directly. Instead, income taxes are paid by the unitholders—those who own units in the trust. The other key feature of the trust is that 85% to 90% of the distributable income is required to be paid to unitholders every year. The units of RE trade on the national stock exchange.

Distributable income is calculated as net income (according to GAAP) before special charges, less a replacement reserve (which is an amount set aside to refurbish assets). RE distributed 127% and 112% of its distributable income in 2017 and 2016, respectively. Management calculates distributable income since this calculation is not defined by GAAP. As at the end of 2017, property and equipment was $1.7 billion compared with $1.9 billion in total assets. Net income for the year was $55 million.

According to the notes to the financial statements, RE accounts for its property, plant, and equipment at amortized cost.

Instructions

Assume the role of the entity's auditors, and discuss any financial reporting issues.

ENABLING COMPETENCIES ## Integrated Cases

(*Hint:* If there are issues here that are new, use the conceptual framework to help you support your analysis with solid reasoning.)

†IC10-1 Iskra Vremec and Colin McFee are experienced scuba divers who have spent many years in the salvage business. About a year ago, they decided to start

†This item was originally published by the *Canadian Institute of Chartered Accountants* (CICA) as a question in the Uniform Final Evaluation (UFE). Adapted with permission of the Chartered Professional Accountants of Canada, Toronto, Canada. Any changes to the original material are the sole responsibility of the publisher and have not been reviewed or endorsed by the Chartered Professional Accountants of Canada.

their own company to recover damaged and sunken vessels and their cargoes off the east coast of Canada. They incorporated Atlantic Explorations Limited (AEL) on February 1, 2016. Iskra (president) and Colin (vice-president) each own 30% of AEL's shares. The remaining 40% of the shares were purchased by a group of 10 investors who contributed $50,000 each so that AEL could acquire the necessary equipment and cover other start-up costs.

AEL carries on two types of activities. The first is a commercial salvage operation. The second is treasure hunting. To date, commercial salvage operations have generated all of AEL's revenues. The demand for these services is strong, and there are few competitors because of the unpredictable nature of the business and the long hours. Colin manages the commercial salvage operations. Customers pay in three instalments, including an upfront fee, a fee payable approximately midway through the contract, and a fee at the end once the items in question have been salvaged (found and brought to land). If the item is never found or AEL cannot bring the item to the surface and to land, then the final payment is not made.

Iskra spends most of her time locating and recovering underwater artifacts and, where possible, sunken treasure. Her research shows that numerous vessels carrying gold, silver, and other valuables to the "Old World" were wrecked off the shores of Nova Scotia. AEL has permits to investigate three target areas. As compensation for the permits, AEL agrees to remit 1% of the fair value of any treasure found. These funds are to be invested in the local economy by AEL (subject to government approval). The company also pays an upfront fee that allows it to search a given area. There has been a discovery in the first of these target areas.

It is now September 5, 2016. AEL has engaged your auditing firm to provide advice on the accounting for the ongoing operations and the discovery that AEL has just made. You (as audit manager) and Alex Green, the partner assigned to the engagement, met with Colin and Iskra.

During your meeting, Iskra said that she believes that finding treasure is like winning a lottery, as all revenues would accrue to AEL and thus should be treated accordingly. If this discovery proves to be as substantial as preliminary results suggest, AEL will require additional financing of $1.5 million to acquire equipment and an on-shore laboratory, and lease a specially equipped vessel needed to salvage the wreck and its treasures. The bank has said that it is not willing to advance further funds. However, Iskra and Colin know of other individuals who are interested in investing in AEL.

AEL receives grants from the government to assist in the process of finding treasure and salvaging sunken vessels. Iskra and Colin have just found out that they are likely to receive a grant in connection with the recent discovery.

Instructions

AUDIT Draft a memo for auditor Alex Green, analyzing all financial reporting issues and providing recommendations.

IC10-2 OG Limited (OG) is in the oil and gas business. It spends quite a bit of money each year exploring for new wells. Currently, it has several wells that are in the production phases. The company's shares trade on the London Stock Exchange. OG is looking to expand its exploration into China and therefore would like to issue more shares next year to fund the exploration. The company's top management is compensated partly with stock options.

One of the company's wells recently exploded, pouring a significant amount of oil into a nearby waterway. It took one month to cap the well, and during that time the company incurred significant costs in capping the well, including costs related to many failed attempts. OG has announced that it will clean up the spilled oil and estimates that it will cost between $5 and $10 million to do so. It has also announced that it will act in a responsible manner when dealing with any losses and complaints that the local farmers may have in connection with the spill.

OG is now being sued in a class action suit brought about by the farmers. They are suing for $100 million in compensation for their land, which is now unusable because of the oil. The company's lawyers feel they can settle for 10% of that amount.

The company capitalizes all costs incurred in connection with searching for new oil and gas wells, even when the exploration does not result in a well that has oil in it. They argue that they must incur those costs in order to find a producing well. In many countries where OG explores and operates, there are no legal requirements to restore the land to its original state once the exploration is complete or a well is depleted. The company does, however, state that it considers this an important activity and will make every effort to restore the site.

When excavating one site, OG came across a significant amount of gold. OG is now mining and selling the gold. Currently, it is trying to decide how to account for the gold inventory and is considering valuing the gold at market price once it has been refined, even though it is not yet sold.

Instructions

AUDIT Assume the role of the company's auditors and analyze the financial reporting issues.

RESEARCH AND ANALYSIS

REAL WORLD EMPHASIS

RA10-1   Magna International Inc.

Access the financial statements of **Magna International Inc.** for the company's year ended December 31, 2014. These are available at www.sedar.com or the company's website. Review the information that is provided and answer the following questions about the company.

Instructions

(a) What business is Magna International in?

(b) Identify the types of tangible capital assets that Magna reports, and indicate whether these assets form a significant portion of the company's total assets at December 31, 2014. Also explain why these assets are classified as property, plant and equipment, and what conditions must exist before Magna reports them on its financial statements.

(c) Identify all the accounting policies disclosed in the notes to the financial statements that explain how the company determines the cost of its property, plant, and equipment.

(d) How much did Magna spend on new capital asset acquisitions in 2013 and 2014 (excluding business acquisitions)? Identify where the company obtained the funds to invest in these additions.

(e) Explain how the company accounts for government assistance.

(f) Compare the percentage increase in fixed asset additions from 2013 to 2014 to the percentage increase in sales. Taking the point of view of an investor or a potential investor, comment on the results of your analysis.

REAL WORLD EMPHASIS

RA10-2   Stora Enso Oyj

Access the annual financial statements of **Stora Enso Oyj** for the company's year ended December 31, 2014. These are available at the company's website, www.storaenso.com. Review the information that is provided and answer the following questions about the company.

Instructions

(a) What major business(es) is Stora Enso Oyj in?

(b) What type of biological assets does the company have? Identify the accounting policies disclosed in the notes to the financial statements that explain how the company accounts for these assets.

(c) What was the amount in the biological assets account at December 31, 2014 and 2013, owned directly by Stora Enso? What caused this account balance to change from 2013 to 2014? Be specific.

(d) How is fair value of the biological assets determined? What kinds of estimates are required to determine fair value?

(e) What was the impact on the net earnings for 2014 and 2013 related to the biological assets valuation?

REAL WORLD EMPHASIS

RA10-3   Empire Company Limited and Loblaw Companies Limited

Companies in the same line of business usually have similar investments and capital structures, and an opportunity for similar rates of return. One of the key performance indicators that is used to assess the profitability of companies is the return on assets ratio. This ratio results from two key relationships—the profit margin and the total asset turnover—and in general terms can be written as follows:

Return on assets = Total asset turnover (or Sales/Total assets) × Profit margin (or Income/Sales)

This says that profitability depends directly on how many sales dollars are generated for each dollar invested in assets (total asset turnover) and on how costs are controlled for each dollar of sales (profit margin). An increase in either ratio results in an increase in the return on assets. As property, plant, and equipment is often the largest single asset on the balance sheet, companies need to have strategies to manage their investment in such assets.

Instructions

Access the financial statements of two companies that are in the food distribution and retail business: **Empire Company Limited** for the year ended May 2, 2015, and **Loblaw Companies Limited** for the year ended January 3, 2015. These are available at www.sedar.com or each company's website. Review the financial statements and answer the following questions.

(a) At each company's year end, determine the percentage of property, plant, and equipment to total assets.

(b) Calculate each company's fixed asset turnover, total asset turnover, and profit margin (using net income) for the most recent year.

(c) Determine the return on assets for each company. Which company is more profitable?

(d) Which company appears to use its total assets more effectively in generating sales? Its fixed assets?

(e) Are there any differences in accounting policies that might explain the differences in the fixed asset turnover ratios?

(f) Examine the leasing note for each company. How might the amount of assets that are leased affect the above asset turnover ratios?

(g) Which company has better control over its expenses for each dollar of sales? How do you explain the asset turnover ratios and the profit ratio comparisons?

RA10-4   Brookfield Asset Management Inc.

REAL WORLD EMPHASIS

Access the financial statements of **Brookfield Asset Management Inc.** for the company's year ended December 31, 2014. These are included at the end of the book. Review the information that is provided and answer the following questions about the company.

Instructions

(a) What business is Brookfield Asset Management in? Identify the types of tangible capital assets the company includes on its balance sheet. (*Hint:* See Notes 1 and 2 to the financial statements.)

(b) Indicate what accounting model is used to measure and report each type of tangible capital asset identified in part (a).

(c) Review the company's Statement of Operations, Statement of Comprehensive Income, and relevant notes to the financial statements to identify the effect on net income and on other comprehensive income of each accounting model used for its tangible capital assets.

(d) For the assets identified in part (b) that were measured using fair values, explain how the company determined their fair values; that is, what methods were used and what type of key assumptions were required.

RA10-5   Extractive Industry

REAL WORLD EMPHASIS

Access the financial statements of **BHP Billiton plc** for the company's year ended June 30, 2014. Also access the financial statements of **Newfield Exploration Company** for the company's year ended December 31, 2014. These are available at the companies' websites. Review the information that is provided and answer the following questions about the companies.

Instructions

(a) What business is BHP Billiton plc in? What business is Newfield Exploration Co. in?

(b) How does BHP Billiton account for exploration, evaluation, and development expenditures related to its mineral reserves and resources? What specific costs are included?

(c) How does Newfield account for exploration, evaluation, and development expenditures related to its mineral reserves and resources? What specific costs are included?

(d) Using the two companies as examples, discuss the similarities and differences between the successful efforts method and the full cost method.

(e) One method for reporting these assets that is being contemplated by IFRS is the fair value method. What assumptions would be required to determine the fair value of mineral or oil and gas reserves? What are some drawbacks to using the fair value method to value these types of assets?

(f) From a user's perspective, which method(s) discussed above would provide the most faithful representation and relevant information?

RA10-6   Acquisition and Installation Costs

ETHICS

A machine's invoice price is $40,000. Various other costs relating to the acquisition and installation of the machine—including transportation, electrical wiring, a special base, and so on—amount to $7,500. The machine has an estimated life of 10 years, with no residual value at the end of that period.

The owner-manager of the company that you work for as an accountant suggests that the incidental costs of $7,500 be charged to expense immediately for the following reasons:

- If the machine is ever sold, these costs cannot be recovered in the sale price.
- The inclusion of the $7,500 in the machinery account on the books will not necessarily result in a closer approximation of this asset's market price over the years, because demand and supply levels could change.
- Charging the $7,500 to expense immediately will reduce income taxes.

Instructions

Prepare a memo to the owner-manager that addresses each of the issues assuming that the company follows ASPE.

RA10-7   Government Funding

Hotel Resort Limited is a company that builds world-class resorts in tourist areas around the globe. When the company decided to build a resort in Yellowknife, the federal government agreed to provide a forgivable loan in the amount of $50 million to help fund the construction of the tourist facilities anticipated to cost about $700 million. The loan will be forgiven provided the tourist facility is operated for at least 15 years. If the resort is closed or sold before 15 years have elapsed, the amount of the loan must be repaid in full, along with interest at the prevailing market rate.

In addition, the federal government also agreed to provide annual funding to cover 70% of the related costs of payroll and room and board for 50 summer students, provided the students were hired to work for four full months. The company would receive this annual funding once it proved the costs incurred for these students.

Instructions

Prepare a memo that would be suitable to present to the Hotel Resort Limited board of directors in which you explain how the receipt of the government funding is expected to affect the company's reported total assets and earnings. Also, draft the related note disclosure that would be required.

(Adapted from AICPA.)

RA10-8   Capitalizing Costs for Self-Constructed Assets

Gomi Medical Labs Inc. began operations five years ago producing a new type of instrument it hoped to sell to doctors, dentists, and hospitals. The demand for the new instrument was much higher than had been planned for, and the company was unable to produce enough of them to meet demand. The company was manufacturing its product on equipment that had been built at the start of its operations.

To meet demand, more efficient equipment was needed. The company decided to design and build the equipment because the equipment currently available on the market was unsuitable for producing this product.

In 2017, a section of the plant was devoted to developing the new equipment and expert employees were hired. Within six months, a machine, developed at a cost of $714,000, increased production dramatically and reduced labour costs substantially. Thrilled by the new machine's success, the company built three more machines of the same type for its own use, at a cost of $441,000 each.

Instructions

(a) In general, what costs should be capitalized for self-constructed equipment?

(b) Discuss whether the capitalized cost of self-constructed assets should include the following:

1. The increase in overhead that results from the company's own construction of its fixed assets

2. A proportionate share of overhead on the same basis as what is applied to goods that are manufactured for sale

(c) Discuss the proper accounting treatment of the $273,000 cost amount ($714,000 – $441,000) that was higher for the first machine than the cost of the subsequent machines.

ENDNOTES

[1] For details, see "Guide to Accounting for and Reporting Tangible Capital Assets: Guidance for Local Governments and Local Government Entities that Apply the Public Sector Handbook" (available on-line at: http://www.frascanada.ca/standards-for-public-sector-entities/resources/reference-materials/item14603.pdf).

[2] See http://www.infrastructure.gc.ca/plan/plan-eng.html for details.

[3] If a company is involved in a significant amount of self-construction activity, some of its fixed overhead costs may be considered "directly attributable."

[4] Sometimes a standard will specify that another amount will be the asset's **deemed cost**. The deemed cost is the amount recognized under the specific requirements of a particular standard, such as IFRS 1 *First Time Adoption of International Financial Reporting Standards*, where fair value can be used in the opening statement of financial position when a company first adopts IFRS (IFRS 1.30).

[5] IFRS 2 *Share-based Payment* is considerably more complex than is indicated here. The recognition and measurement guidance depends on what is being acquired as well as whether the payment is in shares directly or in cash with the amount based on the share price, or whether there is a choice of cash-based settlement or settlement in shares.

[6] Keep in mind that IFRS 2 *Share-based Payment* "uses the term 'fair value' in a way that differs in some respects from the definition of fair value in IFRS 13 Fair Value Measurement. Therefore, when applying IFRS 2 an entity measures fair value in accordance with IFRS 2, not IFRS 13." Copyright © IFRS Foundation. All rights reserved. Reproduced by John Wiley & Sons Canada, Ltd. with the permission of the IFRS Foundation®. Reproduction and use rights are strictly limited. No permission granted to third parties to reproduce or distribute.

[7] For example, if a company exchanges inventory held for sale for other similar merchandise for sale in order to facilitate a sale to a customer, it would be difficult to justify the claim that the company's economic position has changed significantly. In fact, ASPE discusses this type of situation as an exception to the use of fair value in a nonmonetary exchange.

[8] IAS 20 *Accounting for Government Grants and Disclosure of Government Assistance* indicates that, while government grants in the form of nonmonetary assets are usually measured at their fair value, an entity may record both the asset and the grant at a nominal amount (see IAS 20.23).

[9] While a credit to Other Comprehensive Income (OCI) may seem like a valid option, accounting standards tend to be prescriptive about what can bypass net income and be recognized directly in OCI. This option is not provided in either IFRS or ASPE for government grants.

[10] Investment property includes land or buildings or part of a building or both under IAS 40, and could be property held under a finance lease or directly owned.

[11] See IAS 40.11 for further details.

[12] IFRS 13 *Fair Value Measurement*, Paragraph 9. Copyright © IFRS Foundation. All rights reserved. Reproduced by John Wiley & Sons Canada, Ltd. with the permission of the IFRS Foundation®. Reproduction and use rights are strictly limited. No permission granted to third parties to reproduce or distribute.

[13] Chapter 3 includes a discussion of the meaning of fair value and ways in which fair values are determined, and Appendix B of IFRS 13 provides detailed guidance relating to the fair value measurement approach under IFRS.

[14] This method is easy to apply when fair values are based on an index of specific prices, such as a construction price index. It also has the benefit of providing additional information to users about the relative age of the assets because the accumulated depreciation continues.

[15] IAS 16 discusses the revaluation model in more detail, including the two alternatives for transferring the revaluation surplus to retained earnings (see IAS 16.41).

[16] Note that, to the extent these ordinary expenditures are classified as factory overhead, the costs are included as an inventory (product) cost before being charged to the income statement as an expense—cost of goods sold.

[17] Unlike investment income earned on the temporary investment of asset-specific borrowings, IAS 23 *Borrowing Costs* does not discuss whether investment income earned on general-purpose debt should reduce the borrowing costs eligible to be capitalized or not. The principles set out in this IFRS and the company-specific circumstances would have to be assessed to determine the best approach in each case.

11 | DEPRECIATION, IMPAIRMENT, AND DISPOSITION

REFERENCE TO THE CPA COMPETENCY MAP	LEARNING OBJECTIVES
	After studying this chapter, you should be able to:
1.1.1, 1.1.2, 1.1.4	1. Understand the importance of depreciation, impairment, and disposition from a business perspective.
1.2.1, 1.2.2	2. Explain the concept of depreciation and identify the factors to consider when determining depreciation charges.
1.2.1, 1.2.2	3. Identify how depreciation methods are selected; calculate and recognize depreciation using the straight-line, decreasing charge, and activity methods.
1.1.2, 1.2.1, 1.2.2, 1.2.3, 5.4.1, 5.4.2	4. Explain the accounting issues for depletion of mineral resources.
1.2.1, 1.2.2	5. Explain and apply the accounting procedures for partial periods and a change in depreciation rate.
1.1.2, 1.1.4, 1.2.1, 1.2.3, 5.4.1	6. Explain the issues and apply the accounting standards for capital asset impairment under both IFRS and ASPE.
1.2.1, 1.2.2, 1.2.3	7. Account for derecognition of property, plant, and equipment and explain and apply the accounting standards for long-lived assets that are held for sale.
1.1.2, 1.3.2, 1.4.1	8. Describe the types of disclosures required for property, plant, and equipment.
1.4.2, 1.4.4, 5.1.1	9. Analyze a company's investment in assets.
1.1.4	10. Identify differences in accounting between IFRS and ASPE, and what changes are expected in the near future.

After studying Appendix 11A, you should be able to:

1.2.1, 1.2.2, 1.2.3, 6.1.2, 6.1.4	11. Calculate capital cost allowance in routine and non-routine situations.

A "GOLDEN" ACCOUNTING RULE

As you've seen in previous chapters, the cost of any asset must be allocated to various accounting periods. Most tangible assets are known as property, plant, and equipment, and their cost allocation is called depreciation. Intangible assets are amortized, while mineral resource properties are depleted. But the accounting treatments for these various types of assets differ in more than just terminology.

Take mineral resource properties as an example. Other types of tangible, long-lived assets are depreciated over their estimated useful lives. The costs are usually presented as a depreciation expense on the statement of comprehensive income. But mineral resources are different. Companies with mineral resources deplete them

Courtesy Alacer Gold Corp.

via charges that are accumulated in inventory prior to being charged to expense.

An example is Alacer Gold Corp., a Canadian company with an 80% interest in a gold mine in Turkey. Its mineral resources that have not yet been fully processed are considered work-in-process inventory. Its work-in-process inventory represents the costs of converting ores into partially refined precious metals. "Costs capitalized to work-in-process inventory include costs incurred to that stage of the mining process such as direct and indirect materials and consumables; direct labor; repairs and maintenance; utilities; depreciation, depletion and amortization of mineral property, plant and equipment; and site support costs. Costs are removed from work-in-process inventory and transferred to finished goods inventory as ounces are produced based on the average cost per recoverable ounce," Alacer said in its 2014 annual report.

When the company sells refined gold, it transfers costs from inventory and reports them as cost of goods sold on its income statement (which it calls the consolidated statement of profit (loss)). As at December 31, 2014, the company reported $42.3 million in work-in-process inventories in the notes to the financial statements, and depreciation, depletion, and amortization costs of $54.0 million as part of total cost of goods sold of $174.6 million on its income statement.

Another difference in accounting for mineral resource properties is that their inventory levels are sometimes difficult to estimate. To recover gold from ore, Alacer uses a leaching process, where a chemical solution dissolves the gold contained in the ore. "The nature of the leaching process inherently limits the ability to precisely monitor inventory levels. As a result, estimates are refined based on actual results and engineering studies over time. The ultimate recovery of gold from leach pads will not be known until the leaching process is concluded at the end of the mine life," the annual report stated.

Sources: Alacer Gold Corp. 2014 annual report; Alacer Gold corporate website, www.alacergold.com; "Financial Reporting in the Mining Industry," PricewaterhouseCoopers, June 2007.

PREVIEW OF CHAPTER 11

Capital assets can be a major investment for companies. It is therefore important that you have a firm understanding of this chapter's topics. For example, you should be aware of the alternatives that exist for charging these capital costs to operations and the potential for impairment in their values. Some critics argue that financial statement readers do not need to be concerned with non-cash expenses such as depreciation, so it is important to understand the purpose of charging depreciation and the difference between cost allocation and valuation. It is also important to understand rules governing allocation of capital costs for calculating income taxes. The appendix outlines key aspects of the capital cost allowance system that is required for income tax purposes.

The chapter is organized as follows:

DEPRECIATION, IMPAIRMENT, AND DISPOSITION						
The Importance of Depreciation, Impairment, and Disposition from a Business Perspective	Depreciation—a Method of Allocation	Impairment	Held for Sale and Derecognition	Presentation, Disclosure, and Analysis	IFRS/ASPE Comparison	Appendix 11A—Depreciation and Income Tax
	▪ Factors considered in the depreciation process ▪ Depreciation—methods of allocation and calculation ▪ Depletion of mineral resources ▪ Other depreciation issues	▪ Indicators of impairment ▪ Impairment—recognition and measurement models ▪ Asset groups and cash-generating units	▪ Long-lived assets to be disposed of by sale ▪ Derecognition	▪ Presentation and disclosure ▪ Analysis	▪ A comparison of IFRS and ASPE ▪ Looking ahead	▪ Capital cost allowance method

THE IMPORTANCE OF DEPRECIATION, IMPAIRMENT, AND DISPOSITION FROM A BUSINESS PERSPECTIVE

Objective 1
Understand the importance of depreciation, impairment, and disposition from a business perspective.

The economic benefits of property, plant, and equipment (PP&E) are typically consumed as the items are used by the organization. Because PP&E is used over multiple periods, companies must find an appropriate method for allocating the benefits as the assets' capacity and expected output are used up. Businesses usually cannot determine exactly how long a long-lived asset will be used productively. However, they are generally able to make a reasonable estimate of useful life. Several factors may have an impact on the asset's useful life and residual value. These factors include the asset's planned repairs and maintenance, its expected technical or commercial obsolescence, and legal or other limits on its use (such as lease terms).[1]

By allocating the cost of property, plant, and equipment over its useful life, businesses are better able to match the costs and benefits of the assets to the revenues that they help generate. This also ensures that businesses do not have to record a disproportionate amount of expense in the year the asset is acquired. Similarly, if PP&E is not depreciated or expensed, businesses might need to record large losses in the year of disposition.

WHAT DO THE NUMBERS MEAN?

REAL WORLD EMPHASIS

Under IFRS, determining a reasonable basis for depreciation has become even more of a challenge for many businesses. For example, **Ontario Power Generation** (OPG) had planned to adopt IFRS starting in 2012. The delay to 2012, when most businesses adopted IFRS in 2011, was due partly to the complications involving organizations whose rates are regulated by the government, such as OPG. With its PP&E having a carrying amount of more than $17.6 billion at the end of 2014 (and $13.6 billion at the end of 2010), OPG has to consider matters such as the impact of IFRS's focus on individual components of PP&E. This affects items such as OPG's nuclear, hydroelectric, and thermal generating stations. The switch to IFRS was to come just a few years after a significant change in the estimated useful life of its Darlington nuclear generating station, which was extended from 2019 to 2051 after the organization announced the station's refurbishment. This change in estimate was largely responsible for a decrease of $62 million in OPG's depreciation expense between 2009 and 2010. Starting in 2012, OPG decided to adopt U.S. GAAP instead of IFRS to minimize the differences from "old" Canadian GAAP, which was followed until 2011. Assuming OPG continues to have rate-regulated activities, it has an exemption from the Ontario Securities Commission that allows it to continue to use U.S. GAAP until the earlier of January 1, 2019, and the effective date under IFRS for the mandatory application of an IFRS standard specific to entities with rate-regulated activities.[2]

Depreciation helps businesses ensure that assets are carried at an amount no higher than what is expected to be recoverable for the asset. However, over time, the asset could still end up being carried at too high an amount. What if the asset's carrying value exceeds its recoverable amount, due to poor estimates of useful life, residual value, or other factors such as unexpected obsolescence? In that case, the carrying amount should be reduced.[3] Companies therefore need to regularly assess their PP&E for signs of impairment. If there are signs, companies should re-estimate how much will be recoverable. This should help them better understand their business, along with complying with GAAP.

DEPRECIATION—A METHOD OF ALLOCATION

Many people at one time or another buy and sell a vehicle. The automobile dealer and the buyer typically discuss what the old car's trade-in value is. Also, they may talk about what the new car's trade-in value will be in several years. In both cases, the decline in value is generally referred to as depreciation.

To accountants, however, depreciation is not a matter of valuation (determining an asset's declining value). **Depreciation**—or amortization, as it is also called—**is a means of cost allocation**. It is the process of allocating the depreciable amount of a PP&E asset to expense in a systematic manner to those periods expected to benefit from its use. As explained in this chapter, the depreciable amount is the asset's cost less its residual amount. (There could, however, be a substitute value used instead of cost, such as that used when the revaluation model is applied.)

It is true that an asset's value changes between the time it is purchased and the time it is sold or scrapped. Most companies use a cost allocation approach rather than a valuation approach, however. This is because objectively measuring the changes in their assets' values every reporting period is often difficult and usually costly.

As mentioned above, the terms **amortization** and **depreciation** are almost interchangeable. **Amortization** is the general process of allocating the carrying amount of any long-lived asset to the accounting periods that benefit from its use. It can also specifically refer to this process for **intangible assets**. The term **depreciation** is reserved for property, plant, and equipment, and **depletion** is used only with natural resource assets.

Factors Considered in the Depreciation Process

Objective 2
Explain the concept of depreciation and identify the factors to consider when determining depreciation charges.

Before calculating the dollar amount of depreciation expense, a company has to answer four basic questions:

1. What asset components are depreciated separately?

2. What is the asset's depreciable amount?

3. Over what period is the asset depreciated?

4. What pattern best reflects how the asset's economic benefits are used up?

As you might expect, judgement and estimates are needed to answer these questions. This means that the resulting **depreciation is an estimate**. A perfect measure of items affecting depreciation expense, such as useful life and residual value, is often impossible.

Asset Components

As mentioned in Chapter 10, management has to develop a **componentization** policy; that is, a policy to guide decisions on which fixed asset components to recognize separately. What individual parts of multi-component assets, such as a building, should be pulled out and recorded separately? And when should numerous small PP&E assets, such as small tools, be combined and accounted for together? Determining the unit of account is the first step in the depreciation process.

The following principles guide the componentization decision:

- Identify each part of a PP&E asset whose cost is a significant portion of the total asset cost as a separate component.

- Group together significant components with similar useful lives and patterns of providing economic benefits.

- Add together the costs of the remaining parts of the asset, none of which is individually significant. These may be depreciated as a single component, taking into account the nature of the different parts.

- Group together individual minor assets to depreciate as one component based on the similarity of their useful life and pattern of consumption.

REAL WORLD EMPHASIS

Air Canada indicates that its aircraft and flight equipment are componentized into aircraft frames, engines, and cabin interior equipment and modifications. Cabin interior equipment and modifications are depreciated over a much shorter period of time (eight years) than its airframes and engines (20 to 25 years). Similarly, **British Airways plc** reports that the cabin interior modifications of its aircraft fleet are recognized and depreciated separately from the aircraft themselves (typically five years for cabin interior modifications versus 18 to 25 years for its fleet aircraft).

Both IFRS and ASPE require entities to recognize separate components for the purpose of depreciation, but the international standards are more fully developed and more strictly applied.

Depreciable Amount

The amount of an asset that is to be depreciated—its **depreciable amount**—is the difference between the asset's cost (or revalued amount, if the revaluation model is being used) and its residual value.[4] The **residual value** is defined as the estimated amount a company would **receive today** if it disposed of the asset, less any related disposal costs, if the asset were at the **same age and condition expected at the end of its useful life**.[5] It is the amount the company depreciates the asset to over its useful life. For example, Illustration 11-1 shows that, if an asset has a cost (or net revalued amount) of $10,000 and a residual value of $3,600, only $6,400 of its cost is depreciated.

In some cases, the residual value may be so low as to be immaterial. Some long-lived assets, however, have substantial net realizable values at the end of their useful lives to a specific enterprise. As long as the residual value is less than the asset's carrying amount, depreciation is recognized on the asset. If the residual value increases so it is more than the asset's carrying amount, no depreciation is taken until this situation reverses. It is important that the residual value be reviewed regularly, but particularly whenever changes in the environment occur that might affect its estimate. Under IFRS, this review is required at least at each year end.

Original cost (or amount substituted for "cost")	$10,000
Less: residual value	3,600
Depreciable amount	$ 6,400

Illustration 11-1
Calculation of Amount to Be Depreciated

A more technical and conservative policy is required under ASPE where, to ensure that charges to the income statement are adequate, the depreciation charge is based on the higher of two amounts:

1. the cost less salvage value over the life of the asset, and

2. the cost less residual value over the asset's useful life.

The **salvage value** is the estimate of the asset's net realizable value at the end of its life, rather than its value at the end of its useful life to the entity. The salvage value is usually an insignificant amount. In practice, the residual value is most commonly used to calculate depreciation.

So, for the example in Illustration 11-1, assume the asset is a machine with a cost of $10,000, an estimated useful life of eight years, and a residual value of $3,600. Its depreciation under IFRS would be $800 if it uses straight-line depreciation. However, if the total expected life of the asset is 10 years with no salvage value, under ASPE the minimum depreciation charge would be $1,000 per year. Journal entries to record the depreciation under IFRS versus ASPE are provided in Illustration 11-2.

IFRS
A	=	L	+	SE
−800				−800

Cash flows: No effect

ASPE
A	=	L	+	SE
−1,000				−1,000

Cash flows: No effect

To record depreciation of the machine:	IFRS[a]	ASPE[b]
Depreciation Expense	800	1,000
Accumulated Depreciation—Machinery	800	1,000

[a]IFRS depreciation ($10,000 − $3,600)/8 = $800
[b]ASPE depreciation is the greater of ($10,000 − $3,600)/8 = $800 or ($10,000 − $0)/10 = $1,000

Illustration 11-2
Accounting for Depreciation (IFRS versus ASPE)

Depreciation Period

As indicated above, to calculate depreciation, we need an estimate of the asset's **useful life**. An asset's useful life is the period during which the asset is expected to be available for use by the entity based on factors such as the asset's expected capacity. Alternatively, useful life can be stated in terms of the number of units of product or service that the asset is expected to produce or provide over this period.

Depreciation begins when the asset is available for use; that is, when it is in place and in the condition necessary for it to be able to operate as management intends. The **depreciation process ends** when the asset is derecognized (removed from the accounts), or when it is classified as held for sale, if earlier. **Depreciation continues** even if the asset is idle or has been taken out of service, unless it is fully depreciated, of course.

Useful or service life and physical life are often not the same. A piece of machinery may be physically capable of producing a specific product for many years past its useful life in a particular organization, but the equipment may not be used for all of those years due to **economic factors** such as obsolescence. The useful lives of Air Canada's aircraft components, described earlier, are likely determined through discussions with others in the organization, such as engineering and manufacturing specialists. New processes or techniques or improved machines may provide the same product or service at lower cost or with higher quality. Changes needed in the product or service itself may shorten an asset's service life. Environmental factors and asset management policies also influence asset retirement decisions.

Physical factors set the outside limit for an asset's service life. Physical factors relate to such things as decay or wear and tear that result from use of the asset and the passage of time. Whenever the asset's physical nature is the main factor that determines its useful life, a company's maintenance policies play a vital role—the better the maintenance, the longer the life of the asset.[6] An asset's **legal life** may also limit its useful life to a specific entity. For example, the benefits of leasehold improvements end when the lease term is over.

To illustrate these concepts, consider a new nuclear power plant. Which is most important in determining its useful life: physical factors, economic factors, or its legal life? The limiting factors seem to be (1) ecological considerations, (2) competition from other power sources, and (3) safety concerns. Physical and legal life do not appear to be primary factors affecting the plant's useful life. While the plant's physical life may be far from over, the plant may be obsolete in 20 years.

The estimate of useful life is often not easy to determine. In some cases, arbitrary lives are selected; in others, sophisticated statistical methods are used. The main basis for estimating an asset's useful life is often judgement and the company's experience with similar assets. In an industrial economy such as Canada's, where research and innovation are so prominent, economic and technological factors have as much effect on the service lives of tangible assets as do physical factors, if not more.

UNDERLYING CONCEPT

Depreciation is a good example of how the matching concept is applied when there is no direct relationship between revenues and costs.

Depreciation—Methods of Allocation and Calculation

Objective 3

Identify how depreciation methods are selected; calculate and recognize depreciation using the straight-line, decreasing charge, and activity methods.

The last major issue in the depreciation process is deciding **which depreciation method is most appropriate**. The underlying principle is that the resulting depreciation should reflect the pattern in which the asset benefits are expected to be used up by the entity. This suggests that the concern is with the pattern in which the physical capacity, wear and tear, technical obsolescence, or legal life are used up as the asset provides service to the company. Four possible patterns are identified in Illustration 11-3.

Pattern (1) is a uniform benefit pattern. This applies to an asset that provides roughly the same level of benefits in each year of its life. A warehouse could be an example. For such assets, a straight-line method is rational because it results in a constant depreciation expense each period.

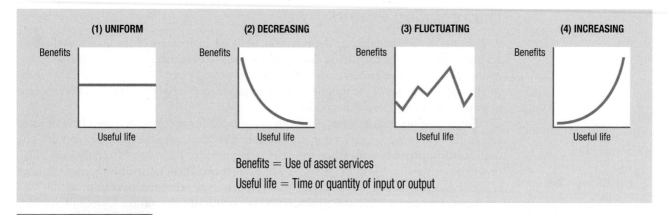

Benefits = Use of asset services
Useful life = Time or quantity of input or output

Illustration 11-3

*Possible Benefit Patterns
for Assets*

**UNDERLYING
CONCEPT**

The accounting profession
is sometimes criticized for
failing to consider the economic consequences that
accounting principles have
for companies. However, the
neutrality concept requires
that the statements be free
from bias in that methods
are not chosen to achieve a
predetermined result.

THEORY

Pattern (2) is a decreasing benefit pattern. An airplane may be an example of an asset with a decreasing benefit pattern. When it is new, it is constantly in service on major routes. As it gets older, its operating efficiency declines—it may be repaired more often and used for less busy routes. Depreciation expense should therefore decline each year.

Pattern (3) is a fluctuating benefit pattern. The use of a truck, in terms of kilometres driven, may fluctuate considerably from period to period, yielding a benefit pattern that varies or fluctuates.

Pattern (4) is an increasing benefit pattern. It is seldom experienced because few assets provide more service potential or generate higher value cash flows as they age. A new hotel might be an example, with lower levels of occupancy in early years and then increasing gradually over time as the hotel's reputation leads to more "repeat business."

Because of the difficulty in some cases in identifying the pattern in which benefits are received, the **simplicity** of each method may be considered. If so, some argue that a straight-line method should be used. However, others may think that the method used for income tax purposes should be used for book purposes **because it eliminates some record-keeping costs**. Canadian companies are required to use the capital cost allowance approach for tax purposes (explained in Appendix 11A), so they may decide to also use this for financial reporting purposes. While this is more common for smaller companies, a larger company is likely to use one method for tax purposes and a different method for financial reporting. This is more reasonable because the objectives of financial reporting differ from those of calculating income tax. One result of using different methods for financial reporting than for taxes is that the entity's financial statement amounts for property, plant, and equipment and for income before taxes will be different from the tax value of capital assets and from taxable income. The financial accounting consequences of such differences are explored in Chapter 18.

Management sometimes appears to choose a depreciation method based on the **perceived economic consequences** of the amounts that will be reported. Companies that want to appear more profitable might be tempted to change from the declining-balance method to a straight-line approach. Because share value tends to be related to reported income, management may feel that such a change favourably affects the firm's market value. In fact, research in this area has found just the opposite: companies that switch to more liberal accounting policies may experience declines in share values. One explanation is that changes like this signal that the company is in trouble and also lead to scepticism about management's attitudes and behaviour.

The choice of a depreciation method affects both the statement of financial position (in terms of the carrying amount of property, plant, and equipment) and the income statement (in terms of the depreciation expense). It follows, therefore, that various ratios are affected by the choice that is made. These ratios include the rate of return on total assets, debt-to-total assets, and total asset turnover. Consequently, contractual commitments based on financial statement ratios, such as agreements related to management compensation plans and bond indentures, are potentially important aspects that tend to be considered when choosing a depreciation method.

How is each of the major depreciation methods applied? Regardless of whether the cost model or the revaluation model is chosen to measure assets after acquisition, the three major systematic methods are:

1. Straight-line method

2. Diminishing balance method

3. Unit of production (or activity) method

To illustrate these choices, assume that a company purchases a crane for heavy construction purposes. Illustration 11-4 presents the relevant data on the purchase of the crane.

Cost of crane	$500,000
Estimated useful life	5 years
Productive life	30,000 hours
Estimated residual value	$ 50,000

UNDERLYING CONCEPT

If the benefits flow evenly over time, there is justification for using the straight-line basis of allocation.

Straight-Line Method

Under the **straight-line method**, depreciation is considered **a function of the passage of time**. This is the most widely used method in practice. Not only is it straightforward to apply, it is often the most conceptually appropriate method as well. When creeping obsolescence is the main reason for a limited service life, the decline in usefulness is likely constant from period to period. The depreciation expense for the crane under the straight-line method is calculated in Illustration 11-5.

Illustration 11-5

Depreciation Calculation, Straight-Line Method—Crane Example

$$\frac{\text{Cost less residual value}}{\text{Estimated useful life}} = \text{Depreciation charge}$$

$$\frac{\$500,000 - \$50,000}{5 \text{ years}} = \$90,000$$

One objection to the straight-line method is that it relies on two assumptions:

1. The asset actually does deliver equal economic benefits each year.

2. Maintenance expense is about the same each period (assuming constant revenue flows).

If these assumptions are not valid, some argue that this method will not give a rational matching of expense with the periods that benefit from the asset.

Another issue with this method (and some of the others) is the distortion that develops in a rate of return analysis (income ÷ assets). Illustration 11-6 indicates how the rate of return increases, assuming one asset and constant income levels, because the asset's book value decreases. The increasing trend in the rate of return can be very misleading as a basis for evaluating the success of operations because the increase is only due to the accounting method used, and not to improvements in underlying economic performance.

Illustration 11-6

Depreciation and Rate of Return Analysis—Crane Example

Year	Depreciation Expense	Undepreciated Asset Balance (net book value)	Income (after depreciation expense)	Rate of Return (income ÷ assets)
0		$500,000		
1	$90,000	410,000	$100,000	24.4%
2	90,000	320,000	100,000	31.2%
3	90,000	230,000	100,000	43.5%
4	90,000	140,000	100,000	71.4%
5	90,000	50,000	100,000	200.0%

UNDERLYING CONCEPT

The matching concept does not justify use of a constant charge to income. If the benefits from the asset decline as it ages, then a decreasing expense better reflects how its benefits are consumed.

Diminishing Balance Method

Diminishing balance methods, often called **decreasing charge methods** or **accelerated amortization,** create a higher depreciation expense in the earlier years and lower charges in later periods. The justification for this approach is that many assets offer their greatest benefits in the early years, so that this method best reflects their pattern of use. Another argument is that repair and maintenance costs are often higher in later periods, and an accelerated method therefore provides a fairly constant total expense (for depreciation plus repairs and maintenance). When Canadian companies use a diminishing balance approach, it is usually a version of what is called the declining-balance method.[7]

The **declining-balance method** uses a depreciation rate that stays constant throughout the asset's life, assuming there is no change in estimate. The depreciation rate is expressed as a percentage and is called the declining-balance rate. This rate is applied each year to the net book value (cost less accumulated depreciation and any accumulated impairment losses) to calculate depreciation expense. For assets accounted for by the revaluation method, the rate is applied to the revalued asset amount less the total of any accumulated depreciation and accumulated impairment losses.

The rate is usually calculated as a multiple of the straight-line rate.[8] Let's look at some examples.

- For an asset with a 10-year life, the double-declining-balance rate is 20% (the straight-line rate of 100% ÷ 10, or 10%, multiplied by 2).

- For an asset with a 20-year life, the double-declining-balance rate is 10% (100% ÷ 20, or 5%, multiplied by 2).

- For an asset with a 20-year life, the triple-declining-balance rate is 15% (the straight-line rate of 100% ÷ 20, or 5%, multiplied by 3).

Unlike other methods, the declining-balance method does not deduct **the asset's residual value** in calculating depreciation expense. Instead, the declining-balance method applies the appropriate rate to the asset's carrying amount at the beginning of each period. Since the asset's book value is reduced each period by the depreciation charge, the rate is applied to a lower and lower carrying amount each period, resulting in a depreciation charge that gets smaller each year. This process continues until the asset's carrying amount is reduced to its estimated residual value. **When the residual value is reached, the asset is no longer depreciated.**

Illustration 11-7 shows how to apply the **double-declining-balance method,** using the crane example.

Illustration 11-7	

Depreciation Calculation, Double-Declining-Balance Method—Crane Example

Year	Book Value of Asset, Beginning of Year	Rate on Declining Balance[a]	Depreciation Expense	Balance of Accumulated Depreciation	Net Book Value, End of Year
1	$500,000	40%	$200,000	$200,000	$300,000
2	300,000	40%	120,000	320,000	180,000
3	180,000	40%	72,000	392,000	108,000
4	108,000	40%	43,200	435,200	64,800
5	64,800	40%	14,800[b]	450,000	50,000

[a] (100% ÷ 5) × 2
[b] Limited to $14,800 because the book value is not reduced below the residual value.

Unit of Production Method

The **unit of production method,** sometimes called the **activity method** or a **variable charge approach,** calculates depreciation **according to usage or productivity** instead of the passage of time. The asset's life is defined in terms of either the output it provides (units produced) or the input required (the number of hours it operates). Conceptually, a better cost association results from using output instead of an input measure such as hours used, but both are widely accepted and used.

The crane's usage in hours is relatively easy to measure. If it is used for 4,000 hours the first year, the depreciation charge is calculated as shown in Illustration 11-8.

Illustration 11-8

Depreciation Calculation, Activity Method—Crane Example

$$\frac{\text{Cost less residual value}}{\text{Total Estimated hours}} = \text{Depreciation expense per hour}$$

$$\frac{\$500,000 - \$50,000}{30,000 \text{ hours}} = \$15 \text{ per hour}$$

First year depreciation expense: 4,000 hours × $15 = $60,000

When the asset's economic benefits are consumed by usage, activity, or productivity, the unit of production method results in the best measure of periodic expense. Companies that adopt this approach have low depreciation during periods of low usage, high charges during high usage, and zero depreciation expense when the asset is available, but idle.

This method's major limitation is that it is appropriate in only a few situations. For example, a building usually suffers a great amount of steady deterioration from the weather (a function of time) regardless of how it is used. In addition, when an asset's useful life is affected by economic or functional factors that have nothing to do with its usage, the activity method is not appropriate. If a company is expanding rapidly, a particular building may soon become obsolete for its intended purpose. The level of activity is irrelevant.

One industry where the activity method is particularly relevant is the extractive industry, which includes mining and oil and gas. Accounting for the depletion of natural resources is discussed in the next section.

Other Methods

Sometimes, because of cost-benefit considerations or because the assets have unique characteristics, an entity may choose not to use one of the more common depreciation methods. Instead, it may use the method required by the Canada Revenue Agency for tax purposes as explained in Appendix 11A, or develop its own tailor-made amortization method. In 2014, the IASB clarified IAS 16 to indicate that using depreciation methods based on revenue generated is not appropriate. Depreciation should be based on the benefits being consumed, not benefits generated by running the business.

WHAT DO THE NUMBERS MEAN?

REAL WORLD EMPHASIS

Some companies try to imply that amortization is not a cost. For example, in their press releases, they often draw more attention to earnings before interest, taxes, depreciation, and amortization (referred to as EBITDA) or pro forma earnings (which may exclude items such as depreciation and restructuring costs) rather than net income as calculated under GAAP.[9] Some companies like the EBITDA figure because it "dresses up" their earnings numbers, and they promote it using the argument that the excluded costs are not operating costs or that amortization and depreciation are non-cash charges. Regardless, when all is said and done, companies must generate enough cash from revenues to cover all their costs, as the amounts they borrow to finance long-term asset acquisitions have to be repaid. Investors need to understand the differences between these various indicators of financial performance.

Consider **Intertape Polymer Group Inc.**'s review of its results for 2014. EBITDA was reported at $103.9 million, while net income under GAAP amounted to $35.8 million. At one time, **Hollinger International Inc.** reported EBITDA of U.S. $111.4 million and a GAAP net loss of U.S. $238.8 million! Because of concerns that investors may be confused or misled by non-GAAP earnings measures, the Canadian Securities Administrators, which is the umbrella group for provincial regulators, issued specific guidance for certain disclosures that are associated with non-GAAP earnings measures. These include requiring that entities present a reconciliation of their non-GAAP measure(s) with audited GAAP results.

While reporting EBITDA and other pro forma numbers has not been prohibited, it appears that the new requirements have made some companies less enthusiastic about reporting these results as prominently as they previously did.

Depletion of Mineral Resources

Objective 4
Explain the accounting issues for depletion of mineral resources.

One industry where the activity method is particularly relevant is the extractive industry. Chapter 10 explains that generally the costs of acquisition, exploration, and development (including asset retirement costs) relating to oil and gas reserves and mineral deposits are capitalized into mineral resource assets using either the full cost or successful efforts method. The amortization of the cost of these reserves, as the wells or ore bodies are put into production, is known as **depletion**. The resulting **depletion expense** is a product cost, and therefore is a part of the direct cost of the minerals or petroleum products (inventory) produced during the period, as we saw in our opening story.

The accounting issues associated with the depletion of mineral resources are similar to those encountered with the amortization of other types of property, plant, and equipment. They include:

1. determining the pattern of depletion (amortization) to be used, and

2. the difficulty in estimating the asset's useful life.

Natural resource companies also have to deal with the associated issue of liquidating dividends, as discussed below.

Pattern of Depletion

Once the company establishes the depletion base—the cost of the mineral resource asset to be amortized—the next step is to determine how these capitalized costs will be allocated to accounting periods. Normally, **depletion is calculated using an activity approach, such as the unit of production method.** This approach is used because of the close association of the resulting expense with the asset benefits consumed in the period. Under this method, the cost of the resource asset is divided by the estimated recoverable reserves (the number of units that are estimated to be in the resource deposit) to obtain a cost per unit of production. The cost per unit is then multiplied by the number of units extracted during the period to determine the depletion charge. **Alacer Gold**, in our opening story, uses a unit of production method based on a calculation of their average cost per recoverable ounce of gold.

For example, assume a mining company acquired the right to use 1,000 hectares of land in the Northwest Territories to mine for gold. The lease cost is $50,000, the related exploration and evaluation costs are $100,000, and development costs incurred in opening the mine are $3,850,000, all of which have been capitalized. Total costs related to the mine before the first ounce of gold is extracted are, therefore, $4 million. The company estimates that the mine will provide approximately 5,000 ounces of gold. The depletion rate is determined in Illustration 11-9.

Illustration 11-9
Calculation of Depletion Rate

$$\frac{\text{Total cost} - \text{residual value}}{\text{Total estimated units available}} = \text{Depletion cost per unit}$$

$$\frac{\$4,000,000}{5,000} = \$800 \text{ per ounce}$$

If 1,250 ounces are extracted in the first year, the depletion for the year is $1 million (1,250 ounces at $800). The entry to record the depletion is:

A = L + SE
0   0   0
Cash flows: No effect

Inventory	1,000,000	
Accumulated Depletion		1,000,000

As shown in our feature story, the depletion charge for the extracted resource (in addition to labour and other direct production costs) is initially charged (debited) to inventory.

When the resource is sold, the inventory costs are transferred to cost of goods sold and matched with the period's revenue. The remaining mineral resource is reported with property, plant, and equipment as a non-current asset, as follows:

Gold mine (at cost)	$4,000,000	
Less: Accumulated depletion	1,000,000	$3,000,000

The equipment used in extracting the resource may also be amortized on a unit of production basis, especially if the equipment's benefits and useful life are directly related to the quantity of ore extracted from that specific deposit. If the equipment is used on more than one job and at more than one site, other cost allocation methods may be more appropriate.

Estimating Recoverable Reserves

Companies often change the estimate of the resource's useful life; that is, the amount of the recoverable reserves. This may result from new information or from the availability of more sophisticated production processes. Natural resources such as oil and gas deposits and some rare metals are the greatest challenges. Estimates of these reserves are largely "knowledgeable guesses."

Accounting for a change in the estimate of reserves is the same as for a change in the useful life of an item of plant and equipment. The procedure, explained later in this chapter, is to revise the depletion rate by dividing the costs remaining on the books less any residual value by the new estimate of the recoverable reserves. Past depletion is not adjusted. This approach has much merit because the required estimates are so uncertain.

WHAT DO THE NUMBERS MEAN?

REAL WORLD EMPHASIS

Husky Energy, a Canadian company in the oil and gas industry, reports in the Accounting Estimates and Key Judgments sections of its 2014 annual report that:

... amounts recorded for depletion, depreciation, amortization and impairment, ARO [asset retirement obligations], assets and liabilities measured at fair value, [and] employee future benefits ... are based on estimates.

Management makes judgments regarding the application of IFRS for each accounting policy. Critical judgments that have the most significant effect on the amounts recognized in the consolidated financial statements include successful efforts and impairment assessments, the determination of cash generating units ("CGUs") ...

Costs directly associated with an exploration well are initially capitalized as exploration and evaluation assets. Expenditures related to wells that do not find reserves or where no future activity is planned are expensed as exploration and evaluation expenses. Exploration and evaluation costs are excluded from costs subject to depletion until technical feasibility and commercial viability is

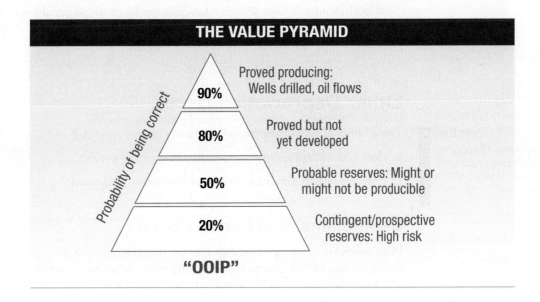

THE VALUE PYRAMID

Probability of being correct

90% Proved producing: Wells drilled, oil flows

80% Proved but not yet developed

50% Probable reserves: Might or might not be producible

20% Contingent/prospective reserves: High risk

"OOIP"

assessed or production commences. At that time, costs are either transferred to property, plant and equipment or their value is impaired. Impairment is charged directly to net earnings.

The Simmons & Company International illustration of the Value Pyramid on the previous page underscores the measurement uncertainty associated with resource quantities, and therefore the depletion expense, recognized by companies in the industry.

"OOIP" refers to the original oil in place, and determining this is the starting point in the calculation of reserves. After this, the amount of the OOIP that

is technically and economically recoverable is then estimated. The percentages indicated in each layer of the pyramid give you some idea of the likelihood of these estimates being correct. The bottom line is that estimating oil and gas reserves may be more an art than a science!

Source: Simmons and Company International. From a presentation given by Matthew R. Simmons to the Standing Group on the Oil Market of the International Energy Agency in Paris, France, March 16, 2004, available at: http://www.simmonsco-intl.com/files/IEA-SOM.pdf, accessed June 2, 2009.

VALUATION
5.4.1, 5.4.2

Liquidating Dividends

A company may own a property from which it plans to extract mineral resources, and have this as its only major asset. If the company does not expect to purchase more properties, it may decide to distribute to shareholders a portion or all of their capital investment by paying a **liquidating dividend**, which is a dividend greater than the amount of accumulated net income. These dividends are usually equal to the accumulated amount of net income (after depletion) **plus the amount of depletion that has been charged.**

The major accounting issue is to distinguish between dividends that are a return **of capital** and those that are not. A company issuing a liquidating dividend reduces the appropriate Share Capital account for the portion of the dividend that is related to the original investment instead of reducing Retained Earnings, because the dividend is a return of part of the investor's original contribution.

To illustrate, assume Callahan Mining Corp. has a retained earnings balance of $1,650,000, accumulated depletion on mineral properties of $2.1 million, and common share capital of $5.4 million. Callahan's board declares and pays a dividend of $3 per share on the 1 million shares outstanding. The company records the dividend as follows:

A   =   L   +   SE
−3,000,000   −3,000,000

Cash flows: ↓ 3,000,000 outflow

Retained Earnings	1,650,000	
Common Shares	1,350,000*	
Cash		3,000,000
*($3,000,000 − $1,650,000)		

Callahan must inform shareholders that the $3 dividend per share represents a $1.65 ($1,650,000/1,000,000) per share **return on investment** and a $1.35 ($1,350,000/1,000,000) per share liquidating dividend, or **return of capital**.

Other Depreciation Issues

Objective 5

Explain and apply the accounting procedures for partial periods and a change in depreciation rate.

Two additional depreciation issues remain:

1. How should depreciation be calculated for partial periods?

2. How are revisions to depreciation rates made and reported?

Depreciation and Partial Periods

Plant assets are rarely purchased on the first day of a fiscal period or disposed of on the last day of a fiscal period, except in accounting texts! A practical question therefore is, "How much depreciation should be charged for partial periods?"

Assume, for example, that an automated drill machine with a five-year life is purchased for $45,000 (no residual value) on June 10, 2017. The company's fiscal year ends December 31, and depreciation is charged for $6\frac{2}{3}$ months during the year. The total depreciation for a full year, assuming the straight-line method, is $9,000 ($45,000 ÷ 5). The depreciation for the first, partial year is therefore:

$$\frac{\$9,000 \times 6^2/_3}{12} = \$5,000$$

Rather than making a precise allocation of cost for a partial period, many companies set a policy to simplify the process. One variation is to take no depreciation in the year of acquisition and a full year's depreciation in the year of disposal. For example, depreciation is calculated for the full period on the opening balance in the asset account, and none for acquisitions in the year. Another variation is to charge a full year's depreciation on assets that are used for a full year and charge a half year of amortization in the years of acquisition and disposal. Alternatively, the company may charge a full year's depreciation in the year of acquisition and none in the year of disposal.

Although not conceptually "correct," companies may adopt one of these fractional-year policies in allocating cost to the first and last years of an asset's life if the method is applied consistently and the resulting effect on the financial statements is not material. For example, for its 2014 fiscal year, **Canadian Pacific Railway Limited** follows a group depreciation policy that applies a single depreciation rate for items within the same class of property. The company accounts for retirements and disposals of items like trains by charging the cost of the property, less any net salvage, to accumulated depreciation. For the illustrations and problem material in this text, depreciation is calculated based on the nearest full month, unless something different is stated. Illustration 11-10 shows depreciation allocated under five different fractional-year policies using the straight-line method on an automated drill machine purchased for $45,000 on June 10, 2017.

REAL WORLD EMPHASIS

Illustration 11-10

Fractional-Year Depreciation Policies, Straight-Line Method

Machine Cost = $45,000	Depreciation Allocated Each Year over 5-Year Life (rounded to the nearest dollar)					
Fractional-Year Policy	2017	2018	2019	2020	2021	2022
1. Nearest fraction of a year	$5,000[a]	$9,000	$9,000	$9,000	$9,000	$4,000[b]
2. Nearest full month	5,250[c]	9,000	9,000	9,000	9,000	3,750[d]
3. Half year in period of acquisition and disposal	4,500	9,000	9,000	9,000	9,000	4,500
4. Full year in period of acquisition, none in period of disposal	9,000	9,000	9,000	9,000	9,000	0
5. None in period of acquisition, full year in period of disposal	0	9,000	9,000	9,000	9,000	9,000

[a]6.667/12 ($9,000)   [b]5.333/12 ($9,000)   [c]7/12 ($9,000)   [d]5/12 ($9,000)

The partial period calculation is relatively simple when a company uses the straight-line method. But how is partial period depreciation handled when using an accelerated method? To illustrate, assume that an asset was purchased for $10,000 on October 1, 2017, with an estimated useful life of five years. The depreciation expense for 2017, 2018, and 2019 using the double-declining-balance method is shown in Illustration 11-11.

Illustration 11-11

Calculation of Partial Period Depreciation, Double-Declining-Balance Method

Annual Calculations	
1st full year	$(40\% \times \$10,000) = \$4,000$
2nd full year	$(40\% \times 6,000) = 2,400$
3rd full year	$(40\% \times 3,600) = 1,440$

Depreciation October 1, 2017, to December 31, 2017:	$3/12 \times \$4,000 = \underline{\underline{\$1,000}}$

Depreciation for 2018:	$9/12 \times \$4,000 = \$3,000$
	$3/12 \times \$2,400 = \underline{600}$
	$\underline{\underline{\$3,600}}$

Depreciation for 2019:	$9/12 \times \$2,400 = \$1,800$
	$3/12 \times \$1,440 = \underline{360}$
	$\underline{\underline{\$2,160}}$

Alternatively:

Depreciation for 2017: $(40\% \times \$10,000) \times 3/12 =$ $\qquad$ $\$1,000$
   Asset carrying amount now = $\$10,000 - \$1,000 = \$9,000$

Depreciation for 2018: $(40\% \times \$9,000) =$ $\qquad$ $\$3,600$
   Asset carrying amount now = $\$9,000 - \$3,600 = \$5,400$

Depreciation for 2019: $(40\% \times \$5,400) =$ $\qquad$ $\$2,160$
   Asset carrying amount now = $\$5,400 - \$2,160 = \$3,240$

As you can see, the depreciation amount is identical whether you proceed through yearly "layers" of depreciation or whether you simply apply the rate to the asset's carrying amount at the start of each year.

Revision of Depreciation Rates

When a plant asset is acquired, depreciation rates are carefully determined based on past experience with similar assets and other pertinent information. Depreciation is only an estimate, however, and the estimates of the expected pattern of consumption of the asset's benefits, useful life, and residual value need to be reviewed regularly and at least at each fiscal year end under IFRS. A change in any one of these variables requires that either the depreciation method or the rate also be changed. Unexpected physical deterioration, unforeseen obsolescence, or changes in the extent or way in which the asset is used may make the asset's useful life less than originally estimated. Improved maintenance procedures, a revision of operating policies, or similar developments may prolong its life beyond what was expected.

When a change in estimate takes place, accounting standards **do not permit companies to go back and "correct" the records, nor to make a "catch-up" adjustment** for any accumulated difference. Instead, a company accounts for a change in estimate **prospectively; that is, in the period of change and in the future, if applicable.** This is because estimates are such an inherent part of the accounting process. As new information becomes available, the changes are incorporated into current and future measurements.

For example, assume that machinery that cost $90,000 was estimated originally to have a 20-year life and a $10,000 residual value. It has already been depreciated for eight years. In year nine, the asset's total life is now expected to be 30 years with a residual value of only $2,000. Depreciation has been recorded on the asset at the rate of 1/20 ($90,000 – $10,000), or $4,000 each year, by the straight-line method. But now a new depreciation schedule has to be prepared for the asset. The new schedule uses the undepreciated costs that remain on the books, along with the most recent estimates of the asset's residual value and remaining useful life. If another depreciation method is more appropriate for the current circumstances, then it will be applied going forward.

Continuing with our example, Illustration 11-12 shows the charges for depreciation in the current and subsequent periods based on revised calculations, assuming the straight-line method is still appropriate.

Illustration 11-12

*Calculation of Depreciation after
Revision of Estimated Life and
Residual Value*

Machinery cost		$90,000
Less: Accumulated depreciation to date: 8 × $4,000/year		32,000
Carrying amount of machinery at end of 8th year		58,000
Less estimated residual value		2,000
Costs to be depreciated		$56,000

Revised depreciation = $56,000 ÷ (30 − 8) years remaining life = $2,545 per year

The entry to record depreciation in each of the remaining 22 years is:

A = L + SE
−2,545   −2,545

Cash flows: No effect

Depreciation Expense	2,545	
Accumulated Depreciation—Machinery		2,545

If the double-declining-balance method had been used initially, the change in estimated life would result in a new depreciation rate to be applied to the book value in the current (ninth) and subsequent years.[10] In this example, a revised remaining life of 22 years results in a revised 100% ÷ 22 or 4.55% straight-line and a 9.09% double-declining rate. As this method initially ignores residual value in determining depreciation expense, a change in residual value is ignored in the revised calculation until such time as book value equals residual value.

TransAlta Corporation is a Canadian power generation and wholesale marketing company operating in Canada, the United States, and Australia. In its quarterly report for the first quarter of 2015, it provided information about a change in the estimated useful life of its Windsor facility. The information, disclosed in Illustration 11-13, also reports the change in its depreciation expense.

**REAL WORLD
EMPHASIS**

Illustration 11-13

*Change in Estimate of Useful
Life and Depreciation Expense*

TransAlta Corporation

Accounting Changes

A. Current Accounting Changes

II. Change in Estimates – Useful Lives

During the quarter, the Corporation's subsidiary TransAlta Cogeneration L.P. ("TA Cogen") executed a new 15-year power supply contract with Ontario's Independent Electricity System Operator for the Windsor facility, which is effective Dec. 1, 2016. Accordingly, the useful life of the Windsor facility was extended prospectively to Nov. 30, 2031. As a result, depreciation expense for the three months ended March 31, 2015 decreased by $1 million and the full year 2015 depreciation expense is expected to be lower by $8 million.

IMPAIRMENT

Objective 6

Explain the issues and apply the accounting standards for capital asset impairment under both IFRS and ASPE.

As indicated in Chapter 10, property, plant, and equipment (PP&E) assets are measured after acquisition by applying the cost model, the revaluation model, or the fair value model. **If an investment property is measured at fair value** and if the asset becomes impaired, the remeasurement of the asset to fair value automatically recognizes this reduction and the associated loss is recognized in income.

Assets measured under the **cost or revaluation model**, however, are not automatically adjusted to fair value. Instead, they are reported at cost (or at fair value at the most recent revaluation date) less accumulated depreciation. Is this amount the appropriate value for the statement of financial position? Or should PP&E assets be valued at **the lower of cost and net realizable value** as most inventory assets are?

It is important to report inventory on the statement of financial position at no more than the net cash the entity expects to receive on its disposal because, as a **current asset**, it is expected to be converted into cash within the operating cycle. Property, plant, and equipment assets, however, are **not held to be directly converted into cash**. They are ordinarily **used in operations over the long term**. For this reason, the same "lower of cost and net realizable value" measure is not appropriate for PP&E assets. However, it is important that any impairment in value be recognized.

WHAT DO THE NUMBERS MEAN?

REAL WORLD EMPHASIS

Even when long-lived capital assets become partially obsolete, accountants have been reluctant to reduce their carrying amount. This is because it is often difficult to arrive at a measure for property, plant, and equipment that is not subjective and arbitrary. For example, **Falconbridge Ltd.** at one time had to decide whether all or a part of its property, plant, and equipment in a nickel-mining operation in the Dominican Republic should be written off. The project had been incurring losses because nickel prices were low and operating costs were high. Only if nickel prices increased by about 33% would the project be reasonably profitable. Whether it was appropriate to recognize an impairment loss depended on the future price of nickel. Even if a decision were made to write down the asset, the amount to be written off would not be obvious. This same issue faced most Canadian companies in the oil and gas industry in 2014 and 2015 as the price of a barrel of oil dropped by more than 50%. For example, **Husky Energy Inc.** reported a non-cash impairment charge of $838 million in 2014 on its oil and natural gas assets located in Western Canada, as a result of decreases in short- and long-term crude oil and natural gas prices.

How do accountants handle this problem? The first step in accounting for **impairments** is for management to be alert to events and circumstances that might indicate that a long-lived asset is **impaired**; in other words, that its carrying amount is higher than its future economic benefits to the company.

Indicators of Impairment

Illustration 11-14 provides examples of possible evidence of impairment.

Illustration 11-14

Potential Indicators of Impairment (see IAS 36.12)

External Indicators	**Internal Indicators**
There are observable indications of a significant reduction in the asset's value.	There is evidence of obsolescence or physical damage of the asset.
A significant change in the technological, market, economic, or legal environment has affected or is expected to adversely affect the entity.	Significant changes with adverse effects have taken place or are expected to take place in how the asset is used (for example, the asset becoming idle or subject to plans for early disposition).
Market rates of return have increased, with a negative effect on the asset's value in use and recoverable amount.	Internal reports about the asset indicate its performance is or will be worse than expected.
The carrying value of the entity's net assets is more than the company's market capitalization.	Costs incurred for an asset's acquisition or operation significantly exceed the amount originally expected.

There may be other factors that suggest that an asset's carrying amount is overstated. The objective is to be open to the possibility of impairment with changes in the internal and external environment. Even if an impairment loss is not evident, a change may be needed in the estimate of the asset's useful life or residual value, or in the depreciation method applied.

IFRS requires that assets be assessed for indications of impairment at the end of each reporting period, while **ASPE** requires this assessment only when events and changes in circumstances indicate that an asset's carrying amount may not be recoverable (at which time the asset is tested for impairment). We describe two different approaches to impairment accounting next.

Impairment—Recognition and Measurement Models

Just as there are different models for measuring capital assets, there are also different models for measuring impairment losses for these assets. One approach, a **cost recovery**

impairment model, concludes that a long-lived asset is impaired only if an entity cannot recover the asset's carrying amount from using the asset and eventually disposing of it. Another approach, a **rational entity impairment model**, assumes that an entity makes rational decisions in managing its long-term assets. A company is likely to continue to use an asset if its use and later disposal earn a higher return than if it is currently disposed of (sold). If current disposal generates a higher return, then management is likely to take this action. This model, therefore, incorporates both these values in the impairment decision.

Cost Recovery Impairment Model

If events or changes in circumstances indicate that an asset's carrying amount may not be recoverable, the cost recovery impairment model uses a **recoverability test** to determine whether an impairment loss needs to be recognized. Two basic assumptions underlie this approach:

1. The asset will continue to be used in operations.

2. As long as the dollars of cost remaining are expected to be recovered by future inflows of dollars, the asset's carrying amount will be recovered and no impairment is evident.

An estimate is made of the future net cash flows that are expected from the use of the asset and its eventual disposal. These cash flows are not discounted. If these **undiscounted** future cash flows are **less than the asset's carrying amount**, the asset is considered impaired. Conversely, if the **undiscounted** future net cash flows are **equal to or greater than the asset's carrying amount**, no impairment has occurred. Essentially, the recoverability test is a screening device to determine whether an asset is impaired.

If the recoverability test indicates that an asset held for use is impaired, an **impairment loss** is calculated. It is the amount by which the asset's carrying amount exceeds its fair value. This is **not the same** as the difference between its carrying amount and its recoverable amount in the recoverability test. **Fair value** under this model is the price that would be agreed upon in an arm's-length transaction between knowledgeable, willing parties who are under no compulsion to act. By its nature, fair value is a discounted or present value measure. It is best measured by quoted market prices in active markets, but if there is no active market—which is often the case—other valuation methods are used.

Example A: Cost Recovery Impairment Model

Step 1: Because of changes in how equipment is being used, it is reviewed for possible impairment.

Step 2: Based on the possibility of impairment, carry out a **recoverability test**. The asset's carrying amount is $600,000 ($800,000 cost less $200,000 accumulated depreciation). The expected future undiscounted net cash flows from the use of the asset and its later disposal are estimated to be $650,000, and the asset's fair value is $525,000. The recoverability test indicates that the $650,000 of expected net cash flows from the asset exceeds its carrying amount of $600,000. As a result, **no impairment is evident** and no further steps are required.

Example B: Cost Recovery Impairment Model

Assume the same facts as in Example A above, except that the expected future net cash flows from the equipment are $580,000 instead of $650,000.

Step 1: Because of changes in how equipment is being used, it is reviewed for possible impairment.

Step 2: Based on the possibility of impairment, carry out a recoverability test. The **recoverability test** indicates that the $580,000 of expected net cash flows from the asset is less than its carrying amount of $600,000. Therefore, the asset is considered impaired.

Step 3: Measure and record the impairment loss. If the asset's fair value is $525,000, the impairment loss is calculated as shown in Illustration 11-15.

Illustration 11-15

*Calculation of Impairment
Loss—Cost Recovery
Impairment Model*

Carrying amount of the equipment	$600,000
Fair value of equipment	525,000
Impairment loss	$ 75,000

The entry to record the impairment loss is as follows:

A = L + SE
−75,000   −75,000

Cash flows: No effect

| Loss on Impairment | 75,000 | |
| Accumulated Impairment Losses—Equipment | | 75,000 |

Notice that the entry credits an Accumulated Impairment Losses account rather than Accumulated Depreciation or the capital asset account itself. Any one of these credits may be and is used in practice. Regardless of which account is credited, the adjusted carrying amount becomes the asset's new "cost" and the writedown is charged to expense. As the asset is considered to have a new cost basis, no reversal of the impairment charge is permitted. After the impairment loss is recorded, the depreciation method chosen for the asset is reviewed, as are the remaining useful life and residual value. Revised depreciation amounts are then calculated.

ASPE uses the cost recovery impairment model.

Rational Entity Impairment Model

Another approach to the recognition and measurement of impairment losses is the **rational entity impairment model**. This approach assumes that an entity makes rational decisions in managing its long-term assets and therefore it compares the asset's book value with a recoverable amount **that differs depending on the circumstances**. If management can earn a higher return from using an asset than from selling it, the company will continue to use it. However, if a higher return is possible from selling the asset, then the rational decision is to sell it. This model, therefore, compares the asset's carrying amount with its **recoverable amount**, defined as the **higher of its value in use and its fair value less costs of disposal**. If the recoverable amount is less than its carrying amount, the impairment loss is equal to the difference. Illustration 11-16 indicates how the loss is calculated.

Illustration 11-16

*Calculation of Impairment
Loss—Rational Entity Model*

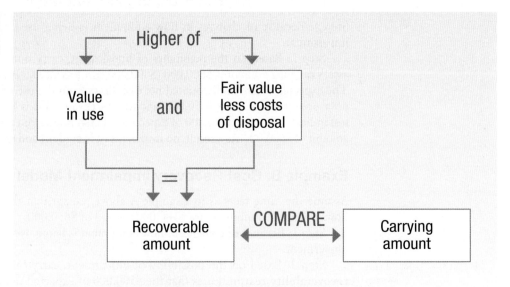

If recoverable amount > carrying amount: no impairment loss

If recoverable amount < carrying amount: impairment loss = difference

Unlike the cost recovery impairment method, there is **no pre-screening test** to determine whether an asset is impaired. Instead, the carrying amount is compared directly with a fair-value-based recoverable amount that is a discounted present value measure.

Value in use is the present value of the future cash flows expected to be derived from the asset's use and subsequent disposal. **Fair value less costs of disposal** is the amount currently expected to be received from the sale of the asset in an orderly transaction between market participants after subtracting incremental costs directly related to the disposal.[11] Fair value is estimated using the fair value hierarchy set out in IFRS 13. The level of the fair value hierarchy used must be disclosed, together with further disclosures if Level 2 or Level 3 measures are used. Disposal costs might include legal costs, transaction taxes, and removal costs, for example, but exclude finance costs and income tax expense. IFRS uses this model.

VALUATION
5.4.1

Example C: Rational Entity Impairment Model

Step 1: As a result of its annual assessment of property, plant, and equipment for indications of impairment, an entity determines that equipment with a carrying amount of $45,000 (cost of $60,000; accumulated depreciation of $15,000) may be impaired due to technological obsolescence.

Step 2: The entity calculates the asset's recoverable amount to be $47,500. This is the higher of its value in use of $47,500 and its fair value less costs of disposal of $40,000. Because the recoverable amount is more than the asset's book value, there is no impairment loss to be recognized.

Example D: Rational Entity versus Cost Recovery Impairment Model

Assume the same facts as in Example C, except that the asset's value in use is determined to be $37,500 and its fair value less costs of disposal (of $2,000) is $40,000. In addition, the expected future undiscounted net cash flows from the use of the asset and its later disposal are estimated to be $43,000. Compare the accounting for impairment under ASPE versus IFRS.

Step 1 (IFRS and ASPE): As a result of its annual assessment of property, plant, and equipment for indications of impairment, an entity determines that equipment with a carrying amount of $45,000 (cost of $60,000; accumulated depreciation of $15,000) may be impaired due to technological obsolescence.

Step 2 (IFRS—rational entity model): The entity calculates the asset's recoverable amount to be $40,000. This is the higher of its value in use of $37,500 and its fair value less costs of disposal of $40,000. Now an impairment loss of $5,000 is indicated, as calculated in Illustration 11-17.

(ASPE—cost recovery impairment model): The recoverability test indicates that the $43,000 of expected net cash flows from the asset is less than the carrying amount of $45,000. As a result, **impairment is evident**, and the impairment loss is calculated in Illustration 11-17.

Illustration 11-17

Calculation of Impairment Loss—Rational Entity Model versus Cost Recovery Impairment Model

	Rational Entity Impairment Model	Cost Recovery Impairment Model
Carrying amount of the equipment	$45,000	$45,000
Recoverable amount (IFRS)/Fair value (ASPE)	40,000	42,000
Impairment loss	$ 5,000	$ 3,000

The entry to record the impairment loss is as follows:

IFRS
A   =   L   +   SE
−5,000   −5,000

Cash flows: No effect

ASPE
A   =   L   +   SE
−3,000   −3,000

Cash flows: No effect

IFRS: Rational Entity Impairment Model		ASPE: Cost Recovery Impairment Model	
Impairment Loss	5,000	Impairment Loss	3,000
Accumulated Impairment		Accumulated Impairment	
Losses—Equipment	5,000	Losses—Equipment	3,000

The loss from the writedown is recognized in net income. However, if the asset is accounted for under the revaluation model, the loss is accounted for on the same basis as a revaluation decrease, explained in Chapter 10: it is charged first through other comprehensive income to any revaluation surplus that exists for that asset, and only the excess is recognized in income. After the impairment loss is recognized, the depreciation method, remaining useful life, and residual value are reviewed, and revised depreciation amounts are determined.

Under the rational entity method, it is important to keep track separately of any impairment losses recognized because, unlike the cost recovery approach, a portion of **the impairment loss may be reversed in the future**. The recoverable amount is considered to be based on estimates that may change in the future. At each reporting date, information that mirrors the original indicators of impairment is assessed to determine whether a previously recognized impairment loss still exists. If the estimates used to determine the asset's value in use and fair value less costs of disposal have changed, then a reversal of the impairment can be recognized.

The reversal amount, however, is limited. The specific asset cannot be increased in value to more than what its book value would have been, net of depreciation, if the original impairment loss had never been recognized.

The method described here as the rational entity model is the one applied under IFRS. What is the core difference between this and the cost recovery impairment method? The IFRS approach better reflects the economic circumstances underlying the asset's usefulness to the entity, capturing both the declines and recoveries in value. The cost recovery (ASPE) approach waits until circumstances indicate that conditions are very bad before recognizing impairment. It does not take into account the time value of money in the recoverability test. It is not neutral because, after recognizing impairment, it does not allow for later recognition of any recovery. That is, no reversals of impairment loss are permitted.

Asset Groups and Cash-Generating Units

The discussion above assumes that recoverable amounts can be determined for each individual asset. However, many assets do not generate cash flows on their own, but only in combination with other assets. (Some examples are in Illustration 11-18.) In this case, the cash flows based on a single asset's value in use cannot be independently determined. Instead, the asset has to be identified with an **asset group** or **cash-generating unit (CGU)** and it is the group whose cash flows are tested for impairment. An asset group or CGU is the smallest identifiable group of assets that generates cash inflows that are predominantly independent of the cash flows from other individual assets or other groups of assets.[12] IAS 36 *Impairment of Assets* provides the examples summarized in Illustration 11-18.

These examples should help provide a basic understanding of what an asset group or CGU is and how each is generally determined. **Both the cost recovery and the rational entity impairment models are then applied as explained above to the groups of assets rather than individual assets.** Any resulting impairment loss is then allocated proportionally (based on relative carrying amounts) to the long-lived assets in the asset group. However, no individual asset is reduced below its fair value (cost recovery impairment model), or the highest of its fair value less costs of disposal, its value in use, or zero (under the rational entity model). This is illustrated in Example E below.

Illustration 11-18

Examples of Cash-Generating Units

Situation	Asset Group or CGU
A mining company owns a private railway to support its mining activities. The railway could be sold for scrap value only. It does not generate cash inflows that are independent of those from the mine's other assets. [IAS 36.67]	It is not possible to estimate the recoverable amount of the private railway alone because its value in use cannot be determined and is probably different from its scrap value. So, the entity should estimate the recoverable amount of the CGU that the private railway belongs to. This is the mine as a whole.
A bus company provides services under contract with a municipality that requires minimum service on each of five separate routes. The assets devoted to each route and the cash flows from each are known. One of the routes operates at a significant loss. [IAS 36.68]	Because the company does not have the option to reduce service on any one bus route, the lowest level of identifiable cash flows that are largely independent of the cash inflows from other assets or groups of assets is represented by the cash flows generated by the five routes together. The CGU for each route is the bus company as a whole.

Example E: Asset Group or CGU

Uni Corp. (UC) is a manufacturer that produces parts for residential telephone sets. Recent indications are that the market for this product is likely to continue to decline significantly and UC is testing equipment used in the production process for impairment. The following assets are used only in the manufacture of these parts (in thousands):

	Cost	Accumulated Depreciation	Carrying Amount
Tools and dies	$10,000	$ 6,000	$ 4,000
Specialized equipment	50,000	35,000	15,000
General equipment	30,000	18,000	12,000
	$90,000	$59,000	$31,000

The tools and dies and specialized equipment cannot be used elsewhere and have no resale value, while the general equipment could be sold today for $15,000. UC plans to continue producing the parts for two more years to fill a commitment to its customer. The net future cash flows from the next two years' production of these parts and the disposal of the equipment are estimated to be $32,000, and the present value of these cash flows is $26,000.

Impairment Loss—Cost Recovery Impairment Model

Because the tools and dies and specialized equipment cannot generate cash flows on their own, they are combined into an asset group with the general equipment. The carrying amount of the asset group is $31,000. The cost recovery impairment model applies a recoverability test to determine if there is an impairment. The book value of $31,000 is compared with the undiscounted future cash flows expected from the use and later disposal of the asset group of $32,000. Because the book value can be recovered, there is no impairment, and no loss is recognized. As mentioned above, if an impairment loss is indicated, it is allocated only to the long-lived assets in the group that are held for use. The allocation is based on the assets' relative carrying amounts, although no asset is written down below its fair value, if known.

Impairment Loss—Rational Entity Model

Under this model, the carrying amount of the cash-generating group of $31,000 is compared with the CGU's recoverable amount. The recoverable amount is $26,000—the higher of the CGU's value in use of $26,000 and its fair value less costs of disposal of $15,000.

Carrying amount of CGU	$31,000
Recoverable amount	26,000
Impairment loss	$ 5,000

The impairment loss is then allocated to the individual assets in the group,[13] but no individual asset can be reduced below the highest of (1) its value in use, (2) its fair value less costs of disposal, or (3) zero. In this case, the only determinable amount is the general equipment's fair value less costs of disposal of $15,000. Because this asset's book value is already less than this, the $5,000 loss is therefore allocated only to the tools and dies and specialized equipment pro rata on the basis of the carrying amount of each asset.

Allocation:	Carrying Amount	Proportion	Loss Allocation
Tools and dies	$ 4,000	4/19	$1,050
Specialized equipment	15,000	15/19	3,950
Total	$19,000		$5,000

The entry to record the impairment is:

A = L + SE
−5,000   −5,000

Cash flows: No effect

Impairment Loss	5,000	
Accumulated Impairment Losses—Tools and Dies		1,050
Accumulated Impairment Losses—Equipment		3,950

HELD FOR SALE AND DERECOGNITION

Long-Lived Assets to Be Disposed of by Sale

Held for Sale

Objective 7

Account for derecognition of property, plant, and equipment and explain and apply the accounting standards for long-lived assets that are held for sale.

What happens if a company intends to dispose of its long-lived assets by sale instead of continuing to use them? Because this is relevant information for financial statement readers, such an asset is classified as **held for sale**, is remeasured at the lower of its carrying amount and fair value less costs of disposal, and is reported separately. A "fair value less costs of disposal" measurement is used if this is less than its book value because it corresponds better to the amount of cash a company expects to generate from the asset. The usefulness of this measurement is increased by the strict criteria for classifying a long-lived asset as held for sale, including the requirement that the asset be disposed of within a short period of time. These criteria were presented in Chapter 4 in the section on discontinued operations.

Assets that are held for sale **are not depreciated while they are held**. The reason is that it would be inconsistent to amortize assets that are not in use, that are likely to be sold, and that are carried at the equivalent of the lower of (amortized) cost and net realizable value. In many respects, these assets are closer to inventory than capital assets.

After being classified as a held-for-sale asset, such an asset continues to be carried at the lower of amortized cost and fair value less costs of disposal. Further losses are recognized if the net amount expected from the asset continues to drop. Gains (that is, loss recoveries) are recognized for any increases in net realizable value, but these are limited to the amount of the cumulative losses previously recognized.

How these assets and gains and losses are reported is governed by the need for users to understand the effects of discontinued operations and disposals of non-current assets. If the long-lived asset is a component of an entity that meets the criteria for being reported as a discontinued operation, the losses and any recoveries are reported as part of discontinued operations on the income statement. Otherwise, they are reported in income from continuing operations. Practice differs on how the PP&E assets held for sale are reported on the statement of financial position. ASPE allows these assets to be reclassified as current assets only if they are sold before the financial statements are completed, and the proceeds to be received qualify as a current asset. Otherwise, they are reported separately as non-current assets. Under IFRS, most non-current assets that meet the stringent requirements for classification as held for sale also meet the criteria for recognition as current assets. In all cases, they are reported separately from other assets on the statement of financial position with note disclosure of the major classes of assets making up the total.

Derecognition

Sale of Property, Plant, and Equipment

Unless an asset has been classified as held for sale, depreciation is taken until the date the asset is **derecognized**; that is, the time when all accounts related to the asset are removed from the accounts. An item of property, plant, and equipment is usually derecognized on the date of disposal, but it could be taken off the books earlier if management thinks it will provide no further economic benefits, from either use or disposal. Ideally, when it is derecognized, the asset's carrying amount would be the same as its disposal value, but this is rarely the case. Therefore, a gain or loss is usually reported.

Under the cost and fair value models, the gain or loss on derecognition is shown on the income statement, but would not be classified as revenue unless the company routinely sells property, plant, and equipment items that it had been renting to others. A gain or loss from the disposal of long-lived assets included in a discontinued business is reported in the discontinued operations section of the statement.

UNDERLYING CONCEPT

The "ideal" treatment of the change in value suggested here is more consistent with a physical concept of capital maintenance.

What happens to the gain or loss on disposal if the asset was accounted for under the revaluation model? Theoretically, there would not be a gain or loss on disposal. This is based on the idea that the asset would be revalued to its fair value at the date of disposal, with the change in value accounted for in the same way as all previous revaluations. If so, there would be no difference between the proceeds on disposal and the carrying amount to recognize on the income statement. Any remaining balance in the Revaluation Surplus account would be adjusted directly to Retained Earnings. However, IAS 16 *Property, Plant, and Equipment* does not address this issue, stating only that gains or losses on derecognition are reported in income. A company could, then, recognize the difference between the asset's most recent carrying amount and the proceeds of disposal on the income statement.

To illustrate the disposal of an asset that is held for use, assume that a machine costing $18,000 has been used for nine years and depreciated at a rate of $1,200 per year. If the machine is sold in the middle of the tenth year for $7,000, the entry to record the half-year's depreciation up to the sale date is:

A = L + SE
−600   −600

Cash flows: No effect

Depreciation Expense	600	
Accumulated Depreciation—Machinery		600

The entry for the asset's sale is:

A = L + SE
+400   +400

Cash flows: ↑ 7,000 inflow

Cash	7,000	
Accumulated Depreciation—Machinery	11,400	
[($1,200 × 9) ÷ $600]		
Machinery		18,000
Gain on Sale of Machinery		400

There is a gain on sale because the $7,000 proceeds on disposal is $400 more than the machinery's carrying amount of $6,600 ($18,000 − $11,400).

If an asset is classified as **held for sale**, it is carried at its fair value less costs of disposal. In this case, the net proceeds from the sale of the asset should be close to the asset's carrying amount and it is likely that only minor gains or losses would be recognized when the actual disposal occurs.

Involuntary Conversion

Sometimes an asset's service ends through an involuntary conversion, such as fire, flood, theft, or expropriation. When this happens, the gains or losses are calculated in the same way as they are for the sale of an item of property, plant, and equipment.[14]

To illustrate, assume that a company is forced to sell its building that stands directly in the path of a planned major highway. For several years, the provincial government has tried to purchase the land on which the building stands, but the company has always resisted. The government ultimately exercises its right to expropriate and the courts have upheld its actions. In settlement, the company receives $500,000, which is much higher than the $100,000 book value of the building (cost of $300,000 less accumulated depreciation of $200,000) and the $100,000 book value of the land. The following entry is made:

A = L + SE
+300,000   +300,000

Cash flows: ↑ 500,000 inflow

Cash	500,000	
Accumulated Depreciation—Buildings	200,000	
Buildings		300,000
Land		100,000
Gain on Disposal of Land and Buildings		300,000

Similar treatment is given to other types of involuntary conversions. The difference between any amount that is recovered, such as through insurance, and the asset's carrying amount is reported as a gain or loss.

Donations of Capital Assets

When a company donates or contributes an asset, the gift is recorded as an expense and is measured at the asset's fair value. The difference between its fair value and its carrying amount is recognized as a gain or loss. To illustrate, assume that Kline Industries donates property with a fair value of $110,000 to the City of Saskatoon for a park. The land's book and fair value is $30,000 and a small building on the site is carried at its cost of $95,000 and accumulated depreciation to the contribution date of $45,000. The entry to record the donation is:

A = L + SE
−80,000   −80,000

Cash flows: No effect

Contribution Expense	110,000	
Accumulated Depreciation—Buildings	45,000	
Buildings		95,000
Land		30,000
Gain on Disposal of Buildings		30,000

Miscellaneous Issues

If an asset is scrapped or abandoned without any cash recovery, the entity recognizes a loss that is equal to the asset's book value. If the asset can be sold for scrap, the gain or loss is the difference between its scrap value and its book value. If a fully depreciated asset is still used, both the asset and its accumulated depreciation remain on the books.

PRESENTATION, DISCLOSURE, AND ANALYSIS

Presentation and Disclosure

Objective 8
Describe the types of disclosures required for property, plant, and equipment.

A significant amount of information needs to be reported about a company's property, plant, and equipment so that users of financial statements can assess the existence and measurement of, and changes in, such assets. The following is a summary of the types of disclosures that are generally required:[15]

- an entity's gross carrying amount of property, plant, and equipment, in investment property, and in biological assets;

- changes in the gross carrying amount and in the accumulated depreciation and impairment;

- the nature and circumstances relating to impairment losses (and any reversal, if applicable);

- how net income is affected by the changes related to depreciation, impairment, and impairment reversals;

- the policies, models, and choices made in measuring PP&E, such as depreciation rates and methods and government grants;

- the existence and amounts of restrictions related to the assets;

- the effects related to each of continuing and discontinued operations;

- changes in assets as a result of fair value remeasurements;

- the carrying amount and other details of capital assets that are not being used because they are under construction or held for sale;

- cash inflows and outflows associated with the exploration and evaluation of mineral resources;

- the fair value of investment property assets;

- the level of fair value hierarchy (per IFRS 13) used to measure fair value less costs of disposal for assets or cash-generating units where an impairment loss has been recognized or reversed during the period;

- any outstanding related contingencies.

The requirement for separate disclosure of both the cost and accumulated depreciation gives financial statement readers more information than if only the net book value is disclosed. As an example, consider two companies, each having capital assets with a carrying amount of $100,000. The first company's assets cost $1 million and have accumulated depreciation of $900,000 charged against them. The second company, on the other hand, has assets with a cost of $105,000, and accumulated depreciation of $5,000. With the additional data, information is provided about the size of the original investment in property, plant, and equipment and its relative age. Information about depreciation rates and methods and accounting policy choices represents important disclosures because these result in material charges to the income statement. Depreciation is often the largest non-cash expense recognized by companies.

Illustration 11-19 provides excerpts from the disclosures for **The Hershey Company**'s property, plant, and equipment on its December 31, 2014 balance sheet. The company is based in the United States and reports amounts in thousands of U.S. dollars. These disclosures are quite similar to those that would be required in Canada under ASPE. You are probably familiar with some of Hershey's products!

REAL WORLD EMPHASIS

Consolidated Balance Sheets at 31 December 2014

	2014	2013
	000's	000's
Assets		
Property, plant and equipment, net	2,151,901	1,805,345

1. SUMMARY OF SIGNIFICANT ACCOUNTING POLICIES (excerpts)

Property, Plant and Equipment

Property, plant and equipment are stated at cost and depreciated on a straight-line basis over the estimated useful lives of the assets, as follows: 3 to 15 years for machinery and equipment; and 25 to 40 years for buildings and related improvements. We capitalize applicable interest charges incurred during the construction of new facilities and production lines and amortize these costs over the assets' estimated useful lives.

We review long-lived assets for impairment whenever events or changes in circumstances indicate that the carrying amount of such assets may not be recoverable. We measure the recoverability of assets to be held and used by a comparison of the carrying amount of long-lived assets to future undiscounted net cash flows expected to be generated. If these assets are considered to be impaired, we measure impairment as the amount by which the carrying amount of the assets exceeds the fair value of the assets. We report assets held for sale or disposal at the lower of the carrying amount or fair value less cost to sell.

We assess asset retirement obligations on a periodic basis and recognize the fair value of a liability for an asset retirement obligation in the period in which it is incurred if a reasonable estimate of fair value can be made. We capitalize associated asset retirement costs as part of the carrying amount of the long-lived asset.

2. BUSINESS ACQUISITIONS AND DIVESTITURES (excerpts, amounts in thousands)

Acquisitions

Acquisitions of businesses are accounted for as purchases and, accordingly, the results of operations of the businesses acquired have been included in the consolidated financial statements since the respective dates of the acquisitions. The purchase price for each of the acquisitions is allocated to the assets acquired and liabilities assumed.

Planned Divestiture

In December 2014, we entered into an agreement to sell the Mauna Loa Macadamia Nut Corporation ("Mauna Loa") for $38,000, subject to a working capital adjustment and customary closing conditions. The sale is expected to be finalized in the first quarter of 2015. As a result of the expected sale, we have recorded an estimated loss on the anticipated sale of $22,256 to reflect the disposal entity at fair value, less an estimate of the selling costs. This amount includes impairment charges totaling $18,531 to write down goodwill and the indefinite-lived trademark intangible asset, based on the valuation of these assets as implied by the agreed-upon sales price. The estimated loss on the anticipated sale is reflected within business realignment and impairment costs in the Consolidated Statements of Income. Mauna Loa is reported within our North America segment. Its operations are not material to our annual net sales, net income or earnings per share.[16]

15. SUPPLEMENTAL BALANCE SHEET INFORMATION (excerpts, amounts in thousands)

The components of certain Consolidated Balance Sheet accounts are as follows:

December 31 Property, plant and equipment	2014	2013
Land	$ 95,913	$ 96,334
Buildings	1,031,050	882,508
Machinery and equipment	2,863,559	2,527,420
Construction in progress	338,085	273,132
Property, plant and equipment, gross	4,328,607	3,779,394
Accumulated depreciation	(2,176,706)	(1,974,049)
Property, plant and equipment, net	$ 2,151,901	$ 1,805,345

Analysis

Because property, plant, and equipment and their related depreciation are so significant on most companies' statements of financial position and income statements, it is important to understand the nature of these long-lived assets, and to ensure that management is generating an acceptable rate of return on their investment in them.

Depreciation and Replacement of Assets

Depreciation is similar to other expenses in that it reduces net income, but is different in that **it does not involve a current cash outflow**. A common misconception about depreciation is that it provides funds to replace capital assets.

To illustrate the fact that depreciation does not provide funds for replacing plant assets, assume that a business starts operating with plant assets of $500,000 with a useful life of five years. The company's statement of financial position at the beginning of the period is:

Plant assets	$500,000	Owners' equity	$500,000

Now if we assume the company earns no revenue over the five years, the income statements are as follows:

	Year 1	Year 2	Year 3	Year 4	Year 5
Revenue	$ –0–	$ –0–	$ –0–	$ –0–	$ –0–
Depreciation	(100,000)	(100,000)	(100,000)	(100,000)	(100,000)
Loss	$(100,000)	$(100,000)	$(100,000)	$(100,000)	$(100,000)

The statement of financial position at the end of the five years is:

Plant assets	$–0–	Owners' equity	$–0–

This extreme example shows that depreciation in no way provides funds to replace assets. Funds for the replacement of assets usually come from new asset inflows represented by revenues. By setting selling prices high enough to recover out-of-pocket costs plus depreciation expense, companies do generate cash flows to help finance replacements. If management wants to accumulate a replacement fund, however, it has to set aside the cash specifically for this purpose.

Efficiency of Asset Use and Return on Investment

Investors are interested in information that tells them how efficiently management uses the long-lived assets it has invested in. Incurring capital costs provides the company with a certain level of operating capacity, and usually creates the need for significant amounts of fixed costs far into the future.

Which ratios provide information about the usage of the assets? Assets can be analyzed in terms of both activity (turnover) and profitability. How efficiently a company uses its assets to generate revenue is measured by the **asset turnover ratio**. This ratio is calculated by dividing net revenue or sales by average total assets for the period. The resulting number represents the dollars of revenue produced by each dollar invested in assets. **For a given level of investment in assets, a company that generates more**

revenue per dollar of investment is more efficient and likely to be more profitable. While this may not be true if the percentage profit on each dollar of revenue is lower than another company's, the asset turnover ratio is one of the key components of return on investment.[17]

REAL WORLD EMPHASIS

To illustrate, the following data are provided from the 2014 financial statements of **Loblaw Companies Limited**. Loblaw is Canada's largest food distributor, with more than 1,100 corporate and franchised stores across the country. Its asset turnover ratio is calculated in Illustration 11-20.

LOBLAW COMPANIES LIMITED	
(in millions)	
Revenues	$42,611
Total assets, January 3, 2015	33,684
Total assets, December 28, 2013	20,741

Illustration 11-20

Asset Turnover Ratio—Loblaw Companies

$$\text{Asset turnover} = \frac{\text{Net revenue}}{\text{Average total assets}}$$

$$= \frac{\$42,611}{\dfrac{\$33,684 + \$20,741}{2}}$$

$$= 1.57$$

The asset turnover ratio shows that Loblaw generated $1.57 of revenue for each dollar invested in assets during 2014. The ratio is affected by Loblaw's acquisition of Shoppers Drug Mart in the second quarter of 2014. (Note the dramatic increase in total assets!) The ratio was 1.82 in 2011. It will be interesting to see if the ratio returns to the 2011 level in future years.

Asset turnover ratios vary considerably among industries. For its fiscal year ending in June 2014, **Open Text Corporation**, a software company, had a ratio of 0.49 times, and a capital-asset-heavy company like Canadian Pacific Railway Limited had a ratio of only 0.39 times.

Using the **profit margin ratio** together with the asset turnover ratio allows us to determine another key indicator: the rate of return earned on total assets. By using the Open Text data for 2014, the profit margin ratio and the rate of return on total assets are calculated as shown in Illustration 11-21 (in thousands of US dollars).

Illustration 11-21

Profit Margin—Open Text Corporation

$$\text{Profit margin} = \frac{\text{Net income}}{\text{Net revenue}}$$

$$= \frac{\$218}{\$1,624}$$

$$= 13.4\%$$

$$\text{Rate of return on assets} = \text{Profit margin} \times \text{Asset turnover}$$

$$= 13.4\% \times 0.49$$

$$= 6.6\%$$

The profit margin indicates how much is left over from each sales dollar after all expenses are covered. In the Open Text example, a profit margin of 13.4% indicates that 13.4 cents of profit remained from each $1 of revenue generated. By combining the profit margin with the asset turnover, it is possible to calculate the rate of return on assets for the period. This makes sense. The more revenue that is generated per dollar invested in assets, the better off the company is. Also, the more of each sales dollar that is profit, the better off the company should be. Combined, the ratio provides a measure of the profitability of the company's investment in assets. To the extent that long-lived assets make up a significant portion of total assets, fixed asset management has a definite effect on profitability.

The **rate of return on assets (ROA)** can also be calculated directly by dividing net income by average total assets. Continuing with the same example, Illustration 11-22 shows the calculation of this ratio.

Illustration 11-22

Rate of Return on Assets—Open Text Corporation

$$\text{Rate of return on assets} = \frac{\text{Net income}}{\text{Average total assets}}$$
$$= \frac{\$218}{\dfrac{\$3,919 + \$2,655}{2}}$$
$$= 6.6\%$$

The 6.6% rate of return calculated in this way is the same as the 6.6% rate calculated by multiplying the profit margin by the asset turnover. The rate of return on assets is a good measure of profitability because it combines the effects of cost control (profit margin) and asset management (asset turnover).

A more sophisticated calculation adds back the after-tax interest expense to net income so that the results are not skewed by how the assets are financed. The ratio can then be used more legitimately for inter-company comparisons. An adjustment should also be made when there are significant assets measured at fair values, with the changes in value bypassing the income statement by being reported directly in Other Comprehensive Income (OCI). To be comparable, either the net income should be compared with the reported assets reduced by the related Accumulated OCI, or total comprehensive income should be compared with the total assets as reported.

Care must be taken in interpreting the numbers, however. A manager who is interested in reporting a high return on assets can achieve this in the short run by not investing in new plant and equipment and by cancelling expenditures such as those for research and development and employee training—decisions that may result in lower long-term corporate value. In the short run, the result is a higher return on investment because the net income number (the numerator) will be higher and the total asset number (the denominator) will be lower.

IFRS/ASPE COMPARISON

A Comparison of IFRS and ASPE

Objective 10

Identify differences in accounting between IFRS and ASPE, and what changes are expected in the near future.

In general, the concept of depreciation and how it is applied is quite similar under IFRS and ASPE, and the same is true for non-current assets held for sale. It is also true, however, that there are minor differences not covered in this chapter that require a thorough reading of the specific detailed standards.

The most significant differences between IFRS and ASPE in Chapter 11 relate to the impairment models, as can be seen in Illustration 11-23.

Illustration 11-23

IFRS and ASPE Comparison Chart

	IFRS—IAS 16, 36, 40, and 41; IFRS 5 and 13	Accounting Standards for Private Enterprises (ASPE)—*CPA Canada Handbook,* Part II, Sections 1505, 3061, 3063, and 3475	References to Related Illustrations and Select Brief Exercises
Depreciation process	Componentization is more common, with parts of assets recognized separately and depreciated over different periods of time.	Practice has been not to recognize asset components to the same extent as under IFRS.	BE11-2
	Depreciation is the allocation of the cost (or other amount) less the residual value over the asset's useful life, including any idle period.	Depreciation is the larger of: (a) cost less salvage value over asset's life, and (b) cost less residual value over asset's useful life.	Illustration 11-2 BE11-3 and BE11-4
Impairment	An assessment of indicators of impairment is required at least at each reporting date.	Evaluation of impairment is required only when events and changes in circumstances indicate that the carrying amount may not be recoverable.	N/A
	Rational entity approach is applied. Asset or cash-generating unit is impaired only if the carrying amount is more than the higher of the value in use and the fair value less costs of disposal. Fair value is based on IFRS 13 (*Fair Value Measurement*).	Cost recovery approach to impairment is applied. An asset or asset group is impaired only if the entity cannot recover the carrying amount with the net future undiscounted cash flows from use and later disposal.	Illustration 11-17 BE11-15
	"Recoverable amount" is defined as the higher of value in use and the fair value less costs of disposal.	"Recoverable test" is based on a comparison of the undiscounted net future cash flows from use and eventual disposal.	Illustration 11-17 BE11-13
	An impairment loss is reversed if there is a change in the estimates used to calculate recoverable amount. It is limited in amount.	Once an asset is written down to its impaired value, this becomes the asset's new cost and no reversal of the write-off is allowed.	BE11-12
Held for sale	Non-current assets may be reclassified as current assets only when they meet the criteria to be classified as held for sale (see IFRS 5.3). This requires that the asset (or disposal group) be available for immediate sale in its present condition and its sale must be highly probable.	Long-lived assets classified as held for sale are classified as current only if sold before the date the financial statements are completed and the proceeds will be received within the period defined for an asset to be a current asset.	BE11-16

(continued)

Disclosure	A reconciliation of the opening to ending balances of the carrying amounts of each class of PP&E asset is required, along with the same reconciliation for its associated accumulated depreciation and accumulated impairment losses.	A reconciliation of the opening to ending balances of the carrying amounts of each class of PP&E asset is not required.	
	Extensive disclosures are required for investment property measured under the fair value model. Even where the cost model is used for investment property, its fair value must be disclosed.	Because the cost model is the only accepted model, there are no disclosure requirements related to revaluation and fair value measurement models.	

Looking Ahead

Few changes are expected in the near future to standards covering the majority of property, plant, and equipment. There is one possible exception: accounting standards related to the upstream extractive activities undertaken by companies in the mining and oil and gas industries.

A Discussion Paper based on the IASB's extractive activities research project was released in 2010. In October 2010 the staff presented a summary of the feedback received in response to the discussion paper entitled *Extractive Activities*. The IASB noted that the project's objective was to analyze the unique financial reporting issues regarding extractive activities and to identify a basis for a possible financial reporting model to address these issues. While the Board planned to use the feedback on the Discussion Paper to help it decide whether to add the project to its active agenda, the project relating to Extractive Activities remained paused as of May 2015. If added to the formal agenda, it would likely take at least two to three years, from the date added, to develop a final standard.

IAS 36 *Impairment of Assets* was amended effective for annual periods starting on or after January 1, 2014, to require additional disclosures for impairment losses recognized or reversed during the period. For example, disclosure of the level of the fair value hierarchy used for fair value measurement under IFRS 13 is now required (and, for Level 2 or 3 measurements, further details of valuation techniques and underlying assumptions used must be provided).

In 2014, the IASB changed IAS 16 (*Property, Plant, and Equipment*) to note that using revenue-based methods to calculate depreciation of an asset is not appropriate. Entities affected by this change were required to apply the amendments prospectively for annual periods starting on or after January 1, 2016.

SUMMARY OF LEARNING OBJECTIVES

1 Understand the importance of depreciation, impairment, and disposition from a business perspective.

The economic benefits of property, plant, and equipment are typically consumed as the items are used by the organization. Because the benefits are consumed over multiple periods, companies use depreciation to allocate the benefits of the PP&E to each period as the capacity of the assets is used up. By allocating the cost of property, plant, and equipment over its useful life, businesses are better able to match the costs and benefits of the assets to the revenues that they help generate. Companies also need to assess their PP&E each year under IFRS for indications of impairment, and if these indications are present, they should re-estimate how much will be recoverable. Following GAAP should also help companies better understand their business.

2   Explain the concept of depreciation and identify the factors to consider when determining depreciation charges.

Depreciation is the process of allocating the cost of property, plant, and equipment assets in a systematic and rational manner to the periods that are expected to benefit from their use. The allocation of the cost of intangible capital assets is termed "amortization" and the allocation of the costs of mineral resource assets is termed "depletion." Four factors involved in determining depreciation expense are (1) the recognition of the appropriate asset components, (2) the amount to be depreciated (depreciable amount), (3) the estimated useful life, and (4) the pattern and method of depreciation.

3   Identify how depreciation methods are selected; calculate and recognize depreciation using the straight-line, decreasing charge, and activity methods.

The depreciation method chosen should amortize an asset in a pattern and at a rate that corresponds to the benefits received from that asset. The choice often involves the use of professional judgement. Tax reporting, simplicity, perceived economic consequences, and impact on ratios are examples of factors that influence such judgements in practice.

The straight-line method assumes that an asset provides its benefits as a function of time. As such, cost less residual value is divided by the useful life to determine the depreciation expense per period. The decreasing charge method provides for a higher depreciation charge in the early years and lower charges in later periods. For this method, a constant rate (such as double the straight-line rate) is multiplied by the net book value (cost less accumulated depreciation and accumulated impairment losses) at the start of the period to determine each period's expense. The main justification for this approach is that the asset provides more benefits in the earlier periods. The activity method assumes that the benefits provided by the asset are a function of use instead of the passage of time. The asset's life is considered in terms of either the output that it provides or an input measure, such as the number of hours it works. The depreciation charge per unit of activity (depreciable amount divided by estimated total units of output or input) is calculated and multiplied by the units of activity produced or consumed in a period to determine the depreciation.

4   Explain the accounting issues for depletion of mineral resources.

After the depletion base has been established through accounting decisions related to the acquisition, exploration and evaluation, development, and restoration obligations associated with mineral resources, these costs are allocated to the natural resources that are removed. Depletion is normally calculated using the unit of production method. In this approach, the resource's cost less residual value, if any, is divided by the number of units that are estimated to be in the resource deposit, to obtain a cost per unit of product. The cost per unit is then multiplied by the number of units withdrawn in the period to calculate the depletion.

5   Explain and apply the accounting procedures for partial periods and a change in depreciation rate.

Because all the variables in determining depreciation are estimates—with the exception, perhaps, of an asset's original cost—it is common for a change in those estimates to result in a change in the depreciation amount. When this occurs, there is no retroactive change and no catch-up adjustment. The change is accounted for in the current and future periods.

6   Explain the issues and apply the accounting standards for capital asset impairment under both IFRS and ASPE.

A capital asset is impaired when its carrying amount is not recoverable. The cost recovery method (ASPE) defines recoverable as the undiscounted cash flows from the asset's use and later disposal. If impaired, the asset is written down to its fair value, and this loss cannot be reversed later if the asset's value recovers. The rational entity model (IFRS) defines recoverable amount as the higher of the asset's value in use and fair value less costs of disposal. Both these values are discounted cash flow amounts. If the recoverable amount subsequently improves, the impairment losses recognized are reversed.

7   Account for derecognition of property, plant, and equipment and explain and apply the accounting standards for long-lived assets that are held for sale.

Assets held for sale are no longer depreciated. They are remeasured to their fair value less costs of disposal at each statement of financial position date. Recoveries in value may be recognized to the extent of previous losses. Held-for-sale items of property, plant, and equipment are separately reported as non-current assets unless they meet the definition of current assets. Under ASPE, assets held for sale are only permitted to be reported in current assets if sold before the financial statements are completed and the proceeds on sale are expected within 12 months from the date of the statement of financial position (or operating cycle, if longer).

Depreciation continues for PP&E assets until they are classified as held for sale or derecognized. At the date of disposal, all accounts related to the retired asset are removed from the books. Gains and losses from the disposal of plant assets are shown on the income statement in income before discontinued operations, unless the conditions for reporting as a discontinued operation are met. For property, plant, and equipment donated to an organization outside the reporting entity, the donation is reported at its fair value with a gain or loss on disposal recognized.

8   Describe the types of disclosures required for property, plant, and equipment.

The type of information required to be disclosed for property, plant, and equipment is governed by the information needs of users. Because users of private entities' financial information are often able to seek further specific information from a company, there are fewer required disclosures than for public companies reporting under IFRS. The required disclosures under IFRS include those relating to measurement, changes in account balances and the reasons for the changes, information about how fair values are determined, and many others.

9 Analyze a company's investment in assets.

The efficiency of use of a company's investment in assets may be evaluated by calculating and interpreting the asset turnover rate, the profit margin, and the rate of return on assets.

10 Identify differences in accounting between IFRS and ASPE, and what changes are expected in the near future.

In most major ways, international and Canadian accounting standards for the depreciation of property, plant, and equipment are similar. Significant differences do exist, however, in the extent of componentization for depreciation, the impairment models applied, and the extent of disclosure. The impairment differences relate to how it is determined whether an asset is impaired, how the impairment is measured, and the ability to recognize recoveries in value.

KEY TERMS

accelerated amortization, p. 634
activity method, p. 634
amortization, p. 629
asset group, p. 646
asset turnover ratio, p. 653
cash-generating unit (CGU), p. 646
componentization, p. 629
cost recovery impairment model, p. 642
declining-balance method, p. 634
decreasing charge methods, p. 634
depletion, p. 629

depreciable amount, p. 630
depreciation, p. 629
derecognized, p. 649
diminishing balance methods, p. 634
double-declining-balance method, p. 634
fair value, p. 643
impaired, p. 642
impairment loss, p. 643
impairments, p. 642
liquidating dividend, p. 638
profit margin ratio, p. 654

rate of return on assets (ROA), p. 655
rational entity impairment model, p. 643
recoverability test, p. 643
recoverable amount, p. 644
residual value, p. 630
salvage value, p. 630
straight-line method, p. 633
sum-of-the-years'-digits method, p. 690
unit of production method, p. 634
useful life, p. 631
value in use, p. 645

APPENDIX 11A

DEPRECIATION AND INCOME TAX

Capital Cost Allowance Method

Objective 11
Calculate capital cost allowance in routine and non-routine situations.

For the most part, issues related to the calculation of income taxes are not discussed in financial accounting courses. However, because the concepts of tax depreciation are similar to those of depreciation for financial reporting purposes, and because the tax method is sometimes adopted for record-keeping purposes, we present an overview of this subject here.

Canadian businesses use the capital cost allowance method to determine depreciation in calculating their taxable income and the tax value of assets, regardless of the method they use for financial reporting purposes. Because companies use this method for tax purposes, some—particularly small businesses—also use it for financial reporting, judging that the benefits of keeping two sets of records are less than the costs of doing this.[18] While keeping only one set of records may be cost-effective, it may not provide a rational measure of expense under GAAP. Therefore, most companies keep a record of capital cost allowance for tax purposes and use another method to determine depreciation for financial reporting purposes.

The **capital cost allowance method** is similar to the declining-balance approach covered in the chapter, except for the following:

1. Instead of being labelled "depreciation expense," it is called **capital cost allowance (CCA)**.

2. The Income Tax Act (Income Tax Regulations, Schedule II) specifies the rate to be used for an asset class. This rate is called the capital cost allowance or CCA rate. The Income Tax Act identifies several different classes of assets and the maximum CCA rate for each class. To determine which class a particular asset falls into, it is necessary to examine the definition of each asset class and the examples given in the act. Illustration 11A-1 provides examples of various CCA classes, the maximum rate for the class, and examples of the types of assets it includes.

Illustration 11A-1

Examples of CCA Classes

Class	Rate	Examples of Assets Included in the Class
1	4%	• most buildings acquired after 1987, including component parts such as plumbing, elevators, sprinkler systems.
8	20%	• property or equipment not included in other specified classes. Also includes furniture, photocopiers, and refrigeration equipment.
10	30%	• automotive equipment, such as motor vehicles and passenger vehicles (unless they meet class 10.1 conditions).
10.1	30%	• passenger vehicles purchased during a company's 2011 fiscal year or thereafter having a cost of more than $30,000. (The amount that can be used for capital cost purposes is limited to $30,000 plus PST and GST, or HST.)

Source: Classes of Depreciable Property Compiled using information available on the CRA website <http://www.cra-arc.gc.ca/tx/bsnss/tpcs/slprtnr/rprtng/cptl/dprcbl-eng.html#class10>. Accessed September 2015.

---

3. CCA is calculated separately for each asset class and can be claimed only on year-end amounts in each class. Assuming there have been no net additions (purchases less proceeds of disposals, if any) to a class during a year, the maximum CCA allowed is the undepreciated capital cost (UCC) at year end multiplied by the CCA rate for the class. In a year when there is a net addition (regardless of when it occurs), the maximum CCA on the net addition is one half of the allowed CCA rate multiplied by the amount of the net addition. This is often referred to as the **half-year rule**. The CCA for the net addition plus the CCA on the remaining UCC is the total CCA for the asset class. If there is only one asset in a class, the maximum CCA allowed in the acquisition year is the acquisition cost multiplied by one half of the CCA rate, even if the asset was purchased one week before year end. (This provides a tax planning opportunity for companies. From a tax planning perspective, it is better to purchase an asset in the last month of the fiscal year instead of the first month of the next year!) No CCA would be allowed in the year of disposal for this single asset, even if it is sold just before year end.

CORPORATE TAX
6.1.2, 6.1.4

4. The government, through the Income Tax Act, requires that any benefits that a company receives from government grants and investment tax credits for the purpose of acquiring a capital asset reduce the cost basis of the capital asset for tax purposes. For investment tax credits deducted or refunded in a tax year, the capital cost of the asset and the UCC of the class of asset are reduced in the next taxation year.

5. CCA can be taken even if it results in a UCC balance that is less than the estimated residual value.

6. Companies are not required to take the maximum rate, or even any CCA, in a particular year, although they normally would as long as they have taxable income. If a company takes less than the maximum CCA in a specific year, it cannot add the remainder to the amount claimed in a subsequent year. In any year, the maximum that can be claimed is limited to the UCC times the specified CCA rate.

Basic CCA and UCC Example

To illustrate depreciation calculations under the CCA system, assume the following facts for a company's March 28, 2016 acquisition of manufacturing equipment, its only asset in this CCA class:

Cost of equipment	$500,000	CCA class	Class 8
Estimated useful life	10 years	CCA rate for Class 8	20%
Estimated residual value	$ 30,000		

Illustration 11A-2 shows how to calculate the CCA for the first three years and the UCC at the end of each of the three years.[19]

Illustration 11A-2

CCA Schedule for Equipment

Class 8—20%	CCA	UCC
January 1, 2016		**0**
Additions during 2016		
Cost of new asset acquisition		$500,000
Disposals during 2016		0
CCA 2016: $500,000 × ½ × 20%	$50,000	(50,000)
December 31, 2016		**$ 450,000**
Additions less disposals, 2017		0
		$450,000
CCA, 2017: $450,000 × 20%	$90,000	(90,000)
December 31, 2017		**$ 360,000**
Additions less disposals, 2018		0
		$360,000
CCA, 2018: $360,000 × 20%	$72,000	(72,000)
December 31, 2018		**$ 288,000**

The **undepreciated capital cost (UCC)** at any point in time is known as the capital asset's **tax value** or **tax basis**. Note that the asset's carrying amount on the statement of financial position will be different from its tax value whenever the depreciation method for financial reporting is not the tax method. The significance of this difference to financial reporting is explained in Chapter 18.

Illustration 11A-3 is a continuation of Illustration 11A-2. It incorporates the following transactions:

1. In 2019, the company bought another Class 8 asset for $700,000.

2. In 2020, the company sold for $300,000 the equipment that it purchased in 2016.

3. In 2021, the company sold the remaining Class 8 asset for $500,000. There are no Class 8 assets remaining after the sale.

Illustration 11A-3

CCA Schedule for Class 8

Class 8—20%		CCA	UCC
December 31, 2018			**$ 288,000**
Additions less disposals, 2019			
Cost of new asset			700,000
CCA, 2019			
$288,000 × 20% =	$57,600		$988,000
$700,000 × ½ × 20% =	70,000	$127,600	(127,600)
December 31, 2019			**$ 860,400**
Additions less disposals, 2020			
Manufacturing equipment originally			
purchased in 2016 (lesser of original			
cost of $500,000 and proceeds			
of disposal of $300,000)			(300,000)
			$560,400
CCA, 2020: $560,400 × 20% =		$112,080	(112,080)
December 31, 2020			**$ 448,320**
Additions less disposals, 2021			
2019 asset acquisition			
(lesser of original cost of			
$700,000 and proceeds of			
disposal of $500,000)			(500,000)
			$ (51,680)
Recaptured CCA, 2021		$ (51,680)	51,680
December 31, 2021			**$ 0**

Additions to an Asset Class

The purchase of another Class 8 asset in 2019 resulted in a **net addition** of $700,000 to the undepreciated capital cost at the end of 2019. Consequently, the balance of the UCC at the end of 2019 prior to calculating CCA is made up of this $700,000 plus the $288,000 UCC of the original equipment. The capital cost allowance for 2019 is therefore 20% of $288,000 ($57,600) plus one half of 20% of the net addition of $700,000 ($70,000) for a total of $127,600.

If a government grant of $35,000 had been received in 2019 to help finance the acquisition of this asset, the addition in 2019 would be reported net of the government grant; that is, at $700,000 – $35,000 = $665,000. If the 2019 acquisition were eligible instead for an investment tax credit (ITC) of $35,000, the tax legislation specifies that the ITC reduces the asset's capital cost and the UCC of the class of assets **in the year following** the year of acquisition.[20] Assuming the Class 8 asset acquired in 2019 in Illustration 11A-3 was eligible for a $35,000 ITC, the $700,000 addition is recognized in 2019, and the UCC is reduced by the $35,000 ITC in 2020 along with the $300,000 proceeds on the original manufacturing equipment that was sold in 2020. The CCA claimed in 2020 is reduced accordingly.

Retirements from an Asset Class, Continuation of Class

While the CCA class is increased by the cost of additions, it is reduced **by the proceeds on the asset's disposal**, not by the asset's cost. However, if the proceeds on disposal are more than the asset's original capital cost, the class is reduced by the cost only. There is a good reason for this. If the proceeds on disposal are more than the original cost, there is a capital gain on the disposal. Capital gains are taxed differently than ordinary business income; thus, the portion that is a capital gain must be identified as being that. Cost, therefore, is the maximum amount to be deducted from the CCA class. It is not common for depreciable assets to be sold for more than their cost.

In 2020, the company sells the original manufacturing equipment for $300,000. Because this is less than its $500,000 capital cost, there is no capital gain on disposal. Therefore, Class 8 is reduced by the proceeds on disposal of $300,000, and the CCA for the year is calculated on the remaining balance in the class.

Retirements from an Asset Class, Elimination of Class

When an asset's disposal eliminates the asset class, either because there are no more assets remaining in the class or because the disposal results in the elimination of the UCC balance of the class, the following may result:

1. There may be a recapture of capital cost allowance, with or without a capital gain.

2. There may be a terminal loss, with or without a capital gain. This occurs only when the last asset in the class is disposed of and a UCC balance still exists in the class after deducting the appropriate amount on the asset disposal.

A **recapture** of CCA occurs when, after deducting the appropriate amount from the class on disposal of an asset, a negative amount is left as the UCC balance. The negative balance is the amount of CCA that must be "recaptured" and included in the calculation of taxable income in the year. It is taxed at the normal income tax rates. When this situation occurs, it suggests that too much CCA was deducted throughout the lives of the assets, and the taxing of the recaptured capital cost allowance therefore adjusts for this. This is what occurred in 2021 in our example. When the proceeds of disposal were deducted from the UCC, the UCC became negative. The excess of $51,680 is therefore added back and included in taxable income in 2021.

As indicated above, if an asset is sold for more than its cost, a **capital gain** results. This may occur whether or not the class is eliminated. For tax purposes, a capital gain is treated differently from a recapture of CCA. Essentially, the **taxable** capital gain (that is, the amount subject to tax) is only a portion of the capital gain as defined above.[21] The taxable capital gain is included with other taxable income.

If the Class 8 asset purchased in 2019 had been sold in 2021 for $750,000, a capital gain and a recapture of CCA would have resulted. The capital gain would be $50,000, but only 50% or $25,000 would be the taxable capital gain. In this case, Class 8 would be reduced by $700,000 and the recapture would be $251,680 ($700,000 less the $448,320 UCC).

A **terminal loss** occurs when a positive balance remains in the class after the appropriate reduction is made to the CCA class from the disposal of the last asset. This remaining balance is a terminal loss that is deductible in full when calculating taxable income for the period. If the remaining equipment had been sold in 2021 for $300,000, a terminal loss of $148,320 would have resulted (the UCC of $448,320 less the $300,000 proceeds).

This example illustrating the basic calculations of capital gains, taxable capital gains, recaptured capital cost allowance, and terminal losses has necessarily been simplified. In essence, the tax rate on taxable capital gains is specified by tax law, which may change from time to time and have other implications (such as a refundable dividend tax on hand). Similarly, the tax rate that applies to recaptured CCA is affected by the particular circumstances of the type of taxable income that is being reported, of which the recaptured amount is a component. These and other technical aspects, including definitions, are beyond the scope of this text. Be warned that specialist knowledge of tax law is often required to determine income taxes payable!

SUMMARY OF LEARNING OBJECTIVE FOR APPENDIX 11A

11 Calculate capital cost allowance in routine and non-routine situations.

"Capital cost allowance" (CCA) is the term used for depreciation when calculating taxable income in income tax returns. The CCA method is similar to the declining-balance method except that rates are specified for asset classes and the amount claimed is based on year-end balances. The half-year rule is applied to net additions in the year, which means that only 50% of the normal rate is permitted. For an asset class, retirements are accounted for under specific rules that govern the calculation of taxable income. Capital gains occur if the proceeds on disposal are more than the asset's original cost. When an asset class is eliminated, a terminal loss or recapture of capital cost allowance can occur.

KEY TERMS

capital cost allowance (CCA), p. 660	half-year rule, p. 660	tax value, p. 661
capital cost allowance method, p. 660	recapture, p. 663	terminal loss, p. 663
capital gain, p. 663	tax basis, p. 661	undepreciated capital cost (UCC), p. 661

Note: All assignment material with an asterisk (*) relates to the appendix to the chapter.

Unless otherwise indicated, depreciation expense should be calculated to the nearest whole month.

Completion of this end-of-chapter material will help develop CPA enabling competencies (such as ethics and professionalism, problem-solving and decision-making and communication) and technical competencies. We have highlighted selected items with an integration icon and material in *WileyPLUS* has been linked to the competencies. All cases emphasize integration, especially of the enabling competencies. The brief exercises, exercises and problems generally emphasize problem-solving and decision-making.

Brief Exercises

(LO 1, 7) BE11-1   Cella Corporation's statement of financial position shows property, plant, and equipment of $100,000. The notes to its financial statements state that the amount is represented by a cost of $600,000, accumulated depreciation of $300,000, and accumulated impairment losses of $200,000. Discuss the usefulness of the information provided, referring to the qualitative characteristics identified in the conceptual framework for financial reporting (discussed in Chapter 2).

(LO 2) BE11-2   On October 1, 2017, Ocean Airways Ltd. purchased a new commercial aircraft for a total cost of $100 million. Included in the total cost are the aircraft's two engines, at a cost of $10 million each, and the aircraft's body, which costs $80 million. The estimated useful life of each of the aircraft's two engines is 10 years, with a residual value of $1 million. The estimated useful life of the aircraft's body is 10 years, with a residual value of $5 million. The entire aircraft's useful life is limited to the life of the aircraft's body. (a) Prepare the journal entries required on October 1, 2017, and December 31, 2017, if Ocean Airways prepares financial statements in accordance with IFRS and uses straight-line depreciation. (b) Explain any differences in the journal entries if Ocean Airways prepares financial statements in accordance with ASPE.

(LO 2) BE11-3   Chong Corp. purchased a machine on July 1, 2017, for $30,000. Chong paid $200 in title fees and a legal fee of $100 related to the machine. In addition, Chong paid $500 in shipping charges for delivery, and paid $400 to a local contractor to build and wire a platform for the machine on the plant floor. The machine has an estimated useful life of 10 years, a total expected life of 12 years, a residual value of $6,000, and no salvage value. Chong uses straight-line depreciation. (a) Calculate the 2017 depreciation expense if Chong prepares financial statements in accordance with IFRS. (b) Calculate the 2017 depreciation expense if Chong prepares financial statements in accordance with ASPE.

(LO 3) BE11-4   Gilles Corp. purchased a piece of equipment on February 1, 2017, for $100,000. The equipment has an estimated useful life of eight years, with a residual value of $25,000, and an estimated physical life of 10 years, with no salvage value. The equipment was delivered to Gilles's factory floor, installed, and in working condition, on March 1, 2017. On April 1, 2017, Gilles's staff used the equipment to produce the first saleable units. (a) Calculate the 2017 depreciation expense if Gilles uses straight-line depreciation and prepares financial statements in accordance with IFRS. (b) Calculate the 2017 depreciation expense if Gilles prepares financial statements in accordance with ASPE.

(LO 3) BE11-5   Odyssey Ltd. purchased machinery on January 1, 2017, for $60,000. The machinery is estimated to have a residual value of $6,000 after a useful life of eight years. (a) Calculate the 2017 depreciation expense using the straight-line method. (b) Calculate the 2017 depreciation expense using the straight-line method, but assuming the machinery was purchased on September 1, 2017.

(LO 3) BE11-6   Use the information for Odyssey Ltd. in BE11-5. (a) Calculate the 2017 depreciation expense using the double-declining-balance method. (b) Calculate the 2018 depreciation expense using the double-declining-balance method, but assuming the machinery was purchased on October 1, 2017. (c) Discuss when it might be more appropriate to use the straight-line method of depreciation and when the double-declining-balance method is more appropriate.

(LO 3) BE11-7   Use the information for Odyssey Ltd. in BE11-5. (a) Calculate the 2017 depreciation expense using the sum-of-the-years'-digits method. (b) Calculate the 2017 depreciation expense using the sum-of-the-years'-digits method, but assuming the machinery was purchased on April 1, 2017.

(LO 3, 11) *BE11-8   Andeo Corporation purchased a truck at the beginning of 2017 for $48,000. The truck is estimated to have a residual value of $3,000 and a useful life of 275,000 km. It was driven for 52,000 km in 2017 and 65,000 km in 2018.

TAXATION

(a) Calculate depreciation expense for 2017 and 2018 using the unit of production method. (b) For tax purposes, the asset is depreciated at a rate of 30%. Calculate the Capital Cost Allowance (CCA) for 2017 and 2018.

(LO 4) **BE11-9** Extract Corporation, a publicly traded mining company, acquires a mine at a cost of $500,000. Capitalized development costs total $125,000. After the mine is depleted, $75,000 will be spent to restore the property, after which it can be sold for $157,500. Extract estimates that 5,000 tonnes of ore can be mined. Assuming that 900 tonnes are extracted in the first year, prepare the journal entry to record depletion.

(LO 5) **BE11-10** Chuckwalla Limited purchased a computer for $7,000 on January 1, 2017. Straight-line depreciation is used for the computer, based on a five-year life and a $1,000 residual value. In 2019, the estimates are revised. Chuckwalla now expects the computer will be used until December 31, 2020, when it can be sold for $500. Calculate the 2019 depreciation expense.

(LO 6) **BE11-11** Qilin Corp., a small company that follows ASPE, owns machinery that cost $900,000 and has accumulated depreciation of $360,000. The undiscounted future net cash flows from the use of the asset are expected to be $500,000. The equipment's fair value is $400,000. Using the cost recovery impairment model, prepare the journal entry, if any, to record the impairment loss.

(LO 6) **BE11-12** Use the information for Qilin Corp. given in BE11-11. By the end of the following year, the machinery's fair value has increased to $490,000. (a) Assuming the machinery continues to be used in production, prepare the journal entry required, if any, to record the increase in its fair value. (b) Explain any differences in your answer to part (a) if Qilin prepares financial statements in accordance with IFRS.

(LO 6) **BE11-13** Hambrecht Corp. is preparing its financial statements for the fiscal year ending November 30, 2017. Certain specialized equipment was scrapped on January 1, 2018. At November 30, 2017, this equipment was being used in production by Hambrecht and had a carrying amount of $1 million. As at November 30, 2017, it was estimated that the asset has undiscounted net future cash flows of $1.1 million, value in use of $800,000, and fair value less costs of disposal of $50,000 (scrap value). (a) If Hambrecht prepares financial statements in accordance with IFRS, what is the recoverable amount of the equipment at November 30, 2017? (b) If Hambrecht prepares financial statements in accordance with ASPE, what is the recoverable amount of the equipment at November 30, 2017?

(LO 6) **BE11-14** Greentree Properties Ltd. is a publicly listed company following IFRS. Assume that on December 31, 2017, the carrying amount of land on the statement of financial position is $500,000. Management determines that the land's value in use is $425,000 and that the fair value less costs to sell is $400,000. (a) Using the rational entity impairment model, prepare the journal entry required, if any, to record the impairment loss. (b) Due to an economic rebound in the area, by the end of the following year the land has a value in use of $550,000 and fair value less costs of disposal of $480,000. Prepare the journal entry required, if any, to record the increase in its recoverable amount.

(LO 6) **BE11-15** Riverbed Ltd. is a manufacturer of computer network equipment and has just recently adopted IFRS. The wireless division is a cash-generating unit or asset group that has the following carrying amounts for its net assets: land, $20,000; buildings, $30,000; and equipment, $10,000. The undiscounted net future cash flows from use and eventual disposal of the wireless division are $70,000, and the present value of these cash flows is $45,000. The land can be sold immediately for $35,000; however, the buildings and equipment are specialized and cannot be used elsewhere and thus have no resale value. Allocate the impairment loss to the net assets of the wireless division using (a) the cost recovery model under ASPE and (b) the rational entity model under IFRS.

(LO 7) **BE11-16** Caley Inc. owns a building with a carrying amount of $1.5 million, as at January 1, 2017. On that date, Caley's management determined that the building's location is no longer suitable for the company's operations and decided to dispose of the building by sale. Caley is preparing financial statements for the fiscal year ending December 31, 2017. As at that date, management had an authorized plan in place to sell the building, the building met all criteria for classification as held for sale, and the building's estimated fair value less costs to sell was $1 million. The building's depreciation expense for 2017 would amount to $200,000. (a) Prepare the journal entry(ies) required on December 31, 2017, if any. (b) Discuss how the building would be classified on the December 31, 2017 statement of financial position if Caley prepared financial statements in accordance with IFRS. (c) Discuss how the building would be classified on the December 31, 2017 statement of financial position if Caley prepared financial statements in accordance with ASPE.

(LO 7) **BE11-17** Volumetrics Corporation owns machinery that cost $20,000 when purchased on January 1, 2017. Depreciation has been recorded at a rate of $3,000 per year, resulting in a balance in accumulated depreciation of $6,000 at December 31, 2018. The machinery is sold on September 1, 2019, for $13,500. Prepare journal entries to (a) update depreciation for 2019 and (b) record the sale.

(LO 7) **BE11-18** Use the information presented for Volumetrics Corporation in BE11-17, but assume that the machinery is sold for $5,200 instead of $13,500. Prepare journal entries to (a) update depreciation for 2019 and (b) record the sale.

(LO 9) BE11-19 In its 2017 annual report, Winkler Limited reports beginning-of-the-year total assets of $1,923 million, end-of-the-year total assets of $2,487 million, total revenue of $2,687 million, and net income of $52 million. (a) Calculate Winkler's asset turnover ratio. (b) Calculate Winkler's profit margin. (c) Calculate Winkler's rate of return on assets (1) using the asset turnover and profit margin, and (2) using net income.

TAXATION

(LO 11) *BE11-20 Fong Limited purchased an asset at a cost of $45,000 on March 1, 2017. The asset has a useful life of seven years and an estimated residual value of $3,000. For tax purposes, the asset belongs in CCA Class 8, with a rate of 20%. Calculate the CCA for each year, 2017 to 2020, assuming this is the only asset in Class 8.

Exercises

(LO 1, 2, 3) E11-1 **(Match Depreciation Method with Assets)** The following assets have been acquired by various companies over the past year:

1. Boardroom table and chairs for a corporate head office

2. Dental equipment in a new dental clinic

3. Long-haul trucks for a trucking business

4. Weight and aerobic equipment in a new health club facility

5. Classroom computers in a new community college

Instructions

For each long-lived asset listed above:

(a) Identify the factors to consider in establishing the useful life of the asset.

(b) Recommend the pattern of depreciation that most closely represents the pattern of economic benefits received by the entity that owns the asset.

(c) Discuss how good estimates of asset useful life would help a company manage its assets.

(LO 2, 3) E11-2 **(Terminology, Calculations—Straight-Line, Double-Declining-Balance)** Diderot Corp. acquired a property on September 15, 2017, for $220,000, paying $3,000 in transfer taxes and a $1,500 real estate fee. Based on the provincial assessment information, 75% of the property's value was related to the building and 25% to the land. It is estimated that the building, with proper maintenance, will last for 20 years, at which time it will be torn down and have zero salvage value. Diderot, however, expects to use it for 10 years only, as it is not expected to suit the company's purposes after that. The company should be able to sell the property for $155,000 at that time, with $40,000 of this amount being for the land. Diderot prepares financial statements in accordance with IFRS. Depreciation expense should be calculated to the nearest half month.

Instructions

Assuming a December 31 year end, identify all of the following:

(a) The building's cost

(b) The building's depreciable amount

(c) The building's useful life

(d) Depreciation expense for 2017, assuming the straight-line method

(e) Depreciation expense for 2018, assuming the double-declining-balance method

(f) The building's carrying amount at December 31, 2018, assuming the double-declining-balance method

(g) Depreciation expense for 2017, assuming the straight-line method and assuming Diderot prepares financial statements in accordance with ASPE

(LO 3) E11-3 **(Depreciation Calculations—Straight-Line, Double-Declining-Balance; Partial Periods)** Gambit Corporation purchased a new plant asset on April 1, 2017, at a cost of $769,000. It was estimated to have a useful life of 20 years and a residual value of $300,000, a physical life of 30 years, and a salvage value of $0. Gambit's accounting period is the calendar year. Gambit prepares financial statements in accordance with IFRS.

Instructions

(a) Calculate the depreciation for this asset for 2017 and 2018 using the straight-line method.

(b) Calculate the depreciation for this asset for 2017 and 2018 using the double-declining-balance method.

(c) Calculate the depreciation for this asset for 2017 and 2018 using the straight-line method and assuming Gambit prepares financial statements in accordance with ASPE.

(d) Discuss when it might be more appropriate to select the straight-line method, and when it might be more appropriate to select the double-declining-balance method.

(e) Assume that additional information has been provided relating to the cost ($769,000). There are three components of the plant asset. Components 1, 2, and 3 have costs of $400,000, $254,000, and $115,000, respectively. The useful lives of components 1, 2, and 3 are 25, 20, and 30 years, respectively. Determine straight-line depreciation expense for 2017 and 2018 for each component under IFRS if the residual value is $100,000 for component 1, $154,000 for component 2, and $46,000 for component 3.

(f) How would your answer in (e) differ if the company prepared financial statements in accordance with ASPE.

(LO 3, 5, 11) ***E11-4 (Depreciation Calculations—Six Methods; Partial Periods)** Jupiter Wells Corp. purchased machinery for $315,000 on May 1, 2017. It is estimated that it will have a useful life of 10 years, residual value of $15,000, production of 240,000 units, and 25,000 working hours. The machinery will have a physical life of 15 years and a salvage value of $3,000. During 2018, Jupiter Wells Corp. used the machinery for 2,650 hours and the machinery produced 25,500 units. Jupiter Wells prepares financial statements in accordance with IFRS.

TAXATION

Instructions

From the information given, calculate the depreciation charge for 2018 under each of the following methods, assuming Jupiter Wells has a December 31 year end.

(a) Straight-line

(b) Unit of production

(c) Working hours

(d) Declining-balance, using a 20% rate

(e) Sum-of-the-years'-digits

(f) CCA at 20%

(g) Assume that Jupiter Wells is a small privately owned company that follows ASPE and uses straight-line depreciation. How would depreciation expense differ, if at all? Provide calculations to support your answer.

DIGGING DEEPER

(h) Assuming that Jupiter Wells follows ASPE, from the perspective of a potential investor in Jupiter Wells, discuss the advantages and disadvantages of Jupiter Wells using the capital cost allowance approach to calculate and record depreciation expense for financial reporting purposes.

(LO 2, 3) **E11-5 (Different Methods of Depreciation)** Jared Industries Ltd., a public company, presents you with the following information:

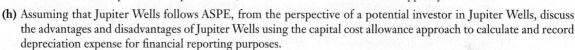

Description	Date Purchased	Cost	Residual Value	Life in Years	Depreciation Method	Accumulated Depreciation to Dec. 31, 2020	Depreciation for 2021
Machine A	Dec. 2, 2019	$142,500	$16,000	10	(1)	$39,900	(2)
Machine B	Aug. 15, 2018	(3)	21,000	5	Straight-line	29,000	(4)
Machine C	July 21, 2017	75,400	23,500	8	Double-declining-balance	(5)	(6)

Instructions

(a) Complete the table for the year ended December 31, 2021. The company depreciates all assets for a half year in the year of acquisition and the year of disposal.

(b) What criteria would you consider in determining whether to select the straight-line or double-declining-balance method?

(LO 3) **E11-6 (Depreciation Computations—Straight-Line, Sum-of-the-Years'-Digits, Double-Declining-Balance)** Deluxe Ezra Company purchases equipment on January 1, 2017, at a cost of $469,000. The asset is expected to have a service life of 12 years and a salvage value of $40,000.

Instructions

(a) Compute the amount of depreciation for each of 2017, 2018, and 2019 using the straight-line depreciation method.

(b) Compute the amount of depreciation for each of 2017, 2018, and 2019 using the sum-of-the-years'-digits method.

(c) Compute the amount of depreciation for each of 2017, 2018, and 2019 using the double-declining-balance method. (In performing your calculations, round constant percentage to the nearest one-hundredth and round dollar amounts to the nearest dollar.)

(LO 3) E11-7 (Depreciation Computations—Five Methods) Jon Seceda Furnace Corp. purchased machinery for $315,000 on May 1, 2017. It is estimated that it will have a useful life of 10 years, salvage value of $15,000, production of 240,000 units, and working hours of 25,000. During 2018, Seceda Corp. uses the machinery for 2,650 hours, and the machinery produces 25,500 units.

Instructions

From the information given, compute the depreciation charge for 2018 under each of the following methods. (Round to the nearest dollar.)

(a) Straight-line

(b) Unit of production

(c) Working hours

(d) Sum-of-the-years'-digits

(e) Declining-balance (use 20% as the annual rate)

(LO 3) E11-8 (Depreciation Calculations—Straight-Line, Double-Declining-Balance) Jiang Company Ltd. purchases equipment on January 1, 2017, for $387,000 cash. The asset is expected to have a useful life of 12 years and a residual value of $39,000. Jiang prepares financial statements under IFRS.

Instructions

(a) Calculate the amount of depreciation for each of 2017, 2018, and 2019 using the straight-line method.

(b) Calculate the amount of depreciation for each of 2017, 2018, and 2019 using the double-declining-balance method. (In performing your calculations, round percentages to the nearest one-hundredth and round dollar amounts to the nearest dollar.)

(c) Assume that the equipment consists of an input device with a cost of $55,000, residual value of $5,000, and useful life of 5 years; a processor with a cost of $132,000, residual value of $12,000, and useful life of 10 years; and an output device with a cost of $200,000, residual value of $22,000, and useful life of 12 years. Prepare the journal entry to record the purchase on January 1, 2017.

(d) Assume the information given in part (c) above. Also assume that the benefits of the input device and processor are expected to flow to Jiang evenly over time, but that the output device is expected to provide the greatest benefits in the early years. Calculate the amount of depreciation for 2017 using the most appropriate methods.

(e) Assume the information given in part (c) above with respect to the cost components. The equipment is expected to provide benefits evenly over time. Also assume that the equipment has a salvage value of $37,000 and a physical life of 14 years. The salvage values of the input device, processor, and output device are $3,000, $10,000, and $19,000, respectively. The physical lives of the input device, processor, and output device are 6 years, 12 years, and 14 years, respectively. Calculate the amount of depreciation for 2017, 2018, and 2019 using the straight-line method. Jiang Company Ltd. prepares financial statements under ASPE.

(LO 3) E11-9 (Depreciation—Conceptual Understanding) Hubbub Company Ltd. acquired equipment at the beginning of Year 1. The asset has an estimated useful life of five years. An employee has prepared depreciation schedules for this asset using two different methods, in order to compare the results of using one method with the results of using the other. Assume that the following schedules have been correctly prepared for this asset using (1) the straight-line method and (2) the double-declining-balance method. Hubbub Company Ltd. prepares its financial statements under IFRS.

Year	Straight-Line	Double-Declining-Balance
1	$12,000	$30,000
2	12,000	18,000
3	12,000	10,800
4	12,000	1,200
5	12,000	–0–
Total	$60,000	$60,000

Instructions

(a) What is the cost of the asset that is being depreciated?

(b) What amount, if any, was used in the depreciation calculations for the residual value of this asset?

(c) Which method will produce the higher net income in Year 1?

(d) Which method will produce the higher charge to income in Year 4?

(e) Which method will produce the higher carrying amount for the asset at the end of Year 3?

(f) Which method will produce the higher cash flow in Year 1? In Year 4?

(g) If the asset were sold at the end of Year 3, which method would yield the higher gain (or lower loss) on disposal of the asset?

(h) Repeat parts (c) through (g) assuming a salvage value of $0 and a physical life of six years using ASPE.

(LO 3) E11-10 (Depreciation for Fractional Periods) On March 10, 2017, Lucas Limited sold equipment that it purchased for $192,000 on August 20, 2010. It was originally estimated that the equipment would have a useful life of 12 years and a residual value of $16,800 at the end of that time, and depreciation has been calculated on that basis. The company uses the straight-line method of depreciation and prepares its financial statements under IFRS.

Instructions

(a) Calculate the depreciation charge on this equipment for 2010 and for 2017, and the total charge for the period from 2011 to 2016, inclusive, under each of the following six assumptions for partial periods:

   1. Depreciation is calculated for the exact period of time during which the asset is owned. (Use 365 days for your base.)

   2. Depreciation is calculated for the full year on the January 1 balance in the asset account.

   3. Depreciation is calculated for the full year on the December 31 balance in the asset account.

   4. Depreciation for a half year is charged on plant assets that are acquired or disposed of during the year.

   5. Depreciation is calculated on additions from the beginning of the month following their acquisition and on disposals to the beginning of the month following the disposal.

   6. Depreciation is calculated for a full period on all assets in use for over half a year, and no depreciation is charged on assets in use for less than half a year. (Use 365 days for your base.)

(b) Briefly evaluate the above methods in terms of basic accounting theory and how simple the methods are to apply.

(c) Calculate straight-line depreciation under ASPE only for assumption 1 if the asset has a physical life of 13 years and a salvage value of $1,000. Round to the nearest dollar.

(LO 3, 5) E11-11 (Error Analysis and Depreciation) Gibbs Inc. purchased a machine on January 1, 2017, at a cost of $60,000. The machine is expected to have an estimated residual value of $5,000 at the end of its five-year useful life. The company capitalized the machine and depreciated it in 2017 using the double-declining-balance method of depreciation. The company has a policy of using the straight-line method to depreciate equipment, as this method best reflects the benefits to the company over the life of its machinery. However, the company accountant neglected to follow company policy when he used the double-declining-balance method. Net income for the year ended December 31, 2017, was $53,000 as a result of depreciating the machine incorrectly. Gibbs has not closed its books for 2017 yet. Gibbs uses IFRS to prepare its financial statements.

Instructions

(a) Using the method of depreciation that the company normally follows, prepare the correcting entry and determine the corrected net income. Assume the books of account have not yet been closed for 2017, and ignore income taxes.

**DIGGING
DEEPER**

(b) Repeat part (a) assuming Gibbs uses ASPE instead of IFRS, the salvage value is $3,000, and the machinery has a physical life of six years.

(c) Discuss the impact on a potential investor if the error is not detected and corrected by Gibbs.

(LO 3, 5) E11-12 (Error Analysis and Depreciation) Wettlauffer Company Ltd. shows the following entries in its Equipment account for 2017. All amounts are based on historical cost.

Equipment			
1/1	Balance	134,750	6/30 Cost of equipment sold
8/10	Purchases of equipment	32,000	(purchased prior to 2017) 23,000
8/12	Freight on equipment purchased	700	
8/25	Installation costs	2,700	
11/10	Repairs	500	

Instructions

(a) Prepare any correcting entries that are necessary.

(b) Assuming that depreciation is to be charged for a full year based on the ending balance in the asset account no matter when acquired, calculate the proper depreciation charge for 2017 under both methods listed below. Assume an estimated life of 10 years for all equipment at the time of acquisition, with no residual value. The equipment included in the January 1, 2017 Equipment balance was purchased in 2015.

1. Straight-line

2. Declining-balance (assume twice the straight-line rate)

(LO 4) E11-13 (Depletion Calculations—Timber) Rachel Timber Inc., a small private company that follows ASPE, owns 9,000 hectares of timberland purchased in 2004 at a cost of $1,400 per hectare. At the time of purchase, the land without the timber was valued at $420 per hectare. In 2005, Rachel built fire lanes and roads, with a physical life of 30 years, at a cost of $84,000 and separately capitalized these costs. Every year, Rachel sprays to prevent disease at a cost of $3,000 per year and spends $7,000 to maintain the fire lanes and roads. During 2006, Rachel selectively logged and sold 700,000 cubic metres of the estimated 3.5 million cubic metres of timber. In 2007, Rachel planted new seedlings to replace the cut trees at a cost of $100,000.

Instructions

(a) Determine the depletion charge and the portion of depletion included in the cost of timber sold in 2006. Provide the journal entries to record the depletion charged to inventory (and subsequently to cost of goods sold) for the year.

(b) Rachel has not logged since 2006. Assume that Rachel logged 900,000 cubic metres of timber in 2017, of which 60% was sold in 2017 and the remainder sold in 2018. The timber cruiser (the appraiser) had estimated a total resource of 5 million cubic metres. Determine the cost of timber sold that relates to the depletion for 2017 and 2018. Provide the journal entries to account for the cost of timber produced in 2017 and subsequently sold in 2017 and 2018.

(c) How would Rachel account for the maintenance costs of the fire lanes and roads and the spraying of the timberland?

DIGGING DEEPER

(d) Discuss the depreciation methods that Rachel could use to depreciate the cost of the fire lanes and roads.

(e) Explain how your answers for parts (a) to (d) would differ if Rachel were a public company and followed IFRS.

(LO 4) E11-14 (Depletion Calculations—Oil) Marmon Drilling Limited leases property on which oil has been discovered. Wells on this property produced 21,000 barrels of oil during the current year, sold at an average of $80 per barrel. The total oil resources of this property are estimated to be 250,000 barrels.

The lease provided for an immediate payment of $5 million to the lessor (owner) before drilling began and an annual rental of $275,000. Development costs of $6,250,000 were incurred before any oil was produced, and Marmon follows a policy of capitalizing these preproduction costs. The lease also specified that each year the lessor would be paid a premium of 5% of the sales price of every barrel of oil that was removed. In addition, the lessee is to clean up all the waste and debris from drilling and to pay the costs of reconditioning the land for farming when the wells are abandoned. It is estimated that the present value of the obligations at the time of the lease for the cleanup and reconditioning for the existing wells is $300,000. All amounts are in Canadian dollars.

Instructions

(a) From the information given, provide the journal entry made by Marmon Drilling Limited to record depletion for the current year, assuming that Marmon applies ASPE.

(b) Assuming that the oil property was acquired at the beginning of the current year, provide the entry to record the acquisition of the asset and the annual rental payment.

(LO 4) E11-15 (Depletion Calculations—Minerals) At the beginning of 2017, Kao Company, a small private company, acquired a mine for $850,000. Of this amount, $100,000 was allocated to the land value and the remaining portion to the minerals in the mine. Surveys conducted by geologists found that approximately 12 million units of ore appear to be in the mine. Kao had $170,000 of development costs for this mine before any extraction of minerals. It also determined that the fair value of its obligation to prepare the land for an alternative use when all of the minerals have been removed was $40,000. During 2017, 2.5 million units of ore were extracted and 2.2 million of these units were sold.

Instructions

Calculate the following information for 2017 (rounding your unit cost answers to three decimal places):

(a) The depletion cost per unit

(b) The total amount of depletion for 2017 (and prepare the required journal entry, if any)

(c) The total amount that is charged as an expense for 2017 for the cost of minerals sold during 2017 (and prepare the required journal entry, if any)

(LO 5) E11-16 (Depreciation—Change in Estimate) Machinery purchased for $56,000 by Wong Corp. on January 1, 2012, was originally estimated to have an eight-year useful life with a residual value of $4,000. Depreciation has been entered for five years on this basis. In 2017, it is determined that the total estimated useful life (including 2017) should have been 10 years, with a residual value of $4,500 at the end of that time. Assume straight-line depreciation and that Wong Corp. uses IFRS for financial statement purposes.

Instructions

(a) Prepare the entry that is required to correct the prior years' depreciation, if any.

(b) Prepare the entry to record depreciation for 2017.

(c) Repeat part (a) assuming Wong Corp. uses ASPE and the machinery is originally estimated to have a physical life of 8.5 years and a salvage value of $0. In 2017 it is determined that the total estimated physical life (including 2017) should have been 11 years, with a residual value of $100 at the end of that time. Round to the nearest dollar.

(d) Repeat part (b) assuming Wong Corp. uses the double-declining-balance method of depreciation.

(LO 5) E11-17 (Depreciation Calculation—Addition, Change in Estimate) In 1988, Lincoln Limited completed the construction of a building at a cost of $1.8 million; it occupied the building in January 1989. It was estimated that the building would have a useful life of 40 years and a residual value of $400,000.

Early in 1999, an addition to the building was constructed at a cost of $750,000. At that time, no changes were expected in its useful life, but the residual value with the addition was estimated to increase by $150,000. The addition would not be of economic use to the company beyond the life of the original building.

In 2017, as a result of a thorough review of its depreciation policies, company management determined that the building's original useful life should have been estimated at 30 years. The neighbourhood where the building is has been going through a renewal, with older buildings being torn down and new ones being built. Because of this, it is now expected that the company's building and addition are unlikely to have any residual value at the end of the 30-year period. Lincoln Limited follows IFRS for its financial statements.

Instructions

(a) Using the straight-line method, calculate the annual depreciation that was charged from 1989 through 1998.

(b) Calculate the annual depreciation that was charged from 1999 through 2016.

(c) Prepare the entry, if necessary, to adjust the account balances because the estimated useful life was revised in 2017.

(d) Calculate the annual depreciation to be charged beginning with 2017.

(e) Comment on the revision of the estimated useful life in 2017, from the perspective of an investor who purchased shares in Lincoln in 2016.

(f) Repeat parts (a) through (d) assuming Lincoln Limited prepares its financial statements using ASPE. The original estimate of the physical life of the building was 44 years, with a salvage value of $216,000. (Ignore the addition in early 1999.) In 2017, the estimated useful life and physical life were both revised to be 30 years, with no residual value/salvage value for the asset at the end of the 30-year period.

(LO 5) E11-18 (Depreciation Replacement—Change in Estimate) Finlay Limited constructed a building at a cost of $2.8 million and has occupied it since January 1997. It was estimated at that time that its life would be 40 years, with no residual value. In January 2017, a new roof was installed at a cost of $370,000, and it was estimated then that the building would have a useful life of 25 years from that date. The cost of the old roof was $190,000 and was capitalized in the Buildings account at that time. Finlay Limited follows IFRS for its financial statements.

Instructions

(a) What amount of depreciation was charged annually for the years 1997 through 2016? (Assume straight-line depreciation.)

(b) What entry should be made in 2017 to record the roof replacement? Is there an alternative entry available under ASPE?

(c) Prepare the entry in January 2017 to record the revision in the building's estimated life, if necessary.

(d) What amount of depreciation should be charged for the year 2017?

(LO 6) E11-19 (Impairment—Cost Recovery Model) The management of Luis Inc., a small private company that uses the cost recovery impairment model, was discussing whether certain equipment should be written down as a charge to current operations because of obsolescence. The assets had a cost of $900,000, and depreciation of $400,000 had been taken to December 31, 2017. On December 31, 2017, management projected the undiscounted future net cash flows from this equipment to be $300,000, and its fair value to be $230,000. The company intends to use this equipment in the future.

Instructions

(a) Prepare the journal entry, if any, to record the impairment at December 31, 2017.

(b) Where should the gain or loss on the impairment, if any, be reported on the income statement?

(c) At December 31, 2018, the equipment's fair value increased to $260,000. Prepare the journal entry, if any, to record this increase in fair value.

(d) Assume instead that as at December 31, 2017, the equipment was expected to have undiscounted future net cash flows of $510,000, and that its fair value was estimated to be $450,000. Prepare the journal entry to record the impairment at December 31, 2017, if any.

(e) Assume instead that as at December 31, 2017, the equipment was expected to have undiscounted future net cash flows of $45,000 per year for each of the next 10 years, and that there is no active market for the equipment. Luis Inc. uses a 10% discount rate in its cash flow estimates. Prepare the journal entry to record impairment at December 31, 2017, if any.

DIGGING DEEPER

(f) Discuss why impairment is tested using undiscounted future cash flows rather than present value of future cash flows.

(LO 6) E11-20   (Impairment—Cash-Generating Units) Perez Corp., a mining company, owns a significant mineral deposit in a northern territory. Perez prepares financial statements in accordance with IFRS. Included in the asset is a road system that was constructed to give company personnel access to the mineral deposit for maintenance and mining activity. The road system cannot be sold separately and separate cash flow information is not available for it. The carrying amounts of two cash-generating units of the mine at June 30, 2017, are as follows:

Machinery	$4,000,000
Mine in the development phase	$9,500,000

The machinery's value in use has been assessed at $4,500,000 while the fair value less costs to sell is $3,800,000. With respect to the mine, the value in use is $9,000,000 while fair value less costs to sell is $9,350,000.

Instructions

(a) How should the road system's recoverable amount be determined?

(b) Determine if the machinery and the mine are impaired and prepare the journal entries, if any, to record the impairment at June 30, 2017.

(LO 6) E11-21   (Impairment—Rational Entity Model and Cash-Generating Units, Cost Recovery Model and Asset Groups) Green Thumb Landscaping Limited has determined that its lawn maintenance division is a cash-generating unit under IFRS. The carrying amounts of the division's assets at December 31, 2017, are as follows:

Land	$ 25,000
Building	50,000
Equipment	30,000
Trucks	15,000
	$120,000

The lawn maintenance division has been assessed for impairment and it is determined that the division's value in use is $108,000, fair value less costs to sell is $75,000, and undiscounted future net cash flows is $144,000.

Instructions

(a) Determine if the cash-generating unit is impaired and prepare the journal entry, if any, to record the impairment at December 31, 2017, assuming that none of the individual assets in the division has a determinable recoverable amount.

(b) Prepare the journal entry, if any, to record the impairment at December 31, 2017, assuming that the division's only individual asset that has a determinable recoverable amount is the building, which has a fair value less costs to sell of $46,000.

(c) Assume that Green Thumb prepares financial statements under ASPE instead, and that the lawn maintenance division is an asset group. Determine if the asset group is impaired and prepare the journal entry, if any, to record the impairment at December 31, 2017, assuming that none of the individual assets in the division has a determinable recoverable amount.

(LO 6) E11-22 (Impairment—Cost Recovery and Rational Entity Models) The information that follows relates to equipment owned by Gaurav Limited at December 31, 2017:

Cost	$10,000,000
Accumulated depreciation to date	2,000,000
Expected future net cash flows (undiscounted)	7,000,000
Expected future net cash flows (discounted, value in use)	6,350,000
Fair value	6,200,000
Costs to sell (costs of disposal)	50,000

Assume that Gaurav will continue to use this asset in the future. As at December 31, 2017, the equipment has a remaining useful life of four years. Gaurav uses the straight-line method of depreciation.

Instructions

(a) Assume that Gaurav is a private company that follows ASPE.

  1. Prepare the journal entry at December 31, 2017, to record asset impairment, if any.

  2. Prepare the journal entry to record depreciation expense for 2018.

  3. The equipment's fair value at December 31, 2018, is $6.5 million. Prepare the journal entry, if any, to record the increase in fair value.

(b) Repeat the requirements in (a) above assuming that Gaurav is a public company that follows IFRS.

(c) Referring to the qualitative characteristics identified in the conceptual framework for financial reporting (discussed in Chapter 2), discuss the differences between the cost recovery impairment model and the rational entity impairment model. Which method is preferred?

(LO 6, E11-23   (Impairment—Cost Recovery and Rational Entity Models) Assume the same information as in E11-22, **7, 8)** except that at December 31, 2017, Gaurav discontinues use of the equipment and intends to dispose of it in the coming year by selling it to a competitor. It is expected that the costs of disposal will total $50,000.

Instructions

(a) Assume that Gaurav is a private company that follows ASPE.

  1. Prepare the journal entry at December 31, 2017, to record asset impairment, if any.

  2. Prepare the journal entry to record depreciation expense for 2018.

  3. Assume that the asset was not sold by December 31, 2018. The equipment's fair value (and recoverable amount) on this date is $6.5 million. Prepare the journal entry, if any, to record the increase in fair value. It is expected that the costs of disposal will total $50,000.

  4. Identify where, and at what amount, the asset will be reported on the December 31, 2018 statement of financial position.

(b) Repeat the requirements in (a) above assuming that Gaurav is a public company that follows IFRS, and that the asset meets all criteria for classification as an asset held for sale.

(LO 2, E11-24   (Depreciation Calculation—Replacement, Trade-in) Onkar Corporation bought a machine on June 1, **3, 7)** 2013, for $31,800, f.o.b. the place of manufacture. Freight costs were $300, and $500 was spent to install it. The machine's useful life was estimated at 10 years, with a residual value of $1,900, while the machine's physical life was estimated at 11 years, with no residual value.

On June 1, 2014, a part that was designed to reduce the machine's operating costs was added to the machine for a cost of $1,980. On June 1, 2017, the company bought a new machine with greater capacity for a cost of $35,000, delivered. A trade-in value was received on the old machine equal to its fair value of $19,000. The cost of removing the old machine from the plant was $75, and the cost of installing the new machine was $1,300. It was estimated that the new machine would have a useful life of 10 years, with a residual value of $4,000.

Instructions

(a) Assuming that depreciation is calculated on the straight-line basis, determine the amount of any gain or loss on the disposal of the first machine on June 1, 2017, and the amount of depreciation that should be provided during the company's current fiscal year, which begins on June 1, 2017. The financial statements are prepared under IFRS.

(b) How would your answer in (a) change when assuming the financial statements were prepared under ASPE?

(LO 3, E11-25   (Depreciation Calculations—Revaluation Model) Jamoka Corporation is a public company that man- **5, 7)** ufactures farm implements, such as tractors, combines, and wagons. Jamoka uses the revaluation model per IAS 16, and records asset revaluations using the elimination method. (This means the balance in the accumulated depreciation account is eliminated against the asset account just prior to revaluation of the asset to fair value.) A piece of manufacturing equipment included in the property, plant, and equipment section on Jamoka's statement of financial position was purchased on December 31, 2016, for a cost of $100,000. The equipment was expected to have a remaining useful life of five years, with benefits being received evenly over the five years. Residual value of the equipment was estimated to be $10,000.

Consider the following two situations:

Situation 1: At December 31, 2017, no formal revaluation is performed, as management determines that the carrying amount of the property, plant, and equipment is not materially different from its fair value.

Situation 2: At December 31, 2017, a formal revaluation is performed and the independent appraisers assess the equipment's fair value to be $89,000. During the revaluation process, it is determined that the remaining useful life of the equipment is four years, with residual value of $11,000.

At December 31, 2018, no formal revaluation is performed, as management determines that the carrying amount of the property, plant, and equipment is not materially different from its fair value. The equipment is sold on March 31, 2019, for $62,000.

Instructions

(a) Prepare any journal entries required under situation 1 described above for: (1) the fiscal year ended December 31, 2017; (2) the fiscal year ended December 31, 2018; and (3) the disposal of the equipment on March 31, 2019.

(b) Prepare any journal entries required under situation 2 described above for: (1) the fiscal year ended December 31, 2017; (2) the fiscal year ended December 31, 2018; and (3) the disposal of the equipment on March 31, 2019.

(c) Assume that Jamoka uses the proportional method to record asset revaluations under the revaluation model. Prepare any journal entries required under situation 2 described above for: (1) the fiscal year ended December 31, 2017; (2) the fiscal year ended December 31, 2018; and (3) the disposal of the equipment on March 31, 2019.

(d) What is the equivalent standard under ASPE?

(LO 7) E11-26   (Entries for Disposition of Assets) Consider the following independent situations for Kwok Corporation. Kwok applies ASPE.

Situation 1: Kwok purchased equipment in 2010 for $120,000 and estimated a $12,000 residual value at the end of the equipment's 10-year useful life. At December 31, 2016, there was $75,600 in the Accumulated Depreciation account for this equipment using the straight-line method of depreciation. On March 31, 2017, the equipment was sold for $28,000.

Situation 2: Kwok sold a piece of machinery for $10,000 on July 31, 2017. The machine originally cost $38,000 on January 1, 2009. It was estimated that the machine would have a useful life of 12 years with a residual value of $2,000, and the straight-line method of depreciation was used.

Situation 3: Kwok sold equipment that had a carrying amount of $3,500 for $5,200. The equipment originally cost $12,000 and it is estimated that it would cost $16,000 to replace the equipment.

Instructions

(a) Prepare the appropriate journal entries to record the disposition of the property, plant, and equipment assets, assuming that Kwok's fiscal year end is December 31 and that Kwok only prepares financial statements and adjusts the accounts annually.

(b) How would the journal entries in (a) change if Kwok Corporation applied IFRS?

(LO 7) E11-27   (Entries for Disposition of Assets) On December 31, 2016, Grey Inc. owns a machine with a carrying amount of $940,000. The original cost and accumulated depreciation for the machine on this date are as follows:

Machine	$1,300,000
Accumulated depreciation	360,000
	$ 940,000

Depreciation is calculated at $60,000 per year on a straight-line basis.

Instructions

A set of independent situations follows. For each situation, prepare the journal entry for Grey Inc. to record the transaction. Ensure that depreciation entries are recorded to update the machine's carrying amount before its disposal. Assume that Grey Inc. uses IFRS for financial statement purposes.

(a) A fire completely destroyed the machine on August 31, 2017. An insurance settlement of $430,000 was received for this casualty. Assume the settlement was received immediately.

(b) On April 1, 2017, Grey sold the machine for $1,040,000 to Dwight Company.

(c) On July 31, 2017, the company donated the machine to the Dartmouth City Council. The machine's fair value at the time of the donation was estimated to be $1.1 million.

(d) Would the treatment of (a) through (c) differ if presented under ASPE instead of IFRS?

(LO 7) E11-28 (Disposition of Assets) On April 1, 2017, Lombardi Corp. was awarded $460,000 cash as compensation for the forced sale of its land and building, which were directly in the path of a new highway. The land and building cost $60,000 and $280,000, respectively, when they were acquired. At April 1, 2017, the accumulated depreciation for the building amounted to $165,000. On August 1, 2017, Lombardi purchased a piece of replacement property for cash. The new land cost $160,000 and the new building cost $410,000. The new building is estimated to have a useful life of 20 years, physical life of 30 years, residual value of $230,000, and salvage value of $75,000. Lombardi prepares financial statements in accordance with IFRS.

Instructions

(a) Prepare the journal entries to record the transactions on April 1 and August 1, 2017.

(b) How would the transactions on April 1 and August 1, 2017, affect the income statement for 2017? Would the effect be different if Lombardi prepared financial statements in accordance with ASPE?

(c) Prepare the journal entries required at December 31, 2017, under (1) IFRS and (2) ASPE.

(LO 9) E11-29 (Ratio Analysis) The 2017 annual report of Trocchi Inc. contains the following information (in thousands):

	Dec. 31, 2017	Dec. 31, 2016
Total assets	$1,071,348	$ 787,167
Total liabilities	626,178	410,044
Consolidated sales	3,374,463	2,443,592
Net income	66,234	49,062

Instructions

(a) Calculate the following ratios for Trocchi Inc. for 2017:

1. Asset turnover ratio

FINANCE

2. Rate of return on assets

3. Profit margin on sales

(b) How can the asset turnover ratio be used to calculate the rate of return on assets?

(c) Briefly comment on the results for the ratios calculated in part (a).

(LO 3, 11) *E11-30 (Depreciation Calculations—Four Methods; Partial Periods) On August 1, 2017, Iroko Corporation purchased a new machine for its assembly process. The cost of this machine was $136,400. The company estimated that the machine would have a trade-in value of $14,200 at the end of its useful life. Its useful life was estimated to be six years and its working hours were estimated to be 18,000 hours. Iroko's year end is December 31. (Round depreciation per unit to three decimal places.) Iroko Corporation prepares its financial statements using IFRS.

Instructions

Calculate the depreciation expense under each of the following:

(a) Straight-line method for 2017

TAXATION

(b) Activity method for 2017, assuming that machine use was 800 hours

(c) Double-declining-balance method for 2017 and 2018

(d) Capital cost allowance method for 2017 and 2018 using a CCA rate of 25%

(LO 11) *E11-31 (CCA) During 2017, Laiken Limited sold its only Class 3 asset. At the time of sale, the balance of the undepreciated capital cost for this class was $37,450. The asset originally cost $129,500.

Instructions

(a) Calculate recaptured CCA, capital gains, and terminal losses, if any, assuming the asset was sold for proceeds of

TAXATION

(1) $132,700, (2) $51,000, and (3) $22,000.

(b) Assume the tax rates are scheduled to increase for 2017. What strategy could Laiken use to reduce its taxes payable that are due to the recapture on the disposal of the asset?

DIGGING DEEPER

(LO 11) *E11-32   (Book versus Tax Depreciation) Barnett Inc. purchased computer equipment on March 1, 2017, for $31,000. The computer equipment has a useful life of five years and a residual value of $1,000. Barnett uses a double-declining-balance method of depreciation for this type of capital asset. For tax purposes, the computer is assigned to Class 10 with a 30% rate.

Instructions

(a) Prepare a schedule of depreciation covering 2017, 2018, and 2019 for financial reporting purposes for the new computer equipment purchased. The company follows a policy of taking a full year's depreciation in the year of purchase and none in the year of disposal.

(b) Prepare a schedule of CCA and Undepreciated Capital Cost (UCC) for this asset covering 2017, 2018, and 2019, assuming it is the only Class 10 asset owned by Barnett.

TAXATION

(c) How much depreciation is deducted over the three-year period on the financial statements? In determining taxable income? What is the carrying amount of the computer equipment on the December 31, 2019 statement of financial position? What is the tax value of the computer equipment at December 31, 2019?

Problems

P11-1   Phoenix Corp. purchased Machine no. 201 on May 1, 2017. The following information relating to Machine no. 201 was gathered at the end of May:

Price	$85,000
Credit terms	2/10, n/30
Freight-in costs	$800
Preparation and installation costs	$3,800
Labour costs during regular production operations	$10,500

It was expected that the machine could be used for 10 years, after which the residual value would be zero. However, Phoenix intends to use the machine for only eight years, and expects to then be able to sell it for $1,500. The invoice for Machine no. 201 was paid on May 5, 2017. Phoenix has a December 31 year end. Depreciation expense should be calculated to the nearest half month. Phoenix follows IFRS for financial statement purposes.

Instructions

(a) Calculate the depreciation expense for the years indicated using the following methods. (Round to the nearest dollar.)

  1. Straight-line method for the fiscal years ended December 31, 2017 and 2018

  2. Double-declining-balance method for the fiscal years ended December 31, 2017 and 2018

*(b) Calculate the capital cost allowance for the 2017 and 2018 tax returns, assuming a CCA class with a rate of 25%.

TAXATION

(c) The president of Phoenix tells you that, because the company is a new organization, she expects it will be several years before production and sales reach optimum levels. She asks you, an accounting policy advisor, to recommend a depreciation method that will allocate less of the company's depreciation expense to the early years and more to later years of the assets' lives. Which method would you recommend? Explain.

DIGGING DEEPER

(d) In your answer to part (c) above, how would cash flows to the new company be affected by the choice of depreciation method? How would current and potential creditors interpret the choice of depreciation method?

(e) Assume that Phoenix selects the double-declining-balance method of depreciation. In 2019, demand for the product produced by the machine decreases sharply, due to the introduction of a new and better competing product on the market. On August 15, 2019, the management of Phoenix meets and decides to discontinue manufacturing the product. On September 15, 2019, a formal plan to sell the machine is authorized. On this date, the machine meets all criteria for classification as held for sale, and the machine's fair value less costs to sell is $65,500. Calculate the depreciation expense for 2019.

P11-2   Alladin Company purchased a large piece of equipment on October 1, 2017. The following information relating to the equipment was gathered at the end of October:

Price	$60,000
Credit terms	2/10, n/30
Engineering costs	$4,800
Maintenance costs during regular production operations	$8,500

It is expected that the equipment could be used for 12 years, after which the salvage value would be zero. Alladin intends to use the equipment for only 10 years, however, after which it expects to be able to sell it for $3,100. The equipment was delivered on October 1 and the invoice for the equipment was paid October 9, 2017. Alladin uses the calendar year as the basis for the preparation of financial statements. Alladin follows IFRS for financial statement purposes.

Instructions

(a) Calculate the depreciation expense for the years indicated using the following methods. (Round to the nearest dollar.) Round all calculations down to the nearest dollar

   1. Straight-line method for 2017

   2. Sum-of-the-years'-digits method for 2018

   3. Double-declining-balance method for 2017

(b) The CEO of Alladin tells you that the company is interested in maintaining a stable level of income, because it plans to expand in the future and does not want to appear unduly risky to potential lenders. He asks you, the company's newly hired CPA, to recommend a depreciation method that will best achieve this goal. You know that because the equipment is new it should have low repairs and maintenance costs for the next few years. However the repairs and maintenance costs are likely to increase steadily during years 3–10 of the life of the equipment. Which method would you recommend? Explain.

P11-3   On June 15, 2014, a second-hand machine was purchased for $77,000. Before being put into service, the equipment was overhauled at a cost of $5,200, and additional costs of $400 for direct material and $800 for direct labour were paid in fine-tuning the controls. The machine has an estimated residual value of $5,000 at the end of its five-year useful life. The machine is expected to operate for 100,000 hours before it will be replaced and is expected to produce 1.2 million units in this time. Operating data for the next six fiscal years are provided below. The company has an October 31 fiscal year end. Depreciation expense should be calculated to the nearest half month.

Year	Hours of Operation	Units Produced
2014	10,000	110,000
2015	20,000	270,000
2016	20,000	264,000
2017	20,000	310,000
2018	18,000	134,000
2019	12,000	112,000

Instructions

(a) Calculate the depreciation charges for each fiscal year under each of the following depreciation methods. Where necessary, round depreciation rate per unit to four decimal places.

   1. Straight-line method

   2. Activity method: based on output

   3. Activity method: based on input

   4. Double-declining-balance method

TAXATION   *****5.** CCA, Class 8, 20%

DIGGING DEEPER

(b) What is the carrying amount of the machine on the October 31, 2017 statement of financial position under the first four methods above?

(c) Compare your answers in (b) with the asset's tax value at the same date.

(d) Which method would the company's management prefer in order to minimize taxes in 2014?

(e) What happens if the actual hours of operation or units produced do not correspond to the numbers that were estimated in setting the rate?

P11-4   Comco Tool Corp. records depreciation annually at the end of the year. Its policy is to take a full year's depreciation on all assets that are used throughout the year and depreciation for half a year on all machines that are acquired or disposed of during the year. The depreciation rate for the machinery is 10%, applied on a straight-line basis, with no estimated scrap or residual value.

The balance of the Machinery account at the beginning of 2017 was $172,300; the Accumulated Depreciation on Machinery account had a balance of $72,900. The machinery accounts were affected by the following transactions that occurred in 2017:

Jan. 15   Machine no. 38, which cost $9,600 when it was acquired on June 3, 2010, was retired and sold as scrap metal for $600.

Feb. 27   Machine no. 81 was purchased. The fair value of this machine was $12,500. It replaced two machines, nos. 12 and 27, which were traded in on the new machine. Machine no. 12 was acquired on February 4, 2005, at a cost of $5,500 and was still carried in the accounts, although it was fully depreciated and not in use. Machine no. 27 was acquired on June 11, 2010, at a cost of $8,200. In addition to these two used machines, Comco paid $9,000 in cash.

Apr. 7   Machine no. 54 was equipped with electric controls at a cost of $940. This machine, originally equipped with simple hand controls, was purchased on December 11, 2013, for $1,800. The new electric controls can be attached to any one of several machines in the shop.

12   Machine no. 24 was repaired at a cost of $720 after a fire caused by a short circuit in the wiring burned out the motor and damaged certain essential parts.

July 22   Machines 25, 26, and 41 were sold for $3,100 cash. The purchase dates and cost of these machines were as follows:

No. 25	May 8, 2009	$4,000
No. 26	May 8, 2009	3,200
No. 41	June 1, 2011	2,800

Instructions

(a) Record each transaction in general journal form.

(b) Calculate and record depreciation for the year. None of the machines currently included in the balance of the account were acquired before January 1, 2009.

DIGGING DEEPER

(c) As an investor of Comco Tool Corp., would you view regular gains on the disposition of equipment favourably? Explain.

P11-5   On January 1, 2015, Dayan Corporation, a small manufacturer of machine tools, acquired new industrial equipment for $1.1 million. The new equipment had a useful life of five years and the residual value was estimated to be $50,000. Dayan estimates that the new equipment can produce 12,000 machine tools in its first year. It estimates that production will decline by 1,000 units per year over the equipment's remaining useful life.

The following depreciation methods may be used: (1) straight-line, (2) double-declining-balance, and (3) unit of production. For tax purposes, the CCA class is Class 10—30%.

Instructions

TAXATION

(a) Which of the three depreciation methods would maximize net income for financial statement reporting purposes for the three-year period ending December 31, 2017? Prepare a schedule showing the amount of accumulated depreciation at December 31, 2017, under the method you chose.

DIGGING DEEPER

*(b) Over the same three-year period, how much capital cost allowance would have been written off for tax purposes?

(c) Which pattern of depreciation do you feel best reflects the benefits that are provided by the new equipment? Explain briefly.

P11-6   The following data relate to the Plant Assets account of Keller Inc. at December 31, 2016:

	A	B	C	D
Original cost	$46,000	$58,000	$68,000	$73,000
Year purchased	2011	2012	2013	2014
Useful life	10 years	17,000 hours	15 years	10 years
Residual value	$3,900	$4,450	$8,000	$4,700
Depreciation method	straight-line	activity	straight-line	double-declining
Accumulated depreciation through 2016	$21,050	$31,600	$12,000	$26,280

Note: In the year an asset is purchased, Keller does not record any depreciation expense on the asset. In the year an asset is retired or traded in, Keller takes a full year's depreciation on the asset.

The following transactions occurred during 2017:

1. On May 5, Asset A was sold for $16,500 cash. The company's bookkeeper recorded this retirement as follows:

| Cash | 16,500 | |
| Asset A | | 16,500 |

2. On December 31, it was determined that Asset B had been used 3,200 hours during 2017.

3. On December 31, before calculating depreciation expense on Asset C, Keller management decided that Asset C's remaining useful life should be nine years as of year end.

4. On December 31, it was discovered that a piece of equipment purchased in 2016 had been expensed completely in that year. The asset cost $31,000, had a useful life of 10 years when it was acquired, and had no residual value. Management has decided to use the double-declining-balance method for this asset, which can be referred to as "Asset E." Ignore income taxes.

Instructions

DIGGING DEEPER

(a) Prepare any necessary adjusting journal entries required at December 31, 2017, as well as any entries to record depreciation for 2017.

(b) As an owner of Keller Inc., do you have any concerns with respect to the bookkeeper's work?

P11-7   Soon after December 31, 2017, the auditor of Morino Manufacturing Corp. asked the company to prepare a depreciation schedule for semi trucks that showed the additions, retirements, depreciation, and other data that affected the company's income in the four-year period from 2014 to 2017, inclusive. The following data were obtained:

Balance of Trucks account, January 1, 2014:	
Truck no. 1, purchased Jan. 1, 2011, cost	$18,000
Truck no. 2, purchased July 1, 2011, cost	22,000
Truck no. 3, purchased Jan. 1, 2013, cost	30,000
Truck no. 4, purchased July 1, 2013, cost	24,000
Balance, January 1, 2014	$94,000

The account Accumulated Depreciation—Trucks had a correct balance of $30,200 on January 1, 2014. (This includes depreciation on the four trucks from the respective dates of purchase, based on a five-year life, with no residual value.) No charges had been made against the account before January 1, 2014.

Transactions between January 1, 2014, and December 31, 2017, and their records in the ledger were as follows:

July 1, 2014	Truck no. 3 was traded for a larger one (no. 5). The agreed purchase price (fair value) was $34,000. Morino Manufacturing paid the automobile dealer $15,000 cash on the transaction. The entry was a debit to Trucks and a credit to Cash, $15,000.
Jan. 1, 2015	Truck no. 1 was sold for $3,500 cash. The entry was a debit to Cash and a credit to Trucks, $3,500.
July 1, 2016	A new truck (no. 6) was acquired for $36,000 cash and was charged at that amount to the Trucks account. (Assume truck no. 2 was not retired.)
July 1, 2016	Truck no. 4 was so badly damaged in an accident that it was sold as scrap for $700 cash. Morino Manufacturing received $2,500 from the insurance company. The entry made by the bookkeeper was a debit to Cash, $3,200, and credits to Gain on Disposal of Trucks, $700, and Trucks, $2,500.

Entries for depreciation were made at the close of each year as follows: 2014, $20,300; 2015, $21,100; 2016, $24,450; and 2017, $27,800.

Instructions

AUDITING

DIGGING DEEPER

(a) For each of the four years, calculate separately the increase or decrease in net income that is due to the company's errors in determining or entering depreciation or in recording transactions affecting the trucks. Ignore income tax considerations.

(b) Prepare one compound journal entry as at December 31, 2017, to adjust the Trucks account to reflect the correct balances according to your schedule, and assuming that the books have not been closed for 2017.

(c) Based on the errors noted, what recommendations, if any, would the auditors likely make? Are there any implications for the auditors' report in detecting errors several years after they have occurred?

P11-8   Linda Monkland established Monkland Ltd. in mid-2016 as the sole shareholder. The accounts on June 30, 2017, the company's year end, just prior to preparing the required adjusting entries, were as follows:

Current assets		$100,000
Capital assets		
Land	$40,000	
Building	90,000	
Equipment	50,000	180,000
Current liabilities		40,000
Long-term bank loan		120,000
Common shares		90,000
Net income prior to depreciation		30,000

All the capital assets were acquired and put into operation in early July 2016. Estimates and usage information on these assets were as follows:

Building: 25-year life, $15,000 residual value

Equipment: Five-year life, 15,000 hours of use, $5,000 residual value. The equipment was used for 1,000 hours in 2016 and 1,400 hours in 2017 up to June 30.

Linda Monkland is now considering which depreciation method or methods would be appropriate. She has narrowed the choices down for the building to the straight-line or double-declining-balance method, and for the equipment to the straight-line, double-declining-balance, or activity method. She has requested your advice and recommendation. In discussions with her, the following concerns were raised:

1. The company acquires goods from suppliers with terms of 2/10, n/30. The suppliers have indicated that these terms will continue as long as the current ratio does not fall below 2 to 1. If the ratio falls lower, no purchase discounts will be given.

2. The bank will continue the loan from year to year as long as the ratio of long-term debt to total assets does not exceed 46%.

3. Linda Monkland has contracted with the company's manager to pay him a bonus equal to 50% of any net income in excess of $14,000. She prefers to minimize or pay no bonus as long as conditions of agreements with suppliers and the bank can be met.

ETHICS

4. In order to provide a strong signal to attract potential investors to join her in the company, Ms. Monkland believes that a rate of return on total assets of at least 5% must be achieved.

Instructions

(a) Prepare a report for Linda Monkland that (1) presents tables, (2) analyzes the situation, (3) provides a recommendation on which method or methods should be used, and (4) justifies your recommendation by considering her concerns and the requirement that the method(s) used be considered generally acceptable accounting principle(s).

(b) What other factors should you discuss with Ms. Monkland to help her in choosing appropriate depreciation methods for her business?

DIGGING DEEPER

(c) Do any ethical issues arise if a depreciation method is chosen in order to manipulate the financial results in a way that will satisfy the constraints listed above? Explain.

P11-9 On April 30, 2017, Oceanarium Corporation ordered a new passenger ship, which was delivered to the designated cruise port and available for use as of June 30, 2017. Overall, the cost of the ship was $97 million, with an estimated useful life of 12 years and residual value of $30 million. Oceanarium expects that the new ship, as a whole, will provide its greatest economic benefits in its early years of operation. After further research and discussion with management, it is determined that the ship consists of major parts with differing useful lives, residual values, and patterns of providing economic benefits:

Part	Cost	Useful life	Residual value	Pattern of benefits	Total output (nautical miles)
Engines (6)	$975,000 per engine	8 years	$120,000 per engine	Varies with activity	7.0 million
Hull	$3,350,000	10 years	$502,000	Highest in early years	7.8 million
Body	$87.8 million	15 years	$15.5 million	Evenly over life of body	12.6 million

The ship's first voyage took place on August 1, 2017. The ship sailed a total of 328,000 nautical miles in 2017. Oceanarium prepares financial statements in accordance with IFRS.

Instructions

(a) Identify the factors to consider in determining how to account for the purchase and depreciation of the ship.

(b) Prepare the journal entry to record the purchase of the ship, assuming that Oceanarium paid cash for the purchase.

(c) Prepare the journal entry(ies) to record depreciation expense for 2017.

(d) Explain any differences in part (a) above if Oceanarium prepares financial statements in accordance with ASPE instead of IFRS.

DIGGING DEEPER

(e) Oceanarium Corporation's banker has requested financial statements prepared under IFRS to determine Oceanarium's ability to repay a long-term loan granted in 2016. What is the benefit to the banker of having each component of the ship depreciated separately?

P11-10 On January 1, 2016, Locke Company, a small machine-tool manufacturer, acquired a piece of new industrial equipment for $1,260,000. The new equipment had a useful life of five years, and the salvage value was estimated to be $60,000. Locke estimates that the new equipment can produce 12,000 machine tools in its first year. It estimates that production will decline by 1,000 units per year over the remaining useful life of the equipment.

The following depreciation methods may be used: (1) straight-line, (2) double-declining-balance, (3) sum-of-the-years'-digits, and (4) unit of output.

Instructions

(a) Which depreciation method would maximize net income for financial statement reporting for the three-year period ending December 31, 2018? Prepare a schedule showing the amount of accumulated depreciation at December 31, 2018, under each method to support the method selected. Ignore present value, income tax, and deferred income tax considerations.

(b) Which depreciation method would minimize net income for the three-year period ending December 31, 2018? Determine the amount of accumulated depreciation at December 31, 2018. Ignore present value considerations.

P11-11 Khamsah Mining Ltd. is a small private company that purchased a tract of land for $720,000. After incurring exploration costs of $83,000, the company estimated that the tract would yield 120,000 tonnes of ore with enough mineral content to make mining and processing profitable. It is further estimated that 6,000 tonnes of ore will be mined in the first and last years and 12,000 tonnes every year in between. The land is expected to have a residual value of $30,000.

The company built necessary bunkhouses and sheds on the site at a cost of $36,000. It estimated that these structures would have a physical life of 15 years but, because they must be dismantled if they are to be moved, they have no residual value. The company does not intend to use the buildings elsewhere. Mining machinery installed at the mine was purchased second-hand at a cost of $60,000. This machinery cost the former owner $150,000 and was 50% depreciated when it was purchased. Khamsah Mining estimated that about half of this machinery would still be useful when the present mineral resources are exhausted, but that dismantling and removing it would cost about as much as it is worth at that time. The company does not intend to use the machinery elsewhere. The remaining machinery is expected to last until about half of the estimated mineral ore has been removed and will then be worthless. Cost is to be allocated equally between these two classes of machinery.

Khamsah also spent another $126,400 in opening up the mine so that the ore could be extracted and removed for shipping. The company estimates that the site reclamation and restoration costs that it is responsible for by contract when the mine is depleted have a present value of $53,600. Khamsah follows a policy of expensing exploration costs and capitalizing development costs.

Instructions

(a) As chief accountant for the company, you are to prepare a schedule that shows the estimated depletion and depreciation costs for each year of the mine's expected life.

DIGGING DEEPER

(b) Prepare the journal entry(ies) to record the transactions for the acquisition of the mining property and related assets during the first year. Also prepare entries to record depreciation and depletion for the first year. Assume that actual production was 5,000 tonnes. Nothing occurred during the year to cause the company engineers to change their estimates of either the mineral resources or the life of the structures and equipment.

(c) Assume that 4,500 tonnes of product were processed and sold during the first year of the mine's expected life. Identify all costs mentioned above that will be included in the first-year income statement of Khamsah Mining Ltd.

AUDITING

(d) As the auditor of Khamsah Mining Ltd., how would you assess the reasonability of the asset retirement obligations established by the client?

P11-12 Conan Logging and Lumber Company, a small private company that follows ASPE, owns 3,000 hectares of timberland on the north side of Mount Leno, which was purchased in 2005 at a cost of $550 per hectare. In 2017, Conan began selectively logging this timber tract. In May 2017, Mount Leno erupted, burying Conan's timberland under 15 centimetres of ash. All of the timber on the Conan tract was downed. In addition, the logging roads, built at a cost of $150,000, were destroyed, as well as the logging equipment, with a carrying amount of $300,000.

At the time of the eruption, Conan had logged 20% of the estimated 500,000 cubic metres of timber. Prior to the eruption, Conan estimated the land to have a value of $200 per hectare after the timber was harvested. Conan includes the logging roads in the depletion base.

Conan estimates it will take three years to salvage the downed timber at a cost of $700,000. The timber can be sold for pulpwood at an estimated price of $3 per cubic metre. The value of the land is unknown, but must be considered nominal due to future uncertainties.

Instructions

(a) Determine the depletion cost per cubic metre for the timber that was harvested prior to the eruption of Mount Leno.

(b) Prepare the journal entry to record the depletion before the eruption.

(c) Determine the amount of the estimated loss before income taxes and show how the losses of roads, machinery, and timber and the timber salvage value should be reported in Conan's financial statements for the year ended December 31, 2017.

(d) As an investor in Conan Logging and Lumber Company, do you have any concerns about the eruption of Mount Leno?

DIGGING
DEEPER

P11-13   Darby Sporting Goods Inc. has been experiencing growth in the demand for its products over the last several years. The last two Olympic Games greatly increased the popularity of basketball around the world. As a result, a European sports retailing consortium entered into an agreement with Darby's Roundball Division to purchase an increasing number of basketballs and other accessories over the next five years.

FINANCE   To be able to meet the quantity commitments of this agreement, Darby had to increase its manufacturing capacity. A real estate firm found an available factory close to Darby's Roundball manufacturing facility, and Darby agreed to purchase the factory and used machinery from Encino Athletic Equipment Company on October 1, 2016. Renovations were necessary to convert the factory for Darby's manufacturing use.

The terms of the agreement required Darby to pay Encino $50,000 when renovations started on January 1, 2017, with the balance to be paid as renovations were completed. The overall purchase price for the factory and machinery was $400,000. The building renovations were contracted to Malone Construction at $100,000. The payments made as renovations progressed during 2017 are shown below. The factory began operating on January 1, 2018.

	Jan. 1	Apr. 1	Oct. 1	Dec. 31
Encino	$50,000	$90,000	$110,000	$150,000
Malone		30,000	30,000	40,000

On January 1, 2017, Darby secured a $500,000 line of credit with a 12% interest rate to finance the purchase cost of the factory and machinery and the renovation costs. Darby drew down on the line of credit to meet the payment schedule shown above; this was Darby's only outstanding loan during 2017.

Bob Sprague, Darby's controller, will capitalize the maximum allowable interest costs for this project, which he has calculated to be $21,000. Darby's policy regarding purchases of this nature is to use the appraisal value of the land for book purposes and pro-rate the balance of the purchase price over the remaining items. The factory had originally cost Encino $300,000 and had a carrying amount of $50,000, while the machinery originally cost $125,000 and had a carrying amount of $40,000 on the date of sale. The land was recorded on Encino's books at $40,000. An appraisal, conducted by independent appraisers at the time of acquisition, valued the land at $290,000, the factory at $105,000, and the machinery at $45,000.

Angie Justice, chief engineer, estimated that the renovated factory would be used for 15 years, with an estimated residual value of $30,000. Justice estimated that the productive machinery would have a remaining useful life of 5 years and a residual value of $3,000. Darby's depreciation policy specifies the 200% declining-balance method for machinery and the 150% declining-balance method for the factory. Half a year's depreciation is taken in the year the factory is placed in service and half a year's depreciation is allowed when the property is disposed of or retired.

Instructions

(a) Determine the amounts to be recorded on the books of Darby Sporting Goods Inc. as at December 31, 2017, for each of the following properties acquired from Encino Athletic Equipment Company: (1) land, (2) factory, and (3) machinery.

(b) Calculate Darby Sporting Goods Inc.'s 2018 depreciation expense, for book purposes, for each of the assets acquired from Encino Athletic Equipment Company.

DIGGING
DEEPER

(c) Discuss the arguments for and against the capitalization of interest costs. Why would the treatment of interest costs matter to a shareholder of a public company, for instance?

P11-14   Roland Corporation uses special strapping equipment in its packaging business. The equipment was purchased in January 2016 for $10 million and had an estimated useful life of eight years with no residual value. In early April 2017, a part costing $875,000 and designed to increase the machinery's efficiency was added. The machine's estimated useful life did not change with this addition. By December 31, 2017, new technology had been introduced that would speed up the obsolescence of Roland's equipment. Roland's controller estimates that expected undiscounted future net cash flows on the equipment would be $6.3 million, and that expected discounted future net cash flows on the equipment would be $5.8 million. Fair value of the equipment at December 31, 2017, was estimated to be $5.6 million. Roland intends to continue using the equipment, but estimates that its remaining useful life is now four years. Roland uses straight-line depreciation. Assume that Roland is a private company that follows ASPE.

Instructions

(a) Prepare the journal entry to record asset impairment at December 31, 2017, if any.

(b) Fair value of the equipment at December 31, 2018, is estimated to be $5.9 million. Prepare any journal entries for the equipment at December 31, 2018.

(c) Repeat part (b), assuming that on December 31, 2018, Roland's management decides to dispose of the equipment. As at December 31, 2018, the asset is still in use and not ready for sale in its current state. In February 2019, Roland's management will meet to outline an active program to find a buyer.

(d) Repeat part (b), assuming that the equipment is designated as "held for sale" as of January 1, 2018, and that the equipment was not in use in 2018 but was still held by Roland on December 31, 2018.

(e) For each situation in (b), (c), and (d), indicate where the equipment will be reported on the December 31, 2018 balance sheet.

(f) Repeat parts (a) and (b), assuming instead that Roland is a public company that prepares financial statements in accordance with IFRS.

DIGGING DEEPER

(g) From the perspective of a financial statement user, discuss the importance of frequent impairment testing in producing relevant and faithfully representative financial statements. Do IFRS and ASPE differ in the required frequency? Explain briefly.

P11-15 The following is a schedule of property dispositions for Shangari Corp.:

SCHEDULE OF PROPERTY DISPOSITIONS

	Cost	Accumulated Depreciation	Cash Proceeds	Fair Market Value	Nature of Disposition
Land	$40,000	—	$31,000	$31,000	Expropriation
Building	15,000	—	3,600	—	Demolition
Warehouse	70,000	$16,000	74,000	74,000	Destruction by fire
Machine	8,000	2,800	900	7,200	Trade-in
Furniture	10,000	7,850	—	3,100	Contribution
Automobile	9,000	3,460	2,960	2,960	Sale

The following additional information is available:

Land

On February 15, land that was being held mainly as an investment was expropriated by the city. On March 31, another parcel of unimproved land to be held as an investment was purchased at a cost of $35,000.

Building

On April 2, land and a building were purchased at a total cost of $75,000, of which 20% was allocated to the building on the corporate books. The real estate was acquired with the intention of demolishing the building, which was done in November. Cash proceeds that were received in November were the net proceeds from the building demolition.

Warehouse

On June 30, the warehouse was destroyed by fire. The warehouse had been purchased on January 2, 2014, and accumulated depreciation of $16,000 had been properly recorded. On December 27, the insurance proceeds and other funds were used to purchase a replacement warehouse at a cost of $90,000.

Machine

On December 26, the machine was exchanged for another machine having a fair market value of $6,300. Cash of $900 was also received as part of the deal.

Furniture

On August 15, furniture was contributed to a registered charitable organization. No other contributions were made or pledged during the year.

Automobile

On November 3, the automobile was sold to Jared Dutoit, a shareholder.

Instructions

(a) Prepare the entries to record the transactions and indicate how these items would be reported on the income statement of Shangari Corp. Assume that Shangari follows ASPE, but also indicate if the reporting would be treated differently under IFRS.

DIGGING DEEPER

(b) As a current creditor of Shangari Corp., if you noted that there are several dispositions of property, plant and equipment, would you have any concerns or questions for management?

(Adapted from AICPA.)

P11-16   Sung Corporation, a manufacturer of steel products, began operations on October 1, 2016. Sung's accounting department has begun to prepare the capital asset and depreciation schedule that follows. You have been asked to assist in completing this schedule. In addition to determining that the data already on the schedule are correct, you have obtained the following information from the company's records and personnel:

1. Depreciation is calculated from the first day of the month of acquisition to the first day of the month of disposition.

2. Land A and Building A were acquired together for $820,000. At the time of acquisition, the land had an appraised value of $90,000 and the building had an appraised value of $810,000.

3. Land B was acquired on October 2, 2016, in exchange for 2,500 newly issued common shares. At the date of acquisition, the shares had a fair value of $30 each. During October 2016, Sung paid $16,000 to demolish an existing building on this land so that it could construct a new building.

4. Construction of Building B on the newly acquired land began on October 1, 2017. By September 30, 2018, Sung had paid $320,000 of the estimated total construction costs of $450,000. It is estimated that the building will be completed and occupied by July 2019.

5. Certain equipment was donated to the corporation by a local university. An independent appraisal of the equipment when it was donated estimated its fair value at $30,000 and the residual value at $3,000.

6. Machine A's total cost of $164,900 includes an installation expense of $600 and normal repairs and maintenance of $14,900. Its residual value is estimated at $6,000. Machine A was sold on February 1, 2018.

7. On October 1, 2017, Machine B was acquired with a down payment of $5,740 and the remaining payments to be made in 11 annual instalments of $6,000 each, beginning October 1, 2017. The prevailing interest rate was 8%. The following data were determined from present-value tables and are rounded:

PV of $1 at 8%		PV of an Ordinary Annuity of $1 at 8%	
10 years	0.463	10 years	6.710
11 years	0.429	11 years	7.139
15 years	0.315	15 years	8.559

SUNG CORPORATION
Capital Asset and Depreciation Schedule
For Fiscal Years Ended September 30, 2017, and September 30, 2018

Assets	Acquisition Date	Cost	Residual Value	Depreciation Method	Estimated Life in Years	Depreciation Expense, Year Ended September 30 2017	2018
Land A	Oct. 1, 2016	$ (1)	N/A	N/A	N/A	N/A	N/A
Building A	Oct. 1, 2016	(2)	$40,000	Straight-line	(3)	$17,450	(4)
Land B	Oct. 2, 2016	(5)	N/A	N/A	N/A	N/A	N/A
Building B	Under construction	$320,000 to date	—	Straight-line	30	—	(6)
Donated Equipment	Oct. 2, 2016	(7)	3,000	150% declining-balance	10	(8)	(9)
Machine A	Oct. 2, 2016	(10)	6,000	Double-declining-balance	8	(11)	(12)
Machine B	Oct. 1, 2017	(13)	—	Straight-line	20	—	(14)

N/A = Not applicable

Instructions

(a) For each numbered item in the schedule, give the correct amount. Round each answer to the nearest dollar.

(b) When would it be appropriate for management to use different depreciation policies as they have done for Machines A and B?

DIGGING DEEPER

P11-17   Consider the following independent situations.

Situation 1: Ducharme Corporation purchased electrical equipment at a cost of $12,400 on June 2, 2014. From 2014 through 2017, the equipment was depreciated on a straight-line basis, under the assumption that it would have a 10-year useful life and a $2,400 residual value. After more experience and before recording 2018's depreciation, Ducharme revised its estimate of the machine's useful life downward from a total of 10 years to 8 years, and revised the estimated residual value to $2,000.

On April 29, 2019, after recording part of a year's depreciation for 2019, the company traded in the equipment on a newer model, and received a $4,000 trade-in allowance, even though the equipment's fair value was only $2,800. The new asset had a list price of $15,300 and the supplier accepted $11,300 cash for the balance. The new equipment was depreciated on a straight-line basis, assuming a seven-year useful life and a $1,300 residual value.

Situation 2: Malcolm Limited acquired a truck to deliver and install its specialized products at the customer's site. The vehicle's list price was $45,000, but customization added another $10,000 in costs. Malcolm took delivery of the truck on September 30, 2017, with a down payment of $5,000, signing a four-year, 8% note for the remainder, payable in equal payments of $14,496 beginning September 30, 2018.

Malcolm expected the truck to be usable for 500 deliveries and installations. After that, the product's technology would have changed and made the vehicle obsolete. In late July 2020, the truck was destroyed when a concrete garage collapsed. Malcolm used the truck for 45 deliveries in 2017, 125 in 2018, 134 in 2019, and 79 in 2020. The company received a cheque for $12,000 from the insurance company and paid what remained on the note.

Situation 3: A group of new machines was purchased on February 17, 2018, under a royalty agreement with the following terms: The purchaser, Keller Corp., is to pay a royalty of $1 to the machinery supplier for each unit of product that is produced by the machines each year. The machines are expected to produce 200,000 units over their useful lives. The machines' invoice price was $75,000, freight costs were $2,000, unloading charges were $1,500, and royalty payments for 2018 were $13,000. Keller uses the unit of production method to depreciate its machinery.

Situation 4: On March 31, 2014, Wayside Corporation purchased a new piece of manufacturing equipment for a cost of $323,000. At that time, the estimated useful life of the equipment was five years, with a residual value of $65,000. On August 1, 2017, due to increased competition causing a decreased selling price for its product, Wayside decided to discontinue manufacturing the product. By December 31, 2017, there was a formal plan in place to sell the equipment, and the equipment qualified for classification as held for sale. At December 31, 2017, the equipment's fair value less costs to sell was $52,000. Due to matters beyond Wayside's control, a potential sale of the equipment fell through in 2018, although consumer confidence in Wayside's product increased significantly because of reported defects in its competitors' products. The equipment remained classified as held for sale at December 31, 2018, when the equipment's fair value less costs to sell increased to $145,000. Wayside uses the straight-line method to depreciate its equipment.

Instructions

(a) For situation 1, determine the amount of depreciation expense reported by Ducharme for each fiscal year for the years ending December 31, 2014, to December 31, 2019.

(b) For situation 2, prepare all entries that are needed to record the events and activities related to the truck, including the depreciation expense on the truck each year. Assume that Malcolm uses an activity approach to depreciate the truck, and bases it on deliveries.

(c) For situation 3, prepare journal entries to record the purchase of the new machines, the related depreciation for 2018, and the royalty payment.

(d) For situation 4, prepare all journal entries required for the years ending December 31, 2017, and December 31, 2018.

(e) You are an employee of Wayside Corporation receiving a bonus based on income from continuing operations. If a loss results from the equipment classified as held for sale, how will you be affected under IFRS?

DIGGING DEEPER

*P11-18 Munro Limited reports the following information in its tax files covering the five-year period from 2015 to 2019. All assets are Class 10 with a 30% maximum CCA, and no capital assets had been acquired before 2015.

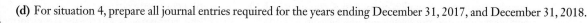

2015	Purchased assets A, B, and C for $20,000, $8,000, and $1,200, respectively.
2016	Sold asset B for $7,000; bought asset D for $4,800.
2017	Purchased asset E for $5,000; received an investment tax credit of $1,000.
2018	Sold asset A for $9,900 and asset C for $1,800.
2019	Asset D was destroyed by fire and was uninsured; asset E was sold to an employee for $500.

TAXATION

Instructions

(a) Prepare a capital cost allowance schedule for Class 10 assets covering the 2015 to 2019 period.

(b) Identify any capital gains, terminal losses, or recapture of CCA and indicate how each would be taxed.

(c) You have been hired as the tax advisor of Munro Limited. Munro is anticipating low income levels, possibly losses, over the next couple of years due to restructuring. However, management anticipates that income levels will be substantially higher than historical levels in the subsequent three to four years. Munro also anticipates purchasing a number of new assets at the beginning of fiscal 2025, as management had been told that assets must be purchased

DIGGING DEEPER

in the first half of the year to take advantage of the half-year rule. Munro is a private company following ASPE. Provide advice, if any, with respect to the company's CCA policy.

TAXATION

*P11-19 Kitchigami Limited was attracted to the Town of Mornington by the town's municipal industry commission. Mornington donated a plant site to Kitchigami, and the provincial government provided $180,000 toward the cost of the new manufacturing facility. The total cost of plant construction came to $380,000, and it was ready for use in early October 2017. Kitchigami expects the plant to have a useful life of 15 years before it becomes obsolete and is demolished. The company uses the straight-line method of depreciation for buildings and is required to include the plant in Class 6 (10% rate) for tax purposes.

Instructions

(a) Prepare the entry(ies) that are required in 2017 to record the payment to the contractor for the building and the receipt of the provincial government assistance. Assume that the company treats the assistance as a reduction of the asset's cost. Also prepare any adjusting entries that are needed at the company's year ends, December 31, 2017 and 2018.

(b) Repeat (a), but assume instead that the company treats the government assistance as a deferred credit.

(c) If Kitchigami reports 2018 income of $79,000 before depreciation on the plant and government assistance, what income before tax will the company report assuming (a) above? Assuming (b) above?

(d) What is the building's tax value at December 31, 2018?

DIGGING DEEPER

(e) Which method of accounting for government assistance would better represent Kitchigami Limited to a lender? Also, which method would result in higher net income?

Integrated Cases

AUDITING

Refer to the Case Primer to help you answer these cases.

(*Hint*: If there are issues here that are new, use the conceptual framework to help you support your analysis with solid reasoning.)

IC11-1 ClubLoop Corporation (CL) is a large owner, operator, and developer of golf courses and resorts. The company is privately owned by several wealthy individuals. During the current year, according to the draft financial statements, revenues increased by 7.2% and net operating income increased by 13% to $22.5 million. Net income dropped from $2.9 million to $822,000. The decrease was largely due to two events: a change in accounting policy and costs related to the settlement of a lawsuit.

One of the company's objectives is to always ensure that capital resources are readily available to meet approved capital expenditures and to take advantage of growth opportunities. According to the draft year-end financial statements, the company has current assets of $12 million and current liabilities of $28 million, resulting in a working capital deficit. Included in the current liabilities are long-term debts that are currently due. The company is working with the financial institutions in question to renew or replace these facilities. CL has received unsolicited expressions of interest from several financial institutions concerning these facilities, and management believes that these facilities will be replaced—hopefully before the current financial statements are issued.

The company owns most of the land on which CL's golf courses are developed. Currently, the company follows a rigorous "weed and feed" program in order to keep the grass on the golf courses in top shape. The chemicals in these fertilizers, herbicides, and insecticides are felt by some people in the local community to be toxic to the environment. The company has met with several community groups and has agreed to study the issue further. In a current meeting of the board of directors, the CEO committed the company to spending $1 million to limit any potential damage. As at year end, none of this amount has yet been spent. There is a concern that the community groups are going to launch legal proceedings and the company feels that this move will help CL's position if there ends up being a lawsuit. Part of the money is for landscaping to limit the spread of the sprayed chemicals and part of it is for advertising to promote the company as a good corporate citizen.

The company is currently developing new golf courses. All direct costs related to the acquisition, development, and construction of these properties, including interest and management costs, are capitalized. For one of the new locations, which was just purchased and developed in the current year, the company has run into a small problem. After CL spent several million dollars on development, the planned golf course is being blocked by environmental groups. The costs to develop the land have been capitalized as previously mentioned, on the basis that they would be recoverable from future membership revenues. However, the company has now decided to sell the land to a real estate developer.

CL's stock-based compensation plan consists of stock options. The company does not recognize any expense for this plan when stock options are issued to employees. It has been company policy to repurchase any shares issued under these stock option plans, although this year the company has indicated that it might not do this since it is planning to redesign the stock-based compensation system.

On July 1, the government tax department issued notices of assessment to the company regarding a dispute over the recognition of revenues. Although the outcome of an appeal of the assessment cannot be determined, the company believes that it will owe $8.7 million if its appeal is unsuccessful.

Instructions

Adopt the role of the company's auditor and prepare an analysis of the financial reporting issues.

IC11-2 MA Hydro (MH) is a private company that owns and operates all of Ontario's electricity transmission systems. It is deciding whether it should follow IFRS or ASPE in the upcoming year. The company must choose now and is looking to do an analysis of the impact of following IFRS or ASPE. Each year, MH must prepare and submit audited financial statements to the government.

The company generates and sells electricity to residential and commercial customers. It is committed to the following:

- Identifying and providing innovative solutions that will improve the reliability and efficiency of electrical delivery
- Sustainability (including not only profitability but also environmental sustainability)—in this regard, MH has a publicly available environmental policy against which the company is measured by the government

The company has just finished a new project to install smart meters in all residential houses. The meters allow residents to track usage and power supply and demand. Each unit is very expensive and will likely become technologically obsolete in three years. MH decided to pursue this strategy nonetheless due to its commitment to sustainability. The company wants all customers to think about using electricity wisely and the meters help with this. The company generally requires a security deposit (amounting to the cost of the meter) when a customer signs up to receive electricity or when the meter is first installed. The value of the meter declines over time and after three years it is worthless. If customers cancel their electricity delivery contract early, they get the full amount back once they return their meters. Otherwise, at the end of three years, MH retains the security deposit and has no obligation to return the cash.

MH is rate-regulated. This means that it must ask for government approval whenever it wants to raise the rates that it charges for electricity. Generally, the government allows the company to recover all costs incurred in generating the electricity plus a reasonable profit margin. Therefore, rates are set as being equal to "cost plus reasonable profit margin." This means that, once approved, the company is able to charge revenues equal to all costs incurred plus a reasonable profit. Under ASPE, special "rate-regulated accounting" exists. One of the features of this special accounting is that companies following rate-regulated accounting are able to defer any losses that are incurred on disposition of assets, on the basis that they can recover these losses from future revenues. IFRS does not allow this.

Sometimes MH signs supply contract agreements with other suppliers of electricity to ensure that power supplies to MH customers are not disrupted. Under the terms of these contracts, MH locks in the quantity and price of electricity. However, the contracts do not explicitly include net settlement provisions. Because electricity is a commodity, the contracts may be bought and sold on the regional commodities exchange.

MH is concerned about maintaining a consistent supply of electricity to its customers, since many of its generating stations are getting very old and the incidence of breakdown and generating station closures due to the age of the equipment is increasing. There is no market for these old generating stations (and MH would probably replace the capacity with newer, greener forms of electricity, such as wind or solar). Often the land that these stations are sitting on is polluted with chemicals. Technically, since this pollution occurred many years ago in most cases, there are no laws in place to force cleanup. Currently, the company is doing a voluntary land assessment and remediation program to identify the extent of this pollution. The company expects that it would recover all of the cleanup costs it might incur from future revenues through increased customer rates. However, there is always the chance that future governments might change the ability to build these costs into the rates charged to customers.

Some of the generating stations are located on lands held by First Nations. The company is negotiating to obtain legal title to the lands but understands that it may have to relocate the assets. The assets in question are material.

MH obtains much of its financing through bonds and commercial paper issuances. Therefore, it is important that it retain its good credit ratings. Currently, it has a very good credit rating, awarded by both S&P and Moody's credit rating agencies. This good rating helps keep costs (and therefore customer rates) down. There are debt covenants in the debt agreements that limit the amount of debt as a percentage of total capitalization (total assets). Debt may not exceed 75% of total assets under these covenants. (Currently, the actual debt to total assets ratio is 65%.)

Instructions

Assume the role of an accounting consultant hired to determine which set of accounting standards to follow. Discuss the financial reporting issues relating to the above. Use the case analysis framework presented in class, including an overview, analysis, and recommendations.

FINANCE

RESEARCH AND ANALYSIS

RA11-1   Brookfield Asset Management Inc.

Brookfield Asset Management Inc. is a global publicly traded Canadian company. Brookfield's financial statements for its year ended December 31, 2014, are included at the end of this book.

Instructions

Access Brookfield's financial statements for the year ended December 31, 2014, review the notes to the statements, and answer the following questions.

(a) What business is Brookfield Asset Management Inc. in?

(b) Identify the accounting model or method used for the following Brookfield operating segment property, plant, and equipment assets: renewable energy assets, infrastructure assets, property, and private equity (other) assets. Summarize the changes in each of the types of assets in the property, plant, and equipment group, explaining how the balances changed over the 2014 year. How is the company growing?

(c) Comment on the extent to which fair values are used in measuring and reporting property, plant, and equipment assets. What methods and types of assumptions has the company used to determine fair values for these assets measured at fair value?

(d) Brookfield also reports significant investment properties on its balance sheet as well as sustainable resources. What measurement models are used for these two types of long-term assets? If any are based on fair value, what methods and types of assumptions are made when measuring them?

(e) What other methods are available to determine fair value? Which methods are most reliable from a user's perspective? Base your answer on IFRS 13 and what it indicates about fair value measurement to determine what level of fair value measurement the company has used to determine fair values.

RA11-2   Canadian Tire Corporation, Limited

Canadian Tire Corporation, Limited is one of Canada's best-known retailers. Obtain a copy of Canadian Tire's financial statements for the year ended January 3, 2015, through SEDAR (www.sedar.com) or on the company's website. To answer the following questions, you may also want to include the 10-year financial review that is produced as supplementary information in the annual report.

Instructions

(a) How significant is Canadian Tire's investment in property, plant, and equipment, including any investment property, compared with its total investment in assets? Compare this

with sample companies in other industries, such as financial services (AGF Management Limited), real estate management and development (Brookfield Office Properties Inc.), and technology (Amaya Inc.). Comment.

(b) Calculate Canadian Tire's total asset turnover for fiscal years 2014, 2013, and 2012.

(c) Calculate the company's profit margin for the same three years.

(d) Calculate the company's return on assets for the same three years by using the ratios calculated in (b) and (c) above.

(e) Based on your calculations in (d), suggest ways in which Canadian Tire might increase the return that it earns on its investment in assets.

RA11-3   Canadian National Railway Company and Canadian Pacific Railway Limited

Two well-known company names in the transportation industry in Canada are **Canadian National Railway Company** and **Canadian Pacific Railway Limited**. Go to either SEDAR (www.sedar.com) or each company's website to gain access to the financial statements of these companies for their year ended December 31, 2014.

Instructions

(a) How significant are the investments made by these companies in property, plant, and equipment? Express the size of these investments as a percentage of total assets.

(b) Compare the types of property, plant, and equipment that each company reports.

(c) Do the companies follow similar policies in what they capitalize as part of property, plant, and equipment?

(d) What methods of depreciation are used by each company?

(e) For assets that are similar at both companies, compare their useful lives or rates of depreciation. Are these similar or would applying them result in differences in the reported results for each year? Explain briefly.

RA11-4   Changes in Depreciation Policies and Impairment Testing

Nickel Strike Mines is a nickel mining company with mines in northern Ontario, Colombia, and Australia. It is a publicly traded company and follows IFRS, and has historically followed industry practice and used unit of production as its depreciation policy for all of its mines. During 2017, the price of nickel declined significantly, even below the costs of production for the Ontario mines. Consequently, the company has had the Ontario mines closed since early January 2017. It has continued to produce in its Colombian and Australian mines. It is now December 2017 and the controller is trying to decide what accounting issues there are related to the Ontario mines. Since it was a very bad year for the company, and investors are expecting the worst, the controller is considering switching to the declining-balance method of depreciation for the Ontario mines only. This would create a significant depreciation charge for 2017, but in the future, the depreciation costs related to the mines would decrease, resulting in higher net income. In addition, since there were no units produced in the Ontario mines for the year, no depreciation is taken. The controller believes that this is wrong, and that some amount of depreciation should be recorded.

Additionally, the controller is also considering taking as large an impairment loss as possible on all the mines. The controller will do this by assuming a very low nickel price, which will cause the recoverable amounts to be below carrying values for all mines. This impairment loss will likely reverse in the following years, since nickel prices are expected to climb dramatically over the next year, as supplies diminish and as demand from Asian countries increases. With the reversal of the impairment in 2018, this would show a significant improvement in the company's net income.

Instructions

You are a Nickel Strike Mines board member and have just heard the controller's comments on these issues. Comment on the controller's suggestions. Include in your discussion how the impairment test would be completed and the assumptions required. Also discuss the note disclosure that would be required related to all of these issues and any ethical issues that may arise.

RA11-5 Depreciation under ASPE and IFRS

Realtor Inc. is a company that owns five large office buildings that are leased out to tenants. Most of the leases are for 10 years or more with renewal clauses for an additional 5 years. Currently, Realtor Inc. is a private company that follows ASPE. Recently Rita Mendoza was hired as a new controller. Ms. Mendoza has suggested to Habib Ganem, the owner and sole shareholder of the company, that the company should consider switching to IFRS. She explained that under ASPE, the buildings are recorded at cost and then depreciated and tested for impairment when events occur that might indicate a decline in value. However, under IFRS, she explained, the buildings could be classified as investment properties and adjusted to fair value every year. In addition, there is no impact on the income statement, since no depreciation is recorded on the investment properties. Finally, Ms. Mendoza stated that there is no impairment testing required for investment properties under IFRS, so there would never be any impairment losses to be recognized.

Mr. Ganem was intrigued with this idea. He had just been looking at the calculation of the bank loan covenants and had found that the company's debt to asset ratio was very close to the maximum that would be allowed. He wanted to take this year's annual financial statement, once completed, to the bank and ask for revisions on the covenants, since he was also looking

at the possible purchase of some new properties. He particularly liked the idea of no depreciation having to be recorded on these assets, which would also improve the company's times interest earned ratio (calculated as Earnings before interest and taxes/Interest expense). Mr. Ganem decided to call his banker to discuss this change and get her thoughts.

Instructions

You are the loans officer at the bank. What comments would you make to Mr. Ganem about the controller's suggestions? In particular, explain the impact on the balance sheet and the income statement under both the cost model and the fair value model and the resulting impact on the existing covenants. From a banker's point of view, which method for reporting the investment properties would be most useful? Make a final recommendation to Mr. Ganem.

RA11-6 PPE–Transition to IFRS

Howeven Inc. is a private company that expects to "go public" and become publicly traded soon. Accordingly, it expects to be adopting IFRS by 2017. It is a manufacturing company with extensive investments in property, plant, and equipment. The company currently has a profit sharing plan that is based on 30% of earnings after depreciation, but before interest and taxes. There is also a debt to fixed asset ratio covenant that must be maintained for the bank loan.

The controller has been learning about IFRS and has determined that there are three different treatments that the property, plant, and equipment can have upon the transition to IFRS.

1. The first option is to continue using the cost model, as the company has been doing. The company currently uses the straight-line method of depreciation for all of its assets.

2. The second option is for the company, on transition at January 1, 2017, to elect to revalue all of its property, plant, and equipment to fair value. This is a one-time increase in value that is allowed for first-time adopters of IFRS. The company would still use the cost model to depreciate this new value (which becomes the deemed cost) in subsequent years.

3. The third option is to adopt the revaluation model for just the "property and plant" assets. The company would continue to use the cost model for the equipment, as fair market values are not readily available for this type of asset.

The controller has estimated the following numbers at January 1, 2017 (debt is expected to be $1,700 million):

	Remaining Useful Life	Carrying Amount	Estimated Fair Value at Jan. 1, 2017
Property and plant	25 years	$2,500 million	$3,250 million
Equipment	10 years	$1,300 million	$1,400 million

Instructions

FINANCE

You are the Vice-President Finance and must prepare a memo to the board explaining these options. Using the numbers in the table to assist you, discuss the implications of the three options for the balance sheet, income statement, bonuses, and the debt to fixed asset covenant.

RA11-7   Air France-KLM Group and Air Canada

Air France-KLM Group and **Air Canada** are both global airline companies. Both companies report under IFRS. Access the financial statements of Air France-KLM for its year ended December 31, 2014, and Air Canada for the same period, from each company's website.

Instructions

(a) What amounts are reported on the statements of financial position for capital assets for Air France-KLM and for Air Canada at December 31, 2014? What percentage of total assets does each company invest in these types of assets? What else might be considered in developing and interpreting these ratios?

(b) For Air France-KLM: What types of capital assets does the company report? What does it include in costs? Is interest capitalized? What depreciation methods are used by the company? How are residual values estimated for aircraft?

(c) For Air Canada: What types of capital assets does the company report? What is included in costs? Is interest capitalized? What depreciation methods are used by Air Canada? How are residual values estimated for aircraft?

(d) Compare the above accounting policies for the two companies. Where are there significant differences between them? What is the likely impact of these differences on the balance sheet and net earnings?

(e) For Air France-KLM, how are the assets tested for impairment? Were any impairment losses recorded for the year, and if so, how much? What did these relate to? Was there any reversal of impairment losses from previous years?

(f) For Air Canada, how have the assets been tested for impairment and were any impairment losses recognized in 2014?

(g) Does Air France-KLM have assets held for sale? How much has been reclassified to this account and where is it presented on the balance sheet? What does it relate to? Does Air Canada have any assets designated as held for sale?

RA11-8   The Ethical Accountant

Lian Tang, HK Corporation's controller, is concerned that net income may be lower this year. He is afraid that upper-level management might recommend cost reductions by laying off accounting staff, himself included. Tang knows that depreciation is a major expense for HK. The company currently uses the same method for financial reporting as it uses for tax purposes—that is, a declining-balance method—and he is thinking of changing to the straight-line method.

Tang does not want to draw attention to the increase in net income that would result from switching depreciation methods. He thinks, "Why don't I just increase the estimated useful lives and the residual values of the property, plant, and equipment? They are only estimates anyway. These changes will decrease depreciation expense and increase income. I may be able to save my job and those of my staff." Tang calls his professional accounting body's "Ethics Hotline" and reaches the Ethical Accountant for advice.

Instructions

Discuss. Make sure that you, as the Ethical Accountant providing advice to Tang, identify the objectives of depreciation, who the stakeholders are in this situation, what disclosures are required, whether any ethical issues are involved, and what Tang should do.

ENDNOTES

[1] See IAS 16, paragraphs 56–57 for further discussion.

[2] Ontario Power Generation (OPG) 2010 Annual Report, p. 13 and OPG 2014 consolidated financial statements Note 2 ("Basis of Presentation").

[3] See IAS 36.7-17.

[4] After acquisition, it is the asset's **net carrying amount** and residual value that determine the depreciable amount.

[5] This is the definition in IAS 16 *Property, Plant, and Equipment*. The definition in the *CPA Canada Handbook*, Part II, Section 3061 *Property, Plant, and Equipment* refers only to the asset's net realizable value at the end of its useful life to an entity. These are not necessarily inconsistent. Copyright © IFRS Foundation. All rights reserved. Reproduced by John Wiley & Sons Canada, Ltd. with the permission of the IFRS Foundation®. Reproduction and use rights are strictly limited. No permission granted to third parties to reproduce or distribute.

[6] The airline industry illustrates the type of problem found in estimations. In the past, aircraft were assumed not to wear out; they just became obsolete. However, some jets have been in service for as long as 20 years, and maintenance of these aircraft has become increasingly expensive. As a result, some airlines now replace aircraft, not because of obsolescence, but because of physical deterioration.

[7] There is another systematic decreasing charge approach, called the **sum-of-the-years'-digits method**, but it is rarely used in Canada. Under this method, the depreciable amount is multiplied each year by a decreasing fraction. The **denominator** of the fraction equals the sum of the digits of an asset's useful life. For example, the sum of the digits of the life of an asset with a five-year life is $1 + 2 + 3 + 4 + 5 = 15$. The **numerator** decreases year by year and the denominator stays constant. Because this is a decreasing charge approach, depreciation expense is 5/15 of the depreciable amount in the first year, 4/15 of the depreciable amount in the second year, 3/15 in the third, 2/15 in the fourth, and 1/15 in the fifth year. At the end of the asset's useful life, its net book value is equal to the estimated residual value. Similarly, for an asset with a 10-year life, the sum of the years' digits, 1 through 10, equals 55.

Depreciation in the first year is 10/55 of the depreciable amount, in the second year it is 9/55, and so on. (A short-cut calculation of the denominator is $[(n \times (n + 1)]/2 = (10 \times 11)/2 = 55)$).

[8] The straight-line rate (%) is equal to 100% divided by the estimated useful life of the asset that is being depreciated. A pure form of the declining-balance method (sometimes called the fixed percentage of book value method) has also been suggested as a possibility, but it is not used very much. This approach finds a rate that depreciates the asset to exactly its residual value at the end of its expected useful life. The formula for determining this rate is as follows:

$$\text{Depreciation rate} = 1 - \sqrt[n]{\frac{\text{Residual value}}{\text{Acquisition cost}}}$$

The life in years is *n*. Once the rate is calculated, it is applied to the asset's declining book value from period to period.

[9] Some critics suggest that pro forma earnings may confuse or mislead users. Investopedia.com notes that one nickname for pro forma earnings is EEBS (earnings excluding bad stuff!).

[10] To determine the undepreciated carrying amount to date when using the double-declining-balance method, the following formula can be used:

Book value $= C(1 - r)^n$, where C = cost of asset; r = depreciation rate; and n = number of full years from the asset's acquisition date. For example, if the machinery in the illustration had been depreciated using the double-declining-balance method instead of the straight-line method, C = $90,000; r = $2 \times (100\% \div 20) = 10\%$; and n = 8.

The asset's carrying amount at the end of year 8, therefore, is $90,000(1 - 0.10)^8$, or $38,742.

[11] This definition is based on amendments to IAS 36 *Impairment of Assets* after approval of the IASB's *Fair Value Measurement* standard (IFRS 13). The amendments became effective January 1, 2013. Chapter 2 of this text provides a fuller discussion of fair values and how they are measured.

[12] IAS 36.68. This is quite similar to *CPA Canada Handbook*, Part II, Section 3063.03. Both ASPE Section 3063 and IAS 36 include liabilities in the asset group if cash flows from the group are the only source of cash to meet the obligation.

[13] The impairment loss for a cash-generating unit (CGU) is allocated first to reduce the carrying amount of any goodwill allocated to the CGU, and then to other individual assets. We discuss this further in Chapter 12.

[14] Under U.S. GAAP, the involuntary conversion would typically have been considered an extraordinary item until 2015. However, the FASB announced the elimination of extraordinary items via an FASB Accounting Standards Update dated January 2015. Neither IFRS nor ASPE have recognized extraordinary items separately in income statements for many years.

[15] Refer to the specific IFRS and ASPE standards for complete coverage of the specific disclosures. Because the users of private entity financial statements can generally request additional information if needed, there are many fewer required disclosures under ASPE than under IFRS.

[16] This is an extract from the Business Acquisitions and Divestitures note; the full note is available as part of Hershey's annual report available on-line.

[17] The higher the proportion of property, plant, and equipment to total assets, the more information this turnover ratio provides about the efficiency of capital asset use. Analysts often calculate separate turnover ratios for each major type of asset reported on the balance sheet and analyze each.

[18] The widespread availability of accounting software capable of maintaining detailed records for property, plant, and equipment; the related depreciation expense; and accumulated depreciation under a variety of methods has significantly reduced the cost of record keeping and the likelihood of errors.

[19] CCA is subject to rules set by government legislation and can therefore change from time to time. Furthermore, various provincial governments can have different rules for determining CCA for purposes of calculating the income on which provincial taxes are based. The examples in this chapter are based on the federal income tax regulations for 2014.

[20] The rationale is that the ITC is not calculated until after the company's year end, when the tax return is completed and filed.

[21] The percentage of the capital gain that is taxable has varied in recent years. In 2014, the inclusion rate—the taxable portion—was 50%.

12 | INTANGIBLE ASSETS AND GOODWILL

REFERENCE TO THE CPA COMPETENCY MAP	LEARNING OBJECTIVES
	After studying this chapter, you should be able to:
1.1.1, 1.1.2, 1.1.4	1. Understand the importance of goodwill and intangible assets from a business perspective and describe their characteristics.
1.1.1, 1.1.2, 1.2.1, 1.2.2, 1.2.3	2. Identify and apply the recognition and measurement requirements for purchased intangible assets.
1.1.1, 1.1.2, 1.1.3, 1.2.1, 1.2.2, 1.2.3	3. Identify and apply the recognition and measurement requirements for internally developed intangible assets.
1.1.1, 1.1.2, 1.2.1, 1.2.2, 1.2.3	4. Explain how intangible assets are accounted for after initial recognition.
1.1.1, 1.1.2, 1.2.1, 1.2.2	5. Identify and explain the accounting for specific types of intangible assets.
1.1.1, 1.1.2, 1.2.1, 1.2.2, 1.2.3	6. Explain and account for impairment of limited-life and indefinite-life intangible assets.
1.1.1, 1.1.2, 1.2.1, 1.2.2	7. Explain how goodwill is measured and accounted for after acquisition.
1.1.1, 1.3.2, 1.2.1, 1.2.2, 1.2.3	8. Explain and account for impairment of goodwill.
1.1.1, 1.1.2, 1.4.1, 1.4.2, 1.4.4, 5.1.1, 5.1.2	9. Identify the types of disclosure requirements for intangible assets and goodwill and explain the issues in analyzing these assets.
1.1.4	10. Identify differences in accounting between IFRS and ASPE.
	After studying Appendix 12A, you should be able to:
1.1.1, 1.1.2, 1.2.3, 1.2.4, 1.4.4, 1.4.5, 5.4.1, 5.4.2, 5.4.3	11. Explain and apply basic approaches to valuing goodwill.

GOODWILL IMPAIRMENT MAKES BIG DENT

WHEN CANADIAN PUBLICLY traded companies had to report using IFRS starting in 2011, some of the impacts were huge and are still being analyzed today. For example, the effects of IFRS on goodwill were massive for some companies. IFRS requires goodwill to be tested for impairment annually at the cash-generating unit level, whereas under pre-changeover Canadian GAAP, goodwill was only tested at a higher (reporting unit) level, which often resulted in less impairment being recognized.

A study conducted in 2013 by corporate finance advisory firm Duff & Phelps and the Canadian Financial Executives Research Foundation examined goodwill impairment charges reported by Canadian companies in 2012 for their 2011 fiscal years.

©Istockphoto.com/hocus-focus

Among the 621 Canadian companies that are publicly traded, and that therefore have to report using IFRS, there was a total of $11.0 billion in goodwill impairment charges reported in the 2011 calendar year. The most common reason cited by public companies for the goodwill writedown was an overall market downturn, reported by 22% of public companies. Some 17% of public companies said the main reason they recognized goodwill impairment in 2011 was the changeover to IFRS.

Most of the $11.0 billion in goodwill impairment in 2011 was reported by just three companies: Thomson Reuters ($3.1 billion), Kinross Gold Corporation ($3.0 billion), and Yellow Media Inc. ($2.9 billion). All were affected by organizational and/or external industry challenges. For example, Thomson Reuters, the world's leading provider of business information, blamed its goodwill impairment on weaker than expected performance in its Markets division, which represents its financial and media business. In its 2011 annual report, the company said its U.S. $705-million operating loss was due to the goodwill impairment charge, "which more than offset the benefit of higher revenues, savings from efficiency and integration initiatives, lower integration programs expenses, gains realized from the disposal of businesses as well as favorable fair value adjustments and foreign currency."

The industry whose goodwill impairment was most affected by the adoption of IFRS was energy. Under pre-changeover GAAP in 2010, only 10% of Canadian energy companies reported a goodwill impairment charge, compared with 35% reporting under IFRS in 2011, the study found. (Energy companies reported a total of $1.8 billion in goodwill impairment in 2011.) The proportion of companies in the utilities industry reporting goodwill writedowns rose from 0% in 2010 to 29% in 2011.

There was some good news in the study: 81% of public companies said that they did not expect additional goodwill or other asset impairments during an upcoming interim or annual test.

Sources: Duff & Phelps and the Canadian Financial Executives Research Foundation, "2012 Goodwill Impairment Study Canadian Edition," December 2013; Thomson Reuters 2011 annual report.

PREVIEW OF CHAPTER 12

The valuation of intangible assets and goodwill is not always clear-cut. For example, as discussed in our opening story, in conjunction with the changeover from pre-IFRS GAAP to IFRS, several Canadian companies had very large writedowns relating to goodwill impairment. Goodwill is an asset whose value is typically recognized only when it is acquired in a business combination. This chapter explains the basic conceptual and reporting issues related to intangible assets and their close relative, goodwill.

The chapter is organized as follows:

INTANGIBLE ASSETS AND GOODWILL

The Business Importance and Characteristics of Goodwill and Intangible Assets	Recognition and Measurement of Intangible Assets	Impairment and Derecognition	Goodwill	Presentation, Disclosure, and Analysis	IFRS/ASPE Comparison	Appendix 12A— Valuing Goodwill
▪ Characteristics of goodwill ▪ Characteristics of intangible assets	▪ Recognition and measurement at acquistion ▪ Recognition and measurement of internally developed intangible assets ▪ Recognition and measurement after acquisition ▪ Specific intangibles	▪ Impairment of limited-life intangibles ▪ Impairment of indefinite-life intangibles ▪ Derecognition	▪ Recognition and measurement of goodwill ▪ Bargain purchase ▪ Valuation after acquisition ▪ Impairment of goodwill	▪ Presentation and disclosure ▪ Analysis	▪ A comparison of IFRS and ASPE ▪ Looking ahead	▪ Excess-earnings approach ▪ Total-earnings approach ▪ Other valuation methods

THE BUSINESS IMPORTANCE AND CHARACTERISTICS OF GOODWILL AND INTANGIBLE ASSETS

Objective 1

Understand the importance of goodwill and intangible assets from a business perspective and describe their characteristics.

REAL WORLD EMPHASIS

Lululemon athletica inc.'s and **Roots Canada's** most important asset is not their store fixtures, it is their brand image. In lululemon's 2015 annual report, the company notes that it is a "designer and retailer of technical athletic apparel … marketed under the lululemon athletica and ivivva brand names." It discusses the importance of brand awareness, its "branded stores," and the image of its brand. The annual report also states, "Competition in the athletic apparel industry is principally on the basis of brand image and recognition as well as product quality, innovation, style distribution and price" and that "our success depends on the value and reputation of the lululemon athletica brand." However, if you look at lululemon's 2015 financial statements, the brand name is not listed as a key part of its $26.2 million in recorded intangible assets. The company's financial statements list goodwill and reacquired franchise rights as its two most significant intangible assets.

Similarly, the major asset of **Coca-Cola** is not its plant facilities, it's the secret formula for making Coke. **Bell Canada's** most important asset is not its Internet connection equipment, it's the subscriber base. Our economy is in creasingly dominated by information and service providers, and their major assets are often intangible in nature. Identifying and measuring these intangibles is often difficult. As a result, many intangibles have not been captured on companies' statements of financial position. However, goodwill and intangible assets remain a key focus of companies and standard setters around the globe.

Characteristics of Goodwill

Goodwill is difficult to imagine because it's not a tangible asset, it can only be recognized when a business is acquired, and it cannot be sold separately, it can only be sold when a business is sold. **Goodwill** is "an asset representing the future economic benefits arising from other assets acquired in a business combination that are not individually identified and separately recognized."[1]

How is goodwill calculated? In a business combination where **one company purchases 100% of another business**, the fair value of what is given up by the acquiring entity (the **acquirer**) is allocated to the various assets and liabilities it receives.[2] All identifiable assets acquired and liabilities assumed (the **identifiable net assets**) are recognized at their fair values at the acquisition date. **The difference between the fair value of the consideration transferred to acquire the business and the fair value amounts assigned to the identifiable net assets is the amount recognized as goodwill.** This is shown in Illustration 12-1.

Illustration 12-1

Measurement of Goodwill

Fair value of consideration transferred—any one or a combination of cash, other assets, notes payable at a later date, common or preferred shares or other equity instruments, or contingent consideration

− **Fair value of all identifiable assets acquired and liabilities assumed**, whether or not previously recognized by the acquired entity

= **GOODWILL**

As you can tell from Illustration 12-1, goodwill is an unidentified excess or residual amount, and it can only be calculated in relation to the business as a whole.

Characteristics of Intangible Assets

LAW

What are intangible assets? Broadly defined, **intangible assets** are identifiable nonmonetary assets that lack physical substance. Intangible assets must have these three characteristics—**identifiability**, **non-physical existence**, and a **nonmonetary nature**—so that only appropriate assets are recognized as intangibles.

1. **Intangible assets are identifiable.** An asset is **identifiable** if it has at least one of the following characteristics:

   - It results from contractual or other legal rights.

   - It is separable—it can be separated or divided from the entity and sold, transferred, licensed, rented, or exchanged, either by itself or in combination with another contract, identifiable asset, or liability.[3]

   For example, the right to lease space at a favourable rate arises from a contractual arrangement and the right may or may not be transferable to others. A subscription list of a successful newspaper or magazine has value in contributing to future revenue streams and is saleable. These are examples of identifiable intangibles that are given separate recognition. Note also that, in order to recognize these items as assets, the company has to be able to control access to the future benefits and restrict others' access. One way to control access to the benefits is having legally enforceable rights; another is having the ability to enter into exchange transactions related to the intangible.

   Goodwill and some other non-physical items of value, on the other hand, are not separable from the rest of the entity, and control over the future benefits does not result from contractual or legal rights. For example, the synergies of a combined sales force or a superior management team can be identified as having value. However, these items cannot be recognized separately as intangible assets because they cannot be separated from the entity in order to exchange them with others, nor can they be controlled through contractual or other legal rights. They are therefore considered part of goodwill.

   While it is important to distinguish one identifiable intangible from another, financial reporting objectives are not well met if every identifiable intangible is recognized separately. At a minimum, the ones that have similar characteristics (such as continuity, stability, and risk) are grouped and recognized together. Because knowledge-based and high-technology companies with large investments in such "soft" assets are an important part of our modern economy, how accounting treats such intangibles is a major issue.

2. **Intangible assets lack physical substance.** Unlike assets such as property, plant, and equipment (PP&E), the value of intangible assets comes from the rights and privileges granted to the company using them. Sometimes it is difficult to tell whether a particular asset is tangible and is therefore an item of PP&E, or whether it is intangible and covered by accounting standards for intangible assets. Consider the example of computer software that is used for a key piece of equipment on an assembly line. What is the asset? Is it the intangible software, or is it the related tangible asset of equipment? In general, if the intangible component is needed for the physical component to work, it is treated as an item of PP&E. If the intangible component is not an integral part of the physical object, then it is classified separately as an intangible asset.

3. **Intangible assets are nonmonetary.** Assets such as accounts receivable and long-term loans lack physical substance, but they are not classified as intangible assets. They are **monetary assets** whose value comes from the right (or claim) to receive fixed or determinable amounts of money in the future. Intangible assets do not contain any such right or claim.

In most cases, items that meet the definition of an intangible asset provide **economic benefits** over a period of years. The benefits may be in the form of revenue from selling products or services, a reduction in future costs, or other economies. They are normally classified as long-term assets. Examples include such widely varied assets as patents, copyrights, franchises or licensing agreements, trademarks or trade names, secret formulas, computer software, technological know-how, prepayments, and some development costs. Specific intangibles are discussed later in the chapter.

RECOGNITION AND MEASUREMENT OF INTANGIBLE ASSETS

Recognition and Measurement at Acquisition

Objective 2

Identify and apply the recognition and measurement requirements for purchased intangible assets.

The **recognition criteria** for intangible assets are identical to those for PP&E assets and both are **measured at cost** at acquisition. For example, each type of asset can be recognized only when it meets the same two recognition criteria:

1. It is probable that the entity will receive the expected future economic benefits.

2. The asset's cost can be reliably measured.[4]

In applying these criteria, however, management has to consider that there is often more uncertainty about the future economic benefits associated with intangible assets than with tangible capital assets.

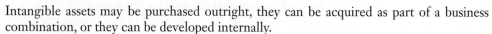

UNDERLYING CONCEPT

The cost concepts introduced in Chapter 10 for property, plant, and equipment are also appropriate for determining the cost of purchased intangible assets.

Purchased Intangibles

Intangible assets may be purchased outright, they can be acquired as part of a business combination, or they can be developed internally.

As indicated above, intangible assets purchased from another party are **measured at cost**. Because the amount paid is based on the company's expectations about receiving future economic benefits from the asset, the "probability" criterion for recognition is met. Cost includes the acquisition cost and all expenditures directly associated with making the intangible ready for its intended use—for example, the purchase price, legal fees, and other direct costs to bring it into working condition. Costs that are **not capitalized** are similar to those for property, plant, and equipment assets: they are those related to product introduction and promotion, conducting business in a new location or with new types of customers, and administration and general overhead. Expenditures incurred after the asset is ready for use as intended and initial operating losses are also excluded.

Similar to other long-lived assets, when direct costs that meet the recognition criteria are incurred after acquisition of the intangible asset, these costs are accounted for as additions or replacements and are capitalized. This is not as common with intangibles, however.

Cost, as was seen in earlier chapters, is the cash cost.

- If there are **delayed payment terms**, any portion of the payments that represents interest is recognized as a financing expense rather than as part of the asset cost.

- If the intangible asset is acquired for shares, cost is the asset's fair value.[5] However, if the fair value of the intangible asset cannot be measured reliably, then the shares' fair value is used. ASPE is not as prescriptive. It allows the more reliable of the fair value of the asset or of the shares to be used.

- If the intangible asset is acquired by giving up **nonmonetary assets**, the cost of the intangible is the fair value of what is given up or the fair value of the intangible asset received, whichever one can be measured more reliably. This assumes that the transaction has **commercial substance** and that fair values can be reliably measured. You may want to review the section in Chapter 10 that discusses this situation and provides examples of transactions and entries for nonmonetary exchanges.

- If the intangible asset is acquired via a government grant, the asset's fair value usually establishes its cost on the books. GAAP does permit a company to recognize a zero or nominal dollar cost in this case. Any other direct costs of acquisition are capitalized into the asset cost, however.

Intangibles Purchased in a Business Combination

When a company purchases an intangible asset as a single asset, such as an acquisition of a specific trademark or patent, the accounting is relatively clear. When several intangibles are bought together in a "basket purchase," the accounting is more complex because the cost has to be allocated to each intangible based on its relative fair value.

A further complication happens when intangibles are acquired in a **business combination**—when one entity acquires control over one or more businesses. This can take place either by directly purchasing the net assets of the business or by acquiring the equity interests (the shares) that control the entity and its net assets. An issue arises because of the variety of assets and liabilities that make up a complete and ongoing business. Even the fact that the business is fully operational instead of being just in the planning stages adds value to it. The entity has to account for all the assets that are acquired, regardless of whether or not they are recognized in the acquired business's accounting records. Many of the assets acquired that contribute to the value of the business are intangible, but only those that are **identifiable** can be separately recognized. Intangibles acquired that are not identifiable assets are considered part of goodwill.

The acquisition cost assigned to each of the identifiable intangible assets acquired as part of a business combination is its fair value.[6] All such assets acquired in this way are recognized, even though they may have been internally generated by the business itself and are not eligible for capitalization under the standards for internally generated intangible assets. Examples include brand names, patents, customer relationships, and **in-process research and development (R&D)**. In-process R&D comes about when one company acquires the business of another company, and one of the identifiable assets acquired is the research work and findings of the acquired company. When the research work and findings meet the requirements for reporting as an asset separate from goodwill, they are recognized as an identifiable intangible.

Prepayments

So far we have seen that, if expenditures for intangibles do not qualify for recognition as an intangible asset or as part of goodwill in a business combination, they must be recognized as an expense when incurred. In some cases, however, a prepaid asset—a **prepaid expense**—can be recognized initially. A prepayment is recognized as an asset only when an entity pays for **goods** before their delivery (or other right of access) or for **services** before receiving those services. The asset is the right to receive the goods or services. When received, this "right to receive" no longer exists and the costs are expensed.

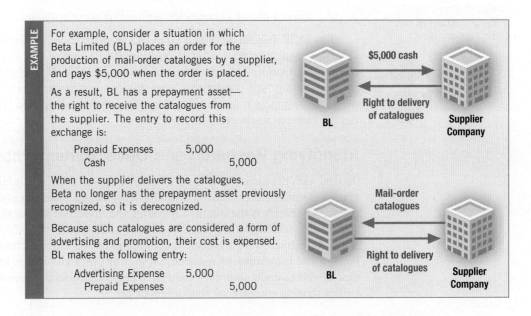

EXAMPLE

For example, consider a situation in which Beta Limited (BL) places an order for the production of mail-order catalogues by a supplier, and pays $5,000 when the order is placed.

As a result, BL has a prepayment asset— the right to receive the catalogues from the supplier. The entry to record this exchange is:

Prepaid Expenses	5,000	
Cash		5,000

When the supplier delivers the catalogues, Beta no longer has the prepayment asset previously recognized, so it is derecognized.

Because such catalogues are considered a form of advertising and promotion, their cost is expensed. BL makes the following entry:

Advertising Expense	5,000	
Prepaid Expenses		5,000

WHAT DO THE NUMBERS MEAN?

Canadian-based **Nortel Networks** filed for bankruptcy protection in January 2009. But unlike many bankrupt companies, Nortel still had some valuable assets to sell: its patents. Two and a half years after declaring bankruptcy, Nortel auctioned off approximately 6,000 patents to Rockstar, a company co-owned by Apple, Microsoft, BlackBerry, Ericsson, and Sony, for $4.5 billion. The patents included products and processes related to 4G wireless networks, Internet and voice technology, semiconductors, and optical equipment. Rockstar filed patent lawsuits against Google, Samsung, HTC, and Huawei in late 2013 relating to these patents. In November 2014, it was reported that Google and Rockstar agreed to settle the patent litigation. Subsequently, the most valuable patents were distributed among the Rockstar consortium members, with the remaining patents being sold to RPX, a patent risk management company, for $900 million.

Sources: Barrie McKenna, "The Ghost of Nortel Continues to Haunt Canada's Tech Sector," *The Globe and Mail*, December 4, 2011; Charles Arthur, "Nortel Patents Sold for $4.5bn," *The Guardian*, July 1, 2011; "Nortel Reports Financial Results for the Fourth Quarter and Full Year 2011," company news release, March 8, 2012; "Nortel Patents at Issue in Suits Against Google, Huawei," cbc.ca/news/business, November 1, 2013; "Google, Rockstar Agree to Settle Patent Litigation," http://re/code.net, November 20, 2014, "Apple-Backed Rockstar Sells Patents to RPX for $900 Million," http://re/code.net, December 23, 2014.

Recognition and Measurement of Internally Developed Intangible Assets

Objective 3

Identify and apply the recognition and measurement requirements for internally developed intangible assets.

It is a more challenging task to decide which costs should be capitalized and recognized as intangible assets when an entity develops such assets internally. The difficulty involves the following recognition and measurement issues.

1. Has an identifiable asset been created that will generate expected future cash flows?

2. What costs should be capitalized? Are the costs incurred just day-to-day operating costs or expenditures related to internally generated goodwill (which are expensed), or are they really additional costs of identifiable assets? How reliably can cost be measured?

How costs associated with internally generated intangible assets should be accounted for has been a controversial issue for many years. The following alternatives have been suggested:

UNDERLYING CONCEPT

The Financial Accounting Standards Board (FASB) in the United States has chosen option (b).

(a) Recognize the costs as internally generated intangible assets when certain criteria are met, and expense all others.

(b) Recognize all costs of internally generated intangible assets as an expense.

(c) Recognize expenditures on all internally generated intangible assets as an expense, with certain specified exceptions.

(d) Allow a choice between the accounting treatments in (a) and (b) above.[7]

The IASB decided on option (a) in IAS 38 *Intangible Assets* while option (d) was selected in *CPA Canada Handbook*, Part II, Section 3064 *Goodwill and Intangible Assets* for private enterprises. Option (a) is illustrated in the next section. Note that the IFRS requirements for recognizing "self-constructed" intangibles are more stringent than those for property, plant, and equipment assets. This is because of the recognition and measurement uncertainties referred to above.

Identifying Research and Development Phase Activities

To deal with the uncertainty of whether an asset should be recognized, the process of generating the intangible is broken down into two parts: a **research phase** and a **development phase**. **Research** is the planned investigation undertaken with the hope of gaining new scientific or technical knowledge and better understanding. The investigation may or may not be directed toward a specific practical aim or application. **Development**, on the other hand, is the translation of research findings or other knowledge into a plan or design for new or substantially improved materials, devices, products, processes, systems, or services before starting commercial production or use.[8]

The **research phase** and the **development phase** are interpreted in the accounting standards as broader terms than implied in the definitions of research and development provided. Examples of activities in each of these phases are set out in Illustration 12-2.

Illustration 12-2

Examples of Research Stage Activities and Development Stage Activities

Activities in the Research Stage	Activities in the Development Stage
Obtaining new knowledge	Designing, constructing, and testing prototypes and models prior to production or use
Searching for, evaluating, and selecting ways to use research findings or knowledge	Designing tools, jigs, moulds, and dies involving new technology
Investigating possible alternatives for existing materials, products, processes, systems, and services	Designing, constructing, and operating pilot plants that are not economically feasible for commercial production
Formulating, designing, evaluating, and choosing possible alternatives for new or existing materials, products, processes, systems, and services	Designing, constructing, and testing chosen alternatives for new or improved materials, products, processes, systems, and services[9]

If there is uncertainty about which phase a particular activity relates to when internally creating an intangible asset, it is classified only as a **research phase** activity.

Accounting for Research Phase Costs

The accounting standards are very clear that no costs incurred on research or during the research phase of an internal project meet the criteria for recognition as an asset. **All such costs are recognized as expenses when they are incurred.** However, if a company has its own research facility consisting of buildings, laboratories, and equipment that are used for general research activities, it accounts for these assets as capitalized property, plant, and equipment. The depreciation and other costs that are related to such facilities are accounted for as research-related expenses.

Sometimes entities conduct research activities for other companies **under a contractual arrangement**. In this case, the contract usually specifies that all direct costs, certain specific indirect costs, and a profit element will be reimbursed to the entity performing the research work. Because reimbursement is expected, such research costs are recorded as inventory or a receivable.

Accounting for Development Phase Costs

An intangible asset can be recognized from the development stage of an internal project, but only when an entity can demonstrate its technical and financial feasibility and the company's intention and ability to generate future economic benefits from it. **All six of the following specific conditions need to be demonstrated** in order to capitalize costs incurred in the development phase:

1. Technical feasibility of completing the intangible asset

2. The entity's intention to complete it for use or sale

3. The entity's ability to use or sell it

4. Availability of technical, financial, and other resources needed to complete it, and to use or sell it

5. The way in which the future economic benefits will be generated: including the existence of a market for the asset if it will be sold, or its usefulness to the entity if it will be used internally

6. The ability to reliably measure the costs associated with and attributed to the intangible asset during its development

Because **all** six criteria must be met, this means that an entity capitalizes development phase costs **only when the future benefits are reasonably certain**. This means that internally generated intangible assets are recognized only in limited situations, and projects may be quite far along in the development stage before all six criteria are met. **Only then do the costs begin to be capitalized.** No expenditures incurred prior to this point and previously expensed are added to the asset's cost, even if the expenditures were in the same accounting period.

Although it is contrary to the usual principles-based approach, several items are specifically identified as not being recognized as internally generated intangible assets. These include brands, mastheads (the front-page or cover banner design of newspapers and magazines), publishing titles, customer lists, and other similar items. They are excluded on the basis that costs incurred to develop them cannot be distinguished from general business development costs.

Costs Included and Excluded

The cost of an internally generated intangible begins to be accumulated at the date when the six criteria in the development process are met. From this point forward, the types of expenditures that are capitalized are familiar: all directly attributable costs needed to create, produce, and prepare the intangible asset to operate in the way intended by management. Examples of such direct costs include:

UNDERLYING CONCEPT

1. Materials and services used or consumed to generate the asset

2. Direct costs of personnel, such as salaries, wages, payroll taxes, and related employee benefit costs

3. Fees needed to register a legal right

4. Amortization of other intangibles needed to generate the new asset

5. Interest or borrowing costs[10]

The requirement that all research-type and most development-type costs be expensed as they are incurred is an example of the old conflict between relevance and reliability, with verifiability or reliability carrying more weight in this case.

Specifically **excluded** as capitalized costs are selling, administrative, and other general overhead costs that cannot be directly linked to preparing the asset for use, costs incurred to train employees, and initial operating losses after the intangible is ready for use.

Generally, the costs of start-up activities such as legal and other costs of incorporation (**organization costs**); pre-opening costs associated with new facilities or businesses; and pre-operating costs for launching new operations, products, or processes are all expensed. Relocation and reorganization costs, and those associated with advertising and promotional activities including mail-order catalogues, are also not capitalized.

To illustrate the accounting treatment of activities associated with intangible items and research and development phases, assume that a company develops, produces, and markets laser machines for medical, industrial, and defence uses. The types of expenditures related to its laser machine activities, along with the recommended IFRS accounting treatment, are listed in Illustration 12-3.

Illustration 12-3

Sample Expenditures and Their Accounting Treatment

Type of Expenditure	Accounting Treatment
1. Construction of long-range research facility (three-storey, 1,000-m² building) for use in current and future projects	Capitalize as PP&E assets; depreciate as a research-type expense.
2. Acquisition of research-related equipment for use on current project only	Capitalize as PP&E asset; depreciate as a research-type expense.
3. Purchase of materials to be used on current and future R&D projects	Capitalize as inventory; expense as a research-type expense as consumed.
4. Salaries of research staff designing new laser bone scanner	Expense immediately as a research-type expense.

(continued)

Illustration 12-3
Sample Expenditures and Their Accounting Treatment (continued)

5. Research costs incurred under contract for customer and billable monthly	Expense as operating expense in period of related revenue recognition.
6. Material, labour, and overhead costs of prototype laser scanner	Capitalize as intangible asset if development criteria are all met; otherwise expense.
7. Costs of testing prototype and design modifications	Capitalize as intangible asset if development criteria are all met; otherwise expense.
8. Legal fees to obtain patent on new laser scanner	Capitalize as patent (intangible asset) provided asset meets recognition criteria; amortize to cost of goods manufactured as used.
9. Executive salaries	Expense as operating expense (general and administrative).
10. Cost of marketing research related to promotion of new laser scanner	Expense as operating expense (selling).
11. Engineering costs incurred to advance the laser scanner to full production stage	Capitalize as intangible asset if development criteria are all met; otherwise expense.
12. Costs of successfully defending patent on laser scanner	Capitalize as intangible asset (patent); amortize to cost of goods manufactured as used.
13. Commissions to sales staff marketing new laser scanner	Expense as operating expense (selling).

Recognition and Measurement after Acquisition

Objective 4
Explain how intangible assets are accounted for after initial recognition.

Items of property, plant, and equipment commonly have parts added to them or replaced, but most intangible assets do not. The nature of intangibles is such that costs incurred after the asset has been acquired are normally made to maintain the asset's benefits and therefore do not meet the recognition criteria for capitalization. Although there are exceptions, most after-acquisition costs are expensed.

Two models have been put forward for measuring intangible assets after initial recognition: a **cost model (CM)** and a **revaluation model (RM)**. The cost model is the most widely used approach by far, and under ASPE, it is the only method allowed.

Why is the RM not widely used? The reason is simply that it can be applied only to intangible assets that have a fair value determined in an **active market**.[11] This limits its use to situations where the items are homogeneous (interchangeable), there is a good supply of willing buyers and sellers, and the prices are available to the public. An active securities market, such as the Toronto Stock Exchange, exists for equity securities, but active markets do not ordinarily exist for intangible assets. Most intangible assets, such as patents, brands, and trademarks, grant unique rights to the entity that holds them. This results in unique pricing when such assets are bought and sold. There are some exceptions. Examples include the prices of quotas for a variety of agricultural products for which the government sets production limits, such as milk or eggs. The revaluation model could also be used where there are transferable fishing or taxi licences, which are available in some jurisdictions.

When the RM is chosen for an intangible asset, all the assets in the same class must also apply the same method. Examples of classes include copyrights, patents, computer software, secret recipes, and designs. If there is no active market for the other assets in the class, then the cost model is applied to these assets.

Accounting under these two models is the same for intangible assets as for property, plant, and equipment. For both PP&E and intangible assets using the revaluation method, there is no requirement for an annual revaluation, only that the carrying amount reported on the statement of financial position not be materially different from its fair value. Instead of repeating the full coverage of this topic provided in Chapters 10 and 11, we summarize the two methods of accounting for limited-life intangible assets in Illustration 12-4.[12] You may want to review the specific examples in the earlier chapters to reinforce this material.

Illustration 12-4

Cost Model and Revaluation Model for Intangible Assets

Cost Model (CM)	
At acquisition	Recognized and measured at cost.
After acquisition	Carried at cost less accumulated amortization and any accumulated impairment losses.
On disposal	Difference between asset's carrying amount and proceeds on disposal is gain or loss reported in net income.

Revaluation Model (RM)	
At acquisition	Recognized and measured at cost.
After acquisition	Carried at fair value at the date of the revaluation less any subsequent accumulated amortization and any subsequent impairment losses.
Revaluation increase	Record credit to Revaluation Surplus (Other Comprehensive Income) unless this reverses a previous decrease recognized in income. If so, recognize the increase in income to the extent of the prior decrease.
Revaluation decrease	Record debit to Revaluation Surplus (Other Comprehensive Income) to the extent there is a balance associated with the same asset. Any remaining amount is recognized as a charge to income.
Revaluation	Apply either the **proportional method** (both asset and accumulated amortization balances continue and are adjusted so that net amount is asset's new fair value) or the **asset adjustment method** (accumulated amortization is closed to the asset account and begins again at zero; asset is revalued to new amount).
On disposal	Either bring asset to its fair value at the date of disposal, account for the revaluation increase or decrease as above, and recognize no gain or loss on disposal, or recognize a gain or loss on disposal in net income equal to the difference between the proceeds on disposal and the asset's carrying amount on the date of disposal.
Revaluation Surplus account balance	Either transfer amounts directly to Retained Earnings each period (equal to the difference between amortization expense determined on the cost model basis and amortization expense determined on the revaluation model basis), or wait until asset is disposed of and transfer balance remaining in the account directly to Retained Earnings.

As suggested above, intangibles are a diverse mix of assets. Some intangibles have values based on rights that are given legally by contract, statute, or similar means. Examples include a Tim Hortons franchise or licences granted by the federal government to broadcasters. Some of these rights have finite or limited legal lives that can be easily renewed; others have lives that are not renewable, and others are renewable only at a significant cost. Some can be sold while others may not be exchangeable. Internally developed intangibles may have a wide range of useful lives. Other intangibles may be granted in perpetuity and have an indefinite life. An **indefinite life** does not mean "infinite"—that the asset will last forever. Instead, it means that, after looking at all relevant factors, there appears to be no foreseeable limit to how long the asset will generate positive net cash flows for the entity.

Accounting standards used to require all intangible assets to be amortized over a period of not more than 40 years. While this simplified the accounting, the reality is that intangibles are diverse, and the approach to their measurement after acquisition should be based on their specific characteristics. Under current standards, if an intangible asset has a finite, or limited, useful life, it is amortized over that useful life. If instead the intangible has an indefinite life, no amortization is taken. Financial reporting is better served by retaining the asset in the accounts until it is determined to be impaired or its life becomes limited.

Limited-Life Intangibles

An intangible asset with a **finite** or **limited life** is amortized by systematic charges to expense over its useful life whether using the cost model or revaluation model. The factors to consider in determining the useful life are similar to the factors for long-lived property, plant, and equipment, and include:

1. The expected use of the asset by the entity, and the expected useful life of other assets that may affect the useful life of the intangible asset (such as mineral rights for depleting assets).

2. Any legal, regulatory, or contractual provisions that may either limit the useful life or allow renewal or extension of the asset's legal or contractual life without the entity having to pay a substantial cost. (If the renewal cost is significant, then the expenditure for the renewal may represent the cost of a new intangible asset.)

3. The effects of obsolescence, demand, competition, and other economic factors. Examples include the stability of the industry, known technological advances, and legislative action that results in an uncertain or changing regulatory environment. Effective January 1, 2016, IAS 38 was clarified to note that expected future reductions in sales prices of items produced using an intangible asset (such as a patent) could indicate expected commercial or technological obsolescence.[13]

4. The level of maintenance expenditure that is needed to obtain the expected future cash flows from the asset.[14]

SIGNIFICANT CHANGE

Amortization expense for a limited-life asset should ideally reflect the pattern in which the asset's economic benefits are used up, if that pattern can be reliably determined. For example, assume that Second Wave, Inc. has purchased a licence to manufacture a limited quantity of a vaccine called Megadose. Because the life of the licence is reduced with each unit produced, the cost of the licence is amortized following the pattern of production of Megadose—a unit of production approach. If the pattern cannot be determined, the straight-line method is used. The amortization charges are usually reported **as expenses**, and the credits are made to **accumulated amortization** accounts. Note that in the Second Wave, Inc. example, the amortization is likely a product cost that is first included in inventory and then expensed on the income statement as part of the cost of goods sold when the product is sold. Effective January 1, 2016, IAS 38.92 was clarified such that there is an underlying assumption that it is inappropriate to use amortization methods based on revenue generated by an activity, including the use of an intangible asset. The standard does allow exceptions, however. An example of an exception would be an intangible asset providing the right to operate a toll road that expires when a preset cumulative toll amount to be collected is reached.

The amount to amortize for an intangible asset is its carrying amount less residual value. Uncertainties about residual values for intangibles are greater than they are for items of property, plant, and equipment. Because of this, an intangible asset's residual value is assumed to be zero. This assumption can be overturned only if the asset is expected to be of use to another entity and a third party commits to purchase the asset at the end of its useful life, or if there is an active market for the asset that is expected to still exist at the end of its useful life to the entity.[15]

There are other similarities between the accounting for limited-life intangibles and property, plant, and equipment assets, as shown in Illustration 12-5.

Illustration 12-5 *Accounting for Intangible Assets with a Limited Life*	**Transaction or Event**	**Accounting Treatment for Intangible Assets with a Limited Life**	**Same as for Most PP&E Assets?**

Transaction or Event	Accounting Treatment for Intangible Assets with a Limited Life	Same as for Most PP&E Assets?
Amortization begins...	...when the asset is in the location and condition to be able to be used as management intends	Yes
Amortization stops...	...at the earlier of when it is derecognized or classified as held for sale	Yes
Review of useful life and amortization method	ASPE: at least annually	PP&E is reviewed "regularly"
	IFRS: at least at the end of each financial year	Yes
Change in estimate of useful life, residual value, amortization method	Accounted for prospectively—as a change in accounting estimate	Yes

Indefinite-Life Intangibles

An intangible asset with an indefinite life **is not amortized**. For example, assume that Double Clik, Inc. acquires a trademark that is used to distinguish a leading consumer product from other such products. The trademark is renewable every 10 years at minimal cost. After evaluating all relevant factors, the evidence indicates that this trademark product will generate net cash flows for an indefinite period of time. Therefore, it has an indefinite life.

Because of the potential effect on the financial statements, it is important for management to review whether events and circumstances continue to support the assessment of an indefinite life. This is required every accounting period under IFRS (and when circumstances indicate possible impairment under ASPE). If the useful life is later considered to be limited instead of indefinite, the change is considered a change in estimate and past results are not affected. Such an assessment may also indicate that the asset's carrying amount is impaired. The accounting treatment for impairment is discussed later in this chapter.

Specific Intangibles

The many different types of intangibles assets are sometimes classified into the following five major categories:[16]

1. Marketing-related

2. Customer-related

3. Artistic-related

4. Contract-based

5. Technology-based

Marketing-Related Intangible Assets

Marketing-related intangible assets are used mainly in the marketing or promotion of products or services and derive their value from the contractual or legal rights that they contain. Examples are trademarks or trade names, newspaper mastheads, Internet domain names, and non-competition agreements.

LAW

A very common form of marketing-related intangible asset is a trademark. A **trademark** or **trade name** is a word, symbol, or design, or combination of these, that is used to distinguish the goods or services of one person or entity from those of others. The terms **brand** and **brand name** are similar but often refer to a group of assets such as a trade name and its related formulas, recipes, and technology. The right to use a trademark, trade name, or brand name in Canada is granted by Industry Canada and the registration system is administered by its Trademarks Office.[17] In order to obtain and maintain this right, the owner must have made prior and continuing use of it. Trade names like Kraft Dinner, Pepsi-Cola, and Kleenex, and brand names such as President's Choice and Canadian Tire create immediate product recognition in our minds, which makes them more marketable. Company names themselves may have value and characteristics that companies are willing to spend money on to develop.[18]

If a mark or name is **purchased**, its capitalizable cost is the purchase price and other direct costs of acquisition. If it is **developed** by the enterprise itself and its future benefits to the company are reasonably assured, the costs may be capitalized, but only from the point in time when all six of the required capitalization criteria are met in its development phase. These costs may include lawyers' fees, registration fees, design costs, consulting fees, successful legal defence costs, expenditures related to securing the mark or name, and other direct development costs. When a trademark, trade name, or brand name's total cost is insignificant or all six capitalization criteria have not been met, the costs are expensed.

Hoping to promote the management of brands in the same financially robust way as other long-term investments, Brand Finance plc published a report entitled the Brand Finance Global 500 2015. The study uses a "royalty relief approach" to value the brands of major companies; that is, the authors determine how much a company would have to pay to license the brand from a third party. The brand's value is the present value of that hypothetical stream of payments.

Apple, Samsung, and **Google** were ranked as having the three most valuable brands in the world, with China's **China Mobile** joining Samsung as the only non–U.S.-based companies in the top 10. The most valuable Canadian brand, according to this report, was the **Royal Bank of Canada**, with an estimated worth of almost $12.5 billion. Most other major Canadian banks were also included in the top 500 world brands, together with other well-known companies and brands like

Bell, Rogers, Telus, Enbridge, McCain, and **Brookfield Asset Management**. The RBC brand, however, does not appear as an asset on the Royal Bank's balance sheet. Why not? Brand value is a function of marketing, advertising, and public relations spending, including customer loyalty and retention programs, which all result in an increased volume of business, retail sales, and shipments. This type of cost is expensed as it is incurred because it cannot be directly related to future benefits.

In an earlier report, Brand Finance contended that "long-term investment decisions about future promotional expenditures, and the host of other activities that combine to build brand value" are better made when management can articulate the arguments in financial terms, as is done for most other investments.

Source: Brand Finance website, http://www.brandfinance.com.

Trademark registrations in Canada last for 15 years, and are renewable at a reasonable cost. Although the legal life of such assets **may be unlimited**, in practice they may only provide benefits to the enterprise over a **finite** period. Trademarks can, however, be determined to provide benefits to an enterprise indefinitely. A brand such as Coca-Cola, worth billions of dollars, may reasonably be expected to have an indefinite useful life. In this case, the intangible asset is not amortized.

Customer-Related Intangible Assets

Customer-related intangible assets result from interactions with outside parties and their value may be derived from legal-contractual rights, or because they are separable. Examples include customer lists, order or production backlogs, and customer contracts or non-contractual relationships.

To illustrate, assume that We-Market Inc. acquires the customer list of a large newspaper for $6 million on January 1, 2017. The customer list is a database that includes customer names, contact information, order history, and demographic information. We-Market expects to benefit from the information on the acquired list for 10 years, and it believes that these benefits will be spread evenly over the 10 years. In this case, assume the customer list is a limited-life intangible that should be amortized on a straight-line basis. The customer list would typically have a limited life due to factors such as people moving into or out of the area and competition from other newspapers and other media sources.

The entries to record the purchase of the customer list and its amortization at the end of each year are as follows:

A = L + SE
0 = 0 + 0
Cash flows: ↓ 6,000,000 outflow

January 1, 2017		
Intangible Assets—Customer List	6,000,000	
Cash		6,000,000

A = L + SE
−600,000 = −600,000
Cash flows: No effect

December 31, 2017, through December 31, 2026		
Amortization Expense	600,000	
Accumulated Amortization—Customer List		600,000

This example assumes that the customer list has no residual value. But what if We-Market determines that it can sell the list for $60,000 to another company at the end of 10 years? In that case, the residual value is subtracted from the cost in order to determine the amortizable amount.

Artistic-Related Intangible Assets

LAW

Artistic-related intangible assets involve ownership rights to plays, literary works, musical works, pictures, photographs, and video and audiovisual material. These ownership rights are protected by copyrights and have value because of the legal-contractual nature of the rights.

A **copyright** is the exclusive right to copy a creative work or allow someone else to do so. It is a federally granted right that applies to all original literary, dramatic, musical, and artistic works, whatever the mode or form of expression. A copyright is acquired automatically when an original work is created, but it can also be registered with the federal Copyright Office (part of the Canadian Intellectual Property Office (CIPO)). The right is granted for the life of the creator plus 50 years, and gives the owner or heirs the exclusive right to reproduce, sell, communicate, or translate an artistic or published work. Copyrights are not renewable. Like trade names, they may be assigned or sold to other individuals.[19] The costs of acquiring and defending a copyright may be capitalized, but research costs that are associated with them are expensed as they are incurred.

Generally, the copyright's useful life is shorter than its legal life. Its useful life depends on the unique facts and circumstances of each case. Consumer habits, market trends, and prior experience all play a part. Because it is so difficult to determine how many periods will benefit from a copyright, companies often choose to write these costs off over a fairly short period of time.

WHAT DO THE NUMBERS MEAN?

Copyrights can be valuable. When Michael Jackson died in mid-2009, he was in dire financial trouble. However, he did have one asset that was extremely valuable: a 50% interest in the **Sony Corp./ATV Music Publishing** joint venture set up in 1995. The partnership owns copyrights to the lyrics and music of tens of thousands of songs by such artists as the Beatles, Roy Orbison, Hank Williams, and Jimi Hendrix.

With its 2012 acquisition of EMI Music Publishing, Sony/ATV is said to have become the world's largest publishing company, with over 2 million songs and revenues in excess of U.S. $1.2 billion, and is estimated to be worth in excess of U.S. $3 billion! Altogether, Sony/ATV Music Publishing owns or administers more than 2 million copyrights for the who's who of the music industry.

Contract-Based Intangible Assets

Contract-based intangible assets are the value of rights that come from contractual arrangements. Examples are licensing arrangements, lease agreements, construction permits, broadcast rights, and service or supply contracts. A very common form of contract-based intangible asset is a franchise.

LAW

When you drive down the street in an automobile purchased from a Toyota dealer, fill your tank at the corner Petro-Canada station, grab a coffee at Tim Hortons, eat lunch at McDonald's, cool off with a Baskin-Robbins cone, work at a Coca-Cola bottling plant, live in a home purchased through a Royal LePage real estate broker, or vacation at a Holiday Inn resort, you are dealing with franchises. A **franchise** is a contractual arrangement under which the franchisor grants the franchisee the right to sell certain products or services; to use certain trademarks, trade names, or brands; or to perform certain functions, usually within a designated geographic area. **Licensing agreements** work in a similar way.

After having developed a unique concept or product, the franchisor protects it through a patent, copyright, trademark, or trade name. The franchisee then acquires the right to take advantage of the franchisor's idea or product by signing a franchise agreement. Another type of franchise is the arrangement that is commonly entered into by a municipality or other government body and a business enterprise that uses public property. In this case, a privately owned enterprise is given permission to use public property in performing its services. Examples are the use of public waterways for a ferry service, the use of public land for telephone or electric lines, the use of city streets for a bus line, or the use of the airwaves for radio or TV broadcasting. Such operating rights are frequently referred to as **licences** or **permits**, and are obtained through agreements with government departments or agencies.

Franchises and licences may be granted for a definite period of time, for an indefinite period of time, or in perpetuity. The enterprise that acquires the franchise or licence recognizes an intangible asset account titled either Franchise or Licence on its books as soon as there are costs (such as a lump-sum payment in advance or legal fees and other expenditures) that are identified with the acquisition of the operating right. The cost of a franchise or licence **with a limited life** is amortized over the lesser of its legal or useful life. A franchise **with an indefinite life, or a perpetual franchise**, is amortized if its **useful life** is deemed to be limited. Otherwise, it is not amortized.

Annual franchise fees paid under a franchise agreement are entered as operating expenses in the period in which they are incurred. They do not represent an asset to the enterprise because they do not relate to future rights.

Another contract-related intangible asset is a **favourable lease**. A **lease** or **lease-hold** is a contractual understanding between a lessor (property owner) and a lessee (property renter) that grants the lessee the right to use specific property, owned by the lessor, for a certain period of time in return for specific, usually periodic, cash payments. A lease contract is an intangible asset to the extent that the terms are more favourable than the usual market terms for such an arrangement. It could be an asset to the lessor or the lessee.[20]

Technology-Based Intangible Assets

LAW

Technology-based intangible assets relate to innovations or technological advances. Examples include Nortel's patents that were sold in 2011 (as discussed above) and patents for technology and trade secrets that are granted by the federal government's Patent Office (also part of CIPO). Patents are granted for products and processes that are new, workable, and ingenious. A **patent** gives the holder the right to exclude others from making, selling, or using a product or process for a period of 20 years from the date the patent application is filed with the Patent Office. Fortunes can be made by holding patents, as companies such as **BlackBerry, Bombardier, IMAX, Polaroid**, and **Xerox** can attest.[21]

If a patent is purchased from an inventor or other owner, the purchase price represents its cost. Other costs that are incurred in connection with securing a patent, including legal fees and unrecovered costs of a successful lawsuit to protect the patent, are capitalized as part of the patent cost. Most research and development costs incurred that result in an internally generated patent are expensed. Only directly attributable costs incurred in the development phase after the six capitalization criteria are met can be included as part of the asset's cost. For this reason, most research and development costs related to developing a product, process, or idea that is subsequently patented are expensed as they are incurred.

The cost of a patent is amortized over its legal life or its useful life to the entity, whichever is shorter. If a patent is owned from the date it is granted, and it is expected to be useful during its entire legal life, it is amortized over 20 years. If it is expected to be useful for a shorter period, its cost is amortized to expense over that shorter period. Changing demand, new inventions replacing old ones, inadequacy, and other factors often limit the useful life of a patent to less than its legal life. For example, the useful life of patents in the pharmaceutical industry is often less than the legal life because of the testing and approval period that follows their issuance. A typical drug patent has five to 11 years knocked off its 20-year legal life. Why? A drug manufacturer spends one to four years on animal tests, four to six years on human tests, and two to three years for government agencies to review the tests—all after the patent is issued but before the product goes on the pharmacist's shelves.

Legal fees and other costs that are associated with a successful defence of a patent are capitalized as part of the asset's cost because lawsuits establish the patent holder's legal rights. Such costs are amortized along with other acquisition costs over the remaining useful life of the patent.

Patent amortization follows a pattern that is consistent with the benefits that are received, if that pattern can be reliably determined. This could be based on time or on units produced. To illustrate, assume that on January 1, 2017, Harcott Ltd. either pays $180,000 to acquire a patent or incurs $180,000 in legal costs to successfully defend an internally developed patent. Further, assume that the patent has a remaining useful life of 12 years and is amortized on a straight-line basis. The entries to record the $180,000 expenditure on January 1, 2017, and the amortization at the end of each year are as follows:

A = L + SE
0   0   0

Cash flows: ↓ 180,000 outflow

January 1, 2017		
Intangible Assets—Patents	180,000	
Cash		180,000
December 31, 2017		
Amortization Expense	15,000	
Accumulated Amortization—Patents		15,000

A = L + SE
−15,000   −15,000

Cash flows: No effect

Although a patent's useful life may be limited by its legal life, small modifications or additions may lead to a new patent and an extension of the life of the old patent.[22] In this case, the entity can apply the unamortized costs of the old patent to the new patent if the new patent provides essentially the same benefits. Alternatively, if a patent's value is reduced because, for example, demand drops for the product, the asset is tested for impairment.[23]

WHAT DO THE NUMBERS MEAN?

REAL WORLD EMPHASIS

Coca-Cola has managed to keep the recipe for the world's best-selling soft drink under wraps for more than 100 years. How has it done so? The company offers almost no information about its lifeblood. The only written copy of the formula is in a vault in the company's own museum in Atlanta, Georgia. This handwritten sheet is not available to anyone except by vote of the Coca-Cola board of directors.

Why is science unable to offer some clues? Coke contains 17 to 18 ingredients. These include the usual caramel colour and corn syrup, as well as a blend of oils known as 7X—rumoured to be a mix of orange, lemon, cinnamon, and others. Distilling natural products like these is complicated since they are made of thousands of compounds. Although the original formula contained trace amounts of cocaine, this is one ingredient that you will not find in today's Coke. When was it removed? That is a secret, too. Experts suggest that the power of this formula and related brand image account for almost U.S. $56 billion of the company's market capitalization of U.S. $180 billion (as of May 2015).

Sources: Reed Tucker, "How Has Coke's Formula Stayed a Secret?" *Fortune*, July 24, 2000, p. 42; David Kiley, "Best Global Brands," *Business Week*, August 6, 2007, p. 59; Gavin Allen, "Bad News Pepsi! After 90 Years Coca-Cola's Secret Recipe Is Finally Out of the Bank Vault for Museum Display... But Rivals Still Won't Get a Peek at the Ingredients," *The Daily Mail*, December 9, 2011; www.forbes.com/powerful-brands/list/ (accessed June 28, 2015).

Another common technology-based intangible relates to **computer software costs**, either for internal use or for sale as a product. Costs that are incurred in the development of software as a potential product **for sale** or those directly attributable to the development, betterment, or acquisition of computer software **for internal use** are covered by the same capitalization criteria required for other intangible assets.

IMPAIRMENT AND DERECOGNITION

Objective 6

Explain and account for impairment of limited-life and indefinite-life intangible assets.

Similar to property, plant, and equipment, the carrying amounts of intangible assets and goodwill have to be reviewed to ensure that they do not exceed the economic benefits the assets are expected to provide in the future. If an item is determined to be **impaired**, its carrying amount will have to be written down and an impairment loss recognized.

Impairment of Limited-Life Intangibles

The same impairment models and standards that apply to **long-lived tangible assets** also apply to **limited-life intangibles**.[24] As indicated in Chapter 11, under ASPE, long-lived assets that a company intends to hold and use are assessed for potential impairment whenever events and circumstances indicate the carrying value may not be recoverable. Under IFRS, these assets are **assessed for impairment** at the end of each reporting period.

Differences between the current fair value and carrying amount are more common among long-term assets, although there can also be significant differences in the current asset category. Cash is obviously not a problem in terms of its value. Receivables are normally fairly close to their current valuation, although adjustments do sometimes need to be made because of inadequate bad debt provisions. The fair values of current liabilities also are usually close to their recorded book values. However, if interest rates have changed since long-term liabilities were issued, their value determined using current interest rates may be quite different from their carrying amount. A careful analysis must also be done to ensure that there are no unrecorded liabilities.

Returning to our example, the $20,000 difference between the fair value and carrying amount of Tractorling's inventories ($62,000 − $42,000) could be due to several factors. One explanation might be that Tractorling acquired significant inventories when the prices were lower and uses specific identification or an average cost valuation, in which ending inventory includes inventory at older costs.

In many cases, the values of long-lived assets such as property, plant, and equipment and intangibles may have increased substantially over the years. This difference could be due to inaccurate estimates of useful lives, continual expensing of small expenditures (say, amounts less than $500), or substantial increases in replacement costs. Alternatively, there may be assets that have not been recognized in the company's books. In Tractorling's case, land was acquired many years ago and its fair value has increased significantly, and internally developed patents have not been recognized in the accounts, yet they have a fair value of $18,000.

Since the investigation indicates that the fair value of the identifiable net assets is $350,000, why would Multi-Diversified pay $400,000? Tractorling might point to the company's established reputation, good credit rating, top management team, well-trained employees, and so on as factors that make the value of the business as a whole greater than $350,000. Multi-Diversified places a premium on the future earning power of these attributes as well as the company's current basic asset structure. At this point in the negotiations, Tractorling's total fair value, and price, may be due to many factors; the most important may be sheer skill at the bargaining table.

Multi-Diversified labels the difference between the fair value of the consideration paid of $400,000 and the fair value of the identifiable net assets of $350,000 as goodwill. Goodwill is viewed as the unidentifiable values plus the value of the identifiable intangibles that do not meet the criteria for separate recognition. The procedure for valuation shown in Illustration 12-9 is referred to as a master valuation approach, because goodwill is assumed to cover all the values that cannot be specifically associated with any identifiable tangible or intangible asset. Note that this method of accounting for a business combination is a fair value approach rather than one based on the cost of the acquisition and cost allocation. For example, acquisition-related costs associated with a business combination are expensed as incurred and are not capitalized as they would be in a cost-based system.

Illustration 12-9

Determination of Goodwill—
Master Valuation Approach

Fair value of consideration transferred:		$400,000
Fair value of identifiable net assets:		
Cash	$ 25,000	
Accounts receivable	35,000	
Inventories	62,000	
Property, plant, and equipment	265,000	
Patents	18,000	
Liabilities	(55,000)	350,000
Value assigned to goodwill:		$ 50,000

Multi-Diversified's entry to record the purchase of Tractorling's net assets, assuming the consideration is $400,000 cash, is as follows:[25]

The internal and external sources of information that may indicate an intangible asset is impaired are the same factors described in Illustration 11-14 in Chapter 11 for items of property, plant, and equipment. Of course, evidence of physical damage would not apply in the assessment of an intangible asset! If an assessment indicates there may be impairment, the asset is formally tested by applying the appropriate impairment model.

A summary of the two models and how they are applied is provided in Illustration 12-6. Remember that the **cost recovery impairment model** is used for **ASPE**, and the **rational entity impairment model** is used for **IFRS**. If you review the section "Impairment—Recognition and Measurement Models" in Chapter 11, it might help to reinforce your understanding of the details of each model.

Illustration 12-6

Summary of Impairment Models
for Limited-Life Intangible Assets

Cost Recovery Impairment Model	
Concept	Assumes asset will continue to be used; it is impaired only if the asset's carrying amount is not recoverable from the future undiscounted cash flows from use and eventual sale.
Recoverability test	If undiscounted future cash flows ≥ carrying amount, asset is not impaired.
	If undiscounted future cash flows < carrying amount, asset is impaired. Proceed to calculate impairment loss.
Impairment loss	Asset's carrying amount − fair value = impairment loss; fair value is a discounted cash flow, market-based concept.
Entry to record loss	Loss on Impairment $XX
	Accumulated Impairment Losses— $XX Licenses (or "-Patents", etc.)
Subsequent amortization	Review carrying amount to be amortized, useful life, and pattern of amortization and determine new periodic amortization charge.
Reversal of impairment loss	Reversal not permitted. The fair value to which the asset is written down becomes the asset's new cost basis.
If no single-asset identifiable cash flows	Combine with other assets into an asset group, test for impairment, and, if impaired, calculate impairment loss using same approach as for an individual asset. Allocate loss only to long-lived assets, based on their relative carrying amounts, within limits.

Rational Entity Impairment Model	
Concept	Assumes management will use the asset or dispose of it currently, whichever results in a higher return to the entity. It is impaired only if its carrying amount is not recoverable from the more profitable, or less costly, of the two options.
Recoverability test	No separate test of undiscounted cash flows.
Impairment loss	Calculate recoverable amount = **higher of** value in use **and** fair value less costs to sell, both of which are discounted cash flow concepts.
	If recoverable amount ≥ carrying amount, no impairment loss.
	If recoverable amount < carrying amount, impairment loss = the difference.
Entry to record loss under cost model	Loss on Impairment $XX
	Accumulated Impairment Losses— $XX Licenses (or "-Patents", etc.)
Subsequent amortization	Review carrying amount to be amortized, useful life, and pattern of amortization and determine new periodic amortization charge.
Reversal of impairment loss	Reversal of loss is required if estimates underlying recoverable amount have changed. Reversal amount is limited.
If no single-asset identifiable cash flows	Combine with other assets into a cash-generating group and calculate impairment loss using same approach as for an individual asset. Allocate loss to assets based on their relative carrying amounts, within limits.

Impairment of Indefinite-Life Intangibles

Accounting for the impairment of intangible assets with an **indefinite life** is a little different than explained above for limited-life intangibles. These differences and the reasons for them are discussed below.

ASPE

An intangible asset with an indefinite life still needs to be tested for impairment only when events and circumstances indicate there might be impairment, but now the test is different. The impairment test for an indefinite-life asset is a **fair value test**. This test compares the **fair value** of the intangible asset with the asset's carrying amount. If its fair value is less than the carrying amount, an impairment loss equal to the difference is recognized.

Why is there a different standard for indefinite-life intangibles? This one-step test is used because it would be relatively easy for many indefinite-life assets to meet the recoverability test. That is, the undiscounted cash flows would extend many years into the future and the total cash to be recovered tends to add up to a large sum. However, the dollars received in periods far into the future have a much lower value today. **As a result, the separate recoverability test is not used**, and the test compares the carrying amount directly with the asset's fair value—a discounted cash flow concept.

To illustrate, assume that Space Corp. (SC) purchases a broadcast licence for $1,150,000, and that the licence is renewable every seven years if the company provides appropriate service and does not violate the rules and regulations of the Canadian Radio-television and Telecommunications Commission (CRTC). The licence is then renewed with the CRTC twice at a minimal cost, and because cash flows are expected to last indefinitely, the licence is reported as an indefinite-life intangible asset. Assume that SC is beginning to question whether the asset might be impaired because advertising revenues are expected to drop with changing demographics in the area covered by the licence. The following information has been gathered about the benefits of the licence:

Undiscounted future net cash flows expected from its use	$1,800,000
Discounted future net cash flows, or fair value	$ 950,000

Is the licence impaired? Yes. Because the carrying amount of $1,150,000 is more than its fair value of $950,000, an impairment loss of $1,150,000 − $950,000 = $200,000 is indicated.

Space Corp. may either set up and credit an accumulated impairment loss account for the licence or credit the asset account itself. The licence is now reported at a net amount of $950,000, and this is its new "cost" for subsequent accounting.

IFRS

There is only a minor difference in the IFRS standard for impairment for indefinite-life intangibles, as compared with those with limited lives. Assets with an indefinite life are **tested for impairment** by comparing their carrying amount and recoverable value **on an annual basis, whether or not there is any indication of impairment**. Why a stronger standard for these assets? The answer lies in the fact that no expense is being charged against income for such assets on a regular basis. For this reason, the assumption of a continuing recoverable value in excess of book value needs to be regularly tested.

Derecognition

An intangible asset is derecognized when it is disposed of or when its continuing use or disposal is not expected to generate any further economic benefits. Similar to property, plant, and equipment assets, a gain or loss is recognized at this time, equal to the difference between the asset's carrying amount and the proceeds on disposal, if any. The gain or loss on disposal is recognized in income in the period of disposal.

GOODWILL

Recognition and Measurement of Goodw

Recognition of Internally Generated Goodwill

Goodwill that is generated internally is not capitalized in the acco the components of internally generated goodwill is simply too comple: costs incurred with future benefits is too difficult. In fact, the future be: may have no relationship to the costs that were incurred to develop it. T plexity, goodwill may even exist when there have been no specific expend it. In addition, because no transaction has taken place with outside parti subjectivity—even misrepresentation—might be involved in trying to m

Purchased Goodwill

As previously indicated, goodwill is recognized only when a business con because the value of goodwill cannot be separated from a business as a wh of determining the proper values to assign to identifiable intangible as: combination is complex because of the many different types of intangib acquired. Because goodwill is a residual amount, every dollar that is assign including identifiable intangible assets, leaves one less dollar to be assign

To illustrate, assume that Multi-Diversified, Inc. decides that it need to supplement its existing tractor distributorship. The president of Mu interested in buying Tractorling Ltd., a small company near Edmonton t lished reputation and is looking to sell its business. Illustration 12-7 sh current statement of financial position.

Illustration 12-7
Tractorling Ltd. Statement of Financial Position

TRACTORLING LTD.
Statement of Financial Position
December 31, 2017

Assets		Liabilities and equity	
Cash	$ 25,000	Current liabilities	
Accounts receivable	35,000	Share capital	
Inventories	42,000	Retained earnings	
Property, plant, and equipment (net)	153,000		
Total assets	$255,000	Total liabilities and equity	

After considerable negotiation, Tractorling Ltd.'s shareholders decide Diversified's offer of $400,000. The two companies might agree on a $4 ment, or $400,000 in value of Multi-Diversified's shares, or other forms How should goodwill, if any, be measured?

The answer is not obvious. The fair values of Tractorling's identifiable ities are not disclosed in its cost-based statement of financial position. It that as the negotiations progressed, Multi-Diversified had a detailed inves Tractorling's underlying assets to determine their fair values. Such an inve done through a purchase audit by Multi-Diversified's auditors, or an indep from some other source. Illustration 12-8 shows the results.

Illustration 12-8
Fair Values of Tractorling Ltd.'s Identifiable Net Assets

Fair Values, December 31, 2017	
Cash	$ 25,000
Accounts receivable	35,000
Inventories	62,000
Property, plant, and equipment (net)	265,000
Patents	18,000
Liabilities	(55,000)
Fair value of identifiable net assets	$350,000

Cash	25,000
Accounts Receivable	35,000
Inventory	62,000
Property, Plant, and Equipment	265,000
Intangible Assets—Patents	18,000
Goodwill	50,000
Liabilities	55,000
Cash	400,000

A = L + SE
+55,000 +55,000
Cash flows: ↓ 375,000 outflow

Bargain Purchase

A **bargain purchase**, resulting in what is sometimes called **negative goodwill**, arises when the total of the fair value of the identifiable net assets acquired is higher than the fair value of the consideration transferred for those net assets. This situation is a result of market imperfection (or a poor decision by the seller) because the seller would be better off to sell the assets individually than in total. However, situations do occur when the value of what is given up is less than the value of the identifiable net assets that are acquired, and this requires accounting for a goodwill "credit."

How should this credit be handled in the accounts? Should it be taken to Retained Earnings directly, to Other Comprehensive Income, to net income in the year of purchase, or amortized to income over a reasonable future period? The accounting standards over the past 45 years or so have taken a variety of approaches to this "bonus," which shows the difficulty there has been in coming to terms with its conceptual nature.

Current standards require the excess to be recognized **as a gain in net income** in the same period that the combination takes place. However, this cannot be done without a thorough reassessment of all the variables, values, and measurement procedures used that resulted in this gain. If a gain still results from the re-examination, then it is recognized in income. While some critics do not agree with recognizing a gain **on the acquisition of assets**, this treatment is not applied lightly and appears to be a practical approach to a situation that rarely occurs.

Valuation after Acquisition

Once goodwill has been recognized in the accounts, how should it be treated in subsequent periods? Three basic approaches have been suggested:

1. **Charge goodwill immediately to expense.** Supporters of this approach justify an immediate write-off because the accounting for goodwill is then consistent whether purchased or created internally. Goodwill created internally is not recognized as an asset. Perhaps the best rationale for charging goodwill against income directly is that identifying the periods over which the future benefits are to be received is so difficult that the result is purely arbitrary.

2. **Amortize goodwill over its useful life.** Others believe that goodwill has value when it is acquired, but that its value eventually disappears. Therefore the asset should be charged to expense over the periods that are affected. To the extent that goodwill represents a wasting asset, this method provides a better matching of the costs of the benefits to revenues than other methods, even though the useful life may be difficult to determine.

3. **Retain goodwill indefinitely unless a reduction in value occurs.** Others believe that goodwill can have an indefinite life and should be kept as an asset until a decline in value occurs. Some form of goodwill should always be an asset because the current costs to maintain or enhance the purchased goodwill are being expensed. Also, unless there is strong evidence that a decline in its value has occurred, a write-off of goodwill is arbitrary and leads to distortions in net income.

Not so long ago, companies were required to amortize goodwill over a period no longer than 40 years. However, as we saw in the opening story, goodwill acquired in a business combination **is now considered to have an indefinite life and is no longer amortized.** Although goodwill may decrease over time, predicting the actual life of goodwill and an appropriate pattern of amortization is extremely difficult. Therefore, it is carried on the statement of financial position at the amount originally recognized in the combination less any subsequent impairment losses. **Income statements are not charged with any amounts paid for the goodwill until the asset is considered impaired.**

WHAT DO THE NUMBERS MEAN?

The opening story to the chapter referred to a study of goodwill impairment conducted by Duff & Phelps and the Canadian Financial Executives Research Foundation. The study also included a summary of a survey of members of the Financial Executives International (FEI Canada). These members stated that the top challenges for companies when performing goodwill impairment tests were developing cash flow projections, identifying cash-generating units (CGUs), determining the discount rate to be used for estimation, and properly identifying impairment indicators for CGUs.

REAL WORLD EMPHASIS

Objective 8

Explain and account for impairment of goodwill.

Impairment of Goodwill

Goodwill is not an identifiable asset and cannot generate cash flows independently of other assets. Because it can be acquired only in combination with other assets making up a business, it has to be assigned to a reporting unit or cash-generating unit (CGU) in order to be tested for impairment. An example of a CGU is the Markets division of Thomson Reuters in our feature story, which recorded goodwill impairment. Other than this specific facet that focuses on the reporting unit or CGU, impairment accounting for goodwill is similar to that for intangibles with an indefinite life. Applying the standards in this area can be complex, but we provide a summary of the basic elements in Illustration 12-10 under both ASPE and IFRS.

Illustration 12-10

Summary of Accounting for Impairment of Goodwill

	ASPE	IFRS
Apply impairment test...	...when events or changes in circumstances indicate	...annually, and whenever there is an indication that the CGU may be impaired
At acquisition date, assign goodwill...	...to a reporting unit: an operating segment or one level below	...to cash-generating unit: smallest identifiable group of assets where goodwill is monitored for management purposes, and no larger than an operating segment
There is an impairment loss...	...when carrying amount of reporting unit including goodwill > fair value of reporting unit. Loss = amount of excess	...when carrying amount of CGU including goodwill > recoverable amount. Loss = amount of excess. Recoverable amount is the higher of value in use and fair value less costs to sell
Impairment loss is allocated...	...to goodwill as a goodwill impairment loss; impairment test for other assets in group is done before goodwill impairment test	...first to goodwill related to the CGU, then remainder to other assets on a relative carrying amount (proportionate) basis
Goodwill impairment reversal...	...is not permitted	...is not permitted

To illustrate impairment accounting for goodwill, assume that Coburg Corporation has three divisions. One division, Pritt Products, was purchased four years ago for $2 million and has been identified as a reporting unit. Unfortunately, it has experienced operating losses over the last three quarters and management is reviewing the reporting unit to determine whether there has been an impairment of goodwill. The carrying amounts of Pritt Division's net assets, including the associated goodwill of $900,000, are listed in Illustration 12-11.

Illustration 12-11

Pritt Reporting Unit—Carrying Amount of Net Assets Including Goodwill

Cash	$ 200,000
Receivables	300,000
Inventory	700,000
Property, plant, and equipment (net)	800,000
Goodwill	900,000
Less: Accounts and notes payable	(500,000)
Net assets, at carrying amounts	$2,400,000

Situation 1: The fair value of the Pritt Division reporting unit as a whole is estimated to be $2.8 million. Management determines that the unit's value in use is $2.9 million and that the company would incur direct costs of $50,000 if the unit were sold.

Under **ASPE**, the goodwill is not impaired. The asset group's $2.4-million carrying value is less than its fair value of $2.8 million. Under **IFRS**, goodwill is not considered impaired either. The recoverable amount of the unit is $2.9 million—the higher of its value in use ($2.9 million) and its fair value less costs to sell ($2,800,000 − $50,000)—and this exceeds the unit's carrying amount of $2.4 million.

Situation 2: The fair value of the Pritt Division cash-generating unit as a whole is $1.9 million, its value in use is $2.1 million, and the direct cost of selling the unit is $50,000.

Under **ASPE**, an impairment loss is indicated:

Carrying amount of unit, including goodwill	$2,400,000
Fair value of unit	1,900,000
Goodwill impairment loss	$ 500,000

Under **IFRS**, an impairment loss is also indicated:

Carrying amount of unit, including goodwill		$ 2,400,000
Recoverable amount of unit: higher of		
Value in use	$2,100,000	
and		(2,100,000)
Fair value less costs to sell	$1,850,000	
Goodwill impairment loss		$ 300,000

The entries to record the losses under ASPE and IFRS are shown in Illustration 12-12.

Illustration 12-12

Entry to Record Impairment of Goodwill under ASPE and IFRS

	ASPE		IFRS	
Loss on Impairment	500,000		300,000	
Accumulated Impairment Losses-Goodwill		500,000		300,000

A	= L +	SE
ASPE		
−500,000		−500,000
IFRS		
−300,000		−300,000

Cash flows: No effect

Because there is a requirement to report the gross amount of goodwill and accumulated impairment losses at the end of the period, the Accumulated Impairment Losses account is credited instead of the Goodwill account so that the required information is retained. The Goodwill's net carrying amount is now $400,000 ($900,000 − $500,000) under ASPE and $600,000 ($900,000 − $300,000) under IFRS.

Illustration 12-13 summarizes the impairment tests for various intangible assets.

Illustration 12-13

Summary of Intangible Asset Impairment Tests

	Impairment Test	
Type of Asset	**ASPE**	**IFRS**
Limited-life intangible	Recoverability test; if failed, write down to fair value	Compare carrying amount with recoverable amount
Indefinite-life intangible	Compare carrying amount with fair value	Compare carrying amount with recoverable amount
Goodwill	Compare carrying amount of reporting unit with its fair value	Compare carrying amount of CGU with its recoverable amount

PRESENTATION, DISCLOSURE, AND ANALYSIS

Objective 9

Identify the types of disclosure requirements for intangible assets and goodwill and explain the issues in analyzing these assets.

REAL WORLD EMPHASIS

A survey indicates that the most common types of intangible assets reported are broadcast rights, publishing rights, trademarks, patents, licences, customer lists, non-competition agreements, franchises, and purchased R&D.[26] These, along with goodwill, have become an increasingly large proportion of companies' reported assets, making intangibles an important contributor to entity performance and financial position. For example, **Corus Entertainment Inc.**, a Canadian-based media and entertainment company, reported indefinite-life broadcast licences and goodwill at August 31, 2014, that amounted to 68.8% of its total assets. There were charges for impairment in both 2014 and 2013, after a period of stability for these intangibles; from 2010 to 2012, there were no impairment charges. The company recognized $83.0 million of impairment losses on these two classes of assets in 2014 ($5.7 million in 2013). The write-offs in 2014 represented about 7% of their opening book value, with the impairment being due, in part, to a soft advertising market and "ratings challenges in some markets." The CGUs affected by the write-offs were predominantly in Ontario for the broadcast licence impairment and in the radio CGU group segment overall for goodwill.

Presentation and Disclosure

Overview

While there are few required disclosures on the face of the statement of financial position and the statement of comprehensive income, a significant amount of information is required in the notes to the financial statements, particularly those prepared under IFRS. As seen in previous chapters, ASPE disclosures are considerably curtailed because most users of their financial statements can request additional information as needed. The goal of disclosure for publicly accountable entities is basically to allow readers to understand the significance of intangibles and goodwill to the operations of the business. To that end, this section summarizes some of the major disclosures required.

For each class of intangible asset, and separately for internally generated intangibles and other intangible assets, the following information is required:

- whether their lives are indefinite or finite (limited), useful life, methods and rates of amortization, and the line where amortization is included on the statement of comprehensive income;

- the carrying amount of intangible assets with an indefinite life, and the reasons supporting an assessment of an indefinite life;

- a reconciliation of the opening and ending balances of their carrying amount and accumulated amortization and impairment losses, separately identifying each reason for an increase or decrease; and

- impairment losses and reversals of impairment losses and where they are reported in the statement of comprehensive income.

For each material impairment loss recognized or reversed in the period, the following is required:

- the circumstances that led to its recognition, the amount recognized, the nature of the asset or cash-generating unit, and information about how the recoverable amount was determined.

For each cash-generating unit or group of units that has a significant amount of goodwill or intangible assets with an indefinite life, the following is required:

- how the unit's recoverable amount was determined, as well as assumptions underlying the calculation of the recoverable amount.

For intangible assets measured using the revaluation model, the following is required:

- their carrying amount, the carrying amounts if the revaluation model had not been applied, the date of the revaluation, the amount of the associated revaluation surplus and changes in that account, and the methods and assumptions used in estimating fair values.

This list identifies only some of the disclosures. The best source of the specific requirements is the standards themselves.

REAL WORLD EMPHASIS

Illustration of Disclosures

Excerpts from the financial statements of Corus Entertainment for its year ended August 31, 2014, are provided in Illustration 12-14. These disclosures are based on IFRS, which the company adopted in 2012 and are similar to ASPE. This company, reporting in millions of Canadian dollars, operates through two main lines of business: television and radio. Its 24 television networks include YTV, Treehouse, TELETOON, W Network, and HBO Canada.

Illustration 12-14

Selected Excerpts: Notes on Intangible Assets—Corus Entertainment

3. Significant accounting policies

The consolidated financial statements have been prepared on a cost basis, except for derivative and available-for-sale financial assets, which have been measured at fair value.

GOODWILL AND INTANGIBLE ASSETS

Intangible assets acquired separately are measured on initial recognition at cost. Intangible assets acquired in a business combination are measured at fair value as at the date of acquisition. Following initial recognition, intangible assets are carried at cost less accumulated amortization and accumulated impairment charges, if any. Internally generated intangible assets such as goodwill, brands and customer lists, excluding capitalized program and film development costs, are not capitalized and expenditures are reflected in the consolidated statements of income and comprehensive income in the year in which the expenditure is incurred. Intangible assets are recognized separately from goodwill when they are separable or arise from contractual or other legal rights and their fair value can be measured reliably. The useful lives of intangible assets are assessed as either finite or indefinite.

Intangible assets with finite lives are amortized over their useful economic lives and assessed for impairment whenever there is an indication that the intangible assets may be impaired. The amortization period and the amortization method for intangible assets with finite useful lives are reviewed at least at the end of each reporting period. Changes in the expected useful life or the expected pattern of consumption of future economic benefits embodied in the assets are accounted for by changing the amortization period or method, as appropriate, and are treated as changes in accounting estimates. The amortization expense on intangible assets with finite lives is recognized in the consolidated statements of income and comprehensive income in the expense category, consistent with the function of the intangible assets.

Amortization is recorded on a straight-line basis over the estimated useful life of the asset as follows:

Brand names, trademarks and digital rights	Agreement term
Software, patents and customer lists	3–5 years

Intangible assets with indefinite useful lives are not amortized. Broadcast licenses are considered to have an indefinite life based on management's intent and ability to renew the licenses without significant cost and without material modification of the existing terms and conditions of the license. The assessment of indefinite life is reviewed annually to determine whether the indefinite life continues to be supportable. If not, the change in useful life from indefinite to finite is made on a prospective basis.

Goodwill is initially measured at cost, being the excess of the aggregate of the consideration transferred and the amount recognized for non-controlling interest over the net identifiable assets acquired and liabilities assumed. If this consideration is lower than the fair value of the net identifiable assets of the subsidiary acquired, the difference is recognized in profit or loss.

After initial recognition, goodwill is measured at cost less any accumulated impairment losses. For the purpose of impairment testing, goodwill acquired in a business combination is, from the acquisition date, allocated to a CGU or group of CGUs that are expected to benefit from the synergies of the combination, irrespective of whether other assets or liabilities of the acquiree are assigned to those units. The group of CGUs is not larger than the level at which management monitors goodwill or the Company's operating segments.

(continued)

Illustration 12-14

Selected Excerpts: Notes on Intangible Assets—Corus Entertainment (continued)

Where goodwill forms part of a CGU and part of the operation within that unit is disposed of, the goodwill associated with the operation disposed of is included in the carrying amount of the operation when determining the gain or loss on disposal of the operation. Goodwill disposed of in this circumstance is measured based on the relative fair value of the operation disposed of and the portion of the CGU retained.

Broadcast licenses and goodwill are tested for impairment annually or more frequently if events or circumstances indicate that they may be impaired. The Company completes its annual testing during the fourth quarter each year.

Broadcast licenses by themselves do not generate cash inflows and therefore, when assessing these assets for impairment, the Company looks to the CGU to which the asset belongs. The identification of CGUs involves judgment and is based on how senior management monitors operations; however, the lowest aggregations of assets that generate largely independent cash inflows represent CGUs for broadcast license impairment testing.

CGUs for broadcast license impairment testing

For the Television segment, the Company has determined that there are two CGUs: (1) specialty and pay television networks that are operated and managed directly by the Company; and (2) other, as these are the levels at which independent cash inflows have been identified. For the Radio segment, the Company has determined that the CGU is a radio cluster whereby a cluster represents a geographic area, generally a city, where radio stations are combined for the purpose of managing performance. These clusters are managed as a single asset by a general manager and overhead costs are allocated amongst the cluster and have independent cash inflows at the cluster level.

Groups of CGUs for goodwill impairment testing

For purposes of impairment testing of goodwill, the Company has grouped the CGUs within the Television and Radio operating segments and is performing the test at the operating segment level. This is the lowest level at which management monitors goodwill for internal management purposes.

Gains or losses arising from derecognition of an intangible asset are measured as the difference between the net disposal proceeds and the carrying amount of the asset and are recognized in the consolidated statements of income and comprehensive income when the asset is derecognized.

9. Broadcast licenses and goodwill

Broadcast licenses and goodwill are tested for impairment annually as at August 31 or more frequently if events or changes in circumstances indicate that they may be impaired. At August 31, 2014, the Company concluded that interim impairment tests were required for goodwill for the Radio segment and for broadcast licenses for certain Radio CGUs. As a result of these tests, the Company recorded goodwill and broadcast license impairment charges of $65.5 million and $17.5 million in fiscal 2014, respectively, as certain radio CGUs had actual results that fell short of previous estimates and the outlook for these markets was less robust.

At August 31, 2014, the Company performed its annual impairment test for fiscal 2014 and determined that there were no further impairments, other than those recorded in the second and third quarters of fiscal 2014, for the year then ended. The changes in the book value of goodwill were as follows:

	Total
Balance—August 31, 2012	646,045
Balance—August 31, 2013	646,045
Acquisitions (note 26)	354,363
Impairments (note 10)	(65,549)
Balance—August 31, 2014	934,859

The changes in the book value of broadcast licenses for the period ended August 31, 2014, were as follows:

	Total
Balance—August 31, 2012	520,770
Impairments	(5,734)
Balance—August 31, 2013	515,036
Acquisitions (note 26)	482,399
Impairments (note 10)	(17,451)
Balance—August 31, 2014	979,984

At August 31, 2013 the Company performed its annual impairment test for fiscal 2013. As certain CGUs had actual results that fell short of previous estimates and the outlook for these markets was less robust, impairment losses of $5,734 were recorded for certain Radio broadcast licenses.

Broadcast licenses and goodwill are located primarily in Canada.

The internal and external sources of information that may indicate an intangible asset is impaired are the same factors described in Illustration 11-14 in Chapter 11 for items of property, plant, and equipment. Of course, evidence of physical damage would not apply in the assessment of an intangible asset! If an assessment indicates there may be impairment, the asset is formally tested by applying the appropriate impairment model.

A summary of the two models and how they are applied is provided in Illustration 12-6. Remember that the **cost recovery impairment model** is used for **ASPE**, and the **rational entity impairment model** is used for **IFRS**. If you review the section "Impairment— Recognition and Measurement Models" in Chapter 11, it might help to reinforce your understanding of the details of each model.

Illustration 12-6

Summary of Impairment Models for Limited-Life Intangible Assets

Cost Recovery Impairment Model	
Concept	Assumes asset will continue to be used; it is impaired only if the asset's carrying amount is not recoverable from the future undiscounted cash flows from use and eventual sale.
Recoverability test	If undiscounted future cash flows ≥ carrying amount, asset is not impaired.
	If undiscounted future cash flows < carrying amount, asset is impaired. Proceed to calculate impairment loss.
Impairment loss	Asset's carrying amount − fair value = impairment loss; fair value is a discounted cash flow, market-based concept.
Entry to record loss	Loss on Impairment $XX
	Accumulated Impairment Losses— $XX Licenses (or "-Patents", etc.)
Subsequent amortization	Review carrying amount to be amortized, useful life, and pattern of amortization and determine new periodic amortization charge.
Reversal of impairment loss	Reversal not permitted. The fair value to which the asset is written down becomes the asset's new cost basis.
If no single-asset identifiable cash flows	Combine with other assets into an asset group, test for impairment, and, if impaired, calculate impairment loss using same approach as for an individual asset. Allocate loss only to long-lived assets, based on their relative carrying amounts, within limits.

Rational Entity Impairment Model	
Concept	Assumes management will use the asset or dispose of it currently, whichever results in a higher return to the entity. It is impaired only if its carrying amount is not recoverable from the more profitable, or less costly, of the two options.
Recoverability test	No separate test of undiscounted cash flows.
Impairment loss	Calculate recoverable amount = **higher of** value in use **and** fair value less costs to sell, both of which are discounted cash flow concepts.
	If recoverable amount ≥ carrying amount, no impairment loss.
	If recoverable amount < carrying amount, impairment loss = the difference.
Entry to record loss under cost model	Loss on Impairment $XX
	Accumulated Impairment Losses— $XX Licenses (or "-Patents", etc.)
Subsequent amortization	Review carrying amount to be amortized, useful life, and pattern of amortization and determine new periodic amortization charge.
Reversal of impairment loss	Reversal of loss is required if estimates underlying recoverable amount have changed. Reversal amount is limited.
If no single-asset identifiable cash flows	Combine with other assets into a cash-generating group and calculate impairment loss using same approach as for an individual asset. Allocate loss to assets based on their relative carrying amounts, within limits.

Impairment of Indefinite-Life Intangibles

Accounting for the impairment of intangible assets with an **indefinite life** is a little different than explained above for limited-life intangibles. These differences and the reasons for them are discussed below.

ASPE

An intangible asset with an indefinite life still needs to be tested for impairment only when events and circumstances indicate there might be impairment, but now the test is different. The impairment test for an indefinite-life asset is a **fair value test**. This test compares the **fair value** of the intangible asset with the asset's carrying amount. If its fair value is less than the carrying amount, an impairment loss equal to the difference is recognized.

Why is there a different standard for indefinite-life intangibles? This one-step test is used because it would be relatively easy for many indefinite-life assets to meet the recoverability test. That is, the undiscounted cash flows would extend many years into the future and the total cash to be recovered tends to add up to a large sum. However, the dollars received in periods far into the future have a much lower value today. **As a result, the separate recoverability test is not used**, and the test compares the carrying amount directly with the asset's fair value—a discounted cash flow concept.

To illustrate, assume that Space Corp. (SC) purchases a broadcast licence for $1,150,000, and that the licence is renewable every seven years if the company provides appropriate service and does not violate the rules and regulations of the Canadian Radio-television and Telecommunications Commission (CRTC). The licence is then renewed with the CRTC twice at a minimal cost, and because cash flows are expected to last indefinitely, the licence is reported as an indefinite-life intangible asset. Assume that SC is beginning to question whether the asset might be impaired because advertising revenues are expected to drop with changing demographics in the area covered by the licence. The following information has been gathered about the benefits of the licence:

Undiscounted future net cash flows expected from its use	$1,800,000
Discounted future net cash flows, or fair value	$ 950,000

Is the licence impaired? Yes. Because the carrying amount of $1,150,000 is more than its fair value of $950,000, an impairment loss of $1,150,000 − $950,000 = $200,000 is indicated.

Space Corp. may either set up and credit an accumulated impairment loss account for the licence or credit the asset account itself. The licence is now reported at a net amount of $950,000, and this is its new "cost" for subsequent accounting.

IFRS

There is only a minor difference in the IFRS standard for impairment for indefinite-life intangibles, as compared with those with limited lives. Assets with an indefinite life are **tested for impairment** by comparing their carrying amount and recoverable value **on an annual basis, whether or not there is any indication of impairment**. Why a stronger standard for these assets? The answer lies in the fact that no expense is being charged against income for such assets on a regular basis. For this reason, the assumption of a continuing recoverable value in excess of book value needs to be regularly tested.

Derecognition

An intangible asset is derecognized when it is disposed of or when its continuing use or disposal is not expected to generate any further economic benefits. Similar to property, plant, and equipment assets, a gain or loss is recognized at this time, equal to the difference between the asset's carrying amount and the proceeds on disposal, if any. The gain or loss on disposal is recognized in income in the period of disposal.

GOODWILL

Objective 7

Explain how goodwill is measured and accounted for after acquisition.

Recognition and Measurement of Goodwill

Recognition of Internally Generated Goodwill

Goodwill that is generated internally is not capitalized in the accounts. Measuring the components of internally generated goodwill is simply too complex, and associating costs incurred with future benefits is too difficult. In fact, the future benefits of goodwill may have no relationship to the costs that were incurred to develop it. To add to the complexity, goodwill may even exist when there have been no specific expenditures to develop it. In addition, because no transaction has taken place with outside parties, a great deal of subjectivity—even misrepresentation—might be involved in trying to measure it.

Purchased Goodwill

As previously indicated, goodwill is recognized only when a business combination occurs, because the value of goodwill cannot be separated from a business as a whole. The problem of determining the proper values to assign to identifiable intangible assets in a business combination is complex because of the many different types of intangibles that might be acquired. Because goodwill is a residual amount, every dollar that is assigned to other assets, including identifiable intangible assets, leaves one less dollar to be assigned to goodwill.

To illustrate, assume that Multi-Diversified, Inc. decides that it needs a parts division to supplement its existing tractor distributorship. The president of Multi-Diversified is interested in buying Tractorling Ltd., a small company near Edmonton that has an established reputation and is looking to sell its business. Illustration 12-7 shows Tractorling's current statement of financial position.

Illustration 12-7

Tractorling Ltd. Statement of Financial Position

TRACTORLING LTD. Statement of Financial Position December 31, 2017			
Assets		**Liabilities and equity**	
Cash	$ 25,000	Current liabilities	$ 55,000
Accounts receivable	35,000	Share capital	20,000
Inventories	42,000	Retained earnings	180,000
Property, plant, and equipment (net)	153,000		
Total assets	$255,000	Total liabilities and equity	$255,000

After considerable negotiation, Tractorling Ltd.'s shareholders decide to accept Multi-Diversified's offer of $400,000. The two companies might agree on a $400,000 cash payment, or $400,000 in value of Multi-Diversified's shares, or other forms of consideration. How should goodwill, if any, be measured?

The answer is not obvious. The fair values of Tractorling's identifiable assets and liabilities are not disclosed in its cost-based statement of financial position. It is likely, though, that as the negotiations progressed, Multi-Diversified had a detailed investigation done of Tractorling's underlying assets to determine their fair values. Such an investigation may be done through a purchase audit by Multi-Diversified's auditors, or an independent appraisal from some other source. Illustration 12-8 shows the results.

Illustration 12-8

Fair Values of Tractorling Ltd.'s Identifiable Net Assets

Fair Values, December 31, 2017	
Cash	$ 25,000
Accounts receivable	35,000
Inventories	62,000
Property, plant, and equipment (net)	265,000
Patents	18,000
Liabilities	(55,000)
Fair value of identifiable net assets	$350,000

Differences between the current fair value and carrying amount are more common among long-term assets, although there can also be significant differences in the current asset category. Cash is obviously not a problem in terms of its value. Receivables are normally fairly close to their current valuation, although adjustments do sometimes need to be made because of inadequate bad debt provisions. The fair values of current liabilities also are usually close to their recorded book values. However, if interest rates have changed since long-term liabilities were issued, their value determined using current interest rates may be quite different from their carrying amount. A careful analysis must also be done to ensure that there are no unrecorded liabilities.

Returning to our example, the $20,000 difference between the fair value and carrying amount of Tractorling's inventories ($62,000 − $42,000) could be due to several factors. One explanation might be that Tractorling acquired significant inventories when the prices were lower and uses specific identification or an average cost valuation, in which ending inventory includes inventory at older costs.

In many cases, the values of long-lived assets such as property, plant, and equipment and intangibles may have increased substantially over the years. This difference could be due to inaccurate estimates of useful lives, continual expensing of small expenditures (say, amounts less than $500), or substantial increases in replacement costs. Alternatively, there may be assets that have not been recognized in the company's books. In Tractorling's case, land was acquired many years ago and its fair value has increased significantly, and internally developed patents have not been recognized in the accounts, yet they have a fair value of $18,000.

Since the investigation indicates that the fair value of the identifiable net assets is $350,000, why would Multi-Diversified pay $400,000? Tractorling might point to the company's established reputation, good credit rating, top management team, well-trained employees, and so on as factors that make the value of the business as a whole greater than $350,000. Multi-Diversified places a premium on the future earning power of these attributes as well as the company's current basic asset structure. At this point in the negotiations, Tractorling's total fair value, and price, may be due to many factors; the most important may be sheer skill at the bargaining table.

Multi-Diversified labels the difference between the fair value of the consideration paid of $400,000 and the fair value of the identifiable net assets of $350,000 as goodwill. Goodwill is viewed as the unidentifiable values plus the value of the identifiable intangibles that do not meet the criteria for separate recognition. The procedure for valuation shown in Illustration 12-9 is referred to as a master valuation approach, because goodwill is assumed to cover all the values that cannot be specifically associated with any identifiable tangible or intangible asset. Note that this method of accounting for a business combination is a fair value approach rather than one based on the cost of the acquisition and cost allocation. For example, acquisition-related costs associated with a business combination are expensed as incurred and are not capitalized as they would be in a cost-based system.

	Illustration 12-9	
Determination of Goodwill— Master Valuation Approach		

Fair value of consideration transferred:		$400,000
Fair value of identifiable net assets:		
Cash	$ 25,000	
Accounts receivable	35,000	
Inventories	62,000	
Property, plant, and equipment	265,000	
Patents	18,000	
Liabilities	(55,000)	350,000
Value assigned to goodwill:		$ 50,000

Multi-Diversified's entry to record the purchase of Tractorling's net assets, assuming the consideration is $400,000 cash, is as follows:[25]

Cash	25,000	
Accounts Receivable	35,000	
Inventory	62,000	
Property, Plant, and Equipment	265,000	
Intangible Assets—Patents	18,000	
Goodwill	50,000	
Liabilities		55,000
Cash		400,000

A = L + SE
+55,000 +55,000
Cash flows: ↓ 375,000 outflow

Bargain Purchase

A **bargain purchase**, resulting in what is sometimes called **negative goodwill**, arises when the total of the fair value of the identifiable net assets acquired is higher than the fair value of the consideration transferred for those net assets. This situation is a result of market imperfection (or a poor decision by the seller) because the seller would be better off to sell the assets individually than in total. However, situations do occur when the value of what is given up is less than the value of the identifiable net assets that are acquired, and this requires accounting for a goodwill "credit."

How should this credit be handled in the accounts? Should it be taken to Retained Earnings directly, to Other Comprehensive Income, to net income in the year of purchase, or amortized to income over a reasonable future period? The accounting standards over the past 45 years or so have taken a variety of approaches to this "bonus," which shows the difficulty there has been in coming to terms with its conceptual nature.

Current standards require the excess to be recognized **as a gain in net income** in the same period that the combination takes place. However, this cannot be done without a thorough reassessment of all the variables, values, and measurement procedures used that resulted in this gain. If a gain still results from the re-examination, then it is recognized in income. While some critics do not agree with recognizing a gain **on the acquisition of assets**, this treatment is not applied lightly and appears to be a practical approach to a situation that rarely occurs.

Valuation after Acquisition

Once goodwill has been recognized in the accounts, how should it be treated in subsequent periods? Three basic approaches have been suggested:

1. **Charge goodwill immediately to expense.** Supporters of this approach justify an immediate write-off because the accounting for goodwill is then consistent whether purchased or created internally. Goodwill created internally is not recognized as an asset. Perhaps the best rationale for charging goodwill against income directly is that identifying the periods over which the future benefits are to be received is so difficult that the result is purely arbitrary.

2. **Amortize goodwill over its useful life.** Others believe that goodwill has value when it is acquired, but that its value eventually disappears. Therefore the asset should be charged to expense over the periods that are affected. To the extent that goodwill represents a wasting asset, this method provides a better matching of the costs of the benefits to revenues than other methods, even though the useful life may be difficult to determine.

3. **Retain goodwill indefinitely unless a reduction in value occurs.** Others believe that goodwill can have an indefinite life and should be kept as an asset until a decline in value occurs. Some form of goodwill should always be an asset because the current costs to maintain or enhance the purchased goodwill are being expensed. Also, unless there is strong evidence that a decline in its value has occurred, a write-off of goodwill is arbitrary and leads to distortions in net income.

Not so long ago, companies were required to amortize goodwill over a period no longer than 40 years. However, as we saw in the opening story, goodwill acquired in a business combination **is now considered to have an indefinite life and is no longer amortized**. Although goodwill may decrease over time, predicting the actual life of goodwill and an appropriate pattern of amortization is extremely difficult. Therefore, it is carried on the statement of financial position at the amount originally recognized in the combination less any subsequent impairment losses. **Income statements are not charged with any amounts paid for the goodwill until the asset is considered impaired.**

WHAT DO THE NUMBERS MEAN?

The opening story to the chapter referred to a study of goodwill impairment conducted by Duff & Phelps and the Canadian Financial Executives Research Foundation. The study also included a summary of a survey of members of the Financial Executives International (FEI Canada). These members stated that the top challenges for companies when performing goodwill impairment tests were developing cash flow projections, identifying cash-generating units (CGUs), determining the discount rate to be used for estimation, and properly identifying impairment indicators for CGUs.

REAL WORLD EMPHASIS

Objective **8**

Explain and account for impairment of goodwill.

Impairment of Goodwill

Goodwill is not an identifiable asset and cannot generate cash flows independently of other assets. Because it can be acquired only in combination with other assets making up a business, it has to be assigned to a reporting unit or cash-generating unit (CGU) in order to be tested for impairment. An example of a CGU is the Markets division of Thomson Reuters in our feature story, which recorded goodwill impairment. Other than this specific facet that focuses on the reporting unit or CGU, impairment accounting for goodwill is similar to that for intangibles with an indefinite life. Applying the standards in this area can be complex, but we provide a summary of the basic elements in Illustration 12-10 under both ASPE and IFRS.

Illustration 12-10

Summary of Accounting for Impairment of Goodwill

	ASPE	IFRS
Apply impairment test...	...when events or changes in circumstances indicate	...annually, and whenever there is an indication that the CGU may be impaired
At acquisition date, assign goodwill...	...to a reporting unit: an operating segment or one level below	...to cash-generating unit: smallest identifiable group of assets where goodwill is monitored for management purposes, and no larger than an operating segment
There is an impairment loss...	...when carrying amount of reporting unit including goodwill > fair value of reporting unit. Loss = amount of excess	...when carrying amount of CGU including goodwill > recoverable amount. Loss = amount of excess. Recoverable amount is the higher of value in use and fair value less costs to sell
Impairment loss is allocated...	...to goodwill as a goodwill impairment loss; impairment test for other assets in group is done before goodwill impairment test	...first to goodwill related to the CGU, then remainder to other assets on a relative carrying amount (proportionate) basis
Goodwill impairment reversal...	...is not permitted	...is not permitted

To illustrate impairment accounting for goodwill, assume that Coburg Corporation has three divisions. One division, Pritt Products, was purchased four years ago for $2 million and has been identified as a reporting unit. Unfortunately, it has experienced operating losses over the last three quarters and management is reviewing the reporting unit to determine whether there has been an impairment of goodwill. The carrying amounts of Pritt Division's net assets, including the associated goodwill of $900,000, are listed in Illustration 12-11.

Illustration 12-11

Pritt Reporting Unit—Carrying Amount of Net Assets Including Goodwill

Cash	$ 200,000
Receivables	300,000
Inventory	700,000
Property, plant, and equipment (net)	800,000
Goodwill	900,000
Less: Accounts and notes payable	(500,000)
Net assets, at carrying amounts	$2,400,000

Situation 1: The fair value of the Pritt Division reporting unit as a whole is estimated to be $2.8 million. Management determines that the unit's value in use is $2.9 million and that the company would incur direct costs of $50,000 if the unit were sold.

Under **ASPE**, the goodwill is not impaired. The asset group's $2.4-million carrying value is less than its fair value of $2.8 million. Under **IFRS**, goodwill is not considered impaired either. The recoverable amount of the unit is $2.9 million—the higher of its value in use ($2.9 million) and its fair value less costs to sell ($2,800,000 − $50,000)—and this exceeds the unit's carrying amount of $2.4 million.

Situation 2: The fair value of the Pritt Division cash-generating unit as a whole is $1.9 million, its value in use is $2.1 million, and the direct cost of selling the unit is $50,000.

Under **ASPE**, an impairment loss is indicated:

Carrying amount of unit, including goodwill	$2,400,000
Fair value of unit	1,900,000
Goodwill impairment loss	$ 500,000

Under **IFRS**, an impairment loss is also indicated:

Carrying amount of unit, including goodwill		$ 2,400,000
Recoverable amount of unit: higher of		
Value in use	$2,100,000	
and		(2,100,000)
Fair value less costs to sell	$1,850,000	
Goodwill impairment loss		$ 300,000

The entries to record the losses under ASPE and IFRS are shown in Illustration 12-12.

Illustration 12-12

Entry to Record Impairment of Goodwill under ASPE and IFRS

A = L + SE
ASPE
−500,000   −500,000
IFRS
−300,000   −300,000
Cash flows: No effect

	ASPE	IFRS
Loss on Impairment	500,000	300,000
Accumulated Impairment Losses-Goodwill	500,000	300,000

Because there is a requirement to report the gross amount of goodwill and accumulated impairment losses at the end of the period, the Accumulated Impairment Losses account is credited instead of the Goodwill account so that the required information is retained. The Goodwill's net carrying amount is now $400,000 ($900,000 − $500,000) under ASPE and $600,000 ($900,000 − $300,000) under IFRS.

Illustration 12-13 summarizes the impairment tests for various intangible assets.

Illustration 12-13

Summary of Intangible Asset Impairment Tests

	Impairment Test	
Type of Asset	ASPE	IFRS
Limited-life intangible	Recoverability test; if failed, write down to fair value	Compare carrying amount with recoverable amount
Indefinite-life intangible	Compare carrying amount with fair value	Compare carrying amount with recoverable amount
Goodwill	Compare carrying amount of reporting unit with its fair value	Compare carrying amount of CGU with its recoverable amount

PRESENTATION, DISCLOSURE, AND ANALYSIS

Objective 9

Identify the types of disclosure requirements for intangible assets and goodwill and explain the issues in analyzing these assets.

REAL WORLD EMPHASIS

A survey indicates that the most common types of intangible assets reported are broadcast rights, publishing rights, trademarks, patents, licences, customer lists, non-competition agreements, franchises, and purchased R&D.[26] These, along with goodwill, have become an increasingly large proportion of companies' reported assets, making intangibles an important contributor to entity performance and financial position. For example, **Corus Entertainment Inc.**, a Canadian-based media and entertainment company, reported indefinite-life broadcast licences and goodwill at August 31, 2014, that amounted to 68.8% of its total assets. There were charges for impairment in both 2014 and 2013, after a period of stability for these intangibles; from 2010 to 2012, there were no impairment charges. The company recognized $83.0 million of impairment losses on these two classes of assets in 2014 ($5.7 million in 2013). The write-offs in 2014 represented about 7% of their opening book value, with the impairment being due, in part, to a soft advertising market and "ratings challenges in some markets." The CGUs affected by the write-offs were predominantly in Ontario for the broadcast licence impairment and in the radio CGU group segment overall for goodwill.

Presentation and Disclosure

Overview

While there are few required disclosures on the face of the statement of financial position and the statement of comprehensive income, a significant amount of information is required in the notes to the financial statements, particularly those prepared under IFRS. As seen in previous chapters, ASPE disclosures are considerably curtailed because most users of their financial statements can request additional information as needed. The goal of disclosure for publicly accountable entities is basically to allow readers to understand the significance of intangibles and goodwill to the operations of the business. To that end, this section summarizes some of the major disclosures required.

For each class of intangible asset, and separately for internally generated intangibles and other intangible assets, the following information is required:

- whether their lives are indefinite or finite (limited), useful life, methods and rates of amortization, and the line where amortization is included on the statement of comprehensive income;

- the carrying amount of intangible assets with an indefinite life, and the reasons supporting an assessment of an indefinite life;

- a reconciliation of the opening and ending balances of their carrying amount and accumulated amortization and impairment losses, separately identifying each reason for an increase or decrease; and

- impairment losses and reversals of impairment losses and where they are reported in the statement of comprehensive income.

For each material impairment loss recognized or reversed in the period, the following is required:

- the circumstances that led to its recognition, the amount recognized, the nature of the asset or cash-generating unit, and information about how the recoverable amount was determined.

For each cash-generating unit or group of units that has a significant amount of goodwill or intangible assets with an indefinite life, the following is required:

- how the unit's recoverable amount was determined, as well as assumptions underlying the calculation of the recoverable amount.

For intangible assets measured using the revaluation model, the following is required:

- their carrying amount, the carrying amounts if the revaluation model had not been applied, the date of the revaluation, the amount of the associated revaluation surplus and changes in that account, and the methods and assumptions used in estimating fair values.

This list identifies only some of the disclosures. The best source of the specific requirements is the standards themselves.

Illustration of Disclosures

Excerpts from the financial statements of Corus Entertainment for its year ended August 31, 2014, are provided in Illustration 12-14. These disclosures are based on IFRS, which the company adopted in 2012 and are similar to ASPE. This company, reporting in millions of Canadian dollars, operates through two main lines of business: television and radio. Its 24 television networks include YTV, Treehouse, TELETOON, W Network, and HBO Canada.

Illustration 12-14

Selected Excerpts: Notes on Intangible Assets—Corus Entertainment

---

3. Significant accounting policies

The consolidated financial statements have been prepared on a cost basis, except for derivative and available-for-sale financial assets, which have been measured at fair value.

GOODWILL AND INTANGIBLE ASSETS

Intangible assets acquired separately are measured on initial recognition at cost. Intangible assets acquired in a business combination are measured at fair value as at the date of acquisition. Following initial recognition, intangible assets are carried at cost less accumulated amortization and accumulated impairment charges, if any. Internally generated intangible assets such as goodwill, brands and customer lists, excluding capitalized program and film development costs, are not capitalized and expenditures are reflected in the consolidated statements of income and comprehensive income in the year in which the expenditure is incurred. Intangible assets are recognized separately from goodwill when they are separable or arise from contractual or other legal rights and their fair value can be measured reliably. The useful lives of intangible assets are assessed as either finite or indefinite.

Intangible assets with finite lives are amortized over their useful economic lives and assessed for impairment whenever there is an indication that the intangible assets may be impaired. The amortization period and the amortization method for intangible assets with finite useful lives are reviewed at least at the end of each reporting period. Changes in the expected useful life or the expected pattern of consumption of future economic benefits embodied in the assets are accounted for by changing the amortization period or method, as appropriate, and are treated as changes in accounting estimates. The amortization expense on intangible assets with finite lives is recognized in the consolidated statements of income and comprehensive income in the expense category, consistent with the function of the intangible assets.

Amortization is recorded on a straight-line basis over the estimated useful life of the asset as follows:

Brand names, trademarks and digital rights	Agreement term
Software, patents and customer lists	3–5 years

Intangible assets with indefinite useful lives are not amortized. Broadcast licenses are considered to have an indefinite life based on management's intent and ability to renew the licenses without significant cost and without material modification of the existing terms and conditions of the license. The assessment of indefinite life is reviewed annually to determine whether the indefinite life continues to be supportable. If not, the change in useful life from indefinite to finite is made on a prospective basis.

Goodwill is initially measured at cost, being the excess of the aggregate of the consideration transferred and the amount recognized for non-controlling interest over the net identifiable assets acquired and liabilities assumed. If this consideration is lower than the fair value of the net identifiable assets of the subsidiary acquired, the difference is recognized in profit or loss.

After initial recognition, goodwill is measured at cost less any accumulated impairment losses. For the purpose of impairment testing, goodwill acquired in a business combination is, from the acquisition date, allocated to a CGU or group of CGUs that are expected to benefit from the synergies of the combination, irrespective of whether other assets or liabilities of the acquiree are assigned to those units. The group of CGUs is not larger than the level at which management monitors goodwill or the Company's operating segments.

(continued)

Where goodwill forms part of a CGU and part of the operation within that unit is disposed of, the goodwill associated with the operation disposed of is included in the carrying amount of the operation when determining the gain or loss on disposal of the operation. Goodwill disposed of in this circumstance is measured based on the relative fair value of the operation disposed of and the portion of the CGU retained.

Broadcast licenses and goodwill are tested for impairment annually or more frequently if events or circumstances indicate that they may be impaired. The Company completes its annual testing during the fourth quarter each year.

Broadcast licenses by themselves do not generate cash inflows and therefore, when assessing these assets for impairment, the Company looks to the CGU to which the asset belongs. The identification of CGUs involves judgment and is based on how senior management monitors operations; however, the lowest aggregations of assets that generate largely independent cash inflows represent CGUs for broadcast license impairment testing.

CGUs for broadcast license impairment testing

For the Television segment, the Company has determined that there are two CGUs: (1) specialty and pay television networks that are operated and managed directly by the Company; and (2) other, as these are the levels at which independent cash inflows have been identified. For the Radio segment, the Company has determined that the CGU is a radio cluster whereby a cluster represents a geographic area, generally a city, where radio stations are combined for the purpose of managing performance. These clusters are managed as a single asset by a general manager and overhead costs are allocated amongst the cluster and have independent cash inflows at the cluster level.

Groups of CGUs for goodwill impairment testing

For purposes of impairment testing of goodwill, the Company has grouped the CGUs within the Television and Radio operating segments and is performing the test at the operating segment level. This is the lowest level at which management monitors goodwill for internal management purposes.

Gains or losses arising from derecognition of an intangible asset are measured as the difference between the net disposal proceeds and the carrying amount of the asset and are recognized in the consolidated statements of income and comprehensive income when the asset is derecognized.

9. Broadcast licenses and goodwill

Broadcast licenses and goodwill are tested for impairment annually as at August 31 or more frequently if events or changes in circumstances indicate that they may be impaired. At August 31, 2014, the Company concluded that interim impairment tests were required for goodwill for the Radio segment and for broadcast licenses for certain Radio CGUs. As a result of these tests, the Company recorded goodwill and broadcast license impairment charges of $65.5 million and $17.5 million in fiscal 2014, respectively, as certain radio CGUs had actual results that fell short of previous estimates and the outlook for these markets was less robust.

At August 31, 2014, the Company performed its annual impairment test for fiscal 2014 and determined that there were no further impairments, other than those recorded in the second and third quarters of fiscal 2014, for the year then ended. The changes in the book value of goodwill were as follows:

	Total
Balance—August 31, 2012	646,045
Balance—August 31, 2013	646,045
Acquisitions (note 26)	354,363
Impairments (note 10)	(65,549)
Balance—August 31, 2014	934,859

The changes in the book value of broadcast licenses for the period ended August 31, 2014, were as follows:

	Total
Balance—August 31, 2012	520,770
Impairments	(5,734)
Balance—August 31, 2013	515,036
Acquisitions (note 26)	482,399
Impairments (note 10)	(17,451)
Balance—August 31, 2014	979,984

At August 31, 2013 the Company performed its annual impairment test for fiscal 2013. As certain CGUs had actual results that fell short of previous estimates and the outlook for these markets was less robust, impairment losses of $5,734 were recorded for certain Radio broadcast licenses.

Broadcast licenses and goodwill are located primarily in Canada.

Analysis

Missing Values

REAL WORLD EMPHASIS

The requirement that most research and development phase costs incurred for internally developed intangibles be expensed immediately is a conservative, practical solution that ensures consistency in practice and uniformity among companies. But the practice of immediately writing off expenditures that are made in the expectation of benefiting future periods cannot always be justified on the grounds that it is good accounting theory.

Since the 1990s, the conventional financial-accounting model has been increasingly criticized for its inability to capture many of the attributes that give a business value. In July 2015, for example, Apple Inc. had a total book value of approximately U.S. $129 billion, while its market capitalization (the market value of its outstanding shares) was over U.S. $700 billion.[27] Why such a significant difference?

UNDERLYING CONCEPT

These decisions represent some of the older trade-offs between relevance and reliability. With a growing emphasis on faithful representation over verifiability, standard setters may be taking another look at existing standards.

The answer is that financial accounting does not capture and report many of the assets that contribute to future cash flows, and this is seen by some critics as the greatest challenge facing the accounting profession today. Many of the missing values belong to unrecognized, internally developed intangible assets known as **knowledge assets** or **intellectual capital**. These include the value of key personnel (not only Tim Cook, the CEO successor to Apple co-founder Steve Jobs, but the many creative and technologically proficient employees in general), the investment in products from research and development and their potential, organizational adaptability, customer retention, strategic direction, brands, flexible and innovative management, customer service capability, and effective advertising programs, to name only a few types of knowledge assets. When a company is not allowed to capitalize many of these expenditures, this excludes from its statement of financial position what may be its most valuable assets.

These indicators of longer-term value that are created in an organization will ultimately result in realized values through future transactions and, therefore, are relevant information for financial statement readers. Companies increasingly disclose more of this "soft" information in annual reports outside the financial statements, in news releases, and in interviews with market analysts. While some observers believe that standard setters should work to ensure that more of these intangibles are captured on the statement of financial position, others believe that new frameworks for reporting performance need to be developed together with—or that they should even replace—the current financial reporting model.

FINANCIAL ANALYSIS AND PLANNING
5.1.1, 5.1.2

Our conventional accounting model captures the results of past transactions. This has been considered a very significant benefit because it is what makes it possible to verify the reported measures and therefore add to the reliability of the financial statements. In most cases, the intellectual capital and knowledge assets identified above cannot be measured in financial terms with enough reliability to give them accounting recognition. Some cannot be included as assets because of the enterprise's inability to control access to the benefits. Investments that are made in employee education and development, for example, can walk out the door when employees leave the company to work elsewhere. Others argue that the amount of costs charged to expense in each accounting period is about the same whether there is immediate expensing or capitalization followed by amortization, because most companies continuously invest in a variety of research, development, and other activities.

THEORY

Others opposed to increased capitalization of costs point to the decline in market value of technology shares—in particular, from early 2000 to 2001. **Microsoft**, a key company in the high-tech sector, lost over 60% of its value in this period, bringing it much closer to its book value. Some use this as an argument that the historical cost model still has much to recommend it! The "truth," of course, lies somewhere in between. While inflated market values are not reliable enough to support the recognition of previously unrecognized intangible asset value, the historical-cost, transactions-based model certainly fails to capture many of the things at the heart of corporate value. Much research is being carried out in the search for solutions to the discrepancies between what gets reported as having value on the financial statements and what the capital markets perceive as having value and therefore reflect in share prices.

Comparing Results

When comparing the operating results of companies—either of one company over time or between companies—it is not only important to pay close attention to which set of GAAP each applies. It is also important to examine how deferred charges, intangible assets, and goodwill have been accounted for and how any changes in related accounting policies have been handled. This is important because the standards for intangibles have changed significantly in recent years and may continue to change. Montreal-based communications company **Quebecor Inc.**, for example, like other companies when they first adopted IFRS, was required to review its existing goodwill and was permitted to recognize any impairment as an adjustment to its opening balance of retained earnings. So, when IFRS was first applied, Quebecor recognized a goodwill impairment loss of $2.2 billion—a charge that bypassed the income statement completely, and went straight against retained earnings! Quebecor thus took a "big bath" writedown—writing down goodwill that it had previously reported as an asset. This means that these costs will never flow through the company's income statement, and future operating statements are freed from them.[28] Care has to be taken when calculating and interpreting any ratios that include earnings and asset numbers, especially when the results of different years are being compared.

IFRS/ASPE COMPARISON

A Comparison of IFRS and ASPE

Objective **10**
Identify differences in
accounting between
IFRS and ASPE.

With a few specific exceptions, accounting for intangible assets and goodwill under IFRS and ASPE is very similar. Illustration 12-15 identifies the relevant standards that apply to intangible assets and goodwill for both and the areas of difference that exist.

Illustration 12-15

*IFRS and ASPE Comparison
Chart*

		IFRS—IAS 23, 36, and 38; IFRS 2, 3, and 13	**Accounting Standards for Private Enterprises (ASPE)— CPA *Canada Handbook*, Part II, Sections 1582, 3063, 3064, 3475, and 3831**	**References to Related Illustrations and Select Brief Exercises**
Measurement at acquisition		Borrowing costs directly attributable to the acquisition, construction, or development of qualifying assets are capitalized.	Interest costs directly attributable to the acquisition, construction, or development of an intangible asset, once it meets the criteria to be capitalized, may be capitalized or expensed, depending on the entity's accounting policy.	BE12-3
		Costs associated with the development of internally generated intangible assets are capitalized when six specific conditions are met in the development stage.	Costs associated with the development of internally generated intangible assets that meet the six specific conditions in the development stage may be capitalized or expensed, depending on the entity's accounting policy.	BE12-9
Measurement after acquisition		Intangible assets are accounted for under the cost model or the revaluation model. The latter is used only when the asset has an active market fair value.	Intangible assets are accounted for according to the cost model.	Illustration 12-4 and BE12-15

(continued)

Illustration 12-15

IFRS and ASPE Comparison Chart (continued)

Impairment of intangible assets	Assess limited-life intangible assets for potential impairment at the end of each reporting period; for those with an indefinite life, this includes calculating the (IFRS) recoverable amount and comparing it with book value.	Test both limited and indefinite-life intangibles for potential impairment whenever events and changing circumstances indicate the carrying value may not be recoverable.	Illustration 12-6
	For limited-life intangibles, apply the rational entity impairment model.	For limited-life intangibles, apply the cost recovery impairment model.	Illustrations 12-6 and 12-13 BE12-15, BE12-16, and BE12-17
	For indefinite-life intangibles, apply the rational entity impairment model.	For indefinite-life intangibles, impairment test is comparison of carrying amount with asset's fair value; loss is equal to the difference when fair value is lower.	Illustration 12-13 BE12-18
	Impairment losses are reversed for recoveries related to economic changes.	Impairment losses are not reversed.	
Impairment of goodwill	Similar to impairment of indefinite-life intangible assets, except that there is no reversal of an impairment loss for goodwill. See also Illustration 12-10.	Similar to impairment of indefinite-life intangible assets. See also Illustration 12-10.	Illustrations 12-10, 12-12, and 12-13 BE12-20 and BE12-21
Disclosures	Significant disclosures are required including detailed reconciliations between opening and ending balances for each type of intangible and goodwill. Considerable information is also required whenever fair values are used to explain how they are determined, as well as background information about impairment losses on goodwill and intangibles.	Basic disclosures are required about the balance of intangible assets and goodwill on the balance sheet with additional details by classes and whether or not they are amortized. Details explaining each impairment loss and where each is reported on the income statement are also required.	Illustration 12-14

Looking Ahead

Whether recognized or not, intangible assets are an increasingly important aspect of what gives an entity value, and existing standards do not do a very good job of reporting these assets to users of the financial statements. Current standards significantly restrict the intangibles that can be recognized, and after acquisition, only intangibles with fair values determined in an active market can use the revaluation model under IFRS. Also, there are inconsistent treatments of intangible assets developed internally and those acquired in a business combination, as well as of internally developed property, plant, and equipment assets.

As discussed in Chapter 11, IAS 36 *Impairment of Assets* was amended for annual periods starting on or after January 1, 2014, to require additional disclosures for impairment losses recognized or reversed during the period. For example, the level of the fair value hierarchy used for fair value measurements under IFRS 13 must be disclosed.

Effective January 1, 2016, IAS 38.92 was clarified such that there is an underlying assumption (which the IASB refers to as a "rebuttable presumption") that amortization methods based on revenue generated by an activity that includes the use of an intangible asset are inappropriate.

The AcSB (in May 2014) agreed with the Private Enterprise Advisory Committee's recommendation to undertake research on alternative approaches to accounting for goodwill, but such research is only expected to begin when staff resources become available after considering higher-priority projects.

The IASB considered a proposal for a joint project with the FASB relating to accounting for identifiable intangible assets, but in December 2007 the IASB decided not to add the project to its agenda. With so many other possible projects competing for time and resources, it is unlikely that there will be changes in the intangible asset standards in the short to medium term.

SUMMARY OF LEARNING OBJECTIVES

1 Understand the importance of goodwill and intangible assets from a business perspective and describe their characteristics.

We have an economy that is increasingly dominated by information and service providers, and their major assets are often intangible in nature. Identifying and measuring intangible assets tends to be difficult, and as a result many intangibles are not captured on companies' statements of financial position. However, intangible assets and goodwill remain critically important for companies, and are a key focus of standard setters in North America and internationally.

Intangible assets have three characteristics: (1) they are identifiable, (2) they lack physical substance, and (3) they are nonmonetary in nature. Goodwill represents the difference between the fair value of the identifiable assets acquired and liabilities assumed and the consideration given when a company acquires another business.

2 Identify and apply the recognition and measurement requirements for purchased intangible assets.

A purchased intangible asset is recognized when it is probable that the entity will receive the expected future economic benefits and when its cost can be measured reliably. It is measured initially at cost. When several intangibles, or a combination of intangibles and other assets, are acquired in a business combination, the cost of each intangible asset is its fair value. When acquired in a business combination, the identifiable intangibles are recognized separately from the goodwill component.

3 Identify and apply the recognition and measurement requirements for internally developed intangible assets.

No costs are capitalized unless they meet the general recognition criteria concerning future benefits and measurability. Costs incurred in the research phase of developing an intangible asset internally are expensed. Costs incurred in the development phase of a project are also expensed unless the entity can demonstrate that it meets six stringent criteria. These criteria are designed to provide evidence that the asset is technically and financially feasible and that the company has the intent and ability to generate future economic benefits from it. Under ASPE, entities have a choice whether to capitalize or expense costs that meet the six criteria.

4 Explain how intangible assets are accounted for after initial recognition.

Under ASPE, intangible assets are accounted for using the cost model, whereas IFRS also allows the revaluation model to be used if the asset's fair value is determined in an active market. This is not often used. An intangible with a finite or limited useful life is amortized over its useful life to the entity. Except in unusual and specific circumstances, the residual value is assumed to be zero. The amount to report for amortization expense should reflect the pattern in which the asset is consumed or used up if that pattern can be reliably determined. Otherwise, a straight-line approach is used. An intangible with an indefinite life is not amortized until its life is determined to no longer be indefinite. All intangibles are tested for impairment.

5 Identify and explain the accounting for specific types of intangible assets.

Major types of intangibles include the following: (1) marketing-related intangibles that are used in the marketing or promotion of products or services, (2) customer-related intangibles that result from interactions with outside parties, (3) artistic-related intangibles that involve ownership rights to such items as plays and literary works, (4) contract-related intangibles that represent the value of rights that arise from contractual arrangements, and (5) technology-related intangible assets that relate to innovations or technological advances.

6 Explain and account for impairment of limited-life and indefinite-life intangible assets.

Under ASPE, impairment is determined and applied by using the cost recovery impairment model. Impairment for *limited-life* intangible assets is based first on a recoverability test. If the carrying amount is higher than the asset's (undiscounted) net recoverable amount, then an impairment loss must be measured and recognized, based on the asset's fair value. No reversals of such losses are permitted. The procedures are the same as for property, plant, and equipment. *Indefinite-life* intangibles use only a fair value test. Under IFRS, the rational entity impairment model is used. An intangible asset is impaired only if its carrying amount is higher than its recoverable amount. The recoverable amount is defined as the greater of the asset's value in use and its fair value less costs to sell. The impairment loss is the difference between the carrying amount and the recoverable amount, if lower. The loss is reversed subsequently if economic conditions change and the recoverable amount increases. The same approach is used for both limited-life and indefinite-life intangible assets.

7 Explain how goodwill is measured and accounted for after acquisition.

Goodwill is unique because, unlike all other assets, it can be identified only with the business as a whole. It is not an identifiable asset. Goodwill is recorded only when a business is purchased. To calculate goodwill in a 100% acquisition, the fair value of the identifiable assets that are acquired and liabilities that are assumed is compared with the fair value of the consideration transferred for the acquired business. The difference is goodwill. After acquisition, it is not amortized but is regularly assessed for impairment.

8 Explain and account for impairment of goodwill.

Goodwill is assigned to a cash-generating group or reporting unit and the group is tested for impairment. Under ASPE, a goodwill impairment loss is recognized if the fair value of the asset group is lower than the group's carrying amount, and the loss is equal to the difference. Under IFRS, there is a goodwill impairment loss if the recoverable amount of the cash-generating unit is less than its carrying amount. The loss is equal to the difference and is applied to goodwill first. Under **both** ASPE and IFRS, goodwill impairment losses are not reversed.

9 Identify the types of disclosure requirements for intangible assets and goodwill and explain the issues in analyzing these assets.

Disclosures under ASPE are limited because users can typically access additional information. Under IFRS, significant details are required to be disclosed. The disclosures allow a reader to determine how amounts invested in classes of intangibles (and goodwill) have changed over the period, with substantial information provided when fair values are used, such as under the revaluation model and all impairment calculations. For intangibles that are not amortized, companies must indicate the amount of any impairment losses that have been recognized as well as information about the circumstances that led to the write-down. Goodwill must be separately reported, as must the major classes of intangible assets. Because it is difficult to measure intangibles, some resources, such as intellectual capital and other internally developed intangible assets, do not get captured on the statement of financial position. Other intangibles are recognized, but with a relatively high level of measurement uncertainty. For these reasons and because of recent changes in the accounting policy related to intangibles, care must be taken when analyzing financial statement information related to earnings and total assets.

10 Identify differences in accounting between IFRS and ASPE.

There are few, but significant, differences between ASPE and IFRS regarding intangible assets and goodwill. One major difference is the accounting treatment for costs incurred in the development phase of internally generated intangible assets that meet the six stringent criteria for capitalization. Under ASPE, entities can choose whether to capitalize these costs or expense all costs associated with internally generated intangibles. Under IFRS, these costs are capitalized. The other major difference is the impairment models applied: the cost recovery model for ASPE, and the rational entity model for IFRS.

KEY TERMS

acquirer, p. 694

active market, p. 701

artistic-related intangible assets, p. 706

bargain purchase, p. 713

brand, p. 704

brand name, p. 704

business combination, p. 697

computer software costs, p. 708

contract-based intangible assets, p. 706

copyright, p. 706

cost recovery impairment model, p. 709

customer-related intangible assets, p. 705

development, p. 698

development phase, p. 698

economic benefits, p. 695

favourable lease, p. 707

finite life, p. 702

franchise, p. 706

goodwill, p. 694

identifiable, p. 695

identifiable net assets, p. 694

impaired, p. 708

indefinite life, p. 702

in-process research and development (R&D), p. 697

intangible assets, p. 695

intellectual capital, p. 719

knowledge assets, p. 719

lease, p. 707

leasehold, p. 707

licences, p. 706

licensing agreements, p. 706

limited life, p. 702

marketing-related intangible assets, p. 704

monetary assets, p. 695

negative goodwill, p. 713

organization costs, p. 700

patent, p. 707

permits, p. 706

prepaid expense, p. 697

rational entity impairment model, p. 709

research, p. 698

research phase, p. 698

technology-based intangible assets, p. 707

trademark, p. 704

trade name, p. 704

APPENDIX 12A

VALUING GOODWILL

Objective 11
Explain and apply basic approaches to valuing goodwill.

In this chapter, we discussed the method of measuring and recording goodwill when one entity acquires 100% of another business **as the excess of the fair value of the consideration given up by the acquirer over the fair value of the identifiable assets acquired and liabilities assumed in a business acquisition**. Determining the fair value of the consideration transferred and the fair value of the assets and liabilities acquired is an inexact process, and therefore, so is the calculation of the amount of goodwill. As the chapter suggests, it is usually possible to determine the fair value of specifically identifiable assets, but the question remains, "How does a buyer value intangible factors such as superior management, a good credit rating, and so on?"

Excess-Earnings Approach

VALUATION
5.4.1, 5.4.2, 5.4.3

One method to estimate the amount of goodwill in a business is the **excess-earnings approach**. This approach works as follows:

1. Calculate the average annual "normalized" earnings that the company is expected to earn in the future.

2. Calculate the annual average earnings that the company would be expected to earn if it generated the same return on investment as the average firm in the same industry. The return on investment is the percentage that results when income is divided by the net assets or shareholders' equity invested to generate that income.

3. Calculate the excess annual earnings: the difference between what the specific company and the average firm in the industry are expected to earn in the future. The ability to generate a higher income indicates that the business has an unidentifiable value that provides this greater earning power. This ability to earn a higher rate of return than the industry is considered to be the heart of what goodwill really is.

4. Estimate the value of the goodwill based on the future stream of excess earnings.

This approach is a systematic and logical way to calculate goodwill because its value is directly related to what makes a company worth more than the sum of its parts. We will use the Tractorling Ltd. example referred to in Illustration 12-8 again here to explain each of the four steps above. As indicated above, we first:

1. **Calculate the average annual "normalized" earnings that the company is expected to earn in the future.** Because the past often provides useful information about the future, the past earnings are a good place to start in estimating a company's likely future earnings. Going back three to six years is usually adequate.

Assume that Tractorling's net income amounts for the last five years and the calculation of the company's average earnings over this period are as given in Illustration 12A-1.

Earnings History—Tractorling Limited	
2012	$ 60,000
2013	55,000
2014	110,000[a]
2015	70,000
2016	80,000
Total for 5 years	$375,000
Average earnings $375,000 ÷ 5 years = $75,000	

[a]Includes gain on discontinued operation of $25,000

Based on the average annual earnings of $75,000 and the fair value of the company's identifiable net assets of $350,000 from Illustration 12-8, a return on investment of approximately 21.4% is initially indicated: $75,000 ÷ $350,000. Before we go further, however, we need to know whether $75,000 is representative of Tractorling's **future earnings**. A company's past earnings need to be analyzed to determine whether any adjustments are needed in estimating expected future earnings. This process is often called "normalizing earnings" and the income that results is termed **normalized earnings**.

First, **the accounting policies applied should be consistent with those of the purchaser**. For example, assume that the purchasing company measures inventory using the FIFO cost formula rather than average cost, which Tractorling uses. Further assume that the use of average cost had the effect of reducing Tractorling's net income by $2,000 each year below a FIFO-based net income. In addition, Tractorling uses accelerated depreciation while the purchaser uses straight-line. As a result, the reported earnings are $3,000 lower each year than they would have been on a straight-line basis.

Second, because the purchaser will pay current prices for the company, **future earnings should be based on the net assets' current fair values** rather than the carrying amount on Tractorling's books. That is, differences between the assets' carrying amounts and fair values may affect reported earnings in the future. For example, internally developed patent costs of $18,000 not previously recognized as an asset would be recognized on the purchase of Tractorling and are included in the $350,000 fair value of identifiable assets. This asset will need to be amortized, say, at the rate of $1,000 per year.

Finally, because we are trying to estimate future earnings, **amounts that are not expected to recur should be adjusted out of our calculations**. The 2014 gain on discontinued operations of $25,000 is an example of such an item. Illustration 12A-2 shows the analysis that can now be made of what the purchaser expects the annual future earnings of Tractorling to be.

Average past earnings of Tractorling (from Illustration 12A-1)		$75,000
Add		
Adjustment for change from average cost to FIFO	$2,000	
Adjustment for change from accelerated to straight-line depreciation	3,000	5,000
		80,000
Deduct		
Gain on discontinued operation ($25,000 ÷ 5)	5,000	
Patent amortization on straight-line basis	1,000	6,000
Expected future annual earnings of Tractorling		$74,000

Note that it was necessary to divide the gain on the discontinued operation of $25,000 by five years to adjust it correctly. The whole $25,000 was included in the total income earned over the five-year history, but only one fifth of it, or $5,000, is included in the average annual earnings.[29]

2. **Calculate the annual average earnings that the company would be expected to earn if it generated the same return on investment as the average firm in the same industry.** Determining the industry's average rate of return earned on net assets requires

an analysis of companies that are similar to the enterprise being examined. An industry average may be determined by examining annual reports or data from statistical services. Assume that a rate of 15% is found to be average for companies in Tractorling's industry. **This is the level of earnings that is expected from a company without any goodwill.** In this case, the estimate of what Tractorling's earnings would be if based on the norm for the industry is calculated in Illustration 12A-3.

Illustration 12A-3

Tractorling's Earnings at the Average Rate for the Industry

Fair value of Tractorling's identifiable net assets	$350,000
Industry average rate of return	15%
Tractorling's earnings if no goodwill	$ 52,500

The net assets' fair value—not their carrying amount—is used to calculate Tractorling's level of earnings at the industry average rate of return. Fair value is used because the cost of the net identifiable assets to any company that is interested in purchasing Tractorling will be their fair value, not their carrying amount on Tractorling's books. This makes fair value the relevant measure.

3. **Calculate the excess annual earnings: the difference between what the specific company and the average firm in the industry are expected to earn in the future.** The next step is to calculate how much of the company's expected earnings exceed the industry norm. This is what gives the company value in excess of the fair value of its identifiable net assets. Tractorling's excess earnings are determined in Illustration 12A-4.

Illustration 12A-4

Calculation of Excess Earnings

Expected future earnings of Tractorling	$74,000
Tractorling's earnings if no goodwill	52,500
Tractorling's excess annual earnings	$21,500

4. **Estimate the value of the goodwill based on the future stream of excess earnings.** Because the excess earnings are expected to continue for several years, they are discounted back to their present value to determine how much a purchaser would pay for them now. A discount rate must be chosen, as well as the length of the discount period.

Discount Rate

The choice of discount rate is relatively subjective.[30] The lower the discount rate, the higher the goodwill value and vice versa. To illustrate, assume that the excess earnings of $21,500 are expected to continue indefinitely. If the excess earnings are capitalized at a rate of 25% in perpetuity, for example, the results are as indicated in Illustration 12A-5.

Illustration 12A-5

Capitalization of Excess Earnings at 25% in Perpetuity

Capitalization at 25%

$$\frac{\text{Excess earnings}}{\text{Capitalization rate}} = \frac{\$21,500}{0.25} = \$86,000$$

As indicated in Illustration 12A-6, if the excess earnings are capitalized in perpetuity at a somewhat lower rate, say 15%, a much higher goodwill figure results.[31]

Illustration 12A-6

Capitalization of Excess Earnings at 15% in Perpetuity

Capitalization at 15%

$$\frac{\text{Excess earnings}}{\text{Capitalization rate}} = \frac{\$21,500}{0.15} = \$143,333$$

What do these numbers mean? In effect, if a company pays $86,000 over and above the fair value of Tractorling's identifiable net assets because the company generates earnings above the industry norm, and Tractorling actually does generate these excess profits in perpetuity, the $21,500 of extra earnings per year represents a 25% return on the amount invested. That is, there is a $21,500 return on the $86,000 invested.

If the purchaser invests $143,333 for the goodwill, the extra $21,500 represents a 15% return on investment: $21,500 relative to the $143,333 invested.

Because it is uncertain—risky—that excess profits will continue, a conservative or risk-adjusted rate (higher than the normal rate) tends to be used. Factors that are considered in determining the rate are the stability of past earnings, the speculative nature of the business, and general economic conditions.

Discount Period

Determining the period over which excess earnings are expected to continue is perhaps the most difficult problem in estimating goodwill. The perpetuity examples above assume that the excess earnings will last indefinitely. Usually, however, the excess earnings are assumed to last a limited number of years. The earnings are then discounted over the shorter period.

Assume that the company interested in purchasing Tractorling's business believes that the excess earnings will last only 10 years and, because of general economic uncertainty, chooses 25% as an appropriate rate of return. The present value of a 10-year annuity of excess earnings of $21,500 discounted at 25% is $76,766.[32] This is the amount that a purchaser should be willing to pay above the fair value of the identifiable net assets—that is, for goodwill—given the assumptions stated.

Total-Earnings Approach

Another way to estimate goodwill that is similar may help to increase your understanding of the process and resulting numbers. Under this approach—the **total-earnings approach**—the value of the company as a whole is determined, based on the total expected earnings, not just the excess earnings. The fair value of the identifiable net assets is then deducted from the value of the company as a whole. The difference is goodwill. The calculations under both approaches are provided in Illustration 12A-7, assuming the purchaser is looking for a 15% return on the amounts it will invest in Tractorling, and the earnings are expected to continue into perpetuity.

Illustration 12A-7			

Total Earnings Approach to the Calculation of Goodwill

	Assumptions:	Expected future earnings	$74,000
		Normal or industry-level earnings	$52,500
		Expected excess future earnings	$21,500
		Discount rate	15%
		Discount period	perpetuity, ∞
Excess-earnings approach:	Goodwill	= present value of the annuity of excess future earnings	
		= present value of annuity of $21,500 ($n = \infty$, $i = 0.15$)	
		= $\dfrac{\$21,500}{0.15}$	= $143,333
Total-earnings approach:	Goodwill	= difference between the fair value of the company and the fair value of its identifiable net assets	
	Fair value of company	= present value of the annuity of future earnings	
		= present value of annuity of $74,000 ($n = \infty$, $i = 0.15$)	
		= $\dfrac{\$74,000}{0.15}$	= $493,333
	Fair value of identifiable net assets	= present value of the annuity of industry-level earnings	
		= present value of annuity of $52,500 ($n = \infty$, $i = 0.15$)	
		= $\dfrac{\$52,500}{0.15}$	= (350,000)
	Goodwill	=	$143,333

Other Valuation Methods

There are several other methods of valuing goodwill: some are very basic and others are very sophisticated. The methods illustrated here are some of the least complex approaches. Others include simply multiplying excess earnings by the number of years that the excess earnings are expected to continue. This method, often referred to as the **number of years method**, provides a rough measure of goodwill. The approach has the advantage only of simplicity; it does not consider the time value of money because the future cash flows are not discounted.

An even simpler method is one that relies on multiples of average yearly earnings that are paid for other companies in the same industry. If Skyward Airlines was recently acquired for five times its average yearly earnings of $50 million, or $250 million, then Worldwide Airways, a close competitor with $80 million in average yearly earnings, would be worth $400 million.

VALUATION
5.4.1, 5.4.2, 5.4.3

Another method (similar to discounting excess earnings) is the **discounted free cash flow method**, which involves projecting the company's free cash flow over a long period, typically 10 or 20 years. The method first projects into the future a dozen or so important financial variables, including production; prices; and noncash expenses such as amortization, taxes, and capital outlays—all adjusted for inflation. The objective is to determine the amount of operating cash flow that will be generated beyond the amount needed to maintain existing capacity. The present value of the free cash flow is then calculated. This amount represents the value of the business.

For example, if Magnaputer Ltd. is expected to generate $1 million a year of free cash flow for 20 years, and the buyer's rate-of-return objective is 15%, the buyer would be willing to pay about $6,260,000 for Magnaputer. (The present value of $1 million to be received for 20 years discounted at 15% is $6,259,330.) The goodwill, then, is the difference between the $6,260,000 and the fair value of the company's identifiable net assets.

In practice, prospective buyers use a variety of methods to produce a valuation curve or range of prices. But the actual price that ends up being paid may be more a factor of the buyer's or seller's ego and negotiating skill.

Valuation of a business—determining how much to pay for it—and its inherent goodwill is at best a highly uncertain process.[33] The estimated value of goodwill depends on a number of factors, all of which are tenuous and subject to bargaining. It ends up accounted for as the difference between the fair value of what you give up to acquire the business and the fair value of the identifiable net assets acquired.

SUMMARY OF LEARNING OBJECTIVE FOR APPENDIX 12A

11 Explain and apply basic approaches to valuing goodwill.

One method of valuing goodwill is the excess-earnings approach. Using this approach, the value of goodwill is based on discounting expected future earnings in excess of the industry average to their present value. Another method involves determining the total value of the business by capitalizing total earnings, and then deducting the fair values of the identifiable net assets. The number of years method of valuing goodwill simply multiplies the excess earnings by the number of years of expected excess earnings. Another method of valuing goodwill is the discounted free cash flow method, which projects the future operating cash that will be generated over and above the amount needed to maintain current operating levels. The present value of the free cash flows is today's estimate of the firm's value.

KEY TERMS

discounted free cash flow method, p. 728   normalized earnings, p. 725   total-earnings approach, p. 727

excess-earnings approach, p. 724   number of years method, p. 728

Note: All assignment material with an asterisk (*) relates to the appendix to the chapter.

Unless otherwise indicated, amortization expense should be calculated to the nearest whole month.

Completion of this end-of-chapter material will help develop CPA enabling competencies (such as ethics and professionalism, problem-solving and decision-making and communication) and technical competencies. We have highlighted selected items with an integration icon and material in *WileyPLUS* has been linked to the competencies. All cases emphasize integration, especially of the enabling competencies. The brief exercises, exercises and problems generally emphasize problem-solving and decision-making.

Brief Exercises

(LO 1) **BE12-1** Wholesome Foods Corporation is a producer of gourmet organic cookies. The company was established three years ago when its founder and president, Martha Spencer, purchased the trademark "Healthy Originals" and its six patented cookie recipes. Martha soon discovered that there was a specialty market for the cookies, and began marketing them as hand-decorated and personalized gourmet organic cookies for special occasions such as birthdays and bridal and baby showers. Nearly all of the company's sales are through the company's internally developed website (**www.healthyoriginals.com**), where customers can enter personalized orders for batches of individually decorated and wrapped cookies.

(a) Provide examples of intangible assets that may appear on the company's balance sheet.

(b) Discuss the importance of the intangible assets to the company's business.

(c) Referring to the conceptual framework (discussed in Chapter 2), discuss the importance of recording the intangible assets on the company's statement of financial position.

(LO 1, 2, 3) **BE12-2** For each independent scenario outlined below, discuss whether the three criteria required for an asset to be classified as an intangible are fulfilled:

(a) Software purchased specifically for a manufacturing machine that cannot operate without that software

(b) Software purchased for a hotel reservation system that is not essential to the related ancillary hardware equipment

(c) Software developed internally for eventual sale to customers

(d) Software purchased for eventual resale to customers

(LO 2, 3, 10) **BE12-3** E-Learning Educational Services Inc. incurred the following costs associated with its research facilities. Indicate whether these items are capitalized or expensed in the current year, assuming the company reports under ASPE. Where applicable, indicate how your answer would change under IFRS.

(a) Executive salaries

(b) Costs of testing prototypes

(c) Market research to prepare for the product launch

(d) Sales commissions

(e) Salaries of research staff investigating alternatives for existing products

(f) Borrowing costs directly attributable to the development of a qualifying intangible asset

(LO 2, 3, 4) **BE12-4** Azure Industries Ltd. acquired two copyrights during 2017. One copyright was on a textbook that was developed internally at a cost of $36,000. This textbook is estimated to have a useful life of three years from July 1, 2017, the date it was published. The second copyright is for a history research textbook and was purchased from University Press on October 1, 2017, for $54,000. This textbook seems to have an indefinite useful life. How should these two copyrights be reported on Azure's statement of financial position as at December 31, 2017?

(LO 2) **BE12-5** Sunny Valley Inc. purchased an Internet domain name by issuing a $220,000, five-year, non–interest-bearing note to Ti-Mine Corp. with an effective yield of 12%. The note is repayable in five annual payments of $44,000 each. Prepare the journal entry to record the purchase of the intangible asset.

(LO 2, 3, 5) **BE12-6** Bountiful Industries Ltd. had one patent recorded on its books as at January 1, 2017. This patent had a book value of $365,000 and a remaining useful life of eight years. During 2017, Bountiful incurred research costs of $140,000 and brought a patent infringement suit against a competitor. On December 1, 2017, Bountiful received the good news that its patent was valid and that its competitor could not use the process Bountiful had patented. The company spent $106,000 to defend this patent. At what amount should the patent be reported on the December 31, 2017 statement of financial position, assuming monthly straight-line amortization of patents?

(LO 2, 3) **BE12-7** Programming for Kids Ltd. decided that it needed to update its computer programs for its supplier relationships. It purchased an off-the-shelf program and modified it internally to link it to Programming for Kids' other programs. The following costs may be relevant to the accounting for the new software:

Net carrying amount of old software	$2,000
Purchase price of new software	7,500
Training costs	4,000
General and administrative costs	2,480
Direct cost of in-house programmer's time spent on modifying software	1,480

Prepare journal entries to record the software replacement.

(LO 2, 3, 5, 10) **BE12-8** Indicate whether the following items are capitalized or expensed in the current year, assuming IFRS was used to prepare financial statements. Assume that any items that may qualify for capitalization have met all six "development phase" criteria.

(a) The purchase cost of a patent from a competitor

(b) Product research costs

(c) Organization costs

(d) Costs that are incurred internally to create goodwill

(e) Costs that are incurred internally to create a secret recipe

(f) Legal costs to successfully support trademark

(g) Pre-operating costs to launch new products

(h) Relocation of manufacturing activities

(i) Corporate reorganization costs

(j) Costs incurred to develop computer software

How would the answer differ if ASPE were used to prepare financial statements?

(LO 2, 3, 4, 10) **BE12-9** Sweet Tooth, Inc., a private company that applies ASPE, incurred $15,000 in materials and $12,000 in direct labour costs between January and March 2017 to develop a new product. In May 2017, the criteria required to capitalize development costs were met. A further $45,000 was spent for materials, $15,000 for direct labour costs, $2,000 for borrowing costs, and $72,000 for directly related legal fees. Discuss any options that may be available to Sweet Tooth for recording these expenditures. In addition, prepare the appropriate journal entries.

How would your answer change if Sweet Tooth were a public company following IFRS?

(LO 2, 4, 5) **BE12-10** Darrien Corporation purchased a trade name, customer list, and manufacturing equipment for a lump sum of $800,000. The fair market values of each asset are $280,000, $290,000, and $320,000, respectively. There were initial operating losses of $14,500 during the first four months after the assets were put into use. Prepare the journal entry to record the treatment of these costs.

(LO 3) **BE12-11** Using the data provided in BE12-10, assume that Darrien also spent $12,500 to promote and launch the product that the manufacturing equipment is used to produce. Explain the accounting for these costs.

(LO 3, 4, 10) **BE12-12** Green Earth Corp. has capitalized software costs of $450,000 on a product to be sold externally. During its first year, sales of this product totalled $195,000. Green Earth expects to earn $1,250,000 in additional future revenue from this product, which is estimated to have an economic life of four years. Calculate the amount of software amortization, assuming that amortization is based on the pattern in which Green Earth receives benefits from the software program and Green Earth uses IFRS. How would your answer differ under ASPE?

(LO 2, 4) **BE12-13** Lakeshore Corporation purchased a patent from MaFee Corp. on January 1, 2017, for $87,000. The patent had a remaining legal life of 16 years. Prepare Lakeshore's journal entries to record the 2017 patent purchase and amortization.

(LO 2, 4) **BE12-14** Use the information in BE12-13 and assume that in January 2019, Lakeshore spends $26,000 successfully defending a patent suit. In addition, Lakeshore now feels the patent will be useful only for another seven years. Prepare the journal entries to record the 2019 expenditure and amortization.

(LO 2, 4, 10) **BE12-15** On December 31, 2017, Convenient Cabs Incorporated was granted 10 taxi licences by the City of Somerdale, at a cost of $1,000 per licence. It is probable that Convenient Cabs will receive the expected future economic benefits of the taxi licences. There is an active market for taxi licences in Somerdale.

(a) Prepare the journal entry to record the costs incurred.

(b) Discuss how the licences are accounted for after initial recognition if Convenient Cabs follows ASPE.

(c) Discuss how the licences are accounted for after initial recognition if Convenient Cabs follows IFRS.

(LO 6, 10) **BE12-16** Coffee Time Limited has a trademark with a carrying amount of $83,750, and expected useful life of 15 years. As part of an impairment test on December 31, 2017, due to a change in customer tastes, Coffee Time gathered the following data about the trademark for the purposes of an impairment test: fair value $45,000; fair value less costs to sell $40,000; value in use $95,200; and undiscounted future cash flows $125,000. Assume that Coffee Time is reporting under ASPE. Determine if the trademark is impaired on December 31, 2017.

(LO 6, 10) **BE12-17**   Use the data provided in BE12-16. How would your response change if Coffee Time were a public company reporting under IFRS?

(LO 6, 10) **BE12-18**   Use the data provided in BE12-16, except assume that useful life is expected to be unlimited. How would your response change if Coffee Time reported under (a) ASPE or (b) IFRS?

(LO 7) **BE12-19**   On September 1, 2017, Pipeline Corporation acquired Tunneling Limited for a cash payment of $954,000. At the time of purchase, Tunneling's statement of financial position showed assets of $780,000, liabilities of $420,000, and owners' equity of $360,000. The fair value of Tunneling's assets is estimated to be $1,140,000. Calculate the amount of goodwill acquired by Pipeline.

(LO 8, 10) **BE12-20**   Using the data from BE12-19, assume that Pipeline Corporation is a public company and that the goodwill was allocated entirely to one cash-generating unit (CGU). Two years later, information about the CGU is as follows: carrying amount $3,740,000; value in use $3,680,000; and fair value less costs to sell $3,575,000. Determine if the goodwill is impaired, and calculate the goodwill impairment loss, if any.

(LO 8, 10) **BE12-21**   Using the data from BE12-19, assume that Pipeline Corporation is a private entity. Explain how goodwill will be tested for impairment. If the unit's carrying amount (including goodwill) is $3,581,000 and its fair value is $3,474,000, determine the amount of impairment loss, if any, under ASPE.

(LO 11) ***BE12-22**   Nigel Corporation is interested in purchasing Lau Company Ltd. The total of Lau's net income amounts over the last five years is $750,000. During one of those years, Lau reported a gain on discontinued operations of $94,000. The fair value of Lau's net identifiable assets is $690,000. A normal rate of return is 15%, and Nigel wants to capitalize excess earnings at 20%. Calculate the estimated value of Lau's goodwill.

FINANCE

Exercises

(LO 2, 5, 10) **E12-1**   **(Classification Issues—Intangibles)** The following is a list of items that could be included in the intangible assets section of the statement of financial position:

1. An investment in a subsidiary company
2. Timberland
3. The cost of an engineering activity that is required to advance a product's design to the manufacturing stage
4. A lease prepayment (six months of rent paid in advance)
5. The cost of equipment obtained under a capital lease
6. The cost of searching for applications for new research findings
7. Costs incurred in forming a corporation
8. Operating losses incurred in the start-up of a business
9. Training costs incurred in the start-up of a new operation
10. The purchase cost of a franchise
11. Goodwill generated internally
12. The cost of testing in the search for product alternatives
13. Goodwill acquired in the purchase of a business
14. The cost of developing a patent
15. The cost of purchasing a patent from an inventor
16. Legal costs incurred in securing a patent
17. Unrecovered costs of a successful legal suit to protect a patent
18. The cost of conceptual formulation of possible product alternatives
19. The cost of purchasing a copyright
20. Product development costs
21. Long-term receivables

22. The cost of developing a trademark

23. The cost of purchasing a trademark

24. The cost of an annual update of payroll software

25. A five-year advertising contract for rights of advertising by a top hockey player in Canada

26. Borrowing costs specifically identifiable with an internally developed intangible asset

Instructions

(a) Indicate which items on the list would be reported as intangible assets on the statement of financial position.

(b) Indicate how, if at all, the items that are not reportable as intangible assets would be reported in the financial statements.

(c) Identify any differences between ASPE and IFRS with respect to capitalization of such items as intangible assets.

(LO 2, 5, 7, 10) **E12-2** **(Classification Issues—Intangibles)** Selected account information follows for Entertainment Inc. as at December 31, 2017. All the accounts have debit balances. Assume the company uses IFRS when preparing financial statements.

Cable Television Franchises	Film Contract Rights
Music Copyrights	Customer Lists Acquired in a Business Combination
Research Costs	Prepaid Expenses
Goodwill	Covenants Not to Compete
Cash	Brand Names
Accounts Receivable	Notes Receivable
Property, Plant, and Equipment	Investments in Affiliated Companies
Leasehold Improvements	Organization Cost
Annual Franchise Fee Paid	Land
In-Process Research and Development Acquired in a Business Combination	Excess of Purchase Price over Fair Value of Identifiable Net Assets, X Corp.

Instructions

(a) Identify which items should be classified as intangible assets. For the items that are not classified as intangible assets, indicate where they would be reported in the financial statements.

(b) How would the answer differ if ASPE were followed instead of IFRS?

(LO 2, 3, 5, 7, 10) **E12-3** **(Classification Issues—Intangibles)** Berrie Electric Inc. has the following amounts included in its general ledger at December 31, 2017:

Organization costs	$ 34,000
Purchased trademarks	17,500
Development phase activities (meet all six development phase criteria)	29,000
Deposits with advertising agency for ads to promote goodwill of company	8,000
Excess of cost over fair value of identifiable net assets of acquired subsidiary	81,000
Cost of equipment acquired for research and development projects; the equipment has an alternative future use	125,000
Costs of researching a secret formula for a product that is expected to be marketed for at least 20 years	75,000
Payment for a favourable lease; lease term of 10 years	15,000

Instructions

(a) Based on the information provided, calculate the total amount for Berrie to report as intangible assets on its statement of financial position at December 31, 2017. Assume Berrie uses IFRS to prepare its financial statements.

(b) If an item should not be included in intangible assets, explain the proper treatment for reporting it.

(c) Indicate which amounts might be reported differently if ASPE were followed instead of IFRS.

(LO 2, 3, 4, 10) **E12-4** **(Intangible Amortization)** Selected information follows for Mount Olympus Corporation for three independent situations:

1. Mount Olympus purchased a patent from Bakhshi Co. for $1.8 million on January 1, 2015. The patent expires on January 1, 2025, and Mount Olympus is amortizing it over the 10 years remaining in its legal life. During 2017, Mount Olympus determined that the patent's economic benefits would not last longer than six years from the date of acquisition.

2. Mount Olympus bought a perpetual franchise from Carmody Inc. on January 1, 2017, for $650,000. Its carrying amount on Carmody's books at January 1, 2017, was $750,000. Assume that Mount Olympus can only provide evidence of clearly identifiable cash flows for 25 years, but thinks the franchise could have value for up to 60 years.

3. On January 1, 2015, Mount Olympus incurred development costs (meeting all required criteria) of $375,000. Mount Olympus is amortizing these costs over five years.

Instructions

(a) In situation 1, what amount should be reported in the statement of financial position for the patent, net of accumulated amortization, at December 31, 2017?

(b) In situation 2, what amount of amortization expense should be reported for the year ended December 31, 2017?

(c) In situation 3, what amount, if any, should be reported as unamortized development costs as at December 31, 2017? How might the accounting treatment change if Mount Olympus were using ASPE?

(LO 2, 3, 4, 10) E12-5 (Correct Intangible Asset Account) As the recently appointed auditor for Daleara Corporation, you have been asked to examine selected accounts before the six-month financial statements of June 30, 2017, are prepared. The controller for Daleara Corporation mentions that only one account is kept for intangible assets. The entries in Intangible Assets since January 1, 2017, are as follows:

INTANGIBLE ASSETS

			Debit	Credit	Balance
Jan.	4	Research costs	1,050,000		1,050,000
	5	Legal costs to obtain patent	45,000		1,095,000
		Payment of seven months' rent on property leased by Daleara (February to August)	49,000		1,144,000
Feb.	11	Proceeds from issue of common shares		296,000	848,000
Apr.	30	Promotional expenses related to start-up of business	157,000		1,005,000
June	1	Development stage costs (meet all six development stage criteria)	215,000		1,220,000
	30	Start-up costs for first six months	316,000		1,536,000

Instructions

Prepare the entry or entries that are necessary to correct this account. Assume that the patent has a useful life of 10 years and that Daleara Corporation follows IFRS.

(LO 2, 3, 4, 5) E12-6 (Recognition and Amortization of Intangibles) Institute Limited organized late in 2016 and set up a single account for all intangible assets. The following summary shows the entries in 2017 (all debits) that have been recorded in Intangible Assets since then:

Jan.	2	Purchased patent (8-year life)	$ 320,000
Mar.	31	Costs to search for new ways to apply patent that was purchased on Jan. 2	21,000
Apr.	1	Purchased goodwill (indefinite life)	310,000
July	1	Purchased franchise with 10-year life; expiration date July 1, 2027	250,000
	1	Promotional costs to increase the future economic benefit of the goodwill that was purchased on Apr. 1	33,000
Aug.	1	Payment for copyright (5-year life)	140,000
	1	Purchased trademark (3-year life)	15,000
	1	Purchased customer list (2-year life)	10,000
Sept.	1	Research costs	239,000
			$1,338,000

Instructions

(a) Prepare the necessary entries to clear the Intangible Assets account and to set up separate accounts for distinct types of intangibles.

(b) Make the entries as at December 31, 2017, for any necessary amortization so that all balances are accurate as at that date.

(c) Provide the asset amounts reported on the December 31, 2017 statement of financial position.

(LO 2, 3, 4, 5) **E12-7** **(Accounting for Trade Name)** In early January 2017, FJS Corporation applied for and received approval for a trade name, incurring legal costs of $52,500. In early January 2018, FJS incurred $28,200 in legal fees in a successful defence of its trade name.

Instructions

(a) Management determines that this asset has a limited useful life. Identify the variables that must be considered in determining the appropriate amortization period for this trade name.

(b) Calculate amortization for 2017; carrying amount at December 31, 2017; amortization for 2018; and carrying amount at December 31, 2018, if the company amortizes the trade name over its 15-year legal life.

(c) Repeat part (b), assuming a useful life of six years.

(d) Assume the trade name is assessed as having an indefinite life upon initial acquisition. Explain the accounting implications.

DIGGING DEEPER

(e) Assume the role of a potential investor in FJS. Comment on the estimated useful life of the trade name, and its effects on the company's financial statements.

(LO 3, 4, 10) **E12-8** **(Internally Generated Intangibles)** Oakville Corp. incurred the following costs during 2017 in connection with its research and development phase activities:

Cost of equipment acquired for use in research and development projects over the next five years (straight-line depreciation used)	$240,000
Materials consumed in research projects	61,000
Materials consumed in the development of a product committed for manufacturing in the first quarter of 2018	32,000
Consulting fees paid in the last quarter of 2017 to outsiders for research and development projects, including $4,500 for advice related to the $32,000 of materials used above	95,000
Personnel costs of persons involved in research and development projects	108,000
Indirect costs reasonably allocated to research and development projects	25,000
General borrowing costs on the company's line of credit	12,000
Training costs for a new customer service software program	17,500

Instructions

(a) Calculate the amount to be reported as research and development expense by Oakville on its income statement for 2017. Assume the equipment is purchased at the beginning of the year. Assume the company follows IFRS for financial reporting purposes.

(b) Explain the treatment of training costs and borrowing costs incurred after the six development phase capitalization criteria are met.

(c) Explain how the answer may be the same or differ if ASPE were followed.

(LO 3, 4, 5, 10) **E12-9** **(Internally Generated Intangibles)** In 2017, Inventors Corp. spent $392,000 on a research project, but by the end of 2017 it was impossible to determine whether any benefit would come from it. Inventors prepares financial statements in accordance with IFRS.

Instructions

(a) What account should be charged for the $392,000, and how should it be shown in the financial statements for fiscal 2017?

(b) The research project is completed in 2018, and a successful patent is obtained. The research phase costs to complete the project are $71,000. The administrative and legal expenses incurred in obtaining patent number 481-761-0092 on January 3, 2018, total $10,000. The patent has an expected useful life of five years. Inventors Corp. will now begin investigating applications that use or apply the knowledge obtained on this project. Record these costs in journal entry form. Also, record patent amortization for a full year in 2018.

(c) In January 2019, the company successfully defended the patent in litigation at a cost of $12,400. The victory extended the patent's life to December 31, 2026. What is the proper way to account for this cost? Also, record patent amortization for a full year in 2019.

(d) By early September 2019, and at an additional cost of $101,000, Inventors Corp. had a product design that was technologically and financially feasible. Additional engineering and consulting costs of $66,000 were incurred in October 2019 to advance the design of the new product to the manufacturing stage. Discuss the proper accounting treatment for the 2019 costs incurred.

(LO 2, 3, 4, 5, 10) **E12-10** **(Accounting for Patents, Franchises, and R&D)** Tennessee Corp., reporting under ASPE, has provided the following information regarding its intangible assets:

1. A patent was purchased from Marvin Inc. for $1.2 million on January 1, 2016. Tennessee estimated the patent's remaining useful life to be 10 years. The patent was carried in Marvin's accounting records at a carrying amount of $1,350,000 when Marvin sold it to Tennessee. On January 1, 2017, because of recent events in the field, Tennessee estimates that the remaining life of this patent is only five years from January 1, 2017.

2. During 2017, a franchise was purchased from Burr Ltd. for $290,000. As part of the deal, Burr must also be paid 5% of revenue from the franchise operations. Revenue from the franchise for 2017 was $1.4 million. Tennessee estimates the franchise's useful life to be 10 years and takes a full year's amortization in the year of purchase.

3. Tennessee incurred the following research costs in 2017:

Materials and equipment	$ 81,000
Personnel	111,000
Indirect costs	55,000
	$247,000

Instructions

(a) Prepare a schedule showing the intangibles section of Tennessee's balance sheet at December 31, 2017. Show supporting calculations in good form.

(b) Prepare a schedule showing the income statement effect for the year ended December 31, 2017, as a result of the facts above. Show supporting calculations in good form.

(c) Explain how the accounting would differ if Tennessee were a public company.

(Adapted from AICPA.)

(LO 3, 4, 6, 10) **E12-11 (Internally Developed Intangibles)** During 2017, Saskatchewan Enterprises Ltd., a private entity, incurred $4.7 million in costs to develop a new software product called Dover. Of this amount, $1.8 million was spent before establishing that the product was technologically and financially feasible. Dover was completed by December 31, 2017, and will be marketed to third parties. Saskatchewan expects a useful life of eight years for this product, with total revenues of $12 million. During 2018, Saskatchewan realized revenues of $2.7 million from sales of Dover.

Instructions

(a) Assuming Saskatchewan reports under ASPE, prepare the journal entries that are required in 2017 to record the above.

(b) Prepare the entry to record amortization at December 31, 2018.

(c) At what amount should the software costs be reported in the December 31, 2018 balance sheet?

(d) Could the net realizable value of this asset at December 31, 2018, affect your answer? Explain how limited-life assets are tested for impairment.

(e) How would your response to (d) change if Saskatchewan Enterprises Ltd. were a public company?

(LO 2, 4, 6, 10) **E12-12 (Revaluation Model)** Blue and White Town Taxi Incorporated applied for several taxi licences for its taxicab operations in the Town of Somerville and, on August 31, 2017, incurred costs of $12,500 in the application process. The outcome of applying for taxi licences in the town was uncertain, as Somerville has been known to limit the number of issued taxi licences in an effort to encourage use of public transportation.

The application was successful and on June 30, 2018, Blue and White was granted 30 freely transferable taxi licences for a registration fee of $3,750 per licence. According to management, each licence will have a useful life of only five years from the date of registration, because demand for taxi services in Somerville is expected to decrease significantly after the town's subway system is expanded. There is an active market for taxi licences in Somerville.

In 2019, in an effort to decrease traffic congestion in its downtown, the town did not issue any new taxi licences, and the fair value of each taxi licence held by Blue and White was $4,200 as at December 31, 2019. In 2021, due to a severe shortage of taxis in the town, Somerville decreased the registration fee and issued many new taxi licences. As at December 31, 2021, each taxi licence had value in use of $5,400, fair value of $3,800, and costs to sell of $200. Blue and White amortizes intangible assets using the straight-line method, and prepares financial statements in accordance with IFRS.

Instructions

(a) Prepare the entry to record the costs incurred on August 31, 2017.

(b) Prepare the entry to record the costs incurred on June 30, 2018.

(c) Assume that after initial recognition, Blue and White uses the cost model to measure its intangible assets. Prepare the entries required on December 31, 2019, December 31, 2020, and December 31, 2021, and calculate the carrying amount of the intangible asset, if any, as at December 31, 2021.

(d) Assume that after initial recognition, Blue and White uses the revaluation model (asset adjustment method) to measure its intangible assets. Prepare the entries required on December 31, 2019, December 31, 2020, and December 31, 2021, and calculate the carrying amount of the intangible asset, if any, as at December 31, 2021. Assume revaluation adjustments are made on December 31, 2019, and December 31, 2021.

DIGGING
DEEPER

(e) From the perspective of Blue and White's auditor, discuss the criteria that must be met for the intangible asset to be measured using the revaluation model. Discuss under which financial reporting standards the revaluation model can be applied.

(LO 6, 10) E12-13   (Impairment Testing) At the end of 2017, Dayton Corporation owns a licence with a remaining life of 10 years and a carrying amount of $530,000. Dayton expects undiscounted future cash flows from this licence to total $535,000. The licence's fair value is $425,000 and disposal costs are estimated to be nil. The licence's discounted cash flows (that is, value in use) are estimated to be $475,000. Dayton prepares financial statements in accordance with IFRS.

Instructions

(a) Determine if the licence is impaired at the end of 2017 and prepare any related entries that are necessary.

(b) Assume the recoverable amount is calculated to be $450,000 at the end of 2018. Determine if the licence is impaired at the end of 2018 and prepare any related entries that are necessary.

(c) Explain how the answer to part (b) would change if the licence's fair value were $500,000 at the end of 2018.

(LO 6, 10) E12-14   (Impairment Testing)

Instructions

Repeat E12-13, but now assume that Dayton prepares financial statements in accordance with ASPE, and that the recoverable amount under ASPE (undiscounted future cash flows) is calculated to be $500,000 at the end of 2018.

(LO 6, 10) E12-15   (Impairment Testing)

Instructions

Repeat E12-13, but now assume that the licence was granted in perpetuity and has an indefinite life.

(LO 6, 10) E12-16   (Impairment Testing)

Instructions

Repeat E12-13, but now assume that the licence was granted in perpetuity and has an indefinite life, and that Dayton prepares financial statements in accordance with ASPE.

(LO 6, 10) E12-17   (Intangible Impairment) The following information is for a copyright owned by Lighting Designs Corp., a private entity, at December 31, 2017. Lighting Designs Corp. applies ASPE.

Cost	$4,300,000
Carrying amount	2,150,000
Expected future net cash flows (undiscounted)	2,000,000
Fair value	1,600,000

Assume that Lighting Designs Corp. will continue to use this copyright in the future. As at December 31, 2017, the copyright is estimated to have a remaining useful life of 10 years.

Instructions

(a) Prepare the journal entry, if any, to record the asset's impairment at December 31, 2017.

(b) Prepare the journal entry to record amortization expense for 2018 related to the copyright.

(c) The copyright's fair value at December 31, 2018, is $2.2 million. Prepare the journal entry, if any, to record the increase in fair value.

DIGGING
DEEPER

(d) Using the information from part (a), discuss whether the copyright would be amortized in 2017 before the impairment test is conducted. Would the asset be tested for impairment before or after amortizing the copyright in 2017?

(LO 6, 10) E12-18   (Intangible Impairment) Refer to the information provided in E12-17, but now assume that Lighting Designs Corp. is a publicly accountable company. At December 31, 2017, the copyright's value in use is $1,850,000 and its selling costs are $100,000.

Instructions

(a) Prepare the journal entry, if any, to record the asset's impairment at December 31, 2017.

(b) Prepare the journal entry to record amortization expense for 2018 related to the copyright.

(c) The copyright's fair value at December 31, 2018, is $2.2 million. Prepare the journal entry, if any, to record the increase in fair value.

(LO 7) E12-19 **(Accounting for Goodwill)** Fred Moss, owner of Medici Interiors Inc., is negotiating for the purchase of Athenian Galleries Ltd. The condensed statement of financial position of Athenian follows in an abbreviated form:

ATHENIAN GALLERIES LTD.
Statement of Financial Position
As at December 31, 2017

Assets		Liabilities and Shareholders' Equity		
Cash	$118,000	Accounts payable		$ 92,000
Land	70,000	Long-term notes payable		351,000
Building (net)	244,000	Total liabilities		443,000
Equipment (net)	185,000	Common shares	$200,000	
Copyright (net)	98,000	Retained earnings	72,000	272,000
Total assets	$715,000	Total liabilities and shareholders' equity		$715,000

Medici and Athenian agree that the land is undervalued by $40,000 and the business equipment is overvalued by $12,000. Athenian agrees to sell the business to Medici for $382,000.

Instructions

Prepare the entry to record the purchase of the business's net assets on Medici's books.

(LO 7, 8, E12-20 **(Accounting for Goodwill)** On July 1, 2017, Zoe Corporation purchased the net assets of Soorya Company
10) by paying $415,000 cash and issuing a $50,000 note payable to Soorya Company. At July 1, 2017, the statement of financial position of Soorya Company was as follows:

Cash	$ 75,000	Accounts payable	$300,000
Accounts receivable	102,000	Soorya, capital	239,000
Inventory	98,000		$539,000
Land	50,000		
Buildings (net)	75,000		
Equipment (net)	90,000		
Trademarks (net)	49,000		
	$539,000		

The recorded amounts all approximate current values except for land (worth $60,000), inventory (worth $125,000), and trademarks (worthless). The receivables are shown net of an allowance for doubtful accounts of $12,000. The amounts for buildings, equipment, and trademarks are shown net of accumulated amortization of $14,000, $23,000, and $47,000, respectively.

Instructions

(a) Prepare the July 1, 2017 entry for Zoe Corporation to record the purchase.

(b) Assume that Zoe is a private entity and tested its goodwill for impairment on December 31, 2018. Management determined that the reporting unit's carrying amount (including goodwill) was $500,000 and that the reporting unit's fair value (including goodwill) was $450,000. Determine if there is any impairment and prepare any necessary entry on December 31, 2018. Zoe applies ASPE.

(c) Repeat part (a), assuming that the purchase price was $204,000, all paid in cash.

(d) Based on part (a), assume now that Zoe is a public entity and tested its goodwill for impairment on December 31, 2018. The cash-generating unit's values (including goodwill) are as follows:

Carrying amount	$500,000
Value in use	475,000
Fair value	450,000
Disposal costs	25,000

DIGGING
DEEPER

Determine if there is any impairment and prepare any necessary entry on December 31, 2018.

(e) Based on part (a), discuss factors that Zoe may have considered in deciding to pay total consideration of $465,000 for Soorya.

(LO 8, 10) E12-21   (Goodwill Impairment) The following is net asset information for the Dhillon Division of Klaus, Inc.:

NET ASSETS
as of December 31, 2017
(in millions)

	Book Value	Fair Value Excluding Goodwill
Cash	$ 50	$ 50
Accounts receivable	216	216
Property, plant, and equipment (net)	2,618	2,760
Goodwill	206	
Less: Notes payable	(2,700)	(2,700)
Net assets	$ 390	

The purpose of the Dhillon Division (also identified as a reporting unit or cash-generating unit) is to develop a nuclear-powered aircraft. If successful, travelling delays that are associated with refuelling could be greatly reduced, and operational efficiency would increase significantly.

To date, management has not had much success and is deciding whether a writedown is appropriate at this time. Management has prepared the following estimates for the reporting unit or cash-generating unit:

1. Undiscounted future net cash flows is approximately $400 million.

2. Future value in use is approximately $385 million.

3. Sale of the unit would yield $346 million and selling costs would total $5 million.

Instructions

(a) Under ASPE, determine if there is any impairment and prepare any necessary entry on December 31, 2017.

(b) On December 31, 2018, it is estimated that the reporting unit's fair value has increased to $400 million. Under ASPE, prepare the journal entry, if any, to record the increase in fair value.

(c) Under IFRS, determine if there is any impairment and prepare any necessary entry on December 31, 2017.

(d) On December 31, 2018, it is estimated that the cash-generating unit's fair value has increased to $400 million. Under IFRS, prepare the journal entry, if any, to record the increase in fair value.

(LO 11) *E12-22   (Calculate Normalized Earnings) Rotterdam Corporation's pre-tax accounting income of $725,000 for the year 2017 included the following items:

Amortization of identifiable intangibles	$147,000
Depreciation of building	115,000
Loss from discontinued operations	44,000
Unusual, non-recurring gains	152,000
Profit-sharing payments to employees	65,000

FINANCE

Ewing Industries Ltd. would like to purchase Rotterdam Corporation. In trying to measure Rotterdam's normalized earnings for 2017, Ewing determines that the building's fair value is triple the book value and that its remaining economic life is double the life that Rotterdam is using. Ewing would continue the profit-sharing payments to employees, with the payments being based on income from continuing operations before amortization and depreciation.

Instructions

Calculate the 2017 normalized earnings amount of Rotterdam Corporation that Ewing would use to calculate goodwill.

(LO 11) *E12-23   (Calculate Goodwill) Net income figures for Belgian Ltd. are as follows:

FINANCE

2013—$75,000	2016—$87,000
2014—$53,000	2017—$69,000
2015—$84,000	

Future income is expected to continue at the average amount of the past five years. The company's identifiable net assets are appraised at $460,000 on December 31, 2017. The business is to be acquired by Mooney Corp. in early 2015. The normal rate of return on net assets for the industry is 7%.

Instructions

What amount should Mooney Corp. pay for goodwill, and for Belgian Ltd. as a whole, if:

(a) goodwill is equal to average excess earnings capitalized at 23%?

(b) a perpetual 18% return is expected on any amount paid for goodwill?

(c) goodwill is equal to five years of excess earnings?

(d) goodwill is equal to the present value of five years of excess earnings capitalized at 15%?

(LO 11) *E12-24 (Calculate Goodwill) Aswan Corporation is interested in acquiring Richmond Plastics Limited. Richmond has determined that its excess earnings have averaged approximately $175,000 and feels that such an amount should be capitalized over an unlimited period at a 15% rate. Aswan feels that, because of increased competition, the excess earnings of Richmond Plastics will continue for seven years at the most and that a 12% discount rate is appropriate.

FINANCE

Instructions

(a) How far apart are the positions of these two parties?

(b) Is there really a difference in the two approaches being used by the parties to evaluate Richmond Plastics' goodwill? Explain.

(LO 11) *E12-25 (Calculate Goodwill) As the president of Niagara Wineries Corp., you are considering purchasing Grimsby Wine Accessories Limited, whose statement of financial position is summarized as follows:

Current assets	$ 240,000	Current liabilities	$ 210,000
Plant and equipment (net)	825,000	Long-term liabilities	550,000
Other assets	285,000	Common shares	440,000
		Retained earnings	150,000
Total	$1,350,000	Total	$1,350,000

FINANCE

The current assets' fair value is $80,000 higher than their carrying amount because of inventory undervaluation. All other assets and liabilities have book values that approximate their fair value. The normal rate of return on net assets for the industry is 15%. The expected annual earnings for Grimsby are $140,000.

Instructions

Assuming that the excess earnings are expected to continue for five years, how much would you be willing to pay for goodwill, and for the company? (Estimate goodwill by the present value method.)

(LO 11) *E12-26 (Calculate Fair Value of Identifiable Assets) Louvre Inc. bought a business that is expected to give a 25% annual rate of return on the investment. Of the total amount paid for the business, $75,000 was deemed to be goodwill, and the rest was attributed to the identifiable net assets. Louvre Inc. estimated that the annual future earnings of the new business would be equal to the average ordinary earnings per year of the business over the past three years. The total net income over the past three years was $375,000. This amount included a loss on discontinued operations of $25,000 in one year and an unusual and non-recurring gain of $95,000 in one of the other two years.

FINANCE

Instructions

Calculate the fair value of the identifiable net assets that Louvre Inc. purchased in this transaction.

Problems

P12-1 Guiglano Inc. is a large, publicly held corporation. The following are six selected expenditures that were made by the company during the fiscal year ended April 30, 2017. The proper accounting treatment of these transactions must be determined in order to ensure that Guiglano's annual financial statements are prepared in accordance with IFRS.

1. Guiglano spent $3 million on a program that is designed to improve relations with its dealers. Dealers responded well to the project and Guiglano's management believes that it will therefore result in significant future benefits. The program was conducted during the fourth quarter of the 2016–17 fiscal year.

2. A pilot plant was constructed during 2016–17 at a cost of $5.5 million to test a new production process. The plant will be operated for approximately five years. After the five years, the company will make a decision about the

economic value of the production process. The pilot plant is too small for commercial production, so it will be dismantled when the test is over.

3. During the year, Guiglano began a new manufacturing operation in Newfoundland, its first plant east of Montreal. To get the plant into operation, the following costs were incurred: (i) $100,000 to make the building fully wheelchair-accessible; (ii) $41,600 to outfit the new employees with Guiglano uniforms; (iii) $12,700 for the reception to introduce the company to others in the industrial mall where the plant is located; and (iv) $64,400 in payroll costs for the new employees while they were being trained.

4. Guiglano purchased Eagle Company for $6 million cash in early August 2016. The fair value of Eagle's net identifiable assets was $5.2 million.

5. The company spent $14 million on advertising during the year. Of that, $2.5 million was spent in April 2017 to introduce a new product to be released during the first quarter of the 2018 fiscal year and $200,000 was used to advertise the opening of the new plant in Newfoundland. The remaining expenditures were for recurring advertising and promotion coverage.

6. During the first six months of the 2016–17 fiscal year, $400,000 was spent on legal work on a successful patent application. The patent became effective in November 2016. The patent's legal life is 20 years and its economic life is expected to be approximately 10 years.

Instructions

For each of the six items presented, determine and justify the following:

(a) The amount, if any, that should be capitalized and included on Guiglano's statement of financial position prepared as at April 30, 2017.

(b) The amount that should be included in Guiglano's statement of income for the year ended April 30, 2017.

P12-2   Information for Naples Corporation's intangible assets follows:

1. On January 1, 2017, Naples signed an agreement to operate as a franchisee of Copy Service, Inc., for an initial franchise fee of $75,000. Of this amount, $35,000 was paid when the agreement was signed and the balance is payable in four annual payments of $10,000 each, beginning January 1, 2018. The agreement provides that the down payment is not refundable and no future services are required of the franchisor. The present value at January 1, 2017, of the four annual payments discounted at 8% (the implicit rate for a loan of this type) is $33,121. The agreement also provides that 5% of the franchisee's revenue must be paid to the franchisor each year. The franchisor requires that Naples provide it with some form of assurance verifying the revenue amount used to determine the 5% payment. Naples's revenue from the franchise for 2017 was $800,000. Naples estimates that the franchise's useful life will be 10 years.

2. Naples incurred $45,000 in experimental costs in its laboratory to develop a patent, and the patent was granted on January 2, 2017. Legal fees and other costs of patent registration totalled $13,600. Naples estimates that the useful life of the patent will be six years.

3. A trademark was purchased from Shanghai Company for $28,600 on July 1, 2014. The legal costs to successfully defend the trademark totalled $8,160 and were paid on July 1, 2017. Naples estimates that the trademark's useful life will be 15 years from the acquisition date.

Assume that Naples reports using ASPE.

Instructions

(a) Prepare a schedule showing the intangible assets section of Naples' statement of financial position at December 31, 2017. Show supporting calculations in good form.

(b) Prepare a schedule showing all expenses resulting from the transactions that would appear on Naples's income statement for the year ended December 31, 2017. Show supporting calculations in good form.

(c) How would your response change under IFRS?

(d) What type of report could Naples provide to the franchisor to verify the revenue amount provided?

(Adapted from AICPA.)

DIGGING DEEPER

P12-3   Gelato Corporation, a private entity reporting under ASPE, was incorporated on January 3, 2016. The corporation's financial statements for its first year of operations were not examined by a public accountant. You have been engaged to audit the financial statements for the year ended December 31, 2017, and your audit is almost complete. The corporation's trial balance is as follows:

AUDITING

GELATO CORPORATION
Trial Balance
December 31, 2017

	Debit	Credit
Cash	$ 57,000	
Accounts receivable	87,000	
Allowance for doubtful accounts		$ 1,500
Inventory	60,200	
Machinery	82,000	
Equipment	37,000	
Accumulated depreciation		26,200
Intangible assets—patents	128,200	
Leasehold improvements	36,100	
Prepaid expenses	13,000	
Goodwill	30,000	
Intangible assets—licensing agreement No. 1	60,000	
Intangible assets—licensing agreement No. 2	56,000	
Accounts payable		93,000
Unearned revenue		17,280
Common shares		300,000
Retained earnings, January 1, 2017		173,020
Sales		720,000
Cost of goods sold	475,000	
Selling expenses	180,000	
Interest expense	29,500	
Totals	$1,331,000	$1,331,000

The following information is for accounts that may still need adjustment:

1. Patents for Gelato's manufacturing process were acquired on January 2, 2017, at a cost of $87,500. An additional $35,000 was spent in July 2017 and $5,700 in December 2017 to improve machinery covered by the patents and was charged to the Intangible Assets—Patents account. Depreciation on fixed assets was properly recorded for 2017 in accordance with Gelato's practice, which is to take a full year of depreciation for property on hand at June 30. No other depreciation or amortization was recorded. Gelato uses the straight-line method for all amortization and amortizes its patents over their legal life, which was 17 years when the patent was granted. Accumulate all amortization expense in one income statement account.

2. At December 31, 2017, management determined that the undiscounted future net cash flows that are expected from the use of the patent would be $80,000, the value in use was $75,000, the resale value of the patent was approximately $55,000, and disposal costs would be $5,000.

3. On January 3, 2016, Gelato purchased licensing agreement no. 1, which management believed had an unlimited useful life. Licences similar to this are frequently bought and sold. Gelato could only clearly identify cash flows from agreement no. 1 for 15 years. After the 15 years, further cash flows are still possible, but are uncertain. The balance in the Licences account includes the agreement's purchase price of $57,000 and expenses of $3,000 related to the acquisition. On January 1, 2017, Gelato purchased licensing agreement no. 2, which has a life expectancy of five years. The balance in the Licences account includes its $54,000 purchase price and $6,000 in acquisition expenses, but it has been reduced by a credit of $4,000 for the advance collection of 2018 revenue from the agreement. In late December 2016, an explosion caused a permanent 60% reduction in the expected revenue-producing value of licensing agreement no. 1. In January 2018, a flood caused additional damage that rendered the agreement worthless.

4. The balance in the Goodwill account results from legal expenses of $30,000 that were incurred for Gelato's incorporation on January 3, 2016. Management assumes that the $30,000 cost will benefit the entire life of the organization, and believes that these costs should be amortized over a limited life of 30 years. No entry has been made yet.

5. The Leasehold Improvements account includes the following:

(i) There is a $15,000 cost of improvements that Gelato made to premises that it leases as a tenant. The improvements were made in January 2016 and have a useful life of 12 years.

(ii) Movable assembly-line equipment costing $15,000 was installed in the leased premises in December 2017.

(iii) Real estate taxes of $6,100 were paid by Gelato in 2017, but they should have been paid by the landlord under the terms of the lease agreement.

Gelato paid its rent in full during 2017. A 10-year non-renewable lease was signed on January 3, 2016, for the leased building that Gelato uses in manufacturing operations. No amortization or depreciation has been recorded on any amounts related to the lease or improvements.

6. Included in selling expenses are the following costs incurred to develop a new product. Gelato hopes to establish the technical, financial, and commercial viability of this project in fiscal 2018.

Salaries of two employees who spend approximately 50% of their time on research and development initiatives (this amount represents their full salary)	$110,000
Materials consumed	35,000

Instructions

(a) Prepare an eight-column work sheet to adjust the accounts that require adjustment and include columns for an income statement and a statement of financial position. A separate account should be used for the accumulation of each type of amortization. Formal adjusting journal entries and financial statements are not required.

(b) Prepare Gelato's statement of financial position and income statement for the year ended December 31, 2017, in proper form.

(c) Explain how the accounting would differ if Gelato were reporting under IFRS.

(Adapted from AICPA.)

P12-4   Monsecours Corp., a public company incorporated on June 28, 2016, set up a single account for all of its intangible assets. The following summary discloses the debit entries that were recorded during 2016 and 2017 in that account:

INTANGIBLE ASSETS—MONSECOURS

July 1, 2016	8-year franchise; expiration date of June 30, 2024	$ 35,000
Oct. 1	Advance payment on leasehold (2-year lease)	25,000
Dec. 31	Net loss for 2016 including incorporation fee, $1,000; related legal fees of organizing, $5,000; expenses of recruiting and training staff for start-up of new business, $3,800	17,000
Feb. 15, 2017	Patent purchased (10-year life)	65,400
Mar. 1	Direct costs of acquiring a 5-year licensing agreement	86,000
Apr. 1	Goodwill purchased (indefinite life)	287,500
June 1	Legal fee for successful defence of patent (see above)	13,350
Dec. 31	Costs of research department for year	75,000
31	Royalties paid under licensing agreement (see above)	2,775

The new business started up on July 2, 2016. No amortization was recorded for 2016 or 2017. The goodwill purchased on April 1, 2017, includes in-process development costs that meet the six development stage criteria, valued at $175,000. The company estimates that this amount will help it generate revenues over a 10-year period.

Instructions

DIGGING DEEPER

(a) Prepare the necessary entries to clear the Intangible Assets account and to set up separate accounts for distinct types of intangibles. Make the entries as at December 31, 2017, and record any necessary amortization so that all balances are appropriate as at that date. State any assumptions that you need to make to support your entries.

(b) In what circumstances should goodwill be recognized? From the perspective of an investor, does the required recognition and measurement of goodwill provide useful financial statement information?

P12-5   Fields Laboratories holds a valuable patent (No. 758-6002-1A) on a precipitator that prevents certain types of air pollution. Fields does not manufacture or sell the products and processes it develops. Instead, it conducts research and develops products and processes that it patents, and then assigns the patents to manufacturers on a royalty basis. Occasionally it sells one of its patents. The history of Fields patent number 758-6002-1A is as follows.

Date	Activity	Cost
2008–2009	Research conducted to develop precipitator	$384,000
Jan. 3, 2010	Design and construction of a prototype	87,600
Mar. 15, 2010	Testing of models	42,000
Jan. 4, 2011	Fees paid to engineers and lawyers to prepare patent application; patent granted June 30, 2011	59,500
Nov. 30, 2012	Engineering activity necessary to advance the design of the precipitator to the manufacturing stage	81,500
Dec. 31, 2013	Legal fees paid to successfully defend precipitator patent	42,000
Apr. 15, 2014	Research aimed at modifying the design of the patented precipitator	43,000
July 31, 2018	Legal fees paid in unsuccessful patent infringement suit against a competitor	34,000

Fields assumed a useful life of 17 years when it received the initial precipitator patent. On January 1, 2016, it revised its useful life estimate downward to five remaining years. The company's year ends December 31. Fields follows IFRS for reporting purposes.

Instructions

Calculate the carrying value of patent No. 758-6002-1A on each of the following dates:

(a) December 31, 2011

(b) December 31, 2015

(c) December 31, 2018

How would your answer differ if ASPE were followed?

P12-6   During 2015, Medicine Hat Tools Ltd., a Canadian public company, purchased a building site for its product development laboratory at a cost of $61,000. Construction of the building started in 2015. The building was completed in late December 2016 at a cost of $185,000 and placed in service on January 2, 2017. The building's estimated useful life for depreciation purposes is 15 years. The straight-line method of depreciation is used and there is no estimated residual value. After the building went into service, several projects were begun and many are still in process.

Management estimates that about 50% of the development projects will result in long-term benefits (for at least 10 years) to the corporation. The other projects either benefited the current period or were abandoned before completion. A summary of the different projects, their number, and the direct costs that were incurred for development activities in 2017 appears in the table that follows.

On the recommendation of its research and development group, Medicine Hat Tools Ltd. acquired a patent for manufacturing rights at a cost of $102,500. The patent was acquired on April 1, 2016, and has an economic life of 10 years.

	Number of Projects	Salaries and Employee Benefits	Other Expenses (Excluding Building Depreciation Charges)
Development of viable products (management intent and capability, financial, technical, and commercial viability criteria were met)	15	$125,000	$ 81,000
Abandoned projects or projects that benefit the current period only	10	87,000	21,000
Projects in process—results uncertain	5	52,500	18,500
Total	30	$264,500	$120,500

Instructions

(a) How should the items above that relate to product development activities be reported under IFRS on the company's income statement and statement of financial position at December 31, 2017? Be sure to give account titles and amounts, and briefly justify your presentation.

(b) Outline the criteria that would have to be met for any development costs to qualify as an intangible asset.

(Adapted from CMA.)

P12-7   In 2017, Aquaculture Incorporated applied for several commercial fishing licences for its commercial fishing vessels. The application was successful and on January 2, 2017, Aquaculture was granted 22 commercial fishing licences for a registration fee of $18,700 per licence. According to management, each licence had a useful life of eight years from the date of registration. After the eight years, further cash flows might still be possible, but they are uncertain. There is an active market for Aquaculture's licences, which are freely transferable.

In 2018, due to an oil spill in the bordering ocean and severe commercial fishing restrictions, the value of Aquaculture's licences decreased. As at December 31, 2018, each licence had a value in use of $9,500, fair value of $8,300, and costs to sell of $200. In 2020, due to much higher demand and restricted issuance of commercial fishing licences, the value of Aquaculture's licences increased. As at December 31, 2020, each licence had a value in use of $14,900, fair value of $17,000, and costs to sell of $200. Aquaculture amortizes intangible assets using the straight-line method, revalues the licences at the end of 2018 and 2020, and prepares financial statements in accordance with IFRS.

Instructions

(a) Prepare the entry to record the costs incurred on January 2, 2017.

(b) Assume that after initial recognition, Aquaculture uses the revaluation model (asset adjustment method) to measure its intangible assets. Prepare the entries required on December 31, 2018, December 31, 2019, and December 31, 2020, and calculate the carrying amount of the intangible asset, if any, as at December 31, 2020.

(c) Assume that after initial recognition, Aquaculture uses the revaluation model (proportionate method) to measure its intangible assets. Prepare the entries required on December 31, 2018, December 31, 2019, and December 31, 2020, and calculate the carrying amount of the intangible asset, if any, as at December 31, 2020.

(d) Would an investor prefer Aquaculture to use the asset adjustment method or the proportionate method to apply the revaluation model?

P12-8   Meridan Golf and Sports was formed on July 1, 2017, when Steve Powerdriver purchased Old Master Golf Corporation. Old Master provides video golf instruction at kiosks in shopping malls. Powerdriver's plan is to make the instruction business part of his golf equipment and accessory stores. Powerdriver paid $650,000 cash for Old Master. At the time of purchase, Old Master's balance sheet reported assets of $550,000 and liabilities of $100,000 (shareholders' equity was $450,000). The fair value of Old Master's identifiable assets was estimated to be $700,000. Included in the identifiable assets was the Old Master trade name with a fair value of $15,000 and a copyright on some instructional books with a fair value of $25,000. The trade name had a remaining legal life of five years and can be renewed indefinitely at nominal cost. The copyright had a remaining life of 40 years.

Instructions

Assume that Meridan Golf and Sports is a private company reporting under ASPE.

(a) Prepare the intangible assets section of Meridan Golf and Sports at December 31, 2017. How much amortization expense is included in Meridan's income for the year ended December 31, 2017? Show all supporting calculations.

(b) Prepare the journal entry to record the amortization expense for 2018. Prepare the intangible assets section of Meridan Golf and Sports at December 31, 2018. (No impairment needs to be recorded in 2018.)

(c) At the end of 2019, Powerdriver is evaluating the results of the instructional business. Due to fierce competition from Internet sites and television, the Old Master reporting unit has been losing money and has a carrying amount (including goodwill) of $450,000 and fair value (including goodwill) of $430,000.

Powerdriver has collected the following information about the company's intangible assets:

Intangible Asset	Expected Cash Flows (Undiscounted)	Fair Value
Trade name	$11,000	$ 8,000
Copyright	30,000	25,000

Prepare the required journal entries, if any, to record impairment on Meridan's intangible assets. (Assume that amortization for 2019 has been recorded.) Show supporting calculations.

P12-9   Use the data provided in P12-8. Assume instead that Meridan Golf and Sports is a public company. The relevant information for the impairment test on December 31, 2019, is as follows:

	Carrying Amount	Future Net Cash Flows (Undiscounted)	Value in Use	FV–Selling Costs
Trade name	$ 15,000	$ 11,000	$ 7,000	$ 7,500
Copyright	23,438	30,000	27,000	24,000
Cash-generating unit to which goodwill was allocated	450,000	470,000	440,000	420,000

Instructions

Provide the calculations for the impairment test and any associated journal entry.

P12-10   Six examples of purchased intangible assets follow. They are reported on the consolidated statement of financial position of Powers Enterprises Limited and include information about their useful and legal lives. Powers prepares financial statements in accordance with IFRS.

Intangible 1(i) is the trade name for one of the company's subsidiaries. The trade name has a remaining legal life of 16 years, but it can be renewed indefinitely at a very low cost. The subsidiary has grown quickly and been very successful, and its name is well known to Canadian consumers. Powers management has concluded that it can identify positive cash flows from the use of the trade name for another 25 years, and assumes the cash flows will continue even longer.

Intangible 1(ii) is the trade name as identified in 1(i), but assume instead that Powers Enterprises expects to sell this subsidiary in three years, since the subsidiary operates in an area that is not part of Powers' core activities.

Intangible 2 is a licence granted by the federal government to Powers that allows Powers to provide essential services to a key military installation overseas. The licence expires in five years, but is renewable indefinitely at little cost.

Because of the profitability associated with this licence, Powers expects to renew it indefinitely. The licence is very marketable and will generate cash flows indefinitely.

Intangible 3 is a magazine subscription list. Powers expects to use this subscriber list to generate revenues and cash flows for at least 25 years. It has determined the cash flow potential of this intangible by analyzing the subscribers' renewal history, the behaviour of the group of subscribers, and their responses to questionnaires.

Intangible 4 is a non-competition covenant. Powers acquired this intangible asset when it bought out a major owner-managed competitor. The seller signed a contract in which he agreed not to set up or work for another business that was in direct or indirect competition with Powers. The projected cash flows resulting from this agreement are expected to continue for at least 25 years.

Intangible 5 is medical files. One of Powers' subsidiary companies owns several dental clinics. A recent purchase of a retiring dentist's practice required a significant payment for the practice's medical files and clients. Powers considers that this base will benefit the business for as long as it exists, providing cash flows indefinitely.

Intangible 6 is a favourable lease. Powers acquired a sublease on a large warehouse property that requires an annual rental amount that is 50% below competitive rates in the area. The lease extends for 35 years.

Instructions

For each intangible asset and situation described above, do the following:

(a) Identify the appropriate method of accounting for the asset subsequent to acquisition, and justify your answer.

(b) Provide an example of a specific situation that would cause you to test the intangible asset for impairment.

P12-11 In late July 2017, Mona Ltd., a private company, paid $2 million to acquire all of the net assets of Lubello Corp., which then became a division of Mona. Lubello reported the following statement of financial position at the time of acquisition:

Current assets	$ 415,000	Current liabilities	$ 300,000
Non-current assets	1,335,000	Long-term liabilities	265,000
		Shareholders' equity	1,185,000
	$1,750,000		$1,750,000

It was determined at the date of the purchase that the fair value of the identifiable net assets of Lubello was $1.7 million. Over the next six months of operations, the new division had operating losses. In addition, it now appears that it will generate substantial losses for the foreseeable future. At December 31, 2017, the fair value of the Lubello Division is $1,850,000, and the division reports the following statement of financial position information:

Current assets	$ 462,000
Non-current assets (including goodwill recognized in purchase)	2,400,000
Current liabilities	(703,500)
Long-term liabilities	(530,000)
Net assets	$1,628,500

Assume that Mona Ltd. prepares financial statements in accordance with ASPE.

Instructions

(a) Calculate the amount of goodwill, if any, that should be recognized in late July 2017.

(b) Determine the impairment loss, if any, to be recognized on December 31, 2017.

(c) Assume that the fair value of the Lubello Division on December 31, 2017, is $1.5 million. Determine the impairment loss, if any, that would be recognized.

(d) Prepare the journal entry to record the impairment loss, if any, in (b) and (c) and indicate where the loss would be reported in the income statement.

(e) Explain how the accounting would differ under IFRS.

(f) Shortly after Mona purchased Lubello, Lubello incurred losses and its future does not look promising. What advice can you provide to Mona's management team for any future acquisitions the company may be considering?

DIGGING DEEPER

P12-12 On September 1, 2017, Madonna Lisa Corporation, a public company, acquired Jaromil Enterprises for a cash payment of $763,000. At the time of purchase, Jaromil's statement of financial position showed assets of $850,000, liabilities of $430,000, and owners' equity of $420,000. The fair value of Jaromil's identifiable assets is estimated to be $1,080,000.

Instructions

(a) Calculate the amount of goodwill acquired by Madonna Lisa.

(b) Assume that the goodwill was allocated entirely to one cash-generating unit (CGU), as indicated below. The CGU's value in use at the statement of financial position date was $3,850,000 and the fair value less costs to sell was $4,250,000. Determine if the goodwill is impaired.

	Plant A CGU
Assets (other than goodwill)	$4,500,000
Goodwill	113,000
Total carrying value of CGU	$4,613,000

(c) Explain how a future reversal of impairment is accounted for under IFRS.

*P12-13   Macho Inc. has recently become interested in acquiring a South American plant to handle many of its production functions in that market. One possible candidate is De Fuentes SA, a closely held corporation, whose owners have decided to sell their business if a proper settlement can be obtained. De Fuentes's statement of financial position is as follows:

Current assets	$125,000
Fair value—net income investments	55,000
Buildings (net)	405,000
Total assets	$585,000
Current liabilities	$ 85,000
Notes payable	105,000
Share capital	225,000
Retained earnings	170,000
Total equities	$585,000

FINANCE

Macho has hired Yardon Appraisal Corporation to determine the proper price to pay for De Fuentes SA. The appraisal firm finds that the fair value—net income investments have a fair value of $75,000 and that inventory is understated by $40,000. All other assets and liabilities have book values that approximate their fair values. An examination of the company's income for the last four years indicates that the net income has steadily increased. In 2017, the company had a net operating income of $110,000, and this income should increase by 15% each year over the next four years. Macho believes that a normal return in this type of business is 15% on net assets. The asset investment in the South American plant is expected to stay the same for the next four years.

Instructions

(a) Yardon Appraisal Corporation has indicated that the company's fair value can be estimated in several ways. Prepare estimates of the value of De Fuentes SA, with the value based on each of the following independent assumptions:

1. Goodwill is based on the purchase of average excess earnings over the next four years.

2. Goodwill is equal to the capitalization of average excess earnings of De Fuentes SA at 30%.

3. Goodwill is equal to the present value of the average excess earnings over the next four years discounted at 15%.

4. The value of the business is based on the capitalization of future excess earnings of De Fuentes SA at 16%.

(b) De Fuentes SA is willing to sell the business for $1 million. What advice should Yardon Appraisal give Macho in regard to this offer?

(c) If Macho were to pay $850,000 to purchase the assets and assume the liabilities of De Fuentes SA, how would this transaction be reflected on Macho's books?

*P12-14   The president of Plain Corp., Joyce Lima, is thinking of purchasing Balloon Bunch Corporation. She thinks that the offer sounds fair but she wants to consult a professional accountant to be sure. Balloon Bunch Corporation is asking for $85,000 in excess of the fair value of the identifiable net assets. Balloon Bunch's net income figures for the last five years are as follows:

2013—$67,000		2016—$80,000	
2014—$50,000		2017—$72,000	
2015—$81,000			

FINANCE   The company's identifiable net assets were appraised at $400,000 on December 31, 2017.

You have done some initial research on the balloon industry and discovered that the normal rate of return on identifiable net assets is 15%. After analyzing such variables as the stability of past earnings, the nature of the business, and general economic conditions, you have decided that the average excess earnings for the last five years should be capitalized at 20% and that the excess earnings will continue for about six more years. Further research led you to discover that the Happy Balloon Corporation, a competitor of similar size and profitability, was recently sold for $450,000, five times its average yearly earnings of $90,000.

Instructions

(a) Prepare a schedule that includes the calculation of Balloon Bunch Corporation's goodwill and purchase price under at least three methods.

(b) Write a letter to Joyce Lima that includes all of the following:

1. An explanation of the nature of goodwill.

2. An explanation of the different acceptable methods of determining the fair value of goodwill. (Include with your explanation the rationale for how each method arrives at a goodwill value.)

3. Advice for Joyce Lima on how to determine her purchase price.

4. Considerations before relying on the earnings figure used to determine the purchase price.

 P12-15 On July 31, 2017, Mexico Company paid $3,000,000 to acquire all of the common shares of Conchita Incorporated, which became a division of Mexico. Conchita reported the following balance sheet at the time of the acquisition.

CONCHITA INC.
Statement of Financial Position
As at July 31, 2017

Current assets	$ 800,000	Current liabilities	$ 600,000
Non-current assets	2,700,000	Long-term liabilities	500,000
Total assets	$3,500,000	Shareholders' equity	2,400,000
		Total liabilities and shareholders' equity	$3,500,000

It was determined at the date of the purchase that the fair value of the identifiable net assets of Conchita was $2,750,000. Over the next six months of operations, the newly purchased division experienced operating losses. In addition, it now appears that it will generate substantial losses for the foreseeable future. At December 31, 2017, Conchita reports the following balance sheet information:

Current assets	$ 450,000
Non-current assets (including goodwill recognized in purchase)	2,400,000
Current liabilities	(700,000)
Long-term liabilities	(500,000)
Net assets	$1,650,000

It is determined that the fair value of the Conchita Division as at December 31, 2017, is $1,850,000. The recorded amount for Conchita's net assets (excluding goodwill) is the same as fair value, except for property, plant, and equipment, which has a fair value $150,000 above the carrying value. Assume that Mexico follows ASPE for financial reporting purposes.

Instructions

(a) Calculate the amount of goodwill recognized, if any, on July 31, 2017.

(b) Determine the impairment loss, if any, to be recorded on December 31, 2017.

(c) Assume that fair value of the Conchita Division is $1,600,000 instead of $1,850,000. Determine the impairment loss, if any, to be recorded on December 31, 2017.

(d) Prepare the journal entry to record the impairment loss, if any, and indicate where the loss would be reported in the income statement.

Integrated Cases

ENABLING COMPETENCIES

Refer to the Case Primer on the Student Website and in *WileyPLUS* to help you answer these cases.

(*Hint:* If there are issues here that are new, use the conceptual framework to help you support your analysis with solid reasoning.)

IC12-1   Dr. Gary Morrow, a former surgeon, is the president and owner of Morrow Medical (MM), a private Ontario company that focuses on the design and implementation of various medical and pharmaceutical products. With the recent success of various products put to market by MM, Dr. Morrow has decided that this would be a good opportunity to sell his company and retire to the Arizona desert. Dr. Morrow has located a potential buyer for the business and an agreement has been put in place that would see MM being sold at five times the December 31, 2016 net income. The potential buyer is extremely interested in an MM product that is currently in the development stage—the MM Surgical Drill.

During 2016, MM launched into production a special latex glove for use during surgery. This glove is laced with a special antibacterial agent that significantly reduces the risk of infection during surgery. The product had been in the development phase since 2013, and in early 2015, it was approved by Health Canada for production and use.

Dr. Morrow was pleased with the initial demand for the product after trial runs conducted by surgeons during late 2015. After the success of the trial testing, MM landed contracts with several hospitals in the province and early feedback was favourable. Dr. Morrow was surprised, however, with how small the quantity of orders placed by hospitals actually was. He was certain that hospitals would quickly run out of the gloves and was beginning to fear that they would buy a competitor's product.

Since Dr. Morrow wanted to prevent hospitals from buying elsewhere, as it would result in a loss of sales for MM, for each purchase order received from a hospital, Dr. Morrow shipped several more units than were ordered. He was certain that all of the extra inventory would eventually be consumed and this was MM's way of avoiding the hospitals' running out of inventory. To prevent hospitals from returning the extra inventory, he allowed them eight months to either pay for the entire shipment or return any unused gloves in excess of the initial amount that

AUDIT

was ordered. Dr. Morrow's first priority is always getting the product out of the warehouse and into the hospitals. Orders are generally filled and shipped within two days of receipt of a purchase order. Because MM is dealing with hospitals, there is little concern over collectibility.

During 2013, under the supervision of Dr. Morrow, MM began the research and development of a special surgical drill (the MM Surgical Drill mentioned above) that would allow for more precise handling by surgeons than any other drill currently on the market. The development of this product grew from various market surveys conducted in hospitals throughout Ontario that showed that surgeons were unhappy with the drills that were currently available.

The following costs were incurred in 2016:

Cost of setting up production lab	$ 30,000
Testing of Surgical Drill	100,000
Design of the moulds involved in Surgical Drill technology	17,500
Testing to evaluate product alternatives	12,000
Marketing and promotion costs in connection with launching the surgical gloves	15,000

Dr. Morrow intends to capitalize all of these costs for the December 31 year end. In addition, $25,000 of tool design costs that were expensed in 2015 will be capitalized in 2016.

MM has the technical resources available to complete the Surgical Drill project and, since testing to date has been successful, management intends to bring this product to market in early 2018. MM has been faced with cash flow problems in the last few months but hopes that once MM is sold, additional funding will be available to see this product into its production stage.

In early 2016, an engineer testing the Surgical Drill was severely injured as a result of a product malfunction. This glitch was subsequently identified and fixed. MM has recently been sued. The claim is for $500,000 and alleges that MM was responsible for the engineer's injuries. MM's lawyer's best estimate of what the company will end up paying is $100,000 to $200,000. As the trial does not begin until 2017, MM has no intention of recording this in its December 31, 2016 financial statements.

Instructions

Adopt the role of the auditor hired by MM's potential buyer and analyze the financial reporting issues.

IC12-2   Biofuel Inc. (BI) is a private company that just started up this year. The company's owner, Sarah Biorini, created a process whereby carbon dioxide (CO_2) emissions are converted into biofuel. Specifically, the CO_2 is pumped into a pond where algae are grown. The algae feed on the CO_2 and release oxygen. The algae are harvested, dried, and sold as fuel. The fuel is used by cement manufacturing companies to heat their kilns (ovens). Sarah contributed the prototype and idea to the newly formed company in return for common shares. She esti-

mated that the prototype was worth about $500,000. BI spent the first year developing the idea and by year end was producing and selling the fuel to several cement production companies. Cement companies not only produce large amounts of CO_2, but also need large amounts of fuel to heat their kilns.

One of the critical success factors for BI is that the algae-producing pond should be close to the source of CO_2. This reduces transportation costs. After much consideration, BI decided to build pipelines to pump CO_2

from the source (the cement company) into an adjacent algae-filled pond. The pond is excavated by BI but it sits on the cement company's land (close to the source of CO_2). Once a month, BI harvests the algae and ships them to its manufacturing plant to process them into biofuel. It then sells the biofuel back to the cement companies.

The cost of constructing the pipelines is funded by the bank, as is the excavation of the ponds. The construction is done by BI and generally takes about three to six months. The finished biofuel made from the algae is priced to recover patent costs and the cost of building the pipe and the ponds, as well as any other costs. It is sold back to the cement companies. The

cement companies are both customers and suppliers of the CO_2.

The bank is quite happy to continue funding additional projects as long as BI sends its financial statements to the bank every quarter, starting next year. In addition, the bank would like to see audited annual financial statements beginning with the current year. The bank and BI have agreed that the debt to equity ratio cannot exceed 3:1, or the loans become immediately due. BI's accountant is looking to produce the annual financial statements for the first year of operations. He has not yet decided whether to follow IFRS or ASPE and is interested in the differences between the two.

Instructions

Assume the role of BI's accountant and discuss the financial reporting issues relating to the above. Use the case analysis framework presented in class, including an overview, analysis, and recommendations.

IC12-3   As a recent graduate and newly hired financial analyst for the local branch office of a national brokerage firm, you are excited to get your first assignment, allowing you to use your accounting expertise. Your supervisor provides you with updated data for the most recent quarter for three companies that the firm has been recommending to its clients as "buys." All three companies are publicly traded and use IFRS for financial reporting purposes. Each of the companies made one significant acquisition in the past that expanded their markets in their respective industries. The companies all put a high intrinsic value on the potential that these new markets would bring to the acquiring company. Each of the acquisitions was brought into the acquiring company as a new division. The new acquisitions represent at least 25% of the operations of the companies that acquired them.

The return on assets for each of the companies as a whole has outperformed their industry cohorts in the past.

But, given recent challenges in their markets, coupled with unsteady performance overall in the marketplace, there is concern that the companies may experience operating challenges and lower earnings. In particular, each of the acquisitions has not performed as expected and has resulted in quarterly net losses to the companies' bottom line.

As shown by the data summarized below, each newly acquired division's market value is now lower than its corresponding book value. Your supervisor wants to understand what, if any, implications this may have for each company's future prospects, given the significance of the divisions to the overall operations of each company.

The book value reported in the table below includes the carrying value of goodwill assigned to each division at the time of its acquisition. For each company, there has been no impairment of the carrying value of goodwill previously recorded for these divisions.

(All numbers in millions, except return on assets.)

Company Name and Division	Market Value (B)	Book Value (Net Assets) (C)	Carrying Value of Goodwill (D)	Value in Use (E)	Costs to Sell (F)	ROA for the Company (%) (G)
ABC Limited, Division 1	$36,200	$51,500	$30,200	$32,300	$1,000	3.5
DEF Limited, Division H	12,700	22,200	9,000	16,500	500	2.6
XYZ Limited, Division XX	1,800	4,000	900	3,000	200	5.2

FINANCE

Your supervisor suspects that the companies will need to record goodwill impairment for the acquired divisions in the near future, but is unsure about the goodwill impairment rules. She would like to know if it is likely that these companies will recognize impairment. If they will, your supervisor would like you to estimate the amount for each and explain to her where the impairment loss would be recorded. In addition, she would like to know how this might impact the overall return on assets ratio for each company and the impact on the "buy" recommendations.

Your supervisor would also like to know if these companies can reverse the impairment losses recorded once the market improves and the prospect of these divisions looks promising. If a reversal is possible, the supervisor has suggested that the current year impairments may have less impact than if no reversal were available.

Your supervisor would like you to respond within two days, as the brokerage firm's clients are nervous about their portfolios and are anxious to hear about any good "buy" recommendations.

Instructions

Adopt the role of the newly hired finanwcial analyst and prepare the report for your supervisor.

RESEARCH AND ANALYSIS

REAL WORLD EMPHASIS

RA12-1 British Airways

Access the annual report for **British Airways plc (BA)** for the year ended December 31, 2014, from its parent company's website (www.iagshares.com). British Airways is now a part of the International Airlines Group. Use the amounts in and notes to BA's group (i.e., consolidated) financial statements to answer the following questions.

Instructions

(a) Does British Airways plc report any intangible assets or goodwill in its 2014 financial statements and accompanying notes? Identify all such accounts, describe their nature, their reported balance sheet amounts at December 31, 2014, and the accounting policies that are applied to these assets, including any general impairment policies. Are there any situations where there are discrepancies with IFRS standards?

(b) What additions were made to the landing rights and software for 2014? Do you expect the landing rights are mainly for use within the EU or outside the EU? Explain briefly.

(c) How is goodwill tested for impairment? Provide details on the methods and key assumptions used by the company. Is information provided on the recoverable amounts determined? Were there any impairment losses recorded in 2014? What assumptions would make the recoverable amount equal to the carrying amount for the network airline operations?

(d) Why is the information provided in (c) considered helpful to users?

REAL WORLD EMPHASIS

RA12-2 Rights to Use Sports Celebrities' Names

Since 1996, **Nike, Inc.**, has had endorsement contracts with Tiger Woods and some of the world's best-known athletes. For example, Nike has been able to gain the rights to use top golfers' names in advertising promotions and on Nike Golf apparel, footwear, golf balls, and golf equipment. Recently, Rory McIlroy's name has been added to its list.

Instructions

Conduct research on the Internet to determine the nature of the endorsement contracts that Nike has with top athletes, such as Rory McIlroy. What form do Nike's payments for such rights take? Using Nike, Inc.'s most recent financial statements (which can be found in their Form-10K filing), determine how Nike reports the cost of endorsement contracts. Does the cost qualify as an intangible asset under IAS 38? Explain briefly.

RA12-3 Intangible Issues

Kolber Manufacturing Limited designs, manufactures, and distributes safety boots. In January 2017, Kolber purchased another business that manufactures and distributes safety shoes, to complement its existing business. The total purchase price was $10 million in cash paid immediately and another $5 million in cash to be paid in one year's time. The company's current interest cost was 6%. The assets and liabilities purchased include accounts receivable, finished goods inventories, land and plant, manufacturing equipment and office equipment, accounts payable, and a loan that is secured by the manufacturing equipment. In addition, a trademark was included (which has six years remaining on its current legal life), as well as existing customer relationships (although there are no outstanding contracts with these customers), and a non-compete agreement with the existing owners that they will not start any similar business for the next five years. The company reports under IFRS.

Instructions

You are the controller of Kolber and have been given the task of recording the purchase in the company's books.

(a) Outline how you might go about determining how to allocate the purchase price to the intangible assets and any goodwill purchased. In addition, consider how each of these assets is subsequently reported and what the effect will be on net earnings in subsequent years given your decisions now.

(b) If this company reported under ASPE, explain how the impairment test for goodwill would differ from the IFRS method.

(To assist you with this question, you may want to read the following article: "From Intangible to Tangible," by Andrew Michelin, *CA Magazine*, June/July 2008.)

(Adapted from AICPA.)

AUDIT

RA12-4 Websites

Weaver Limited is a company that distributes hard-to-find computer supplies, such as hardware parts and cables. It sells and ships products all over the world. Recently, the board of directors approved the plan and a budget for the company to design its own website. The website has two sections. One is for general information and can be accessed by anyone. On this part of the site, the company has information about what it does and pictures of all the products sold. The other part of the website is accessible only by logging in. Customers are given passwords to enter this part of the site, where they can place their orders, which are then reviewed by the order clerks and sent on to shipping. The IT manager has been put in charge of managing the website project, keeping track of and approving all costs incurred.

The company has incurred the following costs to develop the site: the IT manager's salary for the six months required to supervise the project; legal fees to register the domain name; consulting costs for a feasibility study; purchase of the hardware; software developers to develop the code for the application, installation, and testing of the software; graphic artist to design the layout and colour for the web pages; photographers to take pictures of the products to be shown on the site; staff time to upload all the information to the site, including the company and product descriptions; and the data required to place an order, including prices, data entry screens, and shipping options. Finally, the company has incurred costs to train the employees on using the software. Ongoing costs include updating product prices and content, adding new functions, and backing up the data.

Instructions

(a) You are an external auditor and have been hired by Weaver to explain how these costs should be reported. Using IAS 38 and SIC 32—Intangible Assets—Web Site Costs (an Interpretation under International Financial Reporting Standards that is accessible via an Internet search), discuss the treatment of these costs, referring to the general principles in IAS 38 to support your analysis. Explain how the company must report costs incurred once the website is operating.

(b) As Weaver's external auditor, what might you be concerned about in addition to the GAAP financial accounting and reporting of the internally developed intangible asset website?

RA12-5   Goodwill

FINANCE

Echo Corp., a retail propane gas distributor, has increased its annual sales volume to a level that is three times greater than the annual sales of a dealer that it purchased in 2016 in order to begin operations. The board of directors of Echo Corp. recently received an offer to negotiate the sale of the company to a large competitor. As a result, the majority of the board members want to increase the stated value of goodwill on the balance sheet to reflect the larger sales volume that it developed through intensive promotion and the product's current market price. A few of the board members, however, would prefer to eliminate goodwill from the balance sheet altogether in order to prevent possible misinterpretations. Goodwill was recorded properly at the start of fiscal 2016.

Instructions

(a) Discuss the meaning of the term "goodwill."

(b) Why are the book and fair values of Echo Corp.'s goodwill different?

(c) Discuss the appropriateness of each of the following:

   1. Increasing the stated value of goodwill prior to the negotiations

   2. Eliminating goodwill completely from the balance sheet
                      (Adapted from AICPA.)

RA12-6   Comparative Analysis

REAL WORLD EMPHASIS

Instructions

From the SEDAR website (www.sedar.com) choose one company from each of four different industry classifications. Choose from a variety of industries, such as real estate (e.g., Crombie Real Estate Investment Trust), food stores—merchandising (e.g., Loblaw Companies Limited), biotechnology and pharmaceuticals (e.g., AEterna Zentaris Inc.), or communications and media (e.g., Quebecor Inc.). From the companies' financial statements for their 2014 fiscal year, identify the year-end amounts reported for goodwill, intangibles, and total assets, and the accounting policies for goodwill and each type of intangible asset reported.

(a) What net amounts were reported for goodwill and for intangible assets by each company? What are the amounts of accumulated amortization reported for the intangible assets? Identify any impairment losses reported in the current period.

(b) What percentage of total assets does each company have invested in goodwill and intangible assets?

(c) Does the type of intangible assets differ depending on the type of industry? Does the relative size of the investment in this category of asset differ among industries? Comment.

(d) Do the policies differ by type of intangible? By type of industry?

(e) Describe the type of disclosure provided for those companies that reported impairment losses.

RA12-7   Regulated Assets

When Canadian public companies were required to apply IFRS beginning in 2011, one of the major issues faced by some entities, particularly those whose revenues were regulated by an independent body, concerned the accounting for regulatory assets. This issue remains unresolved.

Instructions

Research the financial accounting issues related to rate regulation, beginning with the IASB website (www.ifrs.org) and the "Work plan for IFRSs" link. Answer the following questions.

(a) Provide a brief history of the IASB's rate regulation project, and explain where the project currently stands and what the future plans are for this issue.

(b) Identify the type of companies that are considered rate-regulated, and explain what regulatory assets are.

(c) Explain what the current accounting issues are with respect to reporting these assets.

(d) What choice, if any, does the IASB have for settling this issue? Identify any progress that has been made since September 2015 in reaching a decision.

ENDNOTES

[1] *CPA Canada Handbook*, Part II, 1582.03(j) and IFRS 3 Appendix A. Copyright © 2015 IFRS Foundation. All rights reserved. Reproduced by Wiley Canada with the permission of the IFRS Foundation®. No permission granted to third parties to reproduce or distribute.

[2] When less than a 100% interest is acquired or the controlling interest is acquired in stages, the calculation of goodwill is more complex. This topic is left to a course in advanced financial accounting.

[3] See *Business Combinations* in *CPA Canada Handbook*, Part II, Section 1582.03(k) and IFRS 3, Appendix A.

[4] IAS 38, paragraph 21 and *CPA Canada Handbook*, Part II, Section 3064.21.

[5] IFRS 2 *Share-based Payment* is considerably more complex than is indicated here. In addition, the term "fair value" used in IFRS 2 differs from the definition of fair value in IFRS 13 *Fair Value Measurement*. When applying IFRS 2, an entity measures fair value in accordance with the definition in IFRS 2, not IFRS 13. (See IFRS 2, paragraphs 6A and 16-18.)

[6] If control over the assets is acquired through the acquisition of voting shares, the fair value of all the identifiable assets and liabilities (identifiable net assets) is assigned as their cost through the consolidation process. Refer to Chapter 3 for a discussion of how fair values are determined.

[7] IAS 38, *Basis for Conclusions*: BCZ29.

[8] *CPA Canada Handbook*, Part II, Section 3064.08.

[9] *CPA Canada Handbook*, Part II, Section 3064.39 and .43; IAS 38.56 and .59.

[10] Under ASPE, interest or borrowing costs would be included only if it is the accounting policy chosen by the entity. See Chapter 10 for a fuller discussion of the capitalization of borrowing costs.

[11] See Chapter 3 for a fuller discussion of fair value measurement.

[12] For indefinite-life intangible assets, the same accounting applies except that there would be no amortization or accumulated amortization amounts.

[13] See IAS 38.92 for further details. Copyright IFRS Foundation. All rights reserved. Reproduced by John Wiley & Sons Canada, Ltd. with the permission of the IFRS Foundation®. Reproduction and use rights are strictly limited. No permission granted to third parties to reproduce or distribute.

[14] *CPA Canada Handbook*, Part II, Section 3064.61.

[15] *CPA Canada Handbook*, Part II, Section 3064.59 and IAS 38.100. Per IAS 38.100, an active market is based on the definition found in IFRS 13.

[16] This classification framework is used in IFRS 3 *Business Combinations:* Illustrative Examples IE16–IE44 to describe identifiable intangible assets acquired in a business combination. This same classification was previously used in superseded *CPA Canada Handbook*, Part II, Section 1581 *Business Combinations*, Appendix A.

[17] Canadian Intellectual Property Office: http://www.ic.gc.ca.

[18] To illustrate how various intangibles might arise from a specific product, consider what the Canadian creators of the highly successful game Trivial Pursuit did to protect their creation. First, they copyrighted the 6,000 questions that are at the heart of the game. Then they shielded the Trivial Pursuit name by applying for a registered trademark. As a third mode of protection, the creators obtained a design patent on the playing board's design because it represents a unique graphic creation.

[19] Canadian Intellectual Property Office: http://www.ic.gc.ca.

[20] Accounting for lease contracts themselves is in the midst of change. Under existing standards, a lease that transfers the risks and rewards of ownership to the lessee is usually treated as an item of property, plant, and equipment, not an intangible asset. This may change before long. An exposure draft was issued by the IASB in 2010, and based on comments received, a re-exposure draft was issued in 2013 and a new standard was planned for late 2015. With a change in concept to a lease being a "right of use" asset being considered, more contracts will likely fall within the intangible asset category.

[21] Consider the opposite result: Sir Alexander Fleming, who discovered penicillin, decided not to use a patent to protect his discovery. He hoped that companies would produce it more quickly to help save sufferers. Companies, however, refused to develop it because they did not have the protection of a patent and, therefore, were afraid to make the investment.

[22] The Canadian Intellectual Property Office website indicates in its "A Guide to Patents, Part 1" that 90% of patents are for improvements to existing patented inventions.

[23] **Eli Lilly**'s well-known drug Prozac, which is used to treat depression, accounted for 43% of the company's U.S. sales in 1998. The patent on Prozac expired in 2001 and the company was unable to extend its protection with a second-use patent for the use of Prozac to treat appetite disorders. Sales of Prozac went down substantially in 2001 as generic equivalents entered the market.

[24] *CPA Canada Handbook*, Part II, Section 3063 *Impairment of Long-lived Assets* and IAS 36 *Impairment of Assets*.

[25] In reality, the Cash amounts would be netted and only $375,000 would be transferred. If Multi-Diversified gained control over Tractorling by purchasing all of that company's shares instead of buying all the individual assets and liabilities making up the business, the entry would be:

Investment in Shares of Tractorling	400,000	
Cash		400,000

When Multi-Diversified prepares consolidated financial statements, the Investment account is removed from the balance sheet and is replaced with the underlying assets and liabilities that the Investment balance represents. Regardless of the transaction's legal form, the goodwill appears on the investor's consolidated GAAP balance sheet.

[26] Nadi Chlala, Diane Paul, Louise Martel, and Andrée Lavigne, *Financial Reporting in Canada, 2007* (CICA, 2007), p. 343, and Clarence Byrd, Ida Chen, and Joshua Smith, *Financial Reporting in Canada, 2005* (CICA, 2005), p. 256.

[27] Based on estimates from Yahoo Finance, which quoted Apple's March 2015 quarterly financial statements as compared with its market capitalization on July 14, 2015.

[28] A "big bath" in accounting occurs when a company decides that, if a loss has to be reported, it might as well report a very large loss. Any loss is seen as negative but the advantage of reporting a bigger loss is that fewer costs remain in the accounts to be reported as future expenses.

[29] If you find this unclear, try the following approach: Start with the total earnings of $375,000 over the past five years and make the necessary adjustments. First add 5 × $2,000 for the average cost/FIFO adjustment and 5 × $3,000 for the depreciation, and then deduct 5 × $1,000 for the patent amortization and $25,000 for the gain on discontinued operations. The adjusted total five-year earnings of $370,000 are then divided by 5 to get the expected future annual earnings. The result is $74,000.

[30] The following illustrates how the capitalization or discount rate might be calculated for a small business:

A Method of Selecting a Capitalization Rate

	%
Long-term Canadian government bond rate	4
Add: Average premium return on small company shares over government bonds	5
Expected total rate of return on small publicly held shares	9
Add: Premium for greater risk and illiquidity	6
Total required expected rate of return, including inflation component	15
Deduct: Consensus long-term inflation expectation	3
Capitalization rate to apply to current earnings	12

Adapted from Warren Kissin and Ronald Zulli, "Valuation of a Closely Held Business," *The Journal of Accountancy*, June 1988, p. 42.

[31] Why do we divide by the capitalization or discount rate to arrive at the goodwill amount? Recall that the present value of an ordinary annuity is equal to:

$$P\overline{n}|i = [1 - 1 \div (1 + i)^n] \div i$$

When a number is capitalized in perpetuity, $(1 + i)^n$ becomes so large that $1/(1 + i)^n$ essentially equals zero, which leaves $1/i$ or, as in the case above, $21,500/0.25$ or $21,500/0.15$.

[32] The present value of an annuity of $1 received in a steady stream for 10 years in the future discounted at 25% is $3.57050. The present value of an annuity of $21,500, therefore, is $21,500 × 3.57050 = $76,765.75.

[33] Business valuation is a specialist field. The Canadian Institute of Chartered Business Valuators oversees the granting of the specialist designation, Chartered Business Valuator (CBV), to professionals who meet the education, experience, and examination requirements.

Task-Based Simulation and Cumulative Coverage: Chapters 10 to 12

Templates to complete this task-based simulation are available in WileyPLUS and on the instructor website.

Fit Fixtures Incorporated (FFI) is a manufacturer of exercise equipment such as treadmills, stair climbers, and elliptical machines. The company has a December 31 year end and uses ASPE. The accounting staff member who normally looks after the capital asset accounts was on maternity leave for the year, and the company put all transactions in a temporary account called Asset Additions and Disposals, which has a current balance of $2,844,000.

The company policy on calculating depreciation for partial periods of ownership is to take 50% of the normal amount of depreciation in the year of addition or disposal. Due to the staff member's maternity leave, no depreciation or amortization expense has yet been taken in 2017.

1. The company completed construction of a new plant in Saskatchewan on December 15, 2017, to help it better meet the needs of its customers west of Ontario. The costs associated with this construction project were as follows:

Land	$ 500,000
Construction contract: building, 20 years of useful life, residual value of $50,000	1,500,000
Manufacturing equipment	(See below)
Office equipment	250,000
Training costs (employees learning to use equipment)	45,000
Avoidable interest calculated at 8% on financing of project from inception until put in use	75,000

Manufacturing equipment: The equipment purchased for the new plant was purchased on a deferred payment contract signed on December 1. FFI issued a $5-million, five-year, non–interest-bearing note payable to the equipment supplier at a time when the annual market rate of interest was 6%. The note will be repaid with five equal payments made on December 1 of each year, beginning in 2018.

2. FFI purchased a used computer and a printer at an auction for $2,500. The printer needed a new drum. The cost of the new drum was $500. The used computer's fair market value was $2,000 if purchased separately. The printer was worth $1,000 without a drum and $1,500 with the drum replaced.

3. On July 1, 2017, FFI sold a delivery truck for $10,000. The truck originally cost $25,000, and accumulated depreciation on the truck to December 31, 2016, was $10,000. The truck was amortized on a straight-line basis over a five-year period, with no residual value. The sale was recorded as a debit to Cash and a credit to Asset Additions and Disposals. No amortization was recorded in the current year.

4. Due to an office redesign in the Ontario building, FFI traded some old office equipment for different office equipment with a similar life and value in use. The fair value of the equipment disposed of was $5,000. The cost of this equipment was $7,000, and the accumulated depreciation on the equipment at December 31, 2016, was $3,000. This transaction was not recorded in the books of account. No entry was made to record the exchange.

5. Shortly after the new factory was completed, vandals attacked the building and significant damage was done. The costs to correct the damage, which were not covered by insurance, included:

New paint to cover graffiti	$ 4,000
Glass for broken windows	10,000
Improved security system	25,000

6. During the year, the company developed a new piece of exercise equipment that has a built-in video game. It was the policy to amortize development costs on a straight-line basis over three years, with 50% of the normal amount in the year of development. The costs associated with product development included:

Costs to determine how a video game would work with exercise equipment	$ 50,000
Design, testing, and construction of prototype equipment	350,000
Costs to determine the best production process for the new equipment	40,000
Advertising costs to alert customers about the new product	47,000

7. The company has goodwill and an intangible asset as follows:

Asset	Details	Carrying Value as at December 31, 2016	Accumulated Amortization as at December 31, 2016	Amortization Method
Goodwill	Recorded in 2012 when the company took over the business of its predecessor	$500,000	$0	Not applicable
Customer list	Purchased in 2012 when the company took over the business of its predecessor	$250,000	$112,500	Straight-line over 10 years

The customer list has lost value and will not provide benefits through to 2022, as was originally predicted. It is now expected to provide undiscounted future cash flows of $50,000 in total over the next two years. There are no estimated costs to sell the list, as it will not be sold, and the value in use is $46,000. Goodwill has a recoverable value of $700,000 as at December 31, 2017.

Instructions

Part A: New Saskatchewan plant

Determine whether each expenditure related to the new Saskatchewan plant must be capitalized or expensed or whether it could be either (depends on policy choice). Place the dollar amount in the appropriate column in the table below.

	Capitalize	Expense	Policy Choice to Capitalize or Expense
Land			
Building			
Manufacturing equipment			
Office equipment			
Training costs			
Avoidable interest			

Part B: Used equipment purchased at auction

Allocate the expenditure related to the used computer and printer bundle to each component, and identify whether each component must be capitalized or expensed or whether it could be either (depends on policy choice). Place the dollar amount of the amount allocated to each component in the appropriate column in the table below.

	Capitalize	Expense	Policy Choice to Capitalize or Expense
Computer			
Printer			

Part C: Delivery truck disposition

Account for the disposition of the delivery truck by preparing a journal entry in good form

Part D: Office equipment swap

Determine the impact on the company's assets, liabilities, and net income of measuring the transaction with the carrying value versus the fair value. Write "increase," "decrease," or "no impact" in each space.

	Carrying Value	Fair Value
Assets		
Liabilities		
Net income		

Part E: Vandal attack

Determine the impact on the company's assets, liabilities, and net income of the three expenditures related to the vandal attack. Write "increase," "decrease," or "no impact" in each space.

	Paint	Glass	Security System
Assets			
Liabilities			
Net income			

Part F: Research and development costs

Determine whether each expenditure is clearly a research cost or could potentially be a development cost (if the six criteria are met at the point when the costs are incurred). Place the dollar amount of each expenditure in the Research and Other Expenses or Potentially Development cost column.

	Research and Other Expenses	Potentially Development
Costs to determine how a video game would work with exercise equipment		
Design, testing, and construction of prototype equipment		
Costs to determine the best production process for the new equipment		
Advertising costs to alert customers about the new product		

Part G: Intangible assets

Determine whether the intangible assets are impaired, and if so, the amount of the writedown. Place an X in the Impaired or Not Impaired column for both intangible assets (only one X per asset). If the asset is impaired, enter the amount of the writedown in the Writedown Required column.

	Not Impaired (X)	Impaired (X)	Writedown Required ($)
Customer list			
Goodwill			

SPECIMEN FINANCIAL STATEMENTS

Brookfield Asset Management

The following pages contain the financial statements, extracts from selected notes, and other information from the 2014 annual financial statements of Brookfield Asset Management. The complete annual report is available on *WileyPLUS* and the student website. The corporate profile below is taken from the company annual report.

PART 1 – OVERVIEW AND OUTLOOK

OUR BUSINESS

Brookfield is a global alternative asset manager with over $200 billion in assets under management. For more than 100 years we have owned and operated assets on behalf of shareholders and clients with a focus on property, renewable energy, infrastructure and private equity.

We manage a wide range of investment funds and other entities that enable institutional and retail clients to invest in these assets. We earn asset management income including fees, carried interests and other forms of performance income for doing so. As at December 31, 2014, our managed funds and listed partnerships represented $89 billion of invested and committed fee bearing capital. These products include publicly listed partnerships that are listed on major stock exchanges as well as private institutional partnerships that are available to accredited investors, typically pension funds, endowments and other institutional investors. We also manage portfolios of listed securities through a series of segregated accounts and mutual funds.

We align our interests with clients' by investing alongside them and have $27 billion of capital invested in our listed partnerships and private funds, based on IFRS carrying values.

Our business model is simple: (i) raise pools of capital from ourselves and clients that target attractive investment strategies, (ii) utilize our global reach to identify and acquire high-quality assets at favourable valuations, (iii) finance them on a long-term basis, (iv) enhance the cash flows and values of these assets through our operating platforms to earn reliable, attractive long-term total returns, and (v) realize capital from asset sales or refinancings when opportunities arise.

Organization Structure

Our operations are organized into five principal groups ("operating platforms"). Our property, renewable energy, infrastructure and private equity platforms are responsible for operating the assets owned by our various funds and investee companies. The equity capital invested in these assets is provided by a series of listed partnerships and private funds which are managed by us and are funded with capital from ourselves and our clients. A fifth group operates our public markets business, which manages portfolios of listed securities on behalf of clients.

We have formed a large capitalization listed partnership entity in each of our property, renewable energy and infrastructure groups, which serves as the primary vehicle through which we invest in each respective segment. As well as owning assets directly, these partnerships serve as the cornerstone investors in our private funds, alongside capital committed by institutional investors. This approach enables us to attract a broad range of public and private investment capital and the ability to match our various investment strategies with the most appropriate form of capital. Our private equity business is conducted primarily through private funds with capital provided by institutions and ourselves.

Our balance sheet capital is invested primarily in our three flagship listed partnerships, Brookfield Property Partners L.P. ("BPY" or "Brookfield Property Partners"); Brookfield Renewable Energy Partners L.P. ("BREP" or "Brookfield Renewable Energy Partners"); and Brookfield Infrastructure Partners L.P. ("BIP" or "Brookfield Infrastructure Partners"), our private equity funds, and in several directly held investments and businesses.

The following chart is a condensed version of our organizational structure:

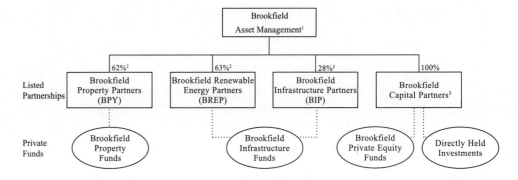

1.   Includes asset management and corporate activities
2.   Economic ownership interest, see page 34 for further details
3.   Privately held, includes private equity, residential development and service activities

MANAGEMENT'S RESPONSIBILITY FOR THE FINANCIAL STATEMENTS

The accompanying consolidated financial statements and other financial information in this Annual Report have been prepared by the company's management which is responsible for their integrity, consistency, objectivity and reliability. To fulfill this responsibility, the company maintains policies, procedures and systems of internal control to ensure that its reporting practices and accounting and administrative procedures are appropriate to provide a high degree of assurance that relevant and reliable financial information is produced and assets are safeguarded. These controls include the careful selection and training of employees, the establishment of well-defined areas of responsibility and accountability for performance, and the communication of policies and code of conduct throughout the company. In addition, the company maintains an internal audit group that conducts periodic audits of the company's operations. The Chief Internal Auditor has full access to the Audit Committee.

These consolidated financial statements have been prepared in conformity with International Financial Reporting Standards as issued by the International Accounting Standards Board and, where appropriate, reflect estimates based on management's judgment. The financial information presented throughout this Annual Report is generally consistent with the information contained in the accompanying consolidated financial statements.

Deloitte LLP, the Independent Registered Public Accounting Firm appointed by the shareholders, have audited the consolidated financial statements set out on pages 83 through 149 in accordance with Canadian generally accepted auditing standards and the standards of the Public Company Accounting Oversight Board (United States) to enable them to express to the board of directors and shareholders their opinion on the consolidated financial statements. Their report is set out on the following page.

The consolidated financial statements have been further reviewed and approved by the Board of Directors acting through its Audit Committee, which is comprised of directors who are not officers or employees of the company. The Audit Committee, which meets with the auditors and management to review the activities of each and reports to the Board of Directors, oversees management's responsibilities for the financial reporting and internal control systems. The auditors have full and direct access to the Audit Committee and meet periodically with the committee both with and without management present to discuss their audit and related findings.

J. Bruce Flatt
Chief Executive Officer

Brian D. Lawson
Chief Financial Officer

March 26, 2015
Toronto, Canada

REPORT OF INDEPENDENT REGISTERED PUBLIC ACCOUNTING FIRM

To the Board of Directors and Shareholders of Brookfield Asset Management Inc.

We have audited the accompanying consolidated financial statements of Brookfield Asset Management Inc. and subsidiaries (the "Company"), which comprise the consolidated balance sheets as at December 31, 2014 and December 31, 2013, and the consolidated statements of operations, consolidated statements of comprehensive income, consolidated statements of changes in equity and consolidated statements of cash flows for the years then ended, and a summary of significant accounting policies and other explanatory information.

Management's Responsibility for the Consolidated Financial Statements

Management is responsible for the preparation and fair presentation of these consolidated financial statements in accordance with International Financial Reporting Standards as issued by the International Accounting Standards Board, and for such internal control as management determines is necessary to enable the preparation of consolidated financial statements that are free from material misstatement, whether due to fraud or error.

Auditor's Responsibility

Our responsibility is to express an opinion on these consolidated financial statements based on our audits. We conducted our audits in accordance with Canadian generally accepted auditing standards and the standards of the Public Company Accounting Oversight Board (United States). Those standards require that we comply with ethical requirements and plan and perform the audit to obtain reasonable assurance about whether the consolidated financial statements are free from material misstatement.

An audit involves performing procedures to obtain audit evidence about the amounts and disclosures in the consolidated financial statements. The procedures selected depend on the auditor's judgment, including the assessment of the risks of material misstatement of the consolidated financial statements, whether due to fraud or error. In making those risk assessments, the auditor considers internal control relevant to the entity's preparation and fair presentation of the consolidated financial statements in order to design audit procedures that are appropriate in the circumstances. An audit also includes evaluating the appropriateness of accounting policies used and the reasonableness of accounting estimates made by management, as well as evaluating the overall presentation of the consolidated financial statements.

We believe that the audit evidence we have obtained in our audits is sufficient and appropriate to provide a basis for our audit opinion.

Opinion

In our opinion, the consolidated financial statements present fairly, in all material respects, the financial position of Brookfield Asset Management Inc. and subsidiaries as at December 31, 2014 and December 31, 2013, and their financial performance and their cash flows for the years then ended in accordance with International Financial Reporting Standards as issued by the International Accounting Standards Board.

Other Matter

We have also audited, in accordance with the standards of the Public Company Accounting Oversight Board (United States), the Company's internal control over financial reporting as of December 31, 2014, based on the criteria established in *Internal Control – Integrated Framework (2013)* issued by the Committee of Sponsoring Organizations of the Treadway Commission and our report dated March 26, 2015 expressed an unqualified opinion on the Company's internal control over financial reporting.

Deloitte LLP

Chartered Professional Accountants, Chartered Accountants
Licensed Public Accountants

March 26, 2015
Toronto, Canada

CONSOLIDATED FINANCIAL STATEMENTS
CONSOLIDATED BALANCE SHEETS

(MILLIONS)	Note	Dec. 31, 2014	Dec. 31, 2013
Assets			
Cash and cash equivalents	6	$ 3,160	$ 3,663
Other financial assets	6	6,285	4,947
Accounts receivable and other	7	8,399	6,666
Inventory	8	5,620	6,291
Assets classified as held for sale	9	2,807	—
Equity accounted investments	10	14,916	13,277
Investment properties	11	46,083	38,336
Property, plant and equipment	12	34,617	31,019
Sustainable resources	13	446	502
Intangible assets	14	4,327	5,044
Goodwill	15	1,406	1,588
Deferred income tax assets	16	1,414	1,412
Total Assets		$ 129,480	$ 112,745
Liabilities and Equity			
Accounts payable and other	17	$ 10,408	$ 10,316
Liabilities associated with assets classified as held for sale	9	1,419	—
Corporate borrowings	18	4,075	3,975
Non-recourse borrowings			
Property-specific mortgages	19	40,364	35,495
Subsidiary borrowings	19	8,329	7,392
Deferred income tax liabilities	16	8,097	6,164
Subsidiary equity obligations	20	3,541	1,877
Equity			
Preferred equity	21	3,549	3,098
Non-controlling interests	21	29,545	26,647
Common equity	21	20,153	17,781
Total equity		53,247	47,526
Total Liabilities and Equity		$ 129,480	$ 112,745

On behalf of the Board:

Frank J. McKenna, Director

George S. Taylor, Director

CONSOLIDATED STATEMENTS OF OPERATIONS

YEARS ENDED DECEMBER 31 (MILLIONS, EXCEPT PER SHARE AMOUNTS)	Note		2014		2013
Revenues	22	$	**18,364**	$	20,093
Direct costs	23		**(13,118)**		(13,928)
Other income and gains	24		**190**		1,262
Equity accounted income	10		**1,594**		759
Expenses					
Interest			**(2,579)**		(2,553)
Corporate costs			**(123)**		(152)
Fair value changes	25		**3,674**		663
Depreciation and amortization			**(1,470)**		(1,455)
Income taxes	16		**(1,323)**		(845)
Net income		$	**5,209**	$	3,844
Net income attributable to:					
Shareholders		$	**3,110**	$	2,120
Non-controlling interests			**2,099**		1,724
		$	**5,209**	$	3,844
Net income per share:					
Diluted	21	$	**4.67**	$	3.12
Basic	21	$	**4.79**	$	3.21

CONSOLIDATED STATEMENTS OF COMPREHENSIVE INCOME

YEARS ENDED DECEMBER 31
(MILLIONS)

	Note	2014	2013
Net income		$ 5,209	$ 3,844
Other comprehensive income (loss)			
Items that may be reclassified to net income			
Financial contracts and power sales agreements		(301)	442
Available-for-sale securities		(105)	(24)
Equity accounted investments	10	(22)	8
Foreign currency translation		(1,717)	(2,429)
Income taxes	16	22	(114)
		(2,123)	(2,117)
Items that will not be reclassified to net income			
Revaluation of property, plant and equipment		2,998	825
Revaluation of pension obligations	29	(77)	26
Equity accounted investments	10	245	231
Income taxes	16	(632)	(166)
		2,534	916
Other comprehensive income (loss)		411	(1,201)
Comprehensive income		$ 5,620	$ 2,643
Attributable to:			
Shareholders			
Net income		$ 3,110	$ 2,120
Other comprehensive income (loss)		301	(795)
Comprehensive income		$ 3,411	$ 1,325
Non-controlling interests			
Net income		$ 2,099	$ 1,724
Other comprehensive income (loss)		110	(406)
Comprehensive income		$ 2,209	$ 1,318

CONSOLIDATED STATEMENTS OF CHANGES IN EQUITY

YEAR ENDED DECEMBER 31, 2014 (MILLIONS)	Common Share Capital	Contributed Surplus	Retained Earnings	Ownership Changes[1]	Accumulated Other Comprehensive Income — Revaluation Surplus	Currency Translation	Other Reserves[2]	Common Equity	Preferred Equity	Non-controlling Interests	Total Equity
Balance as at December 31, 2013	$ 2,899	$ 159	$ 7,159	$ 2,354	$ 5,165	$ 190	$ (145)	$17,781	$ 3,098	$26,647	$47,526
Changes in year:											
Net income	—	—	3,110	—	—	—	—	3,110	—	2,099	5,209
Other comprehensive income	—	—	—	—	1,094	(670)	(123)	301	—	110	411
Comprehensive income	—	—	3,110	—	1,094	(670)	(123)	3,411	—	2,209	5,620
Shareholder distributions											
Common equity	—	—	(388)	—	—	—	—	(388)	—	—	(388)
Preferred equity	—	—	(154)	—	—	—	—	(154)	—	—	(154)
Non-controlling interests	—	—	—	—	—	—	—	—	—	(2,428)	(2,428)
Other items											
Equity issuances, net of redemptions	132	(18)	(69)	—	—	—	—	45	451	2,505	3,001
Share-based compensation	—	44	(7)	—	—	—	—	37	—	16	53
Ownership changes	—	—	51	(375)	(126)	39	(168)	(579)	—	596	17
Total change in year	132	26	2,543	(375)	968	(631)	(291)	2,372	451	2,898	5,721
Balance as at December 31, 2014	$ 3,031	$ 185	$ 9,702	$ 1,979	$ 6,133	$ (441)	$ (436)	$20,153	$ 3,549	$29,545	$53,247

1. Includes gains or losses on changes in ownership interests of consolidated subsidiaries
2. Includes available-for-sale securities, cash flow hedges, actuarial changes on pension plans and equity accounted other comprehensive income, net of associated income taxes

YEAR ENDED DECEMBER 31, 2013 (MILLIONS)	Common Share Capital	Contributed Surplus	Retained Earnings	Ownership Changes[1]	Accumulated Other Comprehensive Income — Revaluation Surplus	Currency Translation	Other Reserves[2]	Common Equity	Preferred Equity	Non-controlling Interests	Total Equity
Balance as at December 31, 2012	$ 2,855	$ 149	$ 6,813	$ 2,088	$ 5,289	$ 1,405	$ (449)	$18,150	$ 2,901	$23,287	$44,338
Changes in year:											
Net income	—	—	2,120	—	—	—	—	2,120	—	1,724	3,844
Other comprehensive loss	—	—	—	—	101	(1,183)	287	(795)	—	(406)	(1,201)
Comprehensive income	—	—	2,120	—	101	(1,183)	287	1,325	—	1,318	2,643
Shareholder distributions											
Common equity	—	—	(1,287)	—	—	(32)	17	(1,302)	—	906	(396)
Preferred equity	—	—	(145)	—	—	—	—	(145)	—	—	(145)
Non-controlling interests	—	—	—	—	—	—	—	—	—	(910)	(910)
Other items											
Equity issuances, net of redemptions	44	(12)	(331)	—	—	—	—	(299)	197	1,675	1,573
Share-based compensation	—	22	(31)	—	—	—	—	(9)	—	45	36
Ownership changes	—	—	20	266	(225)	—	—	61	—	326	387
Total change in year	44	10	346	266	(124)	(1,215)	304	(369)	197	3,360	3,188
Balance as at December 31, 2013	$ 2,899	$ 159	$ 7,159	$ 2,354	$ 5,165	$ 190	$ (145)	$17,781	$ 3,098	$26,647	$47,526

1. Includes gains or losses on changes in ownership interests of consolidated subsidiaries
2. Includes available-for-sale securities, cash flow hedges, actuarial changes on pension plans and equity accounted other comprehensive income, net of associated income taxes

CONSOLIDATED STATEMENTS OF CASH FLOWS

YEARS ENDED DECEMBER 31
(MILLIONS)

	Note	2014	2013
Operating activities			
Net income		$ 5,209	$ 3,844
Other income and gains	24	(190)	(1,820)
Share of undistributed equity accounted earnings		(920)	(307)
Fair value changes	25	(3,674)	(663)
Depreciation and amortization		1,470	1,455
Deferred income taxes	16	1,209	686
Investments in residential inventory		57	(378)
Net change in non-cash working capital and other balances		(587)	(539)
		2,574	2,278
Financing activities			
Corporate borrowings arranged		454	949
Corporate borrowings repaid		—	(224)
Commercial paper and bank borrowings, net		(88)	(35)
Property-specific mortgages arranged		10,939	11,073
Property-specific mortgages repaid		(8,650)	(10,029)
Other debt of subsidiaries arranged		5,463	6,781
Other debt of subsidiaries repaid		(3,191)	(6,115)
Subsidiary equity obligations issued		1,947	541
Subsidiary equity obligations redeemed		(342)	(343)
Capital provided from non-controlling interests		5,733	3,218
Capital repaid to non-controlling interests		(3,228)	(1,543)
Preferred equity issuances		706	191
Preferred equity redemption		(268)	—
Common shares issued		108	85
Common shares repurchased		(63)	(388)
Distributions to non-controlling interests		(2,345)	(910)
Distributions to shareholders		(542)	(541)
		6,633	2,710
Investing activities			
Acquisitions			
Investment properties		(1,970)	(1,835)
Property, plant and equipment		(1,098)	(1,374)
Sustainable resources		(27)	(53)
Equity accounted investments		(1,645)	(2,326)
Other financial assets		(3,877)	(2,745)
Acquisition of subsidiaries		(5,999)	(2,960)
Dispositions			
Investment properties		2,192	948
Property, plant and equipment		313	98
Equity accounted investments		471	657
Other financial assets		3,651	1,502
Disposition of subsidiaries		161	4,057
Restricted cash and deposits		(1,768)	(10)
		(9,596)	(4,041)
Cash and cash equivalents			
Change in cash and cash equivalents		(389)	947
Foreign exchange revaluation		(114)	(134)
Balance, beginning of year		3,663	2,850
Balance, end of year	31	$ 3,160	$ 3,663

NOTES TO THE CONSOLIDATED FINANCIAL STATEMENTS

1. CORPORATE INFORMATION

Brookfield Asset Management Inc. ("Brookfield" or the "company") is a global alternative asset management company. The company owns and operates assets with a focus on property, renewable energy, infrastructure and private equity. The company is listed on the New York, Toronto and Euronext stock exchanges under the symbols BAM, BAM.A and BAMA, respectively. The company was formed by articles of amalgamation under the Business Corporations Act (Ontario) and is registered in Ontario, Canada. The registered office of the company is Brookfield Place, 181 Bay Street, Suite 300, Toronto, Ontario, M5J 2T3.

2. SIGNIFICANT ACCOUNTING POLICIES

a) Statement of Compliance

These consolidated financial statements have been prepared in accordance with International Financial Reporting Standards ("IFRS") as issued by the International Accounting Standards Board ("IASB").

These financial statements were authorized for issuance by the Board of Directors of the company on March 26, 2015.

b) Adoption of Accounting Standards

IFRIC 21, *Levies* ("IFRIC 21") provides guidance on when to recognize a liability for a levy imposed by a government, both for levies that are accounted for in accordance with IAS 37, *Provisions, Contingent Liabilities and Contingent Assets*, and those where the timing and amount of the levy is certain. IFRIC 21 identifies the obligating event for the recognition of a liability as the activity that triggers the payment of the levy in accordance with the relevant legislation. A liability is recognized progressively if the obligating event occurs over a period of time or, if an obligation is triggered on reaching a minimum threshold, the liability is recognized when that minimum threshold is reached. IFRIC 21 became effective on January 1, 2014. The adoption of IFRIC 21 did not have a material effect on the company's consolidated financial statements.

c) Future Changes in Accounting Standards

Property, Plant, and Equipment and Intangible Assets

IAS 16 *Property, Plant, and Equipment* ("IAS 16") and IAS 38 *Intangible Assets* ("IAS 38") were both amended by the IASB as a result of clarifying the appropriate amortization method for intangible assets of service concession arrangements under IFRIC 12 *Service Concession Arrangements* ("SCAs"). The IASB determined that the issue does not only relate to SCAs but all tangible and intangible assets that have finite useful lives. Amendments to IAS 16 prohibit entities from using a revenue-based depreciation method for items of property, plant, and equipment. Similarly, the amendment to IAS 38 introduces a rebuttable presumption that revenue is not an appropriate basis for amortization of an intangible asset, with only limited circumstances where the presumption can be rebutted. Guidance is also introduced to explain that expected future reductions in selling prices could be indicative of a reduction of the future economic benefits embodied in an asset. The amendments apply prospectively and are effective for annual periods beginning on or after January 1, 2016, with earlier application permitted. The company has not yet determined the impact of the amendments to IAS 16 or IAS 38 on its consolidated financial statements.

Revenue from Contracts with Customers

IFRS 15, *Revenue from Contracts with Customers* ("IFRS 15") specifies how and when revenue should be recognized as well as requiring more informative and relevant disclosures. This standard supersedes IAS 18 *Revenue*, IAS 11 *Construction Contracts* and a number of revenue-related interpretations. Application of the Standard is mandatory and it applies to nearly all contracts with customers; the main exceptions are leases, financial instruments and insurance contracts. IFRS 15 is effective for periods beginning on or after January 1, 2017 with early application permitted. The company has not yet determined the impact of IFRS 15 on its consolidated financial statements.

Financial Instruments

In July 2014, the IASB issued the final publication of IFRS 9, *Financial Instruments* ("IFRS 9"), superseding IAS 39, *Financial Instruments*. IFRS 9 establishes principles for the financial reporting of financial assets and financial liabilities that will present relevant and useful information to users of financial statements for their assessment of the amounts, timing and uncertainty of an entity's future cash flows. This new standard also includes a new general hedge accounting standard which will align hedge accounting more closely with risk management. It does not fully change the types of hedging relationships or the requirement to measure and recognize ineffectiveness, however, it will provide more judgment to assess the effectiveness of a hedging relationship. The standard has a mandatorily effective date for annual periods beginning on or after January 1, 2018 with early adoption permitted. The company has not yet determined the impact of IFRS 9 on its consolidated financial statements.

d) Basis of Presentation

The financial statements are prepared on a going concern basis.

i. Subsidiaries

The consolidated financial statements include the accounts of the company and its subsidiaries, which are the entities over which the company exercises control. Control exists when the company has the power to direct the relevant activities, exposure or rights to variable returns from involvement with the investee, and the ability to use its power over the investee to affect the amount of its returns. Subsidiaries are consolidated from the date the control is obtained, and continue to be consolidated until the date when control is lost. The company continually reassesses whether or not it controls an investee, particularly if facts and circumstances indicate there is a change to one or more of the control criteria previously mentioned. In certain circumstances when the company has less than a majority of the voting rights of an investee, it has power over the investee when the voting rights are sufficient to give it the practical ability to direct the relevant activities of the investee unilaterally. The company considers all relevant facts and circumstances in assessing whether or not the company's voting rights are sufficient to give it power.

Non-controlling interests in the equity of the company's subsidiaries are included within equity on the Consolidated Balance Sheets. All intercompany balances, transactions, unrealized gains and losses are eliminated in full.

Gains or losses resulting from changes in the company's ownership interest of a subsidiary that do not result in a loss of control are accounted for as equity transactions and are recorded within ownership changes as a component of equity. When control of a subsidiary is lost, the difference between the carrying value and the proceeds from disposition is recognized within other income and gains in the Consolidated Statements of Operations.

Transaction costs incurred in connection with the acquisition of control of a subsidiary are expensed immediately within fair value changes in the Consolidated Statements of Operations.

Refer to Note 4 for additional information on subsidiaries of the company with significant non-controlling interests.

ii. Associates and Joint Ventures

Associates are entities over which the company exercises significant influence. Significant influence is the power to participate in the financial and operating policy decisions of the investee but without control or joint control over those policies. Joint ventures are joint arrangements whereby the parties that have joint control of the arrangement have the rights to the net assets of the joint arrangement. Joint control is the contractually agreed sharing of control over an arrangement, which exists only when decisions about the relevant activities require unanimous consent of the parties sharing control. The company accounts for associates and joint ventures using the equity method of accounting within equity accounted investments on the Consolidated Balance Sheets.

Interests in associates and joint ventures accounted for using the equity method are initially recognized at cost. At the time of initial recognition, if the cost of the associate or joint venture is lower than the proportionate share of the investment's underlying fair value, the company records a gain on the difference between the cost and the underlying fair value of the investment in net income. If the cost of the associate or joint venture is greater than the company's proportionate share of the underlying fair value, goodwill relating to the associate or joint venture is included in the carrying amount of the investment. Subsequent to initial recognition, the carrying value of the company's interest in an associate or joint venture is adjusted for the company's share of comprehensive income and distributions of the investee. Profit and losses resulting from transactions with an associate or joint venture are recognized in the consolidated financial statements based on the interests of unrelated investors in the investee. The carrying value of associates or joint ventures is assessed for impairment at each balance sheet date. Impairment losses on equity accounted investments may be subsequently reversed in net income. Further information on the impairment of long-lived assets is available in Note 2j).

iii. Joint Operations

A joint operation is a joint arrangement whereby the parties that have joint control of the arrangement have rights to the assets, and obligations for the liabilities, related to the arrangement. Joint control is the contractually agreed sharing of control of an arrangement, which exists only when decisions about the relevant activities require unanimous consent of parties sharing control. The company recognizes only its assets, liabilities and share of the results of operations of the joint operation. The assets, liabilities and results of joint operations are included within the respective line items of the Consolidated Balance Sheets, Consolidated Statements of Operations and Consolidated Statements of Comprehensive Income.

e) Foreign Currency Translation

The U.S. dollar is the functional and presentation currency of the company. Each of the company's subsidiaries, associates, joint ventures and joint operations determines its own functional currency and items included in the financial statements of each subsidiary, associate, joint venture and joint operation are measured using that functional currency.

Assets and liabilities of foreign operations having a functional currency other than the U.S. dollar are translated at the rate of exchange prevailing at the reporting date and revenues and expenses at average rates during the period. Gains or losses on translation are accumulated as a component of equity. On the disposal of a foreign operation, or the loss of control, joint

Depreciation on renewable energy generating assets is calculated on a straight-line basis over the estimated service lives of the assets, which are as follows:

(YEARS)	Useful Lives
Dams	Up to 115
Penstocks	Up to 60
Powerhouses	Up to 115
Hydroelectric generating units	Up to 115
Wind generating units	Up to 22
Other assets	Up to 60

Cost is allocated to the significant components of power generating assets and each component is depreciated separately.

The depreciation of property, plant and equipment in our Brazilian renewable energy operations is based on the duration of the authorization or the useful life of a concession. The weighted average remaining duration at December 31, 2014 is 15 years (2013 – 16 years). Land rights are included as part of the concession or authorization and are subject to depreciation.

iv. Sustainable Resources

Sustainable resources consist of standing timber and other agricultural assets and are measured at fair value after deducting the estimated selling costs and are recorded in sustainable resources on the Consolidated Balance Sheets. Estimated selling costs include commissions, levies, delivery costs, transfer taxes and duties. The fair value of standing timber is calculated using the present value of anticipated future cash flows for standing timber before tax and terminal dates of 20 to 28 years. Fair value is determined based on existing, sustainable felling plans and assessments regarding growth, timber prices and felling and silviculture costs. Changes in fair value are recorded in net income in the period of change. The company determines fair value of its standing timber using external valuations on an annual basis.

Harvested timber is included in inventory and is measured at the lower of fair value less estimated costs to sell at the time of harvest and net realizable value.

Land under standing timber, bridges, roads and other equipment used in sustainable resources production are accounted for using the revaluation method and included in property, plant and equipment. These assets are depreciated over their useful lives, generally 3 to 35 years.

v. Infrastructure

Utilities, transport and energy assets within our infrastructure operations as well as assets under development classified as property, plant and equipment are accounted for using the revaluation method. The company determines the fair value of its utilities, transport and energy assets using a discounted cash flow model, which includes estimates of forecasted revenue, operating costs, maintenance and other capital expenditures. Valuations are performed internally on an annual basis. Discount rates are selected for each asset, giving consideration to the volatility and geography of its revenue streams.

Depreciation on utilities and transport and energy assets is calculated on a straight-line basis over the estimated service lives of the components of the assets, which are as follows:

(YEARS)	Useful Lives
Buildings and district energy systems	Up to 50
Machinery, equipment, transmission stations and towers	Up to 40
Rail and transport assets	Up to 40

The fair value and the estimated remaining service lives are reassessed on an annual basis.

Public service concessions that provide the right to charge users for a service in which the service and fee is regulated by the grantor are accounted for as intangible assets.

vi. Hotel Assets

Hotel operating assets within our property operations are classified as property, plant and equipment and are accounted for using the revaluation method. The company determines the fair value for these assets by discounting the expected future cash flows. The company determines fair value using internal valuations. The company uses external valuations to assist in determining fair value, but external valuations are not necessarily indicative of fair value.

Depreciation on hotel assets is calculated on a straight-line basis over the estimated service lives of the components of the assets, which range from 3 to 50 years for buildings and 3 to 10 years for other equipment.

---

control or significant influence, the component of accumulated other comprehensive income relating to that foreign operation is reclassified to net income. Gains or losses on foreign currency denominated balances and transactions that are designated as hedges of net investments in these operations are reported in the same manner.

Foreign currency denominated monetary assets and liabilities of the company and its subsidiaries are translated using the rate of exchange prevailing at the reporting date and non-monetary assets and liabilities measured at fair value are translated at the rate of exchange prevailing at the date when the fair value was determined. Revenues and expenses are measured at average rates during the period. Gains or losses on translation of these items are included in net income. Gains or losses on transactions which hedge these items are also included in net income. Foreign currency denominated non-monetary assets and liabilities, measured at historic cost, are translated at the rate of exchange at the transaction date.

f) Cash and Cash Equivalents

Cash and cash equivalents include cash on hand, demand deposits and highly liquid short-term investments with original maturities of three months or less.

g) Related Party Transactions

In the normal course of operations, the company enters into various transactions on market terms with related parties, which have been measured at their exchange value and are recognized in the consolidated financial statements. Related party transactions are further described in Note 30. The company's subsidiaries with significant non-controlling interests are described in Note 4 and its associates and joint ventures are described in Note 10.

h) Operating Assets

i. Investment Properties

The company uses the fair value method to account for real estate classified as an investment property. A property is determined to be an investment property when it is principally held to earn either rental income or capital appreciation, or both. Investment properties also include properties that are under development or redevelopment for future use as investment property. Investment property is initially measured at cost including transaction costs. Subsequent to initial recognition, investment properties are carried at fair value. Gains or losses arising from changes in fair value are included in net income during the period in which they arise. Fair values are primarily determined by discounting the expected future cash flows of each property, generally over a term of 10 years, using discount and terminal capitalization rates reflective of the characteristics, location and market of each property. The future cash flows of each property are based upon, among other things, rental income from current leases and assumptions about rental income from future leases reflecting current conditions, less future cash outflows relating to such current and future leases. The company determines fair value using internal valuations. The company uses external valuations to assist in determining fair value, but external valuations are not necessarily indicative of fair value.

ii. Revaluation Method for Property, Plant and Equipment

The company uses the revaluation method of accounting for certain classes of property, plant and equipment. Property, plant and equipment as well as certain assets which are under development for future use as property, plant and equipment. Property, plant and equipment measured using the revaluation method is initially measured at cost and subsequently carried at its revalued amount, being the fair value at the date of the revaluation less any subsequent accumulated depreciation and any accumulated impairment losses. Revaluations are performed on an annual basis, commencing in the first year subsequent to the date of acquisition, unless there is an indication that assets are impaired. Where the carrying amount of an asset increases as a result of a revaluation, the increase is recognized in other comprehensive income and accumulated in equity in revaluation surplus, unless the increase reverses a previously recognized impairment recorded through net income, in which case that portion of the increase is recognized in net income. Where the carrying amount of an asset decreases, the decrease is recognized in other comprehensive income to the extent of any balance existing in revaluation surplus in respect of the asset, with the remainder of the decrease recognized in net income. Depreciation of an asset commences when it is available for use. On loss of control or partial disposition of an asset measured using the revaluation method, all accumulated revaluation surplus or the portion disposed of, respectively, is transferred into retained earnings or ownership changes, respectively.

iii. Renewable Energy Generation

Renewable energy generating assets, including assets under development, are classified as property, plant and equipment and are accounted for using the revaluation method. The company determines the fair value of its renewable energy generating assets using a discounted cash flow model, which includes estimates of forecasted revenue, operating costs, maintenance and other capital expenditures. Discount rates are selected for each facility giving consideration to the expected proportion of contracted to un-contracted revenue and markets into which power is sold.

Generally, the first 20 years of cash flow are discounted with a residual value based on the terminal value cash flows. The fair value and estimated remaining service lives are reassessed on an annual basis. The company determines fair value using internal valuations. The company uses external appraisers to review fair values of our renewable energy generating assets, but external valuations are not necessarily indicative of fair value.

vii. **Other Property, Plant and Equipment**

The company accounts for its other property, plant and equipment using the revaluation method or the cost model, depending on the nature of the asset and the operating segment. Other property, plant and equipment measured using the revaluation method is initially measured at cost and subsequently carried at its revalued amount, being the fair value at the date of the revaluation less any subsequent accumulated depreciation and any accumulated impairment losses. Under the cost method, assets are initially recorded at cost and are subsequently depreciated over the assets' useful lives, unless an impairment is identified requiring a write-down to estimated fair value.

viii. **Residential Development**

Residential development lots, homes and residential condominium projects are recorded in inventory. Residential development lots are recorded at the lower of cost, including pre-development expenditures and capitalized borrowing costs, and net realizable value, which the company determines as the estimated selling price of the inventory in the ordinary course of business in its completed state, less estimated expenses, including holding costs, costs to complete and costs to sell.

Homes and other properties held for sale, which include properties subject to sale agreements, are recorded at the lower of cost and net realizable value in inventory. Costs are allocated to the saleable acreage of each project or subdivision in proportion to the anticipated revenue.

ix. **Other Financial Assets**

Other financial assets are classified as either fair value through profit or loss or available-for-sale based on their nature and use within the company's business. Changes in the fair values of financial instruments classified as fair value through profit or loss and available-for-sale are recognized in net income and other comprehensive income, respectively. The cumulative changes in the fair values of available-for-sale securities previously recognized in accumulated other comprehensive income are reclassified to net income when the security is sold, or there is a significant or prolonged decline in fair value or when the company acquires a controlling or significant interest in the underlying investment and commences equity accounting or consolidating the investment. Other financial assets are recognized on their trade date and initially recorded at fair value with changes in fair value recorded in net income or other comprehensive income in accordance with their classification. Fair values for financial instruments are determined by reference to quoted bid or ask prices, as appropriate. Where bid and ask prices are unavailable, the closing price of the most recent transaction of that instrument is used.

The company assesses the carrying value of available-for-sale securities for impairment when there is objective evidence that the asset is impaired. When objective evidence of impairment exists, the cumulative loss in other comprehensive income is reclassified to net income.

Other financial assets also include loans and notes receivable which are recorded initially at fair value and, with the exception of loans and notes receivable designated as fair value through profit or loss, are subsequently measured at amortized cost using the effective interest method, less any applicable provision for impairment. A provision for impairment is established when there is objective evidence that the company will not be able to collect all amounts due according to the original terms of the receivables. Loans and receivables designated as fair value through profit or loss are recorded at fair value, with changes in fair value recorded in net income in the period in which they arise.

i)   Fair Value Measurement

Fair value is the price that would be received to sell an asset or paid to transfer a liability in an orderly transaction between market participants at the measurement date, regardless of whether that price is directly observable or estimated using another valuation technique. In estimating the fair value of an asset or a liability, the company takes into account the characteristics of the asset or liability if market participants would take those characteristics into account when pricing the asset or liability at the measurement date.

Fair value measurement is disaggregated into three hierarchical levels: Level 1, 2 or 3. Fair value hierarchical levels are directly based on the degree to which the inputs to the fair value measurement are observable. The levels are as follows:

Level 1 – Inputs are unadjusted, quoted prices in active markets for identical assets or liabilities at the measurement date.

Level 2 – Inputs (other than quoted prices included in Level 1) are either directly or indirectly observable for the asset or liability through correlation with market data at the measurement date and for the duration of the asset's or liability's anticipated life.

Level 3 – Inputs are unobservable and reflect management's best estimate of what market participants would use in pricing the asset or liability at the measurement date. Consideration is given to the risk inherent in the valuation technique and the risk inherent in the inputs in determining the estimate.

Further information on fair value measurements is available in Notes 6, 11, 12 and 13.

j)   Impairment of Long-Lived Assets

At each balance sheet date the company assesses whether its assets, other than those measured at fair value with changes in value recorded in net income, have any indication of impairment. An impairment is recognized if the recoverable amount, determined as the higher of the estimated fair value less costs of disposal and the discounted future cash flows generated from use and eventual disposal from an asset or cash-generating unit, is less than their carrying value. Impairment losses are recorded as fair value changes within the Consolidated Statements of Operations. The projections of future cash flows take into account the relevant operating plans and management's best estimate of the most probable set of conditions anticipated to prevail. Where an impairment loss subsequently reverses, the carrying amount of the asset or cash-generating unit is increased to the lesser of the revised estimate of its recoverable amount and the carrying amount that would have been recorded had no impairment loss been recognized previously.

k)   Accounts Receivable

Trade receivables are recognized initially at fair value and subsequently measured at amortized cost using the effective interest method, less any allowance for uncollectability.

l)   Intangible Assets

Finite life intangible assets are carried at cost less any accumulated amortization and any accumulated impairment losses, and are amortized on a straight-line basis over their estimated useful lives. Amortization is recorded within depreciation and amortization in the Consolidated Statements of Operations.

Certain of the company's intangible assets have an indefinite life, as there is no foreseeable limit to the period over which the asset is expected to generate cash flows. Indefinite life intangible assets are recorded at cost unless an impairment is identified which requires a write-down to its recoverable amount.

Indefinite life intangible assets are evaluated for impairment annually or more often if events or circumstances indicate there may be an impairment. Any impairment of the company's indefinite life intangible assets is recorded in net income in the period in which the impairment is identified. Impairment losses on intangible assets may be subsequently reversed in net income.

m)   Goodwill

Goodwill represents the excess of the price paid for the acquisition of an entity over the fair value of the net identifiable tangible and intangible assets and liabilities acquired. Goodwill is allocated to the cash-generating unit to which it relates. The company identifies cash-generating units as identifiable groups of assets that are largely independent of the cash inflows from other assets or groups of assets.

Goodwill is evaluated for impairment annually or more often if events or circumstances indicate there may be an impairment. Impairment is determined for goodwill by assessing if the carrying value of a cash-generating unit, including the allocated goodwill, exceeds its recoverable amount determined as the greater of the estimated fair value less costs to sell and the value in use. Impairment losses recognized in respect of a cash-generating unit are first allocated to the carrying value of goodwill and any excess is allocated to the carrying amount of assets in the cash-generating unit. Any goodwill impairment is recorded in income in the period in which the impairment is identified. Impairment losses on goodwill are not subsequently reversed. On disposal of a subsidiary, any attributable amount of goodwill is included in determination of the gain or loss on disposal.

n)   Subsidiary Equity Obligations

Subsidiary equity obligations include subsidiary preferred equity units, subsidiary preferred shares and capital securities, limited-life funds and redeemable fund units.

Subsidiary preferred equity units and capital securities are preferred shares that may be settled by a variable number of common equity units upon their conversion by the holders or the company. These instruments, as well as the related accrued distributions, are classified as liabilities on the Consolidated Balance Sheets. Dividends or yield distributions on these instruments are recorded as interest expense. To the extent conversion features are not closely related to the underlying liability the instruments are bifurcated into debt and equity components.

Limited-life funds represent the interests of others in the company's consolidated funds that have a defined maximum fixed life where the company has an obligation to distribute the residual interests of the fund to fund partners based on their proportionate share of the fund's equity in the form of cash or other financial assets at cessation of the fund's life.

Redeemable fund units represent interests of others in consolidated subsidiaries that require the company to deliver cash or other financial assets to the holders of the units upon receiving a redemption notice.

Limited-life funds and redeemable fund units are classified as liabilities and recorded at fair value within subsidiary equity obligations on the Consolidated Balance Sheets. Changes in the fair value are recorded in net income in the period of the change.

o) Revenue Recognition

i. Asset Management

Asset management revenues consist of base management fees, advisory fees, incentive distributions and performance-based incentive fees which arise from the rendering of services. Revenues from base management fees, advisory fees and incentive distributions are recorded on an accrual basis based on the amounts receivable at the balance sheet date and are recorded within revenues in the Consolidated Statements of Operations.

Revenues from performance-based incentive fees are recorded on the accrual basis based on the amount that would be due under the incentive fee formula at the end of the measurement period established by the contract where it is no longer subject to adjustment based on future events, and are recorded within revenues in the Consolidated Statements of Operations.

ii. Property Operations

Property revenues primarily consist of rental revenues from leasing activities and interest and dividends from unconsolidated real estate investments.

Property rental income is recognized when the property is ready for its intended use. Office and retail properties are considered to be ready for their intended use when the property is capable of operating in the manner intended by management, which generally occurs upon completion of construction and receipt of all occupancy and other material permits.

The company has retained substantially all of the risks and benefits of ownership of its investment properties and therefore accounts for leases with its tenants as operating leases. Revenue recognition under a lease commences when the tenant has a right to use the leased asset. The total amount of contractual rent to be received from operating leases is recognized on a straight-line basis over the term of the lease; a straight-line or free rent receivable, as applicable, is recorded as a component of investment property for the difference between the amount of rental revenue recorded and the contractual amount received. Rental revenue includes percentage participating rents and recoveries of operating expenses, including property, capital and similar taxes. Percentage participating rents are recognized when tenants' specified sales targets have been met. Operating expense recoveries are recognized in the period that recoverable costs are chargeable to tenants.

Revenue from land sales is recognized at the time that the risks and rewards of ownership have been transferred, possession or title passes to the purchaser, all material conditions of the sales contract have been met, and a significant cash down payment or appropriate security is received.

Revenue from hotel operations are recognized when the services are provided and collection is reasonably assured.

iii. Renewable Energy Operations

Renewable energy revenues are derived from the sale of electricity and is recorded at the time power is provided based upon the output delivered and capacity provided at rates specified under either contract terms or prevailing market rates. Costs of generating electricity are recorded as incurred.

iv. Sustainable Resources Operations

Revenue from timberland operations is derived from the sale of logs and related products. The company recognizes sales to external customers when the product is shipped, title passes and collectability is reasonably assured. Revenue from agricultural development operations is recognized at the time that the risks and rewards of ownership have transferred.

v. Utility Operations

Revenue from utility operations is derived from the distribution and transmission of energy as well as from the company's coal terminal. Distribution and transmission revenue is recognized when services are rendered based upon usage or volume during that period. Terminal infrastructure charges are charged at set rates per tonne of coal based on each customer's annual contracted tonnage and is then recognized on a pro rata basis each month. The company's coal terminal also recognizes variable handling charges based on tonnes of coal shipped through the terminal.

vi. Transport Operations

Revenue from transport operations consists primarily of freight and transportation services revenue. Freight and transportation services revenue is recognized at the time of the provision of services.

vii. Energy Operations

Revenue from energy operations consists primarily of energy transmission, distribution and storage income. Energy revenue is recognized when services are provided and are rendered based upon usage or volume throughout the period.

viii. Private Equity Operations

Revenue from our private equity operations primarily consists of revenues from the sale of goods and rendering of services. Sales are recognized when the product is shipped, title passes and collectability is reasonably assured. Services revenues are recognized when the services are provided.

ix. Residential Developments Operations

Revenue from residential land sales is recognized at the time that the risks and rewards of ownership have been transferred, which is generally when possession or title passes to the purchaser, all material conditions of the sales contract have been met, and a significant cash down payment or appropriate security is received.

Revenue from the sale of homes and residential condominium projects is recognized upon completion, when title passes to the purchaser upon closing and at which time all proceeds are received or collectability is reasonably assured.

x. Service Activities

Revenues from construction contracts are recognized using the percentage-of-completion method once the outcome of the construction contract can be estimated reliably, in proportion to the stage of completion of the contract, and to the extent to which collectability is reasonably assured. The stage of completion is measured by reference to actual costs incurred as a percentage of estimated total costs of each contract. When the outcome cannot be reliably determined, contract costs are expensed as incurred and revenue is only recorded to the extent that the costs are determined to be recoverable. Where it is probable that a loss will arise from a construction contract, the excess of total expected costs over total expected revenue is recognized as an expense immediately. Other service revenues are recognized when the services are provided.

xi. Investments in Financial Assets

Dividend and interest income from other financial assets are recorded within revenues when declared or on an accrual basis using the effective interest method.

Revenue from loans and notes receivable, less a provision for uncollectible amounts, is recorded on the accrual basis using the effective interest method.

xii. Other Income and Gains

Other income and gains represent the excess of proceeds over carrying values on the disposition of subsidiaries, investments or assets, or the settlement of liabilities for less than carrying values.

p) Derivative Financial Instruments and Hedge Accounting

The company and its subsidiaries selectively utilize derivative financial instruments primarily to manage financial risks, including interest rate, commodity and foreign exchange risks. Derivative financial instruments are recorded at fair value within the company's consolidated financial statements. Hedge accounting is applied when the derivative is designated as a hedge of a specific exposure and there is assurance that it will continue to be effective as a hedge based on an expectation of offsetting cash flows or fair values. Hedge accounting is discontinued prospectively when the derivative no longer qualifies as a hedge or the hedging relationship is terminated. Once discontinued, the cumulative change in fair value of a derivative that was previously recorded in other comprehensive income by the application of hedge accounting is recognized in net income over the remaining term of the original hedging relationship. The assets or liabilities relating to unrealized mark-to-market gains and losses on derivative financial instruments is recorded in accounts receivable and other or accounts payable and other, respectively.

i. Items Classified as Hedges

Realized and unrealized gains and losses on foreign exchange contracts, designated as hedges of currency risks relating to a net investment in a subsidiary or an associate, are included in equity and net income in the period in which the subsidiary or associate is disposed of or, to the extent partially disposed and control is not retained. Derivative financial instruments that are designated as hedges to offset corresponding changes in the fair value of assets and liabilities and cash flows are measured at their estimated fair value with changes in fair value recorded in net income or as a component of equity, as applicable.

Unrealized gains and losses on interest rate contracts designated as hedges of future variable interest payments are included in equity as a cash flow hedge when the interest rate risk relates to an anticipated variable interest payment. The periodic exchanges of payments on interest rate swap contracts designated as hedges of debt are recorded on an accrual basis as an adjustment to interest expense. The periodic exchanges of payments on interest rate contracts designated as hedges of future interest payments are amortized into net income over the term of the corresponding interest payments.

Unrealized gains and losses on electricity contracts designated as cash flow hedges of future power generation revenue are included in equity as a cash flow hedge. The periodic exchanges of payments on power generation commodity swap contracts designated as hedges are recorded on a settlement basis as an adjustment to power generation revenue.

ii. Items Not Classified as Hedges

Derivative financial instruments that are not designated as hedges are carried at their estimated fair value, and gains and losses arising from changes in fair value are recognized in net income in the period in which the change occurs. Realized and unrealized gains and losses on equity derivatives used to offset the change in share prices in respect of vested Deferred Share Units and Restricted Share Units are recorded together with the corresponding compensation expense. Realized and unrealized gains on other derivatives not designated as hedges are recorded in revenues, direct costs or corporate costs, as applicable. Realized and unrealized gains and losses on derivatives which are considered economic hedges, and where hedge accounting is not able to be elected, are recorded in fair value changes in the Consolidated Statements of Operations.

In making estimates and judgments management relies on external information and observable conditions where possible, supplemented by internal analysis as required. These estimates have been applied in a manner consistent with prior periods and there are no known trends, commitments, events or uncertainties that the company believes will materially affect the methodology or assumptions utilized in making these estimates in these consolidated financial statements.

i. Critical Estimates

The significant estimates used in determining the recorded amount for assets and liabilities in the consolidated financial statements include the following:

a. Investment Properties

The critical assumptions and estimates used when determining the fair value of commercial properties are: the timing of rental income from future leases reflecting current market conditions, less assumptions of future cash flows in respect of current and future leases; maintenance and other capital expenditures; discount rates; terminal capitalization rates; and terminal valuation dates. Properties under development are recorded at fair value using a discounted cash flow model which includes estimates in respect of the timing and cost to complete the development.

Further information on investment property estimates is provided in Note 11.

b. Revaluation Method for Property, Plant and Equipment

When determining the carrying value of property, plant and equipment using the revaluation method, the company uses the following critical assumptions and estimates: the timing of forecasted revenues, future sales prices and margins; future sales volumes; future regulatory rates; maintenance and other capital expenditures; discount rates; terminal capitalization rates; terminal valuation dates; useful lives; and residual values. Determination of the fair value of property, plant and equipment under development includes estimates in respect of the timing and cost to complete the development.

Further information on estimates used in the revaluation method for property, plant and equipment is provided in Note 12.

c. Sustainable Resources

The fair value of standing timber and agricultural assets is based on the following critical estimates and assumptions: the timing of forecasted revenues and prices; estimated selling costs; sustainable felling plans; growth assumptions; silviculture costs; discount rates; terminal capitalization rates; and terminal valuation dates.

Further information on estimates on estimates used for sustainable resources is provided in Note 13.

d. Financial Instruments

Estimates and assumptions used in determining the fair value of financial instruments are: equity and commodity prices; future interest rates; the credit worthiness of the company relative to its counterparties; the credit risk of the company's counterparties; estimated future cash flows; the amount of the liability and equity components of compound financial instruments; discount rates and volatility utilized in option valuations.

Further information on estimates used in determining the carrying value of financial instruments is provided in Notes 6, 26 and 27.

e. Inventory

The company estimates the net realizable value of its inventory using estimates and assumptions about future development costs, costs to hold and future selling costs.

f. Other

Other estimates and assumptions utilized in the preparation of the company's consolidated financial statements are: the assessment or determination of net recoverable amounts; depreciation and amortization rates and useful lives; estimation of recoverable amounts of cash-generating units for impairment assessments of goodwill and intangible assets; ability to utilize tax losses and other tax measurements; fair value of assets held as collateral and the percentage of completion for construction contracts.

ii. Critical Judgments

Management is required to make critical judgments when applying its accounting policies. The following judgments have the most significant effect on the consolidated financial statements:

a. Control or Level of Influence

When determining the appropriate basis of accounting for the company's investees, the company makes judgments about the degree of influence that the company exerts directly or through an arrangement over the investees' relevant activities. This may include the ability to elect investee directors or appoint management. Control is obtained when the company has the power to direct the relevant investing, financing and operating decisions of an entity and does so in its capacity as principal of the operations, rather than as an agent for other investors. Operating as a principal includes having sufficient capital at risk in any investee and exposure to the variability of the returns generated by the decisions of the company as principal. Judgment is used

---

q) Income Taxes

Current income tax assets and liabilities are measured at the amount expected to be paid to tax authorities, net of recoveries, based on the tax rates and laws enacted or substantively enacted at the balance sheet date. Current and deferred income tax relating to items recognized directly in equity are also recognized in equity. Deferred income tax liabilities are provided for using the liability method on temporary differences between the tax bases and carrying amounts of assets and liabilities. Deferred income tax assets are recognized for all deductible temporary differences, and carry forward of unused tax credits and unused tax losses, to the extent that it is probable that deductions, tax credits and tax losses can be utilized. The carrying amount of deferred income tax assets is reviewed at each balance sheet date and reduced to the extent it is no longer probable that the income tax assets will be recovered. Deferred income tax assets and liabilities are measured using the tax rates that are expected to apply to the year when the asset is realized or the liability settled, based on the tax rates and laws that have been enacted or substantively enacted at the balance sheet date.

r) Business Combinations

Business combinations are accounted for using the acquisition method. The cost of a business acquisition is measured at the aggregate of the fair values at the date of exchange of assets given, liabilities incurred or assumed, and equity instruments issued in exchange for control of the acquiree. The acquiree's identifiable assets, liabilities and contingent liabilities are recognized at their fair values at the acquisition date, except for non-current assets that are classified as held-for-sale which are recognized and measured at fair value less costs to sell. The interest of non-controlling shareholders in the acquiree is initially measured at the non-controlling shareholders' proportion of the net fair value of the identifiable assets, liabilities and contingent liabilities recognized.

To the extent the fair value of consideration paid exceeds the fair value of the net identifiable tangible and intangible assets, the excess is recorded as goodwill. To the extent the fair value of consideration paid is less than the fair value of net identifiable tangible and intangible assets, the excess is recognized in net income.

When a business combination is achieved in stages, previously held interests in the acquired entity are re-measured to fair value at the acquisition date, which is the date control is obtained, and the resulting gain or loss, if any, is recognized in net income, other than amounts transferred directly to retained earnings. Amounts arising from interests in the acquiree prior to the acquisition date that have previously been recognized in other comprehensive income are reclassified to net income. Transaction costs are recorded as an expense within fair value changes in the Consolidated Statements of Operations.

s) Other Items

i. Capitalized Costs

Capitalized costs related to assets under development and redevelopment include all eligible expenditures incurred in connection with the acquisition, development and construction of the asset until it is available for its intended use. These expenditures consist of costs that are directly attributable to these assets.

Borrowing costs are capitalized when such costs are directly attributable to the acquisition, construction or production of a qualifying asset. A qualifying asset is an asset that takes a substantial period of time to prepare for its intended use.

ii. Share-based Payments

The company and its subsidiaries issue share-based awards to certain employees and non-employee directors. The cost of equity-settled share-based transactions, comprised of share options, restricted shares and escrowed shares, is determined as the fair value of the award on the grant date using a fair value model. The cost of equity-settled share-based transactions is recognized as each tranche vests and is recorded in contributed surplus as a component of equity. The cost of cash-settled share-based transactions, comprised of Deferred Share Units and Restricted Share Units, is measured as the fair value at the grant date, and expensed on a proportionate basis consistent with the vesting features over the vesting period with the recognition of a corresponding liability. The liability is measured at each reporting date at fair value with changes in fair value recognized in net income.

iii. Pensions and other post-employment benefits

The company offers pension and other post-employment benefit plans to employees of certain of its subsidiaries, with certain of these subsidiaries offering defined benefit plans. Defined benefit pension expense, which includes the current year's service cost, is included in Direct costs. For each defined benefit plan, we recognize the present value of our defined benefit obligations less the fair value of the plan assets, as a defined benefit liability reported in Accounts payable and other on our Consolidated Balance Sheets. The company's obligations under its defined benefit pension plans are determined periodically through the preparation of actuarial valuations.

t) Critical Judgments and Estimates

The preparation of financial statements requires management to make estimates and judgments that affect the carried amounts of certain assets and liabilities, disclosure of contingent assets and liabilities and the reported amounts of revenues and expenses recorded during the period. Actual results could differ from those estimates.

[...]

in determining the sufficiency of the capital at risk or variability of returns. In making these judgments, the company considers the ability of other investors to remove the company as a manager or general partner in a controlled partnership.

b.   Investment Properties

When applying the company's accounting policy for investment properties, judgment is applied in determining whether certain costs are additions to the carrying amount of the property and, for properties under development, identifying the point at which practical completion of the property occurs and identifying the directly attributable borrowing costs to be included in the carrying value of the development property.

c.   Property, Plant and Equipment

The company's accounting policy for its property, plant and equipment requires critical judgments over the assessment of carrying value, whether certain costs are additions to the carrying amount of the property, plant and equipment as opposed to repairs and maintenance, and for assets under development the identification of when the asset is capable of being used as intended and identifying the directly attributable borrowing costs to be included in the asset's carrying value.

For assets that are measured using the revaluation method, judgment is required when estimating future prices, volumes and discount and capitalization rates. Judgment is applied when determining future electricity prices considering market data for years that a liquid market is available and estimates of electricity prices from renewable sources that would allow new entrants into the market in subsequent years.

d.   Common Control Transactions

The purchase and sale of businesses or subsidiaries between entities under common control fall outside the scope of IFRS and accordingly, management uses judgment when determining a policy to account for such transactions taking into consideration other guidance in the IFRS framework and pronouncements of other standard-setting bodies. The company's policy is to record assets and liabilities recognized as a result of transfers of businesses or subsidiaries between entities under common control at carrying value. Differences between the carrying amount of the consideration given or received and the carrying amount of the assets and liabilities transferred are recorded directly in equity.

e.   Indicators of Impairment

Judgment is applied when determining whether indicators of impairment exist when assessing the carrying values of the company's assets, including: the determination of the company's ability to hold financial assets; the estimation of a cash-generating unit's future revenues and direct costs; and the determination of discount and capitalization rates, and when an asset's carrying value is above the value derived using publicly traded prices which are quoted in a liquid market.

f.   Income Taxes

The company makes judgments when determining the future tax rates applicable to subsidiaries and identifying the temporary difference that relate to each subsidiary. Deferred income tax assets and liabilities are measured at the tax rates that are expected to apply during the period when the assets are realized or the liabilities settled, using the tax rates and laws enacted or substantively enacted at the consolidated balance sheet dates. The company measures deferred income taxes associated with its investment properties based on its specific intention with respect to each asset at the end of the reporting period. Where the company has a specific intention to sell a property in the foreseeable future, deferred taxes on the building portion of an investment property are measured based on the tax consequences following from the disposition of the property. Otherwise, deferred taxes are measured on the basis the carrying value of the investment property will be recovered substantially through use. Judgment is required in determining the manner in which the carrying amount of each investment property will be recovered.

g.   Classification of Non-controlling Interests in Limited-Life Funds

Non-controlling interests in limited-life funds are classified as liabilities (subsidiary equity obligations) or equity (non-controlling interests) depending on whether an obligation exits to distribute residual net assets to non-controlling interests on liquidation in the form of cash or another financial asset or assets delivered in kind. Judgment is required to determine whether the governing documents of each entity convey a right to cash or another financial asset, or if assets can be distributed on liquidation.

h.   Other

Other critical judgments include the determination of effectiveness of financial hedges for accounting purposes; the likelihood and timing of anticipated transactions for hedge accounting; and the determination of functional currency.

6.   FAIR VALUE OF FINANCIAL INSTRUMENTS

The following tables list the company's financial instruments by their respective classification as at December 31, 2014 and 2013:

AS AT DECEMBER 31, 2014 (MILLIONS) FINANCIAL INSTRUMENT CLASSIFICATION	FVTPL[1] (Fair Value)	Available-for-Sale (Fair Value)	Loans and Receivables/Other Financial Liabilities (Amortized Cost)	Total
MEASUREMENT BASIS				
Financial assets[2]				
Cash and cash equivalents	$ —	$ —	$ 3,160	$ 3,160
Other financial assets				
Government bonds	66	31	—	97
Corporate bonds and debt instruments	60	867	—	927
Fixed income securities	684	185	—	869
Common shares and warrants	3,023	442	—	3,465
Loans and notes receivable	49	—	878	927
	3,882	1,525	878	6,285
Accounts receivable and other[3]	1,369	—	5,755	7,124
	$ 5,251	$ 1,525	$ 9,793	$ 16,569
Financial liabilities				
Corporate borrowings	$ —	$ —	$ 4,075	$ 4,075
Property-specific mortgages	—	—	40,364	40,364
Subsidiary borrowings	—	—	8,329	8,329
Accounts payable and other[3]	1,922	—	8,486	10,408
Subsidiary equity obligations	1,423	—	2,118	3,541
	$ 3,345	$ —	$ 63,372	$ 66,717

1.   Financial instruments classified as fair value through profit or loss
2.   Total financial assets include $2,014 million of assets pledged as collateral
3.   Includes derivative instruments which are elected for hedge accounting totalling $1,121 million included in accounts receivable and other and $1,459 million of derivative instruments included in accounts payable and other, of which changes in fair value are recorded in other comprehensive income

The following table provides the carrying values and fair values of financial instruments as at December 31, 2014 and December 31, 2013:

(MILLIONS)	Dec. 31, 2014		Dec. 31, 2013	
	Carrying Value	Fair Value	Carrying Value	Fair Value
Financial assets				
Cash and cash equivalents	$ 3,160	$ 3,160	$ 3,663	$ 3,663
Other financial assets				
Government bonds	97	97	179	179
Corporate bonds	927	927	319	319
Fixed income securities	869	869	212	212
Common shares and warrants	3,465	3,465	2,758	2,758
Loans and notes receivable	927	927	1,479	1,479
	6,285	6,285	4,947	4,947
Accounts receivable and other	7,124	7,124	5,176	5,176
	$ 16,569	$ 16,569	$ 13,786	$ 13,786
Financial liabilities				
Corporate borrowings	$ 4,075	$ 4,401	$ 3,975	$ 4,323
Property-specific mortgages	40,364	41,570	35,495	36,389
Subsidiary borrowings	8,329	8,546	7,392	7,225
Accounts payable and other	10,408	10,408	10,316	10,316
Subsidiary equity obligations	3,541	3,558	1,877	1,898
	$ 66,717	$ 68,483	$ 59,055	$ 60,151

The current and non-current balances of other financial assets are as follows:

(MILLIONS)	Dec. 31, 2014	Dec. 31, 2013
Current	$ 1,234	$ 942
Non-current	5,051	4,005
Total	$ 6,285	$ 4,947

Hedging Activities

The company uses derivatives and non-derivative financial instruments to manage or maintain exposures to interest, currency, credit and other market risks. For certain derivatives which are used to manage exposures, the company determines whether hedge accounting can be applied. When hedge accounting may be applied, a hedge relationship may be designated as a fair value hedge, cash flow hedge or a hedge of foreign currency exposure of a net investment in a foreign operation. To qualify for hedge accounting, the derivative must be highly effective in accomplishing the objective of offsetting changes in the fair value or cash flows attributable to the hedged risk both at inception and over the life of the hedge. If it is determined that the derivative is not highly effective as a hedge, hedge accounting is discontinued prospectively.

i. Cash Flow Hedges

The company uses the following cash flow hedges: energy derivative contracts to hedge the sale of power; interest rate swaps to hedge the variability in cash flows or future cash flows related to a variable rate asset or liability; and equity derivatives to hedge the long-term compensation arrangements. For the year ended December 31, 2014, pre-tax net unrealized losses of $224 million (2013 – gains of $29 million) were recorded in other comprehensive income for the effective portion of the cash flow hedges. As at December 31, 2014, there was an unrealized derivative liability balance of $128 million relating to derivative contracts designated as cash flow hedges (2013 – $30 million asset). The unrealized losses on cash flow hedges are expected to be realized in net income by 2024.

ii. Net Investment Hedges

The company uses foreign exchange contracts and foreign currency denominated debt instruments to manage its foreign currency exposures arising from net investments in foreign operations. For the year ended December 31, 2014, unrealized pre-tax net gains of $312 million (2013 – gain of $1 million) were recorded in other comprehensive income for the effective portion of hedges of net investments in foreign operations. As at December 31, 2014, there was an unrealized derivative asset balance of $307 million relating to derivative contracts designated as net investment hedges (2013 – $70 million liability).

AS AT DECEMBER 31, 2013 (MILLIONS) FINANCIAL INSTRUMENT CLASSIFICATION MEASUREMENT BASIS	FVTPL[1] (Fair Value)	Available-for-Sale (Fair Value)	Loans and Receivables/Other Financial Liabilities (Amortized Cost)	Total
Financial assets²				
Cash and cash equivalents	$ —	$ —	$ 3,663	$ 3,663
Other financial assets				
Government bonds	75	104	—	179
Corporate bonds and debt instruments	36	283	—	319
Fixed income securities	68	144	—	212
Common shares and warrants	2,493	265	—	2,758
Loans and notes receivable	31	—	1,448	1,479
	2,703	796	1,448	4,947
Accounts receivable and other³	1,163	—	4,013	5,176
	$ 3,866	$ 796	$ 9,124	$ 13,786
Financial liabilities				
Corporate borrowings	$ —	$ —	$ 3,975	$ 3,975
Property-specific mortgages	—	—	35,495	35,495
Subsidiary borrowings	—	—	7,392	7,392
Accounts payable and other	1,305	—	9,011	10,316
Subsidiary equity obligations³	1,086	—	791	1,877
	$ 2,391	$ —	$ 56,664	$ 59,055

1. Financial instruments classified as fair value through profit or loss
2. Total financial assets include $1,626 million of assets pledged as collateral
3. Includes derivative instruments which are elected for hedge accounting totalling $752 million included in accounts receivable and other and $792 million of derivative instruments included in accounts payable and other, of which changes in fair value are recorded in other comprehensive income

Gains or losses arising from changes in the fair value of fair value through profit or loss financial assets are presented in the Consolidated Statements of Operations in the period in which they arise. Dividends on fair value through profit or loss and available-for-sale financial assets are recognized when the company's right to receive payment is established. Interest on available-for-sale financial assets is calculated using the effective interest method.

During the year ended December 31, 2014, $14 million of net deferred gains (2013 – $35 million) previously recognized in accumulated other comprehensive income were reclassified to net income as a result of the disposition of available-for-sale securities.

Included in cash and cash equivalents is $2,650 million (2013 – $3,128 million) of cash and $510 million of short-term deposits at December 31, 2014 (2013 – $535 million).

Available-for-sale securities are recorded on the balance sheet at fair value, and are assessed for impairment at each reporting date. As at December 31, 2014, the unrealized gains and losses relating to the fair value of available-for-sale securities amounted to $24 million (2013 – $60 million) and $124 million (2013 – $41 million), respectively.

Financial assets and liabilities are offset with the net amount reported in the Consolidated Balance Sheet where the company currently has a legally enforceable right to offset and there is an intention to settle on a net basis or realize the asset and settle the liability simultaneously.

The following table summarizes the valuation techniques and significant unobservable inputs used in the fair value measurement of Level 3 financial instruments:

(MILLIONS) Type of asset/liability	Carrying value Dec. 31, 2014	Valuation technique(s)	Significant unobservable input(s)	Relationship of unobservable input(s) to fair value
Fixed income securities	$ 773	Discounted cash flows	• Future cash flows	• Increases (decreases) in future cash flows increase (decrease) fair value
			• Discount rate	• Increases (decreases) in discount rate decrease (increase) fair value
Investment in common shares	1,297	Net asset valuation	• Forward exchange rates (from observable forward exchange rates at the end of the reporting period)	• Increases (decreases) in the forward exchange rate increase (decrease) fair value
			• Discount rate	• Increases (decreases) in discount rate decrease (increase) fair value
Warrants	1,398	Black-Scholes model	• Volatility	• Increases (decreases) in volatility increase (decrease) fair value
Limited-life funds (subsidiary equity obligations)	1,337	Discounted cash flows	• Future cash flows	• Increases (decreases) in future cash flows increase (decrease) fair value
			• Discount rate	• Increases (decreases) in discount rate decrease (increase) fair value
			• Terminal capitalization rate	• Increases (decreases) in terminal capitalization rate decrease (increase) fair value
			• Investment horizon	• Increases (decreases) in the investment horizon increase (decrease) fair value
Derivative assets/ Derivative liabilities (accounts receiveable/payable)	147/ (92)	Discounted cash flows	• Future cash flows	• Increases (decreases) in future cash flows increase (decrease) fair value
			• Forward exchange rates (from observable forward exchange rates at the end of the reporting period)	• Increases (decreases) in the forward exchange rate increase (decrease) fair value
			• Discount rate	• Increases (decreases) in discount rate decrease (increase) fair value

Fair Value Hierarchy Levels

Assets and liabilities measured at fair value on a recurring basis include $3,627 million (2013 – $2,729 million) of financial assets and $1,429 million (2013 – $1,089 million) of financial liabilities which are measured at fair value using unobservable valuation inputs or based on management's best estimates. The following table categorizes financial assets and liabilities, which are carried at fair value, based upon the fair value hierarchy levels:

(MILLIONS)	Dec. 31, 2014			Dec. 31, 2013		
	Level 1	Level 2	Level 3	Level 1	Level 2	Level 3
Financial assets						
Other financial assets						
Government bonds	$ 28	$ 69	$ —	$ 41	$ 138	$ —
Corporate bonds	768	159	—	20	299	113
Fixed income securities	57	39	773	44	55	113
Common shares and warrants	765	5	2,695	838	1	1,919
Loans and notes receivables	—	37	12	—	23	8
Accounts receivable and other	—	1,222	147	131	343	689
	$ 1,618	$ 1,531	$ 3,627	$ 1,074	$ 859	$ 2,729
Financial liabilities						
Accounts payable and other	$ —	$ 1,830	$ 92	$ 117	$ 1,046	$ 142
Subsidiary equity obligations	—	86	1,337	—	139	947
	$ —	$ 1,916	$ 1,429	$ 117	$ 1,185	$ 1,089

There were no transfers between Level 1, Level 2 and Level 3 in 2014 or 2013.

Fair values for financial instruments are determined by reference to quoted bid or ask prices, as appropriate. Where bid and ask prices are unavailable, the closing price of the most recent transaction of that instrument is used. In the absence of an active market, fair values are determined based on prevailing market rates for instruments with similar characteristics and risk profiles or internal or external valuation models, such as option pricing models and discounted cash flow analysis, using observable market inputs.

Level 2 financial assets and financial liabilities include foreign currency forward contracts, interest rate swap agreements, energy derivatives, and redeemable fund units.

The following table summarizes the valuation techniques and key inputs used in the fair value measurement of Level 2 financial instruments:

(MILLIONS) Type of asset/liability	Carrying value Dec. 31, 2014	Valuation technique(s) and key input(s)
Derivative assets/Derivative liabilities (accounts receivable/ payable)	$ 1,222/ (1,830)	Foreign currency forward contracts – discounted cash flow model – forward exchange rates (from observable forward exchange rates at the end of the reporting period) and discounted at credit adjusted rate
		Interest rate contracts – discounted cash flow model – forward interest rates (from observable yield curves) and applicable credit spreads discounted at a credit adjusted rate
		Energy derivatives – quoted market prices, or in their absence internal valuation models corroborated with observable market data
Redeemable fund units (subsidiary equity obligations)	86	Aggregated market prices of underlying investments
Other financial assets	309	Valuation models based on observable market data

Fair values determined using valuation models (Level 3 financial assets and liabilities) require the use of unobservable inputs, including assumptions concerning the amount and timing of estimated future cash flows and discount rates. In determining those unobservable inputs, the company uses observable external market inputs such as interest rate yield curves, currency rates, and price and rate volatilities, as applicable, to develop assumptions regarding those unobservable inputs.

The following table presents the change in the balance of financial assets and liabilities classified as Level 3 as at December 31, 2014 and December 31, 2013:

	Financial Assets		Financial Liabilities	
(MILLIONS)	2014	2013	2014	2013
Balance at beginning of year	$ 2,729	$ 2,334	$ 1,089	$ 680
Fair value changes recorded in net income	788	(24)	110	(35)
Fair value changes recorded in other comprehensive income[1]	(114)	104	(59)	36
Additions, net of disposals	224	315	289	408
Balance at end of year	$ 3,627	$ 2,729	$ 1,429	$ 1,089

1. Includes foreign currency translation

The following table categorizes liabilities measured at amortized cost, but for which fair values are disclosed:

	Dec. 31, 2014			Dec. 31, 2013		
(MILLIONS)	Level 1	Level 2	Level 3	Level 1	Level 2	Level 3
Corporate borrowings	$ 4,401	$ –	$ –	$ 4,323	$ –	$ –
Property-specific mortgages	1,054	14,461	26,055	922	12,640	22,827
Subsidiary borrowings	2,172	2,342	4,032	1,836	1,980	3,409
Subsidiary equity obligations	–	–	2,135	–	–	812

Fair values for Level 2 and Level 3 liabilities measured at amortized cost but for which fair values are disclosed are determined using valuation techniques such as adjusted public pricing and discounted cash flows.

7. ACCOUNTS RECEIVABLE AND OTHER

(MILLIONS)	Note	Dec. 31, 2014	Dec. 31, 2013
Accounts receivable	(a)	$ 3,110	$ 3,220
Prepaid expenses and other assets		2,644	2,569
Restricted cash	(b)	2,645	877
Total		$ 8,399	$ 6,666

The current and non-current balances of accounts receivable and other are as follows:

(MILLIONS)	Dec. 31, 2014	Dec. 31, 2013
Current	$ 6,312	$ 4,840
Non-current	2,087	1,826
Total	$ 8,399	$ 6,666

a) Accounts Receivable

Accounts receivable includes $228 million (2013 – $592 million) of unrealized mark-to-market gains on energy sales contracts and $718 million (2013 – $764 million) of completed contracts and work-in-progress related to contracted sales from the company's residential development operations.

b) Restricted Cash

Restricted cash in 2014 includes $1.8 billion of deposits restricted for a subsidiary of the company's bid to acquire the remaining interest in Canary Wharf Group plc ("Canary Wharf") that it did not already own, as part of a joint venture. On March 5, 2015, the joint venture's bid for the additional interest became compulsory to the remaining outstanding shareholders that had not yet accepted the prior offers.

The remaining $845 million (2013 – $877 million) of restricted cash relates to the company's property, renewable energy, service activities and residential development financing arrangements including defeasement of debt obligations, debt service accounts and deposits held by the company's insurance operations.

8. INVENTORY

(MILLIONS)	Dec. 31, 2014	Dec. 31, 2013
Residential properties under development	$ 2,468	$ 2,785
Land held for development	2,176	2,541
Completed residential properties	519	443
Forest products and other	457	522
Total	$ 5,620	$ 6,291

The current and non-current balances of inventory are as follows:

(MILLIONS)	Dec. 31, 2014	Dec. 31, 2013
Current	$ 2,815	$ 2,839
Non-current	2,805	3,452
Total	$ 5,620	$ 6,291

During the year ended December 31, 2014, the company recognized as an expense $3,091 million (2013 – $5,388 million) of inventory relating to cost of goods sold and $147 million (2013 – $33 million) relating to impairments of inventory. The carrying amount of inventory pledged as security at December 31, 2014 was $2,284 million (2013 – $2,462 million).

9. HELD FOR SALE

The following is a summary of the assets and liabilities that were classified as held for sale as at December 31, 2014:

(MILLIONS)	Property	Infrastructure	Total
Assets			
Accounts receivables and other	$ 68	$ 4	$ 72
Investment properties	2,173	–	2,173
Property, plant and equipment	–	218	218
Equity accounted investments	–	311	311
Intangible assets	–	33	33
Assets classified as held for sale	$ 2,241	$ 566	$ 2,807
Liabilities			
Accounts payable and other	$ 55	$ 11	$ 66
Property-specific mortgages	1,165	145	1,310
Deferred income tax liabilities	–	43	43
Liabilities associated with assets classified as held for sale	$ 1,220	$ 199	$ 1,419

During the year ended December 31, 2014 the company classified seven separate asset groups or investments as held for sale.

i. Property

As at December 31, 2014, a subsidiary of the company classified a group of commercial office properties in Washington D.C. as held for sale based on approved plans to sell a controlling interest in these properties. The Washington D.C. office properties have assets of $1,334 million and total liabilities of $687 million. In addition, the subsidiary also agreed to sell office properties in Toronto and Seattle and multifamily assets in Virginia and Maryland and has therefore classified these assets as held for sale. Total assets and liabilities of the office and multifamily assets to be disposed of are $907 million and $533 million, respectively.

ii. Infrastructure

At December 31, 2014, a subsidiary of the company has initiated a plan to dispose its interest in its New England electricity transmission operations and its North American natural gas transmission business during 2015. The New England electricity transmission operation's total assets are $255 million and total liabilities are $199 million. The company's North American natural gas transmission investment is equity accounted with a carrying value of $311 million.

10. EQUITY ACCOUNTED INVESTMENTS

The following table presents the voting interests and carrying values of the company's investments in associates and joint ventures, all of which are accounted for using the equity method:

(MILLIONS)	Investment Type	Voting Interest Dec. 31 2014	Voting Interest Dec. 31 2013	Carrying Value Dec. 31 2014	Carrying Value Dec. 31 2013
Property					
General Growth Properties	Associate	29%	28%	$ 6,887	$ 6,044
245 Park Avenue¹	Joint Venture	51%	51%	708	653
Grace Building	Joint Venture	50%	50%	538	695
Rouse Properties	Associate	34%	39%	408	399
Other property joint ventures¹	Joint Venture	25 – 75%	25 – 75%	1,736	1,586
Other property investments¹	Associate	20 – 75%	20 – 75%	266	366
Renewable energy					
Other renewable energy investments	Associate	14 – 50%	14 – 50%	273	290
Infrastructure					
Brazilian toll road	Associate	49%	49%	1,237	1,203
South American transmission operations	Associate	28%	28%	724	717
Brazilian rail and port operations	Associate	27%	—	767	—
Other infrastructure investments	Associate	26 – 50%	26 – 50%	816	694
Other joint ventures	Joint Venture	25 – 50%	25 – 50%	403	343
Other investments	Associate	28 – 50%	28 – 50%	153	287
Total				$ 14,916	$ 13,277

1. Investments in which the company's ownership interest is greater than 50% represent investments in equity accounted joint ventures or associates where control is either shared or does not exist resulting in the investment being equity accounted

The following table presents the change in the balance of investments in associates and joint ventures:

YEARS ENDED DECEMBER 31 (MILLIONS)	2014	2013
Balance at beginning of year	$ 13,277	$ 11,618
Additions, net of disposals (including reclassifications to held for sale)	1,011	1,099
Acquisitions through business combinations	—	350
Share of net income	1,345	1,283
Impairments of equity accounted investments	249	(524)
Share of other comprehensive income	223	239
Distributions received	(674)	(452)
Foreign exchange	(515)	(336)
Balance at end of year	$ 14,916	$ 13,277

The following table presents current and non-current assets as well as current and non-current liabilities of the company's investments in associates and joint ventures:

(MILLIONS)	Dec. 31, 2014 Current Assets	Non-Current Assets	Current Liabilities	Non-Current Liabilities	Dec. 31, 2013 Current Assets	Non-Current Assets	Current Liabilities	Non-Current Liabilities
Property								
General Growth Properties	$ 1,108	$ 40,631	$ 830	$ 17,985	$ 1,132	$ 38,335	$ 754	$ 16,224
245 Park Avenue	30	2,167	13	795	20	2,057	14	791
Grace Building	47	1,930	19	882	15	1,742	369	—
Rouse Properties	107	2,823	76	1,618	99	2,449	66	1,455
Other property investments	290	7,417	805	2,853	603	8,217	855	1,999
Renewable energy								
Other renewable energy investments	42	782	27	254	54	958	27	405
Infrastructure								
Brazilian toll road	683	5,867	666	1,495	805	4,758	532	2,578
South American transmission operation	244	5,513	155	3,361	1,254	4,543	1,189	2,055
Brazilian rail and port operations	787	3,337	240	883	542	8,087	383	6,229
Other infrastructure investments	330	3,374	230	1,730	1,579	1,024	459	654
Other	1,430	544	860	248				
Total	$ 5,098	$ 74,385	$ 3,921	$ 32,104	$ 6,103	$ 72,170	$ 4,648	$ 32,390

Certain of the company's investments in associates are subject to restrictions over the extent to which they can remit funds to the company in the form of cash dividends, or repayment of loans and advances as a result of borrowing arrangements, regulatory restrictions and other contractual requirements.

The following table presents total revenues, net income, and other comprehensive income ("OCI") of the Company's investments in associates and joint ventures and dividends received by the company from these investments:

YEARS ENDED DECEMBER 31 (MILLIONS)	2014 Revenue	Net Income	OCI	Dividends Received	2013 Revenue	Net Income	OCI	Dividends Received
Property								
General Growth Properties	$ 3,188	$ 2,556	$ (5)	$ 158	$ 3,079	$ 2,835	$ 64	$ 107
245 Park Avenue	149	164	—	17	145	55	—	29
Grace Building	106	191	—	252	100	154	—	—
Rouse Properties	304	87	8	14	263	146	—	11
Other property investments	645	381	—	72	921	448	—	128
Renewable energy								
Other renewable energy investments	109	6	115	27	110	20	—	18
Infrastructure								
Brazilian toll road	1,056	88	41	28	1,125	113	(193)	68
South American transmission operation	434	65	335	—	446	(15)	264	—
Brazilian rail and port operations	459	58	—	—	—	—	—	—
Australian energy distribution	—	—	—	—	308	206	(45)	19
Other infrastructure investments	929	26	72	36	1,459	(1,032)	204	34
Other	1,523	169	(7)	70	488	178	(18)	38
Total	$ 8,902	$ 3,791	$ 559	$ 674	$ 8,444	$ 3,108	$ 276	$ 452

Certain of the company's investments are publicly listed entities with active pricing in a liquid market. The fair value based on the publicly listed price of these equity accounted investments in comparison to the company's carrying value is as follows:

11. INVESTMENT PROPERTIES

(MILLIONS)	Dec. 31, 2014		Dec. 31, 2013	
	Public Price	Carrying Value	Public Price	Carrying Value
General Growth Properties	$ 7,183	$ 6,887	$ 5,125	$ 6,044
Rouse Properties	359	408	430	399
Other	28	17	31	23
	$ 7,570	$ 7,312	$ 5,586	$ 6,466

At December 31, 2014, the Company reviewed the valuation of its investment in General Growth Properties Inc. ("GGP" or "General Growth Properties") to determine whether the impairment recognized in 2013 of $249 million, or any portion thereof, may no longer be required. Based on the published price of GGP common stock as at December 31, 2014 the recoverable amount of the investment in GGP had increased to an amount that was in excess of the company's carrying value and the impairment loss was reversed. The impairment and subsequent reversal has been recorded within equity accounted income. The Company's investment in GGP at December 31, 2014 includes $552 million of excess of consideration paid over the fair value of the investment at the date of acquisition.

In 2013, the company recognized a $275 million impairment relating to its investment in a North American natural gas transmission operation based on weak market fundamentals in the U.S. market.

The following table presents the change in the fair value of investment properties, all of which are considered Level 3 within the fair value hierarchy:

YEARS ENDED DECEMBER 31 (MILLIONS)	2014	2013
Fair value at beginning of year	$ 38,336	$ 33,161
Additions	2,269	1,835
Acquisitions through business combinations	8,332	5,530
Disposals and reclassifications to assets held for sale	(4,800)	(1,908)
Fair value changes	3,266	1,031
Foreign currency translation	(1,320)	(1,313)
Fair value at end of year	$ 46,083	$ 38,336

Investment properties include the company's office, retail, multifamily, industrial and other properties as well as higher-and-better use land within the company's sustainable resource operations. Investment properties generated $3,679 million (2013 – $3,093 million) in rental income, and incurred $1,729 million (2013 – $1,302 million) in direct operating expenses.

Significant unobservable inputs (Level 3) are utilized when determining the fair value of investment properties. The significant Level 3 inputs include:

Valuation technique(s)	Significant unobservable input(s)	Relationship of unobservable input(s) to fair value
Discounted cash flow models	• Future cash flows primarily driven by net operating income	• Increases (decreases) in future cash flows increase (decrease) fair value
	• Discount rate	• Increases (decreases) in discount rate decrease (increase) fair value
	• Terminal capitalization rate	• Increases (decreases) in terminal capitalization rate decrease (increase) fair value
	• Investment horizon	• Increases (decreases) in the investment horizon increase (decrease) fair value

Key valuation metrics of the company's investment properties are presented in the following table on a weighted-average basis:

	Office		Retail		Multifamily, Industrial and Other		Weighted Average	
AS AT DECEMBER 31	2014	2013	2014	2013	2014	2013	2014	2013
Discount rate	7.1%	7.4%	9.2%	9.2%	6.7%	8.6%	7.1%	7.7%
Terminal capitalization rate	6.0%	6.3%	7.2%	7.6%	7.3%	7.5%	6.1%	6.6%
Investment horizon (years)	10	11	10	10	10	10	10	11

12. PROPERTY, PLANT AND EQUIPMENT

(MILLIONS)	Dec. 31, 2014	Dec. 31, 2013
Cost	$ 25,337	$ 23,281
Accumulated fair value changes	13,978	11,574
Accumulated depreciation	(4,698)	(3,836)
Total	$ 34,617	$ 31,019

Accumulated fair value changes include revaluations of property, plant and equipment using the revaluation method, which are recorded in revaluation surplus, as well as unrealized impairment losses recorded in net income.

The company's property, plant and equipment relates to the operating segments as shown in the following table:

		Carried at Fair Value[1]		Carried at Amortized Cost		Total	
(MILLIONS)	Note	Dec. 31, 2014	Dec. 31, 2013	Dec. 31, 2014	Dec. 31, 2013	Dec. 31, 2014	Dec. 31, 2013
Renewable energy	(a)	$ 19,970	$ 16,611	$ —	$ —	$ 19,970	$ 16,611
Infrastructure	(b)	9,061	8,564	—	—	9,061	8,564
Property	(c)	2,872	3,042	—	—	2,872	3,042
Private equity and other	(d)	—	—	2,714	2,802	2,714	2,802
		$ 31,903	$ 28,217	$ 2,714	$ 2,802	$ 34,617	$ 31,019

1. Classified as Level 3 in the fair value hierarchy due to the use of significant unobservable inputs when determining fair value

a) Renewable Energy

Our renewable energy, property, plant and equipment is comprised of the following:

(MILLIONS)	Note	2014	2013
Hydroelectric and other	(i)	$ 16,687	$ 14,148
Wind energy	(ii)	3,283	2,463
		$ 19,970	$ 16,611

Renewable energy assets are accounted for under the revaluation model and the most recent date of revaluation was December 31, 2014. Valuations utilize significant unobservable inputs (Level 3) when determining the fair value of renewable energy assets. The significant Level 3 inputs include:

Valuation technique(s)	Significant unobservable input(s)	Relationship of unobservable input(s) to fair value
Discounted cash flow models	• Future cash flows – primarily driven by future electricity price assumptions	• Increases (decreases) in future cash flows increase (decrease) fair value
	• Discount rate	• Increases (decreases) in discount rate decrease (increase) fair value
	• Terminal capitalization rate	• Increases (decreases) in terminal capitalization rate decrease (increase) fair value

The company's estimate of future renewable power pricing is based on management's estimate of the cost of securing new energy from renewable sources to meet future demand by 2020, which will maintain system reliability and provide adequate levels of reserve generations.

Key valuation metrics of the company's hydro and wind generating facilities at the end of 2014 and 2013 are summarized below.

	United States		Canada		Brazil	
	Dec. 31, 2014	Dec. 31, 2013	Dec. 31, 2014	Dec. 31, 2013	Dec. 31, 2014	Dec. 31, 2013
Discount rate						
Contracted	5.2%	5.8%	4.8%	5.1%	8.4%	9.1%
Uncontracted	7.1%	7.6%	6.7%	6.9%	9.7%	10.4%
Terminal capitalization rate	7.1%	7.1%	6.5%	6.4%	n/a	n/a
Exit date	2034	2033	2034	2033	2029	2029

Terminal values are included in the valuation of hydroelectric assets in the United States and Canada. For the hydroelectric assets in Brazil, cash flows have been included based on the duration of the authorization or useful life of a concession asset without consideration of potential renewal value. The weighted-average remaining duration at December 31, 2014 is 15 years (2013 – 16 years). Consequently, there is no terminal value attributed to the hydroelectric assets in Brazil.

i.   *Renewable Energy – Hydroelectric and Other*

(MILLIONS)	Dec. 31, 2014	Dec. 31, 2013
Cost	$ 7,997	$ 6,647
Accumulated fair value changes	10,877	9,413
Accumulated depreciation	(2,187)	(1,912)
Total	$ 16,687	$ 14,148

The following table presents the changes to the cost of the company's hydroelectric and other energy generation assets:

YEARS ENDED DECEMBER 31 (MILLIONS)	2014	2013
Balance at beginning of year	$ 6,647	$ 5,864
Additions, net of disposals	365	170
Acquisitions through business combinations	1,341	957
Foreign currency translation	(356)	(344)
Balance at end of year	$ 7,997	$ 6,647

As at December 31, 2014, the cost of generating facilities under development includes $126 million of capitalized costs (2013 – $9 million).

The following table presents the changes to the accumulated fair value changes of the company's hydroelectric and other energy generation assets:

YEARS ENDED DECEMBER 31 (MILLIONS)	2014	2013
Balance at beginning of year	$ 9,413	$ 10,031
Fair value changes	1,932	(155)
Foreign currency translation	(468)	(463)
Balance at end of year	$ 10,877	$ 9,413

The following table presents the changes to the accumulated depreciation of the company's hydroelectric and other energy generation assets:

YEARS ENDED DECEMBER 31 (MILLIONS)	2014	2013
Balance at beginning of year	$ (1,912)	$ (1,604)
Depreciation expense	(403)	(413)
Foreign currency translation	128	105
Balance at end of year	$ (2,187)	$ (1,912)

ii.   *Renewable Energy – Wind Energy*

(MILLIONS)	Dec. 31, 2014	Dec. 31, 2013
Cost	$ 3,079	$ 2,137
Accumulated fair value changes	657	645
Accumulated depreciation	(453)	(319)
Total	$ 3,283	$ 2,463

The following table presents the changes to the cost of the company's wind energy assets:

YEARS ENDED DECEMBER 31 (MILLIONS)	2014	2013
Balance at beginning of year	$ 2,137	$ 1,753
Acquisitions through business combinations	1,075	430
Additions, net of disposals	78	16
Foreign currency translation	(211)	(62)
Balance at end of year	$ 3,079	$ 2,137

The following table presents the changes to the accumulated fair value changes of the company's wind energy assets

YEARS ENDED DECEMBER 31 (MILLIONS)	2014	2013
Balance at beginning of year	$ 645	$ 681
Fair value changes	57	5
Foreign currency translation	(45)	(41)
Balance at end of year	$ 657	$ 645

The following table presents the changes to the accumulated depreciation of the company's wind energy assets:

YEARS ENDED DECEMBER 31 (MILLIONS)	2014	2013
Balance at beginning of year	$ (319)	$ (193)
Depreciation expense	(157)	(138)
Foreign currency translation	23	12
Balance at end of year	$ (453)	$ (319)

b)   Infrastructure

Our infrastructure property, plant and equipment is comprised of the following:

(MILLIONS)	Note	2014	2013
Utilities	(i)	$ 3,637	$ 3,624
Transportation	(ii)	2,702	2,941
Energy	(iii)	1,745	1,198
Sustainable resources	(iv)	977	801
		$ 9,061	$ 8,564

i. Infrastructure – Utilities

(MILLIONS)	Dec. 31, 2014	Dec. 31, 2013
Cost	$ 3,122	$ 3,369
Accumulated fair value changes	729	378
Accumulated depreciation	(214)	(123)
Total	$ 3,637	$ 3,624

The company's utilities assets are comprised of terminals and energy transmission and distribution networks, which are operated primarily under regulated rate base arrangements.

Utilities assets are accounted for under the revaluation model, and the most recent date of revaluation was December 31, 2014. The company determined fair value to be the current replacement cost. Valuations utilize significant unobservable inputs (Level 3) when determining the fair value of utility assets. The significant Level 3 inputs include:

Valuation technique(s)	Significant unobservable input(s)	Relationship of unobservable input(s) to fair value
Discounted cash flow model	• Future cash flows – primarily driven by a regulated return on asset base	• Increases (decreases) in future cash flows increase (decrease) fair value
	• Discount rate	• Increases (decreases) in discount rate decrease (increase) fair value
	• Terminal capitalization multiple	• Increases (decreases) in terminal capitalization multiple decrease (increase) fair value
	• Investment horizon	• Increases (decreases) in the investment horizon decrease (increase) fair value

Key assumptions used in the December 31, 2014 valuation process include: discount rates ranging from 8% to 12% (2013 – 8% to 13%), terminal capitalization multiples ranging from 8x to 16x (2013 – 10x to 16x), and an investment horizon between 10 and 20 years (2013 – 10 to 20 years).

The following table presents the changes to the cost of the company's utilities assets:

YEARS ENDED DECEMBER 31 (MILLIONS)	2014	2013
Balance at beginning of year	$ 3,369	$ 3,203
Additions, net of disposals and assets reclassified to held for sale	17	165
Foreign currency translation	(264)	1
Balance at end of year	$ 3,122	$ 3,369

The following table presents the changes to the accumulated fair value changes of the company's utilities assets:

YEARS ENDED DECEMBER 31 (MILLIONS)	2014	2013
Balance at beginning of year	$ 378	$ 113
Fair value changes	449	271
Dispositions and assets reclassified to held for sale	(55)	—
Foreign currency translation	(43)	(6)
Balance at end of year	$ 729	$ 378

The following table presents the changes to the accumulated depreciation of the company's utilities assets:

YEARS ENDED DECEMBER 31 (MILLIONS)	2014	2013
Balance at beginning of year	$ (123)	$ (6)
Depreciation expense	(130)	(121)
Dispositions and assets reclassified to held for sale	28	—
Foreign currency translation	11	4
Balance at end of year	$ (214)	$ (123)

ii. Infrastructure – Transport

(MILLIONS)	Dec. 31, 2014	Dec. 31, 2013
Cost	$ 2,187	$ 2,334
Accumulated fair value changes	725	744
Accumulated depreciation	(210)	(137)
Total	$ 2,702	$ 2,941

The company's transport assets consists of railroads, toll roads and ports.

Transport assets are accounted for under the revaluation model, and the most recent date of revaluation was December 31, 2014. The company determined fair value to be the current replacement cost. Valuations utilize significant unobservable inputs (Level 3) when determining the fair value of transport assets. The significant Level 3 inputs include:

Valuation technique(s)	Significant unobservable input(s)	Relationship of unobservable input(s) to fair value
Discounted cash flow models	• Future cash flows – primarily driven by traffic or freight volumes and tariff rates	• Increases (decreases) in future cash flows increase (decrease) fair value
	• Discount rate	• Increases (decreases) in discount rate decrease (increase) fair value
	• Terminal capitalization multiple	• Increases (decreases) in terminal capitalization multiple decrease (increase) fair value
	• Investment horizon	• Increases (decreases) in the investment horizon decrease (increase) fair value

Key assumptions used in the December 31, 2014 valuation process include: discount rates ranging from 11% to 15% (2013 – 11% to 12%), terminal capitalization multiples ranging from 10x to 12x (2013 – 7x to 11x), and an investment horizon between 10 and 20 years (2013 – 10 years).

The following table presents the changes to the cost of the company's transport assets:

YEARS ENDED DECEMBER 31 (MILLIONS)	2014	2013
Balance at beginning of year	$ 2,334	$ 2,502
Additions, net of disposals	122	160
Foreign currency translation	(269)	(328)
Balance at end of year	$ 2,187	$ 2,334

The following table presents the changes to the accumulated fair value changes of the company's transport assets:

YEARS ENDED DECEMBER 31 (MILLIONS)	2014	2013
Balance at beginning of year	$ 744	$ 519
Fair value changes	8	317
Foreign currency translation	(27)	(92)
Balance at end of year	$ 725	$ 744

The following table presents the changes to the accumulated depreciation of the company's transport assets:

YEARS ENDED DECEMBER 31 (MILLIONS)	2014	2013
Balance at beginning of year	$ (137)	$ (33)
Depreciation expense	(129)	(127)
Foreign currency translation	56	23
Balance at end of year	$ (210)	$ (137)

iii. *Infrastructure – Energy*

(MILLIONS)	Dec. 31, 2014	Dec. 31, 2013
Cost	$ 1,653	$ 1,132
Accumulated fair value changes	210	131
Accumulated depreciation	(118)	(65)
Total	$ 1,745	$ 1,198

The company's energy assets consist of energy transmission, distribution and storage and district energy assets.

Energy assets are accounted for under the revaluation model, and the most recent date of revaluation was December 31, 2014. The company determined fair value to be the current replacement cost.

Valuations utilize significant unobservable inputs (Level 3) when determining the fair value of energy assets. The significant Level 3 inputs include:

Valuation technique(s)	Significant unobservable input(s)	Relationship of unobservable input(s) to fair value
Discounted cash flow models	• Future cash flows – primarily driven by transmission, distribution and storage volumes and pricing	• Increases (decreases) in future cash flows increase (decrease) fair value
	• Discount rate	• Increases (decreases) in discount rate decrease (increase) fair value
	• Terminal capitalization multiple	• Increases (decreases) in terminal capitalization multiple decrease (increase) fair value
	• Investment horizon	• Increases (decreases) in the investment horizon decrease (increase) fair value

Key assumptions used in the December 31, 2014 valuation process include: discount rates ranging from 10% to 13% (2013 – 15% to 16%), terminal capitalization multiples ranging from 8x to 12x (2013 – 8x to 12x), and an investment horizon of 10 years (2013 – 10 years).

The following table presents the changes to the cost of the company's energy assets:

YEARS ENDED DECEMBER 31 (MILLIONS)	2014	2013
Balance at beginning of year	$ 1,132	$ 1,004
Additions, net of disposals	59	33
Acquisitions through business combinations	517	142
Foreign currency translation	(55)	(47)
Balance at end of year	$ 1,653	$ 1,132

The following table presents the changes to the accumulated fair value changes of the company's energy assets:

YEARS ENDED DECEMBER 31 (MILLIONS)	2014	2013
Balance at beginning of year	$ 131	$ 47
Fair value changes	89	83
Foreign currency translation	(10)	1
Balance at end of year	$ 210	$ 131

The following table presents the changes to the accumulated depreciation of the company's energy assets:

YEARS ENDED DECEMBER 31 (MILLIONS)	2014	2013
Balance at beginning of year	$ (65)	$ (25)
Depreciation expense	(56)	(37)
Foreign currency translation	3	(3)
Balance at end of year	$ (118)	$ (65)

iv. *Infrastructure – Sustainable Resources*

Sustainable resources assets represents timberlands and other agricultural land.

(MILLIONS)	2014	2013
Cost	$ 480	$ 469
Accumulated fair value changes	519	349
Accumulated depreciation	(22)	(17)
Total	$ 977	$ 801

Investment properties within our sustainable resources operations are accounted for under the revaluation model and the most recent date of revaluation was December 31, 2014.

Valuations utilize significant unobservable inputs (Level 3) when determining the fair value of sustainable resource assets. The significant Level 3 inputs include:

Valuation technique(s)	Significant unobservable input(s)	Relationship of unobservable input(s) to fair value
Discounted cash flow models	• Future cash flows – primarily driven by avoided cost or future replacement value	• Increases (decreases) in future cash flows increase (decrease) fair value
	• Discount rate	• Increases (decreases) in discount rate decrease (increase) fair value
	• Terminal valuation date	• Increases (decreases) in terminal valuation date decrease (increase) fair value
	• Exit date	• Increases (decreases) in the exit date decrease (increase) fair value

Key valuation assumptions included a weighted average discount rate of 6% (2013 – 7%), and a terminal valuation date of 3 to 30 years (2013 – 3 to 35 years).

The following table presents the changes to the cost of the company's sustainable resources business:

YEARS ENDED DECEMBER 31 (MILLIONS)	2014	2013
Balance at beginning of year	$ 469	$ 1,264
Additions, net of disposals	63	(784)
Foreign currency translation	(52)	(11)
Balance at end of year	$ 480	$ 469

The following table presents the changes to the accumulated fair value changes of the company's sustainable resources business:

YEARS ENDED DECEMBER 31 (MILLIONS)	2014	2013
Balance at beginning of year	$ 349	$ 166
Fair value changes	212	49
Dispositions	—	133
Foreign currency translation	(42)	1
Balance at end of year	$ 519	$ 349

The following table presents the changes to the accumulated depreciation of the company's sustainable resources business:

YEARS ENDED DECEMBER 31 (MILLIONS)	2014	2013
Balance at beginning of year	$ (17)	$ (18)
Depreciation expense	(8)	(3)
Dispositions	—	3
Foreign currency translation	3	1
Balance at end of year	$ (22)	$ (17)

c)   Property

(MILLIONS)	Dec. 31, 2014	Dec. 31, 2013
Cost	$ 2,859	$ 3,168
Accumulated fair value changes	455	170
Accumulated depreciation	(442)	(296)
Total	$ 2,872	$ 3,042

The company's property assets include hotel assets accounted for under the revaluation model, with the most recent revaluation as at December 31, 2014. The company determines fair value for these assets by discounting the expected future cash flows using internal valuations.

Valuations utilize significant unobservable inputs (Level 3) when determining the fair value of property assets. The significant Level 3 inputs include:

Valuation technique(s)	Significant unobservable input(s)	Relationship of unobservable input(s) to fair value
Discounted cash flow models	• Future cash flows – primarily driven by pricing, volumes and direct operating costs	• Increases (decreases) in future cash flows increase (decrease) fair value
	• Discount rate	• Increases (decreases) in discount rate decrease (increase) fair value
	• Terminal capitalization rate	• Increases (decreases) in terminal capitalization rate decrease (increase) fair value
	• Investment horizon	• Increases (decreases) in the investment horizon decrease (increase) fair value

Key valuation assumptions included a weighted average discount rate of 10.0% (2013 – 10.5%), terminal capitalization rate of 7.0% (2013 – 7.6%), and investment horizon of 6 years (2013 – 7 years).

The following table presents the changes to the cost of the company's hotel assets included within its property operations:

YEARS ENDED DECEMBER 31 (MILLIONS)	2014	2013
Balance at beginning of year	$ 3,168	$ 3,130
Additions, net of disposals	(227)	137
Foreign currency translation	(82)	(99)
Balance at end of year	$ 2,859	$ 3,168

The following table presents the changes to the accumulated fair value changes of the company's hotel assets included within its property operations:

YEARS ENDED DECEMBER 31 (MILLIONS)	2014	2013
Balance at beginning of year	$ 170	$ 4
Fair value changes	324	166
Foreign currency translation	(39)	—
Balance at end of year	$ 455	$ 170

The following table presents the changes to the accumulated depreciation of the company's hotel assets included within its property operations:

YEARS ENDED DECEMBER 31 (MILLIONS)	2014	2013
Balance at beginning of year	$ (296)	$ (166)
Depreciation expense	(152)	(130)
Dispositions	4	—
Foreign currency translation	2	—
Balance at end of year	$ (442)	$ (296)

d)   Private Equity and Other

(MILLIONS)	Dec. 31, 2014	Dec. 31, 2013
Cost	$ 3,960	$ 4,025
Accumulated impairments	(194)	(256)
Accumulated depreciation	(1,052)	(967)
Total	$ 2,714	$ 2,802

Other property, plant and equipment includes assets owned by the company's private equity, residential development and service operations held directly or consolidated through funds.

These assets are accounted for under the cost model, which requires the assets to be carried at cost less accumulated depreciation and any accumulated impairment losses. The following table presents the changes to the carrying value of the company's property, plant and equipment assets included in these operations:

YEARS ENDED DECEMBER 31 (MILLIONS)	2014	2013
Balance at beginning of year	$ 4,025	$ 3,928
Additions, net of disposals	73	124
Acquisitions through business combinations	90	86
Foreign currency translation	(228)	(113)
Balance at end of year	$ 3,960	$ 4,025

The following table presents the changes to the accumulated impairment losses of the company's property, plant and equipment within these operations:

YEARS ENDED DECEMBER 31 (MILLIONS)	2014	2013
Balance at beginning of year	$ (256)	$ (162)
Impairment charges	(41)	(99)
Dispositions	75	—
Foreign currency translation	28	5
Balance at end of year	$ (194)	$ (256)

The following table presents the changes to the accumulated depreciation of the company's other property, plant and equipment within these operations:

YEARS ENDED DECEMBER 31 (MILLIONS)	2014	2013
Balance at beginning of year	$ (967)	$ (854)
Depreciation expense	(224)	(217)
Disposals	141	110
Foreign currency translation	(2)	(6)
Balance at end of year	$ (1,052)	$ (967)

13.   SUSTAINABLE RESOURCES

(MILLIONS)	Dec. 31, 2014	Dec. 31, 2013
Timberlands	$ 394	$ 449
Other agricultural assets	52	53
Total	$ 446	$ 502

The company held 1.8 million acres of consumable freehold timberlands at December 31, 2014 (2013 – 1.4 million), representing 39.9 million cubic metres (2013 – 39.9 million) of mature timber and available for harvest. Additionally, the company provides management services to approximately 1.3 million acres (2013 – 1.3 million) of licensed timberlands.

The following table presents the changes to the cost of the company's intangible assets:

YEARS ENDED DECEMBER 31 (MILLIONS)	2014	2013
Cost at beginning of year	$ 5,492	$ 6,166
Disposals, net of additions	(218)	(13)
Acquisitions through business combinations	10	20
Foreign currency translation	(420)	(681)
Cost at end of year	$ 4,864	$ 5,492

The following table presents the changes in the accumulated amortization and accumulated impairment losses of the company's intangible assets:

YEARS ENDED DECEMBER 31 (MILLIONS)	2014	2013
Accumulated amortization and impairment losses at beginning of year	$ (448)	$ (396)
Amortization	(139)	(105)
Disposals	40	39
Foreign currency translation and other	10	14
Accumulated amortization and impairment losses at end of year	$ (537)	$ (448)

The following table presents intangible assets by geography:

(MILLIONS)	Dec. 31, 2014	Dec. 31, 2013
United States	$ 112	$ 180
Canada	119	266
Australia	2,283	2,535
Europe	426	456
Chile	1,093	1,278
Brazil and other	294	329
	$ 4,327	$ 5,044

Intangible assets, including trademarks, concession agreements and conservancy rights, are recorded at amortized cost and are tested for impairment annually or when an indicator of impairment is identified using a discounted cash flow valuation. This valuation utilizes the following significant unobservable inputs assumptions:

Valuation technique	Significant unobservable input(s)	Relationship of unobservable input(s) to fair value
Discounted cash flow models	• Future cash flows	• Increases (decreases) in future cash flows will increase (decrease) the recoverable amount
	• Discount rate	• Increases (decreases) in discount rate will decrease (increase) the recoverable amount
	• Terminal capitalization rate	• Increases (decreases) in terminal capitalization rate will decrease (increase) the recoverable amount
	• Exit date	• Increases (decreases) in the exit date will decrease (increase) the recoverable amount

15. GOODWILL

(MILLIONS)	Dec. 31, 2014	Dec. 31, 2013
Cost	$ 1,579	$ 1,635
Accumulated impairment losses	(173)	(47)
Total	$ 1,406	$ 1,588

The following table presents the change in the balance of timberlands and other agricultural assets:

YEARS ENDED DECEMBER 31 (MILLIONS)	2014	2013
Balance at beginning of year	$ 502	$ 3,516
Additions, net of disposals	62	(2,991)
Fair value adjustments	38	205
Decrease due to harvest	(81)	(186)
Foreign currency changes	(75)	(42)
Balance at end of year	$ 446	$ 502

The carrying values are based on external appraisals that are completed annually as of December 31. The appraisals utilize a combination of the discounted cash flow and sales comparison approaches to arrive at the estimated value. The significant unobservable inputs (Level 3) included in the discounted cash flow models used when determining the fair value of standing timber and agricultural assets include:

Valuation technique(s)	Significant unobservable input(s)	Relationship of unobservable input(s) to fair value
Discounted cash flow models	• Future cash flows	• Increases (decreases) in future cash flows increase (decrease) fair value
	• Growth assessments	• Increases (decreases) in growth assessments increase (decrease) fair value
	• Timber/Agricultural prices	• Increases (decreases) in price increase (decrease) fair value
	• Discount rate/terminal capitalization rate	• Increases (decreases) in discount rate or terminal capitalization rate decrease (increase) fair value

Key valuation assumptions include a weighted average discount and terminal capitalization rate of 5.9% (2013 – 6.9%), and terminal valuation dates of 30 years (2013 – 20 to 28 years). Timber and agricultural asset prices were based on a combination of forward prices available in the market and price forecasts.

14. INTANGIBLE ASSETS

(MILLIONS)	Dec. 31, 2014	Dec. 31, 2013
Cost	$ 4,864	$ 5,492
Accumulated amortization and impairment losses	(537)	(448)
Total	$ 4,327	$ 5,044

Intangible assets are allocated to the following cash-generating units:

(MILLIONS)	Note	Dec. 31, 2014	Dec. 31, 2013
Infrastructure – Utilities	(a)	$ 2,048	$ 2,231
Infrastructure – Transport	(b)	1,427	1,633
Property – Industrial, Multifamily, Hotel and other		309	327
Private equity		156	257
Service activities		266	297
Renewable energy		18	94
Other		103	205
		$ 4,327	$ 5,044

a) Infrastructure – Utilities

The company's Australian regulated terminal operation has access agreements with the users of the terminal which entails 100% take or pay contracts at a designated tariff rate based on the asset value. The concession arrangement has an expiration date of 2051 and the company has an option to extend the arrangement an additional 49 years. The aggregate duration of the arrangement and the extension option represents the remaining useful life of the concession.

b) Infrastructure – Transport

The company's Chilean toll road concession provides the right to charge a tariff to users of the road over the term of the concession. The concession arrangement has an expiration date of 2033, which is the basis for the company's determination of its remaining useful life. Also included within the company's transport operations is $334 million (2013 – $355 million) of indefinite life intangible assets which represent perpetual conservancy rights associated with the company's UK port operation.

The recoverable amounts used in goodwill impairment testing are calculated using discounted cash flow models based on the following significant unobservable inputs:

Valuation technique	Significant unobservable input(s)	Relationship of unobservable input(s) to fair value
Discounted cash flow models	• Future cash flows	• Increases (decreases) in future cash flows will increase (decrease) the recoverable amount
	• Discount rate	• Increases (decreases) in discount rate will decrease (increase) the recoverable amount
	• Terminal capitalization rate	• Increases (decreases) in terminal capitalization rate will decrease (increase) the recoverable amount
	• Exit date	• Increases (decreases) in the exit date will decrease (increase) the recoverable amount

[...]

22. REVENUES

Revenues include $12,338 million (2013 – $12,834 million) from the sale of goods, $5,277 million (2013 – $6,448 million) from the rendering of services, of which $nil (2013 – $558 million) was received in kind, and $749 million (2013 – $811 million) from other activities.

23. DIRECT COSTS

Direct costs include all attributable expenses except interest, depreciation and amortization, taxes and fair value changes and primarily relate to cost of sales and compensation. The following table lists direct costs for 2014 and 2013 by nature:

YEARS ENDED DECEMBER 31 (MILLIONS)	2014	2013
Cost of sales	$ 9,381	$ 10,416
Compensation	1,557	1,125
Selling, general and administrative expenses	1,010	975
Property taxes, sales taxes and other	1,170	1,412
	$ 13,118	$ 13,928

24. OTHER INCOME AND GAINS

Other income and gains in 2013 includes a $525 million gain on the settlement of a long-dated interest rate swap contract as well as a $664 million gain on the sale of a private equity investee company.

In August 2013, the company paid $905 million to terminate the contract, which had accrued to $1,440 million in our Consolidated Financial Statements at the time of settlement. The gain was determined based on the difference between the accrued liability immediately prior to termination and the termination payment amount, adjusted for associated transaction costs and recorded in our corporate activities segment.

25. FAIR VALUE CHANGES

Fair value changes recorded in net income represent gains or losses arising from changes in the fair value of assets and liabilities, including derivative financial instruments, accounted for using the fair value method and are comprised of the following:

YEARS ENDED DECEMBER 31 (MILLIONS)	2014	2013
Investment properties	$ 3,266	$ 1,031
Warrants in General Growth Properties	526	53
Investment in Canary Wharf	319	89
Forest products investment	230	—
Power contracts	(13)	(134)
Other private equity investments	(31)	(94)
Redeemable units	(283)	(20)
Impairments of goodwill and other[1]	(340)	(262)
	$ 3,674	$ 663

1. Other fair value changes includes $74 million (2013 – $33 million) of transaction costs associated with business combinations

---

Goodwill is allocated to the following cash-generating units:

(MILLIONS)	Note	Dec. 31, 2014	Dec. 31, 2013
Services – Construction	(a)	$ 660	$ 720
Residential development – Brazil	(b)	153	277
Services – Property services		54	54
Asset management		323	341
Other		216	196
Total		$ 1,406	$ 1,588

a) Construction

Goodwill in our construction business is tested for impairment using a discounted cash flow analysis with the following valuation assumptions used to determine the recoverable amount: discount rate of 14.5% (2013 – 15.6%), terminal capitalization rate of 10.3% (2013 – 12.1%) and exit date of 2019 (2013 – 2018).

b) Residential Development – Brazil

Goodwill in our Brazilian residential development business is tested for impairment using a discounted cash flow with the following valuation assumptions used to determine the recoverable amount: discount rate of 13.5% (2013 – 14.0%) and terminal capitalization rate of 9.0% (2013 – 9.5%). The current year test resulted in an $87 million impairment of goodwill as a result of the recoverable amount of the business unit being less than our carrying value.

The following table presents the change in the balance of goodwill:

YEARS ENDED DECEMBER 31 (MILLIONS)	2014	2013
Cost at beginning of year	$ 1,635	$ 2,540
Acquisitions through business combinations	78	—
Disposals	(3)	(645)
Foreign currency translation and other	(131)	(260)
Cost at end of year	$ 1,579	$ 1,635

The following table reconciles accumulated impairment losses:

YEARS ENDED DECEMBER 31 (MILLIONS)	2014	2013
Accumulated impairment at beginning of year	$ (47)	$ (50)
Impairment losses	(130)	—
Foreign currency translation	4	3
Accumulated impairment at end of year	$ (173)	$ (47)

The following table presents goodwill by geography:

(MILLIONS)	Dec. 31, 2014	Dec. 31, 2013
United States	$ 314	$ 282
Canada	28	4
Australia	577	625
Brazil	230	397
Europe	26	27
Other	231	253
	$ 1,406	$ 1,588

[...]

27. MANAGEMENT OF RISKS ARISING FROM HOLDING FINANCIAL INSTRUMENTS

The company is exposed to the following risks as a result of holding financial instruments: market risk (i.e., interest rate risk, currency risk and other price risk that impact the fair value of financial instruments); credit risk; and liquidity risk. The following is a description of these risks and how they are managed:

a) Market Risk

Market risk is defined for these purposes as the risk that the fair value or future cash flows of a financial instrument held by the company will fluctuate because of changes in market prices. Market risk includes the risk of changes in interest rates, currency exchange rates and changes in market prices due to factors other than interest rates or currency exchange rates, such as changes in equity prices, commodity prices or credit spreads.

The company manages market risk from foreign currency assets and liabilities and the impact of changes in currency exchange rates and interest rates, by funding assets with financial liabilities in the same currency and with similar interest rate characteristics, and holding financial contracts such as interest rate and foreign exchange derivatives to minimize residual exposures.

Financial instruments held by the company that are subject to market risk include other financial assets, borrowings, and derivative instruments such as interest rate, currency, equity and commodity contracts.

Interest Rate Risk

The observable impacts on the fair values and future cash flows of financial instruments that can be directly attributable to interest rate risk include changes in the net income from financial instruments whose cash flows are determined with reference to floating interest rates and changes in the value of financial instruments whose cash flows are fixed in nature.

The company's assets largely consist of long-duration interest-sensitive physical assets. Accordingly, the company's financial liabilities consist primarily of long-term fixed-rate debt or floating-rate debt that has been swapped with interest rate derivatives. These financial liabilities are, with few exceptions, recorded at their amortized cost. The company also holds interest rate caps to limit its exposure to increases in interest rates on floating rate debt that has not been swapped, and holds interest rate contracts to lock in fixed rates on anticipated future debt issuances and as an economic hedge against the values of long duration interest sensitive physical assets that have not been otherwise matched with fixed rate debt.

The result of a 50 basis-point increase in interest rates on the company's net floating rate financial assets and liabilities would have resulted in a corresponding decrease in net income before tax of $63 million (2013 – $41 million) on an annualized basis.

Changes in the value of fair value through profit or loss interest rate contracts are recorded in other comprehensive income. The impact of a 10 basis-point parallel increase in the yield curve on the aforementioned financial instruments is estimated to result in a corresponding increase in net income of $6 million (2013 – $2 million) and an increase in other comprehensive income of $23 million (2013 – $37 million), before tax for the year ended December 31, 2014.

Currency Exchange Rate Risk

Changes in currency rates will impact the carrying value of financial instruments denominated in currencies other than the U.S. dollar.

The company holds financial instruments with net unmatched exposures in several currencies, changes in the translated value of which are recorded in net income. The impact of a 1% increase in the U.S. dollar against these currencies would have resulted in a $16 million (2013 – $14 million) increase in the value of these positions on a combined basis. The impact on cash flows from financial instruments would be insignificant. The company holds financial instruments to limit its exposure to the impact of foreign currencies on its net investments in foreign operations whose functional and reporting currencies are other than the U.S. dollar. A 1% increase in the U.S. dollar would increase the value of these hedging instruments by $78 million (2013 – $82 million) as at December 31, 2014, which would be recorded in other comprehensive income and offset by changes in the U.S. dollar carrying value of the net investment being hedged.

Other Price Risk

Other price risk is the risk of variability in fair value due to movements in equity prices or other market prices such as commodity prices and credit spreads.

Financial instruments held by the company that are exposed to equity price risk include equity securities and equity derivatives. A 5% decrease in the market price of equity securities and equity derivatives held by the company, excluding equity derivatives that hedge compensation arrangements, would have decreased net income by $193 million (2013 – $126 million) and decreased other comprehensive income by $22 million (2013 – $13 million), prior to taxes. The company's liability in respect of equity compensation arrangements is subject to variability based on changes in the company's underlying common share price. The company holds equity derivatives to hedge almost all of the variability. A 5% change in the common equity price of the company in respect of compensation agreements would increase the compensation liability and compensation expense by $47 million (2013 – $36 million). This increase would be offset by a $47 million (2013 – $37 million) change in value of the associated equity derivatives of which $46 million (2013 – $36 million) would offset the above mentioned increase in compensation expense and the remaining $1 million (2013 – $1 million) would be recorded in other comprehensive income.

The company sells power and generation capacity under long-term agreements and financial contracts to stabilize future revenues. Certain of the contracts are considered financial instruments and are recorded at fair value in the financial statements, with changes in value being recorded in either net income or other comprehensive income as applicable. A 5% increase in energy prices would have decreased net income for the year ended December 31, 2014 by approximately $15 million (2013 – $49 million) and decreased other comprehensive income by $20 million (2013 – $27 million), prior to taxes. The corresponding increase in the value of the revenue or capacity being contracted, however, is not recorded in net income until subsequent periods.

The company held credit default swap contracts with a total notional amount of $848 million (2013 – $800 million) at December 31, 2014. The company is exposed to changes in the credit spread of the contracts' underlying reference asset. A 10 basis-point increase in the credit spread of the underlying reference assets would have increased net income by $2 million (2013 – $2 million) for the year ended December 31, 2014, prior to taxes.

b) Credit Risk

Credit risk is the risk of loss due to the failure of a borrower or counterparty to fulfill its contractual obligations. The company's exposure to credit risk in respect of financial instruments relates primarily to counterparty obligations regarding derivative contracts, loans receivable and credit investments such as bonds and preferred shares.

The company assesses the credit worthiness of each counterparty before entering into contracts and ensures that counterparties meet minimum credit quality requirements. Management evaluates and monitors counterparty credit risk for derivative financial instruments and endeavours to minimize counterparty credit risk through diversification, collateral arrangements, and other credit risk mitigation techniques. The credit risk of derivative financial instruments is generally limited to the positive fair value of the instruments, which, in general, tends to be a relatively small proportion of the notional value. Substantially all of the company's derivative financial instruments involve either counterparties that are banks or other financial institutions in North America, the United Kingdom and Australia, or arrangements that have embedded credit risk mitigation features. The company does not expect to incur credit losses in respect of any of these counterparties. The maximum exposure in respect of loans receivable and credit investments is equal to the carrying value.

c) Liquidity Risk

Liquidity risk is the risk that the company cannot meet a demand for cash or fund an obligation as it comes due. Liquidity risk also includes the risk of not being able to liquidate assets in a timely manner at a reasonable price.

To ensure the company is able to react to contingencies and investment opportunities quickly, the company maintains sources of liquidity at the corporate and subsidiary level. The primary source of liquidity consists of cash and other financial assets, net of deposits and other associated liabilities, and undrawn committed credit facilities.

The company is subject to the risks associated with debt financing, including the ability to refinance indebtedness at maturity. The company believes these risks are mitigated through the use of long-term debt secured by high-quality assets, maintaining debt levels that are in management's opinion relatively conservative, and by diversifying maturities over an extended period of time. The company also seeks to include in its agreements terms that protect the company from liquidity issues of counterparties that might otherwise impact the company's liquidity.

[...]

30. RELATED PARTY TRANSACTIONS

a) Related Parties

Related parties include subsidiaries, associates, joint arrangements, key management personnel, the Board of Directors ("Directors"), immediate family members of key management personnel and Directors, and entities which are, directly or indirectly, controlled by, jointly controlled by or significantly influenced by key management personnel, Directors or their close family members.

b) Key Management Personnel and Directors

Key management personnel are those individuals that have the authority and responsibility for planning, directing and controlling the company's activities, directly or indirectly and consist of the company's Senior Managing Partners. The company's Directors do not plan, direct, or control the activities of the company directly; they provide oversight over the business.

The remuneration of Directors and other key management personnel of the company during the years ended December 31, 2014 and 2013 was as follows:

YEARS ENDED DECEMBER 31 (MILLIONS)	2014	2013
Salaries, incentives and short-term benefits	$ 19	$ 21
Share-based payments	56	41
	$ 75	$ 62

The remuneration of Directors and key executives is determined by the Compensation Committee of the Board of Directors having regard to the performance of individuals and market funds.

c) Related Party Transactions

In the normal course of operations, the company executes transactions on market terms with related parties, which have been measured at exchange value and are recognized in the Consolidated Financial Statements, including, but not limited to: base management fees, performance fees and incentive distributions; loans, interest and non-interest bearing deposits; power purchase and sale agreements; capital commitments to private funds; the acquisition and disposition of assets and businesses; derivative contracts; and the construction and development of assets.

The following table lists the related party balances included within the Consolidated Financial Statements as at and for the years ended December 31, 2014 and 2013:

(MILLIONS)	Dec. 31, 2014	Dec. 31, 2013
Financial assets	$ 1,394	$ 868
Investment and other income, net of interest expense	526	25
Management fees received	29	43

In 2013, the Corporation entered into a $500 million three-year subordinated credit facility with wholly owned subsidiaries of BPY, which was subsequently increased to a notional amount of $1.0 billion in 2014, of which $570 million was drawn on the facility at year end. The terms of the facility, including the interest rate charged by the company, are consistent with market practice given BPY's credit worthiness and the subordination of this facility. All transactions related to this facility have been approved by the independent directors of BPY.

31. OTHER INFORMATION

a) Commitments, Guarantees and Contingencies

In the normal course of business, the company enters into contractual obligations which include commitments to provide bridge financing, letters of credit, operating leases and guarantees provided in respect of power sales contracts and reinsurance obligations. At the end of 2014, the company and its subsidiaries had $1,087 million (2013 – $868 million) of such commitments outstanding.

In addition, the company executes agreements that provide for indemnifications and guarantees to third parties in transactions or dealings such as business dispositions, business acquisitions, sales of assets, provision of services, securitization agreements, and underwriting and agency agreements. The company has also agreed to indemnify its directors and certain of its officers and employees. The nature of substantially all of the indemnification undertakings prevents the company from making a reasonable estimate of the maximum potential amount the company could be required to pay third parties, as in most cases, the agreements do not specify a maximum amount, and the amounts are dependent upon the outcome of future contingent events, the nature and likelihood of which cannot be determined at this time. Neither the company nor its consolidated subsidiaries have made significant payments in the past nor do they expect at this time to make any significant payments under such indemnification agreements in the future.

Table A-1

FUTURE VALUE OF 1

(FUTURE VALUE OF A SINGLE SUM)

$$FVF_{n,\,i} = (1+i)^n$$

(n) periods	2%	2½%	3%	4%	5%	6%	8%	9%	10%	11%	12%	15%
1	1.02000	1.02500	1.03000	1.04000	1.05000	1.06000	1.08000	1.09000	1.10000	1.11000	1.12000	1.15000
2	1.04040	1.05063	1.06090	1.08160	1.10250	1.12360	1.16640	1.18810	1.21000	1.23210	1.25440	1.32250
3	1.06121	1.07689	1.09273	1.12486	1.15763	1.19102	1.25971	1.29503	1.33100	1.36763	1.40493	1.52088
4	1.08243	1.10381	1.12551	1.16986	1.21551	1.26248	1.36049	1.41158	1.46410	1.51807	1.57352	1.74901
5	1.10408	1.13141	1.15927	1.21665	1.27628	1.33823	1.46933	1.53862	1.61051	1.68506	1.76234	2.01136
6	1.12616	1.15969	1.19405	1.26532	1.34010	1.41852	1.58687	1.67710	1.77156	1.87041	1.97382	2.31306
7	1.14869	1.18869	1.22987	1.31593	1.40710	1.50363	1.71382	1.82804	1.94872	2.07616	2.21068	2.66002
8	1.17166	1.21840	1.26677	1.36857	1.47746	1.59385	1.85093	1.99256	2.14359	2.30454	2.47596	3.05902
9	1.19509	1.24886	1.30477	1.42331	1.55133	1.68948	1.99900	2.17189	2.35795	2.55803	2.77308	3.51788
10	1.21899	1.28008	1.34392	1.48024	1.62889	1.79085	2.15892	2.36736	2.59374	2.83942	3.10585	4.04556
11	1.24337	1.31209	1.38423	1.53945	1.71034	1.89830	2.33164	2.58043	2.85312	3.15176	3.47855	4.65239
12	1.26824	1.34489	1.42576	1.60103	1.79586	2.01220	2.51817	2.81267	3.13843	3.49845	3.89598	5.35025
13	1.29361	1.37851	1.46853	1.66507	1.88565	2.13293	2.71962	3.06581	3.45227	3.88328	4.36349	6.15279
14	1.31948	1.41297	1.51259	1.73168	1.97993	2.26090	2.93719	3.34173	3.79750	4.31044	4.88711	7.07571
15	1.34587	1.44830	1.55797	1.80094	2.07893	2.39656	3.17217	3.64248	4.17725	4.78459	5.47357	8.13706
16	1.37279	1.48451	1.60471	1.87298	2.18287	2.54035	3.42594	3.97031	4.59497	5.31089	6.13039	9.35762
17	1.40024	1.52162	1.65285	1.94790	2.29202	2.69277	3.70002	4.32763	5.05447	5.89509	6.86604	10.76126
18	1.42825	1.55966	1.70243	2.02582	2.40662	2.85434	3.99602	4.71712	5.55992	6.54355	7.68997	12.37545
19	1.45681	1.59865	1.75351	2.10685	2.52695	3.02560	4.31570	5.14166	6.11591	7.26334	8.61276	14.23177
20	1.48595	1.63862	1.80611	2.19112	2.65330	3.20714	4.66096	5.60441	6.72750	8.06231	9.64629	16.36654
21	1.51567	1.67958	1.86029	2.27877	2.78596	3.39956	5.03383	6.10881	7.40025	8.94917	10.80385	18.82152
22	1.54598	1.72157	1.91610	2.36992	2.92526	3.60354	5.43654	6.65860	8.14028	9.93357	12.10031	21.64475
23	1.57690	1.76461	1.97359	2.46472	3.07152	3.81975	5.87146	7.25787	8.95430	11.02627	13.55235	24.89146
24	1.60844	1.80873	2.03279	2.56330	3.22510	4.04893	6.34118	7.91108	9.84973	12.23916	15.17863	28.62518
25	1.64061	1.85394	2.09378	2.66584	3.38635	4.29187	6.84847	8.62308	10.83471	13.58546	17.00000	32.91895
26	1.67342	1.90029	2.15659	2.77247	3.55567	4.54938	7.39635	9.39916	11.91818	15.07986	19.04007	37.85680
27	1.70689	1.94780	2.22129	2.88337	3.73346	4.82235	7.98806	10.24508	13.10999	16.73865	21.32488	43.53532
28	1.74102	1.99650	2.28793	2.99870	3.92013	5.11169	8.62711	11.16714	14.42099	18.57990	23.88387	50.06561
29	1.77584	2.04641	2.35657	3.11865	4.11614	5.41839	9.31727	12.17218	15.86309	20.62369	26.74993	57.57545
30	1.81136	2.09757	2.42726	3.24340	4.32194	5.74349	10.06266	13.26768	17.44940	22.89230	29.95992	66.21177
31	1.84759	2.15001	2.50008	3.37313	4.53804	6.08810	10.86767	14.46177	19.19434	25.41045	33.55511	76.14354
32	1.88454	2.20376	2.57508	3.50806	4.76494	6.45339	11.73708	15.76333	21.11378	28.20560	37.58173	87.56507
33	1.92223	2.25885	2.65234	3.64838	5.00319	6.84059	12.67605	17.18203	23.22515	31.30821	42.09153	100.69983
34	1.96068	2.31532	2.73191	3.79432	5.25335	7.25103	13.69013	18.72841	25.54767	34.75212	47.14252	115.80480
35	1.99989	2.37321	2.81386	3.94609	5.51602	7.68609	14.78534	20.41397	28.10244	38.57485	52.79962	133.17552
36	2.03989	2.43254	2.88928	4.10393	5.79182	8.14725	15.96817	22.25123	30.91268	42.81808	59.13557	153.15185
37	2.08069	2.49335	2.98523	4.26809	6.08141	8.63609	17.24563	24.25384	34.00395	47.52807	66.23184	176.12463
38	2.12230	2.55568	3.07478	4.43881	6.38548	9.15425	18.62528	26.43668	37.40434	52.75616	74.17966	202.54332
39	2.16474	2.61957	3.16703	4.61637	6.70475	9.70351	20.11530	28.81598	41.14479	58.55934	83.08122	232.92482
40	2.20804	2.68506	3.26204	4.80102	7.03999	10.28572	21.72452	31.40942	45.25926	65.00087	93.05097	267.86355

Table A-2

PRESENT VALUE OF 1

(PRESENT VALUE OF A SINGLE SUM)

$$PVF_{n,i} = \frac{1}{(1+i)^n} = (1+i)^{-n}$$

(n) periods	2%	2½%	3%	4%	5%	6%	8%	9%	10%	11%	12%	15%
1	.98039	.97561	.97087	.96156	.95238	.94340	.92593	.91743	.90909	.90090	.89286	.86957
2	.96117	.95181	.94260	.92456	.90703	.89000	.85734	.84168	.82645	.81162	.79719	.75614
3	.94232	.92860	.91514	.88900	.86384	.83962	.79383	.77218	.75132	.73119	.71178	.65752
4	.92385	.90595	.88849	.85480	.82270	.79209	.73503	.70843	.68301	.65873	.63552	.57175
5	.90583	.88385	.86261	.82193	.78353	.74726	.68058	.64993	.62092	.59345	.56743	.49718
6	.88797	.86230	.83748	.79031	.74622	.70496	.63017	.59627	.56447	.53464	.50663	.43233
7	.87056	.84127	.81309	.75992	.71068	.66506	.58349	.54703	.51316	.48166	.45235	.37594
8	.85349	.82075	.78941	.73069	.67684	.62741	.54027	.50187	.46651	.43393	.40388	.32690
9	.83676	.80073	.76642	.70259	.64461	.59190	.50025	.46043	.42410	.39092	.36061	.28426
10	.82035	.78120	.74409	.67556	.61391	.55839	.46319	.42241	.38554	.35218	.32197	.24719
11	.80426	.76214	.72242	.64958	.58468	.52679	.42888	.38753	.35049	.31728	.28748	.21494
12	.78849	.74356	.70138	.62460	.55684	.49697	.39711	.35554	.31863	.28584	.25668	.18691
13	.77303	.72542	.68095	.60057	.53032	.46884	.36770	.32618	.28966	.25751	.22917	.16253
14	.75788	.70773	.66112	.57748	.50507	.44230	.34046	.29925	.26333	.23199	.20462	.14133
15	.74301	.69047	.64186	.55526	.48102	.41727.	.31524	.27454	.23939	.20900	.18270	.12289
16	.72845	.67362	.62317	.53391	.45811	.39365	.29189	.25187	.21763	.18829	.16312	.10687
17	.71416	.65720	.60502	.51337	.43630	.37136	.27027	.23107	.19785	.16963	.14564	.09293
18	.70016	.64117	.58739	.49363	.41552	.35034	.25025	.21199	.17986	.15282	.13004	.08081
19	.68643	.62553	.57029	.47464	.39573	.33051	.23171	.19449	.16351	.13768	.11611	.07027
20	.67297	.61027	.55368	.45639	.37689	.31180	.21455	.17843	.14864	.12403	.10367	.06110
21	.65978	.59539	.53755	.43883	.35894	.29416	.19866	.16370	.13513	.11174	.09256	.05313
22	.64684	.58086	.52189	.42196	.34185	.27751	.18394	.15018	.12285	.10067	.08264	.04620
23	.63416	.56670	.50669	.40573	.32557	.26180	.17032	.13778	.11168	.09069	.07379	.04017
24	.62172	.55288	.49193	.39012	.31007	.24698	.15770	.12641	.10153	.08170	.06588	.03493
25	.60953	.53939	.47761	.37512	.29530	.23300	.14602	.11597	.09230	.07361	.05882	.03038
26	.59758	.52623	.46369	.36069	.28124	.21981	.13520	.10639	.08391	.06631	.05252	.02642
27	.58586	.51340	.45019	.34682	.26785	.20737	.12519	.09761	.07628	.05974	.04689	.02297
28	.57437	.50088	.43708	.33348	.25509	.19563	.11591	.08955	.06934	.05382	.04187	.01997
29	.56311	.48866	.42435	.32065	.24295	.18456	.10733	.08216	.06304	.04849	.03738	.01737
30	.55207	.47674	.41199	.30832	.23138	.17411	.09938	.07537	.05731	.04368	.03338	.01510
31	.54125	.46511	.39999	.29646	.22036	.16425	.09202	.06915	.05210	.03935	.02980	.01313
32	.53063	.45377	.38834	.28506	.20987	.15496	.08520	.06344	.04736	.03545	.02661	.01142
33	.52023	.44270	.37703	.27409	.19987	.14619	.07889	.05820	.04306	.03194	.02376	.00993
34	.51003	.43191	.36604	.26355	.19035	.13791	.07305	.05340	.03914	.02878	.02121	.00864
35	.50003	.42137	.35538	.25342	.18129	.13011	.06763	.04899	.03558	.02592	.01894	.00751
36	.49022	.41109	.34503	.24367	.17266	.12274	.06262	.04494	.03235	.02335	.01691	.00653
37	.48061	.40107	.33498	.23430	.16444	.11579	.05799	.04123	.02941	.02104	.01510	.00568
38	.47119	.39128	.32523	.22529	.15661	.10924	.05369	.03783	.02674	.01896	.01348	.00494
39	.46195	.38174	.31575	.21662	.14915	.10306	.04971	.03470	.02430	.01708	.01204	.00429
40	.45289	.37243	.30656	.20829	.14205	.09722	.04603	.03184	.02210	.01538	.01075	.00373

Table A-3

FUTURE VALUE OF AN ORDINARY ANNUITY OF 1

$$FVF\text{-}OA_{n,\,i} = \frac{(1+i)^n - 1}{i}$$

(n) periods	2%	2½%	3%	4%	5%	6%	8%	9%	10%	11%	12%	15%
1	1.00000	1.00000	1.00000	1.00000	1.00000	1.00000	1.00000	1.00000	1.00000	1.00000	1.00000	1.00000
2	2.02000	2.02500	2.03000	2.04000	2.05000	2.06000	2.08000	2.09000	2.10000	2.11000	2.12000	2.15000
3	3.06040	3.07563	3.09090	3.12160	3.15250	3.18360	3.24640	3.27810	3.31000	3.34210	3.37440	3.47250
4	4.12161	4.15252	4.18363	4.24646	4.31013	4.37462	4.50611	4.57313	4.64100	4.70973	4.77933	4.99338
5	5.20404	5.25633	5.30914	5.41632	5.52563	5.63709	5.86660	5.98471	6.10510	6.22780	6.35285	6.74238
6	6.30812	6.38774	6.46841	6.63298	6.80191	6.97532	7.33592	7.52334	7.71561	7.91286	8.11519	8.75374
7	7.43428	7.54743	7.66246	7.89829	8.14201	8.39384	8.92280	9.20044	9.48717	9.78327	10.08901	11.06680
8	8.58297	8.73612	8.89234	9.21423	9.54911	9.89747	10.63663	11.02847	11.43589	11.85943	12.29969	13.72682
9	9.75463	9.95452	10.15911	10.58280	11.02656	11.49132	12.48756	13.02104	13.57948	14.16397	14.77566	16.78584
10	10.94972	11.20338	11.46338	12.00611	12.57789	13.18079	14.48656	15.19293	15.93743	16.72201	17.54874	20.30372
11	12.16872	12.48347	12.80780	13.48635	14.20679	14.97164	16.64549	17.56029	18.53117	19.56143	20.65458	24.34928
12	13.41209	13.79555	14.19203	15.02581	15.91713	16.86994	18.97713	20.14072	21.38428	22.71319	24.13313	29.00167
13	14.68033	15.14044	15.61779	16.62684	17.71298	18.88214	21.49530	22.95339	24.52271	26.21164	28.02911	34.35192
14	15.97394	16.51895	17.08632	18.29191	19.59863	21.01507	24.21492	26.01919	27.97498	30.09492	32.39260	40.50471
15	17.29342	17.93193	18.59891	20.02359	21.57856	23.27597	27.15211	29.36092	31.77248	34.40536	37.27972	47.58041
16	18.63929	19.38022	20.15688	21.82453	23.65749	25.67253	30.32428	33.00340	35.94973	39.18995	42.75328	55.71747
17	20.01207	20.86473	21.76159	23.69751	25.84037	28.21288	33.75023	36.97371	40.54470	44.50084	48.88367	65.07509
18	21.41231	22.38635	23.41444	25.64541	28.13238	30.90565	37.45024	41.30134	45.59917	50.39593	55.74972	75.83636
19	22.84056	23.94601	25.11687	27.67123	30.53900	33.75999	41.44626	46.01846	51.15909	56.93949	63.43968	88.21181
20	24.29737	25.54466	26.87037	29.77808	33.06595	36.78559	45.76196	51.16012	57.27500	64.20283	72.05244	102.44358
21	25.78332	27.18327	28.67649	31.96920	35.71925	39.99273	50.42292	56.76453	64.00250	72.26514	81.69874	118.81012
22	27.29898	28.86286	30.53678	34.24797	38.50521	43.39229	55.45676	62.87334	71.40275	81.21431	92.50258	137.63164
23	28.84496	30.58443	32.45288	36.61789	41.43048	46.99583	60.89330	69.53194	79.54302	91.14788	104.60289	159.27638
24	30.42186	32.34904	34.42647	39.08260	44.50200	50.81558	66.76476	76.78981	88.49733	102.17415	118.15524	184.16784
25	32.03030	34.15776	36.45926	41.64591	47.72710	54.86451	73.10594	84.70090	98.34706	114.41331	133.33387	212.79302
26	33.67091	36.01171	38.55304	44.31174	51.11345	59.15638	79.95442	93.32398	109.18177	127.99877	150.33393	245.71197
27	35.34432	37.91200	40.70963	47.08421	54.66913	63.70577	87.35077	102.72314	121.09994	143.07864	169.37401	283.56877
28	37.05121	39.85990	42.93092	49.96758	58.40258	68.52811	95.33883	112.96822	134.20994	159.81729	190.69889	327.10408
29	38.79223	41.85630	45.21885	52.96629	62.32271	73.63980	103.96594	124.13536	148.63093	178.39719	214.58275	377.16969
30	40.56808	43.90270	47.57542	56.08494	66.43885	79.05819	113.28321	136.30754	164.49402	199.02088	241.33268	434.74515
31	42.37944	46.00027	50.00268	59.32834	70.76079	84.80168	123.34587	149.57522	181.94343	221.91317	271.29261	500.95692
32	44.22703	48.15028	52.50276	62.70147	75.29883	90.88978	134.21354	164.03699	201.13777	247.32362	304.84772	577.10046
33	46.11157	50.35403	55.07784	66.20953	80.06377	97.34316	145.95062	179.80032	222.25154	275.52922	342.42945	644.66553
34	48.03380	52.61289	57.73018	69.85791	85.06696	104.18376	158.62667	196.98234	245.47670	306.83744	384.52098	765.36535
35	49.99448	54.92821	60.46208	73.65222	90.32031	111.43478	172.31680	215.71076	271.02437	341.58955	431.66350	881.17016
36	51.99437	57.30141	63.27594	77.59831	95.83632	119.12087	187.10215	236.12472	299.12681	380.16441	484.46312	1014.34568
37	54.03425	59.73395	66.17422	81.70225	101.62814	127.26812	203.07032	258.37595	330.03949	422.98249	543.59869	1167.49753
38	56.11494	62.22730	69.15945	85.97034	107.70955	135.90421	220.31595	282.62978	364.04343	470.51056	609.83053	1343.62216
39	58.23724	64.78298	72.23423	90.40915	114.09502	145.05846	238.94122	309.06646	401.44778	523.26673	684.01020	1546.16549
40	60.40198	67.40255	75.40126	95.02552	120.79977	154.76197	259.05652	337.88245	442.59256	581.82607	767.09142	1779.09031

Table A-4

PRESENT VALUE OF AN ORDINARY ANNUITY OF 1

$$PVF\text{-}OA_{n,\,i} = \frac{1 - \dfrac{1}{(1+i)^n}}{i}$$

(n) periods	2%	2½%	3%	4%	5%	6%	8%	9%	10%	11%	12%	15%
1	.98039	.97561	.97087	.96154	.95238	.94340	.92593	.91743	.90909	.90090	.89286	.86957
2	1.94156	1.92742	1.91347	1.88609	1.85941	1.83339	1.78326	1.75911	1.73554	1.71252	1.69005	1.62571
3	2.88388	2.85602	2.82861	2.77509	2.72325	2.67301	2.57710	2.53130	2.48685	2.44371	2.40183	2.28323
4	3.80773	3.76197	3.71710	3.62990	3.54595	3.46511	3.31213	3.23972	3.16986	3.10245	3.03735	2.85498
5	4.71346	4.64583	4.57971	4.45182	4.32948	4.21236	3.99271	3.88965	3.79079	3.69590	3.60478	3.35216
6	5.60143	5.50813	5.41719	5.24214	5.07569	4.91732	4.62288	4.48592	4.35526	4.23054	4.11141	3.78448
7	6.47199	6.34939	6.23028	6.00205	5.78637	5.58238	5.20637	5.03295	4.86842	4.71220	4.56376	4.16042
8	7.32548	7.17014	7.01969	6.73274	6.46321	6.20979	5.74664	5.53482	5.33493	5.14612	4.96764	4.48732
9	8.16224	7.97087	7.78611	7.43533	7.10782	6.80169	6.24689	5.99525	5.75902	5.53705	5.32825	4.77158
10	8.98259	8.75206	8.53020	8.11090	7.72173	7.36009	6.71008	6.41766	6.14457	5.88923	5.65022	5.01877
11	9.78685	9.51421	9.25262	8.76048	8.30641	7.88687	7.13896	6.80519	6.49506	6.20652	5.93770	5.23371
12	10.57534	10.25776	9.95400	9.38507	8.86325	8.38384	7.53608	7.16073	6.81369	6.49236	6.19437	5.42062
13	11.34837	10.98319	10.63496	9.98565	9.39357	8.85268	7.90378	7.48690	7.10336	6.74987	6.42355	5.58315
14	12.10625	11.69091	11.29607	10.56312	9.89864	9.29498	8.24424	7.78615	7.36669	6.98187	6.62817	5.72448
15	12.84926	12.38138	11.93794	11.11839	10.37966	9.71225	8.55948	8.06069	7.60608	7.19087	6.81086	5.84737
16	13.57771	13.05500	12.56110	11.65230	10.83777	10.10590	8.85137	8.31256	7.82371	7.37916	6.97399	5.95424
17	14.29187	13.71220	13.16612	12.16567	11.27407	10.47726	9.12164	8.54363	8.02155	7.54879	7.11963	6.04716
18	14.99203	14.35336	13.75351	12.65930	11.68959	10.82760	9.37189	8.75563	8.20141	7.70162	7.24967	6.12797
19	15.67846	14.97889	14.32380	13.13394	12.08532	11.15812	9.60360	8.95012	8.36492	7.83929	7.36578	6.19823
20	16.35143	15.58916	14.87747	13.59033	12.46221	11.46992	9.81815	9.12855	8.51356	7.96333	7.46944	6.25933
21	17.01121	16.18455	15.41502	14.02916	12.82115	11.76408	10.01680	9.29224	8.64869	8.07507	7.56200	6.31246
22	17.65805	16.76541	15.93692	14.45112	13.16800	12.04158	10.20074	9.44243	8.77154	8.17574	7.64465	6.35866
23	18.29220	17.33211	16.44361	14.85684	13.48857	12.30338	10.37106	9.58021	8.88322	8.26643	7.71843	6.39884
24	18.91393	17.88499	16.93554	15.24696	13.79864	12.55036	10.52876	9.70661	8.98474	8.34814	7.78432	6.43377
25	19.52346	18.42438	17.41315	15.62208	14.09394	12.78336	10.67478	9.82258	9.07704	8.42174	7.84314	6.46415
26	20.12104	18.95061	17.87684	15.98277	14.37519	13.00317	10.80998	9.92897	9.16095	8.48806	7.89566	6.49056
27	20.70690	19.46401	18.32703	16.32959	14.64303	13.21053	10.93516	10.02658	9.23722	8.45780	7.94255	6.51353
28	21.28127	19.96489	18.76411	16.66306	14.89813	13.40616	11.05108	10.11613	9.30657	8.60162	7.98442	6.53351
29	21.84438	20.45355	19.18845	16.98371	15.14107	13.59072	11.15841	10.19828	9.36961	8.65011	8.02181	6.55088
30	22.39646	20.93029	19.60044	17.29203	15.37245	13.76483	11.25778	10.27365	9.42691	8.69379	8.05518	6.56598
31	22.93770	21.39541	20.00043	17.58849	15.59281	13.92909	11.34980	10.34280	9.47901	8.73315	8.08499	6.57911
32	23.46833	21.84918	20.38877	17.87355	15.80268	14.08404	11.43500	10.40624	9.52638	8.76860	8.11159	6.59053
33	23.98856	22.29188	20.76579	18.14765	16.00255	14.23023	11.51389	10.46444	9.56943	8.80054	8.13535	6.60046
34	24.49859	22.72379	21.13184	18.41120	16.19290	14.36814	11.58693	10.51784	9.60858	8.82932	8.15656	6.60910
35	24.99862	23.14516	21.48722	18.66461	16.37419	14.49825	11.65457	10.56682	9.64416	8.85524	8.17550	6.61661
36	25.48884	23.55625	21.83225	18.90828	16.54685	14.62099	11.71719	10.61176	9.67651	8.87859	8.19241	6.62314
37	25.96945	23.95732	22.16724	19.14258	16.71129	14.73678	11.77518	10.65299	9.70592	8.89963	8.20751	6.62882
38	26.44064	24.34860	22.49246	19.36786	16.86789	14.84602	11.82887	10.69082	9.73265	8.91859	8.22099	6.63375
39	26.90259	24.73034	22.80822	19.58448	17.01704	14.94907	11.87858	10.72552	9.75697	8.93567	8.23303	6.63805
40	27.35548	25.10278	23.11477	19.79277	17.15909	15.04630	11.92461	10.75736	9.77905	8.95105	8.24378	6.64178

Table A-5

PRESENT VALUE OF AN ANNUITY DUE OF 1

$$PVF-AD_{n,\,i} = 1 + \frac{1 - \dfrac{1}{(1+i)^{n-1}}}{i}$$

(n) periods	2%	2½%	3%	4%	5%	6%	8%	9%	10%	11%	12%	15%
1	1.00000	1.00000	1.00000	1.00000	1.00000	1.00000	1.00000	1.00000	1.00000	1.00000	1.00000	1.00000
2	1.98039	1.97561	1.97087	1.96154	1.95238	1.94340	1.92593	1.91743	1.90909	1.90090	1.89286	1.86957
3	2.94156	2.92742	2.91347	2.88609	2.85941	2.83339	2.78326	2.75911	2.73554	2.71252	2.69005	2.62571
4	3.88388	3.85602	3.82861	3.77509	3.72325	3.67301	3.57710	3.53130	3.48685	3.44371	3.40183	3.28323
5	4.80773	4.76197	4.71710	4.62990	4.54595	4.46511	4.31213	4.23972	4.16986	4.10245	4.03735	3.85498
6	5.71346	5.64583	5.57971	5.45182	5.32948	5.21236	4.99271	4.88965	4.79079	4.69590	4.60478	4.35216
7	6.60143	6.50813	6.41719	6.24214	6.07569	5.91732	5.62288	5.48592	5.35526	5.23054	5.11141	4.78448
8	7.47199	7.34939	7.23028	7.00205	6.78637	6.58238	6.20637	6.03295	5.86842	5.71220	5.56376	5.16042
9	8.32548	8.17014	8.01969	7.73274	7.46321	7.20979	6.74664	6.53482	6.33493	6.14612	5.96764	5.48732
10	9.16224	8.97087	8.78611	8.43533	8.10782	7.80169	7.24689	6.99525	6.75902	6.53705	6.32825	5.77158
11	9.98259	9.75206	9.53020	9.11090	8.72173	8.36009	7.71008	7.41766	7.14457	6.88923	6.65022	6.01877
12	10.78685	10.51421	10.25262	9.76048	9.30641	8.88687	8.13896	7.80519	7.49506	7.20652	6.93770	6.23371
13	11.57534	11.25776	10.95400	10.38507	9.86325	9.38384	8.53608	8.16073	7.81369	7.49236	7.19437	6.42062
14	12.34837	11.98319	11.63496	10.98565	10.39357	9.85268	8.90378	8.48690	8.10336	7.74987	7.42355	6.58315
15	13.10625	12.69091	12.29607	11.56312	10.89864	10.29498	9.24424	8.78615	9.36669	7.98187	7.62817	6.72448
16	13.84926	13.38138	12.93794	12.11839	11.37966	10.71225	9.55948	9.06069	8.60608	8.19087	7.81086	6.84737
17	14.57771	14.05500	13.56110	12.65230	11.83777	11.10590	9.85137	9.31256	8.82371	8.37916	7.97399	6.95424
18	15.29187	14.71220	14.16612	13.16567	12.27407	11.47726	10.12164	9.54363	9.02155	8.54879	8.11963	7.04716
19	15.99203	15.35336	14.75351	13.65930	12.68959	11.82760	10.37189	9.75563	9.20141	8.70162	8.24967	7.12797
20	16.67846	15.97889	15.32380	14.13394	13.08532	12.15812	10.60360	9.95012	9.36492	8.83929	8.36578	7.19823
21	17.35143	16.58916	15.87747	14.59033	13.46221	12.46992	10.81815	10.12855	9.51356	8.96333	8.46944	7.25933
22	18.01121	17.18455	16.41502	15.02916	13.82115	12.76408	11.01680	10.29224	9.64869	9.07507	8.56200	7.31246
23	18.65805	17.76541	16.93692	15.45112	14.16300	13.04158	11.20074	10.44243	9.77154	9.17574	8.64465	7.35866
24	19.29220	18.33211	17.44361	15.85684	14.48857	13.30338	11.37106	10.58021	9.88322	9.26643	8.71843	7.39884
25	19.91393	18.88499	17.93554	16.24696	14.79864	13.55036	11.52876	10.70661	9.98474	9.34814	8.78432	7.43377
26	20.52346	19.42438	18.41315	16.62208	15.09394	13.78336	11.67478	10.82258	10.07704	9.42174	8.84314	7.46415
27	21.12104	19.95061	18.87684	16.98277	15.37519	14.00317	11.80998	10.92897	10.16095	9.48806	8.89566	7.49056
28	21.70690	20.46401	19.32703	17.32959	15.64303	14.21053	11.93518	11.02658	10.23722	9.54780	8.94255	7.51353
29	22.28127	20.96489	19.76411	17.66306	15.89813	14.40616	12.05108	11.11613	10.30657	9.60162	8.98442	7.53351
30	22.84438	21.45355	20.18845	17.98371	16.14107	14.59072	12.15841	11.19828	10.36961	9.65011	9.02181	7.55088
31	23.39646	21.93029	20.60044	18.29203	16.37245	14.76483	12.25778	11.27365	10.42691	9.69379	9.05518	7.56598
32	23.93770	22.39541	21.00043	18.58849	16.59281	14.92909	12.34980	11.34280	10.47901	9.73315	9.08499	7.57911
33	24.46833	22.84918	21.38877	18.87355	16.80268	15.08404	12.43500	11.40624	10.52638	9.76860	9.11159	7.59053
34	24.98856	23.29188	21.76579	19.14765	17.00255	15.23023	12.51389	11.46444	10.56943	9.80054	9.13535	7.60046
35	25.49859	23.72379	22.13184	19.41120	17.19290	15.36814	12.58693	11.51784	10.60858	9.82932	9.15656	7.60910
36	25.99862	24.14516	22.48722	19.66461	17.37419	15.49825	12.65457	11.56682	10.64416	9.85524	9.17550	7.61661
37	26.48884	24.55625	22.83225	19.90828	17.54685	15.62099	12.71719	11.61176	10.67651	9.87859	9.19241	7.62314
38	26.96945	24.95732	23.16724	20.14258	17.71129	15.73678	12.77518	11.65299	10.70592	9.89963	9.20751	7.62882
39	27.44064	25.34860	23.49246	20.36786	17.86789	15.84602	12.82887	11.69082	10.73265	9.91859	9.22099	7.63375
40	27.90259	25.73034	23.80822	20.58448	18.01704	15.94907	12.87858	11.72552	10.75697	9.93567	9.23303	7.63805

Glossary

Accelerated amortization A depreciation method that creates a higher depreciation expense in the earlier years and lower charges in the later periods. An example is the *Diminishing balance method*.

Account An individual accounting record of increases and decreases in a specific asset, liability, or shareholders' equity item.

Accounting cycle A series of steps followed by accountants in preparing financial statements.

Accounting information system The system of collecting and processing transaction data and communicating financial information to interested parties.

Accounting Standards Board (AcSB) The group primarily responsible for setting GAAP in Canada, which publishes the *CPA Canada Handbook* and other authoritative documents.

Accounting Standards for Private Enterprises (ASPE) The financial reporting standards applicable to private entities in Canada. Private entities may also use IFRS.

Accounting Standards Oversight Council (AcSOC) The group that provides oversight to AcSB activities such as setting the agenda, reporting to the public, and raising funds for standard setting.

Accrual basis The most commonly used basis of accounting whereby revenue is recognized when it is earned and expenses are recognized in the period incurred, without regard to the time of receipt or payment of cash. Also known as "accrual-basis accounting."

Accrual-basis accounting See *Accrual basis*.

Accrued expenses Expenses incurred, but not yet paid at the statement date.

Accrued revenues Revenues earned, but not yet received in cash at the statement date.

Accumulated other comprehensive income The cumulative total of all past charges and credits to OCI up to the statement of financial position date. It is similar to retained earnings, but it is for OCI items.

Acquirer A company that purchases another business.

Active market A level of trading of a particular security or asset where there is a good supply of willing buyers and sellers.

Activity method A method of calculating depreciation whereby depreciation is determined as a function of the use or productivity of the asset.

Activity ratios Ratios that measure how effectively a company uses its assets, and the liquidity of certain assets such as inventory and receivables.

Additions Increases or extensions of existing assets.

Adjunct account An account that increases either an asset, a liability, or an owners' equity account.

Adjusted trial balance A list of all open accounts in the ledger and their balances taken immediately after all adjusting entries have been posted.

Adjusting entries Journal entries made at the end of the accounting period to ensure that the revenue recognition and matching principles are followed.

Adverse selection A result of information asymmetry whereby the capital marketplace may attract the wrong types of companies (that is, those that have the most to gain from having information that others do not).

Aggressive accounting A bias that exists in financial reporting that focuses more on the positive information about a company and its financial position and operations; for example, a company may overstate net income or net assets.

Aging method A method of estimating the percentage of outstanding receivables that will become uncollectible based on past experience using the percentage-of-receivables approach.

Aging schedule A schedule to organize accounts receivable that indicates which accounts require special attention for collection by providing the age of such accounts receivable.

All-inclusive approach An income measurement approach that indicates that most items, including irregular ones, are recorded in income.

Allowance method A method of estimating uncollectible accounts receivable whereby bad debt expense is recorded in the same period as the sale to obtain a proper matching of expenses and revenues, and to achieve a proper carrying value for accounts receivable.

Amortization The process of allocating the cost of an asset to expense over its useful life in a rational and systematic manner. Also known as *Depreciation*.

Amortized cost The acquisition cost adjusted for the amortization of the discount or premium.

Amortized cost model A model applied to investments in debt securities and long-term notes and loans receivable that measures the difference between the initial amount recognized and the maturity value and allocates it to income over time.

Arm's-length transaction A transaction that has been carried out between parties that are not related (resulting in terms that are fairly bargained and that represent market terms).

Artistic-related intangible assets Ownership rights over the reproduction of a creative work. They are protected by copyright and have value because of their legal-contractual nature.

Asset group See *Cash-generating unit (CGU)*.

Asset retirement costs Costs recognized at the same time that the liability associated with the retirement of an asset is recognized.

Asset turnover ratio A measurement of how efficiently a company uses its total assets to generate revenue. It is calculated by dividing net sales by average total assets.

Asset-backed financing The use of receivables as collateral to generate immediate cash for a company, either through secured borrowings or sales of receivables.

Asset-backed securities Securities that represent ownership claims to a pool of individual loans that have been securitized; that is, repackaged into asset pools in which ownership interest has been sold.

Asset-liability approach A revenue recognition approach that focuses on changes in contractual rights and contractual obligations created by contracts with customers.

Assets Probable future economic benefits obtained or controlled by a particular entity as a result of past transactions or events.

Associate An entity that an investor has significant influence over that is neither a subsidiary nor a joint venture.

Assurance-type warranty A type of warranty that provides assurance as to the quality of the product sold at the point of sale and for a reasonable period thereafter.

Available for sale investments A type of investment that is not otherwise classified under IAS 39 as held to maturity, loans and receivables, or at fair value through profit or loss.

Average days to sell inventory A variable of the inventory turnover ratio that represents the average age of the inventory on hand based on the number of days it takes to sell inventory once purchased.

Avoidable borrowing costs The actual borrowing costs that would not have been incurred by a company borrowing funds to finance a specific qualifying asset if the expenditures for the qualifying asset had not been made.

Bad debts Impaired trade receivables. Also known as "uncollectible accounts."

Balance sheet A financial statement that shows a company's financial condition at the end of a period (under ASPE). Also known as *Statement of financial position*.

Bank overdrafts What occurs when cheques are written for more than the amount in the cash account.

Bank reconciliation A schedule explaining any differences between the bank's and the company's records of cash.

Bargain purchase The purchase of an investment or asset at a price that is lower than its fair value. Also known as "negative goodwill" in a business combination.

Barter transactions Transactions where few or no monetary assets are received as consideration when goods or services are purchased or sold. Also known as *Nonmonetary transactions*.

Basic elements Financial reporting terms that constitute the language of accounting and business, such as "assets," "liabilities," and "equity."

Basic loan features Contractual terms that result in cash flows that are payments of principal and interest.

Basket purchase The purchase of a group of units with different characteristics at a single lump-sum price.

Beneficial interest A debt or equity claim to the cash flows of the party that acquired the receivables, arising when a company sells a receivable.

Biological assets Any living asset, such as livestock or trees.

Bill-and-hold arrangement A type of business arrangement where goods are sold but the seller does not deliver the goods right away.

Book value The amount at which an asset is recognized in the statement of financial position. Also known as *Carrying amount*.

Boot The payment or receipt of a significant amount of cash or other monetary asset when assets are exchanged or traded in.

Borrowing costs Interest and other costs that a company incurs in connection with the borrowing of funds.

Brand A group of assets such as a trade name and its related formulas, recipes, and technology that are used to distinguish a particular company or product.

Brand name See *Brand*.

Bright-line tests Quantitative thresholds in financial reporting standards that act as a benchmark to dictate how something is to be accounted for.

Bundled sales Contracts involving the sale of multiple goods and/or services for one price. Also known as "multiple deliverables."

Business combination What results when one entity acquires control over the net assets of another business, either by acquiring the net assets directly, or by acquiring the equity interest representing control over the net assets.

Business component A component of an entity being disposed of where the operations, cash flows, and financial elements are clearly distinguishable from the rest of the entity.

Business model The manner in which a company adds value. Different business models include manufacturing, retail selling, providing services, exploration and development, and others.

Canadian Institute of Chartered Accountants (CICA) The predecessor organization of Chartered Professional Accountants Canada (CPA Canada).

Canadian Public Accountability Board (CPAB) The regulatory oversight body that ensures that certain standards are met regarding quality controls and independence.

Capital allocation The process by which accounting enables investors and creditors to assess the relative returns and risks associated with investment opportunities and thereby channel resources more effectively.

Capital approach A method of accounting for contributions of assets from an owner where the increase in assets is treated as contributed (donated) capital (a Contributed Surplus account) rather than as earned revenue.

Capital cost allowance (CCA) The amount of depreciation allowed to be deducted for tax purposes in tax returns.

Capital cost allowance method The method used in calculating depreciation for tax purposes and calculating the tax value of an asset by Canadian businesses, regardless of the method used for reporting purposes.

Capital expenditure An expenditure that increases an asset's useful life, increases the quantity of units produced from the asset, or enhances the quality of units produced.

Capital gain The result when the proceeds on disposal of a capital asset are greater than the original cost of the asset.

Capitalization period The time period during which interest may be capitalized. It begins when three conditions are present: (1) expenditures for the asset have been made, (2) activities that are necessary to get the asset ready for its intended use are in progress, and (3) interest cost is being incurred.

Capitalization rate A weighted-average borrowing rate on general borrowings, used to determine avoidable borrowing costs on non–asset-specific debt.

Capitalized Recorded in asset accounts and then depreciated, as is appropriate for expenditures for items with useful lives greater than one year.

Carrying amount The amount at which an asset is recognized in the statement of financial position. Also known as *Book value*.

Cash Cash on hand and demand deposits.

Cash and cash equivalents Cash, demand deposits, and short-term highly liquid investments that are readily convertible into known amounts of cash and that are subject to insignificant risk of changes in value.

Cash debt coverage ratio A long-run measure of financial flexibility that indicates a company's ability to repay its liabilities from net cash provided by operating activities, without having to liquidate the assets used in its operations.

Cash discounts Sales discounts that are offered to induce prompt payment.

Cash equivalents Short-term, highly liquid investments that are readily converted to known amounts of cash and are subject to an insignificant risk of change in value.

Cash-generating unit (CGU) The smallest identifiable group of assets that generates cash inflows that are largely independent of the cash flows from other assets or groups of assets. Also known as an "asset group."

Change in accounting principle A change that occurs when an accounting principle adopted is different from the one previously used.

Chartered Professional Accountants Canada (CPA Canada) The main professional accounting body for chartered accountants that also has primary responsibility for setting GAAP in Canada through the Accounting Standards Board.

Closing entries The journal entries that close the temporary accounts in order to start a new financial reporting period. After closing revenue and expense accounts, the related Income Summary amounts are posted to retained earnings.

Closing process The procedure generally followed to reduce the balance of temporary accounts to zero in order to prepare the accounts for the next period's transactions.

Collectibility A threshold relating to revenue recognition dealing with the company's ability to collect cash from a sale to a customer.

Commercial substance An exchange of assets where there is a significant change in the company's expected future cash flows relative to the fair values of the assets exchanged.

Comparability What occurs when information that has been measured and reported in a similar manner for different companies is considered comparable.

Compensating balances That portion of any demand deposit (or any time deposit or certificate of deposit) maintained by a company that constitutes support for existing borrowing arrangements of the company with a lending institution.

Completed-contract method The revenue recognition method in which revenues and gross profit are recognized only when the contract is completed.

Completeness The quality of accounting information that makes it reliable by including all information necessary to provide an accurate portrayal of events and transactions.

Componentization Decisions regarding which fixed asset components to recognize separately.

Compound interest Interest that is earned on the principal amount invested and on any accrued interest.

Comprehensive income A measure of income under IFRS that includes net income plus other comprehensive income.

Computer software costs A technology-based intangible asset, either developed for internal use or for sale as a product.

Conceptual framework A coherent system of interrelated objectives and fundamentals that can lead to consistent standards and that prescribes the nature, function, and limits of financial accounting and financial statements.

Conservatism A constraint of financial reporting stipulating that, in doubtful situations, the solution that will least likely overstate assets and income should be chosen.

Conservative accounting A bias that exists in financial reporting that ensures that, where uncertainty exists and judgement is needed, net income and/or net assets are understated rather than being overstated.

Consigned goods Goods that are sold on consignment yet remain the consignor's property and therefore must be included in inventory.

Consignee The party in a consignment arrangement that displays goods for sale (where legal title remains with the supplier/consignor).

Consignment A type of transaction where one party, who does not have legal title to goods, presents them to customers for sale and earns a commission when the customer buys the goods.

Consignor The party in a consignment arrangement that has legal title to goods for sale but allows the goods to be displayed for sale by another party (consignee).

Consistency What occurs when a company applies the same accounting treatment to similar events from period to period.

Consolidation The process of treating both parent and subsidiary companies as a single economic entity.

Constructive obligation A type of performance obligation not stated in a contract that is created through a past practice or by signalling something to potential customers, such as a "100% satisfaction guaranteed" policy.

Contingency "An existing condition or situation involving uncertainty as to a possible gain or loss to an enterprise that will ultimately be resolved when one or more future events occur or fail to occur," as defined under ASPE.

Contra account An account on the statement of financial position that reduces an asset, a liability, or an owners' equity account.

Contra asset account An account that is offset against an asset account on the statement of financial position.

Contract A legally binding arrangement between two or more parties.

Contract assets Assets that arise through contractual rights.

Contract liability Liabilities that arise through contractual obligations.

Contract modification Where a contract is subsequently changed.

Contract-based intangible assets The value of rights that arise from contractual arrangements, such as licensing agreements, lease agreements, and broadcast rights.

Contractual yield basis A model of managing a long-term receivables contract involving the holding of instruments for their principal and interest flows.

Control Under ASPE, the continuing power to determine the strategic operating, financing, and investing policies of another entity without the co-operation of others. Under IFRS, the power to direct the activities of another entity to generate returns, either positive or negative, for the investor.

Conventional retail inventory method A method to value inventory that uses the cost-to-retail ratio incorporating net markups but excluding net markdowns. This method is designed to approximate the lower of average cost and market.

Conversion costs A type of product cost that includes labour and variable production overhead costs incurred in processing materials into finished goods.

Copyright A federally granted right that all authors, painters, musicians, sculptors, and other artists have in their creations, whatever mode or form of expression. It is an exclusive right to reproduce and sell an artistic or published work.

Cost All expenditures needed to acquire an item of property, plant, and equipment and bring it to its location and ready it for use.

Cost formula A method of assigning inventory costs incurred during the accounting period to inventory that is still on hand at the end of the period. The three acceptable formulas are specific identification; first-in, first-out (FIFO); and weighted average cost.

Cost model (CM) The model that measures property, plant, and equipment assets after acquisition at their cost, less accumulated depreciation and any accumulated impairment losses.

Cost of goods available for sale or use The total of (1) the cost of goods on hand at the beginning of the period and (2) the cost of the goods acquired or produced during the period.

Cost of goods manufactured The total cost of items that have been manufactured including raw materials and related processing costs.

Cost of goods sold The difference between those goods available for sale during the period and those on hand at the end of the period.

Cost recovery impairment model A model of measuring impairment losses whereby a long-lived asset is impaired only if a company cannot recover the asset's carrying amount from using the asset and eventually disposing of it.

Cost reduction method An income approach method for accounting for government assistance, whereby the asset cost and future depreciation are reduced by the amount of government assistance received.

Cost-benefit relationship A constraint of financial reporting that the costs of obtaining and providing information should not be higher than the benefits that are gained by providing it.

Cost-to-cost basis The process by which the percentage of completion is measured by comparing costs incurred to date with the most recent estimate of the total costs to complete the contract.

Cost-to-retail ratio A ratio used in the retail inventory method determined by dividing goods available for sale at cost, by the goods available for sale at retail.

Coupon rate See *Stated interest rate.*

Coverage ratios Ratios that measure the degree of protection for long-term creditors and investors. Also known as *Solvency ratios.*

CPA Canada Handbook A set of principles and guidelines for accounting and assurance.

Credit The right side of a general ledger account.

Credit risk The likelihood of loss because of the failure of the other party in a transaction to fully pay the amount owed.

Current assets Cash and other assets ordinarily realizable within one year from the date of the balance sheet or within the normal operating cycle where that is longer than a year.

Current cash debt coverage ratio The ratio of net cash provided by operating activities to average current liabilities, indicating how well a company can address its current obligations from internally generated cash flow.

Current liabilities Amounts due within one year from the date of the statement of financial position or within the normal operating cycle, where this is longer than a year.

Current operating performance approach An income measurement approach that argues that the most useful income measure will reflect only regular and recurring revenue and expense elements.

Current ratio The ratio of total current assets to total current liabilities.

Customer-related intangible assets Intangible assets that occur as a result of interactions between company employees and systems with outside parties interested in buying goods and services.

Cut-off schedule A schedule prepared by the accountant for the end of the period to ensure that goods received from suppliers around the end of the year are recorded in the appropriate period.

Debit The left side of a general ledger account.

Debt instruments Financial instruments that have contractual cash flows including principal and interest.

Debt securities Financial instruments that have contractual cash flows including principal and interest whose prices are generally quoted in an active market.

Decision-usefulness approach Approach to financial reporting whereby the amount and types of information to be disclosed and the format in which information should be presented involves determining which alternative provides the most useful information for decision-making purposes.

Declining-balance method A depreciation method that uses a depreciation rate that remains a constant percentage throughout the asset's useful life and reduces the book value each year to determine depreciation expense.

Decreasing charge method A depreciation method that provides for a higher depreciation expense in the earlier years and lower charges in the later periods on the basis that more depreciation should be charged in earlier years if that is when the asset offers the greatest benefits.

Deferral method The method of recording the amount of government assistance received as a deferred credit, amortizing it to revenue over the life of the related assets.

Deferred income tax assets The future tax consequence due to deductible temporary differences. Also known as *Future income tax assets* under ASPE.

Deferred income tax liabilities The future tax consequences associated with taxable temporary differences. Also known as *Future income tax liabilities* under ASPE.

Depletion The amortization of natural resources.

Depletion base A natural resource's capitalized costs of acquisition, exploration, development, and restoration.

Deposits in transit End-of-month deposits of cash recorded in the depositor's books one month and received and recorded by the bank the following month.

Depreciable amount The difference between the asset's cost, or revalued amount if the revaluation model is being used, and its residual value.

Depreciation The cost of tangible capital assets allocated to the accounting periods benefiting their use; generally used to describe tangible assets. Also known as *Amortization.*

Derecognition The process of removing an item from a company's statement of financial position or income statement.

Derecognized Describing an asset after all of its related items have been removed from a company's accounts.

Development The translation of research findings or other knowledge into a plan or design for new or substantially improved materials, devices, products, processes, systems, or services prior to the start of commercial production or use.

Development phase A broad category of development activities where costs are capitalized only when future benefits are reasonably certain.

Diminishing balance method A depreciation method that applies a constant percentage rate to net book value to calculate depreciation expense over the useful life of the asset. A type of *Accelerated amortization*.

Direct method A method of recording inventory used when revaluing inventory to reflect net realizable value under the lower of cost and net realizable value method where the Inventory account is revalued.

Direct write-off method A method for recording uncollectible accounts receivable where no entry is made until a specific account has definitely been established as uncollectible.

Discontinued operations The operations of an identifiable business segment that has been sold, abandoned, shut down, or otherwise disposed of, or that is the subject of a formal plan of disposal.

Discount What occurs when a bond sells at less than face value.

Discounted cash flow model A model for measuring fair value that deals with uncertainty and the time value of money. It has two approaches: the traditional approach and the expected cash flow approach.

Discounted free cash flow method A method to value goodwill that involves a projection of the company's free cash flow over a long period.

Double-declining-balance method A depreciation method that uses a rate (which is the straight-line percentage rate multiplied by two) that is applied to the net book value every year, resulting in a declining depreciation expense year after year.

Double-entry accounting System of accounting requiring the equality of debits and credits when recording transactions, which helps prove the accuracy of the recorded amounts.

Due process A method used in standard setting in order to ensure that standard-setting bodies operate in full view of the public by giving those who are interested ample opportunity to make their views known.

Earnings approach An approach to revenue recognition whereby revenues are recognized when performance is substantially complete and collection is reasonably assured.

Earnings management The process of targeting certain earnings levels (whether current or future) or desired earnings trends and working backwards to determine what has to be done to ensure that these targets are met.

Earnings multiple A number calculated by dividing the market price of a share by earnings per share.

Earnings per share Net income available to common shareholders divided by the weighted average number of common shares outstanding.

Economic benefits Benefits provided by assets, such as increased revenues from sales of products or services and reductions in future costs.

Economic entity assumption An assumption that a company's business activity can be kept separate and distinct from its owners and any other business units. Economic activity can therefore be identified with a particular degree of accountability.

Economic substance The underlying economic reality reported on a representationally faithful document.

Effective interest method A method of amortization whereby the current market rate of interest at the time of investment is used to calculate interest income by applying it to the carrying amount (book value) of the investment for each interest period. The note's carrying amount changes as it is increased by the amount of discount amortized.

Effective interest rate The interest rate actually earned. Also known as *Market rate* or *Yield rate*.

Efficient markets hypothesis A theory that states that, if information is available, it will be incorporated into decisions made by market participants.

Elements of financial statements Basic items that are presented in the financial statements.

Entity perspective The viewpoint that companies are viewed as separate and distinct from their owners and therefore financial reporting should focus on the needs of the main users and not just the owners.

Equitable obligations Commitments that arise from moral or ethical considerations.

Equity The residual interest in the assets of a company that remains after deducting its liabilities.

Equity instruments Any contract that evidences a residual interest in the assets of a company after deducting all of its liabilities; examples are common and certain preferred shares.

Equity method A method of accounting for investments where a significant influence relationship is acknowledged between the investor and the investee. The investment is originally recorded at its cost, but is subsequently adjusted each period for changes in the investee's net assets.

Equity pickup What occurs when an investor "picks up" its share of income or loss under the equity method.

Ethical dilemmas Problems where there are no set guidelines to follow in order to resolve a situation. These are the grey areas where one has to ask "Is it right or wrong?"

Event Something of consequence that happens, which is generally the source of changes in asset, liability, and equity balances. An event may be internal or external.

Excess-earnings approach A method used to value goodwill that calculates the "normal" earnings generated by companies in the same industry. If a company earns a higher rate of return than the industry average, this excess is goodwill.

Executory contract An agreement requiring future, continuing performance by both parties.

Exit price A measure of fair value that represents the amount that a company would receive on selling an asset or transferring a liability.

Expected cash flow approach An approach to the discounted cash flow model where a risk-free discount rate is used to discount cash flows that have been adjusted for uncertainty. The discount rate is the risk-free rate and the cash flow uncertainty is dealt with by using probabilities.

Expected loss impairment model A model of accounting for impairment where estimates of future cash flows used to determine the present value of the investment are made on a continuous basis.

Expenses Decreases in economic resources, either by outflows or reductions of assets or incurrence of liabilities resulting from a company's ordinary revenue-generating activities.

Face rate See *Stated interest rate*.

Face value The fair value of an interest-bearing note or loan receivable when the stated interest rate is equal to the effective (market) rate.

Factoring receivables When a company sells its accounts receivable to banks or finance companies that buy receivables from businesses for a fee and then collect the remittances directly from the customers.

Fair value An estimate of the price a company would have received if it had sold the asset or would have paid, if it had been relieved of the liability, on the measurement date in an arm's-length exchange motivated by normal business considerations.

Fair value hierarchy A model that categorizes inputs to valuation methods (and the items being valued) by quality of information.

Fair value loss impairment model A model of impairment whereby the impairment loss is the difference between the asset's fair value and its current carrying amount assuming the fair value is less than the carrying amount.

Fair value model (FVM) A method of accounting for investment property, under which it is recognized on the statement of financial position after acquisition at its fair value.

Fair value option The option given to companies allowing them to use fair value for most financial instruments. Under IFRS, certain conditions must be met.

Fair value principle The GAAP principle that provides guidance regarding how to measure financial statement elements using best estimates of market values.

Fair value through net income (FV-NI) A method of measuring the fair value of financial instruments where the carrying amount is adjusted to its current fair value at each reporting date such that all holding gains and losses are reported in net income along with any dividends or interest income earned. Also known as "fair value through profit or loss (FVTPL)."

Fair value through other comprehensive income (FV-OCI) A model where the carrying amount of each FV-OCI investment is adjusted to its current fair value at each reporting date, and the holding gains and losses are recognized in other comprehensive income.

Fair value through profit or loss (FVTPL) See *Fair value through net income (FV-NI)*.

Favourable lease A lease that is considered an intangible asset when the terms are more favourable than the usual market terms.

Feedback/confirmatory value The notion that relevant information helps users confirm or correct prior expectations.

Financial accounting The process that culminates in the preparation of financial reports for the company as a whole for use by both internal and external parties. Also known as *Financial reporting*.

Financial Accounting Standards Board (FASB) The major standard-setting body in the United States.

Financial asset A receivable that represents contractual rights to receive cash or other financial assets from another party.

Financial components approach A method of recording a sale of receivables transaction whereby each party to the sale of an account receivable recognizes the components (assets and liabilities) that it controls after the sale and derecognizes the assets and liabilities that were sold or extinguished.

Financial engineering A process whereby a business arrangement or transaction is structured legally such that it meets the company's financial reporting objective (for example, to maximize earnings, minimize a debt-to-equity ratio, or other).

Financial flexibility The measurement of a company's ability to take effective actions to alter the amounts and timing of cash flows so it can respond to unexpected needs and opportunities.

Financial instruments Contracts that give rise to both a financial asset for one party and a financial liability or equity instrument for another.

Financial reporting The process that culminates in the preparation of financial reports for the company as a whole for use by both internal and external parties. Also known as *Financial accounting*.

Financial statements The principal means through which financial information is communicated to those outside a company. They provide a company's history, quantified in money terms.

Financing activities Activities resulting in changes in the size and composition of the company's equity capital and borrowings.

Finished goods inventory The reporting of the costs associated with the completed but unsold units at the end of the fiscal period.

Finite life A type of asset that has a foreseeable limit to its useful life, and that is amortized by systematic charges to expense over the useful life using the cost model or revaluation model. Also known as "limited life."

First principles Foundational principles from which decisions stem, making decisions theoretically consistent if they stem from the same foundational reasoning.

First-in, first-out (FIFO) cost formula The method that assigns costs to inventory assuming that goods are used in the order in which they are purchased.

Fixed assets Tangible capital assets that are acquired for use in operations and not for resale, are long-term in nature, are usually subject to depreciation, and possess physical substance. Also known as *Plant assets* or *Property, plant, and equipment*.

f.o.b. destination Shipping designation meaning that the legal title of an asset does not pass to the buyer until the goods reach the customer's location.

f.o.b. shipping point Shipping designation meaning that the legal title of an asset belongs to the buyer when the goods leave the shipping company's dock.

Franchise A contractual arrangement under which the franchisor grants the franchisee the right to sell certain services, to use certain trademarks or trade names, or to perform certain functions, usually within a designated geographical area. Also known as *Licensing agreement*.

Free cash flow An indicator of financial flexibility that uses information provided on the cash flow statement. Free cash flow is net operating cash flows reduced by the capital expenditures needed to sustain the current level of operations.

Freedom from material error A measure of the reliability of reported information, assuring that the relevant information is accurate and unaffected by the opinions of stakeholders.

Full disclosure principle Financial reporting of any information significant enough to influence the judgement of an informed reader.

Function (of expense) The type of activity, such as cost of goods sold, selling and distribution, and research and development, used as a way of classifying and presenting expenses on the statement of income.

Future income tax assets The future tax consequences due to deductible temporary differences. Also known as *Deferred income tax assets* under IFRS.

Future income tax liabilities The future tax consequences associated with taxable temporary differences. Also known as *Deferred income tax liabilities* under IFRS.

GAAP hierarchy Guidance that notes that primary sources of GAAP should be used first, followed by other relevant and reliable sources, including the conceptual framework and professional judgement.

Gains Increases in equity (net assets) from a company's peripheral or incidental transactions and from all other transactions and other events and circumstances affecting the company during a period, except those that result from revenues or investments by owners.

General journal A chronological listing of transactions and other events expressed in terms of debits and credits to particular accounts.

General ledger A collection of all asset, liability, shareholders' equity, revenue, and expense accounts and their respective balances.

General-purpose financial statements Basic GAAP financial statements that provide information that meets the needs of external users (normally investors and creditors).

Generally accepted accounting principles (GAAP) The common set of standards and procedures used to prepare financial statements with the expectation that the majority of users' needs will be met.

Going concern assumption The assumption of most accounting methods that the company will have a long life.

Goodwill An asset representing the future economic benefits arising from other assets acquired in a business combination that are not individually identified or separately recognized.

Gross method A method of recording inventory whereby the use of a Purchase Discounts account indicates that the company is reporting its purchases and accounts payable at the gross amount.

Gross profit method A method for estimating inventory where taking a physical count is impractical or impossible. It is based on three premises: (1) the beginning inventory plus purchases equal total goods to be accounted for; (2) goods not sold must be on hand; (3) and when the net sales, reduced to cost, are deducted from the total goods to be accounted for, the result is the ending inventory.

Gross profit percentage The gross profit expressed as a percentage of sales.

Half-year rule A requirement of the income tax regulation that in the year a capital asset is acquired, only half the usual capital cost allowance can be claimed for tax purposes.

Held for sale Describing assets where a formal, detailed plan exists to sell the assets, normally within a year.

Held for trading investments Investments that are traded for short-term profit taking and are bought and sold on a regular basis.

Held to maturity investments Investments that a company has the intent and ability to hold until they mature.

Highest and best use A concept for valuing assets that assumes the highest value that the market would place on the asset, considering uses that are possible, legally permissible, and financially feasible.

Historical cost principle An accounting principle that provides guidance on how to measure transactions and balances on the basis of acquisition price.

Identifiable (intangible asset) A characteristic of intangible assets that either results from contractual or other legal rights, or can be separated and divided from the company and sold, transferred, licensed, rented, or exchanged, either by itself or with another contract, identifiable asset, or liability.

Identifiable net assets What arise when a company's purchase price is allocated among all the assets and liabilities to which a value can be attributed; refers to all net assets except goodwill.

IFRS Advisory Council A group that provides strategic advice to the IASB.

IFRS Foundation A group that raises finances and provides strategic direction and oversight to the IASB.

Impaired The state when a long-lived asset's carrying amount is higher than its future economic benefits to the company.

Impairment loss The amount by which the asset's carrying amount exceeds its fair value.

Impairments A decrease in the carrying value of a long-term asset to an amount that is less than the amount shown under the cost principle.

Implicit interest rate The discount rate that corresponds to the lessor's internal rate of return on the lease.

Imprest system A petty cash system where the custodian is responsible for the amount of funds on hand at all times, whether the amount is in cash or signed receipts.

Imputed interest rate The actual interest rate realized on a bond, which is different from the stated rate when there is a discount or premium.

In-process research and development (R&D) An identifiable intangible asset involving the research work and findings of a company, acquired when the company purchases another. It must be separable from goodwill to be reported separately.

Income approach A method to account for contributions of assets that requires the amount received to be deferred and recognized over the period that the related assets are employed.

Income statement A report that measures the success of a company's operations used for a specific time period (under ASPE).

Incurred loss impairment model A model where investments are recognized as impaired when there is no longer reasonable assurance that the future cash flows associated with them will be collected in their entirety when due. It accounts for credit losses triggered by specific events that occurred by the balance sheet date.

Indefinite life An asset's useful life where there appears to be no foreseeable limit to how long the asset will generate positive net cash flows to the company.

Indirect method A method used to revalue inventory to reflect net realizable value under the lower of cost and net realizable value method whereby a contra Inventory account is used to revalue inventory.

Information asymmetry The state that exists when one party (such as management) has access to more information than the other party (for example, investors).

Information overload The phenomenon that too much information may result in a situation where the user is unable to digest or process the information.

Information symmetry The state that exists when both parties have access to the same information.

Input measures Costs incurred that measure efforts devoted to a contract.

Inspection An organized formal evaluation of property, plant, and equipment that is considered a type of recurring cost after acquisition.

Institutional investors Large corporations or corporate investors such as pension funds or mutual funds.

Intangible assets Nonmonetary assets that lack physical substance and usually have a higher degree of uncertainty concerning their future benefits.

Intellectual capital See *Knowledge assets*.

Interest-bearing notes Notes that have a stated rate of interest that is payable over and above the face value of the note.

International Accounting Standards Board (IASB) The group responsible for setting IFRS with the goal of increasing the transparency of financial reporting by achieving a single, global method of accounting.

International Financial Reporting Interpretation Committee (IFRIC) A committee that studies and provides recommendations on issues not covered by the IASB.

International Financial Reporting Standards (IFRS) The internationally recognized common set of financial reporting standards and procedures.

International Integrated Reporting Committee (IIRC) A group that looks at a broader view of financial reporting that includes management information, governance and compensation, and sustainability reporting.

Intraperiod tax allocation The approach to allocating taxes within the financial statements of the current period.

Inventories Assets that are held for sale in the ordinary course of business.

Inventory turnover ratio A ratio that measures the number of times, on average, the inventory was sold during the period.

Investing activities Activities covering the acquisition and disposal of long-term assets and other investments not included in cash equivalents.

Investment property Property held to generate rentals and/or appreciate in value rather than to sell in the ordinary course of business or to use in production, administration, or in supplying goods and services.

Joint cost A single cost of purchasing or producing multiple items.

Joint venture A type of equity investment characterized by joint control, rather than unilateral control by one party.

Journal The book of original entry where transactions and selected other events are initially recorded.

Knowledge assets Unrecognized intangible assets related to the creativity and knowledge of key employees that create value for a company. Also known as "intellectual capital."

Laid-down costs Any cost incurred to get the asset in place and ready for use (whether it is for sale or to generate income through use). Also known as "out-of-pocket costs."

Last-in, first-out (LIFO) cost formula A method no longer permitted under ASPE and IFRS that assigns inventory costs on the basis that the cost of the most recent purchase is the first cost to be charged to cost of goods sold.

Lease A contractual agreement between a lessor (property owner) and a lessee (property renter) that gives the lessee the right to use specific property, owned by the lessor, for a specified time in return for stipulated, and generally periodic, cash payments (rents). Also known as "leasehold."

Leasehold See *Lease*.

Leasehold improvements Improvements made to the leased property by the lessee.

Legal title A right meaning that a good is legally owned; not the same as possession.

Liabilities "Obligations of an enterprise arising from past transactions or events, the settlement of which may result in the transfer of assets, provisions of services or other yielding of economic benefits in the future," as described in the *CPA Canada Handbook*.

Licences Operating rights obtained through agreements with governmental units or agencies, such as the use of airwaves for radio or television broadcasting. Also known as *Permits*.

Licensing agreement A contractual arrangement under which a government body or a business entity grants a business enterprise the right to sell certain services, to use certain trademarks or trade names, or to perform certain functions, usually within a designated geographical area. Also known as a *Franchise*.

Limited life See *Finite life*.

Liquidating dividend A dividend greater than accumulated net income, which represents a return of a shareholder's investment rather than profits of the company.

Liquidity A company's ability to convert assets into cash to pay off its current liabilities in the ordinary course of business.

Liquidity ratios Ratios that measure the company's short-run ability to pay its maturing obligations.

Loans and receivables Financial assets that result from the delivery of cash or other assets by a lender to a borrower in return for a promise to pay an amount on specified dates or on demand, usually with interest.

Loans receivable An agreement where one party advances cash or other assets in exchange for a promise to be repaid later.

Long-term liabilities Obligations that are not reasonably expected to be liquidated within the greater of one year or the normal operating cycle, but instead are payable at some date beyond that time.

Losses Decreases in equity (net assets) from a company's peripheral or incidental transactions and from all other transactions and other events and circumstances affecting the company during a period, except those that result from expenses or distributions to owners.

Lower of cost and market See *Lower of cost and net realizable value (LC&NRV) standard* and *market*.

Lower of cost and net realizable value A basis for stating inventory at the lower of its original cost and the net realizable value at the end of the period.

Lower of cost and net realizable value (LC&NRV) standard A principle used for ensuring that inventory is not overstated by comparing carrying cost and the amount that could be received if the inventory were disposed of and measuring the inventory at the lower of the two. Also known as "lower of cost and market."

Lump-sum price The price paid when several assets are purchased together for a single price.

Major overhauls Substantial repairs or replacements of equipment, or renovations to property. Treated as a recurring component of cost after acquisition.

Management best estimate Assumptions made by management in light of their knowledge and familiarity with the company, the industry, and the economy.

Management bias The presentation by management of information about their company in its best light in order to make their company look as successful as possible.

Managerial accounting The process of identifying, measuring, analyzing, and communicating financial information to internal decision-makers.

Markdown A decrease in price below the original selling price.

Markdown cancellations What occurs when markdowns are offset by an increase in the prices of goods that had been previously marked down.

Market Net realizable value in the context of the LC&NRV principle, as defined by ASPE and IFRS. Can also refer to net realizable value, replacement cost, or net realizable value less a normal profit margin.

Market rate The interest rate actually earned. Also known as *Effective interest rate* or *Yield rate*.

Marketing-related intangible assets Intangible assets related primarily to the marketing or promotion of products or services.

Markup An increase in the price above the original selling price.

Markup cancellations What occurs when markups are offset by a decrease in the prices of goods that had been previously marked up.

Markup on cost What occurs when the selling price is determined by a rate being equal to the gross profit as a percentage of cost.

Matching The accounting principle that dictates that efforts (expenses) be matched with accomplishments (revenues) whenever reasonable and practicable.

Materiality The constraint that relates to an item's impact on a company's overall financial operations. An item is material if its inclusion or omission would influence or change the judgement of a reasonable person.

Measurement uncertainty What occurs when there is a variance between the recognized amount and another reasonably possible amount.

Merchandise inventory Inventory purchased in a form ready for sale.

Mineral resource properties Capitalized costs that are associated with the acquired rights, and the exploration, evaluation, and development of these minerals.

Mineral resources Minerals and oil and gas resources that do not regenerate. Also known as "wasting assets."

Minority interest The percentage of the net assets not owned (reported as a liability on the balance sheet), or the percentage of the net income that does not accrue to the parent company (reported as a deduction from the combined net income on the income statement). Also known as *Noncontrolling interest*.

Modified cash basis A mixture of cash basis and accrual basis accounting often followed by professional service firms.

Monetary assets Money or claims to future cash flows that are fixed in amounts and timing by contract or other arrangement.

Monetary unit assumption The assumption that money is the common denominator of economic activity and provides an appropriate basis for accounting measurement and analysis.

Moral hazard The risk that certain parties who have additional information not accessible to others will act in their own self-interest.

Most advantageous market A concept used for measuring fair value that considers the value based on the market that would pay the most for the asset.

Moving-average cost formula An inventory pricing method that prices inventory items based on the moving-average cost of the goods available for sale in the period.

Multiple deliverables See *Bundled sales*.

Multiple-step income statement An income statement format that recognizes a separation between operating transactions and non-operating transactions and matches the relevant costs and expenses with their related revenues.

Nature (of expense) The type of expense, such as payroll, depreciation, and cost of raw materials, as classified and presented on the statement of income.

Negative goodwill See *Bargain purchase*.

Net income Revenues less expenses (including gains and losses) other than those defined under IFRS as other comprehensive income.

Net markdowns Markdowns less markdown cancellations.

Net markups Markups less markup cancellations.

Net method A recording method whereby purchases and accounts payable are recorded at an amount net of cash discounts.

Net realizable value (NRV) The net amount expected to be received in cash for an asset.

Neutrality The quality of accounting information that makes it reliable by being reasonably free of error and bias.

Non-current investments Long-term investments that will not be realized within one year or during the current operating cycle.

Non-GAAP earnings An adjusted net income number derived from GAAP net income plus or minus any nonrecurring or non-operating items.

Non–interest-bearing notes Notes that include interest, equal to the difference between the amount borrowed (the proceeds) and the face amount paid back. Also known as "zero-interest-bearing notes."

Non-reciprocal transfers Transfers of assets in one direction only, such as donations, gifts, or government grants, where nothing is given in exchange.

Noncontrolling interest The percentage of the net assets not owned (reported as a liability on the balance sheet), or the percentage of the net income that does not accrue to the parent company (reported as a deduction from the combined net income on the income statement). Also known as *Minority interest*.

Nonmonetary assets Items whose value in terms of the monetary unit may change over time.

Nonmonetary, non-reciprocal transactions A type of transaction where there is no exchange (such as a donation), making it difficult to determine cost or fair value.

Nonmonetary transactions Transactions where few or no monetary assets are received as consideration when goods or services are purchased or sold. Also known as *Barter transactions*.

Nontrade receivables Written promises entitling a company to receive a certain sum of money, arising from a variety of transactions that are not part of normal business operations.

Normal production capacity The usual amount of goods that a company can produce in a year, and the basis for allocating fixed production costs.

Normalized earnings Adjusted past earnings that reflect expected annual future earnings.

Not-sufficient-funds (NSF) cheque A cheque that is written or deposited and the corresponding money for payment does not exist at the time of the deposit.

Notes receivable Written promises entitling a company to receive a certain sum of money on a specified future date.

Notes to financial statements Information that is linked to the financial statements that generally amplifies or explains the items presented in the main body of the statements in order to complete the picture of a company's performance and position.

Number of years method A method of valuing goodwill whereby the excess earnings are multiplied by the number of years they are expected to continue.

Objective of financial reporting The goal "to communicate information that is useful to investors, members, contributors, creditors, and other users in making their resource allocation decisions and/or assessing management stewardship," as laid out in the *CPA Canada Handbook*.

On margin Investments in shares where the investor pays only part of the purchase price to acquire the shares, and the broker covers the difference.

Onerous contract A contract where the unavoidable costs of completing the contract are higher than the benefits expected from receiving the contracted goods or services. A loss provision is recognized for such a contract under IFRS, though such a provision is not stipulated under ASPE.

Ontario Securities Commission (OSC) A group that regulates companies listed on the Toronto Stock Exchange (TSX) by reviewing and monitoring their financial statements with a view to assessing whether the statements present fairly the financial position and results of operations.

Operating activities "The enterprise's principal revenue-producing activities and other activities that are not investing or financing activities," as defined under IFRS and ASPE.

Operating income Income from ongoing revenues after deducting expenses.

Ordinary repairs Expenditures made to maintain plant assets in operating condition, which are charged to an expense account in the period in which they are incurred.

Organization costs Costs incurred in the formation of a corporation.

Other assets Assets that are not included in any other category and are generally not individually material.

Other comprehensive income (OCI) Items of revenues, expenses, gains, and losses that are required by IFRS to be included in comprehensive income, but excluded from net income.

Output measures The output of a contract, or the process that is used to measure results.

Outstanding cheques Cheques written by a depositor and recorded when written but that may not be recorded or cleared by the bank until a following month.

Owners' equity The residual amount, or net assets, of a company, composed of capital shares, contributed surplus, retained earnings, and accumulated other comprehensive income.

Patent A right to use, manufacture, and sell a product or process for a period of 20 years from the date of application without influence or infringement by others.

Percentage-of-completion method A revenue recognition method that recognizes revenue, costs, and gross profit as progress is made toward completion of a long-term contract.

Percentage-of-receivables approach The process whereby receivables are recorded on the statement of financial position at their net realizable value.

Percentage-of-sales approach A method of estimating bad debt expense.

Performance obligation An obligation that arises when a company promises to deliver something or provide a service in the future.

Period costs Costs, such as selling and administrative, that are not considered directly related to the acquisition or production of goods and, therefore, are not considered a part of inventory.

Periodic inventory system The inventory recording system where a Purchases account is used and the Inventory account is unchanged during the period. Cost of goods sold is determined by adding the beginning inventory to the net purchases and deducting ending inventory.

Periodicity assumption The accounting assumption that implies that a company's economic activities can be divided into artificial time periods.

Permanent accounts All of the asset, liability, and equity accounts that appear on the balance sheet. Also known as "real accounts."

Permits Operating rights obtained through agreements with governmental units or agencies. Also known as *Licences*.

Perpetual inventory system The inventory recording system where purchases and sales are recorded in the Inventory account as they occur.

Petty cash A method of keeping cash on hand to cover small amounts where it would not be practical to issue cheques, such as for office supplies and taxi fares.

Plant assets Tangible capital assets that are acquired for use in operations and not for resale, are long-term in nature, are usually subject to depreciation, and possess physical substance. Also known as *Fixed assets* or *Property, plant, and equipment*.

Possession The physical control over a good, but not the legal title to the good.

Post-closing trial balance A trial balance taken immediately after closing entries have been posted.

Posting The process whereby items entered in a general journal must be transferred to the general ledger.

Predictive value A characteristic of accounting information that helps users make predictions about the ultimate outcome of past, present, and future events.

Premium What occurs when a bond sells at more than face value.

Prepaid expenses Expenses paid in cash and recorded as assets before they are used or consumed.

Price risk The risk that the value of an asset will change due to changes in market conditions.

Principal market The market that the company normally uses to buy and sell or transfer things, used for measuring fair value.

Principal-agent relationship Companies act either as principals or agents in selling transactions. When acting as a principal, the company generally has the risks and rewards of ownership of the item being sold. When acting as an agent, the company does not.

Product costs Those costs that "attach" to the inventory and are recorded in the Inventory account.

Professional judgement The process by which professional accountants with significant education and experience apply the *CPA Canada Handbook*'s "general principles" appropriately as they see fit, which is important in Canada because IFRS and ASPE are based primarily on general principles rather than specific rules.

Profit margin ratio A ratio that indicates how much is left over from each sales dollar after all expenses are covered.

Profitability ratios Ratios that measure the financial performance of a given company or division for a given period of time.

Promissory note A written promise that supports a note receivable to pay a certain sum of money at a specified future date.

Property, plant, and equipment Tangible capital assets that are acquired for use in operations and not for resale, are long-term in nature, are usually subject to depreciation, and possess physical substance. Also known as *Fixed assets* or *Plant assets*.

Proprietary perspective The viewpoint that financial reporting should focus on the needs of the owners of the company.

Provincial securities commissions The groups that oversee and monitor the provincial capital marketplaces. They ensure that the participants in the capital markets adhere to securities legislation, and thus that the marketplace is fair.

Provision A liability that has an uncertain timing or amount (under IFRS).

Provision matrix A matrix-based calculation that multiplies age-based groupings of accounts receivable by the historical observed default rates over the expected life of the trade receivables. The default rates used are adjusted at each reporting date for changes in forward-looking estimates due to matters such as changes in economic conditions.

Public Company Accounting Oversight Board (PCAOB) The regulatory oversight body in the United States that ensures that certain standards are met regarding quality controls and independence.

Purchase commitments Arrangements under which a company agrees to buy inventory weeks, months, or even years in advance.

Purchase discounts A reduction in the price of inventory in order to induce prompt payment.

Qualifying assets Assets that require substantial time to get ready for sale or their intended use and qualify for capitalization of interest.

Qualitative characteristics The characteristics defined by the conceptual framework that distinguish more useful information from less useful information for decision-making purposes.

Quality of earnings How well reported earnings reflects the sustainability of earnings and underlying business fundamentals without bias.

Quantities only system A system of tracking inventory that records increases and decreases in quantities only—not dollar amounts.

Rate of return on assets (ROA) Net income expressed as a percentage of average total assets.

Ratio analysis An analysis based on relationships among selected financial statement data.

Rational entity impairment model A model for measuring impairment losses that assumes that an entity makes rational decisions in managing its long-term assets and therefore it compares the asset's book value with a recoverable amount that differs depending on what leads to a higher return for the entity.

Raw materials inventory The costs assigned to goods and materials on hand, but not yet placed into production.

Realizable (revenue) Revenue from assets received or sold that can be readily converted into cash or claims to cash.

Realized (revenue) Revenue from products (goods or services), merchandise, or other assets that are exchanged for cash.

Rearrangement and reinstallation costs Expenditures intended to benefit future periods and to facilitate future production by the movement of assets from one location to another.

Recapture The recovery of capital cost allowance when, after deducting the appropriate amount from the class on disposition of the last asset, a negative amount is left as the undepreciated capital cost balance.

Receivables turnover ratio A ratio calculated to evaluate the liquidity of a company's accounts receivable. It measures the number of times, on average, receivables are collected during the period.

Reciprocal exchange A two-way exchange.

Recognition The process of recording a transaction in a company's statement of financial position or income statement.

Recoverability test A test to determine whether an impairment loss needs to be recognized for a long-lived asset.

Recoverable amount The higher of an asset's value in use and its fair value less costs to sell.

Related party transaction A transaction in which one of the transacting parties has the ability to significantly influence the policies of the other, or in which a nontransacting party has the ability to influence the policies of the two transacting parties.

Relative sales value method A method used to apportion a total cost or sales amount to individual components using fair values. Commonly used whenever there is a joint product cost that needs to be allocated or in a "basket" purchase or sale.

Relevance A qualitative characteristic of accounting information that indicates that it must make a difference in a decision.

Replacement The substitution of one asset for a similar asset.

Representational faithfulness A qualitative characteristic of accounting information that represents economic reality. It must be transparent, complete, neutral, and free from material error and bias.

Repurchase agreements Arrangements between a company and customer where a sale is completed but the company also agrees to repurchase the items sold at a later date.

Research A planned investigation undertaken with the hope of gaining new scientific or technical knowledge and understanding.

Research phase A broad category of research activities where costs are recognized as expenses when they are incurred.

Residual value An estimate of the amount that a company would obtain from the disposal of an asset at the end of its useful life.

Restricted cash Cash that is segregated from "regular" cash for reporting purposes because it needs to be set aside for a particular purpose.

Retail inventory method A method of valuing inventory when necessary, where inventory taken at its selling price (retail) can be converted to inventory at cost by applying the cost-to-retail formula.

Revaluation model (RM) A model for accounting for a long-lived asset that carries the asset at its fair value at the date of revaluation less any subsequent accumulated depreciation and impairment losses.

Revenue expenditure An expenditure where the benefit is in the period in which the expenditure occurred.

Revenue recognition principle The accounting principle that sets guidelines as to when revenue should be reported.

Revenues Increases in economic resources, either by inflows or other enhancements of a company's assets or settlement of its liabilities resulting from its ordinary activities.

Reversing entries A journal entry made at the beginning of the next accounting period that is the exact opposite of the related adjusting journal entry made in the previous period.

Right of return A right given by a company to a customer that allows the customer to return items that have been purchased.

Risk management The identification, assessment, and mitigation of potential risks to a company.

Risk/return trade-off An economic concept that notes that the higher the risk, the greater the return or compensation that is required to take that risk.

Sales discounts Cash discounts that are offered by the seller to induce prompt payment.

Sales returns and allowances An amount of sales involving large amounts near the end of the accounting period that should be anticipated and recognized in the period of the sale to avoid distorting the current period's income statement.

Salvage value The asset's estimated net realizable value at the end of its life.

Secured borrowing When a creditor requires that a debtor designate (assign) or pledge receivables or other assets as security for the loan, but the assets remain under the control of the borrowing company.

Securities and Exchange Commission (SEC) The U.S. counterpart of the Ontario Securities Commission, which regulates the U.S. capital markets and supports the FASB by indicating that financial statements conforming with FASB standards will be presumed to have substantial authoritative support.

Securitization What occurs when a pool of assets is taken, such as credit card receivables, mortgage receivables, or car loan receivables, and shares are sold in these pools of interest and principal payments. The effect is to create securities backed by these pools of assets.

Self-constructed assets Assets built by a company and assigned all relevant costs to be capitalized.

Service-type warranty A type of warranty whereby the company agrees to fix or replace products that subsequently break or cease to work over an extended period.

Servicing asset component An asset that is recognized if the benefits of servicing (such as servicing fees under contract and late charges) are greater than the estimated cost of the obligation.

Servicing liability component An obligation that is recorded if the transferor receives no reimbursements for servicing the receivables, or receives less than the estimated cost of doing so.

Significant influence What an investor has when it owns roughly 20% to 50% of a company and/or there is investor representation on the board of directors, participation in policy-making processes, material inter-company transactions, interchange of managerial personnel, or provision of technical information.

Simple interest Interest paid or received on only the initial investment (the principal).

Single-step income statement A simplified income statement that lists all income first followed by all expenses.

Solvency A company's ability to pay its debts and related interest.

Solvency ratios Measures of the degree of protection for long-term creditors and investors or a company's ability to meet its long-term obligations. Also known as *Coverage ratios*.

Special journals Journals that summarize transactions possessing a similar characteristic.

Specific identification A cost formula whereby each inventory item is identified separately, the costs of the specific item sold are included in cost of goods sold, and the cost of the specific items on hand is included in inventory.

Stakeholders Parties who rely on and use financial statements and other financial documents to make decisions.

Standard cost system A system that predetermines unit costs for material, labour, and manufacturing overhead based on costs that should be incurred at normal levels of efficiency and capacity.

Stated interest rate The interest rate written in the terms of the bond indenture. Also known as "coupon rate" or "face rate."

Statement of cash flows A financial statement that provides information about the cash inflows (receipts) and outflows (payments) for a specific period of time. It is divided into operating activities, investing activities, and financing activities, and allows users to assess a company's capacity to generate cash and cash equivalents and its needs for cash resources.

Statement of changes in shareholders' equity The financial statement that reconciles the balance of the Retained Earnings account, common shares, and other shareholders' equity accounts from the beginning to the end of the period (under IFRS).

Statement of comprehensive income The financial statement that reconciles net income to comprehensive income; reconciling items include unrealized gains and losses on certain financial instruments, and debits/credits from related party or other transactions not recognized in net income (under IFRS). Some companies provide a combined statement of income and comprehensive income.

Statement of financial position The financial statement that shows a company's financial condition at the end of a period. Also known as *Balance sheet* under ASPE.

Statement of income/earnings The main financial statement that reports a company's financial performance during the period.

Statement of retained earnings The financial statement that reconciles the balance of the Retained Earnings account from the beginning to the end of the period (under ASPE).

Stewardship Management's responsibility to manage assets with care and trust, which is described as its fiduciary relationship.

Straight-line method A method of depreciation (or amortization) where depreciation is considered a function of the passage of time.

Strict cash basis A basis of reporting whereby revenues and expenses are recorded only when cash is received or paid out.

Subsequent events Events that occur after the balance sheet date, but before the financial statements are issued.

Subsidiary A corporation that is being controlled by another corporation.

Subsidiary ledger A ledger that contains the details related to a given general ledger account.

Sum-of-the-years'-digits method A decreasing charge depreciation method where the depreciable amount is multiplied each year by a decreasing fraction related to the number of years in the asset's useful life.

Supplementary information Information that may include details or amounts that presents a different perspective from that adopted in the financial statements.

Tangible capital assets Assets that are acquired for use in operations and not for resale, are long-term in nature, are usually subject to depreciation, and possess physical substance.

Tax basis See *Tax value*.

Tax value The undepreciated capital cost of a capital asset at any point in time. Also known as "tax basis."

Technology-based intangible assets Innovations or technological advances such as patented technology and trade secrets.

Temporary accounts Revenue, expense, and dividend accounts; except for dividends, they appear on the statement of comprehensive income. Temporary accounts are closed at the end of each fiscal year; permanent accounts are left open. Also known as "nominal accounts."

Terminal loss What occurs when the disposition of the last asset in its class results in a positive balance remaining in the capital cost allowance class.

Timeliness A characteristic of relevance that states that information must be available for decision-makers before it loses its capacity to influence their decisions.

Toronto Stock Exchange (TSX) The largest stock exchange in Canada.

Total-earnings approach A method of valuing goodwill where the value of the company as a whole is determined based on the total expected earnings, not just the excess earnings.

Trade discounts A reduction in the catalogue price used to avoid frequent changes in catalogues, to quote different prices for different quantities purchased, or to hide the true invoice price from competitors.

Trade name One or more words, or a series of letters or numbers, or a design or shape that distinguishes a particular company or product. Also known as *Trademark*.

Trade receivables Amounts owed by customers for goods and services rendered as part of the normal course of business operations.

Trademark One or more words, or a series of letters or numbers, or a design or shape that distinguishes a particular company or product. Also known as *Trade name*.

Trading The act of buying and selling for profit in the short term.

Traditional discounted cash flow approach An approach to the discounted cash flow model where the discount rate reflects all risks in the cash flows but the cash flows are assumed to be certain. The stream of contracted cash flows is discounted, and the discount rate is adjusted to accommodate their riskiness.

Transaction An external event involving a transfer or exchange between two or more entities or parties.

Transaction costs Costs associated with the acquisition of financial instruments, such as fees, commissions, or transfer taxes.

Transaction price The amount of consideration that a company expects to receive from a customer.

Transparency A goal of financial reporting such that the information provided reflects the underlying transactions and events and their effects on a company. Is one of the characteristics of representational faithfulness.

Trial balance A list of all open accounts in the ledger and their balances.

Undepreciated capital cost (UCC) The amount of a class of assets' cost less total capital cost allowance (for tax purposes).

Understandability The quality of information that permits reasonably informed users to perceive its significance.

Unearned revenues Revenues received in cash and recorded as liabilities until they are earned.

Unit of measure The level at which an asset such as property, plant, and equipment is recognized (that is, the extent to which separate components are measured and recorded).

Unit of production method A method of calculating depreciation whereby depreciation is determined as a function of use or productivity of the asset.

Unrealized holding gains or losses The difference between the fair value and cost (carrying amount) of an asset still held (owned) by the investor.

Upfront fees Amounts collected from a customer in advance of the goods or services being shipped or provided.

Useful life The term of service provided by a capital asset, often many years long.

Value in use The present value of the future cash flows expected to be derived from an asset's use and subsequent disposal.

Vendor rebate A retroactive discount on goods if the buyer meets certain criteria, such as purchasing a target quantity within a year.

Verifiability The quality of information that demonstrates that independent measurers, using the same measurement methods, obtain similar results.

Warranty An arrangement with a customer to replace or fix goods that have been sold.

Weighted average cost formula A cost formula that determines the average cost of inventory weighted by the number of units purchased at each unit cost. It is calculated as the cost of goods available for sale divided by the number of units available for sale.

Weighted-average accumulated expenditures A calculation of construction expenditures that is weighted by the amount of time that interest cost could be incurred on the expenditure.

With recourse Describes receivables sold via a third party, where the transferor guarantees payment to the seller if the customer fails to pay.

Without recourse Describes receivables sold via a third party, where the buyer assumes the risk of collection and absorbs any credit losses.

Work sheet A spreadsheet that is used to adjust the account balances and prepare the financial statements.

Work-in-process inventory The cost of the raw materials on which production has been started but not completed, plus the direct labour cost applied specifically to this material, and an applicable share of manufacturing overhead costs.

Working capital The excess of total current assets over total current liabilities.

Yield rate The interest rate actually earned. Also known as *Effective interest rate* or *Market rate*.

Zero-interest-bearing notes See *Non–interest-bearing notes*.

Some conventions to note when using this glossary: Terms listed but **not** defined refer to *defined synonyms* as "See…." Terms listed and defined refer to *listed synonyms* as "Also known as" with the synonyms in italics. Terms listed and defined refer to *unlisted synonyms* as "Also known as" with the synonyms in quotation marks.

Company Index

A

Adelphia Communications Corp., 580
AEterna Zentaris Inc., 751
Air Canada, 39, 73, 87, 215–216, 228–229, 238–239, 269, 488, 612–613, 629–630, 690
Air France-KLM Group, 690
Airbnb, 148–149
Airbus Group NV, 335, 410
Alacer Gold Corp., 627, 636
American Accounting Association, 59
American Institute of Certified Public Accountants, 59
Andrew Peller Limited, 385, 481
Apple Inc., 705, 719
Arthur Andersen, 3
Atlas Cold Storage Income Trust, 580
ATS Automation Tooling Systems Inc., 158

B

Bank of Montreal, 31, 206
Bank of Nova Scotia, 31
Baskin-Robbins, 706
BCE Inc., 206, 335, 371–373, 385, 562
Becker Milk Company Limited, 392
Bell Aliant, 342
Bell Canada, 694, 705
Bennett Environmental Inc., 72
BHP Billiton plc, 624
Biovail Corporation, 222
BlackBerry Ltd., 218–219, 268, 278, 707
Bloomberg, 31
Bombardier Inc., 266, 707
Borealis Infrastructure, 485
BP plc, 584–585
Bre-X Minerals, 72
Brick Brewing Company Limited, 168–170
British Airways plc, 215, 630, 750
British Columbia Securities Commission, 16
Brookfield Asset Management Inc., 146, 266, 335, 481, 551, 556–557, 578, 624, 688, 705
Brookfield Office Properties Inc., 205, 267–268

C

Cameco Corporation, 166–167, 175
Canada Life Financial Corporation, 488, 520–523
Canada Revenue Agency, 172, 434
Canadian Coalition for Good Governance (CCGG), 29, 31
Canadian Derivatives Exchange, 31

Canadian Financial Executives Research Foundation, 692
Canadian Imperial Bank of Commerce, 31
Canadian Institute of Chartered Accountants (CICA), 13
Canadian Institute of Chartered Business Valuators, 753
Canadian National Railway Company, 688
Canadian Pacific Railway Limited, 639, 654, 688
Canadian Radio-television and Telecommunications Commission (CRTC), 338, 710
Canadian Securities Administrators (CSA), 19, 31–32, 208–209
Canadian Tire Bank, 365
Canadian Tire Corporation, Limited, 217, 355, 365–367, 405, 423, 481, 688
Canadian Utilities Limited, 373
CDNX Stock Market, 31
Cendant, 18
Chartered Professional Accountants Canada (CPA Canada), 13, 33, 47, 55, 446, 454, 558
China Mobile, 705
CIBC, 264
ClubLink, 220, 488
Coca-Cola Company, 336, 694, 706, 708
Corus Entertainment Inc., 716–718
CPA Canada. See Chartered Professional Accountants Canada (CPA Canada)

D

Daimler-Benz (DaimlerChrysler), 29
DiagnoCure Inc., 166
Dominion Bond Rating Service, 31
Dominion Diamond Corporation, 160–162, 164
Duff & Phelps, 692

E

Eastman Kodak Company, 212
Eli Lilly and Company, 411, 752
EMI Music Publishing, 706
Empire Company Limited, 224, 346–347, 406, 482, 623
Enbridge, 705
Enron Corp., 3, 18, 42, 48, 75, 264
European Aeronautic Defence and Space Company (EADS NV), 335

F

Falconbridge Ltd., 642
Financial Executives International, 59
Ford Motor Corporation, 457

G

General Electric Company, 31
Glacier Credit Card Trust, 366
Glencore PLC, 439
Goldcorp Inc., 266
Google, 705

H

HBC. See Hudson's Bay Company (HBC)
Hershey Company, The, 651–652
Holiday Inn, 706
Hollinger International Inc., 635
Honeywell International Inc., 31
Hudson's Bay Company (HBC), 340, 409, 450
Husky Energy Ltd., 637, 642

I

IBI Group Inc., 217–218, 268
IMAX, 707
Imperial Metals Corporation, 561
Indigo Books & Music Inc., 418–419, 488
Institute of Internal Auditors, 59
Institute of Management Accountants, 59
Intel, 113
Intertape Polymer Group Inc., 635
Investopedia.com, 691

J

Jean Coutu Group (PJC) Inc., The, 410

K

Kimberly-Clark Corporation, 31
Kinross Gold Corporation, 693
Kobo Inc., 418

L

Livent Inc., 18, 40, 50, 580
Loblaw Companies Limited, 41, 232, 243, 406, 426, 482, 623, 654, 751
Lord & Taylor, 409
Lucent Technologies, 297
lululemon athletica inc., 694

M

Mackenzie Financial Corp., 31
Macy's, Inc., 152
Magna International Inc., 340, 623
Magnotta Winery Corporation, 294–295
Mainstreet Equity Corp., 205
Manufacturers Hanover Trust Co., 378
Maple Leaf Foods Inc., 205, 266, 405
MasterCard, 365
McCain, 705
McDonald's Corporation, 31, 299, 706
Microsoft Corp., 113, 719

Montreal Exchange (MX), 31
Moody's, 31
Moxie Retail, 409

N

NASDAQ (National Association of
    Securities Dealers Automated
    Quotation), 15, 31
National Association of Accountants, 59
Newfield Exploration Company, 624
Nike, Inc., 750
Nortel Networks Inc., 27, 698
North West Company Inc., 450
Nutreco N.V., 440–442
NYSE (New York Stock Exchange), 15

O

OfficeMax Incorporated, 423
Ontario Municipal Employees Retirement
    System (OMERS), 484–485, 487
Ontario Power Generation, 628
Ontario Securities Commission (OSC), 2,
    12, 16, 31–32, 40, 177
Open Text Corporation, 654
OSC. *See* Ontario Securities Commission
    (OSC)
Oxford Properties, 485

P

PepsiCo, 336
Petro-Canada, 573, 706
Polaroid, 707
Potash Corporation of Saskatchewan Inc.,
    355, 410, 551
Priceline.com, 300
Procter & Gamble Company, The, 335
Province of Ontario, 19

Q

Quebecor Inc., 267, 720, 751

R

Rakuten Inc., 418
RBC Global Asset Management Inc., 31
Real Estate Investment Trust, 751
Repsol SA, 225
Research In Motion. *See* BlackBerry Ltd.
Rite Aid, 18, 299
Rockwell Collins, Inc., 31
Rogers Communications, 338–339,
    342, 705
Roots Canada, 694
Royal Bank of Canada, 31, 205–206, 488,
    551, 705
Royal LePage, 706

S

Saks Fifth Avenue, 409
Samsung, 705
Sears Canada Inc., 366, 410, 445–446, 450
SEC. *See* Securities and Exchange
    Commission (SEC)
Securities and Exchange Commission
    (SEC), 15, 16, 18, 31, 59
SEDAR, 266, 267, 406, 481, 751
Simmons & Company International, 638
Sobeys, 488
Sony Corp./ATV Music Publishing, 706
Sponsoring Organizations of the
    Treadway Commission (COSO), 59
Standard & Poor's, 31, 173
Stantec Inc., 355
Stora Enso Oyj, 481, 623
Sunbeam, 18, 297
Suncor Energy, 341

T

Talisman Energy Inc., 225
Target Canada Co., 77
Target Corporation, 76–77
TD Asset Management Inc., 31

Teck Resources Limited, 73
TELUS Corporation, 164–165, 185, 335,
    402–403, 705
Thompson Creek Metals Company,
    344–345
Thomson Reuters Corporation, 267, 693
Tim Hortons, 706
TMX Group, 2–3
Toronto Dominion Bank, 31
Toronto Stock Exchange (TSX), 2, 16,
    31, 33
Torstar Corporation, 170–171
Toyota Motor Corporation, 410, 706
TransAlta Corporation, 561, 641
TSX Private Markets, 2, 31
TSX Venture Exchange, 2, 31
TWC Enterprises Limited, 220–221

V

Valeant Pharmaceuticals International,
    222
Vermilion Energy Inc., 150–152
Visa, 365

W

Walmart Stores Inc., 41,
    150–152, 457
WestJet, 87
WorldCom Inc., 3, 30, 580

X

Xerox, 707

Y

Yellow Media Inc., 693

Z

Zellers, 76
Zynga Inc., 272–273

Subject Index

A

abnormal shortages, 454
abnormal terms, 277
accelerated amortization, 634
account, 78
  see also specific types of accounts
  contra account, 349
  crediting the account, 79
  debiting the account, 79
  writing off an account, 353–354
accountants' role, 58
accounting
  accrual-basis accounting, 8, 50,
    181–185
  aggressive accounting, 10
  and capital allocation, 4–5
  challenges and opportunities, 18–23
  conservative accounting, 10
  defined, 4
  essential characteristics of, 4
  financial accounting, 4
  goals and purposes, 36–37
  language of, 43
  managerial accounting, 4
accounting cycle, 80, 81
  adjusting entries, 84–92
  adjustments. *See* adjusting entries
  closing process, 94–97
  financial statements, 93
  identification of transactions and
    other events, 80–81
  journalizing, 81–82
  ownership structure, 93
  posting, 82–83
  recording transactions and other
    events, 80–81
  reversing entries, 96–97
  trial balance, 83
accounting equation, 79–80
  basic accounting equation, 79
  expanded basic equation, 80
accounting guidelines, 16
accounting information system, 23, 78
  see also accounting cycle
  accounting equation, 79–80
  basic terminology, 78–79
accounting oversight board, 18
accounting policies, 176, 227
accounting policy changes, 174
accounting standards, 11–12
  see also Accounting Standards for
    Private Enterprises (ASPE);
    International Financial Reporting
    Standards (IFRS); standard setting
Accounting Standards Board (AcSB),
  12–13, 17, 20, 375
  conceptual framework, 36

goodwill, 722
private entities, 43
Accounting Standards for Private
  Enterprises (ASPE), 12
  see also generally accepted accounting
    principles (GAAP); IFRS-ASPE
    comparison
  accounting policy changes, 174
  amortization method not
    specified, 358
  asset retirement costs, 562
  associates, investments in,
    512, 523
  biological assets and agricultural
    produce, 439–440
  buildings, 572
  capitalization of costs, 560
  cash equivalents, 344
  completed-contract method, 311
  components, 559, 630
  contingencies, 223, 226
  control, 48, 517
  cost model, 701
  cost recovery impairment model,
    644, 709
  current assets, 519
  depreciation, 630
  derecognition of receivables, 367–368,
    369, 375
  disclosure, 716
  earnings approach, 280, 293,
    307–308
  expenses, 170
  fair value, 54
  fair value option, 54
  financial assets, 350
  financial instruments, 214
  financial statements, names of, 78
  full cost method, 574
  future income tax assets, 222
  goodwill, 714, 715
  held for sale, 649
  impairment, 507, 510–511, 642
  income, 156
  income statement, 163
  indefinite life, 704
  indefinite-life intangibles, 710
  inventory, 412
  inventory cost, 422
  investment measurement models,
    505–506
  investment property, 573
  investments, 495
  liabilities, recognition of, 227
  limited-life intangibles, 709
  principles-based approach,
    21, 57

"probable," 46
product costs, 424
professional judgement, 17
rearrangement and reinstallation
  costs, 584
receivables, 367–369, 371
replacements, major overhauls, and
  inspections, 584
retained earnings statement, 173
sales returns and allowances, 349
sales revenues, and returns, 296
share-based payments, 566
significant influence, 513, 516
straight-line method, 361, 492
transaction costs, 358
Accounting Standards Oversight Council
  (AcSOC), 13
accounting theory, 10
account sales, 300
accounts receivable, 213, 347
  see also receivables
  aging method, 351
  aging schedule, 351
  allowance method, 352–354
  cash discounts, 348–349
  direct write-off method, 356
  effects on accounts, 354–355
  estimating uncollectible trade accounts
    receivable, 350–351
  expected credit losses, 351, 375
  extensive accounts receivable, 340
  gross average accounts receivable
    (GAAR), 355
  impairment, 350–356
  lifetime expected credit losses, 350
  management of, 341
  measurement, 347–350
  measurement after acquisition, 350
  monitoring, 341
  net realizable value (NVR), 351
  nonrecognition of interest
    element, 350
  percentage-of-receivables
    approach, 351
  percentage-of-sales approach, 353
  previously written off account, 354
  provision matrix, 351
  recognition, 347–350
  sales discounts, 348–349
  sales returns and allowances,
    349–350
  securitization, 339
  trade discounts, 348
  types of, 341
  written off, 353–354
accrual basis, 181
  see also accrual-basis accounting

accrual-basis accounting, 8, 50
    accrued expenses, 89
    conversion from cash basis, 182–183
    equity method, 514
    and estimates, 154
    operating expense calculation, 183–184
    service revenue calculation, 183
    vs. cash basis accounting, 181–185
accruals, 84
    accrued expenses, 84, 89–91
    accrued revenues, 84, 89
    adjusting entries, 88–91
    reversing entries, 96
accrued expenses, 84, 89
    accrued interest, 90
    accrued salaries, 90–91
    adjusting entries, 89–91
accrued interest, 90
accrued revenues, 84, 89
accrued salaries, 90–91
Accumulated Depreciation account, 576
accumulated other comprehensive
        income, 93, 173, 224
Accumulated Other Comprehensive
        Income account, 94, 104, 157
acid test ratio, 211, 244
acquirer, 694
acquisition cost, 52, 573
AcSB. *See* Accounting Standards
        Board (AcSB)
active market, 701
activity method, 634–635
activity ratios, 211, 243–244
actual use, 86
additions, 580–581
adjunct account, 230
adjusted EBITDA, 206–207
adjusted EBITDA margin, 206–207
adjusted market assessment approach, 289
adjusted net earnings, 207
adjusted trial balance, 78
adjusting entries, 78, 84–92
    accruals, 84, 88–91
    estimated items, 84, 91–92
    prepayments, 84–88
    types of, 84
    when required, 84
    work sheet, 107–108
advances, 345–346
adverse selection, 10, 37
aggressive accounting, 10
aging method, 351
aging schedule, 351
agricultural produce, 439–440, 456
all-inclusive approach, 156
allocation technique, 49
allowance account, 352–354
allowance for credit losses, 355
allowance method, 352–354, 437
amortization, 86, 558, 626, 629
    see also depreciation
    accelerated amortization, 634
    accumulated amortization, 703
    expenses, 703

finite or limited life, 702–703
    intangible assets, 629, 702
    prepaid expenses, 86
amortized cost, 358
amortized cost model, 491–495, 505
    debt securities of other entities,
        491–495
    income under, 492–494
    sale of investments, 494–495
analysis
    accounting policies, 176
    cash flow statement, 176
    comparison of operating results, 720
    financial statements, 176
    goodwill, 719–720
    income statement, 176
    information-rich analysis, 243
    intangible assets, 719–720
    investments, 523–524
    measurement uncertainty, 176
    missing values, 719
    notes to financial statements, 176
    property, plant, and equipment,
        653–655
    ratio analysis. *See* ratio analysis
    receivables, 373–374
    statement of financial position, 176, 210
    transactions, 80
annuities, 118–121
arm's-length transaction, 52, 275
articles, 17
artificial time periods, 51
artistic-related intangible assets, 706
ASPE. *See* Accounting Standards for
        Private Enterprises (ASPE)
asset account, 79
asset adjustment method, 702
asset-backed financing, 365
asset-backed securities, 365
asset class, 662–663
asset exchanges, 566–570
asset groups, 646–648
asset-liability approach, 280–293,
        307–308, 584
    allocation of transaction price to
        separate performance
        obligations,
        289–291
    determination of transaction price,
        285–288
    example, 281
    identification of separate performance
        obligations, 283–285
    identification of the contract with
        customers, 282–283
    recognition of revenue when each
        performance obligation satisfied,
        291–292
    summary of process, 292–293
asset retirement costs, 424, 562
assets, 43
    see also specific types of assets
    biological assets, 34–35, 309, 439–440,
        456, 574, 578
    classes, 575

classification in statement of financial
        position, 213
    contract assets, 304–305
    contractual rights to receive cash, 214
    contributed assets, 570–572
    current assets, 216–220, 641
    current *vs.* non-current classification, 52
    deferred income tax assets, 222
    disposal of assets. *See* disposition
    exploration and evaluation assets, 637
    financial assets, 214, 218, 342
    fixed assets, 558
    function, 213
    future income tax assets, 222
    held for sale, 158–159
    historical cost, 212
    identifiable, 695
    identifiable net assets, 694
    impairment, 101
    intangible assets. *See* intangible assets
    knowledge assets, 719
    liquidation approach, 52
    long-lived assets, 648–649
    monetary assets, 213, 566, 695
    net assets, 214
    nonmonetary assets, 213, 566, 696
    other assets, 222
    plant assets, 558
    property, plant, and equipment.
        See property, plant, and equipment
    qualifying assets, 590
    recognized from costs incurred to
        fulfill a contract, 306
    on statement of financial position, 214
    tangible capital assets, 99, 558
    useful life, 86
    valuation of assets, 34–35
    wasting assets, 573
asset turnover, 244
associates, 512–516, 523
assurance-type warranty, 300, 308
audit, 6
audit committees, 18
auditing standards, 38
auditors, 6, 39
authorized plan to sell, 158–159
available for sale investments, 488, 500
    see also fair value through other
        comprehensive income (FV-OCI)
average days to sell inventory, 446
avoidable borrowing costs, 561, 591,
        592–593

B

bad debt expense, 352–353
bad debts, 84, 92, 350
balance sheet, 4, 78, 211
    see also statement of financial position
        (balance sheet)
balance sheet approach, 49
bank accounts, 378–379
bank charges, 381
bank credits, 381
bank drafts, 342

bank errors, 381
bank overdrafts, 344–345
bank reconciliation, 380–383
bargain purchase, 713
barter transactions, 53, 276
basic elements, 43
basic terminology, 78–79
basket purchase, 425, 697
bearer plants, 34–35, 588
beginning inventory, 95
beneficial interests, 370
benefits, 43
benefits of ownership, 294
best-quality fair value measure, 103
bias
    in financial reporting, 10–11, 154, 279
    management bias, 10–11, 19
    motivation to bias information, 11
    revenue numbers, biased, 279
"big bath" writedown, 720
bill-and-hold arrangement, 277,
    298, 303
biological assets, 34, 309, 439–440, 456,
    574, 578
bona fide, 276
bonds, 223
bonuses, 18
book value, 87
book value per share, 244
boot, 568
borrowing costs, 424, 561–562,
    590–595
brand, 704
brand name, 704
bright-line tests, 21
brokerage commissions, 552
budgets, 59
buildings, 572
bundled sales, 274
burden, 561
business combination, 697
business component, 159
business environment, 58
business models, 150–153, 162, 242
business perspective, 274
    depreciation, 628
    disposition, 628
    impairment, 628
    property, plant, and equipment,
        557–558
    sales transaction, 274
    statement of cash flows, 210–211
    statement of financial position
        (balance sheet), 210–211
business risks, 242–243
buyback agreements, 415

C

Canadian Accounting Standards Board
    (AcSB). *See* Accounting Standards
    Board (AcSB)
Canadian dollar, 344
Canadian Institute of Chartered
    Accountants (CICA), 13

Canadian Intellectual Property Office
    (CIPO), 706
Canadian Public Accountability Board
    (CPAB), 19
Canadian Securities Administrators (CSA),
    19, 208–209
capital
    allocation of, 4–5
    sources of capital, 5
Capital account, 93, 94
capital allocation, 5
capital allocation process, 5
capital approach, 571
capital cost allowance (CCA), 660
capital cost allowance method, 659–663
    additions to an asset class, 662
    basic CCA and UCC example, 661
    half-year rule, 660
    recapture, 663
    retirements from asset class,
        continuation of class, 662
    retirements from asset class, elimination
        of class, 663
    terminal loss, 663
    undepreciated capital cost (UCC),
        660, 661
capital expenditure, 580
capital gain, 663
capital-intensive, 220
capitalization of costs, 305–306, 560,
    590–595
capitalization period, 590–591
capitalization rate, 592
capitalized, 559
capital maintenance, 649
capital maintenance theory, 207
capital marketplace
    oversight in, 18–19
    signals to, 55
capital market risks, 243
capital markets, 10
capital shares, 224
carrying amount, 87, 498, 519
cash, 217, 235, 342–343
    bank overdrafts, 344–345
    compensating balances, 345
    control of, 340
        see also cash controls
    as financial asset, 214
    in foreign currencies, 344
    IFRS-ASPE comparison, 374
    management, 37, 340
        see also cash controls
    measurement, 342–345
    net cash provided by operating
        activities, 235
    and operations, 153
    recognition, 342–345
    and recurring obligations, 343
    reporting cash, 341–345
    restricted cash, 343
    summary of cash-related items, 345
cash and cash equivalents, 217
    see also cash; cash equivalents

cash basis accounting
    conversion to accrual basis, 182–183
    modified cash basis, 182
    strict cash basis, 181
    theoretical weaknesses of, 185
    vs. accrual basis accounting, 181–185
cash controls, 378–383
    bank accounts, 378–379
    imprest petty cash system, 379–380
    internal control, 378
    physical protection of cash balances,
        380
    reconciliation of bank balances,
        380–383
cash cost, 563
cash crunch, 236
cash debt coverage ratio, 237, 244
cash discounts, 288, 348–349, 563
cash equivalents, 343–344
cash flow per share, 239
cash flows
    cash flow patterns, 237
    discounting the future cash flows, 115
    estimates, 99
    free cash flow, 238–239
    interest cash flows, 362
    prospects, 8
cash flow statement, 4, 176
    see also statement of cash flows
cash-generating unit (CGU),
    646–648, 714
cashier's cheques, 342
cash inflows, 231
cash outflows, 231
cash payments
    ending prepaid expenses, 183
    operating expenses, conversion to
        accrual basis, 183–184
    service revenue, conversion to accrual
        basis, 183
cash price equivalent, 563
cash rebates, 423
cause and effect relationship, 49
CCA rate, 660
certificates of deposit, 342
certified cheques, 342
challenges for accounting profession,
    18–23
change funds, 343
changes in accounting principle, 174
Chartered Professional Accountants
    Canada (CPA Canada), 13, 33, 47,
    55, 446, 454, 558
checks and balances, 7
cheques
    not-sufficient-funds (NSF) cheques, 381
    outstanding cheques, 381
    postdated cheques, 343, 345
classified statement of financial position
    (balance sheet), 215–226
    see also statement of financial position
        (balance sheet)
clearing account, 94
closing entries, 78, 94–95

closing process, 94–97
  inventory and cost of goods sold, 95
  post-closing trial balance, 95–96
  preparation of closing entries, 94–95
code of ethics, 18
codification project, 21–22
collectibility, 306
collection float, 378
collections received in advance, 223
combined statement of income/
        comprehensive income, 164–165
commercial paper, 344
commercial substance, 276, 567, 569, 696
commissions, 300
commodity broker-traders, 456
Common Shares account, 93
communication of information about
        performance, 153
comparability, 41, 57
compensating balances, 343, 345
completed-contract method, 308, 311,
        315–316
completeness, 39
componentization, 559, 629–630
compound interest, 114–115
comprehensive income, 45, 156, 179
computer software costs, 708
conceptual framework, 17, 18, 35, 157
  development of, 36–37
  elements of financial statements, 37,
        43–45
  expanded conceptual framework, 56
  Exposure Drafts (EDs), 60, 105,
        179, 240
  foundational principles, 45–57
  objective of financial reporting, 36, 37
  overview of, 36–37
  qualitative characteristics, 37–42, 154
  rationale for, 35–36
  universally accepted conceptual
        framework, 36
"Conceptual Framework for Financial
        Accounting and Reporting:
        Elements of Financial Statements
        and Their Measurement"
        (FASB), 36
concessionary terms, 276–278
condensed financial statements, 168–169
conditional right to receive
        consideration, 304
confirmatory value, 38
  see also feedback
conservatism, 53, 74
conservative accounting, 10
consideration, 275, 283
  conditional right to receive
        consideration, 304
  noncash consideration, 288
  paid or payable to customers, 288
  present value of, 563
  unconditional right to receive
        consideration, 304
  variable consideration, 285–286, 308
consigned goods, 414

consignee, 300
consignments, 300–301, 303
consignor, 300
consistency, 42, 57, 174
consolidation, 48, 518
constructive obligations, 44, 279
contingencies, 223, 226–227
contingent gains, 227
contra account, 87, 229–230, 349
contra asset account, 87
contract, 282
  basic accounting, 282
  consideration. See consideration
  contract modification, 283
  costs to obtain and/or fulfill a contract,
        305–306
  criteria for revenue guidance, 282
  with customers, 306
  executory contract, 416
  financing component, 286
  long-term contracts, 310–317
  new and separate contract, 283
  non-cancellable purchase
        contracts, 416
  onerous contract, 416
  performance, need for, 282–283
  unprofitable contract, 317
contract assets, 304–305
contract-based approach. See asset-
        liability approach
contract-based intangible assets, 706–707
contract law, 278–279
contract liability, 305
contract modification, 283
contractual obligations to pay, 214
contractual rights to receive cash, 214
contractual situations, 227
contractual yield basis, 358
contra items, 229–230
contributed assets, 570–572
contributed surplus, 224, 225
Contributed Surplus account, 93
control, 46–48, 281, 291, 293, 517
conventional retail inventory method,
        452–454
conversion costs, 424
copyright, 706
Copyright Office, 706
corporate scandals, 18
corporate strategy, 487
corporation, 46–47
  equity section accounts, 93
  shareholders' equity account, 94
cost-based measures, 97
cost-benefit relationship, 42
cost formulas, 218, 428–434
  choice of, 412, 433
  first-in, first-out (FIFO) cost formula,
        432–433, 454
  last-in, first-out (LIFO) cost formula,
        41, 433–434
  moving-average cost formula, 430
  specific identification, 429–430
  weighted average cost, 430–432

cost model, 490–495, 505, 574–575, 641,
        701–702
cost of goods available for sale or use, 411
cost of goods manufactured, 417–418
cost of goods sold, 412
cost recovery impairment model, 642–644,
        645–646, 709
cost reduction method, 571
costs, 560
  acquisition cost, 52, 573
  asset retirement costs, 424, 562
  borrowing costs, 424, 561–562,
        590–595
  capitalization of, 305–306, 560
  cash cost, 563
  change in estimated costs, 314
  computer software costs, 708
  conversion costs, 424
  deemed cost, 625
  demolition cost, 572
  development phase costs, 699–700
  directly attributable costs, 561
  dismantling costs, 562
  disposal costs, 645
  excluded from inventory, 425
  exit costs, 77
  flow of costs, 417–418
  freight costs, 454
  historical cost principle, 52–53, 86
  historical costs, 575
  IAS 16 definition, 563
  incremental costs, 305
  inventory costs. See inventory costs
  joint cost, 425
  kinds of costs, 42
  laid-down costs, 52
  to obtain and/or fulfill a contract,
        305–306, 307
  organization costs, 700
  period costs, 50, 425
  product costs, 50, 424–425
  property, plant, and equipment,
        560–562
  rearrangement and reinstallation costs,
        580, 584
  replacement cost, 434–435
  research phase costs, 699
  restoration costs, 562
  of service providers' work in progress,
        425
  that expire with passage of time, 84
  transaction costs, 358, 489
cost-to-cost basis, 292, 312–314
cost-to-retail ratio, 450
coupon rate, 358
coupons, 288
covenants, 223
coverage ratios, 211, 243–244
CPA Canada. See Chartered Professional
        Accountants Canada (CPA Canada)
CPA Canada Handbook, 13, 16, 412, 558,
        698
  see also Accounting Standards for
        Private Enterprises (ASPE)

credible financial statements, 40
credit, 78–79
crediting the account, 79
creditors, 7, 236
credit policy, 277
credit rating agencies, 5
credit risk, 276, 306, 339, 350, 358
creditworthiness, 210–211
critical event, 294
cross-references, 229–230
current assets, 216–220, 641
    cash, 217
    inventories, 218–219
    prepaid expenses, 219
    receivables, 217–218
    short-term investments, 217
current cash debt coverage ratio, 211,
    236–237, 244
current liabilities, 222–223
current operating performance
    approach, 156
current ratio, 211, 215, 244, 419, 421
customer acceptance conditions, 277
customer-related intangible assets, 705
cut-off schedule, 414

D
debit, 78–79
debit/credit rules and effects, 80
debiting the account, 79
debt
    long-term debt, 223–224
    valuation of company's own debt, 104
debt instruments, 486
debt market, 5
debt securities, 486, 491–495
debt to equity ratios, 104, 215
debt to total assets, 244
decision usefulness, 37
decision-usefulness approach, 8
declining-balance method, 634
decreasing charge methods, 634
deemed cost, 625
deferral method, 571
deferred income tax assets, 222
deferred income tax liabilities, 223–224
deferred payment terms, 563–564
deficit, 225
deflation, 51
delayed payment terms, 345,
    415–416, 696
demolition cost, 572
depletion, 558, 626, 629, 636
    estimate of recoverable reserves, 637
    liquidating dividend, 638
    pattern of depletion, 636–637
depletion base, 574
depletion expense, 636
depositor errors, 381
deposits in transit, 381
depreciable amount, 630
depreciation, 86, 97, 558, 626, 629
    see also amortization
    allocation methods, 631–635

asset components, 629–630
assets held for sale, 648
business perspective, 628
calculation, 631–635
declining-balance method, 634
depreciable amount, 630
depreciation period, 631
diminishing balance methods, 634
double-declining-balance method,
    634, 641
estimate, 629
factors considered in depreciation
    process, 629–631
IFRS-ASPE comparison, 655–656
and income tax, 659–663
as means of cost allocation, 629
partial periods, 638–640
prepaid expenses, 86
and replacement of assets, 653
residual value, 630
revalued amount, 575, 596
revision of depreciation rates,
    640–641
salvage value, 630
straight-line method, 633
tax purposes, 635
unit of production method, 634–635
derecognition, 46
    disposition, 649–650
    IFRS-ASPE comparison, 375
    intangible assets, 710
    receivables, 364–370
derivatives, 99, 223
deterioration due to elements, 86
development, 698
development expenses, 220
development phase, 698–700
differentiation strategy, 153
digital economy, 272
diminishing balance methods, 634
directly attributable costs, 561
direct method, 235, 436–437
direct write-off method, 356
disclosure
    accounting methods, 154
    assets recognized from costs incurred
        to fulfill a contract, 306
    borrowing costs, 595
    contract with customers, 306
    contra items, 229–230
    cross-references, 229–230
    of date financial statement authorized
        for issue, 239
    disaggregation of revenue, 307
    estimates, use of, 227
    full disclosure principle, 55–57, 163,
        223, 278
    goodwill, 716–718
    greater disclosures, 19
    IASB research project, 60
    increased disclosure under IFRS, 57
    intangible assets, 716–718
    inventories, 444–445
    investments, 518–523

Management Discussion and Analysis
    (MD&A), 55–56
note disclosures, 4
notes to financial statements, 176,
    228–229
parenthetical explanations, 228
property, plant, and equipment,
    651–652
receivables, 371–373
reconciliation of contract
    balances, 307
remaining performance
    obligations, 307
restatement of, 18
revenue recognition, 306–307
sale of receivables, 370
significant judgements, 306
supporting schedule, 230
techniques, 228–230
discontinued operations,
    158–162
    assets held for sale, 158–159
    measurement, 159–160
    presentation, 159–162
    separate component, 158
discount, 288, 291, 362
    cash discounts, 288, 348–349, 563
    employee discounts, 454
    prompt settlement discounts, 288
    purchase discounts, 422, 454
    sales discounts, 348–349, 454
    trade discounts, 348
discounted cash flow model, 100
discounted free cash flow
    method, 728
discounting the future cash flows, 115
discount period, 727
discount rate, 100, 308, 726–727
discrete earnings process, 294
discussion papers (DPs), 15
dismantling costs, 562
disposal costs, 645
disposition, 158
    see also sale
    business perspective, 628
    derecognition, 649–650
    donations of capital assets, 650
    held for sale, 648–650
    IFRS-ASPE comparison, 656
    involuntary conversion, 650
    long-lived assets to be disposed of by
        sale, 648–649
    miscellaneous issues, 650
    sale of property, plant, and equipment,
        649–650
dividends, 638
Dividends account, 93
dividends receivable, 345
donations of capital assets, 650
double-declining-balance method,
    634, 641
double-entry accounting, 79
double-entry bookkeeping, 79
due process, 13

E

earnings
  adjusted net earnings, 207
  all-inclusive approach, 156
  earnings process, 49
  higher-quality earnings, 155
  non-GAAP earnings, 177
  normalized earnings, 725
  presentation, 155
  quality of, 153–156, 210
  retained earnings, 224
  sustainability of, 154
earnings approach, 280, 293–295, 307–308
earnings before interest, taxes,
    depreciation, and amortization
    (EBITDA), 635
earnings management, 155, 580
earnings multiple, 178
earnings per share (EPS), 156–157,
    172–173, 244
earnings process, 294
economic activity, 46
economic benefits, 695
economic consequences argument, 40
economic entity, 47–48, 518
economic entity assumption, 46–48
economic environment, 58
economic factors, 631
economic resources, 44, 214
economics of sales transactions, 274–278
economic substance, 39
economic theory, 10
effective interest method, 97, 360–361,
    492, 493
effective interest rate, 358
efficiency of asset use, 653–655
efficient markets hypothesis, 10
efficient use of resources, 4
elements of financial statements, 37,
    43–45, 81
  assets, 43
  basic elements, 43
  equity, 44
  expenses, 44
  fair value, measurement of, 102–104
  gains, 44
  liabilities, 43–44
  losses, 44
  measurement of, 97–104
  present value-based accounting
    measurements, 99
  recognition, 46–49
  revenues, 44
  valuation techniques, 98–101
  value in use measurements, 101–102
employee discounts, 454
enforceable promise, 278
enhancing qualitative characteristics,
    41–42
entity concept, 46
entity perspective, 8
entity-specific measure, 53, 101
environmental liabilities, 99
E.O.M. (end of the month), 348

equipment, 573
equitable obligations, 44
equity, 44, 214
equity claims, 518
equity instruments, 213, 214, 486
equity investments, 344
equity market, 5
equity method, 513–516, 517
equity pickup, 513
equity securities, 498
error
  bank or depositor errors, 381
  freedom from material error, 40–41
  inventory errors, 419–421
estimated items, 84
  adjusting entries, 91–92
  bad debts, 84, 92
  unrealized holding gain or loss, 92
estimates
  and accrual accounting, 154
  cash flow estimates, 99
  change in, 314, 640
  depreciation, 629
  disclosure of use of, 227
  for income measurement, 154
  inventories, 442–444
  recoverable reserves, 637
  in statement of financial position, 212
  uncollectible trade accounts receivable,
    350–351
  for unperformed work, 315
  useful life, 631
  variable consideration, 285–286
ethical dilemmas, 19
ethical sensitivity, 19
ethics
  biased revenue numbers, 279
  centrality of ethics, 19
  code of ethics, 18
  cost deferrals, 50
  earnings management, 155, 580
  ethical dilemmas, 19
  ethical sensitivity, 19
  principles-based GAAP, 57
  and professional judgement, 227
  structured financings, 60
European Financial Reporting Advisory
    Group, 20
event, 78
  see also transaction
excess-earnings approach, 724–727
exchange price, 347, 563
executory contract, 416
exit costs, 77
exit price, 53
expected cash flow approach, 100
expected cost plus a margin, 289
expected credit losses, 351, 375
expected loss impairment model,
    508–511
expected present value technique, 100–101
expected value, 285
expenditures, major types of, 580–584
expense account, 79

expenses, 44
  see also specific expenses
  accrued expenses, 84, 89–91
  development expenses, 220
  function, 169–171
  IFRS-ASPE comparison, 178
  nature, 169–171
  operating expenses, 183–184, 220
  prepaid expenses, 84, 85–87, 219
  presentation, 169–171
  in single-step income statements, 165
  supplementary schedules, 168
exploration and evaluation assets, 637
Exposure Drafts (EDs), 15
  conceptual framework, 60, 105, 179,
    240
  *Disclosure Initiative: Proposed Amendments
    to IAS 7*, 267
  financial statement presentation, 240
  proposed amendments to IAS 7, 240
extended payment terms, 287
extended warranties, 301–302
extensible business reporting language
    (XBRL), 22
external users, 4
extractive industries, 587–588, 657

F

face rate, 358
face value, 358–359
factoring receivables, 365
fair value, 575, 643
  best-quality fair value measure, 103
  company's own debt, 104
  "cost" on the books, 570
  estimate of, 53
  less costs of disposal, 645
  less costs to sell, 574, 578
  loans receivable, 357–358, 364
  measurement, using IFRS 13, 102–104
  nonmonetary transactions, 567
  not equal to cash consideration, 364
  notes receivable, 357–358
  property, plant, and equipment,
    575–576
  relative fair value, 309
  and revenue recognition, 288
fair value hierarchy, 103
fair value less costs to sell, 439–442
fair value loss impairment model,
    510–511
fair value model (FVM), 575, 578–579,
    584
fair value option, 54, 214, 505
fair value principle, 53–54
fair value standard, 566–568
fair value test, 710
fair value through net income (FV-NI),
    92, 495–499, 505
fair value through other comprehensive
    income (FV-OCI), 92, 157,
    500–506
  income from FV-OCI investments
    (debt instruments), 503–504

fair value through other comprehensive
     income (FV-OCI) (*continued*)
   income from FV-OCI investments
        (shares), 501–502
   investments in debt instruments of
        other entities, 503–506
   investments in shares of other entities,
        500–502
   sale of FV-OCI investments (debt
        instruments), 504–506
   sale of FV-OCI investments
        (shares), 502
   with recycling, 500
   without recycling, 500
fair value through profit or loss
     (FVTPL), 527
favourable lease, 707
feedback, 38, 153
feedback value, 156, 167
financial accounting, 4
Financial Accounting Standards Board
     (FASB), 12, 15–16
   conceptual framework, 36
   derecognition of receivables, 375
   financial statement presentation, 240
   intangible assets, 722
   last-in, first-out (LIFO) accounting, 41
   nonmonetary exchange, 567
   performance reporting project, 179
financial assets, 214, 218, 342, 350
financial calculators, 117–118, 120–121
financial components approach, 369
financial crisis, 7–8, 18
financial engineering, 58
financial flexibility, 211–213, 223, 237
financial institutions, 5, 7
financial instruments, 213–216, 456
financial ratios. *See* ratio analysis
financial reporting, 4
   bias in, 10–11, 154, 279
   conceptual framework. *See* conceptual
        framework
   decision-usefulness approach, 8
   economic or business environment, 58
   entity perspective, 8
   financial engineering, 58
   fraudulent financial reporting, 58–59
   integrated reporting, 22–23
   issues, 57–59
   objective of financial reporting, 8–9, 57
   other pressures, 59
   proprietary perspective, 8
   stakeholders, 5–7
   well-reasoned and supported analysis, 58
financial risks, 243, 519
financial statements, 4, 55, 78, 93
   see also specific types of financial
        statements
   analysis. *See* analysis
   basic elements, 43
   basic presentation requirements, 163
   condensed financial statements, 168–169
   consolidation, 48, 518
   credible financial statements, 40

elements of financial statements, 37,
     43–45, 81, 97–104
general-purpose financial statements, 8, 36
IFRS-ASPE comparison, 104
measurement of financial statement
     elements, 97–104
note disclosures, 4
notes to financial statements, 55, 176
as point estimates, 153
preparation from work sheet, 110–112
presentation. *See* presentation
supplementary information, 55
users, 4, 6, 37, 274
financing activities, 150, 231, 234
finished goods inventory, 410
finite life, 221, 702–703
first-in, first-out (FIFO) cost formula,
     432–433, 454
first principles, 57
five-step revenue recognition process
   allocation of transaction price to
        separate performance obligations,
        289–291
   determination of transaction price,
        285–288
   example, 281
   identification of separate performance
        obligations, 283–285
   identification of the contract with
        customers, 282–283
   recognition of revenue when each
        performance obligation satisfied,
        291–292
   summary of, 292–293
fixed assets, 558
   see also property, plant, and equipment
flexibility, 57
f.o.b. destination, 278, 414
f.o.b. shipping point, 278, 414
foreign currencies, 344
formal plan to sell, 159
forms of organization, 46–47
foundational principles, 45–57
   measurement, 50–54
   presentation and disclosure, 55–57
   recognition and derecognition, 46–49
franchise, 706–707
fraudulent financial reporting, 58–59
*Fraudulent Financial Reporting:
     1998–2007*, 59
Freakonomics (Levitt and Dubner), 11
free cash flow, 238–239
freedom from material error, 40–41
freight costs, 454
full cost method, 574
full disclosure principle, 55–57, 163, 223, 278
function, 169–171, 213
fundamental qualitative characteristics,
     38–41
future income tax assets, 222
future income tax liabilities, 223–224
FV-OCI model. *See* fair value through
     other comprehensive income
     (FV-OCI)

G
GAAP. *See* generally accepted accounting
     principles (GAAP)
GAAP hierarchy, 16–17
gains, 44
   contingent gains, 227
   realized, 489
   unrealized holding gains or
        losses, 84, 489
   unusual gains, 163
   vs. revenues, 163
general and administrative expenses, 425
general chequing account, 378
general journal, 82–83
general ledger, 78, 81
generally accepted accounting principles
     (GAAP), 6, 12
   see also Accounting Standards for Private
        Enterprises (ASPE)
   in absence of specific GAAP
        guidance, 57
   comprehensive income, 156
   conceptual framework, 17
   consolidated statements, 47
   CPA Canada Handbook, 13, 16
   disclosure of accounting methods, 154
   entities responsible for GAAP, 12
   GAAP hierarchy, 16–17
   under IFRS, 17
   not always optimal, 154
   other sources of GAAP, 16–17
   primary sources, 16–17, 45
   principles-based approach, 21, 57
   principles *vs.* rules, 21
   professional judgement, 17–18
   rational and systematic allocation
        policy, 49
   rules-based approach, 21
   sources of GAAP, 16–17
   U.S. GAAP, 15, 21–22, 434
   see also Financial Accounting
        Standards Board (FASB)
general-purpose financial statements, 8, 36
going concern assumption, 52
goods, 274
   consigned goods, 414
   distinct goods, 283
   physical goods, 413–417
   sale of goods, 294–295
   see also sales transaction
   sales of *vs.* sales of services, 274
goods in transit, 414
goodwill, 222, 694
   analysis, 719–720
   bargain purchase, 713
   business importance, 694
   characteristics, 694
   disclosure, 716–718
   discounted free cash flow method, 728
   excess-earnings approach, 724–727
   IFRS, effects of, 692–693
   IFRS-ASPE comparison, 721
   impairment, 714–715
   internally generated goodwill, 711

goodwill (*continued*)
  measurement, 694, 711–712
  negative goodwill, 713
  number of years method, 728
  presentation, 716–717
  present value-based accounting
    measurements, 99
  purchased goodwill, 711–712
  recognition, 711–712
  total-earnings approach, 727
  valuation after acquisition, 713–714
  valuation of goodwill, 713–714,
    724–728
government grants, 570–572, 588
Great Depression, 12
gross average accounts receivable
    (GAAR), 355
gross margin, 299
gross method, 299, 348–349, 422
gross profit margins, 170, 299
gross profit method, 442
gross profit percentage, 443

H
half-year rule, 660
hard numbers, 41, 154, 212
held for sale, 158–159, 648–650, 656
held for trading instruments, 488, 505
held to maturity instruments, 490, 505
highest and best use, 102
historical cost-based model, 53
historical cost measures, 97–98
historical cost principle, 52–53
  depreciable assets, 86
  on statement of financial position, 212
historical costs, 575
holder, 365
horizontal analysis, 268
human behaviour, 10
hyperinflation, 52

I
IASB. *See* International Accounting
    Standards Board (IASB)
identifiable, 695
identifiable net assets, 694
IFRS. *See* International Financial
    Reporting Standards (IFRS)
IFRS Advisory Council, 14
IFRS-ASPE comparison
  see also Accounting Standards for Private
    Enterprises (ASPE); International
    Financial Reporting Standards
    (IFRS)
  accounting changes, 179
  cash and cash equivalents, 374
  cash flow per share information, 239
  current *vs.* non-current liabilities, 239
  depreciation, 655–656
  derecognition, 375
  disclosure, property, plant, and
    equipment, 657
  disclosure of date financial statement
    authorized for issue, 239

discontinued operations, 178
earnings per share, 179
expenses, 178
financial statements, 104
fundamental similarities, 59
goodwill, 721
held for sale, 656
impairment, 375, 655–656
intangible assets, 720–721
inventories, 446–447
investments, 524–525
measurement issues, 104–105
other comprehensive income/
    comprehensive income, 179
"probable," and recognition of losses
    and liabilities, 46
property, plant, and equipment,
    585–587
receivables, 375
revenue recognition, 307–309
statement of cash flows, 239
statement of changes in shareholders'
    equity, 179
statement of financial position (balance
    sheet), 239
statement of income/comprehensive
    income (income statement),
    178–179
statement of retained earnings, 179
IFRS Foundation, 14, 34
impaired, 642
impairment, 641–642
  accounts receivable, 350–356
  asset groups, 646–648
  business perspective, 628
  cash-generating unit (CGU), 646–648
  cost recovery impairment model,
    642–644, 645–646, 709
  goodwill, 714–715
  IFRS-ASPE comparison, 375, 655–656
  indefinite-life intangibles, 710
  indicators of impairment, 642
  limited-life intangibles, 708–709
  rational entity impairment model, 643,
    643–646, 709
  recognition and measurement models,
    642–646
  recoverable amount, 644
  in value, equity method, 516
impairment loss, 507, 643–646,
    647–648
impairment models, 507–511
  expected loss impairment model,
    508–511
  fair value loss impairment model,
    510–511
  incurred loss impairment model,
    507–508, 510–511
  summary of, 510–511
implicit interest rate, 359
imprest bank accounts, 378
imprest system, 379–380
imputation, 363
imputed interest rate, 363

incidental transactions, 44, 167
income
  all-inclusive approach, 156
  under amortized cost model, 492–494
  comprehensive income, 45, 156
  from continuing operations, 207
  measurement, 154
  multiple view of income, 157
  net income. *See* net income
  nonrecurring income or losses, 167
  numbers, and accounting methods, 154
  operating income, 153, 156
  other comprehensive income. *See* other
    comprehensive income (OCI)
  sustainability of, 155
income approach, 571
income models, 98
income statement, 4, 78, 150, 176
  see also statement of income/
    comprehensive income (income
    statement)
Income Summary account, 94
Income Tax Act, 660
income taxes
  capital cost allowance method, 659–663
  depreciation, 659–663
  work sheet, 108–109
incremental costs, 305
incurred loss impairment model, 507–508,
    510–511
indefinite life, 221, 702, 704, 707, 710, 714
indirect method, 235, 437
industries, 150–153
industry practice, 17
inflation, 51
inflation accounting, 52
information
  integrity of, 154
  quality of, 153–156
information asymmetry, 9–11, 37
  adverse selection, 10, 37
  moral hazard, 10, 37
information overload, 55
information symmetry, 9
in-process research and development
    (R&D), 697
input measures, 292, 312
inspections, 580–584
institutional investors, 8–9, 484–485
insurance, 85–86, 219
insurance claims, 345
intangible assets, 221–222, 695
  at acquisition, 696–697
  after acquisition, 701–704
  amortization, 629, 702
  analysis, 719–720
  artistic-related intangible assets, 706
  business combination, 697
  business importance, 694
  characteristics, 695
  contract-based intangible assets,
    706–707
  customer-related intangible assets, 705
  derecognition, 710

intangible assets *(continued)*
  development phase, 698–700
  disclosure, 716–718
  finite life, 221
  IFRS-ASPE comparison, 720–721
  impairment of indefinite-life
    intangibles, 710
  impairment of limited-life intangibles,
    708–709
  indefinite life, 221, 702, 704, 710
  internally developed intangible assets,
    222, 698–701
  limited-life intangibles, 702–703,
    708–709
  marketing-related intangible assets,
    704–705
  measurement, 696–704
  measurement difficulties, 222
  prepayments, 697
  presentation, 716–717
  purchased intangibles, 696
  recognition, 696–704
  research phase, 698–699
  technology-based intangible assets,
    707–708
  useful life, 221
  valuation difficulties, 222
integrated reporting, 22–23
intellectual capital, 719
interest, 563
  accrued interest, 90
  capitalization of interest, 561–562
  compound interest, 114–115
  nature of, 113
  nonrecognition of interest element, 350
  notes receivable, 356
  simple interest, 114
interest-bearing investment, 492
interest-bearing notes, 356, 361–363
interest rates
  calculation of, 122–123
  effective interest rate, 358
  implicit interest rate, 359
  imputed interest rate, 363
  market rate, 358, 362–363
  present value calculations, 122
  stated interest rate, 358, 362–363
  yield rate, 358
interest receivable, 345
internal control, 378
internal control systems, 18
internal users, 4
International Accounting Standards
  (IAS), 17
  see also International Financial
    Reporting Standards (IFRS)
  agriculture, 34–35, 439, 574, 588
  bearer plants, 34–35
  biological assets and agricultural
    produce, 34–35, 309, 446
  borrowing costs, 561
  cost, 563
  depreciation, 635
  disclosure, 444

fair value through other comprehensive
  income, 157
financial instruments, 407
government grants and disclosure of
  government assistance, 588
hyperinflation, 52, 575
impairment of assets, 657, 721
intangible assets, 698, 703, 722
inventories, 440, 446
investment measurement models,
  505–506
investment property, 573, 579
markdowns, 454
property, plant, and equipment, 34, 558,
  573, 649, 657
provisions, contingent liabilities, and
  contingent assets, 416
revenue, 209
statement of cash flows, 240
International Accounting Standards Board
  (IASB), 12–16, 20
  see also International Financial
    Reporting Standards (IFRS)
  adoption date for IFRS, 15, 309
  biological assets, 34
  conceptual framework, 36, 60, 105, 157
  derecognition of receivables, 375
  disclosures, 60
  extractive industries, 587–588, 657
  financial statement presentation, 240
  intangible assets, 722
  materiality, 60
  performance reporting project, 179
  reporting entity, defining, 48
  revenue recognition, 280
International Accounting Standards
  Committee (IASC), 14
International Financial Reporting
  Interpretation Committee
  (IFRIC), 14, 17
International Financial Reporting
  Standards (IFRS), 12
  see also generally accepted accounting
    principles (GAAP); IFRS-ASPE
    comparison; International
    Accounting Standards (IAS);
    International Accounting
    Standards Board (IASB)
  accounts receivable, 350, 351
  all-inclusive approach, 156
  asset impairment, 101
  asset-liability approach, 280, 307–308
  asset retirement costs, 562
  associates, investments in, 512, 523
  balance sheet approach, 49
  biological assets and agricultural
    produce, 440–441
  capitalization of costs, 560
  cash equivalents, 344
  combined statement of income/
    comprehensive income, 164–165
  components, 559, 630
  comprehensive income, 45
  control, 48, 517

current assets, 518–519
depreciation, 630
derecognition of receivables,
  367–369
disclosure, 716
effective interest method, 358, 360, 492
evolution of a new or revised IFRS, 15
expenses, 169–170
fair value, 53, 101–104, 645,
  657, 721
fair value option, 54
financial assets, 350, 506
financial instruments, 214
GAAP under IFRS, 17
goodwill, 692–693, 714–715
held for sale, 649
held-for-sale assets and liabilities, 160
impairment, 375, 507, 509–511,
  519–520, 642
income, 156
increased disclosure, 57
indefinite life, 704
indefinite-life intangibles, 710
intangible assets, 698, 700–701
inventory, 41, 412, 444
inventory cost, 422
investment measurement models,
  505–506
investment property, 573, 575
investments, 495, 501
liabilities, recognition of, 227
lifetime expected credit losses,
  350, 509
limited-life intangibles, 709
mineral resources, 588
other comprehensive income, 45,
  157, 172
principles-based approach, 21, 57
"probable," 46
product costs, 424
professional judgement, 17
provisions, 223, 227
rational entity impairment model, 709
rational entity model, 645
receivables, 367–369, 371, 375
refund liability, 349–350
replacements, major overhauls, and
  inspections, 584
revaluation model, 702
revaluation of company's own debt, 104
revenue from contracts with customers,
  49, 280
revenue recognition, 295
sales revenue, 349
share-based payment, 566
significant influence, 516
statement of changes in equity,
  173–175
statement of income/comprehensive
  income, 163–165, 169–170
transaction costs, 358
United States, and IFRS, 21–22
vs. U.S. GAAP, 21–22
zero-profit method, 311

International Integrated Reporting
    Committee (IIRC), 23
Internet, 11, 22
intraperiod tax allocation, 172
inventories, 413
    accounting definition, 413
    analysis, 446
    basket purchases and joint product
        costs, 425
    beginning inventory, 95
    categories, 410
    change in control, 417
    companies with inventory, 410
    consigned goods, 414
    and cost of goods sold, 95
    costs. See inventory costs
    as current asset, 218–219
    disclosure, 444–445
    ending inventory, 95, 419–420
    estimates, 442–444
    finished goods inventory, 410
    goods in transit, 414
    IFRS-ASPE comparison, 446–447
    information for decision-making,
        411–412
    inventory errors, 419–421
    inventory tracking, 408–409
    last-in, first-out (LIFO) cost
        formula, 41
    manufacturing inventory, 218
    measurement, 411, 421–444
    merchandise inventory, 410
    physical count, 95
    physical goods, 413–417
    planning and control, 410–411
    presentation, 444–445
    purchase commitments, 416–417
    purchase discounts, 422
    purchases and inventory misstated,
        420–421
    raw materials inventory, 410
    recognition, 412–421
    risks and rewards, 417
    sales with buyback agreements, 415
    sales with delayed payment terms,
        415–416
    sales with high rates of return, 415
    types of inventory, 456
    understatement of, 414
    vendor rebate, 422–423
    vs. property, plant, and equipment,
        558–559
    work-in-process inventory, 410
inventory accounting systems
    periodic inventory system, 95, 427–428,
        432, 437
    perpetual inventory system, 95,
        426–428, 430, 432, 437
    quantities only system, 428
inventory costs, 421–422, 450–455
    borrowing costs, 424
    cost formula. See cost formulas
    cost of service providers' work in
        progress, 425

costs excluded from inventory, 425
exceptions to lower of cost and net
    realizable value model, 438–442
fair value less costs to sell, 439–442, 441
flow of costs, 417–418
lower of cost and market (LCM), 434
lower of cost and net realizable value,
    434–438
net realizable value, 438–439
product costs, 424–425
retail inventory method, 450–455
standard cost system, 424
inventory errors, 419–421
inventory turnover ratio, 244, 446
investee, 487
investing activities, 150, 231, 235, 237
investment property, 573, 575
investments
    amortized cost model, 491–495
    analysis, 523–524
    application of accounting models, 490
    associates, investments in, 512–516, 523
    available for sale, 488
    cost model, 490–495
    in debt instruments of other entities,
        503–506
    disclosure, 518–523
    equity investments, 344
    expected loss impairment model,
        508–511
    fair value loss impairment model,
        510–511
    fair value through net income (FV-NI),
        495–499
    fair value through other comprehensive
        income (FV-OCI), 500–506
    held for trading, 488, 505
    held to maturity investments, 490, 505
    IFRS-ASPE comparison, 524–525
    impairment models, 507–511
    incurred loss impairment model,
        507–508, 510–511
    information for decision-making, 488
    long-term investments, 220
    on margin, 489
    measurement, 489–511
    non-current investments, 220
    presentation, 518–523
    present value-based accounting
        measurements, 99
    recoverable amount, 516
    returns, 487
    in shares of other entities, 500–502
    short-term investments, 217, 343
    significant influence investments, 513
    strategic investments, 511–518
    subsidiaries, investments in, 517–518
    types of companies, 487–488
    types of investments, 486
    without significant influence or control,
        518–523
investors, 7–9, 487
involuntary conversion, 650
IOUs, 343, 345

irregular activities, 167
irregular items, 156, 172
item-by-item approach, 436

J
joint cost, 425
joint venture, 512
journal entries, 78
    see also specific journal entries
journalizing, 81–82
journals, 17, 78
    general journal, 82–83
    special journal, 82
judgement. See professional judgement

K
knowledge assets, 719

L
laid-down costs, 52
language of accounting and business, 43
last-in, first-out (LIFO) cost formula, 41,
    433–434
leasehold, 707
leasehold improvements, 572–573
leases, 707
    favourable lease, 707
    present value-based accounting
        measurements, 99
ledger, 78
    general ledger, 78, 81
    subsidiary ledger, 78
legal control, 512
legal entity, 47
legal life, 631
legal title, 274, 277–278, 295, 414
lenient return or payment policy, 277
liabilities, 43–44
    classification in statement of financial
        position, 213
    contract liability, 305
    contractual obligations to pay, 214
    current liabilities, 222–223
    current vs. non-current classification, 52
    deferred income tax liabilities, 223–224
    environmental liabilities, 99
    and financial flexibility, 213
    future income tax liabilities, 223–224
    held for sale, 160
    historical cost, 212
    liquidation approach, 52
    monetary liabilities, 213
    nonmonetary liabilities, 213
    recognition, 227
    on statement of financial position, 214
liability account, 79
licences, 706–707
licensing agreements, 706
lifetime expected credit losses, 350, 509
limited liability partnerships (LLPs), 47
limited life, 702–703, 707–709
limited resources, 4
liquidating dividend, 638
liquidation approach, 52

liquidity, 12, 210–211, 215, 236–237
liquidity ratios, 211–212, 243–244
liquidity risk, 212
loans, 346, 358
loans receivable, 341, 346–347
   see also notes receivable
   fair value, 357–358, 364
   long-term loans receivable, 357–364
   short-term loans receivable, 356–357
   transaction costs, 358
lockbox accounts, 378–379
longer-term returns, 487
long-lived assets, 648–649
long-term contracts, 310–317
   completed-contract method,
      315–316
   losses on, 316–317
   loss in current period, 316–317
   loss on unprofitable contract, 317
   percentage-of-completion method,
      311–315
   progress billings, 311
long-term debt, 223–224
long-term investments, 220
long-term liabilities, 223–224
long-term loans receivable, 357–364
long-term notes receivable, 357–364
losses, 44
   allowance for credit losses, 355
   in current period, 316–317
   expected credit losses for accounts
      receivable, 351
   on long-term contracts, 316–317
   nonrecurring income or losses, 167
   realized, 489
   on unprofitable contract, 317
   unrealized holding gains or losses,
      84, 489
   unusual losses, 163
loss events, 507
low-cost/high-volume strategy, 153
lower of cost and market (LCM), 434
lower of cost and net realizable value,
   434–438, 454, 456, 641–642
lower of cost and net realizable value
   (LC&NRV) standard, 435–436
lump-sum price, 565

M
major overhauls, 580–584
maker, 356
management best estimate, 40
management bias, 10–11, 19
Management Discussion and Analysis
   (MD&A), 55–56
managerial accounting, 4
manufacturing inventory, 218
markdown cancellations, 451
markdowns, 451
market, 434
   capital markets, 10
   debt market, 5
   efficient markets hypothesis, 10
   equity market, 5

most advantageous market, 102
   principal market, 102
market-based measure, 53
marketing-related intangible assets,
   704–705
market models, 98
market participant view, 101
market rate, 358, 362–363
market valuation model, 53
market value, 87
markup, 451
markup cancellations, 451
markup on cost, 443
matching, 49–50
   and adjusting entries, 84
   depreciable assets, 86
   depreciation, 631
   estimate of bad debts, 92
   percentage-of-sales approach, 353
materiality, 38–39, 60, 163, 278, 580
material right, 285
*MD&A: Guidance on Preparation and
   Disclosure* (CPA Canada), 55
measurement, 50–54
   accounts receivable, 347–350
   cash, 342–345
   of company performance, 4–5
   at cost, 696
   cost-based measures, 97
   current value measures, 97
   discontinued operations, 159–160
   entity-specific measure, 53, 101
   fair value principle, 53–54
   of fair value using IFRS 13, 102–104
   financial assets, 350
   going concern assumption, 52
   goodwill, 694, 711–712
   historical cost principle, 52–53
   hybrid measures, 97
   IFRS-ASPE comparison, 104–105
   impairment, 642–646
   income measurement, 154
   intangible assets, 222, 696–704
   inventory, 411, 421–444
   investments, 489–511
   items recognized in financial
      statements, 81
   long-term loans receivable, 357–364
   long-term notes receivable, 357–364
   market-based measure, 53
   measurement uncertainty, 51, 53
   monetary unit assumption, 51–52
   non-GAAP measures, 177
   other key measures, 177–178
   periodicity assumption, 51
   present value-based accounting
      measurements, 99
   property, plant, and equipment—after
      acquisition, 574–579
   property, plant, and equipment—cost,
      563–574
   receivables, 347–370
   and recognition, 50–51
   remeasurement, 159

   of revenue, 280–295
   short-term loans receivable, 356–357
   short-term notes receivable, 356–357
   statement of income/comprehensive
      income, 156–157
   tools, 51
   value in use measurements, 101–102
measurement uncertainty, 51, 53, 176
merchandise inventory, 410
mineral resource properties, 573–574,
   587–588, 626–627
   see also depletion
mineral resources, 573
   see also depletion
minority interest, 518
mixed valuation model, 53
modified cash basis, 182
monetary assets, 213, 566, 695
monetary liabilities, 213
monetary unit assumption, 51–52
money, 217
money-market funds, 342, 344
money orders, 342
moral hazard, 10, 37
most advantageous market, 102
most likely amount, 285
moving-average cost formula, 430
multiple deliverables, 274
multiple performance obligations,
   289–290
multiple-step income statement, 166–168

N
natural resources, 573–574
   see also mineral resources
nature, 169–171
negative goodwill, 713
negotiable instruments, 342
net approach, 299
net assets, 214
net carrying amount, 690
net cash inflows, 153
net income, 51, 156, 235, 299
   accrual-based net income, 185
   income approach, 571
   losses, 84
   significantly higher than cash flows
      from operations, 210
   work sheet, 110
net income per share. *See* earnings per
   share (EPS)
net markdowns, 451
net markups, 451
net method, 348–349, 422
net realizable value (NVR), 52, 351,
   434–439
net working capital, 223
neutrality, 40, 57, 74, 632
non-cancellable purchase contracts, 416
noncash consideration, 288
noncontrolling interest, 518
non-current investments, 220
non-GAAP earnings, 177
non-GAAP measures, 177

non–interest-bearing investment, 492, 497
non–interest-bearing notes, 356–357
nonmonetary, non-reciprocal transactions, 53
nonmonetary assets, 213, 566, 696
nonmonetary liabilities, 213
nonmonetary transactions, 53, 276, 566–570
non-operating transactions, 166
non-reciprocal transfers, 570
nonrecurring income or losses, 167
non-refundable upfront fees, 302–303
nontrade receivables, 341, 346
normal business practices, 278
normalized earnings, 725
normal production capacity, 424
normal selling terms, 277
normal shortages, 454
Norwalk Agreement, 16
note disclosures, 4
notes receivable, 213, 346–347
    face value, 358–359
    fair value, 357–358
    interest-bearing notes, 356, 361–363
    long-term notes receivable, 357–364
    non–interest-bearing notes, 356–357
    received for property, goods, or services, 361–362
    short-term notes receivable, 356–357
    transaction costs, 358
    zero-interest-bearing notes, 356, 359–361
notes to financial statements, 55, 176, 228–229
    present value-based accounting measurements, 99
not-sufficient-funds (NSF) cheques, 381
number of years method, 728

O
objective of financial reporting, 8–9, 36–37, 57
obsolescence, 86, 631, 642
off–balance sheet, 212
oil and gas properties, 574, 587–588
one-line consolidation, 516
onerous contract, 416
on margin, 489
Ontario Securities Commission (OSC), 2, 12, 16, 31, 32, 40, 177
operating activities, 150, 231, 233–235
operating expenses, 183–184, 220
operating income, 153, 156
operating items, 156
operating risk, 243
operating transactions, 166
opportunities, 150
opportunities for accounting profession, 18–23
ordinary activities, 44, 163
ordinary enterprise operations, 223
ordinary repairs, 584

ordinary revenue-generating activities, 44
ordinary trade accounts, 217
organization costs, 700
original oil in place, 638
other assets, 222
other comprehensive income (OCI), 45, 157
    accumulated other comprehensive income, 93
    IFRS-ASPE comparison, 179
    revaluation of company's own debt, 104
    unrealized holding gain or loss, 84
output measures, 312
outstanding cheques, 381
overhead, 561
oversight in capital marketplace, 18–19
Owners' Drawings account, 93
owners' equity, 93–94, 224–225
ownership
    ownership interest, 44
    ownership structure, 93
    risk of, 294

P
parent corporation, 517
parenthetical explanations, 228
parking transactions, 415
partial periods, and depreciation, 638–640
partnership, 46–47, 93–94
patent, 707
Patent Office, 707
payee, 356
payment policy, 277
payout ratio, 244
pensions, 99
percentage-of-completion method, 308, 311–315
percentage-of-receivables approach, 351
percentage-of-sales approach, 353
performance
    business models, 150–153
    communication of information about performance, 153
    industries, 150–153
    quality of earnings/information, 153–156
performance obligations, 49, 283
    allocation of transaction price, 289–291
    identification of, 283–285
    remaining performance obligations, 307
    satisfaction of, 291–292
period costs, 51, 425
periodic inventory system, 95, 427–428, 432, 437
periodicity assumption, 51
periodic payment, 123–124
peripheral activities, 163
peripheral transactions, 44
permanent account, 78
permits, 706
perpetual franchise, 707
perpetual inventory system, 95, 426–428, 430, 432, 437
petty cash, 379–380

petty cash funds, 343–345
physical count, 95
physical factors, 631
physical goods, 413–417
physical life, 631
plant assets, 558
    see also property, plant, and equipment
point of delivery, 294
political environment, standard setting in, 20
possession, 274, 278, 295
postage stamps, 343, 345
post-closing trial balance, 78, 95–96
postdated cheques, 343, 345
posting, 78, 82–83
post-retirement benefits, 99
predictive value, 38, 53, 153, 155–156, 167
preferred shares, 344
premium, 363
prepaid expenses, 84, 219, 697
    adjusting entries, 85–87
    depreciation/amortization, 86
    expiration of, 85
    insurance, 85–86
    vs. unearned revenues, 87–88
prepayments, 84
    adjusting entries, 85–88
    alternative method for adjusting, 88
    as current assets, 219
    intangible assets, 697
    prepaid expenses, 84–87, 697
    unearned revenues, 84–85, 87–88
presentation, 55–57
    basic presentation requirements, 163
    contract assets, 304–305
    discontinued operations, 159–162
    of earnings, 155
    expenses, 169–171
    Exposure Draft, "staff draft" of, 240
    goodwill, 716–717
    intangible assets, 716–717
    inventories, 444–445
    investments, 518–523
    issues, 239
    multiple-step income statement, 166–168
    ordinary vs. peripheral activities, 163
    percentage-of-completion method, 314–315
    property, plant, and equipment, 651–652
    receivables, 371–373
    revenues and revenue recognition, 304–306
    single-step income statements, 165–166
    statement of cash flows, 232–235
    statement of changes in equity, 174–176
    statement of financial position (balance sheet), 215–226
    statement of income/comprehensive income, 162–173
    statement of retained earnings, 173–174
present obligations, 214

present value, 113–124
  calculation methods, 115–122
  compound interest, 114–115
  of consideration, 563
  exchange price, 563
  expected present value technique, 100
  financial assets, 350
  financial calculators, 117–118, 120–121
  fundamental variables, 113–115
  interest, nature of, 113
  interest rate calculation, 122–123
  interest rates and time periods, 122
  notes, 357–358, 360
  periodic payment, calculation of,
    123–124
  present value formula, 115–116,
    119–120
  present value tables, 116–117, 120
  series of future cash flows (annuities),
    118–121
  simple interest, 114
  single future amount, 115–118
  spreadsheets, 118, 121
  value in use, 101–102
present value-based accounting
    measurements, 99
present value factor, 360
price
  cash price equivalent, 563
  exchange price, 347, 563
  lump-sum price, 565
  stand-alone selling price, 289
  transaction price, 285–291
price earnings ratio, 178, 244
price-level change, 51–52
price risk, 276
primary sources of GAAP, 16–17,
    45, 439
principal-agent relationship, 298–299, 303
principal market, 102
principles-based approach, 21, 57
principles *vs.* rules, 21
private companies, 13
Private Enterprise Advisory
    Committee, 722
private entity GAAP. *See* Accounting
    Standards for Private Enterprises
    (ASPE)
product costs, 50, 424–425
product market risks, 243
professional corporations, 47
professional judgement, 17–18, 57, 212,
    227, 306
profitability ratios, 243–244
profit margin on sales, 244
profit margin ratio, 654–655
profit margins, 167, 170
profits, 18
pro forma numbers, 635
promise, 278
promissory note, 356–357
  see also loans receivable; notes receivable
prompt settlement discounts, 288
pronouncements, 17

property, plant, and equipment,
    220–221, 558
  additions, 580–581
  analysis, 653–655
  asset exchanges, 566–570
  biological assets, 574
  borrowing costs, 561–562
  buildings, 572
  business perspective, 557–558
  cash discounts, 563
  cash not exchanged at acquisition,
    563–572
  characteristics, 558–559
  contributed assets, 570–572
  cost elements, 560–562
  cost model (CM), 574–575
  costs associated with specific assets,
    572–574
  costs incurred after acquisition, 580–585
  deferred payment terms, 563–564
  definition, 58
  depreciation. *See* depreciation
  disclosure, 651–652
  dismantling and restoration costs, 562
  disposal. *See* disposition
  economic benefits, 628
  efficiency of asset use, 653–655
  equipment, 573
  expenditures, major types of, 580–584
  fair value model (FVM), 575,
    578–579, 584
  fair value standard, 566–568
  government grants, 570–572
  IFRS-ASPE comparison, 585–587, 657
  impairment. *See* impairment
  inspections, 580–584
  investment property, 573
  leasehold improvements, 572–573
  lump-sum purchases, 565
  major overhauls, 580–584
  measurement after acquisition, 574–579
  measurement of cost, 563–574
  natural resource properties, 573–574
  net basis, 234
  nonmonetary exchanges, 565–570
  nonmonetary transactions, 566–570
  presentation, 651–652
  rearrangement and reinstallation costs,
    580, 584
  recognition principle, 559
  repairs, 580, 584
  replacement of assets, 653
  replacements, 580–584
  return on investment, 653–655
  revaluation model (RM),
    574–578, 584
  sale of, 649–650
  self-constructed assets, 561
  share-based payments, 565–566
  vs. inventory, 558–559
proportional method, 702
proprietary perspective, 8
provincial securities commissions, 12, 16
provision matrix, 351

provisions, 223, 227
public companies, 13
Public Company Accounting Oversight
    Board (PCAOB), 18
Public Sector Accounting Handbook, 558
purchase allowances, 454
purchase commitments, 416–417
purchase discounts, 422, 454
purchase returns, 454
purchasers of receivables, 365

Q
qualifying assets, 590–592
qualitative characteristics, 37–42, 154
  comparability, 41
  cost-benefit relationship, 42
  elements of financial statements, 37
  enhancing qualitative characteristics,
    41–42
  fundamental, 38–41
  relevance, 38–39, 42
  representational faithfulness,
    38–42
  timeliness, 41
  trade-offs, 42
  understandability, 41–42
  verifiability, 41
quality of earnings, 153–156, 210
quantitative data, 51
quantitative factors, 39
quantities only system, 428
quick ratio, 211, 244

R
radio-frequency identification (RFID),
    408–409
rate of return on assets (ROA), 244, 655
rate of return on common share equity,
    244
ratio analysis, 177–178, 243
  acid-test ratio, 211, 244
  activity ratios, 211, 243–244
  asset turnover, 244
  average days to sell inventory, 446
  benchmarking, 244–245
  book value per share, 244
  business risks, 242–243
  cash debt coverage ratio, 237, 244
  cost-to-retail ratio, 450
  coverage ratios, 211, 243–244
  current cash debt coverage ratio, 211,
    236–237, 244
  current ratio, 211, 215, 244, 419, 421
  debt to equity ratios, 104, 215
  debt to total assets, 244
  earnings per share (EPS), 156–157,
    172–173, 244
  inventory turnover ratio, 244, 446
  liquidity ratios, 211–212, 243–244
  major types of ratios, 243
  misclassification, effect of, 239
  payout ratio, 244
  price earnings ratio, 178, 244
  profitability ratios, 243–244

ratio analysis (continued)
  profit margin on sales, 244
  profit margin ratio, 654–655
  quick ratio, 211, 244
  rate of return on assets, 244
  rate of return on assets (ROA), 244, 655
  rate of return on common share equity, 244
  receivables turnover ratio, 373–374
  solvency ratios, 212
rational entity impairment model, 643–646, 709
ratios. See ratio analysis
raw materials inventory, 410
realizable (revenue), 49
realized (gains and losses), 489
realized (revenue), 49
real-time financial information, 51
rearrangement and reinstallation costs, 580, 584
reasonable knowledge, 41
rebates, 288
recapture, 663
receivables, 346
  see also accounts receivable
  analysis, 373–374
  as current asset, 217–218
  definition, 346
  derecognition, 364–370
  disclosure, 370–373
  estimated uncollectible receivables, 92
  factoring receivables, 365
  IFRS-ASPE comparison, 375
  loans receivable. See loans receivable
  measurement, 347–370
  nontrade receivables, 341, 346
  notes receivable. See notes receivable
  presentation, 371–373
  recognition, 347–370
  with recourse, 369–370
  reporting, 347
  sale of receivables, 365–370
  sale without recourse, 369
  secured borrowings, 365
  trade receivables, 341, 346
receivables management, 341
receivables turnover ratio, 244, 373–374
reciprocal exchange, 52
reciprocal transaction, 275–276
reclassification adjustment, 502
reclassified items, 157
recognition, 46–49
  accounts receivable, 347–350
  cash, 342–345
  control, 46–48
  economic entity assumption, 46–48
  estimated uncollectible receivables, 92
  goodwill, 711–712
  impairment, 642–646
  intangible assets, 696–704
  inventory, 412–421
  liabilities, 227
  long-term loans receivable, 357–364

long-term notes receivable, 357–364
matching principle, 49–50
and measurement, 50–54
property, plant, and equipment, 559
realized and realizable, 49
receivables, 347–370
revenue recognition. See revenue recognition
short-term loans receivable, 356–357
short-term notes receivable, 356–357
when to recognize an item, 81
reconciliation of bank balances, 380–383
recording process
  adjusting entries, 84–92
  closing process, 94–97
  identification of transactions and other events, 80–81
  journalizing, 81–82
  posting, 82–83
  recording transactions and other events, 80–81
  reversing entries, 96–97
  trial balance, 83
recoverability test, 643, 710
recoverable amount, 644
recoverable reserves, 637
recycled items, 157
recycling, 500–501
refund liability, 349–350
regular activities, 167
regular-way purchase or sale, 552
reinstallation, 580, 584
related party transactions, 53, 217
relative fair value, 309
relative sales value method, 425
relevance, 38–39, 42, 163, 719
reliability, 719
rental real estate, 573
repairs, 580, 584
replacement cost, 434–435
replacements, 580–584, 653
reporting entity, 48
representational faithfulness, 38–42, 150, 575
repurchase agreements, 296–297, 303
research, 698
research phase, 698–699
research studies, 17
reserves, 155
residual approach, 289
residual interest, 44, 214
residual value, 630, 634
residual value method, 309
resources
  allocation of, 4–5, 37, 41
  economic resources, 44, 214
  efficient use of resources, 4–5
  evaluations of alternatives, 41
  successful use of, 166–167
  transfer of, 5
restoration costs, 562
restricted cash, 343
restrictions, 223

retail inventory method, 450–455
  conventional retail inventory method, 452–454
  evaluation of, 455
  special items, 454–455
  terminology, 451
retained earnings, 224
Retained Earnings account, 93–94
retrospective restatement, 174–175
returnable items, 345
return on investment, 487, 653–655
return policy, 277
return rates, 415
revaluation adjustment on property, plant, and equipment, 164
revaluation model (RM), 574–578, 584, 596–597, 641, 701–702
Revaluation Surplus account, 104, 576, 578
revenue account, 79
revenue constraint, 287
revenue expenditure, 580
revenue recognition
  approaches to, 280–295
  asset-liability approach, 280–293
  bill-and-hold arrangement, 298, 303
  consignments, 300, 301, 303
  disclosure, 306–307
  earnings approach, 280, 293–295
  five-step revenue recognition process, 281–293
  gross method, 299
  IFRS-ASPE comparison, 307–309
  key concepts, 280
  long-term contracts, 310–317
  misrepresentation in financial statements, 279–280
  net approach, 299
  non-refundable upfront fees, 302–303
  presentation, 304–306
  principal-agent relationship, 298–299, 303
  repurchase agreements, 296–297, 303
  revenue recognition principle, 49, 84
  right of return, 295–296, 303
  situations, 284
  warranties, 300–303
revenue recognition principle, 49, 84, 295
revenues, 44
  accrued revenues, 84, 89
  basic revenue transaction, 282–283
  biased revenue numbers, 279
  collectibility, 306
  collectible revenues, 49
  contract assets and liabilities, 304–305
  from contracts with customers, 49
  costs to obtain and/or fulfill a contract, 305–306, 307
  disaggregation of revenue, 307
  measurement, 280–295
  and operations, 153
  presentation, 304–306
  realizable (revenue), 49
  realized (revenue), 49

revenues (*continued*)
 recognition. *See* revenue recognition
 reconciliation of contract balances, 307
 remaining performance obligations, 307
 sales revenues, 349
 service revenue, 183
 in single-step income statements, 165
 unearned revenues, 84, 87–88
 vs. gains, 163
reversing entries, 78, 96–97
rewards of ownership, 294
right of return, 295–296, 303, 309, 349
risk, 150
 of bankruptcy, 211
 business model, and various related
  risks, 242
 business risks, 242–243
 capital market risks, 243
 credit risk, 276, 306, 339, 350, 358
 financial risks, 243, 519
 inputs to income models, 99
 liquidity risk, 212
 operating risk, 243
 of ownership, 294
 price risk, 276
 product market risks, 243
 risks and rewards, 49
risk-free discount rate, 100
risk management, 150
risk profile, 276
risk/return trade-off, 150
ROA. *See* rate of return on assets (ROA)
royalty relief approach, 705
rules-based approach, 21

S
sale
 of goods, 294–295
  see also sales transaction
 property, plant, and equipment, 649–650
 of receivables, 365–370
 regular-way purchase or sale, 552
 of services, 295
sales discounts, 348–349, 454
sales returns and allowances, 349–350, 454
sales revenues, 349
sales transaction
 business perspective, 274
 concessionary terms, 276–278
 constructive obligation, 279
 contract law, 278–279
 economics of, 274–278
 fundamentals of understanding sales
  transactions, 274–275
 information for decision-making,
  279–280
 legalities of, 278–279
 reciprocal nature, 275–276
 revenue recognition. *See* revenue
  recognition
salvage value, 630
Sarbanes-Oxley Act (SOX), 18–19
secured borrowings, 365, 367
Securities Act, 19

Securities and Exchange Commission
  (SEC), 12, 15–16, 18, 59
securitization, 7, 339, 365–366, 374
self-constructed assets, 561
self-interest, 7
selling expenses, 425
selling transactions. *See* sales transaction
sensitive numbers on financial statements,
  38–39
service contracts, 274
service life. *See* useful life
service revenue, 183
services, 274
 additional services, 277
 distinct services, 283
 ongoing services, 277
 performance of the service, 295
 sale of services, 295
 virtual services, 272–273
 vs. sales of goods, 272–273
service-type warranty, 301–302
servicing asset component, 370
servicing liability component, 370
share-based payments, 565–566
shared advertising, 288
shareholders' equity, 224–225
short-term financing, 223
short-term investments, 217, 343
short-term liquidity ratios, 211
short-term loans receivable, 356–357
short-term notes receivable, 356–357
short-term paper, 342–343, 345
short-term returns, 487
significant influence, 512
significant influence investments, 513
significant judgements, 306
simple interest, 114
single-step income statements, 165–166
soft numbers, 41, 50, 154, 212
sole proprietorship, 46–47, 93–94
solvency, 12, 211, 215
solvency ratios, 211–212, 243
special journal, 82
special purpose entity (SPE), 7, 48, 366
specific identification, 429–430
spreadsheets, 118, 121
stable dollar, 51
stakeholders, 5–7
stand-alone selling price, 289
standard cost system, 424
standard setting
 Accounting Standards Board
  (AcSB), 13
 challenge for, 21
 and conceptual framework, 35–36
 Financial Accounting Standards
  Board (FASB), 15–16
 funding, 20
 International Accounting Standards
  Board (IASB), 13–15
 need for standards, 11–12
 parties involved in standard setting, 12
 in political environment, 20
 provincial securities commissions, 16

Securities and Exchange Commission
  (SEC), 15–16
standard-setting organizations, 12
Standards Interpretation Committee
  (SIC), 17
stated interest rate, 358, 362–363
statement of cash flows, 78, 176, 230
 cash flow patterns, 237
 cash inflows and outflows, 231
 content, 230–231
 direct method, 235
 financial flexibility, 237
 financing activities, 231, 234–235
 format, 231–232
 free cash flow, 238–239
 IFRS-ASPE comparison, 239
 indirect method, 235
 investing activities, 231, 235
 liquidity, 236–237
 operating activities, 231, 233–235
 perspectives, 237–239
 preparation of, 232–235
 purpose, 230
 usefulness from business perspective,
  210–211
 usefulness of, 235–236
statement of changes in equity, 4, 173,
  174–176
 see also statement of retained earnings
statement of changes in shareholders'
  equity, 78, 110
statement of comprehensive income,
  78, 150
 see also income statement
 preparation from work sheet, 110
 unrealized holding gain or loss, 92
statement of financial position (balance
  sheet), 4, 78, 211
 accounting policies, 227
 additional detail, 227
 additional information reported,
  226–228
 analysis of, 210
 assets, 214
 cash, 217
 classification, 213–216
 classified statement of financial position,
  215–226
 comparative, 233
 contingencies, 226–227
 contractual situations, 227
 contra items, 229–230
 cross-references, 229–230
 current assets, 216–220
 current liabilities, 222–223
 disclosure techniques, 228–230
 elements of, 214
 financial assets, 218
 financial instruments, 213–216
 format, 225–226
 IFRS-ASPE comparison, 239
 intangible assets, 221–222
 inventories, 218–219
 leaving out items of relevance, 212

statement of financial position (balance sheet) (*continued*)
  liabilities, 214
  limitations, 212
  long-term investments, 220
  long-term liabilities, 223–224
  monetary *vs.* non-monetary assets and liabilities, 213
  non-current investments, 220
  notes to financial statements, 228–229
  off–balance sheet, 212
  other assets, 222
  owners' equity, 224–225
  parenthetical explanations, 228
  prepaid expenses, 219
  preparation from work sheet, 110–111
  preparation of, 215–226
  property, plant, and equipment, 220–221
  provisions, 227
  receivables, 217–218
  short-term investments, 217
  standard format, 214
  subsequent events, 228
  supporting schedule, 230
  terminology, 230
  usefulness, 210–212
statement of income/comprehensive income (income statement), 4, 151–152
  see also income statement
  basic presentation requirements, 163
  combined statement of income/comprehensive income, 164–165
  condensed, 168–169
  continuing operations, 168
  conversion of statement of cash receipts and disbursements to income statement, 184
  detail, level of, 168
  discontinued operations, 158–162, 168
  earnings per share, 172–173
  expenses, 169–171
  IFRS-ASPE comparison, 178–179
  income tax section, 168
  intraperiod tax allocation, 172
  measurement, 156–157
  multiple-step income statement, 166–168
  non-operating section, 168
  operating section, 168
  ordinary *vs.* peripheral activities, 163
  other comprehensive income, 168
  as point estimates, 153
  presentation, 162–173
  sections, 168
  single-step income statements, 165–166
statement of income/earnings, 150
  see also income statement; statement of income/comprehensive income (income statement)
statement of retained earnings, 4, 78, 173–174
  see also statement of changes in equity

Statements of Financial Accounting Concepts, 36
stewardship, 11, 37
stock market crash, 12
straight-line amortization, 493
straight-line method, 361, 363, 492, 633
strategic investments, 511–518
  associates, investments in, 512–516
  equity method, 513–516, 517
  subsidiaries, investments in, 517–518
strategy
  corporate strategy, 487
  differentiation strategy, 153
  low-cost/high-volume strategy, 153
strict cash basis, 181
structured financings, 58
studies, 17
subjective values, 53
subprime mortgages, 7
subsequent events, 228
subsidiary, 517–518
subsidiary ledger, 78
substantial completion or performance, 294
successful efforts method, 574
sum-of-the-years'-digits method, 690–691
supplementary information, 55
supplementary schedules, 168
supporting schedule, 230

T
tangible capital assets, 99, 558
  see also property, plant, and equipment
taxation
  capital gain, 663
  deferred income tax assets, 222
  deferred income tax liabilities, 223–224
  and depreciation, 659–663
  future income tax assets, 222
  future income tax liabilities, 223–224
  income taxes, 108–109
  intraperiod tax allocation, 172
tax basis, 661
tax rebates receivable, 345
tax value, 661
technology, impact of, 22
technology-based intangible assets, 707–708
telecom companies, 338–339
temporary account, 78
temporary use of land during construction, 560
10-column work sheet, 107
terminal loss, 663
textbooks, 17
timeliness, 41
time periods, 122
times interest earned, 244
time value concepts, 113, 356
  see also present value
time value of money, 99, 286–287
Toronto Stock Exchange (TSX), 2, 16, 31, 33

total-earnings approach, 727
trade discounts, 348
trade-in allowance, 568
trademark, 704
trade name, 704
trade-offs, 42
trade receivables, 341, 346
trading, 487
traditional discounted cash flow approach, 100
transaction, 78
  see also event
  analysis of, 80
  arm's-length transaction, 53, 275
  barter transactions, 53, 276
  incidental transactions, 44, 167
  nonmonetary, non-reciprocal transactions, 53
  nonmonetary transactions, 53, 276
  peripheral transactions, 44
  related party transactions, 53
  revenue transaction, 282–283
  sales transaction. *See* sales transaction
transaction costs, 358, 489
transaction price, 285–291, 308
transfers-in, 454
transparency, 39, 278
travel advances, 345
treasury bills, 344
treasury stock, 225
trend analysis, 268
trial balance, 78, 83
trigger events, 507
tuition fees, 87
turnover ratio, 211
typical business activities, 163

U
uncertainty
  acceptable level of uncertainty, 51
  inputs to income models, 99
  measurement uncertainty, 51, 53, 176
uncollectible accounts, 350
  see also bad debts
uncollectible trade accounts receivable, 350–351
unconditional right to receive consideration, 304
undepreciated capital cost (UCC), 660–661
understandability, 41–42
unearned revenues, 84–85
  adjusting entries, 87–88
  vs. prepaid expenses, 87–88
unearned sales revenue, 305
unearned service revenue, 305
United States, and IFRS, 21–22
unit of accountability, 46
unit of measure, 559
unit of production method, 634–635
units-of-delivery method, 292
unprofitable contract, 317
unrealized holding gains or losses, 84, 92, 489

unrecorded items, 84
unusual gains and losses, 163
unusual items, 217
upfront fees, 302–303
U.S. dollar, 344
U.S. GAAP, 15, 21–22, 434
    see also Financial Accounting Standards
        Board (FASB)
U.S. stock markets and exchanges, 15
useful life, 86, 221, 559, 631, 703, 707
users of financial information, 4, 6, 37, 274

V
valuation
    goodwill, 713–714, 724–728
    intangible assets, 222
valuation premise, 102
valuation techniques, 98–101
    choice of model, 98–99
    discounted cash flow model, 100
    income models, 98
    inputs, 99
    market models, 98
    quality of the measurement, 100

value in use, 645
value in use measurements, 101–102
variable charge approach, 634–635
variable consideration, 285–286, 308
vendor rebate, 422–423
verifiability, 41, 575
vertical analysis, 268
virtual services, 272–273
volume rebates, 288

W
warranties, 223, 275, 300–303, 308
wasting assets, 573
weighted-average accumulated
    expenditures, 591
weighted average cost, 430–432
without recourse, 369
with recourse, 369–370
working capital, 223, 227, 419
work-in-process inventory, 410
work sheet, 107
    adjusted trial balance columns, 108
    adjustments, 107–108
    adjustments columns, 108

columns, 108
completion of, 108–110
income taxes, 108–109
net income, 110
preparation of financial statements,
    110–112
statement of comprehensive income
    columns, 108
statement of financial position columns,
    108
10-column work sheet, 107
trial balance columns, 108
using a work sheet, 107–112
writing off an account, 353–354

Y
yield rate, 358

Z
zero-interest-bearing notes, 356, 359–361
zero-profit method, 311, 315

A SUMMARY OF THE CASE PRIMER*

Case analysis is important in accounting education. It mirrors the complexities of real-life in-context decision-making, and it encourages critical thinking and the development of judgement. It also allows students to test how deeply they know their theory and technical material. Knowledge of the *CPA Canada Handbook*, various accounting methods, bookkeeping, financial statement analysis, discounting, and fair value estimation methods is important to a good accounting education. These are crucial building blocks, but, at the same time, they are only a means to an end. The real goal is to develop judgement and insight into the issues that are faced by individuals and society in relation to accounting.

FRAMEWORK FOR CASE ANALYSIS

Decision-making must be done in the context of the situation at hand. We have to consider the accounting body of knowledge (*CPA Canada Handbook*, accounting methods, etc.) and must do this within a specific scenario. Who is in charge of preparing the financial information? Who will be using the information (and for what purpose)? Are there any circumstances either inside the company or outside it that may lead to bias?

STAGES

Case analysis can be seen as having three main stages:

1. Assessment of the reporting environment/ framework/overview

2. Identification and analysis of the financial reporting issues

3. Recommendations

A short version of the case primer follows. A more detailed version is available in *WileyPLUS* and on the Student Website <www.wiley.com/go/kiesocanada> accompanying *Intermediate Accounting*, Eleventh Canadian Edition.

1. **Assessment of the reporting environment/ framework/overview**

   a. Potential for bias (Look for sensitive numbers and/or financial statement items. Identify and articulate the bias and related key numbers.)

   i. **Users and the decisions** they are making. Who is using the information and for what purpose? Are there any key numbers/ratios that will be the focus of these users? Are there any contracts that refer to the financial reporting (such as debt covenants, payout ratios, etc.)?

   ii. **Financial statement preparers.** Consider management compensation such as bonuses that are based on net income, stock options that are based on the value of the stock (and are affected by the financial information), the need to obtain financing, etc.

   iii. **Business/economic reporting environment.** Is the company experiencing a decline in profitability or cash flows due to increased competition, less demand for services, internal problems, etc.? What are the key numbers/ratios that users focus on to assess the financial health of the company?

   b. GAAP constraint
   If the company's shares trade on a stock exchange, there is normally a legal requirement to follow IFRS. Otherwise, the GAAP constraint would depend on what the users want from the statements. As a general rule, GAAP statements, by definition, are reliable, relevant, comparable, consistent, and understandable. Private entities may choose to follow ASPE or IFRS.

   c. Overall conclusion on financial reporting objective
   Based on your role in the case and the above information, conclude on whether the financial reporting will be more aggressive or conservative or somewhere in between. Note that aggressive accounting tends to overstate net income/assets and present the company in the best light. Conservative accounting ensures that net income/assets are not overstated and that all pertinent information (positive or negative) is disclosed.

This primer is a summary of the case primer document on the Student Website and in WileyPLUS.